WSP
70924-1/$5.95 U.S./$7.95 CAN./REFERENCE/WASHINGTON SQUARE PRESS

ROMANOV'S RUSSIAN-ENGLISH ENGLISH-RUSSIAN Dictionary

Over 35,000 vocabulary entries
plus a pronunciation guide for Russian and English. Special grammatical tables, lists of geographical names, abbreviations, weights and measures. An indispensable aid for students, teachers, home and office libraries.
Two volumes in one • Over 500 pages

ROMANOV'S РУССКО-АНГЛИЙСКИЙ АНГЛО-РУССКИЙ СЛОВАРЬ

А.С. РОМАНОВА

0-671-70924-0

НОВИНКА

АВТОРИТЕТНЫЙ СПРАВОЧНИК

Вот недорогой

русско-английский

англо-русский

словарь — лучший из когда-либо

вышедших из печати

Предназначенный для широкого круга лиц, интересующихся обоими языками, этот словарь будет особенно выгодным и ценным справочником как для учащихся и учителей, так и в частных и конторских библиотеках. Он содержит более 35 000 заглавных слов в алфавитном порядке с указанием правильного произношения, таблицы флексий, списки географических названий, сокращений, имен числительных, мер веса и длины и т. д.

Русско-английский/англо-русский словарь Романова подготовлен сотрудниками фирмы Лангеншейдта, самого известного в мире издательства двуязычных словарей. Он отличается сжатостью и достоверностью и является необходимым справочником исключительной ценности.

The above text appears in English on the back cover

А. С. РОМАНОВ

Карманный
РУССКО-АНГЛИЙСКИЙ
и
АНГЛО-РУССКИЙ
словарь

с учетом
американского произношения и правописания

Обе части в одном томе

Составили:

д-р Э. Ведель (ч. 1)

А. С. Романов (ч. 2)

WASHINGTON SQUARE PRESS
PUBLISHED BY POCKET BOOKS
New York London Toronto Sydney Tokyo Singapore

ROMANOV'S

Pocket

RUSSIAN-ENGLISH ENGLISH-RUSSIAN Dictionary

With special emphasis on American English

Two Volumes in One

Part I by E. Wedel, Ph. D.

Part II by A. S. Romanov

WASHINGTON SQUARE PRESS
PUBLISHED BY POCKET BOOKS
New York London Toronto Sydney Tokyo Singapore

A Washington Square Press Publication of
POCKET BOOKS, a division of Simon & Schuster Inc.
1230 Avenue of the Americas, New York, NY 10020

Published by arrangement with Langenscheidt KG, Publishing House

ISBN: 0-671-70924-0

First Pocket Books printing August 1964

27 26 25 24 23 22 21 20

Printed in the U.S.A.

Contents

Оглавление

Preface

This Russian-English dictionary has been compiled with the same care and diligence as all other publications of Langenscheidt Publishers, which have been appreciated as standard works for many decades.

The dictionary is meant to be used in all walks of life and at school. In its two parts it contains more than 35,000 vocabulary entries with many translations and idioms as well as their phonetic transcriptions. Americanisms have received special consideration, and in the Russian-English part cases of particular American usage are even cited in the first place, being followed by their respective British semantic (or orthographic) equivalents.

English pronunciation follows that laid down by Daniel Jones in his *An English Pronouncing Dictionary* (1953). In the Russian-English part pronunciation is only given after those Russian words and parts of words which deviate from the basic rules of pronunciation. Generally speaking, Russian words can be pronounced properly if the place of the accent is known. Therefore every Russian word has been given its stress. Shift of stress, as far as it takes place within the inflection, is also indicated. A detailed account of Russian pronunciation with the help of the symbols of I. P. A.'s phonetic transcription can be found on pages 21—27.

References to full-length inflection tables in the supplement to the dictionary, as given after nouns, adjectives and verbs, enable the user to employ the words in question in all their modifications.

In addition to the vocabulary this dictionary contains lists of geographical names (American and British), abbreviations, numerals, measures and weights and a survey of the most important differences between British and American spelling and pronunciation.

Publishers and editors hope of this book that it may contribute to the mutual understanding between nations and thus help to deepen their cultural relations.

Предисловие

Настоящий словарь русского и английского языков составлен с такой же тщательностью и аккуратностью, как и все издания Лангеншейдта, зарекомендовавшие себя образцовыми трудами на протяжении многих десятков лет.

Словарь предназначается преимущественно для работников разных профессий и учащихся. Он содержит в обеих частях более 35000 заглавных слов в алфавитном порядке, с указанием произношения, переводом и устойчивыми оборотами речи, причём учитываются в должной мере особенности американского варианта английского языка.

Английское произношение даётся по словарю Daniel Jones, An English Pronouncing Dictionary (1953).

К словнику прилагаются: списки географических названий (американских и английских), сокращений, имён числительных, мер длины и веса, грамматические таблицы, а также перечень важнейших различий между языком британцев и американцев в отношении правописания и произношения.

Издательство и сотрудники надеются изданием настоящего словаря способствовать взаимопониманию и укреплению культурных связей между народами.

ROMANOV'S
POCKET
Russian-English
English-Russian
DICTIONARY

Careful reading and observation of the following preliminary notes will both facilitate the use and help to open up the full value of the dictionary.

Preliminary Notes

1. Arrangement. Material in this dictionary has been arranged in alphabetical order. In the Russian-English part, proper names (Christian, geographical, etc.) as well as abbreviations appear in their individual alphabetical order within the vocabulary itself. In the case of a number of prefixed words, especially verbs, not explicitly listed because of the limited size of the dictionary, it may prove useful to drop the prefix, which is often but a sign of the perfective aspect (see below), and look up the primary (imperfective) form thus obtained.

Compounds not found in their alphabetical places should be reduced to their second component in order to find out their main meaning, e. g.:
термоя́дерный → я́дерный = nuclear.

To save space with the aim of including a maximum of material, compounds, derivatives, and occasionally just similar words, have, wherever possible, been arranged in groups, the vertical stroke (|) in the first entry word of such a group separating the part common to all following items of the group, and the tilde (**~**) in the run-on words replacing the part preceding the vertical stroke in the first entry and consequently not repeated in the other articles of the group. The tilde may also stand for the whole first entry, which then has no separation mark since it is entirely repeated in the run-on items of the group.

Besides the bold-faced tilde just mentioned, the same mark in standard type (~) is employed within a great number of entries to give phrases and idioms of which the entry word or any component of its inflection system forms part.

A tilde with circlet (2) indicates a change in the initial letter (capital to small and vice versa) of a run-on word.

Examples: **Аме́рик|а** ...; **2а́нский** = **америка́нский**
англи́|йский ...; **'2я** = **'Англия** (for stress see below, 3).

Within brackets: square [ ], round ( ), acute-angled ⟨ ⟩, instead of the tilde a hyphen (-) with the same function (mark of repetition) has been used, e. g.:

то́лстый [14; толст, -á, -о] = [14; толст, толстá, то́лсто]
брать [беру́, -рёшь; брал, -á, -о] = [беру́, берёшь; брал, брала́, бра́ло]
весели́ть ...; (**-ся**) = **весели́ться**
cf. **убира́ть** ..., ⟨убра́ть⟩ ...; **-ся** = **убира́ться**, ⟨убра́ться⟩
проси́ть ..., ⟨по-⟩ = ⟨попроси́ть⟩.

Of the two main aspects of a Russian verb the imperfective form appears first, in boldface type, followed, in acute-angled brackets ⟨ ⟩ and in standard type, by its perfective counterpart. Verbs occurring only as perfective aspects (or whose imperfective or iterative aspect is hardly ever used) bear the mark *pf.*; those used only in the imperfective aspect have no special designation at all; verbs whose perfective aspect coincides with the imperfective are marked thus: *(im)pf.*

If in a certain meaning (or meanings) only one member of an aspect pair may be used, the cases concerned are preceded by the abbreviations *impf.* or *pf.* respectively and thus separated from the meanings to which both aspects apply, these latter being always given in the first place. Similarly in a noun the abbreviation *pl.* (or *sg.*) after one or more translation items designates the word(s) following it as referring only to the plural (or singular) form of the entry otherwise used in both numbers. Number differences between a Russian entry and its English counterpart(s) are indicated by adding the abbreviation *pl.* or *sg.* behind the latter, whereas a noun used only in the plural bears the mark *pl.* right after the entry itself, i. e. where usually the gender is given (see below).

In the English equivalents of Russian verbs the particle 'to' of the infinitive has been omitted for reasons of space economy.

Also, a number of quite similar international words, particularly nouns terminating in **-áция, -ѝция** or **-ѝзм, -ѝст** = -ation, -ition, -ism, -ist, or likewise obvious cases such as **тайфýн** 'typhoon' have not been included in the dictionary, especially since there are no stress or inflectional peculiarities about the Russian nouns in question nor is there, on the whole, any difficulty in deducing their semantic values.

Moreover, English adjectives used as nouns (and nouns used as adjectives) alike have, in connection with successive pertinent entries, been given but once, whereas the Russian words naturally appear in their different forms, i. e. parts of speech; e. g.:

> **америк|áнец** *m* ..., **~áнка** *f* ..., **~áнский** ... = American (i. e. man, woman, *adj.*)
> **квадрáт** *m* ..., **~ный** ... square = square (*su.*) & square (*adj.*)
> *cf.* **лимѝт** *m* ..., **~ѝровать** ... *(im)pf.* = limit (*su.*) & limit (*vb.*).

Otherwise the adjectival use of an English noun (and occasionally other parts of speech) corresponding to a Russian adjective has as a rule been noted by adding dots (...) to the noun, etc. form concerned, irrespective of the mode of its orthographic combination with another noun, i. e. whether they are spelled in one word, hyphenated or written separately.

2. Pronunciation. As a rule pronunciation in individual Russian entry words has been given only in cases and places that differ from the standard pronunciation of Russian vowel and consonant letters (for this cf. pp. 21—27), e. g.:

> **г** = ɡ, but in **лёгкий** = (-x-)
> **ч** = tʃ, but in **что** = (ʃ-)
> **не** = ɲɛ, but in (the loan word) **пенснé** = (-ˈnɛ)

To transcribe Russian sounds and (Cyrillic) letters, the alphabet of the International Phonetic Association (I.P.A.) has been used.

3. Stress. The accent mark (ˊ) is placed above the stressed vowel of a Russian entry (or any other) word having more than one syllable and printed in full, as well as of run-on words, provided their accentuated vowel is not covered by the tilde or hyphen (= marks of repetition), e. g.:

дока́з|ывать, ⟨~а́ть⟩ = ⟨доказа́ть⟩. Since ё is always stressed the two dots over it represent implicitly the accent mark.

Wherever the accent mark precedes the tilde ('~) the **last syllable but one** of the part for which the tilde stands is stressed.

Examples: **уведом|ля́ть** ..., ⟨'~ить⟩ = ⟨уве́домить⟩.
выполн|я́ть ..., ⟨'~ить⟩ = ⟨вы́полнить⟩.

An accent mark over the tilde (~́) implies that the **last** (or sole) syllable of the part replaced by the tilde is to be stressed.

Examples: **наход|и́ть** ...; ~́ка = нахо́дка
прода|ва́ть ..., ⟨~́ть⟩ = ⟨прода́ть⟩
по́езд ...; ~́ка = пое́здка
труб|а́ ...; ~́ка = тру́бка.

In special cases of **phonetic transcription**, however, the accent mark precedes the stressed syllable, cf. **анте́нна** [-ˈten-], this usage being in accordance with I.P.A. rules.

Two accents in a word denote two equally possible modes of stressing it, thus:

и́на́че = ина́че *or* и́наче
загр|ужа́ть ..., ⟨~узи́ть⟩ [... -у́зи́шь] = [... загру́зишь *or* загрузи́шь]
нали|ва́ть ..., ⟨~́ть⟩ [... на́ли́л ...] = [... на́лил *or* нали́л ...].

Quite a number of **predicative** (or short) **adjectives** show a shift, or shifts, of stress as compared with their attributive forms. Such divergences are recorded as follows:

хоро́ший [17; хоро́ш, -а́] = [17; хоро́ш, хороша́, хорошо́ (*pl.* хороши́)]
плохо́й [16; плох, -а́, -о] = [16; плох, плоха́, пло́хо (*pl.* пло́хи)]
до́брый [14; добр, -а́, -о, до́бры́] = [14; добр, добра́, до́бро (*pl.* до́бры *or* добры́)].

The same system of stress designation applies, by the way, to accent shifts in the preterite forms of a number of verbs, e. g.:

да|ва́ть ..., ⟨~ть⟩ [... дал, -а́, -о; ...(дан, -а́)] = [... дал, дала́, да́ло (*pl.* да́ли); ... (дан, дана́, дано́, даны́)].

Insertion of "epenthetic" о, е between the two last stem consonants in masculine short forms has been noted in all adjectives concerned.

Examples: **лёгкий** [16; лёгок, легка́; *a.* лёгки] = [16; лёгок, легка́, легко́ (*pl.* легки́ *or* лёгки)]
бе́дный [14; -ден, -дна́, -о; бе́дны́] = [14; бе́ден, бедна́, бе́дно (*pl.* бе́дны *or* бедны́)]
больно́й [14; бо́лен, больна́] = [14; бо́лен, больна́, больно́ (*pl.* больны́)]
по́лный [14; по́лон, полна́, по́лно́] = [14; по́лон, полна́, по́лно *or* полно́ (*pl.* по́лны *or* полны́)].

If the stress in all short forms conforms to that of the attributive adjective the latter is merely provided with the abbreviation *sh.* (for *short form*) that indicates at the same time the possibility of forming such predicative forms, e. g.:

бога́тый [14 *sh.*] = [14; бога́т, бога́та, бога́то, бога́ты]
паху́чий [17 *sh.*] = [17; паху́ч, паху́ча, паху́че, паху́чи]
сво́йственный [14 *sh.*] = [14; сво́йствен, сво́йственна, сво́йственно, сво́йственны].

4. Inflected forms. All Russian inflected parts of speech appearing in the dictionary are listed in their respective basic forms, i. e. nominative singular (nouns, adjectives, numerals, certain pronouns) or infinitive (verbs). The gender of Russian nouns is indicated by means of one of three abbreviations in italics (*m*, *f*, *n* — cf. list, pp. 487—488) behind the entry word.* Each inflected entry is followed, in square brackets [ ], by a figure, which serves as reference to a definite paradigm within the system of conjugation and declension as tabulated at the end of the book, pp. 483—491. Any variants of these paradigms are stated after the reference figure of each entry word in question.

Examples: **ло́жка** *f* [5; *g/pl.*: -жек], like **ло́жа** *f* [5], is declined according to paradigm 5, except that the former example inserts in the genitive plural "epenthetic" е between the two last stem consonants: ло́жек; cf. **ло́дка** *f* [5; *g/pl.*: -док] = [*g/pl.*: ло́док]. **кусо́к** *m* [1; -ска́] = "epenthetic" о is omitted in the oblique cases of the singular and in all cases of the plural; cf. **коне́ц** *m* [1; -нца́] = [конца́, концу́, etc.].

го́род *m* [1; *pl.*: -да́, *etc. e.*] = the example stresses its stem in the singular, but the endings in the plural, the nominative plural being in -а́ (instead of in -ы́): города́, городо́в, etc.

край *m* [3; в -аю́; *pl.*: -ая́, *etc. e.*] = declined after paradigm 3, but the ending of the prepositional singular, with prepositions в, на, is in -ю́ (stressed); as for the plural, see го́род, above. Cf. also **печь** *f* [8; в -чи́; *from g/pl e.*], where, in addition to the stressed ending of the prepositional singular (after в, на), the accent shifts onto the ending in the genitive plural and all following cases of that number.

кури́ть [13; курю́, ку́ришь] = conjugated after paradigm 13, except that stress shifts onto the stem syllable in the 2nd and all following persons (singular and plural).

As the prefixed forms of a verb follow the same inflection model and (with the exception of perfective aspects having the stressed prefix вы́-) mode of accentuation as the corresponding unprefixed verb, differences in stress, etc. have in cases of such aspect pairs been marked but once, viz. with the imperfective form.

---

* For users of part II: Any Russian noun ending in a **consonant** *or* **-й** is of masculine gender;
those ending in **-а** *or* **-я** are of feminine gender;
those ending in **-о** *or* **-е** are of neuter gender.
In case of deviation from this rule, as well as in nouns terminating in **-ь**, the gender is indicated.

5. Government. Government, except for the accusative, is indicated with the help of Latin and Russian abbreviations (cf. list, pp. 33—35). Emphasis has been laid on differences between the two languages, including the use of prepositions. Whenever a special case of government applies only to one of several meanings of a word, this has been duly recorded in connection with the meaning concerned. To ensure a clear differentiation of person and thing in government, the English and Russian notes to that effect show the necessary correspondence in sequence.

6. Semantic distinction. If a word has different meanings and, at the same time, different forms of inflection or aspect, such significations have been differentiated by means of figures (e. g. бить, коса́, коси́ть); otherwise a semicolon separates different meanings, a comma mere synonyms. Italicized additions serve to specify individual shades of meaning, e. g. **поднима́ть** ... take up (*arms*); hoist (*flag*); set (*sail*); give (*alarm*); make (*noise*); scare (*game*); **приёмный** ... reception (*day*; *room* ...); ... office (*hours*); entrance (*examination*); foster (*father* ...). For further definitions with the help of illustrative symbols and abbreviations cf. list below, pp. 33—35.

In a number of Russian verbs the perfective aspect indicated (particularly with the prefixes ⟨за-⟩ and ⟨по-⟩) has, strictly speaking, the connotations "to begin to do s. th." (the former) and "to do s. th. a (little) while" (the latter); but since these forms are very often rendered into English by means of the equivalent verb without any such additions they have occasionally been given as simple aspect counterparts without further indication as to their aforesaid semantic subtlety.

7. Orthography. In both the Russian and English parts newest spelling standards have been applied, and in the latter differences between American and British usage noted wherever possible and feasible.

A hyphen at the end of a line and at the beginning of the next one denotes a hyphenated word.

In parts of words or additions given in brackets a hyphen is placed within the respective bracket.

Полноценное пользование словарём возможно лишь при точном соблюдении нижеследующих указаний!

Предварительные замечания

1. Порядок. Все заглавные слова, включая и неправильные производные формы отдельных частей речи, расположены в алфавитном порядке, напр.: *bore, born, borne* от *bear*; *men* от *man*; в русско-английской части: лучше, лучший от хороший.

Американские и английские географические названия, а также сокращения даны в особых списках на стр. 493—505.

Тильда (~ ~) служит в гнёздах слов знаком повторения. Жирная тильда (~) заменяет или всё заглавное слово или же его составную часть, стоящую перед вертикальной чертой (|). Светлая тильда (~) заменяет: а) непосредственно предыдущее заглавное слово, которое уже само может быть образовано посредством жирной тильды; б) в указании произношения произношение всего предыдущего заглавного слова. Чёрточка (-) в указании произношения даётся вместо повторения неизменяемой части заглавного слова.

При изменении начальной буквы (прописной на строчную или наоборот) вместо простой тильды ставится соответствующая тильда с кружком ₂ (₂).

Примеры: abandon [ə'bændən], ~ment [-mənt = ə'bændənmənt]; certi|ficate, ~fication, ~fy, ~tude.

2. Произношение. Произношение сложных английских слов как правило не указывается, если каждая из их составных частей приводится в алфавитном порядке как самостоятельное заглавное слово с указанием произношения.

3. Дополнения **курсивом** служат только для уточнения отдельных английских значений.

Дальнейшие пояснения даны в виде **условных знаков и сокращений** (см. стр. 33—35).

4. Точка с запятой отделяет различные оттенки значений; синонимы даны через запятую.

5. Прибавление (**~ally**) к английскому имени прилагательному означает, что его наречие образуется посредством добавления ~ally к заглавному слову, напр.: dramatic (~ally = dramatically).

6. Переносный знак в конце строчки и в начале последующей означает, что данное английское слово пишется через чёрточку, напр.: air-conditioned = air-‑conditioned.

The Russian Alphabet

Printed	Written	Russian name	Transcribed	Printed	Written	Russian name	Transcribed
А а	А а	а	a	П п	П п	пэ	pɛ
Б б	Б б	бэ	bɛ	Р р	Р р	эр	ɛr
В в	В в	вэ	vɛ	С с	С с	эс	ɛs
Г г	Г г	гэ	gɛ	Т т	Т т	тэ	tɛ
Д д	Д д д	дэ	dɛ	У у	У у	у	u
Е е	Е е	е	jɛ	Ф ф	Ф ф	эф	ɛf
Ё ё	Ё ё	ё	jɔ	Х х	Х х	ха	xa
Ж ж	Ж ж	жэ	ʒɛ	Ц ц	Ц ц	цэ	tsɛ
З з	З з з	зэ	zɛ	Ч ч	Ч ч	че	tʃe
И и	И и	и	i	Ш ш	Ш ш	ша	ʃa
Й й	Й й	и[1])		Щ щ	Щ щ	ща	ʃtʃa
К к	К к	ка	ka	Ъ ъ	- ъ	[2])	
Л л	Л л	эль	ɛl̡	Ы ы	- ы	ы[3])	ɨ
М м	М м	эм	ɛm	Ь ь	- ь	[4])	
Н н	Н н	эн	ɛn	Э э	Э э	э[5])	e
О о	О о	о	ɔ	Ю ю	Ю ю	ю	ju
				Я я	Я я	я	ja

[1]) и кра́ткое short i [2]) твёрдый знак hard sign, jer [3]) *or* еры́
[4]) мягкий знак soft sign, jer̡ [5]) э оборо́тное reversed e
Until 1918 in addition the following letters were used in Russia:
і, ѵ = и, ѣ = е, ѳ = ф.

Explanation of Russian Pronunciation with the Help of Phonetic Symbols

Объяснение русского произношения при помощи фонетических знаков

I. Vowels

1. All vowels in stressed position are half-long in Russian.
2. In unstressed position Russian vowels are very short, except in the first pretonic syllable, where this shortness of articulation is less marked. Some vowel letters (notably о, е, я), when read in unstressed position, not only differ in length (quantity), but also change their timbre, i. e. acoustic quality.

Russian letter	Explanation of its pronunciation		Transcription symbol
а	stressed	= a in 'father': мáма ('mamə) 'mamma, mother'	a
	unstressed	1. = a in the above examples, but shorter – in first pretonic syllable: [illegible]	a
		2. = a in 'ago, about' – in post-tonic or second, etc. pretonic syllable(s): атáка (a'takə) 'attack' абрикóс (əbŗi'kɔs) 'apricot'	ə
		3. = i in 'sit' – after ч, щ in first pretonic syllable: часы́ (tʃɪ'sɨ) 'watch, clock' щади́ть (ʃ[t]ʃɪ'ḑiţ) 'spare'	ɪ
е	Preceding consonant (except ж, ш, ц) is soft, i. e. palatalized.		
	stressed	1. = ye in 'yet' – in initial position, i. e. at the beginning of a word, or after a vowel, ъ, ь (if not ё) before a hard consonant: ем (jɛm) '[I] eat' бытиé (bɨţi'jɛ) 'being' съел (sjɛɫ) 'ate [up]' премьéр (pŗɪ'mjɛr) 'premier'	jɛ
		2. = e in 'set' – after consonants, soft or hard (ж, ш, ц), before a hard consonant, as well as in final position, i. e. at the end of a word, after consonants: нет (ŋɛt) 'no' шест (ʃɛst) 'pole' цел (tsɛɫ) 'whole, sound' в странé (fstra'ŋɛ) 'in the country' на лицé (nəli'tsɛ) 'on the face'	ɛ
		3. = ya in 'Yale' (but without the i-component) – in initial position or after a vowel, ъ, ь, both before a soft consonant: ель (jeḷ) 'fir' биéние (ḅi'jeɲe) 'palpitation, throb' съесть (sjeşţ) 'to eat [up]'	je

Russian letter	Explanation of its pronunciation		Transcription symbol
		4. = a in 'pale' – after consonants, soft or hard (ж, ш, ц), before a soft consonant: петь (p̡eţ) 'to sing' сесть (şeşţ) 'to sit down' шесть (ʃeşţ) 'six' цель (tseḽ) 'aim'	e
	unstressed	1. = ɪ in 'sɪt', but preceded by (j) – in initial position, i. e. also after a vowel: ещё (jɪ'ʃ̡[t]ʃ̡ɔ) 'still, yet' зна́ет ('znajɪt) '[he, she, it] knows'	jɪ
		2. = ɪ in 'sɪt' – after soft consonants: река́ (ŗɪ'ka) 'river'	ɪ
		3. = ы (cf.) after ж, ш, ц: жена́ (ʒɨ'na) 'wife' пшено́ (pʃɨ'nɔ) 'millet' цена́ (tsɨ'na) 'price'	ɨ
ё	*Preceding consonant (except ж, ш, ц) is soft.*		
	only stressed	1. = ya in 'yacht' or yo in 'beyond' – in initial position, i. e. also after a vowel, ъ, ь, before a hard consonant, or in final position: ёлка ('jɔɫkə) 'Christmas tree' даёт (da'jɔt) '[he, she, it] gives' подъём (pad'jɔm) 'rise' бельё (ḅɪ'ḽjɔ) 'linen'	jɔ
		2. = o in 'cost' – after both soft and hard consonants before hard consonants: лёд (ḽɔt) 'ice' шёлк (ʃɔɫk) 'silk'	ɔ
и	*Preceding consonant (except ж, ш, ц) is soft.*		
	stressed	= ee in 'seen': и́ва ('ivə) 'willow' юри́ст (ju'ŗist) 'lawyer'	i
	Note:	In the instr/sg. of он/оно́ and the oblique forms of они́ initial и- may be pronounced (ji-): их (ix *or* jix) 'of them'.	i/ji
	unstressed	1. = ee in 'seen', but shorter – in *first pretonic* syllable: мину́та (m̡i'nutə) 'minute'	i
		2. = ɪ in 'sɪt' – in *post-tonic* or *second, etc. pretonic* syllable(s): хо́дит ('xɔḑɪt) '[he, she, it] goes' приписа́ть (p̡ŗɪp̡i'saţ) 'to ascribe'	ɪ
	stressed & unstressed	= ы (cf.) after ж, ш, ц: жить (ʒɨţ) 'to live' ши́рма ('ʃɨrmə) 'screen' цили́ндр (tsɨ'ḽindr) 'cylinder'	ɨ
о	stressed	= o in 'cost': том (tɔm) 'volume'	ɔ

Russian letter	Explanation of its pronunciation		Tran-scription symbol
	unstressed	1. = a in 'father', but shorter – in **first pretonic** syllable: вода́ (va'da) 'water' Москва́ (ma'skva) 'Moscow'	a
		2. = a in 'ago', 'about' – in **post-tonic** or **second**, etc. **pretonic** syllable(s): го́род ('gɔrət) 'town, city' огоро́д (əga'rɔt) 'kitchen garden'	ə
	Note:	In foreign words unstressed o is pronounced (ɔ) in final position, cf.: ра́дио ('raḑiɔ) 'radio', кака́о (ka'kaɔ) 'cocoa' as against Russian (native) ма́сло ('masłə) 'butter'.	ɔ
у	stressed & unstressed	= oo in 'boom': бу́ду ('budu) '[I] will (*Brt.* shall) be'	u
ы	stressed & unstressed	a retracted variety of i, as in 'hill'; no English equivalent: вы (vɨ) 'you' ро́зы ('rɔzɨ) 'roses'	ɨ
э	stressed & unstressed	1. = e in 'set' – before a hard consonant: э́то ('ɛtə) 'this' эпо́ха (ɛ'pɔxə) 'epoch'	ɛ
		2. resembles the English sound a in 'pale' (but without the i-component) or é in French 'été' – before a soft consonant: э́ти ('eţı) 'these' элеме́нт (eļı'm̡ɛnt) 'element'	e
ю	Preceding consonant is soft.		
	stressed & unstressed	1. like yu in 'yule', but shorter – in initial position, i. e. also after a vowel, and after ь: юг (juk) 'south' зна́ю ('znaju) '[I] know' вью́га ('v̡jugə) 'snowstorm'	ju
		2. = u in 'rule' – after consonants: рю́мка ('ŗumkə) 'wineglass' люблю́ (ļu'b̡ļu) '[I] like, love'	u
я	Preceding consonant is soft.		
	stressed	1. = ya in 'yard', but shorter – in initial position, i. e. also after a vowel and ъ, as well as after ь: я́ма ('jamə) 'pit' мая́к (ma'jak) 'lighthouse' изъя́н (iz'jan) 'defect' статья́ (sta'ţja) 'article' рья́ный ('ŗjanɨj) 'zealous'	ja
		2. = a in 'father' – after a consonant and before a hard consonant: мя́со ('m̡asə) 'meat; flesh'	a
		3. = a in 'bad' – in interpalatal position, i. e. between soft consonants: пять (p̡æţ) 'five'	æ

Russian letter	Explanation of its pronunciation	Transcription symbol
	unstressed 1. = i in 'sit', but preceded by (j) – in initial position, i. e. also after a vowel and ъ: язы́к (jɪ'zɨk) 'tongue; language' та́ять ('tajɪţ) 'to thaw' изъяви́ть (ɪzjɪ'ɣiţ) 'to express, show'	jɪ
	2. = i in 'sit' – after soft consonants: мясни́к (ɱɪş'ɳik) 'butcher' Ряза́нь (ŗɪ'zaɳ) 'Ryazan [town]'	ɪ
	3. = a in 'ago' (preceded by j after vowels) – in final position: ня́ня ('ɳaɳə) '(wet) nurse' а́рмия ('arɱɪjə) 'army'	(j)ə
	II. Semivowel	
й	1. = y in 'yet' – in initial position, i. e. also after a vowel, in loan words: (Нью-)Йо́рк (jɔrk) '(New) York' майо́р (ma'jɔr) 'major'	j
	2. in the formation of diphthongs as their second element:	j
ай	= (ɪ) of (aɪ) in 'time': май (maj) 'May'	aj
ой	= [stressed] oi in 'noise': бой (bɔj) 'fight', большо́й (baļ'ʃɔj) 'big'	ɔj
	= [first pretonic] i in 'time': война́ (vaj'na) 'war'	aj
	= [post-tonic] a in 'ago' + y in 'yet': но́вой ('nɔvəj) 'of/to the new'	əj
уй	= u in 'rule' + (j): бу́йвол ('bujvəɫ) 'buffalo'	uj
ый	= ы (cf.) + (j): вы́йти ('vɨjţɪ) 'to go out', кра́сный ('krasnɨj) 'red'	ɨj
ий	= и (cf.) + (j): кий (ķij) 'cue', си́ний ('şiɳɪj) 'blue'	ij ɪj
ей	(j +) a in 'pale' ей (jej) 'to her', пей (ɳej) 'drink!', нейтро́н (ɳej'trɔn) 'neutron'	(j)ej
юй	= ю (cf.) + (j): плюй (pļuj) 'spit!'	(j)uj
яй	= [stressed] (j +) a in bad + (j): я́йца ('jæjtsə) 'eggs' = [unstressed] yi in Yiddish: яйцо́ (jɪ'tsɔ) 'egg'	(j)æj jɪ

III. Consonants

1. As most Russian consonants may be palatalized (or 'softened') there is, beside the series of normal ('hard') consonants, a nearly complete set of 'soft' parallel sounds. According to traditional Russian spelling, in writing or printing this 'softness' is marked by a combination of such palatalized consonants with the vowels е, ё, и, ю, я or, either in final position or before a consonant, the so-called 'soft sign' (ь). In phonetic transcription palatalized

consonants are indicated by means of a small hook, or comma, attached to them. As a rule a hard consonant before a soft one remains hard; only з, с may be softened before palatalized з, с, д, т, н.

2. Always hard are ж, ш, ц.
3. Always soft are ч, щ.
4. The voiced consonants б, в, г, д, ж, з are pronounced voicelessly (i. e. = п, ф, к, т, ш, с) in final position.
5. The voiced consonants б, в, г, д, ж, з, when followed by (one of) their voiceless counterparts п, ф, к, т, ш, с, are pronounced voicelessly (regressive assimilation) and vice versa: voiceless before voiced is voiced (except that there is no assimilation before в).
6. The articulation of doubled consonants, particularly those following a stressed syllable, is marked by their lengthening.

Russian letter	Explanation of its pronunciation	Transcription symbol
б	hard = b in 'bad': бок (bɔk) 'side'	b
	soft as in 'Albion': бéлка ('ḅełkə) 'squirrel'	ḅ
в	hard = v in 'very': вóдка ('vɔtkə) 'vodka'	v
	soft as in 'view': вéра ('ṿɛrə) 'faith, belief'	ṿ
г	hard = g in 'gun': горá (ga'ra) 'mountain'	g
	soft as in 'argue': гимн (g̦imn) 'anthem'	g̦
	Notes 1. = (v) in endings -ого, -его: больнóго (baḷ'nɔvə) 'of the sick, ill' рабóчего (ra'bɔtʃıvə) 'of the worker'	v
	2. = (x) in бог (bɔx) 'God' and in the combinations -гк-, -гч-: мя́гкий ('ṃaxķij) 'soft' мя́гче ('ṃaxtʃı) 'softer'	x
д	hard = d in 'door': дáма ('damə) 'lady'	d
	soft as in 'dew': дя́дя ('ḍæḍə) 'uncle'	ḍ
	-здн- – in this combination д is mute: пóздно ('pɔznə) 'late'	
ж	hard = s in 'measure', but hard: жáжда ('ʒaʒdə) 'thirst'	ʒ
	-жж- may also be soft: вóжжи ('vɔʒ̦ʒ̦ı) 'reins'	ʒ̦ʒ̦
	-жч- = щ: мужчи́на (mu'ʃ[t]ʃinə) 'man'	ʃ[t]ʃ
з	hard = z in 'zoo': зал (zał) 'hall'	z
	soft as in 'presume': зéркало ('ẓerkələ) 'mirror'	ẓ
	-зж- = hard or soft doubled ж: пóзже ('pɔʒʒɛ *or* 'pɔʒ̦ʒ̦ɛ) 'later'	ʒʒ/ʒ̦ʒ̦
	-зч- = щ: извóзчик (iz'vɔʃ[t]ʃık) 'coachman'	ʃ[t]ʃ
к	hard = c in 'come': как (kak) 'how, as'	k
	soft like k in 'key': кирпи́ч (ķir'pitʃ) 'brick'	ķ
л	hard = ll in General American 'call': лáмпа ('łampə) 'lamp'	ł
	soft = ll in English 'million': ли́лия ('ḷiḷijə) 'lily'	ḷ
м	hard = m in 'man': мак (mak) 'poppy'	m
	soft as in 'mute': мир (ṃir) 'world; peace'	ṃ

Russian letter	Explanation of its pronunciation	Transcription symbol
н	hard = n in 'noise': нос (nɔs) 'nose'	n
	soft = n in 'new': нет (n̡ɛt) 'no'	n̡
п	hard = p in 'part': пол (pɔɫ) 'floor'	p
	soft as in 'scorpion': пить (p̡it̡) 'to drink'	p̡
р	hard = trilled r: рот (rɔt) 'mouth'	r
	soft as in 'Orient': ряд (r̡at) 'row'	r̡
с	hard = s in 'sad': сад (sat) 'garden'	s
	soft as in 'assume': сюда́ (s̡u'da) 'hither, here'	s̡
	-сч- = щ: сча́стье ('ʃ̡[t]ʃ̡æs̡t̡jɪ) 'happiness; luck'	ʃ̡[t]ʃ̡
т	hard = t in 'tent': там (tam) 'there'	t
	soft as in 'tune': тюльпа́н (t̡ul̡'pan) 'tulip'	t̡
	-стн-, -стл- – in these combinations -т- is mute: ле́стница ('l̡es̡n̡ɪtsə) 'staircase' счастли́вый (ʃ̡[t]ʃ̡ɪs'l̡ivɨj) 'happy; lucky'	
ф	hard = f in 'far': фа́брика ('fabr̡ɪkə) 'factory'	f
	soft as in 'few': фильм (f̡il̡m) 'film'	f̡
х	hard = ch in Scotch 'loch': холм (xɔɫm) 'hill'	x
	soft like ch in German 'ich'; no English equivalent: хи́мия ('x̡im̡ɪjə) 'chemistry'	x̡
ц	hard = ts in 'tsar': царь (tsar̡) 'tsar, czar'	ts
ч	soft = ch in 'cheek': час (tʃ̡as) 'hour'	tʃ̡
ш	hard = sh: шум (ʃum) 'noise'	ʃ
щ	soft = sh + ch in 'cheek', cf. fresh cheeks, or = doubled (ʃ̡ʃ̡) as in 'sure': щека́ (ʃ̡[t]ʃ̡ɪ'ka) 'cheek', щи (ʃ̡[t]ʃ̡i) 'cabbage soup'	ʃ̡[t]ʃ̡
	IV. 'Surds'	
ъ	The *jer* or 'hard sign' separates a hard (final) consonant of a prefix and the initial vowel, preceded by (j), of the following root, thus marking both the hardness of the preceding consonant and the distinct utterance of (j) before the vowel: предъяви́ть (pr̡ɪdjɪ'v̡it̡) 'to show, produce' съезд (sjɛst) 'congress'. *Note*: Until 1918 the 'hard sign' was also used at the end of a word terminating in a hard consonant: братъ (brat) 'brother'.	

Russian letter	Explanation of its pronunciation	Transcription symbol
ь	The *jeŗ* or 'soft sign' serves to represent the palatal or soft quality of a (preceding) consonant in final position or before another consonant, cf.: брат (brat) 'brother' and брать (braţ) 'to take' по́лка ('pɔłkə) 'shelf' and по́лька ('pɔļkə) 'polka, Pole (= Polish woman)'.	¸
	It is also used before vowels to indicate the softness of a preceding consonant as well as the pronunciation of (j) with the respective vowel, e. g.:	
	семья́ (şɪm̧'ja) 'family' – *cf.* се́мя ('şem̧ə) 'seed',	j̧
	and in foreign words, such as батальо́н (bəta'ļjɔn) 'battalion'.	j̧

Объяснение английского произношения при помощи фонетических знаков

Explanation of English Pronunciation with the Help of Phonetic Symbols

А. Гласные и дифтонги

В английском языке существуют краткие и долгие гласные, независимо от ударения.

[ɑ:] — долгий, глубокий и открытый звук «а», как в слове «мама».

[ʌ] — краткий, неясный звук, похожий на русский неударный звук «о», который слышится в слове «Москва», или «а» в слове «варить».
Английский звук [ʌ] встречается главным образом в ударном слоге.

[æ] — звонкий, не слишком краткий звук, средний между «а» и «э», более открытый, чем «э». При произнесении рот широко открыт.

[ɛə] — дифтонг, напоминающий не слишком долгий открытый звук, близкий к русскому «э» (в слове «этот»), за которым следует неясный гласный [ə] (примерно эа).

[ai] — этот дифтонг похож на русское «ай»; его первый элемент близок к русскому «а» в слове «два». Второй элемент — очень краткий звук [i].

[au] — этот дифтонг похож на русское «ау» (в слове «пауза»). Его первый элемент тот же, что и в [ai]; однако этот звук переходит постепенно в очень краткий звук [u].

[ei] — дифтонг, напоминающий русское «эй». Он состоит из звука [e] и очень краткого звука [i].

[e] — краткий звук, напоминающий «э» в слове «эти», но короче.

[ə] — нейтральный, неясный, безударный гласный звук, напоминающий русский беглый гласный в словах: «комната», «водяной» (в первом слоге).

[i:] — долгий гласный звук, похожий на русское протяжное «и» в словах: «ива», «вижу».

[i] — короткий открытый гласный, напоминающий средний звук между «и» и «ы», похожий на «и» в слове «шить».

[iə] — дифтонг, состоящий из полуоткрытого, полудолгого звука [i] и неясного звука [ə].

[ou] — дифтонг, напоминающий русское «оу». Первый его элемент — полуоткрытый звук «о» — переходит в слабое «у», причём губы слегка округляются, а язык остается неподвижным.

[ɔ:] — открытый, долгий гласный, похожий на протяжное русское «о» в слове «бор».
При произнесении этого гласного губы округлены (но не выпячены), положение рта почти как при русском «а», однако язык отодвинут назад.

[ɔ] — краткий открытый звук, похожий на русское «о».
При произнесении этого звука надо открыть рот как при «а» и, отодвигая язык назад, не выпячивая губ, произнести «о».

[o] — закрытый, краткий (близкий к «у») звук «о» в безударных слогах.

[ə:] — В русском языке нет звука, похожего на [ə:]. При его произнесении надо рот приоткрыть только слегка, губы растянуть, а язык оставить в нейтральном положении.
В закрытом слоге этот гласный орфографически представлен сочетаниями -er, -ir и -ur.

[ɔi] — дифтонг, состоящий из звука [ɔ] и очень краткого [i].

[u:] — долгий гласный, напоминающий протяжно произнесенное русское «у» под ударением, напр.: сук, губка.

При произнесении этого звука губы вперёд не выдвигаются.

[uə] — дифтонг, состоящий из звука [u] и неясного гласного [ə].

[u] — краткий звук, похожий на русский неударный звук «у» в словах: «тупой», «сума». При произнесении этого звука губы не выдвигаются.

Б. Согласные

Согласные: [b] — б, [f] — ф, [g] — г, [k] — к, [m] — м, [p] — п, [s] — с, [v] — в, [z] — з почти не отличаются от соответствующих русских.

Английские звонкие согласные, в противоположность русским, сохраняют на конце слова свою звонкость и произносятся чётко и энергично.

[r] — произносится только перед гласными, в конце слова только, если следующее слово начинается с гласного. При произнесении этого звука кончик языка поднят к нёбу и только слегка прикасается к нему выше альвеол. Английское [r] произносится, в отличие от соответствующего русского звука «р», без раскатистой вибрации языка.

[ʒ] — звук, похожий на смягченное русское «ж».

[ʃ] — звук, похожий на смягченное русское «ш».

[θ] — аналогичного звука в русском языке нет. Для получения этого согласного пропускается струя воздуха между кончиком языка и краем верхних зубов; этот звук приближается к русскому «с» в слове «сын», если его произнести с чуть высунутым языком.

[ð] — отличается от [θ] только присутствием голоса. Следует избегать звука, похожего на русское «з».

[s] — соответствует русскому «с».

[z] — соответствует русскому «з».

[ŋ] — носовой заднеязычный согласный. В русском языке аналогичного звука нет. (Чтобы научиться произносить этот звук, надо с открытым ртом задней частью спинки языка попробовать произнести «м» так, чтобы воздух проходил не через рот, а через нос.)

[ŋk] — согласный звук, отличающийся от [ŋ] только присутствием [k].

[w] — согласный, похожий на очень краткое русское «у». При произнесении этого звука воздух проходит между губами, которые сначала слегка вытягиваются вперёд, а затем быстро занимают положение, нужное для следующего гласного звука.

[h] — простой, безголосный выдох.

[j] — звук, похожий на русский «й».

[f] — соответствует русскому согласному «ф».

[v] — соответствует русскому согласному «в».

Ударение в английских словах обозначается знаком (ˈ) и ставится перед ударным слогом, напр.: onion (ˈʌnjən).

В английском языке, кроме слов с ударением на одном слоге, бывают слова с одинаково сильным ударением на двух слогах, напр.: unsound (ˈʌnˈsaund), а также (длинные слова) с главным и побочным ударением, напр.: conglomeration (kənˈglɔməˈˈreiʃn).

Две точки (:) обозначают **долготу звука**, напр.: ask (ɑ:sk), astir (əsˈtə:).

Английский алфавит

a (ei), b (bi:), c (si:), d (di:), e (i:), f (ef), g (dʒi:), h (eitʃ), i (ai), j (dʒei), k (kei), l (el), m (em), n (en), o (ou), p (pi:), q (kju:), r (ɑ:, *Am.* ɑ:r), s (es), t (ti:), u (ju:), v (vi:), w (ˈdʌblju:), x (eks), y (wai), z (zed, *Am.* zi:).

Американская орфография

отличается от британской главным образом следующим:

1. Вместо ...our пишется ...or, напр.: hon*or* = honour, lab*or* = labour.
2. Окончанию ...re соответствует ...er, напр.: cent*er* = centre, theat*er* = theatre, meag*er* = meagre; исключения представляют og*re* и слова, оканчивающиеся на ...cre, напр.: massa*cre*, nac*re*.
3. Вместо ...ce пишется ...se, напр.: defen*se* = defence, licen*se* = licence.
4. Во всех словах, производных от глаголов, оканчивающихся на ...l и ...p, согласная на конце не удваивается, напр.: travel — trave*l*ed — trave*l*er — trave*l*ing, worship — worshi*p*ed — worshi*p*er — worshi*p*ing. Также и в некоторых других словах вместо двойной пишется одна согласная, напр.: wagon = waggon, woo*l*en = woollen.
5. В некоторых случаях немое e опускается, напр.: abridg*m*ent = abridg*e*ment, acknowled*gm*ent = acknowledg*e*ment, jud*gm*ent = judg*e*ment, ax = ax*e*, good-by = good-by*e*.
6. В некоторых словах написанию приставки en... предпочитается in..., напр.: *in*close = enclose, *in*snare = ensnare.
7. Написания æ и œ часто заменяются простым e, напр.: an*e*mia = anæmia, diarrh*e*a = diarrhœa.
8. Немой конечный слог в словах французского происхождения часто опускается, напр.: catalog = catalog*ue*, program = program*me*, prolog = prolog*ue*.
9. Особые случаи: st*a*nch = staunch, m*o*ld = mould, m*o*lt = moult, gr*a*y = grey, pl*ow* = plough, ski*ll*ful = skilful, t*i*re = tyre.

Американское произношение

отличается от английского главным образом следующим:

1. ɑ: произносится как протяжное æ: в словах ask (æ:sk = ɑ:sk), castle (kæ:sl = kɑ:sl), grass (græ:s = grɑ:s), past (pæ:st = pɑ:st) и т. д.; так же в словах branch (bræ:ntʃ = brɑ:ntʃ), can't (kæ:nt = kɑ:nt), dance (dæ:ns = dɑ:ns) и т. д.
2. ɔ произносится как ɑ в таких словах: common ('kɑmən = 'kɔmən), not (nɑt = nɔt), on (ɑn = ɔn), rock (rɑk = rɔk), bond (bɑnd = bɔnd) и во многих других.
3. ju: произносится как u:, напр.: due (du: = dju:), duke (du:k = dju:k), new (nu: = nju:).
4. r произносится между предшествующим гласным и последующим согласным звонко, коротко, причём кончик языка оттягивается назад и касается твёрдого нёба несколько выше альвеол, напр.: clerk (klə:rk = klɑ:k), hard (hɑ:rd = hɑ:d); так же и в конце слова, напр.: far (fɑ:r = fɑ:), her (hə:r = hə:).
5. Глухие p, t, k в начале безударного слога (следующего за ударным слогом) произносятся звонко, т. е. как b, d, g, напр.: property, water, second.
6. Разница между слогами с сильным и слабым ударением выражена гораздо меньше; в более длинных словах слышится ясно второстепенное ударение, напр.: dictionary (ˌˈdikʃəˈnɛri = ˈdikʃənri), ceremony (ˌˈserəˈmouni = ˈseriməni), inventory (ˌˈinvenˈtouri = ˈinvəntri), secretary (ˌˈsekrəˈtɛri = ˈsekrətri).
7. Перед, а часто также и после носовых согласных (m, n, ŋ) гласные и дифтонги произносятся с носовым оттенком, напр.: stand, time, small.

Symbols and Abbreviations

Условные знаки и сокращения

1. Symbols — Знаки

□ после английского имени прилагательного или причастия указывает на возможность правильного образования от них наречий путем прибавления суффикса ...*ly* или изменения ...*le* на ...*ly* или ...*y* на ...*ily*, напр.: rich □ = *richly*; acceptable □ = *acceptably*; happy □ = *happily*.

□ after an English adjective or participle means that from it an adverb may be formed regularly by adding ...*ly*, or by changing ...*le* into ...*ly* or ...*y* into ...*ily*; as: rich □ = *richly*; acceptable □ = *acceptably*; happy □ = *happily*.

F *familiar* = *colloquial language* разговóрный язы́к.

P *popular* просторéчие.

⁂ *rare, little used* рéдко, малоупотреби́тельно.

† *obsolete* устарéвшее слóво, выражéние.

🕮 *scientific term* наýчный тéрмин.

⚘ *botany* ботáника.

⊕ *handicraft, engineering* тéхника.

⚒ *mining* гóрное дéло.

⚔ *military term* воéнное дéло.

⚓ *nautical term* судохóдство.

☨ *commercial term* торгóвля.

🚂 *railroad, railway* железнодорóжное дéло.

✈ *aviation* авиáция.

✉ *postal affairs* пóчта.

♪ *musical term* мýзыка.

△ *architecture* архитектýра.

⚡ *electrical engineering* электротéхника.

⚖ *jurisprudence* юриспрудéнция.

Å *mathematics* математи́ка.

🌾 *farming* сéльское хозя́йство.

⚗ *chemistry* хи́мия.

⚕ *medicine* медици́на.

& *and* и.

= *equal to* равнó.

2. Abbreviations — Сокращения

a. *also* тáкже.

abbr. *abbreviation* сокращéние.

acc. *accusative* (*case*) вини́тельный падéж.

adj. *adjective* и́мя прилагáтельное.

adv. *adverb* нарéчие.

Am. *Americanism* американи́зм.

anat. *anatomy* анатóмия

art. *article* арти́кль, член.

ast. *astronomy* астронóмия.

attr. *attributively* атрибути́вное употреблéние (т. е. в кáчестве определéния).

biol. *biology* биолóгия.

Brt. *British* (*English*) *usage* бритáнское (англи́йское) словоупотреблéние.

b. s. *bad sense* в дурнóм смы́сле.

cap. *capitalized* с большóй бýквы.

cf. *compare* сравни́.
ch. *chess* ша́хматы.
cj. *conjunction* сою́з.
co. *comic(ally)* шутли́во.
coll. *collective (noun)* собира́тельное и́мя (существи́тельное).
com. *commonly* обыкнове́нно.
comp. *comparative (degree)* сравни́тельная сте́пень.
compd(s). *compound(s)* сло́жное сло́во (сло́жные слова́).
cond. *conditional* усло́вное наклоне́ние.
contp. *contemptuously* пренебрежи́тельно.
cook. *cookery* кулина́рия.

dat. *dative (case)* да́тельный паде́ж.
dem. *demonstrative pronoun* указа́тельное местоиме́ние.
dim. *diminutive* уменьши́тельная фо́рма.

e. *endings stressed (throughout)* ударе́ние (сплошь) на оконча́ниях.
eccl. *ecclesiastical term* церко́вное выраже́ние.
econ. *economy* эконо́мика.
educ. *education* шко́ла, шко́льное де́ло, педаго́гика.
e. g. *for example* наприме́р.
esp. *especially* осо́бенно.
etc. *et cetera (and so on)* и т. д. (и так да́лее).

f *feminine (gender)* же́нский род.
fenc. *fencing* фехтова́ние.
fig. *figuratively* в перено́сном значе́нии.
form. *formerly* пре́жде.
f/pl. *feminine plural* мно́жественное число́ же́нского ро́да.
fr. *French* францу́зское сло́во, выраже́ние.
ft. *future (tense)* бу́дущее вре́мя.

gen. *genitive (case)* роди́тельный паде́ж.
geogr. *geography* геогра́фия.
geol. *geology* геоло́гия.
geom. *geometry* геоме́трия.
ger. *gerund* геру́ндий.
g/pl. *genitive plural* роди́тельный паде́ж мно́жественного числа́.
g. pr. *(pt.) present (past) gerund* дееприча́стие настоя́щего (проше́дшего) вре́мени.
gr. *grammar* грамма́тика.

hist. *history* исто́рия.
hunt. *hunting* охо́та.

imp. *imperative* повели́тельное наклоне́ние.
impers. *impersonal (form), -ly* безли́чная фо́рма, безли́чно.
impf. *imperfective (aspect)* несоверше́нный вид.
(im)pf. *imperfective and perfective (aspect)* несоверше́нный и соверше́нный вид.
ind(ecl). *indeclinable word* несклоня́емое сло́во.
inf. *infinitive* инфинити́в, неопределённая фо́рма глаго́ла.
instr. *instrumental (case)* твори́тельный паде́ж.
int. *interjection* междоме́тие.
interr. *interrogative(ly)* вопроси́тельная фо́рма, вопроси́тельно.
iro. *ironically* ирони́чески.
irr. *irregular* непра́вильный.
iter. *iterative, frequentative (aspect)* многокра́тный вид.

ling. *linguistics* лингви́стика, языкозна́ние.
lit. *literary* кни́жное выраже́ние.

m *masculine (gender)* мужско́й род.
metall. *metallurgy* металлу́ргия.
min. *mineralogy* минерало́гия.
mot. *motoring* автомобили́зм.
m/pl. *masculine plural* мно́жественное число́ мужско́го ро́да.
mst *mostly* бо́льшей ча́стью.

n *neuter (gender)* сре́дний род.
no. *number* но́мер.
nom. *nominative (case)* имени́тельный паде́ж.
n/pl. *neuter plural* мно́жественное число́ сре́днего ро́да.
npr. *proper name (or noun)* и́мя со́бственное.

o. a. one another друг дру́га, друг дру́гу.

obj. *objective* (*case*) объе́ктный паде́ж.

obl. *oblique* (*cases*) ко́свенные падежи́.

oft. *often* ча́сто.

once *semelfactive* (*aspect*) однокра́тный вид.

op. *opposite* противополо́жно.

opt. *optics* о́птика.

o. s. oneself себя́, себе́, -ся.

p. *participle* прича́стие.

p. person лицо́.

P. *person* челове́к.

paint. *painting* жи́вопись.

parl. *parliamentary term* парла́ментское выраже́ние.

part. 1. *particle* части́ца; 2. *particular*(*ly*) осо́бенно.

part. g. *partitive genitive* роди́тельный раздели́тельный.

pers. *pers. person*(*al form*) лицо́ (ли́чная фо́рма).

pf. *perfective* (*aspect*) соверше́нный вид.

pharm. *pharmacy* фармаце́втика.

phon. *phonetics* фоне́тика.

phot. *photography* фотогра́фия.

phys. *physics* фи́зика.

pl. *plural* мно́жественное число́.

poet. *poetic* поэти́ческое сло́во, выраже́ние.

pol. *politics* поли́тика.

poss. *possessive* (*form*) притяжа́тельная фо́рма.

p. pr. a. (*p.*) *present participle active* (*passive*) действи́тельное (страда́тельное) прича́стие настоя́щего вре́мени.

p. pt. a. (*p.*) *past participle active* (*passive*) действи́тельное (страда́тельное) прича́стие проше́дшего вре́мени.

pr. *present* (*tense*) настоя́щее вре́мя.

pred(*ic.*) *predicative* предикати́вное употребле́ние (т. е. в ка́честве именно́й ча́сти сказу́емого).

pref. *prefix* приста́вка.

pr(*e*)*s.* *present* (*tense*) настоя́щее вре́мя.

pron. *pronoun* местоиме́ние.

prov. *proverb*(*ial saying*) посло́вица, погово́рка.

prp. *preposition* предло́г.

prpos. *prepositional* (*case*) предло́жный паде́ж.

psych. *psychology* психоло́гия.

pt. *preterite, past* (*tense*) проше́дшее вре́мя.

rad. *radio* ра́дио.

refl. *reflexive* (*form*) возвра́тная фо́рма.

rel. *relative* (form) относи́тельная фо́рма.

rhet. *rhetoric* рето́рика.

s. *see* смотри́.

s. b. somebody кто́- (кого́-, кому́-) -нибудь.

s. b.'s somebody's че́й-нибудь.

sg. *singular* еди́нственное число́.

sh. *short* (*predicative*) *form* кра́ткая фо́рма.

sl. *slang* жарго́н.

Sov. *Soviet term* выраже́ние сове́тского пери́ода.

st. *stem stressed* (*throughout*) ударе́ние (сплошь) на осно́ве.

s. th. something что́-либо.

su. *substantive* и́мя существи́тельное.

sup. *superlative* превосхо́дная сте́пень.

surv. *surveying* топогра́фия.

tel. *telegraphy* телегра́ф.

teleph. *telephony* телефо́н.

text. *textiles* тка́ни.

th. *thing* вещь, предме́т.

thea. *theater* теа́тр.

typ. *typography* типогра́фское де́ло.

univ. *university* университе́т.

usu. *usually* обы́чно.

v/aux. *auxiliary verb* вспомога́тельный глаго́л.

vb. *verb* глаго́л.

vet. *veterinary* ветерина́рия.

v/i. *verb intransitive* неперехо́дный глаго́л.

voc. *vocative* (*case*) зва́тельный паде́ж.

v/refl. *verb reflexive* возвра́тный глаго́л.

v/t. *verb transitive* перехо́дный глаго́л.

zo. *zoology* зооло́гия.

Russian Abbreviations — Русские сокращения

И **имени́тельный паде́ж nominative (case).**

Р **роди́тельный паде́ж genitive (case).**

Д **да́тельный паде́ж dative (case).**

В **вини́тельный паде́ж accusative (case).**

Т **твори́тельный паде́ж instrumental (case).**

П **предло́жный паде́ж prepositional *or* locative (case).**

и т. д. **(и так да́лее) *etc.* (*et cetera*).**

и т. п. **(и тому́ подо́бное) *and the like.***

лат. **лати́нский язы́к Latin.**

тж. **та́кже *also.***

PART ONE

RUSSIAN-ENGLISH VOCABULARY

A

а 1. *cj.* but, and; а то or else; а что? why so?; **2.** *int.* ah!; **3.** *part.* F eh?

аб|ажу́р *m* [1] lamp shade; **~ба́т** *m* [1] abbot; **~ба́тство** *n* [9] abbey; **~за́ц** *m* [1] paragraph; **~онеме́нт** *m* [1] subscription; **~оне́нт** *m* [1] subscriber; **~orда́ж** ⚓ *m* [1] grappling, boarding; **~о́рт** *m* [1] abortion; **~рико́с** *m* [1] apricot; **~солю́тный** [14; -тен, -тна] absolute; **~стра́ктный** [14; -тен, -тна] abstract; **~су́рд** *m* [1] absurdity; **~су́рдный** [14; -ден, -дна] absurd; **~сце́сс** *m* [1] abscess.

аван|га́рд *m* [1] advance guard; vanguard; **~по́ст** *m* [1] outpost; **∠с** *m* [1] advance(d money); **∠сом** (*payment*) in advance; **~тю́ра** *f* [5] adventure; **~тюри́ст** *m* [1] adventurer; **~тюри́стка** *f* [5; *g/pl.*: -ток] adventuress.

авар|и́йный [14] emergency...; **∠ия** *f* [7] accident; wreck.

а́вгуст *m* [1] August.

авиа|ба́за *f* [5] air base; **~бо́мба** *f* [5] air bomb; **~констру́ктор** *m* [1] aircraft designer; **~ли́ния** *f* [7] airline; **~ма́тка** *f* [5; *g/pl.*: -ток], **~но́сец** *m* [1; -сца] aircraft carrier; **~по́чта** *f* [5] air mail; **~тра́сса** *f* [5] air route; **~цио́нный** [14] air(craft)...; **∠ция** *f* [7] aviation; aircraft *pl.*; **~шко́ла** *f* [5] flying school.

аво́сь F perhaps, maybe; на ~ at random.

австр|али́ец *m* [1; -и́йца], **~али́йка** *f* [5; *g/pl.*: -и́ек], **~али́йский** [16] Australian; **2а́лия** *f* [7] Australia; **~и́ец** *m* [1; -и́йца], **~и́йка** *f* [5; *g/pl.*: -и́ек], **~и́йский** [16] Austrian; **'2ия** *f* [7] Austria.

автобиогр|афи́ческий [16], **~афи́чный** [14; -чен, -чна] autobiographic(al); **~а́фия** *f* [7] autobiography.

авто́бус *m* [1] (motor) bus.

авто|го́нки *f/pl.* [5; *gen.*: -нок] (car) race; **∠граф** *m* [1] autograph; **~жи́р** *m* [1] autogiro; **~заво́д** *m* [1] car factory, automobile plant; **~кра́тия** *f* [7] autocracy; **~магистра́ль** *f* [8] highway; **~ма́т** *m* [1] automaton; slot machine; submachine gun; **~мати́ческий** [16], **~мати́чный** [14; -чен, -чна] automatic; **~ма́тчик** *m* [1] submachine gunner; **~маши́на** *f* [5] *s.* ~моби́ль; **~мобили́ст** *m* [1] motorist; **~моби́ль** *m* [4] (motor-) car; го́ночный ~моби́ль *m* racing car, racer; **~но́мия** *f* [7] autonomy.

а́втор *m* [1] author; **~изова́ть** [7] (*im*)*pf.* authorize; **~ите́т** *m* [1] authority; **~ский** [16] author's; ~ское пра́во *n* copyright; **~ство** *n* [9] authorship.

авто|ру́чка *f* [5; *g/pl.*: -чек] fountain pen; **~стра́да** *f* [5] (motor, super)highway.

ага́ (a'ha) aha!; (oh,) I see!

Ага́фья *f* [6; *g/pl.*: -фий] Agatha.

аге́нт *m* [1] agent; **~ство** *n* [9], **~у́ра** *f* [5] agency.

агит|ацио́нный [14] agitation..., propaganda...; **~и́ровать** [7], ⟨с-⟩ agitate; **∠ка** F *f* [5; *g/pl.*: -ток] (agitation) leaflet; **~про́п** (агитацио́нно-пропаганди́стский отде́л) *m* [1] *pol.* agitation and propaganda department; **~пу́нкт** *m* [1] (*local*) agitation center (*Brt.* -tre).

агра́рный [14] agrarian.

агресс|и́вный [14; -вен, -вна] agressive; **∠ия** *f* [7] aggression.

агрикульту́ра *f* [5] agriculture.

агро|но́м *m* [1] agriculturist; **~номи́ческий** [16] agronomi(cal); **~но́мия** *f* [7] agronomy.

ад *m* [1; в -у́] hell.

Ада́м *m* [1] Adam.

ада́птер (-tɛr) ⚡ *m* [1] pickup.

адвока́т *m* [1] lawyer; attorney (at law), *Brt.* barrister; solicitor; **~у́ра** *f* [5] ⚖ bar.

адми|нистрати́вный [14] administrative; **~нистра́ция** *f* [7] administration; **~ра́л** *m* [1] admiral; **~ралте́йство** *n* [9] admiralty.

а́дрес *m* [1; *pl.*: -á, *etc. e.*] address (не по Д at wrong); **~а́т** *m* [1], **~а́тка** *f* [5; *g/pl.*: -ток] addressee; consignee; **~ный** [14]: ~ный стол *m* register-office; **~ова́ть** [7] (*im*)*pf.* address, direct.

адриати́ческий [16] Adriatic...

а́дский [16] hellish, infernal.

адъюта́нт *m* [1] aide-de-camp.

аз *m* [1 *e.*]: **~ы́** *pl.* elementaries; F с ~о́в from scratch.

аза́рт *m* [1] passion, vehemence; hazard; войти́ в ~ get excited; **~ный** [14; -тен, -тна] hot-tempered, hazardous; venturesome.

а́збу|ка *f* [5] alphabet; **~чный** [14] alphabetic(al); ~чная и́стина *f* truism.

азербайджа́н|ец *m* [1, -нца] Azerbaijanian; **~ский** [16] Azerbaijan.

ази|а́т *m* [1], **~а́тка** *f* [5; *g/pl.*: -ток], **~а́тский** [16] Asian; Asiatic; **'2я** *f* [7] Asia; Ма́лая '2я Asia Minor.

азо́вский [16] Asov...

азóт *m* [1] nitrogen; **~ный** [14] nitric.
áист *m* [1] stork; **~овый** [14] stork...
ай ah!, oh!
айвá *f* [5] quince.
академ|ик *m* [1] academician; graduate; **~ический** [16] academic; **~ия** *f* [7] academy; **2ия наýк** Academy of Sciences; **2ия худóжеств** Academy of Arts.
акáция *f* [7] acacia.
акварéль *f* [8] water colo(u)r.
акклиматизи́ровать [7] (*im*)*pf*. acclimatize.
аккомпан|емéнт ♪ *m* [1] accompaniment; **~и́ровать** ♪ [7] accompany.
аккóрд ♪ *m* [1] chord; **~ный** [14]: **~ная** рабóта *f* piecework.
аккредит|и́в *m* [1] letter of credit; **~овáть** [7] (*im*)*pf*. accredit.
аккурáтный [14; -тен, -тна] accurate, punctual; tidy, neat.
акт *m* [1] act(ion); *thea.* act; document; *parl.* bill; **~ёр** *m* [1] actor.
акти́в *m* [1] asset(s); body of active functionaries; **~ный** [14; -вен, -вна] active.
актри́са *f* [5] actress.
актуáльный [14; -лен, -льна] topical.
акýла *f* [5] shark.
акýст|ика *f* [5] acoustics; **~и́ческий** [16] acoustic(al).
акушéр|ка *f* [5; *g*/*pl*.: -рок] midwife; **~ство** *n* [9] midwifery.
акцéнт *m* [1] accent; stress.
акцептовáть ✝ [7] (*im*)*pf*. accept.
акци|онéр *m* [1] stockholder, *Brt.* shareholder; **~онéрный** [14] joint-stock (*company*); **'~я** *f* [7] share; *pl. a.* stock.
албáн|ец *m* [1; -нца], **~ка** *f* [5; *g*/*pl*.: -нок], **~ский** [16] Albanian.
áлгебра *f* [5] algebra.
алебáстр *m* [1] alabaster.
Алексéй *m* [3] Alexis.
алéть [8] blush, grow crimson; glow.
Алжи́р *m* [1] Algeria; Algiers.
алимéнты *m*/*pl*. [1] alimony.
алкогóл|ик *m* [1] alcoholic; **~ь** *m* [4] alcohol.
аллегори́ческий [16] allegorical.
аллéя *f* [6; *g*/*pl*.: -éй] avenue, alley.
алмáз *m* [1], **~ный** [14] diamond.
алтáрь *m* [4 *e*.] altar.
алфави́т *m* [1] alphabet; **~ный** [14] alphabetical.
áлчн|ость *f* [8] greed(iness); **~ый** [14; -чен, -чна] greedy (of, for к [Д]).
áлый [14 *sh*.] crimson.
альбóм *m* [1] album; sketchbook.
альманáх *m* [1] almanac.
альпини́|зм *m* [1] mountain climbing, Alpinism; **~ст** *m* [1], **~стка** *f* [5; *g*/*pl*.: -ток] climber, Alpinist.
'Альпы *f*/*pl*. [5] Alps.
альт *m* [1 *e*.] alto.
áльф|а *f* [5]: от **~ы** до омéги from beginning to end.
алюми́ний *m* [3] aluminium.
Аля́ска *f* [5] Alaska.
амбáр *m* [1] barn; granary.
амбразýра *f* [5] embrasure.
амбулатóр|ия *f* [7] ambulance station, dispensary; **~ный** [14]: **~ный** больнóй *m* outpatient.
Амéрик|а *f* [5] America; **2áнец** *m* [1; -нца], **2áнка** *f* [5; *g*/*pl*.: -нок], **2áнский** [16] American.
ами́нь amen.
амнист|и́ровать [7] (*im*)*pf*., **~ия** *f* [7] amnesty.
амортиз|áция *f* [7] amortization; **~и́ровать** [7] (*im*)*pf*. amortize, pay off.
áмпула *f* [5] ampoule.
ампут|áция *f* [7] amputation; **~и́ровать** [7] (*im*)*pf*. amputate.
амуни́ция *f* [7] ammunition.
амфи́бия *f* [7] amphibian.
амфитеáтр *m* [1] amphitheater (*Brt*. -tre); *thea.* circle.
анáлиз *m* [1] analysis; **~и́ровать** [7] (*im*)*pf*., ⟨про-⟩ analyze (*Brt*. -se).
ана|логи́чный [14; -чен, -чна] analogous, similar; **~лóгия** *f* [7] analogy; **~нáс** *m* [1] pineapple; **~рхия** *f* [7] anarchy.
анатом|и́ровать [7] (*im*)*pf*. anatomize; **~и́ческий** [16] anatomical; **~ия** *f* [7] anatomy.
ангáр *m* [1] hangar.
áнгел *m* [1] angel.
анги́на *f* [5] quinsy, tonsillitis.
англи́|йский [16] English; **~чáнин** *m* [1; *pl*.: -чáне, -чáн] Englishman; **~чáнка** *f* [5; *g*/*pl*.: -нок] Englishwoman; **'2я** *f* [7] England.
Андрéй *m* [3] Andrew.
'Анды *f*/*pl*. [5] Andes.
анекдóт *m* [1] anecdote.
ане|ми́я *f* [7] anemia; **~стези́я** (-nɛstɛ-) *f* [7] anesthesia.
ани́с *m* [1] anise.
Анкарá *f* [5] Ankara.
анкéта *f* [5] questionnaire; form.
аннекс|и́ровать [7] (*im*)*pf*. annex; **~ия** *f* [7] annexation.
аннули́ровать [7] (*im*)*pf*. annul.
анóд *m* [1] anode; **~ный** [14] anodic.
аномáлия *f* [7] anomaly.
анони́мный [14; -мен, -мна] anonymous.
ансáмбль *m* [4] ensemble.
антагони́зм *m* [1] antagonism.
Антаркт|и́да *f* [5] Antarctica; **~ика** *f* [5], **2и́ческий** [16] Antarctic.
антéнна (-'tɛn-) *f* [5] aerial; *zo.* antenna.
антиквáр *m* [1] antiquary; dealer in antiquarian goods; **~ный** [14] antiquarian.
антилóпа *f* [5] antelope.
анти|пати́чный [14; -чен, -чна] antipathetic; **~пáтия** *f* [7] antipathy; **~санитáрный** [14] insani-

tary; **~се́птика** *f* [5] antisepsis; antiseptic; **~те́за** *f* [5] antithesis.
анти́чн|ость *f* [8] antiquity; **~ый** [14] antique.
антоло́гия *f* [7] anthology.
Анто́н *m* [1] Anthony; **~и́на** *f* [5] Antonia.
антра́кт *m* [1] intermission, *Brt.* interval; interlude.
антропо́л|ог *m* [1] anthropologist; **~о́гия** *f* [7] anthropology.
анчо́ус *m* [1] anchovy.
апат|и́чный [14; -чен, -чна] apathetic; **~ия** *f* [7] apathy.
апелл|и́ровать [7] (*im*)*pf.* appeal (to к Д); **~яцио́нный** [14] (*court*) of appeal; **~яцио́нная жа́лоба** *f* = **~я́ция** ⚖ *f* [7] appeal.
апельси́н *m* [1] orange.
аплоди́|ровать [7], ‹за-› applaud; **~сме́нты** *m/pl.* [1] applause.
апоге́й *m* [3] apogee.
аполити́чн|ость *f* [8] indifference toward(s) politics; **~ый** [14; -чен, -чна] indifferent to politics.
апологи́ческий [16] apologetic.
апопле́ксия *f* [7] apoplexy.
апо́стол *m* [1] apostle.
апофео́з *m* [1] apotheosis.
аппара́т *m* [1] apparatus; camera.
аппе́нд|икс *m* [1] *anat.* appendix; **~ици́т** *m* [1] appendicitis.
аппети́т *m* [1] appetite; прия́тного ~а! bon appétit!; **~ный** [14; -и́тен, -и́тна] appetizing.
апре́ль *m* [4] April.
апте́ка *f* [5] drugstore, *Brt.* chemist's shop; **~рь** *m* [4] druggist, *Brt.* (pharmaceutical) chemist.
ара́|б *m* [1], **~бка** *f* [5; *g/pl.*: -бок] Arab; **~бский** [16] (*a.* **~ви́йский** [16]) Arabian, Arabic; Arab (*Ligue, etc.*); **~п** † *m* [1] Moor, Negro.
арби́тр *m* [1] arbiter; umpire; **~а́ж** ⚖ *m* [1] arbitration.
арбу́з *m* [1] watermelon.
Аргенти́н|а *f* [5] Argentina; **♀ец** *m* [1; -нца], **♀ка** *f* [5; *g/pl.*: -нок], **♀ский** [16] Argentine.
арго́ *n* [*indecl.*] argot.
аргуме́нт *m* [1] argument; **~и́ровать** [7] (*im*)*pf.* argue.
аре́на *f* [5] arena; sphere.
аре́нд|а *f* [5] lease, rent; сдава́ть (брать) в ~у lease (rent); **~а́тор** *m* [1] lessee; tenant; **~ова́ть** [7] (*im*)*pf.* rent.
аре́ст *m* [1] arrest; **~а́нт** *m* [1], **~а́нтка** *f* [5; *g/pl.*: -ток] prisoner; **~о́вывать** [1], ‹~ова́ть› [7] arrest.
аристокра́тия *f* [7] aristocracy.
арифме́т|ика *f* [5] arithmetic; **~и́ческий** [16] arithmetic(al).
а́рия *f* [7] aria; air.
а́рка *f* [5; *g/pl.*: -рок] arc; arch.
арка́да *f* [5] arcade.
'Аркти|ка *f* [5] Arctic (Zone); **♀ческий** (-'ţi-) [16] arctic.
армату́ра *f* [5] fittings, armature.
Арме́ния *f* [7] Armenia.
а́рмия *f* [7] army.
армян|и́н *m* [1; *pl.*: -мя́не, -мя́н], **~ка** *f* [5; *g/pl.*: -нок], **~ский** [16] Armenian.
арома́т *m* [1] aroma, perfume, fragrance; **~и́ческий** [16], **~ный** [14; -тен, -тна] aromatic, fragrant.
арсена́л *m* [1] arsenal.
арте́ль *f* [8] workmen's cooperative association.
арте́рия *f* [7] artery.
артилле́р|ия *f* [7] artillery; **~и́ст** *m* [1] artilleryman; **~и́йский** [16] artillery...
арти́ст *m* [1] artist(e); actor; **~ка** *f* [5; *g/pl.*: -ток] artist(e); actress.
артишо́к *m* [1] artichoke.
а́рфа *f* [5] harp.
археолог *m* [1] archeologist; **~и́ческий** [16] archeologic(al); **~ия** *f* [7] archeology.
архи́в *m* [1] archives *pl.*
архиепи́скоп *m* [1] archbishop.
архипела́г *m* [1] archipelago.
архите́кт|ор *m* [1] architect; **~у́ра** *f* [5] architecture; **~у́рный** [14] architectonic.
арши́н *m* [1; *g/pl.*: арши́н] arshine (†, = *0.711 m.* = *2 ft. 4 in.*).
арьерга́рд *m* [1] rear guard.
асбе́ст *m* [1] asbestos.
асе́птика (-'sɛ-) *f* [5] asepsis.
аспира́нт *m* [1] candidate (*for university teacher's/researcher's career*).
ассамбле́я *f* [6; *g/pl.*: -ле́й]: Генера́льная ♀ Организа́ции Объединённых На́ций United Nations, General Assembly.
ассигнова́|ть [7] (*im*)*pf.* assign, allocate, allot; **~ние** *n* [12] assignment, allocation, allotment.
ассимил|и́ровать [7] (*im*)*pf.* assimilate (-ся o. s.); **~я́ция** *f* [7] assimilation.
ассисте́нт *m* [1], **~ка** *f* [5; *g/pl.*: -ток] assistant.
ассортиме́нт *m* [1] assortment.
ассоци|а́ция *f* [7] association; **~и́ровать** [7] (*im*)*pf.* associate.
АССР (Автоно́мная Сове́тская Социалисти́ческая Респу́блика *f*) Autonomous Soviet Socialist Republic.
а́стра *f* [5] aster.
астроно́м *m* [1] astronomer; **~и́ческий** [16] astronomic(al); **~ия** *f* [7] astronomy.
асфа́льт *m* [1] asphalt.
ата́к|а *f* [5] attack, charge; **~ова́ть** [7] (*im*)*pf.* attack, charge.
атама́н *m* [1] hetman.
ателье́ (-tɛ-) *n* [*indecl.*] studio, atelier.
атланти́ческий [16] Atlantic...
а́тлас[1] *m* [1] atlas.
атла́с[2] *m* [1] satin.
атле́т *m* [1] athlete; **~ика** *f* [5] athletics; **~и́ческий** [16] athletic.
атмосфе́р|а *f* [5] atmosphere; **~ный** [16] atmospheric.
а́том *m* [1] atom; **~ный** [14] atomic.

аттестáт *m* [1] certificate.
ауди|éнция *f* [7] audience; **~тóрия** *f* [7] lecture hall; audience.
аукциóн *m* [1] auction (by с P).
Афанáсий *m* [3] Athanasius.
Афганистáн *m* [1] Afghanistan.
афéр|а *f* [5] speculation, fraud, shady deal; **~íст** *m* [1], **~íстка** *f* [5; *g/pl.*: -ток] speculator, swindler.
Афíны *f/pl.* [5] Athens.
афíша *f* [5] playbill, poster.
афорíзм *m* [1] aphorism.
'Африка *f* [5] Africa.
африкáн|ец *m* [1; -нца], **~ка** *f* [5; *g/pl.*: -нок], **~ский** [16] African.
ах ah!; **~ать** [1], *once* ⟨**~нуть**⟩ [20] groan, lament; be amazed.
ацетилéн *m* [1] acetylene.
аэро|динáмика *f* [5] aerodynamics; **~дрóм** *m* [1] airdrome (*Brt.* aero-); **~навигáция** *f* [7] aerial navigation; **~плáн** *m* [1] airplane (*Brt.* aero-); **~пóрт** *m* [1] airport; **~пóчта** *f* [5] air mail; **~снíмок** *m* [1; -мка] aerial view; **~стáт** *m* [1] balloon; **~(фото)съёмка** *f* [5; *g/pl.*: -мок] aerial photography.

Б

б *s.* бы; б. *abbr.*: бы́вший.
бáб|а *f* [5] (country)woman; peasant's wife; *fig.* milksop; снéжная **~а** snowman; **~а-ягá** *f* [5] old witch, hag; **~ий** [18] womanish, effeminate; **~ье** лéто *n* Indian summer; **~ьи** скáзки *f/pl.* old wives' tales; **~ка** *f* [5; *g/pl.*: -бок] grandmother; повивáльная **~ка** midwife; *pl.* knucklebones; **~очка** *f* [5; *g/pl.*: -чек] butterfly; **~ушка** *f* [5; *g/pl.*: -шек] grandmother; granny; вот тебé **~ушка** и 'Юрьев день! a pretty business this!
багáж *m* [1*e.*] baggage, *Brt.* luggage; ручнóй ~ small baggage; сдать в ~ check one's baggage, *Brt.* register one's luggage; **~ный** [14]: **~ный** вагóн *m* baggage car, *Brt.* luggage van.
багров|éть [8], ⟨по-⟩ become purple, redden; **~ый** [14 *sh.*] purple.
бадья́ *f* [6] bucket, pail, tub.
бáза *f* [5] base, basis, foundation.
базáр *m* [1] market, bazaar; F revel, row; **~ный** [14] market...; *fig.* vulgar, cheap.
бáзис *m* [1] basis.
байдáрка *f* [5; *g/pl.*: -рок] canoe.
бáйка *f* [5] baize.
Байкáл *m* [1] (Lake) Baikal.
бак *m* [1] ⚓ forecastle; container, receptacle; tank; boiler.
бакал|éйный [14]: **~éйный** магазíн *m*, **~éйная** лáвка *f* grocery, grocer's store (*Brt.* shop); **~éйные** товáры *m/pl.* = **~éя**; **~éйщик** *m* [1] grocer; **~éя** *f* [6] groceries *pl.*
бáк|ен *m* [1] beacon; **~енбáрды** *f/pl.* [5], **~и** *m/pl.* [1; *gen.*: бак] whiskers.
баклажáн *m* [1] eggplant.
баклу́ш|а *f* [5]: бить **~и** F idle, dawdle, fool (away).
бактериóлог *m* [1] bacteriologist; **~íческий** [16] bacteriological; **~ия** *f* [7] bacteriology.
бактéрия *f* [7] bacterium.
бал *m* [1; на -у́; *pl. e.*] ball (at на П).
балагáн *m* [1] booth, show.
балагу́р F *m* [1] joker; **~ить** F [13] joke, crack jokes.
балалáйка *f* [5; *g/pl.*: балалáек] balalaika.
баламу́тить F [15], ⟨вз-⟩ trouble, stir up.
балáнс *m* [1] balance (*a.* ✝); торгóвый ~ balance of trade; **~íровать** [7] balance; **~овый** [14] balance...
балбéс *m* [1] simpleton, booby.
балдá *m/f* [5] blockhead, dolt.
балдахíн *m* [1] canopy.
бале|рíна *f* [5] (female) ballet dancer; **~т** *m* [1] ballet.
бáлка *f* [5; *g/pl.*: -лок] beam; hollow.
балкáнский [16] Balkan...
балкóн *m* [1] balcony.
балл *m* [1] grade, mark; point.
балáда *f* [5] ballad.
балáст *m* [1] ballast.
баллистíческий [16] ballistic.
баллóн *m* [1] balloon.
баллотíр|овать [7] ballot; **~óвка** *f* [5; *g/pl.*: -вок] vote, poll.
балóв|анный F [14 *sh.*] spoilt; **~áть** [7] (*a.* **-ся**) be naughty; trifle; ⟨из-⟩ spoil, coddle; **'~ень** *m* [4; -вня] darling, pet; **~ník** *m* [1 *e.*] urchin, brat; **~нíца** *f* [5] tomboy; **~ствó** *n* [9] naughtiness, spoiling, trifling.
балтíйский [16] Baltic...
бальзáм *m* [1] balm; **~íровать** [7], ⟨на-⟩ embalm.
балюстрáда *f* [5] balustrade.
бамбу́к *m* [1] bamboo.
банáль|ность *f* [8] banality; commonplace; **~ный** [14; -лен, льна] banal, trite.
банáн *m* [1] banana.
бáнда *f* [5] gang.
бандáж *m* [1*e.*] bandage; truss.
бандерóль *f* [8] (postal) wrapper.
бандíт *m* [1] bandit, gangster.
банк *m* [1] bank; **~а** *f* [5; *g/pl.*: -нок] jar; can, *Brt.* tin.
банкéт *m* [1] banquet.
банкíр *m* [1] banker.
банкнóт *m* [1], **~а** *f* [5] bank note.

банкрóт *m* [1] bankrupt; **~иться** [15], ⟨о-⟩ go bankrupt; **~ство** *n* [9] bankruptcy.
бант *m* [1] bow.
бáнщ|ик *m* [1], **~ица** *f* [5] attendant (at baths).
бáня *f* [6] bath(s).
бар *m* [1] saloon, (snack) bar.
барабáн *m* [1] drum; **~ить** [13], ⟨про-⟩ (beat the) drum; **~ный** [14]: **~ный** бой *m* beat of the drum; **~ная** перепóнка *f* eardrum; **~щик** *m* [1] drummer.
барáк *m* [1] barracks, hut.
барáн *m* [1] wether; ⚔ ram; **~ий** [18] wether...; согнýть в **~ий** рог bully, intimidate; **~ина** *f* [5] mutton; **~ка** *f* [5; *g/pl.*: -нок] (*kind of*) round cracknel.
барахлó *n* [9] junk, *Brt.* lumber.
барáхтаться F [1] flounce, flounder.
барáшек *m* [1; -шка] lamb(skin).
барбари́с *m* [1] barberry.
барельéф *m* [1] bas-relief.
Бáренцово [19]: ~ мóре *n* Barents Sea.
бáржа *f* [5] barge.
бáрий *m* [3] barium.
бáрин *m* [1; *pl.*: бáре *or* бáры, бар] nobleman; landlord; master; sir.
баритóн *m* [1] baritone.
бáрка ⚓ *f* [5; *g/pl.*: -рок] bark, barque; **∠с** ⚓ *m* [1] launch.
бaрóметр *m* [1] barometer.
баррикáда *f* [5] barricade.
барс *m* [1] panther.
бáр|ский [16] lordly; manorial; жить на **~скую** нóгу live in grand style; **~ство** *n* [9] the noble class; gentility; idleness; haughtiness.
барсýк *m* [1*e.*] badger.
бáрхат *m* [1] velvet; **~ный** [14] velvet(y).
бáрщина *f* [5] statute labo(u)r, corvée.
бáрын|я *f* [6] lady; mistress; madam, ma'am.
бары́ш *m* [1*e.*] profit, gain(s); **~ник** *m* [1] forestaller; horsedealer; **~ничать** [1] buy up, practise usury; **~ничество** *n* [9] forestallment.
бáрышня *f* [6; *g/pl.*: -шень] young lady; miss.
барьéр *m* [1] barrier.
бас ♪ *m* [1; *pl. e.*] bass.
баск *m* [1] Basque.
баскетбóл *m* [1] basketball.
басно|пи́сец *m* [1; -сца] fabulist; **~слóвный** [14; -вен, -вна] fabulous, incredible.
бáсня *f* [6; *g/pl.*: -сен] fable.
басóн *m* [1] galloon, lace.
бассéйн *m* [1] basin; region; ~ для плáвания swimming-pool.
бáста that will do; no more of this!
бастáрд *m* [1] bastard; hybrid.
бастиóн *m* [1] bastion.
бастовáть [7], ⟨за-⟩ (be ⟨go⟩ on) strike.
батальóн *m* [1] battalion; **~ный** [14] battalion...; **~ный** (командúр) battalion commander.
батарé|йка *f* [5; *g/pl.*: -рéек] flashlight (*Brt.* torch, pocket lamp); **~я** ⚡, ⚔ *f* [6; *g/pl.*: -éй] battery.
бати́ст *m* [1] cambric; **~овый** [14] of cambric.
батрáк *m* [1 *e.*] day labo(u)rer, farm hand.
бáтюшк|а *m* [5; *g/pl.*: -шек] father, papa; priest; (F *address*) dear friend, old boy; как вас по **~е**? what's your father's name?; **~и** (мои́)!, **~и** свéты! good gracious!, o(h) dear!
бахвáл P *m* [1] braggart; **~иться** [13] boast, brag; **~ьство** *n* [9] brag(ging), vaunt.
бахромá *f* [5] fringe.
бахчевóдство *n* [9] melon-growing.
баци́лла *f* [5] bacillus.
бáшенка *f* [5; *g/pl.*: -нок] turret.
башкá P *f* [5] head, noddle.
башлы́к *m* [1 *e.*] (*kind of*) hood.
башмáк *m* [1 *e.*] shoe; clog; drag; быть под **~óм** be henpecked.
бáшня *f* [6; *g/pl.*: -шен] tower; ⚔ turret, cupola.
баю́кать [1], ⟨у-⟩ lull.
баян *m* [1] (*kind of*) accordion.
бдéние *n* [12] wake(fulness); care.
бди́тель|ность *f* [8] vigilance; **~ный** [14; -лен, -льна] vigilant, watchful.
бег *m* [1; на бегý] run(ning); *pl.* [бегá, *etc. e.*] race(s); escape; барьéрный ~ hurdle race; эстафéтный ~ relay race; на **~ý** while running; *s.* бегóм.
бéганье *n* [12] running (*a. for. s. th., on business*); ~ на конькáх skating.
бéгать [1], ⟨по-⟩ run (around); F shun (*a.* p. от P); *fig.* run after (*a* p. за T); ~ взáпуски F race, vie in a run.
бегемóт *m* [1] hippopotamus.
беглéц *m* [1 *e.*] runaway.
бéгл|ость *f* [8] fluency, agility; cursoriness; **~ый** [14] fluent, agile; cursory; fugitive.
бег|овóй [14] race...; **~óм** in full career; **~отня́** F *f* [6] running about, bustle; **∠ство** *n* [9] flight (put to обрати́ть в B), escape, stampede.
бегýн *m* [1 *e.*] runner; trotter.
бед|á *f* [5; *pl.*: бéды] misfortune, disaster, mischief; что за **~á**? what does it matter?; не **~á** it doesn't matter; **~á** не великá there's no harm in that; в тóм-то и **~á** that's the trouble; на **~ý** F unluckily; **~á** как F awfully; **∠ненький** [16] poor, pitiable; **~нéть** [8], ⟨о-⟩ grow (become) poor; **∠ность** *f* [8] poverty; **~нотá** *f* [5] the poor *coll.*; **∠ный** [14; -ден, -днá, -дно] poor (in T); **~ня́га** F [5], **~ня́жка** *m/f* [5; *g/pl.*: -жек] poor fellow, wretch; **~ня́к** *m* [1 *e.*] poor man, pauper; small farmer.

бедро́ *n* [9; *pl.*: бёдра, -дер, -драм] thigh; hip; loin.
бе́дств|енный [14 *sh.*] disastrous, miserable; ~енное положе́ние *n* distress, emergency; **~ие** *n* [12] distress, disaster; **~овать** [7] suffer want, live in misery.
бежа́ть [4; бегу́, бежи́шь, бегу́т; беги́!; бегу́щий], ⟨по-⟩ (be) run (-ning, *etc.*); flee; avoid, shun (*a.* p. от P); ~ сломя́ го́лову F run for one's life *or* head over heels.
бе́жевый [14] beige.
бе́жен|ец *m* [1; -нца], **~ка** *f* [5; *g/pl.*: -нок] refugee.
без, **~о** (P) **1.** without, ...less; out of (*work*); **2.** less (*with quantities*); **3.** to (*with time*): ~о всего́ without anything; ~ вас ... *a.* ... while you were out.
безала́берный F [14; -рен, -рна] slovenly, disorderly.
безалкого́льный [14] nonalcoholic.
безапелляцио́нный [14; -о́нен, -о́нна] unappealable; peremptory.
безбе́дный [14; -ден, -дна] well off.
безбиле́тный [14]: ~ пассажи́р *m* [1] stowaway.
безбо́ж|ие *n* [12], **~ность** *f* [8] atheism, ungodliness; **~ник** *m* [1], **~ница** *f* [5] atheist; **~ный** [14; -жен, -жна] atheistic, godless, impious; unscrupulous; F awful.
безболе́зненный [14 *sh.*] painless.
безборо́дый [14] beardless.
безбоя́зненный [14 *sh.*] fearless.
безбра́ч|ие *n* [12] celibacy; **~ный** [14; -чен, -чна] unmarried.
безбре́жный [14; -жен, -жна] shoreless, boundless.
безве́рие *n* [12] unbelief.
безве́стный [14; -тен, -тна] unknown.
безве́тр|енный [14 *sh.*] **~ие** *n* [12] calm.
безви́нный [14; -и́нен, -и́нна] guiltless, innocent.
безвку́с|ие *n* [12], **~ица** *f* [5] tastelessness, bad taste; **~ный** [14; -сен, -сна] tasteless, insipid.
безвла́стие *n* [12] anarchy.
безво́дный [14; -ден, дна] arid.
безвозвра́тный [14; -тен, -тна] irretrievable.
безвозду́шный [14] void of air.
безвозме́здный [-mezn-) [14] gratuitous; without compensation.
безволо́сый [14] hairless, bald.
безво́льный [14; -лен, -льна] lacking willpower, weak-willed.
безвре́дный [14; -ден, -дна] harmless.
безвре́менный [14] premature.
безвы́ездный [14] (-jiznyj) permanent.
безвы́ходный [14; -ден, -дна] **1.** continual; **2.** desperate, hopeless.
безголо́вый [14] headless; stupid; forgetful.
безгра́мотн|ость *f* [8] illiteracy, ignorance; **~ый** [14; -тен, -тна] illiterate; faulty.
безграни́чный [14; -чен, -чна] boundless, unlimited.
безда́рный [14; -рен, -рна] untalented, dull; bungling.
безде́йств|ие *n* [12] inactivity; **~овать** [7] be inactive, idle.
безде́л|ица *f* [5], **~ка** *f* [5; *g/pl.*: -лок], **~у́шка** *f* [5; *g/pl.*: -шек] trifle; (k)nick-(k)nack.
безде́ль|е *n* [12] idleness; **~ник** *m* [1], **~ница** *f* [5] idler; good-for-nothing; **~ничать** [1] idle, lounge.
безде́нежье *n* [10] want of money.
безде́тный [14; -тен, -тна] childless.
безде́ятельный [14; -лен, -льна] inactive.
бе́здна *f* [5] abyss; *fig.* F lots (of).
бездо́мный [14; -мен, -мна] homeless.
бездо́нный [14; -до́нен, -до́нна] bottomless; *fig.* unfathomable.
бездоро́ж|ье *n* [12] impassability; **~ный** [14; -жен, -жна] impassable.
бездохо́дный [14; -ден, -дна] unprofitable.
безду́шный [14; -шен, -шна] soulless; heartless.
безжа́лостный (bizʒ-sn-) [14; -тен, -тна] ruthless.
безжи́зненный (bizʒ-) [14 *sh.*] lifeless; *fig.* dull.
беззабо́тный [14; -тен, -тна] careless; carefree.
беззаве́тный [14; -тен, -тна] unselfish; unreserved.
беззако́н|ие *n* [12] lawlessness; anarchy; **~ность** *f* [8] illegality; **~ный** [14; -о́нен, -о́нна] illegal; lawless.
беззасте́нчивый [14 *sh.*] shameless; impudent; unscrupulous.
беззащи́тный [14; -тен, -тна] defenseless; unprotected.
беззвёздный (-zn-) [14; -ден, -дна] starless.
беззву́чный [14; -чен, -чна] soundless; silent; mute.
безземе́льный [14] landless.
беззло́бный [14; -бен, -бна] good-natured.
беззу́бый [14] toothless.
безли́чный [14; -чен, -чна] impersonal.
безлю́дный [14; -ден, -дна] deserted, uninhabited.
безме́рный [14; -рен, -рна] immeasurable; immense.
безмо́зглый F [14] brainless, stupid.
безмо́лв|ие *n* [12] silence; **~ный** [14; -вен, -вна] silent.
безмяте́жный [14; -жен, -жна] quiet, calm; undisturbed.
безнадёжный [14; -жен, -жна] hopeless.
безнадзо́рный [14; -рен, -рна] uncared for.

безнака́занный [14 *sh.*] unpunished, with impunity.
безнали́чный [14]: ~ расчёт *m* ✝ cashless settlement.
безнра́вственный [14*sh.*] immoral.
безоби́дный [14; -ден, -дна] inoffensive; harmless.
безо́блачный [14; -чен, -чна] cloudless; serene.
безобра́з|не *n* [12] ugliness; deformity; mess; disgrace; ~ие! scandalous!, shocking!; **~ничать** [1] behave in an improper *or* mischievous manner; **~ный** [14; -зен, -зна] ugly; deformed; shameful, disgusting, abominable; indecent, mischievous.
безоговоро́чный [14; -чен, -чна] unconditional.
безопа́с|ность *f* [8] safety; security; Сове́т Ձности Security Council; **~ный** [14; -сен, -сна] safe, secure (from от P); ~ная бри́тва *f* safety razor.
безору́жный [14; -жен, -жна] unarmed; defenseless.
безостано́вочный [14; -чен, -чна] continuous; nonstop...
безотве́тный [14; -тен, -тна] without response; humble; dumb.
безотве́тственный [14 *sh.*] irresponsible.
безотлага́тельный [14; -лен, -льна] undelayable, urgent.
безотра́дный [14; -ден, -дна] desolate, wretched.
безотчётный [14; -тен, -тна] unaccountable; unconscious, involuntary.
безоши́бочный [14; -чен, -чна] faultless.
безрабо́т|ица *f* [5] unemployment; **~ный** [14] unemployed.
безразли́ч|ие *n* [12] (к Д) indifference (to, toward); **~ный** [14; -чен, -чна] indifferent; э́то мне ~но it is all the same to me.
безрассу́дный [14; -ден, -дна] thoughtless, reckless, rash.
безрезульта́тный [14; -тен, -тна] futile, vain.
безро́потный [14; -тен, -тна] humble, meek, submissive.
безрука́вка *f* [5; *g/pl.:* -вок] sleeveless jacket, waistcoat.
безуда́рный [14; -рен, -рна] unstressed.
безу́держный [14; -жен, -жна] unrestrained; impetuous.
безукори́зненный [14 *sh.*] irreproachable, unobjectionable.
безу́м|ец *m* [1; -мца] madman, lunatic; madcap; **~ие** *n* [12] madness, folly; **~ный** [14; -мен, -мна] mad, insane; nonsensical, absurd; rash.
безумо́лчный [14; -чен, -чна] incessant, uninterrupted.
безу́мство *n* [9] folly.
безупре́чный [14; -чен, -чна] blameless, irreproachable.
безусло́в|но certainly, surely; **~ный** [14; -вен, -вна] absolute, unconditional.
безуспе́шный [14; -шен, -шна] unsuccessful.
безуста́нный [14; -а́нен, -а́нна] incessant; indefatigable.
безуте́шный [14; -шен, -шна] disconsolate, inconsolable.
безуча́стный [14; -тен, -тна] indifferent.
безымя́нный [14] anonymous; ~ па́лец *m* ring finger.
безыску́сственный [14 *sh.*] unaffected, unsophisticated.
безысхо́дный [14; -ден, -дна] hopeless, desperate.
бейсбо́л *m* [14] baseball.
бека́с *m* [1] snipe.
белёсый [14] whitish.
беле́ть [8], ⟨по-⟩ grow *or* turn white; *impf.* (*a.* **-ся**) appear *or* show white.
белизна́ *f* [5] whiteness.
бели́ла *n/pl.* [9] ceruse.
бели́ть [13; белю́, бе́лишь; белённый] **1.** ⟨вы́-⟩ bleach; **2.** ⟨на-⟩ paint (white); **3.** ⟨по-⟩ whitewash.
бе́лка *f* [5; *g/pl.:* -лок] squirrel.
беллетри́стика *f* [5] fiction.
бело|боро́дый [14] white-bearded; **~бры́сый** F [14] flaxen-haired.
белова́тый [14 *sh.*] whitish.
бело|ви́к *m* [1 *e.*], **~во́й** [14]: ~вой экземпля́р *m* fair copy; **~воло́сый** [14] white-haired; **~гварде́ец** *m* [1; -е́йца] White Guard (*member of troops fighting against the Red Guards and the Red Army in the Civil War 1918-1920*); **~голо́вый** [14] white-headed.
бело́к *m* [1; -лка́] albumen; white [(*of egg or eye*).]
бело|кали́льный [14] white hot; **~кро́вие** *n* [12] leukemia; **~ку́рый** [14 *sh.*] blond, fair; **~ру́с** *m* [1], **~ру́ска** *f* [5; *g/pl.*: -сок] Byelorussian, White Russian; **Ձру́ссия** *f* [7] Byelorussia, White Russia; **~ру́сский** [16] Byelorussian; **~сне́жный** [14; -жен, -жна] snow-white; **~шве́йка** *f* [5; *g/pl.*: -шве́ек] seamstress.
белу́га *f* [5] sturgeon.
бе́л|ый [14; бел, -á, -о] white; light, fair; secular; ~ый свет *m* (wide) world; ~ые стихи́ *m/pl.* blank verse; средь ~а дня F in broad day-light.
бель|ги́ец *m* [1; -ги́йца], **~ги́йка** *f* [5; *g/pl.*: -ги́ек], **~ги́йский** [16] Belgian; 'Ձгия *f* [7] Belgium.
бельё *n* [12] linen; ни́жнее ~ underwear.
бельм|о́ ✗ *n* [9; *pl.:* бе́льма, бельм] wall-eye; *pl.* goggle-eyes; вы́пучить ~а F stare; он у меня́ как ~о́ на глазу́ he is an eyesore to me.
бельэта́ж *m* [1] *thea.* dress circle; second (*Brt.* first) floor.

бемо́ль ♪ *m* [4] flat.
бенефи́с *m* [1] benefit(-night).
бензи́н *m* [1] benzine; gasoline, *Brt.* petrol.
бензо|ба́к *m* [1] gasoline *or* petrol tank; **~коло́нка** (*a.* ~запра́вочная коло́нка) *f* [5; *g/pl.:* -нок] filling station; **~л** *m* [1] benzol.
бенуа́р *m* [1] *thea.* parterre box.
бе́рег *m* [1; на -гу́; *pl.*: -га́, *etc. e.*] bank, shore, coast; land; вы́йти (вы́ступить) из ~о́в overflow the banks; приста́ть к ~у land; **~ово́й** [14] coast(al), shore... ~ово́е судохо́дство *n* coasting.
бережли́вый [14 *sh.*] economical.
бе́режный [14; -жен, -жна] cautious, careful.
берёза *f* [5] birch.
берёзовый [14] birch(en).
бере́йтор *m* [1] horse-breaker.
бере́мен|ная [14] pregnant; **~ность** *f* [8] pregnancy.
бере́т *m* [1] cap, beret.
бере́чь [26 г/ж: берегу́, бережёшь] **1.** ⟨по-⟩ guard, watch (over); **2.** ⟨по-, с-⟩ spare, save, take care of; **3.** ⟨с-⟩ [сбережённый] keep; preserve; **-ся** take care (of o. s.); берегѝсь! take care!, look out!, attention!
Бе́рингов [19]: ~ проли́в *m* Bering Strait; ~о мо́ре *n* Bering Sea.
берло́га *f* [5] bear's lair; den.
берцо́|вый [14]: ~вая кость *f* shinbone.
бес *m* [1] demon.
бесе́д|а *f* [5] conversation, talk; conference, discussion; **~ка** *f* [5; *g/pl.*: -док] arbo(u)r, summerhouse; **~овать** [7] converse.
бесёнок *m* [2; -нка; *pl.*: бесеня́та] imp.
беси́ть F [15], ⟨вз-⟩ [взбешённый] enrage, madden; **-ся** (fly into a) rage; romp.
бесконе́ч|ность *f* [8] infinity; до ~ности endlessly; **~ный** [14; -чен, -чна] endless, infinite; unlimited, boundless; eternal; ~но ма́лый 𝔄 infinitesimal.
бескоры́ст|ие *n* [12] unselfishness; **~ный** [14; -тен, -тна] disinterested.
бескро́в|ие *n* [12] an(a)emia; **~ный** [14; -вен, -вна] an(a)emic; bloodless.
бесновá|тый [14] possessed, demoniac; **~ться** [7] rage, rave.
бeсо́вщина *f* [5] devilry.
беспа́мят|ность *f* [8] forgetfulness; **~ный** [14; -тен, -тна] forgetful; unconscious; **~ство** *n* [9] unconsciousness, swoon.
беспарти́йный [14] (*pol.*) independent; non-party (man).
беспере6о́йный [14; -бо́ен, -бо́йна] uninterrupted, smooth.
беспереме́нный [14] invariable; unalterable.
беспереса́дочный [14] through...
беспе́ч|ность *f* [8] carelessness; **~ный** [14; -чен, -чна] careless.
беспла́т|ный [14; -тен, -тна] free (of charge), gratuitous; ~но gratis.
беспло́д|ие *n* [12] sterility; **~ный** [14; -ден, -дна] sterile; fruitless, vain.
бесповоро́тный [14; -тен, -тна] unalterable, irrevocable.
бесподо́бный [14; -бен, -бна] incomparable, matchless.
беспозвоно́чный [14] invertebrate.
беспок|о́ить [13], ⟨(п)о-⟩ upset, worry; disturb, bother, trouble; **-ся** worry, be anxious (about о П); **~о́йный** [14; -ко́ен, -ко́йна] restless; uneasy; **~о́йство** *n* [9] unrest; trouble; anxiety; прости́те за ~о́йство sorry to (have) trouble(d) you.
бесполе́зный [14; -зен, -зна] useless.
беспо́мощный [14; -щен, -щна] helpless.
беспоро́чный [14; -чен, -чна] blameless, irreproachable.
беспоря́до|к *m* [1; -дка] disorder, mess; *pl.* disorders; **~чный** [14; -чен, -чна] disorderly, incoherent.
беспоса́дочный [14]: ~ перелёт nonstop flight.
беспо́шлинный [14] duty-free.
беспоща́дный [14; -ден, -дна] pitiless, ruthless, relentless.
беспреде́льный [14; -лен, -льна] boundless, infinite, unlimited.
беспрекосло́вный [14; -вен, -вна] absolute, unquestioning, implicit.
беспрепя́тственный [14 *sh.*] unhampered, unhindered.
беспреры́вный [14; -вен, -вна] uninterrupted, continuous.
беспреста́нный [14; -а́нен, -а́нна] incessant, continual.
беспри́быльный [14; -лен, -льна] unprofitable.
беспризо́рн|ик *m* [1] waif, stray; **~ый** [14; -рен, -рна] homeless, uncared-for.
бесприме́рный [14; -рен, -рна] unprecedented, unparalleled.
беспринци́пный [14; -пен, -пна] unprincipled, unscrupulous.
беспристра́ст|ие *n* [12] impartiality; **~ный** (-sn-) [14; -тен, -тна] impartial, unprejudiced, unbias(s)ed.
беспричи́нный [14; -и́нен, -и́нна] groundless; unfounded.
бесприю́тный [14; -тен, -тна] homeless.
беспробу́дный [14; -ден, -дна] deep (*about sleep*); unrestrained.
беспро́волочный [14] wireless.
беспросве́тный [14; -тен, -тна] pitch-dark; *fig.* hopeless.
беспроце́нтный [14] without charge for interest.
беспу́тный [14; -тен, -тна] dissolute.

бессвя́зный [14; -зен, -зна] incoherent, rambling.
бессерде́чный [14; -чен, -чна] heartless, unfeeling, callous.
бесси́|лие *n* [12] debility; impotence; **~льный** [14; -лен, -льна] weak, powerless, impotent.
бессла́вный [14; -вен, -вна] infamous, disgraceful, inglorious.
бессле́дный [14; -ден, -дна] without leaving a trace, entire.
бесслове́сный [14; -сен, -сна] speechless, dumb; taciturn.
бессме́рт|ие *n* [12] immortality; **~ный** [14; -тен, -тна] immortal.
бессмы́сл|енный [14 *sh.*] senseless; dull; **~ица** *f* [5] nonsense.
бессо́вестный [14; -тен, -тна] unscrupulous.
бессодержа́тельный [14; -лен, -льна] empty, insipid, dull.
бессозна́тельный [14; -лен, -льна] unconscious.
бессо́нн|ица *f* [5] insomnia; **~ый** [14] sleepless.
бесспо́рный [14; -рен, -рна] indisputable; doubtless, certain.
бессро́чный [14; -чен, -чна] termless, not limited in time.
бесстра́ст|ие *n* [12] dispassionateness, calmness; **~ный** [14; -тен, -тна] dispassionate, composed.
бесстра́ш|ие *n* [12] fearlessness; **~ный** [14; -шен, -шна] fearless, intrepid.
бессты́д|ный [14; -ден, -дна] shameless, impudent; indecent; **~ство** *n* [9] impudence, insolence.
бессчётный [14] innumerable.
бесталанный [14; -а́нен, -а́нна] 1. untalented; 2. ill-fated.
бе́стия *f* [7] brute, beast; artful dodger.
бестолко́в|щина *f* [5] nonsense; mess; confusion; **~ый** [14 *sh.*] absurd, confused.
бестре́петный [14; -тен, -тна] intrepid, undaunted.
бесхи́тростный [14; -тен, -тна] artless, naïve, ingenuous, unsophisticated.
бесхозя́йствен|ность *f* [8] mismanagement; **~ный** [14] thriftless.
бесцве́тный [14; -тен, -тна] colo(u)rless.
бесце́льный [14; -лен, -льна] aimless.
бесце́н|ный [14; -е́нен, -е́нна] invaluable, priceless; **~ок**: за **~ок** F for a song *or* a trifling sum.
бесцеремо́нный [14; -о́нен, -о́нна] unceremonious, bold, inconsiderate.
бесчелове́ч|ие *n* [12], **~ность** *f* [8] inhumanity; **~ный** [14; -чен, -чна] inhuman, cruel.
бесче́ст|ный [14; -тен, -тна] dishonest; dishono(u)rable; **~ье** *n* [10] dishono(u)r, disgrace.
бесчи́нство *n* [9] excess, outrage; **~вать** [7] behave outrageously.
бесчи́сленный [14 *sh.*] innumerable, countless.
бесчу́вств|енный (bi'ʃtʃustv-) [14 *sh.*] insensible, callous, hard-hearted; **~ие** *n* [12] insensibility; unconsciousness, swoon.
бесшаба́шный F [14; -шен, -шна] reckless, careless; wanton.
бесшу́мный [14; -мен, -мна] noiseless, quiet.
бето́н *m* [1] concrete; **~и́ровать** [7], ⟨за-⟩ concrete; **~ный** [14] concrete...
бечёвка *f* [5; *g/pl.*: -вок] string.
бе́шен|ство *n* [9] 1. ⚕ hydrophobia; 2. fury, rage; **~ый** [14] 1. rabid; 2. furious, frantic, wild; 3. enormous.
библе́йский [16] Biblical; Bible...
библиографи́ческий [16] bibliographic(al).
библиоте́|ка *f* [5] library; **~карь** *m* [4] librarian; **~чный** [14] library...
би́блия *f* [7] Bible.
бив(у)а́к *m* [1] bivouac; стоя́ть **~ом** *or* на **~ах** bivouac.
би́вень *m* [4; -вня] tusk.
бидо́н *m* [1] can.
бие́ние *n* [12] beat, throb.
бизо́н *m* [1] bison.
биле́т *m* [1] ticket; card; note, bill; обра́тный ~ round-trip ticket, *Brt.* return-ticket.
биллио́н *m* [1] billion, *Brt.* milliard.
билья́рд *m* [1] billiards.
бино́кль *m* [4] binocular(s); glass; театра́льный ~ opera glasses; полево́й ~ field glass.
бинт *m* [1 *e.*] bandage; **~ова́ть** [7], ⟨за-⟩ bandage, dress.
био́граф *m* [1] biographer; **~и́ческий** [16] biographic(al); **~ия** *f* [7] biography.
био́лог *m* [1] biologist; **~и́ческий** [16] biological; **~ия** *f* [7] biology.
биохи́мия *f* [7] biochemistry.
бипла́н *m* [1] biplane.
би́ржа *f* [5] (stock) exchange; ~ труда́ labor registry office, *Brt.* labour exchange.
бирже|ви́к *m* [1 *e.*], stockbroker; **~во́й** [14]: **~во́й** ма́клер = **~ви́к**.
Би́рм|а *f* [5] Burma; **2а́нец** *m* [1; -нца], **2а́нка** *f* [5; *g/pl.*: -нок], **2а́нский** [16] Burmese.
бирюза́ *f* [5] turquoise.
бис encore!
би́сер *m* [1] *coll.* (glass) beads *pl.*
бискви́т *m* [1] sponge cake.
би́тва *f* [5] battle.
бит|ко́м *s.* наби́тый; **~о́к** *m* [1; -тка́] (mince)meat ball.
бить [бью, бьёшь; бей!; би́тый] 1. ⟨по-⟩ beat; churn (*butter*); 2. ⟨про-⟩ [про́бил, -би́ла, про́било] strike (*clock*); 3. ⟨раз-⟩ [разобью́, -бьёшь] break, smash; 4. ⟨у-⟩ shoot, kill; trump (*card*); 5. *no pf.* spout; ~ в глаза́ strike the eye; ~ в наба́т,

~ трево́гу sound the alarm (bell) (отбо́й the retreat); ~ ключо́м 1. bubble; 2. boil over; 3. sparkle; 4. abound in vitality; про́бил его́ час his hour has struck; би́тый час *m* one solid hour; **-ся** fight; beat (*heart*); drudge, toil; -ся голово́й о(б) сте́ну dash against the rock; -ся об закла́д bet; он бьётся как ры́ба об лёд he exerts himself in vain.

бифште́кс *m* [1] (beef)steak.

бич *m* [1 *e.*] whip; *fig.* scourge; **~е-ва́ть** [7] lash, scourge.

благови́дный [14; -ден, дна] attractive; *fig.* seemly.

благово|ле́ние *n* [12] benevolence, goodwill; **~ли́ть** [13] wish (a. p. к Д) well, be kind (to a. p.); deign.

благово́н|ие *n* [12] fragrance; **~ный** [14] fragrant.

благовоспи́танный [14 *sh.*] well--bred.

благогого|ве́йный [14; -ве́ен, -ве́йна] devout, reverent, respectful; **~ве́ние** *n* [12] awe (of), reverence, respect (for) (пе́ред Т); **~ве́ть** [8] (пе́ред Т) worship, venerate.

благодар|и́ть [13], ‹по-, от-› (В/за В) thank (a p. for s. th.); **∠ность** *f* [8] gratitude; thanks; не сто́ит ∠ности you are welcome, *Brt.* don't mention it; **∠ный** [14; -рен, -рна] grateful, thankful (to a p. for s. th. Д/за В); **~я́** (Д) thanks *or* owing to.

благода́т|ный [14]; -тен, -тна] blessed; **~ь** *f* [8] blessing.

благоде́тель *m* [4] benefactor; **~ница** *f* [5] benefactress; **~ный** [14; -лен, -льна] beneficent; beneficial.

благодея́ние *n* [12] benefit.

благоду́ш|ие *n* [12] good nature, kindness; **~ный** [14; -шен, -шна] kindhearted, benign.

благожела́тель|ность *f* [8] benevolence; **~ный** [14; -лен, -льна] benevolent.

благозву́ч|ие *n* [12], **~ность** *f* [8] euphony, sonority; **~ный** [14; -чен, -чна] sonorous, harmonious.

благонадёжный [14; -жен,-жна] reliable, trustworthy.

благонаме́ренный [14 *sh.*] well--meaning, well-meant.

благонра́вный [14; -вен, -вна] well-mannered, modest.

благообра́зный [14; -зен, -зна] attractive, comely, sightly.

благополу́ч|ие *n* [12] well-being, prosperity, happiness; **~ный** [14; -чен, -чна] happy; safe.

благоприя́т|ный [14; -тен, -тна] favo(u)rable, propitious; **~ствовать** [7] (Д) favo(u)r, promote.

благоразу́м|ие *n* [12] prudence, discretion; **~ный** [14; -мен, -мна] prudent, judicious.

благоро́д|ный [14; -ден, -дна] noble; high-minded, distinguished; lofty; precious; **~ство** *n* [9] nobility.

благосклóнный [14; -óнен, -óнна] favo(u)rable, well-disposed (to [-ward(s)] a p. к Д).

благосло|ве́ние *n* [12] benediction, blessing; **~вля́ть** [28], ‹**~ви́ть**› [14 *e.*; -влю́, -ви́шь] bless.

благосостоя́ние *n* [12] prosperity.

благотвори́тельный [14] beneficent, charitable.

благотво́рный [14; -рен, -рна] wholesome, salutary.

благоустро́енный [14 *sh.*] well--furnished, comfortable.

благоуха́|ние *n* [12] fragrance, odo(u)r; **~ть** [1] scent, exhale fragrance.

благочести́вый [14 *sh.*] pious.

блаже́н|ный [14 *sh.*] blissful; **~ство** *n* [9] bliss; **~ствовать** [7] enjoy felicity.

блаж|и́ть P [16 *e.*; -жу́, -жи́шь] be capricious, cranky; **~но́й** P [14] capricious; preposterous; **~ь** F *f* [8] caprice, whim, freak, fancy; folly.

бланк *m* [1] form; letterhead.

блат P *m* [1] profitable connections; по ∠у on the quiet, illicitly, through good connections; **~но́й** P [14] trickster, rogue; **~но́й язы́к** *m* thieves' slang, cant.

бледне́ть [8], ‹по-› turn pale.

бледно|ва́тый [14 *sh.*] palish; **~ли́цый** [14 *sh.*] with a pale face.

бле́д|ность *f* [8] pallor; **~ный** [14; -ден, -дна́, -о] pale.

блёк|лый [14] faded, withered; **~нуть** [21], ‹по-› fade, wither.

блеск *m* [1] luster, shine, brilliance, glitter, splendo(u)r.

блест|е́ть [11; *a.* бле́щешь], *once* ‹блесну́ть› [20] shine, glitter; flash; не всё то зо́лото, что ~и́т all is not gold that glitters; **~ки** ('bʲlɔski) *f/pl.* [5; *gen.*: -ток] spangle; **~я́щий** [17 *sh.*] brilliant.

блеф *m* [1] bluff.

бле́ять [27], ‹за-› bleat.

ближ|а́йший [17] (*s.* бли́зкий) the nearest, next; **∠е** nearer; **∠ний** [15] near(-by); *su.* fellow creature.

близ (P) near, close; **∠иться** [15; *3rd p. only*], ‹при-› approach (a p. к Д); **∠кий** [16; -зок, -зка́, -о; *comp.*: бли́же], (к Д) near, close; ∠кие *pl.* folk(s), one's family, relatives; ∠ко от (P) close to, not far from; **~лежа́щий** [17] nearby, neighbo(u)ring.

близне́ц *m* [1 *e.*] twin.

близору́кий [16 *sh.*] short-sighted.

бли́зость *f* [8] nearness, proximity; intimacy.

блин *m* [1 *e.*] pancake.

блиста́тельный [14; -лен, -льна] brilliant, splendid, magnificent.

блиста́ть [1] shine, beam.

блок *m* [1] 1. bloc, coalition; 2. pulley.
блок|áда *f* [5] blockade; **~и́ровать** [7] (*im*)*pf*. blockade, block up.
блокнóт *m* [1] notebook.
блонди́н *m* [1] blond; **~ка** *f* [5; *g*/*pl*.: -нок] blonde.
блохá *f* [5; *nom*/*pl*. *st*.: блóхи] flea.
блуд *m* [1] licentiousness; **~и́ть** P 1. [15] roam, wander; 2. [15 *e*.; -жý, -ди́шь] debauch; **~ли́вый** [14 F *sh*.], **~ный** [14] wanton; **~ный сын** *m* prodigal son.
блуждá|ть [1], ⟨про-⟩ roam, wander; **~ющий огонёк** *m* will-o'--the-wisp; **~ющая пóчка** *f* floating kidney.
блýз|а *f* [5] blouse, smock; **~ка** *f* [5; *g*/*pl*.: -зок] (ladies') blouse.
блю́дечко *n* [9; *g*/*pl*.: -чек] saucer.
блю́до *n* [9] dish; course.
блю́дце *n* [11; *g*/*pl*.: -дец] saucer.
блюсти́ [25], ⟨со-⟩ observe, preserve, maintain; watch; **~тель** *m* [4], **~тельница** *f* [5] keeper, guardian.
бля́ха *f* [5] metal plate, badge.
боá [*indecl*.] 1. *m* *zo*. boa; 2. *n* boa (*wrap*).
боб *m* [1 *e*.] bean; haricot; остáться на **~áх** have one's trouble for nothing.
бобёр *m* [1; -брá] beaver (*fur*).
боби́на *f* [5] bobbin, spool, reel.
бобóв|ый [14]: **~ые растéния** *n*/*pl*. legumes.
бобр *m* [1 *e*.], **~óвый** [14] beaver.
бóбслей *m* [3] bobsleigh.
бобы́ль *m* [4 *e*.] landless peasant; *fig*. solitary man, (old) bachelor.
бог (bɔx) *m* [1; *voc*.: бóже; *from g*/*pl*. *e*.] God; god, idol; ~ весть, ~ (егó) знáет F God knows; бóже (мой)! oh God!, good gracious!; дай ~ God grant; I (let's) hope (so); ей **~у**! by a God!; рáди **~а** for God's (goodness') sake; сохрани́ (не дай, избáви, упаси́) ~ (бóже) God forbid!
богат|éть [8] ⟨раз-⟩ grow (become) rich; **~ство** *n* [9] wealth; **~ый** [14 *sh*.; *comp*.: богáче] rich (in T), wealthy.
богаты́рь *m* [4 *e*.] hero; athlete.
богáч *m* [1 *e*.] rich man.
Богéм|ия *f* [7] Bohemia; **2ский** [16] Bohemian.
боги́ня *f* [6] goddess.
богомáтерь *f* [8] the Blessed Virgin.
бого|мóлец *m* [1; -льца], **~мóлка** *f* [5; *g*/*pl*.: -лок] devotee; pilgrim; **~мóлье** *n* [10] prayer; pilgrimage.
богоотстýпник *m* [1] atheist.
богорóдица *f* [5] the Blessed Virgin, Our Lady.
богослóв *m* [1] theologian; **~ие** *n* [12] theology, divinity; **~ский** [16] theological.
богослужéние *n* [12] divine service.
боготвори́ть [13] adore, deify.
богохýль|ник *m* [1] blasphemer; **~ничать** [1] blaspheme; **~ный** [14] blasphemous; **~ство** *n* [9] blasphemy; **~ствовать** [7] = богохýльничать.
бодáть [1], ⟨за-⟩, *once* ⟨боднýть⟩ [20] (*a*. **~ся**) butt, gore (*a*. *o*.*a*.).
бóдр|ость *f* [8] vivacity, sprightliness; **~ствовать** [20] be awake; **~ый** [14; бодр, -á, -о] awake; sprightly, vivacious, brisk; vigorous.
боеви́к *m* [1 *e*.] hit, draw.
боевóй [14] battle..., fighting, war-..., military; live (*shell*, *etc*.); pugnacious, militant; ~ пáрень *m* dashing fellow; ~ поря́док *m* battle array.
бое|припáсы *m*/*pl*. [1] ammunition; **~спосóбный** [14; -бен, -бна] effective.
боéц *m* [1; бойцá] soldier, fighter.
бóже *s*. бог; **~ский** [16] godlike, divine; **~ственный** [14 *sh*.] divine; **~ствó** *n* [9] deity, divinity.
бóжий [18] God's, divine.
божи́ться [16 *e*.; -жýсь, -жи́шься], ⟨по-⟩ swear.
бой *m* [3; бóя, в бою́; *pl*.: бои́, боёв, *etc*. *e*.] battle, combat, fight; брать (взять) бóем *or* с бóю take by assault (storm); рукопáшный ~ close fight; ~ часóв the striking of a clock; **~кий** [16; бóек, бойкá, бóйко; *comp*.: бóйч(é)е] brisk, lively, busy; smart, quick, sharp; voluble, glib; **~кость** *f* [8] liveliness, smartness.
бойкоти́ровать [7] (*im*)*pf*. boycott.
бойни́ца *f* [5] loophole, embrasure.
бóйня *f* [6; *g*/*pl*.: бóен] slaughterhouse; *fig*. massacre, slaughter.
бок *m* [1; на бокý; *pl*.: бокá, *etc*. *e*.] side; нá ~, **~ом** sideways; ~ ó ~ side by side; пóд **~ом** F close by; барáний ~ leg of mutton.
бокáл *m* [1] wineglass.
боковóй [14] lateral.
бокс *m* [1] boxing; **~ёр** *m* [1] boxer; **~и́ровать** [7] box.
болвáн *m* [1] dolt, blockhead.
болгáр|ин *m* [4; *pl*.: -ры, -р] Bulgarian; **2ия** *f* [7] Bulgaria; **~ка** *f* [5; *g*/*pl*.: -рок], **~ский** [16] Bulgarian.
бóлее (*s*. бóльше) more (than P); ~ высóкий higher; ~ и́ли мéнее more or less; не ~ at (the) most.
болéзненный [14 *sh*.] sickly, ailing, morbid; painful.
болéзнь *f* [8] sickness (on the score of по Д), illness; disease; (*mental*) disorder; sick (*leave* ... по Д).
болéльщик *m* [1] *sport*: fan.
болéть 1. [8] be sick, ill (with T); be anxious (for, about за В о П), apprehensive; 2. [9; *3rd p*. *only*] hurt, ache; у меня́ боли́т головá (зуб, гóрло) I have a headache (a toothache, a sore throat).
болóт|истый [14 *sh*.] boggy

swampy; ~ный [14] bog..., swamp-...; ~о *n* [9] bog, swamp.
болт *m* [1 *e.*] bolt.
болтáть [1] **1.** ⟨вз-⟩ shake up; **2.** (-ся) dangle; **3.** F ⟨по-⟩ [20] chat (-ter); ~ся F loaf *or* lounge about.
болтли́вый [14 *sh.*] talkative.
болтовня́ F *f* [6] idle talk, gossip.
болту́н *m* [1; -нá], ~ья *f* [6] babbler, chatterbox.
боль *f* [8] pain, ache.
больни́|ца *f* [5] hospital; ~чный [14] hospital...; ~чная кáсса *f* sick-fund; ~чный листóк *m* medical certificate.
бóльн|о painful(ly); P very; мне ~о it hurts me; глазáм ~о my eyes smart; ~óй [14; бóлен, больнá] sick, ill (*a. su.*), sore; patient, invalid; *fig.* delicate, burning; tender.
бóльше bigger; more; ~ всегó most of all; above all; ~ не ... no more *or* longer; как мóжно ~ as much as possible; ~ви́зм *m* [1] Bolshevism; ~ви́к *m* [1 *e.*], ~ви́чка *f* [5; *g/pl.:* -чек] Bolshevik; ~ви́стский (-'ɣisskij) [16] Bolshevist(ic).
бóльш|ий [17] bigger, greater; ~инствó *n* [9] majority; most; ~óй [16] big, large, great; grownup.
бóмб|а *f* [5] bomb; ~ардировáть [7] bomb, shell; bombard (*a. fig.*); ~ардирóвка *f* [5; *g/pl.:* -вок] bombardment, bombing; ~ардирóвщик *m* [1] bomber; ~ёжка F *f* [5; *g/pl.:* -жек] = ~ардирóвка; ~и́ть [14 *e.*; -блю́, -би́шь; (раз-) бомблённый], ⟨раз-⟩ bomb.
бомбо|вóз *m* [1] = бомбардирóвщик; ~убéжище *n* [11] air-raid shelter.
бонбоньéрка *f* [5; *g/pl.:* -рок] bonbonnière, box for candies.
бóндáрь *m* [4 & 4 *e.*; *pl. a.* -ря́, *etc. e.*] cooper.
бор *m* [1] **1.** [в бору́] pine wood *or* forest; **2.** ⚗ boron.
бордó *n* [*indecl.*] claret.
бордю́р *m* [1] border, trimming.
борéц *m* [1; -рцá] fighter; wrestler; *fig.* champion, partisan.
бор|зóй [14] swift, fleet (*dog*); ~зáя (собáка) *f* borzoi, greyhound.
бóрзый [14; борз, -á, -о] brisk, swift.
Бори́с *m* [1] Boris (*masc. name*).
бормотáть [3], ⟨про-⟩ murmur, mutter.
бóров *m* [1; *from g/pl. e.*] boar.
бородá *f* [5; *ac/sg.:* бóроду; *pl.:* бóроды, борóд, -дáм] beard.
бородáвка *f* [5; *g/pl.:* -вок] wart.
бородá|тый [14 *sh.*] bearded; ~ч *m* [1 *e.*] bearded man.
борóдка *f* [5; *g/pl.:* -док] small beard; bit (*key*).
борозд|á *f* [5; *pl.:* бóрозды, борóзд -дáм] furrow; ~и́ть [15 *e.*; -зжу́ -зди́шь], ⟨вз-⟩ furrow.
боро|нá *f* [5; *ac/sg.:* бóрону; *pl.:* бóроны, борóн, -нáм] harrow; ~ни́ть [13], ~новáть [7], ⟨вз-⟩ harrow.
борóться [17; боря́сь] fight, struggle (for за В); wrestle.
борт *m* [1; на -ту́; *nom/pl.:* -тá] **1.** braid, lace; border; **2.** board; на ~у́ су́дна on board a ship; брóсить зá ~ throw overboard; человéк за ~ом! man overboard!; ~овóй [14] board...
борщ *m* [1 *e.*] borsch(t), red-beet soup.
Бóря *m* [6] *dim. of* Бори́с.
босикóм barefoot.
босóй [14; бос, -á, -о] barefooted; на бóсу́ нóгу = босикóм.
босонóгий [16] = босóй.
Босфóр *m* [1] Bosporus.
бося́к *m* [1 *e.*] tramp, vagabond.
ботáни|к *m* [1] botanist; ~ка *f* [5] botany; ~ческий [16] botanic(al).
боти́нок *m* [1; *g/pl.:* -нок] shoe, *Brt.* (lace-)boot.
ботфóрты *m/pl.* [1] jackboots.
бóты *m/pl.* [1; *g/pl. a.* бот] overshoes.
бóцман *m* [1] boatswain.
бочáр *m* [1 *e.*] cooper.
бóчка *f* [5; *g/pl.:* -чек] cask, tun.
бочкóм sideway(s), sidewise.
бочóно|к *m* [1; -нка] (small) barrel; ~чный [14]: ~чное пи́во *n* draught beer.
боязли́вый [14 *sh.*] timid, fearful.
боя́знь *f* [8] fear, dread.
боя́р|ин *m* [4; *pl.:* -ре, -р], ~ыня *f* [6] boyar(d) (*member of old nobility in Russia*).
боя́рышник *m* [1] hawthorn.
боя́ться [бою́сь, бои́шься; бóйся, бóйтесь!], ⟨по-⟩ be afraid (of P), fear; бою́сь сказáть I don't know exactly, I'm not quite sure.
брáвый [14] brave, courageous.
бразды́ *f/pl.* [5] *fig.* reins.
брази́|лец [1; -льца] Brazilian; **2**-лия *f* [7] Brazil; ~льский [16], ~льянка *f* [5; *g/pl.:* -нок] Brazilian.
брак *m* [1] **1.** marriage; matrimony; **2.** (*no pl.*) defective articles, spoilage.
браковáть [7], ⟨за-⟩ scrap, reject.
бракосочетáние *n* [12] wedding.
брани́ть [13], ⟨по-, вы́-⟩ scold, rebuke, abuse; -ся quarrel, wrangle; swear, curse.
брáнный [14] **1.** abusive; **2.** battle-..., military.
бранчли́вый [14 *sh.*] quarrelsome.
брань *f* [8] **1.** abuse, quarrel([l]ing); invective; **2.** battle, fight.
браслéт *m* [1] bracelet.
брат *m* [1; *pl.:* брáтья, -тьев, -тьям] brother; (*address:*) old boy!; ваш ~ F of your kind; наш ~ F (such as) we.
братá|ние *n* [12] fraternization; ~ться [1], ⟨по-⟩ fraternize.
брáтец *m* [1; -тца] dear brother; (*address:*) old fellow!, dear friend!

бра́тия *f* [7] fraternity; friary; нищая ~ beggary.
брато|уби́йство *n* [9], **~уби́йца** *m/f* [5] fratricide.
бра́т|ский [16; *adv.*: (по-)бра́тски] brotherly, fraternal; **~ство** *n* [9] brotherhood, fraternity, fellowship.
брать [беру́, -рёшь; брал, -á, -o; '...бранный], ⟨взять⟩ [возьму́, -мёшь; взял, -á, -o; взя́тый (взят, -á, -o)] take; ~ напрока́т hire; ~ приме́р (с P) take (a p.) for a model; ~ верх над (T) be victorious over, conquer; ~ на пору́ки be (-come) bail (for B); ~ сло́во take (have) the floor; ~ (с P) сло́во make (s. o.) promise; ~ (свои́ слова́) обра́тно withdraw (one's words); ~ себя́ в ру́ки *fig.* collect o.s., pull o.s. together; ~ на себя́ assume; ~ за пра́вило make it a rule; его́ взяла́ охо́та писа́ть he took a fancy to writing; он взял да сказа́л F he said it without further consideration; возьми́те напра́во! turn (to the) right!; *s. a.* взима́ть; **-ся** [бра́лся, -ла́сь, -ло́сь], ⟨взя́ться⟩ [взя́лся, -ла́сь, взя́ло́сь, взя́ли́сь] (за B) undertake; set about; take hold of seize; ~ за́ руки join hands; ~ за кни́гу (рабо́ту) set about *or* start reading a book (working); отку́да э́то берётся? where does that come from?; отку́да у него́ де́ньги беру́тся? wherever does he get his money from?; отку́да ни возьми́сь all of a sudden.
бра́чный [14] matrimonial, conjugal.
брев|е́нчатый [14] log...; **~но́** *n* [9; *pl.*: брёвна, -вен, -внам] log; beam.
бред *m* [1] delirium; **∠ить** [15], ⟨за-⟩ rave, talk deliriously (about T); **∠ни** *f/pl.* [6; *gen.*: -ней] nonsense, fantasies; raving.
бре́зг|ать [1] (T) disdain; **~ли́вость** *f* [8] squeamishness, disgust; **~ли́вый** [14 *sh.*] squeamish, fastidious (in к Д).
брезе́нт *m* [1] tarpaulin.
бре́зжить [16], **-ся** glimmer; dawn.
бре́мя *n* [13; *no pl.*] burden, load.
бренча́ть [4*e.*; -чу́, -чи́шь], ⟨за-, про-⟩ clink, jingle; strum.
брести́ [25], ⟨по-⟩ drag, lag; grope.
брешь *f* [8] breach; gap.
брига́|да *f* [5] brigade (*a.* ⚔), team, group of workers; уда́рная ~да shock brigade; **~ди́р** *m* [1] brigadier; foreman.
бри́джи *pl.* [*gen.*: -жей] breeches.
бриллиа́нт *m* [1], **~овый** [14] brilliant.
брита́н|ец *m* [1; -нца] Briton, Britisher; **2ия** *f* [7] Britain; **~ский** [16] British; 2ская Импе́рия *f* British Empire; 2ские острова́ *m/pl.* British Isles.

бри́т|ва *f* [5] razor; **~венный** [14]: ~венный прибо́р *m* shaving things.
брить [бре́ю, бре́ешь; бре́й(те)!; бре́я; брил; бри́тый], ⟨вы́-, по-⟩ shave; **-ся** *v/i.* get shaved, (have a) shave; **~ё** *n* [10] shaving.
бров|ь *f* [8; *from g/pl. e.*] eyebrow; хму́рить ∠и frown; он и ∠ью не повёл F he did not turn a hair; попа́сть не в ~ь, а в глаз F hit the nail on the head.
брод *m* [1] ford.
броди́ть [15] **1.** ⟨по-⟩ wander, roam; **2.** (*impers.*) ferment.
бродя́|га *m* [5] tramp, vagabond; **~жничать** F [1] stroll, tramp; **~жничество** *n* [9] vagrancy; **~чий** [17] vagrant.
броже́ние *n* [12] fermentation; *fig.* agitation, unrest.
бром *m* [1] bromine.
бронс|ви́к *m* [1 *e.*] armo(u)red car; **~во́й** [14] armo(u)red; **~но́сец** *m* [1; -сца] battleship; **~по́езд** *m* [1] armo(u)red train; **~та́нковый** [14]: ~та́нковые ча́сти *f/pl.* armo(u)red troops.
бро́нз|а *f* [5] bronze; **~овый** [14] bronzy, bronze...
брони|рова́ть[1] [7], ⟨за-⟩ armo(u)r; **∠ровать**[2] [7], ⟨за-⟩ reserve secure.
бро́нх|и *m/pl.* [1] bronchi *pl.* (*sg.* ~ bronchus); **~и́т** *m* [1] bronchitis.
броня́[1] *f* [6; *g/pl.*: -не́й] armo(u)r.
бро́ня[2] *f* [6; *g/pl.*: -ней] reservation.
броса́ть [1], ⟨бро́сить⟩ [15] throw, (*a.* ⚓) cast, fling (*a.* out) (s. th. at B *or* T/в B); leave, abandon, desert; give up, quit, leave off; (*impers.*) break into, be seized with (в B); lay down (*one's arms*); F waste, squander; брось(те) ...! F (oh) stop ...!; **-ся** dash, rush, plunge, dart (off -ся бежа́ть); fall (up)on (на B); go to (в B); -ся в глаза́ strike the eye.
бро́со|вый [14] catchpenny; under (*price*); ~вый э́кспорт *m* dump.
бросо́к *m* [1; -ска́] hurl, throw.
бро́шка *f* [5; *g/pl.*: -шек] brooch.
брошю́|ра *f* [5] brochure, pamphlet; **~рова́ть** [7], ⟨с-⟩ stitch.
брус *m* [1; *pl.*: бру́сья, бру́сьев, бру́сьям] (square) beam; bar; *pl.* (*a.* паралле́льные ∠ья) (*gymnastics*) parallel bars; **~ко́вый** [14] bar...
брусни́ка *f* [5] red bilberry, -ries *pl.*
брусо́к *m* [1; -ска́] **1.** bar; **2.** (*a.* точи́льный ~) whetstone.
бру́тто [*indecl.*] gross (weight).
бры́з|гать [1 *or* 3] *once* ⟨~нуть⟩ [20] splash, spatter, sprinkle; gush; **~ги** *f/pl.* [5] splash, spray.
брык|а́ть [1], *once* ⟨~ну́ть⟩ [20] (*a.* -ся) kick.
брюз|га́ F *m/f* [5] grumbler, griper, grouch; **~гли́вый** [14 *sh.*] morose, sullen, peevish, grouchy; **~жа́ть**

[4*e.*; -жу́, -жи́шь], ⟨за-⟩ grumble, growl, grouch.
брю́ква *f* [5] turnip.
брю́ки *f/pl.* [5] trousers, pants.
брюне́т *m* [1] brunet; **~ка** *f* [5; *g/pl.:* -ток] brunette.
Брюссе́ль *m* [4] Brussels; **♀ский** [16]: ♀ская капу́ста *f* Brussels sprouts.
брю́хо P *n* [9] belly, paunch.
брюш|и́на *f* [5] peritoneum; **~но́й** [14] abdominal; **~но́й тиф** *m* typhoid fever.
бря́кать [1], *once* ⟨бря́кнуть⟩ [20] 1. *v/i.* clink; 2. *v/t.* plump.
бряца́ть [1] clank, jingle; rattle.
БССР (Белору́сская Сове́тская Социалисти́ческая Респу́блика *f*) Byelorussian Soviet Socialist Republic.
бу́бен *m* [1; -бна; *g/pl.:* бу́бен] (*mst pl.*) tambourine; **~е́ц** *m* [1; -нца́], **~чик** *m* [1] jingle, small bell.
бу́блик *m* [1] (round) cracknel.
бу́бн|ы *f/pl.* [5; *g/pl.:* бубён, -бна́м] (*cards*) diamonds.
буго́р *m* [1; -гра́] hillock.
Будапе́шт *m* [1] Budapest.
бу́дет (*s.* быть) (*impers.*) (it's) enough!, that'll do!
буди́льник *m* [1] alarm clock.
буди́ть [15] 1. ⟨раз-⟩ (a)wake, waken; 2. ⟨про-⟩ [пробуждённый] *fig.* (a)rouse.
бу́дка *f* [5; *g/pl.:* -док] booth, box.
бу́дни *m/pl.* [1; *gen.:* -дней] weekdays; everyday life, monotony; **~чный** [14] everyday; humdrum.
будора́жить [16], ⟨вз-⟩ excite.
бу́дто as if, as though (*a.* ~ бы, ~ б); that; allegedly.
бу́дущ|ее *n* [17] future; **~ий** [17] future (*a. gr.*); **~ность** *f* [8] futurity, future.
бу́ер *m* [1; *pl.:* -ра́, *etc. e.*] iceboat.
буза́ P *f* [5] row, shindy.
бузина́ *f* [5] elder.
буй *m* [3] buoy.
бу́йвол *m* [1] buffalo.
бу́йный [14; бу́ен, буйна́, -о] impetuous, violent, vehement; unbridled; exuberant.
бу́йство *n* [9] mischief, rage, outrage, violence; **~вать** [7] behave outrageously, rage.
бук *m* [1] beech.
бу́к|ва *f* [5] letter; прописна́я (строчна́я) ~ва capital (small) letter (with с P); **~ва́льный** [14] literal, verbal; **~ва́рь** *m* [4*e.*] ABC book, primer; **~вое́д** *m* [1] pedant.
букини́ст *m* [1] second-hand bookseller
бу́ковый [14] beechen, beech...
букс *m* [1] box(wood).
букси́р *m* [1] tug(boat); tow; взять на ~ take in tow; **~ный** [14] tug...; **~овать** [7] tow, tug.
була́вка *f* [5; *g/pl.:* -вок] pin; англи́йская ~ safety pin.
була́ный [14] dun (*horse*).
була́т *m* [1] Damascus steel; **~ный** [14] steel...; damask...
бу́лка *f* [5; *g/pl.:* -лок] small loaf; roll.
бу́лоч|ка *f* [5; *g/pl.:* -чек] roll; bun; **~ная** *f* [14] bakery; **~ник** *m* [1] baker.
булы́жник *m* [1] cobblestone.
бульва́р *m* [1] boulevard, avenue; **~ный** [14] boulevard...; **~ный** рома́н *m* dime novel, *Brt.* penny dreadful; **~ная** пре́сса *f* gutter press.
бу́лькать [1] gurgle.
бульо́н *m* [1] broth, bouillon.
бума́|га *f* [5] paper; document; **~жка** *f* [5; *g/pl.:* -жек] slip of paper; P note (*money*); **~жник** *m* [1] wallet; **~жный** [14] 1. paper...; 2. cotton...; **~зе́я** *f* [6] fustian.
бунт *m* [1] 1. revolt, mutiny, insurrection, uprising; 2. bale, pack; **~а́рь** *m* [4*e.*] = **~овщи́к**.
бунтов|а́ть [7] rebel, revolt; ⟨вз-⟩ instigate; **~ско́й** [14] rebellious, mutinous; **~щи́к** *m* [1 *e.*] mutineer, rebel.
бура́ *f* [5] borax.
бура́в *m* [1 *e.*] drill, auger; **~ить** [14], ⟨про-⟩ bore, drill.
бура́н *m* [1] snowstorm, blizzard.
бурда́ F *f* [5] wash, wish-wash.
бурдю́к *m* [1 *e.*] wineskin.
буреве́стник *m* [1] (stormy) petrel.
буре́ние *n* [12] drilling, boring.
буржуа́ *m* [*indecl.*] bourgeois; **~зи́я** *f* [7] bourgeoisie; **~зный** [14] bourgeois...
буржу́й *contp.* P *m* [3], **~ка** *f* [5; *g/pl.:* -жу́ек] *s.* буржуа́.
бури́ть [13], ⟨про-⟩ bore.
бу́рка *f* [5; *g/pl.:* -рок] felt, cloak.
бурла́к *m* [1 *e.*] (barge) hauler.
бурли́ть [13] rage; seethe.
бурми́стр *m* [1] steward; mayor.
бу́рный [14; -рен, -рна] stormy, storm...; violent, boisterous.
буру́н *m* [1 *e.*] surf.
бурча́|нье *n* [12] grumbling; rumbling; **~ть** [4 *e.*; -чу́, -чи́шь] mumble; grumble; rumble.
бу́ры *m/pl.* [1] Boers.
бу́рый [14] brown, fulvous; ~ у́голь *m* brown coal, lignite.
бурья́н *m* [1] wild grass (*steppe*).
бу́ря *f* [6] storm, tempest.
бу́сы *f/pl.* [5] *coll.* (glass)beads.
бутафо́рия *f* [7] *thea.* properties *pl.*
бутербро́д (-тɛr-) *m* [1] sandwich.
буто́н *m* [1] bud.
бу́тсы *f/pl.* [5] football boots.
буты́л|ка *f* [5; *g/pl.:* -лок] bottle; **~очка** *f* [5; *g/pl.:* -чек] small bottle; **~ь** *f* [8] large bottle; carboy.
буф *m* [1] (*mst pl.*) puff; рука́в (взду́тый) ~ом puffed sleeve.
бу́фер *m* [1; *pl.:* -ра́, *etc. e.*] buffer.
буфе́т *m* [1] sideboard; bar, lunch-

room, refreshment room; **~чик** *m* [1] barkeeper; **~чица** *f* [5] barmaid.
буффо́н *m* [1] buffoon.
бух bounce!, plump!
Бухара́ *f* [5] Bokhara.
Бухаре́ст *m* [1] Bucharest.
буха́нка *f* [5; *g/pl.:* -нок] loaf.
бу́хать [1], *once* ⟨бу́хнуть⟩ plump.
бухга́лтер (bu'ha-) *m* [1] bookkeeper; **~ия** *f* [7] bookkeeping; **~ский** [16] bookkeeper('s)..., bookkeeping...
бу́хнуть [21] **1.** ⟨раз-⟩ swell; **2.** *s.* бу́хать.
бу́хта *f* [5] **1.** bay; **2.** coil.
бушева́ть [7; бушу́ю, -у́ешь] roar, rage, storm.
бушла́т *m* [1] (sailor's) jacket.
бушпри́т *m* [1] bowsprit.
буя́н *m* [1] brawler, rowdy, ruffian; **~ить** [13] brawl, riot, kick up a row.
бы, *short* б, *is used to render subjunctive and conditional patterns:* a) *with the preterite, e.g.* я сказа́л ~, е́сли ~ (я) знал I would say it if I knew it; (*similarly*: *should, could, may, might*); b) *with the infinitive, e.g.:* всё ~ ему́ знать he would like to know everything; не вам ~ говори́ть you had better be quiet.
быва́лый [14] experienced; former; common; *cf.* быва́ть.
быва́|ть [1] **1.** occur, happen; как ни в чём не **~ло** as if nothing had happened; он, **~ло,** гуля́л he would (*or* used to) go for a walk; бо́ли как не **~ло** F the pain had (*or* has) entirely disappeared; **2.** ⟨по-⟩ (у P) be (at), visit, stay (with).
бы́вший [17] former, late, ex-...
бык *m* [1 *e.*] **1.** bull; **2.** abutment.
былина *f* [5] Russian epic.
были́нка *f* [5; *g/pl.:* -нок] blade of grass.
бы́ло (*s.* быть) (*after verbs*) already: я уже́ заплати́л ~ де́ньги ... I had already paid the money, (but) ...; almost nearly, was (were) just going to ...; я чуть ~ не сказа́л I was on the point of saying, I nearly said.
был|о́й [14] bygone, former; **~о́е** *n* past; **~ь** *f* [8] true story *or* ocurrence; past.
быстро|но́гий [16] swift(-footed); **~та́** *f* [5] quickness, swiftness, rapidity; **~хо́дный** [14; -ден, -дна] fast.
бы́стрый [14; быстр, -á, -o] quick, fast, swift.
быт *m* [1; в быту́] way of life, manners *pl.*; **~ие́** *n* [12] existence, being; *Bibl.* Genesis; **~ность** *f* [8] stay; в мою **~ность** в (П) during my stay in, while staying in; **~ово́й** [14] of manners, popular, genre; common, everyday.
быть (*3rd p. sg. pr.:* есть, *cf.*; *3rd p. pl.:* † суть; *ft.:* бу́ду, -дешь; будь[те]!; бу́дучи; был, -á, -o; не́ был, -o, -и) be; (*cf.* бу́дет, быва́ть, бы́ло); ~ (Д) ... will (inevitably) be *or* happen; мне бы́ло (бу́дет) ... (го́да *or* лет) I was (I'll be) ... (years old); как (же) ~? what is to be done?; так и ~! I don't care; будь что бу́дет come what may; будь по-ва́шему have it your own way!; бу́дьте до́бры (любе́зны), ... be so kind as ..., would you please ...
бюва́р *m* [1] writing case.
бюдже́т *m* [1], **~ный** [14] budget.
бюллете́нь *m* [4] bulletin; ballot, *Brt.* voting paper; medical certificate.
бюро́ *n* [*indecl.*] office, bureau; спра́вочное ~ inquiry office; information; ~ путеше́ствий travel bureau, *Brt.* tourist(s') office.
бюрокра́т *m* [1] bureaucrat; **~и́зм** *m* [1] red tape; **~и́ческий** [16] bureaucratic; **~ия** *f* [7] bureaucracy.
бюст *m* [1] bust; **~га́льтер** (-'haltɛr) *m* [1] bra(ssière).
бязь *f* [8] cheap cotton goods.

В

в, во 1. (В): (*direction*) to, into; for; в окно́ out of (in through) the window; (*time*) in, at, on, within; в сре́ду on Wednesday; в два часа́ at two o'clock; (*measure, price, etc.*) at, of; в день a *or* per day; длино́й в четы́ре ме́тра four meters long; чай в два рубля́ килогра́мм tea at 2 roubles a kilo(gram); в де́сять раз бо́льше ten times as much; (*promotion*) to the rank of; идти́ в солда́ты become a soldier; **2.** (П): (*position*) in, at, on; (*time*) in; в конце́ (нача́ле) го́да at the end (beginning) of the year; (*distance*) в пяти́ киломе́трах от (Р) five kilometers from.
в. *abbr.*: **век.**
Вавило́н *m* [1] Babylon.
ваго́н 🚂 *m* [1] car(riage, *Brt.*); **~-рестора́н** *m* dining car; **~е́тка** *f* [5; *g/pl.:* -ток] lorry, trolley, truck; **~овожа́тый** *m* [14] streetcar (*Brt.* tram) driver.
ва́жн|ичать [1] put on (*or* give o.s.) airs; **~ость** *f* [8] importance; conceit; **~ый** [14; ва́жен, -жна́, -o, ва́жны] important, significant; haughty; F не**~о** rather bad; э́то не**~о** that doesn't matter *or* is of no importance.
ва́за *f* [5] vase, bowl.
вака́н|сия *f* [7] vacancy; **~тный** [14; -тен, -тна] vacant.

ва́кса *f* [5] (shoe) polish, blacking.
вакци́на *f* [5] vaccine.
вал *m* [1; на -у́; *pl. e.*] 1. rampart; bank; wall; 2. billow; 3. ⊕ shaft, axle.
валёжник *m* [1] brushwood.
ва́ленок *m* [1; -нка] felt boot.
валерья́н|ка F *f* [5], **~овый** [14]: ~овые ка́пли *f/pl.* valerian.
вале́т *m* [1] (*cards*) knave.
ва́лик *m* [1] 1. ⊕ roller 2. bolster.
вал|и́ть [13; валю́, ва́лишь; ва́ленный], ⟨по-, с-⟩ 1. overturn, tumble (down; *v/i.* **-ся**), fell; heap (up), dump; 2. [*3rd p. only*: -и́т] flock, throng; снег ~и́т it is snowing heavily.
валово́й [14] gross, total.
валу́н *m* [1 *e.*] boulder.
ва́льдшнеп *m* [1] woodcock.
вальс *m* [1] waltz; **~и́ровать** [7], ⟨про-⟩ waltz.
вальцева́ть [7] ⊕ roll.
валю́т|а *f* [5] (foreign) currency; золота́я ~а gold standard; **~ный** [14] currency..., exchange...; ~ный курс *m* rate of exchange.
валя́ть [28], ⟨по-⟩ roll; knead; full; P валя́й! go!; ~ дурака́ idle; play the fool; **-ся** wallow, loll; lie about (in disorder).
вани́ль *f* [8] vanilla.
ва́нн|а *f* [5] tub; bath; со́лнечная ~а sun bath; приня́ть ~у take a bath; **~ая** *f* [14] bath(room).
Ва́нька *m* [5] 1. *s.* Ва́ня; 2. ♀-вста́нька *m* [5] tumbler (*toy*).
Ва́ня *m* [6] *dim. of* Ива́н John.
ва́рвар *m* [1] barbarian; **~ский** [16] barbarous; **~ство** *n* [9] barbarity.
Варва́ра *f* [5] Barbara, Babette.
ва́режка *f* [5; *g/pl.*: -жек] mitten.
вар|е́ние *n* [12] = ва́рка; **~е́ник** *m* [1] (*mst pl.*) boiled pieces of paste enclosing curd *or* fruit; **~ёный** [14] cooked, boiled; **~е́нье** *n* [10] jam, preserves *pl.*
Ва́ренька *f* [5] *dim. of* Варва́ра.
вариа́нт *m* [1] variant, version.
вари́ть [13; варю́, ва́ришь; ва́ренный], ⟨с-⟩ 1. cook, boil (*v/i.* **-ся**); brew; 2. digest.
ва́рка *f* [5] cooking, boiling.
Варша́ва *f* [5] Warsaw.
варьете́ *n* (-ˈtɛ) [*indecl.*] vaudeville, *Brt.* variety (*show & theater, -tre*).
варьи́ровать [7] vary.
Ва́р|я *f* [6] *dim. of* ~ва́ра.
варя́г *m* [1] Varangian.
василёк *m* [1; -лька́] cornflower.
Васи́лий *m* [3] Basil.
васса́л *m* [1] vassal.
Ва́ся [6] *dim. of* Васи́лий.
ва́т|а *f* [5] absorbent cotton, *Brt.* cotton wool; wadding; на ~е wadded.
вата́га *f* [5] gang, band, troop.
ватер|ли́ния (-tɛr-) *f* [7] water line; **~па́с** *m* [1] level.
ва́тный [14] cotton(-wool)...; wadded.
ватру́шка *f* [5; *g/pl.*: -шек] curd *or* jam patty.
ва́фля *f* [6; *g/pl.*: -фель] waffle, wafer.
ва́хт|а ⚓ *f* [5] watch; стоя́ть на ~е keep watch; **~енный** [14] sailor on duty; **~ёр** (*a.* ~ёр) *m* [1] guard, watchman.
ваш *m*, **~а** *f*, **~е** *n*, **~и** *pl.* [25] your; yours; по-~ему in your opinion (*or* language); (пусть бу́дет) по-~ему (have it) your own way, (just) as you like; как по-~ему? what do you think?; *cf.* наш.
Вашингто́н *m* [1] Washington.
вая́|ние *n* [12] sculpture; **~тель** *m* [4] sculptor; **~ть** [28], ⟨из-⟩ form, cut, model.
вбе|га́ть [1], ⟨**~жа́ть**⟩ [4; -гу́, -жи́шь, -гу́т] run *or* rush in.
вби|ва́ть [1], ⟨**~ть**⟩ [вобью́, вобьёшь; вбе́й(те)!; вбил; вби́тый] drive (*or* hammer) in; ~ть себе́ в го́лову take it into one's head; **~ра́ть** [1], ⟨вобра́ть⟩ [вберу́, -рёшь] absorb, imbibe.
вблизи́ nearby; close (to P).
вброд: переходи́ть ~ ford.
вв. *or* **в. в.** *abbr.*: века́.
ввал|ивать [1] ⟨~и́ть⟩ [13; ввалю́, вва́лишь; вва́ленный] throw (in[to]), dump; **-ся** fall *or* tumble in; flock in.
введе́ние *n* [12] introduction.
ввезти́ *s.* ввози́ть.
вверг|а́ть [1], ⟨**~нуть**⟩ [21] fling *or* cast (into в B); plunge (*v/i.* **-ся**); ~а́ть в отча́яние drive to despair.
ввер|я́ть [14], ⟨**~ить**⟩ entrust, commit, give in charge.
ввёртывать [1], ⟨ввертéть⟩ [11; вверчу́, вве́ртишь], *once* ⟨ввернýть⟩ [20; ввёрнутый] screw in; *fig.* put in (*a word, etc.*).
вверх up(ward[s]); ~ по ле́стнице upstairs; ~ дном (*or* нога́ми) upside down; ~ торма́шками F headlong; ру́ки ~! hands up!; **~у́** above; overhead.
ввести́ *s.* вводи́ть.
ввиду́ in view (of P), considering; ~ того́, что as, since, seeing that.
вви́н|чивать [1], ⟨**~ти́ть**⟩ [15 *e.*; -нчу́, -нти́шь] screw in.
ввод|и́ть [15], ⟨ввести́⟩ [25] introduce; bring *or* usher (in); ~и́ть в курс де́ла acquaint with an affair; ~и́ть в строй (*or* де́йствие, эксплуата́цию) ⊕ put into operation; **~ный** [14] introductory; ~ное сло́во *or* предложе́ние *n gr.* parenthesis.
ввоз *m* [1] import(s); importation; **~и́ть** [15], ⟨ввезти́⟩ [24] import; **~ный** [14] import...
вво́лю (P) F plenty of; to one's heart's content.
ввя́з|ываться [1], ⟨**~а́ться**⟩ [3] meddle, interfere (with в B); get involved (in).
вглубь inward(s), deep (into).

вгля́д|ываться [1], ⟨~е́ться⟩ [11] (в В) peer (into), look narrowly (at).

вгоня́ть [28], ⟨вогна́ть⟩ [вгоню́, вго́нишь; вогна́л, -а́, -о; во́гнанный (во́гнан, -ана)] drive in(to).

вдава́ться [5], ⟨вда́ться⟩ [вда́мся, вда́шься, *etc. s.* дать] jut out; press in; indulge (in в В), plunge *or* go (into).

вда́в|ливать [1], ⟨~и́ть⟩ [14] press in.

вдал|еке́, **~и́** far off, far (from от Р); **~ь** into the distance.

вдви|га́ть [1], ⟨~нуть⟩ [20] put *or* push in.

вдво́|е twice (as..., *comp.*: ~е бо́льше twice as much *or* many); *vb.* + ~е *a.* double; **~ём** both *or* two (of us, *etc.*, *or* together); **~йне́** twice (as much, *etc.*), doubly.

вде|ва́ть [1], ⟨~ть⟩ [вде́ну, вде́нешь; вде́тый] (в В) thread.

вде́л|ывать, ⟨~ать⟩ [1] set (in).

вдоба́вок in addition (to); into the bargain, to boot.

вдов|а́ *f* [5; *pl. st.*] widow; **~е́ц** *m* [1; -вца́] widower.

вдо́воль (Р) F quite enough; plenty of.

вдо́вый [14 *sh.*] widowed.

вдого́нку after, in pursuit of.

вдоль (Р, по Д) along; lengthwise; ~ и поперёк throughout, far and wide.

вдохнов|е́ние *n* [12] inspiration; **~е́нный** [14; -ве́нен, -ве́нна] inspired; **~ля́ть** [28], ⟨~и́ть⟩ [14 *e.*; -влю́, -ви́шь] inspire; **-ся** get inspired (with *or* by Т).

вдре́безги into smithereens.

вдруг suddenly, all of a sudden.

вду|ва́ть [1], ⟨~ть⟩ [18] blow in.

вду́м|чивый [14 *sh.*] thoughtful; **~ываться**, ⟨~аться⟩ [1] (в В) ponder (over), reflect ([up]on), dive (into).

вдыха́ть [1], ⟨вдохну́ть⟩ [20] inhale; *fig.* inspire (with).

вегета|риа́нец *m* [1; -нца] vegetarian; **~ти́вный** [14] vegetative.

ве́д|ать [1] **1.** † know; **2.** (Т) be in charge of, manage; **~е́ние** *n* [12] running, directing; ~е́ние книг bookkeeping; **~ение** *n* [12] knowledge, lore; authority, charge, competence; **~омо** known; без моего́ ~ома without my knowledge; **~омость** *f* [8; *from g/pl. e.*] list, roll; bulletin; **~омство** *n* [9] department, administration.

ведро́ *n* [9; *pl.*: вёдра, -дер, -драм] bucket, pail; ~ для му́сора garbage can, *Brt.* dust-bin.

вёдро † *n* [9] serene weather.

веду́щий [17] leading; basic.

ведь indeed, sure(ly); why, well; then; you know!; ~ уже́ по́здно it is late, isn't it?

ве́дьма *f* [5] witch, hag.

ве́ер *m* [1; *pl.*: -ра́, *etc. e.*] fan.

ве́жлив|ость *f* [8] politeness; **~ый** [14 *sh.*] polite.

везде́ everywhere.

везти́ [24], ⟨по-, с-⟩ *v/t.* drive (be driving, *etc.*), transport; pull; ему́ (не) везёт F he is (un)lucky.

век *m* [1; на веку́; *pl.*: века́, *etc. e.*] **1.** century; age; **2.** life(time); сре́дние ~а́ *pl.* Middle Ages; на моём ~у́ in my life(time); ~ с тобо́й мы не вида́лись we haven't met for ages.

ве́ко *n* [9; *nom/pl.*: -ки] eyelid.

веково́й [14] secular.

ве́ксель *m* [4; *pl.*: -ля́, *etc. e.*] bill of exchange, promissory note.

веле́ть [9; ве́ленный] (*im*)*pf.*; *pt. pf. only* order, tell (p. s.th. Д/В).

велика́н *m* [1] giant.

вели́к|ий [16; вели́к, -а́] great; (too) large *or* big; от ма́ла до ~а everybody, young and old; ~ая пя́тница *f* Good Friday; Пётр ♀ий Peter the Great.

Велико|брита́ния *f* [7] Great Britain; ♀**ду́шие** *n* [12] magnanimity; ♀**ду́шный** [14; -шен, -шна] magnanimous, generous; ♀**ле́пие** *n* [12] splendo(u)r, magnificence; ♀**ле́пный** [14; -пен, -пна] magnificent, splendid; ♀**ру́с** *m* [1], ♀**ру́сский** [16] (Great) Russian.

велича́|вый [14 *sh.*] sublime, majestic, lofty; **~ть** [1] praise, glorify; style.

вели́ч|ественный [14 *sh.*] majestic, grand, stately; **~ество** *n* [9] Majesty; **~ие** *n* [12] grandeur; **~ина́** *f* [5; *pl. st.*: -чи́ны] size; quantity; celebrity; ~ино́й в *or* с (В) ... big *or* high.

вело|го́нки *f/pl.* [5; *gen.*: -нок] cycle race; **~дро́м** *m* [1] cycling ground.

велосипе́д *m* [1] bicycle; е́здить на ~е cycle; **~и́ст** *m* [1] cyclist; **~ный** [14] (bi)cycle..., cycling...

вельмо́жа *m* [5] magnate.

ве́на *f* [5] **1.** *anat.* vein; **2.** ♀ Vienna.

венгр|е́ц *m* [1; -рца] ~ка *f*, [5; *g/pl.*: -рок], **~ский** [16] Hungarian.

Ве́нгрия *f* [7] Hungary.

венери́ческий [16] venereal.

Венесуэ́ла *f* [5] Venezuela.

вене́ц *m* [1; -нца́] wreath, garland; crown; halo; идти́ под ~ † marry.

венеци|а́нский [16] Venetian; '♀я (-'ɳɛ-) *f* [7] Venice.

ве́нзель *m* [4; *pl.*: -ля́] monogram.

ве́ник *m* [1] broom, besom.

вено́к *m* [1; -нка́] wreath, garland.

вентил|и́ровать [7], ⟨про-⟩ ventilate, air; **~я́тор** *m* [1] ventilator, fan.

венча́|льный [14] wedding...; **~ние** *n* [12] wedding (ceremony); **~ть** [1] **1.** ⟨у-⟩ wreathe, crown; **2.** ⟨об-, по-⟩ marry; **-ся** get married (in church).

ве́ра *f* [5] **1.** faith, belief, trust (in в В); religion; **2.** ♀ Vera.

ве́рба *f* [5] willow.
верблю́|д *m* [1] camel; **\~жий** [18]: \~жья шерсть *f* camel's hair.
ве́рбн|ый [14]: \~ое воскресе́нье *n* Palm Sunday.
вербов|а́ть [7], ⟨за-, на-⟩ enlist, recruit; engage, hire; **\´ка** *f* [5] enlistment; hire; **\´щик** *m* [1] enlister; hirer.
верёв|ка *f* [5; *g/pl.*: -вок] rope; **\~очка** *f* [5; *g/pl.*: -чек] string, cord; **\~очный** [14] rope...
верени́ца *f* [5] file, chain, line.
ве́реск *m* [1] heather.
веретено́ *n* [9; *pl. st.*: -тёна] spindle.
верещ́ать [16 *e.*; -щу́, -щи́шь] chirp.
верзи́ла F *m* [5] big (stupid) fellow, spindlelegs.
ве́рить [13], ⟨по-⟩ believe (in в В); believe, trust (*acc.* Д); \~ на́ слово take on trust; **-ся** (*impers.*) (мне) не ве́рится one (I) can hardly believe (it).
вермише́ль *f* [8] *coll.* vermicelli.
ве́рно *adv.* 1. & 2. *s.* ве́рный 1. & 2.; 3. probably; **\~сть** *f* [8] 1. faith (-fulness), fidelity, loyalty; 2. correctness, accuracy.
верну́ть(ся) [20] *pf.*, *s.* возвраща́ть(ся).
ве́рн|ый [14; -рен, -рна́, -о] 1. faithful, true; loyal; 2. right, correct; accurate, exact; 3. safe, sure, reliable; 4. inevitable, certain; **\~ée** (сказа́ть) or rather.
ве́ро|вание *n* [12] faith, belief; **\~вать** [7] believe (in в В).
вероиспове́дание *n* [12] creed.
вероло́м|ный [14; -мен, -мна] perfidious, treacherous; **\~ство** *n* [9] perfidy, treachery.
вероотсту́пник *m* [1] apostate.
веротерпи́мость *f* [8] toleration.
вероя́т|ие *n* [12] likelihood; **\~ность** *f* [8] probability; по всей \~ности in all probability; **\~ный** [14; -тен, -тна] probable, likely.
ве́рсия *f* [7] version.
верста́ *f* [5; *pl. st.*: вёрсты] verst (= *3500 ft.*); **\~к** *m* [1 *e.*] workbench; **\~ть** [1], ⟨с-⟩ [свёрстанный] *typ.* make up.
ве́рт|ел *m* [1; *pl.*: -ла́] spit; **\~е́ть** [11; верчу́, ве́ртишь], ⟨по-⟩ turn; twist; (-ся) 1. turn, revolve; 2. fidget; 3. loaf; 4. make subterfuges; -ся на языке́ be on the tip of one's tongue; **\~ика́льный** [14; -лен, -льна] vertical; **\~ля́вый** [14 *sh.*] fidgety, restless; **\~олёт** *m* [1] helicopter; **\~у́н** *m* [1 *e.*] fidget; **\~у́шка** [5; *g/pl.*: -шек] light-minded woman.
ве́рующий [17] pious; believer.
верфь *f* [8] dockyard.
верх *m* [1; на -у́; *pl. e.*] 1. top, upper part; 2. right side (*fabric, clothes*); *fig.* 1. summit, apex, pink; 2. upper hand; **\~и́** *pl.* 1. heads, leaders; ... в \~а́х summit ...; 2. ♪ high notes; 3. surface; superficial knowledge; **\´ний** [15] upper.
верхо́в|ный [14] supreme, high; \~ная власть *f* supreme power; \~ный суд *m* supreme court; **\~о́й** [14] riding...; rider, horseman; \~а́я езда́ *f* riding; **\~ье** *n* [10; *g/pl.*: -ьев] upper (course).
верхо́м *adv.* astride; on horseback; е́здить \~ ride, go on horseback.
верху́шка *f* [5; *g/pl.*: -шек] top, crest; the highest ranks.
верши́на *f* [5] peak, summit.
верши́ть [16 *e.*; -шу́, -ши́шь; -шённый], ⟨за-, с-⟩ 1. (re)solve, decide; 2. direct (T); 3. accomplish.
вершо́к *m* [1; -шка́] vershok (†, = *4.45 cm.* = *1.75 in.*).
вес *m* [1] weight; на \~ by weight; уде́льный \~ *phys.* specific gravity; по́льзоваться больши́м \´ом enjoy great credit; \´ом в (В) weighing...
вес|ели́ть [13], ⟨раз-⟩ amuse, divert (-ся o. s., enjoy o. s.); **\~ёлость** *f* [8] gaiety, mirth; **\~ёлый** [14; ве́сел, -а́, -о] gay, merry, cheerful; как \´ело! it's such fun!; ему́ \´ело he enjoys himself, is of good cheer; **\~е́лье** *n* [10] merriment, merrymaking, fun; **\~ельча́к** *m* [1 *e.*] merry fellow.
весе́нний [15] spring...
ве́с|ить [15] *v/i.* weigh; **\~кий** [16; ве́сок, -ска] weighty.
весло́ *n* [9; *pl.*: вёсла, -сел] oar.
весн|а́ *f* [5; *pl.*: вёсны, вёсен] spring (in [the] T); **\~у́шка** *f* [5; *g/pl.*: -шек] freckle.
весов|о́й [14] 1. weight...; balance-...; 2. sold by weight; **\~щи́к** *m* [1 *e.*] weigher.
вести́ [25], ⟨по-⟩ 1. (be) lead(ing, *etc.*), conduct, guide; 2. carry on; 3. keep; 4. drive; \~ (своё) нача́ло spring (from от P); \~ себя́ behave (o.s.); **\~сь** be conducted *or* carried on; так уж у нас ведётся that's a custom among us.
вестибю́ль *m* [4] entrance hall.
Вест-'Индия *f* [7] West Indies.
ве́ст|ник *m* [1] messenger; bulletin; **\~ово́й** ⚔ *m* [14] orderly; **\~ь** *f* [8; *from g/pl. e.*] 1. news, message; 2. gossip, rumo(u)r.
весы́ *m/pl.* [1] scales, balance.
весь *m*, вся *f*, всё *n*, *pl.*: все [31] 1. *adj.* all, the whole; full, life (*size*; at в В); 2. *su. n* all over; everything, *pl. a.* everybody; лу́чше всего́ (всех) best of all, the best; при всём том *or* со всем тем for all that; во всём ми́ре all over the world; по всей стране́ throughout the country; всего́ хоро́шего! good luck!; во всю F *s.* си́ла; 3. всё *adv.* always, all the time; only, just; всё

(ещё) не not yet; всё бо́льше (и бо́льше) more and more; всё же nevertheless, yet.
весьма́ very, extremely; ~ вероя́тно most probably.
ветв|и́стый [14 *sh.*] branchy; ~ь *f* [8; *from g/pl. e.*] branch.
ве́тер *m* [1; -тра] wind; встре́чный ~ contrary *or* head wind; попу́тный ~ fair wind; броса́ть де́ньги (слова́) на ~ waste money (words); держа́ть нос по ве́тру be a timeserver.
ветерина́р *m* [1], ~**ный** [14]: ~ный врач *m* veterinarian.
ветеро́|к [1; -рка́], ~**чек** [1; -чка] *m* light wind, breeze, breath.
ве́тка *f* [5; *g/pl.*: -ток] branch(let), twig; 🚂 branch line.
ве́то *n* [*indecl.*] veto; наложи́ть ~ veto; ~**шь** *f* [8] rags, tatters *pl.*
ве́тр|еный [14 *sh.*] windy (*a. fig.* = flippant); ~**яно́й** [14] wind...; ~яна́я ме́льница *f* windmill; ~**яный** [14]: ~яная о́спа *f* chicken pox.
ве́тх|ий [16; ветх, -а́, -о; *comp.*: ве́тше] old, dilapidated; worn-out, shabby; decrepit; ~**ость** *f* [8] decay, dilapidation; приходи́ть в ~ость fall into decay.
ветчина́ *f* [5] ham.
ветша́ть [1], ‹об-› decay, dilapidate, weaken.
ве́ха *f* [5] landmark; ⚓ spar buoy.
ве́чер *m* [1; *pl.*: -ра́, *etc. e.*] **1.** evening; **2.** evening party; soiree; ~ом in the evening; сего́дня ~ом tonight; вчера́ ~ом last night; по́д ~ toward(s) the evening; ~**е́ть** [8; *impers.*] decline (*of the day*); ~**и́нка** *f* [5; *g/pl.*: -нок] = ве́чер 2.; ~**ко́м** F = ~ом; ~**ний** [15] evening..., night...; ~**ня** *f* [6; *g/pl.*: -рен] vespers *pl.*, evensong; ~**я** *f* [6]: та́йная ~я *or* ~я госпо́дня the Lord's Supper.
ве́чн|ость *f* [8] eternity; (це́лую) ~ость F for ages; ~**ый** [14; -чен, -чна] eternal, everlasting; perpetual.
ве́ша|лка *f* [5; *g/pl.*: -лок] hanger, tab; peg, rack; cloakroom; ~**ть** [1], **1.** ‹пове́сить› [15] hang (up); -**ся** hang o. s.; **2.** ‹взве́сить› [15] weigh.
вещево́й [14]: ~ мешо́к *m* knapsack.
вещ|е́ственный [14] corporeal, real, material, substantial; ~**ество́** *n* [9] matter, substance; ~**и́ца** *f* [8] knickknack; piece; ~**ь** *f* [8; *from g/pl. e.*] thing; object; work, piece, play; *pl.* belongings; baggage, *Brt.* luggage.
ве́я|лка *f* [5; *g/pl.*: -лок] winnowing machine; ~**ние** *n* [12] waft; 🌾 winnowing; *fig.* trend; influence; ~**ть** [27] **1.** *v/i.* breathe; spread; **2.** ‹про-› *v/t.* winnow.
вжи|ва́ться [1], ‹~ться› [-ву́сь, *etc. s.* жить] accustom o.s. (to в В).
взад back(ward[s]); ~ и вперёд back and forth, to and fro; up and down.
взаи́мн|ость *f* [8] reciprocity; ~**ый** [14; -мен, -мна] mutual, reciprocal; спаси́бо, ~о F thanks, the same to you.
взаимо|де́йствие *n* [12] interaction; coöperation; ~**де́йствовать** [7] interact; cooperate; ~**отноше́ние** *n* [12] mutual (*or* inter-, cor)relation; ~**по́мощь** *f* [8] mutual aid; ~**понима́ние** *n* [12] mutual understanding.
взаймы́ on credit *or* loan; брать ~ borrow (from у, от Р); дава́ть ~ lend.
вза|ме́н (Р) instead of, in exchange for; ~**перти́** locked up, under lock and key; ~**пра́вду** Р = впра́вду.
взба́л|мошный F [14; -шен, -шна] extravagant; ~**тывать**, ‹взболта́ть› [1] shake *or* stir up.
взбе|га́ть [1], ‹~жа́ть› [4; взбегу́, -жи́шь, -гу́т] run up.
взбива́ть [1], ‹взбить› [взобью́, -бьёшь; взбил, -а; взби́тый] fluff; whip, froth.
взбира́ться [1], ‹взобра́ться› [взберу́сь, -рёшься; взобра́лся, -ла́сь, -ло́сь] climb (s. th. на В).
взболта́ть *s.* взба́лтывать.
взбудора́живать [1] = будора́жить.
взбух|а́ть [1], ‹~нуть› [21] swell.
взва́ливать [1], ‹взвали́ть› [13; взвалю́, -а́лишь; -а́ленный] load, charge (with на В).
взвести́ *s.* взводи́ть.
взве́|шивать [1], ‹~сить› [15] weigh; -ся weigh o. s.
взви|ва́ть [1], ‹~ть› [взовью́, -вьёшь, *etc. s.* вить] whirl up; -**ся** soar up, rise.
взви́зг|ивать [1], ‹~нуть› [20] squeak, scream.
взви́н|чивать [1], ‹~ти́ть› [15 *e.*; -нчу́, -нти́шь; -и́нченный] excite; raise (*prices*).
взвить *s.* взвива́ть.
взвод *m* [1] platoon.
взводи́ть [15], ‹взвести́› [25] lead up; lift; impute (s. th. to a p. В/на В); ~ куро́к cock (*firearm*).
взволно́|ванный [14 *sh.*] excited; uneasy; ~**ва́ть(ся)** *s.* волнова́ть.
взгля|д *m* [1] look; glance; gaze; stare; *fig.* view, opinion; на ~д in appearance, by sight; на мой ~д in my opinion; на пе́рвый ~д at first sight; с пе́рвого ~да on the face of it; at once; ~**дывать** [1], *once* ‹~ну́ть› [19] (на В) (have a) look, glance (at).
взгромо|жда́ть [1], ‹~зди́ть› [15 *e.*; -зжу́, -зди́шь; -мождённый] load, pile up; -**ся** clamber, perch (on на В).
вздёр|гивать [1], ‹~нуть› [20] jerk up; ~нутый нос *m* pug nose.

вздор *m* [1] nonsense; **∠ный** [14; -рен, -рна] foolish, absurd; F quarrelsome.
вздорожа́|ние *n* [12] rise of price(s); **~ть** *s.* дорожа́ть.
вздох *m* [1] sigh; испусти́ть после́дний ~ give up the ghost; **~ну́ть** *s.* вздыха́ть.
вздра́гивать [1], *once* ⟨вздро́гнуть⟩ [20] start, wince; shudder.
вздремну́ть F [20] *pf.* nap.
взду|ва́ть [1], ⟨~ть⟩ [18] **1.** whirl up; **2.** *v/i.* **-ся** inflate; **3.** F thrash; **∠тие** *n* [12] swelling.
взду́ма|ть [1] *pf.* conceive the idea, take it into one's head; **-ся:** ему́ ~лось = он ~л; как ~ется at one's will.
взды|ма́ть [1] raise, whirl up; **~ха́ть** [1], *once* ⟨вздохну́ть⟩ [20] sigh; ~ха́ть (по, о П) long (for); *pf.* F draw breath, breathe again.
взи|ма́ть [1] levy, raise (from с Р); **~ра́ть** [1] (на В) look (at); не взира́я на without regard to, notwithstanding.
взла́мывать [1], ⟨взлома́ть⟩ [1] break *or* force open.
взлез|а́ть [1], ⟨~ть⟩ [24 *st.*] (на В) climb up.
взлёт *m* [1] ascent, rise.
взлет|а́ть [1], ⟨~е́ть⟩ [11] fly up, soar.
взлом *m* [1] breaking in; **~а́ть** *s.* взла́мывать; **∠щик** *m* [1] burglar.
взмах *m* [1] stroke; sweep; **∠ивать** [1], *once* ⟨~ну́ть⟩ [20] swing.
взмет|а́ть [3], *once* ⟨~ну́ть⟩ [20] whirl *or* throw up; flap.
взмо́рье *n* [10] seashore, seaside.
взнос *m* [1] payment; fee.
взнузд|ывать [1], ⟨~а́ть⟩ bridle.
взобра́ться *s.* взбира́ться.
взойти́ *s.* восходи́ть & всходи́ть.
взор *m* [1] look; gaze; eyes *pl.*
взорва́ть *s.* взрыва́ть.
взро́слый [14] grown-up, adult.
взрыв *m* [1] explosion; detonation; *fig.* outburst; **~а́тель** *m* [4] fuse; **~а́ть** [1], ⟨взорва́ть⟩ [-ву́, -вёшь; взо́рванный] blow up; *fig.* enrage; **-ся** explode; **~но́й** [14], **∠чатый** [14] explosive (*su.:* ∠чатое вещество́).
взрыхля́ть [28] *s.* рыхли́ть.
взъе|зжа́ть [1] ⟨∠хать⟩ [взъе́ду, -дешь; взъезжа́й(те)!] ride *or* drive up; **~ро́шивать** [1], ⟨~ро́шить⟩ [16 *st.*] dishevel, tousle; **-ся** bristle up.
взыва́ть [1], ⟨воззва́ть⟩ [-зову́, -зовёшь; -зва́л, -а́, -о] cry, call; invoke; appeal (to к Д).
взыск|а́ние *n* [12] **1.** levy, collecting; **2.** punishment, reprimand: **~а́тельный** [14; -лен, -льна] exacting, exigent; **∠ивать** [1], ⟨~а́ть⟩ [3] (с Р) **1.** levy, exact; collect; recover (from); **2.** call to account; impose a penalty (on); не взыщи́(те)! no offence!
взя́т|ие *n* [12] seizure, capture; **~ка** *f* [5; *g/pl.:* -ток] **1.** bribe; дать ~ку bribe, P grease; **2.** trick (*cards*); **~очник** *m* [1] bribe taker, corrupt official; **~очничество** *n* [9] bribery; **~ь** *s.* брать.
вибр|а́ция *f* [7] vibration; **~и́ровать** [7] vibrate.
вид *m* [1] **1.** look(s), appearance, air; **2.** sight, view; **3.** kind, sort; species; **4.** *gr.* aspect; в ∠е (Р) in the form of, as, by way of; при ∠е at the sight of; на ~у́ (у Р) in sight; visible (to); с (*or* по) ∠у by sight; judging from one's appearance; ни под каки́м ∠ом on no account; у него́ хоро́ший ~ he looks well; де́лать *or* пока́зывать ~ pretend; (не) теря́ть *or* выпуска́ть из ∠у lose sight of (keep in view); ста́вить на ~ reproach (a p. with Д/В); ∠ы *pl.* prospects (for на В).
вида́ть F [1], ⟨у-; по-⟩ его́ давно́ не ~ I *or* we haven't seen him for a long time; **-ся** (*iter.*) meet, see (o. a.; a p. с Т).
виде́ние *n* [12] vision.
ви́деть [11 *st.*], ⟨у-⟩ see; catch sight of; ~ во сне dream (of В); ви́дишь (-ите) ли? you see?; **-ся** = вида́ться (*but a. once*).
ви́дим|о apparently, evidently; ~о-не~о F lots of, immense quantity; **~ость** *f* [8] **1.** visibility; **2.** appearance; **~ый** **1.** [14 *sh.*] visible; **2.** [14] apparent.
видн|е́ться [8] appear, be seen; **∠о** it can be seen; it appears; apparently; (мне) ничего́ не ∠о I don't *or* can't see anything; **∠ый** **1.** [14; -ден, -дна́, -о] visible; **2.** [14] outstanding, eminent, prominent; F stately, portly.
видоизмен|е́ние *n* [12] variation; variety; **~я́ть** [1], ⟨~и́ть⟩ [13] alter, change.
видоиска́тель *m* [4] (view) finder.
ви́за *f* [5] visa.
визант|и́ец *m* [1; -и́йца], **~и́йка** *f* [5; *g/pl.:* и́ек], **~и́йский** [16] Byzantine; **~и́я** *f* [7] Byzantium.
виз|г *m* [1] scream, shriek; yelp; **~гли́вый** [14 *sh.*] shrill, squeaky; **~жа́ть** [4 *e.*; -жу́, -жи́шь], ⟨за-⟩ shriek; yelp.
визи́ровать [7] (*im*)*pf.* visa.
визи́т *m* [1] visit, call; **~ный** [14]: ~ная ка́рточка *f* calling card.
ви́ка *f* [5] vetch.
ви́л|ка *f* [5; *g/pl.:* -лок] **1.** fork; **2.** (ште́псельная) ~ка ⚡ plug; **~ы** *f/pl.* [5] pitchfork.
виля́ть [28], ⟨за-⟩, *once* ⟨вильну́ть⟩ [20] wag (one's tail хвосто́м); *fig.* prevaricate, shuffle.
вин|а́ *f* [5] **1.** guilt; fault; **2.** reason; вменя́ть в ~у́ impute (to Д); сва́ливать ~у́ lay the blame (on на В); э́то не по мое́й ~е́ it's not my fault.

винегре́т *m* [1] vinaigrette (salad).
вини́т|ельный [14] *gr.* accusative (*case*); **~ь** [13] blame (for за В), accuse (of в П).
ви́н|ный [14] wine...; **~ный ка́мень** *m* tartar; **~ная я́года** *f* (dried) fig; **~о́** *n* [9; *pl. st.*] wine; F vodka.
винова́т|ый [14 *sh.*] guilty (of в П); **~!** sorry!, excuse me!; (I beg your) pardon!; вы в э́том (не) **~ы** it's (not) your fault; я **~** пе́ред ва́ми I must apologize to you, (*a.* круго́м **~**) it's all my fault.
вино́в|ник *m* [1] **1.** culprit; **2.** originator, author; **~ный** [14; -вен, -вна] guilty (of в П).
виногра́д *m* [1] **1.** vine; **2.** *coll.* grapes *pl.*; сбор **~а** vintage; **~арство** *n* [9] winegrowing; **~арь** *m* [4] winegrower; **~ник** *m* [1] vineyard; **~ный** [14] (of) grape(s).
вино|де́лие *n* [12] winemaking; **~ку́ренный** [14]. **~ку́ренный** заво́д *m* distillery; **~торго́вец** [1; -вца] wine merchant.
винт *m* [1 *e.*] screw; **∠ик** *m* [1] small screw; у него́ **∠ика** не хвата́ет F he has a screw loose; **~о́вка** *f* [5; *g/pl.*: -вок] rifle; **~ово́й** [14] screw...; spiral; **~ова́я ле́стница** *f* spiral (winding) stairs.
винье́тка *f* [5; *g/pl.*: -ток] vignette.
виолонче́ль *f* [8] (violon)cello.
вира́ж *m* **1.** [1 *e.*] bend, curve; **2.** [1] *phot.* toning solution.
виртуо́з *m* [1] virtuoso.
ви́селица *f* [5] gallows, gibbet.
висе́ть [11] hang.
ви́ски *n* [*indecl.*] whisk(e)y.
виско́за *f* [5] viscose.
Ви́сла *f* [5] Vistula.
ви́смут *m* [1] bismuth.
ви́снуть F [21], ⟨по-⟩ *v/i.* hang, be suspended.
висо́к *m* [1; -ска́] *anat.* temple.
високо́сный [14]: **~** год *m* leap year.
вися́чий [17] hanging; suspension-...; **~** замо́к *m* padlock.
витами́н *m* [1] vitamin.
вит|а́ть [1] **1.** stay, linger; **2.** soar; **~ева́тый** [14] affected, bombastic.
вито́к *m* [1; -тка́] coil.
витри́на *f* [5] shopwindow; show-case.
вить [вью, вьёшь; ве́й(те)!; вил, -а́, -о; ви́тый (вит, -а́, -о)], ⟨с-⟩ [совью́, совьёшь] wind, twist; build (*nests*); **-ся 1.** wind; spin, whirl; **2.** twine, creep; curl; **3.** hover.
ви́тязь *m* [4] hero.
вихо́р *m* [1; -хра́] forelock.
вихрь *m* [4] whirlwind.
ви́це-... (*in compds.*) vice-...
вишн|ёвый [14] cherry...; **∠я** *f* [6; *g/pl.*: -шен] cherry.
вишь P look, there's; you see.
вка́пывать [1], ⟨вкопа́ть⟩ dig in; drive in; *fig.* как вко́панный stock-still, transfixed.
вка́т|ывать [1], ⟨**~и́ть**⟩ [15] roll in, wheel in.
вклад *m* [1] deposit; *fig.* contribution (to в В); **∠ка** [5; *g/pl.*: -док] insert; **∠чик** *m* [1] depositor; **∠ывать** [1], ⟨вложи́ть⟩ [16] put in, insert, enclose; invest; deposit.
вкле́|ивать [1], ⟨**~ить**⟩ [13] glue *or* paste in; **~йка** *f* [5; *g/pl.*: -е́ек] gluing in; sheet, *etc.*, glued in.
вкли́ни|вать(ся) [1], ⟨'**∠ть(ся)**⟩ [13; *a. st.*] (be) wedge(d) in.
включ|а́ть [1], ⟨**~и́ть**⟩ [16 *e.*; -чу́, -чи́шь; -чённый] include; insert; ⚡ switch *or* turn on; **-ся** join (s. th. в В); **~а́я** including; **~е́ние** *n* [12] inclusion; insertion; ⚡ switching on; **~и́тельно** included.
вкол|а́чивать [1], ⟨**~оти́ть**⟩ [15] drive *or* hammer in.
вконе́ц F completely, altogether.
вкопа́ть *s.* вка́пывать.
вкорен|я́ться [28], ⟨**~и́ться**⟩ [13] take root; **~и́вшийся** established, (deep-)rooted.
вкось askew, aslant, obliquely; вкривь и **~** pell-mell; amiss.
ВКП(б) = Всесою́зная Коммунисти́ческая па́ртия (большевико́в) C.P.S.U.(B.) = Communist Party of the Soviet Union (Bolsheviks); (*since 1952*: КПСС, *cf.*).
вкра́|дчивый [14 *sh.*] insinuating, ingratiating; **~дываться** [1], ⟨**~сться**⟩ [25] creep *or* steal in; *fig.* insinuate o.s.
вкра́тце briefly, in a few words.
вкруту́ю: яйцо́ **~** hard-boiled egg.
вкус *m* [1] **1.** taste; flavo(u)r; **2.** style; прия́тный на **~** savo(u)ry; прия́тно на **~** = **∠но**; быть *or* прийти́сь по **∠у** be to one's taste, relish (*or* like) s. th.; име́ть **~** (P) taste (of); **∠ный** [14; -сен, -сна́, -о] tasty; (э́то) **∠но** it tastes well *or* nice.
вку|ша́ть [1], ⟨**~си́ть**⟩ [15; вкушённый] **1.** taste; **2.** enjoy, experience.
вла́га *f* [5] moisture.
владе́|лец *m* [1; -льца] owner, proprietor, possessor; **~ние** *n* [12] possession (of T); **~тель** *m* [4] **1.** owner; **2.** ruler; **~ть** [8], ⟨за-, о-⟩ (T) own, possess; rule, govern; master, manage; **~ть собо́й** control o.s.
Влади́мир *m* [1] Vladimir.
влады́|ка *m* [5] **1.** lord, sovereign; **2.** archbishop; **~чество** *n* [9] rule, sway.
вла́жн|ость *f* [8] humidity; **~ый** [14; -жен, -жна́, -о] humid, damp.
вла́мываться [1], ⟨вломи́ться⟩ [14] break in.
власт|во́вать [7] rule, dominate; **~ели́н** *m* [1] sovereign; **~и́тель** *m* [4] master, ruler; **~ный** [14; -тен, -тна] imperious, commanding; в э́том я не **~ен** I have no power

over it; **\~ь** *f* [8; *from g/pl. e.*] authority, power; rule, regime; control; *pl.* authorities.
влачи́ть [16 *e.*; -чу́, -чи́шь] drag; eke out.
вле́во (to the) left.
влез|а́ть [1], ⟨\~ть⟩ [24 *st.*] climb *or* get in(to); climb up.
влет|а́ть [1], ⟨\~е́ть⟩ [11] fly in; rush in.
влеч|е́ние *n* [12] inclination; **\~ь** [26], ⟨по-, у-⟩ drag, pull; *fig.* attract, draw; **\~ь** за собо́й involve, entail.
вли|ва́ть [1], ⟨\~ть⟩ [волью́, -льёшь; вле́й(те)!; влил, -а́, -о; вли́тый (-та́, -о)] pour in; **-ся** flow *or* fall in; **\~я́ние** *n* [12] influence; **\~я́тельный** [14; -лен, -льна] influential; **\~я́ть** [28], ⟨по-⟩ (have) influence.
ВЛКСМ (Всесою́зный Ле́нинский Коммунисти́ческий Сою́з Молодёжи) Leninist Young Communist League of the Soviet Union.
вложи́ть *s.* вкла́дывать.
вломи́ться *s.* вла́мываться.
влюб|лённость *f* [8] amorousness; **\~ля́ться** [28], ⟨\~и́ться⟩ [14] fall in love (with в В); \~лённый enamo(u)red; lover; **\~чивый** [14 *sh.*] amorous.
вмен|я́емый ⚖ [14 *sh.*] responsible, accountable; **\~я́ть** [28], ⟨\~и́ть⟩ [13] consider (as в В), impute; **\~я́ть** (себе́) в обя́занность pledge s. o. (o. s.) (to *inf.*).
вме́сте together, along with; \~ с тем at the same time.
вмести́|мость *f* [8] capacity; **\~тельный** [14; -лен, -льна] capacious, spacious; **\~ть** *s.* **вмеща́ть.**
вме́сто (Р) instead, in place (of); as.
вмеш|а́тельство *n* [9] interference, intervention; ⚕ operation; **\~ивать** [1], ⟨\~а́ть⟩ [1] (В/в В) mingle (with); involve (in); **-ся** interfere, intervene, meddle (with в В).
вме|ща́ть [1], ⟨\~сти́ть⟩ [15 *e.*; -ещу́, -missing-ести́шь; -ещённый] **1.** put, place; **2.** hold, contain, accomodate; **-ся** find room; hold.
вмиг in an instant, in no time.
внаём *or* **внаймы́**: отда́ть (сдать) \~ rent, *Brt.* let; взять \~ rent, hire.
внача́ле at first, at the beginning.
вне (Р) out of, outside; beyond; быть \~ себя́ be beside o. s.
внебра́чный [14] illegitimate.
внедр|е́ние *n* [12] introduction; **\~я́ть** [28], ⟨\~и́ть⟩ [13] inculcate; introduce; **-ся** take root.
внеза́пный [14; -пен, -пна] sudden, unexpected.
внекла́ссный [14] out-of-class.
внеочередно́й [14] extra(ordinary).
внес|е́ние *n* [12] entry; **\~ти́** *s.* вноси́ть.
внешко́льный [14] nonschool.
вне́шн|ий [15] outward, external; foreign; **\~ость** *f* [8] appearance; exterior.
вниз down(ward[s]); **\~у́ 1.** (Р) beneath, below; **2.** down(stairs).
вник|а́ть [1], ⟨\~нуть⟩ [19] (в В) penetrate (into), fathom.
внима́|ние *n* [12] attention; care; приня́ть во \~ние take into consideration; принима́я во \~ние in view of, with regard to; оста́вить без \~ния disregard; **\~тельность** *f* [8] attentiveness; **\~тельный** [14; -лен, -льна] attentive; **\~ть** [1], ⟨внять⟩ [*inf. & pt. only*; внял, -а́, -о] (Д) hear *or* listen (to); follow, watch; comply with.
вничью́: сыгра́ть \~ draw (*game*).
вновь 1. again; **2.** newly.
вноси́ть [15], ⟨внести́⟩ [24 -с-: -су́, -сёшь; внёс, внесла́] carry *or* bring in; enter, include; pay (in); contribute; make (*correction*).
внук *m* [1] grandson; *cf.* внуча́та.
вну́тренн|ий [15] inner, inside, internal, interior; inland...; home...; **\~ость** *f* [8] interior; (*esp. pl.*) internal organs, entrails.
внутр|и́ (Р) in(side); within; **\~ь** (Р) in(to), inward(s), inside.
внуч|а́та *m/f pl.* [2] grandchildren; **\~ка** *f* [5; *g/pl.*: -чек] granddaughter.
внуш|а́ть [1], ⟨\~и́ть⟩ [16 *e.*; -шу́, -ши́шь; -шённый] (Д/В) suggest; inspire (a p. with); inculcate (upon); **\~е́ние** *n* [12] suggestion; infusion; reprimand; **\~и́тельный** [14; -лен, -льна] imposing, impressive; **\~и́ть** *s.* \~а́ть.
вня́т|ный [14; -тен, -тна] distinct; intelligible; **\~ь** *s.* внима́ть.
вобра́ть *s.* вбира́ть.
вовл|ека́ть [1], ⟨\~е́чь⟩ [26] drag in; *fig.* involve.
во́время in *or* on time, timely.
во́все quite; \~ не(т) not at all.
вовсю́ F with all one's might.
во-вторы́х second(ly).
вогна́ть *s.* вгоня́ть.
во́гнутый [14 *sh.*] concave.
вод|а́ *f* [5; *ac/sg.*: во́ду; *pl.*: во́ды, вод, во́дам] water; на \~е́ и на су́ше by sea and by land; в му́тной \~е́ ры́бу лови́ть fish in troubled waters; вы́йти сухи́м из \~ы́ come off clear; толо́чь \~у (в сту́пе) beat the air.
водвор|я́ть [28], ⟨\~и́ть⟩ [13] settle; install; (re)establish.
водеви́ль *m* [4] musical comedy.
води́тель *m* [4] driver.
вод|и́ть [15], ⟨по-⟩ **1.** lead, conduct, guide; **2.** drive; **3.** move (Т); **4.** breed; \~и́ть дру́жбу be on friendly terms; **-ся** be (found), live; be customary *or* the custom; (у Р, за Т) have; (с Т) associate

(with); это за ним ̷ится F that's in his way, to be sure!
во́дка *f* [5; *g/pl.:* -док] vodka (*kind of whisky*); дать на во́дку tip.
водо|боя́знь *f* [8] hydrophobia; **~во́з** *m* [1] water carter; **~воро́т** *m* [1] whirlpool, eddy; **~ём** *m* [1] reservoir; **~измеще́ние** ⚓ *n* [12] displacement, tonnage; **~ка́чка** *f* [5; *g/pl.:* -чек] waterworks.
водо|ла́з *m* [1] diver; **~лече́ние** *n* [12] hydropathy, water cure; **~напо́рный** [14]: ~напо́рная ба́шня *f* water tower; **~непроница́емый** [14 *sh.*] watertight; **~но́с** *m* [1] water carrier; **~па́д** *m* [1] waterfall; **~по́й** *m* [3] watering place; watering (*of animals*); **~прово́д** *m* [1] water pipe; **~разде́л** *m* [1] divide, *Brt.* watershed; **~ро́д** *m* [1] hydrogen; **~ро́дный** [14]: ~ро́дная бо́мба *f* hydrogen bomb; **'~росль** *f* [8] alga, seaweed; **~снабже́ние** *n* [12] water supply; **~сто́к** *m* [1] drain(age), drainpipe; **~сто́чный** [14]: ~сто́чная труба́ *f* gutter; **~храни́лище** *n* [11] reservoir.
водру|жа́ть [1], ⟨~зи́ть⟩ [15 *e.*; -ужу́, -узи́шь; -ужённый] set up; hoist.
вод|яни́стый [14 *sh.*] watery; **~я́нка** *f* [5] dropsy; **~яно́й** [14] water...
воева́ть [14], wage *or* carry on war, be at war.
воеди́но together.
военача́льник *m* [1] commander.
военизи|а́ция *f* [7] militarization; **~и́ровать** [7] (*im*)*pf.* militarize.
военно|-возду́шный [14]: ~-возду́шные си́лы *f/pl.* air force; **~-морско́й** [14]: ~-морско́й флот *m* navy; **~пле́нный** [14] prisoner of war; **~-полево́й** [14]: ~-полево́й суд *m* court-martial; **~слу́жащий** [17] military man, soldier.
вое́нн|ый [14] **1.** military, war...; **2.** military man, soldier; ~ый врач *m* medical officer; ~ый кора́бль *m* man-of-war, warship; ~ое положе́ние *n* martial law (under на П); поступи́ть на ~ую слу́жбу enlist, join; ~ые де́йствия *n/pl.* hostilities.
вож|а́к [1 *e.*] guide; leader; **~а́тый** [14] leader, guide; streetcar (*Brt.* tram) driver; **~дь** *m* [4 *e.*] chief (-tain); leader; **̷жи** *f/pl.* [8; *from g/pl. e.*] reins.
воз *m* [1; на -у́; *pl. e.*] cart(load).
возбу|ди́мый [14 *sh.*] excitable; **~ди́тель** *m* [4] exciter; **~жда́ть** [1], ⟨~ди́ть⟩ [15 *e.*; -ужу́, -уди́шь] excite, stir up; arouse; incite; raise; bring, present; **~жда́ющий** [17] stimulating; ~жда́ющее сре́дство *n* stimulant; **~жде́ние** *n* [12] excitement; **~ждённый** [14] excited.
возвели́ч|ивать [1], ⟨~ить⟩ [16] exalt, praise, glorify.
возвести́ *s.* возводи́ть.
возве|ща́ть [1], ⟨~сти́ть⟩ [15 *e.*; -ещу́, -ести́шь; -ещённый] (В/Д *or* о П/Д) announce.
возв|оди́ть [15], ⟨~ести́⟩ [25] (в *or* на В) lead up; raise, elevate; erect; make.
возвра́|т *m* [1] **1.** = ~ще́ние 1. & 2.; **2.** ⚕ relapse; **~ти́ть(ся)** *s.* ~ща́ть (-ся); **~тный** [14] back...; relapsing; *gr.* reflexive; **~ща́ть** [1], ⟨~ти́ть⟩ [15 *e.*; -ащу́, -ати́шь; -ащённый] return; give back; restore, reimburse; recover; **-ся** return, come back (from из *or* с Р); revert (to к Д); **~ще́ние** *n* [12] **1.** return; **2.** restitution.
возв|ыша́ть [1], ⟨~ы́сить⟩ [15] raise, elevate; **-ся** rise; tower (over над Т); **~ыше́ние** *n* [12] rise; elevation; **~ы́шенность** *f* [8] **1.** sublimity, loftiness; **2.** hill (range); **~ы́шенный** [14] elevated, lofty.
возгл|авля́ть [28], ⟨~а́вить⟩ [14] (be at the) head.
во́згла|с *m* [1] exclamation, (out-) cry; **~ша́ть** [1], ⟨~си́ть⟩ [15 *e.*; -ашу́, -аси́шь; -ашённый] proclaim.
возд|ава́ть [5], ⟨~а́ть⟩ [-да́м, -да́шь, *etc. s.* дава́ть] reward; show, do; ~а́ть до́лжное do justice (to Д).
воздвиг|а́ть [1], ⟨̷нуть⟩ [21] erect, construct, raise.
возде́йств|ие *n* [12] influence, impact; **~овать** [7] (*im*)*pf.* (на В) influence; act upon, affect.
возде́л|ывать, ⟨~ать⟩ [1] till.
воздержа́ние *n* [12] abstinence; abstention.
возде́рж|анный [14 *sh.*] *s.* ~ный; **~иваться** [1], ⟨~а́ться⟩ [4] abstain (from от Р); при двух ~а́вшихся *pol.* with two abstentions; **~ный** [14; -жен, -жна] abstemious, temperate.
во́здух *m* [1] air; на (откры́том *or* све́жем) ~е in the open air, outdoors; **~оплава́ние** *n* [12] aeronautics.
возду́ш|ный 1. [14] air...; ~ная трево́га *f* air-raid warning; ~ные за́мки *m/pl.* castles in the air; **2.** [14; -шен, -шна] airy.
воззва́|ние *n* [12] appeal; proclamation; **~ть** *s.* взыва́ть.
вози́ть [15] drive, transport; **-ся** (с Т) busy o.s. (with), mess (around with); dawdle; fidget; romp, frolic.
возл|ага́ть [1], ⟨~ожи́ть⟩ [16] (на В) lay (on); entrust (with); ~ага́ть наде́жды на (В) rest one's hopes upon.
во́зле (Р) by, near, beside.
возложи́ть *s.* возлага́ть.
возлю́блен|ный [14] beloved; *m* lover; ~ная *f* mistress, sweetheart.
возме́здие *n* [12] requital.
возме|ща́ть [1], ⟨~сти́ть⟩ [15 *e.*; -ещу́, -ести́шь; -ещённый] com-

pensate, recompense; **\~ще́ние** *n* [12] compensation, indemnification.
возмо́жн|о it is possible; possibly; о́чень \~о very likely; **\~ость** *f* [8] possibility; chance; по (ме́ре) \~ости as ... (far) as possible; **\~ый** [14; -жен, -жна] possible; сде́лать всё \~ое do one's utmost.
возмужа́лый [14] mature, virile.
возму|ти́тельный [14; -лен, -льна] revolting, shoking; **\~ща́ть**, ⟨**\~ти́ть**⟩ [15 *e.*; -щу́, -ути́шь] revolt; **-ся** be shocked *or* indignant (at T); **\~ще́ние** *n* [12] indignation; revolt; **\~щённый** [14] indignant.
вознагра|жда́ть [1], ⟨**\~ди́ть**⟩ [15 *e.*; -ажу́, -ади́шь; -аждённый] reward, recompense, indemnify; **\~жде́ние** *n* [12] reward, recompense.
вознаме́ри|ваться [1], ⟨**\~ться**⟩ [13] intend, decide.
вознес|е́ние *n* [12] ascension; **\~ти́(сь)** *s.* возноси́ть(ся).
возник|а́ть [1], ⟨**∠нуть**⟩ [21] arise, originate, emerge; **\~нове́ние** *n* [12] rise, origin.
возн|оси́ть [15], ⟨**\~ести́**⟩ [24 -с-: -су́, -сёшь; -нёс, -несла́; -несённый] raise, elevate; exalt; **-ся**, ⟨**-сь**⟩ **1.** rise; **2.** become haughty.
возня́ *f* [6] **1.** fuss, bustle, romp; **2.** trouble, bother.
возобнов|ле́ние *n* [12] renewal; resumption; **\~ля́ть** [28], ⟨**\~и́ть**⟩ [14 *e.*; -влю́, -ви́шь; -влённый] renew; resume.
возра|жа́ть [1], ⟨**\~зи́ть**⟩ [15 *e.*; -ажу́, -ази́шь] **1.** object (to про́тив Р); **2.** return, retort (to на В); (я) не \~жа́ю I don't mind; **\~же́ние** *n* [12] objection; rejoinder.
во́зраст *m* [1] age (at в П); **\~а́ние** *n* [12] growth, increase; **\~а́ть** [1], ⟨**\~и́**⟩ [24 -ст-: -расту́; -ро́с, -ла́; -ро́сший] grow up; increase, rise.
возро|жда́ть [1], ⟨**\~ди́ть**⟩ [15 *e.*; -ожу́, -оди́шь; -ождённый] revive, regenerate (*v/i.*: **-ся**); **\~жде́ние** *n* [12] rebirth, revival; эпо́ха 2\~жде́ния Renaissance.
во́зчик *m* [1] wag(g)oner, carter.
во́ин *m* [1] warrior, soldier; **\~ский** [16] military; \~ская обя́занность († пови́нность) *f* conscription; **∠ственный** [14] martial, bellicose.
вои́стину truly, really.
вой *m* [3] howl(ing), wail(ing).
во́йло|к *m* [1] **\~чный** [14] felt.
войн|а́ *f* [5; *pl. st.*] war (at на П); warfare; идти́ на \~у́ take the field; поджига́тель \~ы́ warmonger; втора́я мирова́я \~а́ World War II.
во́йск|о *n* [9; *pl. e.*] host; army; *pl.* troops, (*land, etc.*) forces.
войти́ *s.* входи́ть.
вокза́л *m* [1] railroad (*Brt.* railway) station, depot.
вокру́г (Р) (a)round; верте́ться \~ да о́коло F beat about the bush.
вол *m* [1 *e.*] ox.
Во́лга *f* [5] Volga.
волды́рь *m* [4 *e.*] blister, swelling.
волейбо́л *m* [1] volleyball.
во́лей-нево́лей willy-nilly.
во́лжский [16] (on the) Volga...
волк *m* [1; *from g/pl. e.*] wolf; смотре́ть ∠ом F scowl.
волн|а́ *f* [5; *pl. st., from dat. a. e.*] wave; ⚡ дли́нные, сре́дние, коро́ткие ∠ы long, medium, short waves; **\~е́ние** *n* [12] agitation, excitement, unrest; *pl.* troubles, riots; **\~и́стый** [14 *sh.*] wavy, undulating; **\~ова́ть** [7], ⟨вз-⟩ (**-ся** be) agitate(d), excite(d); worry; **\~у́ющий** [17] exciting, thrilling.
воло́вий [18] ox...
Воло́дя *m* [6] *dim. of* Влади́мир.
волоки́т|а F [5] **1.** *f* red tape; a lot of fuss and trouble; **2.** *m* lady-killer, ladies' man; **\~ство** *n* [9] flirtation.
волокн|и́стый [14 *sh.*] fibrous; **\~о́** *n* [9; *pl.*: -о́кна, -о́кон, *etc. st.*] fiber, *Brt.* fibre.
волонтёр *m* [1] volunteer.
во́лос *m* [1; *g/pl.*: -ло́с; *from dat. e.*] (*a. pl.*) hair; **\~а́тый** [14 *sh.*] hairy; **\~о́к** *m* [1; -ска́] (small) hair; ⚡ filament; быть на \~о́к (*or* на \~ке́) от сме́рти F be on the verge (within a hair's breadth *or* ace) of death; висе́ть (*or* держа́ться) на \~ке́ hang by *or* on a thread.
во́лость *f* [8; *from g/pl. e.*] district.
волосяно́й [14] hair...
волочи́ть [16], ⟨по-⟩ drag, pull, draw; **-ся** drag o.s., crawl along; F (за T) run after, court.
волхв *m* [1 *e.*] magician, wizard.
во́лчий [18] wolfish; wolf('s)...
волчо́к *m* [1; -чка́] top (*toy*).
волчо́нок *m* [2] wolf cub.
волше́б|ник *m* [1] magician; **\~ница** *f* [5] sorceress; **\~ный** [14] magic, fairy...; [-бен, -бна] *fig.* enchanting; **\~ство́** *n* [9] magic, witchery.
волы́нка *f* [5 *g/pl.*; -нок] bagpipe.
вольно|ду́мец *m* [1; -мца] freethinker; **\~слу́шатель** *m* [4] auditor, irregular student.
во́льн|ость *f* [8] liberty; freedom; **\~ый** [14; -лен, -льна́, -о] free, easy, unrestricted; ⚔ \~о! at ease!
вольт *m* [1] volt.
вольфра́м *m* [1] wolframite.
во́л|я *f* [6] **1.** will; си́ла \~и will power; **2.** liberty, freedom; \~я ва́ша (just) as you like; по до́брой \~е of one's own will; отпусти́ть на \~ю set free; дать \~ю give free rein.
вон 1. F there; \~ там over there; **2.** \~! get out!; пошёл \~! out *or* away (with you)!; вы́гнать \~ turn out; \~ (оно́) что! F you don't say!; oh, that's it!
вонз|а́ть [1], ⟨**\~и́ть**⟩ [15 *e.*; -нжу́,

-зи́шь; -зённый] thrust, plunge, transfix.
вон|ь *f* [8] stench, stink; **~ючий** [17 *sh.*] stinking; **~ючка** *f* [5; *g/pl.*: -чек] skunk; **~я́ть** [28] stink (of T).
вообра|жа́емый [14 *sh.*] imaginary, supposed; **~жа́ть** [1], ⟨**~зи́ть**⟩ [15 *e.*; -ажу́, -ази́шь; -ажённый] (*a.* ~жа́ть себе́) imagine, fancy; ~жа́ть себя́ imagine o. s. (s. b. T); ~жа́ть о себе́ be conceited; **~же́ние** *n* [12] imagination; fancy; **~зи́мый** [14 *sh.*] imaginable.
вообще́ generally, in general; at all.
воодушев|ле́ние *n* [12] enthusiasm; **~ля́ть** [28], ⟨**~и́ть**⟩ [14 *e.*; -влю́, -ви́шь; -влённый] (-ся feel) inspire(d by T).
вооруж|а́ть [1], ⟨**~и́ть**⟩ [16 *e.*; -жу́, -жи́шь; -жённый] 1. arm, equip (with T); 2. stir up (against про́тив P); **~е́ние** *n* [12] armament, equipment.
воо́чию with one's own eyes.
во-пе́рвых first(ly).
вопи́|ть [14 *e.*; -плю́, -пи́шь], ⟨за-⟩ cry out, bawl; lament, wail; **~ющий** [17] crying, flagrant.
вопло|ща́ть [1], ⟨**~ти́ть**⟩ [15 *e.*; -ощу́, -оти́шь; -ощённый] embody, personify; ~щённый *a.* incarnate; **~ще́ние** *n* [12] embodiment, incarnation.
вопль *m* [4] outcry, clamo(u)r; wail.
вопреки́ (Д) contrary to; in spite of.
вопро́с *m* [1] question; под ~ом questionable, doubtful; ~ не в э́том that's not the question; спо́рный ~ point at issue; что за ~! of course!; **~и́тельный** [14] interrogative; ~и́тельный знак *m* question mark.
вор *m* [1; *from g/pl. e.*] thief.
ворва́ться *s.* врыва́ться.
ворко|ва́ть [7], ⟨за-⟩ coo; **~тня́** F *f* [6] grumble.
вороб|е́й *m* [3 *e.*; -бья́] sparrow; ста́рый (*or* стре́ляный) ~е́й F cunning fellow; **~ьи́ный** [14] sparrow('s)...
воров|а́ть [7], ⟨F с-⟩ steal; **∠ка** *f* [5; *g/pl.*: -вок] (female) thief; **~ско́й** [16] thievish; thieves'...; **~ство́** *n* [9] theft, larceny.
ворожи́ть [16 *e.*; -жу́, -жи́шь], ⟨по-⟩ tell fortunes.
во́рон *m* [1] raven; **∠а** *f* [5] crow; воро́н счита́ть F stand gaping about.
воро́нка *f* [5; *g/pl.*: -нок] 1. funnel; 2. crater.
вороно́й [14] black; *su.* *m* black horse.
во́рот *m* [1] 1. collar; 2. windlass; **∠а** *n/pl.* [9] gate; **~и́ть** [15] 1. (*pf.*) F *cf.* возвраща́ть; 2. (*impf.*) P move, roll; turn off, round; 3. *s.* воро́чать 2.; **~ни́к** *m* [1 *e.*] collar; **~ничо́к** *m* [1; -чка] (small) collar.
во́рох *m* [1; *pl.*: -ха́, *etc. e.*] pile, heap.
воро́|чать [1] 1. *s.* ~ти́ть 2.; 2. F manage, boss (T); -ся toss; turn; stir; **~ши́ть** [16 *e.*; -шу́, -ши́шь; -шённый] turn (over).
ворч|а́ние *n* [12] grumbling, growl; **~а́ть** [4 *e.*; -чу́, -чи́шь], ⟨за-, п(р)о-⟩ grumble, growl; **~ли́вый** [14 *sh.*] grumbling, surly; **~у́н** F *m* [1 *e.*], **~у́нья** *f* [6] grumbler.
восвоя́си F home.
восемна́дца|тый [14] eighteenth; **~ть** [35] eighteen; *s.* пять, пя́тый.
во́семь [35; восьми́, *instr.* восемью́] eight; *cf.* пять & пя́тый; **~десят** [35; восьми́десяти] eighty; **~со́т** [36; восьмисо́т] eight hundred; **~ю** eight times.
воск *m* [1] wax.
воскл|ица́ние *n* [12] exclamation. **~ица́тельный** [14] exclamatory; ~ица́тельный знак *m* exclamation mark *or* point; **~ица́ть** [1], ⟨**~и́кнуть**⟩ [20] exclaim.
восково́й [14] wax(en)...
воскр|еса́ть [1], ⟨**~е́снуть**⟩ [21] rise (from из P); recover; Христо́с ~е́с(е)! Christ has arisen! (*Easter greeting*); (*reply*:) вои́стину ~е́с(е)! (He has) truly arisen!; **~есе́ние** *n* [12] Resurrection; **~есе́нье** *n* [10] Sunday (on: в В, *pl.* по Д); **~еша́ть** [1], ⟨**~еси́ть**⟩ [15 *e.*; -ешу́, -еси́шь; -ешённый] resuscitate, revive.
воспал|е́ние *n* [12] inflammation; ~е́ние лёгких (по́чек) pneumonia (nephritis); **~ённый** [14 *sh.*] inflamed; **~и́тельный** [14] inflammatory; **~я́ть** [28], ⟨**~и́ть**⟩ [13] inflame (*v/i.* -ся).
воспе|ва́ть [1], ⟨**∠ть**⟩ [-пою́, -поёшь; -пе́тый] sing of, praise.
воспит|а́ние *n* [12] education, upbringing; **∠анник** *m* [1], **∠анница** *f* [5] foster child; pupil; **∠анный** [14 *sh.*] well-bred; пло́хо ∠анный ill-bred; **~а́тель** *m* [4] educator; (private) tutor; **~а́тельный** [14] educational, pedagogic(al); **∠ывать** [1], ⟨**~а́ть**⟩ bring up; educate.
воспламен|я́ть [28], ⟨**~и́ть**⟩ [13] inflame (*v/i.* -ся).
восполн|я́ть [28], ⟨**∠ить**⟩ [13] fill (up); make up (for).
воспо́льзоваться *s.* по́льзоваться.
воспомина́ние *n* [12] remembrance, recollection, reminiscence; *pl. a.* memoirs.
воспре|ща́ть [1], ⟨**~ти́ть**⟩ [15 *e.*; -ещу́, -ети́шь; -ещённый] prohibit, forbid; вход ~щён! no entrance!; кури́ть ~ща́ется! no smoking!; **~ще́ние** *n* [12] interdiction, prohibition.
воспри|и́мчивый [14 *sh.*] sensitive; susceptible (to к Д); **~нима́ть** [1], ⟨**~ня́ть**⟩ [-приму́, -и́мешь; -и́нял, -а́, -о; -и́нятый] take (up); conceive; **~я́тие** *n* [12] perception.

воспроизв|еде́ние *n* [12] reproduction; **~оди́ть** [15], ‹~ести́› [25] reproduce.
воспря́нуть [20] *pf.* rise, jump up; ~ ду́хом cheer up.
воссоедин|е́ние *n* [12] reun(ification; **~я́ть** [28], ‹~и́ть› [13] reunite.
восста|ва́ть [5], ‹**́~ть**› [-ста́ну, -ста́нешь] (a)rise; revolt.
восстан|а́вливать [1], ‹**~ови́ть**› [14] 1. reconstruct, restore; 2. stir up, dispose **́~ие** *n* [12] insurrection, revolt; **~ови́ть** *s.* **~а́вливать**; **~овле́ние** *n* [12] reconstruction, restoration.
восто́к *m* [1] east; ♀ the East, Orient; Бли́жний (Да́льний) ♀ the Near (Far) East; на ~ (to[ward] the) east, eastward(s); на ~е in the east; с ~а from the east; к ~у от (P) (to the) east of.
восто́р|г *m* [1] delight, rapture; я в ~ге I am delighted (with от P); приводи́ть (приходи́ть) в ~г = **~га́ть(ся)** [1] *impf.* (be) delight(ed) (with T); **~женный** [14 *sh.*] enthusiastic, exalted.
восто́чный [14] east(ern, -erly); oriental.
востре́бова|ние *n* [12]: до ~ния poste restante; **~ть** [7] *pf.* call for.
восхвал|е́ние *n* [12] praise, eulogy; **~я́ть** [28], ‹~и́ть› [13; -алю́, -а́лишь] praise, extol.
восхи|ти́тельный [14; -лен, -льна] delightful; **~ща́ть** [1], ‹~ти́ть› [15 *e.*; -ищу́, -ити́шь; -ищённый] delight, transport; **-ся** (T) be delighted (with), admire; **~ще́ние** *n* [12] admiration, delight; приводи́ть (приходи́ть) в ~ще́ние *s.* ~ща́ть(ся).
восхо́|д *m* [1], **~жде́ние** *n* [12] rise; ascent; ~д со́лнца sunrise; **~ди́ть** [15], ‹взойти́› [взойду́, -дёшь; взошёл, -шла́; взоше́дший] rise, ascend.
восше́ствие *n* [12] ascent; ~ на престо́л accession to the throne.
восьм|ёрка *f* [5; *g/pl.*: -рок] eight (*cf.* дво́йка); **́~еро** [37] eight (*cf.* дво́е).
восьми|деся́тый [14] eightieth; *cf.* пят(идеся́т)ый; **~ле́тний** [14] of eight, aged 8; **~со́тый** [14] eight hundredth; **~часово́й** [14] eight-hour…
восьм|о́й [14] eighth; *cf.* пя́тый; **~у́шка** *f* [5] eighth of lb.; octavo.
вот here (is); there; now; well; that's …; ~ и всё F that's all; ́~ (оно́) как *or* что! you don't say!, is that so?; ́~ те(бе) ра́з *or* на́! there you are!; a pretty business this!; ́~ како́й … such a …; ́~ челове́к! what a man!; ~-~! yes, indeed; ~-́~ every *or* (at) any moment.
воткну́ть *s.* втыка́ть.
во́тум *m* [1] vote.
во́тчина *f* [5] patrimony (*estate*).
воцар|я́ться [28], ‹~и́ться› [13] 1. accede to the throne; 2. set in; be restored.
вошь *f* [8; вши; во́шью] louse.
вощи́ть [16 *e.*], ‹на-› wax.
вою́ющий [17] belligerent.
впа|да́ть [1], ‹~сть› [25; впал, -а] (в В) fall (flow, run) in(to); **~де́ние** *n* [12] flowing into; mouth, confluence; **́~дина** *f* [5] cavity, socket; **́~лый** [14] hollow, sunken; **~сть** *s.* [~да́ть.]
впервы́е for the first time.
вперего́нки́ F *s.* наперего́нки́.
вперёд forward, ahead (of P), on (-ward); in future; in advance, beforehand; *s. a.* зад.
впереди́ in front, ahead (of P) before.
впереме́жку F alternately.
впер|я́ть [28], ‹~и́ть› [13] fix (one's eyes on взор в В).
впечатл|е́ние *n* [12] impression; **~и́тельный** [14; -лен, льна] sensitive.
впи|ва́ть [1], ‹~ть› [вопью́, -пьёшь; впил, -а́, -о] suck in, imbibe; **-ся** (в В) cling to; seize; stick; fix. [insert.]
впи́с|ывать [1], ‹~а́ть› [3] enter,
впи́т|ывать [1], ‹~а́ть› soak up *or* in; absorb, imbibe; **~ь** *s.* впива́ть.
впи́х|ивать [1], *once* ‹~ну́ть› [20] push *or* squeeze in(to) (в В).
вплавь by swimming.
впле|та́ть [1], ‹~сти́› [25 -т-: вплету́, -тёшь] interlace, braid.
вплот|ну́ю (к Д) (quite) close(ly) by, (right) up to; *fig.* F seriously; **~ь** (к Д) (right) up to; even (till).
вполго́лоса in a low voice.
вполз|а́ть [1], ‹~ти́› [24] creep *or* crawl in(to), up.
вполне́ quite, fully, entirely.
впопа́д F to the point, relevantly.
впопыха́х *s.* второпя́х.
впо́ру: быть ~ fit.
впосле́дствии afterward(s), later.
впотьма́х in the dark.
впра́вду F really, indeed.
вправ|ля́ть [28], ‹́~ить› [14] set.
впра́ве: быть ~ have the right.
впра́во (to the) right.
впредь henceforth, in future.
впро́голодь starv(el)ing.
впрок 1. for future use; 2. to a p.'s benefit; э́то ему́ ~ не пойдёт he won't profit by it.
впро́чем by the way; however.
впры́г|ивать [1], *once* ‹~нуть› [20] jump in(to) *or* on; (в, на В).
впры́с|кивание *n* [12] injection; **~кивать** [1], *once* ‹~нуть› [20] inject.
впря|га́ть [1], ‹~чь› [26 г/ж; *cf.* напря́чь] harness, put to (в В).
впус|к *m* [1] admission; **~ка́ть** [1], ‹~ти́ть› [15] let in, admit.
впусту́ю F in vain, to no purpose.
впу́т|ывать [1], ‹~ать› entangle,

involve (in в B); **-ся** become entangled.
впятер|о five times (*cf.* вдвóе); **~óм** five (together).
враг *m* [1 *e.*] enemy; † devil.
вражд|á *f* [5] enmity; **~дéбность** *f* [8] animosity; **~дéбный** [14; -бен, -бна] hostile; **~довáть** [7] be at enmity (with с T); **∠еский** [16], **∠ий** [18] (the) enemy('s)...
вразбрóд F separately, scatteringly.
вразрéз: идтú ~ be contrary (to с T).
вразум|úтельный [14; -лен, -льна] intelligible, clear; **~лять** [1], ⟨**~úть**⟩ [13] bring to reason; instruct, make wise.
врá|ль F *m* [4 *e.*] liar; tattler; **~ньё** *n* [12] lies, fibs *pl.*, idle talk.
врас|плóх unawares, by surprise; **~сыпнýю**: брóситься ~сыпнýю disperse.
враст|áть [1], ⟨**~ú**⟩ [24 -ст-: -стý; врос, -лá] grow in(to); settle *or* subside.
вратáрь *m* [4 *e.*] goalkeeper.
врать F [вру, врёшь; врал, -á, -о], ⟨со-⟩ [сóвранный], lie; make a mistake; be inaccurate; tell (tales).
врач *m* [1 *e.*] doctor, physician; **~éбный** [14] medical.
вращ|áть [1] (B *or* T) turn, revolve, rotate (*v/i.* **-ся**; -ся в П associate with); **~áющийся** revolving, rotatory; **~éние** *n* [12] rotation.
вред *m* [1 *e.*] harm, damage; detriment; **~úтель** *m* [4] ⸗ pest; saboteur; **~úтельство** *n* [9] sabotage; **~úть** [15 *e.*; -ежý, -едúшь], ⟨по-⟩ (do) harm, (cause) damage (to Д); **∠ный** [14; -ден, -днá, -о] harmful, injurious (to Д *or* для P).
врез|áть [1], ⟨**∠ать**⟩ [3] (в B) cut in(to); lay *or* put in(to); **-ся** run in(to); project into; impress (on).
врéмен|ный [14] temporary, transient, provisional; **~щúк** *m* [1 *e.*] favo(u)rite, minion.
врéм|я *n* [13] time; *gr.* tense; weather; ~я гóда season; во ~я (P) during; в настоя́щее ~я at (the) present (moment); от ~ени до ~ени, по ~енáм, ~енáми from time to time, (every) now and then, sometimes; в скóром ~ени soon; в то (же) ~я at that (the same) time; в то ~я как whereas; за послéднее ~я lately, recently; на ~я for a (certain) time, temporarily; in (*the long*) run; со ~енем in the course of time; тем ~енем meanwhile; скóлько ~ени? how long?; what's the time?; хорошó провестú ~я have a good time; **~яисчислéние** *n* [12] chronology; **~я(пре)провождéние** *n* [12] pastime.
врóвень even, abreast (with с T).
врóде like; such as; kind of.
врождённый [14 *sh.*] innate.

вроз(н)ь separately, apart.
врун F *m* [1 *e.*], **∠ья** F *f* [6] lier.
вруч|áть [1], ⟨**~úть**⟩ [16] hand over; entrust.
вры|вáть [1], ⟨**~ть**⟩ [22] dig in; **-ся**, ⟨ворвáться⟩ [-вýсь, -вёшься; -вáлся, -лáсь] rush in(to); enter (by force).
вряд: ~ ли hardly, scarcely.
всáдни|к *m* [1] horseman; **~ца** *f* [5] horsewoman.
всá|живать [1], ⟨**~дúть**⟩ [15] thrust *or* drive in(to), hit; **~сывать** [1], ⟨всосáть⟩ [-сý, -сёшь] suck in *or* up, imbibe.
всё, все *s.* весь.
все|вéдущий [17] omniscient; **~возмóжный** [14] of all kinds *or* sorts.
всегдá always; **~шний** [15] constant, habitual.
всегó (-ˈvɔ) altogether, in all; sum total; ~ (тóлько, лишь, -нáвсего) only, merely; прéжде ~ above all.
всел|éнная *f* [14] universe, world; **~ять** [28], ⟨**~úть**⟩ [13] settle, move in(to) (*v/i.* **-ся**); *fig.* inspire.
все|мéрный every (*or* all) ... possible; **~мéрно** in every possible way; **~мúрный** [14] world..., universal; **~могýщий** [17 *sh.*] = **~сúльный**; **~нарóдный** [14; -ден, -дна] national, nation-wide; *adv.*: ~нарóдно in public; **∠нощная** *f* [14] vespers *pl.*; **~óбщий** [17] universal, general; **~объéмлющий** [17 *sh.*] universal; **~россúйский** [16] All-Russian.
всерьёз F in earnest, seriously.
все|сúльный [14; -лен, -льна] omnipotent, almighty; **~сою́зный** [14] All-Union, ... of the U.S.S.R.; **~сторóнний** [15] all-round.
всё-таки nevertheless, (but) still.
всеуслы́шание: во ~ in public.
всецéло entirely, wholly.
вскá|кивать [1], ⟨вскочúть⟩ [16] jump *or* leap (up/on на B); start (from с P); F rise *or* swell; **~пывать**, ⟨вскопáть⟩ [1] dig up.
вскарáбк|иваться, ⟨**~аться**⟩ [1] (на B) climb (up).
вскáрмливать [1], ⟨вскормúть⟩ [14] raise, rear *or* bring up.
вскачь at full gallop.
вскип|áть [1], ⟨**~éть**⟩ [10 *e.*; -плю́, -пúшь] boil (up); *fig.* fly into a passion.
вскло́(кó)|чивать [1], ⟨**~чить**⟩ [16] tousle; ~ченные *or* ~чившиеся вóлосы *m/pl.* dishevel(l)ed hair.
всколы́х|ивать [1], ⟨**~áть**⟩ [3 *st.* & 1], *once* ⟨**~нýть**⟩ [20] stir up, rouse.
вскóльзь in passing, cursorily.
вскопáть *s.* вскáпывать.
вскóре soon, before long.
вскормúть *s.* вскáрмливать.
вскочúть *s.* вскáкивать.
вскрú|кивать [1], ⟨**~чáть**⟩ [4 *e.*

-чу́, -чи́шь], *once* ‹~кнуть› [20] cry out, scream.
вскружи́ть [16; -жу́, -у́жи́шь] *pf.*; ~ (Д) го́лову turn a p.'s head.
вскры|ва́ть [1], ‹~ть› [22] **1.** open; reveal; **2.** dissect; **-ся 1.** open; be disclosed; **2.** break (up); **∠тие** *n* [12] **1.** opening; disclosure; **2.** dissection, autopsy; **3.** breaking up.
всласть F to one's heart's content.
вслед (за T; Д) (right) after, behind, following; **∠ствие** (P) in consequence of, owing to; **∠ствие э́того** consequently.
вслепу́ю F blindly, at random.
вслух aloud.
вслу́ш|иваться [1], ‹~аться› (в B) listen attentively (to).
всма́триваться [1], ‹всмотре́ться› [9; -отрю́сь, -о́тришься] (в B) peer, look narrowly (at).
всмя́тку: яйцо́ ~ soft-boiled egg.
всо́|вывать [1], ‹всу́нуть› [20] put, slip (into в B); **~са́ть** *s.* вса́сывать.
вспа́|хивать [1], ‹~ха́ть› [3] plow (*Brt.* plough) *or* turn up; **~шка** *f* [5] tillage.
всплес|к [1] splash; **∠кивать** [1], ‹~ну́ть› [20] splash; **~ну́ть рука́ми** throw up one's arms.
всплы|ва́ть [1], ‹~ть› [23] rise to the surface, emerge.
всполоши́ть F [16 *e.*; -шу́, -ши́шь; -шённый] *pf.* startle (*v/i.* **-ся**).
вспом|ина́ть [1], ‹∠нить› [13] (B *or* о П) remember, recall; (Д + **-ся** = И + *vb.*); **~ога́тельный** [14] auxiliary; **~яну́ть** P [19] = ∠нить.
вспорхну́ть [20] *pf.* fly up.
вспры́г|ивать [1], *once* ‹~нуть› [20] jump *or* spring (up/on на B).
вспры́с|кивать [1], ‹~нуть› [20] sprinkle; wet; inject.
вспу́г|ивать [1], *once* ‹~ну́ть› [20] start, frighten away.
вспух|а́ть [1], ‹∠нуть› [21] swell.
вспыл|и́ть F [13] *pf.* get angry; **∠ьчивость** *f* [8] irascibility; **∠ьчивый** [14 *sh.*] quick-tempered.
вспы́|хивать [1], ‹~хнуть› [20] **1.** flare up, flash; blush; **2.** burst into a rage; break out; **~шка** *f* [5; *g/pl.*: -шек] flare, flash, outburst, outbreak.
вста|ва́ть [5], ‹~ть› [вста́ну, -нешь] stand up; get up, rise (from с P); arise; **∠вка** *f* [5; *g/pl.*: -вок] setting in, insertion, inset; **~вля́ть** [28], ‹∠вить› [14] set *or* put in, insert; **~вно́й** [14] (to be) put in; **~вны́е зу́бы** *m/pl.* false teeth.
встрепену́ться [20] *pf.* start, shudder, shake up.
встрёпк|а P *f* [5] reprimand; **зада́ть ~у** (Д) P bowl out, blow up (a p).
встре́|тить(ся) *s.* **~ча́ть(ся)**; **~ча** *f* [5] meeting, encounter; reception; **тёплая ~ча** warm welcome; **~ча́ть** [1], ‹~тить› [15 *st.*] **1.** meet (*v/t.*, with B), encounter; come across; **2.** meet, receive, welcome; **~ча́ть Но́вый год** celebrate the New Year; **-ся 1.** meet (*v/i.*, o. a., with с T); **2.** (*impers.*) occur, happen; there are (were); **~чный** [14] counter..., (coming from the) opposite (direction), (s. b. *or* s. th.) on one's way; **пе́рвый ~чный** the first comer.
встря́|ска *f* [5; *g/pl.*: -сок] **1.** F shock; **2.** P = встрёпка; **~хивать** [1], *once* ‹~хну́ть› [20] shake (up); stir (up); (**-ся** *v/i.*, o. s.).
вступ|а́ть [1], ‹~и́ть› [14] (в B) enter, join; set one's foot, step (into); begin, enter *or* come into, assume; **~и́ть в брак** contract marriage; **~и́ть на трон** accede to the throne; **-ся** (за B) intercede (for), protect; take a p.'s side; **~и́тельный** [14] introductory; opening; entrance...; **~ле́ние** *n* [12] entry, entrance; accession; beginning; introduction.
всу́|нуть *s.* всо́вывать; **~чивать** F [1], ‹~чи́ть› [16] foist (s.th. on B/Д).
всхлип *m* [1], **∠ывание** *n* [12] sob(bing); **∠ывать** [1], *once* ‹∠нуть› [20 *st.*] sob.
всход|и́ть [15], ‹взойти́› [взойду́, -дёшь; взошёл, -шла́; взоше́дший; *g. pt.*: взойдя́] **1.** go *or* climb ([up]on на B), ascend, rise; come up, sprout; **2.** = входи́ть; **∠ы** *m/pl.* [1] standing *or* young crops.
всхрапну́ть F [20] *pf.* nap.
всып|а́ть [1], ‹∠ать› [2 *st.*] pour *or* put (into в B); P thrash (a p. Д).
всю́ду everywhere, all over.
вся́|кий [16] **1.** any, every; any-, everybody (*or* -one); **2.** = **~ческий** [16] all kinds *or* sorts of, sundry; every possible; **~чески** in every way; **~чески стара́ться** take great pains; **~чина** F *f* [5]: **~кая ~чина** whatnot(s), hodgepodge.
вта́|йне in secret; **~лкивать** [1], ‹втолкну́ть› [20] push *or* shove in(to); **~птывать** [1], ‹втопта́ть› [3] tramp(le) in(to); **~скивать** [1], ‹~щи́ть› [16] pull *or* drag in, up.
вте|ка́ть [1], ‹~чь› [26] flow in(to).
втере́ть *s.* втира́ть.
втир|а́ть [1], ‹втере́ть› [12; вотру́, -рёшь; втёр] rub in; worm; **~а́ть очки́** (Д) throw dust in (p.'s) eyes; **-ся** F worm into; **∠скивать** [1], ‹∠снуть› [20] press *or* squeeze in.
втихомо́лку F on the quiet.
втолкну́ть *s.* вта́лкивать.
втоптать *s.* вта́птывать.
втор|га́ться [1], ‹∠гнуться› [21] (в B) intrude, invade, penetrate; meddle (with); **~же́ние** *n* [12] invasion, incursion; **∠ить** [13] ♪ sing (*or* play) the second part; echo, repeat; **~и́чный** [14] second, repeated; secondary; **~и́чно** once more,

for the second time; **∠ник** *m* [1] Tuesday (on: во В, *pl.*: по Д); **~óй** [14] second; upper; из **~ы́х** рук second hand; *cf.* пе́рвый & пя́тый; **~оку́рсник** *m* [1] sophomore.
второпя́х in a hurry, being in a great haste, hastily.
второстепе́нный [14; -е́нен, -е́нна] secondary, minor.
в-тре́тьих third(ly).
втри́дорога F very dearly.
втро́|е three times (as ..., *comp.*; *cf.* вдвóе); *vb.* + **~е** *a.* treble; **~ём** three (of us, *etc.*, *or* together); **~йне́** three times (as much, *etc.*), trebly.
втуз *m* [1] (вы́сшее техни́ческое учéбное заведе́ние *n*) technical college, institute of technology.
вту́лка *f* [5; *g/pl.*: -лок] plug.
втуне in vain; without attention.
втыка́ть [1], ⟨воткну́ть⟩ [20] put *or* stick in(to).
втя́|гивать [1], ⟨**~ну́ть**⟩ [19] draw *or* pull in(to), on; envolve, engage; **-ся** (в В) fall in; enter; (become) engage(d) in; get used (to).
вуа́ль *f* [8] veil.
вуз *m* [1] (вы́сшее учéбное заведе́ние *n*) university, college; **∠овец** *m* [1; -вца] college student.
вулка́н *m* [1] volcano; **~и́ческий** [16] volcanic.
вульга́рный [14; -рен, -рна] vulgar.
вход *m* [1] entrance; пла́та за ~ entrance *or* admission fee.
входи́ть [15], ⟨войти́⟩ [войду́, -дёшь; вошёл, -шла́; воше́дший; *g. pt.*: войдя́] (в В) enter, go, come *or* get in(to); go in(to), have room *or* hold; run into (*debts, etc.*); penetrate into; be included in; ~ во вкус (P) take a fancy to; ~ в дове́рие (ми́лость) к (Д) gain a p.'s confidence (favo[u]r); ~ в положе́ние (P) appreciate a p.'s position; ~ в привы́чку *or* быт (посло́вицу) become a habit (proverbial); ~ в (состáв [P]) form part (of), belong (to).
входно́й [14] entrance..., admission...
вцеп|ля́ться [28], ⟨**~и́ться**⟩ [14] (в В) grasp, catch hold of.
ВЦСПС (Всесою́зный Центра́льный Сове́т Профессиона́льных Сою́зов) the All-Union Central Council of Trade Unions.
вчера́ yesterday; **~шний** [15] yesterday's, (of) yesterday.
вчерне́ in the rough; in a draft.
вче́тверо four times (as ..., *comp.*; *cf.* вдвóе); **∠м** four (of us, *etc.*).
вчи́т|ываться [1], ⟨**~а́ться**⟩ (в В) become absorbed in *or* familiar with s.th. by reading.
вше́стеро six times (*cf.* вдвóе).
вши|ва́ть [1], ⟨**~ть**⟩ [вошью́, -шьёшь; *cf.* шить] sew in(to); **∠вый** [14] lousy; **~ть** *s.* **~ва́ть**.

въе|да́ться [1], ⟨**∠сться**⟩ [*cf.* есть[1]] eat (in[to]).
въе|зд *m* [1] entrance, entry; ascent; разреше́ние на ~зд entry permit; **~зжа́ть** [1], ⟨**∠хать**⟩ [въе́ду, -дешь; въезжа́й(те)!] enter, ride *or* drive in(to), up/on (в, на В); move in(to); **∠сться** *s.* **~да́ться**.
вы [21] you (*polite form a.* ♀); ~ с ним you and he; у вас (был) ... you have (had) ...
выб|а́лтывать F [1], ⟨**∠олтать**⟩ blab *or* let out; **~ега́ть** [1], ⟨**∠ежать**⟩ [4; вы́бегу, -ежишь] run out; **~ива́ть** [1], ⟨**∠ить**⟩ [вы́бью, -бьешь, *etc.*, *cf.* бить] **1.** beat *or* knock out; break; smash; drive out; hollow out; **2.** stamp, coin; **-ся** break out *or* forth; -ся из сил be(come) exhausted, fatigued; -ся из колей come off the beaten track; **~ира́ть** [1], ⟨**∠рать**⟩ [вы́беру, -решь; -бранный] choose, pick out; elect; take out; find; **-ся** get out; move (out); **∠ить** *s.* **~ива́ть**.
вы́бор *m* [1] choice, selection; на ~ (*or* по ~у) at a p.'s discretion; random (*test*); *pl.* election(s); всеóбщие ~ы *pl.* general election; дополни́тельные ~ы by-election; **~ка** *f* [5; *g/pl.*: -рок] selection; *pl.* excerpts; **~ный** [14] electoral; *su.* delegate.
вы́бр|а́сывать [1], ⟨**~осить**⟩ [15] throw (out *or* away); thrust (out); discard *or* dismiss; exclude, omit; strand; **~а́сывать** (зря) де́ньги waste money; **-ся** throw o. s. out; **~ать** *s.* выбира́ть; **~ить** [-ею, -еешь; -итый] *pf.* shave clean; (*v/i.* -ся); **~осить** *s.* **~а́сывать**.
выб|ыва́ть [1] ⟨**∠ыть**⟩ [-уду, -удешь] leave, withdraw, drop out.
выв|а́ливать [1], ⟨**∠алить**⟩ [13] discharge, throw out; P stream; **-ся** fall out; stream out; **~а́ривать** [1], ⟨**∠арить**⟩ [13] extract; boil down; **~е́дывать**, ⟨**∠едать**⟩ [1] find out, (try to) elicit; **∠езти** *s.* **~ози́ть**; **~ёртывать** [1], ⟨**∠ерпуть**⟩ [20] unscrew; tear out; dislocate; turn (inside out); *v/i.* **-ся**; slip out, extricate o. s.
вы́вес|ить *s.* выве́шивать; **~ка** *f* [5; *g/pl.*: -сок] sign(board); **~ти** *s.* выводи́ть.
выв|е́тривать [1], ⟨**∠етрить**⟩ [13] (remove by) air(ing); **-ся** weather; **~е́шивать** [1], ⟨**∠есить**⟩ [15] hang out *or* put up; **~и́нчивать** [1], ⟨**∠интить**⟩ [15] unscrew.
вы́вих *m* [1] dislocation; **~нуть** [20] *pf.* dislocate, sprain (one's ... себе́ В).
вы́вод *m* [1] **1.** withdrawal; **2.** breeding, cultivation; **3.** derivation, conclusion; сде́лать ~ draw a conclusion; **~и́ть** [15], ⟨вы́вести⟩ [25] **1.** take, lead *or* move (out, to);

2. derive, conclude; 3. hatch; cultivate; 4. construct; 5. remove, extirpate; 6. write *or* draw carefully; 7. depict; ~ить (В) из себя make s. b. lose his temper; -ся, ⟨-сь⟩ disappear; ~ок *m* [1; -дка] brood.
вывоз *m* [1] export(s); ~ить [15], ⟨вывезти⟩ [24] remove, get *or* take *or* bring out; export; ~ной [14] export...
выв|орачивать F [1], ⟨~оротить⟩ [15] = вывёртывать, вывернуть.
выг|адывать, ⟨~адать⟩ [1] gain *or* save (s. th. from В/на П).
выгиб *m* [1] bend, curve; ~ать [1], ⟨выгнуть⟩ [20] arch, curve.
выгля|деть [11 *st.*] *impf.* look (s. th. Т, like как); как она ~дит? what does she look like?; он ~дит моложе своих лет he doesn't look his age; ~дывать [1], *once* ⟨~нуть⟩ [20 *st.*] look *or* peep out (of в В, из Р).
выгнать *s.* выгонять.
выгнуть *s.* выгибать.
выгов|аривать [1], ⟨'~орить⟩ [13] 1. pronounce; utter; 2. F stipulate; 3. *impf.* F (Д) rebuke; '~ор *m* [1] 1. pronunciation; 2. reproof, reprimand.
выгод|а *f* [5] profit; advantage; ~ный [14; -ден, -дна] profitable; advantageous (to Д, для Р).
выгон *m* [1] pasture; ~ять [28], ⟨выгнать⟩ [выгоню, -нишь] turn *or* drive out; expel *or* fire.
выгор|аживать [1], ⟨'~одить⟩ [15] enclose; P exculpate, free from blame; ~ать [1], ⟨'~еть⟩ [9] 1. burn down; 2. fade; 3. F click, come off.
выгр|ужать [1], ⟨~узить⟩ [15] unload; discharge; disembark; (*v/i.* -ся); ~узка [5; *g/pl.*: -зок] unloading; disembarkation.
выдавать [5], ⟨выдать⟩ [-дам, -дашь, *etc. cf.* дать] 1. give (out), pay (out); distribute; 2. draw *or* issue; 3. betray; 4. extradite; ~ (себя) за (В) [make] pass (o.s. off) for; ~ (замуж) за (В) give (*a girl*) in marriage to; -ся 1. stand out; 2. F happen *or* turn out.
выд|авливать [1], ⟨~авить⟩ [14] press *or* squeeze out; ~албливать [1], ⟨~олбить⟩ [14] hollow out.
выда|ть *s.* ~вать; ~ча *f* [5] 1. distribution; delivery; payment; 2. issue; grant; 3. betrayal; 4. extradition; день ~чи зарплаты payday; ~ющийся [17; -щегося, *etc.*] outstanding, distinguished.
выдви|гать [1], ⟨'~нуть⟩ [20] 1. pull out; 2. put forward, propose, promote; -ся 1. step forth, move forward; 2. project; 3. advance; 4. *impf. s.* ~жной; ~женец *m* [1; -нца] promoted worker; ~жной [14] pull-out..., sliding.
выд|еление *n* [12] separation, detachment; discharge, secretion; ~елка *f* [5; *g/pl.*: -лок] manufacture; workmanship; ~елывать, ⟨~елать⟩ [1] work, make; elaborate; curry (*leather*); ~елять [28], ⟨~елить⟩ [13] 1. separate, detach; 2. mark (out); emphasize; 3. ⚖ allot; satisfy (*coheirs*); 4. ⚗ secrete; 5. 🜍 evolve; -ся *v/i.* 1,4; stand out, come forth; rise above, excel; ~ёргивать, ⟨~ернуть⟩ [20] pull out.
выдерж|ивать [1], ⟨'~ать⟩ [4] stand, bear, endure; pass (*exam.*); observe (*size, etc.*); '~ать характер be firm; '~анный self-restrained; consistent; mature; '~ка *f* [5; *g/pl.*: -жек] 1. self-control; 2. extract, quotation 3. *phot.* exposure; на '~ку at random.
выд|ирать F [1], ⟨~рать⟩ [-деру, -ерешь] tear out; pull; *pf.* thrash; ~олбить *s.* ~албливать; ~охнуть *s.* ~ыхать; ~ра *f* [5] otter; ~рать *s.* ~ирать; ~умка *f* [5; *g/pl.*: -мок] invention; ~умывать, ⟨~умать⟩ [1] invent, contrive, devise.
выд|ыхать [1], ⟨~охнуть⟩ [20] breathe out; -ся become stale; *fig.* exhaust o.s.
выезд *m* [1] departure; drive, ride; exit; gateway; visit.
выезжать[1] [1], ⟨выехать⟩ [выеду, -едешь; -езжай(те)!] *v/i.* (из, с Р) 1. leave, depart; 2. drive *or* ride out, on(to); 3. (re)move (from); 4. (begin to) visit (*social affairs, etc.*); ~[2] *a.* выезживать [1], ⟨выездить⟩ [15] *v/t.* break in (*a horse*).
выемка *f* [5; *g/pl.*: -мок] excavation; hollow.
выехать *s.* выезжать.
выж|ать *s.* ~имать; ~дать *s.* ~идать; ~ивать [1], ⟨~ить⟩ [-иву, -ивешь; -итый] survive; go through; stay; F oust; ~ить из ума be in one's dotage; ~игать [1], ⟨~ечь⟩ [26 г/ж: -жгу, -жжешь, -жгут; -жег, жгла; -жженный] burn out, down *or* in; brand; ~идать [1], ⟨~дать⟩ [-жду, -ждешь; -жди(-те)!] (Р *or* В) wait for *or* till (after); ~имать [1], ⟨~ать⟩ [-жму, -жмешь; -жатый] squeeze, press *or* wring out; *sport* lift; ~ить *s.* ~ивать.
вызвать *s.* вызывать.
выздор|авливать [1], ⟨'~оветь⟩ [10] recover; ~авливающий [17] convalescent; ~овление *n* [12] recovery.
выз|ов *m* [1] call; summons; invitation; challenge; ~убривать [1] = зубрить; ~ывать [1], ⟨~вать⟩ [-ову, -овешь] 1. call (to; for *thea.*; up *tel.*; [up]on *pupil*); send for; 2. summon (to к Д; before a court в суд); 3. challenge (to на В); 4. rouse, cause; evoke; -ся undertake *or* offer; ~ывающий [17] defiant, provoking.

выи́гр|ывать, ⟨'~ать⟩ [1] win (from y P), gain, benefit; **'~ыш** *m* [1] win(ning[s]), gain(s); prize; profit; быть в '~ыше have won (profited); **'~ышный** [14] advantageous, profitable; lottery...
вы́йти *s.* выходи́ть.
вык|а́зывать F [1], ⟨~азать⟩ [3] show, prove; display; **~а́лывать** [1], ⟨~олоть⟩ [17] put out; cut out; **~а́пывать,** ⟨~опать⟩ [1] dig out *or* up; **~ара́бкиваться,** ⟨~арабкаться⟩ [1] scramble *or* get out; **~а́рмливать** [1], ⟨~ормить⟩ [14] bring up, rear, breed; **~а́тывать** [1] **1.** ⟨~атать⟩ [1] mangle; roll; **2.** ⟨~атить⟩ [15] push *or* move out; ~атить глаза́ P stare.
выки́|дывать [1], *once* ⟨'~инуть⟩ [20] **1.** throw out *or* away, discard; omit; strand; stretch (out); **2.** hoist (up); **3.** miscarry; **4.** F play (*trick*); **'~идыш** *m* [1] miscarriage, abortion.
вы́кл|адка *f* [5; *g/pl.*: -док] laying out, spreading; exposition; border, trimming; computation, calculation; ⚔ outfit; **~а́дывать** [1], ⟨вы́ложить⟩ [16] **1.** take *or* lay out, spread; set forth; **2.** border; **3.** brick *or* mason; **4.** compute.
выклика́ть [1] call up(on *or*, F, out).
выключ|а́тель *m* [4] ⚡ switch; **~а́ть** [1], ⟨'~ить⟩ [16] **1.** switch *or* turn off; stop; **2.** exclude; **~е́ние** *n* [12] switching off, stopping.
вык|о́вывать [1], ⟨~овать⟩ [7] forge; *fig.* mo(u)ld; **~ола́чивать** [1], ⟨~олотить⟩ [15] beat *or* knock out; dust; P exact (*debts, etc.*); **~олоть** *s.* ~а́лывать; **~опать** *s.* ~а́пывать; **~ормить** *s.* ~а́рмливать; **~орчёвывать** [1], ⟨~орчевать⟩ [7] root up *or* out.
выкр|а́ивать [1], ⟨~оить⟩ [13] cut out; F hunt (up), spare; **~а́шивать** [1], ⟨~асить⟩ [15] paint, dye; **~и́кивать** [1], *once* ⟨~икнуть⟩ [20] cry *or* call (out); **~оить** *s.* ~а́ивать; **~ойка** *f* [5; *g/pl.*: -оек] pattern.
выкр|ута́сы F *m/pl.* [1] flourishes, scrolls; dodges, subterfuges; **~у́чивать** [1], ⟨~утить⟩ [15] twist; wring (out); F unscrew; **-ся** F slip out.
вы́куп *m* [1] redemption; ransom; **~а́ть¹** [1], ⟨~ить⟩ [14] redeem; ransom; **~ать²** *s.* купа́ть.
выку́р|ивать [1], ⟨'~ить⟩ [13] **1.** smoke (out); **2.** distill.
выл|а́вливать [1], ⟨~овить⟩ [14] fish out *or* up; **~азка** *f* [5; *g/pl.*: -зок] **1.** ⚔ sally; **2.** excursion, outing; **~а́мывать,** ⟨~омать⟩ [1] break out.
выл|еза́ть [1], ⟨~езть⟩ [24] climb *or* get out; fall out (*hair*); **~епля́ть** [28], ⟨~епить⟩ [14] model.
вы́лет *m* [1] ✈ start, taking off; flight; **~а́ть** [1], ⟨~еть⟩ [11] fly out; ✈ start, take off (for в B); rush out *or* up; fall out; slip (a p.'s memory ~еть из головы́).
выл|е́чивать [1], ⟨~ечить⟩ [16] cure, heal (*v/i.* **-ся**); **~ива́ть** [1] ⟨~ить⟩ [-лью, -льешь; *cf.* лить] pour (out); **~итый** [14] poured out; ⊕ cast; F just like (s.b. И).
вы́л|овить *s.* ~а́вливать; **~ожить** *s.* выкла́дывать; **~омать** *s.* ~а́мывать; **~упля́ть** [28], ⟨~упить⟩ [14] shell; **-ся** hatch.
вым|а́зывать [1], ⟨~азать⟩ [3] smear; soil (**-ся** o.s.) (with T); **~а́ливать** [1], ⟨~олить⟩ [13] get *or* obtain by entreaties; **~а́нивать** [1], ⟨~анить⟩ [13] lure (out of из P); coax *or* cheat (a p. out of s. th. y P/B); **~а́ривать** [1], ⟨~орить⟩ [13] extirpate; ~а́ривать го́лодом starve (out); **~а́рывать,** ⟨~арать⟩ [1] **1.** soil; **2.** delete, cross out; **~а́чивать** [1], ⟨~очить⟩ [16] drench, soak *or* wet; **~а́щивать** [1], ⟨~остить⟩ [15] pave; **~е́нивать** [1], ⟨~енять⟩ [28] exchange (for на B); **~ереть** *s.* ~ира́ть; **~ета́ть** [1], ⟨~ести⟩ [25 -т- *st.*: -ету, -етешь] sweep (out); **~еща́ть** [1], ⟨~естить⟩ [15] avenge o.s. (on Д); vent (on p. на П); **~ира́ть** [1], ⟨~ереть⟩ [12] die out, become extinct.
вымога́т|ельство *n* [9] blackmail, extortion; **~ь** [1] extort (s.th. from B *or* P/y P).
вым|ока́ть [1], ⟨~окнуть⟩ [21] wet through, get wet; **~олвить** [14] *pf.* utter, say; **~олить** *s.* ~аливать; **~орить** *s.* ~аривать; **~остить** *s.* ~ащивать; **~очить** *s.* ~ачивать.
вы́мпел *m* [1] pennant, pennon.
вым|ыва́ть [1], ⟨~ыть⟩ [22] wash (out, up); ~ыть го́лову (Д) F bawl out, blow up; **~ысел** *m* [1; -сла] invention; falsehood; **~ыть** *s.* ~ыва́ть; **~ышля́ть** [28], ⟨~ыслить⟩ [15] invent; **~ышленный** *a.* fictitious.
вы́мя *n* [13] udder.
вын|а́шивать [1], ⟨~осить⟩ [15] **1.** wear out; **2.** evolve, bring forth; **3.** train; **4.** nurse; **~ести** *s.* ~оси́ть.
вын|има́ть [1], ⟨~уть⟩ [20] take *or* draw out, produce.
вын|оси́ть¹ [15], ⟨~ести⟩ [24 -с-: -су, -сешь; -с, -сла] **1.** carry *or* take out (away), remove; transfer; **2.** endure, bear; **3.** acquire; **4.** submit; express (*gratitude*); pass (*a.* ⚖); **~осить²** *s.* ~а́шивать; **~оска** *f* [5; *g/pl.*: -сок] marginal note, footnote; **~о́сливость** *f* [8] endurance; **~о́сливый** [14 *sh.*] enduring, sturdy, hardy, tough.
вын|ужда́ть [1], ⟨~удить⟩ [15] force, compel; extort (s. th. from B/y *or* от P); **~ужденный** [14 *sh.*] forced; of necessity.

вы́нырнуть [20] *pf.* emerge.

вы́па|д *m* [1], **~де́ние** *n* [12] falling out; *fenc.* lunge; *fig.* thrust, attack; **~да́ть** [1], ⟨**~сть**⟩ [25] **1.** fall *or* drop (out); slip out; **2.** fall (to Д, *a.* на до́лю to a p.'s share *or* lot), devolve on; **3.** lunge.

вып|а́ливать [1], ⟨**~алить**⟩ [13] blurt out; F shoot (with из P); **~а́лывать** [1], ⟨**~олоть**⟩ [17] weed (out); **~а́ривать** [1], ⟨**~арить**⟩ [13] steam; evaporate.

вып|ека́ть [1], ⟨**~ечь**⟩ [26] bake; **~ива́ть** [1], ⟨**~ить**⟩ [-пью, -пьешь; *cf.* пить] drink (up); F booze; **~ить** (ли́шнее) F overdrink o.s.; **~ить** ча́шку ча́ю have a cup of tea; **~ивка** F *f* [5; *g/pl.*: -вок] booze; **~ивший** [17] drunk; tipsy.

вы́п|иска *f* [5; *g/pl.*: -сок] **1.** writing out, copying; **2.** extract; † statement (of account из счёта); **3.** order, subscription; **4.** discharge; notice of departure; **~и́сывать** [1], ⟨**~исать**⟩ [3] **1.** write out (*or* down); copy; **2.** *s.* выводи́ть 6.; **3.** order, subscribe; **4.** discharge, dismiss; **-ся** register one's departure; **-ся** из больни́цы leave hospital.

вы́пла|вка *f* [5] smelting; **~кать** [3] *pf.* weep (one's eyes глаза́) out; F obtain by weeping; **~та** *f* [5] payment; **~чивать** [1], ⟨**~тить**⟩ [15] pay (out *or* off).

выпл|ёвывать [1], *once* ⟨**~юнуть**⟩ [20] spit out; **~ёскивать** [1] ⟨**~ескать**⟩ [3], *once* ⟨**~еснуть**⟩ [20] dash *or* splash (out).

выпл|ыва́ть [1], ⟨**~ыть**⟩ [23] emerge, come out, appear.

выпол|а́скивать [1], ⟨**'~оскать**⟩ [3] rinse; gargle; **~за́ть** [1], ⟨**'~зти**⟩ [24] creep or crawl out; **~не́ние** *n* [12] fulfil(l)ment, execution, realization; **~ня́ть** [1], ⟨**'~нить**⟩ [13] carry out, fulfil(l); make (up); **'~оть** *s.* выпа́лывать.

вы́пр|авка *f* [5; *g/pl.*: -вок] **1.** correction; **2.** carriage (*of a soldier*); **~авля́ть** [28], ⟨**~авить**⟩ [14] set right *or* straight; correct; **~а́шивать** [1], ⟨**~осить**⟩ [15] (try to) obtain by request; **~ова́живать** F [1], ⟨**~оводить**⟩ [15] see out; **2.** turn out; **~ы́гивать** [1], ⟨**~ыгнуть**⟩ [20] jump out *or* off; **~яга́ть** [1], ⟨**~ячь**⟩ [26 г/ж: -ягу, -яжешь; -яг] unharness; **~ямля́ть** [28], ⟨**~ямить**⟩ [14] straighten; **-ся** erect o.s.

вы́пуклый [14] convex; prominent; *fig.* expressive, distinct.

вы́пуск *m* [1] letting out; omission; ⊕ output; † issue; publication; instal(l)ment; (age) class of graduates; **~а́ть** [1], ⟨**вы́пустить**⟩ [15] let out (*or* go); ⚖ release; ⊕ produce; issue; publish; omit, leave out; graduate; **~а́ть** в прода́жу put on sale; **~ни́к** *m* [1 *e.*] graduate; **~но́й** [14] graduate ..., graduation ..., final, leaving; ⊕ discharge-...; outlet ...

вып|у́тывать, ⟨**~утать**⟩ [1] disentangle *or* extricate (o. s. **-ся**); **~у́чивать** [1], ⟨**~учить**⟩ [16] **1.** bulge; **2.** P *s.* тара́щить.

вып|ы́тывать, ⟨**~ытать**⟩ [1] find out, (try to) elicit.

выпя́|ливать P [1], ⟨**'~лить**⟩ [13] *s.* тара́щить; **~чивать** F [1], ⟨**'~тить**⟩ [15] protrude.

выраб|а́тывать, ⟨**'~отать**⟩ [1] manufacture, produce; elaborate, work out; develop; earn, make; **'~отка** *f* [5; *g/pl.*: -ток] manufacture, production; output, performance; elaboration.

выр|а́внивать [1], ⟨**~овнять**⟩ [28] level, ⊕ plane; smooth (*a. fig.*); **-ся** straighten; ⚔ dress; develop, grow up.

выра|жа́ть [1], ⟨**'~зить**⟩ [15] express, show; **~жа́ть** слова́ми put into words; **~же́ние** *n* [12] expression; **~зи́тельный** [14; -лен, -льна] expressive; F significant.

выр|аста́ть [1], ⟨**~асти**⟩ [24 -ст-: -асту; *cf.* расти́] **1.** grow (up); increase; develop into; **2.** emerge, appear; **~а́щивать** [1], ⟨**~астить**⟩ [15] grow; breed; bring up; *fig.* train; **~вать 1.** *s.* **~ыва́ть**[1]; **2.** *s.* рвать 3.

вырез|а́ть [1], ⟨**'~ать**⟩ [15] **1.** cut out, clip; **2.** carve; engrave; **3.** slaughter; **'~ка** *f* [5; *g/pl.*: -зок] cutting (out), clipping; carving; engraving; tenderloin; **~но́й** [14] carved.

вы́ро|док *m* [1; -дка] degenerate; monster; **~жда́ться** [1], ⟨**~диться**⟩ [15] degenerate; **~жде́ние** *n* [12] degeneration.

вы́ро|нить [13] *pf.* drop; **~сший** [17] grown.

выр|уба́ть [1], ⟨**~убить**⟩ [14] **1.** cut down *or* fell; **2.** cut out *or* carve; **~уча́ть** [1], ⟨**~учить**⟩ [16] **1.** help, rescue, relieve; redeem; **2.** † gain; **~учка** *f* [5] rescue, relief, help (to на В); † proceeds.

выр|ыва́ть[1] [1], ⟨**~вать**⟩ [-ву, -вешь] **1.** pull out; tear out; **2.** snatch away; extort (s.th. from a p. В/у Р); **-ся** break away, rush (out); escape; **~ыва́ть**[2], ⟨**~ыть**⟩, [22] dig out, up.

вы́с|адка *f* [5; *g/pl.*: -док] disembarkation, landing; **~а́живать** [1], ⟨**~адить**⟩ [15] **1.** land, disembark; **2.** help out; make *or* let a p. get out; **3.** (trans)plant; **-ся** = 1. *v/i.*; *a.* get out, off.

выс|а́сывать [1], ⟨**~осать**⟩ [-осу, -осешь] suck out; **~ве́рливать** [1], ⟨**~верлить**⟩ [13] bore, drill; **~вобожда́ть** [1], ⟨**~вободить**⟩ [15] free.

выс|ева́ть [1], ‹**∠еять**› [27] sow; **~ека́ть** [1], ‹**∠ечь**› [26] **1.** hew, carve; strike (*fire*); **2.** *s.* сечь[2]; **~еле́ние** *n* [12] expulsion, eviction; transfer; **~еля́ть** [28], ‹**∠елить**› [13] expel, evict; transfer, move; **∠еять** *s.* **~е́ивать**; **~я́живать** [1], ‹**∠идеть**› [11] sit (out), stay; hatch.

выск|а́бливать [1], ‹**∠облить**› [13] scrub clean; erase; **~а́зывать** [1], ‹**∠азать**› [3] express, tell, give; **-ся** express o.s.; express one's opinion, thoughts, *etc.* (about о П); declare o.s. (for за В; against про́тив Р); **~а́кивать** [1], ‹**∠очить**› [16] jump, leap *or* rush out; **~а́льзывать, ~ользá́ть** [1], ‹**∠ользнуть**› [20] slip out; **∠облить** *s.* **~а́бливать**; **∠очить** *s.* **~а́кивать**; **∠очка** *m/f* [5; *g/pl.:* -чек] upstart; F forward pupil; **~реба́ть** [1], ‹**∠рести**› [25 -б-; *cf.* скрести́] scrub clean; scratch out.

вы́сл|ать *s.* высыла́ть; **~е́живать** [1], ‹**~едить**› [15] track down; **~у́живать** [1], ‹**~ужить**› [16] F serve; obtain by *or* for service; **-ся** advance, rise; insinuate o.s.; **~у́шивать**, ‹**~ушать**› [1] listen (to), hear; ⚕ auscultate.

высм|е́ивать [1], ‹**∠еять**› [27] deride, ridicule.

выс|о́вывать [1], ‹**∠унуть**› [20 *st.*] put out; -ся lean out.

высо́кий [16; высо́к, -á, -со́ко́; *comp.*: вы́ше] high; tall (*a.* ~ ро́стом); *fig.* lofty.

высоко|благоро́дие *n* [12] (Right) Hono[u]r(able); **~ка́чественный** [14] (of) high quality; **~квалифици́рованный** [14] highly skilled; **~ме́рие** *n* [12] haughtiness; **~ме́рный** [14; -рен, -рна] haughty, arrogant; **~па́рный** [14; -рен, -рна] bombastic, high-flown; **~превосходи́тельство** *n* [9] Excellency; **~уважа́емый** [14] dear (*polite address*).

вы́сосать *s.* выса́сывать.

высо|та́ *f* [5; *pl.:* -о́ты, *etc. st.*] height; (✈, *astr.*, *geogr.*) altitude; hill; level; *fig.* climax; **~то́й** в (В) ... *or* ... в **~ту́** ... high.

вы́сох|нуть *s.* высыха́ть; **~ший** [17] dried up, withered.

выс|оча́йший [17] highest; supreme, imperial; **~о́чество** *n* [9] Highness; **∠паться** *s.* высыпа́ться.

вы́спренний [15] bombastic.

выстав|ить *s.* **~ля́ть**; **~ка** *f* [5; *g/pl.:* -вок] exhibition, show; **~ля́ть** [28], ‹**~ить**› [14] **1.** put (take) out, put forward (*a. fig.*); **2.** exhibit, display, expose; (re)present (o.s. себя́); **3.** mark, provide (*with date, no.*); ⚔ post; P turn out; **~ля́ть** напока́з show off; **-ся** come out, emerge; **~очный** [14] (of the) exhibition, show...

выстр|а́ивать(ся) [1] *s.* стро́ить (-ся); **∠ел** *m* [1] shot; (*noise*) report; на (расстоя́ние, -ии) **∠ел(а)** within gunshot; **∠елить** *s.* стреля́ть.

высту́к|ивать, ‹**'~ать**› F [1] strike, [tap; ⚕ percuss.

вы́ступ *m* [1] projection; **~а́ть** [1], ‹**~ить**› [14] **1.** step forth, forward; come *or* stand out; appear; **2.** set out, march off; **3.** speak (sing, play) in public; **~а́ть** с ре́чью (в пре́ниях) deliver a speech (take the floor); **~а́ть** в похо́д ⚔ take the field; **~ле́ние** *n* [12] **1.** appearance; **2.** departure; *pol.* speech, declaration; *thea.* performance, turn.

вы́сунуть(ся) *s.* высо́вывать(ся).

высу́ш|ивать [1], ‹**'~ить**› [16] dry (up); drain, *fig.* exhaust.

вы́сш|ий [17] highest, supreme; higher (*a. educ.*), superior; **~ая** ме́ра наказа́ния supreme penalty, capital punishment.

выс|ыла́ть [1], ‹**∠лать**› [вы́шлю, -лешь] send forward; send out, away; banish; **∠ылка** *f* [15] dispatch; exile; **~ыпа́ть** [1], ‹**∠ыпать**› [2] pour out *or* in, on; *v/i.* swarm forth, out; **~ыпа́ться** [1], ‹**вы́спаться**› [-сплюсь, -спишься] sleep one's fill (*or* enough), have a good night's rest; **~ыха́ть** [1], ‹**∠охнуть**› [21] dry up, wither; **~ь** *f* [8] height.

выт|а́лкивать, F ‹**∠олкать**› [1], *once* ‹**∠олкнуть**› [20 *st.*] push out; **~а́пливать** [1], ‹**∠опить**› [14] **1.** heat; **2.** melt (down); **~а́скивать** [1], ‹**∠ащить**› [16] take *or* pull out; F pilfer.

выт|ека́ть [1], ‹**∠ечь**› [26] flow out; *fig.* follow, result; **∠ереть** *s.* **~ира́ть**; **∠ерпеть** [14] *pf.* endure, bear; F не **∠ерпел** couldn't help; **~есня́ть** [28], ‹**∠еснить**› [13] force, push out; oust, expel; **∠ечь** *s.* **~ека́ть**.

выт|ира́ть [1], ‹**∠ереть**› [12] dry, wipe (o. s. **-ся**); wear out.

вы́точенный [14] well-turned.

вы́тр|ебовать [7] *pf.* ask for, demand, order, summon; obtain on demand; **~яса́ть** [1], ‹**∠ясти**› [24 -с-] shake out.

выть [22], ‹вз-› howl.

выт|я́гивать [1], ‹**∠януть**› [20 *st.*] draw, pull *or* stretch (out); drain; F elicit; endure, bear; **-ся** stretch, extend (o.s.); ⚔ come to attention; F grow (up); **∠яжка** *f* [5] drawing, stretching (out); ⚗ extract; на **∠яжку** ⚔ at attention.

выу́|живать [1], ‹**'~дить**› [15] fish out (*a. fig.*).

выу́ч|ивать [1], ‹**'~ить**› [16] learn, memorize; (В + *inf.* *or* Д) teach (a p. to ... *or* s.th.); **-ся** learn (s.th. from Д/у Р).

вых|а́живать F [1], ‹**∠одить**› [15] **1.** rear, bring up; nurse, restore to

health; 2. go (all) over, through; ~вáтывать [1], ‹~ватить› [15] snatch away, from, out; snap up, off.
вы́хлоп *m* [1] exhaust; ~ной [14] exhaust...; ~отать [1] *pf.* obtain.
вы́ход *m* [1] 1. exit; way out (*a. fig.*); outlet; 2. departure; withdrawal, retirement; 3. appearence, publication; *thea.* entrance (*on the stage*), performance; 4. yield, output; ~ зáмуж marriage (*of women*); ~ в отстáвку retirement, resignation; ~ец *m* [1; -дца] immigrant, native of; come *or* originate from.
выходи́ть[1] [15], ‹вы́йти› [вы́йду, -дешь; вы́шел, -шла; вы́шедший; вы́йдя] 1. go *or* come out, leave; get out, off; withdraw, retire; 2. appear, be published *or* issued; 3. come off; turn out, result; happen, arise, originate; 4. spend, use up, run out of; † become due; F вы́шло! it's clicked!; вы́йти в офицéры rise to the rank of an officer; ~ в отстáвку (на пéнсию) retire, resign; ~ за предéлы (P) transgress the bounds of; ~ (зáмуж) за (B) marry (*v/t.*; *of women*); ~ из себя́ be beside o.s.; ~ из терпéния lose one's temper (patience); окнó вы́ходит на у́лицу the window faces the street; ~ из стрóя fall out, be out of action; из негó вы́шел ... he has become ...; из э́того ничегó не вы́йдет nothing will come of it.
вы́ход|ить[2] *s.* выхáживать; ~ка [5; *g/pl.:* -док] trick, prank; excess; ~ной [14] exit...; outlet...; holiday-...; festive; ~нóй день *m* holiday, day off; (have one's быть T).
вы́холенный [14] well-groomed.
выцве|тáть [1], ‹'~сти› [25 -т-: -ету] fade, wither.
выч|ёркивать [1], ‹~еркнуть› [20] strike out, obliterate; ~éрпывать, ‹~ерпать› [1], *once* ‹~ерпнуть› [20 *st.*] scoop; dredge (out); ~есть *s.* ~итáть; ~ет *m* [1] deduction.
вычисл|éние *n* [12] calculation; ~я́ть [1], ‹'~ить› [13] calculate, compute.
вы́чи|стить *s.* ~щáть; ~тáемое *n* [14] subtrahend; ~тáние *n* [12] subtraction; ~тáть [1], ‹вы́честь› [25 -т-: -чту; -чел, -чла; *g. pt.*: вы́чтя] deduct; & subtract; ~щáть [1], ‹~стить› [15] clean, scrub, brush, polish.
вы́чурный [14; -рен, -рна] ornate, flowery; fanciful.
вы́швырнуть [20 *st.*] *pf.* turn out.
вы́ше higher; above; beyond; он ~ меня́ he is taller than I (am); э́то ~ моегó понимáния that's beyond my reach.
вы́ше... above..., afore...
выш|ибáть F [1], ‹~ибить› [-бу, -бешь; -б, -бла; -бленный] knock *or* throw out; ~ивáние *n* [12] embroidery; ~ивáть [1], ‹~ить› [-шью, -шьешь] embroider; ~ивка *f* [5; *g/pl.:* -вок] embroidery.
вышинá *f* [5] height; *cf.* высотá.
вы́шка *f* [5; *g/pl.:* -шек] tower.
выяв|ля́ть [28], ‹'~ить› [14] discover, uncover, reveal.
выясн|éние *n* [12] clarification; ~я́ть [28], ‹'~ить› [13] clear up, find out, ascertain; -ся turn out; come to light.
вью|га *f* [5] snowstorm; ~к *m* [1] pack, bale, load; ~н *m* [1 *e.*] loach (*fish*); ~чить [16], ‹на-› load; ~чный [14] pack...; ~щийся [17] curly; ~щееся растéние *n* creeper.
вя́жущий [17] astringent.
вяз *m* [1] elm.
вязáн|ка *f* [5; *g/pl.:* -нок] fag(g)ot; '~ый [14] knitted; ~ье *n* [10] (*a.* ~ие *n* [12]) knitting; crochet.
вяз|áть [3], ‹с-› 1. tie, bind (together); 2. knit; (крючкóм) crochet; -ся *impf.* match, agree, be in keeping; F make sense; work (well), get on; ~кий [16; -зок, -зкá, -о] viscous, sticky; swampy, marshy; ~нуть [21], ‹за-, у-› sink in, stick.
вя́лить [13], ‹про-› dry, sun.
вя́|лый [14 *sh.*] withered, faded; flabby; *fig.* sluggish; dull (*a.* †); ~нуть [20], ‹за-, у-› wither, fade; droop, flag.

Г

г *abbr.*: грамм.
г. *abbr.:* 1. год; 2. гóрод; 3. господи́н.
га 1. ha(h)!; 2. *abbr.*: гектáр.
Гаáга *f* [5] The Hague.
Гавáна *f* [5] 1. Havana; 2. ♀ Havana cigar.
гáвань *f* [8] harbo(u)r.
Гаври|и́л *m* [1], P ~ла [5] Gabriel.
гáга *f* [5] *zo.* eider.
гад *m* [1] reptile (*a. fig.*).
гадá|лка *f* [5; *g/pl.:* -лок] fortuneteller; ~ние *n* [12] fortunetelling; guessing, conjecture; ~ть [1] 1. ‹по-› tell fortunes; (by cards на кáртах); 2. *impf.* guess, conjecture.
гáд|ина F *f* [5] = гад; ~ить [15] 1. ‹на-, за-› F soil; (Д) P harm; 2. ‹из-› P spoil, botch; ~кий [16; -док, -дкá, -о] nasty, ugly, disgusting, repulsive; ~ли́вый [14 *sh.*] squeamish; ~ость F *f*[8] vermin; villainy, ugly thing (act, word); ~ю́ка *f* [5] *zo.* viper (*a.*, P, *fig.*), adder.
газ *m* [1] 1. gas; свети́льный ~

coal gas; дать ~ *mot.* step on the gas; на по́лном ~е (~у́) at full speed (throttle); *pl.* ⚕ flatulences; **2.** gauze.

газе́ль *f* [8] gazelle.

газе́т|а *f* [14] newspaper; **~ный** [14] news...; ~ный кио́ск *m* newsstand, *Brt.* news stall; **~чик** *m* [1] newsman, newsboy.

газиро́ван|ный [14]: **~ная** вода́ *f* soda water.

га́з|овый [14] **1.** gas...; **~овый** счётчик *m* = **~оме́р**; **~овая** педа́ль *f* *mot.* accelerator (pedal); **2.** gauze...; **~оме́р** *m* [1] gas meter; **~о́метр** *m* [1] gasometer.

газо́н *m* [1] lawn.

газо|обра́зный [14; -зен, -зна] gaseous; **~прово́д** *m* [1] gas pipe line.

га́йка *f* [5; *g/pl.:* га́ек] ⊕ nut.

галантер|е́йный [14]: **~е́йный** магази́н *m* notions store, *Brt.* haberdashery; ~е́йные това́ры *m/pl.* = **~е́я** *f* [6] notions *pl.*, dry goods *pl.*, *Brt.* fancy goods *pl.*

галд|ёж P *m* [1 *e.*] row, hubbub; **~е́ть** P [11], ⟨за-⟩ clamo(u)r, din.

гал|ере́я *f* [6] gallery; **~ёрка** F *f* [5] *thea.* gallery.

галифе́ *pl. indecl.* ⚔ breeches.

га́лка *f* [5; *g/pl.:* -лок] jackdaw.

гало́п *m* [1] gallop; **~ом** at a gallop; **~и́ровать** [7] gallop.

гало́ши *f/pl.* [5] galoshes, rubbers.

га́лстук *m* [1] (neck)tie.

галу́н *m* [1 *e.*] galloon, braid.

гальван|изи́ровать [7] (*im*)*pf.* galvanize; **~и́ческий** [16] galvanic.

га́лька *f* [5; *g/pl.:* -лек] pebble.

гам F *m* [1] din, row, rumpus.

гама́к *m* [1 *e.*] hammock.

гама́ши *f/pl.* [5] gaiters.

га́мма *f* [5] ♪ scale; range.

ган|гре́на ⚕ *f* [5] gangrene; **~дика́п** *m* [1] handikap; **~те́ли** (-'tɛ-) *f/pl.* [8] dumbbells.

гара́ж *m* [1 *e.*] garage.

гарант|и́ровать [7] (*im*)*pf.*, **∠ия** *f* [7] guarantee, warrant.

гардеро́б *m* [1] wardrobe; (*a.* **~ная** *f* [14]) check-, cloakroom; **~щик** *m* [1], **~щица** *f* [5] cloakroom attendant.

гарди́на *f* [5] curtain.

гармо́|ника *f* [5] (*kind of*) accordion; губна́я ~ника mouth organ, harmonica; **~ни́ровать** [20] harmonize, be in harmony (with с T); **~ни́ст** *m* [1] accordionist; harmonist; **~ни́ческий** [16] harmonic; *a.* = **~ни́чный** [14; -чен, -чна] harmonious; **~ния** *f* [7] harmony; F *a.* = **~нь** F *f* [8], **~шка** *f* [5; *g/pl.:* -шек] = ~ника.

гарни|зо́н *m* [1] garrison; **∠р** *m* [1], **∠ровать** [7] (*im*)*pf.*, *cook.* garnish; **~ту́р** *m* [1] set.

гарпу́н *m* [1 *e.*], **~ить** [13] harpoon.

гарцева́ть [7] prance.

гарь *f* [8] (s. th.) burnt, char.

гаси́ть [15], ⟨по-, за-⟩ extinguish, put *or* blow out; slake.

га́снуть [21], ⟨по-, у-⟩ go out, die away; *fig.* fade, wither.

гастрол|ёр *m* [1] guest actor *or* artist, star; **~и́ровать** [7] tour, give performance(s) on a tour; **∠ь** *f* [8] starring (performance).

гастроно́м *m* [1] **1.** gastronome(r); gourmet; **2.** *a.* = **~и́ческий** магази́н *m* delicatessen, (dainty) food store *or* shop; **~и́ческий** [16] gastronomic(al); *cf.* ~ 2.; **~ия** *f* [7] gastronomy; dainties, delicacies *pl.*

гауптва́хта *f* [5] guardhouse.

гвалт F *m* [1] rumpus, din.

гвард|е́ец *m* [1; -е́йца] guardsman; **∠ия** *f* [7] Guards *pl.*

гво́зд|ик *dim. of* **~ь**, *cf.*; **~и́ка** *f* [5] carnation, pink, (*spice*) clove; **~ь** *m* [4 *e.*; *pl.:* гво́зди, -де́й] nail; *fig.* main feature, hit.

гг. *or* **г.г.** *abbr.:* **1.** го́ды; **2.** господа́.

где where; F *s.* куда́ F; ~-~ = ко́е-где́, *cf.*; *cf.* ни; ~ F = **∠-либо**, **∠-нибудь**, **∠-то** any-, somewhere; ∠-то здесь hereabout(s).

ГДР *cf.* герма́нский.

гей! F heigh!

гекта́р *m* [1] hectare.

гектоли́тр *m* [1] hectoliter.

ге́ли|й *m* [3] helium; **~копте́р** (-'tɛ) *m* [1] *s.* вертолёт; **~отерапи́я** *f* [7] heliotherapy.

генеало́гия *f* [7] genealogy.

генера́|л *m* [1] general; **~л-майо́р** *m* major general; **~льный** [14] general; ~льная репети́ция *f* dress rehearsal; **~тор** *m* [1] generator.

ген|иа́льный [14; -лен, -льна] of genius; ingenious; **∠ий** *m* [3] genius.

гео́|граф *m* [1] geographer; **~графи́ческий** [16] geographic(al); **~гра́фия** *f* [7] geography; **~лог** *m* [1] geologist; **~ло́гия** *f* [7] geology; **~ме́трия** *f* [7] geometry.

Гео́рг|ий *m* [3] George; **♀и́н(а** *f* [5]) *m* [1] dahlia.

гера́нь *f* [8] geranium.

Гера́сим *m* [1] Gerasim (*m. name*).

герб *m* [1 *e.*] (coat of) arms; emblem; **∠овый** [14] stamp(ed).

Герма́н|ия *f* [7] Germany; Федерати́вная Респу́блика ~ии (ФРГ) Federal Republic of Germany; **♀ский** [16] German; ~ская Демократи́ческая Респу́блика (ГДР) German Democratic Republic (*Eastern Zone of Germany*).

гермети́ческий [16] hermetic.

геро|и́зм *m* [1] heroism; **~и́ня** *f* [6] heroine; **~и́ческий** [16] heroic; **∠й** *m* [3] hero; **∠йский** [16] heroic.

ге́тры *f/pl.* [5] gaiters.

г-жа *abbr.:* госпожа́.

гиаци́нт *m* [1] hyacinth.

ги́бель *f* [7] ruin, destruction; loss;

⚓ wreck; death; P immense number, lots of; **~ный** [14; -лен, -льна] disastrous, fatal.
ги́бк|ий [16; -бок, -бка́, -о] supple, pliant, flexible (*a. fig.*); **~ость** *f* [8] flexibility.
ги́б|лый P [14] ruinous; **~нуть** [21], ⟨по-⟩ perish.
Гибралта́р *m* [1] Gibraltar.
гига́нт *m* [1] giant; **~ский** [16] gigantic, huge.
гигие́н|а *f* [5] hygiene; **~и́ческий** [16], **~и́чный** [14; -чен, -чна] hygienic.
гид *m* [1] guide.
гидравли́ческий [16] hydraulic.
гидро|пла́н, ~самолёт *m* [1] seaplane, hydroplane; **~(электро)ста́нция** *f* [7] hydroelectric power station.
гие́на *f* [5] hyena.
гик *m* [1], **∠анье** *n* [10] whoop(ing).
ги́льза *f* [5] (*cartridge*) case; shell.
Гимала́и *m/pl.* [3] The Himalayas.
гимн *m* [1] hymn; anthem.
гимна|зи́ст *m* [1] pupil *of* **∠зия** *f* [7] high school, *Brt.* grammar school; **∠ст** *m* [1] gymnast; **~стёрка** *f* [5; *g/pl.:* -рок] ⚔ blouse, *Brt.* tunic; **∠стика** *f* [5] gymnastics; **~сти́ческий** [16] gymnastic.
гипе́рбол|а *f* [5] hyperbole; ⅌ hyperbola; **~и́ческий** [16] hyperbolic, exaggerated.
гипно́|з *m* [1] hypnosis; **~тизи́ровать** [7], ⟨за-⟩ hypnotize.
гипо́теза *f* [5] hypothesis.
гиппопота́м *m* [1] hippopotamus.
гипс *m* [1] *min.* gypsum; ⊕ plaster of Paris; **∠овый** [14] gypsum..., plaster...
гирля́нда *f* [5] garland.
ги́ря *f* [6] weight.
гита́ра *f* [5] guitar.
глав|а́ [5; *pl. st.*] **1.** *f* head; top, summit; cupola; chapter (*in books*); (быть, стоя́ть) во **~е́** (be) at the head; lead (by с Т); **2.** *m/f* head, chief; **~а́рь** *m* [4 *e.*] (ring) leader, chieftain.
главе́нство *n* [9] priority, hegemony; **~вать** [7] (pre)dominate.
главнокома́ндующий *m* [17]: ~ commander in chief; Верхо́вный ~ Commander in Chief; Supreme Commander.
гла́вн|ый [14] chief, main, principal, central; head...; ... in chief; **~ая** кни́га *f* ✝ ledger; **~ое** (де́ло) *n* the main thing; above all; **~ый** го́род *m* capital; **~ым** о́бразом mainly, chiefly.
глаго́л *m* [1] *gr.* verb; † word, speech; **~ьный** [14] verb(al).
глад|и́льный [14] ironing; **∠ить** [15] **1.** ⟨вы́-⟩ iron, press; **2.** ⟨по-⟩ stroke, caress; F **∠ить** по голо́вке treat with indulgence *or* favo(u)r; **∠кий** [16; -док, -дка́, -о] smooth (*a. fig.*); lank (*hair*); plain (*fabric*); P well-fed; **∠кость, ~ь** *f* [8] smoothness.
глаз *m* [1; в -у́; *pl.*: -а́, глаз, -а́м] eye; look; (eye)sight; F heed, care; в **~а́** (Д) to s.b.'s face; (*strike*) the eye; в мои́х **~а́х** in my view *or* opinion; за **~а́** in s.b.'s absence, behind one's back; plentifully; на ~ approximately, by eye; на **~а́х** (*poss. or* у Р) in s.b.'s presence, sight; с **∠у** на ~ privately, tête-à-tête; просты́м (невооружённым) **∠ом** with the naked eye; темно́, хоть ~ вы́коли F it is pitch-dark; **~а́стый** F [14 *sh.*] goggle-eyed; sharp-sighted; **~е́ть** P [8] stare *or* gape (around); **~но́й** [14] eye..., optic; **~но́й** врач *m* oculist; **~о́к** *m* [1; -зка́] **1.** [*pl. st.*: -зки, -зок] *dim. of* ~; аню́тины **∠ки** *pl.* pansy; **2.** [*pl. e.*: -зки́, -зко́в] ⚘ bud; *zo.* ocellus, eye; peephole.
глазоме́р *m* [1]: на ~ estimate(d) by the eye; (*sure, etc.*) eye.
глазу́нья *f* [6] fried eggs *pl.*
глазур|ова́ть [7] (*im*)*pf.* glaze; **∠ь** *f* [8] glaze.
гла|си́ть [15 *e*; *3. p. only*] say, read, run; **∠сность** *f* [8] public(ity); **∠сный** [14] public; (*a. su.*) vowel; *su.* council(l)or; **~ша́тай** *m* [3] town crier; *fig.* herald.
гле́тчер *m* [1] glacier.
гли́н|а *f* [5] loam; clay; **~истый** [14 *sh.*] loamy; **~озём** *m* [1] *min.* alumina; **~яный** [14] earthen; loamy.
глист *m* [1 *e.*], **~а́** *f* [5] (intestinal) worm; (ле́нточный) ~ tapeworm.
глицери́н *m* [1] glycerine.
гло́бус *m* [1] globe.
глода́ть [3], ⟨об-⟩ gnaw (at, round).
глот|а́ть [1], ⟨про**~**и́ть⟩ [15], *once* ⟨**~**ну́ть⟩ [20] swallow; F devour; **∠ка** *f* [5; *g/pl.*: -ток] throat; во всю **∠ку** *s.* го́лос; **~о́к** *m* [1; -тка́] draught, gulp (at Т).
гло́хнуть [21] **1.** ⟨о-⟩ grow deaf; **2.** ⟨за-⟩ fade, die away, out; go out; grow desolate.
глуб|ина́ *f* [5] depth; remoteness (*past*); *fig.* profundity; *thea.* background; Т/в (В) ..., *or* ... в В ... deep; **~о́кий** [16; -бо́к, -бока́, -бо́ко́] deep; low; remote; *fig.* profound; complete; great (*age*); **~о́кой** зимо́й (но́чью) in the dead of winter (late at night).
глубоко|мы́сленный [14 *sh.*] thoughtful, sagacious; **~мы́слие** *n* [12] thoughtfulness; **~уважа́емый** [14] dear (*polite address*).
глубь *f* [8] *s.* глубина́.
глум|и́ться [14 *e.*; -млю́сь, -ми́шься] sneer, mock, scoff (at над Т); **~ле́ние** *n* [12] mockery.
глуп|е́ть [8], ⟨по-⟩ become stupid; **~е́ц** *m* [1; -пца́] fool, blockhead; **~и́ть** F [14 *e.*; -плю́, -пи́шь] fool; **∠ость** *f* [8] stupidity; foolery; non-

sense; ∠ый [14; глуп, -á, -o] foolish, silly, stupid.

глух|áрь *m* [4 *e.*] capercailie, wood grouse; ~óй [14; глух, -á, -o; *comp.*: глýше] deaf (*a. fig.*; к Д to; *cf.* слепóй); dull, vague; desolate, wild; out-of-the-way; ⚠ tight, solid, blind; late, the dead of; *gr.* voiceless; **~онемóй** [14] deaf-mute; **~отá** *f* [5] deafness.

глуш|йтель ⊕ *m* [4] muffler; **~йть** [16 *e.*; -шý, -шйшь; -шённый] **1.** ⟨о-⟩ deafen, stun; **2.** ⟨за-⟩ deafen; deaden; muffle; smother, suppress (*a.*✿); ⊕ switch off, throttle; ⚡ jam; **~ь** *f* [8] thicket; wilderness; solitude, lonely spot, nook.

глы́ба *f* [5] lump, clod; block.

гля|дéть [11; глядя], ⟨по-⟩, *once* ⟨∠нуть⟩ [20] look, glance (at на В); F look after, take care of (за Т); peep (out of, from из Р); F **~дй** very likely; look out!; тогó и **~дй** ... may + *inf.* (unexpectedly); кудá глазá **~дят** at random; after one's nose.

глян|ец *m* [1; -нца] polish; luster; **~цев(йт)ый** [14 (*sh.*)] glossy, lustrous; glazed *paper*; **~уть** *s.* глядéть.

г-н *abbr.*: господйн.

гнать [гоню́, гóнишь; гонймый; гнал, -á -o; '...гнанный], ⟨по-⟩ **1.** *v/t.* (be) drive (-ving, *etc.*); F send; float; **2.** distil; **3.** pursue, chase; (*a.* **-ся** за Т; *fig.* strive for); **4.** *v/i.* speed along.

гнев *m* [1] anger; **∠аться** [1], ⟨раз-, про-⟩ be(come) angry (with на В); **∠ный** [14; -вен, -вна́, -o] angry.

гнедóй [14] sorrel, chestnut (*horse*).

гнезд|йться [15] nest; **~ó** *n* [9; *pl.*: гнёзда, *etc. st.*] nest, aerie.

гнёт *m* [1] press(ure); oppression.

гни|éние *n* [12] putrefaction; **~лóй** [14; гнил, -á, -o] rotten, putrid; wet; **~ль** *f* [8] rottenness; **~ть** [гнию́, -ёшь; гнил, -á, -o], ⟨с-⟩ rot, putrefy.

гно|éние *n* [12] suppuration; **~йть** (**-ся**) [13] fester; **~й** *m* [3] pus; **∠йный** [14] purulent.

гнусáвить [14] snuffle, twang.

гнýсн|ость *f* [8] meanness; **~ый** [14; -сен, -сна́, -o] vile, mean, base.

гнуть [20], ⟨со-⟩ bend, curve; bow; F drive (at к Д); *fig.* bully.

гнушáться [1], ⟨по-⟩ (Р *or* Т) scorn, despise, disdain.

говé|нье *n* [12] fast; **~ть** [1] fast.

гóвор *m* [1] talk, hum, murmur; rumo(u)r; accent; dialect, patois; **~йть** [13], ⟨по-; сказáть⟩ [3] speak *or* talk (about, of о П, про В; to *or* with *p.* с Т); say, tell; **~ят**, **~йтся** they say, it is said; **~йть** по-рýсски speak Russian; инáче **~я** in other words; не **~я** ужé о (П) let alone; по прáвде (сóвести) **~я** to tell the truth; что вы **~йте**! you don't say!; что (как) ни **~й** whatever you (one) may say; что и **~йть**, и не **~й**(те)! yes, of course, sure!; **~лйвый** [14 *sh.*] talkative.

говя́|дина *f* [5], **~жий** [18] beef.

гóгот *m* [1], **~áть** [3], ⟨за-⟩ cackle; P roar (with laughter).

год *m* [1; *pl.*: -ды & -дá, *from g/pl. e.* & лет, *etc.* 9 *e.*] year (в ~ a *or* per year); в э́том (прóшлом) **~ý** this (last) year; из ∠а в ∠ year in year out; ∠ óт **~у** year by year; крýглый ~ all the year round; (с) **~áми** for (after a number of) years; *cf.* пят(и-десят)ый.

годйт|ься [15 *e.*; гожýсь, годйшься], ⟨при-⟩ be of use (for для Р, к Д, на В), do; fit; *pf.* come in handy; э́то (никудá) не **~ся** that's no good (for anything), that won't do, it's (very) bad.

годйчный [14] annual.

гóдный [14; -ден, -днá, -o, гóдны́] fit, suitable, useful, good, ⚔ able(-bodied) (to, *a.* + *inf.*, for для Р, к Д, на В); ни на чтó не ~ good-for-nothing.

годов|óй [14] annual; one year (old); **~щйна** *f* [5] anniversary.

гол *m* [1] goal; забйть ~ score.

гол|енйще *n* [11] bootleg; **∠ень** *f* [8] shank.

голлáнд|ец *m* [1; -дца] Dutchman; **Ωия** *f* [7] Holland; **~ка** *f* [5; *g/pl.*: -док] Dutchwoman; **~ский** [16] Dutch.

голов|á [5; *pl.*: гóловы, голóв, -вáм] **1.** *f* [*ac/sg.*: '**~у**] head; **2.** *m* head, chief; **~á** сáхару sugar loaf; как снег нá **~у** all of a sudden; с **~ы** до ног from head to foot; в **~áх** at the head; на свою́ '**~у** F to one's own harm; повéсить '**~у** become discouraged *or* despondent; **~á** идёт крýгом (у Р s.b.'s) thoughts are in a whirl; **∠ка** *f* [5; *g/pl.*: -вок] small head; head (*pin, nail, etc.*); bulb, clove (*onion, garlic*); **~нóй** [14] head...; ⚔ advance...; **~нáя** боль *f* headache.

голово|кружéние *n* [12] giddiness; **~кружйтельный** [14] dizzy, giddy; **~лóмка** *f* [5; *g/pl.*: -мок] puzzle; **~мóйка** *f* [5; *g/pl.*: -мóек] F blowup; **~рéз** F *m* [1] daredevil; cutthroat, thug; **~тя́п** F *m* [1] booby, bungler.

гóлод *m* [1] **1.** hunger; **2.** *s.* **~óвка**; **~áть** [1] starve; **∠ный** [14; гóлоден, -днá, -o, гóлодны́] hungry; starv(el)ing; **~óвка** *f* [5; *g/pl.*: -вок] starvation; famine; hunger strike.

гололéдица *f* [5] ice-crusted ground.

гóлос *m* [1; *pl.*: -cá, *etc. e.*] voice; vote; прáво **~a** suffrage; во весь ~ at the top of one's voice; в оди́н ~ unanimously; **~á** зá и прóтив the yeas (ayes) & noes; **~йть** P [15 *e.*; -ошý, -осйшь] bawl; **~лóвный**

[14; -вен, -вна] unfounded; empty; **~ова́ние** *n* [12] voting, poll(ing); закры́тое ~ова́ние secret vote; **~ова́ть** [7], ⟨про-⟩ vote; **~ово́й** [14] vocal (cords свя́зки *f/pl*).

голуб|е́ц *m* [1; -бца́] stuffed cabbage; **~о́й** [14] (sky) blue; **∠(уш)ка** *f* [5; *g/pl.*: -бок (-шек)], **∠чик** *m* [1] (F *address*) (my) dear; **'~ь** *m* [4] pigeon; **~я́тня** *f* [6; *g/pl.*: -тен] dovecote.

го́л|ый [14; гол, -á, -о] naked, nude; bare (*a. fig.*); poor, miserable; **~ь** *f* [8] poverty; waste (land).

гомеопа́тия *f* [7] homeopathy.

гомин(ь)да́н *m* [1] Kuomintang.

го́мон F *m* [1] din, hubbub.

гондо́ла *f* [5] gondola (*a.* ✈).

гон|е́ние *n* [12] persecution; **~е́ц** *m* [1; -нца́] courier; **∠ка** *f* [5; *g/pl.*: -нок] rush; chase; F haste; ⚗ distil(l)ment; *pl.* race(s), ⚓ regatta; F blowup; ∠ка вооруже́ний arms race.

Гонко́нг *m* [1] Hong Kong.

го́нор *m* [1] airs *pl.*; **~а́р** *m* [1] fee.

го́ночный [14] race..., racing.

гонт *m* [1] *coll.* shingles.

гонча́р *m* [1 *e.*] potter; **~ный** [14] potter's; ~ные изде́лия *n/pl.* pottery.

го́нчая *f* [17] (*a.* ~ соба́ка) hound.

гоня́ть(ся) [1] drive, *etc.*, *s.* гнать.

гор|á *f* [5; *ac/sg.*: го́ру; *pl.*: го́ры, гор, гора́м] mountain; heap, pile; (*a. pl.*) (toboggan) slide; в ∠у *or* нá ~у uphill; *fig.* up(ward); по́д ~у *or* с ~ы́ downhill; под ~о́й at the foot of a hill (*or* mountain); не за ~а́ми not far off; пир ~о́й F sumptuous feast; стоя́ть ~о́й (за В) defend s.th. *or* s.b. with might & main; у меня́ ~á с плеч свали́лась F a load's been (*or* was) taken off my mind.

гора́здо *used with the comp.* much, far; P quite.

горб *m* [1 *e.*; на -у́] hump, hunch; **~а́тый** [14 *sh.*] humpbacked; curved; aquiline (*nose*); **∠ить** [14], ⟨с-⟩ stoop, bend, curve (*v/i.* -ся); **~у́н** *m* [1 *e.*] hunchback; **~у́шка** *f* [5; *g/pl.*: -шек] top crust, heel (*bread*).

горд|ели́вый [14 *sh.*] haughty, proud; **~е́ц** *m* [1 *e.*] proud man; **~и́ться** [15 *e.*; горжу́сь, горди́шься], ⟨воз-⟩ be(come) proud (of T); **∠ость** *f* [8] pride; **∠ый** [14; горд, -á, -о] proud (of T).

го́р|е *n* [10] grief, distress; trouble; misfortune, disaster; с ~я out of grief; ~е мне! woe is me!; ему́ и ~я ма́ло F he doesn't care a bit; с ~ем попола́м F hardly, with difficulty; **~ева́ть** [6], ⟨по-⟩ grieve; regret (s. th. о П).

горе́л|ка *f* [5; *g/pl.*: -лок] burner; **~ый** [14] burnt.

горемы́ка F *m/f* [5] poor wretch.

го́рест|ный [14; -тен, -тна] sad, sorrowful; **~ь** *f* [8] *cf.* го́ре.

гор|е́ть [9], ⟨с-⟩ burn (*a. fig.*), be on fire; glow, gleam; не ~и́т F there's no hurry; де́ло ~и́т (в рука́х у Р) F the matter is top urgent (makes good progress).

го́рец *m* [1; -рца] mountaineer.

го́речь *f* [8] bitter taste (*or* smell); *fig.* bitterness; grief, affliction.

горизо́нт *m* [1] horizon; **~а́льный** [14; -лен, -льна] horizontal, level.

гори́стый [14 *sh.*] mountainous; hilly.

го́рка *f* [5; *g/pl.*: -рок] *dim. of* горá, *s.*; hill; whatnot, small cupboard.

горла́нить P [13], ⟨за-, про-⟩ bawl.

го́рл|о *n* [9] throat; gullet; (*vessel*) neck (*a.* **~ышко** *n* [9; *g/pl.*: -шек]); по ~о F up to the eyes; я сыт по ~о F I've had my fill (*fig.* I'm fed up with [T]); во всё ~о *s.* го́лос.

горн *m* [1] **1.** ⊕ (*a.* **~и́ло** *n* [9]) furnace, forge; crucible (*a. fig.*); **2.** ♪ horn, bugle; **~и́ст** *m* [1] bugler.

го́рничная *f* [14] parlo(u)rmaid.

горно|заво́дский [16], **~промы́шленный** [14] mining, metallurgical; **~рабо́чий** *m* [17] miner.

горноста́й *m* [3] ermine.

го́рн|ый [14] mountain(ous), hilly; *min.* rock...; ⊕ mining; ~ый про́мысел *m*, ~ое де́ло *n* mining; ~ое со́лнце *n* sun lamp; **~я́к** *m* [1 *e.*] miner.

го́род *m* [1; *pl.*: -дá, *etc. e.*] town; city (*large town*; F *down town*); зá ~(ом) *go* (*live*) out of town; **~и́ть** P [15], ⟨на-⟩ (вздор, *etc.*) talk nonsense; **~о́к** *m* [1; -дкá] small town; quarter; **~ско́й** [14] town..., city..., municipal; *s. a.* горсове́т.

горожа́н|ин *m* [1; *pl.*: -жа́не, -жа́н] townsman; *pl.* townspeople; **~ка** *f* [5; *g/pl.*: -нок] townswoman.

горо́|х *m* [1] pea (*plant*); *coll.* peas (*seeds*) *pl.*; **~ховый** [14] pea(s)...; pea green; чу́чело ~ховое *n*, шут ~ховый *m* F *fig.* scarecrow; boor, merry-andrew; **~шек** *m* [1; -шка] *coll.* (small) peas *pl.*; **~шин(к)а** *f* [5 (*g/pl.*: -нок)] pea; dot.

горсове́т (городско́й сове́т) *m* [1] city *or* town soviet (council).

го́рст|очка *f* [5; *g/pl.*: -чек] *dim.* of **~ь** *f* [8; *from g/pl. e.*] hollow (*hand*); handful (*a. fig.*).

горта́н|ный [14] guttural; **~ь** *f* [8] larynx.

горчи́ца *f* [5] mustard.

горшо́к *m* [1; -шкá] pot.

го́рьк|ий [16; -рек, -рькá, -о; *comp.*: го́рче] bitter (*a. fig.*); *f su.* vodka, bitters *pl.*; ~ий пья́ница *m* dipsomaniac.

горю́ч|ее *n* [17] (engine) fuel; gasoline, *Brt.* petrol; **~ий** [17 *sh.*] combustible; P bitter (*tears*).

горя́ч|ий [17; горя́ч, -á] hot (*a. fig.*); fiery, hot-tempered; ardent, passionate; violent; warm (*scent*); cordial; hard, busy; **~и́ть** [16 *e.*;

-чу́, -чи́шь], ⟨раз-⟩ heat (*a. fig.*); -ся get *or* be excited; ~ка *f* [5] fever (*a. fig.*); ~ность *f* [8] vehemence, hot temper.

гос = госуда́рственный state... (*of the U.S.S.R.*); ♀ба́нк *m* [1] State Bank; ♀изда́т (♀уда́рственное изда́тельство) *m* [1] State Publishing House; ♀пла́н (♀уда́рственный пла́новый комите́т) *m* [1] State Planning Committee.

го́спиталь *m* [4] ⚔ hospital.

господ|и́н *m* [1; *pl.*: -пода́, -по́д, -да́м] gentleman; master (*a. fig.*); Mr. (*with name or title*); (ladies &) gentlemen (*a. address*); *pl.* (*servants*:) master & mistress; уважа́емые ~а́ dear Sirs (*in letters, a.* †); я сам себе́ ~и́н I am my own master; ∠ский [16] seignorial, (land)lord's, master's; manor (house); ∠ство *n* [9] rule; supremacy; ∠ствовать [7] rule, reign; (pre)dominate, prevail (over над Т); command (*region*); ∠ь *m* [го́спода, -ду; *voc.*: -ди] Lord, God (*a. as int., cf.* бог).

госпожа́ *f* [5] lady; mistress; Mrs. *or* Miss (*with name*).

гостеприи́м|ный [14; -мен, -мна] hospitable; ~ство *n* [9] hospitality.

гост|и́ная *f* [14] drawing room; ~и́нец *m* [1; -нца] present, gift; ~и́ница *f* [5] hotel; inn; ~и́ть [15 *e.*; гощу́, гости́шь] be on a visit, stay with (у Р); ~ь *m* [4; *from g/pl. e.*] guest; visitor (*f* ∠ья [6]); идти́ (е́хать) в ∠и go to see (s.b. к Д); быть в ~я́х (у Р) = и́ть.

госуда́рственный [14] state...; national; ⚖ public; high (*treason*); ~ переворо́т *m* coup d'état; ~ стро́й *m* political system, regime; *s. a.* ГПУ.

госуда́р|ство *n* [9] state; ~ь *m* [4] sovereign; Czar; ми́лостивый ~ь (dear) Sir (*a. pl., in letters, a.* †).

готова́льня *f* [6; *g/pl.*: -лен] (case of) drawing utensils *pl.*

гото́в|ить [14] **1.** ⟨при-⟩ prepare (o.s. *or* get ready for -ся к Д); **2.** ⟨под-⟩ prepare, train; **3.** ⟨за-⟩ store up; lay in (*stock*); ~ность *f* [8] readiness; willingness; ~ый [14 *sh.*] ready (for к Д *or inf.*), on the point of; finished; willing; ready-made (*clothes*); будь ~! — всегда́ ~! be ready! — always ready! (*slogan of pioneers, cf.* пионе́р).

ГПУ (Госуда́рственное полити́ческое управле́ние) G.P.U. = Political State Administration (*predecessor, 1922—35, of* НКВД, [*cf.*).

гр. *abbr.*: граждани́н.

граб *m* [1] hornbeam.

граб|ёж *m* [1 *e.*] robbery; ~и́тель *m* [4] robber; ∠ить [14], ⟨о-⟩ rob, plunder.

гра́бли *f/pl.* [6; *gen.*: -бель & -блей] rake.

грав|ёр *m* [1] engraver; ∠ий *m* [3] gravel; ~ирова́ть [7], ⟨вы́-⟩ engrave; ~иро́вка *f* [5; *g/pl.*: -вок] engraving, etching, print (*a.* ~ю́ра *f* [5]).

град *m* [1] hail (*a. fig.* = shower); ~ идёт it is hailing; ∠ом thick & fast, profusely.

гра́дус *m* [1] degree (of в В); под ~ом F tipsy; ~ник *m* [1] thermometer.

гражд|ани́н *m* [1; *pl.*: гра́ждане, -ан], ~а́нка *f* [5; *g/pl.*: -нок] citizen (*U.S.S.R. a.* = [wo]man, & *in address, mst. without name*); ~а́нский [16] civil (*a. war*); civic (*a. right*); ~а́нство *n* [9] citizenship; citizens *pl.*; дать (получи́ть) пра́во ~а́нства (be) accept(ed) (in public); приня́ть ... ~а́нство become a ... citizen.

грамза́пись *f* [8] recording.

грамм *m* [1] gram(me).

грамма́т|ика *f* [5] grammar; ~и́ческий [16] grammatical.

граммофо́н *m* [1] gramophone.

гра́мот|а *f* [5] reading & writing; document; patent; diploma; † letter; вери́тельная ~а credentials; э́то для меня́ кита́йская ~а F it's Greek to me; ~ность *f* [8] literacy; ~ный [14; -тен, -тна] literate; trained, expert.

грана́т *m* [1] pomegranate; *min.* garnet; ~а *f* [5] shell; grenade.

грандио́зный [14; -зен, -зна] mighty; grand.

гранёный [14] facet(t)ed; cut.

грани́т *m* [1] granite.

грани́|ца *f* [5] border, frontier; boundary; *fig.* limit, verge; за ~цу (~цей) *go* (*be*) abroad; из-за ~цы from abroad; ~чить [16] border *or* verge ([up]on с Т).

гра́н|ка *f* [5; *g/pl.*: -нок] *typ.* galley (proof); ~ь *f* [8] *s.* грани́ца; ⅌ plane; facet; edge; *fig.* verge.

граф *m* [1] earl (*Brt.*); count.

граф|а́ *f* [5] column; ∠ик *m* [1] diagram, graph; ∠ика *f* [5] graphic arts.

графи́н *m* [1] decanter, carafe.

графи́ня *f* [6] countess.

графи́|т *m* [1] graphite; ~ть [14 *e.*; -флю, -фи́шь; -флённый], ⟨раз-⟩ line *or* rule (*paper*), draw columns; ~ческий [16] graphic(al).

граци|о́зный [14; -зен, -зна] graceful; '~я *f* [7] grace(fulness).

грач *m* [1 *e.*] rook.

греб|ёнка *f* [5; *g/pl.*: -нок] comb; стри́чь(ся) под ~ёнку (have one's hair) crop(ped); ∠ень *m* [4; -бня] comb; crest; ~е́ц *m* [1; -бца́] oarsman; ~ешо́к *m* [1; -шка́] *s.* ∠ень; ∠ля *f* [6] rowing; ~но́й [14] row(ing)...

грёз|а *f* [5] (day)dream; ~ить ('grę-) [15] *impf.* dream (of о П); ⚘

rave; -ся, ⟨по-, при-⟩: мне гре́зится (И) I dream (of *or* v/t.).
грек *m* [1] Greek.
гре́лка *f* [5; *g/pl.*: -лок] hot-water bottle; электри́ческая ~ heating pad.
грем|е́ть [10 *e.*; гремлю́, -ми́шь], ⟨про-, за-⟩ thunder, peal (*a. voice, bell, etc.*); rattle, clank, tinkle (*sword, chains, keys*); clatter (*dishes*); *fig.* ring; be famous (for, as); **~у́чий** [17] rattling; ⚗ oxyhydrogen; fulminating; ~у́чая змея́ *f* rattlesnake; **~у́шка** *f* [5; *g/pl.*: -шек] rattle (*toy*).
гренки́ *m/pl.* [1 *e.*] toast (*sg.*: -но́к).
Гренла́ндия *f* [7] Greenland.
грести́ [24 -б-: гребу́; грёб, гребла́], ⟨по-⟩ row; scull; rake; scoop.
греть [8; ...гре́тый], ⟨со-, на-, разо-, обо-, подо-⟩ warm (o.s. **-ся**) (up); heat; -ся на со́лнце sun.
грех *m* [1 *e.*] sin; fault; F = грешно́; с **~о́м** попола́м F so-so; *cf.* го́ре; есть тако́й ~ F well, I own it; как на ~ F unfortunately.
Гре́|ция *f* [7] Greece; **♀цкий** [16]: ♀цкий оре́х *m* walnut; **♀ча́нка** *f* [5; *g/pl.*: -нок], **♀ческий** [16] Greek.
греч|и́ха, ∠ка *f* [5] buckwheat; **∠невый** [14] buckwheat...
греш|и́ть [16 *e.*; -шу́, -ши́шь], ⟨со-⟩ sin (*a.* against про́тив Р); **∠ник** *m* [1], **∠ница** *f* [5] sinner; **~но́** (it's a) shame (on Д); **∠ный** [14; -шен, -шна́, -о]; sinful; F *sh.*: sorry.
гриб *m* [1 *e.*] mushroom; **~о́к** [1; -бка́] *dim. of* ~; fungus.
гри́ва *f* [5] mane.
гри́венник F *m* [1] ten-kopeck coin.
Григо́рий *m* [3] Gregory.
грим *m* [1] *thea.* make-up.
грима́с|а *f* [5] grimace; **~ничать** [1] make faces *or* grimaces.
гримирова́ть [7], ⟨за-, на-⟩ make up (*v/i.* **-ся**).
грипп *m* [1] influenza.
гри́фель *m* [4] slate pencil.
Гри́ш(к)а *m* [5] *dim. of* Григо́рий.
гр-ка *abbr.*: гражда́нка.
гроб *m* [1; в -у́; *pl.*: -ы́ & -а́, *etc. e.*] coffin; † grave; **~ни́ца** *f* [5] tomb; **~ово́й** [14] coffin...; tomb...; deadly; **~овщи́к** *m* [1 *e.*] coffin maker.
гроза́ *f* [5; *pl. st.*] (thunder)storm (*a fig.*); disaster; danger, menace; terror.
гро́зд|ь *m* [4; *pl.*: -ди, -де́й, *etc. e.*, & -дья, -дьев] bunch (*grapes*); cluster.
грози́ть [15 *e.*; грожу́, -зи́шь], ⟨по-⟩ threaten (a p. with Д/Т) (*a.* **-ся**).
гро́з|ный [14; -зен, -зна́, -о] menacing; formidable; P severe, cruel; Ива́н ♀ный Ivan the Terrible; **~ово́й** [14] storm(y).
гром *m* [1; *from g/pl.*: *e.*] thunder (*a. fig.*); ~ греми́т it thunders; как **∠ом** поражённый *fig.* thunderstruck.
грома́д|а *f* [5] giant, colossus; mass, heap; **~ный** [14; -ден, -дна] huge, tremendous.
громи́|ть [14 *e.*; -млю́, -ми́шь; -млённый], ⟨раз-⟩ smash, crush; rout.
гро́мк|ий [16; -мок, -мка́, -о; *comp.*: гро́мче] loud; noisy; *fig.* famous, great, noted; notorious; (*words, etc.*) pompous; **~оговори́тель** *m* [4] loud-speaker.
громо|во́й [14] thunder..., thunderous; **~гла́сный** [14; -сен, -сна] roaring; *mst. adv.* in public; **~зди́ть** (**-ся**) [15 *e.*; -зжу́, -зди́шь] *cf.* взгромозжда́ть(ся); **∠здкий** [16; -док, -дка] bulky, cumbersome; **~отво́д** *m* [1] lightning rod *or* conductor.
громыха́ть F [1] rattle.
грот *m* [1] grotto.
гро́х|нуть F [20] *pf.* crash, tumble (*v/i.* **-ся**); **~от** *m* [1] rumble; **~ота́ть** [3], ⟨за-⟩ rumble; P roar.
грош *m* [1 *e.*] half-kopeck; piece; ни **~а́** not a stiver *or* farthing; ~ цена́ *or* ~а́ ло́маного не сто́ит not worth a pin; ни в ~ не ста́вить not care a straw (for В); **~о́вый** [14] worth 1 ~; *fig.* (dirt-)cheap, paltry.
груб|е́ть [8], ⟨за-, о-⟩ harden, become callous; **~и́ть** [14 *e.*; -блю́, -би́шь], ⟨на-⟩ say rude things; **~ия́н** F *m* [1] rude fellow; **∠ость** *f* [8] rudeness; **∠ый** [14; груб, -а́, -о] coarse; rough; rude; gross (*error, etc.*).
гру́да *f* [5] pile, heap, mass.
груд|и́нка *f* [5; *g/pl.*: -нок] brisket; bacon; **~но́й** [14]: ~на́я клё́тка *f* thorax, chest; **~ь** *f* [8; в, на -ди́; *from g/pl. e.*] breast; bosom; стоя́ть **∠ью** (за В) defend bravely.
груз *m* [1] load, freight; ⚓ cargo.
грузи́н *m* [1; *g/pl.*: грузи́н], **~ка** *f* [5; *g/pl.*: -нок] Georgian; **~ский** [16] Georgian.
грузи́ть [15 & 15 *e.*; -ужу́, -у́зишь], ⟨на-, за-, по-⟩ load, embark.
Гру́зия *f* [7] Georgia (*Caucasus*).
гру́з|ный [14; -зен, -зна́, -о] massive, heavy; **~ови́к** *m* [1 *e.*] truck, *Brt.* lorry; **~ово́й** [14] freight..., goods..., ⚓ cargo...; ~ово́й автомоби́ль *m* = ~ови́к; **~оподъёмность** *f* [8] carrying capacity, ⚓ tonnage; **~чик** *m* [1] loader, ⚓ stevedore.
грунт *m* [1] soil; ground (*a. paint.*); **~ово́й** [14] ground...; unpaved.
гру́пп|а *f* [5] group; **~ирова́ть** (**-ся**) [7], ⟨с-⟩ (form a) group.
груст|и́ть [15 *e.*; -ущу́, -сти́шь], F ⟨взгрустну́ть⟩ [20] grieve; long (for) (по П); **∠ный** [14; -тен, -тна́,

-о] sad, sorrowful; dreary; F deplorable; мне ₒно I feel sad; ~ь *f* [8] sadness, grief, melancholy.
гру́ша *f* [5] pear (*a. tree*).
гры́жа *f* [5] hernia, rupture.
грыз|ня́ F *f* [6] squabble; ~ть [24; *pt. st.*], ⟨раз-⟩ gnaw (*a. fig.*), nibble; bite; crack (*nuts*); -ся bite o. a.; F squabble; ~у́н *m* [1 *e.*] *zo.* rodent.
гряд|а́ *f* [5; *nom/pl. st.*] ridge, range (*a. fig.* = line); ✓ bed (*a.* ₒка *f* [5; *g/pl.*: -док]).
гряду́щий [17] future, coming; на сон ~ for a nightcap.
гряз|ево́й [14] mud...; ~езащи́тный [14]: ~езащи́тное крыло́ *n* fender, mudguard; ~елече́бница *f* [5] mud bath; ₒи *f/pl.* [8] (curative) mud; ~ни́ть [13], ⟨за-⟩ soil (*a. fig.*); -ся get dirty; ₒнуть [20], ⟨по-⟩ sink (*mud, etc.*, & *fig.*); ₒный [14; -зен, -зна́, -о, грязны́] dirty (*a. fig.*); muddy; slop... (*pail*); ~ь *f* [8; в -зи́] dirt; mud (*street, etc.*); в ~и́ dirty; не уда́рить лицо́м в ~ь save one's face.
гря́нуть [19 *st.*] *pf.* crash, thunder, (re)sound, ring, roar; break out, burst, start.
губ|а́ *f* [5; *nom/pl. st.*] lip; bay; gulf; ₒа не ду́ра (у P p.'s) taste isn't bad.
губерн|а́тор *m* [1] governor; ₒия *f* [7] government, province.
губи́т|ельный [14; -лен, -льна] pernicious; ~ь [14], ⟨по-, F с-⟩ destroy, ruin; waste (*time*).
гу́б|ка *f* [5; *g/pl.*: -бок] **1.** *dim. of* ~а́; **2.** sponge; ~но́й [14] labial; ~на́я пома́да *f* lipstick.
гуверн|а́нтка *f* [5; *g/pl.*: -ток] governess; ~ёр *m* [1] tutor.
гуд|е́ть [11], ⟨за-⟩ buzz; honk, hoot, whistle; ~о́к *m* [1; -дка́] honk, hoot, signal; horn; siren, whistle.
гул *m* [1] boom, rumble; hum; ₒкий [16; -лок, -лка́, -о] booming, loud; resonant.
гуля́|нье *n* [10] walk(ing); revel(ry), open-air merrymaking, (popular) festival; ~ть [28], ⟨по-⟩ [20] go for a walk (*a.* идти́ ~ть), stroll; *fig.* sweep (*wind, etc.*); make merry.
ГУМ (госуда́рственный универма́г) *m* [1] state department store.
гума́нн|ость *f* [8] humanity, humaneness; ~ый [14; -а́нен, -а́нна] humane.
гумно́ *n* [9; *pl. st., gen.*: -мен & -мён] ✓ floor.
гур|т *m* [1 *e.*] drove (*cattle*); ~то́м F wholesale; ~ьба́ F *f* [5] crowd (in T).
гу́сеница *f* [5] caterpillar (*a.* ⊕).
гуси́ный [14] goose (*a.* flesh ко́жа *f*).
густ|е́ть [8], ⟨за-⟩ thicken; ~о́й [14; густ, -а́, -о] thick, dense; deep, rich (*colo[u]r, sound*); ~ота́ *f* [5] thickness; density; depth.
гус|ь *m* [4; *from g/pl. e.*] goose; *fig.* хоро́ш ~ь F a fine fellow indeed!; как с ₒя вода́ F like water off a duck's back, thick-skinned; ~ько́м in single file.
гу́ща *f* [5] grounds *pl.*; sediment; thicket; *fig.* center (*Brt.* -tre), middle.
ГЭС *abbr.*: гидро(электро)ста́нция.

Д

д. *abbr.*: **1.** дере́вня; **2.** дом.
да 1. *part.* yes; oh (yes), indeed (*a. interr.*); (oh) but, now, well; *imp.* do(n't) ...!; *tags:* aren't, don't, *etc.*; may, let; **2.** *cj.* (*a.* ~ и) and; but; ~ и то́лько continually; ~ что́ вы! you don't say!
дабы́ † (in order) that *or* to.
да|ва́ть [5], ⟨~ть⟩ [дам, дашь, даст, дади́м, дади́те, даду́т ('...-) дал, -а́, -о; ('...)да́нный (дан, -а́)] give; let; bestow; take (*oath*), pledge; make (*way*); ~ва́й(те)! come on!; *with vb.* (*a.* ₒй[те]) let us (me); ни ₒть ни взять exactly like; ~ва́ть ход де́лу set s. th. going *or* further it; -ся let o. s. (*be caught. cheated* в B); (turn out to) be (*e.g. hard*, for Д); (can) master (s. th. И); *pt.* F take to.
дави́ть [14] **1.** ⟨на-⟩ press; squeeze (⟨вы́-⟩ out); **2.** ⟨за-, раз-⟩ crush; run over, knock down; **3.** ⟨по-⟩ oppress; suppress; **4.** ⟨при-, с-⟩ press (down *or* together), jam, compress; throng, crowd; **5.** ⟨у-⟩ strangle; -ся choke; F hang o. s.
да́в|ка F *f* [5] throng, jam; ~ле́ние *n* [12] pressure (*a. fig.*).
да́вн|(и́шн)ий [15] old; ~о́ long ago; for a long time, long since; ~опроше́дший [17] long past; ~опроше́дшее вре́мя *n gr.* past *or* pluperfect; ~ость *f* [8] remoteness; ⚖ limitation; ~ы́м-~о́ F (a) very long (time) ago.
да́же (*a.* ~ и) even; ~ не not even.
да́л|ее *s.* да́льше; и так ~ее and so on (*or* forth); ~ёкий [16; -лёк, -лека́, -леко́ & -лёко; *comp.*: да́лее, да́льше], far, distant (from от P); long (*way*); *fig.* wide (of); strange (to); F smart, clever; ~еко́, ~ёко far (off, away); a long way (to до P); (Д) ~еко́ до (P) F can't match with; ~еко́ не F by no means; ~еко́ за (B) long after; (*age*) well over; ~ь *f* [8; в -ли́] distance; open (space); ~ьне́йший [17] further;

в **~ьнéйшем** later *or* further on; **~ьний** [15] distant (*a. relative*); remote; *s. a.* ~ёкий; **~ьневосточный** [14] Far Eastern.
дально|бóйный ⚔ [14] long range; **~вúдный** [14; -ден, -дна] clear-sighted; **~зóркий** [16; -рок, -рка] far-, long-sighted; **'~сть** *f* [8] remoteness; ⚔, ⊕ (long) range.
дáльше farther; further(more); then, next; (читáйте) ~! go on (reading); не ~ как *or* чем this very; only.
дáм|а *f* [5] lady; partner (*dance*); queen (*card*); **~ский** [16] ladies', women's; **~ба** *f* [5] dam, dike; **~ка** *f* [5; *g/pl.:* -мок] king (*draughts*).
Дани|úл [1], P **∠ла** *m* [5] Daniel.
Дáния *f* [7] Denmark.
дáн|ный [14] given, present, this; **~ная** *f* Ꭿ quantity; **~ные** *pl.* data, facts; statistics.
дантúст *m* [1] dentist.
дань *f* [8] tribute (*a. fig.*).
дар *m* [1; *pl. e.*] gift (*a. fig.*); **~úть** [13], ⟨по-⟩ give (a p. s.th. Д/В), present (a p. with В/Т); **~моéд** F *m* [1] sponger; **~овáние** *n* [12] gift, talent; **~овúтый** [14 *sh.*] gifted, talented; **~овóй** [14] gratis, free.
дáром *adv.* gratis, for nothing; in vain; ~ что (al)though; э́то емý ~ не пройдёт F he will smart for it.
Дáрья *f* [6] Darya (*first name*).
дáт|а *f* [5] date; **~ельный** [14] *gr.* dative (*case*); **~úровать** [7] (*im*)*pf.* (зáдним числóм ante)date.
дáт|ский [16] Danish; **~чáнин** *m* [1; *pl.:* -чáне, -чáн], **~чáнка** *f* [5; *g/pl.:* -нок] Dane.
дать(ся) *s.* давáть(ся).
дáч|а *f* [5] giving; cottage, summer residence, villa; на ~е out of town, in the country; **~ник** *m* [1] summer resident; **~ный** [14] suburban; country...; garden (city посёлок).
Даш([ень]к)а *f* [5] *dim. of* Дáрья.
два *m, n,* две *f* [34] two; *cf.* пять & пя́тый; в ~ счёта F in a jiffy.
двадцат|илéтний [15] twenty-years-old, of 20; **∠ый** [14] twentieth; *cf.* пя́т(идеся́т)ый; **'~ь** [35; -тú] twenty; *cf.* пять.
двáжды twice; ~ два Ꭿ two by two; как ~ два (четы́ре) as sure(ly) as two & two makes four.
двенáдцат|и... (*in compds.*) twelve-...; dodec(a)...; duodecimal, -denary; **~ый** [14] twelfth; *cf.* пя́тый; **~ь** [35] twelve; *cf.* пять.
двер|нóй [14] door...; **∠ца** *f* [5; *g/pl.:* -рец] *dim. of* **~ь** *f* [8; в -рú; *from g/pl. e.*; *instr. a.* -рьмú] door (*a. pl.* ∠и).
двéсти [36] two hundred.
дви|гатель *m* [4] engine, motor; **~гать** [1 & 3], ⟨~нуть⟩ [20] (В & Т) move, push, drive (on); stir; **-ся** move, advance; set out, start; **~жéние** *n* [12] movement (*a. pol.*); stir; *phys.* motion; traffic; *fig.* emotion; *pl.* (light) gymnastics; приводúть (приходúть) в ~жéние set going (start [moving]); **~жимый** [14 *sh.*] movable; **~нуть** *s.* ~гать.
двóе [37] two (*in a group, together*); нас бы́ло ~ we (there) were two (of us); **~брáчие** *n* [12], **~жёнство** *n* [9] bigamy; **~тóчие** *n* [12] colon.
двоúться [13], ⟨раз-⟩ bifurcate.
двóй|ка *f* [5; *g/pl.:* двóек] two (*a. boat*; *team*; P *bus, etc., no. 2*; *cards, a.* deuce); pair; F (*mark*) = плóхо, *cf.*; **~нúк** *m* [1 *e.*] double(ganger); **~нóй** [14] double (*a. fig.*); **~ня** *f* [6; *g/pl.:* двóен] twins *pl.*; **~ственный** [14 *sh.*] double, twofold, -faced; dual (*a. gr.* number числó).
двор *m* [1 *e.*] (court)yard; farm(-stead); court; на ~é outside, outdoors; **~éц** *m* [1; -рцá] palace; **∠ник** *m* [1] janitor, (yard &) street cleaner; F *mot.* windshield (*Brt.* windscreen) wiper; **∠ня** *f* [6] *coll.*, † servants, domestics *pl.*; **~я́га** F *f* [5], **~я́жка** F *f* [5; *g/pl.:* -жек] mongrel; watchdog; **~óвый** [14] yard-..., house...; servant...; **~цóвый** [14] court...; palace...; **~янúн** *m* [1; *pl.:* -я́не, -я́н] nobleman; **~я́нка** *f* [5; *g/pl.:* -нок] noblewoman; **~я́нский** [16] noble; **~я́нство** *n* [9] nobility.
двоюроди|ый [14]: ~ый брат *m*, ~ая сестрá *f* cousin.
двоя́к|ий [16 *sh.*] double, twofold; **~о** in two ways.
дву|бóртный [14] double-breasted; **~глáвый** [14] double-headed; **~глáсный** [14] diphthong(al); **~жúльный** P [14] sturdy, tough; **~кóлка** *f* [5; *g/pl.:* -лок] cart; **~крáтный** [14] double; done twice; **~лúчие** *n* [12] duplicity; **~лúчный** [14; -чен, -чна] double-faced; **~ру́шник** *m* [1] double-dealer; **~ру́шничество** *n* [9] double-dealing; **~смы́сленный** [14 *sh.*] ambiguous; **~ствóлка** *f* [5; *g/pl.:* -лок] double-barrel(l)ed gun; **~ствóльный** [14]: ~ствóльное ружьё *n* = ~ствóлка; **~ствóрчатый** [14]: ~ствóрчатая дверь *f* folding doors; **~сторóнний** [15] bilateral; two-way (*traffic*); reversible (*fabric*).
двух... (*cf. a.* дву...): **~днéвный** [14] two days'; **~колéйный** 🚂 [14] double-track; **~колёсный** [14] two-wheel(ed); **~лéтний** [15] two-years-old; two years'; **~мéстный** [14] two-seat(ed); **~мéсячный** [14] two months' *or* two-months-old; **~мотóрный** [14] twin-engine(d); **~недéльный** [14] two weeks', *Brt. a.* a fortnight's; **~сóтый** [14] two hundredth; **~этáжный** [14] two-storied (*Brt.* -reyed).

двуязы́чный [14; -чен, -чна] bilingual.
дебат|и́ровать [7] debate; **~ы** *m/pl.* [1] debate.
дебе́лый F [14 *sh.*] plump, fat.
де́бет † *m* [1] debit; занести́ в ~ = **~ова́ть** [7] (*im*)*pf.* debit (*sum against or* to a p. В/Д).
дебито́р *m* [1] debtor.
дебо́ш *m* [1] riot, row.
де́бри *f/pl.* [8] thicket; wilderness.
дебю́т *m* [1] debut; opening.
де́ва *f* [5]: (ста́рая) ~ (old) maid.
девальва́ция *f* [7] devaluation.
дева́ть [1], ⟨деть⟩ [де́ну, -нешь] put; place; leave, mislay; куда́ ~ *a.* what to do with, how to spend; **-ся** go, get; *vb.* + И = put, leave + *obj.*; be (*pr.*); куда́ мне ~ся? where shall I go *or* stay? куда́ он де́лся? what has become of him?
де́верь *m* [4; *pl.*: -рья́, -ре́й, -рья́м] (*wife's*) brother-in-law.
деви́з *m* [1] motto.
дев|и́ца *f* [5] maid, girl; **~и́чий** [18] maiden, girl's; ~ичий монасты́рь *m* nunnery; **~ка** *f* [5; *g/pl.*: -вок] wench; P maid; P whore; **~очка** *f* [5; *g/pl.*: -чек] (little) girl; **~ственный** [14 *sh.*] maiden; virgin...; primeval; **~ушка** *f* [5; *g/pl.*: -шек] (grown-up) girl; † parlo(u)rmaid; **~чо́нка** F *f* [5; *g/pl.*: -нок] slut; girl.
девя|но́сто [35] ninety; **~но́стый** [14] ninetieth; *cf.* пя́т(идеся́т)ый; **~тисо́тый** [14] ninehundredth; **~тка** *f* [5; *g/pl.*: -ток] nine (*cf.* дво́йка); **~тна́дцатый** [14] nineteenth; *cf.* пять & пя́тый; **~тна́дцать** [35] nineteen; *cf.* пять; **~тый** [14] ninth; *cf.* пя́тый; **'~ть** [35] nine; *cf.* пять; **~тьсо́т** [36] nine hundred; **'~тью** nine times.
дегенера́т *m* [1] degenerate.
дёготь *m* [4; -гтя] tar.
де́д|(ушка *m* [5; *g/pl.*: -шек]) *m* [1] grandfather; old man; *pl.* ~ы *a.* forefathers; ♀ Моро́з *m* Jack Frost; Santa Claus, Father Christmas.
деепричá́стие *n* [12] *gr.* gerund.
дежу́р|ить [13] be on duty; sit up, watch; **~ный** [14] (p.) on duty; **~ство** *n* [9] duty; (night) watch.
дезерти́р *m* [1] deserter; **~овать** [7] (*im*)*pf.* desert; **~ство** *n* [9] desertion.
дезинф|е́кция *f* [7] disinfection; **~ици́ровать** [7] (*im*)*pf.* disinfect.
дезорганиз|ова́ть [7] (*im*)*pf.*, *impf.* *a.* **~о́вывать** [1] disorganize.
де́йств|енный [14 *sh.*] efficient; **~ие** *n* [12] action; activity; ⚔, ⊕, ⅍ operation; *thea.* act; effect; efficacy; influence, impact; ме́сто ~ия scene; свобо́да ~ий free play; **~и́тельно** really; indeed; **~и́тельность** *f* [8] reality; validity; **~и́тельный** [14; -лен, -льна] real, actual; valid; ⚔, *gr.* active (*service*; *voice*); **~овать** [7], ⟨по-⟩ act, work (*a.* upon на В); operate, function; apply; have effect (on на В); get (*on one's nerves*); **~ующий** [17] active; acting; ⚔ field...; ~ующее лицо́ *n* character, personage.
дека́брь *m* [4 *e.*] December.
дека́н *m* [1] dean.
декла|ми́ровать [7], ⟨про-⟩ declaim; **~ра́ция** *f* [7] declaration.
декольт|е́ (dɛ-; -'tɛ) *n* [*indecl.*] décolleté; **~иро́ванный** [14 *sh.*] low-necked.
декора́|тор *m* [1] decorator; **~ция** *f* [7] decoration; *thea.* scenery.
декре́т *m* [1] decree, edict; **~и́ровать** [7] (*im*)*pf.* decree.
де́ла|нный [14 *sh.*] affected, forced; **~ть** [1], ⟨с-⟩ make, do; ~ть не́чего F it can't be helped; **-ся** (Т) become, grow, turn; happen (with, to с Т), be going on; что с ним сде́лалось? what has become of him?
делега́|т *m* [1] delegate; **~ция** *f* [7] delegation.
дел|ёж F *m* [1 *e.*] distribution, sharing; **~е́ние** *n* [12] division (*a.* ⅍); partition; point (*scale*).
деле́ц *m* [1; -льца́] (sharp) businessman, moneymaker.
делика́тн|ость *f* [8] tact(fulness), delicacy; **~ый** [14; -тен, -тна] delicate.
дели́|мое *n* [14] ⅍ dividend; **~тель** *m* [4] ⅍ divisor; **~ть** [13; делю́, де́лишь] **1.** ⟨раз-, по-⟩ (на В) divide (in[to]), *a.* ⅍ (by); **2.** ⟨по-⟩ share (*a.* **-ся** [Т/с Т s.th. with s.b.], exchange; confide [s.th. to], tell; ⅍ be divisible).
дели́шки F *n/pl.* [9; *gen*: -шек] [business.]
де́л|о *n* [9; *pl. e.*] affair, matter, concern; work, business (on по Д), line; art *or* science; deed, act(ion); ⚖ case, (*a. fig.*) cause; file; ⚔ action, battle; говори́ть ~о F talk sense; де́лать ~о *fig.* do serious work; то и ~о continually, incessantly; в чём ~о? what's the matter?; в том то и ~о F that's just the point; что вам за ~о? *or* э́то не ва́ше ~о that's no business of yours; на ~е in practice; на (*or* в) са́мом ~е in reality, in fact; really, indeed; по ~а́м on business; как ~а́? F how are you?; ~о идёт *cf.* идти́.
делов|и́тый [14 *sh.*], **~о́й** [14] businesslike; expert; ~о́й *a.* business...; work(ing).
делопроизводи́тель *m* [4] secre-[tary.]
де́льный [14] competent; sensible.
демаго́г *m* [1] demagogue; **~и́ческий** [16] demagogic(al).
демаркацио́нный [14] (of) demarcation.
демилитаризова́ть [7] (*im*)*pf.* demilitarize.
демобилизова́ть [7] (*im*)*pf.* demobilize.

демокра́т *m* [1] democrat; **~и́ческий** [16] democratic; **~ия** [7] democracy.
демонстр|а́ция *f* [7] demonstration; **~и́ровать** [7] (*im*)*pf*., *a.* ⟨про-⟩ demonstrate; show, project (*film*).
демонта́ж *m* [1] dismantling.
де́нежный [14] money..., monetary, pecuniary; currency...; F rich.
день *m* [4; дня] day; в ~ a *or* per day; в э́тот ~ (on) that day; ∠ за́ ~ day after day; изо дня́ в ∠ day by day; ∠ ото дня́ from day to day; весь ~ all day (long); на (э́тих) днях the other day; one of these days; три часа́ дня 3 p.m., 3 o'clock in the afternoon; *cf.* днём.
де́ньги *f*/*pl.* [*gen*.: де́нег; *from. dat. e.*] money.
департа́мент *m* [1] department.
депе́ша *f* [5] dispatch, wire(less).
депози́т ☨ *m* [1] deposit.
депута́т *m* [1] deputy, delegate; member of the Supreme Soviet.
дёр|гать [1], *once* ⟨~нуть⟩ [20] pull, tug (*a.* за В at), jerk, twist; F press a p. hard, importune.
дерев|ене́ть [8], ⟨за-, о-⟩ stiffen; grow numb; **~е́нский** [16] village-..., country..., rural, rustic; ~е́нский жи́тель *m* villager; ∠**ня** *f* [6; *g*/*pl.*: -ве́нь, *etc. e.*] village; country(side); '~**о** *n* [9; *pl.*: -е́вья, -е́вьев] tree; *sg.* wood; кра́сное '~о mahogany; чёрное '~о ebony; резьба́ по ~у wood engraving; **~я́нный** [14] wooden (*a. fig.*).
держа́ва *f* [5] power; *hist.* orb.
держа́ть [4] hold; keep; support; have (*a.* ☨ in stock; *a. exam.*); read (*proofs*); ~ сто́рону side with; ~ себя́ (кого́-либо) в рука́х (have) control (over) o.s. (a p.); ~ себя́ conduct o.s., behave = **-ся** 1.; 2. ⟨у~ся⟩ (за В; Р) hold (on[to]); *fig.* stick (to); keep; hold out, stand.
дерз|а́ть [1], ⟨~ну́ть⟩ [20] dare, venture; ∠**кий** [16; -зок, -зка́, -о; *comp.*: -зче] impudent, insolent; bold, daring, audacious; (*a.* = † **~нове́нный** [14; -е́нен, -е́нна] & ∠**остный** [14; -тен, -тна]); ∠**ость** *f* [8] impudence, cheek.
дёрн *m* [1] turf; **~уть** *s.* дёргать.
дес|а́нт *m* [1] landing; troops *pl.* landed (авиа... airborne...); **~е́рт** *m* [1] dessert; **~на́** *f* [5; *pl.*: дёсны, -сен, *etc. st.*] gum; ∠**пот** *m* [1] despot.
десяти|дне́вный [14] ten days'; **~кра́тный** [14] tenfold; **~ле́тие** *n* [12] decade; tenth anniversary; **~ле́тка** *f* [5; *g*/*pl.*: -ток] ten-grades (*or* -forms) standard school (*leading to maturity*) (*U.S.S.R.*); **~ле́тний** [15] ten years'; ten-years-old.
десят|и́на *f* [5] †, = *approx.* $2^3/_4$ *acres*; tithe; **~и́чный** [14] decimal; ∠**ка** *f* [5; *g*/*pl.*: -ток] ten (*cf.* дво́йка); ∠**ник** *m* [1] foreman; ∠**ок** *m* [1; -тка] ten; *pl.* dozens of, many; *s.* идти́; не ро́бкого ∠ка F not a craven; ∠**ый** [14] tenth (*a., f*, part; 3,2 — *read:* три це́лых и две ∠ых = 3.2); *cf.* пя́т(идеся́т)ый; из пя́того в ∠ое discursively, in a ramblingmanner; '~**ь** [35 *e.*] ten; *cf.* пять & пя́тый; '~**ью** ten times.
дета́ль *f* [8] detail; ⊕ part; **~но** in detail; **~ный** [14; -лен, -льна] detailed, minute.
дет|вора́ *f* [5] *coll.* F = ∠и; **~ёныш** *m* [1] young one; cub, *etc.*; ∠**и** *n*/*pl.* [-е́й, -ям, -ьми́, -ях] children, kids; дво́е, (тро́е, че́тверо, *etc.*) ~е́й two (three, four) children; *sg.*: дитя́ (*a.* ребёнок), *cf.*; ∠**ский** [16] child(ren)'s, infant(ile); childlike; childish; ∠ский дом *m* (orphan) boarding school; ∠ский сад *m* kindergarten; ∠ская *f* nursery (room); ∠**ство** *n* [9] childhood.
де́ть(ся) *s.* дева́ть(ся).
дефе́ктный [14] defective.
дефици́тный [14; -тен, -тна] unprofitable; scarce.
деш|еве́ть [8], ⟨по-⟩ cheapen, become cheaper; **~еви́зна**, F **~ёвка** *f* [5] cheapness, low price(s); **~ёвый** [14; дёшев, дешева́, дёшево; *comp.*: деше́вле] cheap (*a. fig.*); low (*price*).
де́ятель *m* [4] man; representative; госуда́рственный ~ statesman; нау́чный ~ scientist; обще́ственный ~ public man; полити́ческий ~ politician; **~ность** *f* [8] activity, -ties *pl.*; work; **~ный** [14; -лен, -льна] active.
джу́нгли *f*/*pl.* [*gen.*: -лей] jungle.
диа́|гноз *m* [1] diagnosis; **~гона́ль** *f* [8] diagonal; **~ле́кт** *m* [1] dialect; **~ле́ктный** [14] dialectic(al); **~ле́ктика** *f* [5] dialectic(s); **~лекти́ческий** [16] dialectic(al); **~ло́г** *m* [1] dialogue; **~ма́т** *m* [1] dialectical materialism; **~метр** *m* [1] diameter; **~пазо́н** *m* [1] ♪ diapason (*a. fig.*); ⊕ range; **~позити́в** *m* [1] (lantern) slide; **~фра́гма** *f* [5] diaphragm.
дива́н *m* [1] divan, sofa.
диверс|а́нт *m* [1] saboteur; ∠**ия** *f* [7] sabotage; ⚔ diversion.
диви́зия ⚔ *f* [7] division.
див|и́ться [14 *e.*], ⟨по-⟩ wonder (at Д *or* на В); ∠**ный** [14; -вен, -вна] wonderful; delightful; ∠**о** *n* [9] wonder, miracle, marvel (*a.* it is a ...); на ∠о excellently; что за ∠о! (most) wonderful!; no wonder.
дие́т|а (-'ɛta) *f* [5] diet; **~и́ческий** [16] dietetic(al).
дизентери́я *f* [7] dysentery.
дик|а́рь *m* [4 *e.*] savage (*a. fig.*); F shy person; ∠**ий** [16; дик, -а́, -о] wild, savage (*a. fig.*); odd, bizarre; shy, unsociable; drab; ⚘ proud

(*flesh*); dog (*rose*); ∠ость *f* [8] wildness, savagery, -geness; absurdity.
дикт|áнт *m* [1] *s.* ~óвка; **~áтор** *m* [1] dictator; **~áторский** [16] dictatorial; **~атýра** *f* [5] dictatorship; **~овáть** [7], ⟨про-⟩ dictate; **~óвка** *f* [5; *g/pl.:* -вок] dictation; **∠ор** *m* [1] (radio) announcer.
дилетáнт *m* [1] dilettante; **~ский** [16] dilettant(e)ish.
динáм|ика *f* [5] dynamics; **~и́т** *m* [1] dynamite; **~и́ческий** [16] dynamic; **~о(-машúна** *f* [5]) *n* [*indecl.*] dynamo.
динáстия *f* [7] dynasty.
диплóм *m* [1] diploma; F thesis to degree.
дипломáт *m* [1] diplomat; **~и́ческий** [16] diplomatic; **~ия** *f* [7] diplomacy.
дирек|ти́ва *f* [5] directive; **∠тор** *m* [1; *pl.:* -pá, *etc. e.*] manager, director; (*school*) principal, *Brt.* headmaster; **∠ция** *f* [7] management, directorate.
дириж|áбль *m* [4] airship; **~ёр** *m* [1] ♪ conductor; **~и́ровать** [7] (T) ♪ conduct.
дисгармóния *f* [7] discord.
диск *m* [1] disk; **~óнт** *m* [1], **~онти́ровать** [7] (*im*)*pf.* discount; **~ýссия** *f* [7] discussion.
дисп|ансéр (-'sɛr) *m* [1] dispensary; **~éтчер** *m* [1] dispatcher; 🚂 traffic superintendent; **∠ут** *m* [1] dispute, disputation.
дис|сертáция *f* [7] dissertation, thesis; **~сонáнс** *m* [1] dissonance, discord; **~тáнция** *f* [7] distance; 🚂 section; **~тилли́ровать** [7; -óванный] (*im*)*pf.* distil(l); **~циплúна** *f* [5] discipline.
дитя́ *n* [-я́ти ✎; *pl.* дéти, *cf.*] child.
диф|ирáмб *m* [1] dithyramb; **~тери́т** *m* [1], **~тери́я** *f* [7] diphtheria; **~фамáция** *f* [7] defamation.
дифференц|иáл *m* [1], **~иáльный** [14] ♂, ⊕ differential; **~и́ровать** [7] (*im*)*pf.* differentiate.
дич|áть [1], ⟨о-⟩ run wild; *fig.* grow (**~и́ться** F [16 *e.*; -чýсь, чи́шься] be) shy, unsociable; shun (a p. P); **~ь** *f* [8] game, wild fowl; F wilderness; F nonsense, bosh.
длин|á *f* [5] length; в ~ý (at) full length, lengthwise; ~óй в (В) ... *or* в ~ý ... long; **~но...** (*in compds.*) long...; **∠ный** [14; -и́нен, -иннá, -и́нно] long; too long; F tall.
длит|ельный [14; -лен, -льна] long; protracted, lengthy; **~ься** [13], ⟨про-⟩ last.
для (Р) for, to; because of; ~ тогó, чтóбы (in order) to, that ... may; ~ чегó? wherefore?; я́щик ~ пи́сем mail (*Brt.* letter) box.
Дми́трий *m* [3] Demetrius (*name*).
днев|áльный [14] ⚔ orderly; p. on duty; **~áть** [6] spend the day; have a day of rest; **~ни́к** *m* [1 *e.*] journal, diary (*vb.:* вести́ keep); **~нóй** [14] day('s), daily; day(light свет *m*).
днём by day, during the day.
Днепр *m* [1 *e.*] Dnieper; **2óвский** [16] Dnieper...
дн|о *n* [9; *pl.:* дóнья, -ньев] bottom; золотóе ~о *fig.* gold mine; вы́пить до ~а drain, empty; идти́ ко ~у *v/i.* (пусти́ть на ~о *v/t.*) sink.
до (Р) *place:* to, as far as, up (*or* down) to; *time:* till, until, to; before; *degree:* to, up (*or* even) to; *age:* under; *quantity:* up to; about; ~ тогó so (much); (Д) не ~ F not be interested in *or* disposed for, *or* have no time, *etc.*, for, to.
добáв|ить *s.* **~ля́ть**; **~лéние** *n* [12] addition; supplement; **~ля́ть** [28], ⟨**~ить**⟩ [14] add; **~очный** [14] additional, extra; supplementary.
добе|гáть [1], ⟨**~жáть**⟩ [-егý, -ежи́шь, -егýт] run up to (до Р).
доб|ивáть [1], ⟨**~и́ть**⟩ [-бью́, -бьёшь; -бéй(те)!; -би́тый] beat completely *or* utterly, smash; kill, finish; **-ся** (Р) (try to) get, obtain *or* reach; strive for; find out (about); он ~и́лся своегó he gained his end(s); **~ирáться** [1], ⟨**~рáться**⟩ [-берýсь, -рёшься] get to, reach.
дóблест|ный [14; -тен, -тна] valiant, brave; **~ь** *f* [8] valo(u)r.
добрó[1] *n* [9] good; F property; **~м** F kindly, amicably; **~**[2] F well; ~ бы if only; ~ пожáловать! welcome!; please; **~вóлец** *m* [1; -льца] volunteer; **~вóльный** [14; -лен, -льна] voluntary; **~дéтель** *f* [8] virtue; **~дéтельный** [14; -лен, -льна] virtuous; **~дýшие** *n* [12] good nature; **~дýшный** [14; -шен, -шна] good-natured; **~желáтельный** [14; -лен, -льна] benevolent; **~желáтельство** *n* [9] benevolence; **~кáчественный** [14 *sh.*] (of) good (quality); ⚕ benign; **~сердéчный** [14; -чен, -чна] good-hearted; **~сóвестный** [14; -тен, -тна] conscientious; **~сосéдский** [16] good neighbo(u)rly; **~м** *s.* ~[1].
добр|отá *f* [5] kindness; **~óтный** [14; -тен, -тна] (very) good, solid; **∠ый** [14; добр, -á, -о, дóбры́] kind; good; F solid; ∠ое ýтро *n* (∠ый день *m*, вéчер *m*)! good morning (afternoon, evening)!; в ∠ый час!, всегó ∠ого! good luck!; чегó ∠ого after all; бýдь(те) ~(ы́) will you be so kind.
добы|вáть [1], ⟨**∠ть**⟩ [-бýду, -дешь; дóбы́л, -á, дóбы́ло; дóбы́тый (дóбы́т, добы́та, дóбы́то)] get, obtain, procure; ⚒ extract, mine; *hunt.* bag; **∠ча** *f* [5] procurement; ⚒ extraction, mining; booty, spoil; (*animals'*) prey (*a. fig.*); *hunt.* bag.
довезти́ *s.* довози́ть.

довéр|енность *f* [8] (на В) ⚖ letter of attorney; † = ~ие; **~енный** [14] deputed; proxy, agent; **~ие** *n* [12] confidence, trust (in к Д); **~ить** *s.* ~ять; **~чивый** [14 *sh.*] trusting, trustful; confidential; **~шáть** [1], ⟨~ши́ть⟩ [16 *e.*; -шу́, -ши́шь] finish; complete; **~шéние** *n* [12] completion; в ~шéние *or* к ~шéнию (Р) to complete *or* crown (s.th.); **~я́ть** [28], ⟨~ить⟩ [13] trust (a p. Д); confide *or* entrust (s.th. to В/Д); entrust (a p. with Д/В); **-ся** (Д) *a.* trust, rely (on).

дов|ести́ *s.* ~оди́ть; **~́од** *m* [1] argument; **~оди́ть** [15], ⟨~ести́⟩ [25] (до Р) see (a p. to); lead ([up] to); bring (to); drive (to), make.

довоéнный [14] prewar.

дов|ози́ть [15], ⟨~езти́⟩ [24] (до Р) take *or* bring ([right up] to).

довóль|но enough, sufficient; rather, pretty, fairly; **~ный** [14; -лен, -льна] content(ed), satisfied (with Т); **~ствие** ⚔ *n* [12] ration, allowance; **~ство** *n* [9] contentment, satisfaction; F prosperity; **~ствоваться** [7] content o.s. (with Т).

довы́боры *m/pl.* [1] by-election.

догад|áться *s.* ~́ываться; **~́ка** *f* [5; *g/pl.*: -док] guess, conjecture; **~́ливый** [14 *sh.*] quick-witted; **~́ываться**, ⟨~áться⟩ [1] (о П) guess, surmise.

дóгма *f* [5], **~т** *m* [1] dogma.

догнáть *s.* догоня́ть.

догов|áривать [1], ⟨~ори́ть⟩ [13] finish (speaking), speak; **-ся** (о П) agree (upon), arrange; ~áривающиеся стóроны *f/pl.* contracting parties; **~óр** *m* [1] contract; *pol.* treaty; **~ори́ть(ся)** *s.* ~áривать(ся); **~óрный** [14] contract(ual).

дог|оня́ть [28], ⟨~нáть⟩ [-гоню́, -гóнишь, *cf.* гнать] catch up (with), overtake; drive *or* bring to; *impf.* *a.* pursue, try to catch up, be (on the point of) overtaking; **~орáть** [1], ⟨~орéть⟩ [9] burn down; *fig.* fade, die out.

дод|éлывать, ⟨~éлать⟩ [1] finish, complete; **~у́мываться**, ⟨~у́маться⟩ [1] (до Р) find, reach *or* hit upon (s. th., by thinking).

доезжá|ть [1], ⟨доéхать⟩ [-éду, -éдешь] (до Р) reach; не ~я short of.

дожд|áться *s.* дожидáться; **~еви́к** F *m* [1 *e.*] raincoat; **~евóй** [14] rain(y); ~евóй зóнтик *m* umbrella; ~евóй червь *m* earthworm; **~ли́вый** [14 *sh.*] rainy; **~ь** *m* [4 *e.*] rain (in под Т, на П); ~ь идёт it is raining.

дож|ивáть [1], ⟨~и́ть⟩ [-живу́, -вёшь; дóжил, -á, -о; дóжитый (дóжит, -á, -о)] *impf.* live one's last years, *etc.*; (до Р) *pf.* live (till *or* up to); (live to) see; come to; **~идáться** [1], ⟨~дáться⟩ [-ду́сь, -дёшься; *cf.* ждать] (Р) wait (for, till); *pf.* *a.* see.

дóза *f* [5] dose.

дозво|ля́ть [28], ⟨~́лить⟩ [13] permit, allow; ~́ленный *a.* licit; **~ни́ться** F [13] *pf.* reach (a p. by phone до Р), ring till the door *or* phone is answered.

дознáние ⚖ *n* [12] inquest.

дозóр ⚔ *m* [1], **~ный** ⚔ [14] patrol.

доиск|иваться F [1], ⟨~áться⟩ [3] (Р) (try to) find (out).

дои́ть(ся) [13], ⟨по-⟩ (give) milk.

дойти́ *s.* доходи́ть.

док *m* [1] ⚓ dock.

доказ|áтельство *n* [9] proof, evidence; **~́ывать** [1], ⟨~áть⟩ [3] prove; argue.

док|áнчивать [1], ⟨~óнчить⟩ [16] finish, end.

доклáд *m* [1] report; lecture (on о П); **~нáя** [14] (*a.* запи́ска *f*) memorandum, report; **~чик** *m* [1] lecturer; reporter; **~ывать** [1], ⟨доложи́ть⟩ [16] report (s.th. В *or* on о П); announce (a p. о П).

докóнчить *s.* докáнчивать.

дóктор *m* [1; *pl.* -рá, *etc. e.*] doctor.

доктри́на *f* [5] doctrine.

докумéнт *m* [1] document.

докучáть F [1] = надоедáть.

долби́ть [14 *e.*; -блю́, -би́шь; -блённый] **1.** ⟨вы́-, про-⟩ hollow (out); peck (*bird*); chisel; *impf.* F strike; **2.** P ⟨в-⟩ inculcate; cram.

долг *m* [1; *pl. e.*] debt; *sg.* duty; (last) hono(u)rs *pl.*; в ~ = взаймы́; в ~у́ indebted (*a. fig.*, to у Р, пéред Т); **~́ий** [16; дóлог, долгá, -о] long; **~́о** long, (for) a long time *or* while.

долго|вéчный [14; -чен, -чна] perennial (*a.* ♀), durable; **~вóй** [14]: ~вóе обязáтельство *n* promissory note; **~врéменный** [14] (very) long; **~вя́зый** F [14 *sh.*] lanky; **~игрáющий** [17]: ~игрáющая пласти́нка *f* long-playing record; **~лéтие** *n* [12] longevity; **~лéтний** [15] longstanding; of several years; **~срóчный** [14] long-term; **~тá** *f* [5; *pl.*: -гóты, *etc. st.*] length; *geogr.* longitude; **~терпели́вый** [14 *sh.*] long-suffering.

дóл|ее = ~ьше, *cf.*; **~етáть** [1], ⟨~етéть⟩ [11] (до Р) fly ([up] to), reach; *a.* = доноси́ться.

дóлж|ен *m*, ~нá *f*, ~нó *n* (*cf.* ~нó[2]), ~ны́ *pl.* **1.** must [*pt.*: ~ен был, ~нá былá, *etc.* had to]; **2.** (Д) owe (a p.); **~ни́к** *m* [1 *e.*] debtor; **~но[1]** one (it) must *or* ought to (be ...); proper(ly); **~нó[2]** P = ~нó быть probably, apparently; **~ностнóй** [14] official; **~ность** *f* [8] post; office; **~ный** [14] due (*a. su.* ~ное *n*), proper; ~ным óбразом duly.

доли|вáть [1], ⟨~́ть⟩ [-лью́, -льёшь; *cf.* лить] fill (up), add.

доли́на *f* [5] valley.

до́ллар *m* [1] dollar.
доложи́ть *s.* докла́дывать.
доло́й F off, down; ~ ... (В)! down *or* off with ...!; с глаз ~! out of my sight!
долото́ *n* [9; *pl. st.*: -ло́та] chisel.
до́льше (*comp. of* до́лгий) longer.
до́ля *f* [6; *from g/pl. e.*] lot, fate; grain (*of truth*), spark (*of wit, etc.*); в восьму́ю (четвёртую) до́лю листа́ octavo (quarto), in 8vo (4to).
дом *m* [1; *pl.*: -а́, *etc. e.*] house; home; family; household; вы́йти и́з ~у leave (one's home), go out; на́ ~ = ~о́й; на ~у́ = ﬞ~а at home; как ﬞ~а at one's ease; (у Р) не все ﬞ~а (be) a bit off (one's head), nutty; **~а́шний** [15] home..., house(hold)-...; private; domestic; *pl. su.* folks; ~а́шний стол *m* plain fare; **ﬞ~енный** [14]: ﬞ~енная печь *f* = ﬞ~на; **ﬞ~ик** *m* [1] *dim. of* дом.
домин|ио́н *m* [1] (*Brt.*) dominion; **~и́ровать** [7] (pre)dominate; **~о́** *n* [*indecl.*] domino(es).
домкра́т *m* [1] (lifting) jack.
до́мна *f* [5; *g/pl.*: -мен] blast furnace.
дом|ови́тый [14 *sh.*] thrifty, careful; notable (*housewife*); **~овладе́лец** *m* [1; -льца] house owner; **~о́вый** [14] house...
домога́ться [1] (Р) strive for, solicit.
домо́|й home; **~ро́щенный** [14] homebred; **~се́д** *m* [1] stay-at-home; **~управле́ние** *n* [12] house management; **~ча́дцы** *m/pl.* [1] folks; inmate.
домрабо́тница *f* [5] housemaid.
до́мысел *m* [1; -сла] conjecture.
Дон *m* [1; на -ну́] Don; **~ба́сс** (= Доне́цкий бассе́йн) ⚒ *m* [1] Donets Basin.
доне|се́ние *n* [12] report; **~сти́(сь)** *s.* доноси́ть(ся); **ﬞ~цкий** [14] *s.* Донба́сс.
до́н|изу to bottom; **~има́ть** F [1], ⟨~я́ть⟩ [дойму́, -мёшь; *cf.* заня́ть] press, exhaust (with Т).
доно́с ⚖ *m* [1] denunciation, information (against на В); **~и́ть** [15], ⟨донести́⟩ [24; -су́, -сёшь] carry *or* bring ([up] to); report (s.th., about, on о П); denounce, inform (against на В); ~и́ть *pf.* wear out; *a.* **-ся** (до Р) waft (to), reach, (re-)sound; **~чик** *m* [1] informer.
донско́й [16] (*adj. of* Дон) Don...
доны́не to this day, till now.
доня́ть *s.* донима́ть.
допи|ва́ть [1], ⟨ﬞ~ть⟩ [-пью́, -пьёшь; *cf.* пить] drink up.
допла́|та *f* [5] additional payment, extra (*or* sur)charge; **~чивать** [1], ⟨~ти́ть⟩ [15] pay in addition.
допо́длинный F [14] true, real.
дополн|е́ние *n* [12] addition; supplement; *gr.* object; **~и́тельный** [14] additional, supplementary; extra; *adv. a.* in addition; more; **~я́ть** [28], ⟨ﬞ~ить⟩ [13] add, supply, complete, fill up; enlarge (*edition*).
допото́пный [14] antediluvian.
допр|а́шивать [1], ⟨~оси́ть⟩ [15] ⚖ interrogate, examine; *impf.* question; **~о́с** *m* [1] ⚖ interrogation, examination; F questioning; **~оси́ть** *s.* ~а́шивать.
до́пу|ск *m* [1] access, admittance; **~ска́ть** [1], ⟨~сти́ть⟩ [15] admit (*a.* of), concede; allow; tolerate; suppose; make (*mistake*); **~сти́мый** [14 *sh.*] admissible, permissible; **~ще́ние** *n* [12] admission.
допы́т|ываться [1], ⟨~а́ться⟩ F (try to) find out.
дореволюцио́нный [14] pre-revolutionary, before the revolution.
доро́г|а *f* [5] road, way (*a. fig.*); passage; trip, journey; больша́я ~а highroad; желе́зная ~а railroad, *Brt.* railway; ~ой *or* в (по) ~е on the way; туда́ ему́ и ~а F that serves him right; *cf. a.* путь.
дорого|ви́зна *f* [5] dearness, high price(s); **ﬞ~й** [16; до́рог, -а́, -о; *comp.*: доро́же] dear (*a. fig.*), expensive.
доро́дный [14; -ден, -дна] stout, burly.
дорож|а́ть [1], ⟨вз-, по-⟩ become dearer, rise in price; **~и́ть** [16 *e.*; -жу́, -жи́шь] (Т) esteem (highly), (set a high) value (on).
доро́ж|ка *f* [5; *g/pl.*: -жек] path; бегова́я ~ка race track (*Brt.* -way); лётная ~ка ✈ runway; **~ный** [14] road...; travel(l)ing.
доса́|да *f* [5] vexation; annoyance, fret; F кака́я ~да! how annoying!, what a pity!; **~ди́ть** *s.* ~жда́ть; **~дливый** [14 *sh.*] fretful, peevish; **~дный** [14; -ден, -дна] annoying, vexatious; deplorable; (мне) ~дно it is annoying (annoys me); **~довать** [7] feel *or* be annoyed, vexed (at, with на В); **~жда́ть** [1], ⟨~ди́ть⟩ [15 *e.*; -ажу́, -ади́шь] vex, annoy (a p. with Д/Т).
доск|а́ *f* [5; *ac/sg.*: до́ску; *pl.*: до́ски, до́со́к, доска́м] board, plank; (*a.* кла́ссная ~а́) blackboard; plate; гри́фельная ~а́ slate; от ~и́ до ~и́ (*read*) from cover to cover; на одну́ ﬞ~у on a level.
доскона́льный [14; -лен, -льна] thorough.
досло́вный [14] literal, verbal.
досм|а́тривать [1], ⟨~отре́ть⟩ [9; -отрю́, -о́тришь] see up to *or* to the end (до Р); watch, look after (за Т); не ~отре́ть overlook; **~о́тр** *m* [1] supervision; (customs) examination; **~отре́ть** *s.* ~а́тривать.
доспе́хи *m/pl.* [1] armo(u)r; outfit.
досро́чный [14] preschedule.
дост|ава́ть [5], ⟨~а́ть⟩ [-ста́ну, -ста́нешь] take (out, *etc.*); get; procure; ([до] Р) touch; reach (to); F (Р) suffice, have enough; **-ся** (Д)

fall to a p.'s share; (turn out to) be, cost (*fig.*); F catch it; **~áвить** *s.* **~авля́ть**; **~áвка** *f* [5; *g/pl.*: -вок] delivery; conveyance; с ~áвкой (нá дом) carriage paid; free to the door; **~авля́ть** [28], ⟨**~áвить**⟩ [14] deliver, hand; bring; *fig.* procure, cause, give; **~áток** *m* [1; -тка] prosperity, (good) fortune; F sufficiency; **~áточно** considerably; (P) (be) enough, sufficient; suffice; **~áточный** [14; -чен, -чна] sufficient.

дости|гáть [1], ⟨**∠гнуть**⟩, ⟨**∠чь**⟩ [21 -г-: -сти́гну, -гнешь] (P) reach, arrive at, attain (*a. fig.*); (*prices*) amount *or* run up (to); **~жéние** *n* [12] attainment; achievement; **~жи́мый** [14 *sh.*] attainable.

достовéрный [14; -рен, -рна] authentic, reliable; positive.

достó|инство *n* [9] dignity; merit, advantage; (*money, etc.*) worth, value; **~йный** [14; -óин, -óйна] worthy (*a.* of P); well-deserved; **~пáмятный** [14; -тен, -тна] memorable, notable; **~примечáтельность** *f* [8] (*mst. pl.*) sight(s); **~примечáтельный** [14; -лен, -льна] remarkable, noteworthy; **~я́ние** *n* [12] property (*a. fig.*), fortune.

дóступ *m* [1] access; **∠ный** [14; -пен, -пна] accessible (*a. fig.*); approachable, affable; comprehensible; susceptible; moderate (*price*).

досу́г *m* [1] leisure; на ~е at leisure, during one's leisure hours.

дóс|уха (quite) dry; **∠ы́та** one's fill.

дот ⚔ *m* [1] pillbox.

дотлá completely, utterly; to the ground.

дотр|áгиваться [1], ⟨**~óнуться**⟩ [20] (до P) touch.

дóх|лый [14] dead; **~ля́тина** *f* [5] carrion; **~нуть** [21], ⟨из-, по-⟩ die; P croak, kick off; **~ну́ть** *s.* дышáть.

дохóд *m* [1] income, revenue; proceeds *pl.* **~и́ть** [15], ⟨дойти́⟩ [дойду́, -дёшь; *cf.* идти́] (до P) go *or* come (to), arrive (at), reach: *hist.* come down to; (*price*) rise, run up to; **~ный** [14; -ден, -дна] profitable.

доцéнт *m* [1] lecturer, instructor.

дóчиста (quite) clean; F completely.

дочи́т|ывать, ⟨**~áть**⟩, [1] finish (*book, etc.*) *or* read up to (до P).

дóч|ка *f* [5; *g/pl.*: -чек] F = **~ь** *f* [дóчери, *etc.* = 8; *pl.*: дóчери, -рéй, *etc. e.*; *instr.*: -рьми́] daughter.

дошкóльный *m* [1] preschool.

дощ|áтый [14] of boards, plank...; **~éчка** *f* [5; *g/pl.*: -чек] *dim. of* доскá.

доя́рка *f* [5; *g/pl.*: -рок] milkmaid.

драгоцéнн|ость *f* [8] jewel, gem (*a. fig.*); precious thing *or* possession; **~ый** [14; -цéнен, -цéнна] precious (*a. stone*), costly, valuable.

дразни́ть [13; -ню́, дрáзнишь] **1.** ⟨по-⟩ tease, banter; nickname; **2.** ⟨раз-⟩ excite.

дрáка *f* [5] scuffle, fight.

дракóн *m* [1] dragon.

дрáма *f* [5] drama; **~ти́ческий** [16] dramatic; **~ту́рг** *m* [1] playwright, dramatist.

драп|ировáть [7], ⟨за-⟩ drape; **∠овый** [14] (of thick) cloth (драп).

дра|ть [деру́, -рёшь; драл, -á, -о; '... дранный], ⟨со-⟩ (*cf.* сдирáть) pull (off); tweak (p.'s *ear* B/ за B; F *cf.* выдирáть & раздирáть; **-ся,** ⟨по-⟩ scuffle, fight, struggle; **~чли́вый** [14 *sh.*] pugnacious.

дребе|дéнь F *f* [8] trash; **'~зг** F *m* [1] clash; *cf.* вдрéбезги; **~зжáть** [4; -зжи́т], ⟨за-⟩ rattle.

древ|еси́на *f* [5] wood substance *or* material(s); **~éсный** [14] tree...; wood(y); ~éсный спирт *m* methyl alcohol; ~éсный у́голь *m* charcoal; **∠ко** *n* [9; *pl.*: -ки, -ков] flagpole.

дрéвн|ий [15; -вен, -вня] ancient (*a. su.*), antique; (very) old; **~ость** *f* [8] antiquity (*a. pl.* = -ties).

дрейф ⚓, ✈ *m* [1], **~овáть** [7] drift.

дрем|áть [2], ⟨за-⟩ doze (off), slumber; **~óта** *f* [5] drowsiness; slumber, doze; **~у́чий** [17] dense; ~у́чий лес *m* primeval forest.

дрессировáть [7], ⟨вы́-⟩ train.

дроб|и́ть [14 *e.*; -блю́, -би́шь; -блённый], ⟨раз-⟩ break to pieces, crush; dismember, divide *or* split up; *impf.* F drum; **∠ный** [14; -бен, -бна] fractional; rolling; drumming; **~ь** *f* [8] *coll.* (small) shot; (*drum*) roll; ⅍ [*from g/pl. e.*] fraction; decimal.

дров|á *n/pl.* [9] (fire)wood; **∠ни** *m/pl.* [4; *a. from g/pl. e.*] peasant's sled(ge); **~осéк** *m* [1] lumberman, *Brt.* woodcutter.

дрó|ги *f/pl.* [5] dray; **~гнуть 1.** [21], ⟨про-⟩ shiver *or* shake (*with cold*), chill; **2.** [20 *st.*] *pf.* start; waver, falter; shrink, flinch; **~жáть** [4 *e.*; -жу́, -жи́шь], ⟨за-⟩ tremble, shake, shiver (with от P); flicker, glimmer; dread (s.th. пéред T); be anxious (about за B); guard, save (над T); **~жжи** *f/pl.* [8; *from gen. e.*] yeast, barm; **~жки** *f/pl.* [5; *gen.*: -жек] droshky; **~жь** *f* [8] trembling, shiver; vibration; ripples *pl.*

дро|зд *m* [1 *e.*] thrush; **~к** *m* [1] ⚘ broom; **∠тик** *m* [1] dart, javelin; **~фá** *f* [5; *pl. st.*] *zo.* bustard.

друг[1] *m* [1; *pl.*: друзья́, -зéй, -зья́м] friend; (*address a.*) dear; **~**[2]: ~ **∠**а each (one an)other; ~ за ∠ом one after another; ~ с ∠ом with each other; **~óй** [14] (an)other, different; else, next, second; (н)и тóт (н)и ~óй both (neither); на ~óй день the next day.

дру́ж|ба *f* [5] friendship; **~елю́бный** [14; -бен, -бна] amicable, friendly; **~еский** [16], **~ественный** [14 *sh.*] friendly; **~и́на** *f* [5] bodyguard, retinue; militia; troop, (*fire*) brigade; **~и́ть** [16; -жу́, -у́жишь] be friends, be on friendly terms (with с Т); **~и́ще** *m* F [11] old chap *or* boy; **~ка** [5; *g/pl.*: -жек] **1.** *f* F = друг²; **2.** *m* best man; **~ный** [14; -жен, -жна́, -о, дру́жны́] friendly, on friendly terms; harmonious, concurrent, unanimous; ♀, ⚔ vigorous; *adv. a.* hand in hand, together; at once.

дря́|блый [14; дрябл, -á, -о] limp, flabby; **~зги** F *f/pl.* [5] squabbles; **~нно́й** P [14] wretched, mean, trashy; **~нь** F *f* [8] rubbish, trash (*a. fig.*); P rotten, lousy (thing, p.); **~хлый** [14; дряхл, -á, -о] decrepit; F dilapidated.

дуб *m* [1; *pl. e.*] oak; **~и́льный** [14] tan...; **~и́льня** *f* [6; *g/pl.*: -лен] tannery; **~и́на** *f* [5] club, cudgel; P boor, dolt; **~и́ть** [14 *e.*; -блю́, -би́шь], ⟨вы́-⟩ tan; **~лёр** *m* [1] *thea.* understudy, double; **~ова́тый** F [14 *sh.*] dull; **~о́вый** [14] oak(en); *fig.* dull; **~ра́ва** *f* [5] (oak) wood, forest.

дуг|á *f* [5; *pl. st.*] arc (*a.* ⚡); (shaft) bow (*harness*); ~óй arched; **~ово́й** [14]: ~ова́я ла́мпа *f* arc light.

ду́дк|а *f* [5; *g/pl.*: -док] pipe; F ~и! fudge!, rats!; плясáть под ~у *or* по ~е dance to s.b.'s tune *or* piping.

ду́ло *n* [9] muzzle; barrel (*gun*).

ду́ма *f* [5] **1.** thought; meditation; **2.** (*Russia, prior to 1917*) duma = council; elective legislative assembly; **~ть** [1], ⟨по-⟩ think (about, of о П); reflect, meditate (on над Т, о П); (+ *inf.*) intend, be going to; care (for о П); F suspect (на В); как ты ~ешь? what do you think?; мно́го ~ть о себе́ be conceited; не до́лго ~я without hesitation; **-ся** seem, appear; ([one, you] must, can) think.

Дуна́й *m* [3] Danube.

дун|ове́ние *n* [12] waft, breath; **∠уть** *s.* дуть.

Ду́ня *f* [6] *dim. of* Евдоки́я.

дупло́ *n* [9; *pl. st.*: ду́пла, -пел, -плам] hollow (*tree*); cavity (*tooth*).

ду́р|а *f* [5] silly woman; **~а́к** *m* [1 *e.*] fool, simpleton; ~а́к ~ако́м arrant fool; **~а́цкий** [16] foolish, silly; fool's; **~а́чество** F *n* [9] tomfoolery; **~а́чить** F [16], ⟨о-⟩ fool, hoax; **-ся** fool, play tricks; **~е́ть** F [8], ⟨о-⟩ grow stupid; become stupefied; **~и́ть** F [13] *s.* ~а́читься; be naughty *or* obstinate.

дурма́н *m* [1] jimson weed, thorn apple; *fig.* narcotic; **~ить** [13], ⟨о-⟩ stupefy.

дурн|е́ть [8], ⟨по-⟩ grow plain *or* ugly; **~о́й** [14; ду́рен, -рна́, -о] bad; plain, ugly; P stupid; мне ∠о I feel (am) sick *or* unwell; **~ота́** F *f* [5] giddiness, sickness.

дурь F *f* [8] folly, caprice; trash.

ду́т|ый [14] blown (*glass*); *fig.* inflated; false; **~ь** [18], ⟨по-⟩, *once* ⟨ду́нуть⟩ [20] blow; ду́ет there is a draught (draft); **-ся**, ⟨на-⟩ swell; F sulk, be angry with (на В); P give o.s. airs.

дух *m* [1] spirit; mind; courage; ghost; F breath; P scent; (не) в ∠е in a good (bad) temper *or* in high (low) spirits, ([+ *inf.*] in no mood to); в моём ∠е to my taste; на ~у́ at the confession; P ∠ом in a jiffy *or* trice; at one draught; во весь ~ *or* что́ есть ∠у at full speed, with all one's might; **~и́** *m/pl.* [1 *e.*] perfume.

духов|е́нство *n* [9] *coll.* clergy; **∠ка** *f* [5; *g/pl.*: -вок] oven; **~ни́к** *m* [1 *e.*] (father) confessor; **∠ный** [14] spiritual; mental; ecclesiastical, clerical, religious, sacred; ∠ная *f* (*form.*) testament, will; ∠ный оте́ц *m* = ~ни́к; ∠ное лицо́ *n* clergyman; **~о́й** [14] ♪ wind (*instrument*); ~о́й орке́стр *m* brassband.

духота́ *f* [5] sultriness, sultry air.

душ *m* [1] shower (bath); douche.

душ|á *f* [5; *ac/sg.*: ду́шу; *pl. st.*] soul; mind, disposition; temper (-ament); feeling, emotion; person; *hist.* serf; F *address*: dear, darling; ~á в ∠у in perfect harmony; в глубине́ ~и́ in one's heart of hearts; от (всей) ~и́ from (with all) one's heart; по ~а́м heart-to-heart; ~á в пя́тки ушла́ have one's heart in one's mouth.

душ|евнобольно́й [14] mentally sick *or* deranged (person); **~е́вный** [14] mental, psychic(al); sincere, hearty; **∠енька** F *f* [5] darling; **~ераздира́ющий** [17] heart-rending.

душ|и́стый [14 *sh.*] fragrant; sweet (*peas*); **~и́ть** [16] **1.** ⟨за-⟩ strangle, choke (*a. fig.*); **2.** ⟨на-⟩ perfume (o.s. **-ся**); **∠ный** [14; -шен, -шна́, -о] stuffy; sultry.

дуэ́|ль *f* [8] duel; **~т** *m* [1] duet.

ды́б|ом (*stand*) on end (*hair*); **~ы́**: (встать, *etc.*) на ~ы́ rear (*a.* up, *fig.*), prance.

дым *m* [1] smoke; **~и́ть** [14 *e.*; -млю́, -ми́шь], ⟨на-⟩ *or* **~и́ться** smoke; steam; **∠ка** *f* [5] haze; gauze; **∠ный** [14] smoky; **~ово́й** [14] smoke...; **~о́к** *m* [1; -мка́] small stream *or* puff of smoke; **~охо́д** *m* [1] flue.

ды́ня *f* [6] muskmelon.

дыр|á *f* [5; *pl. st.*], **∠ка** *f* [5; *g/pl.*: -рок] hole; **~я́вый** [14 *sh.*] having a hole *or* full of holes; (*clothes, shoes*)

tattered; F bad (*memory*); ~ая голова́ F forgetful person.
дыха́|ние *n* [12] breath(ing); **~тельный** [14] respiratory; **~тельное го́рло** *n* windpipe.
дыша́ть [4], ⟨по-⟩, F (*a. once*) ⟨дохну́ть⟩ [20] breathe (s.th. T); *a.* devote o.s. to, indulge in; foam with; ~ све́жим во́здухом take the air; е́ле ~ *or* ~ на ла́дан F have one foot in the grave.
ды́шло *n* [9] (*wagon, cart*) pole.
дья́вол *m* [1] devil; **~ьский** [16] devilish.
дья|к, ~чо́к *m* [1; -чка́] clerk & chanter, sexton; **~кон** *m* [1] deacon.
дю́жий P [17; дюж, -а́, -е] sturdy.
дю́жин|а *f* [5] dozen; ~ами, по ~ам by the dozen; **~ный** [14] common(-place), mediocre.
дю|йм *m* [1] inch; **~на** *f* [5] dune.
дюралюми́ний *m* [3] duralumin.
дя́д|ька *m* [5; *g/pl.*: -дек] F & *contp.* = ~я; † tutor, instructor; **~я** *m* [6; *g/pl.*: -дей] uncle (*a. in* F *address*); F (strong) fellow, guy.
дя́тел *m* [1; -тла] woodpecker.

Е

'Ева *f* [5] Eve (*name*).
Ева́нгелие *n* [12] Gospel (♀ *fig.*).
Евге́ни|й *m* [3] Eugene; **~я** *f* [7] Eugenia.
Евдоки́я *f* [7] Eudoxia.
евре́й *m* [3] Jew; **~ка** *f* [5; *g/pl.*: -ре́ек] Jewess; **~ский** [16] Jewish.
Евро́п|а *f* [5] Europe *n*; **♀е́ец** *m* [1; -пе́йца], **♀е́йка** *f* [5; *g/pl.*: -пе́ек], **♀е́йский** [16] European.
е́герь *m* [4; *pl.*: *a.* -ря́, *etc. e.*] hunter; ⚔ chasseur.
Еги́п|ет *m* [1; -пта] Egypt; **♀етский** [16] Egyptian; **♀тя́нин** *m* [1; *pl.*: -я́не, -я́н], **♀тя́нка** *f* [5; *g/pl.*: -нок] Egyptian.
его́ (ji'vɔ) his; its; *cf.* **он.**
Его́р P *m* [1] George.
еда́ *f* [5] food; meal.
едва́ (*a.* ~ ли) hardly, scarcely; *s. a.* е́ле; no sooner; ~ не almost, nearly; ~ ли не perhaps.
един|е́ние *n* [12] unity, union; **~и́ца** *f* [5] ⅍ one; digit; unit; F (*mark*) very bad; *pl.* (a) few; **~и́чный** [14; -чен, -чна] single, isolated.
едино... (*cf. a.* одно...): **~бо́рство** *n* [9] (single) combat, duel; **~вла́стие** *n* [12] autocracy; **~вре́менный** [14] single; † simultaneous; **~гла́сие** *n* [12] unanimity; **~гла́сный** [14; -сен, -сна] unanimous; **~гла́сно** unanimously; **~ду́шие** *n* [12] unanimity; **~ду́шный** [14; -шен, -шна] unanimous; **~ли́чный** [14] individual (*a.* peasant ~ли́чник *m*), personal; **~мы́слящий** [17] like-minded; **~мышленник** *m* [1] like-minded p., associate, confederate; **~обра́зный** [14; -зен, -зна] uniform; **~ро́г** *m* [1] unicorn.
еди́нствен|ный [14 *sh.*] only, single, sole; ~ный в своём ро́де unique; ~ное число́ *n gr.* singular.
еди́н|ство *n* [9] unity; unanimity; **~ый** [14 *sh.*] one, single; only (one), sole; one whole; united; (one and the) same; все до ~ого all to a man.
е́дкий [16; е́док, едка́, -о] caustic.
едо́к *m* [1 *e.*] (F good) eater.
её her; its; *cf.* она́.
ёж *m* [1 *e.*] hedgehog.
ежеви́ка *f* [5] blackberry, -ries *pl.*
еже|го́дный [14] annual; **~дне́вный** [14] daily; everyday; **~ме́сячный** [14] monthly; **~мину́тный** [14] (occuring) every minute; continual; **~неде́льный** [14] weekly; **~ча́сный** [14] hourly.
ёжиться [16], ⟨съ-⟩ shrink; be shy.
ежо́в|ый [14]: держа́ть в ~ых рукави́цах rule with a rod of iron.
езд|а́ *f* [5] ride, drive; **~ить** [15], go (by T), ride, drive; come, visit; travel; **~о́к** *m* [1 *e.*] rider, horseman.
ей: ~(-~) P, ~-бо́гу F really, indeed.
Екатери́на *f* [5] Catherine.
е́ле (*a.* ~-~) hardly, scarcely, barely; slightly; with (great) difficulty.
еле́й *m* [3] (holy) oil; *fig.* unction; **~ный** [14] unctuous.
Еле́на *f* [5] Helen.
Елизаве́та *f* [5] Elizabeth.
ёлка *f* [5; *g/pl.*: ёлок] fir; (рожде́ственская, новогóдняя) ~ Christmas (*Sov.*: New Year's) tree *or* (children's) party (на В to, for; на П at).
ел|о́вый [14] fir(ry); **~ь** *f* [8] fir; **~ьник** *m* [1] fir wood (*or* greens *pl.*).
ёмк|ий [16; ёмок, ёмка] capacious; **~ость** *f* [8] capacity; ме́ра ~ости cubic measure.
Енисе́й *m* [3] Yenisei (*Siber. river*).
ено́т *m* [1] raccoon.
епи́скоп *m* [1] bishop.
ерала́ш F *m* [1] mess, muddle, jumble.
е́ре|сь *f* [8] heresy; **~ти́к** *m* [1 *e.*] heretic.
ёрзать F [1] fidget; slip.
еро́шить [16] = взъеро́шивать, *s.*
ерунда́ F *f* [5] nonsense; trifle(s).
е́сли if, in case; once (*a.* ~ уж[е́]); а *or* и ~ if ever; whereas; ~ и *or*

(да́)же even though; ах *or* о, ~ б(ы) ... oh, could *or* would ...; ~ бы не but for; ~ то́лько provided.
есте́ств|енный [14 *sh.*] natural; **~о** *n* [9] nature; **~ове́д** *m* [1] naturalist, scientist; **~ове́дение, ~озна́ние** *n* [12] natural science; **~оиспыта́тель** *m* [4] *s.* ~ове́д.
есть[1] [ем, ешь, ест, еди́м, еди́те, едя́т; ешь(те)!; ел; ...е́денный] 1. ⟨съ-, по-⟩ eat (*pf. a.* up), have; 2. ⟨разъ-⟩ eat away (*rust*); corrode; bite; 3. F ⟨по-, разъ-⟩ bite, gnaw, sting; P torment.
есть[2] *cf.* быть; am, is, are; there is (are); у меня́ ~ ... I have ...; так и ~ indeed!; ~ тако́е де́ло! F O.K.; ~! ⚔ yes, sir!
ефре́йтор ⚔ *m* [1] private first class, *Brt.* lance-corporal.
е́ха|ть [е́ду, е́дешь; поезжа́й!], ⟨по-⟩ (be) go(ing, *etc.*) (by Т), ride, drive (in, on Т *or* в, на П); come; run; (в, на В) leave (for), go (to); (за Т) go for, fetch; по~ли! *s.* идти́.
ехи́д|ный [14; -ден, -дна] spiteful, malignant; **~ство** *n* [9] spite, malice.
ещё (не) (not) yet; (всё) ~ still (*a. with comp.*); another, more (& more ~ и ~); ~ раз once more; else; already; as early (late, *etc.*) as; possibly, probably; more or less, somewhat; ~ бы! (to be) sure!, I should think so!, of course!; it would be worse still if ...

Ж

ж *s.* же.
жа́б|а *f* [5] toad; грудна́я ~а angina pectoris; **~ра** *f* [5] gill.
жа́воронок *m* [1; -нка] (sky)lark.
жа́дн|ичать F [1], ⟨по-⟩ be greedy *or* avaricious; **~ость** *f* [8] greed (-iness), avarice; **~ый** [14; -ден, -дна́, -о] greedy (of на В, до Р, к Д), avaricious.
жа́жда *f* [5] thirst (*a. fig.* for Р, *or inf.*); **~ть** [-ду, -дешь] thirst, crave (for Р, *or inf.*).
жаке́т *m* [1], F **~ка** *f* [5; *g/pl.*: -ток] jacket.
жале́ть [8], ⟨по-⟩ 1. pity; (о П) regret; 2. (Р *or* В) spare; grudge.
жа́лить [13], ⟨у-⟩ sting, bite.
жа́лк|ий [16; -лок, -лка́, -о; *comp.*: жа́льче] pitiable; miserable, wretched; **~о** *s.* жаль.
жа́ло *n* [9] sting (*a. fig.*).
жа́лоб|а *f* [5] complaint; ⚖ action; **~ный** [14; -бен, -бна] mournful, plaintive; (of) complaint(s).
жа́лова|нье *n* [10] pay, salary; reward; **~ть** [7], ⟨по-⟩ (Т) reward, award; give; appoint (в И *pl.*); F like; come (to see a p. к Д); **-ся** (на В) complain (of); F inform (against); ⚖ sue, go to law.
жа́лост|ливый F [14 *sh.*] compassionate; sorrowful; **~ный** F [14; -тен, -тна] mournful; compassionate; **~ь** *f* [8] pity, compassion.
жаль it is a pity (как ~ what a pity); unfortunately; (Д ~ В): мне ~ его́ I am sorry for (*or* pity) him; *a.* regret; grudge.
жар *m* [1; в -у́] heat; fever; *fig.* ardo(u)r; **~а́** *f* [5] heat, hot weather; **~еный** [14] fried; roast(ed); *s. a.* ~ко́е; **~ить** [13], ⟨за-, из-, P с-⟩ roast; fry; F (*sun*) burn; **~кий** [16; -рок, -рка́, -о; *comp.*: жа́рче] hot; *fig.* ardent. vehement intense; мне ~ко I am hot; **~ко́е** *n* [16] roast meat.
жа́т|ва *f* [5] harvest; crop; **~венный** [14] reaping.
жать[1] [жму, жмёшь; ...жа́тый], ⟨с-⟩, *cf.*, & ⟨по-⟩ press, squeeze (*a.* out); shake (hands with ру́ку Д); pinch (*shoes, etc.*); F *fig.* oppress; **-ся** shrink (with от Р); crowd; snuggle; F vacillate; **~**[2] [жну, жнёшь; ... жа́тый], ⟨с-⟩ [сожну́], ⟨по-⟩ reap, harvest.
жва́ч|ка *f* [5] rumination; cud; P chewing gum (*or* tobacco); **~ный** [14]: ~ные (живо́тные) *n/pl.* ruminants.
жгут *m* [1 *e.*] strap.
жгу́чий [17 *sh.*] burning; poignant.
ж. д. *abbr.*: желе́зная доро́га; *cf.* R. R., Ry.
ждать [жду, ждёшь; ждал, -а́, -о], ⟨подо-⟩ wait (for Р); expect, await; вре́мя не ждёт time presses; ~ не дожда́ться wait impatiently (for Р).
же 1. *conj.* but, and; whereas, as to; 2. = ведь, *cf.*; *a.* do + *vb.*; the (this) very, same (*a.* place, time, *etc.*); just; too; *interr.* ever, on earth; for goodness' sake.
жева́|ть [7 *e.*; жую́, жуёшь] chew; **~тельный** [14] masticatory; chewing.
жезл *m* [1 *e.*] staff, rod, wand.
жела́|ние *n* [12] wish, desire; по (согла́сно) ~нию at, by (as) request(ed); **~нный** [14; -а́нен, -а́нна] desired, long wished for; welcome; beloved; **~тельный** [14; -лен, -льна] desirable; desired; мне ~тельно I am anxious to; **~ть** [1], ⟨по-⟩ wish (a p. s.th. Д/Р), desire; love; **~ющие** *pl.* [17] p.s wishing to ...
желе́ *n* [*indecl.*] jelly (*a. fish, meat*).
железа́ *f* [5; *pl.*: же́лезы, желёз, железа́м] gland.

желез|нодоро́жник *m* [1] railroad (*Brt.* railway-) man; **~нодоро́жный** [14] railroad..., *Brt.* railway...; **~ный** [14] iron...; rail...; **~о** *n* [9] iron; кро́вельное ~о sheet iron; куй ~о, пока́ горячо́ strike while the iron is hot; **~обето́н** *m* [1] reinforced concrete.
жёлоб *m* [1; *pl.:* -бá, *etc. e.*] gutter.
желт|е́ть [8], ⟨по-⟩ grow *or* turn yellow; *impf.* (*a.* **-ся**) appear *or* show yellow; **~изна́** *f* [5] yellow (-ness); **~ова́тый** [14 *sh.*] yellowish; **~о́к** *m* [1; -тка́] yolk; **~у́ха** *f* [5] jaundice.
жёлтый [14; жёлт, -á, -о] yellow.
желу́до|к *m* [1; -дка] stomach; **~чный** [14] gastric, stomachic(al).
жёлудь *m* [4; *from g/pl. e.*] acorn.
жёлч|ный [14] gall...; [жёлчен, -чна, -о] bilious (*a. fig.*); **~ь** *f* [8] bile, gall (*a. fig.*); grief.
жема́н|иться F [13] mince; be prim; **~ница** F *f* [5] prude; **~ный** [14; -а́нен, -а́нна] affected, mincing, prim; **~ство** *n* [9] primness, prudery.
же́мч|уг *m* [1; *pl.:* -гá, *etc. e.*] *coll.* pearls *pl.*; **~у́жина** *f* [5] pearl; **~у́жный** [14] pearl(y).
жен|а́ *f* [5; *pl. st.:* жёны] wife; † woman; **~а́тый** [14 *sh.*] married (*man*; to a p. на П); **~и́ть** [13; женю́, же́нишь] (*im*)*pf.* marry (*a man* to на П); **-ся** marry (*v/t.* на П; *of men*); **~и́тьба** *f* [5] marriage (to на П); **~и́х** [1 *e.*] fiancé; bridegroom; suiter; F marriageable young man; **~олю́б** *m* [1] lady-killer, ladies' man; **~оненави́стник** *m* [1] woman hater **~оподо́бный** [14; -бен, -бна] womanlike; **~ский** [16] female, woman('s) *or* women's; girls'; *gr.* feminine; **~ственный** [14 *sh.*] womanly; womanish, effeminate; **~щина** *f* [5] woman.
жердь *f* [8; *from g/pl. e.*] pole.
жереб|ёнок *m* [2] foal, colt; **~е́ц** *m* [1; -бца́] stallion.
жерло́ *n* [9; *pl. st.*] crater; aperture, mouth; muzzle (*gun, etc.*).
жёрнов *m* [1; *pl. e.:* -вá] millstone.
же́ртв|а *f* [5] sacrifice; (*p.:*) victim; **~овать** [7], ⟨по-⟩ (Т) sacrifice (*v/t.*; o.s. собо́й); (В) give; **~оприноше́ние** *n* [12] offering.
жест *m* [1] gesture; **~икули́ровать** [7] gesticulate.
жёсткий [16; -ток, -ткá, -о; *comp.:* -тче] hard; rough, rude, coarse, harsh (*a. fig.*); tough; stiff, rigid, severe, rigorous; ~ ваго́н (ordinary) passenger car, *Brt.* second-class carriage.
жесто́к|ий [16; жесто́к, -á, -о] cruel; terrible, dreadful, fierce, grim; rigorous, violent; **~осе́рдие** *n* [12] hard-heartedness; **~ость** *f* [8] cruelty; severity.
жест|ь *f* [8] tin (plate); **~я́нка** *f* [5; *g/pl.:* -нок] can, *Brt.* tin; **~яно́й** [14] tin...; **~я́нщик** *m* [1] tinsmith.
жето́н *m* [1] counter; medal; token.
жечь, ⟨с-⟩ [26 г/ж: (со)жгу́, -жжёшь, -жгу́т; (с)жёг, (со)жгла́; сожжённый] burn (*a. fig.*); torment.
живи́т|ельный [14; -лен, -льна] vivifying; crisp (*air*); **~ь** [14 *e.*; живлю́, -ви́шь], ⟨о-⟩ vivify, animate.
жив|о́й [14; жив, -á, -о] living; alive (*pred.*); lively, vivid, vivacious; quick, nimble; real, true; в **~ы́х** alive; ~ и здоро́в safe & sound; ни ~ ни мёртв more dead than alive; заде́ть за **~о́е** sting to the quick; **~опи́сец** *m* [1; -сца] painter; **~опи́сный** [14; -сен, -сна] picturesque; **~опись** *f* [8] painting; **~ость** *f* [8] vivacity; vividness.
живо́т *m* [1 *e.*] P belly; stomach; † life; **~во́рный** [14; -рен, -рна] vivifying; **~новóдство** *n* [9] cattle breeding; **~ное** *n* [14] animal; **~ный** [14] animal; *fig.* brutal.
жив|отрепе́щущий [17] living (*fish*); *fig.* burning; **~у́чий** [17 *sh.*] hardy, tough; enduring; **~ьём** P alive.
жи́дк|ий [16; -док, -дкá, -о; *comp.:* жи́же] liquid, fluid; watery, weak, thin; sparse, scanty; **~ость** *f* [8] liquid; scantiness.
жи́ж|а, ~ица F *f* [5] slush; broth.
жи́зне|нность *f* [8] viability; vitality; vividness; **~нный** 1. [14 *sh.*] (of) life('s), worldly; vivid; living; 2. [14] vital; **~описа́ние** *n* [12] biography; **~ра́достный** [14; -тен, -тна] cheerful, merry; **~спосо́бный** [14; -бен, -бна] viable.
жизн|ь *f* [8] life; practice; в **~ь** (**~и**) не ... never (in one's life); при **~и** in a p.'s lifetime; alive; не на **~ь**, а на смерть of life & death.
жи́л|а *f* [5] F sinew, tendon; vein (*a.* ⚒); **~е́т** *m* [1], **~е́тка** *f* [5; *g/pl.:* -ток] vest, *Brt.* waistcoat; **~е́ц** *m* [1; -льца́] lodger, roomer; inmate; † = жи́тель; **~истый** [14 *sh.*] sinewy, stringy (*a. meat*), wiry; **~и́ще** *n* [11] dwelling, lodging(s); **~и́щный** [14] housing; **~ка** *f* [5; *g/pl.:* -лок] *dim. of* ~а; veinlet; vein (*leaf, wing, marble, & fig.*); **~о́й** [14] dwelling; inhabited; living, *cf.* **~пло́щадь** *f* [8] living space; **~ьё** *n* [10] habitation; F dwelling.
жир *m* [1; в -у́; *pl. e.*] fat; grease; ры́бий ~ cod-liver oil; **~е́ть** [8], ⟨о-, раз-⟩ grow fat; **~ный** [14; -рен, -рнá, -о] fat; (of) grease, greasy; ⚘ fleshy; *fig.* rich; *typ.* bold -(-faced); **~о** † *n* [*indecl.*] endorsement; **~ово́й** [14] fat(ty).
жит|е́йский [16] worldly, (of) life('s); everyday; **~ель** *m* [4], **~ельница** *f* [5] inhabitant, resident;

∠ельство *n* [9] residence; вид на ∠ельство residence (*or* stay) permit; ~не́ *n* [12] life (*a. of a saint*).
жи́тница *f* [5] granary.
жить [живу́, -вёшь; жил, -á, -о; не́ жил(и)] live (T, на B [up]on; T *a.* for); reside, lodge; exist, be; как живёте? how are you (getting on)?; жи́л(и)-бы́л(и) ... once upon a time there was (were) ... (*in fairy tales*); **∠ся:** ему́ хорошо́ живётся he is well off; **~ё(-бытьё)** F *n* [10] life, living; residence, stay; (Д) be well off.
жму́рить [13], ⟨за-⟩ screw up *or* contract (one's eyes **-ся**; blink).
жн|е́йка *f* [5; *g/pl.*: -е́ек], **~ея́** *f* [6] reaping machine, harvester; **~ец** *m* [1 *e.*] reaper; **~ивьё** *n* [10; *pl.*: жни́вья, -вьев] stubble(s); **~и́ца** *f* [5] reaper.
жо́л..., жо́р... *s.* **жёл..., жёр...**
жрать P [жру, жрёшь; жрал, -á, -о], ⟨со-⟩ eat; devour, gorge, gobble.
жре́бий *m* [3] lot (*a. fig.* = destiny); броса́ть (тяну́ть) ~ cast (draw) lots; ~ бро́шен the die is cast.
жрец *m* [1 *e.*] (*pagan*) priest (*a. fig.*).
жужжа́|ние *n* [12], **~ть** [4 *e.*; жужжу́, -и́шь] buzz, hum.
жу|к *m* [1 *e.*] beetle; ма́йский ~к cockchafer; P = **∠лик** F *m* [1] swindler, cheat(er), trickster; filcher, pilferer; **∠льничать** F [1], ⟨с-⟩ cheat, trick.
жу́пел *m* [1] bugaboo, bugbear.
жура́вль *m* [4 *e.*] (*zo., well*) crane.
жури́ть F [13], ⟨по-⟩ scold, rebuke.
журна́л *m* [1] magazine, periodical, journal; diary; ⚓ log(book); **~и́ст** *m* [1] news(paper)man, journalist; **~и́стика** *f* [5] journalism.
журча́|ние *n* [12], **~ть** [-чи́т] purl, murmur.
жу́т|кий [14; -ток, -тка́, -о] weird, uncanny, dismal, sinister; мне ~ко I am terrified; **~кость**, F **~ь** *f* [8] dismay, dread(ful P *pred.*).
жюри́ *n* [*indecl.*] jury (*prizes*).

З

за 1. (B): (*direction*) behind; over, across, beyond; out of; (*distance*) at; (*time*) after; over, past; before (*a.* ~ ... до P); (with)in, for, during; (*object*[*ive*], *favo*[*u*]*r, reason, value, substitute*) for; ~ то, что because; ~ что? what for?, why?; **2.** (T): (*position*) behind; across, beyond; at, over; after (*time & place*); because of; with; ~ мной ... *a.* I owe ...; ко́мната ~ мной I take (reserve) the room.
заба́в|а *f* [5] amusement, entertainment; **~ля́ть** [28], ⟨(по)~ить⟩ [13] amuse (-ся o.s., be amused at T); **~ник** F *m* [1] joker, wag; **~ный** [14; -вен, -вна] amusing, funny.
забасто́в|ка *f* [5; *g/pl.*: -вок] strike, walkout; **~очный** [14] strike ...; **~щик** *m* [1] striker.
забве́ние *n* [12] oblivion.
забе|га́ть [1], ⟨**~жа́ть**⟩ [4; забегу́, -ежи́шь, -егу́т; -еги́!] run in(to), get; run off, away; F drop in (on к Д); ~га́ть вперёд forestall.
заб|ива́ть [1], ⟨**~и́ть**⟩ [-бью́, -бьёшь; *cf.* бить] drive in; nail up; stop up, choke (up); block (up); F outdo, beat; (*fountain*) spout forth; sound (*alarm*); F stuff (*head*); take (*into one's head*); **-ся** F hide, get; *pf.* begin to beat.
заб|ира́ть [1], ⟨**~ра́ть**⟩ [-беру́, -рёшь; *cf.* брать] take (*a.*, F, away); capture, (*a. fig.*) seize; arrest; put (into); turn, steer; (T) close, partition (off); **-ся** climb *or* creep (in, up); steal in, penetrate; hide; get (far off).
заби́|тый [14] browbeaten, cowed, (in)timid(ated); **~ть** *s.* ~ва́ть; **~я́ка** F *m/f* [5] bully, squabbler.
заблаго|вре́менно in (due) time, beforehand; **~вре́менный** [14] preliminary; timely; **~рассу́диться** [15; *impers.*, *with* Д] think fit.
забл|уди́ться [15] *pf.* lose one's way, go astray; **~у́дший** [17] lost; stray; **~ужда́ться** [1] be mistaken, err; **~ужде́ние** *n* [12] error, mistake; ввести́ в ~ужде́ние mislead.
забол|ева́ть [1], ⟨**~е́ть**⟩ [8] fall sick *or* ill (of T), be taken ill with; ache; *su.*: **~ева́ние** *n* [12] *a.* = боле́знь.
забо́р *m* [1] fence; **~ный** [14] fence...; *fig.* vulgar, trashy.
забо́т|а *f* [5] care (about, of о П), concern, anxiety, worry, trouble; без ~ careless; carefree; **~иться** [15], ⟨по-⟩ (о П) care (for), take care of, look after; worry, be anxious (about); **~ливый** [14 *sh.*] careful, provident; attentive; anxious, solicitous.
забр|а́сывать [1] **1.** ⟨**~оса́ть**⟩ (T) fill up; heap (*a. fig.* = overwhelm); pelt (*stones*); bespatter (*dirt*); **2.** ⟨**~о́сить**⟩ [15] throw, fling, (*a. fig.*) cast; neglect, give up; **~а́ть** *s.* забира́ть; **~еда́ть** [1], ⟨**~ести́**⟩ [25] wander *or* get ([in]to, far); **~оса́ть, ~о́сить** *s.* ~а́сывать; **~о́шенный** [14] deserted; unkempt.
забры́згать [1] *pf.* splash, sprinkle.
заб|ыва́ть [1], ⟨**~ы́ть**⟩ [-бу́ду, -дешь] forget (*o.s.* **-ся**; *a.* nap, doze); **~ы́вчивый** [14 *sh.*] forgetful; **~ытьё** *n* [12; в -тьи́] unconscious-

ness, swoon; drowsiness; slumber; reverie; frenzy.

зава́л *m* [1] heap, drift; obstruction, abatis; **~ивать** [1], ⟨~и́ть⟩ [13; -алю́, -а́лишь] fill *or* heap (up); cover; block, obstruct, close; F overburden (*with work, etc.*); **-ся** fall; sink; collapse.

зава́р|ивать [1], ⟨~и́ть⟩ [13; -арю́, -а́ришь] boil (*a.* down), make (*tea*); scald; P *fig.* concoct.

зав|еде́ние *n* [12] establishment, institution; (закры́тое) учёбное ~еде́ние (boarding) school; **~е́довать** [7] (T) be in charge *or* the head (chief) of, manage; **~е́домый** [14] notorious, indubitable; ~е́домо knowingly; admittedly, certainly; **~е́дующий** [17] (T) chief, head; director; **~езти́** *s.* ~ози́ть.

зав|ере́ние *n* [12] assurance; **~е́рить** *s.* ~еря́ть; **~ерну́ть** *s.* ~ёртывать; **~ерте́ть** [11; -ерчу́ -е́ртишь] *pf.* start turning (*v/i.* **-ся**); **~ёртывать** [1], ⟨~ерну́ть⟩ [20] wrap (up); turn (*a.* up; off, screw up); F drop in; **~ерша́ть** [1], ⟨~ерши́ть⟩ [16 *e.*; -шу́, -ши́шь; -шён-ный] finish, complete, accomplish; crown; **~ерше́ние** *n* [12] conclusion, end; completion; **~еря́ть** [28], ⟨~е́рить⟩ [13] assure (a p. of В/в П); attest, authenticate.

заве́|са *f* [5] curtain; screen (*a.* ⚔); *fig.* veil; **~сить** *s.* ~шивать; **~сти́** *s.* заводи́ть.

заве́т *m* [1] legacy; precept, maxim; vow; *Bibl.* (Ве́тхий Old, Но́вый New) ~ Testament; **~ный** [14] sacred; dear, precious; fond; cherished; intimate; † forbidden.

заве́|шивать [1], ⟨~сить⟩ [15] cover, hang with, curtain.

завеща́|ние *n* [12] testament, will; **~ть** [1] (*im*)*pf.* bequeath; instruct, leave as precept.

завзя́тый F [14] inveterate; enthusiastic; true, genuine.

зав|ива́ть [1], ⟨~и́ть⟩ [-вью́, -вьёшь; *cf.* вить] wave, curl; wind round; **~и́вка** *f* [5; *g/pl.:* -вок] waving; холо́дная (шестиме́сячная) ~и́вка water (permanent) wave.

зави́д|ный [14; -ден, -дна] enviable, desirable; envious (of Д/И); **~овать** [7], ⟨по-⟩ envy (a p. a th. Д/в П), be envious (of).

зави́н|чивать [1], ⟨~ти́ть⟩ [15 *e.*; -инчу́, -инти́шь] screw up.

зави́с|еть [11] depend (on от Р); **~имость** *f* [8] dependence; в ~имости от (Р) depending on; **~имый** [14 *sh.*] dependent.

зави́ст|ливый [14 *sh.*] envious, jealous; **'~ь** *f* [8] envy (of, at к Д).

зави|то́й [14] curly; **~то́к** *m* [1; -тка́] curl, ringlet; flourish; **∠ть** *s.* ~ва́ть.

завко́м *m* [1] (заводско́й комите́т) works council.

завлад|ева́ть [1], ⟨~е́ть⟩ [8] (T) take possession *or* hold of, seize.

завл|ека́тельный [14; -лен, -льна] enticing, tempting; **~ека́ть** [1], **~е́чь** [26] (al)lure, entice, tempt; involve; carry away.

заво́д[1] *m* [1] works, factory, plant (at/to на П/В); stud (*a.* ко́нский ~); **~**[2] winding mechanism; *typ.* edition; **~и́ть** [15], ⟨завести́⟩ [25] take, bring, lead; put; establish, set up, found (*business, etc.*); form, contract (*habit, friendship, etc.*); get, procure, acquire (*things*); start (*a. motor*), begin (*talk, dispute, etc.*; *a.* to keep [*animals*]); wind up (*watch, etc.*); **-ся**, ⟨завести́сь⟩ appear; nest; get, have; **~ной** [14] ⊕ starting; mechanical (*toy*); **~ский**, **~ско́й** [16] works…, factory…; stud…

заво|ева́ние *n* [12] conquest; *fig.* (*mst pl.*) achievement(s); **~ева́тель** *m* [4] conqueror; **~ёвывать** [1], ⟨~ева́ть⟩ [6] conquer; win, gain.

зав|ози́ть [15], ⟨~езти́⟩ [24] take, bring, drive; leave, F deliver.

завол|а́кивать [1], ⟨~о́чь⟩ [26] cover, overcast; get cloudy.

завор|а́чивать [1], ⟨~оти́ть⟩ [15] turn (in, up, down, about); direct.

завсегда́тай *m* [3] habitué.

за́втра tomorrow; **~к** *m* [1] breakfast (at за Т; for на В, к Д); (второ́й ~к) lunch; **~кать** [1], ⟨по-⟩ (have, take) breakfast (lunch); **~шний** [15] tomorrow's; ~шний день *m* tomorrow; *fig.* (near) future.

завыва́ть [1], ⟨завы́ть⟩ [22] howl.

зав|яза́ть[1] [3], ⟨~я́знуть⟩ [21] sink in, stick; F *fig.* get stuck *or* involved in; **~яза́ть**[2] *s.* ~я́зывать; **~я́зка** *f* [5; *g/pl.:* -зок] string, tie; beginning, starting point; entanglement, plot; **~я́зывать** [1], ⟨~яза́ть⟩ [3] tie (up), bind, fasten; *fig.* begin, start; entangle, knit (*plot*); **∠язь** ♀ *f* [8] ovary; **~я́нуть** *s.* вя́нуть.

заг|ада́ть *s.* ~а́дывать; **~а́дить** *s.* ~а́живать; **~а́дка** *f* [5; *g/pl.:* -док] riddle, enigma; **~а́дочный** [14; -чен, -чна] enigmatic(al); mysterious; **~а́дывать** [1], ⟨~ада́ть⟩ [1] propose (*a riddle*); try to find out (*by a guess, fortunetelling, etc.*); F fix upon; plan; **~а́живать** F [1], ⟨~а́дить⟩ [15] soil, befoul.

зага́р *m* [1] sunburn, tan.

загво́здка F *f* [5; *g/pl.*: -док] hitch, trouble.

заги́б *m* [1] bend; dog-ear (*page*); *pol.* deviation; **~а́ть** [1], ⟨загну́ть⟩ [20] bend, fold (over), turn (up).

загла́в|ие *n* [12] title (*book, etc.*); **~ный** [14] title…; ~ная бу́ква *f* capital letter.

загла́|живать [1], ⟨~дить⟩ [15] smooth; press, iron; *fig.* make up (*or* amends) for, expiate.

загл|óхнуть *s.* глóхнуть 2.; **~óхший** [17] deserted, desolate; **~ушáть** [1], ‹~ушúть› [16] *s.* глушúть 2.
загля́|дывать [1], ‹~ну́ть› [19] glance; peep; look (through, up); have a look (at); F drop in *or* call (on к Д); **~дываться** [1], ‹~дéться› [11] (на В) gaze, gape *or* stare (at), feast one's eyes *or* gloat ([up]on).
заг|ня́ть *s.* ~оня́ть; **~ну́ть** *s.* ~ибáть; **~овáривать** [1], ‹~оворúть› [13] **1.** *v/i.* begin, start (*or* try) to talk *or* speak; **2.** *v/t.* tire with one's talk; exorcise; **3.** **-ся** F drivel, talk nonsense; be(come) confused; talk (too) long, much; **~óвор** *m* [1] conspiracy, plot; exorcism; составля́ть ~óвор conspire, plot; **~оворúть** *s.* ~овáривать; **~овóрщик** *m* [1] conspirator.
заголóвок *m* [1; -вка] heading, [title.]
загóн *m* [1] enclosure; быть в ~е F suffer neglect; **~я́ть** [28], ‹загнáть› [-гоню́, -гóнишь; *cf.* гнать] drive (in, off); exhaust, fatigue.
загор|áживать [1], ‹~одúть› [15 & 15 *e.*; -рожу́, -рóдишь] enclose, shut in; block (up), bar (*way*); **-ся** fence, protect; **~áть** [1], ‹~éть› [9] become sunburnt; **-ся** catch *or* take fire; light up, kindle, flash; blush, blaze up; *fig.* (get) inflame(d); break out; **~éлый** [14] sunburnt; **~одúть** *s.* ~áживать; **~óдка** F *f* [5; *g/pl.*: -док] fence, enclosure; partition; **'~одный** [14] country (*house, etc.*); out-of-town.
загот|áвливать [1] & **~овля́ть** [28], ‹~óвить› [14] prepare; store up; lay in (*stock*); **~óвка** *f* [5; *g/pl.*: -вок], **~овлéние** *n* [12] storage, laying in (*stocks, supplies*).
загра|дúтельный [14] ⚔ curtain (*fire*), barrage (*a. balloon*); **~ждáть** [1], ‹~дúть› [15 *e.*; -ажу́, -адúшь; -аждённый] block (up), bar; **~ждéние** *n* [12] block(ing), obstruction; прóволочное ~ждéние wire entanglement.
загранú|чный [14] foreign; [abroad.]
загре|бáть [1], ‹~стú› *s.* грестú.
загрóбн|ый [14] sepulchral (*voice*); ~ый мир *m* the other world; ~ая жизнь *f* the beyond.
загромо|ждáть [1], ‹~здúть› [15 *e.*; -зжу́, -здúшь; -мождённый] block (up), (en)cumber, crowd; overload; **~ждéние** *n* [12] blocking; overloading.
загрубéлый [14] callous, coarse.
загр|ужáть [1], ‹~узúть› [15 & 15 *e.*; -ужу́, -у́зишь] (T) load; ⊕ charge; F busy, assign work to; be occupied (*or* taken) by work (*time*); **~у́зка** *f* [5] load(ing, *etc.*), charge; **~ызáть** [1], ‹~ы́зть› [24; *pt. st.*; загры́зенный] bite (*fig.* worry) to death, kill.
загрязн|éние *n* [12] soiling; pollution; infection; **~я́ть** [28], ‹~úть› [13] (**-ся** become) soil(ed), pollute(d) (*water, etc.*), infect(ed) (*air*).
загс *m* [1] (*abbr.*: отдéл зáписей áктов граждáнского состоя́ния) registrar's (registry) office.
зад *m* [1; на -у́; *pl. e.*] back, rear *or* hinder part; posterior(s), rump; *pl.* F things already (well-)known *or* learned; **~ом** наперёд back to front.
зад|áбривать [1], ‹~óбрить› [13] (B) insinuate o.s. (with), gain upon.
зад|авáть [5], ‹~áть› [-дáм, -дáшь, *etc.*, *cf.* дать; зáдал, -á, -о; зáданный (зáдан, -á, -о)] set, assign (*task*); give (*a.* ♪ *keynote*), F dress (down); ask (*question*); **-ся** [*pt.*: -дáлся, -лáсь] цéлью (мы́слью) take it into one's head, set one's mind on doing s.th.; F happen to be.
задáв|ливать [1], ‹~úть› [14] crush; run over, knock down; *fig.* suppress; P strangle, kill.
задáние *n* [12] assignment, task; (com)mission (*a.* ⚔); домáшнее ~ homework.
задáток *m* [1; -тка] earnest money; deposit; *pl.* rudiments.
задá|ть *s.* ~вáть; **~ча** *f* [5] problem (*a.* ♞); task; object(ive), aim, end; **~чник** *m* [1] book of problems.
задв|игáть [1], ‹~úнуть› [20] push (into, *etc.*); shut (*drawer*); draw (*curtain*); slide (*bolt*); **~úжка** [5; *g/pl.*: -жек] bolt; **~ижнóй** [14] sliding (*door*); sash (*window*).
задвóрки *f/pl.* [*gen.*: -рок] backyards.
зад|евáть [1], ‹~éть› [-éну, -éнешь; -éтый] be caught (by за B), brush against, touch (*a. fig.*, [up]on); excite; hurt, wound; ⚕ affect; **~éлывать**, ‹~éлать› [1] stop up, choke (up); wall up.
задёр|гать [1] *pf.* overdrive; F harrass; **~гивать** [1], ‹~нуть› [20] draw (*curtain*); cover.
задержáние *n* [12] arrest.
задéрж|ивать [1], ‹~áть› [4] detain, hold back *or* up, stop; delay, check; arrest; slow down; **-ся** stay; be delayed; linger; stop; be late; **~ка** *f* [5; *g/pl.*: -жек] delay; (*a.* ⊕) trouble, break.
задёрнуть *s.* задёргивать.
задéть *s.* задевáть.
зад|ирáть F [1], ‹~рáть› [-дeру́, -рёшь; *cf.* драть] lift *or* pull (up); stretch; *impf.* provoke, vex, pick a quarrel (with); ~(и)рáть нос be haughty, turn up one's nose.
зáдний [15] back, hind(er); reverse [(*gear*).]
задóлго (до P) long before.
зад|олжáть F [1] *pf.* run into debt; owe (*money*); **~óлженность** *f* [8] debts *pl.*, indebtedness.
зáдом backward(s); *cf.* зад.
задóр *m* [1] fervo(u)r; quick temper;

provocative tone *or* behavio(u)r; **~ный** [14; -рен, -рна] fervent; provoking, teasing; frolicsome.
задрáть *s.* задирáть.
зад|увáть [1], ⟨~ýть⟩ [18] blow out; F begin to blow; *impf.* blow (in).
задý|мать *s.* ~мывать; **~мчивый** [14 *sh.*] thoughtful, pensive; **~мывать** [1], ⟨~мать⟩ conceive; resolve, decide; plan, intend; **-ся** think (about, of о П); reflect, meditate (on над Т); begin to think, (be) engross(ed, lost) in thought(s); hesitate; **~ть** *s.* ~вáть.
задушéвный [14] heart-felt, warm-hearted, affectionate; intimate, in(ner)most.
зад|ыхáться [1], ⟨~охнýться⟩ [21] gasp, pant; choke (*a. fig.*, with от Р).
заéз|дить F [15] *pf.* fatigue, exhaust; **~жáть** [1], ⟨заéхать⟩ [-éду, -éдешь; -езжáй!] call on (*on the way*), drive, go *or* come (to [see, *etc.*] к Д *or* into в В); pick up, fetch (за Т); get; **~жий** [17] visitant.
заём *m* [1; зáйма] loan.
за|éхать *s.* ~езжáть; **~жáть** *s.* ~жимáть; **~жéчь** *s.* ~жигáть.
заж|ивáть [1], ⟨~ить⟩ [-ивý, -вёшь; зáжил, -á, -о] **1.** heal (up); close, skin (over); **2.** *pf.* begin to [live.]
зáживо alive.
зажигá|лка *f* [5; *g/pl.*: -лок] (cigarette) lighter; **~ние** *n* [12] lighting; ignition; **~тельный** [14] incendiary (*bomb, & fig.*); **~ть** [1], ⟨зажéчь⟩ [26 г/ж: -жгý, -жжёшь; *cf.* жечь] light, kindle (*a. fig.*); (*match a.*) strike; turn on (*light*); **-ся** light (up), kindle.
зажим *m* [1] ⊕ clamp; *fig.* suppression; **~áть** [1], ⟨зажáть⟩ [-жмý, -жмёшь; -жáтый] press, squeeze; clutch; *fig.* F (sup)press; stop (*mouth*), hold (*nose*), close (*ears*).
зажи|точный [14; -чен, -чна] prosperous; **~точность** *f* [8] prosperity; **~ть** *s.* ~вáть.
заздрáвный [14] (to s.b.'s) health.
зазевáться F [1] gape (at на В); be (-come) heedless, absent(-minded).
зазем|лéние *n* [12], **~лять** [28], ⟨~лить⟩ [13] ⚡ ground, *Brt.* earth.
зазна|вáться F [5], ⟨~ться⟩ [1] be (-come) presumptuous, put on airs.
заз|óрный †, P [14; -рен, -рна] shameful, scandalous; **~рéние** *n* [12]: без ~рéния (сóвести) without remorse *or* shame.
зазýбр|ивать [1] *s.* зубрить; **~ина** [*f* [5] notch.]
заигрывать F [1], (с Т) flirt, coquet (with), make advances (to); ingratiate o.s. (with).
заик|а *m/f* [5] stutterer; **~áние** *n* [12] stutter; stammer; **~áться** [1], *once* ⟨~нýться⟩ [20] stutter; stammer; F (give a) hint (at о П), suggest, mention; stir; *pf.* stop short.
заимствова|ние *n* [12] borrowing, taking; loan word (*a.* ~нное слóво); **~ть** [7] (*im*)*pf.*, *a.* ⟨по-⟩ borrow, take (over).
заиндевелый [14] frosty.
заинтересóв|ывать(ся) [1], ⟨~áть (-ся)⟩ [7] (be[come]) interest(ed in Т), rouse a p.'s interest (in в П); я ~ан(а) I am interested (in в П).
заискивать [1] ingratiate o.s. (with [у Р).]
зайти *s.* заходить.
зáйчик *m* [1] *dim. of* заяц; F speck(le).
закабал|ять [28], ⟨~ить⟩ [13] enslave.
закавкáзский [16] Transcaucasian.
закадычный F [14] bosom (*friend*).
закáз *m* [1] order; дать ~ (на В/Д) ✝ place an order (for ... with); **~áть** *s.* ~ывать; на ~ = **~нóй** [14] made to order; ~нóй лес (p)reserve; ~нóе (письмó) *n* registered (letter); **~чик** *m* [1] customer; **~ывать** [1], ⟨~áть⟩ [3] order (o.s. себé); † forbid.
закáл *m* [1], **~ка** *f* [5] ⊕ tempering; *fig.* hardening; endurance, hardiness; breed, kind; **~ять** [28], ⟨~ить⟩ [13] ⊕ temper; *fig.* harden; ~ённый tempered (*metal*); *fig.* hardened, tried, experienced.
зак|áлывать [1], ⟨~олóть⟩ [17] kill, slaughter; stab; pin (up); у меня ~олóло в бокý I have a stitch in the side; **~áнчивать** [1], ⟨~óнчить⟩ [16] finish, conclude; **~áпывать** [1], ⟨~опáть⟩ [1] bury; fill up.
закáт *m* [1] sunset; *fig.* decline; end; **~ывать** [1] **1.** ⟨~áть⟩ [1] roll up; **2.** ⟨~ить⟩ [15] roll (into, under, *etc.* в, под В); turn up (*eyes*); **-ся** roll; set (*sun, etc.*); *fig.* end; F burst (out laughing *or* into tears).
заквá|ска *f* [5] ferment; leaven; *fig.* F breed; **~шивать** [1], ⟨~сить⟩ [15] sour.
заки|дывать [1] **1.** ⟨~дать⟩ [1] F fill up, cover; *fig.* ply, assail, pelt (with Т); **2.** ⟨~нуть⟩ [20] throw (in [-to], on, over, behind, *etc.* в, на, за ... В; *a.* out [*net*], back [*head*]); fling, (*a. fig.*) cast.
зак|ипáть [1], ⟨~ипéть⟩ [10; -пит] begin to boil; *cf.* кипéть; **~исáть** [1], ⟨~снуть⟩ [21] turn sour.
заклáд *m* [1] † = залóг; *s. a.* биться; **~ка** *f* [5; *g/pl.*: -док] laying; walling (up); harnessing, putting to; bookmark; **~нóй** [14] pawn...; ~нáя mortgage (bond); **~чик** *m* [1] pawner; pawnbroker; **~ывать** [1], ⟨заложить⟩ [16] put (*a.* in, *etc.*), lay (*a.* out [*garden*], the foundation [stone] of, found), place; F mislay; heap, pile (with Т); wall up; pawn, pledge; harness, put (*horse[s]*) to, get ready (*carriage*); mark, put in (*bookmark*); *impers.* F obstruct (*hearing, nose*), press (*breast*).

закл|ёвывать [1], ‹**~ева́ть**› [6 *е.*; -клюю́, -юёшь] peck to death *or* wound (badly) (by pecking); F wreck, ruin; **~е́ивать** [1], ‹**~е́ить**› [13] glue *or* paste up (over); **~ёпка** *f* [5; *g/pl.*: -пок], **~ёпывать**, ‹**~епа́ть**› [1] rivet.

заклина́|ние *n* [12] conjuration, incantation; exorcism; **~тель** *m* [4] conjurer, exorcist; (*snake*) charmer; **~ть** [1] conjure, adjure.

заключ|а́ть [1], ‹**~и́ть**› [16 *е.*; -чу́, -чи́шь; -чённый] enclose, put; confine, imprison; conclude (= finish, with T; = infer, from из P, по Д — что; *v/t.*: *treaty*, [= make] *peace, etc.*); *impf.* (*a.* в себе́) contain; **~а́ться** [1] consist (in в П); end (with T); **~е́ние** *n* [12[confinement, imprisonment (*a.* тюре́мное); conclusion; **~ённый** [14] prisoner; **~и́тельный** [14] final, concluding.

закля́тый [14] implacable; sworn.

зако́в|ывать [1], ‹**~а́ть**› [7 *е.*; -кую́, куёшь] put in (irons), chain; *fig.* freeze; prick (*horse*).

закол|а́чивать F [1], ‹**~оти́ть**› [15] drive in; nail up; board up; *fig.* beat to death; thrash; **~до́вывать** [1], ‹**~дова́ть**› [7] enchant; bewitch, charm; **~до́ванный** круг *m* vicious circle; **~оти́ть** *s.* **~а́чивать**; **~о́ть** *s.* зака́лывать.

зако́н *m* [1] law; rule; **~** бо́жий (God's) Law; religion (*form. school subject*); объяви́ть вне **~а** outlaw; по (вопреки́) **~у** according (contrary) to law; охраня́емый **~ом** †/⚖ registered; **~ность** *f* [8] legality; law; **~ный** [14; -о́нен, -о́нна] legal, lawful, legitimate.

законо|ве́д *m* [1] jurist, jurisprudent; **~да́тель** *m* [4] legislator; **~да́тельный** [14] legislative; **~да́тельство** *n* [9] legislation; **~ме́рность** *f* [8] regularity; **~ме́рный** [14; -рен, -рна] regular; **~положе́ние** *n* [12] regulation(s); **~прое́кт** *m* [1] bill, draft.

зако́|нчить *s.* зака́нчивать; **~па́ть** *s.* зака́пывать; **~пте́лый** [14] smoky; **~рене́лый** [14] deep-rooted, inveterate,in grained; **~рю́чка** F *f* [5; *g/pl.*: -чек] flourish; trick, ruse; hitch; **~сне́лый** [14] = **~рене́лый**; **~у́лок** *m* [1; -лка] alleyway, (*Brt.*) (narrow) lane; nook; **~чене́лый** [14] (be)numb(ed), stiff.

закра́|дываться [1], ‹**~сться**› [25; *pt. st.*] creep in; **~шивать** [1], ‹**~сить**› [15] paint over.

закреп|ле́ние *n* [12] fastening; strengthening; securing; (за T) assignment (*a.* ⚖); ⚔ fortification; **~ля́ть** [28], ‹**~и́ть**› [14 *е*; -плю́, -пи́шь; -плённый] fasten, (*a. phot.*) fix; strengthen, consolidate, fortify (*a.* ⚔); secure; assign (to за T, *a.* ⚖); ⚒ strut.

закрепо|ща́ть [1], ‹**~сти́ть**› [15 *е.*; -ощу́, -ости́шь; -ощённый] enslave; **~ще́ние** *n* [12] enslavement.

закро́йщи|к *m* [1], **~ца** *f* [5] cutter.

закругл|е́ние *n* [12] rounding (off); curve; **~я́ть** [28], ‹**~и́ть**› [13] round (off).

закру́|чивать [1], ‹**~ти́ть**› [15] turn (round, off, up); twist.

закр|ыва́ть [1], ‹**~ы́ть**› [22] shut, close; lock (up); cover, hide; turn off (*tap*); **~ыва́ть** глаза́ (на B) shut one's eyes (to); **~ы́тие** *n* [12] closing, close; **~ы́ть** *s.* **~ыва́ть**; **~ы́тый** [14] closed; secret; boarding (*school*); high-necked (*dress*); в **~ы́**том помеще́нии indoor(s).

закули́сный [14] (lying *or* passing) behind the scenes; secret.

закуп|а́ть [1], ‹**~и́ть**› [14] buy (*a.* in), purchase; **~́ка** *f* [5; *g/pl.*: -пок] purchase.

заку́пор|ивать [1], ‹**~ить**› [13] cork (up), (*cask*) bung (up); **~ка** *f* [5; *g/pl.*: -рок] corking; ⚕ embolism; constipation.

заку́пщик [1] purchasing agent, buyer.

заку́р|ивать [1], ‹**~и́ть**› [13; -урю́, -у́ришь] light (*cigar, etc.*), begin to smoke; F (blacken with) smoke; **~и́**(те)! have a cigar(ette)!

заку́с|ка *f* [5; *g/pl.*: -сок] snack, lunch; hors d'oeuvres; на **~ку** *a.* for the last bit; **~о́чная** *f* [14] lunchroom, snackbar; **~ывать** [1], ‹**~и́ть**› [15] bite (*a. one's lip*[*s*]); take *or* have a snack, lunch; eat (s.th. [with, after a drink] T); **~и́ть** язы́к stop short, hold one's tongue.

заку́т|ывать, ‹**~ать**› [1] wrap up.

за́л *m* [1], † **~а** *f* [5] hall; room.

зал|ега́ние *n* [12] *geol.* deposit(ion); **~ега́ть** [1], ‹**~е́чь**› [26; -ля́гу, -ля́жешь] lie (down); hide; *fig.* root; ⚕ be obstructed (with phlegm).

заледене́лый [14] icy; numb.

зал|ежа́лый [14] stale, spoiled (by long storage); **~ежа́лый** това́р *m* drug; **~ёживаться** [1], ‹**~ежа́ться**› [4 *е.*; -жу́сь, -жи́шься] lie (too) long (*a. goods, & spoil thus*), stale; **~́ежь** *f* [8] *geol.* deposit; ⚘ fallow.

зал|еза́ть [1], ‹**~е́зть**› [24 *st.*] climb up, in(to), *etc.*; hide; steal *or* get in(to); **~епля́ть** [28], ‹**~епи́ть**› [14] stop, close; glue *or* paste up; stick over; **~ета́ть** [1], ‹**~ете́ть**› [11] fly in(to), up, far off, beyond; come, get; **~ётный** [14] stray(ing); migratory (*bird*); F visitant.

зале́ч|ивать [1], ‹**~и́ть**› [16] heal; F cure to death; **~ь** *s.* **~ега́ть**.

зал|и́в *m* [1] gulf, bay; **~ива́ть** [1], ‹**~и́ть**› [-лью́, -льёшь; за́ли́л, -а́, -о; за́ли́тый] (T) flood, overflow; pour (all) over, cover; fill; extinguish; **-ся** break into *or* shed (*tears* слеза́ми), burst out (laughing сме́хом); trill, warble, roll, quaver;

~ивно́й [14] floodable, flooded; jellied; resonant; **~и́ть** *s.* ~ива́ть.
зал|о́г *m* [1] pledge (*a. fig.*); pawn; security; *gr.* voice; дать в ~о́г pawn, pledge; **~ожи́ть** *s.* закла́дывать; **~о́жник** *m* [1], **~о́жница** *f* [5] hostage.
залп *m* [1] volley; ~ом F (*drink*) at one draught; (*smoke, etc.*) at a stretch; (*read*) at one sitting; blurt out.
зама́|зка *f* [5] putty; **~зывать** [1], ⟨**~зать**⟩ [3] smear, soil; paint over; putty; F *fig.* veil, hush up; **~лчивать** F [1], ⟨замолча́ть⟩ [4 *e.*; -чу́, -чи́шь] conceal, keep secret; **~нивать** [1], ⟨**~ани́ть**⟩ [13; -маню́, -ма́нишь] lure, decoy, entice; **~нчивый** [14 *sh.*] alluring, tempting; **~хиваться** [1], *once* ⟨**~хну́ться**⟩ [20] lift one's arm (*etc.* against Т/на В), threaten (with); **~шка** F *f* [5; *g/pl.*: -шек] habit, manner.
замедл|е́ние *n* [12] delay; **~я́ть** [28], ⟨**~ить**⟩ [13] slow down, reduce; delay, retard (*a.* с Т); не ~я́ть с (Т) (do, *etc.*) soon.
заме́|на *f* [5] substitution (of/for Т/Р), replacement (by Т); ⚖ commutation; substitute; **~ни́мый** [14 *sh.*] replaceable, exchangeable; **~ни́тель** *m* [4] substitute; **~ня́ть** [28], ⟨**~ни́ть**⟩ [13; -меню́, -ме́нишь; -менённый] replace (by Т), substitute (p., th. for Т/В); ⚖ commute (for, into); (И/В) (be) follow(ed).
замере́ть *s.* замира́ть.
замерза́|ние *n* [12] freezing; то́чка ~ния freezing point; **~ть** [1], ⟨замёрзнуть⟩ [21] freeze, congeal; be frozen (to death, *a.* F = feel very cold).
за́мертво (as if) dead, unconscious.
замести́ *s.* замета́ть.
замести́|тель *m* [4] deputy, assistant, vice-...; **~ть** *s.* замеща́ть.
заме|та́ть [1], ⟨**~сти́**⟩ [25 -т-: -мету́] sweep (up); drift, cover; block up (*roads*); wipe out (*tracks*).
заме́|тить *s.* ~ча́ть; **~тка** *f* [5; *g/pl.*: -ток] mark; note; paragraph, (brief) article, item; **~тный** [14; -тен, -тна] noticeable, perceptible; marked, remarkable; ~тно *a.* one (it) can (be) see(n), notice(d); **~ча́ние** *n* [12] remark, observation; *pl.* criticism; reproof, rebuke; досто́йный ~ча́ния worthy of notice; **~ча́тельный** [14; -лен, -льна] remarkable, outstanding; wonderful; noted (for Т); **~ча́ть** [1], ⟨**~тить**⟩ [15] notice; mark; observe, remark; reprove.
замеша́тельств|о *n* [9] confusion, embarrassment; в ~е confused, disconcerted, embarrassed.
зам|е́шивать, ⟨**~еша́ть**⟩ [1] involve, entangle; ~е́шан(а) в (П) *a.* mixed up with; (-ся be) mingle(d) in, with (в В *or* П, ме́жду Т); supervene; **~е́шкаться** F [1] *pf.* be delayed, tarry; **~еща́ть** [1], ⟨**~ести́ть**⟩ [15 *e.*; -щу́, -ести́шь; -ещённый] replace; substitute; act for, deputize; fill (*vacancy*); **~еще́ние** *n* [12] substitution (*a.* ⚗, ♏); replacement; deputizing; filling.
зам|ина́ть F [1], ⟨**~я́ть**⟩ [-мну́, -мнёшь; -мя́тый] crumple; smother, hush up; **-ся** falter, halt, stick, be(come) confused, stop short; flag; **~и́нка** *f* [5; *g/pl.*: -нок] halt, hitch; **~ира́ть** [1], ⟨**~ере́ть**⟩ [12; за́мер, -рла́, -о] be(come) *or* stand stockstill, transfixed (with от Р); stop; fade, die away; у меня́ се́рдце ~ерло my heart stood still.
за́мкнутый [14 *sh.*] closed; secluded; reserved; *cf.* замыка́ть.
за́м|ок[1] *m* [1; -мка] castle; **~о́к**[2] *m* [1; -мка́] lock; америка́нский ~о́к springlock; на ~ке́ *or* под ~ко́м under lock & key.
замо́л|вить [14] *pf.*: ~вить сло́в(е́чк)о F put in a word (for a p. за В, о П); **~ка́ть** [1], ⟨**~кнуть**⟩ [21] become silent, stop (speaking, *etc.*), cease, break off; die away *or* off; **~ча́ть** [4 *e.*; -чу́, -чи́шь] *pf.* **1.** *v/i.* *s.* ~ка́ть; **2.** *v/t.* *s.* зама́лчивать.
замор|а́живать [1], ⟨**~о́зить**⟩ [15] freeze, congeal; **'~озки** *m/pl.* [1] (light morning *or* night) frost; **~ский** [16] (from) oversea; foreign.
за́муж *s.* выдава́ть & выходи́ть; **~ем** married (to за Т, *of women*); **~ество** *n* [9] marriage (*of women*); **~ний** [15]: ~няя (же́нщина) married (woman).
замуро́в|ывать [1], ⟨**~а́ть**⟩ [7] immure; wall up.
заму́ч|ивать [1], ⟨**~ить**⟩ [16] torment to death; fatigue, exhaust.
за́мш|а *f* [5], **~евый** [14] chamois, suede.
замыка́|ние *n* [12]: коро́ткое ~ние ⚡ short circuit; **~ть** [1], ⟨замкну́ть⟩ [20] (en)close; † lock (up); **-ся** isolate o.s. (in в В *or* Т); -ся в себе́ become unsociable.
за́м|ысел *m* [1; -сла] intention, plan, design; conception; **~ы́слить** *s.* ~ышля́ть; **~ыслова́тый** [14 *sh.*] intricate, ingenious; fanciful; **~ышля́ть** [28], ⟨**~ы́слить**⟩ [15] plan, intend; resolve; conceive.
замя́ть(ся) *s.* замина́ть(ся).
за́нав|ес *m* [1] curtain (*a. thea.*); желе́зный ~ес *pol. a.* iron curtain; **~е́сить** *s.* ~е́шивать; **~е́ска** *f* [5; *g/pl.*: -сок] (*window*) curtain; **~е́шивать** [1], ⟨**~е́сить**⟩ [15] curtain.
зан|а́шивать [1], ⟨**~оси́ть**⟩ [15] soil; wear out; **~емо́чь** [26 г/ж: -могу́, -мо́жешь; *cf.* мочь[1]] *pf.* fall sick, *Brt.* ill; **~ести́** *s.* ~оси́ть 1.
занима́|ние *n* [12] borrowing; **~тельный** [14; -лен, -льна] interesting, entertaining, amusing; engaging, captivating; **~ть** [1], ⟨за-

ня́ть⟩ [займу́, -мёшь; за́нял, -á, -о; заня́вший; за́нятый (за́нят, -á, -о)] **1.** borrow (from у Р); **2.** (Т) occupy, (*a. time*) take; employ, busy; reserve, secure (*place*); interest, engross, absorb; entertain; ~ть дух у (Р) F take one's breath away; **-ся** [заня́лся́, -ла́сь] **1.** *v/t.* (& Т) occupy *or* busy o.s. (with); (*a. sport*) engage in; attend (to); learn, study; set about, begin to (read, *etc.*); **2.** *v/i.* blaze *or* flare up; break, dawn; *s. a.* заря́.

за́ново anew, afresh.

зано́|за *f* [5] splinter; **~зи́ть** [15 *e.*; -ожу́, -ози́шь] *pf.* run a splinter (into В).

зано́с *m* [1] drift; **~и́ть** [15] **1.** ⟨занести́⟩ [24 -с-: -су́, -сёшь] bring; carry; note down, enter, register; (*a. impers.*) (be) cast, get; drift, cover, block up; lift, raise (*arm, etc.*), set (*foot*); **2.** *pf., s.* зана́шивать; **~чивый** [14 *sh.*] arrogant, presumptuous.

заня́т|ие *n* [12] occupation, work, business; exercise (of Т); *pl.* F lessons, school, lecture(s) (to на В, at на П); ⚔ capture; **~ный** [14; тен, -тна] F = занима́тельный; **~ь** (**-ся**) *s.* занима́ть(ся); **~о́й** [14] busy; **'~ый** [14; за́нят, -á, -о] occupied, busy, engaged.

заодно́ conjointly; together; at one; F at the same time, besides, too.

заостр|я́ть [28], ⟨~и́ть⟩ [13] point, sharpen (*a. fig.*); **-ся** taper.

зао́чн|ик [1] student of a correspondence school, college, *etc.*; **~ый** [14] in a p.'s absence; behind one's back; ~ое обуче́ние *n* instruction by correspondence; ~ое реше́ние *n* ⚖ judg(e)ment by default.

за́пад *m* [1] west; ♀ the West, Occident; *cf.* восто́к; **~а́ть** [1], ⟨запа́сть⟩ [25; -па́л, -а] fall in, sink; impress (*a.* on на *or* в В); **~ник** *m* [1] *hist.* Westerner; **~ный** [14] west(ern, -erly); occidental.

западня́ *f* [6; *g/pl.*: -не́й] trap.

запа́|здывать, ⟨запозда́ть [1] be late (for на В), be tardy (with с Т); **~ивать** [1], ⟨~я́ть⟩ [28] solder (up); **~ко́вывать** [1], ⟨~кова́ть⟩ [7] pack (up); wrap up.

запа́л *m* [1] ⚔, ⚒ fuse; touchhole; (*horse*) heaves; F fit, passion; **~ьный** [14] touch...; ~ьный шнур *m* match; ~ьная свеча́ *f* ⚡ spark(ing) plug; **~ьчивый** [14 *sh.*] quick-tempered, irascible; provoking.

запа́с *m* [1] stock (*a. fig., of words, etc.* = store, fund), supply, (*a.* ⚔) reserve; в ~е in stock, on hand; про ~ in store *or* reserve; **~а́ть** [1], ⟨~ти́⟩ [24 -с-: -су́, -сёшь]; **-ся**, ⟨~ти́сь⟩ provide o.s. (with Т); **~ливый** [14 *sh.*] provident; **~но́й**, **~ный** [14] spare (*a.* ⊕); reserve... (*a.* ⚔; *su.* reservist), emergency..., side... (*a.* 🚂); **~ть** *s.* запада́ть.

за́п|ах *m* [1] smell, odo(u)r, scent; **~а́хивать** [1] **1.** ⟨~аха́ть⟩ [3] plow (*Brt.* plough) *or* turn up, in; **2.** ⟨~ахну́ть⟩ [20] lap (over), wrap (o.s. **-ся**) up (in в В, Т); F slam; **~а́шка** *f* [5] tillage; **~ая́ть** *s.* ~а́ивать.

запе|ва́ла *m/f* [5] precentor, (*a. fig.*) leader; **~ва́ть** [1] lead (*chorus*); **~ка́нка** *f* [5; *g/pl.*: -нок] baked pudding; spiced brandy; **~ка́ть** [1], ⟨'~чь⟩ [26] bake (in); **-ся** clot, coagulate (*blood*); crack (*lips*); **~ре́ть** *s.* запира́ть; **'~ть** *pf.* [-пою́, -поёшь; -пе́тый] start singing, strike up.

запеча́т|ать *s.* ~ывать; **~лева́ть** [1], ⟨~ле́ть⟩ [8] embody, render; impress (on в П), retain; mark, seal; **~ывать**, ⟨~ать⟩ [1] seal (up); close, glue up.

запе́чь *s.* запека́ть.

запи|ва́ть [1], ⟨'~ть⟩ [-пью́, -пьёшь; *cf.* пить] wash down (with Т), drink *or* take after, thereupon; F take to drink.

зап|ина́ться [1], ⟨~ну́ться⟩ [20] stumble (over, against за *or* о В), falter; pause, hesitate; **~и́нка** *f* [5]: без ~и́нки fluently, smoothly.

запира́|тельство *n* [9] disavowal, denial; **~ть** [1], ⟨запере́ть⟩ [12; за́пер, -ла́, -о; за́пертый (за́перт, -á, -о)] lock (up; *a.* ~ть на ключ, замо́к); ⚔, ⚓ blockade; **-ся** *impf.* F (в П) deny, disavow.

запис|а́ть *s.* '~ывать; **'~ка** *f* [5; *g/pl.*: -сок] note, slip; (brief) letter; memorandum, report; *pl.* notes, memoirs, reminiscences; transactions, proceedings; **~но́й** [14] note...; F inveterate; **'~ывать** [1], ⟨~а́ть⟩ [3] write down, note (down); record (*a. on tape, etc.*); enter, enrol(l), register; ⚖ transfer (to Д, на В, за Т), deed; **-ся** enrol(l), register, matriculate; subscribe (to; for в, на В), book; make an appointment (with a doctor к врачу́); **'~ь** *f* [8] entry; enrol(l)ment; registration; record (-ing); subscription; ⚖ deed.

запи́ть *s.* запива́ть.

запи́х|ивать F [1], ⟨~а́ть⟩ [1], *once* ⟨~ну́ть⟩ [20] push in; cram, stuff.

запла́ка|нный [14 *sh.*] tearful, in tears, tear-stained; **~ть** [3] *pf.* begin to cry.

запла́та [5] patch.

запле́сневелый [14] mo(u)ldy.

запле|та́ть [1], ⟨~сти́⟩ [25 -т-: -плету́, -тёшь] braid, plait; **-ся** F: но́ги ~та́ются totter, stagger; язы́к ~та́ется slur, mumble.

заплы|ва́ть [1], ⟨'~ть⟩ [23] swim (far), get (*by swimming*); (Т) be covered *or* closed (*a. by swelling, with fat*); swell, bloat, puff up.

запну́ться *s.* запина́ться.
запове́д|ник *m* [1] reserve; nursery; **~ный** [14] forbidden, reserved; secret; dear; intimate, inmost; **~овать** [7], ⟨**~ать**⟩ [1] command; **~ь** ('za-) *f* [8] *Bibl.* commandment.
запод|а́зривать († -о́зр-) [1], ⟨**~о́зрить**⟩ [13] suspect (of в П).
запозда́|лый [14] (be)late(d), tardy; out-of-date; **~ть** *s.* запа́здывать.
запо́|й *m* [3] hard drinking; пить **~ем** booze, tipple, be a hard drinker.
заполз|а́ть [1], ⟨**~ти́**⟩ [24] creep (in).
заполн|я́ть [28], ⟨**~ить**⟩ [13] fill (up); (*form*) fill out (*Brt.* in).
запом|ина́ть [1], ⟨**~нить**⟩ [13] remember, keep in mind; memorize; **-ся** (Д) remember, stick to one's memory.
за́понка *f* [5; *g/pl.*: -нок] cuff link; collar button (*Brt.* stud).
запо́р *m* [1] bar, bolt; lock; ⚕ constipation; на **~е** bolted.
запор|а́шивать [1], ⟨**~оши́ть**⟩ [16 *e.*; *3rd p. only*] powder *or* cover (with *snow* Т).
запоте́лый F [14] moist, sweaty.
заправ|и́ла *m* F [5] boss, chief; **~ля́ть** [28], ⟨**~ить**⟩ [14] put, tuck (in); (Т) dress, season (*meals* with); get ready; tank, refuel (*car, plane*); **~ка** *f* [5; *g/pl.*: -вок] refuel(l)ing; seasoning, condiment; **~очный** [14]: **~очная** коло́нка *f* filling (gas) station; **~ский** F [16] true, real.
запр|а́шивать [1], ⟨**~оси́ть**⟩ [15] ask, inquire (with/about у Р/о П); (*a.* Р) request; charge, ask (*excessive price*; с Р).
запре́|т *m* [1] = **~ще́ние**; **~ти́тельный** [14] prohibitive; **~ти́ть** *s.* **~ща́ть**; **~тный** [14] forbidden; **~тная** зо́на *f* prohibited area; **~ща́ть** [1], ⟨**~ти́ть**⟩ [15 *e.*; -ещу́, -ети́шь; -ещённый] forbid, prohibit, interdict; **~ще́ние** *n* [12] prohibition, interdiction.
заприхо́довать [7] *pf.* enter, book.
запроки́|дывать [1], ⟨**~нуть**⟩ [20] F throw back; P overturn.
запро́с *m* [1] inquiry (about о П, *esp.* ⚓ на В); *pl.* demands, requirements, claims, interests; F overcharge; ⚓ цена́ без **~а** fixed price; **~и́ть** *s.* запра́шивать; **'~то** plainly, unceremoniously.
запру́|да *f* [5] dam(ming); **~живать** [1], ⟨**~ди́ть**⟩ 1. [15 & 15 *e.*; -ужу́, -у́ди́шь] dam up; 2. [15 *e.*; -ужу́, -уди́шь] F jam, crowd.
запр|яга́ть [1], ⟨**~я́чь**⟩ [26 г/ж: -ягу́, -яжёшь; *cf.* напря́чь harness; put (*horse[s]*) to (в В); yoke (*oxen*); get ready (*carriage*); **~я́жка** *f* [5; *g/pl.*: -жек] harness(ing); team; **~я́тывать** F [1], ⟨**~я́тать**⟩ [3] hide, conceal; put (away); P confine; **~я́чь** *s.* запряга́ть.
запу́г|ивать, ⟨**~а́ть**⟩ [1] intimidate; **~анный** (in)timid(ated).
за́пус|к *m* [1] start; **~ка́ть** [1], ⟨**~ти́ть**⟩ [15] 1. neglect; disregard; let grow (*beard*); leave untilled (*land*); 2. ⊕ start, set going; fly (*kite*); F (*a.* Т / в В) fling, hurl (s. th. at); put, slip, thrust, drive (into); **~те́лый** [14] desolate; **~ти́ть** *s.* **~ка́ть**.
запу́|тывать, ⟨**~тать**⟩ [1] (-ся become, get) tangle(d, *etc.*); *fig.* confuse, perplex; complicate; F entangle, involve (in в В); **~танный** *a.* intricate; **~щенный** [14] deserted, desolate; neglected, uncared-for, unkempt.
запыха́ться F [1] pant.
запя́стье *n* [10] wrist; † bracelet.
запята́я *f* [14] comma; F hitch, fix.
зараб|а́тывать, ⟨**~о́тать**⟩ [1] earn; **-ся** F overwork o.s.; **'~отный** [14]: **'~отная** пла́та *f* wages *pl.*; salary; pay; **'~оток** *m* [1; -тка] earnings *pl.*; job; на **'~отки** in search of a job; ... to hire o.s. out.
зара|жа́ть [1], ⟨**~зи́ть**⟩ [15 *e.*; -ражу́, -рази́шь; ражённый] infect (*a. fig.*); **-ся** become infected (with Т), catch; **~же́ние** *n* [12] infection; **~же́ние** кро́ви blood poisoning.
зара́з F at once; at the same time.
зара́|за *f* [5] infection; contagion; pest; **~зи́тельный** [14; -лен, -льна] infectious; **~зи́ть** *s.* **~жа́ть**; **~зный** [14; -зен, -зна] infectious, contagious; infected.
зара́нее beforehand, in advance.
зара|ста́ть [1], ⟨**~сти́**⟩ [24; -сту́, -стёшь; *cf.* расти́] be overgrown.
за́рево *n* [9] blaze, glow, gleam.
заре́з *m* [1] slaughter; P ruin; до **~у** F (*need s.th.*) very badly.
заре|ка́ться [1], ⟨**~чься**⟩ [26] forswear, abjure; **~комендова́ть** [7] *pf.* recommend; **~комендова́ть** себя́ (Т) show o. s., prove.
заржа́вленный [14] rusty.
зарисо́вка *f* [5; *g/pl.*: -вок] drawing, sketch.
зарни́ца *f* [5] sheet (heat) lightning.
зар|оди́ть(ся) *s.* **~ожда́ть(ся)**; **~о́дыш** *m* [1] embryo, germ (*a. fig.*); в **~о́дыше** in the bud; **~ожда́ть** [1], ⟨**~оди́ть**⟩ [15 *e.*; -ожу́, -оди́шь; -ождённый] *fig.* engender; † bear; (-ся) arise; (be) conceive(d); **~ожде́ние** *n* [12] origin, rise; conception.
заро́к *m* [1] vow, pledge, promise.
зарони́ть [13; -роню́, -ро́нишь] *pf.* rouse; infuse; F drop, cast; **-ся** impress (on в В).
за́росль *f* [8] underbrush; thicket.
зар|пла́та *f* [5] F *s.* **~або́тный**.
заруб|а́ть [1], ⟨**~и́ть**⟩ [14] kill, cut down; notch, cut in; **~и́(те)** на носу́ (на лбу, в па́мяти)! mark it well!
зарубе́жный [14] foreign.

зар|уби́ть *s.* ~уба́ть; **~у́бка** *f* [5; *g/pl.:* -бок] incision, notch; **~убцева́ться** [7] *pf.* cicatrize.
заруч|а́ться [1], ⟨**~и́ться**⟩ [16 *e.*; -учу́сь, -учи́шься] (T) secure.
зар|ыва́ть [1], ⟨**~ы́ть**⟩ [22] bury.
зар|я́ *f* [6; *pl.*: зо́ри, зорь, заря́м & зо́рям] (у́тренняя) **~я́** (*a. fig.*) dawn (⚔ [*acc.* зо́рю] reveille); вече́рняя **~я́** evening glow; (⚔ tattoo, retreat); на **~е́** at dawn, daybreak (*a.* с **~ёй**); *fig.* at the earliest stage *or* beginning; от **~и́** до **~и́** from morning to night, all day (night); **~я́** занима́ется it dawns.
заря́|д *m* [1] charge (⚔, ⚡); shot; shell, cartridge; *fig.* store; **~ди́ть** *s.* **~жа́ть**; **~дка** *f* [5] ⚔ loading; ⚡ charge, -ging; *sport:* gymnastics *pl.*, bodily exercise; **~дный** [14] charge..., loading; **~дный я́щик** *m* ammunition wag(g)on; **~жа́ть** [1], ⟨**~ди́ть**⟩ [15 & 15 *e.*; -яжу́, -я́ди́шь; -я́женный & -яжённый] ⚔, *phot.* load; ⚡ charge; *fig.* inspire, imbue; *pf.* F (set in &) reiterate *or* go on & on.
заса́|да *f* [5] ambush; попа́сть в **~ду** be ambushed; **~живать** [1], ⟨**~ди́ть**⟩ [15] plant; F confine; compel to (*do s. th.*); **-ся** F, ⟨**засе́сть**⟩ [25; -ся́ду, -дешь; -се́л] sit down; settle, retire, stay; hide, lie in ambush; (за B) set *or* begin to, bury o.s. in (*work*).
заса́л|ивать [1] **1.** ⟨**~ить**⟩ [13] grease, smear; **2.** ⟨**засоли́ть**⟩ [13; -олю́, -о́ли́шь; -о́ленный] salt; corn (*meat*).
зас|а́ривать [1] & **засоря́ть** [28], ⟨**~ори́ть**⟩ [13] litter, soil; stop (up), obstruct (*a. fig.*); ⚕ constipate; be(come) weedy; **~ори́ть** глаз(а́) have (get) s.th. in(to) one's eye(s).
зас|а́сывать [1], ⟨**~оса́ть**⟩ [-су́, -сёшь; -о́санный] suck in; engulf, swallow up.
заса́харенный [14] candied, sugared.
за́свет|ло by daylight; **~и́ть(ся)** [13; -све́тится] *pf.* light (up).
засвиде́тельствовать [7] *pf.* testify; attest, authenticate.
засе́|в *m* [1] sowing; **~ва́ть** [1], ⟨**~ять**⟩ [27] sow.
заседа́|ние *n* [12] session (⚖, *parl.*); meeting; (*prp.*: in, at на П); **~тель** *m* [4] assessor; **~ть** [1] **1.** be in session; sit; meet; **2.** ⟨**засе́сть**⟩ [-ся́ду, -дешь; -се́л] stick.
засе|ка́ть [1], ⟨**~́чь**⟩ [26] **1.** [-се́к, -ла́; -сечённый] notch, mark; stop (*time with stop watch*); **2.** [-се́к, -се́кла; -се́ченный] flog to death.
засел|е́ние *n* [12] colonization; **~я́ть** [28], ⟨**~и́ть**⟩ [13] people, populate; occupy, inhabit.
засе́|сть *s.* заса́живаться & **~да́ть** 2.; **~чь** *s.* **~ка́ть**; **~ять** *s.* **~ва́ть**.
засѝ|живать [1], ⟨**~де́ть**⟩ [11] (**~женный** [му́хами]) flyblow(n); **-ся** sit, stay *or* live (too) long; sit up late.
заскору́злый [14] hardened.
засло́н|ка *f* [5; *g/pl.:* -нок] (stove, *etc.*) door, screen, trap; **~я́ть** [28], ⟨**~и́ть**⟩ [13] protect, screen; shut off, take away (*light*); repress, oust.
заслу́|га *f* [8] merit, desert; он получи́л по **~гам** (it) served him right; **~женный** [14] merited, (well-)deserved, just; meritorious, worthy; hono(u)red (*a. in Sov. titles*); **~живать** [1], ⟨**~жи́ть**⟩ [16] merit, deserve (*impf. a.* P); F earn.
заслу́ш|ивать, ⟨**~ать**⟩ [1] hear; **-ся** listen (to T, P) with delight.
засм|а́триваться [1], ⟨**~отре́ться**⟩ [9; -отрю́сь, -о́тришься] (на B) feast one's eyes *or* gloat ([up]on), look (at) with delight.
засну́ть *s.* засыпа́ть 2.
зас|о́в *m* [1] bar, bolt; **~о́вывать** [1], ⟨**~у́нуть**⟩ [20] put, slip, tuck; F mislay; **~оли́ть** *s.* **~а́ливать** 2.
засор|е́ние *n* [12] obstruction; ⚕ constipation; **~и́ть**, **~я́ть** *s.* заса́ривать.
засоса́ть *s.* заса́сывать.
засо́х|ший [17] dry, dried up; ♀ dead; **~нуть** *s.* засыха́ть.
за́спанный F [14] sleepy.
заста́|ва *f* [5] *hist.* (toll)gate, turnpike; ⚔ frontier post; outpost; **~ва́ть** [5], ⟨**~ть**⟩ [-а́ну, -а́нешь] find, meet with; surprise; take ...; **~вля́ть** [28], ⟨**~вить**⟩ [14] **1.** compel, force, make; **~вить ждать** keep waiting; **~вить замолча́ть** silence; **2.** (T) block (up); fill; **~ре́лый** [14] inveterate, chronic; **~ть** *s.* **~ва́ть**.
заст|ёгивать [1], ⟨**~егну́ть**⟩ [20; -ёгнутый] button (one's coat, *etc.*, *a.* **-ся**, up); buckle, clasp, hook (up); **~ёжка** *f* [5; *g/pl.:* -жек] clasp.
застекл|я́ть [28], ⟨**~и́ть**⟩ [13] glaze.
засте́н|ок *m* [1; -нка] torture chamber; **~чивый** [14 *sh.*] shy, timid.
засти|га́ть [1], ⟨**~́гнуть**⟩, ⟨**~́чь**⟩ [21 -г-: -и́гну, -и́гнешь; -и́г, -и́гла; -и́гнутый] surprise, catch; take...
заст|ила́ть [1], ⟨**~ла́ть**⟩ [-телю́, -те́лешь; за́стланный] cover; cloud.
засто́|й *m* [3] standstill, deadlock; stagnation; **~йный** [14] stagnant; chronic; ✝ unsalable; **~льный** [14] table...; drinking; **~я́ться** [-ою́сь, -ои́шься] *pf.* stand *or* stay too long; be(come) stagnant, stale.
застр|а́ивать [1], ⟨**~о́ить**⟩ [13] build on; build up, encumber; **~ахо́вывать** [1], ⟨**~ахова́ть**⟩ [7] insure; *fig.* safeguard; **~ева́ть** [1], ⟨**~я́ть**⟩ [-я́ну, -я́нешь] stick; F come to a standstill; be delayed; be lost; **~е́ливать** [1], ⟨**~ели́ть**⟩ [13; -елю́, -е́лишь; -е́ленный]

shoot, kill; **~ельщик** *m* [1] ⚔ skirmisher; *fig.* instigator; initiator; **~бить** *s.* **~а́ивать**; **~о́йка** *f* [5; *g/pl.*: -о́ек] building (on); **~я́ть** *s.* **~ева́ть**.
за́ступ *m* [1] spade.
заступ|а́ть [1], ⟨**~и́ть**⟩ [14] take (*s. b.'s place*), relieve; F start (*work* на В); **-ся** (за В) take s.b.'s side; protect; intercede for; **~ник** *m* [1] protector, patron; advocate; **~ница** *f* [5] protectress, patroness; **~ничество** *n* [9] intercession.
засты|ва́ть [1], ⟨**~ть**⟩ [-ы́ну, -ы́нешь] cool down, congeal; stiffen, be(come) *or* stand stockstill; (*a. blood*) freeze (F to death), chill.
засу́нуть *s.* засо́вывать.
за́суха *f* [5] drought.
засу́ч|ивать [1], ⟨**~и́ть**⟩ [16] turn *or* tuck up.
засу́ш|ивать [1], ⟨**~и́ть**⟩ [16] dry (up); F make arid; **~ливый** [14 *sh.*] droughty.
засчи́т|ывать, ⟨**~а́ть**⟩ [1] reckon, (ac)count; credit.
зас|ыпа́ть [1] **1.** ⟨**~ы́пать**⟩ [2] (Т) fill up; cover, drift; *fig.* heap, ply, overwhelm; F pour, strew; **2.** ⟨**~ну́ть**⟩ [20] fall asleep; **~ыха́ть** [1], ⟨**~о́хнуть**⟩ [21] dry up; wither.
зата́|ивать [1], ⟨**~и́ть**⟩ [13] conceal, hide; hold (*breath*); bear (*grudge*); **~ённый** *a.* secret.
зат|а́пливать [1] & **~опля́ть** [28], ⟨**~опи́ть**⟩ [14] **1.** light (make) a fire; **2.** flood; sink; **~а́птывать** [1], ⟨**~опта́ть**⟩ [3] trample, tread (down); **~а́скивать** [1] **1.** F, ⟨**~аска́ть**⟩ [1] wear out; **~а́сканный** worn, shabby; hackneyed; **2.** ⟨**~ащи́ть**⟩ [16] drag, pull (in, *etc.*); mislay.
затв|ердева́ть [1], ⟨**~ерде́ть**⟩ [8] harden; **~е́рживать** [1], ⟨**~ерди́ть**⟩ [15 *e.*; -ржу́, -рди́шь; -ржённый] memorize, learn (by heart).
затво́р *m* [1] bolt, bar; (*a.* ⚔) lock; gate; *phot.* shutter; **~я́ть** [28], ⟨**~и́ть**⟩ [13; -орю́, -о́ришь; -о́ренный] shut, close; **-ся** shut o.s. up.
зат|ева́ть F [1], ⟨**~е́ять**⟩ [27] start, undertake; conceive; resolve; **~е́йливый** [14 *sh.*] fanciful; ingenious, intricate; **~ека́ть** [1], ⟨**~е́чь**⟩ [26] flow (in, *etc.*); swell; be(come) numb, asleep (*limbs*), bloodshot (*eyes*).
зате́м then; for that purpose, that is why; ~ что́бы in order to (*or* that); ~ что † because.
затемн|е́ние *n* [12] ⚔ blackout; obscuration; **~я́ть** [28], ⟨**~и́ть**⟩ [13] darken, overshadow, (*a. fig.*) obscure; ⚔ black out.
затер|е́ть *s.* затира́ть; **~я́ть** F [28] *pf.* lose; **-ся** get *or* be lost; disappear; lie in the midst of.
зате́|чь *s.* затека́ть; **~я** *f* [6] plan, undertaking; invention, freak; diversion; trick; **~ять** *s.* **~ва́ть**.
зат|ира́ть [1], ⟨**~ере́ть**⟩ [12] wipe *or* blot out; jam, block (up); F wear out; efface, stunt; **~иха́ть** [1], ⟨**~и́хнуть**⟩ [21] become silent *or* quiet, stop (speaking, *etc.*); die away *or* off; calm down, abate; **~и́шье** *n* [10] lull, calm; shelter, quiet spot, nook.
заткну́ть *s.* затыка́ть.
затм|ева́ть [1], ⟨**~и́ть**⟩ [14 *e.*; *no 1st. p. sg.*; -ми́шь], **~е́ние** *n* [12] eclipse.
зато́ but (then, at the same time), instead, in return, on the other hand; therefore.
затова́ривание † *n* [12] glut.
затоп|и́ть, ~ля́ть *s.* зата́пливать; **~та́ть** *s.* зата́птывать.
зато́р *m* [1] jam, block, obstruction.
заточ|а́ть [1], ⟨**~и́ть**⟩ [16 *e.*; -чу́; -чи́шь; -чённый] confine, imprison; exile; **-е́ние** *n* [12] confinement, imprisonment; exile.
затра́|вливать [1], ⟨**~ви́ть**⟩ [14] bait (*a. fig.* F), course, chase down; **~гивать** [1], ⟨затро́нуть⟩ [20] touch (*a. fig.*, [up]on); affect; hurt.
затра́|та *f* [5] expense, expenditure; **~чивать** [1], ⟨**~тить**⟩ [15] spend.
затро́нуть *s.* затра́гивать.
затрудн|е́ние *n* [12] difficulty, trouble; embarrassment; в **~е́нии** *a.* at a loss; **~и́тельный** [14; -лен, -льна] difficult, hard, straitened; **~и́тельное положе́ние** *n* predicament; **~я́ть** [28], ⟨**~и́ть**⟩ [13] embarrass, (cause) trouble; render (more) difficult, inconvenience; aggravate, complicate; **-ся** *a.* be at a loss (for в П, Т).
зату|ма́нивать(ся) [1], ⟨**~ма́нить (-ся)**⟩ [13] fog; dim; **~ха́ть** F [1], ⟨**~хнуть**⟩ [21] die out; (*a. radio*) fade; **~шёвывать** [1], ⟨**~шева́ть**⟩ [6] shade; *fig.* F smooth over; **-ся** efface; **~ши́ть** F [16] *s.* туши́ть.
за́тхлый [14] musty, fusty.
зат|ыка́ть [1], ⟨**~кну́ть**⟩ [20] stop (up), (про́бкой) cork (up); F tuck, slip; **~ы́лок** *m* [1; -лка] back of the head; nape (of the neck).
заты́чка *f* F [5; *g/pl.*: -чек] bung, plug.
затя́|гивать [1], ⟨**~ну́ть**⟩ [19] tighten, draw tight; gird, lace, enclose, press; draw in, *etc.*; involve; cover; *impers.*: sink; close, skin (over); protract, delay; begin (to sing); **~жка** *f* [5; *g/pl.*: -жек] drawing tight; protraction; inhalation (*smoking*); **~жно́й** [14] long, lengthy, protracted.
зау|ны́вный [14; -вен, -вна] sad, mournful, melancholy; **~ря́дный** [14; -ден, -дна] common(place), ordinary, mediocre; **~се́ница** *f* [5] agnail.
зау́треня *f* [6] matins *pl.*
зау́ч|ивать [1], ⟨**~и́ть**⟩ [16] memorize.

захва́т *m* [1] seizure, capture; usurpation; **~ывать** [1], ‹**~и́ть**› [15] grasp, grip(e); take (along [with one, *a.* с собо́й]); seize, capture; usurp; absorb, captivate; F catch, snatch, take (away [*breath*], up, *etc.*); **~нический** [16] aggressive; **~чик** *m* [1] invader, aggressor; **~ывать** *s.* **~и́ть.**
захвора́ть F [1] *pf.* fall sick, ill.
захл|ёбываться [1], ‹**~ебну́ться**› [20] choke, stifle (with T, от P); *fig.* be beside o.s.; ⚔, ⊕ break down, stop; **~ёстывать** [1], ‹**~естну́ть**› [20; -хлёстнутый] lash (round, on [-to], together); swamp (*boat, etc.*); *fig.* seize; **~о́пывать(ся)** [1], ‹**~о́пнуть(ся)**› [20] slam, bang.
захо́д *m* [1] (со́лнца sun)set; call (*at a port*); ✈ approach; **~и́ть** [5], ‹зайти́› [зайду́, -дёшь; *g. pt.*: зайдя́; *cf.* идти́] go *or* come in *or* to (see, *etc.*), call *or* drop in (on, at к Д, в В); pick up, fetch (за Т); ⚓ call *or* touch at, enter; get, advance; pass, draw out; (*a.* ✈) approach; ⚔ outflank; turn, disappear, go behind (за В); *ast.* set; речь зашла́ о (П) (we, *etc.*) began (came) to (*or* had a) talk (about).
захолу́ст|ный [14] out-of-the-way, provincial, country...; rustic, boorish; **~ье** *n* [10] solitude, lonely *or* dreary spot (suburb).
захуда́лый [14] down & out; mean.
зацеп|ля́ть [28], ‹**~и́ть**› [14] (*a.* за В) catch, hook on, grapple; fasten; F & **-ся** *s.* задева́ть.
зачаро́в|ывать [1], ‹**~а́ть**› [7] charm.
зачасту́ю F often, frequently.
зача́|тие *n* [12] conception; **~ток** *m* [1; -тка] germ; *pl.* rudiments; **~точный** [14] rudimentary; **~ть** [-чну́, -чнёшь; зача́л, -а́, -о; зача́тый (зача́т, -а́, -о)] conceive.
заче́м why, wherefore, for what (*or* what for); **~-то** for some purpose (reason) (or other).
зач|ёркивать [1], ‹**~еркну́ть**› [20; -чёркнутый] strike out, obliterate; **~е́рпывать** [1], ‹**~ерпну́ть**› [20; -че́рпнутый] scoop, dip; **~ерстве́лый** [14] stale; *fig.* unfeeling; **~е́сть** *s.* **~и́тывать**[1]; **~ёсывать** [1], ‹**~еса́ть**› [3] comb (back); **~ёт** *m* [1] examination, test; F *educ.* credit.
зач|и́нщик *m* [1] instigator; **~исля́ть** [28], ‹**~и́слить**› [13] enrol(l), enlist, engage; † enter; **~и́тывать**[1] [1], ‹**~е́сть**› [25 -т-: -чту́, -чтёшь; *cf.* проче́сть] reckon, charge, account; *educ.* credit; **~и́тывать**[2], ‹**~ита́ть**› [1] read (to, aloud); F thumb, wear out, tear; not return (*borrowed book*); **-ся** be(come) absorbed (in T); read (too) long.
зачумлённый [14 *sh.*] infected with pestilence.
заш|ива́ть [1], ‹**~и́ть**› [-шью́, -шьёшь; *cf.* шить] sew up; **~нуро́вывать** [1], ‹**~нурова́ть**› [7] lace (up); **~то́панный** [14] darned.
защёлк|ивать [1], ‹**~нуть**› [20] snap, catch.
защем|ля́ть [28], ‹**~и́ть**› [14 *e.*; -емлю́, -еми́шь; -емлённый] squeeze (in), pinch, jam; *impers.* *fig.* oppress with grief.
защи́|та *f* [5] defense (*Brt.* -nce), protection, cover; maintenance; **~ти́ть** *s.* **~ща́ть**; **~тник** *m* [1] defender; protector; ⚖ advocate (*a. fig.*), counsel([l]or) for the defense; *sport*: back; **~тный** [14] protective; safety...; khaki ...; crash (*helmet*); **~ща́ть** [1], ‹**~ти́ть**› [15 *e.*; -ищу́, -ити́шь; -ищённый] (от P) defend (from, against); protect (from); vindicate, advocate, (*a. thesis*) maintain, support; *impf.* ⚖ defend, plead (for).
заяв|и́ть *s.* **~ля́ть**; **~ка** *f* [5; *g/pl.*: -вок] application (for на В); claim; request; **~ле́ние** *n* [12] declaration, statement; petition, application (for о П); **~ля́ть** [28], ‹**~и́ть**› [14] (*a.* о П) declare, announce, state; claim, present; enter, lodge; notify, inform; show, manifest.
зая́длый F [14] = завзя́тый.
за́я|ц *m* [1; за́йца] hare; F speck(le); P stowaway; **~чий** [18] hare('s)...; F cowardly; **~чья** губа́ *f* harelip.
зва́|ние *n* [12] rank; title; class; standing; **~ный** [14] invited; **~ный** обе́д (ве́чер) *m* dinner (evening) party; **~тельный** [14] *gr.* vocative (*case*); **~ть** [зову́, зовёшь; звал, -а́, -о; (’...)зва́нный (зван, -а́, -о)] **1.** ‹по-› call; invite (to [*a.* **~ть** в го́сти] к Д, на В); **2.** ‹на-› (Т) F (be) call(ed); как вас зову́т? what is your (first) name?; меня́ зову́т Петро́м *or* Пётр my name is Peter.
звезда́ [5; *pl.* звёзды, *etc. st.*] star (*a. fig.*); морска́я ~ *zo.* starfish.
звёзд|ный [14] star..., stellar; starry (*sky*); starlit (*night*); **~очка** *f* [5; *g/pl.*: -чек] starlet; *print.* asterisk.
звен|е́ть [9], ‹за-, про-› ring, jingle, clink; у меня́ **~и́т** в уша́х my ears ring.
звено́ *n* [9; *pl.*: зве́нья, -ьев] link; *fig.* part, branch; ✈ flight; squad.
звери́н|ец *m* [1; -нца] menagerie; **~ый** [14] animal; feral; *s.* зве́рский.
зверо|бо́й *m* [3] (*seal, walrus, etc.*) hunter; **~ло́в** *m* [1] trapper; hunter.
зве́р|ский [16] *s.* звери́ный; *fig.* brutal, atrocious; F beastly, awful, dog(-*tired*); **~ство** *n* [9] brutality; *pl.* atrocities; **~ь** *m* [4; *from g/pl. e.*] (wild) animal, beast; *fig.* brute.
звон *m* [1] ring, jingle, peal, chime; **~а́рь** *m* [4 *e.*] bell ringer, sexton; **~и́ть** [13], ‹по-› ring (*v/t.* в В), chime, peal; (Д) telephone, call up; **~́кий** [16; зво́нок, -нка́, -о; *comp.*:

звóнче] sonorous, clear; resonant; *gr.* voiced; hard (*cash*); **~óк** *m* [1; -нкá] bell; ring; the bell rings.
звук *m* [1] sound; tone (*a.* ♪); tune; **~овóй** [14] sound...; talking (*picture*); **~онепроницáемый** [14] soundproof; **~оподражáние** *n* [12] onomatopoeia; **~оподражáтельный** [14] onomatopoe(t)ic.
звуч|áние *n* [12] sounding; **~áть** [4 *e.*; *3rd p. only*], ⟨про-⟩ (re)sound; ring; clang; **∠ный** [14; -чен, -чнá, -о] sonorous, clear; resonant.
звя́к|ать [1], ⟨~нуть⟩ [20] clink.
зги: (ни) згú не видáть *or* не вúдно it is pitch-dark.
здáние *n* [12] building.
зде|сь here; local (*on letter*); **~сь!** present!; **∠шний** [15] local; я не ∠шний I am a stranger here.
здорóв|аться [1], ⟨по-⟩ (с T) greet *or* salute (o. a.), welcome; wish good morning, *etc.*; ~аться зá руку shake hands; ~о¹ P hi!, hello!; ′~о² P awfully; well done, dandy; **~ый** [14 *sh.*] healthy (*a. su.*), sound (*a. fig.*); wholesome, salubrious; P strong; in good health; бýдь(те) ~(ы)! good-by(e)!, good luck!; your health!; **~ье** *n* [10] health; кáк вáше ~ье? how are you?; за вáше ~ье! your health!, here's to you!; на ~ье! good luck (health)!; éшь(те) на ~ье! help yourself (-ves), please!
здрáв|ие *n* [12] † = здорóвье; ~ия желáю (-лáем) ⚔ good morning (*etc.*), sir!; **~ица** *f* [5] toast; **~ница** *f* [5] sanatorium; sanitarium; **~омы́слящий** [17] sane, sensible; **~оохранéние** *n* [12] public health service; **~ствовать** [7] be in good health; ~ствуй(те)! hello!, hi!, good morning! (*etc.*); how do you do?; да ~ствует ...! long live ...!; **~ый** [14 *sh.*] † = здорóвый; *fig.* sound, sane, sensible; ~ый смысл *m* common sense; в ~ом умé in one's senses; ~ и невредúм safe & sound.
зев *m* [1] throat, gullet, *anat.* pharynx; † jaws *pl.*; **~áка** F *m/f* [5] gaper; **~áть** [1], *once* ⟨~нýть⟩ [20] yawn; F gape (at на B); ~áть по сторонáм stand gaping around; F dawdle; не ~áй! look out!; **~óк** *m* [1; -вкá] yawn; **~óта** *f* [5] yawning.
зелен|éть [8], ⟨за-, по-⟩ grow, turn *or* be green; *impf.* (*a.* **-ся**) appear *or* show green; **~óй** [14] greengrocer's; **~овáтый** [14 *sh.*] greenish; **~щúк** *m* [1 *e.*] greengrocer.
зелёный [14; зéлен, -á, -о] green (*a. fig.*), verdant; ~ теáтр open-air stage; ~ юнéц F greenhorn.
зéл|ень *f* [8] verdure; green; potherbs, greens *pl.*; **~ье** *n* [10] herb; poison.
земéльный [14] land...; landed.
землевладé|лец *m* [1; -льца] landowner; **~ние** *n* [12] (крýпное great) landed property, (real) estate.
земледéл|ец *m* [1; -льца] farmer; **~ие** *n* [12] agriculture, farming; **~ьческий** [16] agricultural.
земле|кóп *m* [1] digger; *Brt.* navvy; **~мéр** *m* [1] (land) surveyor; **~трясéние** *n* [12] earthquake; **~черпáлка** [5; *g/pl.*: -лок] dredge.
землúстый [14 *sh.*] earthy; ashy.
земл|я́ *f* [6; *ac/sg.*: зéмлю; *pl.*: зéмли, земéль, зéмлям] earth (*as planet* ♁ Я); land; ground, soil; † country; на ∠ю to the ground; **~я́к** *m* [1 *e.*] (fellow) countryman; **~янúка** *f* [5] (wild) strawberry, -ries *pl.*; **~я́нка** *f* [5; *g/pl.*: -нок] (*a.* ⚔) dugout; (mud) hut; **~янóй** [14] earth(en), mud...; land...; ashy; ~янóй орéх *m* peanut; ~янáя грýша *f* (Jerusalem) artichoke.
земновóдный [14] amphibian.
земнóй [14] (of the) earth, terrestrial; earthly; *fig.* earthy.
зéм|ский [16] *hist.* State...; county-...; ⚔ Territorial (*Army*); ~ский собóр *m* diet; ~ский начáльник *m* sheriff, bailiff; **~ство** *n* [9] zemstvo, county council (*1864—1917*).
зенúт *m* [1] zenith (*a. fig.* = climax); **~ный** ⚔ [14] anti-aircraft...
зенúц|а *f* [5] † pupil, eye; берéчь как ~у óка cherish like the apple of one's eye.
зéркал|о *n* [9; *pl. e.*] looking glass, (*a. fig.*) mirror; **∠ьный** [14] *fig.* (dead-)smooth; plate (*glass*).
зерн|úстый [14 *sh.*] grainy, granular; **~ó** *n* [9; *pl.*: зёрна, зёрен, зёрнам] grain (*a. coll.*), corn, (*a. fig.*) seed; **~овóй** [14] grain...; *su. pl.* cereals.
зигзáг *m* [1], **~ообрáзный** [14; -зен, -зна] zigzag.
зим|á *f* [5; *ac/sg.*: зúму; *pl. st.*] winter (in [the] T; for the на B); **∠ний** [15] winter..., wintry; **~овáть** [7], ⟨за-, пере-⟩ winter; hibernate; **~óвка** *f* [5; *g/pl.*: -вок], **~óвье** *n* [10] wintering; hibernation; winter hut.
зия́|ние *n* [12] gaping; *ling.* hiatus; **~ть** [28] gape.
злак *m* [1] herb; grass; *pl.* ⚘ gramineous plants; хлéбные ~и *pl.* cereals.
злато... † *poet.* gold(en).
злить [13], ⟨обо-, разо-⟩ vex, anger *or* make angry, irritate; **~ся** be (-come) *or* feel angry (with на B); *fig.* rage.
зло *n* [9; *pl. gen.* зол *only*] evil.
злóб|а *f* [5] spite; rage; ~а дня topic of the day; **~ный** [14; -бен, -бна] spiteful, malicious; **~одневный** [14; -вен, -вна] topical, burning; **~ствовать** [7] *s.* злúться.
злов|éщий [17 *sh.*] ominous, ill-boding; **~óние** *n* [12] stench; **~óнный** [14; -óнен, óнна] stinking, fetid; **~рéдный** [14; -ден, -дна] malicious, malign(ant).

злоде́|й *m* [3] malefactor, evildoer; criminal; villain; **~йский** [16] vile, villainous, outrageous; malicious; **~йство** *n* [9], **~я́ние** *n* [12] misdeed, outrage, villainy, crime.
злой [14; зол, зла, зло] wicked, (*a. su. n*) evil; malicious, spiteful; angry (with на В); fierce; severe; bad; mordant; ⚕ malignant.
зло|ка́чественный [14 *sh.*] malignant; **~ключе́ние** *n* [12] misfortune; **~наме́ренный** [14 *sh.*] malevolent; **~нра́вный** [14; -вен, -вна] ill-natured; **~па́мятный** [14; -тен, -тна] vindictive; **~полу́чный** [14; -чен, -чна] unfortunate, ill-fated; **~ра́дный** [14; -ден, -дна] mischievous.
злосло́ви|е *n* [12], **~ть** [14] slander.
зло́ст|ный [14; -тен, -тна] malicious, spiteful; malevolent; **~ь** *f* [8] spite; rage.
зло|сча́стный [14; -тен, -тна] *s.* ~полу́чный.
злоумы́шленн|ик *m* [1] plotter; malefactor; **~ый** [14] malevolent.
злоупотреб|ле́ние *n* [12], **~ля́ть** [28], ⟨~и́ть⟩ [14 *e.*; -блю́, -би́шь] (Т) abuse; (make) excessive use.
зме|и́ный [14] snake('s), serpent('s), -tine; **~и́ться** [13] meander, wind (o.s.); **~й** *m* [3] dragon; (*a.* бума́жный ~й) kite; †, P = **~я́** *f* [6; *pl. st.:* зме́и, змей] snake, serpent (*a. fig.*).
знак *m* [1] sign, mark, token; symbol; omen; badge; signal; **∠и** *pl.* препина́ния punctuation marks; в ~ (Р) in (*or* as a) token (sign) of.
знако́м|ить [14], ⟨по-⟩ introduce (a p. to В/с Т); *a.* ⟨о-⟩) acquaint (with с Т); **-ся** (с Т) *p.*: meet, make the acquaintance of, (*a. th.*) become acquainted with; *th.:* familiarize o.s. with, go into; **~ство** *n* [9] acquaintance (-ces *pl.*); **~ый** [14 *sh.*] familiar, acquainted (with с Т); known; *su.* acquaintance; бу́дьте ~ы = ~ьтесь, ..., meet ...
знамена́тель *m* [4] denominator; **~ный** [14; -лен, -льна] memorable, remarkable; significant, suggestive; *gr.* notional.
знаме́н|ие *n* [12] †, *s.* знак; **~и́тость** *f* [8] fame, renown; *p.:* celebrity; **~и́тый** [14 *sh.*] famous, renowned, celebrated (by, for Т).
знам|ено́сец *m* [1; -сца] standard bearer; **∠я** *n* [13; *pl.:* -мёна, -мён] banner, flag; ⚔ standard; colo(u)rs.
зна́ни|е *n* [12] (*a. pl.* ~я) knowledge; со ~ем де́ла with skill *or* competence.
зна́т|ный [14; -тен, -тна́, -о] noble; distinguished, notable, eminent; **~о́к** *m* [1 *e.*] expert; connoisseur.
знать[1] **1.** [1] know; дать ~ (Д) let know; дать себя́ (о себе́) ~ make o.s. felt (send news); то и знай = то и де́ло; кто́ его́ зна́ет goodness knows; **-ся** F associate with (с Т); (get to) know; **2.** P apparently, probably; **~**[2] *f* [8] nobility, notables.
знач|е́ние *n* [12] meaning, sense; significance, importance (*vb.*: име́ть be of); **~и́тельный** [14; -лен, -льна] considerable; large; important; significant, suggestive; **∠ить** [16] mean, signify; matter; **∠ит** consequently, so; well (then); **-ся** be registered; *impers.* (it) say(s); **~о́к** *m* [1; -чка́] badge; sign.
зноби́т|ь: меня́ ~ I feel chilly.
зной *m* [3] heat, sultriness; **∠ный** [14; зно́ен, зно́йна] sultry, hot.
зоб *m* [1] crop, craw; ⚕ goiter, -tre.
зов *m* [1] call; F invitation.
зо́дчество *n* [9] architecture.
зол|а́ *f* [5] ashes *pl.*; **~о́вка** *f* [5; *g/pl.*: -вок] sister-in-law (*husband's sister*).
золоти́|стый [14 *sh.*] golden; **~ть** [15 *e.*; -очу́, -оти́шь], ⟨по-, вы́-⟩ gild.
зо́лот|о *n* [9] gold; на вес ~а worth its weight in gold; **~оиска́тель** *m* [4] gold digger; **~о́й** [14] gold(en) (*a. fig.*); dear; **~ы́х дел ма́стер** *m* † jewel(l)er.
золоту́|ха F *f* [5] scrofula; **~шный** F [14; -шен, -шна] scrofulous.
золочёный [14] gilt, gilded.
зо́н|а *f* [5] zone; **~а́льный** [14] zonal.
зонд *m* [1], **~и́ровать** [7] sound.
зонт, ∠ик *m* [1] umbrella; sunshade.
зоо́|лог *m* [1] zoölogist; **~логи́ческий** [16] zoölogical; **~ло́гия** *f* [7] zoölogy; **~па́рк, ~са́д** *m* [1] zoo (-logical garden).
зо́ркий [16; зо́рок, -рка́, -о; *comp.*: зо́рче] sharp-sighted (*a. fig.*); observant, watchful, vigilant.
зрачо́к *m* [1; -чка́] *anat.* pupil.
зре́л|ище *n* [11] sight; spectacle; show; **~ость** *f* [8] ripeness, maturity; **~ый** [14; зрел, -а́, -о] ripe, mature; deliberate.
зре́ни|е *n* [12] (eye)sight; по́ле ~я range of vision, eyeshot; *fig.* horizon; то́чка ~я point of view, standpoint, angle (*prp.*: с то́чки ~я = под угло́м ~я from ...).
зре́ть 1. [8], ⟨со-, вы́-⟩ ripen, mature; **2.** † [9], ⟨у-⟩ see; look.
зри́тель *m* [4] spectator, onlooker, looker-on; **~ный** [14] visual, optic; ~ный зал *m* hall, auditorium; ~ная труба́ spyglass.
зря F in vain, to no purpose, (all) for nothing; it's no good (use) ...ing.
зря́чий [17] seeing (*one that can see*).
зуб *m* [1; *from g/pl. e.*; ⊕ зу́бья, зу́бьев] tooth; ⊕ *a.* cog, dent; до ~о́в to the teeth; не по ~а́м too tough (*a. fig.*); сквозь ∠ы through clenched teeth; (*mutter*) indistinctly; име́ть *or* точи́ть ~ (на В) have a grudge against; **~а́стый** [14 *sh.*]

large-, sharp-toothed; *fig.* sharp--tongued; **~éц** *m* [1; -бца́] ⊕ = зуб; ⚔ battlement; **~и́ло** *n* [9] chisel; **~но́й** [14] tooth...; dental; ~но́й врач *m* dentist; ~на́я боль *f* toothache; **~очи́стка** *f* [5; *g/pl.*: -ток] toothpick.
зубр *m* [1] bison; *fig.* fossil.
зубр|ёжка F *f* [5] cramming; **~и́ть** 1. [13], ⟨за-⟩ notch; зазу́бренный jagged; 2. F [13; зубрю́, зу́бри́шь], ⟨вы́-, за-⟩ [зазу́бренный] cram, learn by rote.
зубча́тый [14] ⊕ cog(wheel)..., gear...; indented.
зуд *m* [1], **~е́ть** F [9] itch (*a. fig.*).
зы́б|кий [16; зы́бок, -бка́, -о; *comp.*: зы́бче] loose; shaky; unsteady, unstable; swelling, rippled; vague; **~у́чий** [17 *sh.*] = ~кий; **~ь** *f* [8] ripples *pl.*; swell; † wave.
зы́чный [14; -чен, -чна; *comp.*: -чне́е] ringing.
зя́б|кий [16; -бок, -бка́, -о] chilly; **~левый** [14] winter...; **~лик** *m* [1] chaffinch; **~нуть** [21], ⟨(пр)о-⟩ feel chilly; freeze; **~ь** *f* [8] winter tillage.
зять *m* [4; *pl. e.*: зятья́, -ьёв] son- *or* brother-in-law (*daughter's or sister's husband*).

И

и 1. *cj.* and; and then, and so; but; (even) though, much as; (that's) just (what ... is, *etc.*), (this) very *or* same; 2. *part.* oh; too, (n)either; even; и ... и ... both ... and ...
и́бо because, since, as.
и́ва *f* [5] willow.
Ива́н *m* [1] Ivan; John.
и́волга *f* [5] oriole.
игл|а́ *f* [5; *pl. st.*] needle (*a.* ⊕, ⚕, *min.*, ♀); thorn, prickle; quill, spine, bristle; **~и́стый** [14 *sh.*] prickly, thorny; spiny; crystalline.
Игна́|тий *m* [3], F **~т** [1] Ignatius.
игнори́ровать [7] (*im*)*pf.* ignore.
и́го *n* [8] *fig.* yoke.
иго́л|ка *f* [5; *g/pl.*: -лок] *s.* игла́; как на ~ках on tenterhooks; с ~(оч)ки brand-new, spick-and--span; **~ьный** [14] needle('s)...
иго́рный [14] gambling; card...
игра́ *f* [5; *pl. st.*] play; game (of в В); effervescense; sparkle; ~ слов play on words, pun; ~ не сто́ит свеч it isn't worth while *or* doesn't pay; **~лище** *n* [11] sport, plaything; **~льный** [14] playing (*card*); **~ть** [1], ⟨по-, сыгра́ть⟩ play (*sport, cards, chess, etc.*, в В; ♪ на П); gamble; (*storm, etc.*) rage; (*a. wine, etc.*) sparkle; *thea. a.* act.
игри́|вый [14 *sh.*] playful, sportive; equivocal, immodest; **~стый** [14 *sh.*] sparkling.
игро́к *m* [1 *e.*] player, gambler.
игру́шка *f* [5; *g/pl.*: -шек] toy, plaything.
игу́мен *m* [1] abbot, superior.
идеа́л *m* [1] ideal; **~и́зм** *m* [1] idealism; **~и́ст** *m* [1] idealist; **~исти́ческий** [16] idealistic; **~ьный** [14; -лен, -льна] ideal.
иде́йный [14; -е́ен, -е́йна] ideologic(al); ideal; high-principled.
идео́лог *m* [1] ideologist; **~и́ческий** [16] ideologic(al); **~ия** [7] ideology.
иде́я *f* [6] idea.
иди́лл|ия *f* [7] idyl(l); **~и́ческий** [16] idyllic.
идиома́т|ика *f* [5] stock of idioms; idiomology; **~и́ческий** [16] idiomatic(al).
идио́т *m* [1] idiot; **~и́зм** *m* [1] idiocy; **~ский** [16] idiotic.
и́дол *m* [1] idol; *contp.* blockhead.
идти́ [иду́, идёшь; шёл, шла; ше́дший; идя́, F и́дучи; ...дённый], ⟨пойти́⟩ [пойду́, -дёшь; пошёл, -шла́] (be) go(ing, *etc.*; *a. fig.*), walk; come; run, pass, drive, sail, fly, *etc.*; (за Т) follow, *a.* go for, fetch; leave; move (*a. chess*, Т), flow, drift, blow; (в, на В) enter (*school*), join (*army, etc.*), become; proceed, be in progress, take place; be on (*thea., film*); lead (*road; a. card* с Р); (на В) attack; spread (*rumo[u]r*); (be) receive(d); ✝ sell; ⊕ work; (в, на, под В) be used, spent (for); (в В) be sent to; ([к] Д) suit; (за В) marry; ~ в счёт count; ~ на вёслах row; ~ по отцу́ take after one's father; идёт! all right!, done!; пошёл (пошли́)! (let's) go!; де́ло (речь) идёт о (П) the question *or* matter is (whether), it is a question *or* matter (of); ... is at stake; ему́ идёт *or* пошёл шесто́й год (деся́ток) he is over *or* past five (fifty).
иезуи́т *m* [1] Jesuit (*a. fig.*).
иеро́глиф *m* [1] hieroglyph(ic).
Иерусали́м *m* [1] Jerusalem.
иждиве́н|ец *m* [1; -нца] dependent; **~ие** *n* [12]: на ~ии (Р) (*live*) at s.b's. expense, depend on.
из, ~о (Р) from, outof; of; for, through; with; in; by; что ж ~ э́того? what does that matter?
изба́ *f* [5; *pl. st.*] (peasant's) house, hut, cottage; room (*therein*); ~-чита́льня *f* [5/6] village reading room.
избав|и́тель *m* [4] rescuer, saver, deliverer; **~́ить** *s.* ~ля́ть; **~ле́ние** *n* [12] deliverance, rescue; **~ля́ть** [28], ⟨~́ить⟩ [14] (от Р from) deliver,

free; save; relieve; redeem; **-ся** (от P) escape, get rid of.
избало́ванный [14] spoilt.
избе|га́ть [1], ⟨**~жа́ть**⟩ [4; -егу́, -ежи́шь, -егу́т], ⟨**~гнуть**⟩ [21] (P) avoid, shun; escape, evade; **~жа́ние** *n* [12]: во ~жа́ние (P) (in order) to avoid.
изб|ива́ть [1], ⟨**~и́ть**⟩ [изобью́, -бьёшь; *cf.* бить] beat, thrash; † slaughter, extirpate; F damage; **~и́ение** *n* [12] beating; extermination, massacre.
избира́тель *m* [4] voter, elector; *pl. a.* electorate; constituency; **~ный** [14] electoral; election...; ~ный уча́сток *m* polling place; ~ное пра́во *n* franchise; ~ное собра́ние *n* caucus, *Brt.* electoral assembly.
изб|ира́ть [1], ⟨**~ра́ть**⟩ [-беру́, -рёшь; *cf.* брать] choose; elect (B/ в И *pl. or* /T), **~ранный** *a.* select(ed).
изби́|тый [14] *fig.* beaten (*path, etc*); hackneyed, trite; **~ть** *s.* ~ва́ть.
избра́|ние *n* [12] election; **~нник** *m* [1] the elect; **~ть** *s.* избира́ть.
избы́т|ок *m* [1; -тка] superfluity, surplus; abundance, plenty; в ~ке, с ~ком in plenty, plentiful(ly); **~очный** [14; -чен, -чна] superfluous, surplus...
изваяние *n* [12] statue; *s.* вая́ть.
изве́д|ывать, ⟨**~ать**⟩ [1] learn, (come to) know, see; experience.
и́звер|г *m* [1] monster; **~га́ть** [1], ⟨**~гнуть**⟩ [21] cast out (*a. fig.*); vomit; erupt; **~же́ние** *n* [12] ejection, eruption.
изверну́ться *s.* извора́чиваться.
извести́ *s.* изводи́ть.
изве́ст|ие *n* [12] news *sg.*; information; *pl. a.* bulletin; после́дние ~ия *rad.* news(cast); **~и́ть** *s.* извеща́ть.
извёстк|а *f* [5], **~о́вый** [14] lime.
изве́стн|ость *f* [8] notoriety; reputation, fame; по́льзоваться (мирово́й) ~остью be (world-)renowned *or* famous *or* well known; ста́вить (B) в ~ость bring to a p.'s notice (s. th. о П); **~ый** [14; -тен, -тна] known (for T; as как, P за B), familiar; well-known, renowned, famous; notorious; certain; ~ое (P ~о) де́ло of course; (мне) ~о it is known (I know); (ему́) э́то хорошо́ ~о it is a well-known fact (he is well aware of this) [′~ь *f* [8] lime.
извест|ня́к *m* [1 *e.*] limestone;
изве|ща́ть [1], ⟨**~сти́ть**⟩ [15 *e.*; -ещу́, -ести́шь; -ещённый] inform (of о П); notify; † *a.* advise; **~ще́ние** *n* [12] notification, information, notice; ⚖ summons, writ.
изви|ва́ться [1] wind, twist, wriggle, meander; **~лина** *f* [5] bend, curve; turn; **~листый** [14 *sh.*] winding, tortuous.
извин|е́ние *n* [12] pardon; apology, excuse; **~и́тельный** [14; -лен, -льна] pardonable; [*no sh.*] apologetic; **~я́ть** [28], ⟨**~и́ть**⟩ [13] excuse, pardon; forgive (a p. a th. Д/B); ~и́(те)! excuse me!, (I'm) sorry!; нет, (уж) ~и́(те)! oh no!, on no account!; **-ся** apologize (to/for пе́ред T/в П); beg to be excused (on account of T); ~я́юсь! P = ~и́(те)!
извл|ека́ть [1], ⟨**~е́чь**⟩ [26] take *or* draw out; extract (*a.* ℞); derive (*a. profit*); **~ече́ние** *n* [12] extract(ion).
извне́ from outside *or* without.
изводи́ть F [15], ⟨извести́⟩ [25] use up; exhaust, ruin. [cab.
изво́зчик *m* [1] cabman, cab driver;
изво́л|ить [13] please, deign; † want (*or just polite form of respect*); ~ь(те) + *inf.* (would you) please + *vb.*; *a. order, admonition:* (if you) please; *discontent*: how can one ...; F ~ь(те) all right, O. K.; please; *cf.* уго́дно.
извор|а́чиваться [1], ⟨изверну́ться⟩ [20] F dodge; shift; (try to) wriggle out; **~о́тливый** [14 *sh.*] nimble (*a. fig.*), elusive; shifty.
извра|ща́ть [1], ⟨**~ти́ть**⟩ [15 *e.*; -ащу́, -ати́шь; -ащённый] distort; pervert.
изги́б *m* [1] bend, curve, turn; *fig.* shade; **~а́ть** [1], ⟨изогну́ть⟩ [20] bend, curve, crook (*v/i.* **-ся**).
изгла́|живать [1], ⟨**~дить**⟩ [15] (**-ся** be[come]) efface(d), erase(d); smooth out.
изгна́|ние *n* [12] expulsion, banishment; exile; **~нник** *m* [1] exile; **~ть** *s.* изгоня́ть.
изголо́вье *n* [10] head (*bed*); bolster.
изг|оня́ть [28], ⟨**~на́ть**⟩ [-гоню́, -го́нишь; -гна́л, -ла́, -о; и́згнанный] drive out; oust; expel; exile, banish.
и́згородь *f* [8] fence; hedge(row).
изгот|а́вливать [1], **~овля́ть** [28], ⟨**~о́вить**⟩ [14] make, produce, manufacture; F prepare (*food*); **~овле́ние** *n* [12] production, manufacture; making.
изда|ва́ть [5], ⟨**~сть**⟩ [-да́м, -да́шь, *etc., cf.* дать; и́зданный (и́здан, -а́, -о)] publish; edit; (*order*) issue; (*law*) enact; (*sound*) utter, emit.
и́зда|вна at all times; from of old; long since; **~лека́**, **~лёка**, **~ли** from afar; afar off.
изда́|ние *n* [12] publication; edition; issue; **~тель** *m* [4] publisher; editor (*of material*); **~тельство** *n* [9] publishing house, publishers *pl.*; **~ть** *s.* издава́ть.
издева́т|ельство *n* [9] derision (of над T), scorn, scoff; **~ься** [1] jeer, sneer, mock (at над T); bully.
изде́лие *n* [12] make; product(ion), article; (needle)work; *pl. a.* goods.

издерж|ивать [1], ⟨~ать⟩ [4] spend; use up; **-ся** F spend much (*or* run short of) money; **~ки** *f/pl.* [5; *gen.*: -жек] expenses; ⚖ costs.
издыха́|ть [1] *s.* до́хнуть; **~ние** *n* [12] (last) breath *or* gasp.
изж|ива́ть [1], ⟨~и́ть⟩ [-живу́, -вёшь; -жи́тый, F -то́й (изжи́т, -а́, -о)] eliminate, extirpate; complete, end (*life, etc.*); endure; **~и́ть себя́** be(come) outdated, have had one's day; **~о́га** *f* [5] heartburn.
из-за (P) from behind; from; because of; over; for (the sake of); **~ чего́?** what for?; **~ э́того** therefore.
излага́ть [1], ⟨изложи́ть⟩ [16] state, set forth, expound, expose.
излеч|е́ние *n* [12] cure, (medical) treatment; recovery; **~ивать** [1], ⟨~и́ть⟩ [16] cure; **~и́мый** [14 *sh.*] curable.
изл|ива́ть [1], ⟨~и́ть⟩ [изолью́, -льёшь; *cf.* лить] shed; **~и́ть ду́шу, мы́сли** unbosom o.s.; *anger*: vent ... on (на В).
изли́ш|ек *m* [1; -шка] surplus, (*a.* **~ество** *n* [9]) excess, & = избы́ток; **~ний** [15; -шен, -шня, -не] superfluous, excessive; needless.
изл|ия́ние *n* [12] outpouring, effusion; **~и́ть** [28] = **~ива́ть**.
изловчи́ться F [16 *e.*; -чу́сь, -чи́шься] *pf.* contrive.
излож|е́ние *n* [12] exposition, statement; **~и́ть** *s.* излага́ть.
изло́манный [14] broken; angular; spoilt, deformed, unnatural.
излуч|а́ть [1], ⟨~и́ть⟩ [16 *e.*; -чу́, -чи́шь; -чённый] radiate.
излу́чина *f* [5] *s.* изги́б.
излю́бленный [14] favo(u)rite.
изме́н|а *f* [5] (Д to) treason; unfaithfulness; **~е́ние** *n* [12] change, alteration, modification; впредь до **~е́ния** until further notice; **~и́ть** *s.* **~я́ть**; **~ник** *m* [1] traitor; **~чивый** [14 *sh.*] changeable, variable; fickle; **~я́ть** [28], ⟨~и́ть⟩ [13; -ню́, -е́нишь] **1.** *v/t.* change (v/i. **-ся**), alter; modify; vary; **2.** *v/i.* (Д) betray; be(come) unfaithful (to); break, violate (*oath, etc.*); fail (*memory, etc.*), desert.
измер|е́ние *n* [12] measurement; ⩓ dimension; **~и́мый** [14 *sh.*] measurable; **~и́тель** *m* [4] meter, measure, measuring instrument; **~я́ть** [28], ⟨~ить⟩ [13] measure; fathom (*a. fig.*).
измождённый [14 *sh.*] exhausted.
измо́р: взять **~ом** ⚔ starve (out).
и́зморозь *f* [8] rime; mist.
и́зморось *f* [8] drizzle.
изму́чи|вать [1], ⟨~ть⟩ [16] (**-ся** be[come]) fatigue(d), exhaust(ed), wear (worn) out; *refl. a.* pine.
измышл|е́ние *n* [12] invention; **~я́ть** [28], ⟨измы́слить⟩ [13; -ы́шленный] invent; contrive, devise.
изна́нка *f* [5] back, inside; (*fabric*) wrong side; *fig.* seamy side.
изна́шивать [1], ⟨износи́ть⟩ [15] wear out (by use); *v/i.* **-ся**.
изне́женный [14] coddled; effeminate.
изнем|ога́ть [1], ⟨~о́чь⟩ [26 г/ж: -огу́, -о́жешь, -о́гут] be(come) exhausted *or* enervated; collapse; **~ожéние** *n* [12] exhaustion, weariness.
изно́с *m* [1] wear and tear; **~и́ть** *s.* изна́шивать.
изнур|е́ние *n* [12] exhaustion, fatigue; **~и́тельный** [14; -лен, -льна] wearisome, wasting; **~я́ть** [28], ⟨~и́ть⟩ [13] (**-ся** be[come]) fatigue(d), exhaust(ed), waste(d).
изнутри́ from within; within.
изны|ва́ть [1], ⟨~ть⟩ [22] pine (for по Д); *impf. a.* (от Р) die of, be wearied *or* bored to death.
изоби́л|ие *n* [12] abundance, plenty (of P, *a.* в П); **~овать** [7] abound (in T); **~ьный** [14; -лен, -льна] rich, abundant (in T).
изоблич|а́ть [1], ⟨~и́ть⟩ [16 *e.*; -чу́, -чи́шь; -чённый] convict (of в П); unmask; *impf.* reveal, show.
изобра|жа́ть [1], ⟨~зи́ть⟩ [15 *e.*; -ажу́, -ази́шь; -ажённый] represent (*a. impf.* + собо́ю), depict; describe; express; **~жа́ть из себя́** (B) F act, set up for; **~же́ние** *n* [12] representation; description; image, picture; **~зи́тельный** [14; -лен, -льна] graphic, descriptive; (*no sh.*) fine (*arts*).
изобре|сти́ *s.* **~та́ть**; **~та́тель** *m* [4] inventor; **~та́тельный** [14; -лен, -льна] inventive, resourceful; **~та́ть** [1], ⟨~сти́⟩ [25 -т-: -брету́, -тёшь] invent; **~те́ние** *n* [12] invention.
изогну́ть *s.* изгиба́ть.
изо́дранный [14] F = изо́рванный.
изол|и́ровать [7] (*im*)*pf.* isolate; ⚡ *a.* insulate; **~я́тор** *m* [1] ⚡ insulator; ⚕ isolation ward; cell *or* jail (for close solitary confinement); **~я́ция** *f* [7] isolation; ⚡ insulation.
изо́рванный [14] torn, tattered.
изощр|ённый [14] refined, subtle; **~я́ть** [28], ⟨~и́ть⟩ [13] (**-ся** become) refine(d), sharpen(ed); *refl. impf. a.* exert o.s., excel (in в П *or* T).
из-под (P) from under; from; from the vicinity of; буты́лка **~** молока́ milk bottle.
изразе́ц *m* [1; -зца́] (Dutch) tile.
Изра́иль *m* [4] Israel.
и́зредка occasionally; here & there.
изре́з|ывать [1], ⟨~ать⟩ [3] cut up.
изре|ка́ть [1], ⟨~чь⟩ pronounce; **~че́ние** *n* [12] aphorism, maxim.
изруб|а́ть [1], ⟨~и́ть⟩ [14] chop, mince; cut (up, down); saber (-bre).
изря́дный [14; -ден, -дна] (fairly) good *or* big, fair (*amount*).
изуве́р *m* [1] fanatic; monster.
изуве́ч|ивать [1], ⟨~ить⟩ [16] mutilate.

изум|и́тельный [14; -лен, -льна] amazing, wonderful; **~и́ть(ся)** *s.* ~ля́ть(ся); **~ле́ние** *n* [12] amazement; **~ля́ть** [28], ⟨~и́ть⟩ [14 *e*; -млю́, -ми́шь; -млённый] (-ся Д be) amaze(d), astonish(ed), surprise(d at, wonder).
изумру́д *m* [1] emerald.
изу́стный [14] oral.
изуч|а́ть [1], ⟨~и́ть⟩ [16] study, learn; familiarize o. s. with, master; scrutinize; **~е́ние** *n* [12] study.
изъе́з|дить [15] *pf.* travel (all) over, through; **~женный** [14] beaten; bumpy (*road*).
изъяв|и́тельный [14] *gr.* indicative; **~ля́ть** [28], ⟨~и́ть⟩ [14] express, show; (*consent*) give.
изъя́н *m* [1] defect; stain; loss.
изыма́ть [1], ⟨изъя́ть⟩ [изыму́, изы́мешь] withdraw; seize.
изыска́ние *n* [12] investigation, research; survey; ⚒ prospect.
изы́сканный [14 *sh.*] refined, elegant; choice, exquisite; far-fetched.
изы́ск|ивать [1], ⟨~а́ть⟩ [3] find.
изю́м *m* [1] *coll.* raisins *pl.*
изя́щн|ый [14; -щен, -щна] graceful, elegant, (*a.*, †, *arts*) fine; ~ое *n su.* the beautiful; ~ая литерату́ра *f* belles-lettres *pl.*
Иису́с *m* [1; *voc.*: -у́се] Jesus.
ик|а́ть [1], ⟨~ну́ть⟩ [20] hiccup.
ико́|на *f* [5] icon; **~та** *f* [5] hiccup.
икра́ *f* [5] (hard) roe, spawn; caviar; *mst. pl.* [*st.*] calf (*leg*).
ил *m* [1] silt.
и́ли or; or else; ~ ... ~ either ... or.
иллю́|зия *f* [7] illusion; **~мина́ция** *f* [7] illumination; **~миннова́ть** [7] (*im*)*pf.* illuminate; **~стра́ция** *f* [7] illustration; **~стри́ровать** [7] (*im*)*pf.* illustrate.
Ил|ья́ *m* [6], F *dim.* **~ю́ша** [5] Elias.
им. *abbr.*: и́мени, *s.* и́мя.
имби́рь *m* [4 *e.*] ginger.
име́ние *n* [12] estate.
имени́|ны *f*/*pl.* [5] name day; **~тельный** [14] *gr.* nominative; **~тый** [14 *sh.*] eminent, notable.
и́менно just, very (*adj.*), exactly, in particular; (*a.* а ~, и ~) namely, to wit, that is to say; (*a.* вот ~) F indeed.
именова́ть [7], ⟨на-⟩ call, name.
име́ть [8] have, possess; ~ де́ло с (Т) have to do with; ~ ме́сто take place; ~ в виду́ have in view, mean, intend; remember, bear in mind; -ся be at, in *or* on hand; (у Р) have; there is, are, *etc.*
иммигра́нт *m* [1] immigrant.
иммуните́т *m* [1] immunity.
импера́т|ор *m* [1] emperor; **~ри́ца** *f* [5] empress.
империали́|зм *m* [1] imperialism; **~ст** *m* [1] imperialist; **~сти́ческий** [16] imperialist(ic).
импе́рия *f* [7] empire.
и́мпорт *m* [1], **~и́ровать** [7] (*im*)*pf.* import.
импровизи́ровать [7] (*im*)*pf.* & ⟨сымпровизи́ровать⟩ improvise.
и́мпульс *m* [1] impulse.
иму́щ|ество *n* [9] property; belongings *pl.*; (не)дви́жимое ~ество ⚖ (im)movables *pl.*; **~ий** [17] well-to-do.
и́мя *n* [13] (*esp.* first, Christian) name (*a. fig.* & *gr.*; *parts of speech*: = *Lat.* nomen); и́мени: шко́ла им. Че́хова Chekhov school; и́менем, во ~; от и́мени (*all 3*) in the name of (P); на ~ addressed to, for; по и́мени named; in name (only); (*know*) by name.
ина́че differently; otherwise, (or) else; не ~, как just; та́к и́ли ~ one way or another, anyhow.
инвали́д *m* [1] invalid; ~ труда́ (войны́) disabled worker (veteran, *Brt.* ex-serviceman).
инвент|аризá́ция *f* [7] inventory, stock-taking; **~а́рь** *m* [4 *e.*] inventory; (живо́й live)stock; implements, fittings *pl.*
инд|е́ец *m* [1; -е́йца] (*Am.* Red) Indian; **~е́йка** *f* [5; *g*/*pl.*: -е́ек] turkey; **~е́йский** [16] (Red) Indian; ~е́йский пету́х *m* = ~ю́к; **~иа́нка** *f* [5; *g*/*pl.*: -нок] *fem. of* ~е́ец & ~и́ец.
индиви́д, **~уум** *m* [1] individual; **~уа́льный** [14; -лен, -льна] individual.
инди́|ец *m* [1; -и́йца] (East) Indian, Hindu; **~йский** [16] Indian (*a.* Ocean: ♀йский океа́н *m*), Hindu.
'Индия *f* [7] India.
Индо|кита́й *m* [3] Indo-China; **~не́зия** *f* [7] Indonesia; **~ста́н** *m* [1] Hindustan.
инду́с *m* [1], **~ка** *f* [5; *g*/*pl.*: -сок], **~ский** [16] Hindu.
индустриализ|а́ция *f* [7] industrialization (*Brt.* -sa-); **~(и́р)ова́ть** [7] (*im*)*pf.* industrialize (*Brt.* -se).
инд|устриа́льный [14] industrial; **~у́стрия** *f* [7] industry.
индю́к *m* [1 *e.*] turkey cock.
и́ней *m* [3] (white *or* hoar)frost.
ине́р|тный [14; -тен, -тна] inert; **~ция** *f* [7] inertia; по ~ции mechanically.
инжене́р *m* [1] engineer; **~-строи́тель** *m* [1/4] civil engineer; **~ный** [14] (*a.* ⚔ & ~ное де́ло *n*) engineering.
инициа́|лы *m*/*pl.* [1] initials; **~ти́ва** *f* [5] initiative; **~тор** *m* [1] initiator.
иногда́ sometimes, now and then.
иногоро́дний [15] nonresident, foreign.
инозе́м|ец *m* [1; -мца] foreigner; **~ный** [14] foreign.
ино́|й [14] (an)other, different; some, many a; ~й раз sometimes; не кто ~й (не что ~е), как ... nobody (nothing) else but ...

иносказа́тельный [14; -лен, -льна] allegorical.
иностра́н|ец *m* [1; -нца], **~ка** *f* [5; *g/pl.*: -нок] foreigner; **~ный** [14] foreign; *s. a.* министе́рство.
инста́нция *f* [7] ⚖ instance; *pl.* (official) channels; hierarchy.
инсти́нкт *m* [1] instinct; **~и́вный** [14; -вен, -вна] instinctive.
институ́т *m* [1] institute; (*a.* ⚖) institution; *form.* (girls') boarding school (**~ка** *f* [5; *g/pl.*: -ток] pupil *thereof*).
инструме́нт *m* [1] instrument.
инсцени́р|овать [7] (*im*)*pf.* stage, screen; *fig.* feign; **~о́вка** *f* [5; *g/pl.*: -вок] staging, *etc.*; direction; dramatization.
интегра́л *m* [1] integral; **~ьный** [14; *fig.* -лен, -льна] integral.
интеллектуа́льный [14; -лен, -льна] intellectual.
интеллиге́н|т *m* [1] intellectual; **~тность** *f* [8] intelligence; **~тный** [14; -тен, -тна] intelligent; intellectual; **~ция** *f* [7] intelligentsia, intellectuals *pl.*
интенда́нт *m* [1] ⚔ commissary; **~ство** *n* [9] commissariat.
интенси́вный (-tɛn-) [14; -вен, -вна] intense, (*a. econ.*) intensive.
интерва́л *m* [1] interval.
интерве́нция *f* [7] intervention.
интервью́ (-tɛr-) *n* [*indecl.*], **~и́ровать** (-tɛr-) [7] (*im*)*pf.* interview.
интере́с *m* [1] interest (in к Д; be of/to име́ть ~ для P; in the/of в ~ах P); F use; **~ный** [14; -сен, -сна] interesting; F handsome, attractive; **~ова́ть** [7], ‹за-› (**-ся** be[come]) interest(ed, take an interest in T).
интерна́т *m* [1] boarding school; hostel.
Интернациона́л *m* [1] International(e); **♀ьный** [14; -лен, -льна] international.
интерни́рова|ние (-tɛr-) *n* [12] internment; **~ть** (-tɛr-) [7] (*im*)*pf.* intern.
инти́мн|ость *f* [8] intimacy; **~ый** [14; -мен, -мна] intimate.
интри́г|а *f* [5] intrigue; **~а́н** *m* [1] intriguer; **~а́нка** *f* [5; *g/pl.*: -нок] intrigante; **~ова́ть** [7], ‹за-› intrigue.
интуити́вный [14; -вен, -вна] intuitive.
Интури́ст *m* [1] (*Sov.*) State bureau of foreign tourism.
инфе́кция *f* [7] infection.
инфля́ция *f* [7] inflation.
информ|а́ция *f* [7] information; **♀бюро́** *n* [*indecl.*] (Communist) Information Bureau, Cominform; **~и́ровать** [7] (*im*)*pf.* & ‹про-› inform.
и. о. = исполня́ющий обя́занности.
ипподро́м *m* [1] race track (course).
и пр(оч). *abbr.*: и про́чее, *s.* про́чий.
Ира́|к *m* [1] Iraq; **~н** *m* [1] Iran.
ири́дий *m* [3] iridium.
и́рис *m* [1] iris (♀, *anat.*).
ирла́нд|ец *m* [1; -дца] Irishman; **~ка** *f* [5; *g/pl.*: -док] Irishwoman; **~ский** [16] Irish (*a.* Sea: ♀ское мо́ре); **♀ия** *f* [7] Ireland; Eire.
ирон|изи́ровать [7] mock, sneer (at над T); **~и́ческий** [16] ironic(al), derisive; **∠ия** *f* [7] irony.
иск ⚖ *m* [1] suit, action.
иска|жа́ть [1], ‹~зи́ть› [15 *e.*; -ажу́, -ази́шь; -ажённый] distort, disfigure; **~же́ние** *n* [12] distortion.
иска́ть [3], ‹по-› (B) look for; (*mst.* P) seek; ⚖ sue (a p. for с P/B).
исключ|а́ть [1], ‹~и́ть› [16 *e.*; -чу́, -чи́шь; -чённый] exclude, leave out; expel; **~а́я** (P) except(ing); **~ено́** impossible; **~е́ние** *n* [12] exclusion; expulsion; exception (with the за T; as an в ви́де P); **~и́тельный** [14; -лен, -льна] exceptional; exclusive; extraordinary; F excellent; *adv. a.* solely, only; **~и́ть** *s.* **~а́ть**.
иско́мый [14] sought, looked for;
иск|они́ † = и́здавна; **~о́нный** [14] (ab)original, native; arch...
ископа́ем|ый [14] (*a. fig.* & *su. n*) fossil; mined; *pl. su.* minerals; поле́зные **~ые** treasures of the soil.
искорен|я́ть [28], ‹~и́ть› [13] extirpate.
и́скоса askance, asquint.
и́скра *f* [5] spark(le); spangle.
и́скренн|ий [15; -ренен, -ренна, -е & -о, -и & -ы] sincere, frank, candid; **~о** пре́данный Вам Sincerely (*or* Respectfully) yours; **~ость** *f* [8] sincerity, frankness.
искрив|ля́ть [28], ‹~и́ть› [14 *e.*; -влю́, -ви́шь; -влённый] (**-ся** become) bend (-t), crook(ed); distort(ed), disfigure(d).
искр|и́стый [14 *sh.*] sparkling; **∠и́ться** [13] sparkle, scintillate.
искуп|а́ть [1], ‹~и́ть› [14] (B) atone for, expiate; **~ле́ние** *n* [12] atonement, expiation.
иску́с *m* [1] trial (*fig.*); **~и́тель** *m* [4] tempter; **~и́ть** *s.* искуша́ть.
иску́с|ный [14; -сен, -сна] skil(l)ful, skilled; **~ственный** [14 *sh.*] artificial; false (*tooth, etc.*), imitation (*pearls, etc.*); **~ство** *n* [9] art; skill.
иску|ша́ть [1], † ‹~си́ть› [15 *e.*; -ушу́, -уси́шь] tempt; **~ше́ние** *n* [12] temptation; **~шённый** [14] tried; versed, (*a.* **~ённый** о́пытом) experienced.
исла́м *m* [1] Islam.
Исла́ндия *f* [7] Iceland.
испа́н|ец *m* [1; -нца], **~ка** *f* [5; *g/pl.*: -нок] Spaniard; **♀ия** *f* [7] Spain; **~ский** [16] Spanish.
испар|е́ние *n* [12] evaporation; *pl. a.* vapo(u)r(s); **~я́ть** [28], ‹~и́ть› [13] evaporate (*v/i.* **-ся**, *a. fig.*).
испе|пеля́ть [28], ‹~пели́ть› [13] burn to ashes; **~стря́ть** F [28],

⟨~стри́ть⟩ [13], **~щря́ть** [28], ⟨~щри́ть⟩ [13] mottle, speckle, variegate; stud; interlard.
испи́с|ывать [1], ⟨~а́ть⟩ [3] write (*sheet, etc.*), write upon (*on both sides, etc.*), fill (up, *book*); ~ан full of notes, *etc.*; F use up; **-ся** F write o.s. out; be(come) used up (by writing).
испито́й F [14] emaciated.
испове́д|ание *n* [12] confession; creed; ~ать [1] † = ~овать; **~ник** *m* [1] confessor; **~овать** [7] (*im*)*pf.* confess (*v/i.* **-ся,** to a p. пе́ред Т; s.th. в П); profess (*religion*); F interrogate; **~ь** (ˈis-) *f* [8] confession (*eccl.* [*prp.*: на В/П to/at] & *fig.*).
и́спод|воль F gradually; **~ло́бья** frowningly; **~тишка́** F on the quiet.
испоко́н: ~ ве́ку (веко́в) = и́здавна.
исполи́н *m* [1] giant; **~ский** [16] gigantic.
исполко́м *m* [1] (исполни́тельный комите́т) executive committee.
исполн|е́ние *n* [12] execution; fulfil(l)ment, performance; приводи́ть в ~е́ние = ~я́ть; **~и́мый** [14 *sh.*] realizable; practicable; **~и́тель** *m* [4] executor; *thea.*, ♪ performer; ⚖ (court) bailiff; **~и́тельный** [14] executive; [-лен, -льна] industrious; **~я́ть** [28], ⟨~ить⟩ [13] carry out, execute; fulfil(l), do (*duty*); hold, fill (*office, etc.*); keep (*promise*); *thea.*, ♪ perform; **-ся** come true; (*age*) be: ему́ ~илось пять лет he is five; (*period*) pass (since [с тех пор] как).
испо́льзова|ние *n* [12] use, utilization; **~ть** [7] (*im*)*pf.* use, utilize.
испо́р|тить *s.* по́ртить; **~ченный** [14 *sh.*] spoilt, broken; depraved.
исправ|до́м F *m* [1] (~и́тельный дом) reformatory, reform school; **~и́тельный** [14] correctional; *s.* ~дом; **~ле́ние** *n* [12] correction; improvement; reform; **~ля́ть** [28], ⟨~ить⟩ [14] correct; improve; reform; repair; *impf.* hold (*office*); **-ся** reform.
испра́вн|ость *f* [8] intactness; accuracy; в ~ости = **~ый** [14; -вен, -вна] intact, in good order; accurate, correct; diligent, industrious.
испражн|е́ние *n* [12] ⚕ evacuation; *pl.* f(a)eces; **~я́ться** [28], ⟨~и́ться⟩ [13] ⚕ evacuate.
испу́г *m* [1] fright; **~а́ть** *s.* пуга́ть.
испус|ка́ть [1], ⟨~ти́ть⟩ [15] utter; emit; exhale; give up (*ghost*).
испыт|а́ние *n* [12] test, (*a. fig.*) trial; examination (at на П); **~анный** [14] tried; **~а́тельный** [14] test...; **~у́ющий** [17] searching; **~ывать,** ⟨~а́ть⟩ [1] try (*a. fig.*), test; experience, undergo, feel.
иссле́дова|ние *n* [12] investigation, research; exploration; examination; ⚗ analysis; treatise, paper, essay (on по Д); **~тель** *m* [4] research worker, researcher; explorer; **~тельский** [16] research... (*a.* нау́чно-~тельский); **~ть** [7] (*im*)*pf.* investigate; explore; examine (*a.* ⚕); ⚗ analyze; ⚓ sound.
иссо́хнуть *s.* иссыха́ть.
и́сстари = и́здавна, *cf.*
исступл|е́ние *n* [12] ecstasy, frenzy; rage; **~ённый** [14] frantic.
исс|уша́ть [1], ⟨~уши́ть⟩ [16] *v/t.*, **~ыха́ть** [1], ⟨~о́хнуть⟩ [21] *v/i.* & **~яка́ть** [1], ⟨~я́кнуть⟩ [21] *v/i.* dry (*v/i.* up); *fig. a.* exhaust, wear out (*v/i.* o.s. *or* become ...).
ист|ека́ть [1], ⟨~е́чь⟩ [26] flow out; *impf.* spring; elapse (*time*), expire, become due (*date*); dissolve (in *tears* Т); ~ека́ть кро́вью bleed to death; **~е́кший** [17] past, last.
исте́р|ика *f* [5] hysterics *pl.*; **~и́ческий** [16], **~и́чный** [14; -чен, -чна] hysterical; **~и́я** *f* [7] hysteria.
исте́ц *m* [1; -тца́] plaintiff.
истече́ни|е *n* [12] expiration (*date*), lapse (*time*); ⚕ discharge; ~е кро́ви bleeding; по ~и (Р) at the end of.
исте́чь *s.* истека́ть.
и́стин|а *f* [5] truth; **~ный** [14; -инен, -инна] true, genuine; right (*way, fig.*); plain (*truth*).
истл|ева́ть [1], ⟨~е́ть⟩ [8] mo(u)lder, rot, decay; die away.
и́стовый [14] true; grave; zealous.
исто́к *m* [1] source (*a. fig.*).
истолк|ова́ние *n* [12] interpretation; **~о́вывать** [1], ⟨~ова́ть⟩ [7] interpret, expound, (*a.* себе́) explain (to o.s.).
исто́м|а *f* [5] languor; **~ля́ть** [28], ⟨~и́ть⟩ [14 *e.*; -млю́, -ми́шь; -млённый] (**-ся** be[come]) tire(d), fatigue(d), weary (-ied).
истоп|ни́к *m* [1 *e.*] stoker; **~та́ть** F [3] *pf.* trample; wear out.
исторг|а́ть *m* [1], ⟨~нуть⟩ [21] wrest; draw; deliver, save.
исто́р|ик *m* [1] historian; **~и́ческий** [16] historical; **~ия** *f* [7] history; story; F affair, thing; ве́чная ~ия! always the same!
источ|а́ть [1], ⟨~и́ть⟩ [16 *e.*; -чу́, -чи́шь] draw; shed; exhale, emit; **~ник** *m* [1] spring; (*a. fig.*) source.
истощ|а́ть [1], ⟨~и́ть⟩ [16 *e.*; -щу́, -щи́шь; -щённый] (**-ся** be[come]) exhaust(ed), use(d) up.
истра́чивать [1] *s.* тра́тить.
истреб|и́тель *m* [4] destroyer (*a.* ⚓); ✈ pursuit plane, fighter; **~и́тельный** [14] destructive; fighter...; **~и́ть** *s.* ~ля́ть; **~ле́ние** *n* [12] destruction; extermination; **~ля́ть** [28], ⟨~и́ть⟩ [14 *e.*; -блю́, -би́шь; -блённый] destroy, annihilate; exterminate.
истука́н *m* [1] idol; dolt; statue.
и́стый [14] true, genuine; zealous.

истяза́|ние *n* [12], **~ть** [1] torment.
исхо́д *m* [1] end, outcome, result; way out, outlet, vent; † exit; *Bibl.* Exodus; быть на ~е come to an end; run short of; **~и́ть** [15] (из P) come, emanate; originate, proceed; start from; † depart; *pf.* F go all over; *s. a.* истека́ть; **~ный** [14] initial, of departure.
исхуда́лый [14] emaciated, thin.
исцара́пать [1] *pf.* scratch (all over).
исцел|е́ние *n* [12] healing; recovery; **~я́ть** [28], ⟨~и́ть⟩ [13] heal, cure; **-ся** recover.
исчез|а́ть [1], ⟨**´**нуть⟩ [21] disappear, vanish; **~нове́ние** *n* [12] disappearance; **´нуть** *s.* **~а́ть.**
исче́рп|ывать, ⟨~ать⟩ [1] exhaust, use up; settle (*dispute, etc.*); **~ывающий** exhaustive.
исчисл|е́ние *n* [12] calculation; ⅄ calculus; **~я́ть** [28], ⟨**´**ить⟩ [13] calculate.
ита́к thus, so; well, then, now.
Ита́лия *f* [7] Italy.
италья́н|ец *m* [1; -нца], **~ка** *f* [5; *g/pl.*: -нок]; **~ский** [16] Italian; ~ская забасто́вка *f* sit-down strike.
и т. д. *abbr.*: и так да́лее.
ито́г *m* [1] sum, total; result; в ~е in the end; подвести́ ~ sum up; **~о́** (-ˈvɔ) altogether; in all, total.
и т. п. *abbr.*: и тому́ подо́бное.
итти́ *s.* идти́.
их (*a.* jix) their (*a.*, P, **´**ний [15]); *cf.* они́.
ишь P (just) look, listen; there; oh; now.
ище́йка *f* [5; *g/pl.*: -е́ек] bloodhound, sleuthhound.
ию́|ль *m* [4] July; **~нь** *m* [4] June.

Й

йод *m* [1] iodine.
йо́т|а *f* [5]: ни на ~у not a jot.

К

к, ко (Д) to, toward(s); *time a.* by; for.
к. *abbr.*: копе́йка, -ки, -е́ек.
-ка F (*after vb.*) just; will you.
каба́к *m* [1 *e.*] tavern, pub; mess.
кабала́ *f* [5] serfdom, bondage.
каба́н *m* [1 *e.*] (*a.* wild) boar.
ка́бель *m* [4] cable.
каби́н|а *f* [5] cabin, booth; ✈ cockpit; **~е́т** *m* [1] study; office; ⚕ (consulting) room; *pol.* cabinet.
каблу́к *m* [1 *e.*] heel; быть под ~о́м *fig.* be henpecked.
каб|ота́ж *m* [1] coasting; **~ы́** P if.
кавале́р *m* [1] cavalier; knight; **~и́йский** [16] cavalry...; **~и́ст** *m* cavalryman; **~ия** *f* [7] cavalry, horse.
ка́верз|а F *f* [5] intrigue; trick; **~ный** [14] trick(s)y.
Кавка́з *m* [1] Caucasus (*prp.*: на В/П to/in); **2ец** *m* [1; -зца] Caucasian; **2ский** [16] Caucasian.
кавы́чк|и *f/pl.* [5; *gen.*: -чек] quotation marks; в ~ах *iron.* so-called.
кади́|ло *n* [9] cencer; **~ть** [15 *e.*; кажу́, кади́шь] cence.
ка́дка *f* [5; *g/pl.*: -док] tub, vat.
ка́дмий *m* [3] cadmium.
кадр *m* [1] (*mst. pl.*) cadre, key group, van(guard); skilled workers; (*film*) shot; close-up; **´овый** [14] ⚔ regular, active; commanding; skilled.
кады́к F *m* [1 *e.*] Adam's apple.
каждодне́вный [14] dayly.
ка́ждый [14] every, each; either (*of two*); *su.* everybody, everyone.
ка́ж|ется, ~ущийся *s.* каза́ться.
каза́к *m* [1 *e.*; *pl. a.* 1] Cossack.
каза́рма ⚔ *f* [5] barracks *pl.*
каза́|ться [3], ⟨по-⟩ (T) seem, appear, look; мне ка́жется (~лось), что ... it seems (seemed) to me that; он, ка́жется, прав he seems to be right; *a.* apparently; ка́жущийся seeming; ~лось бы one would think.
каза́х *m* [1], **~ский** [16] Kazak(h); **2ская ССР** Kazak Soviet Socialist Republic; **2ста́н** *m* [1] Kazakstan.
каза́|цкий [16], **~чий** [18] Cossack('s)...
каз|ённый [14] state..., government...; official, public; formal, perfunctory; commonplace; на ~ённый счёт *m* gratis; **~на́** *f* [5] treasury, exchequer; **~наче́й** *m* [3] treasurer; ⚔ paymaster.
казн|и́ть [13] (*im*)*pf.* execute, put to death; *impf. fig.* scourge; **~ь** *f* [8] execution; (*a. fig.*) punishment.
Каи́р *m* [1] Cairo.
кайма́ *f* [5; *g/pl.*: каём] border.
как how; as; (as) like; what; but; since; F when, if; (+*su., adv.*) very (much), awfully; (+ *pf. vb.*) suddenly; я ви́дел, как он шёл ... I saw him going ...; ~ бу́дто, ~ бы as if, as it were; ~ бы мне (*inf.*) how am I to ...; ~ ни however; ~ же! sure!; ~ (же) так? you don't say!;

~ ..., так и ... both ... and ...; ~ когда́, *etc.* that depends; ~ не (+ *inf.*) of course ...; ~ мо́жно (нельзя́) скоре́е (лу́чше) as soon as (in the best way) possible.
кака́о *n* [*indecl.*] cocoa.
ка́к-нибу́дь somehow (or other); anyhow; sometime.
како́в [-ва́, -о́] how; what; what sort of; (such) as; ~! just look (at him)!; ~о́? what do you say?; **~о́й** [14] which.
како́й [16] what, which; such as; F any; that; ещё ~! and what ... (*su.*)!; како́е там! not at all!; **~-либо, ~-нибудь** any, some; F no more than, (only) about; **~-то** some, a.
ка́к-то 1. *adv.* somehow; somewhat; F (*a.* ~ раз) once, one day; **2.** *part.* such as.
каламбу́р *m* [1] pun.
каланча́ *f* [5; *g/pl.*: -че́й] watchtower; F maypole.
кала́ч *m* [1 *e.*] small (*padlock-shaped*) white loaf; тёртый ~ *fig.* F cunning fellow.
кале́ка *m/f* [5] cripple.
календа́рь *m* [4 *e.*] calendar.
калёный [14] red-hot; roasted.
кале́чить [16], ⟨ис-⟩ cripple, maim.
ка́лий *m* [3] potassium.
кали́на *f* [5] snowball tree.
кали́тка *f* [5; *g/pl.*: -ток] gate, wicket.
кали́ть [13] **1.** ⟨на-, рас-⟩ heat, incandesce; roast; **2.** ⟨за-⟩ ⊕ temper.
кало́рия *f* [7] calorie.
кало́ши *s.* гало́ши.
ка́льк|а *f* [5; *g/pl.*: -лек] tracing; tracing paper; *fig.* loan translation; **~и́ровать** [7], ⟨с-⟩ trace.
калькул|и́ровать [7], ⟨с-⟩ ✝ calculate; **~я́ция** *f* [7] calculation.
кальсо́ны *f/pl.* [5] drawers, underpants.
ка́льций *m* [3] calcium.
ка́мбала *f* [5] flounder.
камен|е́ть [8], ⟨о-⟩ turn (in)to stone, petrify; **~и́стый** [14 *sh.*] stony; **~ноуго́льный** [14] coal (mining)...; **'~ный** [14] stone...; *fig.* stony; rock (*salt*); '~ный у́голь *m* (pit) coal (*hard & soft*); **~оло́мня** *f* [6; *g/pl.*: -мен] quarry; **~отёс** *m* [1] stonemason; **'~щик** *m* [1] bricklayer, (*a. hist.*) mason; **'~ь** *m* [4; -мня; *from g/pl. e.* (*a.*, ✎, -ме́нья, -ме́ньев)] stone; rock; ⚕ *a.* calculus, gravel; *fig.* weight; ка́мнем like a stone; '~ь преткнове́ния stumbling block.
ка́мер|а *f* [5] (*prison*) cell; ⚕ ward; 🚂 (cloak)room, office; *parl.* (†), ⚖, ⊕, ⚔ chamber; *phot.* camera; bladder (*ball*); tube (*wheel*); **~ный** [14] ♪, ⊕ chamber...
ками́н *m* [1] fireplace.
камка́ *f* [5] damask (*fabric*).
камо́рка *f* [5; *g/pl.*: -рок] closet, small room.
кампа́ния *f* [7] ⚔, *pol.* campaign.
камфара́ *f* [5] camphor.
Камча́т|ка *f* [5] Kamchatka; **♀(н)ый** [14] damask...
камы́ш *m* [1 *e.*], **~о́вый** [14] reed.
кана́ва *f* [5] ditch; gutter; drain.
Кана́д|а *f* [5] Canada; **♀ец** *m* [1; -дца], **♀ка** *f* [5; *g/pl.*: -док]; **♀ский** [16] Canadian.
кана́л *m* [1] canal; (*a. fig.*) channel; pipe; **~иза́ция** *f* [7] canalization; (*town*) severage.
канаре́йка *f* [5; *g/pl.*: -е́ек] canary.
кана́т *m* [1], **~ный** [14] rope, cable.
канва́ *f* [5] canvas; *fig.* basis; outline.
кандалы́ *m/pl.* [1 *e.*] fetters, shackles.
кандида́т *m* [1] candidate; *a. lowest Sov. univ. degree, approx.* = master.
кани́кулы *f/pl.* [5] vacation, *Brt. a.* holidays (during на П, в В).
каните́ль F *f* [8] fuss; trouble; humdrum, monotony.
канон|а́да *f* [5] cannonade; **~е́рка** *f* [5; *g/pl.*: -рок] gunboat.
кану́н *m* [1] eve.
ка́нуть [20] *pf.* sink, fall; как в во́ду ~ disappear without leaving a trace; ~ в ве́чность pass into oblivion.
канцеля́р|ия *f* [7] (secretary's) office, secretariat; **~ский** [16] office...; writing; clerk's; **~щина** *f* [5] red tape.
ка́п|ать [1 & 2], *once* ⟨~нуть⟩ [20] drip, drop, trickle; leak; **~елька** *f* [5; *g/pl.*: -лек] droplet; *sg.* F bit, grain.
капита́л *m* [1] ✝ capital; stock; **~и́зм** *m* [1] capitalism; **~и́ст** *m* [1] capitalist; **~исти́ческий** [16] capitalist(ic); **~овложе́ние** *n* [12] investment; **~ьный** [14] capital; dear, expensive; main; thorough.
капита́н *m* [1] ⚔, ⚓ captain.
капитул|и́ровать [7] (*im*)*pf.* capitulate; **~я́ция** *f* [7] capitulation.
капка́н *m* [1] trap (*a. fig.*).
ка́пл|я *f* [6; *g/pl.*: -пель] drop; *sg.* F bit, grain; **~ями** by drops; как две ~и воды́ (as like) as two peas.
капо́т *m* [1] dressing gown; overcoat; ⊕ hood, *Brt.* bonnet.
капри́з *m* [1] whim, caprice; **~ничать** F [1] be capricious; **~ный** [14; -зен, -зна] capricious, whimsical.
ка́псюль ⚔ *m* [4] percussion cap.
капу́ста *f* [5] cabbage; ки́слая ~ sauerkraut.
капу́т P *m* [*indecl.*] ruin, end.
капюшо́н *m* [1] hood.
ка́ра *f* [5] punishment.
караби́н *m* [1] carbine.
кара́бкаться [1], ⟨вс-⟩ climb.
карава́й *m* [3] (big) loaf.
карава́н *m* [1] caravan.
кара́емый [14 *sh.*] ⚖ punishable.
кара́кул|ь *m* [4], **~евый** [14] astrakhan; **~я** *f* [6] scrawl.

каран|да́ш *m* [1 *e.*] pencil; **~ти́н** *m* [1] quarantine.
карапу́з F *m* [1] tot; hop-o'-my--thumb.
кара́сь *m* [4 *e.*] crucian (*fish*).
кара́|тельный [14] punitive; **~ть** [1], ‹по-› punish.
карау́л *m* [1] sentry, guard; взять (сде́лать) на ~! present arms!; стоя́ть на ~е stand sentinel; F ~! help!, murder!; **~ить** [13], ‹по-› guard, watch (F *a.* for); **~ьный** [14] sentry... (*a. su.*); **~ьная** *f* (*su.*) = **~ьня** *f* [6; *g/pl.*: -лен] guardroom.
карбо́ловый [14] carbolic (*acid*).
карбу́нкул *m* [1] carbuncle.
карбюра́тор *m* [1] carburet(t)or.
каре́л *m* [1] Karelian; **2ия** *f* [7] Karelia; **~ка** *f* [5; *g/pl.*: -лок] Karelian.
каре́та *f* [5] carriage, coach.
ка́рий [15] (dark) brown; bay.
карикату́р|а *f* [5] caricature, cartoon; **~ный** [14] caricature...; [-рен, -рна] comic(al), funny.
карка́с *m* [1] frame(work), skeleton.
ка́рк|ать [1], *once* ‹**~нуть**› [20] croak (*a.*, F, *fig.*), caw.
ка́рлик *m* [1] dwarf, pygmy; **~овый** [14] dwarf...; dwarfish.
карма́н *m* [1] pocket; э́то мне не по ~у F I can't afford that; э́то бьёт по ~у that makes a hole in my (*etc.*) purse; держи́ ~ (ши́ре) that's a vain hope; он за сло́вом в ~ не ле́зет he has a ready tongue; **~ный** [14] pocket...; note(*book*); **~ный** вор *m* pickpocket; *cf.* фона́рик.
карнава́л *m* [1] carnival.
карни́з *m* [1] cornice.
Карпа́ты *f/pl.* [5] Carpathian Mts.
ка́рт|а *f* [5] map; ⚓ chart; (playing) card; menu; ста́вить (всё) на ~у stake (have all one's eggs in one basket); **~а́вить** [14] jar (*or* mispronounce) *Russ.* r &/*or* l (*esp. as uvular* r *or* u, v); **~ёжник** *m* [1] gambler (*at cards*); **~е́ль** (-'tɛl) *f* [8] cartel; **~е́чь** *f* [8] case shot.
карти́н|а *f* [5] picture (in на П); movie, image; painting; scene (*a. thea.*); **~ка** *f* [5; *g/pl.*: -нок] (small) picture, illustration; **~ный** [14] picture...; picturesque, vivid.
карто́н *m* [1] cardboard, pasteboard; † = **~ка** *f* [5; *g/pl.*: -нок] (cardboard) box; hatbox.
картоте́ка *f* [5] card index.
карто́фель *m* [4] *coll.* potatoes *pl.*
ка́рточ|ка *f* [5; *g/pl.*: -чек] card; F ticket; photo; menu; **~ный** [14] card(s)...; **~ная** систе́ма *f* rationing system; **~ный** до́мик *m* house of cards.
карто́шка P *f* [5; *g/pl.*: -шек] potato(es).
карту́з *m* [1 *e.*] cap; † pack(age).
карусе́ль *f* [8] merry-go-round.
ка́рцер *m* [1] dungeon; lockup.
карье́р *m* [1] full gallop (at T); с ме́ста в ~ on the spot; **~а** *f* [5] career; fortune; **~и́ст** *m* [1] careerist.
каса́|тельная ⩓ *f* [14] tangent; **~тельно** ([† до] P) concerning; **~ться** [1], ‹косну́ться› [20] ([до †] P) touch (*a. fig.*); concern; F be about, deal *or* be concerned with; де́ло **~ется** *a.* = де́ло идёт о, *s.* идти́; что **~ется** ..., то as for (to).
ка́ска *f* [5; *g/pl.*: -сок] helmet.
каспи́йский [16] Caspian.
ка́сса *f* [5] pay desk *or* office; (*a.* биле́тная ~) 🚂 ticket window, *Brt.* booking office; *thea.* box office; bank; fund; cash; cash register; money box *or* chest, safe.
кассац|ио́нный [14] *s.* апелляцио́нный; **~ия** ⚖ *f* [7] reversal.
кассе́та *f* [5] *phot.* plate holder.
касси́р *m* [1], **~ша** F *f* [5] cashier.
ка́ста *f* [5] caste (*a. fig.*).
касто́ровый [14] castor (*oil*; *hat*).
кастри́ровать [7] (*im*)*pf.* castrate.
кастрю́ля *f* [6] saucepan; pot.
катало́г *m* [1] catalogue.
ката́нье *n* [10] driving, riding, skating, *etc.* (*cf.* ката́ть[ся]).
катастро́ф|а *f* [5] catastrophe; **~и́ческий** [16] catastrophic.
ката́ть [1] roll (*a.* ⊕); mangle; ‹по-› (take for a) drive, ride, row, *etc.*; **-ся** (go for a) drive, ride (*a.* верхо́м, *etc.*), row (на ло́дке); skate (на конька́х); sled(ge) (на саня́х), *etc.*; roll.
катег|ори́ческий [16] categorical; **~о́рия** *f* [7] category.
ка́тер ⚓ *m* [1; *pl.*: -pá, *etc. e.*] cutter; торпе́дный ~ torpedo boat.
кати́ть [15], ‹по-› roll, drive, wheel (*v/i* **-ся**; sweep; move, flow; *cf. a.* ката́ться).
като́д *m* [1] cathode; **~ный** [14] cathodic.
като́к *m* [1; -тка́] (skating) rink; mangle; ⊕ roll.
като́л|ик *m* [1], **~и́чка** *f* [5; *g/pl.*: -чек], **~и́ческий** [16] (Roman) Catholic.
ка́тор|га *f* [5] hard labo(u)r in (*Siberian*) exile; place of such penal servitude; *fig.* drudgery, misery; **~жа́нин** *m* [1; *pl.*: -а́не, -а́н], **~жник** *m* [1] (exiled) convict; **~жный** [14] hard, penal; *s.* **~га**; *su.* = **~жник**.
кату́шка *f* [5; *g/pl.*: -шек] spool; [⚡ coil.]
Катю́ша [5], **Ка́тя** *f* [6] (*dim. of* Екатери́на) Kitty, Kate.
каучу́к *m* [1] caoutchouc, rubber.
кафе́ (-'fɛ) *n* [*indecl.*] café.
ка́федра *f* [5] platform, pulpit, lecturing desk; chair, cathedra.
ка́фель *m* [4] (Dutch) tile.
кача́|лка *f* [5; *g/pl.*: -лок] rocking chair; **~ние** *n* [12] rocking; swing (-ing); pumping; **~ть** [1] **1.** ‹по-›, *once* ‹качну́ть› [20] rock; swing;

shake (*a.* one's head головóй), toss; ⚓ roll, pitch; (-**ся** *v/i.*; stagger, lurch); **2.** ⟨на-⟩ pump.
качéли *f/pl.* [8] swing.
кáчеств|енный [14] qualitative; **~о** *n* [9] quality; в ~е (P) as, in one's capacity as in the capacity of.
кáч|ка ⚓ *f* [5] rolling (бортовáя *or* боковáя ~ка); pitching (килевáя ~ка); **~нýть(ся)** *s.* ~áть(ся).
кáш|а *f* [5] mush, *Brt.* porridge; gruel; pap; F slush; *fig.* mess, jumble; **~евáр** ⚔ *m* [1] cook.
кáш|ель *m* [4; -шля], **~лять** [28], *once* ⟨~лянуть⟩ [20] cough.
кашнé (-'nɛ) *n* [*indecl.*] neckscarf.
каштáн *m* [1], **~овый** [14] chestnut.
каю́та ⚓ *f* [5] cabin, stateroom.
кáяться [27], ⟨по-⟩ (в П) repent.
кв. *abbr.*: **1.** квадрáтный; **2.** квартúра.
квадрáт *m* [1], **~ный** [14] square.
квáк|ать [1], *once* ⟨~нуть⟩ [20] croak.
квалифи|кáция *f* [7] qualification(s); **~цúрованный** [14] qualified, competent; skilled, trained.
квартáл *m* [1] quarter (= district; 3 months); block, F building (*betw.* 2 *cross streets*); **~ьный** [14] quarter(ly); district... (*a., su., form.*: district inspector).
квартúр|а *f* [5] apartment, *Brt.* flat; ~а в две кóмнаты two-room apt./flat; lodgings *pl.*; ⚔ quarter(s); billet; ~а и стол board and lodging; **~áнт** *m* [1], **~áнтка** *f* [5; *g/pl.*: -ток] lodger, roomer, subtenant; **~ный** [14] housing, house-...; **~ная плáта** = **квартплáта** *f* [5] rent.
квас *m* [1; -а *&* -у; *pl. e.*] quass (*Russ. drink*); **∠ить** [15], ⟨за-⟩ sour.
квасц|óвый [14] aluminous; **~ы́** *m/pl.* [1] alum.
квáшеный [14] sour, leavened.
квéрху up, upward(s).
квит|áнция *f* [7] receipt; check, ticket; **∠(ы)** F quits, even, square.
квóта *f* [5] quota, share.
квт(ч) *abbr.* = kw. (K.W.H.)
кег|ельбáн *m* [1] bowling alley; **∠ля** *f* [6; *g/pl.*: -лей] pin (*pl.*: ninepins), *Brt.* skittle(s).
кедр *m* [1] cedar; сибúрский ~ cembra pine.
кекс *m* [1] cake.
Кёльн *m* [1] Cologne.
кельт *m* [1] Celt; **∠ский** [16] Celtic.
кéлья *f* [6] *eccl.* cell.
кем = T *of* кто, *cf.*
кенгурý *m* [*indecl.*] kangaroo.
кéп|и *n* [*indecl.*], **~ка** *f* [5; *g/pl.*: -пок] cap.
керáм|ика *f* [5] ceramics; **~иковый** [14], **~úческий** [16] ceramic.
керосúн *m* [1], **~овый** [14] kerosene.
кéта *f* [5] Siberian salmon.
кефúр *m* [1] kefir.
кибúтка *f* [5; *g/pl.*: -ток] tilt cart (*or* sledge).
кив|áть [1], *once* ⟨~нýть⟩ [20] nod; beckon; point (to на В); **∠ер** *m* [1; *pl.*: -рá, *etc. e.*] shako; **~óк** *m* [1; -вкá] nod.
кидá|ть(ся) [1], *once* ⟨кúнуть(ся)⟩ [20] *s.* бросáть(ся); меня́ ~ет в жар и хóлод I'm hot and cold all over (have a shivering fit).
Кúев *m* [1] Kiev; **♀ля́нин** *m* [1; *pl.*: -я́не, -я́н], **♀ля́нка** *f* [5; *g/pl.*: -нок] Kiever; **♀ский** [16] Kiev...
кий *m* [3; кия́; *pl.*: кий, киёв] cue.
килó *n* [*indecl.*] = ~грáмм; **~вáтт -(-чáс)** *m* [1; *g/pl.*: -вáтт] kilowatt(-hour); **~грáмм** *m* [1] kilogram (-me); **~мéтр** *m* [1] kilometer (*Brt.* -tre).
киль *m* [4] keel; **~вáтер** (-tɛr) *m* [1] wake; **∠ка** *f* [5; *g/pl.*: -лек] sprat.
КИМ *m* [1] *abbr.*: Communist Youth International (*1919—1943*).
кинематóгр|аф *m* [1] cinema(tograph), movie theater; **~áфия** *f* [7] cinematography.
кинжáл *m* [1] dagger.
кинó *n* [*indecl.*] movie, motion picture, *Brt.* the pictures, cinema (to/at в В/П); *coll.* screen, film; **~актёр** *s.* ~артúст; **~актрúса** *s.* ~артúстка; **~артúст** *m* [1] screen (*or* film) actor; **~артúстка** *f* [5; *g/pl.*: -ток] screen (*or* film) actress; **~ательé** (-tɛ-) *n* [*indecl.*] (film) studio; **'~варь** *f* [8] cinnabar; **~журнáл** *m* [1] newsreel; **~звездá** F *f* [5; *pl.*: -звёзды] filmstar; **~картúна** *f* [5] film; **~лéнта** *f* [5] reel, film (copy); **~оперáтор** *m* [1] cameraman; **~плёнка** *f* [5; *g/pl.*: -нок] film (strip); **~режиссёр** *m* [1] film director; **~сеáнс** *m* [1] show, performance; **~сценáрий** *m* [3] scenario; **~съёмка** *f* [5; *g/pl.*: -мок] shooting (of a film), filming; **~теáтр** *m* [1] movie theater, cinema; **~хрóника** *f* [5] newsreel.
кúнуть(ся) *s.* кидáть(ся).
киóск *m* [1] kiosk, stand, stall.
киóт *m* [1] *eccl.* image case, shrine.
кúпа *f* [5] pile, stack; bale, pack.
кипарúс *m* [1] cypress.
кипé|ние *n* [12] boiling; тóчка ~ния boiling point; **~ть** [10 *e.*; -плю́, -пúшь], ⟨за-, вс-⟩ boil; seethe; surge (up), rage, overflow, teem with; be in full swing (*work, war*).
Кúпр *m* [1] Cyprus.
кипýчий [17 *sh.*] seething; lively, vigorous, exuberant, vehement; busy.
кипят|úть [15 *e.*; -ячý, -ятúшь], ⟨вс-⟩ boil (up; *v/i.* -ся); F be(come) excited; **~óк** *m* [1; -ткá] boiling *or* boiled (hot) water.
киргúз *m* [1], **~ский** [16] Kirghiz.
Кирúлл *m* [1] Cyril; **♀ица** *f* [5] Cyrillic alphabet.

кирка́ *f* [5; *g/pl.*: -ро́к] pick(ax[e]), mattock.
кирпи́ч *m* [1 *e.*], **~ный** [14] brick.
кисе́ль *m* [4 *e.*] (*kind of*) jelly.
кисе́т *m* [1] tobacco pouch.
кисея́ *f* [6] muslin.
кисл|ова́тый [14 *sh.*] sourish; **~оро́д** *m* [1] oxygen; **~ота́** *f* [5; *pl. st.*: -о́ты] acid; **~ый** [14; -сел, -сла́, -о] sour, (*a.* ⚗) acid...
ки́снуть [21], ‹с-, про-› turn sour; F *fig.* get rusty.
ки́ст|очка *f* [5; *g/pl.*: -чек] (*paint, shaving*) brush; tassel; *dim. of* **~ь** *f* [8; *from g/pl. e.*] brush; tassel; cluster, bunch; hand.
кит *m* [1 *e.*] whale.
кита́|ец *m* [1; -та́йца], Chinese; **2й** *m* [3] China; **~йский** [16] Chinese; **2йская Наро́дная Респу́блика** (КНР) Chinese People's Republic; **~я́нка** *f* [5; *g/pl.*: -нок] Chinese.
ки́тель *m* [4; *pl.* -ля́, *etc. e.*] jacket.
китобо́й *m* [3], **~ный** [14] whaler.
кич|и́ться [16 *e.*; -чу́сь, -чи́шься] put on airs; boast (of T); **~ли́вый** [14 *sh.*] haughty, conceited.
кише́ть [киши́т] teem, swarm (with T; *a.* кишмя́ ~).
киш|е́чник *m* [1] bowels, intestines *pl.*; **~е́чный** [14] intestinal, enteric; digestive (*tract*); **~ка́** *f* [5; *g/pl.*: -шо́к] intestine (small то́нкая, large то́лстая), gut; *pl.* F bowels; hose.
кла́виш *m* [1], **~а** *f* [5] ♪, ⊕ key.
клад *m* [1] treasure (*a. fig.*); **~бище** *n* [11] cemetery; **~ка** *f* [5] laying, (*brick-, stone*)work; **~ова́я** *f* [14] pantry, larder; stock- *or* storeroom; **~овщи́к** *m* [1 *e.*] stockman, storekeeper; **~ь** *f* [8] freight, load.
кла́ня|ться [28], ‹поклони́ться› [13; -оню́сь, -о́нишься] (Д) bow (to); greet; **~йтесь ему́ от меня́** give him my regards; F cringe (to пе́ред T); present (a p. s. th. Д/T).
кла́пан *m* [1] ⊕ valve; ♪ key, stop.
класс *m* [1] class; *shool*: grade, *Brt.* form; classroom; **~ик** *m* [1] classic; **~ифици́ровать** [7] (*im*)*pf.* class(ify); **~и́ческий** [16] classic(al); **~ный** [14] class(*room, etc.*); **~овый** [14] class (*struggle, etc.*).
класть [кладу́, -дёшь; клал] **1.** ‹положи́ть› [16] (в, на, *etc.*, В) put, lay (down, on, *etc.*), deposit; apply, spend; take (*as a basis* в В); F fix; rate; make; leave (*mark*); **2.** ‹сложи́ть› [16] lay (down); erect.
клева́ть [6 *e.*; клюю́, клюёшь], *once* ‹клю́нуть› [20] peck, pick; bite (*fish*); ~ но́сом F nod.
кле́вер *m* [1] clover, trefoil.
клевет|а́ *f* [5], **~а́ть** [3; -вещу́, -ве́щешь], ‹о-› *v/t.*, ‹на-› (на В) slander; **~ни́к** *m* [1 *e.*] slanderer; **~ни́ческий** [16] slanderous.
клевре́т *m* [1] accomplice.
клеён|ка *f* [5], **~чатый** [14] oil-[cloth.]
кле́|ить [13], ‹с-› glue, paste; **-ся** stick; F work, get on *or* along; **~й** *m* [3; на клею́] glue, paste; ры́бий **~й** isinglass; **~йкий** [16; клёек, клёйка] sticky, adhesive.
клейм|и́ть [14 *e.*; -млю́, -ми́шь], ‹за-› brand; *fig. a.* stigmatize; **~о́** *n* [9; *pl. st.*] brand; *fig.* stigma, stain; фабри́чное **~о́** trademark.
клён *m* [1] maple.
клепа́ть [1], ‹за-› rivet; hammer.
клёпка *f* [5; *g/pl.*: -пок] riveting; stave.
клет|ка *f* [5; *g/pl.*: -ток] cage; square, check; *biol.* (*a.* **~очка**) cell; в **~**(оч)ку (**~**[оч]ками) check(er)ed, *Brt.* chequered; **~ча́тка** *f* [5] cellulose; cellular tissue; **~чатый** [14] checkered (*Brt.* chequered); cellular.
кле|шня́ *f* [6; *g/pl.*: -не́й] claw (*of the crayfish*); **~щи́** *f/pl.* [5; *gen.*: -ще́й, *etc. e.*] pincers.
клие́нт *m* [1] client.
клизма *f* [5] enema.
клик *m* [1] cry, shout; shriek; **~а** *f* [5] clique; **~ать** [3], *once* ‹**~нуть**› [20] shriek; P call.
клима́т *m* [1] climate; **~и́ческий** [16] climatic.
клин *m* [3; *pl.*: кли́нья, -ьев] wedge; gusset; **~ом** pointed (*beard*); свет не **~ом** сошёлся the world is large; there is always a way out.
кли́ника *f* [5] clinic.
клино́к *m* [1; -нка́] blade.
клич *m* [1] call; cry; **~ка** *f* [5; *g/pl.*: -чек] (*dog's, etc.*) name; nickname.
клише́ *n* [*indecl.*] cliché (*a. fig.*).
клок *m* [1 *e.*; *pl.*: -о́чья, -ьев & клоки́, -ко́в] tuft; shred, rag, tatter, piece, frazzle.
клокота́ть [3] seethe, bubble.
клон|и́ть [13; -оню́, -о́нишь], ‹на-, с-› bend, bow; *fig.* incline; drive (*or* aim) at (к Д); † cast down; меня́ **~и́т** ко сну I am (feel) sleepy; (**-ся** *v/i.*; *a.* decline; approach).
клоп *m* [1 *e.*] bedbug, *Brt.* bug.
кло́ун *m* [1] clown.
клочо́к *m* [1; -чка́] wisp; scrap.
клуб[1] *m* [1; *pl. a. e.*] cloud, puff (*smoke, etc.*); *s. a.* **~о́к**; **~**[2] [1] club (-house); **~ень** *m* [4; -бня] tuber, bulb; **~и́ть** [14 *e.*; *3rd p. only*] puff (up), whirl, coil (*v/i.* **-ся**).
клубни́ка *f* [5] strawberry, -ries *pl.*
клубо́к *m* [1; -бка́] clew; tangle.
клу́мба *f* [5] (flower) bed.
клык *m* [1 *e.*] tusk; canine, fang.
клюв *m* [1] beak, bill.
клю́ка *f* [5] crutch(ed stick), staff.
клю́ква *f* [5] cranberry, -ries *pl.*
клю́нуть *s.* клева́ть.
ключ *m* [1 *e.*] key (*a. fig.*, clue; *a.* ⊕ [га́ечный ~] = wrench; англи́йский ~ monkey wrench); ♪ clef; spring, source; ⚠ keystone; **~и́ца** *f* [5] clavicle, collarbone; **~ница** *f* [5] housekeeper.

клю́шка *f* [5; *g/pl.*: -шек] club.

кля́кса *f* [5] blot.

кля́нчить F [16] beg for.

кляп *m* [1] gag.

кля|сть [-яну́, -нёшь; **-ял, -á, -о**] = проклина́ть, *cf.*; **-ся,** ⟨покля́сться⟩ swear (s. th. в П; by T); **∠тва** *f* [5] oath; дать ∠тву (*or* ∠твенное обеща́ние) take an oath, swear; **~твопреступле́ние** *n* [12] perjury.

кля́уза *f* [5] intrigue, denunciation; † captious suit; pettifoggery.

кля́ча *f* [5] jade.

кни́г|а *f* [5] book (*a.* †); *teleph.* directory; register; **~опеча́тание** *n* [12] (book) printing, typography; **~опрода́вец** *m* [1; -вца] bookseller; **~охрани́лище** *n* [11] archives, storerooms *pl.*; library.

кни́ж|ка *f* [5; *g/pl.*: -жек] book (-let); notebook; passport; **~ный** [14] book...; bookish; **~о́нка** *f* [5; *g/pl.*: -нок] trashy book.

кни́зу down, downward(s).

кно́пка *f* [5; *g/pl.*: -пок] thumbtack, *Brt.* drawing pin; ⚡ (push) button; patent (*or* snap) fastener.

кнут *m* [1 *e.*] whip, knout, scourge.

княгíня

кня|ги́ня *f* [6] princess (*prince's consort*; *daughter*: **~жна́** *f* [5; *g/pl.*: -жо́н]); **~зь** *m* [4; *pl.*: -зья́, -зе́й] prince; вели́кий **~зь** grand duke.

коа|лицио́нный [14] coalition ...; **~ли́ция** *f* [7] coalition.

ко́бальтовый [14] cobaltic.

кобура́ *f* [5] holster; saddlebag.

кобы́ла *f* [5] mare; *sport:* horse.

ко́ваный [14] wrought (*iron*).

кова́р|ный [14; -рен, -рна] artful, guileful, insidious; **~ство** *n* [9] craft, guile, wile.

кова́ть [7 *e.*; кую́, куёшь] **1.** ⟨**вы́-**⟩ forge; **2.** ⟨под-⟩ shoe (*horse*).

ковёр *m* [1; -вра́] carpet, rug.

кове́ркать [1], ⟨ис-⟩ distort, deform; mutilate; murder (*fig.*).

ко́в|ка *f* [5] forging; shoeing; **~кий** [16; -вок, -вка́, -о] malleable.

коври́жка *f* [5; *g/pl.*: -жек] gingerbread.

ковче́г *m* [1] ark; Но́ев **~** Noah's Ark.

ковш *m* [1 *e.*] scoop; bucket; haven.

ковы́ль *m* [4 *e.*] feather grass.

ковыля́ть [28] toddle; stump, limp.

ковыря́ть [28], ⟨по-⟩ pick, poke.

когда́ when; F if; ever; sometimes; *cf.* ни; **~-либо, ~-нибудь** (at) some time (or other), one day; *interr.* ever; **~-то** once, one day, sometime.

ко́|готь *m* [4; -гтя; *from g/pl. e.*] claw; **~д** *m* [1] code.

ко́е|-где́ here & there, in some places; **~-ка́к** anyhow, somehow; with (great) difficulty; **~-како́й** [16] some; any; **~-когда́** off & on; **~-кто́** [23] some(body); **~-куда́** here & there, (in)to some place(s), somewhere; **~-что́** [23] something, some things.

ко́ж|а *f* [5] skin; leather; из **~и** (во́н) лезть F do one's utmost; **~аный** [14] leather...; **~е́венный** [14] leather...; **~е́венный заво́д** *m* tannery; **~е́вник** *m* [1] tanner; **~ица** *f* [5] peel; rind (*a.* **~ура́** *f* [5]); cuticle.

коз|а́ *f* [5; *pl. st.*] (she-)goat; **~ёл** *m* [1; -зла́] (he-)goat; **∠ий** [18] goat...; **~лёнок** *m* [2] kid; **∠лы** *f/pl.* [5; *gen.*: -зел] (coach) box; trestle.

ко́зни *f/pl.* [8] intrigues, plots.

козу́ля *f* [6] roe (deer).

коз|ырёк *m* [1; -рька́] peak (*cap*); **∠ырь** *m* [4; *from g/pl. e.*] trump; **~ыря́ть** F [28], *once* ⟨**~ырну́ть**⟩ [20] trump; boast; ⚔ salute.

ко́йка *f* [5; *g/pl.*: ко́ек] cot; bed.

коке́т|ка *f* [5; *g/pl.*: -ток] coquette; **~ливый** [14 *sh.*] coquettish; **~ничать** [1] coquet, flirt; **~ство** *n* [9] coquetry.

коклю́ш *m* [1] whooping cough.

ко́кон *m* [1] cocoon.

кок|о́с *m* [1] coco; **~о́совый** [14] coco(nut)...; **~с** *m* [1] coke.

кол *m* **1.** [1 *e.*; *pl.*: ко́лья, -ьев] stake, pale; **2.** [*pl.* 1 *e.*] P *s.* едини́ца; ни **~а́** ни двора́ neither house nor home.

колбаса́ *f* [5; *pl. st.*: -а́сы] sausage.

колд|ова́ть [7] conjure; **~овство́** *n* [9] magic, sorcery; **~у́н** *m* [1 *e.*] sorcerer, magician, wizard; **~у́нья** *f* [6] sorceress, enchantress.

колеб|а́ние *n* [12] oscillation; vibration; *fig.* vacillation, hesitation; (*a.* †) fluctuation; **~а́ть** [2 *st.*: -е́блю, *etc.*; -е́бли(те)!; -е́бля], ⟨по-⟩, *once* ⟨**~нуть**⟩ [20] shake (*a. fig.*); **-ся** shake; (*a.* †) fluctuate; waver, vacillate, hesitate; oscillate, vibrate.

коле́н|о *n* [*sg.*: 9; *pl.*: 4] knee; стать на **~и** kneel; [*pl.*: -нья, -ньев] ⚘ joint, knot; [*pl. a.* 9] bend; ⊕ crank; [*pl.* 9] degree, branch (*pedigree*); P ♪ pas(sage); trick; **~чатый** [14] *biol.* geniculate; ⊕ crank(*shaft*).

колес|и́ть F [15 *e.*; -ешу́, -еси́шь] travel (much); take a roundabout way; **~ни́ца** *f* [5] chariot; **~о́** *n* [9; *pl. st.*: -лёса] wheel; кружи́ться как бе́лка в **~е́** fuss, bustle about; вставля́ть па́лки в колёса (Д) put a spoke in a p.'s wheel; но́ги **~о́м** bowlegged.

колея́ *f* [6; *g/pl.*: -ле́й] rut, (*a.* 🚂) track (*both a. fig.*).

коли́бри *m/f* [*indecl.*] hummingbird.

ко́лики *f/pl.* [5] colic, gripes.

коли́честв|енный [14] quantitative; *gr.* cardinal (*number*); **~о** *n* [9] quantity; number; amount; по **~у** quantitatively.

ко́лка *f* [5] splitting, chopping.

ко́лк|ий [16; ко́лок, колка́, -о]

prickly; biting, pungent; ~ость *f* [8] sarcasm, gibe.
коллéг|а *m* /*f* [5] colleague; **~ия** *f* [7] board, staff; college.
коллектив *m* [1] collective, group, body; **~изáция** *f* [7] collectivization; **~ный** [14] collective.
коллéк|тор *m* [1] ⚡ collector; **~ционéр** *m* [1] (*curiosity*) collector; **~ция** *f* [7] collection.
колóд|а *f* [5] block; trough; pack, deck (*cards*); **~ец** [1; -дца] well; shaft, pit; **~ка** *f* [5; *g/pl.*: -док] last; (foot) stock(s); ⊕ (*brake*) shoe; **~ник** *m* [1] convict (*in stocks*).
кóлок|ол *m* [1; *pl.*: -лá, *etc. e.*] bell; **~óльня** *f* [6; *g/pl.*: -лен] bell tower, belfry; **~óльчик** *m* [1] (little) bell; ⚘ bellflower.
колони|áльный [14] colonial; **~зáция** *f* [7] colonization; **~з(úр)овáть** [7] (*im*)*pf.* colonize; **'~я** [7] colony.
колóн|ка *f* [5; *g/pl.*: -нок] *typ.* column; (*gas*) station; water heater, *Brt.* geyser; *a. dim. of* **~на** *f* [5] column (⚠ *a.* pillar; *typ.* †).
кóлос *m* [1; *pl.*: -лóсья, -ьев], **~úться** [15 *e.*; *3rd p. only*] ear; **~ник** *m* [1 *e.*] grate.
колотúть [15] knock (at, on в В, по Д).
колóть [17] 1. ‹рас-› split, cleave; break (*sugar*); crack (*nuts*); 2. ‹на-› chop (*firewood*); кóлотый lump (*sugar*); 3. ‹у-›, *once* ‹кольнýть› [20] prick, sting; *fig.* F taunt; 4. ‹за-› stab; kill, slaughter (*animals*); *impers.* have a stitch; ~ глазá (Д) be a thorn in one's side.
колпáк *m* [1 *e.*] cap; shade; bell glass.
колхóз *m* [1] collective farm, kolkhoz; **~ный** [14] kolkhoz...; **~ник** *m* [1], **~ница** *f* [5] collective farmer.
колчáн *m* [1] quiver.
колчедáн *m* [1] pyrites.
колыбéль *f* [8] cradle; **~ный** [14]: ~ная (пéсня) *f* lullaby.
колых|áть [3 *st.*: -ы́шу, *etc.*, *or* 1], ‹вс-›, *once* ‹~нýть› [20] sway, swing; stir; heave; flicker; **-ся** *v/i.*
кóлышек *m* [1; -шка] peg.
кольнýть *s.* колóть 3. & *impers.*
коль|цевóй [14] ring...; circular; **~цó** *n* [9; *pl. st., gen.*: колéц] ring; circle; **~чýга** *f* [5] mail.
колю́ч|ий [17 *sh.*] thorny, prickly; barbed (*wire*); *fig. s.* кóлкий; **~ка** *f* [5; *g/pl.*: -чек] thorn, prickle; barb.
Кóля *m* [6] (*dim. of* Николáй) Nick.
коля́ска *f* [5; *g/pl.*: -сок] carriage, victoria; baby carriage, *Brt.* perambulator.
ком *m* [1; *pl*: кóмья, -ьев] lump, clod; снéжный ~ snowball.
комáнд|а *f* [5] command; detachment; ⚓ crew; *sport:* team; (*fire*) company (*or* department), *Brt.* brigade; F gang.
командúр *m* [1] commander; **~овáть** [7] (*im*)*pf.*, *a.* ‹от-› send (on a mission); detach; **~óвка** *f* [5; *g/pl.*: -вок] mission; sending.
комáнд|ный [14] command(ing); team...; **~ование** *n* [12] command; **~овать** [7] ([над] Т) command (*a.* = [give] order, ‹с-›); F domineer; **~ующий** [17] (Т) commander.
комáр *m* [1 *e.*] mosquito, gnat.
комбáйн ⚒ *m* [1] combine.
комбин|áт *m* [1] combine of complementary industrial plants (*Sov.*); **~áция** *f* [7] combination; **~úровать** [7], ‹с-› combine.
комéдия *f* [7] comedy; F farce.
комендá|нт *m* [1] commandant; superintendent; **~тýра** *f* [5] commandant's office.
комéта *f* [5] comet.
ком|úзм *m* [1] comicality; **∠ик** *m* [1] comedian, comic (actor).
Коминтéрн *m* [1] (Third) Communist International (*1919—1943*).
комиссáр *m* [1] commissar (*Sov.*); commissioner; **~иáт** *m* [1] commissariat.
коми|ссиóнный [14] commission (*a.* †; *pl. su.* = *sum*); **∠ссия** *f* [7] commission (*a.* †), committee; **~тéт** *m* [1] committee
комúч|еский [16], **~ный** [14; -чен, -чна] comic(al), funny.
кóмкать [1], ‹ис-, с-› crumple.
коммент|áрий *m* [3] comment(ary); **~áтор** *m* [1] commentator; **~úровать** [7] (*im*)*pf.* comment (on).
коммер|сáнт *m* [1] (wholesale) merchant; **∠ческий** [16] commercial.
коммýн|а *f* [5] commune; **~áльный** [14] municipal; **~úзм** *m* [1] communism; **~икáция** *f* [7] communication (*pl.* ⚔); **~úст** *m* [1], **~úстка** *f* [5; *g/pl.*: -ток], **~истúческий** [14] communist (*a. cap.*, *cf.* КПСС).
коммутáтор *m* [1] commutator; *teleph.* switchboard; operator(s' room).
кóмнат|а *f* [5] room; **~ный** [14] room...; ⚘ indoor.
комó|д *m* [1] bureau, *Brt.* chest of drawers; **~к** *m* [1; -мкá] lump, clod.
компáн|ия *f* [7] company (*a.* †); водúть ~ию с (Т) associate with; **~ьóн** *m* [1] † partner; F companion.
компáртия *f* [7] Communist Party.
кóмпас *m* [1] compass.
компенс|áция *f* [7] compensation; **~úровать** [7] (*im*)*pf.* compensate.
компетéн|тный [14; -тен, -тна] competent; **~ция** *f* [7] competence; line.
кóмплек|с *m* [1], **~сный** [14] complex; **∠т** *m* [1] (complete) set; **∠тный** [14], **~товáть** [7], ‹у-› complete.
комплимéнт *m* [1] compliment.

компо|зи́тор *m* [1] composer; **~сти́ровать** [7], ⟨про-⟩ punch; **~́т** *m* [1] sauce, *Brt.* stewed fruit.
компре́сс *m* [1] compress.
компром|ети́ровать [7], ⟨с-⟩, **~и́сс** *m* [1] compromise (*v/i. a.* идти́ на ~и́сс).
комсомо́л *m* [1] Komsomol, *cf.* ВЛКСМ; **~ец** *m* [1; -льца], **~ка** *f* [5; *g/pl.*: -лок], **~ьский** [16] Young Communist.
комфо́рт *m* [1] comfort, convenience; **~а́бельный** [14; -лен, -льна] comfortable, convenient.
конве́йер *m* [1] (belt) conveyor; assembly line.
конве́нция *f* [7] convention.
конве́рт *m* [1] envelope.
конв|ои́р *m* [1], **~ои́ровать** [7], **~о́й** *m* [3], **~о́йный** [14] convoy.
конгре́сс *m* [1] congress.
конденс|а́тор (-dɛ-) *m* [1] condenser; **~и́ровать** [7] (*im*)*pf.* condense; evaporate (*milk*).
конди́тер *m* [1] confectioner; **~ская** *f* [16] confectioner's shop; **~ские** изде́лия *pl.* confectionery.
Кондра́т|ий *m* [3], ~ P [1] Conrad.
конду́ктор *m* [1; *pl. a.* -á, *etc. e.*] conductor (🚂 *Brt.* guard).
конево́дство *n* [9] horse breeding.
конёк *m* [1; -нька́] skate; F hobby.
кон|е́ц *m* [1; -нца́] end; close; point; ⚓ rope; F distance; part; case; без ~ца́ endless(ly); в ~е́ц (до ~ца́) completely; в ~це́ (P) at the end of; в ~це́ ~цо́в at long last; в оди́н ~е́ц one way; в о́ба ~ца́ there & back; на худо́й ~е́ц at (the) worst; под ~е́ц in the end; тре́тий с ~ца́ last but two.
коне́чно (-ʃnə) of course, certainly.
коне́чности *f/pl.* [8] extremities.
коне́чн|ый [14; -чен, -чна] *philos.*, ♧ finite; final, terminal; ultimate.
конкре́тный [14; -тен, -тна] concrete.
конкур|е́нт *m* [1] competitor; **~е́нция** † *f* [7] competition; **~и́ровать** [7] compete; **'~с** *m* [1] competition; † bankruptcy.
ко́нн|ица *f* [5] cavalry; **~ый** [14] horse...; (of) cavalry.
конопа́тить [15], ⟨за-⟩ calk.
конопля́ *f* [6] hemp; **~ный** [14] hempen.
коносаме́нт *m* [1] bill of lading.
консерв|ати́вный [14; -вен, -вна] conservative; **~ато́рия** *f* [7] conservatory, *Brt.* school of music, conservatoire; **~и́ровать** [7] (*im*)*pf.*, *a.* ⟨за-⟩ conserve, preserve; can, *Brt.* tin; **~́ный** [14]: **~́ная** фа́брика *f* cannery; **~́ы** *m/pl.* [1] canned (*Brt.* tinned) goods; safety goggles.
ко́нский [16] horse(*hair, etc.*).
конспе́кт *m* [1] summary, abstract; sketch; **~и́вный** [14; -вен, -вна] concise, sketchy; **~и́ровать** [7], ⟨за-⟩ outline, epitomize.
конспир|ати́вный [14; -вен, -вна] secret; **~а́ция** *f* [7] conspiracy.
конст|ати́ровать [7] (*im*)*pf.* state; find; **~иту́ция** *f* [7] constitution.
констр|уи́ровать [7] (*im*)*pf.*, *a.* ⟨с-⟩ design; **~у́ктор** *m* [1] designer; **~у́кция** *f* [7] design; construction.
ко́нсул *m* [1] consul; **~ьский** [16] consular; **~ьство** *n* [9] consulate; **~ьта́ция** *f* [7] consultation; advice; advisory board; **~ьти́ровать** [7], ⟨про-⟩ advise; **-ся** consult (with с Т).
конта́кт *m* [1] contact.
континге́нт *m* [1] contingent, quota.
контине́нт *m* [1] continent.
конто́р|а *f* [5] office; **~ский** [16] office...; ~ский слу́жащий *m*, **~щик** *m* [1] clerk.
контраба́нд|а *f* [5] contraband; занима́ться ~ой smuggle; **~и́ст** *m* [1] smuggler.
контр|аге́нт *m* [1] contractor; **~-адмира́л** *m* [1] rear admiral.
контра́кт *m* [1] contract.
контра́ст *m* [1], **~и́ровать** [7] contrast.
контрата́ка *f* [5] counterattack.
контрибу́ция ⚔ *f* [7] contribution.
контрол|ёр *m* [1] (ticket) inspector (🚂 *a.* ticket collector); **~и́ровать** [7], ⟨про-⟩ control, check; **~́ь** *m* [4] control, checkup; **~́ьный** [14] control ..., check...; **~́ьная** рабо́та *f* test (paper).
контр|разве́дка *f* [5] counterespionage, secret service; **~револю́ция** *f* [7] counterrevolution.
конту́з|ить [15] *pf.* bruise, contuse; **~ия** *f* [7] contusion, bruise.
ко́нтур *m* [1] contour, outline.
конура́ *f* [5] kennel.
ко́нус *m* [1] cone; **~ообра́зный** [14; -зен, -зна] conic(al).
конфере́нция *f* [7] conference (at на П).
конфе́та *f* [5] candy, *Brt.* sweet(s).
конфи|денциа́льный [14; -лен, -льна] confidential; **~скова́ть** [7] (*im*)*pf.* confiscate.
конфли́кт *m* [1] conflict.
конфу́з|ить [15], ⟨с-⟩ (**-ся** be [-come]) embarrass(ed), confuse(d); **~ливый** F [14 *sh.*] bashful, shy.
конц|ентрацио́нный [14] *s.* ~ла́герь; **~ентри́ровать** [7], ⟨с-⟩ concentrate (**-ся** *v/i.*); **~е́рт** *m* [1] concert (at на П); ♪ concerto; **~ла́герь** *m* [4] concentration camp.
конч|а́ть [1], ⟨**~́ить**⟩ [16] finish, end (**-ся** *v/i.*); graduate from; P stop; **~́ено!** F enough!; **~́ик** *m* [1] tip; end; **~и́на** *f* [5] decease.
конь *m* [4 *e.*; *nom/pl. st.*] horse; *poet.* steed; *chess*: knight; **~ки́** *m/pl.* [1] (ро́ликовые roller) skates; **~кобе́-**

жец *m* [1; -жца] skater; **~кобе́жный** [14] skating.
конья́к *m* [1 *e.*; *part. g.*: -у́] cognac.
ко́н|юх *m* [1] groom, (h)ostler; **~ю́шня** *f* [6; *g/pl.*: -шен] stable.
коопер|ати́в *m* [1] coöperative (store); **~а́ция** *f* [7] coöperation.
координи́ровать [7] *(im)pf.* coördinate.
копа́ть [1], ⟨вы-⟩ dig (up); **-ся** dig, root; rummage (about); dawdle.
копе́йка *f* [5; *g/pl.*: -е́ек] kopeck.
ко́пи *f/pl.* [8] mine, pit.
копи́лка *f* [5; *g/pl.*: -лок] money box.
копир|ова́льный [14]: **~ова́льная** бума́га *f* carbon paper; **~ова́ть** [7], ⟨с-⟩ copy; **~о́вщик** *m* [1] copyist.
копи́ть [14], ⟨на-⟩ save; store up.
ко́п|ия *f* [7] copy (*vb.* снять **~ию** с P); **~на́** *f* [5; *pl.*: ко́пны, -пён, -пна́м] stack.
ко́поть *f* [8] soot, lampblack.
копоши́ться [16 *e.*; -шу́сь, -ши́шься], ⟨за-⟩ swarm; F stir; mess around.
копти́ть [15 *e.*; -пчу́, -пти́шь; -пчённый], ⟨за-⟩ smoke; soot.
копы́то *n* [9] hoof.
копьё *n* [10; *pl. st.*] spear.
кора́ *f* [5] bark; crust.
кораб|лекруше́ние *n* [12] shipwreck; **~лестрое́ние** *n* [12] shipbuilding; **~ль** *m* [4 *e.*] ship; nave (*church*).
кора́лл *m* [1] coral; **~овый** [14] coral..., coralline.
Кордилье́ры *f/pl.* [5] Cordilleras.
коре́|ец *m* [1; -е́йца], **~йский** [16] Korean.
корен|а́стый [14 *sh.*] thickset, stocky; **~и́ться** [13] root; **~но́й** [14] native, aboriginal; fundamental, radical; molar (*tooth*); **'~ь** *m* [4; -рня; *from g/pl. e.*] root; в ко́рне totally; пусти́ть ко́рни take root; вы́рвать с ко́рнем pull up by the roots; **~нья** *n/pl.* [*gen.*: -ьев] roots.
корешо́к *m* [1; -шка́] rootlet; stalk (*mushroom*); back (*book*); stub, *Brt.* counterfoil.
Коре́|я *f* [6] Korea; **⁲я́нка** *f* [5; *g/pl.*: -нок] Korean.
корзи́н(к)а *f* [5 (*g/pl.*: -нок)] basket.
коридо́р *m* [1] corridor, passage.
кори́нка *f* [5; *g/pl.*: -нок] currant.
корифе́й *m* [3] *fig.* luminary, coryphеus, leader.
кори́ца *f* [5] cinnamon.
кори́чневый [14] brown.
ко́рка *f* [5; *g/pl.*: -рок] crust; rind, peel.
корм *m* [1; *pl.*: -ма́, *etc. e.*] fodder; seed; **~а́** *f* [5] stern.
корм|и́лец *m* [1; -льца] breadwinner; **~и́лица** *f* [5] wet nurse; **~и́ть** [14], ⟨на-, по-⟩ feed; **~и́ть** гру́дью nurse; F board; ⟨про-⟩ *fig.* maintain, support; **-ся** live on (T); **~ле́ние** *n* [12] feeding; nursing; **~ово́й** [14] feed(ing), fodder...; ⚓ stern...
корнепло́ды *m/pl.* [1] edible roots.
ко́роб *m* [1; *pl.*: -ба́, *etc. e.*] basket; **~е́йник** *m* [1] hawker; **~ить** [14], ⟨по-⟩ warp; *fig.* offend, sicken: **~ка** *f* [5; *g/pl.*: -бок] box, case.
коро́в|а *f* [5] cow; до́йная **~а** milch cow; **~ий** [18] cow...; **~ка** *f* [5; *g/pl.*: -вок]: бо́жья **~ка** ladybird; **~ник** *m* [1] cowshed.
короле́в|а *f* [5] queen; **~ский** [16] royal, regal; **~ство** *n* [9] kingdom.
корол|ёк *m* [1; -лька́] wren: **~ь** *m* [4 *e.*] king.
коромы́сло *n* [9; *g/pl.*: -сел] yoke; (*a. scale*) beam; dragonfly.
коро́н|а *f* [5] crown; **~а́ция** coronation; **~ка** *f* [5; *g/pl.*: -нок] (*tooth*) crown; **~ова́ние** *n* [12] coronation; **~ова́ть** [7] *(im)pf.* crown.
коро́ста *f* [5] scab, scabies.
корот|а́ть F [1], ⟨с-⟩ while away, beguile; **~кий** [16; ко́ро́ток, -тка́, ко́ротко́, ко́ротки́; *comp.*; коро́че] short, brief; *fig.* intimate, в **~ких** слова́х in a few words; коро́че (говоря́) in a word, in short (brief); **'~ко** и я́сно (quite) plainly; до́лго ли, **~ко** ли sooner or later.
ко́рпус *m* [1] body; [*pl.*: -са́, *etc. e.*] frame, case; building; (*a.* ⚔) corps.
коррект|и́в *m* [1] correction; **~и́ровать** [7], ⟨про-⟩ correct; *typ.* proofread; **~ный** [14; -тен, -тна] correct, proper; **~ор** *m* [1] proofreader; **~у́ра** *f* [5] proof(reading); держа́ть **~у́ру** *s.* **~и́ровать** (*typ.*).
корреспонд|е́нт *m* [1] correspondent; **~е́нция** *f* [7] correspondence.
корсе́т *m* [1] corset, *Brt. a.* stays *pl.*
ко́ртик *m* [1] cutlass, hanger.
ко́рточк|и *f/pl.* [5; *gen.*: -чек]: сесть (сиде́ть) на **~и** (**~ах**) squat.
корчева́|ние *n* [12] rooting out; **~ть** [7], ⟨вы́-, рас-⟩ root out.
ко́рчить [16], ⟨с-⟩ *impers.* (& **-ся**) writhe (with pain от бо́ли); convulse; (*no pf.*) F make (*faces*); (*a.* **~** из себя́) play, pose, put on airs, set up for.
ко́ршун *m* [1] vulture.
коры́ст|ный [14; -тен, -тна] selfish, self-interested; *a.* = **~олюби́вый** [14 *sh.*] greedy (of gain), mercenary; **~олю́бие** *n* [12] self-interest, greed; **~ь** *f* [8] gain, profit; use; greed.
коры́то *n* [9] trough.
корь *f* [8] measles.
коря́вый [14 *sh.*] knotty, gnarled; rugged, rough; crooked; clumsy.
коса́ *f* [5; *ac/sg.*: ко́су; *pl. st.*] **1.** plait, braid; **2.** [*ac/sg. a.* косу́] scythe; spit (of land); **~рь** *m* [4 *e.*] mower.
ко́свенный [14] oblique, indirect (*a. gr.*); ⚖ circumstantial (*evidence*).
коси́|лка *f* [5; *g/pl.*: -лок] mowing machine; **~ть**, ⟨с-⟩ **1.** [15; кошу́,

ко́сишь] mow; **2.** *a.* ⟨по-⟩ [15 *e.*; -кошу́, коси́шь] squint; twist (*mouth*), be(come) (a)wry; **-ся,** ⟨по-⟩ *v/i.*; *a.* look askance (at на В); **~чка** *f* [5; *g/pl.*: -чек] *dim.* of коса́ 1.
косма́тый [14 *sh.*] shaggy.
косм|е́тика *f* [5] cosmetics *pl.*; **~ети́ческий** [16] cosmetic; **~и́ческий** [16] cosmic; **~она́вт** *m* [1] astronaut.
косн|е́ть [8], ⟨за-⟩ persist, sink, fossilize (*fig.*); **∠ость** *f* [8] sluggishness, indolence; stagnation; **~у́ться** *s.* каса́ться; **∠ый** [14; -сен, -сна] sluggish, dull; stagnant, fossil.
косо|гла́зый [14 *sh.*] squint-eyed; **~го́р** *m* [1] slope; **∠й** [14; кос, -а́, -о] slanting, oblique; squint -(-eyed); F wry; **~ла́пый** [14 *sh.*] bandy-legged; F *s.* неуклю́жий.
костене́ть [8], ⟨о-⟩ ossify; stiffen, grow numb; be(come) transfixed.
костёр *m* [1; -тра́] (camp)fire, bonfire; pile, stake; meeting.
кост|и́стый [14 *sh.*] bony; **~ля́вый** [14 *sh.*] scrawny, raw-boned; **∠очка** *f* [5; *g/pl.*: -чек] bone; ⚘ stone; stay.
косты́ль *m* [4 *e.*] crutch; ⊕ spike.
кост|ь *f* [8; в -ти́; *from g/pl. e.*] bone; die; F бе́лая **~ь** blue blood; игра́ть в **∠и** (play at) dice.
костю́м *m* [1] suit; costume; **~иро́ванный** [14]: **~иро́ванный** бал *m* fancy(-dress) ball.
костя́|к *m* [1 *e.*] skeleton; framework; **~но́й** [14] bone...
косу́ля *f* [6] roe (deer).
косы́нка *f* [5; *g/pl.*: -нок] kerchief.
косьба́ *f* [5] mowing.
коса́к *m* [1 *e.*] lintel; slant; felloe; herd; flock; shoal.
кот *m* [1 *e.*] tomcat; *s. a.* ко́тик; купи́ть **~а́** в мешке́ buy a pig in a poke; **~** напла́кал F very little.
кот|ёл *m* [1; -тла́] boiler, caldron; kitchen; **~ело́к** *m* [1; -лка́] kettle, pot; ⚔ mess kit; derby, *Brt.* bowler.
котёнок *m* [2] kitten.
ко́тик *m* [1] *dim. of* кот; fur seal; seal(skin; *adj.*: **~овый** [14]).
котле́та *f* [5] rissole (*without paste*); cutlet, chop.
котлови́на *f* [5] hollow, basin.
кото́мка *f* [5; *g/pl.*: -мок] knapsack; bag.
кото́р|ый [14] which; who; that; what; many a; P some; one; **~ый** раз how many times; **~ый** час? what time is it?; в **~ом** часу́? (at) what time?; **~ый** ему́ год? how old is he?
ко́фе *m* [*indecl.*] coffee; **∠йник** *m* [1] coffee pot; **∠йница** *f* [5] coffee mill; coffee box; **∠йный** [14] coffee...; **∠йная** *f* = **∠йня** *f* [6; *g/pl.*: -ée н] coffee house, café.
ко́фт|а *f* [5] (woman's) jacket; blouse; (вя́заная **~а**) jersey, cardigan; **~очка** *f* [5; *g/pl.*: -чек] blouse.
коча́н *m* [1 *e.*] head (of cabbage).
кочев|а́ть [7] wander, roam; F move; travel; **∠ник** *m* [1] nomad; **~о́й** [14] nomadic.
кочега́р *m* [1] fireman, stoker.
кочене́ть [8], ⟨за-, о-⟩ grow numb, stiffen.
кочерга́ *f* [5; *g/pl.*: -рёг] poker.
ко́чка *f* [5; *g/pl.*: -чек] mound, hillock.
коша́чий [18] cat('s); feline.
кошелёк *m* [1; -лька́] purse.
ко́шка *f* [5; *g/pl.*: -шек] cat.
кошма́р *m* [1] nightmare; **~ный** [14; -рен, -рна] dreadful, horrible; F awful.
кощу́нств|енный [14 *sh.*] blasphemous; **~о** *n* [9] blasphemy; **~овать** [7] blaspheme (*v/t.* над Т).
коэффицие́нт *m* [1] coefficient.
КПСС (Коммунисти́ческая па́ртия Сове́тского Сою́за) Communist Party of the Soviet Union.
кра́деный [14] stolen (goods *n su.*).
краеуго́льный [14] *fig.* corner (*stone*); fundamental.
кра́жа *f* [5] theft; **~** со взло́мом burglary.
край *m* [3; с кра́ю; в -аю́; *pl.*: -ая́, -аёв, *etc. e.*] edge; (b)rim; brink (*a. fig.* =) edge; end; fringe, border, outskirt; region, land, country; **∠ний** [15] outermost, (*a. fig.*) utmost, extreme(ly, utterly, most, very, badly **∠не**); в **∠нем** слу́чае as a last resort; in case of emergency; **∠ность** *f* [8] extreme; extremity; до **∠ности** = **∠не**, *s.*; впада́ть в (доходи́ть до) **∠йности** go *or* run to extremes.
крамо́ла † *f* [5] sedition, revolt.
кран *m* [1] tap; ⊕ crane.
кра́пать [1 *or* 2 *st.*] drop, drip.
крапи́в|а *f* [5] nettle; **~ник** *m* [1] wren; **~ный** [14] nettle (*a.*, ⚕, *rash*).
кра́пинка *f* [5; *g/pl.*: -нок] speckle, spot.
крас|а́ *f* [5] † *s.* **~ота́**; **~а́вец** *m* [1; -вца] handsome man; **~а́вица** *f* [5] beauty, beautiful woman; **~и́вый** [14 *sh.*] beautiful; handsome; *a. iron.* fine.
крас|и́льный [14] dye...; **~и́льня** *f* [6; *g/pl.*: -лен] dye shop; **~и́льщик** *m* [1] dyer; **~и́тель** *m* [4] dye(stuff); **∠ить** [15], ⟨(п)о-, вы́-, рас-⟩ paint, colo(u)r, dye; F ⟨на-⟩ paint, make up; rouge; **∠ка** *f* [5; *g/pl.*: -сок] colo(u)r, paint, dye.
красне́ть [8], ⟨по-⟩ redden, grow *or* turn red; blush; *impf.* be ashamed; (*a.* **-ся**) appear, show red.
красно|арме́ец *m* [1; -ме́йца] Red Army man; **~ба́й** *m* [3] glib talker; **~ва́тый** [14 *sh.*] reddish; **~знамённый** [14] decorated with the Order of the Red Banner; **~ко́жий** [17] redskin(ned); **~речи́вый** [14 *sh.*] eloquent; **~ре́чие** *n* [12] eloquence;

~та́ *f* [5] redness; ruddiness; **~фло́тец** *m* [1; -тца] Red Navy man; **~щёкий** [16 *sh.*] ruddy.
красну́ха *f* [5] German measles.
кра́с|ный [14; -сен, -сна́, -о] red (*a. fig.*); † *s.* **~и́вый**; ♣ coniferous; **~ный** зверь *m* deer; **~ная** строка́ *f typ.* paragraph, new line; **~ная** цена́ *f* † F outside price; **~ное** словцо́ *n* F witticism; проходи́ть **~ной** ни́тью stand out.
красова́ться [7] shine, show (off).
красота́ *f* [5; *pl. st.*: -со́ты] beauty.
красть [25 *pt. st.*; кра́денный], ⟨у-⟩ steal (**-ся** *v/i.*, *impf.*; *a.* prowl slink).
кра́тк|ий [16; -ток, -тка́, -о; *comp.*: кра́тче] short, brief, concise; й **~ое** *or* й с **~ой** *the letter* й; *cf. a.* коро́ткий; **~овре́менный** [14; -енен, -енна] short; passing; **~осро́чный** [14; -чен, -чна] short; short-dated; short-term; **~ость** *f* [8] brevity.
кра́тный [14; -тен, -тна] divisible; *n su.* multiple; ...**~** ...fold.
крах *m* [1] failure, crash, ruin.
крахма́л *m* [1], **~ить** [13], ⟨на-⟩ starch; **~ьный** [14] starch(ed).
кра́шеный [14] painted; dyed.
креди́т *m* [1] credit; в **~** on credit; **~ный** [14], **~ова́ть** [7] (*im*)*pf.* credit; **~о́р** *m* [1] creditor; **~оспосо́бный** [14; -бен, -бна] solvent.
кре́йс|ер *m* [1] cruiser; **~ерство** *n* [9] cruise; **~и́ровать** [7] cruise; ply.
крем *m* [1] cream.
креме́нь *m* [4; -мня́] flint.
кремл|ёвский [16], **♀ь** *m* [4 *e.*] Kremlin.
кре́мн|ий [3] silicon; **~и́стый** [14 *sh.*] gravelly, stony; siliceous.
крен ⚓, ✈ *m* [1] list, careen.
кренде́ль *m* [4] cracknel.
крен|и́ть [13], ⟨на-⟩ list (**-ся** *v/i.*).
креп *m* [1] crepe, crape.
креп|и́ть [14 *e.*; -плю́, -пи́шь] fix, secure; reinforce; ⚓ belay; furl; *fig.* strengthen; **-ся** take courage; F persevere; **∠кий** [16; -пок, -пка́, -о; *comp.*: кре́пче] strong; firm, solid, sound; robust; hard; affectionate; **∠ко** *a.* fast; deep(ly); **∠нуть** [21], ⟨о-⟩ grow strong(er).
крепост|ни́чество *n* [9] serfdom; **~но́й** [14] (of, in) bond(age); *su.* serf; **~но́е** пра́во *s.* **~ни́чество**; (of a) fortress; **'~ь** *f* [8; *from g/pl. e.*] fortress; strength; firmness; ⚖ deed.
кре́сло *n* [9; *g/pl.*: -сел] armchair; *pl. thea.* † stall.
крест *m* [1 *e.*] cross (*a. fig.*); **~**-на́**~** crosswise; **~и́ны** *f/pl.* [5] baptism, christening; **~и́ть** [15; -щённый] (*im*)*pf.*, ⟨о-⟩ baptize, christen; godfather, godmother, sponsor; ⟨пере-⟩ cross (o.s. **-ся**); **∠ник** *m* [1] godson; **∠ница** *f* [5] goddaughter; **∠ный** [14] **1.** (of the) cross; **2.** ('kṛɔs-) **~ный** (оте́ц) *m* godfather; **~ная** (мать) *f* godmother.

крестья́н|ин *m* [1; *pl.*: -я́не, -я́н] peasant, farmer; **~ка** *f* [5; *g/pl.*: -нок] countrywoman, country girl; farmer's wife; **~ский** [16] farm (-er['s]), peasant...; country...; **~ство** *n* [9] peasantry.
креще́ние *n* [12] baptism (⚔ боево́е **~** baptism of fire), christening; ♀ Epiphany.
крив|а́я ⅋ *f* [14] curve; **~изна́** *f* [5] crookedness, curvature; **~и́ть** [14 *e.*; -влю́, -ви́шь; -влённый], ⟨по-, с-⟩ (**-ся** be[come]) crook(ed); twist(ed); **~и́ть** душо́й (со́вестью) palter; **~ля́ние** *n* [12] grimacing, twisting; **~ля́ться** [28] (make) grimace(s); mince; **~о́й** [14; крив, -а́, -о] crooked (*a. fig.*), wry; curve(d); F one-eyed; **~оно́гий** [16 *sh.*] bandy-legged; **~о́толки** *m/pl.* [1] rumo(u)rs, gossip; **~оши́п** ⊕ *m* [1] crank.
кри́зис *m* [1] crisis.
крик *m* [1] cry, shout; bawl, outcry; (*fashion*) cri; **~ли́вый** [14 *sh.*] shrill; clamorous; (*a. dress, etc.*) loud; **∠нуть** *s.* крича́ть; **~у́н** F *m* [1 *e.*], **~у́нья** F *f* [6] bawler, clamo(u)rer; tattler.
кри|мина́льный [14] criminal; **~ста́лл** *m* [1] crystal; **~ста́льный** [14; -лен, -льна] crystalline.
крите́рий *m* [3] criterion.
кри́ти|к *m* [1] critic; **~ка** *f* [5] criticism; critique, review; **~кова́ть** [7] criticize; **∠ческий** [16], **∠чный** [14; -чен, -чна] critical.
крича́ть [4 *e.*; -чу́, -чи́шь], ⟨за-⟩, *once* ⟨кри́кнуть⟩ [20] cry (out), shout (at на В); scream.
кров *m* [1] shelter; home; † roof.
крова́|вый [14 *sh.*] bloody, sanguinary; **~ть** *f* [8] bed; bedstead.
кро́вельщик *m* [1] tiler; slater.
кровено́сный [14] blood (*vessel*).
кро́вля *f* [6; *g/pl.*: -вель] roof(ing).
кро́вный [14] (*adv.* by) blood; full-blooded, pure-, thoroughbred; vital; arch...
крово|жа́дный [14; -ден, -дна] bloodthirsty; **~излия́ние** ⚕ *n* [12] extravasation, hemorrhage; **~обраще́ние** *n* [12] circulation of the blood; **~пи́йца** *m/f* [5] bloodsucker; **~подтёк** *m* [1] bruise; **~проли́тие** *n* [12] bloodshed; **~проли́тный** [14; -тен, -тна] *s.* крова́вый; **~пуска́ние** *n* [12] bloodletting; **~смеше́ние** *n* [12] incest; **~тече́ние** *n* [12] bleeding; *s.* **~излия́ние**; **~точи́ть** [16 *e.*; -чи́т] bleed.
кров|ь *f* [8; в -ви́; *from g/pl. e.*] blood (*a. fig.*); **~яно́й** [14] blood...
кро|и́ть [13; кро́енный], ⟨вы́-, с-⟩ cut (out); **∠йка** *f* [5] cutting (out).
крокоди́л *m* [1] crocodile.
кро́лик *m* [1] rabbit.
кро́ме (Р) except, besides (*a.* **~** того́), apart (*or* aside) from; but.

кромса́ть [1], ⟨ис-⟩ hack, mangle.
кро́на *f* [5] crown.
кропи́ть [14 *e.*; -плю́, -пи́шь; -плённый], ⟨о-⟩ sprinkle.
кропотли́вый [14 *sh.*] laborious, toilsome; painstaking, assiduous.
кроссво́рд *m* [1] crossword puzzle.
крот *m* [1 *e.*] *zo.* mole.
кро́ткий [16; -ток, -тка́, -о; *comp.*: кро́тче] gentle, meek.
кро|ха́ *f* [5; *ac/sg.*: кро́ху; *from dat/pl. e.*] crumb; bit; **⁓хотный** F [14; -тен, -тна], **⁓шечный** F [14] tiny; **⁓ши́ть** [16], ⟨на-, по-, ис-⟩ crumb(le); P crush; **⁓шка** *f* [5; *g/pl.*: -шек] crumb; bit; F baby, little one.
круг 1. *m* [1; в, на -у́; *pl. e.*] circle (*a. fig.*); sphere, range; orbit; F average; slice; **⁓лова́тый** [14 *sh.*] roundish; **⁓лоли́цый** [14 *sh.*] chubby-faced; **⁓лый** [14; кругл, -а́, -о] round; F perfect, complete; **⁓ово́й** [14] circular; mutual (*responsibility*); **⁓оворо́т** *m* [1] circulation; succession; **⁓озо́р** *m* [1] horizon, scope; **⁓о́м** round; around, round about; **⁓о́м!** ⚔ about face (*Brt.* turn)!; F entirely; **⁓ооборо́т** *m* [1] circulation; **⁓ообра́зный** [14; -зен, -зна] circular; **⁓осве́тный** [14] round the world; ⚓ circum...
кру́ж|ево *n* [9; *pl. e.*; *g/pl.*: кру́жев] lace **⁓и́ть** [16 & 16 *e.*; кружу́, кру́жи́шь], ⟨за-, вс-⟩ turn (round), whirl; circle; rotate, revolve, spin; stray about; (**-ся** *v/i.*); голова́ **⁓ится** (у Р) feel giddy, **⁓ка** *f* [5; *g/pl.*: -жек] mug; box.
кру́жный F [14] roundabout.
кружо́к *m* [1; -жка́] (small) circle, disk; *fig.* circle; slice.
круп *m* [1] (⚕ & *horse*) croup.
круп|а́ *f* [5] grits, groats *pl.*; sleet; **⁓и́нка** *f* [5; *g/pl.*: -нок] grain (*a. fig.* = **⁓и́ца** *f* [5]).
кру́пный [14; -пен, -пна́, -о] coarse(-grained), gross; big, large(-scale), great; outstanding; † wholesale; (*film*) close(*up*); F ⁓ разгово́р *m* high words.
крутизна́ *f* [5] steep(ness).
крути́ть [15], ⟨за-, с-⟩ twist; twirl; roll (up); turn; whirl; P *impf.* trick.
круто́|й [14; крут, -а́, -о; *comp.*: кру́че] steep, sharp, abrupt, sudden; hard (*a.*-boiled); harsh; **′⁓сть** *f* [8] steepness; harshness.
кру́ча *f* [5] *s.* крутизна́.
кручи́на P *f* [5] grief, affliction.
круше́ние *n* [12] 🚂 accident; ⚓ wreck; ruin, breakdown.
крыжо́вник *m* [1] gooseberry, -ries *pl.*
крыл|а́тый [14 *sh.*] winged (*a. fig.*); **⁓о́** *n* [9; *pl.*: кры́лья, -льев] wing (*a.* ✈, ⚠, ⚔, *pol.*); sail (*windmill*); splashboard; **⁓ьцо́** *n* [9; *pl.*: кры́льца, -ле́ц, -льца́м] steps *pl.*, (outside) staircase, porch.
Крым *m* [1; в -у́] Crimea; **′⁓ский** [16] Crimean.
кры́с|а *f* [5] rat; **⁓ий** [18] rat('s).
крыть [22], ⟨по-⟩ cover; coat; trump; **-ся** *impf.* lie *or* consist in (в П); be at the bottom of.
кры́ш|а *f* [5] roof; **⁓ка** *f* [5; *g/pl.*: -шек] lid, cover; P (Д р.'s) end, ruin.
крюк *m* [1 *e.*; *pl. a.* крю́чья, -ьев] hook; F detour.
крюч|кова́тый [14 *sh.*] hooked; **⁓котво́рство** *n* [9] pettifoggery; **⁓о́к** *m* [1; -чка́] hook; crochet needle; flourish; F hitch.
кряж *m* [1] range; chain of hills.
кря́к|ать [1], *once* ⟨**⁓нуть**⟩ [20] quack.
кряхте́ть [11] groan, moan.
кста́ти to the point (*or* purpose); opportune(ly), in the nick of time; apropos; besides, too, as well; incidentally, by the way.
кто [23] who; ⁓ ..., ⁓ ... some ..., others ...; ⁓ бы ни whoever; ⁓ бы то ни́ был who(so)ever it may be; ⁓ F = **⁓-либо**, **⁓-нибудь**, **⁓-то** [23] any-, somebody (*or* -one).
куб *m* [1] ⅄ cube; boiler.
ку́барем F head over heels.
ку́би|к *m* [1] (small) cube; block (*toy*); **⁓ческий** [16] cubic(al).
ку́бок *m* [1; -бка] goblet; *prize*: cup.
кубоме́тр *m* [1] cubic meter (-tre).
куве́рт † *m* [1] cover; envelope.
кувши́н *m* [1] jug; pitcher.
кувырк|а́ться [1], *once* ⟨**⁓ну́ться**⟩ [20] somersault, tumble; **⁓о́м** *s.* ку́барем.
куда́ where (... to); what ... for; F (*a.* ⁓ как[о́й], *etc.*) very, awfully, how; at all; by far, much; (*a.* + Д [& *inf.*]) how can ...; (*a.* ⁓ тут, там) (that's) impossible!, certainly not!, what an idea!, (*esp.* ⁓ тебе́!) rats!; ⁓ ..., ⁓ ... to some places ..., to others ...; ⁓ вы (*i. e.* идёте)? where are you going?; хоть ⁓ P tiptop, smart; *cf.* ни; ⁓ F = **⁓-либо**, **⁓-нибудь**, **⁓-то** any-, somewhere.
куда́хтать [3] cackle, cluck.
куде́сник *m* [1] wizard.
ку́др|и *f/pl.* [-е́й, *etc. e.*] curls; **⁓я́вый** [14 *sh.*] curly(-headed); tufty; ornate.
Кузба́сс ⚒ *m* [1] Kuznetsk Basin.
кузн|е́ц *m* [1 *e.*] (black)smith; **⁓е́чик** *m* [1] *zo.* grasshopper; **⁓ица** *f* [5] smithy.
ку́зов *m* [1; *pl.*: -ва́, *etc. e.*] body; box.
кукаре́кать [1] crow.
ку́киш P *m* [1] fig, fico.
ку́к|ла *f* [5; *g/pl.*: -кол] doll; **⁓олка** *f* [5; *g/pl.*: -лок] **1.** *dim. of* ⁓ла; **2.** *zo.* chrysalis; **⁓ольный** [14] doll('s); dollish; **⁓ольный теа́тр** *m* puppet show.

кукуру́за *f* [5] corn, *Brt.* maize.
куку́шка *f* [5; *g/pl.*: -шек] cuckoo.
кула́|к *m* [1 *e.*] fist; ⊕ cam; kulak; **~цкий** [16] kulak...; **~чество** *n* [9] kulaks *pl.*; **~чный** [14] boxing (*match*); club (*law*); ⊕ cam...
кулёк *m* [1; -лька́] (paper) bag.
кули́к *m* [1 *e.*] curlew; snipe.
кули́са *f* [5] wing, side scene; за ~ми behind the scenes.
кули́ч *m* [1 *e.*] Easter cake.
кулуа́ры *m/pl.* [1] lobbies.
куль *m* [4 *e.*] sack, bag.
культ *m* [1] cult; **~иви́ровать** [7] cultivate; **~рабо́та** *f* [5] cultural & educational work (*Sov.*); **~у́ра** *f* [5] culture; **~у́рный** [14 *sh.*] cultural; cultured, civilized; polite, well-bred.
кум *m* [1; *pl.*: -мовья́, -овьёв] godfather; **~а́** *f* [5] godmother; gossip.
кума́ч *m* [1 *e.*] red bunting.
куми́р *m* [1] idol.
кумовство́ *n* [9] sponsorship, friendship; *fig.* nepotism.
кумы́с *m* [1] k(o)umiss.
куни́ца *f* [5] marten.
купа́|льный [14] bathing (~льный костю́м *m* bathing suit, *Brt.* bathing costume); **~льня** *f* [6; *g/pl.*: -лен] (swimming) bath, bathhouse; **~льщик** *m* [1] bather; **~ть(ся)** [1], ‹вы́-, F ис-› (take a) bath; bathe.
купе́ (-ˈpɛ) [*ind.*] 🚃 *n* compartment.
купе́|ц *m* [1; -пца́] merchant; **~ческий** [16] merchant('s); **~чество** *n* [9] merchants *pl.*
купи́ть *s.* покупа́ть.
купле́т *m* [1] couplet, stanza; song.
ку́пля *f* [6] purchase.
ку́пол *m* [1; *pl.*: -ла́] cupola, dome.
купоро́с *m* [1] vitriol.
ку́пчая *f* [14] purchase deed.
курга́н *m* [1] burial mound, barrow.
ку́р|ево P *n* [9] tobacco, smoke; *a.* = **~е́ние** *n* [12] smoking; **~и́льщик** *m* [1] smoker.
кури́|ный [14] chicken...; hen's; F short (*memory*); night... (*blindness*).
кури́|тельный [14] smoking; **~ть** [13; курю́, ку́ришь], ‹по-, вы-› smoke (**-ся** *v/i.*); distil(l).
ку́рица *f* [5; *pl.*: ку́ры, *etc. st.*] hen; chicken, fowl.
курно́сый F [14 *sh.*] snub-nosed.
куро́к *m* [1; -рка́] cock (*gun*).
куропа́тка *f* [5; *g/pl.*: -ток] partridge.
куро́рт *m* [1] health resort.
курс *m* [1] course (⚓, ✈; 🎓; *educ.*; держа́ть ~ на [B] head for; *univ. a.* year); ✝ rate of exchange; *fig.* line, policy; держа́ть (быть) в ~е (P) keep (be) (well) posted on; **~а́нт** *m* [1] student; ⚔ cadet; **~и́в** *m* [1] *typ.* italics; **~и́ровать** [7] ply.
ку́ртка *f* [5; *g/pl.*: -ток] jacket.
курча́вый [14 *sh.*] curly(-headed).
курь|ёз *m* [1] fun(ny thing); curiosity; **~е́р** *m* [1] messenger; courier; **~е́рский** [16]: ~е́рский по́езд *m* express (train).
куря́тник *m* [1] hen house.
куря́щий *m* [18] smoker.
кус|а́ть [1], ‹укуси́ть› [15] bite (**-ся** *v/i., impf.*), sting; **~ково́й** [14] lump (*sugar*); **~о́к** *m* [1; -ска́] piece, bit, morsel; scrap; lump (*sugar*); cake (*soap*); slice; ~ка́ми by the piece; на ~ки́ to pieces; ~о́к хле́ба F living; **~о́чек** *m* [1; -чка] *dim. of* ~о́к.
куст *m* [1 *e.*] bush, shrub; **~а́рник** *m* [1] bush(es), shrub(s); *pl. a.* underwood.
куста́р|ный [14] handicraft...; home(-made); *fig.* homespun; **~ь** *m* [4 *e.*] (handi)craftsman.
ку́тать(ся) [1], ‹за-› muffle, wrap.
кут|ёж *m* [1 *e.*], **~и́ть** [15] carouse.
кух|а́рка *f* [5; *g/pl.*: -рок] cook; **~ня** *f* [6; *g/pl.*: ку́хонь] kitchen; cuisine, cookery; **~онный** [14] kitchen...
ку́цый [14 *sh.*] dock-tailed; short.
ку́ч|а *f* [5] heap, pile; a lot of; ~ами in heaps *or* in crowds; класть в ~у pile up; **~ер** *m* [1; *pl.*: -ра́, *etc. e.*] coachman; **~ка** *f* [5; *g/pl.*: -чек] *dim. of* ~а; group.
куш *m* [1] stake; F lot, sum.
куша́к *m* [1 *e.*] belt, girdle.
ку́ша|нье *n* [10] dish; meal; food; **~ть** [1], ‹по-› eat (up ‹с-›); drink.
куше́тка *f* [5; *g/pl.*: -ток] lounge.

Л

лабири́нт *m* [1] labyrinth.
лаборато́рия *f* [7] laboratory.
ла́ва *f* [5] lava.
лави́на *f* [5] avalanche.
лави́ровать [7] tack (⚓ & *fig.*).
ла́в|ка *f* [5; *g/pl.*: -вок] bench; (small) store, *Brt.* shop; **~очник** *m* [1] store-, shopkeeper; **~р** *m* [1] laurel; **~ро́вый** [14] (of) laurel(s).
ла́гер|ь 1. [4; *pl.*: -ря́, *etc. e.*] camp (*a., pl.*: -ри, *etc. st., fig.*); располага́ться (стоя́ть) ~ем camp (out); **~ный** [14] camp...
лад *m* [1; в -у́; *pl. e.*] F harmony, concord; order; way; tune; (не) в ~у́ (~а́х) *s.* (не) ~ить; идти́ на ~ work (well), get on *or* along; **~ан** *m* [1] incense; **~ить** F [15], ‹по-, с-› get along *or* on (well), *pf. a.* make it up; manage; fix; tune; не ~ить *a.* be at odds *or* variance; out of keeping; **-ся** F *impf. s.* идти́ на ~ & ~ить;

ˏно F well, all right, O. K.; **ˏный** F [14; -ден, -дна́, -о] harmonious; fine, good(-looking).
ла́дожск|ий [16]: ≗ое о́зеро *n* Lake Ladoga.
ладо́|нь *f* [8], **~ша** P *f* [5] palm; как на ~ни (*lie*) spread before the eyes; бить в ~ши clap (one's hands).
ладья́ *f* [6] boat; *chess*: rook.
лазаре́т ⚔ *m* [1] hospital.
лаз|е́йка *f* [5; *g/pl.*: -е́ек] loophole; **ˏить** [15] climb (*v/t.* на В); creep.
лазу́|рный [14; -рен, -рна], **~рь** *f* [8] azure; **~тчик** *m* [1] scout, spy.
лай *m* [3] bark(ing), yelp; **ˏка** *f* [5; *g/pl.*: ла́ек] **1.** Eskimo dog; **2.** kid (*leather*); **ˏковый** [14] kid...
лак *m* [1] varnish, laquer; **ˏовый** [14] varnish(ed), laquer(ed); patent leather...; **~а́ть** [1], ⟨вы́-⟩ lap.
лаке́й *m* [3] footman, lackey; flunk(e)y; **~ский** [16] lackey('s); *fig.* servile.
лакирова́ть [7], ⟨от-⟩ laquer; varnish.
ла́ком|иться [14], ⟨по-⟩ (Т) enjoy, relish (*a. fig.*). eat with delight; be fond of dainties; **~ка** F *m/f* [5] lover of dainties; быть ~кой *a.* have a sweet tooth; **~ство** *n* [9] dainty, delicacy; *pl.* sweetmeats, *Brt.* sweets; **~ый** [14 *sh.*] dainty; † (*a.* ~ый до Р) fond of (dainties); ~ый кусо́(че)к *m* tidbit, *Brt.* titbit.
лакони́ч|еский [16], **~ный** [14; -чен, -чна] laconic(al).
Ла-Ма́нш *m* [1] English Channel.
ла́мп|а *f* [5] lamp; *rad.* tube, *Brt.* valve; **~а́д(к)а** *f* [5 (*g/pl.*: -док)] (*icon*) lamp; **~овый** [14] lamp...; **~очка** *f* [5; *g/pl.*: -чек] bulb.
ландша́фт *m* [1] landscape.
ла́ндыш *m* [1] lily of the valley.
лань *f* [8] fallow deer; hind, doe.
ла́п|а *f* [5] paw; *fig.* clutch; **~оть** *m* [4; -птя; *from g/pl. e.*] bast shoe.
лапша́ *f* [5] noodles *pl.*; noodle soup.
ларёк *m* [1; -рька́] stand, *Brt.* stall.
ларе́ц [1; -рца́] box, chest, casket.
ла́ск|а *f* **1.** [5] caress; F affection; **2.** [5; *g/pl.*: -сок] weasel; **~а́тельный** [14] endearing, pet; † flattering; *s. a.* ~овый; **~а́ть** [1], ⟨при-⟩ caress; pet, fondle; *impf.* cherish; flatter (o.s. with себя́ Т); **-ся** endear o.s. (to к Д); fawn (*dog*); † (Т) cherish; **~овый** [14 *sh.*] affectionate, tender; caressing.
ла́сточка *f* [5; *g/pl.*: -чек] swallow.
лата́ть P [1], ⟨за-⟩ patch, mend.
латви́йский [16] Latvian.
лати́нский [16] Latin.
ла́тка P *f* [5; *g/pl.*: -ток] patch.
лату́к *m* [1] lettuce.
лату́нь *f* [8] brass.
ла́ты *f/pl.* [5] armo(u)r.
латы́нь *f* [13] Latin.
латы́ш *m* [1 *e.*], **~ка** *f* [5; *g/pl.*: -шек] Lett; **~ский** [16] Lettish.
лауреа́т *m* [1] prize winner.
лафе́т *m* [1] gun carriage.
лачу́га *f* [5] hovel, hut.
ла́ять [27], ⟨за-⟩ bark.
лгать [лгу, лжёшь, лгут; лгал, -а́, -о] **1.** ⟨со-⟩ lie; tell a p. (Д, пе́ред Т) a lie; **2.** ⟨на-⟩ (на В) defame.
лгун *m* [1 *e.*], **ˏья** *f* [6] liar.
лебёдка *f* [5; *g/pl.*: -док] windlass.
лебе|ди́ный [14] swan...; **'~дь** *m* [4; *from g/pl. e.*] (*poet. a. f*) swan; **~зи́ть** F [15 *e.*; -бежу́, -бези́шь] fawn (upon пе́ред Т).
лев *m* [1; льва] lion; ♌ Leo.
лев|ша́ *m/f* [5; *g/pl.*: -ше́й] left-handed person; **ˏый** [14] left (*a. fig.*), left-hand; wrong (*side*; on с Р).
лега́льный [14; -лен, -льна] legal.
леге́нд|а *f* [5] legend; **~а́рный** [14; -рен, -рна] legendary.
легио́н *m* [1] legion.
лёгкий (-xk-) [16; лёгок, легка́; *a.* лёгки] light (*a. fig.*); easy; slight; F lucky; (Д) легко́ + *inf.* it is very well for ... + *inf.*; лёгок на поми́не F talk of the devil!
легко|ве́рный (-xk-) [14; -рен, -рна] credulous; **~ве́сный** [14; -сен, -сна] light; *fig.* shallow; **~во́й** [14]: ~во́й автомоби́ль *m* (*a.* ~ва́я [авто]маши́на *f*) auto(mobile), car.
лёгкое (-xk-) *n* [16] lung.
легкомы́сл|енный (-xk-) [14 *sh.*] light-minded, frivolous; thoughtless; **~ие** *n* [12] levity; frivolity; flippancy.
лёгкость (-xk-) *f* [8] lightness; easiness; ease.
лёд *m* [1; льда; на льду́] ice.
лед|ене́ть [8], ⟨за-, о-⟩ freeze, ice; grow numb (with cold); chill; **~ене́ц** *m* [1; -нца́] (sugar) candy; **~ени́ть** [13], ⟨о(б)-⟩ freeze, ice; chill; **ˏник**[1] *m* [1] ice cellar; refrigerator, icebox; **~ни́к**[2] *m* [1 *e.*] glacier; **~нико́вый** [14] glacial; ice...; **~око́л** *m* [1] icebreaker; **~охо́д** *m* [1] ice drift; **~яно́й** [14] ice...; icy (*a. fig.*); chilly.
лежа́лый [14] stale, old, spoiled.
лежа́|ть [4 *e.*; лёжа] lie; be (situated); rest, be incumbent; form (*the basis* в П); **~чий** [17] lying; (*a.* ⚘) prostrate; turndown (*collar*).
ле́звие *n* [12] edge.
лезть [24 *st.*: ле́зу; лезь!; лез, -ла], ⟨по-⟩ (be) climb(ing, *etc.*; *v/t.* на В); creep; penetrate; F reach into; (к Д [с Т]) importune, press; fall out (*hair*); (на В) fit (*v/t.*); P meddle.
лейбори́ст *m* [1] Labo(u)rite.
ле́й|ка *f* [5; *g/pl.*: ле́ек] watering pot, can; **~тена́нт** *m* [1] (second) lieutenant.

лека́р|ственный [14] medicinal, curative; **~ство** *n* [9] medicine, remedy (against, for от, про́тив P); **'~ь** † & P *m* [4; *from g/pl. e.*] doctor.
ле́ксика *f* [5] vocabulary.
ле́к|тор *m* [1] lecturer; **~ция** *f* [7] lecture (at на П; *vb.*: слу́шать [чита́ть] attend [give, deliver]).
леле́ять [27] cherish, fondle.
ле́ме́х *m* [1 & 1 *e*; *pl.*: -ха́, *etc. e.*] plowshare (*Brt.* plough-share).
лён *m* [1; льна] flax.
лени́в|ец *m* [1; -вца] *s.* лентя́й; **~ица** *f* [5] *s.* лентя́йка; **~ый** [14 *sh.*] lazy, idle; sluggish.
Ленингра́д *m* [1] Leningrad; **2ец** *m* [1; -дца] Leningrader.
ле́нин|ец *m* [1; -нца], **~ский** [16] Leninist.
лени́ться [13; леню́сь, ле́нишься], be lazy.
ле́нта *f* [5] ribbon; band; ⊕ tape.
лентя́й F *m* [3], **~ка** *f* [5; *g/pl.*: -я́ек] lazybones; **~ничать** F [1] idle.
лень *f* [8] laziness, idleness; listlessness; F (мне) ~ I hate, don't want, won't.
лепе|сто́к *m* [1; -тка́] petal; **'~т** *m* [1], **~та́ть** [4], ⟨про-⟩ babble, prattle.
лепёшка *f* [5; *g/pl.*: -шек] scone; lozenge.
леп|и́ть [14], ⟨вы́-, с-⟩ sculpture, model, mo(u)ld; F ⟨на-⟩ stick (to на B); **∠ка** model(l)ing, mo(u)lding; F sculpture; **~но́й** [14] plastic.
ле́пта *f* [5] mite.
лес *m* [1; из лесу & из ле́са; в лесу́; *pl.*: леса́, *etc. e.*] wood, forest; lumber, *Brt.* timber; *pl.* scaffold(ing); **∠ом** through a (the) wood; как в ~у́ F *fig.* at sea; **∠а́** *f* [5; *pl.*: лёсы, *etc. st.*] (fishing) line; **~и́стый** [14 *sh.*] woody, wooded; **∠ка** *f* [5; *g/pl.*: -сок] *s.* ∠а́; **~ни́к** *m* [1 *e.*] ranger; **~ни́чество** *n* [9] forest district; **~ни́чий** *m* [17] forester; **~но́й** [14] forest...; wood(y); lumber...; *Brt.* timber...
лесо|во́дство *n* [9] forestry; **~насажде́ние** *n* [12] afforestation; (af)forested tract; wood; **~пи́лка** F *f* [5; *g/pl.*: -лок], **~пи́льный** [14]: ~пи́льный заво́д *m* = **~пи́льня** *f* [6; *g/pl.*: -лен] sawmill; **~ру́б** *m* [1] lumberman, woodcutter.
ле́стница *f* [5] (-șŋ-) (flight of) stairs *pl.*, staircase; ladder; *fig.* scale.
ле́ст|ный [14; -тен, -тна] flattering; **~ь** *f* [8] flattery.
лёт *m* [1] flight; на лету́ in the air, on the wing; F *fig.* in haste; instantly, quickly.
лета́, лет *s.* ле́то; *cf. a.* год.
лета́тельный [14] flying.
лета́ть [1] fly.
лете́ть [11], ⟨по-⟩ (be) fly(ing).
ле́тний [15] summer...
лётный [14] flying; run...
ле́т|о *n* [9; *pl. e.*] summer (in [the] T; for the на B); *pl.* years, age (at в B); ско́лько вам ~? how old are you? (*cf.* быть); в ~а́х elderly, advanced in years; **~опи́сец** *m* [1; -сца] chronicler; **~о́пись** *f* [8] chronicle; **~осчисле́ние** *n* [12] chronology; era.
лету́ч|ий [17 *sh.*] flying; fleeting; offhand, short; ⚗ volatile; **~ая мышь** *f zo.* bat; ~ий листо́к = **~ка** F *f* [5; *g/pl.*: -чек] leaflet.
лётчи|к *m* [1], **~ца** *f* [5] aviator, flier, pilot, air(wo)man.
лече́бн|ица *f* [5] clinic, hospital; **~ый** [14] medic(in)al.
леч|е́ние ⚕ *n* [12] treatment; **~и́ть** [16] treat; **-ся** undergo treatment, be treated; treat (one's ... от P).
лечь *s.* ложи́ться; *cf. a.* лежа́ть.
ле́ший *m* [17] satyr; P Old Nick.
лещ *m* [1 *e.*] *zo.* bream.
лж|е... false; pseudo...; **~ец** *m* [1 *e.*] liar; **~и́вость** *f* [8] mendacity; **~и́вый** [14 *sh.*] false, lying; mendacious.
ли, (*short, after vowels, a.*) ль **1.** (*interr. part.*:) зна́ет ~ он ...? (= он зна́ет ...?) does he know ...?; **2.** (*cj.*:) whether, if; ... ~, ... ~ whether ..., or ...
либера́л *m* [1], **~ьный** [14; -лен, -льна] liberal.
ли́бо or; ~ ..., ~ ... either ... or ...
Лива́н *m* [1] Lebanon.
ли́вень *m* [4; -вня] downpour.
ливре́я *f* [6; *g/pl.*: -ре́й] livery.
ли́га *f* [5] league.
ли́дер *m* [1] (*pol.*, *sport*) leader.
Ли́за(очк)а *f* [5] Liz(zy), Lise.
лиз|а́ть [3], *once* ⟨~ну́ть⟩ lick.
лик *m* [1] face; countenance; image.
ликвиди́ровать [7] (*im*)*pf.* liquidate.
ликова́ть [7], ⟨воз-⟩ exult.
ли́лия *f* [7] lily.
лило́вый [14] lilac(-colo[u]red).
лими́т *m* [1], **~и́ровать** [7] (*im*)*pf.* limit.
лимо́н *m* [1] lemon; **~а́д** *m* [1] lemonade.
ли́мфа *f* [5] lymph.
лингви́стика *f* [5] *s.* языкозна́ние.
лине́й|ка *f* [5; *g/pl.*: -е́ек] line; ruler; slide rule; † carriage; **~ный** [14] linear; ⚔ (of the) line; ⚓ battle...
ли́н|за *f* [5] lens; **~ия** *f* [7] line (*a. fig.*; in по Д); **~ко́р** *m* [1] battleship; **~ова́ть** [7], ⟨на-⟩ rule.
Линч: зако́н (*or* суд) ∠а lynch law; **2ева́ть** [7] (*im*)*pf.* lynch.
линь *m* [4 *e.*] *zo.* tench; ⚓ line.
ли́н|ька *f* [5] mo(u)lt(ing); **~ю́чий** F [17 *sh.*] fading, faded; mo(u)lting;

~ялый F [14] faded; mo(u)lted; **~ять** [28], ⟨вы-, по-⟩ fade; mo(u)lt.
ли́па *f* [5] linden, lime tree.
ли́п|кий [16; -пок, -пка́, -о] sticky; sticking (*plaster*); **~нуть** [21], ⟨при-⟩ stick.
ли́р|а *f* [5] lyre; **~ик** *m* [1] lyric poet; **~ика** *f* [5] lyric poetry; **~и́ческий** [16], **~и́чный** [14; -чен, -чна] lyric(al).
лис|(и́ц)а́ *f* [5; *pl. st.*] fox (silver… серебри́стая, черно-бу́рая); **∠ий** [18] fox…; foxy.
лист *m* 1. [1 *e.*] sheet; certificate; ⚖ deed; *typ.* leaf (= 16 pp.); 2. [1 *e.*; *pl. st* : ли́стья, -ьев] ♣ leaf; *a.* = **~ва́**; **~а́ть** F [1] leaf, thumb (through); **~ва́** *f* [5] foliage, leaves *pl.*; **∠венница** *f* [5] larch; **∠венный** [14] foliose, leafy; deciduous; **∠ик** *m* [1] *dim. of* ~; **~о́вка** *f* [5; *g/pl.*: -вок] *pol.* leaflet; **~о́к** *m* [1; -тка́] *dim. of* ~; slip; (news)paper; **~ово́й** [14] leaf(y); sheet…; folio…
Литва́ *f* [5] Lithuania.
лите́й|ная *f* [14], **~ный** [14]: **~ный заво́д** *m* foundry; **~щик** *m* [1] founder.
ли́тер|а *f* [5] letter, type; **~а́тор** *m* [1] man of letters; writer; **~ату́ра** *f* [5] literature; **~ату́рный** [14; -рен, -рна] literary.
лито́в|ец *m* [1; -вца], **~ка** *f* [5; *g/pl.*: -вок], **~ский** [16] Lithuanian.
лито́й [14] cast.
литр *m* [1] liter (*Brt.* -tre; = *approx.* 1qt.).
лить [лью, льёшь; лил, -а́, -о; ле́й(-те)! ли́тый (лит, -а́, -о)] pour; shed; ⊕ cast; дождь льёт как из ведра́ it's raining cats and dogs; **-ся** flow, pour; spread; sound; **~ё** *n* [10] founding, cast(ing).
лифт *m* [1] elevator, *Brt.* lift; **~ёр** *m* [1] elevator boy, *Brt.* lift man.
ли́фчик *m* [1] waist, bodice; bra(ssière).
лих|о́имец † *m* [1; -мца] usurer; bribe taker; **~о́й** [14; лих, -а́, -о] bold, daring; dashing; nimble; smart; **~ора́дка** *f* [5] fever; **~ора́дочный** [14; -чен, -чна] feverish; **∠ость** *f* [8] bravery; smartness.
лицев|а́ть [7], ⟨пере-⟩ face; turn; **~о́й** [14] face…; front…; right (*side*).
лицеме́р *m* [1] hypocrite; **~ие** *n* [12] hypocricy; **~ный** [14; -рен, -рна] hypocritical; **~ить** [13] dissemble.
лице́нзия *f* [7] license (for на В).
лиц|о́ *n* [9; *pl. st.*] face; countenance (*change v/t.* в П); front; person, individual(ity); в **~о́** by sight; to s. b.'s face; от **~а́** (Р) in the name of; **~о́м** к **~у́** face to face; быть (Д) к **~у́** suit *or* become a p.; нет **~а́** (на П) be bewildered; *s. a.* де́йствующий.
личи́н|а *f* [5] mask, guise; **~ка** *f* [5; *g/pl.*: -нок] larva; maggot.
ли́чн|ый [14] personal; **~ость** *f* [8] personality; identity (*card*).
лиша́й *m* [3 *e.*] ♣ lichen (*a.* **~ник**); ⚕ herpes.
лиш|а́ть [1], ⟨**~и́ть**⟩ [16 *e.*; -шу́, -ши́шь; -шённый] deprive, bereave, strip (of Р); **~а́ть (себя́) жи́зни** commit murder (upon В) (suicide); **~ённый** *a.* devoid of, lack(-ing); **-ся** (Р) lose; **~и́ться чувств** faint; **~е́ние** *n* [12] (de)privation; loss; *pl.* privations, hardships; **~е́ние прав** disfranchisement; **~е́ние свобо́ды** imprisonment; **~и́ть(ся)** *s.* **~а́ть(ся)**.
ли́шн|ий [15] superfluous, odd, excessive, over…, sur…; spare; extra; needless, unnecessary; outsider; **~ее** *n* undue (things, *etc.*), (*a.* a glass) too much; … с **~им** over …; **~ий раз** *m* once again; (Д) не **~е** *inf.* (р.) had better.
лишь (*a.* + то́лько) only; merely, just; as soon as, no sooner … than, hardly; ~ бы if only.
лоб *m* [1; лба; во, на лбу́] forehead.
ло́бзик *m* [1] fret saw.
ло́б|ный *anat.*, **~ово́й** [14] ⚔ frontal.
лови́ть [14], ⟨пойма́ть⟩ [1] catch; (en)trap; grasp, seize; ~ на сло́ве take at one's word.
ло́вк|ий [16; ло́вок, ловка́, -о] dexterous, adroit, deft; **~ость** *f* [8] adroitness, dexterity.
ло́в|ля *f* [6] catching; fishing; **~у́шка** *f* [5; *g/pl.*: -шек] trap; snare.
логари́фм *m* [1] logarithm.
ло́ги|ка *f* [5] logic; **∠ческий** [16], **∠чный** [14; -чен, -чна] logical.
ло́гов|ище *n* [11], **~о** *n* [9] lair, den.
ло́д|ка *f* [5; *g/pl.*: -док] boat; **~очник** *m* [1] boatman.
лоды́жка *f* [5; *g/pl.*: -жек] ankle.
ло́дырь F *m* [4] idler, loafer.
ло́жа *f* [5] *thea.* box; lodge; stock.
ложби́на *f* [5] hollow.
ло́же *n* [11] couch, bed; stock.
ложи́ться [16 *e.*; -жу́сь, -жи́шься], ⟨лечь⟩ [26 г/ж: ля́гу, ля́жешь, ля́гут; ля́г(те)!; лёг, легла́] lie down; ~ в (В) go to (*bed, a.* ~ [спать]); fall.
ло́жка *f* [5; *g/pl.*: -жек] spoon.
ло́ж|ный [14; -жен, -жна] false; **~ный путь** *m* wrong tack; **~ь** *f* [8; лжи; ло́жью] lie, falsehood.
лоза́ *f* [5; *pl. st.*] vine; switch ♣.
ло́зунг *m* [1] slogan, watchword.
локализова́ть [7] (*im*)*pf.* localize.
локо|моти́в *m* [1] locomotive, engine; **'~н** *m* [1] curl, lock; **'~ть** *m* [4; -ктя; *from g/pl. e.*] elbow.
лом *m* [1; *from g/pl. e.*] crowbar, pry; scrap (metal); **∠аный** [14] broken; **~а́ть** [1], ⟨с-⟩ break (*a.* up); pull (down), tear; **~а́ть го́лову** rack one's brains (over над Т); **-ся** break; Р clown, jest; mince, be prim.

ломба́рд *m* [1] pawnshop.
лом|и́ть [14] F = **∼а́ть**; *impers.* ache, feel a pain in; **-ся** bend, burst; F force (*v/t.* в В), break (into); **∠ка** *f* [5] breaking (up); **∠кий** [16; ло́мок, ломка́, -о] brittle, fragile; **∼ово́й** [14] breaking; scrap...; cart(er)...; **∼о́та** *f* [5] acute pains *pl.*; **∼о́ть** *m* [4; -мтя́] slice; **∠тик** *m* [1] *dim. of* **∼о́ть**.
ло́но *n* [9] lap; bosom (in на П).
ло́па|сть *f* [8; *from g/pl. e.*] blade; vane, fan; **∠та** *f* [8] shovel, spade; **∠тка** *f* [5; *g/pl.*: -ток] **1.** *dim. of* **∠та**; **2.** shoulder blade.
ло́п|аться [1], ⟨**∼нуть**⟩ [20] burst; crack, break; tear; F be exhausted.
лопу́х *m* [1 *e.*] burdock.
лоск *m* [1] luster, gloss, polish.
лоску́т *m* [1 *e.*; *pl. a.*: -ку́тья, -ьев] rag, shred, scrap, frazzle.
лос|ни́ться [13] be glossy *or* sleek, shine; **∠о́сь** *m* [4] salmon.
лось *m* [4; *from g/pl. e.*] elk.
лот *m* [1] plummet, lead.
лотере́я *f* [6] lottery.
лото́к *m* [1; -тка́] hawker's stand, tray.
лоха́н|ка *f* [5], **∼ь** *f* [8] tub.
лохм|а́тый [14 *sh.*] shaggy, dishevel(l)ed; **∼о́тья** *n/pl.* [*gen.*: -ьев] rags.
ло́цман ⚓ *m* [1] pilot.
лошад|и́ный [14] horse...; **∼и́ная** си́ла *f* horsepower; **'∼ь** *f* [8; *from g/pl. e., instr.*: -дьми́ & -дя́ми] horse.
лоша́к *m* [1 *e.*] hinny.
лощи́|на *f* [5] hollow, valley; **∼ть** [16 *e.*; -щу́, -щи́шь; -щённый] ⟨на-, вы́-⟩ gloss, polish.
лоя́льн|ость *f* [8] loyalty; **∼ый** [14; -лен, -льна] loyal.
лу|бо́к *m* [1; -бка́] ⚕ splint; cheap popular print (*or* literature).; **∼г** *m* [1; на -у́; *pl.* -а́, *etc. e.*] meadow.
луди́ть [15] tin.
лу́ж|а *f* [5] puddle, pool; сесть в **∼у** F be in a pretty pickle (*or* fix).
лужа́йка *f* [5; *g/pl.*: -а́ек] (small) glade.
лук *m* [1] **1.** onion(s); **2.** bow.
лука́в|ить [14], ⟨с-⟩ dissemble, dodge; **∼ство** *n* [9] cunning, slyness, ruse; **∼ый** [14 *sh.*] crafty, wily.
лу́ковица *f* [5] bulb; onion.
лун|а́ *f* [5] moon; **∼а́тик** *m* [1] sleepwalker; **∠ный** [14] moon(lit); *astr.* lunar.
лу́па *f* [5] magnifier, magnifying glass.
лупи́ть [14], ⟨об-⟩ peel (*v/i.* -ся).
луч *m* [1 *e.*] ray, beam; **∼ево́й** [14] radial; **∼еза́рный** [14; -рен, -рна] radiant; **∼еиспуска́ние** *n* [12] radiation; **∼и́на** *f* [5] (burning) chip, spill; **∼и́стый** [14 *sh.*] radiant.
лу́чш|е *adv.*, *comp. of* хорошо́; **∼ий** [17] better; best (at ... в **∼ем** слу́чае).
лущи́ть [16 *e.*; -щу́, -щи́шь], ⟨вы́-⟩ shell, husk.

лы́ж|а *f* [5] ski (*vb.*: ходи́ть, *etc.*, на **∼ах**); **∼ник** *m* [1], **∼ница** *f* [5] skier; **∼ный** [14] ski...
лы́ко *n* [9; *nom/pl.*: лы́ки] bast.
лы́с|ый [14] bald; **∼ина** *f* [5] bald head; blaze.
ль *s.* ли.
льви́|ный [14] lion's; **∼ный** зев ⚘ *m* snapdragon; **∼ца** *f* [5] lioness.
льго́т|а *f* [5] privilege; **∼ный** [14; -тен, -тна] privileged; reduced; favo(u)rable.
льди́на *f* [5] ice floe.
льну́ть [20], ⟨при-⟩ cling, nestle.
льняно́й [14] flax(en); linen...
льст|е́ц *m* [1 *e.*] flatterer; **∼и́вый** [14 *sh.*] flattering; **∼ить** [15], ⟨по-⟩ (Д) flatter (o.s. with себя́ Т).
любе́зн|ичать F [1] (с Т) court, flirt, spoon; **∼ость** *f* [8] amiability, kindness; favo(u)r; *pl.* compliments; **∼ый** [14; -зен, -зна] amiable, kind; dear; *su.* sweetheart; F lovely.
люби́м|ец *m* [1; -мца], **∼ица** *f* [5] favo(u)rite, pet; **∼ый** [14] beloved, darling; favo(u)rite, pet.
люби́тель *m* [4], **∼ница** *f* [5] lover, fan; amateur; **∼ский** [16] amateur (-ish).
люби́ть [14] love; like, be (⟨по-⟩ grow) fond of; *pf.* fall in love with.
любов|а́ться [7], ⟨по-⟩ (Т *or* на В) admire, (be) delight(ed) (in); **∠ник** *m* [1] lover; **∠ница** *f* [5] mistress; **∠ный** [14] love...; loving, affectionate; **∠ная** связь *f* amour; **∠ь** *f* **1.** [8; -бви́; -бо́вью] love (of, for к Д); **2.** ♀ [8] *fem. name* (*cf.* Amanda).
любо|зна́тельный [14; -лен, -льна] inquisitive, curious; inquiring; **∠й** [14] any(one *su.*); **∼пы́тный** [14; -тен, -тна] curious, inquisitive; interesting; мне **∼пы́тно** ... I wonder ...; **∼пы́тство** *n* [9] curiosity; interest.
лю́бящий [17] loving, affectionate.
люд *m* [1] *coll.* F, **∠и** *pl.* [-е́й, -ям, -дьми́, -ях] people; † servants; вы́йти в **∠и** arrive, make one's way in life (*or* fortune); на **∠ях** in public; **∠ный** [14; -ден, -дна] populous; crowded; **∼ое́д** *m* [1] cannibal; ogre; **∼ско́й** [16] man...; man's; human(e); servants' (room *su. f*).
люк *m* [1] hatch(way).
лю́лька *f* [5; *g/pl.*: -лек] cradle.
лю́стра *f* [5] chandelier, luster.
лю́тик *m* [1] buttercup.
лю́тый [14; лют, -а́, -о; *comp.*: -те́е] fierce, cruel, grim.
люце́рна *f* [5] alfalfa, *Brt.* lucerne.
ляг|а́ть(ся) [1], ⟨**∼ну́ть**⟩ [20] kick.
лягу́шка *f* [5; *g/pl.*: -шек] frog.
ля́жка *f* [5; *g/pl.*: -жек] thigh; haunch.
лязг *m* [1], **∠ать** [1] clank, clang, chatter.
ля́мк|а *f* [5; *g/pl.*: -мок] strap; тяну́ть **∼у** F drudge, toil.

М

мавзоле́й *m* [3] mausoleum.
магази́н *m* [1] store, *Brt.* shop.
магистра́ль *f* [8] main (✈ air) line 🚂 (✈ *a.* route) *or* waterway; thoroughfare; trunk (line); main.
маг|и́ческий [16] magic(al); **~нети́ческий** [16] magnetic(al).
ма́гний *m* [3] magnesium.
магни́т *m* [1] magnet.
магомета́н|ин *m* [1; *pl.*: -а́не, -а́н], **~ка** *f* [5; *g/pl.*: -нок] Mohammedan.
мадья́р *m* [1], **~ский** [16] Magyar.
маёвка *f* [5; *g/pl.*: -вок] May Day meeting, outing *or* picnic.
ма́з|анка *f* [5; *g/pl.*: -нок] mud hut; **~ать** [3] **1.** ⟨по-, на-⟩ smear; rub (in); anoint; spread, butter; whitewash; **2.** ⟨с-⟩ oil, lubricate; **3.** F ⟨за-⟩ soil; *impf.* daub; **~ня́** F *f* [6] daub(ing); **~о́к** *m* [1; -зка́] touch, stroke; ⚕ swab; **~ь** *f* [8] ointment; grease.
май *m* [3] May; **∠ка** *f* [5; *g/pl.*: ма́ек] sleeveless sports shirt; **~о́р** *m* [1] major; **∠ский** [16] May(-Day)...
мак *m* [1] poppy.
мак|а́ть [1], *once* ⟨**~ну́ть**⟩ [20] dip.
маке́т *m* [1] model; dummy.
ма́клер *m* [1] broker.
макну́ть *s.* мака́ть.
макре́ль *f* [8] mackerel.
максима́льный [14; -лен, -льна] maximum.
маку́шка *f* [5; *g/pl.*: -шек] top; crown.
мала́|ец *m* [1; -ла́йца], **~йка** *f* [5; *g/pl.*: ла́ек], **~йский** [16] Malay(an).
малева́ть F [6], ⟨на-⟩ paint, daub.
мале́йший [17] least, slightest.
ма́ленький [16] little, small; short; trifling, petty.
мали́н|а *f* [5] raspberry, -ries *pl.*; **~овка** *f* [5; *g/pl.*: -вок] robin (redbreast); **~овый** [14] raspberry-...; crimson; soft, sonorous.
ма́ло little (*a.* ~ что); few (*a.* ~ кто); a little; not enough; less; ~ где in few places; ~ когда́ seldom; F ~ ли что much, many things, anything; (*a.* ~ что) yes, but ...; that doesn't matter, even though; ~ того́ besides, and what is more; ~ того́, что not only (that).
мало|ва́жный [14; -жен, -жна] insignificant, trifling; **~ва́то** F little, not (quite) enough; **~вероя́тный** [14; -тен, -тна] unlikely; **~во́дный** [14; -ден, -дна] shallow; **~говоря́щий** [17] insignificant; **~гра́мотный** [14; -тен, -тна] uneducated, ignorant; faulty; **~ду́шный** [14; -шен, -шна] pusillanimous; **~зна́чащий** [17 *sh.*], **~значи́тельный** [14; -лен, -льна] *s.* **~ва́жный**; **~иму́щий** [17 *sh.*] poor; **~кро́вие** *n* [12] an(a)emia; **~кро́вный** [14; -вен, -вна] an(a)emic; **~ле́тний** [15] minor, underage; little (one); **~лю́дный** [14; -ден, -дна] poorly populated (*or* attended); **~-ма́льски** F a little bit; somewhat; **~общи́тельный** [14; -лен, -льна] unsociable; **~о́пытный** [14; -тен, -тна] inexperienced; **~-пома́лу** F gradually, little by little; **~ро́слый** [14 *sh.*] undersized; **~содержа́тельный** [14; -лен, -льна] vapid.
ма́л|ость *f* [8] smallness; F trifle; a bit; **~оце́нный** [14; -е́нен, -е́нна] inferior; **~очи́сленный** [14 *sh.*] small (in number), few; **~ый** [14; мал, -а́; *comp.*: ме́ньше] small, little; short; *cf.* **~енький**; *su.* fellow, guy; lad; без **~ого** almost, just shtor of; ~ и стар young & old; с **~ых** лет from (one's) childhood; **~ы́ш** F *m* [1 *e.*] kid(dy).
ма́льч|ик *m* [1] boy; lad; **~и́шеский** [16] boyish; mischievous; **~и́шка** F *m* [5; *g/pl.*: -шек] urchin; greenhorn; **~уга́н** F *m* [1] *s.* малы́ш; *a.* = **~и́шка**.
малю́тка *m/f* [5; *g/pl.*: -ток] baby, infant; *fig.* pygmy..., miniature...
маля́р *m* [1 *e.*] (house) painter.
маляри́я *f* [7] malaria.
ма́м|а *f* [5] ma(mma), mum, mother; **~а́ша** F *f* [5], F **~енька** *f* [5; *g/pl.*: -нек] mammy, mummy.
мандари́н *m* [1] mandarin.
манда́т *m* [1] mandate.
ман|ёвр *m* [1], **~еври́ровать** [7] maneuver, manoeuvre; 🚂 shunt, switch; **~еке́н** *m* [1] mannequin.
мане́р|а *f* [5] manner; **~ка** *f* [5; *g/pl.*: -рок] canteen, *Brt.* water bottle; **~ный** [14; -рен, -рна] affected.
манже́т(к)а *f* [5 (*g/pl.*: -ток)] cuff.
манипули́ровать [7] manipulate.
мани́ть [13; маню́, ма́нишь], ⟨по-⟩ (T) beckon; (al)lure, entice, tempt.
ман|и́шка *f* [5; *g/pl.*: -шек] dick(e)y; **∠ия** *f* [7] (вели́чия megalo)mania; **~ки́ровать** [7] (*im*)*pf.* (T) neglect.
ма́нная [14]: ~ крупа́ *f* semolina.
мануфакту́ра *f* [5] textiles *pl.*
мара́ть F [1], ⟨за-⟩ soil, stain; ⟨на-⟩ scribble, daub; ⟨вы́-⟩ delete.
ма́рганец *m* [1; -нца] manganese.
маргари́тка *f* [5; *g/pl.*: -ток] daisy.
маринова́ть [7], ⟨за-⟩ pickle.
ма́рк|а *f* [5; *g/pl.*: -рок] stamp; mark; counter; make; brand, trademark; **~и́за** *f* [5] awning; **~си́стский** [16] Marxist, Marxian.
ма́рля *f* [6] gauze.
мармела́д *m* [1] fruit candy (*or* drops).
март *m* [1], **∠овский** [16] March.

мар|ты́шка *f* [5; *g/pl.*: -шек] marmoset; '♀фа Martha.
марш *m* [1], **~ирова́ть** [7] march; **~ру́т** *m* [1] route.
ма́ск|а *f* [5; *g/pl.*: -сок] mask; **~ара́д** *m* [1] (*a.* бал-~ара́д) masked ball, masquerade; **~ирова́ть** [7], ⟨за-⟩, **~иро́вка** *f* [5; *g/pl.*: -вок] mask; disguise, camouflage.
ма́сл|еница *f* [5] (last week of) carnival; F feast; **~ёнка** *f* [5; *g/pl.*: -нок] butter dish; lubricator; **~еный** [14] *s.* ~яный; **~и́на** *f* [5] olive; **~и́чный** [14] olive...; oil ...; **~о** *n* [9; *pl.*: -сла́, -сел, -сла́м] (*a.* коро́вье, сли́вочное ~о) butter; (*a.* расти́тельное ~о) oil; как по ~у *fig.* (*go*) on wheels; **~обо́йка** *f* [5; *g/pl.*: -бек] churn; oil mill; **~яный** [14] oil(y); butter(y); greasy, unctuous.
ма́сс|а *f* [5] mass; bulk; multitude; **~а́ж** *m* [1], **~и́ровать** [7] (*pt.a.pf.*) massage; **~и́в** *m* [1] massif; **~и́вный** [14; -вен, -вна] massive; **~овый** [14] mass...
ма́стер *m* [1; *pl.*: -ра́, *etc. e.*] master; foreman; craftsman; expert; ~ на все ру́ки jack-of-all-trades; **~и́ть** F [13], ⟨с-⟩ work; make; **~ска́я** *f* [16] workshop; atelier, studio; **~ско́й** [16] masterly (*adv.* ~ски́); **~ство́** *n* [9] mastery, skill; trade, handicraft.
масти́тый [14 *sh.*] venerable.
масть *f* [8; *from g/pl. e.*] colo(u)r; suit.
масшта́б *m* [1] scale (on в П); *fig.* scope; caliber (*Brt.* -bre); repute; standard.
мат *m* [1] mat; (check)mate.
Матве́й *m* [6] Matthew.
матема́ти|к *m* [1] mathematician; **~ка** *f* [5] mathematics; **~́ческий** [16] mathematical.
материа́л *m* [1] material; **~и́зм** *m* [1] materialism; **~и́ст** *m* [1] materialist; **~исти́ческий** [16] materialistic; **~ьный** [14; -лен, -льна] material; economic; financial.
матери́к *m* [1 *e.*] continent.
матери́|нский [16] mother('s), motherly, maternal; **~нство** *n* [9] maternity; **'~я** *f* [7] matter; fabric, material; stuff.
ма́тка *f* [5; *g/pl.*: -ток] *zo.* female; queen (*bee*); *anat.* uterus.
ма́товый [14] dull, dim, mat.
матра́|с, ~ц *m* [1] mattress.
ма́трица *f* [5] *typ.* matrix; stencil.
матро́с *m* [1] sailor.
матч *m* [1] match (*sport*).
мать *f* [ма́тери, *etc.* = 8; *pl.*: ма́тери, -ре́й, *etc. e.*] mother.
мах *m* [1] stroke, flap; с (одного́) ~́у at one stroke *or* stretch; at once; дать ~́у miss one's mark, make a blunder; **~а́ть** [3, F 1], *once* ⟨~ну́ть⟩ [20] (T) wave; wag; strike, flap; *pf.* F jump, go; ~ну́ть руко́й на (B) give up; **~ови́к** *m* [1 *e.*], **~ово́й** [14]: ~ово́е колесо́ *n* flywheel.
махо́рка *f* [5] (poor) tobacco.
ма́чеха *f* [5] stepmother.
ма́чта *f* [5] mast.
Ма́ш([ень]к)а [5] *dim. of* Мари́я.
маши́н|а *f* [5] machine; engine; F car, bike, *etc.*; **~а́льный** [14; -лен, -льна] mechanical, perfunctory; **~и́ст** *m* [1] machinist; 🚂 engineer, *Brt.* engine driver; **~и́стка** *f* [5; *g/pl.*: -ток] (girl) typist; **~ка** *f* [5; *g/pl.*: -нок] (small) machine; typewriter; clipper (под ~ку cropped); **~ный** [14] machine..., engine...; *cf.* МТС; **~опись** *f* [8] typewriting; **~острое́ние** *n* [7] mechanical engineering.
мая́к *m* [1 *e.*] lighthouse.
ма́я|тник *m* [1] pendulum; **~ться** P [27] drudge; **~́чить** F [16] loom.
МВД *abbr.*: Министе́рство вну́тренних дел (*s.* министе́рство).
мгл|а *f* [5] darkness; mist, haze; **~и́стый** [14 *sh.*] hazy, misty.
мгнове́н|ие *n* [12] moment; instant, twinkling; **~ный** [14; -е́нен, -е́нна] momentary, instantaneous.
ме́бе|ль *f* [8] furniture; **~лирова́ть** [7] (*im*)*pf.*, ⟨об-⟩ furnish (with T); **~лиро́вка** *f* [5] furnishing(s).
мёд *m* [1; *part. g.*: мёду; в меду́; *pl. e.*] honey; mead.
меда́ль *f* [8] medal; **~о́н** *m* [1] locket.
медве́|дица *f* [5] she-bear; *astr.* ♀дица Bear; **~дь** *m* [4] bear (F *a. fig.*); **~жий** [18] bear('s, -skin); bad (*service*); **~жо́нок** *m* [2] bear cub.
ме́ди|к *m* [1] medical man (F student); **~каме́нты** *m/pl.* [1] medicaments, medical supplies; **~ци́на** *f* [5] medicine; **~ци́нский** [16] medical; medicinal.
ме́дл|енный [14 *sh.*] slow; **~и́тельный** [14; -лен, -льна] sluggish, slow, indolent; **~ить** [14], ⟨про-⟩ delay, linger, be slow *or* tardy, hesitate.
ме́дный [14] copper(y); brazen.
медо́вый [14] honey(ed).
мед|осмо́тр *m* [1] medical examination; **~пу́нкт** *m* [1] first-aid post; **~сестра́** *f* [5; *pl. st.:* -сёстры, -сестёр, -сёстрам] nurse.
медь *f* [8] copper; жёлтая ~ brass.
меж *s.* ~́ду; **~а́** *f* [5; *pl.*: ме́жи, меж, межа́м] border; balk; **~доме́тие** *n* [12] *gr.* interjection; **~доусо́бный** [14] internal, civil (*war, etc.*).
ме́жду (T; *a.* P *pl.* †) between; among(st); ~ тем meanwhile, (in the) meantime; ~ тем как whereas, while; **~горо́дный** [14] *teleph.* long-distance..., *Brt.* trunk... (*e. g. exchange, su. f*); interurban; **~наро́дный** [14] international; **~ца́рствие** *n* [12] interregnum.
межплане́тный [14] interplanetary.

Ме́ксик|а *f* [5] Mexico; **2а́нец** *m* [1; -нца], **2а́нка** *f* [5; *g/pl.*: -нок], **2а́нский** [16] Mexican.
мел *m* [1; в -у́] chalk; whitewash.
меланхо́л|ик *m* [1] melancholiac; **~и́ческий** [16], **~и́чный** [14; -чен, -чна] melancholy, melancholic; **~ия** *f* [7] melancholy.
меле́ть [8], ⟨об-⟩ (grow) shallow.
ме́лк|ий [16; -лок, -лка́, -о; *comp.*: ме́льче] small, little; petty; fine, shallow; flat (*plate*); **~ий** дождь *m* drizzle; **~ово́дный** [14; -ден, -дна] shallow; **~ость** *f* [8], F **~ота́** *f* [8] shallowness; **~ота́** *a.* = ме́лочь *coll.*
мелоди́|ческий [16] melodic; melodious; **~чный** [14; -чен, -чна] melodious; **'~я** *f* [7] melody.
ме́лоч|ность *f* [8] pettiness, paltriness; **~ный** & **~но́й** [14; -чен, -чна] petty, paltry; **~ь** *f* [8; *from g/pl. e.*] trifle; trinket; *coll.* small fry, (small) change; *pl.* details, particulars.
мел|ь *f* [8] shoal, sandbank; на **~и́** aground; F in a fix.
мельк|а́ть [1], ⟨**~ну́ть**⟩ [20] flash; gleam; flit; fly (past); loom; turn up; **¿ом** in passing.
ме́льни|к *m* [1] miller; **~ца** *f* [5] mill.
мельч|а́ть [1], ⟨из-⟩ become (**~и́ть** [16 *e.*; -чу́, чи́шь] make) small(er) *or* shallow(er).
мелюзга́ F *f* [5] *s.* ме́лочь *coll.*
мемуа́ры *m/pl.* [1] memoirs.
ме́на *f* [5] exchange; barter.
ме́нее less; **~** всего́ least of all; тем не **~** nevertheless.
менов*о́й* [14] exchange...; *cf.* ме́на.
ме́ньш|е less; smaller; *s. a.* ме́нее; **~еви́к** *m* [1 *e.*] Menshevik; **~ий** [17] smaller, lesser; smallest, least; F (= † **~о́й**) youngest; **~инство́** *n* [9] minority.
меню́ *n* [*indecl.*] menu, bill of fare.
меня́ть [28], ⟨по-, об-⟩ exchange, barter (for на B); change (*cf.* пере~); **-ся** *v/i.* (s. th. with T/cT).
ме́р|а *f* [5] measure; degree; way; по **~е** (P) *or* того́ как according as, to (*a.* в **~у** P); as far as; while the ..., the ... (+ *comp.*); по кра́йней (ме́ньшей) **~е** at least.
мере́щиться F [16], ⟨по-⟩ (Д) seem (*to hear, etc.*); appear; loom.
мерз|а́вец F *m* [1; -вца] rascal; **¿кий** [16; -зок, -зка́, -о] vile, odious.
мёрз|лый [14] frozen; **~нуть** [21], ⟨за-⟩ freeze; be cold, numb.
ме́рзость *f* [8] meanness; nasty thing.
мери́ло *n* [9] standard; criterion.
ме́рин *m* [1] gelding.
ме́р|ить [13], ⟨с-⟩ measure; ⟨при-, по-⟩ F try on; **~иться**, ⟨по-⟩ cope, try conclusions with (с T); **~ка** *f* [5; *g/pl.*: -рок] measure(s) (to по Д).
ме́ркнуть [21], ⟨по-⟩ fade, darken.
мерлу́шка *f* [5; *g/pl.*: -шек] astrakhan.
ме́р|ный [14; -рен, -рна] measured; **~оприя́тие** *n* [12] measure, action.
ме́ртв|енный [14 *sh.*] deadly (pale); **~е́ть** [8], ⟨о-⟩ deaden; grow *or* turn numb (pale, desolate); **~е́ц** *m* [1 *e.*] corpse; **~е́цкая** F *f* [14] mortuary.
мёртв|ый [14; мёртв, мертва́, мёртво; *fig.*: мертво́, мертвы́] dead; **~ый** час *m* after-dinner rest; **~ая** то́чка *f* ⊕ dead center; *fig.* deadlock (at на П).
мерца́|ние *n* [12], **~ть** [1] twinkle.
меси́ть [15], ⟨за-, с-⟩ knead.
мести́ [25 -т-: мету́, метёшь; мётший], ⟨под-⟩ sweep.
ме́стн|ость *f* [8] region, district, locality, place; **~ый** [14] local; **~ый** жи́тель *m* native.
ме́ст|о *n* [9; *pl. e.*] place, spot; seat; F job, post; passage; package; *pl. a.* = **~ность**; о́бщее (*or* изби́тое) **~о** commonplace; (заде́ть за) больно́е **~о** tender spot (touch on the raw); (не) к **~у** in (out of) place; не на **~е** in the wrong place; **~а́ми** in (some) places, here & there; **~ожи́тельство** *n* [9] residence; **~оиме́ние** *n* [12] *gr.* pronoun; **~онахожде́ние**, **~оположе́ние** *n* [12] location, position; **~опребыва́ние** *n* [12] whereabouts; residence; **~орожде́ние** *n* [12] deposit, field.
месть *f* [8] revenge.
ме́ся|ц *m* [1] month; moon; в **~ц** a month, per month; **~чный** [14] month's; monthly; moon...
мета́лл *m* [1] metal; **~и́ст** *m* [1] metalworker; **~и́ческий** [16] metal(lic); **~у́ргия** *f* [7] metallurgy.
мет|а́тельный [14] missile; **~а́ть** [3], *once* ⟨**~ну́ть**⟩ [20] throw; bring forth; keep (*bank*); baste; **~а́ть** икру́ spawn; **-ся** toss, jerk; rush about.
мете́л|ица *f* [5], **~ь** [8] snowstorm.
метеоро́лог *m* [1] meteorologist; **~и́ческий** [16] meteorological; **¿ия** *f* [7] meteorology.
ме́т|ить [15], ⟨по-⟩ mark; (в, на B) aim, drive at, mean; **~ка** [5; *g/pl.*: -ток] mark(ing); **~кий** [16; -ток, -тка́, -о] well-aimed; good (*shot*); keen, accurate, steady; pointed; neat; ready(-witted).
мет|ла́ *f* [5; *pl. st.*: мётлы, мётел; мётлам] broom; **~ну́ть** *s.* мета́ть.
ме́тод *m* [1] method; **~и́ческий** [16] methodic(al), systematic(al).
метр *m* [1] meter, *Brt.* metre.
ме́трика *f* [5] certificate of birth; metrics.
метро́ *n* [*ind.*], **~полите́н** (-'tɛn) *m* [1] subway, *Brt.* tube, underground.
мех *m* [1] **1.** [*pl. e.*] (*often pl.*) bellows *pl.*; **2.** [*pl.*: -xа́, *etc.*, *e.*] fur; (wine)skin; на **~у́** fur-lined.
механ|изи́ровать [7] (*im*)*pf.* mechanize; **~и́зм** *m* [1] mechanism; **¿ик**

m [1] mechanic(ian); ∠ика *f* [5] mechanics; ~и́ческий [16] mechanical propelling (*pencil*).
мехов|о́й [14] fur...; **~щи́к** *m* [1 *e.*] furrier.
меч *m* [1 *e.*] sword.
мече́ть *f* [8] mosque.
мечта́ *f* [5] dream, daydream, reverie; **~ние** *n* [12] 1. = ~; 2. dreaming; **~тель** *m* [4] (day)dreamer; **~тельный** [14; -лен, -льна] dreamy; **~ть** [1] dream (of о П).
меша́|ть [1], ⟨раз-⟩ stir; ⟨с-, пере-⟩ mix, mingle; † confuse; ⟨по-⟩ (Д) disturb; hinder, impede, prevent; вам не **~ет** (**~ло** бы) you'd better; **-ся** meddle, interfere (with в В); не **~йтесь** не в своё де́ло! mind your own business!
ме́шк|ать F [1], ⟨про-⟩ = ме́длить; **~ова́тый** [14 *sh.*] baggy; clumry.
мешо́к *m* [1; -шка́] sack, bag.
мещан|и́н *m* [1; *pl.*: -а́не, -а́н], **∠ский** [16] (petty) bourgeois, Philistine; **∠ство** *n* [9] petty bourgeoisie, lower-middle class; Philistinism, Babbittry.
миг *m* [1] moment, instant; **∠ом** F in a trice (flash); **~а́ть** [1], *once* ⟨**~ну́ть**⟩ [20] blink, wink; twinkle.
мигре́нь *f* [8] sick headache.
мизе́рный [14; -рен, -рна] paltry.
мизи́нец *m* [1; -нца] little finger.
ми́ленький F [16] lovely; dear; darling.
милици|оне́р *m* [1] militiaman; policeman (*Sov.*); **'~я** *f* [7] militia; police (*Sov.*).
милли|а́рд *m* [1] billion, *Brt.* milliard; **~ме́тр** *m* [1] millimeter (*Brt.* -tre); **~о́н** *m* [1] million.
ми́ловать [7] pardon; spare.
мило|ви́дный [14; -ден, -дна] lovely, sweet; **~се́рдие** *n* [12] charity, mercy; **~се́рдный** [14; -ден, -дна] charitable, merciful; **'~стивый** [14 *sh.*] gracious, kind; **'~стыня** *f* [6] alms; **'~сть** *f* [8] mercy; favo(u)r; pardon, ⚔ quarter; kindness; **'~сти** про́сим! welcome!; *iron.* скажи́(те) на **'~сть** just imagine.
ми́л|ый [14; мил, -а́, -о] nice, lovely, sweet; (my) dear, darling.
ми́ля *f* [6] mile.
ми́мо (Р) past, by; beside (*mark*); бить ~ miss; **~лётный** [14; -тен, -тна] fleeting, passing; **~хо́дом** in passing; incidentally.
ми́на *f* [5] ⚔, ⚒ mine; look, air.
минда́|лина *f* [5] almond; *anat.* tonsil; **~ль** *m* [4 *e.*] almond(s); **~льничать** F [1] spoon; trifle.
минерало́гия *f* [7] mineralogy.
миниатю́рный [14; -рен, -рна] miniature...; *fig.* tiny, diminutive.
минист|е́рство *n* [9] ministry; **~е́рство** иностра́нных (вну́тренних) дел Ministry of Foreign (Internal) Affairs (*U.S.S.R.*), State Department (Dept. of the Interior) (*U.S.*), Foreign (Home) Office (*Brt.*); **∠р** *m* [1] minister, secretary.
мин|ова́ть [7] (*im*)*pf.*, ⟨**~у́ть**⟩ [20] pass; leave out *or* aside, not enter into; (Р) escape; (Д) **∠уло** *s.* испо́лниться; **~у́вший**, **~у́вшее** *su.* past.
миноно́сец *m* [1; -сца] torpedo boat; эска́дренный ~ destroyer.
ми́нус *m* [1] minus; defect.
мину́т|а *f* [5] minute; moment, instant (at в В; for на В); сию́ **~у** at once, immediately; at this moment; с **~ы** на **~у** (at) any moment; *cf.* пя́тый & пять; **~ный** [14] minute('s); moment('s), momentary; **~ь** *s.* минова́ть.
мир *m* [1] 1. peace; 2. [*pl. e.*] world, universe; planet; † (peasants') community (meeting); ~ во всём **∠е** world peace; ходи́ть (пусти́ть) по́ **~у** go begging (bring to beggary).
мир|и́ть [13], ⟨по-, при-⟩ reconcile (to с Т); **-ся** make it up, be(come) reconciled; ⟨при-⟩ resign o. s. to; put up with; **∠ный** [14; -рен, -рна] peace... peaceful.
мировоззре́ние *n* [12] Weltanschauung, world view; ideology.
мирово́й [14] world('s), world-wide, universal; peaceful, peaceable, of peace; F *su. f* arrangement.
миро|люби́вый [14 *sh.*] peaceful; peace loving; **~созерца́ние** *n* [12] world view, outlook.
мирско́й [16] worldly; common.
ми́ска *f* [5; *g/pl.*: -сок] dish, tureen; bowl.
мисси|оне́р *m* [1] missionary; **'~я** *f* [7] mission; legation.
ми́стика *f* [5] mysticism.
Ми́тя *m* [6] *dim. of* Дми́трий.
миф *m* [1] myth; **~и́ческий** [16] mythic(al); **~оло́гия** *f* [7] mythology.
Ми|ха́йл *m* [1] Michael; **∠ша** *m* [5] (*dim. of* **~ха́йл**) Mike.
мише́нь *f* [8] target.
мишура́ *f* [5] tinsel, spangle.
младе́н|ец *m* [1; -нца] infant, baby; **~чество** *n* [9] infancy.
мла́дший [17] younger, youngest; junior.
млекопита́ющее *n* [17] mammal.
млеть [8] die, faint, sink, droop.
мле́чный [14] milky (*a.* ♋, *ast.*).
мне́ние *n* [12] opinion (in по Д).
мни́|мый [14 *sh.*, *no m*] imaginary; supposed, pretended, would-be, sham; **~тельный** [14; -лен, -льна] suspicious; hypochondriac(al).
мно́гие *pl.* [16] many (people, *su.*).
мно́го (Р) much, many; a lot (*or* plenty) of; more; ~-~ at (the) most; **~ва́то** F rather much (many); **~во́дный** [14; -ден, -дна] abounding in water, deep; **~гра́нный** [14; -а́нен, -а́нна] many-sided;

~жёнство *n* [9] polygamy; **~значи́тельный** [14; -лен, -льна] significant; **~зна́чный** [14; -чен, -чна] of many places (⅍) *or* meanings; **~кра́тный** [14; -тен, -тна] repeated, frequent(ative *gr.*); ⅍ multiple; **~ле́тний** [15] longstanding, of many years; long-lived; long-term ...; ⚘ perennial; **~лю́дный** [14; -ден, -дна] crowded; populous; mass ...; **~обеща́ющий** [17] (very) promising; **~обра́зный** [14; -зен, -зна] varied, manifold; **~речи́вый** [14 *sh.*], **~сло́вный** [14; -вен, -вна] talkative; wordy; **~сторо́нний** [15; -о́нен, -о́нняя] many-sided; **~страда́льный** [14; -лен, -льна] long-suffering; **~то́чие** *n* [12] dots *pl.*; **~уважа́емый** [14] dear (*address*); **~цве́тный** [14; -тен, -тна] multicolo(u)red; **~чи́сленный** [14 *sh.*] numerous; **~эта́жный** [14] many-storied (*Brt.*-reyed); **~язы́чный** [14; -чен, -чна] polyglot.

мно́ж|ественный [14 *sh.*] plural; **~ество** *n* [9] multitude; **~имое** *n* [14] multiplicand; **~итель** *m* [4] multiplier; **~ить**, ⟨по-⟩ *s.* умножа́ть.

мобилизова́ть [7] (*im*)*pf.* mobilize.

моги́л|а *f* [5] grave; **~ьный** [14] tomb...; **~ьщик** *m* [1] grave digger.

могу́|чий [17 *sh.*], **~щественный** [14 *sh.*] mighty, powerful; **~щество** *n* [9] might.

мо́д|а *f* [5] fashion, vogue; **~е́ль** (-ˈdɛl) *f* [8] model; ⊕ mo(u)ld; **~ернизи́ровать** (-dɛr-) [7] (*im*)*pf.* modernize; **~и́стка** *f* [5; *g*/*pl.*: -ток] milliner; **~ифици́ровать** [7] (*im*-)*pf.* modify; **~ный** [14; -ден, -дна́, -о] fashionable, stylish; [*no sh.*] fashion...

мо́ж|ет быть perhaps, maybe; **~но** (мне, *etc.*) one (I, *etc.*) can *or* may; it is possible; *cf.* как.

моза́ика *f* [5] mosaic.

мозг *m* [1; -а (-у); в -у́; *pl. e.*] brain; marrow; (*spinal*) cord; **~ово́й** [14] cerebral.

мозо́|листый [14 *sh.*] horny, callous; **~лить** [13]: **~лить** глаза́ (Д) F be an eyesore to; **~ль** *f* [8] callosity; corn.

мо|й *m*, **~я́** *f*, **~ё** *n*, **~и́** *pl.* [24] my; mine; *pl. su.* F my folks; *s.* ваш.

мо́кко *m* [*ind.*] mocha.

мо́к|нуть [21], ⟨про-⟩ become wet; soak; **~ро́та**[1] *f* [5] phleghm; **~рота́**[2] F *f* [5] wet(ness), humidity; **~рый** [14; мокр, -а́, -о] wet; moist.

мол *m* [1] jetty, mole.

молв|а́ *f* [5] rumo(u)r; talk; **~ить** † [14] (*im*)*pf.*, ⟨про-⟩ say, utter.

молдава́н|ин *m* [1; *pl.*: -ва́не, -а́н], **~ка** *f* [5; *g*/*pl.*: -нок] Moldavian.

моле́бен *m* [1; -бна] thanksgiving (service), Te Deum.

моле́кул|а *f* [5] molecule; **~я́рный** [14] molecular.

моли́т|ва *f* [5] prayer; **~венник** *m* [1] prayer book; **~ь** [13; молю́, мо́лишь] (о П) implore (s. th.), entreat, beseech (for); **~ься**, ⟨по-⟩ pray (to Д; for о П).

молни|ено́сный [14; -сен, -сна] flash-like; blazing; thunder (*cloud*); violent; ⚔ blitz...; **ˈ~я** *f* [7] lightning; flash; zipper, zip fastener.

молод|ёжь *f* [8] youth, young people *pl.*; **~е́ть** [8], ⟨по-⟩ grow (look) younger; **~е́ц** F *m* [1; -дца́] fine fellow, brick; well done!; **~е́цкий** F [16] brave, valiant; smart; **~и́ть** [15 *e.*; -ложу́, -лоди́шь] rejuvenate; **~ня́к** *m* [1 *e.*] offspring; underwood; saplings *pl.*; **~ожёны** *m*/*pl.* [1] newly wedded couple; **~о́й** [14; мо́лод, -а́, -о; *comp.*: моло́же] young; new; *pl. a.* = **~ожёны**; **ˈ~ость** *f* [8] youth, adolescence; **~цева́тый** [14 *sh.*] smart.

моложа́вый [14 *sh.*] youthful, young-looking.

моло́к|и *f*/*pl.* [5] milt; **~о́** *n* [9] milk; **~осо́с** F *m* [1] greenhorn.

мо́лот *m* [1] (large) hammer; **~и́лка** *f* [5; *g*/*pl.*: -лок] threshing machine; **~и́ть** [15], ⟨с-⟩ thresh; **~о́к** *m* [1; -тка́] hammer; с **~ка́** by auction; **∠ь** [17; мелю́, ме́лешь; меля́], ⟨пере-, с-⟩ grind; P *impf.* talk; **~ьба́** *f* [5] threshing (time).

моло́чн|ая *f* [14] dairy, creamery; **~ик** *m* [1] milk jug; F milkman; **~ый** [14] milk...; dairy...

мо́лча silently, tacitly; **~ли́вый** [14 *sh.*] taciturn; **∠ние** *n* [12] silence; **∠ть** [4 *e.*; мо́лча], be (*or* keep) silent; (за)молчи́! shut up!

моль *f* [8] moth; [*ind. adj.*] ♪ minor.

мольба́ *f* [5] entreaty; prayer.

моме́нт *m* [1] moment, instant (at в В); **~а́льный** [14] momentary, instantaneous; snap (*shot*).

мона́рхия *f* [7] monarchy.

мона|сты́рь *m* [4 *e.*] monastery, convent; **∠х** *m* [1] monk; **∠хиня** *f* [6] nun (*a.*, F, **∠шенка** *f* [5; *g*/*pl.*: -нок]); **∠шеский** [16] monastic; monk's.

монго́льский [16] Mongolian.

моне́т|а *f* [5] coin; money, cash; той же **~ой** in a p.'s own coin; за чи́стую **~у** in good faith; **~ный** [14] monetary; **~ный** двор *m* mint.

моно|ло́г *m* [1] monologue; **~полизи́ровать** [7] (*im*)*pf.* monopolize; **~по́лия** *f* [7] monopoly; **~то́нный** [14; -то́нен, -то́нна] monotonous.

монт|а́ж *m* [1] assembling, assemblage; cutting (*film*); montage; **~ёр** *m* [1] assembler, mechanic(ian); electrician; **~и́ровать** [7], ⟨с-⟩ assemble, install; cut (*film*).

мора́ль *f* [8] morals *pl.*; morality; moral; F lecture, lecturing; **~ный**

[14; -лен, -льна] moral; ~ное состояние *n* morale.
морг|áть [1], ‹~нýть› [20] blink (T).
мóрда *f* [5] muzzle, snout.
мóре *n* [10; *pl. e.*] sea; seaside (at на П); ~м by sea; зá ~м overseas; ~плáвание *n* [12] navigation; ~плáватель *m* [4] seafarer.
морж *m* [1 *e.*], ~óвый [14] walrus.
морúть [13], ‹за-, у-› exterminate; ~ гóлодом starve; torment, exhaust.
моркóвь *f* [8] carrot(s).
морóженое *n* [14] ice cream.
морóз *m* [1] frost; ~ить [15], ‹за-› freeze; ~ный [14; -зен, -зна] frosty.
моросúть [15; -сúт] drizzle.
морóчить F [16] fool, beguile.
морск|óй [14] sea..., maritime; naval; nautical; seaside...; ~óй волк *m* old salt; ~óй флот *m* navy.
мóрфий *m* [3] morphine, morphia.
морфолóгия *f* [7] morphology.
морщú|на *f* [5] wrinkle; ~нистый [14 *sh.*] wrinkled; '~ть [16], ‹на-, с-› wrinkle, frown (*v/i.* -ся); distort.
моря́к *m* [1 *e.*] seaman, sailor.
москатéльный [14] drug(gist's).
Моск|вá *f* [5] Moscow; ♀вúч *m* [1 *e.*] ♀вúчка *f* [5; *g/pl.*: -чек] Moscower; ♀óвский [16] Moscow...
москúт *m* [1] mosquito.
мост *m* [1 & 1 *e.*; на -ý; *pl. e.*] bridge; ~úть [15 *e.*; мощý, мостúшь; мощённый], ‹вы́-› pave; ~кú *m/pl.* [1 *e.*] planked footway, footbridge; ~овáя *f* [14] pavement; ~овóй [14] bridge...; ~овщúк *m* [1 *e.*] pavio(u)r.
мот *m* [1] spendthrift, prodigal.
мот|áть [1], ‹на-, с-› reel, wind; F ‹по-›, *once* ‹~нýть› shake, wag; beckon, point; jerk; F ‹про-› squander, waste; -ся F *impf* dangle; P knock about.
мотúв *m* [1] motiv, motif; ~úровать [7] (*im*)*pf.* motivate.
мотовствó *n* [9] extravagance.
мотóк *m* [1; -ткá] skein.
мотóр *m* [1] motor, engine; ~изовáть [7] (*im*)*pf.* motorize.
мотоцúкл, ~éт *m* [1], motorcycle; ~úст *m* [1] motorcyclist.
моты́га *f* [8] hoe, mattock.
мотылёк [1; -лькá] butterfly.
мох *m* [1; мха & мóха, во (на) мхý; *pl.*: мхи, мхов] moss.
мохнáтый [14 *sh.*] shaggy, hairy.
моховóй [14] mossy.
моч|á *f* [5] urine; ~áлка *f* [5; *g/pl.*: -лок] bast whisp; ~евóй [14]: ~евóй пузы́рь *m* (urinary) bladder; ~úть [16], ‹на-, за-› wet, moisten; soak, step (*v/i.* -ся; *a.* urinate); ∠ка *f* [5; *g/pl.*: -чек] lobe (*of the ear*).
мочь[1] [26 г/ж: могý, мóжешь, мóгут; мог, -лá; могýщий], ‹с-› can, be able; may; я не могý не + *inf.* I can't help ...ing; не могý знать ... I don't know (,sir); не мóжет быть! that's impossible!
моч|ь[2] P *f* [8]: во всю ~ь, изо всей ∠и, что есть ∠и with all one's might; ∠и нет impossible, I, *etc.*, can't; awfully.
мошéнни|к *m* [1] swindler, cheat (-er); ~чать [1], ‹с-› swindle; ~ческий [16] fraudulent; ~чество *n* [9] swindle, fraud.
мóшка *f* [5; *g/pl.*: -шек] midge.
мощёный [14] paved.
мóщи *f/pl.* [*gen.*: -щéй, *etc. e.*] relics.
мóщ|ность *f* [8] power; ~ный [14; мóщен, -щнá, -o] powerful, mighty; ~ь *f* [8] power, might; strength.
м. пр. *abbr.*: мéжду прóчим.
мрак *m* [1] dark(ness); gloom.
мракобéс *m* [1] obscurant; ~ие *n* [12] obscurantism.
мрáмор *m* [1] marble.
мрачн|éть [8], ‹по-› darken; ∠ый [14; -чен, -чнá, -o] dark; obscure; gloomy, somber (*Brt.*-bre).
мстú|тель *m* [4] avenger; ~тельный [14; -лен, -льна] revengeful; ~ть [15], ‹ото-› revenge o.s., take revenge (on Д); (за В) avenge a p.
МТС (машúнно-трáкторная стáнция) machine and tractor station.
мудр|ёный F [14; -ён, -енá; -енée] difficult, hard, intricate; fanciful; queer; ~ёного нет (it's) no wonder; ~éц *m* [1 *e.*] sage; ~úть F [13], ‹на-, с-› subtilize; quibble; trick; (над T) bully; ∠ость *f* [8] wisdom; зуб ∠ости wisdom tooth; F trick; ∠ствовать F [7] *s.* ~úть; ∠ый [14; мудр, -á, -o] wise, sage.
муж *m* 1. [1; *pl.*: -жья́, -жéй, -жья́м] husband; 2. † [1; *pl.*: -жú, -жéй, -жáм] man; ~áть [1], ‹воз-› mature, grow; -ся *impf.* take courage; ∠ественный [14 *sh.*] courageous; manly; ∠ество *n* [9] courage, spirit; ~úк † *m* [1 *e.*] peasant; P boor; man; ~úцкий [16], P ~úчий [18] peasant's, rustic; ~скóй [16] male, (*a. gr.*) masculine; (gentle-) man('s); ~чúна *m* [5] man.
музéй *m* [3] museum.
мýзык|а *f* [5] music; P business; ~áльный [14; -лен, -льна] musical; ~áнт *m* [1] musician.
мýка[1] *f* [5] pain, torment, suffering, torture(s); F harassment.
мукá[2] *f* [5] flour; meal.
мул *m* [1] mule.
мýмия *f* [7] mummy.
мундúр *m* [1] uniform; картóшка в ~е F potatoes in their jackets *or* skin.
мундштýк (-nʃ-) *m* [1 *e.*] cigarette holder; tip; mouthpiece.
муравá *f* [5] (young) grass; glaze.
мурав|éй *m* [3; -вья́; *pl.*: -вьú, -вьёв] ant; ~éйник *m* [1] ant hill; ~ьúный [14] ant...
мурáшки: (от P) ~ бéгают по спинé (у P) F (s. th.) gives (a p.) the shivers.
мурлы́кать [3 & 1] purr; F hum.
мускáт *m* [1], ~ный [14] nutmeg.

му́скул *m* [1] muscle; **~истый** [14 *sh.*], **~ьный** [14] muscular.
му́скус *m* [1] musk.
му́сор *m* [1] rubbish, refuse; **~ный** [14]: **~ный я́щик** *m* ash can, *Brt.* dust bin; **~щик** *m* [1] ashman.
муссо́н *m* [1] monsoon.
мусульма́н|ин *m* [1; *pl.*: -а́не, -а́н], **~ка** *f* [5; *g/pl.*: -нок] Moslem.
мут|и́ть [15; мучу́, му́тишь], ⟨вз-, по-⟩ trouble, muddle; fog; меня́ **~и́т** F I feel sick; **-ся** = **~не́ть** [8], ⟨по-⟩ grow turbid; blur; **∠ный** [14; -тен, -тна́, -о] muddy, (*a. fig.*) troubled (*waters*); dull; blurred; foggy; uneasy; **~о́вка** *f* [5; *g/pl.*: -вок] twirling stick; **~ь** *f* [8] dregs *pl.*; mud; blur; haze; dazzle.
му́фта *f* [5] muff; ⊕ socket, sleeve.
му́х|а *f* [5] fly; **~оло́вка** *f* [5; *g/pl.*: -вок] flycatcher; **~омо́р** *m* [1] toadstool.
муч|е́ние *n* [12] *s.* му́ка; **∠еник** *m* [1] martyr; **~и́тель** *m* [4] tormentor; **~и́тельный** [14; -лен, -льна] painful, agonizing; **∠ить** [16], P **∠ать** [1], ⟨за-, из-⟩ torment, torture; vex, worry; **-ся** agonize, suffer torments; toil; **~но́й** [14] flour(y), mealy.
му́шка *f* [5; *g/pl.*: -шек] midge; beauty spot; speck; (Spanish) fly; (fore)sight (*gun*).
муштр(о́вк)а́ ⚔ *f* [5] drill.
мча́ть(ся) [4], ⟨по-⟩ rush, whirl *or* speed (along).
мши́стый [14 *sh.*] mossy.
мще́ние *n* [12] vengeance.
мы [20] we; ~ с ним he and I.
мы́л|ить [13], ⟨на-⟩ soap; **~ить** го́лову (Д) F blow up, scold; **~о** *n* [9; *pl. e.*] soap; lather; **~оваре́ние** *n* [12] soap boiling; **~ьница** *f* [5] soap dish; **~ьный** [14] soap(y).
мыс *m* [1] cape.
мы́сл|енный [14] mental; **~имый** [14 *sh.*] conceivable; **~и́тель** *m* [4] thinker; **~ить** [13] think (of, about о П); imagine; **~ь** *f* [8] thought, idea (of о П); intention.
мыта́рство *n* [9] toil, drudgery.
мыть(ся) [22], ⟨по-, у-, вы́-⟩ wash.
мыча́ть [4 *e.*; -чу́, -чи́шь] moo, low; F mumble.
мышело́вка *f* [5; *g/pl.*: -вок] mouse trap.
мы́шечный [14] muscular.
мы́шка *f* [5; *g/pl.*: -шек] **1.** armpit; arm; **2.** *dim. of* мышь.
мышле́ние *n* [12] thougt, thinking
мы́шца *f* [5] muscle.
мышь *f* [8; *from g/pl. e.*] mouse.
мышья́к *m* [1 *e.*] arsenic.
мя́гк|ий (-xk-) [16; -гок, -гка́, -о; *comp.*: мя́гче] soft; smooth, sleek; tender; mild, gentle; lenient; easy (*chair*); **~ий** ваго́н 🚃 first-class coach *or* car(riage); **~осерде́чный** [14; -чен, -чна] soft-hearted; **~ость** *f* [8] softness; **~оте́лый** [14] chubby; *fig.* fladdy, spineless.
мягчи́|тельный (-xtʃ-) [14] lenitive; **~ть** [16; -чи́т] soften.
мяк|и́на *f* [5] chaff; **∠иш** *m* [1] crumb; **∠нуть** [21], ⟨на-, раз-⟩ become soft; **∠оть** *f* [8] flesh, pulp.
мя́млить P [13] mumble; dawdle.
мяс|и́стый [14 *sh.*] fleshy, pulpy; F fat, chubby; **~ни́к** *m* [1 *e.*] butcher; **~но́й** [14] meat...; butcher's; **∠о** *n* [9] meat; flesh, pulp; (*cannon*) fodder; **~oру́бка** *f* [5; *g/pl.*: -бок] mincing machine; *fig.* slaughter.
мя́та *f* [8] mint.
мяте́ж *m* [1 *e.*] rebellion, mutiny; **~ник** *m* [1] rebel; **~ный** [14] rebellious.
мять [мну, мнёшь; мя́тый], ⟨с-, по-, из-⟩ [сомну́; изомну́] (c)rumple, press; knead, wrinkle; trample; **-ся** F waver.
мяу́к|ать [1], *once* ⟨**~нуть**⟩ mew.
мяч *m* [1 *e.*] ball; **∠ик** [1] *dim. of* ~.

Н

на[1] **1.** (В): (*direction*) on, onto; to, toward(s); into, in; (*duration, value, purpose, etc.*) for; till; ℞ by; ~ что? what for?; **2.** (П): (*position*) on, upon; in, at; with; for; ~ ней ... she has ... on.
на́[2] F there, here (you are, *a.* ∠ тебе).
наба́в|ка F = надба́вка; **~ля́ть** [28], ⟨**~ить**⟩ [14] raise; add.
наба́т *m* [1] alarm bell, tocsin.
набе́|г *m* [1] incursion, raid; **~га́ть** [1], ⟨**~жа́ть**⟩ [4; -егу́, -ежи́шь, -егу́т; -еги́(те)!] run (against *or* on на В); cover; gather.
набекре́нь F aslant, cocked.
на́бело (*make*) a fair copy.
на́бережная *f* [14] quay, wharf.
наби|ва́ть [1], ⟨**∠ть**⟩ [-бью́, -бьёшь; *cf.* бить] stuff, fill; fix on (*a.* many, much); shoot; print (*calico*); **∠вка** *f* [5; *g/pl.*: -вок] stuffing, padding.
набира́ть [1], ⟨набра́ть⟩ [-беру́, -рёшь; *cf.* брать] gather; enlist, recruit; *teleph.* dial; *typ.* set; take (too many, much); gain (*speed, height*); be, have; **-ся** *a.*, (Р), pluck *or* screw up; F catch; acquire.
наби́|тый [14 *sh.*] (Т) packed; P arrant (*fool*); битко́м **~тый** F crammed full; **~ть** *s.* **~ва́ть**.
наблюд|а́тель *m* [4] observer; **~а́тельный** [14; -лен, -льна] observant, alert; observation (*post*); **~а́ть** [1] (*v/t.* & за Т) observe; watch;

see after *or* to (it that); **~éние** *n* [12] observation; supervision.
нáбожный [14; -жен, -жна] pious, devout.
нáбок to *or* on one side.
наболéвший [16] sore; burning.
набóр *m* [1] enlistment, levy; enrol(l)ment; set; typesetting; taking; **~щик** *m* [1] typesetter, compositor.
набр|áсывать [1] **1.** ⟨~осáть⟩ [1] sketch, design, draft; throw (up); **2.** ⟨~óсить⟩ [15] throw over, on (на В); **-ся** fall (up)on.
набрáть *s.* набирáть.
набрести́ F [25] *pf.* come across (на В).
набрóсок *m* [1; -ска] sketch, draft.
набух|áть [1], ⟨~нуть⟩ [21] swell.
навáл|ивать [1], ⟨~и́ть⟩ [13; -алю́, -áлишь; -áленный] heap; load; **-ся** press; fall (up)on, go at.
навéд|ываться, ⟨~аться⟩ F [1] call on (к Д); inquire after, about (о П).
навéк, **~и** forever, for good.
навéрн|о(е) probably; for certain, definitely; (*a.*, F, **~яка́**) without fail.
навёрстывать, ⟨наверстáть⟩ [1] make up for.
навéрх up(ward[s]); upstairs; **~ý** above, on high; upstairs.
навéс *m* [1] awning; shed.
навеселé F tipsy, drunk.
навести́ *s.* наводи́ть.
навести́ть *s.* навещáть.
навéтренный [14] windward.
навéчно forever, for good.
наве|щáть[1], ⟨~сти́ть⟩[15*e.*; -ещý, -ести́шь; -ещённый] call on.
нáвзничь on one's back.
навзры́д: плáкать ~ sob.
навис|áть [1], ⟨~нуть⟩ [21] hang (over); impend; **~ший** beetle (*brow*).
навле|кáть [1], ⟨~чь⟩ [26] incur.
наводи́ть [15], ⟨навести́⟩ [25] (на В) direct (to); point (at), turn (to); lead (to), bring on *or* about, cause, raise (*cf.* нагоня́ть); apply (*paint, etc.*); make; construct; ~ спрáвки inquire (after о П).
наводн|éние *n* [12] flood, inundation; **~я́ть** [28], ⟨~и́ть⟩ [13] flood, inundate.
наводя́щий [17] leading.
навóз *m* [1], **~ить** [15], ⟨у-⟩ dung, manure; **~ный** [14] dung...; **~ная** жи́жа *f* liquid manure.
нáволочка *f* [5; *g/pl.*: -чек] pillowcase.
навостри́ть [13] *pf.* prick up (*one's ears*).
навря́д (ли) F hardly, scarcely.
навсегдá forever; (*once*) for all.
навстрéчу toward(s); идти́ ~ (Д) go to meet; *fig.* meet halfway.
навы́ворот P topsy-turvy, inside out, wrongly; дéлать ши́ворот-~ put the cart before the horse.
нáвык *m* [1] experience, skill (in к Д, на В, в П); habit.
навы́кат(е) goggle (*eye[d]*).
навы́лет (*shot*) through.
навы́тяжку at attention.
навя́з|ывать [1], ⟨~áть⟩ [3] tie (to, on на В), fasten; knit; impose, obtrude ([up]on Д; *v/i.* **-ся**); **~чивый** [14 *sh.*] obtrusive; fixed.
нагáйка *f* [5; *g/pl.*: -гáек] whip.
нагáр *m* [1] snuff (*candle*).
наг|ибáть [1], ⟨~нýть⟩ [20] bend, bow, stoop (*v/i.* **-ся**).
нагишóм F naked, nude.
наглáзник *m* [1] blinder.
нагл|éц *m* [1 *e.*] impudent fellow; **~ость** *f* [8] impudence, insolence; **~ухо** tightly; **~ый** [14; нагл, -á, -о] impudent, insolent, F cheeky.
нагляд|éться [11] *pf.* (на В) feast one's eyes (upon); не **~éться** never get tired of looking (at); **~ный** [14; -ден, -дна] vivid, graphic; obvious; direct; object (*lesson*); visual (*aid*).
нагнáть *s.* нагоня́ть.
нагнетá|тельный [14] force; (*pump*); **~ть** [1], ⟨нагнести́⟩ [25 -т-] pump.
нагноéние *n* [12] suppuration.
нагнýть *s.* нагибáть.
нагов|áривать [1], ⟨~ори́ть⟩ [13] say, tell, talk ([too] much *or* many ...); F slander (a p. на В, о П); conjure; record; **~ори́ться** *pf.* talk one's fill; не **~ори́ться** never ge tired of talking.
нагóй [14; наг, -á, -о] nude, naked, [bare.]
нáгол|о clean(-*shaven*); **~ó** naked.
нáголову (*defeat*) totally.
нагон|я́й F *m* [3] blowup; **~я́ть** [28], ⟨нагнáть⟩ [-гоню́, -гóнишь; *cf.* гнать] overtake, catch up (with); make up (for); drive (together); F **~я́ть** страх, скýку, *etc.* (на В) frighten, bore, *etc.*
наготá *f* [5] nudity; bareness.
нагот|áвливать [1] [28], ⟨~óвить⟩ [14] prepare; lay in; **~óве** (at the) ready.
награ́бить [14] *pf.* rob, plunder (a lot of).
нагрá|да *f* [5] reward (as a в В), recompense; decoration; **~ждáть** [1], ⟨~ди́ть⟩ [15 *e.*; -ажý, -ади́шь; -аждённый] (Т) reward; decorate; *fig.* endow.
нагревáт|ельный [14] heating; **~ь** [1], *s.* греть.
нагромо|ждáть [1], ⟨~зди́ть⟩ [15 *e.*; -зжý, -зди́шь; -ождённый] pile up.
нагрýдник *m* [1] bib; plastron.
нагру|жáть [1], ⟨~зи́ть⟩ [15 & 15 *e.*; -ужý, -ýзишь; -ужённый] load (with Т); F *a.* burden, busy, assign (*work to*); **~зка** *f* [5; *g/pl.*: -зок] load(ing); F *a.* burden, job, assignment.
нагря́нуть [20] *pf.* appear, come (upon) suddenly, unawares; break out (*war*); take by surprise (на В).

над, ~о (Т) over, above; at; about; with.
надáв|ливать [1], ‹~и́ть› [14] (*a.* на В) press; push; press out (much).
надбáв|ка *f* [5; *g/pl.:* -вок] raise, increase; extra charge; **~ля́ть** [28], ‹~ить› [14] F, *s.* набавля́ть.
надви|гáть [1], ‹~́нуть› [20] push; pull; **-ся** approach, draw near; cover.
нáдвое in two (parts *or* halves).
надгрóбный [14] tomb..., grave...
наде|вáть [1], ‹~́ть› [-éну, -éнешь; -éтый] put on.
надéжд|а *f* [5] hope (of на В); подавáть ~ы show promise; 2а *fem. name, cf.* Hope.
надёжный [14; -жен, -жна] reliable, dependable; firm; safe; sure.
надéл ⚒ *m* [1] lot, plot, allotment.
надéл|ать [1] *pf.* make; do, cause, inflict; **~я́ть** [28], ‹~и́ть› [13] allot (s. th. to Т/В); give; endow.
надéть *s.* надевáть.
надéяться [27] (на В) hope (for); rely (on).
надзéмный [14] overground; 🚂 elevated, *Brt.* high-level...
надз|ирáтель *m* [4] supervisor; inspector; jailer; **~óр** *m* [1] supervision; surveillance.
надл|áмывать, ‹~омáть› [1] F, ‹~оми́ть› [14] crack, break; shatter.
надлежá|ть [4; *impers.*] (Д) have to, be to be + *p. pt.*; **~щий** [17] appropriate, suitable: ~щим óбразом properly, duly.
надлóм *m* [1] crack, fissure; *fig.* crisis; **~áть, ~и́ть** *s.* надлáмывать.
надмéнный [14; -éнен, -éнна] haughty.
нáдо it is necessary (for Д); (Д) (one) must (*go, etc.*); need; want; так емý и ~ it serves him right; **~бность** *f* [8] need (of, for в П), necessity; affair, matter (in по Д).
надо|едáть [1], ‹~éсть› [-éм, -éшь, *etc.*, *s.* есть[1]] (Д/Т) tire; bother, molest; мне ~éл ... I'm tired (of), fed up (with); **~éдливый** [14 *sh.*] tiresome; troublesome, annoying.
надóлго for (a) long (time).
надорвáть *s.* надрывáть.
надпи́|сывать [1], ‹~сáть› [3] superscribe; † endorse; **'~сь** *f* [8] inscription; † endorsement.
надрéз *m* [1] cut, incision; **~áть** & **~ывать** [1], ‹~ать› [3] cut, incise.
надругáтельство *n* [9] outrage.
надры́в *m* [1] rent, tear; strain, burst; **~áть** [1], ‹надорвáть› [-вý, -вёшь; надорвáл, -á, -о; -óрванный] tear; shatter, break, undermine; injure; (over)strain (o. s. себя́, **-ся**; be[come] worn out, exhausted; labo[u]r); ~áть живóтики, ~áться (có смеху) split one's sides (with laughing).
надсмóтр *m* [1] supervision (of над, за Т); **~щик** *m* [1] supervisor.
надстр|áивать [1], ‹~óить› [13] overbuild; raise; **~óйка** *f* [5; *g/pl.:* -рóек] superstructure.
наду|вáть [1], ‹~́ть› [18] inflate, swell; drift, blow; F dupe; ~́ть гýбы pout; **-ся** *v/i.*; **~внóй** [14] inflatable, air...; ~́ть *s.* ~вáть.
надýм|анный [14] far-fetched, strained; **~ать** F [1] *pf.* think (of, out), devise; make up one's mind.
надýтый [14] swollen; sulky.
Нáдя *f* [6] *dim. of* Надéжда.
наедáться [1], ‹наéсться› [-éмся, -éшься, *etc.*, *s.* есть[1]] eat one's fill.
наедине́ alone, in private; tête-à-tête.
наéзд *m* [1] (~ом on) short *or* flying visit(s), run; **~ник** *m* [1] horseman, equestrian; (*horse*) trainer.
нае|зжáть [1], ‹~́хать› [5] (на В) run into, knock against; come across; F come (occasionally), call on (к Д); run (up, down to в В).
наём *m* [1; нáйма] hire; rent; **~ник** *m* [1] hireling, mercenary; **~ный** [14] hired, rent(ed); hackney, mercenary.
наé|сться *s.* ~дáться; **~хать** *s.* ~зжáть.
нажáть *s.* ~имáть.
наждá|к *m* [1*e.*], **~чный** [14] emery.
нажи́|ва *f* [5] profit(s), gain(s); *a.* = ~вка; **~вáть** [1], ‹~ть› [-живý, -вёшь; нáжил, -á, -о; нажи́вший; нáжитый (нáжит, -á, -о)] earn, gain, profit(eer), amass; make (*a fortune; enemies*); get, catch; **~вка** *f* [5; *g/pl.:* -вок] bait.
нажи́м *m* [1] pressure; stress, strain; **~áть** [1], ‹нажáть› [-жмý, -жмёшь; -жáтый] (*a.* на В) press, push (*a.*, F, *fig.* = urge, impel; influence); stress.
нажи́ть *s.* наживáть.
назáвтра F the next day; tomorrow.
назáд back(ward[s]); ~! get back!; томý ~ ago; **~и́** F behind.
назвá|ние *n* [12] name; title; **~ть** *s.* называ́ть.
назéмный [14] land..., ground...
нáземь F to the ground (*or* floor).
назидá|ние *n* [12] edification (for p.'s в В/Д); instruction; **~тельный** [14; -лен, -льна] edifying, instructive.
нáзлó (Д) to (*or* for) spite (s. b.).
назнач|áть [1], ‹~́ить› [16] appoint (p. s. th. В/Т), designate; fix, settle; prescribe; destine; F assign; **~éние** *n* [12] appointment; assignment; prescription; destination.
назóйливый [14 *sh.*] importunate.
назре|вáть [1], ‹~́ть› [8] ripen; swell; ⚕ gather; *fig.* mature; be imminent *or* impending.
назубóк F by heart, thoroughly.
называ́|ть [1], ‹назвáть› [-зовý, -зовёшь; -звáл, -á, -о; нáзван-

ный (на́зван, -а́, -о)] call, name; mention; ~ть себя́ introduce o. s.; F invite; ~ть ве́щи свои́ми имена́ми call a spade a spade; -ся call o. s., be called; как ~ется ...? what is (or do you call) ...?
наи... *in compds.* ... of all, very; ~**бо́лее** most, ...est of all.
наи́вн|ость *f* [12] naïveté; ~**ый** [14; -вен, -вна] naïve, ingenuous; unsophisticated.
наизна́нку inside out.
наизу́сть by heart.
наиме́нее least... of all.
наименова́ние *n* [12] name; title.
на́искос|ь, F ~**о́к** obliquely, aslant.
наи́тие *n* [12] inspiration; intuition.
найдёныш *m* [1] foundling.
наймит *m* [1] hireling, mercenary.
найти́ *s.* находи́ть.
нака́з *m* [1] order; mandate.
наказ|а́ние *n* [12] punishment (as a в В); penalty; F nuisance; ~**у́емый** [14 *sh.*] punishable; ∠**ывать** [1], ⟨~а́ть⟩ [3] punish; † order.
нака́л *m* [1] incandescence; ~**ивать** [1], ⟨~и́ть⟩ [13] incandesce; ~**ённый** incandescent, red-hot.
нак|а́лывать [1], ⟨~оло́ть⟩ [17] pin, fix; chop, break; prick; kill.
накану́не the day before; ~ (Р) on the eve (of).
нак|а́пливать [1] & ~**опля́ть** [28], ⟨~опи́ть⟩ [14] accumulate, amass; collect, gather.
наки́|дка *f* [5; *g/pl.:* -док] cape, cloak; ~**дывать** [1] **1.** ⟨~да́ть⟩ [1] throw (up); **2.** ⟨~нуть⟩ [20] throw upon; F add; raise; -ся (на В) F fall (up)on.
на́кипь *f* [8] scum; scale, deposit.
наклад|на́я *f* [14] waybill; ~**но́й** [14] laid on; plated; false; ✝ overhead; ∠**ывать** & **налага́ть** [1], ⟨наложи́ть⟩ [16] (на В) lay (on), apply (to); put (on), set (to); impose; leave (*trace*); fill; pack, load.
накле́|ивать [1], ⟨~ить⟩ [13; -е́ю] glue *or* paste on; stick on, affix; ~**йка** *f* [5; *g/pl.:* -е́ек] label.
накло́н *m* [1] inclination; slope; ~**е́ние** *n* [12] *s.* ~; *gr.* mode, mood; ~**и́ть** *s.* ~я́ть; ~**ный** [14] inclined, slanting; ~**я́ть** [28], ⟨~и́ть⟩ [13; -оню́, -о́нишь; -онённый] bend, tilt; bow, stoop; † incline; -ся *v/i.*
накова́льня *f* [6; *g/pl.:* -лен] anvil.
нако́жный [14] skin..., cutaneous.
наколо́ть *s.* нака́лывать.
наконе́|ц (~ц-то oh) at last, finally; at length; ~**чник** *m* [1] ferrule; tip, point.
накоп|ле́ние *n* [12] accumulation; ⚔ concentration; ~**ля́ть**, ~**и́ть** *s.* нака́пливать.
накра|хма́ленный [14] starched; ∠**шенный** [14] painted, rouged.
на́крепко fast, tightly, firmly.
на́крест crosswise.
накры|ва́ть [1], ⟨∠ть⟩ [22] cover; (*a.* на) lay (*the table*); serve (*meal*); ⚔ hit; P catch, trap; dupe.
накуп|а́ть [1], ⟨~и́ть⟩ [14] (P) buy.
наку́р|ивать [1], ⟨~и́ть⟩ [13; -урю́, -у́ришь; -у́ренный] (fill with) smoke *or* perfume, scent.
налага́ть *s.* накла́дывать.
нала́|живать [1], ⟨~дить⟩ [15] put right *or* in order, get straight, fix; set going; establish; tune.
нале́во to *or* on the left; *s.* напра́во.
нале|га́ть [1], ⟨∠чь⟩ [26 г/ж: -ля́гу, -ля́жешь, -ля́гут; -лёг, -легла́; -ля́г(те)!] (на В) press (against, down), *fig.* opress; apply o. s. (to); lie; sink, cover; F stress.
налегке́ F (-хк-) with light *or* no baggage (luggage); lightly dressed.
налёт *m* [1] flight; blast; ⚔, ✈ raid, attack; ⚘ fur; (*a. fig.*) touch; с ~а on the wing, with a swoop; *cf.* лёт; ~**а́ть** [1], ⟨~е́ть⟩ [11] (на В) fly (at, [*a.* knock, strike] against); swoop down; raid, attack; fall ([up]on); rush, squall; ~**чик** *m* [1] bandit.
нале́чь *s.* налега́ть.
нали|ва́ть [1], ⟨∠ть⟩ [-лью́, -льёшь; -ле́й(те)!; нали́л, -а́, -о; -ли́вший; на́литый (на́ли́т, -а́, -о)] pour (out); fill; ripen; *p. pt. p.* (*a.* ~то́й) ripe; plump; sappy; (-ся *v/i.*; *a.* swell; ∠ться кро́вью become bloodshot); ∠**вка** *f* [5; *g/pl.:* -вок] (fruit) liqueur; ~**вно́й** [14] *s.* ~ва́ть *p. pt. p.*; ~вно́е су́дно *n* tanker; ∠**м** *m* [1] burbot.
налито́й, нали́ть *s.* налива́ть.
налицо́ present, on hand.
нали́ч|ие *n* [12] presence; ~**ность** *f* [8] stock; cash; *a.* = ~ие; в ~ности = налицо́; ~**ный** [14] (*a. pl., su.*) cash (*a.* down T), ready (*money*); present, on hand; за ~ные (against) cash (down).
нало́г *m* [1] tax, duty, levy; ~**оплате́льщик** *m* [1] taxpayer.
нало́ж|енный [14]: ~енным платежо́м cash (*or* collect) on delivery; ~**и́ть** *s.* накла́дывать.
налюбова́ться [7] *pf.* (T) admire to one's heart's content; не ~ never get tired of admiring (o. s. собо́й).
нама́|зывать [1] *s.* ма́зать; ~**тывать** [1] *s* мота́ть.
наме́дни P recently, the other day.
нам|ёк *m* [1] (на В) allusion (to), hint (at); ~**ека́ть** [1], ⟨~екну́ть⟩ [20] (на В) allude (to), hint (at).
намер|ева́ться [1] intend = (я I, *etc.*) ∠ен(а); ∠**ение** *n* [12] intention, design, purpose (on с T); ∠**енный** [14] intentional, deliberate.
наме́стник *m* [1] governor.
намета́ть *s.* намётывать.
наме́тить *s.* намеча́ть.
нам|ётка *f* [5; *g/pl.:* -ток], ~**ёты**-

вать [1], ⟨**~етáть**⟩ [3] draft, plan; tack; *s. a.* метáть.
наме|чáть [1], ⟨**~́тить**⟩ [15] mark, trace; design, plan; select; nominate.
намнóго much, (by) far.
намок|áть [1], ⟨**~́нуть**⟩ [21] get wet.
намóрдник *m* [1] muzzle.
нанести́ *s.* наноси́ть.
нани́з|ывать [1], ⟨**~áть**⟩ [3] string.
нан|имáть [1], ⟨**~я́ть**⟩ [найму́, -мёшь; нáнял, -á, -о; -я́вший; нáнятый (нáнят, -á, -о)] hire, engage, rent; F lodge; **-ся** *a.* hire out (as в И*pl.* *or* Т).
нáново anew, (over) again.
нанóс *m* [1] alluvium; **~и́ть** [15], ⟨нанести́⟩ [24 -с-: -несу́, -сёшь; -нёс, -неслá] bring (much, many); carry, waft, deposit, wash ashore; heap; enter, mark; lay on, apply; inflict (on Д), cause; pay (*visit*); deal (*blow*); **~ный** [14] alluvial; *fig.* casual, assumed.
наня́ть(ся) *s.* нанимáть(ся).
наоборóт the other way round, vice versa, conversely; on the contrary.
наобу́м F at random, haphazardly.
наотрéз bluntly, categorically.
напа|дáть [1], ⟨**~́сть**⟩ [25; *pt. st.:* -пáл, -а; -пáвший] (на В) attack, fall (up)on; come across *or* upon; hit on; overcome; **~дáющий** *m* [17] assailant; (*sport*) forward; **~дéние** *n* [12] attack; aggression; forwards *pl.*; **~́дки** *f/pl.* [5; *gen.:* -док] accusations, cavils; carping, faultfinding *sg.*
нап|áивать [1], ⟨**~ои́ть**⟩ [13] give to drink; make drunk; imbue.
напá|сть 1. F *f* [8] misfortune, bad luck; **2.** *s.* **~дáть**.
напé|в *m* [1] melody, tune; **~вáть** [1] **1.** hum, sing; **2.** ⟨**~ть**⟩ [-пою́, -поёшь; -пéтый] record.
напере|бóй F vying with each other; **~вéс** atilt; **~гóнки́** F: бежáть ~гóнки́ (run a) race; chase each other; **~д** (-ˈrʹɔt) F *s.* вперёд; **~ди́** P *s.* спéреди; **~кóр** (Д) in spite *or* defiance (of), contrary (to); **~рéз** (in a) short cut, cutting (across *or* s.b.'s way Д, Р); **~ры́в** F = **~бóй**; **~чёт** each and all; few.
напéрсник *m* [1] favo(u)rite; pet.
напёрсток *m* [1; -тка] thimble.
напи|вáться [1], ⟨**~́ться**⟩ [-пью́сь, -пьёшься; -пи́лся, -пилáсь; -пéйся, -пéйтесь!] drink, quench one's thirst, have enough (Р); get drunk.
напи́льник *m* [1] file.
напи́|ток *m* [1; -тка] drink, beverage; **~ться** *s.* **~вáться**.
напи́т|ывать, ⟨**~áть**⟩ [1] (Т) (**-ся** become) saturate(d), soak(ed), imbue(d).
напи́х|ивать, ⟨**~áть**⟩ F [1] cram.
наплы́|в *m* [1] rush; deposit; excrescence; **~вáть** [1], ⟨**~ть**⟩ [23] swim (against на В), run (on); flow; deposit; approach, cover; waft, reach; gather; **~вно́й** [14] *s.* нанóсный.
наповáл (*kill, etc.*) outright.
напoдóбие (Р) like, resembling.
напои́ть *s.* напáивать.
напокáз for show; *cf.* выставля́ть.
наполн|я́ть [28], ⟨**~́ить**⟩ [13] (Т) fill; crowd; imbue; *p.pt.p.* a. full.
наполови́ну half; (*do*) by halves.
напом|инáние *n* [12] reminder; dun(ning); **~инáть** [1], ⟨**~́нить**⟩ [13] remind (a p. of Д/о П), dun.
напóр *m* [1] pressure; charge; F rush, push, vigo(u)r.
напослéдок F ultimately.
напр. *abbr.*: напримéр.
напрáв|ить(ся) *s.* **~ля́ть(ся)**; **~лéние** *n* [12] direction (in в П, по Д); trend; *fig.* current, school; assignment; **~ля́ть** [28], ⟨**~́ить**⟩ [14] direct; refer; send; assign, detach; **-ся** go, head for; turn (to на В).
напрáво (от Р) to *or* on the (s.b.'s) right; ~! ⚔ right face!
напрáсн|ый [14; -сен, -сна] vain; groundless, idle; **~о** in vain, wrongly.
напр|áшиваться [1], ⟨**~оси́ться**⟩ [15] (на В) (pr)offer (o.s. for), solicit; provoke; fish (for); suggest o.s.
напримéр for example *or* instance.
напро|кáт for hire; **~лёт** F (all) ... through[out]; on end; **~лóм** F: идти́ ~лóм force one's way.
напроси́ться *s.* напрáшиваться.
напрóтив (Р) opposite; on the contrary; *s. a.* наперекóр & наоборóт.
напря|гáть [1], ⟨**~́чь**⟩ (-ˈrʹe-) [26 г/ж: ягу́, -яжёшь; -пря́г (-ˈrʹɔk), -яглá; -яжённый] strain (*a. fig.*); exert; stretch; bend (*bow*); **~жéние** *n* [12] tension (*a.* ⚡; voltage), strain, exertion; effort; close attention; **~жённый** [14 *sh.*] strained; (in-) tense; keen, close.
напрями́к F straight on; outright.
напря́чь *s.* напрягáть.
напу́ганный [14] scared, frightened.
напус|кáть [1], ⟨**~ти́ть**⟩ [15] let in, fill; set at (на В); fall; F (~кáть на себя́) put on (*airs*); P cause; **-ся** F fall (up)on (на В); **~кнóй** [14] affected.
напу́тств|енный [14] farewell..., parting; **~ие** *n* [12] parting words.
напы́щенный [14 *sh.*] pompous.
наравнé (с Т) on a level with; equally; together (*or* along) with.
нараспáшку F unbuttoned; (душá) ~ frank, candid; in grand style.
нараспéв with a singing accent.
нараст|áть [1], ⟨**~и́**⟩ [24; -стёт; *cf.* расти́] grow; accrue.
нарасхвáт F greedily; like hot cakes.
нарез|áть [1], ⟨**~́ать**⟩ [3] cut; carve; ⊕ thread; **~́ка** *f* [5; *g/pl.*: -зок] ⊕ thread; **~́ывать** = **~áть**.
нарекáние *n* [12] blame, censure.

наре́чие *n* [12] dialect; *gr.* adverb.
нар|ица́тельный [14] *gr.* common; ✝ nominal; **~ко́з** *m* [1] narcosis.
наро́д *m* [1] people, nation; **~ность** *f* [8] nationality; **~ный** [14] people's, popular, folk...; national; public; **~онаселе́ние** *n* [12] population.
наро|жда́ться [1], ⟨**~ди́ться**⟩ [15] arise, spring up; F be born; grow.
наро́ст *m* [1] (out)growth.
нароч|и́тый [14 *sh.*] deliberate, intentional; *adv.* = **∠но** (-ʃn-) *a.* on purpose; specially, expressly; F in fun; F *a.* = на́зло́; **'~ный** [14] courier.
на́рты *f/pl.* [5] sledge.
нару́ж|ность *f* [8] appearance; exterior; **~ный** [14] external, outward; outdoor, outside; **~у** out(-side), outward(s), (*get*) abroad *fig.*
наруш|а́ть [1], ⟨**∠ить**⟩ [16] disturb; infringe, violate; break (*oath*; *silence*); **~е́ние** *n* [12] violation, transgression, breach; disturbance; **~и́тель** *m* [4] trespasser; disturber; **∠ить** *s.* **~а́ть**.
на́ры *f/pl.* [5] plank bed.
нары́в *m* [1] abcess; *cf.* гнои́ть.
наря́|д *m* [1] attire, dress; assignment, commission, order; ⚔ fatigue (on в П); detachment; **~ди́ть** *s.* **~жа́ть**; **~дный** [14; -ден, -дна] smart, trim, elegant; order...
наряду́ (с T) together *or* along with, beside(s); side by side; *s. a.* наравне́.
наря|жа́ть [1], ⟨**~ди́ть**⟩ [15 & 15 *e.*; -яжу́, -я́ди́шь; -я́женный & -яжённый] dress (up) (*v/i.* **-ся**); disguise; ⚔ detach; assign; † set up.
наса|жда́ть [1], ⟨**~ди́ть**⟩ [15] (im)plant (*a. fig.*); *cf. a.* **∠живать**; **~жде́ние** *n* [12] planting; (im-)plantation; trees, plants *pl.*; **∠живать**, ⟨**~жа́ть**⟩ [1], ⟨**~ди́ть**⟩ [15] plant (many); F set, put, place.
насви́стывать [1] whistle.
насе|да́ть [1], ⟨**∠сть**⟩ [25; -ся́ду, -ся́дешь; *cf.* сесть] set; sit down; cover; press; **∠дка** *f* [5; *g/pl.*: -док] brood hen.
насеко́мое *n* [14] insect.
насел|е́ние *n* [12] population; **~я́ть** [28], ⟨**~и́ть**⟩ [13] people, populate; *impf.* inhabit, live in.
насе́|ст *m* [1] roost; **~сть** *s.* **~да́ть**; **~чка** *f* [5; *g/pl.*: -чек] notch, cut.
наси́|живать [1], ⟨**~де́ть**⟩ [11] brood, hatch; **~женный** *a.* snug, habitual, long-inhabited.
наси́|лие *n* [12] violence, force, coercion; rape; **~ловать** [7], ⟨из-⟩ violate, force; rape; **~лу** F *s.* е́ле; **~льно** by force; forcedly; **~льственный** [14] forcible, forced; violent.
наск|а́кивать [1], ⟨**~очи́ть**⟩ [16] (на B); fall (up)on; run *or* strike against, come across.
наскво́зь through(out); F through and through.
наско́лько as (far as); how (much).
на́скоро F hastily, in a hurry.
наскочи́ть *s.* наска́кивать.
наску́чить F [16] *pf.*, *s.* надоеда́ть.
насла|жда́ться [1], ⟨**~ди́ться**⟩ [15 *e.*; -ажу́сь, -ади́шься] (T) enjoy (o.s.), (be) delight(ed); **~жде́ние** *n* [12] enjoyment; delight; pleasure.
насле́д|ие *n* [12] heritage, legacy; *s. a.* **~ство**; **~ник** *m* [1] heir; **~ница** *f* [5] heiress; **~ный** [14] crown...; *s. a.* **~ственный**; **~овать** [7] (*im*)*pf.*, ⟨у-⟩ inherit; (Д) succed; **~ственность** *f* [8] heredity; **~ственный** [14] hereditary, inherited; **~ство** *n* [9] inheritance; *s. a.* **~ие**; *vb.* + в **~ство** (*or* по **~ству**) inherit.
наслое́ние *n* [12] stratification.
насл|у́шаться [1] *pf.* (P) listen to one's heart's content; не мочь **~у́шаться** never get tired of listening to; *a.* = **~ы́шаться** F [4] (P) hear a lot (of), much; *cf.* понаслы́шке.
на́смерть to death; mortal(ly *fig.* P).
насме|ха́ться [1] mock, jeer; sneer (at над T); **∠шка** *f* [5; *g/pl.*: -шек] mockery, sneer; **∠шливый** [14 *sh.*] (fond of) mocking; **∠шник** *m* [1], **∠шница** *f* [5] scoffer, mocker.
на́сморк *m* [1] cold (in the head).
насмотре́ться [9; -отрю́сь, -о́тришься] *pf.* = нагляде́ться, *cf.*
насо́с *m* [1] pump.
на́спех hurriedly, in a hurry.
наста|ва́ть [5], ⟨**∠ть**⟩ [-ста́нет] come; **~ви́тельный** [14; -лен, -льна] instructive; preceptive; **∠вить** *s.* **~вля́ть**; **~вле́ние** *n* [12] instruction; admonition; lecture, lesson *fig.*; **~вля́ть** [28], ⟨**∠вить**⟩ [14] put, place, set (many P); piece (on), add; aim, level (at на B); instruct; teach (s. th. Д, в П); **∠вник** *m* [1] tutor, mentor, preceptor; **∠ивать** [1], ⟨настоя́ть⟩ [-стою́, -стои́шь] insist (on на П); draw, extract; настоя́ть на своём have one's will; **∠ть** *s.* **~ва́ть**.
на́стежь wide (open).
насти|га́ть [1], ⟨**∠гнуть**⟩ & ⟨**∠чь**⟩ [21 -г-: -и́гну] overtake; find, catch.
наст|ила́ть [1], ⟨**~ла́ть**⟩ [-телю́, -те́лешь; на́стланный] lay, spread; plank, pave.
насто́й *m* [3] infusion, extract; **~ка** *f* [5; *g/pl.*: -о́ек] liqueur; *a.* = **~**.
насто́йчивый [14 *sh.*] persevering, pertinacious; persistent; obstinate.
насто́ль|ко so (*or* as [much]); **~ный** [14] table...; reference...
настор|а́живаться [1], ⟨**~ожи́ться**⟩ [16 *e.*; -жу́сь, -жи́шься] prick up one's ears; **~оже́** on the alert, on one's guard.
настоя́|ние *n* [12] insistence, urgent request (at по Д); **~тельный**

[14; -лен, -льна] urgent, pressing, instant; ~ть s. наста́ивать.
настоя́щ|ий [17] present (*a. gr.*; at ... *time* в В); true, real, genuine; по- ~ему properly.
настр|а́ивать [1], ⟨~о́ить⟩ [13] build (many P); tune (up, in); set against; *s. a.* нала́живать; **~о́го** F most strictly; **~о́ение** *n* [12] mood, spirits *pl.*, frame (of mind); disposition; **~о́ить** *s.* ~а́ивать; **~о́йка** *f* [5; *g/pl.*: -о́ек] superstructure; tuning.
наступ|а́тельный [14] offensive; **~а́ть** [1], ⟨~и́ть⟩ [14] tread *or* step (on на В); come, set in; *impf.* attack, advance; press (hard); approach; **~ле́ние** *n* [12] offensive, attack, advance; beginning, ...break, ...fall (at с Т).
насу́пить(ся) [14] *pf.* frown.
на́сухо *adv.* dry.
насу́щный [14; -щен, -щна] vital; daily.
насчёт (P) F concerning, about.
насчи́т|ывать, ⟨~а́ть⟩ [1] count, number; **-ся** *impf.* there is/are.
насып|а́ть [1], ⟨~ать⟩ [2] pour; strew, scatter; fill; throw up, raise; **'~ь** *f* [8] embankment, mound.
насы|ща́ть [1], ⟨~тить⟩ [15] satisfy; saturate; **~ще́ние** *n* [12] saturation.
нат|а́лкивать [1], ⟨~олкну́ть⟩ [20] (на В) push (against, on); F prompt, suggest; **-ся** strike against; come across.
натвори́ть F [13] *pf.* do, cause.
nате́льный [14] under(*clothes*).
нат|ира́ть [1], ⟨~ере́ть⟩ [12] (Т) rub (*a.* sore); get (*corn*); wax, polish.
на́т|иск *m* [1] press(ure), rush; onslaught, charge; urge.
наткну́ться *s.* натыка́ться.
натолкну́ть(ся) *s.* ната́лкиваться.
натоща́к on an empty stomach.
натра́в|ливать [1], ⟨~и́ть⟩ [14] set (on, at на В), incite.
на́трий *m* [3] natrium.
нату́|га F *f* [5] strain, effort; **'~го** F tight(ly); **~живать** F [1], ⟨~жить⟩ [16] strain, exert (o.s. **-ся**).
нату́р|а *f* [5] nature; model (= **~щик** *m* [1], **~щица** *f* [5]); **~ой**, в ~е in kind; с ~ы from nature *or* life; **~а́льный** [14; -лен, -льна] natural.
нат|ыка́ться [1], ⟨~кну́ться⟩ [20] (на В) run against, (*a.* come) across.
натя́|гивать [1], ⟨~ну́ть⟩ [19] stretch, (*a. fig.*) strain; pull (on на В); draw in (*reins*); **~жка** *f* [5; *g/pl.*: -жек] strain(ing); affectation, forced *or* strained argument(ation), detail, trait, *etc.*; с ~жкой *a.* with great reserve; **~нутый** [14] strained, forced, affected, far-fetched; tense, bad; **~ну́ть** *s.* ~гивать.
нау|га́д, **~да́чу** at random.
нау́ка *f* [5] science; lesson.
наутёк F (*take*) to one's heels.
нау́тро the next morning.
науч|а́ть [1], ⟨~и́ть⟩ [16] teach (a p. s. th. В/Д); **-ся** learn (s.th. Д).
нау́чный [14; -чен, -чна] scientific.
нау́шник F *m* [1] informer; **~и** *m/pl.* [1] earflaps; headphones.
наха́л *m* [1] impudent fellow; **~ьный** [14; -лен, -льна] impudent, insolent; **~ьство** *n* [12] impudence, insolence.
нахва́т|ывать, ⟨~а́ть⟩ F [1] (P) snatch (up), pick up (a lot of, a smattering of; hoard; *a.* **-ся**).
нахлы́нуть [20] *pf.* rush (up [to]).
нахму́ривать [1] = хму́рить, *cf.*
наход|и́ть [15], ⟨найти́⟩ [найду́, -дёшь; нашёл, -шла́; -ше́дший; на́йденный; *g. pt.*: найдя́] find (*a. fig.* = think, consider); come (across на В); cover; be seized (F wrong) with; *impf.* take (*pleasure*); (**-ся**, ⟨найти́сь⟩) be (found, there, [*impf.*] situated, located); happen to have; not to be at a loss; **~ка** *f* [5; *g/pl.*: -док] find; F discovery; бюро́ ~ок lost-property office; **~чивый** [14 *sh.*] resourceful; ready-witted, smart.
национал|из(и́р)ова́ть [7] (*im*)*pf.* nationalize (*Brt.* -ise); **~ьность** *f* [8] nationality; **~ьный** [14; -лен, -льна] national.
нача́|ло *n* [9] beginning (at в П); source, origin; basis; principle; *pl.* rudiments; **~льник** *m* [1] chief, superior; ⚔ commander; 🚂 (*station*) master, agent; **~льный** [14] initial, first; opening; elementary, primary; **~льство** *n* [9] command(er[s], chief[s], superior[s]); authority, -ties *pl.*; **~льствовать** [7] (над Т) command; manage; **~тки** *m/pl.* [1] *s.* ~ло *pl.*; **~ть(ся)** *s.* начина́ть(ся).
начеку́ on the alert, on one's guard.
на́черно roughly, (in) a draft.
начерта́|ние *n* [12] tracing; pattern; outline; **~тельный** [14] descriptive; **~ть** [1] *pf.* trace, design.
начина́|ние *n* [12] undertaking; † beginning; **~ть** [1], ⟨нача́ть⟩ [-чну́, -чнёшь; на́чал, -а́, -о; нача́вший; на́чатый (на́чат, -а́, -о)] begin, start (with с Р, Т); **-ся** *v/i.*; **~ющий** [17] beginner.
начи́н|ка *f* [5; *g/pl.*: -нок] filling; **~я́ть** [28], ⟨~и́ть⟩ [13] fill (with Т).
начисле́ние *n* [12] extra fee.
на́чисто clean; *s.* на́бело; outright.
начи́т|анный [14 *sh.*] well-read; **~а́ться** [1] (Р) read (a lot of); have enough (of); не мочь ~а́ться never get tired of reading.
наш *m*, **~а** *f*, **~е** *n*, **~и** *pl.* [25] our; ours; по-~ему in our way *or* opinion *or* language; ~а взяла́! we've won!
нашаты́р|ный [14]: ~ный спирт *m* aqueous ammonia; **~ь** *m* [4 *e.*] sal ammoniac, ammonium chloride.
наше́ствие *n* [12] invasion, inroad.

наши|ва́ть [1], ⟨**∠ть**⟩ [-шью́, -шьёшь; *cf.* шить] sew on (на В *or* П) *or* many …; **∠вка** *f* [5; *g/pl.*: -вок] galloon, braid; ⚔ stripe.
нащу́п|ывать, ⟨**~ать**⟩ [1] grope, fumble; *fig.* sound; detect, find.
наяву́ in reality; waking.
не not; no; ~ то F (or) else.
неаккура́тный [14; -тен, -тна] careless; inaccurate; unpunctual.
небез… rather …, not without …
небе́сный [14] celestial, heavenly; of heaven; divine; *cf.* небосво́д.
неблаго|ви́дный [14; -ден, -дна] unseemly; **~да́рность** *f* [8] ingratitude; **~да́рный** [14; -рен, -рна] ungrateful; **~надёжный** [14; -жен, -жна] unreliable; **~полу́чный** [14; -чен, -чна] unfortunate, adverse, bad; *adv.* not well, wrong; **~прия́тный** [14; -тен, -тна] unfavo(u)rable, negative; **~разу́мный** [14; -мен, -мна] imprudent; unreasonable; **~ро́дный** [14; -ден, -дна] ignoble; indelicate; **~скло́нный** [14; -о́нен, -о́нна] unkindly; unfavo(u)rable.
не́бо[1] *n* [9; *pl.*: небеса́, -е́с] sky (in на П); heaven(s); air (in the *open* под Т).
нёбо[2] *n* [9] palate.
небога́тый [14 *sh.*] (of) modest (means); poor.
небольш|о́й [17] small; short; … с ~и́м … odd.
небо|сво́д *m* [1] firmament; *a.* **~скло́н** *m* [1]; horizon; **~скрёб** *m* [1] skyscraper.
небо́сь F I suppose; sure.
небре́жный [14; -жен, -жна] careless, negligent.
небы|ва́лый [14] unheard-of, unprecedented; **~ли́ца** *f* [5] tale, fable, invention.
небью́щийся [17] unbreakable.
Нева́ *f* [5] Neva.
нева́жный [14; -жен, -жна́, -о] unimportant, trifling; F poor, bad.
невдалеке́ not far off, *or* from (от Р).
неве́|дение *n* [12] ignorance; **~домый** [14 *sh.*] unknown; **~жа** *m/f* [5] boor; **~жда** *m/f* [5] ignoramus; **~жество** *n* [9] ignorance; **~жливость** *f* [8] incivility; **~жливый** [14 *sh.*] impolite, uncivil.
неве́р|ие *n* [12] unbelief; **~ный** [14; -рен, -рна́, -о] incorrect; false; unfaithful; unsteady; *su.* infidel; **~о́ятный** [14; -тен, -тна] incredible; **~ующий** [17] unbelieving.
невесо́мый [14 *sh.*] imponderable.
неве́ст|а *f* [5] fiancée, bride; F marriageable girl; **~ка** *f* [5; *g/pl.*: -ток] daughter-in-law; sister-in-law (*brother's wife*).
невз|го́да *f* [5] adversity, misfortune; affliction; **~ирая** (на В) in spite of, despite; without respect (of p.'s); **~нача́й** F unexpectedly, by chance; **~ра́чный** [14; -чен, -чна] plain, homely, mean; **~ыска́тельный** [14; -лен, -льна] unpretentious.
неви́д|анный [14] singular, unprecedented; **~имый** [14 *sh.*] invisible.
неви́нный [14; -и́нен, -и́нна] innocent; virgin.
невку́сный [14; -сен, -сна́, -о] insipid.
невме|ня́емый [14 *sh.*] irresponsible; **~ша́тельство** *n* [9] nonintervention.
невнима́тельный [14; -лен, -льна] inattentive.
невня́тный [14; -тен, -тна] indistinct, inarticulate; unintelligible.
не́вод *m* [1] seine.
невоз|врати́мый [14 *sh.*], **~вра́тный** [14; -тен, -тна] irretrievable, irreparable; **~враще́нец** *m* [1; -нца] non-returnee; **~де́ржанный** [14 *sh.*] intemperate; unbridled, uncontrolled; **~мо́жный** [14; -жен, -жна] impossible; **~мути́мый** [14 *sh.*] imperturbable.
нево́л|ить [13] force, compel; **~ьник** *m* [1] slave; captive; **~ьный** [14; -лен, -льна] involuntary; forced; **~я** *f* [6] captivity; bondage; need, necessity.
невоо|брази́мый [14 *sh.*] unimaginable; **~ружённый** [14] unarmed.
невоспи́танный [14 *sh.*] ill-bred.
невпопа́д F *s.* некста́ти.
невреди́мый [14 *sh.*] sound, unhurt.
невы́|годный [14; -ден, -дна] unprofitable; disadvantageous; **~держанный** [14 *sh.*] unbalanced, uneven; unseasoned; **~носи́мый** [14 *sh.*] unbearable, intolerable; **~полне́ние** *n* [12] nonfulfillment; **~полни́мый** *s.* неисполни́мый; **~рази́мый** [14 *sh.*] inexpressible, ineffable; **~рази́тельный** [14; -лен, -льна] inexpressive; **~со́кий** [16; -со́к, -а́, -со́ко́] low, small; short; inferior, slight.
не́га *f* [5] luxury, comfort; bliss, delight; affection.
не́где there is no(where *or* room *or* place to [… from] *inf.*; Д for).
негла́сный [14; -сен, -сна] secret, private.
негод|ный [14; -ден, -дна́, -о] useless; unfit; F nasty; **~ова́ние** *n* [12] indignation; **~ова́ть** [7] be indignant (with на В); **~я́й** *m* [3] scoundrel, rascal.
негр *m* [1] Negro; **~∠амотность** *s.* безгра́мотность; **∠а́мотный** *s.* безгра́мотный; **~итя́нка** *f* [5; *g/pl.*: -нок] Negress; **~итя́нский** [16] Negro…
неда́|вний [15] recent; с **~вних** (**~вней**) пор(ы́) of late; **~вно**

recently; **~лёкий** [16; -ёк, -екá, -екó & -ёко] near(by), close; short; not far (off); recent; dull, stupid; **~льнови́дный** [14; -ден, -дна] short-sighted; **~ром** not in vain, not without reason; justly.
недви́жи́мый [14 *sh.*] immovable.
неде|йстви́тельный [14; -лен, -льна] invalid, void; ineffective, ineffectual; **~ли́мый** [14] indivisible.
недéл|ьный [14] a week's, weekly; **~я** *f* [6] week; в **~ю** a *or* per week; на э́той (про́шлой, бу́дущей) **~е** this (last, next) week.
недобро|желáтельный [14; -лен, -льна] unkindly, ill-natured; **~кáчественный** [14 *sh.*] inferior, off-grade; **~со́вестный** [14; -тен, -тна] unfair; unprincipled; careless.
недо́брый [14; -до́бр, -á, -о] unkind(ly), hostile; evil, bad, ill(-boding).
недовéр|ие *n* [12] distrust; **~чи́вый** [14 *sh.*] distrustful (of к Д).
недово́ль|ный [14; -лен, -льна] (T) dissatisfied, discontented; **~ство** *n* [9] discontent, dissatisfaction.
недогáдливый [14 *sh.*] slow-witted.
недоедá|ние *n* [12] malnutrition; **~ть** [1] not eat enough (*or* one's fill).
недои́мки *f/pl.* [5; *gen.*: -мок] arrears.
недо́лго not long, short; F easily.
недомогáть [1] be unwell, sick.
недомо́лвка *f* [5; *g/pl.*: -вок] omission.
недоно́сок *m* [1; -ска] abortion.
недооцéн|ивать [1], ⟨**~и́ть**⟩ [13] underestimate, undervalue.
недо|пусти́мый [14 *sh.*] inadmissible; intolerable, impossible; **~рáзвитый** [14 *sh.*] underdeveloped; **~разумéние** *n* [12] misunderstanding (through по Д); **~рого́й** [16; -до́рог, -á, -о] inexpensive.
нéдо|росль *m* [4] greenhorn; ignoramus; **~слы́шать** [1] *pf.* fail to hear.
недосмо́тр *m* [1] oversight, inadvertence (through по Д); **~éть** [9; -отрю́, -о́тришь; -о́тренный] *pf.* overlook (*s. th.*).
недост|авáть [5], ⟨**~áть**⟩ [-стáнет] *impers.*: (Д) (be) lack(ing), want(-ing), be short *or* in want of (P); miss; э́того ещё **~авáло**! and that too!; **~áток** *m* [1; -тка] want (for за T, по Д), lack, shortage (of P, в П); deficiency; defect, shortcoming; privation; **~áточный** [14; -чен, -чна] insufficient, deficient, inadequate; *gr.* defective; **~áть** *s.* **~авáть**.
недо|стижи́мый [14 *sh.*] unattainable; **~сто́йный** [14; -о́ин, -о́йна] unworthy; **~сту́пный** [14; -пен, -пна] inaccessible.
недосу́г F *m* [1] lack of time (for за T, по Д); мне **~** I have no time.
недо|сягáемый [14 *sh.*] unattainable; **~у́здок** *m* [1; -дка] halter.
недоум|евáть [1] (be) puzzle(d, perplexed); **~éние** *n* [12] bewilderment; в **~éнии** at a loss.
недочёт *m* [1] deficit; defect.
нéдра *n/pl.* [9] bosom, entrails.
недружелю́бный [14; -бен, -бна] unfriendly.
неду́г *m* [1] ailment, infirmity.
недурно́й [14; -ду́рен & -рён, -рнá, -о] not bad, pretty, nice, handsome.
недю́жинный [14] remarkable.
неестéственный [14 *sh.*] unnatural; affected, forced.
нежелá|ние *n* [12] unwillingness; **~тельный** [14; -лен, -льна] undesirable.
нéжели † = чем than.
неженáтый [14] single, unmarried.
нежи́зненный [14 *sh.*] impracticable; unreal.
нежило́й [14] uninhabited; deserted, desolate; store...
нéж|ить [16] coddle, pamper, fondle; **-ся** loll, lounge; **~ничать** F [1] indulge in caresses; **~ность** *f* [8] tenderness; fondness; civility; **~ный** [14; -жен, -жнá, -о] tender, fond; delicate; soft; sentimental.
незаб|вéнный [14 *sh.*], **~ывáемый** [14 *sh.*] unforgettable; **~у́дка** *f* [5; *g/pl.*: -док] forget-me-not.
независи́м|ость *f* [8] independence; **~ый** [14 *sh.*] independent.
незадáчливый F [14 *sh.*] unlucky.
незадо́лго shortly (before до P).
незако́нный [14; -о́нен, -о́нна] illegal, unlawful, illegitimate; illicit.
незаме|ни́мый [14 *sh.*] irreplaceable; **∠тный** [14; -тен, -тна] imperceptible, unnoticeable; plain, ordinary, humdrum; **∠ченный** [14] unnoticed.
неза|мысловáтый F [14 *sh.*] simple, plain; dull; **~пáмятный** [14] immemorial; **~тéйливый** [14 *sh.*] plain, simple; **~ря́дный** [14; -ден, -дна] remarkable.
нéзачем there is no need *or* point.
незвáный [14] uninvited.
нездоро́в|иться [14]: мне **~ится** I feel (am) sick *or* ill, unwell; **~ый** [14 *sh.*] sick; morbid.
незло́бивый [14 *sh.*] gentle, placid.
незнако́м|ец *m* [1; -мца], **~ка** *f* [5; *g/pl.*: -мок] stranger; *a.*, F, **~ый** [14], unknown, strange; unacquainted.
незнá|ние *n* [12] ignorance; **~чи́тельный** [14; -лен, -льна] insignificant.
незр|éлый [14 *sh.*] unripe; immature; **~и́мый** [14 *sh.*] invisible.
незы́блемый [14 *sh.*] firm; unshakable.
неиз|бéжный [14; -жен, -жна] inevitable; **~вéданный** [14 *sh.*] *s.*

~ве́стный [14; -тен, -тна] unknown; *su. a.* stranger; **~глади́мый** [14 *sh.*] indelible; **~лечи́мый** [14 *sh.*] incurable; **~ме́нный** [14; -е́нен, -е́нна] invariable; permanent; true; **~мери́мый** [14 *sh.*] immense; **~ъясни́мый** [14 *sh.*] inexplicable.

неим|е́ние *n* [12]: за ~е́нием (P) for want of; **~ове́рный** [14; -рен, -рна] incredible; **~у́щий** [17] poor.

неи́с|кренний [15; -енен, -енна] insincere; **~ку́сный** [14; -сен, -сна] unskillful; **~полне́ние** *n* [12] nonfulfillment; **~полни́мый** [14 *sh.*] impracticable.

неиспр|ави́мый [14 *sh.*] incorrigible; **~а́вность** *f* [8] ⊕ disrepair; **~а́вный** [14; -вен, -вна] out of repair *or* order, broken, defective; careless, faulty; inaccurate; unpunctual.

неиссяка́емый [14 *sh.*] inexhaustible.

неи́стов|ство *n* [9] rage, frenzy; atrocity; **~ствовать** [7] rage; **~ый** [14 *sh.*] frantic, furious.

неис|тощи́мый [14 *sh.*] inexhaustible; **~треби́мый** [14 *sh.*] ineradicable; **~цели́мый** [14 *sh.*] incurable; **~черпа́емый** [14 *sh.*] *s.* ~тощи́мый; **~числи́мый** [14 *sh.*] innumerable.

нейтрал|ите́т *m* [1] neutrality; **~ьный** [14; -лен, -льна] neutral.

неказѝстый F [14 *sh.*] = невзра́чный.

не́|кий [24 *st.*] a certain, some; **~когда** there is (мне ~когда I have) no time; once; **~кого** [23] there is (мне ~кого I have) nobody *or* no one (to *inf.*); **~который** [14] some (*pl.* of из P); **~краси́вый** [14 *sh.*] homely, ugly; mean.

некроло́г *m* [1] obituary.

некста́ти inopportunely; inappropriately, malapropos, off the point.

не́кто somebody, -one; a certain.

не́куда there is no(where *or* room *or* place to *inf.*; Д for); *s. a.* не́зачем; F could not be (*better, etc.*).

неку|льту́рный [14; -рен, -рна] uncultured; ill-mannered; **~ря́щий** [17] nonsmoker, nonsmoking.

нел|а́дный F [14; -ден, -дна] wrong, bad; **~ега́льный** [14; -лен, -льна] illegal; **~е́пый** [14 *sh.*] absurd; F awkward.

нело́вкий [16; -вок, -вка́, -о] awkward, clumsy; inconvenient, embarrassing.

нельзя́ (it is) impossible, one (мне I) cannot, must not; ~! no!; как ~ лу́чше in the best way possible, excellently; ~ не *s.* (не) мочь.

нелюди́мый [14 *sh.*] unsociable.

нема́ло (P) a lot, a great deal (of).

неме́дленный [14] immediate.

неме́ть [8], ‹о-› grow dumb, numb.

не́м|ец *m* [1; -мца], **~е́цкий** [16], **~ка** *f* [5; *g/pl.*: -мок] German.

немилосе́рдный [14; -ден, -дна] unmerciful, ruthless.

неми́лост|ивый [14 *sh.*] ungracious; **~ь** *f* [8] disgrace.

неминуе́мый [14 *sh.*] inevitable.

немно́|гие *pl.* [16] (a) few, some; **~го** a little; slightly, somewhat; *s. a.* ~гие; **~гое** *n* [16] little; **~гим** a little; **~ж(еч)ко** F a (little) bit.

немо́й [14; нем, -а́, -о] dumb, mute.

немо|лодо́й [14; -мо́лод, -а́, -о] elderly; **~та́** *f* [5] muteness.

не́мощный [14; -щен, -щна] infirm.

немы́слимый [14 *sh.*] inconceivable.

ненави́|деть [11], ‹воз-› hate; **~стный** [14; -тен, -тна] hateful, odious; **~сть** ('ne-) *f* [8] hatred (against к Д).

нена|гля́дный [14] dear, beloved; **~дёжный** [14; -жен, -жна] unreliable; unsafe, insecure; **~до́лго** for a short while; **~ме́ренный** [14] unintentional; **~паде́ние** *n* [12] nonagression; **~руши́мый** [14 *sh.*] inviolable; **~́стный** [14; -тен, -тна] rainy, foul; **~́стье** *n* [10] foul weather; **~сы́тный** [14; -тен, -тна] insatiable.

нен|орма́льный [14; -лен, -льна] abnormal; F (mentally) deranged; **~у́жный** [14; -жен, -жна́, -о] unnecessary.

необ|ду́манный [14 *sh.*] rash, hasty; **~ита́емый** [14 *sh.*] uninhabited; desert; **~озри́мый** [14 *sh.*] immense, vast; **~осно́ванный** [14 *sh.*] unfounded; **~рабо́танный** [14] uncultivated; crude, unpolished; **~у́зданный** [14 *sh.*] unbridled, unruly.

необходи́м|ость *f* [8] necessity (of по Д), need (of, for P, в П); **~ый** [14 *sh.*] necessary (for Д; для P), essential; *cf.* ну́жный.

необ|щи́тельный [14; -лен, -льна] unsociable, reserved; **~ъясни́мый** [14 *sh.*] inexplicable; **~ъя́тный** [14; -тен, -тна] immense, vast, huge; **~ыкнове́нный** [14; -е́нен, -е́нна], **~ы́ч(а́й)ный** [14; -ч(а)ен, ч(а́й)на] unusual, uncommon; **~яза́тельный** [14; -лен, -льна] optional.

неограни́ченный [14 *sh.*] unrestricted.

неод|нокра́тный [14] repeated; **~обре́ние** *n* [12] disapproval; **~обри́тельный** [14; -лен, -льна] disapproving; **~оли́мый** *s.* непреодоли́мый; **~ушевлённый** [14] inanimate.

неожи́данн|ость *f* [8] surprise; **~ый** [14 *sh.*] unexpected, sudden.

нео́н *m* [1] neon; **~овый** [14] neon-...

неоп|ису́емый [14 *sh.*] indescribable; **~ла́ченный** [14 *sh.*] unpaid, unsettled; **~ра́вданный** [14] unjustified; **~ределённый** [14; -ёнен, -ённа] indefinite (*a. gr.*), uncertain, vague; *gr.* (*vb.*) infinitive; **~ровержи́мый** [14 *sh.*] irrefutable; **~ы́тный** [14; -тен, -тна] inexperienced.

неос|ла́бный [14; -бен, -бна] unremitting, unabated; **~мотри́тельный** [14; -лен, -льна] imprudent; **~нова́тельный** [14; -лен, -льна] unfounded, baseless; **~пори́мый** [14 *sh.*] incontestable; **~торо́жный** [14; -жен, -жна] careless, incautious; imprudent; **~уществи́мый** [14 *sh.*] impracticable; **~яза́емый** [14 *sh.*] intangible.

неот|врати́мый [14 *sh.*] unavoidable; fatal; **~вя́зный** [14; -зен, -зна], **~вя́зчивый** [14 *sh.*] obtrusive, importunate; **~ёсанный** [14 *sh.*] unhewn; F rude; **′~куда** *s.* не́где; **~ло́жный** [14; -жен, -жна] pressing, urgent; **~лу́чный** *s.* неразлу́чный & постоя́нный; **~рази́мый** [14 *sh.*] irresistible; **~сту́пный** [14; -пен, -пна] persistent; importunate; **~чётливый** [14 *sh.*] indistinct; **~ъе́млемый** [14 *sh.*] integral; inalienable.

неохо́т|а *f* [5] listlessness; reluctance; (мне) **~а** F I (*etc.*) am not in the mood; **~но** unwillingly.

не|оцени́мый [14 *sh.*] invaluable; **~перехо́дный** [14] intransitive; **~платёж** *m* [1 *e.*] nonpayment; **~платёжеспосо́бный** [14; -бен, -бна] insolvent.

непо|беди́мый [14 *sh.*] invincible; **~воро́тливый** [14 *sh.*] clumsy, slow; **~го́да** *f* [5] foul weather; **~греши́мый** [14 *sh.*] infallible; **~далёку** not far (away *or* off); **~да́тливый** [14 *sh.*] unyielding, refractory.

непод|ви́жный [14; -жен, -жна] motionless, (*a. ast.*) fixed; sluggish; **~де́льный** [14; -лен, -льна] genuine, true; sincere; **~ку́пный** [14; -пен, -пна] incorruptible; **~обаю́щий** [17] improper, unbecoming; undue; **~ража́емый** [14 *sh.*] inimitable; **~ходя́щий** [17] unsuitable; **~чине́ние** *n* [12] insubordination.

непо|зволи́тельный [14; -лен, -льна] improper, unbecoming; **~колеби́мый** [14 *sh.*] firm, steadfast; unflinching; imperturbable; **~ко́рный** [14; -рен, -рна] intractable; **~ла́дка** F *f* [5; *g/pl.*: -док] defect, trouble; strife; **~́лный** [14; -лон, -лна́, -о] incomplete; short; **~ме́рный** [14; -рен, -рна] excessive, exorbitant.

непоня́т|ливый [14 *sh.*] slow-witted; **~ный** [14; -тен, -тна] unintelligible, incomprehensible; strange, odd.

непо|прави́мый [14 *sh.*] irreparable; **~ро́чный** [14; -чен, -чна] chaste, immaculate; virgin...; **~ря́дочный** [14; -чен, -чна] dishono(u)rable, disreputable; **~се́дливый** [14 *sh.*] fidgety; **~си́льный** [14; -лен, -льна] beyond one's strength; **~сле́довательный** [14; -лен, -льна] inconsistent; **~слу́шный** [14; -шен, -шна] disobedient.

непо|сре́дственный [14 *sh.*] immediate, direct; spontaneous; **~стижи́мый** [14 *sh.*] inconceivable; **~стоя́нный** [14; -я́нен, -я́нна] inconstant, unsteady, fickle; **~хо́жий** [17 *sh.*] unlike, different (from на B).

непра́в|да *f* [5] untruth, lie; (it is) not true; ... и **~дами** (*by hook*) or by crook; **~доподо́бный** [14; -бен, -бна] improbable; **~едный** [14; -ден, -дна] unjust; sinful; **~ильный** [14; -лен, -льна] incorrect, wrong; irregular (*a. gr.*); improper (*a.* ⚕); **~ота́** *f* [5] wrong(fulness); **~ый** [14; непра́в, -а́, -о] wrong; unjust.

непре|взойдённый [14 *sh.*] unsurpassed; **~дви́денный** [14] unforeseen; **~дубеждённый** [14] unbias(s)ed; **~кло́нный** [14; -о́нен, -о́нна] uncompromising; steadfast; **~ло́жный** [14; -жен, -жна] inviolable, invariable; incontestable; **~ме́нный** [14; -е́нен, -е́нна] indispensable; permanent; **~ме́нно** *s.* обяза́тельно; **~одоли́мый** [14 *sh.*] insuperable; irresistible; **~река́емый** [14 *sh.*] indisputable; **~ры́вный** [14; -вен, -вна] continuous; **~ста́нный** [14; -а́нен, -а́нна] incessant.

непри|вы́чный [14; -чен, -чна] unaccustomed; unusual; **~гля́дный** [14; -ден, -дна] homely, mean; **~го́дный** [14; -ден, -дна] unfit; useless; **~е́млемый** [14 *sh.*] unacceptable; **~коснове́нный** [14; -е́нен, -е́нна] inviolable; untouched, untouchable; **~кра́шенный** [14] unvarnished; **~ли́чный** [14; -чен, -чна] indecent, unseemly; **~ме́тный** [14; -тен, -тна] imperceptible, unnoticeable; plain; **~мири́мый** [14 *sh.*] irreconcilable, implacable; **~нуждённый** [14 *sh.*] (free and) easy, at ease; **~сто́йный** [14; -о́ен, -о́йна] obscene, indecent; **~сту́пный** [14; -пен, -пна] inaccessible; impregnable; unapproachable, haughty; **~тво́рный** [14; -рен, -рна] sincere, unfeigned; **~тяза́тельный** [14; -лен, -льна] unpretentious, modest, plain.

неприя́|зненный [14 *sh.*] hostile, unkind(ly); **~знь** *f* [8] dislike; **~тель** *m* [4] enemy; **~тельский**

[16] enemy('s); **~тность** *f* [8] trouble; **~тный** [14; -тен, -тна] disagreeable, unpleasant.
непро|гля́дный [14; -ден, -дна] pitch-dark; **~должи́тельный** [14; -лен, -льна] short, brief; **~е́зжий** [17] impassable; **~зра́чный** [14; -чен, -чна] opaque; **~изводи́тельный** [14; -лен, -льна] unproductive; **~изво́льный** [14; -лен, -льна] involuntary; **~мока́емый** [14 *sh.*] waterproof; **~ница́емый** [14 *sh.*] impenetrable, impermeable, impervious; **~сти́тельный** [14; -лен, -льна] unpardonable; **~ходи́мый** [14 *sh.*] impassable; F complete; **∠чный** [14; -чен, -чна́, -о] flimsy, unstable.
нера́бочий [17] free, off (*day*).
нера́в|енство *n* [9] inequality; **~номе́рный** [14; -рен, -рна] uneven; **~ный** [14; -вен, -вна́, -о] unequal.
неради́вый [14 *sh.*] careless, listless.
нераз|бери́ха F *f* [5] mess; **~бо́рчивый** [14 *sh.*] illegible; unscrupulous; **~вито́й** [14; -ра́звит, -а́, -о] undeveloped; **~де́льный** [14; -лен, -льна] indivisible, integral; undivided; **~личи́мый** [14 *sh.*] indistinguishable; **~лу́чный** [14; -чен, -чна] inseparable; **~реши́мый** [14 *sh.*] insoluble; **~ры́вный** [14; -вен, -вна] indissoluble; **~у́мный** [14; -мен, -мна] injudicious.
нерас|положе́ние *n* [12] dislike; **~суди́тельный** [14; -лен, -льна] imprudent.
нерв *m* [1] nerve; **~и́ровать** [7] make nervous; **∠ничать** [1] be nervous; **~нобольно́й** [14] neurotic; **∠(о́з)ный** [14; -вен, -вна́, -о (-зен, -зна)] nervous; high-strung.
нереши́тельн|ость *f* [8] indecision; в **~ости** at a loss; **~ый** [14; лен, -льна] irresolute.
неро́|бкий [16; -бок, -бка́, -о] brave; **~вный** [14; -вен, -вна́, -о] uneven.
неруши́мый [14 *sh.*] inviolable.
неря́|ха *m/f* [5] sloven; **~шливый** [14 *sh.*] slovenly; careless.
несамостоя́тельный [14; -лен, -льна] dependent (on, *or* influenced by, others).
несбы́точный [14; -чен, -чна] unrealizable.
не|све́дущий [17 *sh.*] ignorant (of в П); **~своевре́менный** [14; -енен, -енна] untimely; tardy; **~свя́зный** [14; -зен, -зна] incoherent; **~сгора́емый** [14] fireproof; **~сде́ржанный** [14 *sh.*] unrestrained; **~серьёзный** [14; -зен, -зна] frivolous; **~сказа́нный** [14 *sh.*, *no m*] indescribable; **~скла́дный** [14; -ден, -дна] ungainly, unwieldy; incoherent; **~склоня́емый** [14 *sh.*] indeclinable.
не́сколько [32] a few, some, several; somewhat.
не|скро́мный [14; -мен, -мна́, -о] immodest; **~слы́ханный** [14 *sh.*] unheard-of; awful; **~слы́шный** [14; -шен, -шна] inaudible, noiseless; **~сме́тный** [14; -тен, -тна] innumerable.
несмотря́ (на В) in spite of, despite, notwithstanding; (al)though.
несно́сный [14; -сен, -сна] intolerable.
несо|блюде́ние *n* [12] nonobservance; **~вершеннолéтие** *n* [12] minority; **~верше́нный** [14; -е́нен, -е́нна] imperfect(ive *gr.*); **~верше́нство** *n* [8] imperfection; **~вмести́мый** [14 *sh.*] incompatible; **~гла́сие** *n* [12] disagreement; **~гла́сный** [14; -сен, -сна] discordant; inconsistent; **~измери́мый** [14 *sh.*] incommensurable; **~круши́мый** [14 *sh.*] indestructible; **~мне́нный** [14; -е́нен, -е́нна] doubtless; **~мне́нно** *a.* undoubtedly, without doubt; **~обра́зный** [14; -зен, -зна] incompatible; absurd, foolish; **~отве́тствие** *n* [12] discrepancy; **~разме́рный** [14; -рен, -рна] disproportionate; **~стоя́тельный** [14; -лен, -льна] needy; insolvent; unsound, baseless.
несп|око́йный [14; -о́ен, -о́йна] restless, uneasy; **~осо́бный** [14; -бен, -бна] incapable (of к Д, на В), unfit (for); **~раведли́вость** *f* [8] injustice; wrong; **~раведли́вый** [14 *sh.*] unjust, wrong; **~роста́** F *s.* недаро́м.
несравне́нный [14; -е́нен, -е́нна] incomparable.
нестерпи́мый [14 *sh.*] intolerable.
нести́ [24 -с-: -су́], <по-> (be) carry(ing, *etc.*); bear; bring; suffer (*loss*); do (*duty*); drift, waft, speed (along) (**-сь** *v/i.*; *a.* be heard; spread); <с-> lay (eggs **-сь**); F talk (*nonsense*); smell (of Т); несёт there's a draught.
не|строево́й [14] noncombatant; **~стро́йный** [14; -о́ен, -ойна́, -о] ungainly; discordant; disorderly; **~сура́зный** F [14; -зен, -зна] foolish, absurd; ungainly; **~схо́дный** [14; -ден, -дна] unlike, different (from с Т).
несча́ст|ный [14; -тен, -тна] unhappy, unlucky; F paltry; **~ье** *n* [12] misfortune; disaster; accident; к **~ью** *or* на **~ье** unfortunately.
несчётный [14; -тен, -тна] innumerable.
нет **1.** *part.*: no; ~ ещё not yet; **2.** *impers. vb.* [*pt.* не́ было, *ft.* не бу́дет] (Р): there is (are) no; у меня́ (*etc.*) ~ I (*etc.*) have no(ne); его́ (её) ~ (s)he is not (t)here *or* in.
нетерп|ели́вый [14 *sh.*] impatient;

~éние *n* [12] impatience; **~и́мый** [14 *sh.*] intolerant; intolerable.
не|тле́нный [14; -éнен, -éнна] imperishable; **~тре́звый** [14; -тре́зв, -á, -o] drunk (*a.* в ~тре́звом ви́де); **~тро́нутый** [14 *sh.*] untouched; **~трудоспосо́бный** [14; -бен, -бна] disabled.
нет|то ('nɛ-) [*ind.*] net; **∠у** F = нет 2.
неу|важе́ние *n* [12] disrespect (for к Д); **~ве́ренный** [14 *sh.*] uncertain; **~вяда́емый** [14 *sh.*] unfading; **~гаси́мый** [14 *sh.*] inextinguishable; **~гомо́нный** [14; -óнен, -óнна] restless, unquiet; untiring.
неуда́ч|а *f* [5] misfortune; failure; **~ливый** [14 *sh.*] unlucky; **~ник** *m* [1] unlucky fellow; **~ный** [14; -чен, -чна] unsuccessful, unfortunate.
неуд|ержи́мый [14 *sh.*] irrepressible; **~иви́тельно** (it is) no wonder.
неудо́б|ный [14; -бен, -бна] inconvenient; uncomfortable; improper; **~ство** *n* [9] inconvenience.
неудов|летвори́тельный [14; -лен, -льна] unsatisfactory; **~о́льствие** *n* [12] displeasure.
неуже́ли really?, is it possible?
неу|жи́вчивый [14 *sh.*] unsociable, unaccomodating; **~кло́нный** [14; -óнен, -óнна] unswerving, firm; **~клю́жий** [17 *sh.*] clumsy, awkward; **~кроти́мый** [14 *sh.*] indomitable; **~лови́мый** [14 *sh.*] elusive; imperceptible; **~ме́лый** [14 *sh.*] unskillful, awkward; **~ме́ние** *n* [12] inability; **~ме́ренный** [14 *sh.*] intemperate, immoderate; **~ме́стный** [14; -тен, -тна] inappropriate; **~моли́мый** [14 *sh.*] inexorable; **~мы́шленный** [14 *sh.*] unintentional; **~потреби́тельный** [14; -лен, -льна] not in use; **~рожа́й** *m* [3] bad harvest; **~ро́чный** [14] unseasonable; **~спе́х** *m* [1] failure; **~ста́нный** [14; -áнен, -áнна] incessant; constant; *s. a.* ~томи́мый; **~сто́йка** *f* [5; *g/pl.*: -óек] forfeit; **~сто́йчивый** [14 *sh.*] unstable; unsteady; **~страши́мый** [14 *sh.*] intrepid, dauntless; **~сту́пчивый** [14 *sh.*] uncomplying, tenacious; **~сы́пный** [14; -пен, -пна] incessant, unremitting; *s. a.* ~томи́мый; **~те́шный** [14; -шен, -шна] disconsolate, inconsolable; **~толи́мый** [14 *sh.*] unquenchable; insatiable; **~томи́мый** [14 *sh.*] tireless, indefatigable, untiring.
не́уч F *m* [1] ignoramus; **~ёный** [14] illiterate; **~е́нье** *n* [10] ignorance.
неу|чти́вый [14 *sh.*] uncivil; **~ю́тный** [14; -тен, -тна] uncomfortable; **~язви́мый** [14 *sh.*] invulnerable.
нефт|еналивно́й *s.* наливно́й; **~епрово́д** *m* [1] pipe line; **~ь** *f* [8] (mineral) oil; **~яно́й** [14] oil...
не|хва́тка F *f* [5; *g/pl.*: -ток] shortage; **~хоро́ший** [17; -ро́ш, -á] bad; **∠хотя** unwillingly; **~цензу́рный** [14; -рен, -рна] *s.* ~присто́йный; **~ча́янный** [14] unexpected; accidental, casual.
не́чего [23]: (мне, *etc.*) ~ + *inf.* (there is *or* one can) (I have) nothing to ...; (one) need not, (there is) no need; (it is) no use; stop ...ing.
не|челове́ческий [16] inhuman; superhuman; **~чести́вый** [14 *sh.*] ungodly; **~че́стность** *f* [8] dishonesty; **~че́стный** [14; -тен, -тнá, -o] dishonest; **∠чет** F *m* [1] *s.* нечётный; **~чётный** [14] odd (*number*).
нечист|опло́тный [14; -тен, -тна] uncleanly, dirty; **~ота́** *f* [5; *pl. st.*: -óты] unclean(li)ness; *pl.* sewage; **∠ый** [14; -чи́ст, -á, -o] unclean, dirty; impure; evil, vile, bad, foul.
не́что something.
не|чувстви́тельный [14; -лен, -льна] insensitive; insensible; **~ща́дный** [14; -ден, -дна] unmerciful; **~я́вка** *f* [5] nonappearance; **~я́ркий** [16; -я́рок, -яркá, -o] dull, dim; mediocre; **~я́сный** [14; -сен, -снá, -o] not clear; *fig.* vague.
ни not a (single оди́н); ~ ..., ~ neither ... nor; ... ever (*e. g.* кто [бы] ~ whoever); кто (что, когда́, где, куда́) бы то ∠ был(о) whosoever (what-, when-, wheresoever); как ~ + *vb. a.* in spite *or* for all + *su.*; как бы (то) ∠ было be that as it may; ~ за что ~ про что for nothing.
ни́ва *f* [5] field (*a. fig.*; in на П).
нигде́ nowhere.
Нидерла́нды *pl.* [1] The Netherlands.
ни́ж|е below, beneath, under; lower; shorter; **~еподписа́вшийся** *m* [17] the undersigned; **~ний** [15] lower; under...; ground *or* first (*floor*).
низ *m* [1; *pl. e.*] bottom, lower part; *pl. a.* masses; **~а́ть** [3], ⟨на-⟩ string.
низвер|га́ть [1], ⟨∠гнуть⟩ [21]; **~же́ние** *n* [12] (over)throw.
низи́на *f* [5] hollow, lowland.
ни́зк|ий [16; -зок, -зкá, -o; *comp.*: ни́же] low; mean, base; short; **~опокло́нник** *m* [1] groveler; **~опокло́нничать** [1] grovel, fawn, cringe.
ни́зменн|ость *f* [8] lowland, plain; **~ый** [14 *sh.*] low(er).
низо|во́й [14] lower; local; **∠вье** *n* [10; *g/pl.*: -ьев] lower (course); **~йти́** *s.* нисходи́ть; **'~сть** *f* [8] meanness.
ника́к by no means, not at all; **~о́й** [16] no (at all F); ни в како́м слу́чае on no account; *s. a.* ~.
ни́кел|евый [14], **~ь** *m* [4] nickel.
никогда́ never.
Никола́й [3] Nicholas.

ни|кой *s.* никак(ой); **\~ктó** [23] nobody, no one, none; **\~кудá** nowhere; *cf. a.* годиться, гóдный; **\~кчёмный** F [14] good-for-nothing; **\~мáло** *s.* \~скóлько; **\~откýда** from nowhere; **\~почём** F very cheap, easy, *etc.*; **\~скóлько** not in the least, not at all.
нисходя́щий [17] descending.
нит|ка *f* [5; *g/pl.:* -ток], **\~ь** [8] thread; string; cotton; \~ь *a.* filament; до (послéдней) \~ки F to the skin; (как) по \~ке straight; шитó бéлыми \~ками be transparent, на живýю \~ку carelessly, superficially.
ниц: пáдать \~ prostrate o. s.
ничегó (-'vo) nothing; \~ (себé) not bad; so-so; no(t) matter; \~! never mind!, that's all right!
нич|éй *m*, **\~ья́** *f*, **\~ьё** *n*, **\~ьи́** *pl.* [26] nobody's; *su. f* draw (*games*).
ничкóм prone; *s. a.* ниц.
ничтó [23] nothing; *s.* ничегó; **\~жество** *n* [9], **\~жность** *f* [8] nothingness, vanity, nonentity; **\~жный** [14; -жен, -жна] insignificant, tiny; vain.
нич|ýть F *s.* нискóлько; **\~ья́** *s.* \~éй.
ни́ша *f* [5] niche.
ни́щ|ая *f* [17], **\~енка** F [5; *g/pl.:* -нок] beggar woman; **\~енский** [16] beggarly; **\~енство** *n* [9] begging; beggary; **\~енствовать** [7] beg; **\~етá** *f* [5] poverty, destitution; **\~ий** 1. [17; нищ, -á, -е] beggarly; 2. *m* [17] beggar.
НКВД (Нарóдный комиссариáт внýтренних дел) People's Commissariat of Internal Affairs (*1935 to 1946*; *since 1946* МВД, *cf.*).
но but, yet.
новáтор *m* [1] innovator.
новéлла *f* [5] short story.
нóв|енький [16; -нек] (brand-) new; **\~изнá** *f* [5], **\~и́нка** [5; *g/pl.:* -нок] novelty; news; **\~ичóк** *m* [1; -чкá] novice, tyro; newcomer.
ново|брáнец *m* [1; -нца] recruit; **\~брáчный** [14] newly married; **\~введéние** *n* [12] innovation; **\~гóдний** [15] New Year's (Eve \~гóдний вéчер *m*); **\~лýние** *n* [12] new moon; **\~прибы́вший** [17] newly arrived; newcomer; **\~рождённый** [14] newborn (child) ; **\~сéлье** *n* [10] new home; housewarming; **\~стрóйка** *f* [5; *g/pl.:* -óек] new building (project).
нóв|ость *f* [8] (piece of) news; novelty; **\~шество** *n* [9] innovation, novelty; **\~ый** [14; нов, -á, -о] new; novel; recent; modern; Ⓝый год *m* New Year's Day; с Ⓝым гóдом! a happy New Year!; \~ый мéсяц *m* crescent; что \~ого? what's (the) new(s *Brt.*)?; **\~ь** *f* [8] virgin soil.
ног|á *f* [5; *ac/sg.:* нóгу; *pl.:* нóги, ног, ногáм, *etc. e.*] foot, leg; идти́ в ⁀у march in (*or* keep) step; со всех \~ with all one's might, at full speed; стать нá \~и recover; become independent; положи́ть ⁀у нá \~у cross one's legs; на ... \~é *or* ⁀у on ... terms *or* a ... footing; in (*grand*) style; ни \~óй (к Д) not visit (a p.); (éле) ⁀и унести́ (have a narrow) escape; в \~áх at the foot (*cf.* головá); под \~áми underfoot.
нóготь *m* [4; -гтя; *from g/pl. e.*] nail.
нож *m* [1 *e.*] knife; на \~áх at daggers drawn; **⁀ик** *m* [1] F = нож; **⁀ка** *f* [5; *g/pl.:* -жек] *dim. of* ногá, *s.*; leg (*chair, etc.*); **⁀ницы** *f/pl.* [5] (pair of) scissors; disproportion; **\~нóй** [14] foot...; **⁀ны́** *f/pl.* [5; *g/pl.;* -жен & -жóн] sheath.
ноздря́ [6; *pl.:* нóздри, ноздрéй, *etc. e.*] nostril.
ноль & нуль *m* [4 *e.*] naught; zero.
нóмер *m* [1; *pl.:* -pá, *etc. e.*] number ([with] за Т); size; (*hotel*) room; item, turn, trick; (*a., dim.,* **\~óк** *m* [1; -ркá]) tag, plate.
номинáльный [14; -лен, -льна] nominal.
норá *f* [5; *ac/sg.:* -рý; *pl.st.*] hole, burrow.
Норвé|гия *f* [7] Norway; **Ⓝжец** *m* [1; -жца], **Ⓝжка** *f* [5; *g/pl.:* -жек], **Ⓝжский** [16] Norwegian.
нóрка *f* [5; *g/pl.:* -рок] 1. *dim. of* норá; 2. *zo.* mink.
нóрм|а *f* [5] norm, standard; rate; **\~áльный** [14; -лен, -льна] normal; **\~ировáть** [7] (*im*)*pf.* standardize.
нос *m* [1; в, на носý; *pl. e.*] nose; beak; prow; F spout; в \~ (*speak*) through one's nose; зá \~ (*lead*) by the nose; на \~ý (*time*) at hand; у меня́ идёт кровь ⁀ом my nose is bleeding; **⁀ик** *m* [1] *dim. of* \~; spout.
нося́|лки *f/pl.* [5; *gen.:* -лок] stretcher, litter; **\~льщик** *m* [1] porter; **\~тель** *m* [4] bearer; carrier; **\~ть** [15] carry, bear, *etc., s.* нести́; wear (*v/i.* -ся); F -ся (с Т) *a.* have one's mind occupied with.
носовóй [14] nasal; prow ...; \~ платóк *m* handkerchief.
носóк *m* [1; -скá] sock; toe; *a.* = нóсик.
носорóг *m* [1] rhinoceros.
нóта *f* [5] note; *pl. a.* music.
нотáриус *m* [1] notary (public).
нотáция *f* [7] reprimand, lecture.
ноч|евáть [7], ‹пере-› pass (*or* spend) the night; **\~ёвка** *f* [5; *g/pl.:* -вок] overnight stop (*or* stay *or* rest); *a.* = \~лéг; **\~лéг** *m* [1] night's lodging, night quarters; *a.* = \~ёвка; **\~нóй** [14] night(ly), (*a.* ♀, *zo.*) nocturnal; \~нáя бáбочка *f* moth; **\~ь** *f* [8; в ночи́; *from g/pl. e.*] night; ⁀ью at (*or* by) night (= *a.* в \~ь, по \~áм); \~ь под ... (В) ... night.
нóша *f* [5] load, burden.
ноя́брь *m* [4 *e.*] November.

нрав *m* [1] disposition, temper; *pl.* customs; (не) по ∠у (Д) (not) to one's liking; **∠иться** [14], ⟨по-⟩ please (a p. Д); он мне ∠ится I like him; **~оуче́ние** *n* [12] moral(ity), moral teaching; **~оучи́тельный** [14] moral(izing); **∠ственность** *f* [8] morals *pl.*, morality; **~ственный** [14 *sh.*] moral.

ну (*a.* ∠-ка) well *or* now (then же)!, come (on)!, why!, what!; the deuce (take him *or* it ~ его́)!; (*a.* да ~?) indeed?, really?, you don't say!; ha?; ~ да of course, sure; ~ + *inf.* begin to; ~ так что́ же? what about it?

ну́дный F [14; ну́ден, -днá, -о] tedious, humdrum.

нужд|á *f* [5; *pl. st.*] need, want (of в П); necessity (of из Р, по Д); F request; concern; ~ы́ нет it doesn't matter; **~áться** [1] (в П) (be in) need (of), be hard up, needy.

ну́жн|ый [14; ну́жен, -жнá, -о, ну́жны́] necessary (for Д); (Д) ~о + *inf.* must (*cf.* нáдо).

нуль = ноль.

ну́мер = но́мер; **~áция** *f* [7] numeration; **~овáть** [7], ⟨за-, про-⟩ number.

ны́н|е now(adays), today; **~ешний** F [15] present, this; actual, today's; **~че** F = ~е.

ныр|я́ть [28], *once* ⟨~ну́ть⟩ [20] dive.

ныть [22] ache; whimper; F lament.

Нью-Йо́рк *m* [1] New York.

н. э. (нáшей э́ры) A. D.

нэп (но́вая экономи́ческая поли́тика) NEP (New Economic Policy. *Sov., from 1922 to 1928*).

нюх *m* [1] flair, scent; **∠ательный** [14]: ∠ательный табáк *m* snuff; **∠ать** [1], ⟨по-⟩ smell; scent; snuff.

ня́н|чить [16] nurse, tend (*a.* **-ся**; F fuss over, busy o. s. with [с Т]); **~я** *f* [6] (F **~ька** [5; *g/pl.*: -нек]) nurse, *Brt. a.* nanny.

О

о, об, обо **1.** (П) about, of; on; with; **2.** (В) against, (up)on; by, in.

о! oh!, o!

о́б|а *m & n*, **~е** *f* [37] both.

обагр|я́ть [28], ⟨~и́ть⟩ [13] redden, purple; stain (with Т); steep.

обанкро́титься *s.* банкро́титься.

обая́|ние *n* [12] spell, charm; **~тельный** [14; -лен, -льна] fascinating.

обвáл *m* [1] collapse; landslide; avalanche; **~иваться** [1], ⟨~и́ться⟩ [13; обвáлится] fall in *or* off; **~я́ть** [1] *pf.* roll.

обвари́ть [13; -арю́, -áришь] scald.

обвёр|тывать [1], ⟨~ну́ть⟩ [20] wrap (up), envelop.

обве́|сить [15] F = ~шать.

обвести́ *s.* обводи́ть.

обве́тренный [14 *sh.*] weather-beaten.

обветшáлый [14] decayed.

обве́ш|ивать, ⟨~ать⟩ [1] hang (with Т).

обви|вáть [1], ⟨∠ть⟩ [обовью́, -вьёшь; *cf.* вить] wind round; embrace (with Т).

обвин|е́ние *n* [12] accusation, charge; indictment; prosecution; **~и́тель** *m* [4] accuser; prosecutor; **~и́тельный** [14] accusatory; of 'guilty'; ~и́тельный акт *m* indictment; **~я́ть** [28], ⟨~и́ть⟩ [13] (в П) accuse (of), charge (with); find guilty; ~я́емый accused; defendant.

обви́слый F [14] flabby.

обви́|ть *s.* ~вáть.

обводи́ть [13], ⟨обвести́⟩ [25] lead, see *or* look (round, about); enclose, encircle *or* border (with Т); draw out; F turn (*a p. round one's finger*).

обвор|áживать [1], ⟨~ожи́ть⟩ [16 *e.*; -жу́, -жи́шь; -жённый] charm, fascinate; **~ожи́тельный** [14; -лен, -льна] charming, fascinating; **~ожи́ть** *s.* ~áживать.

обвя́з|ывать [1], ⟨~áть⟩ [3] tie up *or* round; dress; hang.

обгоня́ть [28], ⟨обогнáть⟩ [обгоню́, -о́нишь; обогнáл, -á, -о; обо́гнанный] (out)distance, outstrip.

обгор|áть [1], ⟨~е́ть⟩ [9] scorch.

обгрыз|áть [1], ⟨∠ть⟩ [24; *pt. st.*] gnaw (at, round, away).

обда|вáть [5], ⟨∠ть⟩ [-áм, -áшь; *cf.* дать; о́бдал, -á, -о; о́бданный (о́бдан, -á, -о)] pour over; scald; bespatter; wrap up; seize.

обде́л|ать *s.* ~ывать; **~и́ть** *s.* ~я́ть; **~ывать**, ⟨~ать⟩ [1] work; lay out; cut (*gem*); F manage, wangle; **~я́ть** [28], ⟨~и́ть⟩ [13; -елю́, -е́лишь] deprive of one's due share (of Т).

обдирáть [1], ⟨ободрáть⟩ [обдеру́, -рёшь; ободрáл, -á, -о; обо́дранный] bark, peel; tear (off).

обду́м|ать *s.* ~ывать; **~анный** [14 *sh.*] deliberate; **~ывать**, ⟨~ать⟩ [1] consider, think over.

обе́д *m* [1] dinner (at за Т; for на В, к Д), lunch; F noon; до (по́сле) ~а in the morning (afternoon); **~ать** [1], ⟨по-⟩ have dinner (lunch), dine; **~енный** [14] dinner..., lunch...

обедне́вший [17] impoverished.

обе́дня *f* [6; *g/pl.*: -ден] mass.

обез|бо́ливание *n* [12] an(a)esthetization; **~вре́живать** [1], ⟨~вре́дить⟩ [15] neutralize; **~глáвли-**

вать [1], ‹~гла́вить› [14] behead; ~до́ленный [14] wretched, miserable; ~зара́живание n [12] disinfection; ~ли́чивать [1], ‹~ли́чить› [16] deprive of personal character, assignment or responsibility; ~лю́деть [8] pf. become deserted; ~надёживать [1], ‹~надёжить› [16] bereave of hope; ~обра́живать [1], ‹~обра́зить› [15] disfigure; ~опа́сить [15] pf. secure (against от P); ~ору́живать [1], ‹~ору́жить› [16] disarm; ~у́меть [8] pf. lose one's senses, go mad.

обезья́н|а f [5] monkey; ape; ~ий [18] monkey('s); apish, apelike; ~ничать F [1] ape.

обер|ега́ть [1], ‹~е́чь› [26 г/ж: -гу́, -жёшь] guard (v/i. -ся), protect (o. s.; against, from от P).

оберну́ть(ся) s. обёртывать(ся).

обёрт|ка f [5; g/pl.: -ток] cover; (book) jacket; ~очный [14] wrapping (or brown paper); ~ывать [1], ‹оберну́ть› [20] wrap (up); wind; turn (a. F, cf. обводи́ть F); -ся turn (round, F back); F wangle.

обескура́ж|ивать [1], ‹~ить› [16] discourage, dishearten.

обеспе́ч|ение n [12] securing; security (on под B), guarantee; maintenance; (social) security; ~енность f [8] (adequate) provision; prosperity; ~енный [14] well-to-do; ~ивать [1], ‹~ить› [16] provide (for; with T); secure, guarantee; protect.

обесси́л|еть [8] pf. become enervated; ~ивать [1], ‹~ить› [13] enervate.

обессме́ртить [13] pf. immortalize.

обесцве́|чивать [1], ‹~тить› [15] discolo(u)r, make colo(u)rless.

обесце́н|ивать [1], ‹~ить› [13] depreciate.

обесче́стить [15] pf. dishono(u)r.

обе́т m [1] vow, promise; ~ова́нный [14] Promised (Land).

обеща́|ние n [12], ~ть [1] (im)pf., F a. ‹по-› promise.

обжа́лование ⚖ n [12] appeal.

обж|ига́ть [1], ‹~е́чь› [26 г/ж: обожгу́, -жжёшь, обожгу́т; обжёг, обожгла́; обожжённый] burn; scorch; ⊕ bake, calcine (cf. ~ига́тельная печь f kiln); -ся burn o. s. (F one's fingers).

обжо́р|а F m/f [5] glutton; ~ливый F [14 sh.] gluttonous; ~ство F n [9] gluttony.

обзав|оди́ться [15], ‹~естись› [25] provide o. s. (with T), acquire, get.

обзо́р m [1] survey; review.

обзыва́ть [1], ‹обозва́ть› [обзову́, -ёшь; обозва́л, -а́, -о; обо́званный] call (names T).

оби|ва́ть [1], ‹~ть› [обобью, обобьёшь; cf. бить] upholster; strike off; F wear out; ~ва́ть поро́ги (у P) importune; ~вка f [5] upholstery.

оби́|да f [5] insult; не в ~ду будь ска́зано no offence meant; не дать в ~ду let not be offended; ~деть (-ся) s. ~жа́ть(ся); ~дный [14; -ден, -дна] offensive, insulting; (мне) ~дно it is a shame or vexing (it offends or vexes me; I am sorry [for за B]); ~дчивый [14 sh.] touchy; ~дчик F m [1] offender; ~жа́ть [1], ‹~деть› [11] (-ся be) offend(ed), hurt (a. be angry with or at на B); wrong; overreach (cf. a. обделя́ть); ~женный [14 sh.] offended (s. a. ~жа́ть[ся]).

оби́л|ие n [12] abundance, wealth; ~ьный [14; -лен, -льна] abundant (in T), plentiful, rich.

обиня́к m [1 e.]: говори́ть ~а́ми speak in a roundabout way.

обира́ть F [1], ‹обобра́ть› [оберу́, -ёшь; обобра́л, -а́, -о; обо́бранный] rob; P gather.

обита́|емый [14 sh.] inhabited; ~тель m [4] inhabitant; ~ть [1] live, dwell, reside.

оби́ть s. обива́ть.

обихо́д m [1] use, custom, way; дома́шний ~ household; ~ный [14; -ден, -дна] everyday; colloquial.

обкла́д|ка f [5] facing; ~ывать [1], ‹обложи́ть› [16] lay round; face, cover; 🝖 fur; pf. besiege; s. облага́ть.

обко́м m [1] (областно́й комите́т) regional committee Sov.).

обкра́дывать [1], ‹обокра́сть› [25; обкраду́, -дёшь; pt. st. обкра́денный] rob.

обла́ва f [5] battue; raid.

облага́ть [1], ‹обложи́ть› [16] impose (tax, fine T); tax; fine.

облагор|а́живать [1], ‹~о́дить› [15] ennoble, refine; finish.

облада́|ние n [12] possession (of T); ~ть [1] (T) possess; command; (health) be in; ~ть собо́й control o. s.

о́блако n [9; pl.: -ка́, -ко́в] cloud.

обл|а́мывать [1], ‹~ома́ть› [1] & ‹~оми́ть› [14] break off.

обласка́ть [1] pf. treat kindly.

област|но́й [14] regional; '~ь f [8; from g/pl. e.] region; province, sphere, field (fig.).

обла́тка f [5; g/pl.: -ток] wafer; capsule.

обла|че́ние n [12] eccl. vestments [pl.]

о́блачный [14; -чен, -чна] cloudy.

обле|га́ть [1], ‹~́чь› [26 г/ж; cf. лечь] cover; fit (close).

облегч|а́ть (-xtʃ-) [1], ‹~и́ть› [16e.; -чу́, -чи́шь; -чённый] lighten; facilitate; ease, relieve.

обледене́лый [14] ice-covered.

облёзлый F [14] mangy, shabby.

обле|ка́ть [1], ‹~́чь› [26] dress; invest (with T); put, express; -ся put on (в B); be(come) invested.

облеп|ля́ть [28], ⟨**~и́ть**⟩ [14] stick all over (*or* round); besiege.
облет|а́ть [1], ⟨**~е́ть**⟩ [11] fly round (*or: all over*, past, in); fall.
облéчь [1], *s.* облегáть & облекáть.
обли|вáть [1], ⟨**∠ть**⟩ [оболью́, -льёшь; облéй!; óбли́л, -á, -о; óбли́тый (óбли́т, -á, -о)] pour (s. th. T) over, wet; flood; soak; **-ся** [*pf.*: -и́лся, -илáсь, -и́лóсь] (T) pour over o. s.; shed (*tears*); be dripping (*with sweat*) *or* covered (*with blood*); bleed (*heart*).
облигáция *f* [7] bond.
облиз|ывать [1], ⟨**~áть**⟩ [3] lick (off); **-ся** lick one's lips (*or* o. s.).
óблик *m* [1] face, look; figure.
обли́|ть(ся) *s.* **~вáть(ся)**; **~цóвывать** [1], ⟨**~цевáть**⟩ [7] face.
облич|áть [1], ⟨**~и́ть**⟩ [16 *е.*; -чу́, -чи́шь; -чённый] unmask; reveal; convict (of в П); **~éние** *n* [12] exposure; conviction; **~и́тельный** [14; -лен, -льна] accusatory, incriminating; **~и́ть** *s.* **~áть**.
облож|éние *n* [12] taxation; ⚔ siege; **~и́ть** *s.* обклáдывать & облагáть; **∠ка** [5; *g/pl.*: -жек] cover, (book) jacket.
облок|áчиваться [1], ⟨**~оти́ться**⟩ [15 & 15 *е.*; -кочу́сь, -кóти́шься] lean one's elbows (on на В).
облом|áть, **~и́ть** *s.* облáмывать; **∠ок** *m* [1; -мка] fragment; *pl.* debris, wreckage.
облуч|áть [1], ⟨**~и́ть**⟩ [16 *е.*; -чу́, -чи́шь; -чённый] ray.
облучóк *m* [1; -чкá] (coach) box.
облюбовáть [7] *pf.* take a fancy to.
обмáз|ывать [1], ⟨**~ать**⟩ [3] besmear; plaster, coat, cement.
обмáк|ивать [1], ⟨**~ну́ть**⟩ [20] dip.
обмáн *m* [1] deception; deceit, fraud; ~ зрéния optical illusion; **~ный** [14] deceitful, fraudulent; **~у́ть(ся)** *s.* **~ывать(ся)**; **~чивый** [14 *sh.*] deceptive; **~щик** *m* [1], **~щица** *f* [5] cheat, deceiver; **~ывать** [1], ⟨**~у́ть**⟩ [20] (**-ся** be) deceive(d), cheat; (be mistaken in в П).
обм|áтывать, ⟨**~отáть**⟩ [1] wind (round); **~áхивать** [1], ⟨**~ахну́ть**⟩ [19] wipe, dust; fan.
обмéн *m* [1] exchange (in/for в В/на В); interchange (of T, P); **~ивать** [1], ⟨**~я́ть**⟩ [28] & F ⟨**~и́ть**⟩ [13; -еню́, -éнишь; ~енённый] exchange (for на В; **-ся** s. th. T).
обм|ерéть *s.* **~ирáть**; **~етáть** [1], ⟨**~ести́**⟩ [25 -т-: обмету́] sweep (off), dust; **~ирáть** F [1], ⟨**~ерéть**⟩ [12; обомру́, -рёшь; óбмер, -рлá, -о; обмéрший] be struck *or* stunned (with *fear* от Р).
обмóлв|иться [14] *pf.* make a slip (in speaking); (T) mention, say; **~ка** *f* [5; *g/pl.*: -вок] slip of the tongue.
обмолóт *m* [1] thresh(ing).
обморóзить [15] *pf.* frostbite.
óбморок *m* [1] faint, swoon (*vb.*: пáдать, *pf.* упáсть в ~).
обмот|áть *s.* обмáтывать; **∠ка** *f* [5; *g/pl.*: -ток] ⚡ winding; *pl.* puttees.
обмундировá|ние *n* [12], **~ть** [7] *pf.* uniform, outfit.
обмы|вáть [1], ⟨**∠ть**⟩ [22] wash (off); **~вáние** *n* [12] *a.* ablution.
обнадёж|ивать [1], ⟨**~ить**⟩ [16] (re)assure, encourage, raise hopes.
обнаж|áть [1], ⟨**~и́ть**⟩ [16 *е.*; -жу́, -жи́шь; -жённый] bare, strip; lay bare; uncover; unsheathe.
обнарóдовать [7] *pf.* promulgate.
обнару́ж|ивать [1], ⟨**~ить**⟩ [16] disclose, show, reveal; discover, detect; **-ся** appear, show; come to light; be found, discovered.
обнести́ *s.* обноси́ть.
обн|имáть [1], ⟨**~я́ть**⟩ [обниму́, обни́мешь; óбнял, -á, -о; óбнятый (óбнят, -á, -о)] embrace, hug, clasp.
обнищáлый [14] impoverished.
обнóв|(к)а F *f* [5; (*g/pl.*: -вок)] new thing, novelty; **~и́ть** *s.* **~ля́ть**; **~лéние** *n* [12] renewal; renovation; **~ля́ть** [28], ⟨**~и́ть**⟩ [14 *е.*; -влю́, -ви́шь; -влённый] renew; renovate.
обн|оси́ть [15], ⟨**~ести́**⟩ [24 -с-: -су́] carry (round); serve; pass by; (T) fence in, enclose; **-ся** F *impf.* wear out one's clothes.
обнюх|ивать, ⟨**~ать**⟩ [1] smell at.
обня́ть *s.* обнимáть.
обобрáть *s.* обирáть.
обобщ|áть [1], ⟨**~и́ть**⟩ [16 *е.*; -щу́, -щи́шь; -щённый] generalize; **~ествля́ть** [28], ⟨**~естви́ть**⟩ [14 *е.*; -влю́, -ви́шь; -влённый] socialize; **~и́ть** *s.* **~áть**.
обога|щáть [1], ⟨**~ти́ть**⟩ [15 *е.*; -ащу́, -ти́шь; -ащённый] enrich.
обогнáть *s.* обгоня́ть.
обогну́ть *s.* огибáть.
обоготворя́ть [28] *s.* боготвори́ть.
обогревáть [1] *s.* греть.
óбод *m* [1; *pl.*: обóдья, -дьев] rim, felloe; **~óк** *m* [1; -дкá] rim.
обóдр|анный F [14 *sh.*] ragged, shabby; **~áть** *s.* обдирáть; **~éние** *n* [12] encouragement; **~я́ть** [28], ⟨**~и́ть**⟩ [13] encourage; **-ся** take courage.
обожáть [1] adore, worship.
обождáть F = подождáть.
обожеств|ля́ть [28], ⟨**~и́ть**⟩ [14 *е.*; -влю́, -ви́шь; -влённый] deify.
обожжённый [14; -ён, -енá] burnt.
обóз *m* [1] train (*a.* ⚔), carts *pl.*
обозвáть *s.* обзывáть.
обознач|áть [1], ⟨**∠ить**⟩ [16] denote, designate, mark; **-ся** appear; **~éние** *n* [12] designation.
обозр|евáть [1], ⟨**~éть**⟩ [9], **~éние** *n* [12] survey; review.
обó|и *m/pl.* [3] wallpaper; **~йти́(сь)**

s. обходи́ть(ся); **~йщик** *m* [1] upholsterer; **~кра́сть** *s.* обкра́дывать.
оболо́чка *f* [5; *g/pl.*: -чек] cover(-ing), envelope; *anat.* membrane; ⊕ jacket, casing; ра́дужная ~ iris.
оболь|сти́тель *m* [4] seducer; **~сти́тельный** [14; -лен, -льна] seductive; **~щать** [1], ⟨~сти́ть⟩ [15 *e.*; -льщу́, -льсти́шь; -льщённый] seduce; (-ся be) delude(d; flatter o. s.); **~ще́ние** *n* [12] seduction; delusion.
обомле́ть F [8] *pf.* be stupefied.
обоня́ние *n* [12] (sense of) smell.
обора́чивать(ся) *s.* обёртывать(-ся).
оборв|а́нец F *m* [1; -нца] ragamuffin; **∠анный** [14 *sh.*] ragged; **~а́ть** *s.* обрыва́ть.
обо́рка *f* [5; *g/pl.*: -рок] frill, ruffle.
оборо́н|а *f* [5] defense (*Brt.* defence); **~и́тельный** [14] defensive, defense...; **~ный** [14] defense..., armament...; **~оспосо́бность** *f* [8] defensive capacity; **~я́ть** [28] defend.
оборо́т *m* [1] revolution; rotation; circulation; turn; turnover; transaction; back, reverse; (см.) на ~е p. t. o.; в ~ F(*take*) to task; **~и́ть(ся)** P [15] *pf. s.* оберну́ть(ся); **~ливый** F [14 *sh.*] sharp, smart; **~ный** [14] back, reverse, seamy (*side*); ✝ circulating.
обору́дова|ние [12] equipment; **~ть** [7] (*im*)*pf.* equip; fit out.
обосн|ова́ние *n* [12] substantiation; ground(s); **~о́вывать** [1], ⟨~ова́ть⟩ [7] prove, substantiate; -ся settle down.
обос|обля́ть [28], ⟨~о́бить⟩ [14] segregate, isolate, detach.
обостр|я́ть [28], ⟨~и́ть⟩ [13] (-ся become) aggravate(d), strain(ed); refine(d).
обою́д|ный [14; -ден, -дна] mutual; **~оо́стрый** [14 *sh.*] double-edged.
обраб|а́тывать, ⟨~о́тать⟩ [1] work, process; ✓ till; elaborate, finish, polish; treat; adapt; F work; *p. pr. a.* ⊕ manufacturing; **~о́тка** *f* [5; *g/pl.*: -ток] processing; ✓ cultivation; elaboration; adaptation.
о́браз *m* [1] manner, way (in T), mode; form; figure, character; image; [*pl.*: ~а́, *etc. e.*] icon; каки́м (таки́м) ~ом how (thus); нико́им ~ом by no means; **~е́ц** *m* [1; -зца́] specimen, sample; model, example; pattern; fashion, way (in на В); **~ный** [14; -зен, -зна] graphic, vivid; **~ова́ние** *n* [12] formation; constitution; education; **~о́ванный** [14 *sh.*] educated; **~ова́тельный** [14; -лен, -льна] (in)formative; **~о́вывать** [1], ⟨~ова́ть⟩ [7] form (*v/i.* -ся; arise); constitute; educate; cultivate; **~у́мить(ся)** F [14] *pf.* bring (come) to one's senses; **~цо́вый** [14] exemplary, model...; **∠чик** *m* [1] *s.* ~е́ц.
обрам|ля́ть [28], ⟨∠ить⟩ [14 *st.*], *fig.* ⟨~и́ть⟩ [14 *e.*; -млю́, -ми́шь; -млённый] frame.
обраст|а́ть [1], ⟨~и́⟩ [24 -ст-: -сту́; обро́с, -ла́] overgrow; be overgrown.
обра|ти́ть *s.* ~ща́ть; **∠тный** [14] back, return...; reverse, (*a.* ⅍) inverse; ⚖ retroactive; ∠тно back; conversely; **~ща́ть** [1], ⟨~ти́ть⟩ [15 *e.*; -ащу́, -ати́шь; -ащённый] turn; direct; convert; employ; draw *or* pay *or* (на себя́) attract (*attention*; to на В); не ~ща́ть внима́ния (на В) disregard; -ся turn (to в В); address o. s. (to к Д), apply (to; for за Т); appeal; take (to *flight* в В); *impf.* (с Т) treat, handle; circulate; **~ще́ние** *n* [12] conversion; transformation; circulation; (с Т) treatment (of), management; manners *pl.*; address; appeal.
обре́з *m* [1] edge; **~а́ть** [1], ⟨~ать⟩ [3] cut off; cut short; **~ок** *m* [1; -зка] scrap; **~ывать** [1] *s.* ~а́ть.
обре|ка́ть [1], ⟨∠чь⟩ [26] doom (to на В, Д).
обремен|и́тельный [14; -лен, -льна] burdensome; **~я́ть** [28], ⟨~и́ть⟩ [13] burden.
обре|чённый [14] doomed (to на В); **∠чь** *s.* ~ка́ть.
обрисо́в|ывать [1], ⟨~а́ть⟩ [7] outline, sketch; -ся loom, appear.
обро́к *m* [1] (quit)rent, tribute.
обро́сший [17] overgrown.
обруб|а́ть [1], ⟨~и́ть⟩ [14] hew (off), lop; **∠ок** *m* [1; -бка] stump, block.
о́бруч *m* [1; *from g/pl. e.*] hoop; **~а́льный** [14] engagement...; **~а́ть** [1], ⟨~и́ть⟩ [16 *e.*; -чу́, -чи́шь; -чённый] affiance, betroth; -ся be(come) engaged (to с Т); **~е́ние** *n* [12] betrothal; **~ённый** [14] fiancé(e ~ённая *f*).
обру́ш|ивать [1], ⟨~ить⟩ [16] demolish; cast; -ся fall in, collapse; fall (up)on (на В).
обры́в *m* [1] precipice, steep; **~а́ть** [1], ⟨оборва́ть⟩ [-ву́, -вёшь; -ва́л, -вала́, -о; обо́рванный] tear *or* pluck (off, round); break off, cut short; -ся *a.* fall (from с Р); **~истый** [14 *sh.*] steep; abrupt; **~ок** *m* [1; -вка] scrap, shred; **~очный** [14; -чен, -чна] scrappy.
обры́зг|ивать, ⟨~ать⟩ [1] sprinkle.
обрю́зглый [14] flabby, bloated.
обря́д *m* [1] ceremony, rite.
об|са́живать [1], ⟨~сади́ть⟩ [15] plant (with Т); **~сева́ть** [1], ⟨~се́ять⟩ [27] sow; stud (with Т).
обсервато́рия *f* [7] observatory.
обсле́дова|ние *n* [12] (Р) inspection (of), inquiry (into), investiga-

tion (of); ~ть [7] (*im*)*pf.* inspect, examine, investigate.

обслу́ж|ивание *n* [12] service; operation; ~ивать [1], ⟨~и́ть⟩ [16] serve, attend; operate; supply (B/T).

обсо́хнуть *s.* обсыха́ть.

обста|вля́ть [28], ⟨~вить⟩ [14] surround; furnish, fit out (with T); F arrange, settle; ~но́вка *f* [5; *g/pl.*: -вок] furniture; *thea.* scenery; situation, conditions *pl.*

обстоя́тель|ный [14; -лен, -льна] detailed, circumstantial; F solid, thorough; ~ственный [14] adverbial; ~ство *n* [9] circumstance (under, in при П, в П; for по Д); *gr.* adverb.

обстоя́ть [-ои́т] be, stand; как обстои́т де́ло с (T)? what about ...?

обстре́л *m* [1] bombardment, fire; ~ивать [1], ⟨~я́ть⟩ [28] fire on, shell; *p. pt. p.* F tried.

обступ|а́ть [1], ⟨~и́ть⟩ [14] surround.

об|сужда́ть [1], ⟨~суди́ть⟩ [15; -ждённый] discuss; ~сужде́ние *n* [12] discussion; ~суши́ть [16] *pf.* dry; ~счита́ть [1] *pf.* cheat; -ся miscalculate.

обсып|а́ть [1], ⟨~ать⟩ [2] strew.

обс|ыха́ть [1], ⟨~о́хнуть⟩ [21] dry.

обт|а́чивать [1], ⟨~очи́ть⟩[16] turn; ~ека́емый [14] streamline...; ~ере́ть *s.* ~ира́ть; ~ёсывать [1], ⟨~еса́ть⟩ [3] hew; ~ира́ть [1], ⟨~ере́ть⟩ [12; оботру́; обтёр; *ger. pt. a.*: -тёрши & -терёв] rub off *or* down, wipe (off), dry; F fray.

обточи́ть *s.* обта́чивать.

обтрёпанный [14] shabby, frayed.

обтя́|гивать [1], ⟨~ну́ть⟩ [19] cover (with T); *impf.* fit close; ~жка *f* [5]: в ~жку close-fitting.

обу|ва́ть [1], ⟨~ть⟩ [18] put (-ся one's) shoes on; F shoe; '~вь *f* [8] footwear, shoes *pl.*

обу́гл|ивать [1], ⟨~ить⟩ [13] char.

обу́за *f* [5] burden, load.

обу́зд|ывать [1], ⟨~а́ть⟩ [1] bridle.

обусло́в|ливать [1], ⟨~ить⟩ [14] condition (on T); cause.

обу́ть(ся) *s.* обува́ть(ся).

о́бух *m* [1] butt; F thunder(*struck*).

обуч|а́ть [1], ⟨~и́ть⟩ [16] teach (s. th. Д), train; -ся (Д) learn, be taught; ~е́ние *n* [12] instruction, training; education.

обхва́т *m* [1] arm's span; circumference; ~ывать [1], ⟨~и́ть⟩ [15] clasp (in T), embrace, infold.

обхо́|д *m* [1] round, beat (be on де́лать); detour; *vb.* + в ~д *s.* ~ди́ть; evasion; ~ди́тельный [14; -лен, -льна] affable, amiable; ~ди́ть [15], ⟨обойти́⟩ [обойду́, -дёшь; *cf.* идти́] go *or* pass round; travel through (many) *or* over; visit (all [one's]); ⚔ outflank; avoid; pass over (in T); (-ся, ⟨-сь⟩) cost (me мне); manage; do without (без P); there is (*no* ... *without*); treat (s.b. с T); ~дный [14] roundabout; ~жде́ние *n* [12] treatment, manners *pl.*

обш|а́ривать [1], ⟨~а́рить⟩ [13] rummage (around); ~ива́ть [1], ⟨~и́ть⟩ [обошью́, -шьёшь; *cf.* шить] sew round, border (with T); plank, face, sheath; F clothe; ~и́вка; *f* [5] trimming, *etc.* (*s. vb.*).

обши́|рный [14; -рен, -рна] vast, extensive; numerous; ~ть *s.* ~ва́ть.

обща́ться [1] associate (with с T).

обще|досту́пный [14; -пен, -пна] popular; *s. a.* досту́пный; ~жи́тие *n* [12] hostel, home; social intercourse *or* (way of) life; ~изве́стный [14; -тен, -тна] well-known.

обще́ние *n* [12] intercourse.

общепри́нятый [14 *sh.*] generally accepted, common.

обще́ств|енность *f* [8] community, public (opinion); ~енный [14] social, public; common; '~о *n* [9] society; company; association; community; ~ове́дение *n* [12] social science.

общеупотреби́тельный [14; -лен, -льна] current, common, widespread.

о́бщ|ий [17; общ, -а́, -е] general; common (in ~его); public; total, (в ~ем on the) whole; (*table*) d'hôte; ~ина *f* [5] community; † *a.* = ~ество; ~и́тельный [14; -лен, -льна] sociable, affable; ~ность *f* [8] community; commonness.

объе|да́ть [1], ⟨~сть⟩ [-е́м, -е́шь, *etc. s.* есть[1]] eat *or* gnaw round, away; -ся overeat o.s.

объедин|е́ние *n* [12] association, union; unification; ~я́ть [28], ⟨~и́ть⟩ [13] unite (*cf. a.* ООН), join (-ся *v/i.*); rally.

объе́дки F *m/pl.* [1] leavings.

объе́|зд *m* [1] detour, by-pass; *vb.* + в ~зд = ~зжа́ть [1] **1.** ⟨~хать⟩ [-е́ду, -е́дешь] go, drive round; travel through *or* over; visit (all [one's]); **2.** ⟨~здить⟩ [15] break in; F *s.* 1.; ~кт *m* [1] object; ~кти́вный [14; -вен, -вна] objective.

объём *m* [1] volume; size; extent, range; ~истый [14 *sh.*] voluminous,

объе́сть(ся) *s.* объеда́ть(ся).

объе́хать *s.* объезжа́ть 1.

объяв|и́ть *s.* ~ля́ть; ~ле́ние *n* [12] announcement, notice; advertisement; declaration; ~ля́ть [28], ⟨~и́ть⟩ [14] declare (s. th. *a.* о П; s.b. [to be] s.th. B/T), tell; announce, proclaim; advertise; express.

объясн|е́ние *n* [12] explanation; declaration (of *love* в П); ~и́мый [14 *sh.*] explicable, accountable; ~и́тельный [14] explanatory; ~я́ть [28], ⟨~и́ть⟩ [13] explain, illustrate; account for; -ся explain o.s.; be

accounted for; declare o.s.; *impf.* make o.s. understood (by T).
объятия *n/pl.* [12] embrace (*vb.*: заключить в ~); (*with open*) arms.
обыватель *m* [4], inhabitant; Philistine; **~ский** [16] Philistine...
обыгр|ывать, ⟨**~ать**⟩ [1] beat; win.
обыденный [14] everyday, ordinary.
обыкновен|ие *n* [12] habit; по ~ию as usual; **~ный** [14; -енен, -енна] ordinary, usual, habitual.
обыск *m* [1], **~ивать** [1], ⟨**~ать**⟩ [3] search.
обыч|ай *m* [3] custom; F habit; **~ный** [14; -чен, -чна] customary, usual, habitual.
обязанн|ость *f* [8] duty; ⚔ service; исполняющий ~ости (P) acting; **~ый** [14 *sh.*] obliged; indebted, owe; responsible.
обязатель|ный [14; -лен, -льна] obligatory, compulsory; **~но** without fail, certainly; **~ство** *n* [9] obligation; liability; engagement.
обяз|ывать [1], ⟨**~ать**⟩ [3] oblige; bind, commit; **-ся** engage, undertake, pledge o.s.
овдовевший [17] widowed.
овёс *m* [1; овса] oats *pl.*
овечий [18] sheep('s).
овлад|евать [1], ⟨**~еть**⟩ [8] (T) seize, take possession of; get control over; master.
овощ|и *m/pl.* [1; *gen.*: -щей, *etc. e.*] vegetables; **~ной** [14]: ~ной магазин *m* greengrocery.
овраг *m* [1] ravine.
овсянка *f* [5; *g/pl.*: -нок] oatmeal.
овц|а *f* [5; *pl. st.*; *g/pl.*: овец] sheep; **~еводство** *n* [9] sheep breeding.
овчарка *f* [5; *g/pl.*: -рок] sheep dog.
овчина *f* [5] sheepskin.
огарок *m* [1; -рка] candle end.
огибать [1], ⟨обогнуть⟩ [20] turn *or* bend (round); ⚓ double.
оглавление *n* [12] table of contents.
огла|ска *f* [5] publicity; **~шать** [1], ⟨**~сить**⟩ [15 *e.*; -ашу, -асишь -ашённый] announce; divulge; publish (the banns of); fill, resound; **-ся** ring; **~шение** [12] announcement; publication; banns *pl.*
оглобля *f* [6; *g/pl.*: -бель] shaft.
оглуш|ать [1], ⟨**~ить**⟩ [16 *e.*; -шу, -шишь; -шённый] deafen, stun; **~ительный** [14; -лен, -льна] deafening, stunning.
огля|дка F *f* [5]: без ~дки headlong, hastily; **~дывать** [1], ⟨**~деть**⟩ [11] examine, take a view of; **-ся 1.** look round; **2.** *pf.*: ⟨**~нуться**⟩ [20] look back (at на B).
огне|вой [14] fire...; fiery; **~дышащий** [17] volcanic; **~мёт** *m* [1] flame thrower; **'~нный** [14] fiery; **~опасный** [14; -сен, -сна] inflammable; **~стойкий** [16; -оек, -ойка] *s.* ~упорный; **~стрельный** [14] fire(*arm*); **~тушитель** *m* [4] fire extinguisher; **~упорный** [14; -рен, -рна] fireproof; fire (*clay, etc.*).
огниво *n* [9] (fire) steel, stone.
огов|аривать [1], ⟨**~орить**⟩ [13] slander; stipulate; *a.* = **-ся** make a reservation; *s. a.* обмолвиться; **~ор** F *m* [1] slander; **~орка** *f* [5; *g/pl.*: -рок] reservation, reserve, proviso; *a.* = обмолвка, *cf.*
огол|ять [28], ⟨**~ить**⟩ [13] bare.
огонёк *m* [1; -нька] light; spark.
огонь *m* [4; огня] fire (*a. fig.*); light; из огня да в полымя out of the frying pan into the fire; сквозь ~ и воду through thick & thin.
огор|аживать [1], ⟨**~одить**⟩ [15 & 15 *e.*; -ожу, -одишь; -оженный] enclose, fence (in); **~од** *m* [1] kitchen garden; **~одник** *m* [1] trucker, market *or* kitchen gardener; **~одничество** *n* [9] trucking, market gardening.
огорч|ать [1], ⟨**~ить**⟩ [16 *e.*; -чу, -чишь; -чённый] grieve (**-ся** *v/i.*), (be) afflict(ed), vex(ed), distress(ed with T); **~ение** *n* [9] grief, affliction, trouble; **~ительный** [14; -лен, -льна] grievous; vexatious.
огра|бление *n* [12] robbing, robbery; **~да** *f* [5] fence; wall; **~ждать** [1], ⟨**~дить**⟩ [15 *e.*; -ажу, -адишь; -аждённый] enclose; guard, protect; **~ждение** *n* [12] enclosure; protection.
огранич|ение *n* [12] limitation; restriction; **~енный** [14 *sh.*] confined; limited; narrow(-minded); **~ивать** [1], ⟨**~ить**⟩ [16] confine, limit, restrict (o.s. **-ся**; to T; content o.s. with; not go beyond); **~ительный** [14]; -лен, -льна] restrictive.
огромный [14; -мен, -мна] huge, vast; enormous, tremendous.
огрубелый [14] coarse, hardened.
огрыз|аться F [1], *once* ⟨**~нуться**⟩ [20] snap; **~ок** *m* [1; -зка] bit, end; stump, stub.
огульный F [14; -лен, -льна] wholesale, indiscriminate; unfounded; *adv. a.* in the lump.
огурец *m* [1; -рца] cucumber.
одалживать [1], ⟨одолжить⟩ [16 *e.*; -жу, -жишь] lend (a. p. s. th. Д/B); borrow; oblige (a p. by B/T).
одар|ённый [14 *sh.*] gifted; **~ивать** [1], ⟨**~ить**⟩ [13] present, gift; (with T); *fig.* (*impf.* **~ять** [28]) endow (with T).
оде|вать [1], ⟨**~ть**⟩ [-ену, -енешь; -етый) dress (**-ся** *v/i.*); **~жда** *f* [5] clothes *pl.*, clothing.
одеколон *m* [1] cologne.
одел|ять [28], ⟨**~ить**⟩ [13] *s.* одаривать.
одеревенелый [14] numb.
одерж|ивать [1], ⟨**~ать**⟩ [4] gain,

win; ~и́мый [14 *sh.*] (T) obsessed (by), afflicted (with).
оде́ть(ся) *s.* одева́ть(ся).
одея́ло *n* [9] blanket, cover(let).
оди́н *m*, одна́ *f*, одно́ *n*, одни́ *pl.* [33] one; alone; only; a, a certain, some; одно́ *su.* one thing, thought, *etc.*; ~ на ~ face to face; tête-à--tête; hand to hand; все до одного́ (*or* все как ~) all to a (*or* the last) man; *cf.* пять & пя́тый.
один|а́ковый [14 *sh.*] equal, identical, the same; **~ёшенек** [-нька] F quite alone; **∠надцатый** [14] eleventh; *cf.* пя́тый; **∠надцать** [35] eleven; *cf.* пять; **~о́кий** [16 *sh.*] lonely; single; lonesome; **~о́чество** *n* [9] solitude, loneliness; **~о́чка** *m/f* [5; *g/pl.*: -чек] lone person; individualist; one-man boat (*or* F cell); ~о́чкой, в ~о́чку alone; **~о́чный** [14] single, solitary; individual; one-man...
одича́лый [14] (run) wild.
одна́жды once, one day.
однако, (*a.* ~ ж[е]) however, yet, still.
одно́... : **~бо́ртный** [14] single--breasted; **~вре́ме́нный** [14] simultaneous; **~гла́зый** [14] one--eyed; **~дне́вный** [14] one-day; **~зву́чный** [14; -чен, -чна] monotonous; **~зна́чный** [14; -чен, -чна] synonymous (*a.* **~зна́чащий** [17]); & simple, of one place; **~имённый** [14; -ёнен, -ённа] of the same name; **~кла́ссник** *m* [1] classmate; **~коле́йный** [14] single-track; **~кра́тный** [14; -тен, -тна] occuring once, single; *gr.* momentary; **~ле́тний** [15] one-year(-old); ⚘ annual; **~ле́ток** *m* [1; -тка] coeval; **~ме́стный** [14] single-seated; **~обра́зный** [14; -зен, -зна] monotonous; **~ро́дный** [14; -ден, -дна] homogeneous; **~ру́кий** [16] one-armed; **~сло́жный** [14; -жен, -жна] monosyllabic; **~сторо́нний** [15; -о́нен, -о́ння] one-sided (*a. fig.*); unilateral; **~фами́лец** *m* [1; -льца] namesake; **~цве́тный** [14; -тен, -тна] monochromatic; plain; **~эта́жный** [14] one-storied (*Brt.* -reyed).
одобр|е́ние *n* [12] approval, approbation; **~и́тельный** [14; -лен, -льна] approving; **~я́ть** [28], ⟨∠ить⟩ [13] approve (of).
одол|ева́ть [1], ⟨~е́ть⟩ [8] overcome, defeat; F exhaust; master.
одолж|е́ние *n* [12] favo(u)r; **~и́ть** *s.* ода́лживать.
одр † *m* [1 *e.*] bed, couch; bier.
одува́нчик *m* [1] dandelion.
оду́м|ываться, ⟨~аться⟩ [1] change one's mind.
одур|ма́нивать [1], ⟨~ма́нить⟩ [13] stupefy; **'~ь** F [8] stupor; **~я́ть** F [28] stupefy.
одутлова́тый [14 *sh.*] puffed up.
одухотвор|я́ть [28], ⟨~и́ть⟩ [13] inspire.
одушев|лённый [14] *gr.* animate; **~ля́ть** [28], ⟨~и́ть⟩ [14 *e.*; -влю́, -ви́шь; -влённый] animate, inspire.
одышка *f* [5] short wind.
ожере́лье *n* [10] necklace.
ожесточ|а́ть [1], ⟨~и́ть⟩ [16 *e.*; -чу́, чи́шь; чённый] harden; exasperate; **~е́ние** *n* [12] exasperation; bitterness; **~ённый** [14 *sh.*] *a.* violent, fierce, bitter.
ожи|ва́ть [1], ⟨∠ть⟩ [-иву́, -ивёшь; о́жил, -а́, -о] revive; **~ви́ть(ся)** *s.* ~вля́ть(ся); **~вле́ние** *n* [12] animation; **~влённый** [14 *sh.*] animated, lively; bright; **~вля́ть** [28], ⟨~ви́ть⟩ [14 *e.*; -влю́, -ви́шь, -влённый] enliven, animate, resuscitate; **-ся** quicken, revive; brighten.
ожида́|ние *n* [12] expectation; зал ~ния waiting room; **~ть** [1] wait (for P); expect, await.
ожи́ть *s.* ожива́ть.
ожо́г *m* [1] burn; scald.
озабо́|чивать [1], ⟨~тить⟩ [15] disquiet, alarm; **-ся** attend to (T); **~ченный** [14 *sh.*] anxious, solicitous (about T); preoccupied.
озагла́в|ливать [1], ⟨~ить⟩ [14] entitle, supply with a title.
озада́ч|ивать [1], ⟨~ить⟩ [16] puzzle, perplex.
озар|я́ть [28], ⟨~и́ть⟩ [13] (**-ся** be[come]) illuminate(d), light (lit) up; brighten, lighten.
озвере́ть [8] *pf.* become brutal.
оздоров|ля́ть [1], ⟨~и́ть⟩ [14] reorganize, reform, improve (the health of).
о́зеро *n* [9; *pl.*: озёра, -ёр] lake.
ози́мый [14] winter (*crops*).
озира́ться [1] look (round *or* back).
озлоб|ля́ть [28], ⟨∠ить⟩ [14] (**-ся** become) exasperate(d), embitter(ed); **~ле́ние** *n* [12] exasperation.
ознак|омля́ть [28], ⟨~о́мить⟩ [14] familiarize (o.s. **-ся**, с T with).
ознамен|ова́ние *n* [12] commemoration (in в B); **~о́вывать** [1], ⟨~ова́ть⟩ [7] mark, commemorate, celebrate.
означа́ть [1] signify, mean.
озно́б *m* [1] chill.
озор|ни́к *m* [1 *e.*], **~ни́ца** *f* [5] F *s.* шалу́н(ья); P ruffian; **~нича́ть** [1] F *s.* шали́ть; P behave outrageously; **~но́й** F [14] mischievous, naughty; **~ство́** F *n* [9] mischief; outrage, excess.
ой oh! o dear!; ~ како́й F awful.
ока́з|ывать [1], ⟨~а́ть⟩ [3] show; render, do; exert (*influence*); give (*preference*); **-ся** (T) turn out (to be), be found; find o.s.; be (shown, rendered, given).
окайм|ля́ть [1], ⟨~и́ть⟩ [14 *e.*; -млю́, -ми́шь, -млённый] border.
окамене́лый [14] petrified.

ока́нчивать [1], ‹око́нчить› [16] finish, end (-ся *v/i.*).
ока́пывать [1], ‹окопа́ть› [1] dig round; entrench (o.s. -ся).
окая́нный [14] damned, cursed.
океа́н *m* [1], **~ский** [16] ocean.
оки́|дывать [1], ‹~нуть› [20] (взгля́дом) take a view of, look at.
окис|ля́ть [28], ‹~ли́ть› [13] oxidize; **'~ь** *f* [8] oxide.
оккуп|ацио́нный [14] occupation-...; **~и́ровать** [7] (*im*)*pf.* occupy.
окла́д *m* [1] salary; tax rate.
окла́дистый [14 *sh.*] full (*beard*).
окле́и|вать [1], ‹~ть› [13] paste; paper.
о́клик *m* [1], **~а́ть** [1], ‹**~**нуть› [20] call, hail.
окно́ *n* [9; *pl. st.*: о́кна, о́кон, о́кнам] window (*look* through в В).
о́ко ↖ [9; *pl.*: о́чи, оче́й, *etc. e.*] eye.
оков|а́ть *s.* **~**ывать; **~ы** *f/pl.* [5] fetters; **~ывать** [1], ‹~а́ть› [7 *e.*; окую́, окуёшь; око́ванный] bind; fetter.
околдова́ть [7] *pf.* bewitch.
окол|ева́ть [1], ‹~е́ть› [8] die.
око́лица *f* [5] *s.* окра́ина *&* обиня́к.
о́кол|о (P) about, around; by, at, near(ly); nearby; **~ыш** *m* [1] cap-band; **~ьный** [14] roundabout.
око́нный [14] window...
оконч|а́ние *n* [12] end(ing *gr.*), close, termination, completion ([up]on по П), conclusion; **~а́тельный** [14; -лен, -льна] final, definitive; **~ить** *s.* ока́нчивать.
око́п *m* [1] trench; **~а́ть(ся)** *s.* ока́пывать(ся).
о́корок *m* [1; *pl.*: -ка́, *etc. e.*] ham.
око|стене́лый [14] ossified; hardened; *a.* = **~чене́лый** [14] numb (with cold).
око́ш|ечко *n* [9; *g/pl.*: -чек], **~ко** *n* [9; *g/pl.*: -шек] *dim. of* окно́.
окра́ина *f* [5] outskirts *pl.*
окра́|ска *f* [5] painting; dyeing; tinge; **~шивать** [1], ‹~сить› [15] paint; dye; tinge.
окре́стн|ость (*often pl.*) *f* [8] environs *pl.*, neighbo(u)rhood; **~ый** [14] surrounding; in the vicinity.
окрова́вленный [14] bloodstained.
о́круг *m* [1; *pl.*: -га́, *etc. e.*] district; избира́тельный ~ constituency.
округл|я́ть [28], ‹~и́ть› [13] round (off); **~ый** [14 *sh.*] roundish.
окруж|а́ть [1], ‹~и́ть› [16 *e.*; -жу́, -жи́шь; -жённый] surround; **~а́ющий** [17] surrounding; **~е́ние** *n* [12] environment; environs *pl.*, neighbo(u)rhood; encirclement; circle, company; **~и́ть** *s.* **~**а́ть; **~но́й** [14] district...; circular; **~ность** *f* [8] circumference; circle; † vicinity.
окрыл|я́ть [28], ‹~и́ть› [13] *fig.* wing, encourage.
октя́брь *m* [4 *e.*], **~ский** [16] October.
окули́ровать [7] (*im*)*pf.* graft.
окун|а́ть [1], ‹~у́ть› [20] dip, plunge (*v/i.* -ся; dive, *a. fig.*).
о́кунь *m* [4; *from g/pl. e.*] perch.
окуп|а́ть [1], ‹~и́ть› [14] (-ся be) offset, recompense(d), compensate(d).
оку́рок *m* [1; -рка] cigarette end, cigar stub.
оку́т|ывать, ‹~ать› [1] wrap (up).
ола́дья *f* [6; *g/pl.*: -дий] fritter.
оледене́лый [14] frozen, iced.
оле́нь *m* [4] deer; се́верный ~ reindeer.
оли́в|а *f* [5], **~ка** *f* [5; *g/pl.*: -вок], **~ковый** [14] olive.
олимп|иа́да *f* [5] Olympiad; **~и́йский** [16] Olympic.
олицетвор|е́ние *n* [12] personification, embodiment; **~я́ть** [28], ‹~и́ть› personify, embody.
о́лов|о *n* [8], **~я́нный** [14] tin.
о́лух P *m* [1] blockhead, dolt.
ольх|а́ *f* [5], **~о́вый** [14] alder.
ома́р *m* [1] lobster.
оме́ла *f* [5] mistletoe.
омерз|е́ние *n* [12] abhorrence, loathing; **~и́тельный** [14; -лен, -льна] abominable, detestable, loathsome; F lousy.
омертве́лый [14] numb; dead.
омле́т *m* [1] omelet(te).
омоложе́ние *n* [12] rejuvenation.
омо́ним *m* [1] *ling.* homonym.
омрач|а́ть [1], ‹~и́ть› [16 *e.*; -чу́, -чи́шь; -чённый] darken, sadden (*v/i.* -ся).
о́мут *m* [1] whirlpool, vortex; deep.
омы|ва́ть [1], ‹**~**ть› [22] wash.
он *m*, **~а́** *f*, **~о́** *n*, **~и́** *pl.* [22] he, she, it, they.
онеме́лый [14] numb; F dumb.
оне́жск|ий [16]: **2**ое о́зеро *n* Lake Onega.
ону́ча *f* [5] *s.* портя́нка.
ООН (Организа́ция Объединённых На́ций) U.N.O. (United Nations Organization).
опа|да́ть [1], ‹**~**сть› [25; *pt. st.*] fall (off); diminish, decrease.
опа́|здывать, ‹опозда́ть› [1] be late (for на В, к Д), arrive (5 min.) late (на пять мину́т); miss (*train* на В); **~ла** *f* [5] disgrace, ban; **~льный** [14] disgraced.
опал|я́ть [28], ‹~и́ть› [13] singe.
опас|а́ться [1] (P) fear, apprehend; beware (of); **~е́ние** *n* [12] fear, apprehension, anxiety; **~ливый** [14 *sh.*] wary; anxious; **~ность** *f* [8] danger, peril, jeopardy; risk (at/of с Т/для Р); **~ный** [14; -сен, -сна] dangerous (to для Р); **~ть** *s.* опада́ть.
опе́к|а *f* [5] guardianship, (*a. fig.*) tutelage; trusteeship; **~а́ть** [1] be guardian (trustee) to; patronize; **~а́емый** [14] ward; **~у́н** *m* [1 *e.*], **~у́нша** *f* [5] guardian; trustee.
опер|ати́вный [14] operative; surgical; executive; ⚔ front..., war...;

~áтор *m* [1] operator (*a.* ⚕ = surgeon); **~ациóнный** [14] operating.
опере|жáть [1], ‹~дúть› [15] outstrip (*a. fig.* = outdo, surpass); **∠ние** *n* [12] plumage; **∠ться** *s.* опирáться.
оперúровать [7] (*im*)*pf.* operate.
óперный [14] opera(tic).
опер|úться [28], ‹~úться› [13] fledge.
опечáт|ка *f* [5; *g/pl.*: -ток] misprint, erratum; **~ывать**, ‹~ать› [1] seal (up).
опúлки *f/pl.* [5; *gen.*: -лок] sawdust.
опирáться [1], ‹оперéться› [12; обопрýсь, -рёшься; опёрся, оперлáсь] lean (against, on на В), *a. fig.* = rest, rely ([up]on).
опис|áние *n* [12] description; **~áтельный** [14] descriptive; **~áть** *s.* ∠ывать; **∠ка** *f* [5; *g/pl.*: -сок] slip of the pen; **∠ывать** [1], ‹~áть› [3] describe (*a.* ⚖); make (*an inventory* [of]); distrain (upon); **-ся** make a slip of the pen; **′~сь** *f* [8] list, inventory; distraint.
оплáк|ивать [1], ‹~ать› [3] bewail, deplore, mourn (over).
оплá|та *f* [5] pay(ment); settlement; **~чивать** [1], ‹~тúть› [15] pay (for); remunerate; settle.
оплеýха F *f* [5] box on the ear.
оплодотвор|éние *n* [12] fertilization; **~úть** [28], ‹~úть› [13 [fertilize, fecundate.
оплóт *m* [1] bulwark, stronghold.
оплóшность *f* [8] blunder.
опове|щáть [1], ‹~стúть› [15 *e.*; -ещý, -естúшь; -ещённый] notify; inform, ✝ *a.* advise (of о П).
опоздá|ние *n* [12] delay; *vb.* + с ~нием = ~ть, *s.* опáздывать.
опозн|авáтельный [14] distinctive; **~авáть** [5], ‹~áть› [1] identify.
óползень *m* [4; -зня] landslide.
ополч|áться [1], ‹~úться› [16 *e.*; -чýсь, -чúшься; -чённый] rise in arms; **~éние** *n* [12] militia; Territorial Army; **~éнец** *m* [1; -нца] militiaman.
опóмниться [13] *pf.* come to *or* recover one's senses, come round.
опóр *m* [1]: во весь ~ at full speed, at a gallop; **~а** *f* [5] support, prop, rest; **~ный** [14] strong, of support.
опорó|жнить [13] *pf.* empty; **~чивать** [1], ‹~чить› [16] defile.
опошл|úть [28], ‹∠ить› [13] vulgarize.
опоя́с|ывать [1], ‹~ать› [3] gird.
оппозициóнный [14] opposition...
оппонúровать [7] (Д) oppose.
опрáва *f* [5] setting; rim, frame.
оправд|áние *n* [12] justification, excuse; ⚖ acquittal; **~áтельный** [14] justificatory; of 'not guilty'; ~áтельный докумéнт *m* voucher; **∠ывать** [1], ‹~áть› [1] justify, excuse; acquit; **-ся** *a.* prove (*or* come) true.
оправ|ля́ть [28], ‹∠ить› [14] put in order; set; **-ся** recover (*a.* o.s.); put one's dress, hair in order.
опрáшивать [1], ‹опросúть› [15] interrogate, question.
определ|éние *n* [12] determination; definition; designation (to, for на В); ⚖ decision; *gr.* attribute; **~ённый** [14; -ёнен, -ённа] definite; fixed; certain, positive; **~я́ть** [28], ‹~úть› [13] determine; define; designate (to, for на В, к Д); appoint, fix; **-ся** take shape; enter, enlist (in[to] на В).
опров|ергáть [1], ‹~éргнуть› [21] refute; deny; **~ержéние** *n* [12] refutation; denial.
опрокú|дывать [1], ‹~нуть› [20; overturn, upset, capsize (**-ся** *v/i.*)] overthrow, throw (down, over).
опро|мéтчивый [14 *sh.*] rash, precipitate; **′~метью** headlong, at top speed.
опрóс *m* [1] interrogation, inquiry; **~úть** *s.* опрáшивать; **~ный** [14]: ~ный лист *m* questionnaire.
опры́ск|ивать, ‹~ать› [1] sprinkle.
опря́тный [14; -тен, -тна] tidy.
óптик *m* [1] optician; **~а** *f* [5] optics.
оптó|вый [14], **′~м** *adv.* wholesale.
опубликов|áние *n* [12] publication; **∠ывать** [1] *s.* публиковáть.
опус|кáть [1], ‹~тúть› [15] lower; cast down; hang; drop; draw (down); ~тúть рýки lose heart; **-ся** sink; fall; go down; *fig.* come down (in the world); *p. pt a.* down & out.
опуст|éлый [14] deserted; **~úть** (**-ся**) *s.* опускáть(ся); **~ошáть** [1], ‹~ошúть›[16 *e.*; -шý, -шúшь; -шённый] devastate; **~ошéние** *n* [12] devastation; **~ошúтельный** [14; -лен, -льна] devastating.
опýт|ывать, ‹~ать› [1] wrap (up), muffle (in); *fig.* entangle.
опух|áть [1], ‹∠нуть› [21] swell; **′~оль** *f* [8] swelling, tumo(u)r.
опý|шка *f* [5; *g/pl.*: -шек] edge, border; **~щéние** *n* [12] ommission.
опыл|úть [28], ‹~úть› [13] pollinate.
óпыт *m* [1] experiment; attempt; essay; [*sg.*, *pl.* †] experience; **~ный** [14] experiment(al); empirical; [-тен, -тна] experienced.
опьянéние *n* [12] intoxication.
опя́ть again (*a.*, F, ~-таки; and ..., too).
орáва P *f* [5] gang, horde, mob.
орáкул *m* [1] oracle.
орáнже|вый [14] orange...; **~рéя** *f* [6] greenhouse.
орáть F [орý, орёшь] yell, bawl.
орбúта *f* [5] orbit.
óрган¹ *m* [1] organ.
оргáн² ♪ *m* [1] organ.
организ|áтор *m* [1] organizer; **∠м** *m* [1] organism; constitution; **~овáть** [7] (*im*)*pf.* (*impf. a.* **~óвывать** [1]) organize (*v/i.* **-ся**).

органи́ческий [16] organic.
о́ргия *f* [7] orgy.
орда́ *f* [5; *pl. st.*] horde.
о́рден *m* [1; *pl.*: -на́, *etc. e.*] order, decoration.
о́рдер *m* [1; *pl.*: -ра́, *etc. e.*] warrant.
ордина́р|ец ⚔ *m* [1; -рца] orderly.
орёл *m* [1; орла́] eagle; ~ или ре́шка? heads or tails?
орео́л *m* [1] halo, aureole.
оре́х *m* [1] nut; лесно́й ~ hazel (-nut); **~овый** [14] (wal)nut...
оригина́льный [14; -лен, -льна] original.
ориенти́р|оваться [7] (*im*)*pf.* orient o. s. (to на В), take one's bearings; familiarize o. s.; **~о́вка** *f* [5; *g*/*pl.*: -вок] orientation, bearings *pl.*; **~о́вочный** [14; -чен, -чна] approximate, tentative.
орке́стр *m* [1] orchestra; band.
орли́ный [14] aquiline.
оро|ша́ть [1], ‹~си́ть› [15 *e.*; -ошу́, -оси́шь; -ошённый] irrigate; **~ше́ние** *n* [12] irrigation.
ору́д|ие *n* [12] tool, instrument, implement; ⚔ gun; **~и́йный** [14] gun...; **~овать** F [7] (T) handle, operate.
оруж|е́йный [14] arms...; **∠ие** *n* [12] weapon(s), arm(s); (*cold*) steel.
орфогра́ф|ия *f* [7] spelling; **~и́ческий** [16] orthographic(al).
орхиде́я *f* [6] orchid.
оса́ *f* [5; *pl. st.*] wasp.
оса́|да *f* [5] siege; **~ди́ть** *s.* ~жда́ть & ~живать; **~дный** [14] of siege *or* martial law; **~док** *m* [1; -дка] sediment; *fig.* aftertaste; **~дки** *pl.* precipitations; **~жда́ть** [1], ‹~ди́ть› [15 & 15 *e.*; -ажу́, -а́ди́шь; -аждённый] besiege; ⚗ precipitate; F importune; **~живать** [1], ‹~ди́ть› [15] check, snub.
оса́н|истый [14 *sh.*] dignified, stately; **~ка** *f* [5] bearing.
осв|а́ивать [1], ‹~о́ить› [13] master; open up; ⚘ acclimate (*Brt.* -tize); **-ся** accustom o. s. (to в П); familiarize o. s. (with с Т).
осведом|ля́ть [28], ‹'~ить› [14] inform (of о П); **-ся** inquire (after, for; about о П); **~лённый** [14] informed; versed.
освеж|а́ть [1], ‹~и́ть› [16 *e.*; -жу́, -жи́шь; -жённый] refresh; freshen *or* touch up; brush up; **~и́тельный** [14; -лен, -льна] refreshing.
осве|ща́ть [1], ‹~ти́ть› [15 *e.*; -ещу́, -ети́шь; -ещённый] light (up), illuminate; *fig.* elucidate, illustrate.
освиде́тельствова|ние *n* [12] examination; **~ть** [7] *pf.* examine.
освист|ывать [1], ‹~а́ть› [3] hiss.
освобо|ди́тель *m* [4] liberator; **~ди́тельный** [14] emancipatory; **~жда́ть** [1], ‹~ди́ть› [15*e.*; -ожу́, -оди́шь; -ождённый] (set) free, release; liberate, deliver; emancipate; exempt, excuse; clear; vacate, quit; **~жде́ние** *n* [12] liberation; release; emancipation; exemption.
осво|е́ние *n* [12] mastering; opening up; **∠ить(ся)** *s.* осва́ивать(ся).
освя|ща́ть [1], ‹~ти́ть› [15 *e.*; -ящу́, -яти́шь; -ящённый] consecrate.
осе|да́ть [1], ‹∠сть› [25; ося́дет; осе́л; *cf.* сесть] subside, settle; **∠длый** [14] settled.
осёл *m* [1; осла́] donkey, (*a. fig.*) ass.
осени́ть *s.* осеня́ть.
осе́н|ний [15] autumnal, fall...; **'~ь** *f* [8] fall, *Brt.* autumn (in [the] T).
осен|я́ть [28], ‹~и́ть› [13] shade; invest; bless, make (*cross*); flash on.
осе́сть *s.* оседа́ть.
осётр *m* [1 *e.*] sturgeon.
осе́чка *f* [5; *g*/*pl.*: -чек] misfire.
оси́ли|вать [1], ‹~ть› [13] *s.* одолева́ть.
оси́н|а *f* [5] asp; **~овый** [14] asp(en).
оси́пнуть [21] *pf.* grow hoarse.
осироте́лый [14] orphan(ed).
оска́ли|вать [1], ‹~ть› [13] show.
оскверн|я́ть [28], ‹~и́ть› [13] profane, desecrate, defile.
оско́лок *m* [1; -лка] splinter.
оскорб|и́тельный [14; -лен, -льна] offensive, insulting; **~ле́ние** *n* [12] insult, offence; **~ля́ть** [28], ‹~и́ть› [14 *e.*; -блю́, -би́шь; -блённый] (**-ся** feel) offend(ed), insult.
оскуд|ева́ть [1], ‹~е́ть› [8] become poor *or* scanty.
ослаб|ева́ть [1], ‹~е́ть› [8] grow weak *or* feeble, languish; slacken; abate; **∠ить** *s.* ~ля́ть; **~ле́ние** *n* [12] weakening; relaxation; **~ля́ть** [28], ‹∠ить› [14] weaken, enfeeble; relax, slacken, loosen.
ослеп|и́тельный [14; -лен. -льна] dazzling; **~ля́ть** [28], ‹~и́ть› [14 *e.*; -плю́, -пи́шь; -плённый] blind; dazzle.
осложн|е́ние *n* [12 complication; **~я́ть** [28], ‹~и́ть› [13] (**-ся** be[come]) complicate(d).
ослу́ш|иваться, ‹~аться› [1] disobey; **~ник** *m* [1] disobedient p.
ослы́шаться [4] *pf.* hear amiss.
осм|а́тривать [1], ‹~отре́ть› [9; -отрю́, -о́тришь; -о́тренный] view, examine; inspect; see (*sights*); **-ся** look round; take a view of (в П).
осме́|ивать [1], ‹~я́ть› [27 *e.*; -ею́, -еёшь; -е́янный] laugh at, ridicule, deride.
осме́ли|ваться [1], ‹~ться› [13] dare, venture; beg *to*.
осмея́|ние *n* [12] ridicule, derision; **~ть** *s.* осме́ивать.
осмо́тр *m* [1] examination, inspection; (*sight*)seeing; visit (to P); **~е́ть(ся)** *s.* осма́тривать(ся); **~и́тельность** *f* [8] circumspection, prudence; **~и́тельный** [14; -лен, -льна] circumspect, prudent.

осмы́сл|енный [14 *sh.*] sensible; intelligent; **~ивать** [1] & **~я́ть** [28], ⟨**~ить**⟩ [13] comprehend, conceive; grasp, make sense of.
осна́|стка *f* [5] rigging (out, up); **~ща́ть** [1], ⟨**~сти́ть**⟩ [15 *e.*; -ащу́, -асти́шь; -ащённый] rig (out, up); **~ще́ние** *n* [12] equipment.
осно́в|а *f* [5] basis, foundation; fundamental, essential principle; *gr.* stem; *text.* warp; **~а́ние** *n* [12] foundation, basis; ⚗, 🜂, ⚒ base; fundamental; ground(s), reason; argument; **~а́тель** *m* [4] founder; **~а́тельный** [14; -лен, -льна] valid; sound, solid; thorough; **~а́ть** *s.* **~ывать**; **~но́й** [14] fundamental, basic, principal, primary; ✝ original (*stock*); **~оположник** *m* [1] founder; **~ывать** [1], ⟨**~а́ть**⟩ [7] found; establish; **-ся** be based, rest; settle.
осо́ба *f* [5] person; personage.
осо́бенн|ость *f* [8] peculiarity; **~ый** [14] (e)special, particular, peculiar.
особня́к *m* [1 *e.*] villa, private residence; **~о́м** apart; aloof; separate (-ly).
осо́б|ый [14] *s.* **~енный**; separate.
осозн|ава́ть [5], ⟨**~а́ть**⟩ [1] realize.
осо́ка *f* [5] sedge.
о́сп|а *f* [5] smallpox; **~оприви́ва́ние** *n* [12] vaccination.
осп|а́ривать [1], ⟨**~о́рить**⟩ [13] contest, dispute; contend (for).
остава́ться [5], ⟨оста́ться⟩ [-а́нусь, -а́нешься] (T) remain, stay; be left; keep; stick (to); be(come); have to; go, get off; ~ (за T) get, win; reserve, take; owe; ~ без (P) lose, have no (left); ~ с но́сом F get nothing.
остав|ля́ть [28], ⟨**~ить**⟩ [14] leave; give up; drop, stop; let (*alone*); keep; **~ля́ть** за собо́й reserve to o. s.
остально́|й [14] remaining; *pl. a.* the others; *n* & *pl. a. su.* the rest (в **~м** as for the rest).
остан|а́вливать [1], ⟨**~ови́ть**⟩ [14] stop, bring to a stop; fix; **-ся** stop; put up (at в П); dwell (on на П); **~ки** *m/pl.* [1] remains; **~ови́ть(ся)** *s.* **~а́вливать(ся)**; **~о́вка** *f* [5; *g/pl.*: -вок] stop(page); break; **~о́вка** за ... (T) (*only*) ... is wanting.
оста́|ток *m* [1; -тка] remainder (*a.* ⚗), rest; remnant; *pl.* remains; **~ться** *s.* **~ва́ться**.
остекл|я́ть [28], ⟨**~и́ть**⟩ [13] glaze.
остервене́лый [14] furious.
остер|ега́ться [1], ⟨**~е́чься**⟩ [26 г/ж: -егу́сь, -ежёшься, -егу́тся] (P) beware of, be careful of.
о́стов *m* [1] skeleton, framework.
остолбене́лый F [14] stunned.
остоло́п F *contp. m* [1] dolt, dunce.
осторо́жн|ость *f* [8] caution, heed; **~ый** [14; -жен, -жна] cautious, careful, wary; prudent; **~о!** look out!; with care!
остри|га́ть [1], ⟨**~чь**⟩ [26 г/ж: -игу́, -ижёшь, -игу́т] (**-ся** have one's hair) cut; crop; shear; pare; **~ё** *n* [12; *g/pl.*: -иёв] point; edge; **~ть** [13], ⟨за-⟩ sharpen; ⟨с-⟩ joke, be witty; **~чь(ся)** *s.* **~га́ть(ся)**.
о́стров *m* [1; *pl.*: -ва́, *etc. e.*] island; isle; **~итя́нин** *m* [1; *pl.*: -я́не, -я́н] islander; **~о́к** *m* [1; -вка́] islet.
остро́г *m* [1] prison; *hist.* burg.
остро|гла́зый F [14 *sh.*] sharp-sighted; **~коне́чный** [14; -чен, -чна] pointed; **~та́** *f* [5; *pl. st.*: -о́ты] sharpness, keenness, acuteness; witticism; joke; **~у́мие** *n* [12] wit; sagacity; **~у́мный** [14; -мен, -мна] witty; ingenious.
о́стр|ый [14; остр (F *a.* остёр), -а́, -о] sharp, pointed; keen; acute; critical; **~я́к** *m* [1 *e.*] wit(ty fellow).
оступ|а́ться [1], ⟨**~и́ться**⟩ [14] stumble.
остыва́ть [1] *s.* сты́нуть.
осу|жда́ть [1], ⟨**~ди́ть**⟩ [15; -уждённый] condemn; doom (to на B); **~жде́ние** *n* [12] condemnation; conviction.
осу́нуться [20] *pf.* grow lean.
осуш|а́ть [1], ⟨**~и́ть**⟩ [16] drain; dry (up); empty.
осуществ|и́мый [14 *sh.*] practicable; **~ля́ть** [28], ⟨**~и́ть**⟩ [14 *e.*; -влю́, -ви́шь; -влённый] realize; **-ся** be carried out; come true; **~ле́ние** *n* [12] realization.
осчастли́вить [14] *pf.* make happy.
осып|а́ть [1], ⟨**~ать**⟩ [2] strew(over); stud; *fig.* heap; **-ся** crumble; fall.
ось *f* [8; *from g/pl. e.*] axis; axle.
осяза́|емый [14 *sh.*] tangible; **~ние** *n* [12] sense of touch; **~тельный** [14] of touch; [-лен, -льна] palpable; **~ть** [1] touch, feel.
от, ото (P) from; of; off; against; for, with; in; on behalf
ота́пливать [1], ⟨отопи́ть⟩ [14] heat.
отбав|ля́ть [28], ⟨**~ить**⟩ [14] take away *or* off; diminish.
отбе|га́ть [1], ⟨**~жа́ть**⟩ [4; -бегу́, -бежи́шь, -бегу́т] run off.
отби|ва́ть [1], ⟨**~ть**⟩ [отобью́, -бьёшь; *cf.* бить] beat, strike (*or* kick) off; ⚔ repel; deliver; snatch away (from у P); break off; **-ся** ward off (от P); get lost, drop behind; break off; F get rid.
отбира́ть [1], ⟨отобра́ть⟩ [отберу́, -рёшь; отобра́л, -а́, -о; ото́бранный] take away *or* off; select, pick out; collect.
отби́ть(ся) *s.* отбива́ть(ся).
о́тблеск *m* [1] reflection; vestige.
отбо́й *m* [3] ⚔ retreat; all clear (*signal*); *teleph.* ring off.
отбо́р *m* [1] selection, choice; **~ный** [14] select, choice, picked.
отбр|а́сывать [1], ⟨**~о́сить**⟩ [15] throw off *or* away; ⚔ throw back; reject; **~о́сы** *m/pl.* [1] refuse, waste.
отбы|ва́ть [1], ⟨**~ть**⟩ [-бу́ду, -бу́-

дешь; óтбыл, -á, -о] 1. *v/i.* leave, depart (for в В); 2. *v/t.* serve; do; **ˏтие** *n* [12] departure.
отвá|га *f* [5] bravery, valo(u)r; **~живаться** [1], ⟨**~житься**⟩ [16] venture, dare; **~жный** [14; -жен, -жна] valiant, brave.
отвáл: до **~а** F one's fill; **~иваться** [1], ⟨**~и́ться**⟩ [13; -áлится] fall off.
отварнóй [14] boiled.
отвé|дывать, ⟨**~дать**⟩ [1] (*a.* Р) taste; **~зти́** *s.* отвози́ть.
отверг|áть [1], ⟨**ˏнуть**⟩ [21] reject, repudiate.
отвердевáть [1] *s.* тверде́ть.
отвéрженный [14] outcast.
отвернýть(ся) *s.* отвёртывать & отворáчивать(ся).
отвёр|тка [5; *g/pl.*: -ток] screwdriver; **~тывать** [1], ⟨отвернýть⟩ [20; отвёрнутый], ⟨отверте́ть⟩ F [10] turn off.
отвéс *m* [1] plummet; **~ить** *s.* отвéшивать; **~ный** [14; -сен, -сна] plumb; sheer; **~ти́** *s.* отводи́ть.
отвéт *m* [1] answer, reply (в ~ на В in reply to); responsibility.
ответвл|éние *n* [12] branch, offshoot; **~я́ться** [28] branch off.
отвé|тить *s.* **~чáть**; **~тственность** *f* [8] responsibility; **~тственный** [14 *sh.*] responsible (to пéред Т); **~тчик** *m* [1] defendant; **~чáть** [1], ⟨**~тить**⟩ [15] (на В) answer, reply (to); (за В) answer, account (for); (Д) answer, suit.
отвé|шивать [1], ⟨**~сить**⟩ [15] weigh out; make (*a bow*).
отви́н|чивать [1], ⟨**~ти́ть**⟩ [15 *е.*; -нчý, -нти́шь; -и́нченный] unscrew, unfasten.
отвис|áть [1], ⟨**ˏнуть**⟩ [21] hang down, lop; **ˏлый** [14] loppy.
отвле|кáть [1], ⟨**ˏчь**⟩ [26] divert, distract; abstract; **~чённый** [14 *sh.*] abstract.
отвóд *m* [1] allotment; rejection; **~и́ть** [15], ⟨отвести́⟩ [25] lead, get, take (off); turn off, avert; parry; reject; allot; **~и́ть** дýшу F unburden one's heart; **~ный** [14] drain ...
отво|ёвывать [1], ⟨**~евáть**⟩ [6] (re)conquer, win; **~зи́ть** [15], ⟨отвезти́⟩ [24] take, get, drive (off).
отворáчивать [1], ⟨отвернýть⟩ [20] turn off; **-ся** turn away.
отвори́ть(ся) *s.* отворя́ть(ся).
отворóт *m* [1] lapel; (*boot*) top.
отвор|я́ть [28], ⟨**~и́ть**⟩ [13; -орю́, -óришь; -óренный] open (*v/i.* **-ся**).
отвра|ти́тельный [14; -лен, -льна] disgusting, abominable; **~щáть** [1], ⟨**~ти́ть**⟩ [15 *е.*; -ащý, -ати́шь; -ащённый] avert; **~щéние** *n* [12] aversion, disgust (for, at к Д).
отвык|áть [1], ⟨**ˏнуть**⟩ [21] (от Р) wean (from), leave off, become disaccustomed (to).
отвя́з|ывать [1], ⟨**~áть**⟩ [3] (**-ся** [be]come) untie(d), undo(ne); F get rid of (от Р); let a person alone.
отгáд|ывать, ⟨**~áть**⟩ [1] guess; **~ка** *f* [5; *g/pl.*: -док] solution.
отгибáть [1], ⟨отогнýть⟩ [20] unbend; turn up (*or* back).
отгов|áривать [1], ⟨**~ори́ть**⟩ [13] dissuade (from от Р); **-ся** pretend (s. th. Т), extricate o. s.; **~óрка** *f* [5; *g/pl.*: -рок] excuse, pretext.
отголóсок *m* [1; -ска] *s.* óтзвук.
отгоня́ть [28], ⟨отогнáть⟩ [отгоню́, -óнишь; отóгнанный; *cf.* гнать] drive (*or* frighten) away; *fig.* banish.
отгор|áживать [1], ⟨**~оди́ть**⟩ [15 & 15 *е.*; -ожý, -óди́шь; -óженный] fence in; partition off.
отгру|жáть [1], ⟨**~зи́ть**⟩ [15 & 15 *е.*; -ужý, -ýзи́шь; -ýженный & -ужённый] load, ship.
отгрыз|áть [1], ⟨**ˏть**⟩ [24; *pt. st.*] gnaw (off), pick.
отда|вáть [5], ⟨**ˏть**⟩ [-дáм, -дáшь, *etc.*, *cf.* дать; óтдал, -á, -о] give back, return; give (away); send (to в В); devote; deliver, (*baggage*) check, *Brt.* book; put; pay; marry; make (*bow*); cast (*anchor*); recoil (*gun*); **~вáть** честь (Д) ⚔ salute; F sell; *impf.* smell *or* taste (of Т); **-ся** devote o. s.; surrender, give o. s. up; resound; be reflected.
отдáв|ливать [1], ⟨**~и́ть**⟩ [14] crush.
отдал|éние *n* [12] removal; estrangement; distance; **~ённый** [14 *sh.*] remote; **~я́ть** [28], ⟨**~и́ть**⟩ [13] move away, remove; put off, postpone; alienate; **-ся** move away (from от Р); become estranged.
отдá|ть(ся) *s.* **~вáть(ся)**; **~ча** *f* [5] delivery; recoil; return.
отдéл *m* [1] department; office; section; **~ать(ся)** *s.* **~ывать(ся)**; **~éние** *n* [12] separation; secretion; department, division; branch (office); ⚔ squad; compartment; (police) station; **~и́мый** [14 *sh.*] separable; **~и́ть(ся)** *s.* **~я́ть(ся)**; **~ка** *f* [5; *g/pl.*: -лок] finishing; trimming; **~ывать**, ⟨**~ать**⟩ [1] finish, put the final touches on; trim; **-ся** get rid of (от Р); get off, escape (with Т); **~ьность** *f* [8]: в **~ьности** individually; **~ьный** [14] separate; individual, single; **~я́ть** [28], ⟨**~и́ть**⟩ [13; -елю́, -éлишь] separate (*v/i.* **-ся** from от Р; come off); secrete.
отдёр|гивать [1], ⟨**~нуть**⟩ [20] draw back; draw open.
отдирáть [1], ⟨отодрáть⟩ [отдерý, -рёшь; отодрáл, -á, -о; отóдранный] tear (off); *pf.* F thrash; pull.
отдохнýть *s.* отдыхáть.
отдýшина *f* [5] vent (*a. fig.*).
óтдых *m* [1] rest, relaxation; дом **~а** rest home, sanatorium; **~áть** [1], ⟨отдохнýть⟩ [20] rest, relax.
отдышáться [4] *pf.* recover breath.

отёк *m* [1] edema.
оте|ка́ть [1], ⟨**́чь**⟩ [26] swell; become dropsical.
оте́ц *m* [1; отца́] father.
оте́че|ский [16] fatherly; paternal; **~ственный** [14] native, home...; patriotic (*war*); **~ство** *n* [9] motherland, fatherland, one's (native) country.
оте́чь *s.* отека́ть.
отжи|ва́ть [1], ⟨**́ть**⟩ [-живу́, -вёшь; о́тжил, -а́, -о; о́тжи́тый (о́тжи́т, -а́, -о)] (have) live(d, had) (one's time *or* day); become obsolete, die out.
о́тзвук *m* [1] echo, repercussion; response; reminiscence.
о́тзыв *m* [1] response; opinion (in по Д *pl.*), reference; comment, review; recall; password; **~а́ть** [1], ⟨отозва́ть⟩ [отзову́, -вёшь; отозва́л, -а́, -о; ото́званный] take aside; recall; **-ся** respond, answer; speak (of о П); (re)sound; call forth (s. th. Т); affect (s. th. на П); *impf.* smack (of Т); **́чивый** [14 *sh.*] responsive, sympathetic.
отка́з *m* [1] refusal, denial, rejection (of в П, Р); renunciation (of от Р); ⊕ breakdown; ♪ natural; без **~а** smoothly; до **~а** to the full; получи́ть **~** be refused; **~ывать** [1], ⟨**~а́ть**⟩ [3] refuse, deny (a p. s. th. Д/в П); (от Р) dismiss; ⊕ break; **-ся** (от Р) refuse, decline, reject; renounce, give up; would(*n't*) mind.
отка́|лывать [1], ⟨отколо́ть⟩ [17] cut *or* chop off; unfasten; **-ся** come off; secede; **~пывать**, ⟨откопа́ть⟩ [1] dig up, unearth; **~рмливать** [1], ⟨откорми́ть⟩ [14] feed, fatten; **~тывать** [1], ⟨**~ти́ть**⟩ [15] roll (aside, away) (**-ся** *v/i.*); **~чивать**, ⟨**~ча́ть**⟩ [1] pump out; **~шливаться** [1], ⟨**~шляться**⟩ [28] clear one's throat.
откид|но́й [14] folding, tip-up; **́дывать** [1], ⟨**́нуть**⟩ [20] throw (off; back); turn down; drop, leave; **-ся** recline.
откла́|дывать [1], ⟨отложи́ть⟩ [16] lay aside; save; put off, defer, postpone; **~няться** [28] *pf.* take one's leave.
откле́|ивать [1], ⟨**~ить**⟩ [13] unstick; **-ся** come unstuck.
о́тклик *m* [1] response; comment; suggestion; *s. a.* о́тзвук; **~а́ться** [1], ⟨**́нуться**⟩ [20] (на В) respond (to), answer; comment (on).
отклон|е́ние *n* [12] deviation, defection; digression; rejection; **~я́ть** [28], ⟨**~и́ть**⟩ [13; -оню́, -о́нишь] deflect; decline, reject; divert, dissuade; **-ся** deviate, deflect; digress.
отк|оло́ть *s.* **~а́лывать**; **~опа́ть** *s.* **~а́пывать**; **~орми́ть** *s.* **~а́рмливать**.
отко́с *m* [1] slope, slant, (e)scarp.
открове́н|ие *n* [12] revelation; **~ный** [14; -е́нен, -е́нна] frank, candid, open(-hearted), outspoken.
откры|ва́ть [1], ⟨**́ть**⟩ [22] open; turn on; discover; disclose; reveal; unveil; inaugurate; **-ся** open; declare *or* unbosom o. s.; **́тие** *n* [12] opening; discovery; revelation; inauguration; unveiling; **́тка** *f* [5; *g/pl.*: -ток] (с ви́дом picture) post card; **́тый** [14] open; public; **́ть(ся)** *s.* **~ва́ть(ся)**.
отку́да where from?; wherefrom; P why; *a.*, F, = **~-нибудь**, **~-то** (from) somewhere *or* anywhere.
о́ткуп *m* [1; *pl.*: -па́, *etc. e.*] *hist.* lease; **~а́ть** [1], ⟨**~и́ть**⟩ [14] buy (up); take on lease; **-ся** ransom o. s.
отку́пори|вать [1], ⟨**~ть**⟩ [13] uncork; open.
отку́с|ывать [1], ⟨**~и́ть**⟩ [15] bite off; pinch off.
отлага́тельство *n* [9] delay.
отлага́ться [1], ⟨отложи́ться⟩ [16] be deposited; secede, fall away.
отла́мывать, ⟨отлома́ть⟩ [1], ⟨отломи́ть⟩ [14] break off (*v/i.* **-ся**).
отл|епи́ть(ся) [14] *pf.*, *s.* откле́ить (-ся); **~ёт** *m* [1] ✈ start; **~ета́ть** [1], ⟨**~ете́ть**⟩ [11] fly away *or* off; F come off.
отли́|в *m* [1] ebb (tide); shimmer; **~ва́ть** [1], ⟨**~ть**⟩ [отолью́, -льёшь; о́тли́л, -а́, -о; *cf.* лить] pour off, in, out (some ... Р); ⊕ found, cast; *impf.* (Т) shimmer, play.
отлич|а́ть [1], ⟨**~и́ть**⟩ [16 *e.*; -чу́, -чи́шь; -чённый] distinguish (from от Р); decorate; **-ся** *a.*, *impf.*, differ; be noted (for Т); **́ие** *n* [12] distinction, difference; в **́ие** от (Р) as against; зна́ки **́ия** decorations; **~и́тельный** [14] distinctive; **́ник** *m* [1], **́ница** *f* [5] excellent pupil, *etc.*; **́ный** [14; -чен, -чна] excellent, perfect; different; *adv. a.* very good, A (*mark*, *cf.* пятёрка).
отло́гий [16 *sh.*] sloping.
отлож|е́ние *n* [12] deposit; **~и́ть** (**-ся**) *s.* откла́дывать отлага́ться; **~но́й** [14] turndown (*collar*).
отлом|а́ть, **~и́ть** *s.* отла́мывать.
отлуч|а́ть [1], ⟨**~и́ть**⟩ [16 *e.*; -чу́, -чи́шь; -чённый] separate; wean; **~и́ть** от це́ркви excommunicate; **-ся** (из Р) leave, absent o. s. (from); **́ка** *f* [5] absence.
отма́лчиваться [1] keep silence.
отма́|тывать [1], ⟨отмота́ть⟩ [1] wind *or* reel off, unwind; **~хивать** [1], ⟨**~хну́ть**⟩ [20] drive (*or* brush) away (aside) (*a.* **-ся** от Р; F disregard, dismiss).
о́тмель *f* [8] shoal, sandbank.
отме́н|а *f* [5] abolition; cancellation; countermand; **~ный** [14; -е́нен, -е́нна] *s.* отли́чный; **~я́ть** [28], ⟨**~и́ть**⟩ [13; -еню́, -е́нишь] abolish; cancel; countermand.
отмер|е́ть *s.* отмира́ть; **~за́ть** [1], ⟨отмёрзнуть⟩ [21] be frostbitten.

отмéр|ивать [1] & **~ять** [28], ⟨~ить⟩ [13] measure (off).

отмéстк|а F *f* [5]: в ~у in revenge.

отмé|тка *f* [5; *g/pl.*: -ток] mark, grade; **~чáть** [1], ⟨~тить⟩ [15] mark, note.

отмирáть [1], ⟨отмерéть⟩ [12; отомрёт; óтмер,- рлá, -о; отмéрший] die away *or* out; fade; mortify.

отмор|áживать [1], ⟨~óзить⟩ [15] frostbite.

отмотáть *s.* отмáтывать.

отмы|вáть [1], ⟨∠ть⟩ [22] wash (off); **~кáть** [1], ⟨отомкнýть⟩ [20] unlock, open; **∠чка** *f* [5; *g/pl.*: -чек] picklock.

отнéкиваться F [1] deny, disavow.

отнести́(сь) *s.* относи́ть(ся).

отнимáть [1], ⟨отня́ть⟩ [-нимý, -ни́мешь; óтнял, -á, -о; óтнятый (óтнят, -á, -о)] take away (from у P); take (*time, etc.*); F amputate; ~ от грýди wean; **-ся** grow numb.

относи́тельн|ый [14; -лен, -льна] relative; ~о (P) concerning, about.

отно|си́ть [15], ⟨отнести́⟩ [24 -с-: -есý; -ёс, -еслá] take (to Д, в В); carry (off, away); put; refer to; ascribe; **-ся**, ⟨отнести́сь⟩ (к Д) treat, be; show; speak (of о П); *impf.* concern; refer; belong; date from; be relevant; **~шéние** *n* [12] attitude (toward[s] к Д); treatment; relation; ratio; (official) letter; respect (in, with в П, по Д); по ~шéнию (к Д) as regards, to (-ward[s]); имéть ~шéние concern.

отны́не henceforth, henceforward.

отню́дь: ~ не by no means.

отня́|тие *n* [12] taking (away); amputation; weaning; **~ть(ся)** *s.* отнимáть(ся).

отобра|жáть [1], ⟨~зи́ть⟩ [15 *e.*; -ажý, -ази́шь] (-ся be) reflect(ed); **~жéние** *n* [12] reflection.

ото|брáть *s.* отбирáть; **~всю́ду** from everywhere; **~гнáть** *s.* отгоня́ть; **~гнýть** *s.* отгибáть; **~гревáть** [1], ⟨~грéть⟩ [8; -грéтый] warm (up); **~двигáть** [1], ⟨~дви́нуть⟩ [20 *st.*] move aside, away (*v/i.* -ся); F put off.

отодрáть *s.* отдирáть.

отож(д)еств|ля́ть [28], ⟨~и́ть⟩ [14 *e.*; -влю́, -ви́шь; -влённый] identify.

ото|звáть(ся) *s.* отзывáть(ся); **~йти́** *s.* отходи́ть; **~мкнýть** *s.* отмыкáть; **~мсти́ть** *s.* мсти́ть.

отоп|и́ть [28] *s.* отáпливать; **~лéние** *n* [12] heating.

оторвáть(ся) *s.* отрывáть(ся).

оторопéть F [8] *pf.* be struck dumb.

отослáть *s.* отсылáть.

отпа|дáть [1], ⟨∠сть⟩ [25; *pt. st.*] (от P) fall off; fall away, secede, desert; be dropped; pass.

отпе|вáние *n* [12] burial service; **∠тый** F [14] inveterate, incorrigible; **~рéть(ся)** *s.* отпирáть(ся).

отпечáт|ок *m* [1; -тка] (im)print; mark; stamp; **~ывать**, ⟨~ать⟩ [1] print; type; imprint, impress.

отпи|вáть [1], ⟨∠ть⟩ [отопью́, -пьёшь; óтпил, -á, -о; -пéй(те)!] drink (some ... P); **∠ливать** [1], ⟨~ли́ть⟩ [13] saw off.

отпирáт|ельство *n* [9] disavowel; **~ь** [1], ⟨отперéть⟩ [12; отопрý, -прёшь; óтпер, -рлá, -о; отпёрший; óтпертый (-ерт, -á, -о)] unlock, unbar, open; **-ся** open; (от P) disavow.

отпи́ть *s.* отпивáть.

отпи́х|ивать F [1], *once* ⟨~нуть⟩ [20] push off, away, aside, back.

отплá|та *f* [5] repayment, requital; **~чивать** [1], ⟨~ти́ть⟩ [15] (re)pay, requite.

отплы|вáть [1], ⟨∠ть⟩ [23] sail, leave; swim (off); **∠тие** *n* [12] sailing off, departure.

óтповедь *f* [8] rebuff, snub.

отпóр *m* [1] repulse, rebuff.

отпорóть [17] *pf.* rip (off).

отправ|и́тель *m* [4] sender; **∠ить** (-ся) *s.* ~ля́ть(ся); **∠ка** F *f* [5] dispatch; **~лéние** *n* [12] dispatch; departure; exercise, practice; function; **~ля́ть** [28], ⟨∠ить⟩ [14] send, dispatch, forward; mail, *Brt.* post; exercise, perform; **-ся** go; leave, set off (for в, на В); *impf.* (от P) start from (*fig.*); **~нóй** [14] starting.

отпрáшиваться [1], ⟨отпроси́ться⟩ [15] ask (and get) leave (*to go ...*).

отпры́г|ивать [1], *once* ⟨~нуть⟩ [20] jump back (*or* aside); rebound.

óтпрыск *m* [1] offshoot.

отпря|гáть [1], ⟨∠чь⟩ [26 г/ж: -ягý, -яжёшь] unharness; **∠нуть** [20 *st.*] *pf.* recoil.

отпýг|ивать [1], ⟨~нуть⟩ [20] scare.

óтпуск *m* [1; *pl.* -кá, *etc. e.*] leave, vacation (on: *go* в В; *be* в П: *a.*, F, в ~ý); sale; supply; allotment; **~áть** [1], ⟨отпусти́ть⟩ [15] let go; release, set free; dismiss; sell; provide; allot; slacken; remit; grow; F crack; **~ни́к** *m* [1 *e.*] vacationist; **~нóй** [14] vacation..., holiday...; selling (*price*).

отпущéн|ие *n* [12] remission; козёл ~ия scapegoat.

отраб|áтывать, ⟨~óтать⟩ [1] work off; finish work; *p. pt. p. a.* waste.

отрáв|а *f* [5] poison; *fig.* bane; **~лéние** *n* [12] poisoning; **~ля́ть** [28], ⟨~и́ть⟩ [14] poison; spoil.

отрáд|а *f* [5] comfort, joy, pleasure; **~ный** [14; -ден, -дна] pleasant, gratifying, comforting.

отра|жáть [1], ⟨~зи́ть⟩ [15 *e.*; -ажý, -ази́шь; -ажённый] repel, ward off; refute; reflect, mirror (*v/i.* **-ся**; на П affect; show).

óтрасль *f* [8] branch.

отра|стáть [1], ⟨~сти́⟩ [24 -ст-:

-сту́; *cf.* расти́] grow; grow again; **∠щивать** [1], ⟨**~сти́ть**⟩ [15 *e.*; -ащу́, -асти́шь; -ащённый] grow.
отре́бье *n* [10] rubbish; rabble.
отре́з *m* [1] pattern, length (*of material*); **~а́ть** & **~ывать** [1], ⟨**~ать**⟩ [3] cut off; F cut short.
отрезв|ля́ть [28], ⟨**~и́ть**⟩ [14 *e.*; -влю́, -ви́шь; -влённый] sober; *fig.* disillusion.
отре́з|ок *m* [1; -зка] piece; stretch; ⅄ segment; **~ывать** *s.* **~а́ть**.
отре|ка́ться [1], ⟨**∠чься**⟩ [26] (от P) disown, disavow; renounce; **∠чься** от престо́ла abdicate.
отре́нье *n* [10] *coll.* rags *pl.*
отре|че́ние *n* [12] (от P) disavowal; renunciation; abdication; **∠чься** *s.* **~ка́ться**; **~ша́ть** [1], ⟨**~ши́ть**⟩ [16 *e.*; -шу́, -ши́шь; -шённый] dismiss; release; **-ся** relinquish; **~ше́ние** *n* [12] dismissal, removal; renunciation (of от P).
отрица́|ние *n* [12] negation, denial; **~тельный** [14; -лен, -льна] negative; **~ть** [1] deny.
отро́|г *m* [1] spur; **'~ду** F from birth; in one's life; **~дье** F *n* [10] spawn; **'~к** † *m* [1] boy; **~сток** *m* [1; -тка] ♣ shoot; *anat.* appendix; **'~чество** *n* [9] boyhood; adolescence.
отруб|а́ть [1], ⟨**~и́ть**⟩ [14] cut off.
о́труби *f/pl.* [8; *from g/pl. e.*] bran.
отры́в *m* [1] separation; disengagement (*a.* ⚔); alienation; interruption; **~а́ть** [1] **1.** ⟨оторва́ть⟩ [-ву́, -вёшь; -ва́л, -а́, -о; ото́рванный] tear (*or* pull, turn) off, away; separate; **-ся** (от P) come off; turn (tear o. s.) away; lose contact (with); ⚔ disengage; не **~а́ясь** without rest; **2.** ⟨отры́ть⟩ [22] dig up, out, away; F disinter; **~истый** [14 *sh.*] abrupt; **~но́й** [14] sheet *or* block (*calendar*); **~ок** *m* [1; -вка] fragment; extract, passage; **~очный** [14; -чен, -чна] fragmentary; scrappy.
отры́жка *f* [5; *g/pl.*: -жек] belch (-ing); F survival.
отры́ть *s.* отрыва́ть.
отря́|д *m* [1] detachment; squadron; troop; ♣, *zo.* class; **~жа́ть** [1], ⟨**~ди́ть**⟩ [15 *e.*; -яжу́, -яди́шь; -яжённый] detach; **~хивать** [1], *once* ⟨**~хну́ть**⟩ [20] shake off.
отсве́чивать [1] shimmer (with T).
отсе́|ивать [1], ⟨**~ять**⟩ [27] sift; *fig.* eliminate; **~ка́ть** [1], ⟨**~чь**⟩ [26; *pt.*: -се́к, -секла́; -сечённый] cut off; **~че́ние** *n* [12] cutting off.
отск|а́кивать [1], ⟨**~очи́ть**⟩ [16] jump off, back; rebound; F fall off.
отслу́ж|ивать [1], ⟨**~и́ть**⟩ [16] serve (one's time); be worn out; hold.
отсове́т|овать [1] *pf.* dissuade (from).
отсохну́ть *s.* отсыха́ть.
отсро́ч|ивать [1], ⟨**~ить**⟩ [16] postpone; respite; **~ка** *f* [5; *g/pl.*: -чек] delay; respite; prolongation.
отста|ва́ть [5], ⟨**∠ть**⟩ [-а́ну, -а́нешь] (от P) lag, fall *or* remain behind; *clock*: be slow (5 min. на пять мину́т); desert; leave off; come (*or* fall) off; F *pf.* leave alone.
отста́в|ка *f* [5] resignation, retirement; dismissal; в **~ке** = **~ной**; **~ля́ть** [28], ⟨**~ить**⟩ [14] remove, set aside; dismiss; F countermand; **~но́й** [14] retired.
отст|а́ивать [1], ⟨**~оя́ть**⟩ [-ою́, -ои́шь] defend, save; maintain, assert; push; F stand; tire; *pf.* be away; **-ся** settle.
отста́|лость *f* [8] backwardness; **~лый** [14] backward; **~ть** *s.* **~ва́ть**.
отстёгивать [1], ⟨отстегну́ть⟩ [20; -ёгнутый] unbutton, unfasten.
отстоя́ть(ся) *s.* отста́ивать(ся).
отстр|а́ивать [1], ⟨**~о́ить**⟩ [13] build (up); **~аня́ть** [28], ⟨**~ани́ть**⟩ [13] push aside, remove; dismiss; debar; **-ся** (от P) dodge; shirk; **~о́ить** *s.* **~а́ивать**.
отступ|а́ть [1], ⟨**~и́ть**⟩ [14] step back; retreat, fall back; recoil; *fig.* recede; deviate; indent; **-ся** renounce (s. th. от P); **~ле́ние** *n* [12] retreat; deviation; digression; **∠ник** *m* [1] apostate; **~но́е** *n* [14] smart money.
отсу́тств|ие *n* [12] absence (in в B; in the/of за T/P); lack; в **~ии** absent; **~овать** [7] be absent; be lacking.
отсчи́т|ывать, ⟨**~а́ть**⟩ [1] count.
отсыл|а́ть [1], ⟨отосла́ть⟩ [-ошлю́, -шлёшь; ото́сланный] send (off, back); refer (to к Д); **∠ка** *f* [5; *g/pl.*: -лок] dispatch; reference.
отсып|а́ть [1], ⟨**∠ать**⟩ [2] pour (out).
отсы|ре́лый [14] damp; **~ха́ть** [1], ⟨отсо́хнуть⟩ [21] wither (off).
отсю́да from here; hence.
отта́|ивать [1], ⟨**~ять**⟩ [27] thaw; **~лкивать** [1], ⟨оттолкну́ть⟩ [20] push off, away, aside; repel; **~лкивающий** [17] repellent; **~скивать** [1], ⟨**~щи́ть**⟩ [16] pull off, away, aside; **~чивать** [1], ⟨отточи́ть⟩ [16] sharpen; **~ять** *s.* **~ивать**.
отте́н|ок *m* [1; -нка] shade, nuance, tinge; **~я́ть** [28], ⟨**~и́ть**⟩ [13] shade; set off, emphasize.
о́ттепель *f* [8] thaw.
оттесн|я́ть [28], ⟨**~и́ть**⟩ [13] push off, aside; ⚔ drive back; F oust.
о́ттис|к *m* [1] impression, reprint; **∠кивать** [1], ⟨**∠нуть**⟩ [20] print (off).
отто|го́ therefore, (*a.* **~го́** и) that's why; **~го́** что because; **~лкну́ть** *s.* отта́лкивать; **~пы́рить** F [13] *pf.* bulge, protrude (*v/i.* **-ся**); **~чи́ть** *s.* отта́чивать.
отту́да from there.

оття́|гивать [1], ⟨~ну́ть⟩ [20; -я́нутый] draw off (back); delay.
отуч|а́ть [1], ⟨~и́ть⟩ [16] disaccustom (to от P), cure (of); -ся leave off.
отхлы́нуть [20] *pf.* rush away, back.
отхо́д *m* [1] departure; ⚔ withdrawal; deviation; rupture; **~и́ть** [15], ⟨отойти́⟩ [-ойду́, -дёшь; отошёл, -шла́; отоше́дший; отойдя́] go (away, aside); leave; deviate; ⚔ withdraw; turn away; come (*or* fall) off; thaw; recover; expire; *impers.* be relieved; **~ы** *m/pl.* [1] waste.
отцве|та́ть [1], ⟨~сти́⟩ [25 -т-: -ету́] fade, wither.
отцеп|ля́ть [28], ⟨~и́ть⟩ [14] unhook; uncouple; F remove.
отцо́в|ский [16] paternal; fatherly; **~ство** *n* [9] paternity.
отча́|иваться [1], ⟨~яться⟩ [27] despair (of в П), despond.
отча́ли|вать [1], ⟨~ть⟩ [13] unmoor; push off; sail away.
отча́сти partly, in part.
отча́я|ние *n* [12] despair; **~нный** [14 *sh.*] desperate; **~ться** *s.* отча́иваться.
о́тче: ~ наш Our Father; Lord's Prayer.
отчего́ why; ~-то for some reason.
отчека́н|ивать [1], ⟨~ить⟩ [13] coin; say distinctly.
о́тчество *n* [9] patronymic.
отчёт *m* [1] account (of о, в П), report (on); return; (от)дава́ть себе́ ~ в П realize *v/t.*; **~ливый** [14 *sh.*] distinct, clear; precise; **~ность** *f* [8] accounting; F accounts *pl.*; **~ный** [14] of account.
отчи́|зна *f* [5] fatherland; **′~й** [17] paternal; **′~м** *m* [1] stepfather.
отчисл|е́ние *n* [12] deduction; subscription; dismissal; **~я́ть** [28], ⟨~́ить⟩ [13] deduct; allot; dismiss.
отчи́т|ывать F, ⟨~а́ть⟩ [1] blow up, rebuke; -ся give *or* render an account (to пе́ред Т).
от|чужда́ть [1] alienate, expropriate; **~шатну́ться** [20] *pf.* start *or* shrink back; **~швырну́ть** F [20] *pf.* hurl (away); **~ше́льник** *m* [1] hermit.
отшиб|а́ть F [1], ⟨~и́ть⟩ [-бу́, -бёшь; -ши́б(ла); -ши́бленный] strike (off).
отщепе́нец *m* [1; -нца] renegade.
отъе́|зд *m* [1] departure; **~зжа́ть** [1], ⟨~́хать⟩ [-е́ду, -е́дешь] drive (off), depart.
отъя́вленный [14] notorious, arch.
оты́гр|ывать, ⟨~а́ть⟩ [1] win back, regain (one's [lost] money -ся).
оты́ск|ивать [1], ⟨~а́ть⟩ [3] find.
отяго|ща́ть [1], ⟨~ти́ть⟩ [15 *e.*; -щу́, -оти́шь; -ощённый] (over-) burden.

офиц|е́р *m* [1] officer; **~е́рский** [16] office(r's, -s'); **~иа́льный** [14; -лен, -льна] official; **~иа́нт** *m* [1] waiter; **~ио́зный** [14; -зен, -зна] semiofficial.
оформ|ля́ть [28], ⟨~́ить⟩ [14] form, shape; get up (*book*); mount (*play*); legalize; adjust.
ох oh!, ah!; **~́анье** *n* [10] groan(s).
оха́пка *f* [5; *g/pl.*: -пок] armful; fagot.
о́х|ать [1], *once* ⟨~нуть⟩ [20] groan.
охва́т|ывать [1], ⟨~и́ть⟩ [15] seize, grasp; embrace; envelop.
охла|дева́ть, ⟨~де́ть⟩ [8] cool down; **~жда́ть** [1], ⟨~ди́ть⟩ [15 *e.*; -ажу́, -ади́шь; -аждённый] cool; **~жде́ние** *n* [12] cooling.
охмел|я́ть [28], ⟨~и́ть⟩ [13] (**~еть** F [8] become) intoxicate(d).
о́хнуть *s.* о́хать.
охо́т|а *f* [5] (на В, за Т) hunt(ing) (of, for); chase (after); (к Д) F desire (for), mind (to); **~а** Д + *inf.*! what do(es) ... want + *inf.* for?; **~иться** [15] (на В, за Т) hunt; chase (after); **~ник** *m* [1] hunter; volunteer; lover (of до Р); **~ничий** [18] hunting, shooting; hunter's (-s'); **~но** willingly, gladly, with pleasure; **~нее** rather; **~нее** всего́ best of all.
охра́н|а *f* [5] guard(s); protection; **~е́ние** *n* [12] protection; ⚔ outpost (-s); **~я́ть** [28], ⟨~и́ть⟩ [13] guard, protect (from, against от Р).
охри́п|лый F [14], **~ший** [17] hoarse.
оце́н|ивать [1], ⟨~и́ть⟩ [13; -еню́, -е́нишь] value (at в В), appraise, estimate; appreciate; **~ка** *f* [5; *g/pl.*: -нок] valuation, appraisal; estimation, appreciation; mark.
оцепене́|лый [14] benumbed; stupefied; **~ние** *n* [12] numbness.
оцеп|ля́ть [28] ⟨~и́ть⟩ [14] encircle.
оча́г *m* [1 *e.*] fireplace, (*a. fig.* = home) hearth; *fig.* center (-tre), seat.
очаров|а́ние *n* [12] charm, fascination; **~а́тельный** [14; -лен, -льна] charming; **~́ывать** [1], ⟨~а́ть⟩ [7] charm, fascinate, enchant.
очеви́д|ец *m* [1; -дца] eyewitness; **~ный** [14; -ден, -дна] evident.
о́чень very, (very) much.
очередно́й [14] next (in turn); regular; foremost; latest.
о́черед|ь *f* [8; *from g/pl. e.*] turn (in; by turns по ~ди); order, succession; line (*Brt.* queue); ⚔ volley; ва́ша ~ь *or* ~ь за ва́ми it is your turn; на ~и next; в свою́ ~ь in (for) my, *etc.*, turn (part).
о́черк *m* [1] sketch; outline; essay.
очерня́ть [28] *s.* черни́ть.
очерстве́лый [14] hardened.
очер|та́ние *n* [12] outline, contour; **~́чивать** [1], ⟨~ти́ть⟩ [15] outline, sketch; **~тя́** го́лову F headlong.
очи́|стка *f* [5; *g/pl.*: -ток] clean(s)-

ing; clearance; *pl.* peelings; **\~щáть** [1], ⟨\~стить⟩ [15] clean(se); clear; peel; purify; evacuate, quit; empty.
очк|и́ *n/pl.* [1] spectacles, glasses; **\~ó** *n* [9; *pl.*: -кú, -кóв] *sport*: point; *cards*: spot, *Brt.* pip; ⚘, ⊕ eye; **\~овтирáтельство** F *n* [9] eyewash, humbug.
очнýться [20] *pf.*, *s.* опóмниться.
очумéлый P [14] crazy, mad.
очути́ться [15; *1st. p. sg. not used*] get, find o. s.
ошалéлый F [14] crazy, mad.
ошéйник *m* [1] collar (*on a dog only*).
ошелом|ля́ть [28], ⟨\~и́ть⟩ [14 *e.*; -млю́, -ми́шь; -млённый] stun, stupefy.
ошиб|áться [1], ⟨\~и́ться⟩ [-бýсь, -бёшься; -и́бся, -и́блась] be mistaken, make a mistake (-s), err; miss; **\´\~ка** *f* [5; *g/pl.*: -бок] mistake (by по Д), error, fault; **\´\~очный** [14; -чен, -чна] erroneous, mistaken.
ошпáр|ивать [1], ⟨\~ить⟩ [13] scald.
ощýп|ывать, ⟨\~ать⟩ [1] feel, touch; **'\~ь** *f* [8]: на '\~ь to the touch; **'\~ью** *adv.* gropingly.
ощу|ти́мый [14 *sh.*], **\~ти́тельный** [14; -лен, -льна] palpable, tangible; felt; not(ice)able; **\~щáть** [1], ⟨\~ти́ть⟩ [15 *e.*; -ущý, -ути́шь; -ущённый] feel, sense; **-ся** be felt; **\~щéние** *n* [12] sensation; feeling.

П

Пáвел *m* [1; -вла] Paul.
павиáн *m* [1] baboon.
павильóн *m* [1] pavilion; (*fair*) hall; (*film*) studio.
павли́н *m* [1], **\~ий** [18] peacock.
пáводок *m* [1; -дка] flood.
пá|губный [14; -бен, -бна] pernicious; **\~даль** *f* [8] carrion.
пáда|ть [1] **1.** ⟨упáсть⟩ [25; *pt. st.*] fall; **2.** ⟨пасть⟩ *fig.* fall; die; **\~ть** дýхом lose courage (*or* heart).
пад|éж[1] *m* [1 *e.*] *gr.* case; **\~ёж**[2] *m* [1 *e.*] (*cattle*) plague, rinderpest; **\~éние** *n* [12] fall; downfall, overthrow; ☨ slump; **\´\~кий** [16; -док, -дка] (на В) greedy (of, for), mad (after); **\~ýчая** *f* [17] epilepsy.
пáдчерица *f* [5] stepdaughter.
паёк *m* [1; пайкá] ration.
пáзуха *f* [5] bosom (in за В); cavity.
пай *m* [3; *pl. e.*: паи́, паёв] share; **\´\~щик** *m* [1] shareholder.
пакéт *m* [1] parcel, package, packet; dispatch; paper bag.
пáкля *f* [6] tow, oakum.
паковáть [7], ⟨у-, за-⟩ pack.
пáк|ость *f* [8] filth, smut, dirt(y trick); **\~т** *m* [1] pact, treaty.
палáт|а *f* [5] chamber; *parl.* house; board; ward; оружéйная **\~а** armo(u)ry; **\~ка** *f* [5; *g/pl.*: -ток] tent; booth.
палáч *m* [1 *e.*] hangman, executioner.
Палести́на *f* [5] Palestine.
пáл|ец *m* [1; -льца] finger; toe; смотрéть сквозь **\~ьцы** wink (at на В); знать как свой пять **\~ьцев** have at one's fingertips; **\~исáдник** *m* [1] (small) front garden
пали́тра *f* [5] palette.
пали́ть [13] **1.** ⟨с-⟩ burn, scorch; **2.** ⟨о-⟩ singe; **3.** ⟨вы́-⟩ fire, shoot.
пáл|ка *f* [5; *g/pl.*: -лок] stick; cane; club; из-под **\~ки** F under *or* in constraint; **\~очка** *f* [5; *g/pl.*: -чек] (small) stick; ♪ baton; wand; ⚕ bacillus.
палóмни|к *m* [1] pilgrim; **\~чество** *n* [9] pilgrimage.
пáлуба *f* [5] deck.
пальбá *f* [5] firing, fire.
пáльма *f* [5] palm (tree).
пальтó *n* [*indecl.*] (over)coat.
пáмят|ник *m* [1] monument; memorial; **\~ный** [14; -тен, -тна] memorable; unforgettable; **\~ь** *f* [8] memory (in/of на В/о П); remembrance; recollection (of о П); на **\~ь** *a.* by heart; без **\~и** unconscious; F mad (about от Р).
Панáмский [16]: \~ проли́в *m* Panama Canal.
панéль *f* [8] pavement; wainscot.
пáника *f* [5] panic.
панихи́да *f* [5] requiem, dirge.
пансиóн *m* [1] boarding house; boarding school.
панталóны *m/pl.* [5] drawers, pants.
пантéра *f* [5] panther.
пáнцирь *m* [4] coat of mail.
пáпа[1] F *m* [5] papa; dad(dy).
пáпа[2] *m* [5] pope.
пáперть *f* [8] porch (*of a church*).
папильóтка *f* [5; *g/pl.*: -ток] hair curler.
папирóса *f* [5] cigarette.
пáпка *f* [5; *g/pl.*: -пок] folder; cardboard.
пáпоротник *m* [1] fern.
пар *m* [1; в -ý; *pl. e.*] **1.** steam; **2.** fallow; **\´\~а** *f* [5] pair; couple.
Парагвáй *m* [4] Paraguay.
парáграф *m* [1] paragraph.
парáд *m* [1] parade; **\~ный** [14] full (dress); front (door).
парашю́т (-'ʃut) *m* [1] parachute; **\~и́ст** *m* [1] parachutist; ⚔ paratrooper.
парéние *n* [12] soar(ing), hover.
пáрень *m* [4; -рня; *from g/pl. e.*] lad, guy.

пари́ *n* [*indecl.*] bet, wager (*vb.*: держа́ть ~); (идёт) ~? what do you bet?
Пари́ж *m* [1] Paris; **2а́нин** *m* [1; *pl.*: -а́не, -а́н], **2а́нка** *f* [5; *g/pl.*: -нок] Parisian.
пари́к *m* [1 *e.*] wig; **~ма́хер** *m* [1] hairdresser, barber; **~ма́херская** *f* [16] hairdressing saloon, barber's (shop).
пари́|ровать [7] (*im*)*pf.*, *a.* ⟨от-⟩ parry; **~ть**[1] [13] soar, hover.
па́рить[2] [13] steam (*in a bath*: **-ся**).
парла́мент *m* [1] parliament; **~а́рий** *m* [3] parliamentarian; **~ский** [16] parliamentary.
парни́к *m* [1 *e.*], **~о́вый** [14] hotbed.
парни́шка F *m* [5; *g/pl.*: -шек] guy, lad, youngster.
парно́й [14] fresh (*milk, meat*).
па́рный [14] paired; twin...
паро|во́з *m* [1] 🚂 engine; **~во́й** [14] steam...; **~ди́ровать** [7] (*im*)*pf.*, **∠дия** *f* [7] parody.
паро́ль *m* [4] password, parole.
паро́м *m* [1] ferry(boat); **~щик** *m* [1] ferryman.
парохо́д *m* [1] steamer; **~ный** [14] steamship...; **~ство** *n* [9] (steamship) line.
па́рт|а *f* [5] (*school*) bench, *Brt. a.* form; **~акти́в** *m* [1] = **~и́йный** акти́в; **~биле́т** *m* [1] = **~и́йный** биле́т; **~е́р** (-ˈtɛr) *m* [1] parterre, *Brt.* pit; **~и́ец** F *m* [1; -и́йца] Party man *or* member (*Sov.*); **~иза́н** *m* [1] guerilla, partisan; **~и́йность** *f* [8] Party membership; partisanship; Party discipline (*Sov.*); **~и́йный** [14] party...; *su.* = **~и́ец**; **~иту́ра** *f* [5] ♪ score; **~ия** *f* [7] party; ☤ parcel, lot, consignment; ⚔ detachment; batch; game, set; match; ♪ part; ☤ **~иями** in lots; **~нёр** *m* [1], **~нёрша** *f* [5] partner; **~о́рг** *m* [1] Party organizer (*Sov.*).
па́рус *m* [1; *pl.*: -са́, *etc. e.*] sail; на всех **~а́х** under full sail; **~и́на** *f* [5] sailcloth, canvas, duck; **~и́новый** [14] canvas...; **~ник** *m* [1] = **~ное** су́дно *n* [14/9] sailing ship.
парфюме́рия *f* [7] perfumery.
парч|а́ *f* [5] brocade; **~о́вый** [14] brocade(d).
парши́вый [14 *sh.*] mangy.
пас *m* [1] pass (*sport, cards*).
па́сквиль *m* [4] lampoon.
паску́дный P [14; -ден, -дна] foul, filthy.
па́смурный [14; -рен, -рна] dull; gloomy.
пасова́ть [7] pass (*sport*; *cards*, ⟨с-⟩); F yield (to пе́ред T).
па́спорт *m* [1; *pl.*: -та́, *etc. e.*], **~ный** [14] passport.
пассажи́р *m* [1], **~ка** *f* [5; *g/pl.*: -рок], **~ский** [16] passenger.
пасси́в *m* [1] ☤ liabilities *pl.*; **~ный** [14; -вен, -вна] passive.
па́ста *f* [5] paste.
па́ст|бище *n* [11] pasture; **~ва** *f* [5] *eccl.* flock; **~и́** [24 -с-] graze (*v/i.* **-сь**), pasture; **~у́х** *m* [1 *e.*] herder (*Brt.* herdsman), shepherd; **~у́шка** *f* [5; *g/pl.*: -шек] shepherdess; **~у́ший** [18] shepherd's; **~ырь** *m* [4] pastor; **~ь 1.** *s.* па́дать; **2.** *f* [8] jaws *pl.*, mouth.
па́сха *f* [5] Easter (for на В; on на П); Easter cake; Passover; **∠льный** [14] Easter...
па́сынок *m* [1; -нка] stepson.
пате́нт *m* [1], **~ова́ть** [7] (*im*)*pf.*, *a.* ⟨за-⟩ patent.
патефо́н *m* [1] record player.
па́тока *f* [5] molasses, *Brt. a.* treacle.
патр|ио́т *m* [1]; patriot; **~иоти́ческий** [16] patriotic; **~о́н** *m* [1] **1.** cartridge, shell; (lamp) socket; **2.** patron; **3.** pattern; **~онта́ш** *m* [1] cartridge belt, pouch; **~ули́ровать** [7], **~у́ль** *m* [4 *e.*] patrol.
па́уза *f* [5] pause.
пау́к *m* [1 *e.*] spider.
паути́на *f* [5] cobweb.
па́фос *m* [1] pathos; verve, vim.
пах *m* [1; в -у́] *anat.* groin; **∠арь** *m* [4] plowman, *Brt.* ploughman; **~а́ть** [3], ⟨вс-⟩ plow (*Brt.* plough), till.
па́хн|уть[1] [20] smell (of T); **~у́ть**[2] F [20] *pf.* puff.
па́хот|а *f* [5] tillage; **~ный** [14] arable.
паху́чий [17 *sh.*] fragrant.
пацие́нт *m* [1], **~ка** *f* [5; *g/pl.*: -ток] patient.
па́че F: тем ~ all the more.
па́чка *f* [5; *g/pl.*: -чек] pack(et), package; batch.
па́чкать [1], ⟨за-, ис-, вы́-⟩ soil.
па́шня *f* [6; *g/pl.*: -шен] tillage, field.
паште́т *m* [1] pie.
пая́льник *m* [1] soldering iron.
пая́сничать F [1] play the fool.
пая́ть [28], ⟨за-⟩ solder.
пая́ц *m* [1] buffoon, merry-andrew.
ПВО = противовозду́шная оборо́на.
пев|е́ц *m* [1; -вца́], **~и́ца** *f* [5] singer; **~у́чий** [17 *sh.*] melodious; **∠чий** [17] singing (*bird*); *su.* chorister, choirboy.
пе́гий [16 *sh.*] piebald.
педаго́г *m* [1] pedagogue, teacher; **~ика** *f* [5] pedagogics; **~и́ческий** [16], **~и́чный** [14; -чен, -чна] pedagogic(al).
педа́ль *f* [8] treadle, pedal.
педа́нт *m* [1] pedant, **~и́чный** [14; -чен, -чна] pedantic(al).
пейза́ж *m* [1] landscape.
пека́р|ня *f* [6; *g/pl.*: -рен] bakery; **ʹ~ь** *m* [4; *pl. a.* -ря́, *etc. e.*] baker.
пелен|а́ *f* [5] shroud; **~а́ть** [1], ⟨за-, с-⟩ swaddle; **~ка** (-ˈlɔn-) *f* [5; *g/pl.*: -нок] swaddling band (*pl.* clothes), diaper, *Brt. a.* napkin.

пельме́ни *m/pl.* [*gen.:* -ней] ravioli.
пе́на *f* [5] foam, froth; lather.
пена́л *m* [1] pen case.
пе́ние *n* [12] singing; crow.
пе́н|истый [14 *sh.*] foamy, frothy; **~иться** [13], ⟨вс-⟩ foam, froth; sparkle, mantle; **~ка** *f* [5; *g/pl.:* -нок] scum; froth.
пе́нсия *f* [7] pension.
пенсне́ (-'nɛ) *n* [*indecl.*] pince-nez, eyeglasses *pl.*
пе́нь *m* [4; пня] stump; blockhead.
пеньк|а́ *f* [5] hemp; **~о́вый** [14] hemp(en).
пе́ня *f* [6; *g/pl.:* -ней] fine.
пеня́ть F [28], ⟨по-⟩ blame (a p. for Д *or* на В/за В).
пе́пел *m* [1; -пла] ashes *pl.*; **~и́ще** *n* [11] the ashes; *s. a.* пожа́рище; **~ьница** *f* [5] ash tray; **~ьный** [14] ashy.
пе́рвен|ец *m* [1; -нца] first-born; **~ство** *n* [9] primogeniture; superiority; championship.
перви́чный [14; -чен, -чна] primary.
перво|бы́тный [14; -тен, -тна] primitive, primeval; **~исто́чник** *m* [1] (first) source, origin; **~кла́ссный** [14] first-rate *or* -class; **~ку́рсник** *m* [1] freshman; **~-на́перво** P first of all; **~нача́льный** [14; -лен, -льна] original; primary; **~о́браз** *m* [1] prototype; **~осно́вы** *f/pl.* [5] elements; **~очередно́й** [14] top-priority; **~со́ртный** = **~**кла́ссный; **~степе́нный** [14; -е́нен, -е́нна] paramount, supreme.
пе́рв|ый [14] first; chief, main; *Brt.* ground (*floor*); *thea.* dress (*circle*); **~**ое *n* first course (*meal*; for на В); **~**ым де́лом (до́лгом) *or* в **~**ую о́чередь first of all, first thing; **~**е́йший the very first; first-rate; *cf.* пя́тый.
перга́мент *m* [1] parchment.
переб|ега́ть [1], ⟨**~**ежа́ть⟩ [4; -егу́, -ежи́шь, -егу́т] run over (*or* across); desert; **~е́жчик** *m* [1] deserter; turncoat; **~ива́ть** [1], ⟨**~**и́ть⟩ [-бью́, -бьёшь, *cf.* бить] interrupt; break; kill; **-ся** break; F rough it.
переб|ира́ть [1], ⟨**~**ра́ть⟩ [-беру́, -рёшь; -бра́л, -а́, -о; -е́бранный] look a th. over; sort (out); *impf.* ♪ finger; tell (one's beads); **-ся** move (into на, в В); cross (*v/t.* че́рез В).
переб|и́ть *s.* **~**ива́ть; **~о́й** *m* [3] stoppage, break; irregularity; **~оро́ть** [17] *pf.* overcome, master.
перебр|а́нка F *f* [5; *g/pl.:* -нок] wrangle; **~а́сывать** [1], ⟨**~**о́сить⟩ [15] throw over; ⚔, ✝ transfer, shift; lay (*bridge*); **-ся** exchange (*v/t.* Т); **~а́ть(ся)** *s.* перебира́ть (-ся); **~о́ска** *f* [5; *g/pl.:* -сок] transference.
перева́л *m* [1] pass; **~ивать** [1], ⟨**~**и́ть⟩ [13; -алю́, -а́лишь; -а́ленный] tumble, turn (over; *v/i.* **-ся**; *impf.* waddle); F pass; *impers.* (Д) **~**и́ло за (В) (p.) is past ...
перева́р|ивать [1], ⟨**~**и́ть⟩ [13; -арю́, -а́ришь; -а́ренный] digest.
пере|везти́ *s.* **~**вози́ть; **~вёртывать** [1], ⟨**~**верну́ть⟩ [20; -вёрнутый] turn over (*v/i.* **-ся**); overturn; turn; **~ве́с** *m* [1] preponderance; **~вести́(сь)** *s.* переводи́ть(ся); **~ве́шивать** [1], ⟨**~**ве́сить⟩ [15] hang (elsewhere); reweigh; outweigh; **-ся** hang *or* bend over; **~вира́ть** F [1], ⟨**~**вра́ть⟩ [-вру́, -врёшь; -е́вранный] misquote, distort.
перево́д *m* [1] transfer(ence); translation (from/into с Р/на В); remittance; (*money*) order; **~и́ть** [15], ⟨перевести́⟩ [25] lead; transfer; translate (from/into с Р/на В), turn; interpret; remit; set (*watch, clock*; *usu.* стре́лку); **~**и́ть дух take breath; (**-ся**, ⟨-сь⟩) transfer; die out; (у Р/И) run out/of; **~ный** [14] translated; (*a.* ✝) transfer...; **~**ный ве́ксель *m* draft; **~чик** *m* [1], **~чица** *f* [5] translator; interpreter.
перево́з *m* [1] ferriage, ferry; *a.* = **~**ка; **~и́ть** [15], ⟨перевезти́⟩ [24] transport, convey; remove; ferry (over); **~ка** *f* [5; *g/pl.:* -зок] transport(ation), conveyance; **~чик** *m* [1] ferryman.
пере|вооруже́ние *n* [12] rearmament; **~вора́чивать** [1] = **~**вёртывать; **~воро́т** *m* [1] revolution; **~воспита́ние** *n* [12] reëducation; **~вра́ть** *s.* **~**вира́ть; **~вы́боры** *m/pl.* [1] reëlection.
перевыполн|е́ние *n* [12] overfulfil(l)ment (*Sov.*); **~я́ть** [28], ⟨'**~**ить⟩ [13] exceed, surpass.
перевя́з|ка *f* [5; *g/pl.:* -зок] dressing, bandage; **~очный** [14] dressing; **~ывать** [1], ⟨**~**а́ть⟩ [3] tie up; dress, bandage.
переги́б *m* [1] bend, fold; dog-ear; **~а́ть** [1], ⟨перегну́ть⟩ [20] bend; **-ся** lean over.
перегля́|дываться [1], *once* ⟨**~**нуться⟩ [19] exchange glances.
пере|гна́ть *s.* **~**гоня́ть; **~гно́й** *m* [3] humus; **~гну́ть(ся)** *s.* **~**гиба́ть(ся).
перегов|а́ривать [1], ⟨**~**ори́ть⟩ [13] talk (s. th.) over (о Т), discuss; **~о́ры** *m/pl.* [1] negotiations; ⚔ parley.
перег|о́нка *f* [5] distillation; **~оня́ть** [28], ⟨**~**на́ть⟩ [-гоню́, -го́нишь; -гна́л, -а́, -о; -е́гнанный] (out)distance, outstrip; surpass, outdo; ⚗ distil.
перегор|а́живать [1], ⟨**~**оди́ть⟩ [15 & 15 *e.*; -рожу́, -ро́ди́шь] partition (off); **~а́ть** [1], ⟨**~**е́ть⟩ [9] (*lamp*) burn out; (*fuse, etc.*) blow

(out); ~óдка f [5; g/pl.: -док] partition.
перегр|евáть [1], ‹~éть› [8; -éтый] overheat; **~ужáть** [1], ‹~узи́ть› [15 & 15 e.; -ужу́, -у́зишь], **~у́зка** f [5; g/pl.: -зок] overload; overwork; **~уппировáть** [7] pf. regroup; **~уппирóвка** f [5; g/pl.: -вок] regrouping; **~ызáть** [1], ‹~ы́зть› [24; pt. st.; -ы́зенный] gnaw through.
пéред¹, ~o (T) before, in front of.
перёд² m [1; пéреда; pl.: -дá, etc. e.] front.
перед|авáть [5], ‹~áть› [-дáм, -дáшь, etc., cf. дать; pt. пéредал, -á, -o] pass, hand (over), deliver; give (a. regards); broadcast; transmit; reproduce; render; tell; take a message (for Д, on the phone); † endorse; -ся ⚕ be communicated; **~áточный** [14] transmissive; **~áтчик** m [1] transmitter; **~áть(ся)** s. ~авáть(ся); **~áча** f [5] delivery, handing over; transfer; broadcast, (a. ⊕) transmission; gear; ⚕ communication; reproduction; package.
передв|игáть [1], ‹~и́нуть› [20] move, shift; **~ижéние** n [12] movement; transportation; **~и́жка** f [5; g/pl.: -жек], **~ижнóй** [14] travel(l)ing, mobile, itinerant.
передéл m [1] repartition; **~ка** f [5; g/pl.: -лок] alteration; recast; F mess; **~ывать**, ‹~ать› [1] recast; make over, alter.
перéдн|ий [15] front..., fore...; **~ик** m [1] apron; **~яя** f [15] hall, antechamber.
передов|и́к m [1 e.] best worker or farmer (Sov.); **~и́ца** f [5] leading article, editorial; **~óй** [14] progressive; leading, foremost; front (line); ~óй отря́д m vanguard.
пере|дóк m [1; -дкá] front; ⚔ limber; **~дохну́ть** [20] pf. take breath or rest; **~дрáзнивать** [1], ‹~дразни́ть› [13; -азню́, -áзнишь] mimic; **~дря́га** F f [5] fix, scrape; **~ду́мывать**, ‹~ду́мать› [1] change one's mind; F s. обду́мать; **~ды́шка** f [5; g/pl.: -шек] respite.
переé|зд m [1] passage; crossing; move, removal (в, на В [in]to); **~зжáть** [1], ‹~хать› [-éду, -éдешь; -езжáй] 1. v/i. cross (v/t. чéрез В); (re)move (в, на В [in]to); 2. v/t. run over.
переж|дáть s. ~идáть; **~ёвывать** [1], ‹~евáть› [7 e.; -жую́, -жуёшь] chew (well); F repeat over and over again; **~ивáние** n [12] experience; **~ивáть** [1], ‹~и́ть› [-живу́, -вёшь; пéрежил, -á, -o; пéрежитый (пéрежит, -á, -o)] experience; go through, endure; survive, outlive; **~идáть** [1], ‹~дáть› [-жду́, -ждёшь; -ждáл, -á, -o] wait (till s. th. is over); **~и́ток** m [1; -тка] survival.
перезрéлый [14] overripe.
переиз|бирáть [1], ‹~брáть› [-беру́, -рёшь; -брáл, -á, -o; -и́збранный] reëlect; **~брáние** n [12] reëlection; **~давáть** [5], ‹~дáть› [-дáм, -дáшь, etc. cf. дать; -дáл, -á, -o] republish; **~дáние** n [12] reëdition; **~дáть** s. ~давáть.
переименовáть [7] pf. rename.
переинáчи|вать F [1], ‹~ть› [16] alter, modify; distort.
перейти́ s. переходи́ть.
переки́|дывать [1], ‹~нуть› [20] throw over (чéрез В); upset; -ся exchange (v/t. T).
перeки|пáть [1], ‹~пéть› [10 e.; 3rd. p. only] boil over; **~сь** ('pe-) f [8] peroxide.
переклáд|ина f [5] crossbar, crossbeam; **~ывать** [1], ‹переложи́ть› [16] put, lay or pack (elsewhere), shift; interlay (with T); cf. перелагáть.
перекл|икáться [1], ‹~и́кнуться› [20] shout to o.a.; reëcho (v/t. с T); **~и́чка** f [5; g/pl.: -чек] roll call.
переключ|áть [1], ‹~и́ть› [16 e.; -чу́, -чи́шь; -чённый] switch over (v/i. -ся); **~éние** n [12] switching over; **~и́ть** s. ~áть.
перековáть [7 e.; -кую́, -куёшь] pf. shoe over again; fig. reëducate, remake.
перекóшенный [14] wry.
перекр|áивать [1], ‹~óить› [13; -óенный] cut again; remake.
перекрёст|ный [14] cross (fire, -examination); **~ок** m [1; -тка] crossroad(s).
перекрои́ть s. перекрáивать.
перекр|ывáть [1], ‹~ы́ть› [22] (re-)cover; exceed, surpass; **~ы́тие** n [12] covering.
перекýс|ывать [1], ‹~и́ть› [15] bite through; F take a bite.
перел|агáть [1], ‹~ожи́ть› [16] transpose; arrange.
перел|áмывать [1] 1. ‹~оми́ть› [14] break in two; overcome; 2. ‹~омáть› [1] break to pieces.
перел|езáть [1], ‹~éзть› [24 st.; -лéз] climb over (чéрез В).
перел|ёт m [1] passage (birds); ✈ flight; **~етáть** [1], ‹~етéть› [11] fly (across); pass, migrate; flit; **~ётный** [14] (bird) of passage.
перели́|в m [1] ♪ run, roulade; play (colo[u]rs); **~вáние** ⚕ n [12] transfusion; **~вáть** [1], ‹~ть› [-лью́, -льёшь, etc., cf. лить] decant, pour; ⚕ transfuse; ~вáть из пустóго в порóжнее mill the wind; -ся overflow; impf. ♪ warble, roll; (colo[u]rs) play, shimmer.
перели́ст|ывать, ‹~áть› [1] turn over (pages); look through.
перели́ть s. переливáть.

перелицева́ть [7] *pf.* turn (*clothes*).
перелож|е́ние *n* [12] transposition; arrangement; setting to music; **~и́ть** *s.* перекла́дывать & перелага́ть.
перело́м *m* [1] fracture; crisis, turning point; **~а́ть, ~и́ть** *s.* перела́мывать.
перем|а́лывать [1], ‹~оло́ть› [17; -мелю́, -ме́лешь; -меля́] grind, mill; **~ежа́ть(ся)** [1] alternate; intermit.
переме́н|а *f* [5] change; recess, break (*school*); **~и́ть(ся)** *s.* **~я́ться**; **~ный** [14] variable; ⚡ alternating; **~чивый** F [14] changeable, variable; **~я́ть** [28], ‹~и́ть› [13; -еню́, -е́нишь] change (*v/i.* **-ся**); exchange.
переме|сти́ть(ся) *s.* **~ща́ть(ся)**; **~́шивать**, ‹~ша́ть› [1] mix (up); confuse; **~ща́ть** [1], ‹~сти́ть› [15 *e.*; -ещу́, -ести́шь; -ещённый] move, shift (*v/i.* **-ся**); **~щённый** [14]: **~щённые** ли́ца *pl.* displaced persons.
переми́рие *n* [12] armistice, truce.
перемоло́ть *s.* перема́лывать.
перенаселе́ние *n* [12] overpopulation.
перенести́ *s.* переноси́ть.
перен|има́ть [1], ‹~я́ть› [-ейму́, -мёшь; пе́ренял, -а́, -о; пе́ренятый (пе́ренят, -а́, -о)] adopt, take over.
перено́с *m* [1] transfer, carrying over; sum carried over; syllabification; **~и́ть** [15], ‹перенести́› [24 -с-] transfer, carry over; bear, endure, stand; postpone, put off (till на В); **~ица** *f* [5] bridge (*of nose*).
перено́с|ка *f* [5; *g/pl.:* -сок] carrying, transport(ation); **~ный** [14] portable; figurative.
переня́ть *s.* перенима́ть.
переобору́дова|ть [7] (*im*)*pf.* reëquip; **~ние** *n* [12] reëquipment.
переод|ева́ться [1], ‹~е́ться› [-е́нусь, -нешься] change (one's clothes); **~е́тый** [14 *sh.*] *a.* disguised.
переоце́н|ивать [1], ‹~и́ть› [13; -еню́, -е́нишь] overestimate, overrate; revalue; **~ка** *f* [5; *g/pl.:* -нок] overestimation; revaluation.
пе́репел *m* [1; *pl.:* -ла́, *etc. e.*] quail.
перепеча́т|ка *f* [5; *g/pl.:* -ток] reprint; **~ывать**, ‹~ать› [1] reprint; type.
перепи́с|ка *f* [5; *g/pl.:* -сок] copying; typing; correspondence; **~чик** *m* [1] copyist; **~ывать** [1], ‹~а́ть› [3] copy; type; list; enumerate; **-ся** *impf.* correspond (with с T); **~ь** ('пе-) *f* [8] census.
перепла́|чивать [1], ‹~ти́ть› [15] overpay.
перепл|ета́ть [1], ‹~ести́› [25 -т-] bind (*book*); interlace, intertwine (*v/i.* **-ся**, ‹-сь›); **~ёт** *m* [1] binding, book cover; **~ётчик** *m* [1] bookbinder; **~ыва́ть** [1], ‹~ы́ть› [23] swim *or* sail (across че́рез В).
переполз|а́ть [1], ‹~ти́› [24] creep, crawl (over).
перепо́лн|енный [14 *sh.*] overcrowded; overflowing; **~я́ть** [28], ‹~ить› [13] overfill (*v/i.* **-ся**), cram; overcrowd.
переполо́|х *m* [1] tumult, turmoil; dismay, fright; **~ши́ть** F [16 *e.*; -шу́, -ши́шь; -шённый] *pf.* (**-ся** get) alarm(ed), perturb(ed).
перепо́нка *f* [5; *g/pl.:* -нок] membrane; web.
перепра́в|а *f* [5] crossing, passage; ford; temporary bridge; **~ля́ть** [28], ‹~ить› [14] carry (over), convey; **-ся** cross, pass.
перепрод|ава́ть [5], ‹~а́ть› [-да́м, -да́шь, *etc.*, *cf.* дать; *pt.:* -о́да́л, -ла́, -о] resell; **~а́жа** *f* [5] resale.
перепры́г|ивать [1], ‹~нуть› [20] jump (over).
перепу́г F *m* [1] fright (for с ~у); **~а́ть** [1] *pf.* (**-ся** get) frighten(ed).
перепу́тывать [1] *s.* пу́тать.
перепу́тье *n* [10] crossroad(s).
перераб|а́тывать, ‹~о́тать› [1] work (up), process; remake; **~о́тка** *f* [5; *g/pl.:* -ток] working (up), processing; remaking.
перерас|та́ть [1], ‹~ти́› [24 -ст-; -ро́с, -сла́] grow, develop; overgrow; **~хо́д** *m* [1] excess expenditure.
перерез|а́ть & **~́ывать** [1], ‹~́ать› [3] cut (through); cut off; kill.
перero|жда́ться [1], ‹~ди́ться› [15 *e.*; -ожу́сь, -оди́шься; -ождённый] regenerate; degenerate.
переруб|а́ть [1], ‹~и́ть› [14] hew *or* cut through.
переры́в *m* [1] interruption; stop, break, interval; (*lunch*) time.
переса́|дка *f* [5; *g/pl.:* -док] transplanting; grafting; 🚂 change; **~живать** [1], ‹~ди́ть› [15] transplant; graft; make change seats; **-ся**, ‹пересе́сть› [25; -ся́ду, -дешь; се́л] take another seat, change seats; change (*trains*).
пересд|ава́ть [5], ‹~а́ть› [-да́м, -да́шь, *etc.*, *cf.* дать] repeat (*exam.*).
пересе|ка́ть [1], ‹~́чь› [26; *pt.* -се́к, -секла́] cut (through, off); intersect, cross (*v/i.* **-ся**).
пересел|е́нец *m* [1; -нца] (re-) settler; **~е́ние** *n* [12] (e)migration; removal, move; **~я́ть** [28], ‹~и́ть› [13] (re)move (*v/i.* **-ся**; [e]migrate).
пересе́сть *s.* переса́живаться.
пересе|че́ние *n* [12] intersection; **~́чь** *s.* **~ка́ть**.
переси́ли|вать [1], ‹~ть› [13] overpower, master, subdue.
переска́з *m* [1] retelling; **~ывать** [1], ‹~а́ть› [3] retell.
переск|а́кивать [1], ‹~очи́ть› [16] jump (over че́рез В); skip.

переслáть *s.* пересылáть.
пересм|áтривать [1], ⟨**~отрéть**⟩ [9; -отрю́, -óтришь; -óтренный] reconsider, revise; ⚖ review; **~óтр** *m* [1] reconsideration, revision; ⚖ review.
пересо|ли́ть [13; -солю́, -óли́шь] *pf.* oversalt; **~хнуть** *s.* пересыхáть.
пересп|áшивать [1], ⟨**~осить**⟩ [15] repeat one's question.
перессóриться [13] *pf.* quarrel.
перест|авáть [5], ⟨**~áть**⟩ [-áну, -áнешь] stop, cease, quit; **~авля́ть** [28], ⟨**~áвить**⟩ [14] put (elsewhere), (*a. clock*) set, move; rearrange; transpose; convert (into на В); ⅋ permute; **~анóвка** *f* [5; *g/pl.*: -вок] shift, move; rearrangement; transposition; conversion (into на В); ⅋ permutation; **~áть** *s.* **~авáть**.
перестр|áивать [1], ⟨**~óить**⟩ [13] rebuild, reconstruct; reorganize; regroup (*v/i.* -ся; adapt o. s., change one's views); **~éливаться** [1], **~éлка** *f* [5; *g/pl.*: -лок] skirmish; **~óить** *s.* **~áивать**; **~óйка** *f* [5; *g/pl.*: -óек] rebuilding, reconstruction; reorganization.
переступ|áть [1], ⟨**~и́ть**⟩ [14] step over, cross; *fig.* transgress.
пересу́ды F *m/pl.* [1] gossip.
пересчи́т|ывать, ⟨**~áть**⟩ [1] re-count; (*a.* ⟨перечéсть⟩ [-чту́, -чтёшь; -чёл, -члá]) count (down).
перес|ылáть [1], ⟨**~лáть**⟩ [-ешлю́, -шлёшь; -éсланный] send (over), transmit; forward; **~ы́лка** *f* [5; *g/pl.*: -лок] consignment, conveyance; carriage; **~ыхáть** [1], ⟨**~óхнуть**⟩ [21] dry up; parch.
перетá|скивать [1], ⟨**~щи́ть**⟩ [16] drag *or* carry (over, across чéрез В).
перéт|ь F [12] press, push; **~я́гивать** [1], ⟨**~яну́ть**⟩ [19] draw (*fig.* win) over; outweigh; cord.
переубе|ждáть [1], ⟨**~ди́ть**⟩ [15 *e.*; *no 1st p. sg.*; -ди́шь; -еждённый] make s. o. change his mind.
переу́лок *m* [1; -лка] lane, alleyway, side street.
переутомл|éние *n* [12] overfatigue; **~ённый** [14 *sh.*] overtired.
переучёт *m* [1] inventory; stock-taking.
перехвáт|ывать [1], ⟨**~и́ть**⟩ [15] intercept; embrace; F borrow.
перехитри́ть [13] *pf.* outwit.
перехóд *m* [1] passage; crossing; ⚔ march; *fig.* transition; conversion; **~и́ть** [15], ⟨перейти́⟩ [-йду́, -дёшь; -шёл, -шлá; *cf.* идти́] cross, go over; pass (on), proceed (to); turn ([in]to); exceed, transgress; **~ный** [14] transitional; *gr.* transitive; **~я́щий** [17] challenge (*cup, etc.*).
пéрец *m* [1; -рца] pepper; paprika.
пéречень *m* [4; -чня] list; index.
пере|чёркивать [1], ⟨**~черкну́ть**⟩ [20] cross out; **~чéсть** *s.* **~считывать** & **~чи́тывать**; **~числя́ть** [28], ⟨**~чи́слить**⟩ [13] enumerate; **~чи́тывать**, ⟨**~читáть**⟩ [1] & ⟨**~чéсть**⟩ [-чту́, чтёшь; -чёл, -члá] reread; read (many, all ...); **~чить** F [16] contradict, oppose; **~шагну́ть** [20] *pf.* step over, cross; transgress; **~шéек** *m* [1; -шéйка] isthmus; **~шёптываться** [1] whisper (to one another); **~шивáть** [1], ⟨**~ши́ть**⟩ [-шью́, -шьёшь, *etc.*, *cf.* шить] make over, alter; **~щеголя́ть** F [28] *pf.* outdo.
пери́ла *n/pl.* [9] railing; banisters.
пери́на *f* [5] feather bed.
пери́од *m* [1] period; epoch, age; **~и́ческий** [16] periodic(al); ⅋ circulating.
перифери́я *f* [7] circumference, periphery; outskirts *pl.* (in на П).
перламу́тр *m* [1] mother-of-pearl.
перлóвый [14] pearl (*barley*).
перманéнт *m* [1] permanent wave.
перна́тый [14 *sh.*] feathered, feathery.
перó *n* [9; *pl.*: пéрья, -ьев] feather, plume; pen; вéчное ~ fountain pen; **~чи́нный** [14]: ~чи́нный нóж(ик) *m* penknife.
перрóн *m* [1] 🚂 platform.
перс *m* [1], **~и́дский** [16] Persian; **~ик** *m* [1] peach; **~ия́нин** *m* [1; *pl.*: -я́не, -я́н], **~ия́нка** *f* [5; *g/pl.*: -нок] Persian; **~óна** *f* [5] person; **~онáл** *m* [1] personnel; **~пекти́ва** *f* [5] perspective; *fig.* prospect, outlook.
пéрстень *m* [4; -тня] (*finger*) ring.
пéрхоть *f* [8] dandruff.
перчáтка *f* [5; *g/pl.*: -ток] glove.
пёс *m* [1; пса] dog; F cur.
пéсенка *f* [5; *g/pl.*: -нок] ditty.
песéц *m* [1; песцá] Arctic fox.
пескáрь *m* [4 *e.*] gudgeon.
песн|ь *f* [8] (*poet., eccl.*), **~я** *f* [6; *g/pl.*: -сен] song; F story.
песó|к *m* [1; -скá] sand; granulated sugar; **~чный** [14] sand(y).
пессимисти́ч|еский [16], **~ный** [14; -чен, -чна] pessimistic.
пестр|éть [8] grow (*or* appear, *a.* **~и́ть** [13]) variegated; gleam, glisten; **~óта** *f* [5] motley; gayness; **~ый** ('pɔ-) [14; пёстр, пестрá, пёстро & пестрó] variegated, parti-colo(u)red, motley (*a. fig.*); gay.
песч|áный [14] sand(y); **~и́нка** *f* [5; *g/pl.*: -нок] grain (of sand).
петли́ца *f* [5] buttonhole; tab.
пéтля *f* [6; *g/pl.*: -тель] loop (*a.*, ✈, мёртвая ~); eye; mesh; stitch; hinge.
Пётр *m* [1; Петрá] Peter.
Петру́шка [5; *g/pl.*: -шек] **1.** *m* Punch (and Judy); **2.** ♀ *f* parsley.
петý|х *m* [1 *e.*] rooster, cock; **~ши́ный** [14] cock(s)...
петь [пою́, поёшь; пéтый] **1.** ⟨с-, про-⟩ sing; **2.** ⟨про-⟩ crow.

пехо́т|а *f* [5], **~ный** [14] infantry; **~и́нец** *m* [1; -нца] infantryman.
печа́л|ить [13], ⟨о-⟩ grieve (*v/i.* **-ся**); **~ь** *f* [8] grief, sorrow; F business, concern; **~ьный** [14; -лен, -льна] sad, grieved, sorrowful.
печа́т|ать [1], ⟨на-⟩ print; type; **-ся** *impf.* be in the press; write for, appear in (в П); **~ник** *m* [1] printer; **~ный** [14] printed; printing; **~ь** *f* [8] seal, stamp (*a. fig.*); press; print, type.
печён|ка *f* [5; *g/pl.:* -нок] liver (*food*); **~ый** [14] baked.
пе́чень *f* [8] liver (*anat.*); **∠е** *n* [10] pastry; cookie, biscuit.
пе́чка *f* [5; *g/pl.:* -чек] *s.* печь[1].
печь[1] *f* [8; в -чи́; *from g/pl. e.*] stove; oven; furnace; kiln.
печь[2] [26], ⟨ис-⟩ bake; scorch (*sun*).
пе́чься [26] care (for о П).
пеш|ехо́д *m* [1] pedestrian; **∠ий** [17] unmounted; **∠ка** *f* [5; *g/pl.:* -шек] pawn (*a. fig.*); **~ко́м** on foot.
пеще́ра *f* [5] cave.
пиани́но *n* [*indecl.*] piano.
пивна́я *f* [14] alehouse, bar, saloon.
пи́во *n* [9] beer; ale; **~ва́р** *m* [1] brewer; **~ва́ренный** [14]: **~ва́ренный заво́д** *m* brewery.
пиджа́к *m* [1 *e.*] coat, jacket.
пижа́ма *f* [5] pajamas (*Brt.* py-) *pl.*
пик *m* [1] peak.
пи́ка *f* [5] pike, lance; **∠нтный** [14; -тен, -тна] piquant, spicy (*a. fig.*).
пи́ки *f/pl.* [5] spades (*cards*).
пики́ровать ✈ [7] (*im*)*pf.* dive.
пи́кнуть [20] *pf.* peep; F stir.
пил|а́ *f* [5; *pl. st.*], **~и́ть** [13; пилю́, пи́лишь] saw; **~о́т** *m* [1] pilot.
пилю́ля *f* [6] pill.
пингви́н *m* [1] penguin.
пино́к *m* [1; -нка́] kick.
пинце́т *m* [1] tweezers *pl.*
пионе́р *m* [1] pioneer (*a. member of Communist youth organization in the U.S.S.R.*); **~ский** [16] pioneer...
пир *m* [1; в -у́; *pl. e.*] feast.
пирами́да *f* [5] pyramid.
пирова́ть [7] feast, banquet.
пиро́|г *m* [1 *e.*] pie; **~жник** *m* [1] pastry cook; **~жное** *n* [14] pastry; fancy cake; **~жо́к** *m* [1; -жка́] patty.
пир|у́шка *f* [5; *g/pl.:* -шек] carousal, revel(ry); **∠шество** *n* [9] feast, banquet.
писа́|ние *n* [12] writing; (*Holy*) Scripture; **'~рь** *m* [4; *pl.:* -ря́, *etc. e.*] clerk; **~тель** *m* [4] writer, author; **~тельница** *f* [5] authoress; **~ть** [3], ⟨на-⟩ write; type(write); paint.
писк *m* [1] squeak; **~ли́вый** [14 *sh.*] squeaky; **∠нуть** *s.* пища́ть.
пистоле́т *m* [1] pistol.
писч|ебума́жный [14] stationery (*store, Brt. shop*); **∠ий** [17] note (*paper*).
пи́сьмен|ность *f* [8] literature; **~ный** [14] written; in writing; writing (*a. table*).
письмо́ *n* [9; *pl. st., gen.:* пи́сем] letter; writing (in на П); **~но́сец** *m* [1; -сца] postman, mailman.
пита́|ние *n* [12] nutrition; nourishment, food; board; ⊕ feeding; **~тельный** [14; -лен, -льна] nutritious, nourishing; **~ть** [1] nourish (*a. fig.*), feed (*a.* ⊕); cherish (*hope, etc.*), bear (*hatred, etc.,* against к Д); **-ся** feed *or* live (on T).
пито́м|ец *m* [1; -мца], **~ица** *f* [5] pupil; nursling; **~ник** *m* [1] nursery.
пить [пью, пьёшь; пил, -а́, -о; пе́й(-те)!; пи́тый (пит, -а́, -о)], ⟨вы́-⟩ drink (*pf. a.* up; to за В); have, take; **~ё** *n* [10] drink(ing); **~ево́й** [14] drinking (*water*), drinkable.
пих|а́ть F [1], ⟨**~ну́ть**⟩ [20] shove.
пи́хта *f* [5] fir.
пи́чкать F [1], ⟨на-⟩ stuff (with T).
пи́шущ|ий [17] writing; **~ая маши́нка** *f* typewriter.
пи́ща *f* [5] food; fare, board.
пища́ть [4 *e.*; -щу́, -щи́шь], ⟨за-⟩, *once* ⟨пи́скнуть⟩ [20] peep, squeak, cheep.
пище|варе́ние *n* [12] digestion; **~во́д** *m* [1] *anat.* gullet; **~во́й** [14] food(*stuffs*).
пия́вка *f* [5; *g/pl.:* -вок] leech.
пла́ва|ние *n* [12] swimming; navigation; voyage, trip; **~ть** [1] swim; float; sail, navigate.
плав|и́льный [14] melting; **~и́льня** *f* [6; *g/pl.:* -лен] foundry; **∠ить** [14], ⟨рас-⟩ smelt, fuse; **∠ка** *f* [5] fusion; **~ни́к** *m* [1 *e.*] fin.
пла́вный [14; -вен, -вна] fluent, smooth; *gr.* liquid.
плагиа́т *m* [1] plagiarism.
плака́т *m* [1] poster, placard, bill.
пла́к|ать [3] weep (for от Р; о П), cry; **-ся** F complain (of на В); **~са** F *m/f* [5] crybaby; **~си́вый** F [14 *sh.*] whining.
плам|ене́ть [8] flame; **∠енный** [14] flaming, fiery; *fig. a.* ardent; **∠я** *n* [13] flame; blaze.
план *m* [1] plan; draft; plane; пе́рвый, пере́дний (за́дний) **~** fore(back)ground (in на П).
планёр ✈ *m* [1] glider.
плане́та *f* [5] planet.
плани́ров|ать[1] [7] **1.** ⟨за-⟩ plan; **2.** ⟨с-⟩ ✈ glide; **~а́ть**[2], ⟨рас-⟩ level; **∠ка** *f* [5; *g/pl.:* -вок] planning; level(l)ing.
пла́нка *f* [5; *g/pl.:* -нок] lath.
плано|вый [14] planned; plan(-ning); **~ме́рный** [14; -рен, -рна] systematic, planned.
планта́тор *m* [1] planter.
пласт *m* [1 *e.*] layer, stratum; **∠ика** *f* [5] plastic arts *pl.*; plastic figure; **~и́нка** *f* [5; *g/pl.:* -нок] plate; (*gramophone*) record; **~ма́сса** *f* [5] plastic; **∠ырь** *m* [4] plaster.

плáт|а *f* [5] pay(ment); fee; wages *pl.*; fare; rent; **~ёж** *m* [1 *e.*] payment; **~ёжеспосóбный** [14; -бен, -бна] solvent; **~ёжный** [14] of payment; **~éльщик** *m* [1] payer; **~ина** *f* [5] platinum; **~и́ть** [15], ⟨за-, у-⟩ pay (in T; for за B); settle (*account* по Д); **-ся**, ⟨по-⟩ *fig.* pay (with T); **~ный** [14] paid; to be paid for.

платóк *m* [1; -тка́] (hand)kerchief.

платфóрма *f* [5] platform.

плáт|ье *n* [10; *g/pl.*: -ьев] dress, gown; **~янóй** [14] clothes...

плáха *f* [5] block.

плац|дáрм *m* [1] base; bridgehead; **~кáрта** *f* [5] reserved seat (ticket).

пла|ч *m* [1] weeping; **~чéвный** [14; -вен, -вна] deplorable, pitiable, lamentable; plaintive; **~шмя́** flat.

плащ *m* [1 *e.*] raincoat; cloak.

плебисци́т *m* [1] plebiscite.

плевá *f* [5] membrane; pleura.

плевáт|ельница *f* [5] cuspidor, spittoon; **~ь** [6 *e.*; плюю́, плюёшь], *once* ⟨плю́нуть⟩ [20] spit (out); F not care (for на B).

плéвел *m* [1] weed.

плевóк *m* [1; -вка́] spit(tle).

плеври́т *m* [1] pleurisy.

плед *m* [1] plaid, travel(l)ing rug.

плем|еннóй [14] tribal; brood..., stud...; **∠я** *n* [13] tribe; race; family; generation; breed; F brood.

племя́нни|к *m* [1] nephew; **~ца** *f* [5] niece.

плен *m* [1; в -у́] captivity; взять (попáсть) в ~ (be) take(n) prisoner; **~áрный** [14] plenary; **~и́тельный** [14; -лен, -льна] captivating, fascinating; **~и́ть(ся)** *s.* **~я́ть(ся)**.

плён|ка *f* [5; *g/pl.*: -нок] film; pellicle.

плéн|ник *m* [1], **~ный** *m* [14] captive, prisoner; **~я́ть** [28], ⟨**~и́ть**⟩ [13] (**-ся** be) captivate(d).

плéнум *m* [1] plenary session.

плéсень *f* [8] mo(u)ld.

плеск *m* [1], **~áть** [3], *once* ⟨плеснýть⟩ [20], **-ся** *impf.* splash.

плéсневеть [8], ⟨за-⟩ get mo(u)ldy.

пле|сти́ [25 -т-: плетý], ⟨с-, за-⟩ braid, plait; weave; spin; F twaddle; lie; **-сь** F drag, lag; **~тёный** [14] wicker...; **~тéнь** *m* [4; -тня́] wicker fence.

плётка *f* [5; *g/pl.*: -ток], **плеть** *f* [8; *from g/pl. e.*] lash, scourge.

плеч|ó *n* [9; *pl.*: плéчи, плеч, -чáм] shoulder; back; ⊕ arm; с ~ долóй F be rid of s. th.; с(о всегó) **~á** with all one's might; straight from the shoulder; (И) не по **~ý** (Д) not be equal to a th.; на **~ó!** shoulder arms!; прáвое **~ó** вперёд! ⚔ left turn (*Brt.* wheel)!; *cf. a.* горá F.

плеш|и́вый [14 *sh.*] bald; **~ь** *f* [8] bald patch.

плит|á *f* [5; *pl. st.*] slab, (flag-, *grave-*) stone; plate; (*kitchen*) range; (*gas*) stove; **∠ка** *f* [5; *g/pl.*: -ток] tablet, cake, bar; hot plate.

плов|éц *m* [1; -вца́] swimmer; **~ýчий** [17] floating (*dock*); **~ýчий** маяк *m* lightship; *s. a.* льди́на.

плод *m* [1 *e.*] fruit; **~и́ть** [15 *e.*; пложý, -ди́шь], ⟨рас-⟩ propagate, multiply (*v/i.* **-ся**); **~ови́тый** [14 *sh.*] fruitful, prolific; **~овóдство** *n* [9] fruit growing; **~óвый** [14] fruit...; **~онóсный** [14; -сен, -сна] fructiferous; **~орóдие** *n* [12] fertility; **~орóдный** [14; -ден, -дна] fertile, fruitful, fecund; **~отвóрный** [14; -рен, -рна] fruitful, productive; profitable; favo(u)rable.

плóмб|а *f* [5] (lead) seal; (*tooth*) filling; **~ировáть** [7], ⟨о-⟩ seal; ⟨за-⟩ fill, stop.

плóск|ий [16; -сок, -скá, -о; *comp.*: плóще] flat (*a. fig.* = stale, trite), plain, level; **~огóрье** *n* [10] plateau, tableland; **~огýбцы** *pl.* [1] pliers; **~ость** *f* [8; *from g/pl. e.*] flatness; plane; level (on в П); angle (under в П); platitude.

плот *m* [1 *e.*] raft; **~и́на** *f* [5] dam, dike; **∠ник** *m* [1] carpenter.

плóтн|ость *f* [8] density; solidity; **~ый** [14; -тен, -тнá, -о] compact, solid; dense; close, thick; thickset.

плот|оя́дный [14; -ден, -дна] carnivorous; **∠ский** [16] carnal, fleshly; **~ь** *f* [8] flesh.

плох|óй [16; плох, -á, -о] bad; **∠о** bad(ly); bad, F (*mark*; *cf.* двóйка & едини́ца).

плошáть F [1], ⟨с-⟩ blunder.

площáд|ка *f* [5; *g/pl.*: -док] ground; playground; (*tennis*) court; platform; landing; **~нóй** [14] vulgar; **'~ь** *f* [8; *from g/pl. e.*] square; area (*a.* ⅄); (*living*) space, *s.* жилплóщадь.

плуг *m* [1; *pl. e.*] plow, *Brt.* plough.

плут *m* [1 *e.*] rogue; trickster, cheat; **~áть** F [1] stray; **~овáть** [7], ⟨с-⟩ trick, cheat; **~овскóй** [16] roguish; rogue...; **~овствó** *n* [9] roguery.

плыть [23] (be) swim(ming); float (-ing), sail(ing); *cf.* плáвать.

плюгáвый F [14 *sh.*] shabby.

плю́нуть *s.* плевáть.

плюс (*su. m* [1]) plus; F advantage.

плюш *m* [1] plush.

плющ *m* [1 *e.*] ivy.

пляж *m* [1] beach.

пляс|áть [3], ⟨с-⟩ dance; **∠ка** *f* [5; *g/pl.*: -сок] (folk) dance; dancing; **~овóй** [14] dance..., dancing.

пневмати́ческий [16] pneumatic.

по **1.** (Д) on, along; through; all over; in; by; according to, after; through; owing to; for; over; across; upon; each, at a time (*2, 3, 4 with* B: пó два); **2.** (B) to, up to; till, through; for; **3.** (П) (up)on; ~ мне

for all I care; ~ часу в день an hour a day.
по- (in *compds.*): *cf.* русский; ваш.
побаиваться [1] be (a little) afraid of (P).
побе́г *m* [1] escape, flight; ♀ shoot, sprout; **~у́шки**: быть на ~у́шках F run errands (for у P).
побе́|да *f* [5] victory; **~ди́тель** *m* [4] victor; winner; **~ди́ть** *s.* ~жда́ть; **~дный** [14], **~доно́сный** [14; -сен, -сна] victorious; **~жда́ть** [1], ⟨~ди́ть⟩ [15 *e.*; *1st p. sg. not used*; -ди́шь; -еждённый] be victorious (over B), win (a victory), conquer, vanquish, defeat; overcome; beat.
побере́жье *n* [10] shore, coast.
побла́жка F *f* [5; *g/pl.*: -жек] indulgence.
побли́зости close by; (от P) near.
побо́и *m/pl.* [3] beating; **~ще** *n* [11] (great) battle.
побо́р|ник *m* [1] advocate; **~о́ть** [17] *pf.* conquer; overcome; beat.
побо́чный [14] accessory, incidental, casual; secondary; subsidiary; by-(*product*); illegitimate.
побу|ди́тельный [14]: **~ди́тельная причи́на** *f* motive; **~жда́ть** [1], ⟨~ди́ть⟩ [15 *e.*; -ужу́, -уди́шь; -уждённый] induce, prompt, impel; **~жде́ние** *n* [12] motive, impulse, incentive.
побы́вка F *f* [5; *g/pl.*: -вок] stay, visit (for, on на B [*or* П]).
пова́д|иться F [15] *pf.* fall into the habit (of [visiting] *inf.*); **~ка** *f* [5; *g/pl.*: -док] F habit; P encouragement.
пова́льный [14] epidemic; general.
по́вар *m* [1; *pl.*: -ра́, *etc. e.*] cook; **~енный** [14] culinary; cook(*book*, *Brt.* cookery book); kitchen (*salt*); **~и́ха** *f* [5] cook.
пове|де́ние *n* [12] behavio(u)r, conduct; **~лева́ть** [1] (T) rule; ⟨~ле́ть⟩ [9] (Д) order; command; **~ли́тельный** [14; -лен, -льна] imperative (*a. gr.*).
поверг|а́ть [1], ⟨~нуть⟩ [21] throw *or* cast (down); put into (в B).
пове́р|енный [14] confidant; plenipotentiary; chargé (d'affaires в дела́х); **~ить** *s.* ~я́ть & ве́рить; **~ка** *f* [5; *g/pl.*: -рок] check(up); roll call; **~ну́ть(ся)** *s.* повора́чивать (-ся).
пове́рх (P) over, above; **~ностный** [14; -тен, -тна] superficial; surface...; **~ность** *f* [8] surface.
пове́р|ье *n* [10] legend, popular belief; **~я́ть** [28], ⟨~ить⟩ [13] entrust, confide (to Д); check (up).
пове́с|а F *m* [5] scapegrace; **~ить** (-ся) *s.* ве́шать(ся); **~ничать** F [1] romp, play pranks.
повествова́|ние *n* [12] narration, narrative; **~тель** *m* [4] narrator; **~тельный** [14] narrative; **~тельное предложе́ние** *n gr.* statement; **~ть** [7] narrate (*v/t.* о П).
пове́ст|ка *f* [5; *g/pl.*: -ток] summons; notice; **~ка дня** agenda; **'~ь** *f* [8; *from g/pl. e.*] story, tale; narrative.
пове́шение *n* [12] hanging.
по-ви́димому apparently.
пови́дло *n* [9] jam, fruit butter.
пови́н|ность *f* [8] duty; **~ный** [14; -и́нен, -и́нна] guilty; owing; **~ная** *f* confession; **~ова́ться** [7] (*pt. a. pf.*) (Д) obey; submit (to); **~ове́ние** *n* [12] obedience.
по́вод *m* **1.** [1] cause; occasion (on по Д); по ~у (P) *a.* concerning; **2.** [1; в -ду́; *pl.*: -о́дья, -о́дьев] rein; на ~у́ (у P) in (s.b.'s) leading strings.
пово́зка *f* [5; *g/pl.*: -зок] cart; wag(g)on.
Пово́лжье *n* [10] Volga region.
повор|а́чивать [1], ⟨поверну́ть⟩ [20], F ⟨~оти́ть⟩ [15] turn (*v/i.* -ся; ~а́чивайся! come on!); **~о́т** *m* [1] turn; **~о́тливый** [14 *sh.*] nimble, agile; **~о́тный** [14] turning.
повре|жда́ть [1], ⟨~ди́ть⟩ [15 *e.*; -ежу́, -еди́шь; -еждённый] damage; injure, hurt; spoil; **~жде́ние** *n* [12] damage; injury.
поврем|ени́ть F [13] *pf.* wait a little; **~е́нный** [14] periodical; time...
повсе|дне́вный [14; -вен, -вна] everyday, daily; **~ме́стный** [14; -тен, -тна] general, universal; **~ме́стно** everywhere.
повста́н|ец *m* [1; -нца] rebel, insurgent; **~ческий** [16] rebel(lious).
повсю́ду everywhere.
повтор|е́ние *n* [12] repetition; review; **~и́тельный** [14] repetitive; **~ный** [14] repeated, second; **~я́ть** [28], ⟨~и́ть⟩ [13] repeat (o.s. -ся); review (*lessons, etc.*).
повы|ша́ть [1], ⟨~сить⟩ [15] raise; promote; **-ся** rise; advance; **~ше́ние** *n* [12] rise; promotion; **~шенный** [14] increased, higher.
повя́з|ка *f* [5; *g/pl.*: -зок] bandage; band, armlet; **~ывать** [1], ⟨~а́ть⟩ [3] bind (up); put on.
пога|ша́ть [1], ⟨~си́ть⟩ [15] put out, extinguish; discharge (*debt*).
погиб|а́ть [1], ⟨~нуть⟩ [21] perish; **~ель** † *s.* ги́бель; **~ший** [17] lost.
погло|ща́ть [1], ⟨~ти́ть⟩ [15; -ощу́; -ощённый] swallow up, devour; absorb; **~ще́ние** *n* [12] absorption.
погля́дывать [1] look (F *a.* after).
погов|а́ривать [1] speak; say; **~о́рка** [5; *g/pl.*: -рок] saying, proverb.
пого́|да *f* [5] weather (in в B, при П); **~ди́ть** F [15 *e.*; -гожу́, -годи́шь] *pf.* wait; **~дя́** later; **~ло́вный** [14] general, universal; **~ло́в-**

но without exception; **~ло́вье** *n* [10] livestock.
пого́н *m* [1] epaulet, shoulder strap; **~щик** *m* [1] drover; **~я** *f* [6] pursuit (of за Т); pursuers *pl.*; **~я́ть** [28] drive *or* urge (on), hurry (up).
пого|ре́лец *m* [1; -льца] burnt down p.; **∠ст** [1] churchyard.
пограни́чн|ый [14] frontier...; **~ик** *m* [1] frontier guard.
по́гре|б *m* [1; *pl.*: -бá, *etc. e.*] cellar; (*powder*) magazine; **~ба́льный** [14] funeral; **~ба́ть** [1], ⟨~сти́⟩ [24 -б-: -бу́] bury, inter; **~бе́ние** *n* [12] burial; funeral; **~му́шка** *f* [5; *g/pl.*: -шек] rattle; **∠шность** *f* [8] error, fault.
погру|жа́ть [1], ⟨~зи́ть⟩ [15 & 15 *e.*; -ужу́, -у́зишь; -у́женный & -ужённый] immerse; sink, plunge, submerge (*v/i.* **-ся**); ~жённый *a.* absorbed, lost (in в В); load, ship; **~же́ние** *n* [12] immersion; **∠зка** [5; *g/pl.*: -зок] loading, shipment.
погряз|а́ть [1], ⟨∠нуть⟩ [21] sink.
под[1], **~о** 1. (В): (*direction*) under; toward(s), to; (*age, time*) about; on the eve of; à la, in imitation of; for, suitable as; 2. (Т): (*position*) under, below, beneath; near, by, (*battle*) of; (used) for, with; по́ле ~ ро́жью rye field; **~**[2] *m* [1; на -у́] hearth, floor.
подава́льщица *f* [5] waitress.
пода|ва́ть [5], ⟨∠ть⟩ [-да́м, -да́шь, *etc., cf.* дать] give; serve (*a. sport*); drive up, get ready; move (in); hand (*or* send) in; lodge (*complaint*), bring (*action*); set (*example*); render; raise (*voice*); не ~ва́ть ви́ду *s.* пока́зывать; **-ся** move; yield.
подав|и́ть *s.* ~ля́ть; **~и́ться** *pf.* choke, suffocate; **~ле́ние** *n* [12] suppression; **~ля́ть** [28], ⟨~и́ть⟩ [14] suppress; repress; depress; crush; ~ля́ющий *a.* overwhelming.
пода́вно F so much *or* all the more.
пода́гра *f* [5] gout; podagra.
пода́льше F rather far off.
пода́|рок *m* [1; -рка] present, gift; **~тель** *m* [4] bearer; petitioner; **~тливый** [14 *sh.*] (com)pliant; **′~ть** *f* [8; *from g/pl. e.*] tax; **~ть(ся)** *s.* ~ва́ть(ся); **~ча** *f* [5] giving; serving; serve; presentation; rendering; supply; ~ча го́лоса voting; **~чка** *f* [5; *g/pl.*: -чек] charity, gift; **~я́ние** *n* [12] alms.
подбе|га́ть [1], ⟨~жа́ть⟩ [4; -бегу́, -бежи́шь, -бегу́т] run up (to к Д).
подби|ва́ть [1], ⟨∠ть⟩ [подобью́, -бьёшь, *etc., cf.* бить] line, fur; (re)sole; hit, injure; F instigate, incite; ∠тый F black (*eye*).
под|бира́ть [1], ⟨~обра́ть⟩ [подберу́, -рёшь; подобра́л, -á, -o; подо́бранный] pick up; tuck up; draw in; pick out, select; **-ся** sneak up (to к Д); **~би́ть** *s.* ~бива́ть; **~бо́р** *m* [1] picking up *or* out; selection; assortment; на ~бо́р chosen, select.
подборо́док *m* [1; -дка] chin.
подбр|а́сывать [1], ⟨~о́сить⟩ [15] throw (up); jolt; add; foist, palm (on Д).
подва́л *m* [1] basement; cellar.
подвезти́ *s.* подвози́ть.
подвер|га́ть [1], ⟨∠гнуть⟩ [21] subject, expose; **-ся** undergo; be exposed; run (*risk*); **∠женный** [14 *sh.*] subject; **~же́ние** *n* [12] subjection.
подве́с|ить *s.* подве́шивать; **~но́й** [14] hanging (*lamp*); ⊕ suspension.
подвести́ *s.* подводи́ть.
подве́тренный [14] leeward.
подве́|шивать [1], ⟨~сить⟩ [15] hang (under; on); fix.
по́двиг *m* [1] feat, exploit, deed.
подви|га́ть [1], ⟨∠нуть⟩ [20] move (*v/i.* **-ся**; advance, get on); push (on, ahead); **~жно́й** [14] mobile; movable; nimble; 🚂 rolling (*stock*); **∠жность** *f* [8] mobility; agility; **~за́ться** [1] be active; **∠нуть(ся)** *s.* ~га́ть(ся).
подв|ла́стный [14; -тен, -тна] subject; **~о́да** *f* [5] cart; wag(g)on.
подводи́ть [15], ⟨подвести́⟩ [25] lead ([up] to); bring, get; lay; build; make (up); F let a p. down.
подво́дн|ый [14] submarine ~ая ло́дка *f* submarine; ~ый ка́мень *m* reef.
подво́з *m* [1] supplies *pl.*; **~и́ть** [15], ⟨подвезти́⟩ [24] bring, get; give a p. a lift.
подвы́пивший F [17] tipsy, drunk.
подвя́з|ка *f* [5; *g/pl.*: -зок] garter; **~ывать** [1], ⟨~а́ть⟩ [3] tie (up).
под|гиба́ть [1], ⟨~огну́ть⟩ [20] tuck (under); bend; **-ся** fail.
подгля́д|ывать [1], ⟨~е́ть⟩ [11] peep, spy.
подгов|а́ривать [1], ⟨~ори́ть⟩ [13] instigate, talk a p. into.
под|гоня́ть [28], ⟨~огна́ть⟩ [подгоню́, -го́нишь; *cf.* гнать] drive *or* urge on, hurry (up); fit, adapt.
подгор|а́ть [1], ⟨~е́ть⟩ [9] burn.
подготов|и́тельный [14] preparatory; **∠ка** *f* [5; *g/pl.*: -вок] preparation (for к Д); training; ⚔ drill; **~ля́ть** [28], ⟨∠ить⟩[14] prepare.
подда|ва́ться [5], ⟨∠ться⟩ [-да́мся, -да́шься, *etc., cf.* дать] yield; не ~ва́ться (Д) defy (*description*).
подда́к|ивать F [1], ⟨~нуть⟩ [20] say yes (to everything), consent.
по́дда|нный *m* [14] subject; **~нство** *n* [9] nationality, citizenship; **∠ться** *s.* ~ва́ться.
подде́л|ка *f* [5; *g/pl.*: -лок] forgery, counterfeit; **~ывать**, ⟨~ать⟩ [1] forge; **~ьный** [14] counterfeit...; sham...
подде́рж|ивать [1], ⟨~а́ть⟩ [4] support; back up; uphold; maintain;

~ка *f* [5; *g/pl.*: -жек] support; approval.
поде́л|ать F [1] *pf.* do; ничего́ не ~аешь there's nothing to be done; *cf. a.* де́лать F; **~о́м** F rightly; ~о́м ему́ it serves him right; **~ывать** F [1]: что (вы) ~ываете? what are you doing (now)?
подёржанный [14] second-hand; worn, used.
поджа́р|ивать [1], ‹~ить› [13] roast, brown; toast; **~ый** [14 *sh.*] lean.
поджа́ть *s.* поджима́ть.
под|же́чь *s.* ~жига́ть; **~жига́тель** *m* [4] incendiary; **~жига́ть** [1], ‹~же́чь› [26; подожгу́, -жжёшь; поджёг, подожгла́; подожжённый] set on fire (*or* fire to).
под|жида́ть [1], ‹~ожда́ть› [-ду́, -дёшь; -а́л, -а́, -о] wait (for P, B).
под|жима́ть [1], ‹~жа́ть› [подожму́, -мёшь; поджа́тый] cross (*legs* under под B); purse (*lips*); draw in (*tail*).
поджо́г *m* [1] arson; burning.
подзаголо́вок *m* [1; -вка] subtitle.
подзадо́р|ивать F [1], ‹~ить› [13] instigate, incite (to на B).
подза|ты́льник *m* [1] cuff on the nape; **~щи́тный** *m* [14] ⚖ client.
подзем|е́лье *n* [10] (underground) vault, cave; dungeon; **∠ный** [14] underground, subterranean; *cf.* метро́.
подзо́рная [14]: ~ труба́ *f* spyglass.
под|зыва́ть [1], ‹~озва́ть› [подзову́, -ёшь; подозва́л, -а́, -о; подо́званный] call, beckon; **~и́** P come (,now); go; try; I suppose.
под|ка́пываться [1], ‹~копа́ться› undermine (*v/t.* под B); **~карау́ливать** F [1], ‹~карау́лить› [13] *s.* подстерега́ть; **~ка́рмливать** [1], ‹~корми́ть› [14] feed, fatten; **~ка́тывать** [1], ‹~кати́ть› [15] roll *or* drive up (under); **~ка́шиваться** [1], ‹~коси́ться› [15] fail.
подки́|дывать [1], ‹~нуть› [20] *s.* подбра́сывать; **~дыш** *m* [1] foundling.
подкла́д|ка *f* [5; *g/pl.*: -док] lining; ⊕ support; **~ывать** [1], ‹подложи́ть› [16] lay (under); add; enclose; foist (on Д).
подкле́|ивать [1], ‹~ить› [13] glue, paste (under).
подко́в|а *f* [5] horseshoe; **~ывать** [1], ‹~а́ть› [7 *e.*; -кую́, -куёшь] shoe; **~анный** *a.* versed.
подко́жный [14] hypodermic.
подко́п *m* [1] sap, mine; **~а́ться** *s.* подка́пываться.
подкоси́ться *s.* подка́шиваться.
подкра́|дываться [1], ‹~сться› [25] steal *or* sneak up (to к Д); **~шивать** [1], ‹~сить› [15] touch up; make up.
подкреп|ля́ть [28], ‹~и́ть› [14 *e.*; -плю́, -пи́шь; -плённый] reinforce, fortify; corroborate; refresh; **~ле́ние** *n* [12] reinforcement; corroboration; refreshment.
по́дкуп *m* [1] bribery; **~а́ть** [1], ‹~и́ть› [14] bribe; win, prepossess; **~но́й** [14] corrupt.
подла́|живаться F [1], ‹~диться› [15] adapt o. s.; make up to.
по́дле (P) beside, by (the side of); nearby.
подлеж|а́ть [4 *e.*; -жу́, -жи́шь] be subject to; be to be; (И) не ~и́т (Д) there can be no (*doubt* about); **~а́щий** [17] subject (to Д); ...able; **~а́щее** *n gr.* subject.
подле|за́ть [1], ‹∠зть› [24 *st.*] creep (under; up); **~та́ть** [1], ‹~те́ть› [11] fly (up).
подле́ц *m* [1 *e.*] scoundrel, rascal.
подли|ва́ть [1], ‹∠ть› [подолью́, -льёшь; подле́й!; по́длил, -а́, -о; по́дли́тый (-ли́т, -а́, -о)] pour, add; **∠вка** *f* [5; *g/pl.*: -вок] gravy; sauce.
подли́з|а *m/f* [5] toady; **~ываться** F [1], ‹~а́ться› [3] flatter, insinuate o. s. (with к Д).
по́длинн|ик *m* [1] original; **~ый** [14; -инен, -инна] original; authentic, genuine; true; pure.
подли́ть *s.* подлива́ть.
по́дличать F [1], ‹с-› act meanly.
подло́|г *m* [1] forgery; **~жи́ть** *s.* подкла́дывать; **~жный** [14; -жен, -жна] spurious, false.
по́дл|ость *f* [8] meanness; low act; **~ый** [14; подл, -а́, -о] mean, base, low.
подма́з|ывать [1], ‹~ать› [3] grease (*a.*, F, *fig.*), smear; F make up; **-ся** F insinuate o. s. (with к Д).
подма́н|ивать [1], ‹~и́ть› [13; -аню́, -а́нишь] beckon.
подмасте́рье *m* [10; *g/pl.*: -ьев] journeyman.
подме́н|а *f* [5] substitution, exchange; **~ивать** [1], ‹~и́ть› [13; -еню́, -е́нишь] substitute (s.th./for T/B) (ex)change.
подме|та́ть [1], ‹~сти́› [25 -т-: -мету́] sweep; **∠тить** *s.* подмеча́ть.
подмётка *f* [5; *g/pl.*: -ток] sole.
подме|ча́ть [1], ‹∠тить› [15] notice, observe, perceive.
подме́ш|ивать, ‹~а́ть› [1] mix (s. th. with s. th. P/в B), adulterate.
подми́г|ивать [1], ‹~ну́ть› [20] wink (at Д).
подмо́га F *f* [5] help, assistance.
подмок|а́ть [1], ‹∠нуть› get wet.
подмо́стки *m/pl.* [1] scaffold; stage.
подмо́ченный [14] wet; F stained.
подмы|ва́ть [1], ‹∠ть› [22] wash (*a.* out, away); F press.
подне|бе́сье *n* [10] firmament; **~во́льный** [14; -лен, -льна] dependent; forced; **~сти́** *s.* подноси́ть.
поднима́ть [1], ‹подня́ть› [-ниму́, -ни́мешь; по́днял, -а́, -о; по́дня-

тый (-нят, -á, -о)] lift; pick up (from с Р); elevate; set (up; off); take up (*arms*); hoist (*flag*); weigh (*anchor*); set (*sail*); give (*alarm*); make (*noise*); scare (*game*); plow (*Brt.* plough) up; ~ нос assume airs; ~ нá ноги alarm; ~ нá смех ridicule; -ся [*pt.*: -ня́лся́, -ла́сь] (с Р from) rise; arise; go up (*stairs* по Д); climb (*hill* на В); set out; get agitated.
подного́тная F *f* [14] ins & outs *pl.*
подно́ж|ие *n* [12] foot, bottom (at у Р); pedestal; **~ка** *f* [5; *g/pl.*: -жек] footboard; *mot.* running board; trip; **~ный** [14] green (*fodder*).
подно́|с *m* [1] tray; **~си́ть** [15], ⟨поднести́⟩ [24 -с-] bring, carry; offer, present (Д); **~ше́ние** *n* [12] gift.
подня́т|ие *n* [12] raise, raising; rise; elevation, *etc.*, *cf.* поднима́ть(ся); **~ь(ся)** *s.* поднима́ть(ся).
подоб|а́ть: ~ает it becomes; ought; **∠ие** *n* [12] resemblance; image (*a. eccl.*); ⅍ similarity; **∠ный** [14; -бен, -бна] similar (to Д); such; и тому́ ∠ное and the like; ничего́ ∠ного nothing of the kind; **~острáстный** [14; -тен, -тна] servile.
подо|бра́ть(ся) *s.* подбира́ть(ся); **~гна́ть** *s.* подгоня́ть; **~гну́ть(ся)** *s.* подгиба́ть(ся); **~грева́ть** [1], ⟨~гре́ть⟩ [8; -е́тый] warm up; **~двига́ть** [1], ⟨~дви́нуть⟩ [20] move ([up] to к Д) (*v/i.* -ся; draw near); **~жда́ть** *s.* поджида́ть & ждать; **~зва́ть** *s.* подзыва́ть.
подозр|ева́ть [1], ⟨заподо́зрить⟩ [13] suspect (of в П); **~е́ние** *n* [12] suspicion; **~и́тельный** [14; -лен, -льна] suspicious.
подойти́ *s.* подходи́ть.
подоко́нник *m* [1] window sill.
подо́л *m* [1] lap, hem.
подо́лгу (for a) long (time).
подо́нки *m/pl.* [1] dregs (*a. fig.*).
подо́пытный [14] test...
подорва́ть *s.* подрыва́ть.
подоро́жн|ая *f* [14] *hist.* post-horse order; **~ик** *m* [1] plantain, ribwort.
подо|сла́ть *s.* подсыла́ть; **~спе́ть** [8] *pf.* come (in time); **~стла́ть** *s.* подстила́ть.
подотде́л *m* [1] sub-division.
подотчётный [14; -тен, -тна] accountable.
подохо́дный [14] income (*tax*).
подо́шва *f* [5] sole; foot, bottom.
подпа|да́ть [1], ⟨∠сть⟩ [25; *pt. st.*] fall (under); **∠ивать** F [1], ⟨подпои́ть⟩ [13] make drunk; **~ли́ть** [13] *pf.* F = подже́чь; singe; **∠сок** *m* [1; -ска] shepherd boy; **∠сть** *s.* ~да́ть.
подпева́ть [1] *s.* вто́рить.
подпира́ть [1], ⟨подпере́ть⟩ [12; подопру́, -прёшь] support, prop.
подпис|а́ть(ся) *s.* ∠ывать(ся); **∠ка** *f* [5; *g/pl.*: -сок] subscription (to; for на В); pledge (take дать); **~но́й** [14] subscription...; **∠чик** *m* [1] subscriber; **∠ывать(ся)** [1], ⟨~а́ть (-ся)⟩ [3] sign; subscribe (to; for на В); **'~ь** *f* [8] signature (for на В); за '~ью (Р) signed by.
подплы|ва́ть [1], ⟨∠ть⟩ [23] swim (under *or* up [to к Д]).
подпо|и́ть *s.* подпа́ивать; **~лза́ть** [1], ⟨~лзти́⟩ [24] creep *or* crawl (under *or* up [to к Д]); **~лко́вник** *m* [1] lieutenant colonel; **∠лье** *n* [10; *g/pl.*: -ьев], **∠льный** [14] underground; **∠р(к)а** *f* [5 (*g/pl.*: -рок)] prop; **∠чва** *f* [5] subsoil; **~я́сывать** [1], ⟨~я́сать⟩ [3] gird.
подпр|у́га *f* [5] girth; **~ы́гивать** [1], *once* ⟨~ы́гнуть⟩ [20] jump up.
подпус|ка́ть [1], ⟨~ти́ть⟩ [15] allow to approach; admit; F add.
подр|а́внивать [1], ⟨~овня́ть⟩ [28] straighten; level; clip.
подража́|ние *n* [12] imitation (in /of в В/Д); **~тель** *m* [4] imitator (of Д); **~ть** [1] imitate, copy (*v/t.* Д); counterfeit.
подраздел|е́ние *n* [12] subdivision; ⚔ unit; **~я́ть** [28], ⟨~и́ть⟩ [13] (-ся be) subdivide(d) (into на В).
подра|зумева́ть [1] mean (by под Т), imply; -ся be implied; ✝ be understood; **~ста́ть** [1], ⟨~сти́⟩ [24 -ст-; -ро́с, -ла́] grow (up); rise.
подрез|а́ть & **∠ывать** [1], ⟨∠ать⟩ [3] cut; crop, clip.
подро́бн|ость *f* [8] detail; **~ый** [14; -бен, -бна] detailed, full-length; **~о** in detail, in full.
подровня́ть *s.* подра́внивать.
подро́сток *m* [1; -стка] teenager; youth, juvenile.
подруб|а́ть [1], ⟨~и́ть⟩ [14] cut; hem.
подру́га [5] (girl) friend; playmate.
по-дру́жески (in a) friendly (way).
подружи́ться [16 *e.*; -жу́сь, -жи́шься] *pf.* make friends (with с Т).
подрумя́нить [13] *pf.* redden.
подру́чный [14] assistant; helper.
подры́|в *m* [1] undermining; blowing up; **~ва́ть** [1] **1.** ⟨~ть⟩ [22] sap, undermine; **2.** ⟨подорва́ть⟩ [-рву́, -рвёшь; -рва́л, -á, -о; подо́рванный] blow up, blast, spring; *fig.* undermine; **~вно́й** [14] blasting, explosive; subversive.
подря́д **1.** *adv.* successive(ly), running; one after another; **2.** *m* [1] contract; **~чик** *m* [1] contractor.
подс|а́живать [1], ⟨~ади́ть⟩ [15] help; plant; -ся, ⟨~е́сть⟩ [25; -ся́ду, -ся́дешь; -се́л] sit down (by к Д).
подсве́чник *m* [1] candlestick.
подсе́сть *s.* подса́живаться.
подска́з|ывать [1], ⟨~а́ть⟩ [3] prompt; **~ка** F *f* [5] prompting.
подскак|а́ть [3] *pf.* gallop (up to к Д); **∠ивать** [1], ⟨подскочи́ть⟩ [16] run ([up] to к Д); jump up.

под|сла́щивать [1], ⟨**~сласти́ть**⟩ [15 *e.*; -ащу́, -асти́шь; -ащённый] sweeten; **~сле́дственный** *m* [14] (prisoner) on trial; **~слепова́тый** [14 *sh.*] weak-sighted; **~слу́шивать**, ⟨**~слу́шать**⟩ [1] eavesdrop, overhear; **~сма́тривать** [1], ⟨**~смотре́ть**⟩ [9; -отрю́, -о́тришь] spy, peep; **~сме́иваться** [1] laugh (at над Т); **~смотре́ть** *s.* **~сма́тривать.**

подсне́жник *m* [1] snowdrop.

подсо́|бный [14] subsidiary, by-..., side..., subordinate; **~вывать** [1], ⟨**подсу́нуть**⟩ [20] push, shove; present; F palm ([off] on Д); **~зна́тельный** [14; -лен, -льна] subconscious; **~лнечник** *m* [1] sunflower; **~хнуть** *s.* подсыха́ть.

подспо́рье F *n* [10] help, support.

подста́в|ить *s.* **~ля́ть**; **~ка** *f* [5; *g/pl.*: -вок] support, prop, stay; stand; saucer; **~ля́ть** [28], ⟨**~ить**⟩ [14] put, place, set (under под В); move up (to [к] Д); expose; ⚗ substitute; **~ля́ть но́гу** *or* **но́жку** (Д) trip (a p.) up; **~но́й** [14] false, straw...; **~но́е лицо́** *n* dummy.

подстан|о́вка ⚗ *f* [5; *g/pl.*: -вок] substitution; **~́ция** *f* [7] substation.

подстер|ега́ть [1], ⟨**~е́чь**⟩ [26 г/ж: -регу́, -режёшь; -рёг, -регла́] lie in wait of; *pf.* trap.

подстил|а́ть [1], ⟨**подостла́ть**⟩ [подстелю́, -е́лешь; подо́стланный & подсте́ленный] spread (under под В); **~́ка** *f* [5; *g/pl.*: -лок] bedding; spreading.

подстр|а́ивать [1], ⟨**~о́ить**⟩ [13] ⌂ build, add; F ♪ tune (to под В); plot.

подстрек|а́тель *m* [4] instigator, monger; **~а́тельство** *n* [9] instigation; **~а́ть** [1], ⟨**~ну́ть**⟩ [20] incite (to на В); stir up, provoke.

подстр|е́ливать [1], ⟨**~ели́ть**⟩ [13; -елю́, -е́лишь] hit, wound; **~ига́ть** [1], ⟨**~и́чь**⟩ [26 г/ж: -игу́, -ижёшь; -и́г, -и́гла; -и́женный] cut, crop, clip; trim, lop; **~о́ить** *s.* подстра́ивать; **~о́чный** [14] interlinear; foot(*note*).

по́дступ *m* [1] approach (*a.* ⚔); **~а́ть** [1], ⟨**~и́ть**⟩ [14] approach (*v/t.* к Д); rise; press.

подсуд|и́мый *m* [14] defendant; **~́ность** *f* [8] jurisdiction.

подсу́нуть *s.* подсо́вывать.

подсч|ёт *m* [1] calculation, computation, cast; **~и́тывать**, ⟨**~ита́ть**⟩ [1] count (up), compute.

подсы|ла́ть [1], ⟨**подосла́ть**⟩ [-шлю́, -шлёшь; -о́сланный] send (secretely); **~па́ть** [1], ⟨**~́пать**⟩ [2] add, pour; **~ха́ть** [1], ⟨**подсо́хнуть**⟩ [21] dry (up).

подта́|лкивать [1], ⟨**подтолкну́ть**⟩ [20] push; nudge; **~со́вывать** [1], ⟨**~сова́ть**⟩ [7] shuffle (trickily); garble; **~чивать** [1], ⟨**подточи́ть**⟩ [16] eat (away); wash (out); sharpen; *fig.* undermine.

подтвер|жда́ть [1], ⟨**~ди́ть**⟩ [15 *e.*; -ржу́, -рди́шь; -рждённый] confirm, corroborate; acknowledge; **-ся** prove (to be) true; **~жде́ние** *n* [12] confirmation; acknowledg(e)ment.

под|тере́ть *s.* **~тира́ть**; **~тёк** *m* [1] bloodshot spot; **~тира́ть** [1], ⟨**~тере́ть**⟩ [12; подотру́; подтёр] wipe (up); **~толкну́ть** *s.* **~та́лкивать**; **~точи́ть** *s.* **~та́чивать.**

подтру́н|ивать [1], ⟨**~и́ть**⟩ [13] tease, banter, chaff (*v/t.* над Т).

подтя́|гивать [1], ⟨**~ну́ть**⟩ [19] pull (up); draw (in *reins*); tighten; raise (*wages*); wind *or* key up, egg on; join in (*song*); **-ся** chin; brace up; improve, pick up; **~жки** *f/pl.* [5; *gen.*: -жек] suspenders, *Brt.* braces.

поду́мывать [1] think (about о П).

подуч|а́ть [1], ⟨**~и́ть**⟩ [16] *s.* учи́ть.

поду́шка *f* [5; *g/pl.*: -шек] pillow; cushion, pad.

подхали́м *m* [1] toady, lickspittle.

подхва́т|ывать [1], ⟨**~и́ть**⟩ [15] catch; pick up; take up; join in.

подхо́д *m* [1] approach (*a. fig.*); **~и́ть** [15], ⟨**подойти́**⟩ [-ойду́, -дёшь; -ошёл; -шла́; *g. pt.* -ойдя́] (к Д) approach, go (up to); arrive, come; (Д) suit, fit; **~я́щий** [17] suitable, fit(ting), appropriate; convenient.

подцеп|ля́ть [28], ⟨**~и́ть**⟩ [14] hook (*a. fig.*); pick up, catch.

подча́с at times, sometimes.

подч|ёркивать [1], ⟨**~еркну́ть**⟩ [20; -ёркнутый] underline; stress.

подчин|е́ние *n* [12] submission; subjection; *gr.* hypotaxis; **~ённый** [14] subordinate; **~я́ть** [28], ⟨**~и́ть**⟩ [13] subject, subdue; subordinate; put under (s.b.'s Д) supervision; **-ся** (Д) submit (to); obey.

под|ше́фный [14] sponsored; **~шива́ть** [1], ⟨**~ши́ть**⟩ [подошью́, -шьёшь; *cf.* шить] sew on (to к Д); hem; file; **~ши́пник** ⊕ *m* [1] bearing; **~ши́ть** *s.* **~шива́ть**; **~шу́чивать** [1], ⟨**~шути́ть**⟩ [15] play a trick (on над Т).

подъе́|зд *m* [1] entrance, porch; drive; approach; **~здно́й** [14] 🚂 branch (*line*); **~зжа́ть** [1], ⟨**~хать**⟩ [-е́ду, -е́дешь] (к Д) drive *or* ride up (to), approach; F drop in (on); make up to.

подъём *m* [1] lift(ing); ascent, rise (*a. fig.*); enthusiasm; instep; лёгок (тяжёл) на ~ nimble (slow); **~ник** *m* [1] elevator, lift, hoist; **~ный** [14]: **~ный мост** *m* drawbridge; **~ная си́ла** *f* carrying capacity; **~ные (де́ньги)** *pl.* travel(l)ing expenses.

подъе́|хать *s.* **~зжа́ть.**

под|ыма́ть(ся) *s.* **~нима́ть(ся).**

поды́ск|ивать [1], ⟨**~а́ть**⟩ [3] *impf.* look for; *pf.* find; choose.

подыто́ж|ивать [1], ⟨**~ить**⟩ [16] sum up.

поеда́ть [1], ⟨пое́сть⟩ *cf.* есть¹.

поеди́нок *m* [1; -нка] duel (with *arms* на П).

по́езд *m* [1; *pl.:* -да́, *etc. e.*] train; **∠ка** *f* [5; *g/pl.:* -док] trip, journey; voyage; tour; **~но́й** 🚂 [14] train...

поéние *n* [12] watering.

пожа́луй maybe, perhaps; I suppose; **~ста** (pa'ʒałustə) please; *cf. a.* (нé за) что; скажи́(те) ~ста! I say!; **~те** come in(to в В), please; ~те сюда́! this way, please; *cf.* жа́ловать & добро́².

пожа́р *m* [1] fire (to/at на В/П); conflagration; **~ище** *n* [11] scene of conflagration; **~ник** *m* [1] fireman; **~ный** [14] fire...; *su.* = **~ник**; *cf.* кома́нда.

пожа́т|ие *n* [12] shake (*of hand*); **~ь** *s.* пожима́ть & пожина́ть.

пожела́ние *n* [12] wish; request.

пожелте́лый [14] yellow, faded.

поже́ртвование *n* [12] donation.

пожи́|ва *f* [5] F = нажи́ва, *s.*; **~ва́ть** [1] F live; как (вы) ~ва́ете? how are you (getting on)?; **~ви́ться** [14*e.*; -влю́сь, -ви́шься] *pf.* F (Т) = нажи́ть; **~зненный** [14] life...; **~ло́й** [14] elderly.

пожи|ма́ть [1], ⟨пожа́ть⟩ [-жму́, -жмёшь; -а́тый] *s.* жать¹; **~ма́ть** плеча́ми shrug one's shoulders; **~на́ть** [1], ⟨пожа́ть⟩ [-жну́, -жнёшь; -жа́тый] *s.* жать²; **~ра́ть** P [1], ⟨пожра́ть⟩ [-жру́, -рёшь; -а́л, -а́, -о] eat up; devour; **∠тки** F *m/pl.* [1] belongings, things; со все́ми ∠тками with bag & baggage.

по́за *f* [5] pose, posture, attitude.

поза|вчера́ the day before yesterday; **~ди́** (Р) behind; past; **~про́шлый** [14] the ... before last.

позвол|е́ние *n* [12] permission (with с Р), leave (by); **~и́тельный** [14; -лен, -льна] permissible; ~и́тельно one may; **~я́ть** [28], ⟨**∠ить**⟩ [13] allow (*a.* of), permit (Д); ~я́ть себе́ venture, presume; † beg *to*; afford; **∠ь(те)** may I; let; I say.

позвоно́|к *m* [1; -нка́] *anat.* vertebra; **~чник** *m* [1] spinal (*or* vertebral) column, spine, backbone; **~чный** [14] vertebral; vertebrate.

по́здн|ий [15] (-ʐŋ-) (**~o** *a.* it is) late.

поздоро́вит|ься F *pf.*: ему́ не ~ся he will (have to) pay for it.

поздрав|и́тель *m* [4] congratulator; **~и́тельный** [14] congratulatory; **∠ить** *s.* ~ля́ть; **~ле́ние** *n* [12] congratulation; *pl.* compliments (of the season с Т); **~ля́ть** [28], ⟨**∠ить**⟩ [14] (с Т) congratulate (on), wish (many happy returns [of the day]); send (*or* give) one's compliments (of the season).

поземе́льный [14] land..., ground...

по́зже later; не ~ (Р) ... at the latest.

позити́вный [14; -вен, -вна] positive.

позици|о́нный [14] trench..., position...; **'~я** *f* [7] position; *pl.* ⚔ line; *fig.* attitude (on по Д).

позна|ва́ть [5], ⟨**∠ть**⟩ [1] perceive; (come to) know; **∠ние** *n* [12] perception; *pl.* knowledge.

позоло́та *f* [5] gilding.

позо́р *m* [1] shame, disgrace, infamy; **~ить** [13], ⟨о-⟩ dishono(u)r, disgrace; **~ный** [14; -рен, -рна] shameful, disgraceful, infamous, ignominious; ~ный столб *m* pillory.

позы́в *m* [1] desire; impulse.

поим|ённый [14] of names; by (roll) call; **~енова́ть**]7] *pf.* name; **~у́щественный** [14] property...

по́ис|ки *m/pl.* [1] search (in в П), quest; **∠тине** truly, really.

по|и́ть [13], ⟨на-⟩ water; give to drink (s. th. Т); **∠йло** *n* [9] swill.

пой|ма́ть *s.* лови́ть; **~ти́** *s.* идти́.

пока́ for the time being (*a.* ~ что); meanwhile; while; ~ (не) until; **~!** F so long!, (I'll) see you later.

пока́з *m* [1] demonstration; showing; **~а́ние** (*usu. pl.*) *n* [12] evidence; ⊕ indication; **~а́тель** *m* [4] 𝔄 exponent; index; figure; **~а́тельный** [14; -лен, -льна] significant; demonstrative; model; show (*trial*); **~а́ть(ся)** *s.* ~ывать(ся); **~но́й** [14] ostentatious; sham...; **~ывать** [1], ⟨~а́ть⟩ [3] show; demonstrate; point (at на В); ⚖ testify, depose (against на В); ⊕ read; ~а́ть себя́ (Т) prove; и ви́ду не ~ывать seem to know nothing; look unconcerned; **-ся** appear (*a.* = seem, Т), turn up.

пока́мест P, *s.* пока́.

пока́т|ость *f* [8] declivity; slope, slant; **~ый** [14 *sh.*] slanting, sloping; retreating (*forehead*).

покая́н|ие *n* [12] penance (do быть на П); penitence; repentance.

поквита́ться F [1] *pf.* settle accounts.

поки|да́ть [1], ⟨**∠нуть**⟩ [20] leave, quit; abandon, desert.

покла|да́я: не ~да́я рук unremittingly; **∠дистый** [14 *sh.*] accommodating; **∠жа** *f* [5] load, lading.

покло́н *m* [1] bow; regards *pl.*; **~е́ние** *n* [12] (Д) worship; deference; **~и́ться** *s.* кла́няться; **~ник** *m* [1] worship(p)er; admirer; **~я́ться** [28] (Д) worship; bow (to).

поко́иться [13] rest, lie; be based.

поко́й *m* [3] rest; repose, peace; calm; † apartment; (оста́вить в П let) alone; **~ник** *m* [1], **~ница** *f* [5] the deceased; ⚖ decedent; **~ницкая** *f* [14] mortuary; **~ный** [14; -о́ен, -о́йна] quiet; calm; easy; the late; *su.* = ~ник, ~ница; *cf.* споко́йный.

поколе́ние *n* [12] generation.

поко́нчить [16] *pf.* ([с] Т) finish;

(с Т) do away with; commit (suicide с собой).
покор|éние *n* [12] conquest; subjugation; **~и́тель** *m* [4] conqueror; **~и́ть(ся)** *s.* **~я́ть(ся)**; **∠ность** *f* [8] submission, obedience; **∠ный** [14; -рен, -рна] obedient; humble, submissive; ∠но *a.* (*thank*) very much; **~я́ть** [28], ‹~и́ть› [13] conquer, subdue; **-ся** submit; resign o. s.
покóс *m* [1] (hay)mowing; meadow.
покри́кивать F [1] shout (at на В).
покрóв *m* [1] cover; hearse cloth.
покрови́тель *m* [4] patron, protector; **~ница** *f* [5] patroness, protectress; **~ственный** [14] patronizing; † protective; **~ство** *n* [9] protection (of Д); patronage; **~ствовать** [7] (Д) patronize; protect.
покрóй *m* [3] cut; kind, breed.
покры|вáло *n* [9] coverlet; veil; **~вáть** [1], ‹**∠ть**› [22] (Т) cover (*a.* = defray); coat; beat, trump; P call *or* run down; **-ся** cover o. s.; be(come) covered; **∠тие** *n* [12] cover(ing); coat(ing); defrayal; **∠шка** *f* [5; *g/pl.*: -шек] (tire) cover; F lid.
покуп|áтель *m* [4], **~áтельница** *f* [5] buyer; customer; **~áтельный** [14] purchasing; **~áть** [1], ‹купи́ть› [14] buy, purchase (from у Р); **∠ка** *f* [5; *g/pl.*: -пок] purchase; package; за ∠ками (*go*) shopping; **~нóй** [14] purchasing; purchase(d).
поку|шáться [1], ‹~си́ться› [15 *e.*; -ушу́сь, -уси́шься] attempt (*v/t.* на В); encroach ([up]on); **~шéние** *n* [12] attempt ([up]on на В).
пол[1] *m* [1; нá ~; на -ý; *pl. e.*] floor.
пол[2] *m* [1; *from g/pl. e.*] sex.
пол[3](...) [*g/sg., etc.*: ~(у)...] half (...).
полá *f* [5; *pl. st.*] skirt, tail.
полагá|ть [1], ‹положи́ть› [16] put; decide; ♪ set (to на В); *impf.* think, suppose, guess; fancy; нáдо ~ть probably; полóжим, что ... suppose, let's assume that; **-ся** rely (on на В); (Д) ~ется must; be due *or* proper; как ~ется properly.
пóл|день *m* [*gen.*: -(ý)дня; *g/pl.*: -дён] noon (at в В); *cf.* обéд; **~днéвный** [14] midday...; **~дорóги** *s.* ~пути́; **~дю́жины** [*gen.*: -удю́жины] half (a) dozen.
пóле *n* [10; *pl. e.*] field (*a. fig.*; in на, в П; across пó Д; Г); ground; *mst. pl.* margin; **~вóй** [14] field...; **∠зный** [14; -зен, -зна] useful, of use; helpful; wholesome; ⊕ effective; net.
полем|изи́ровать [7] polemize; **∠ика** *f* [5], **~и́ческий** [16] polemic.
полéно *n* [9; -нья, -ньев] log.
полёт *m* [1] flight; брéющий ~ low-level flight; слепóй ~ blind flying.
пóлз|ать [1], **~ти́** [24] creep, crawl; **~кóм** on all fours; **~у́чий** [17]: ~у́чее растéние *n* creeper, climber.
поли|вáть [1], ‹**∠ть**› [-лью́, -лёшь; *cf.* лить] water; *pf.* start raining (*or* pouring); **∠вка** *f* [5] watering; flushing.
полигóн *m* [1] (target) range.
полиня́лый [14] faded.
поли|ровáть [7], ‹от-› polish, burnish; **~рóвка** *f* [5; *g/pl.*: -вок] polish(ing); **'~с** *m* [1] (*insurance*) policy.
Полит|бюрó *n* [*indecl.*] Politburo (*Sov.*), Political Bureau; **2грáмота** *f* [5] political primer (*Sov.*); **2éхникум** *m* [1] polytechnic; **2заключённый** *m* [14] political prisoner.
поли́т|ик *m* [1] politician; **~ика** *f* [5] policy; politics *pl.*; **~и́ческий** [16] political; **~рýк** *m* [1] political instructor (*or* commissar[y]) (*Sov.*); **~ýра** *f* [5] polish; **~учёба** *f* [5] political instruction (*Sov.*); **~ь** *s.* поливáть; **~экономия** *f* [7] political economy, economics.
полиц|éйский [16] police(man *su.*); **∠ия** *f* [7] police.
поли́чн|ое *n* [14] corpus delicti; с **~ым** (*catch*) red-handed.
полк *m* [1 *e.*; в -ý] regiment; **∠а** *f* [5; *g/pl.*: -лок] shelf; pan (*gun*).
полкóв|ник *m* [1] colonel; **~óдец** *m* [1; -дца] commander, general; **~óй** [14] regimental.
полнéть [8], ‹по-› grow stout.
пóлно 1. full, to the brim; **2.** F (*a.* ~те) okay, all right; never mind; enough *or* no more (of this); (*a.* ~ Д + *inf.*) stop, quit (that) (...ing)!; **~вéсный** [14; -сен, -сна] weighty; **~влáстный** [14; -тен, -тна] absolute; **~вóдный** [14; -ден, -дна] deep; **~крóвный** [14; -вен, -вна] full-blooded; ⚕ plethoric; **~лýние** *n* [12] full moon; **~мóчие** *n* [12] (full) power; **~мóчный** [14; -чен, -чна] plenipotentiary; *cf.* полпрéд (-ство); **~прáвный** [14; -вен, -вна]: ~прáвный член *m* full member; **~стью** completely, entirely; **~тá** *f* [5] fullness, plenitude; completeness; corpulence; **~цéнный** [14; -éнен, -éнна] full (value)...; *fig.* full-fledged.
пóлночь *f* [8; -(ý)ночи] midnight.
пóлн|ый [14; пóлон, полнá, пóлнó; полнéе] full (of Р *or* Т); complete, absolute; perfect (*a. right*); stout; chubby; **~ым-~ый** F full up, packed (with Р).
полови́к *m* [1 *e.*] mat.
полови́н|а *f* [5] half (by на В); ~а (в ~е) пя́того (at) half past four; два с ~ой two & a half; **~ка** *f* [5; *g/pl.*: -нок] half; leaf (*door*); **~чатый** [14] *fig.* vague, evasive.
полови́ца *f* [5] deal, board.
полово́дье *n* [10] high water (*in spring*).
полов|óй[1] [14] floor...; ~áя тря́пка *f* mop; **~óй**[2] [14] sexual; ~áя зрéлость *f* puberty; **~ые** óрганы *m/pl.* genitals.

по́лог *m* [1] bed curtain.
поло́гий [16; *comp.*: поло́же] slightly sloping, flat.
полож|е́ние *n* [12] position, location; situation; state, condition; standing; regulations *pl.*; thesis; в (интере́сном) ~е́нии F in the family way; **~и́тельный** [14; -лен, -льна] positive; affirmative; **~и́ть** (**-ся**) *s.* класть 1. & полага́ть(ся).
по́лоз *m* [1; *pl.*: -ло́зья, -ло́зьев] runner.
поло́мка *f* [5; *g/pl.*: -мок] breakage.
полоса́ *f* [5; *ac/sg.*: по́лосу́; *pl.*: по́лосы, поло́с, -са́м] stripe, streak; strip; belt, zone; bar; field; period; **~тый** [14 *sh.*] striped.
полоска́ть [3], ⟨про-⟩ rinse; gargle; **-ся** paddle; flap (*flag, etc.*).
по́лость *f* [8; *from g/pl. e.*] cavity.
полоте́нце *n* [11; *g/pl.*: -нец] towel (on T); мохна́тое ~ Turkish towel.
поло́тн|ище *n* [11] width; **~о́** *n* [9; *pl.*: -о́тна, -о́тен, -о́тнам] linen; bunting; 🚂 roadbed; embankment; (*saw*) blade; **~я́ный** [14] linen...
поло́ть [17], ⟨вы́-, про-⟩ weed.
пол|пре́д *m* [1] ambassador; **~пре́дство** *n* [9] embassy (*Sov., till 1941*); **~пути́** halfway (*a.* на ~пути́); **~сло́ва** [9; *gen.*: -(у)сло́ва] half a word; (a few) word(s); на ~(у)сло́ве (*stop*) short; **~со́тни** [6; *g/sg.*: -(у)со́тни; *g/pl.*: -лусо́тен] fifty; **~ти́нник** F *m* [1], P **~ти́на** *f* [5] half (a) ruble, 50 kopecks.
полтор|а́ *m & n*, **~ы́** *f* [*gen.*: -у́тора; -ры (*f*)] one and a half; **~а́ста** [*obl. cases*; -у́тораста] a hundred and fifty.
полу|боти́нки *m/pl.* [1; *g/pl.*: -нок] (low) shoes; **~гла́сный** [14] semivowel; **~го́дие** *n* [12] half year, six months; **~годи́чный**, **~годово́й** [14] semiannual, half-yearly; **~гра́мотный** [14; -тен, -тна] semiliterate; **~́денный** [14] midday...; meridional; **~живо́й** [14; -жи́в, -а́, -о] half dead; **~защи́тник** *m* [1] halfback; **~кру́г** *m* [1] semicircle; **~ме́сяц** *m* [1] half moon, crescent; **~мра́к** *m* [1] twilight, semi-darkness; **~́ночный** [14] midnight...; **~оборо́т** *m* [1] half-turn; **~о́стров** *m* [1; *pl.*: -ва́, *etc. e.*] peninsula; **~све́т** *m* [1] twilight; demimonde; **~спу́щенный** [14] half-mast; **~ста́нок** *m* [1; -нка] 🚂 stop, substation; **~тьма́** *f* [5] = ~мра́к.
получ|а́тель *m* [4] addressee, recipient; **~а́ть** [1], ⟨~и́ть⟩ [16] receive, get; obtain; catch; have; **-ся** come in, arrive; result; prove, turn out; **~е́ние** *n* [12] receipt; getting; **~́чка** F *f* [5; *g/pl.*: -чек] pay (day).
полу|ша́рие *n* [12] hemisphere; **~шу́бок** *m* [1; -бка] short fur coat.
пол|фу́нта [*g/sg.*: -уфу́нта] half pound; **~цены́**: за ~цены́ at half price; **~часа́** *m* [1; *g/sg.*: -уча́са] half (an) hour.
по́лчище *n* [11] horde; mass.
по́лый [14] hollow; high; iceless.
полы́нь *f* [8] wormwood.
полынья́ *f* [6] ice-hole (*on frozen river etc.*).
по́льз|а *f* [5] use; benefit (for на, в В, для Р); profit; advantage; utility; в ~у (Р) in favo(u)r of; **~ова́ть** [7] treat; **-ся**, ⟨вос~оваться⟩ (Т) use, make use of; avail o. s. of; enjoy, have; take (*opportunity*).
по́ль|ка *f* [5; *g/pl.*: -лек] 1. Pole; 2. polka; **~ский** [16] Polish; **2ша** *f* [5] Poland.
полюбо́вный [14] amicable.
по́люс *m* [1] pole; ⚡ *a.* terminal.
поля́|к *m* [1] Pole; **~на** *f* [5] glade; meadow; **~рный** [14] polar.
пома́да *f* [5] pomade; (*lip*)stick.
пома́з|ание *n* [12] unction; **~ывать** [1], ⟨~ать⟩ [3] anoint; *s.* ма́зать.
помале́ньку F so-so; little by little.
пома́лкивать F [1] keep silent.
пома́|рка *f* [5; *g/pl.*: -рок] blot, erasure; **~хивать** [1] wag; flourish.
помести́т|ельный [14; -лен, -льна] spacious; **~ь(ся)** *s.* помеща́ть [(-ся).
поме́стье *n* [10] estate.
по́месь *f* [8] cross breed, mongrel.
поме́сячный [14] monthly.
помёт *m* [1] dung; litter, brood.
поме́|тить *s.* ~ча́ть; **~тка** *f* [5; *g/pl.*: -ток] mark, note; **~ха** *f* [5] hindrance; trouble, disturbance (*a.* ⊕); **~ча́ть** [1], ⟨~́тить⟩ [15] mark, note.
поме́ш|анный [14 *sh.*] crazy; mad (about на П); **~а́тельство** *n* [9] insanity; **~а́ть** *s.* меша́ть; **-ся** *pf.* go mad (*a.* ~а́ться в уме́); F be mad (about на П).
поме|ща́ть [1], ⟨~сти́ть⟩ [15 *e.*; -ещу́, -ести́шь; -ещённый] place; lodge, accommodate; settle; invest; insert, publish; **-ся** settle (o. s.), locate; lodge; find room; hold; be placed *or* invested; *impf.* be (located); **~ще́ние** *n* [12] lodg(e)ment, premise(s), room; investment; **~́щик** *m* [1] landowner, landlord.
помидо́р *m* [1] tomato.
поми́л|ование *n* [12], **~овать** [7] *pf.* pardon; **~у́й(те)!** for goodness' sake; good gracious; ~у́й бог! God forbid!; го́споди ~у́й! God, have mercy upon us.
поми́мо (Р) besides; in spite of; ~ него́ without his knowledge.
поми́н *m* [1] mention (of о П); **~а́ть** [1], ⟨помяну́ть⟩ [19] recollect, remember; speak about, mention; pray for (*a.* о П); commemorate; ~а́й, как зва́ли (be) off and away; не ~а́ть ли́хом bear no ill will (toward[s] a p. В); **~ки** *f/pl.* [5; *gen.*: -нок] commemoration (for the dead); **~у́тно** every minute; constantly.

по́мнит|ь [13], ‹вс-› remember, recollect, think of (*a.* о П); мне **~ся** (as far as) I remember.

помо|га́ть [1], ‹**~чь**› [26 г/ж: -огу́, -о́жешь, -о́гут; -о́г, -огла́] (Д) help; aid, assist; avail.

помо́|и *m/pl.* [3] slops; **~йный** [14] slop, garbage, dust (*hole* =, F, **~йка** *f* [5; *g/pl.*: -о́ек]).

помо́л *m* [1] grind(ing); **~вить** [14] *pf.* affiance (to с T); **~вка** *f* [5; *g/pl.*: -вок] betrothal, engagement.

помо́ст *m* [1] dais; rostrum; scaffold.

по́моч|и F *f/pl.* [8; *from gen. e.*] leading strings (in на П); = подтя́жки; **~ь** *s.* помога́ть.

помо́щ|ник *m* [1], **~ница** *f* [5] assistant; deputy (s. th. P); helper, aid; **'~ь** *f* [8] help, aid, assistance (with с T *or* при П; to one's на В/Д; *call* for на В, о П); ⚕ treatment; relief; каре́та ско́рой **'~и** ambulance.

по́мпа *f* [5] pomp; ⊕ pump.

помрача́ть *s.* омрача́ть.

помутне́ние *n* [12] turbidity.

по́мы|сел *m* [1; -сла] thought; design; **~шля́ть** [28] think (of о П).

помяну́ть *s.* помина́ть.

помя́тый [14] (c)rumpled; trodden.

пона́|добиться [14] *pf.* (Д) need, want; **~пра́сну** F = напра́сно; **~слы́шке** F by hearsay.

поне|во́ле F willy-nilly; against one's will; **~де́льник** *m* [1] Monday (on: в В, *pl.*: по Д).

понемно́|гу, F **~жку** (a) little; little by little, gradually; F *a.* so-so.

пони|жа́ть [1], ‹**~зить**› [15] lower, reduce (*v/i.* -ся; fall, sink); **~же́ние** *n* [12] fall; reduction; decrease; degradation.

поник|а́ть [1], ‹**~нуть**› [21] hang (one's head голово́й); droop; wilt.

понима́|ние *n* [12] comprehension, understanding; conception; **~ть** [1], ‹поня́ть› [пойму́, -ёшь; по́нял, -á, -о; по́нятый (по́нят, -á, -о)] understand, comprehend, see; realize; appreciate; **~ю** (**~ешь**, **~ете** [ли]) I (you) see.

понома́рь *m* [4 *e.*] sexton.

поно́|с *m* [1] diarrhea; **~си́ть** [15], **~ше́ние** *n* [12] abuse.

поно́шенный [14 *sh.*[worn, shabby.

понто́н *m* [1], **~ный** [14] pontoon.

пону|жда́ть [1], ‹**~дить**› [15; -уждённый] force, compel; **~жде́ние** *n* [12] compulsion.

понука́ть [1] urge on, spur.

пону́р|ить [13] hang; **~ый** [14 *sh.*] downcast.

по́нчик *m* [1] doughnut.

поны́не until now.

поня́т|ие *n* [12] idea, notion; concept(ion); comprehension; **~ливый** [14 *sh.*] quick-witted, bright; **~ный** [14; -тен, -тна] intelligible, understandable; clear, plain; **~но** *a.*, F, = коне́чно; **~ь** *s.* понима́ть.

поо́б|даль at some distance; **~ди-но́чке** one by one; **~чередный** [14] alternate.

поощр|е́ние *n* [12] encouragement; **~я́ть** [28], ‹**~и́ть**› [13] encourage.

поп F *m* [1 *e.*] priest.

попа|да́ние *n* [12] hit; **~да́ть** [1], ‹**~сть**› [25; *pt. st.*] (в *or* на В) get, come (*a.* across), fall, find o. s.; hit; catch (*train*); become (в И *pl.*); F (Д *impers.*) get it; не **~сть** miss; как **~ло** anyhow, at random, haphazard; кому́ **~ло** to the first comer (= пе́рвому **~вшемуся**); **-ся** (в В) be caught; fall (into a trap на у́дочку); F (Д + *vb.* + И) come across, chance (up)on, meet; occur, there is (are); strike (a p.'s eye Д на глаза́; не **~да́ться** be out of a p.'s sight).

попадья́ *f* [6] priest's wife.

попа́рно by pairs, in couples.

попа́сть(ся) *s.* попада́ть(ся).

попер|ёк (P) across, crosswise; in (*a p.'s way*); **~еме́нно** by turns; **~е́чный** [14] transverse, transversal; cross...

попеч|е́ние *n* [12] care, charge (in на П); **~и́тель** *m* [4] curator, trustee.

попира́ть [1] trample (on) (*fig.*).

по́пка F *m* [5; *g/pl.*: -пок] parrot.

поплаво́к *m* [1; -вка́] float (*a.* ⊕).

попо́йка F *f* [5; *g/pl.*: -о́ек] booze.

попол|а́м in half; half & half; fifty-fifty; **~знове́ние** *n* [12] mind; pretension (to на В); **~ня́ть** [28], ‹**~нить**› [13] replenish, supplement; enrich; reman, reinforce.

пополу́дни in the afternoon, p. m.

попо́на *f* [5] horsecloth.

попра́в|ить(ся) *s.* **~ля́ть(ся)**; **~ка** *f* [5; *g/pl.*: -вок], **~ле́ние** *n* [12] correction; amendment; improvement; recovery; repair; **~ля́ть** [28], ‹**~ить**› [14] repair; adjust; correct, (a)mend; improve; recover (*v/i.* **-ся**; put on weight, look better).

по-пре́жнему (now) as before.

попрек|а́ть [1], ‹**~ну́ть**› [20] reproach (with T).

по́прище *n* [11] field (in на П).

по́про|сту plainly, unceremoniously; downright; **~ша́йка** F *m/f* [5; *g/pl.*: -áек] beggar.

попуга́й *m* [3] parrot.

популя́рн|ость *f* [8] popularity; **~ый** [14; -рен, -рна] popular.

попус|ти́тельство *n* [9] connivance; **'~т(о́м)у** F in vain, to no purpose.

попу́т|ный [14] fair, favo(u)rable (*wind*); (**~но** in) passing, incidental(ly); **~чик** *m* [1] fellow travel(l)er.

попыт|а́ть F [1] *pf.* try (one's luck сча́стья); **~ка** *f* [5; *g/pl.*: -ток] attempt.

пор|á[1] *f* [5; *ac/sg.*: пóру; *pl. st.*] time; season; weather (in в B); period; F prime; (давнó) ~á it's (high) time (for Д); в (сáмую) ´~у in the nick of time; до ~ы́, до врéмени not last forever; *wait* for one's opportunity; до (с) какúх ~? how long (since when)?; до сих ~ hitherto, so far, up to now (here); до тех ~ (, покá) so (*or* as) long (as); с тех ~ (как) since then (since); на пéрвых ~áх at first, in the beginning; ~óй at times; вечéрней ~óй = вéчером.

пóра[2] *f* [5] pore.

порабо|щáть [1], ⟨~тúть⟩ [15 *e.*; -ощý, -отúшь; -ощённый] enslave, subjugate.

поравня́ться [28] *pf.* overtake (с Т).

пора|жáть [1], ⟨~зúть⟩ [15 *e.*; -ажý, -азúшь; -ажённый] strike (*a. fig.* = amaze, & ⚕ = affect); defeat; ~жéнец *m* [1; -нца] defeatist; ~жéние *n* [12] defeat; ⚕ affection; ⚖ deprivation; striking; ~жéнчество *n* [9] defeatism; ~зúтельный [14; -лен, -льна] striking; ~зúть *s.* ~жáть; ´~нить [13] *pf.* wound, cut.

порвáть(ся) *s.* порывáть(ся).

порéз *m* [1], ~ать [3] *pf.* cut.

порéй *m* [3] leek.

пóристый [14 *sh.*] porous.

порицá|ние *n* [12], ~ть [1] censure.

пóровну (in) equal parts.

порóг *m* [1] threshold; *pl.* rapids.

порó|да *f* [5] breed, species, race; stock; ⚒ rock; layer; ~дистый [14 *sh.*] thoroughbred; racy; ~ждáть [1], ⟨~дúть⟩ [15 *e.*; -ожý, -одúшь; -ождённый] cause, give rise to, entail; ~ждéние *n* [12] brood; production.

порóжний F [15] empty.

пóрознь F separately; one by one.

порóк *m* [1] vice; defect; disease.

поросёнок *m* [2] young pig.

порó|ть [17] **1.** ⟨рас-⟩ undo, unpick; *impf.* F talk (*nonsense*); **2.** F ⟨вы́-⟩ whip, flog; ´~х *m* [1] gunpowder; ~ховóй [14] (gun)powder...

порóч|ить [16], ⟨о-⟩ discredit; defile; ~ный [14; -чен, -чна] vicious.

порошóк *m* [1; -шкá] powder.

порт *m* [1; в -ý; *from g/pl. e.*] port; harbo(u)r; ~атúвный [14; -вен, -вна] portable; ´~ить [15], ⟨ис-⟩ spoil (*v/i.* -ся; break down).

портн|úха *f* [5] dressmaker; ~óй *m* [14] tailor.

портов|úк *m* [1 *e.*] longshoreman, *Brt. a.* docker; ´~ый [14] port..., dock...; ´~ый гóрод *m* seaport.

портсигáр *m* [1] cigar(ette) case.

португáл|ец *m* [1; -льца] Portuguese; ♀ия *f* [7] Portugal; ~ка *f* [5; *g/pl.*: -лок], ~ьский [16] Portuguese.

порт|упéя *f* [6] sword knot; ~фéль *m* [4] brief case; portfolio; ~я́нка *f* [5; *g/pl.*: -нок] foot wrap (rag).

поругáние *n* [12] abuse, affront.

порý|ка *f* [5] bail (on на В *pl.*), security; guarantee; responsibility; ~чáть [1], ⟨~чúть⟩ [16] charge (a p. with Д/В); commission, bid, tell (+ *inf.*); entrust; ~чéние *n* [12] commission; instruction; message; mission; (*a.* †) order (by по Д; *a.* on behalf); ~чик † *m* [1] (first) lieutenant; ~чúтель *m* [4] bail, surety; ~чúть *s.* ~чáть.

порх|áть [1], *once* ⟨~нýть⟩ [20] flit.

пóрция *f* [7] portion, helping.

пóр|ча *f* [5] spoiling, spoilage; damage; ~шень *m* [4; -шня] piston.

поры́в *m* [1] gust, squall; fit, outburst; impulse; ~áть [1], ⟨порвáть⟩ [-вý, -вёшь; -áл, -á, -о; пóрванный] tear; break (off; with с Т); -ся *v/i.*; *impf.* jerk; strive; *s. a.* рвать(ся); ~истый [14 *sh.*] gusty; jerky; impulsive.

порядко|вый [14] current; *gr.* ordinal; ~м F rather; properly.

поря́д|ок *m* [1; -дка] order; way (by в П; in Т), form; course; *pl.* conditions; kind; ~ок дня agenda; по ~ку one after another; current (*no.*); ~очный [14; -чен, -чна] orderly, decent; fair(ly large *or* great).

посáд|ить *s.* сажáть & садúть; ~ка *f* [5; *g/pl.*: -док] planting; embarkation, (*a.* 🚂) boarding; ✈ landing, alighting; ~очный [14] landing...

по-своéму in one's own way.

посвя|щáть [1], ⟨~тúть⟩ [15 *e.*; -ящý, -ятúшь; -ящённый] devote ([o. s.] to [себя́] Д); dedicate; initiate (into в В); (в И *pl.*) ordain; knight; ~щéние *n* [12] dedication; initiation.

посéв *m* [1] sowing; crop; ~нóй [14] sowing (campaign *su. f*).

поседéлый [14] (turned) gray, *Brt.* grey.

посел|éнец *m* [1; -нца] settler; ~éние *n* [12] colony (*a.* **посёлок** *m* [1; -лка]); ~я́ть [28], ⟨~úть⟩ [13] settle (*v/i.* -ся; put up [at в П]); inspire.

посередúне in the middle *or* midst.

посе|тúтель *m* [4], ~тúтельница *f* [5] visitor, caller; ~тúть *s.* ~щáть; ~щáемость *f* [8] attendance; ~щáть [1], ⟨~тúть⟩ [15 *e.*; -ещý, -етúшь; -ещённый] visit, call on; *impf.* attend; ~щéние *n* [12] visit (to P), call.

посúльный [14; -лен, -льна] according to one's strength *or* possibilities, adequate, equal to.

поскользнýться [20] *pf.* slip.

поскóльку inasmuch as, as.

послаблéние *n* [12] indulgence.

послá|ние *n* [12] message; epistle; ~нник *m* [1] envoy; messenger; ~ть *s.* посылáть.

пóсле 1. (P) after (*a.* ~ тогó как + *vb.*); ~ чегó whereupon; **2.** *adv.* after(ward[s]), later (on); **~вое́нный** [14] postwar.

послéдний [15] last; latest; ultimate, final; latter; worst; highest.

послéд|ователь *m* [4] follower; **~овательный** [14; -лен, -льна] consistent; successive; **~ствие** *n* [12] consequence; **~ующий** [17] following.

после|зáвтра the day after tomorrow; **~слóвие** *n* [12] epilogue.

послóвица *f* [5] proverb.

послуш|áние *n* [12] obedience; **∠ник** *m* [1] novice; **∠ный** [14; -шен, -шна] obedient; docile.

посм|áтривать [1] (keep) look (-ing); **~éиваться** [1] chuckle; laugh (in one's sleeve в кулáк; at над Т); **~éртный** [14] posthumous; **~éшище** *n* [11] laughingstock; **~еяние** *n* [12] ridicule.

посóб|ие *n* [12] grant; relief, dole, benefit; aid, means; textbook, manual; **~лять** P [28], ⟨**~ить**⟩ [14 *e.*; -блю, -бишь] (Д) help, remedy.

посóл *m* [1; -слá] ambassador; **~ьство** *n* [9] embassy.

пóсох *m* [1] staff, stick.

поспáть [-сплю, -спишь; -спáл, -á, -о] *pf.* (have a) nap.

поспе|вáть [1], ⟨**∠ть**⟩ [8] ripen; F = успевáть; be done; get ready.

поспéшн|ость *f* [8] haste; **~ый** [14; -шен, -шна] hasty, hurried; rash.

посред|и́(не) (P) amid(st), in the middle; **∠ник** *m* [1] mediator, intermediary, middleman; **∠ничество** *n* [9] mediation; **∠ственность** *f* [8] mediocrity; **∠ственный** [14 *sh.*] middling; mediocre; **∠ственно** *a.* fair, satisfactory, C (*mark*; *cf.* трóйка); **∠ство** *n* [9]: при ∠стве, чéрез ∠ство =**~ством** (P) by means of.

пост *m* [1 *e.*] **1.** post; на ~ý ⚔ *stand* sentinel; **2.** fast; вели́кий ~ Lent.

постáв|ить *s.* ~ля́ть & стáвить; **~ка** *f* [5; *g/pl.*: -вок] delivery (on при П); supply; **~ля́ть** [28], ⟨**~ить**⟩ [14] deliver (*v/t.*; р. Д); supply, furnish; **~щик** *m* [1 *e.*] supplier.

постан|ови́ть *s.* ~овля́ть; **~óвка** *f* [5; *g/pl.*: -вок] erection; staging, production; performance; position; organization; **~овлéние** *n* [12] resolution, decision; decree; **~овля́ть** [28], ⟨**~ови́ть**⟩ [14] decide; decree; **~óвщик** *m* [1] stage manager, director.

посте|ли́ть *s.* стлать; **∠ль** *f* [8] bed; **~пéнный** [14; -éнен, -éнна] gradual.

пости|гáть [1], ⟨∠гнуть⟩ & ⟨∠чь⟩ [21] comprehend, grasp; overtake; **~жи́мый** [14 *sh.*] conceivable.

пост|илáть [1] *s.* стлать; **~и́ться** [15 *e.*; пощýсь, пости́шься] fast; **~и́чь** *s.* ~игáть; **∠ный** [14; -тен, -тнá, -о] fast...; vegetable (*oil*); F lean (*meat*); *fig.* sour; sanctimonious; **~овóй** *m* [14] sentry; **~óй** *m* [3] quarters, billets *pl.*

постóльку insomuch.

посторóнний [15] strange(r *su.*), outside(r), foreign (*a. body*); unauthorized; accessory, secondary.

постоя́лый [14]: ~ двор *m* inn.

постоя́н|ный [14; -я́нен, -я́нна] constant, permanent; continual, continuous; steady; ⚔ standing; ⚡ direct; **~ство** *n* [9] constancy.

пострадáвший [17] injured.

пострéл F *m* [1] scapegrace, rogue.

постри|гáть [1] ⟨∠чь⟩ [26 г/ж: -игý, -ижёшь, -игýт] (-ся have one's hair) cut; make (become) a monk *or* nun.

постро|éние [12], **∠йка** *f* [5; *g/pl.*: -óек] construction; building.

поступ|áтельный [14] progressive; **~áть** [1], ⟨**~и́ть**⟩ [14] act; (с Т) treat, deal (with), handle; (в, на В) enter, join, matriculate; become; come in, be received (for на В); **-ся** (Т) renounce; **~лéние** *n* [12] entrance, entry; matriculation; receipt; **∠ок** *m* [1; -пка] act; behavio(u)r, conduct; **′~ь** *f* [8] gait, step.

посты́|дный [14; -ден, -дна] shameful; **~лый** [14 *sh.*] odious.

посýд|а *f* [5] crockery; (*tea*) service, F things *pl.*; F vessel; **~ный** [14] cup(*board*); dish (*towel*).

посýточный [14] daily; 24 hours'.

посчастли́ви|ться [14; *impers.*] *pf.*: емý ~лось he succeeded (in *inf.*) *or* was lucky (enough).

посыл|áть [1], ⟨послáть⟩ [пошлю́, -шлёшь; пóсланный] send (for за Т); dispatch; **∠ка** *f* [5; *g/pl.*: -лок] dispatch, sending; package, parcel; premise; *cf. a.* побегýшки; **∠ьный** *m* [14] messenger.

посып|áть [1], ⟨∠ать⟩ [2] (be)strew (over; with Т); sprinkle; **∠аться** *pf.* fall down; F shower (down).

посяг|áтельство *n* [9] encroachment; **~áть** [1], ⟨**~нýть**⟩ [20] encroach (on на В), attempt.

пот *m* [1] sweat; весь в ~ý sweating all over.

пота|йнóй [14] secret; **~кáть** F [1] connive (at Д); **~сóвка** F *f* [5; *g/pl.*: -вок] scuffle; thrashing; **∠ш** *m* [1] potash.

потвóрство *n* [9] indulgence, connivance; **~вать** [7] indulge, connive (at Д).

пот|ёмки *f/pl.* [5; *gen.*: -мок] darkness; **~енциáл** (-tɛ-) *m* [1] potential.

потерпéвший [17] (*ship*)wrecked.

потёртый [14 *sh.*] shabby, worn.

потéря *f* [6] loss; waste.
потéть [8], ⟨вс-⟩ sweat (*a.* F = toil; *pane:* ⟨за-⟩), perspire.
потé|ха *f* [5] fun, F lark; **~шáть** [1], ⟨~шить⟩ [16] entertain, amuse; **~шный** [14; -шен, -шна] funny, amusing.
поти|рáть F [1] rub; **~хóньку** F slowly; silently; secretly, on the sly.
пóтный [14; -тен, -тнá; -о] sweaty.
потóк *m* [1] stream; torrent; flow.
потолóк *m* [1; -лкá] ceiling (*a.* ✈).
потóм afterward(s); then; **~ок** *m* [1; -мка] descendant, offspring; **~ственный** [14] hereditary; **~ство** *n* [9] posterity, descendants *pl.*
потомý therefore; ~ что because.
потóп *m* [1] flood, deluge.
потреб|и́тель *m* [4] consumer; buyer; **~и́ть** *s.* **~ля́ть**; **~лéние** *n* [12] consumption; use; **~ля́ть** [28], ⟨~и́ть⟩ [14 *e.*; -блю́, -би́шь; -блённый] consume; use; **~́ность** *f* [8] need, want (of в П), requirement; **~́бный** [14; -бен, -бна] necessary.
потрёпанный F [14] shabby, worn.
потро|хá *m/pl.* [1 *e.*] giblets; bowels; **~ши́ть** [16 *e.*; -шý, -ши́шь; -шённый], ⟨вы́-⟩ draw, disembowel.
потряс|áть [1], ⟨~ти́⟩ [24 -с-] shake (*a. fig.*); **~áющий** [17] tremendous; **~éние** *n* [12] shock, shake; **~ти́** *s.* **~áть.**
потý|ги *f/pl.* [5] travail, labo(u)r; **~пля́ть** [28], ⟨~пить⟩ [14] cast down (*eyes*); hang (*head*); **~хáние** *n* [12] extinction; **~хáть** [1] *s.* тýхнуть.
пóтчевать [7], ⟨по-⟩ F = угощáть.
потя́гивать(ся) *s.* тянýть(ся).
поутрý F early in the morning.
поуч|áть [1] teach (s. th. Д); **~и́тельный** [14; -лен, -льна] instructive; edifying.
похáбный P [14; -бен, -бна] obscene, smutty.
похвал|á *f* [5] praise; commendation; **~́ьный** [14; -лен, -льна] laudable, commendable, praiseworthy; laudatory.
похи|щáть [1], ⟨~́тить⟩ [15; -и́щу; -и́щенный] purloin; kidnap; **~щéние** *n* [12] kidnap(p)ing, abduction.
пох|лёбка *f* [5; *g/pl.:* -бок] soup; skilly; **~мéлье** *n* [10] hang-over.
похóд *m* [1] campaign; march; cruise; крестóвый ~ crusade; **~и́ть** [15] (на В) be like, resemble; **~ка** *f* [5] gait; **~ный** [14] marching; camp-...; battle...
похождéние *n* [12] adventure.
похóж|ий [17 *sh.*] (на В) like, resembling; similar (to); быть **~им** look like; ни на что не **~е** F shocking.
похо|рóнный [14] funeral...; dead (*march*); undertaker's (*office*); **'~рóны** *f/pl.* [5; -óн, -онáм] funeral, burial (at на П); **~тли́вый** [14 *sh.*] lustful, lewd; **'~ть** *f* [8] lust.
поцелýй *m* [3] kiss (on в В).
почáсно hourly.
пóчва *f* [5] soil, (*a. fig.*) ground.
почём F how much (is); how should.
почемý why; ~-то for some reason.
пóчерк *m* [1] handwriting.
почерп|áть [1], ⟨~нýть⟩ [20; -éрпнутый] gather, derive; obtain.
пóчесть[1] *f* [8] hono(u)r.
почéсть[2] *s.* почитáть 2.
почёт *m* [1] hono(u)r, esteem; **~ный** [14; -тен, -тна] honorary; hono(u)rable; (*e. g. guard*) of hono(u)r.
почи|вáть [1], ⟨~́ть⟩ [-и́ю, -и́ешь] rest, repose; F sleep.
почи́н *m* [1] initiative; F ✝ start.
почи́н|ка *f* [5; *g/pl.:* -нок] repair (for в В); **~и́ть** [28] *s.* чини́ть 1 a.
поч|итáть[1] [1] **1.** ⟨~ти́ть⟩ [-чтý, -ти́шь; -чтённый] esteem, respect, hono(u)r; worship; ✝ favo(u)r (with Т); **2.** ⟨~éсть⟩ [25; -чтý, -тёшь; -члá; -чтённый] (Т, за В) esteem, consider; **-ся** be held *or* reputed (to be Т); **~итáть**[2] [1] *pf.* read (a while); **~и́ть** *s.* почивáть; **~́ка** *f* [5; *g/pl.:* -чек] ❦ bud; *anat.* kidney.
пóчт|а *f* [5] mail, *Brt.* post (by по Д, Т); post; *a.* = **~áмт**; **~альóн** *m* [1] mailman, postman; **~áмт** *m* [1] post office (at на П).
почтéн|ие *n* [12] respect (for к Д), esteem, obeisance; F compliments; с совершéнным **~ием** respectfully yours, yours faithfully; **~ный** [14; -éнен, -éнна] respectable; venerable.
почти́ almost, nearly, all but; **~тельность** *f* [8] respect; **~тельный** [14; -лен, -льна] respectful; respectable; **~ть** *s.* почитáть.
почтóв|ый [14] post(al), mail...; post-office; note (*paper*); **~ый я́щик** *m* mail (*Brt.* letter) box; (*abbr.*: п/я) Post Office Box (POB); **~ая мáрка** *f* (postage) stamp.
пóшл|ина *f* [5] custom, duty; **~ость** *f* [8] platitude; **~ый** [14; пошл, -á, -о] common(place), trite, stale.
поштýчный [14] (by the) piece.
пощáда *f* [5] mercy; ⚔ quarter.
пощёчина *f* [5] slap in the face.
поэ́|зия *f* [7] poetry; **~ти́ческий** [16] poetic(al); **~тому** therefore.
появ|и́ться *s.* **~ля́ться**; **~лéние** *n* [12] appearance; **~ля́ться** [28], ⟨~и́ться⟩ [14] appear; emerge.
пóяс *m* [1; *pl.:* -cá, *etc. e.*] belt; zone.
поясн|éние *n* [12] explanation; **~и́тельный** [14] explanatory; **~и́ть** *s.* **~я́ть**; **~и́ца** *f* [5] small of the back; **~óй** [14] belt...; zone...; half-length; **~я́ть** [28], ⟨~и́ть⟩ [13] explain.
прабáбушка *f* [5; *g/pl.:* -шек] great-grandmother.

пра́вд|а *f* [5] truth; (э́то) **~а** it is true; ва́ша **~а** you are right; не **~а** ли? isn't it, (s)he?, aren't you, they?, do(es)n't ... (*etc.*)?; **~и́вый** [14 *sh.*] truthful; **~оподо́бный** [14; -бен, -бна] likely, probable, verisimilar.
пра́ведн|ик *m* [1] (*pl.* the) righteous (man); **~ый** [14; -ден, -дна] just, righteous, godly.
пра́вил|о *n* [9] rule; principle; *pl.* regulations; **~ьный** [14; -лен, -льна] correct, right; regular.
прави́тель *m* [4] ruler; regent; **~ственный** [14] governmental; **~ство** *n* [9] government.
пра́в|ить [14] (T) govern, rule; drive; ⚓ steer; (B) (proof)read; strop; perform; **~ка** *f* [5] proofreading; stropping; **~ле́ние** *n* [12] government; board of directors, managing *or* executive committee; † administration.
пра́внук *m* [1] great-grandson.
пра́во 1. *n* [9; *pl. e.*] right (to на B; of, by по Д); law; justice; *pl.* F license; **2.** *adv.* F indeed, really; **~ве́д** *m* [1] jurist; **~ве́дение** *n* [12] jurisprudence; **~ве́рный** [14; -рен, -рна] orthodox; **~во́й** [14] legal; **~мо́чный** [14; -чен, -чна] authorized; **~писа́ние** *n* [12] orthography, spelling; **~сла́вие** *n* [12] Orthodoxy; **~сла́вный** [14] Orthodox; **~су́дие** *n* [12] (administration of) justice; **~та́** *f* [5] right(fulness), rectitude.
пра́вый [14; *fig.* прав, -á, -o] right (*a. fig.*; *a. side*, on *a.* с P), right-hand.
пра́вящий [17] ruling.
Пра́га *f* [5] Prague.
пра́дед *m* [1] (great-)grandfather.
пра́здн|ик *m* [1] holiday; festival; с **~иком**! compliments *pl.* (of the season)!; **~ичный** [14] festive, holiday...; **~ование** *n* [12] celebration; **~овать** [7], ‹от-› celebrate; **~осло́вие** *n* [12] idle talk; **~ость** *f* [8] idleness; **~ый** [14; -ден, -дна] idle.
пра́кти|к *m* [1] practical man; expert; **~ка** *f* [5] practice (in на П); **~кова́ть** [7] practice, -ise (*v/i.* **-ся**; *a.* be practiced); **∠ческий** [16], **∠чный** [14; -чен, -чна] practical.
пра́порщик † *m* [1] ensign.
прах *m* [1] dust; ashes *pl.* (*fig.*).
пра́ч|ечная (-ʃn-) *f* [14] laundry; **~ка** *f* [5; *g/pl.*: -чек] laundress.
праща́ *f* [5; *g/pl.*: -ще́й] sling.
пребыва́|ние *n* [12], **~ть** [1] stay.
превзойти́ *s.* превосходи́ть.
превоз|мога́ть [1], ‹**~мо́чь**› [26 г/ж: -огу́, -о́жешь, -о́гут; -о́г, -гла́] overcome, subdue; **~носи́ть** [15], ‹**~нести́**› [24 -с-] extol, exalt.
превосх|оди́тельство *n* [9] Excellency; **~оди́ть** [15], ‹превзойти́› [-йду́, -йдёшь, *etc.*, *cf.* идти́; -йдённый] excel, surpass; **~о́дный** [14; -ден, -дна] excellent, splendid; superior; *gr.* superlative; **~о́дство** *n* [9] superiority.
превра|ти́ть(ся) *s.* **~ща́ть(ся)**; **∠тность** *f* [8] vicissitude; wrongness; **∠тный** [14; -тен, -тна] wrong, mis-...; adverse, changeful; **~ща́ть** [1], ‹**~ти́ть**› [15 *e.*; -ащу́, -ати́шь; -ащённый] change, turn, transform (into в B) (*v/i.* **-ся**); **~ще́ние** *n* [12] change; transformation; conversion.
превы|ша́ть [1], ‹**∠сить**› [15] exceed; **~ше́ние** *n* [12] excess.
прегра́|да *f* [5] barrier; obstacle; **~жда́ть** [1], ‹**~ди́ть**› [15 *e.*; -ажу́, -ади́шь; -аждённый] bar, block (up).
прегреш|а́ть [1], ‹**~и́ть**› [16] sin.
пред = пе́ред.
преда|ва́ть [5], ‹**∠ть**› [-да́м, -да́шь, *etc.*, *cf.* -дать; пре́дал, -á, -o; -да́й (-те)!; пре́данный (-ан, -á, -o)] betray; subject, expose; **∠ть** забве́нию bury in oblivion; **-ся** (Д) indulge (in); devote o. s., give o. s. up (to); **∠ние** *n* [12] legend; tradition; **'~нный** [14 *sh.*] devoted, faithful, true; *cf.* и́скренний; **∠тель** *m* [4] traitor; **∠тельский** [16] treacherous; **∠тельство** *n* [9] treason, treachery; **∠ть(ся)** *s.* **~ва́ть(ся)**.
предвар|и́тельно previously, before(hand); **~и́тельный** [14] preliminary; ⚖ *a.* on remand; **~я́ть** [28], ‹**~и́ть**› [13] (B) forestall; advise (of о П).
предве́|стие = предзнаменова́ние; **~стник** *m* [1] harbinger; **~ща́ть** [1] forebode, presage.
предвзя́тый [14 *sh.*] preconceived.
предви́деть [11] foresee.
предвку|ша́ть [1], ‹**~си́ть**› [15] foretaste; **~ше́ние** *n* [12] foretaste.
предводи́тель *m* [4] (ring)leader; † marshal; **~ство** *n* [9] leadership.
предвосх|ища́ть [1], ‹**~и́тить**› [15; -и́щу] anticipate, forestall.
предвы́борный [14] election...
преде́л *m* [1] limit, bound(ary) (within в П); border; *pl.* precincts; **~ьный** [14] limit..., maximum...; utmost, extreme.
предзнаменова́|ние *n* [12] omen, presage, portent; **~ть** [7] *pf.* portend, presage.
предисло́вие *n* [12] preface.
предл|ага́ть [1], ‹**~ожи́ть**› [16] offer (a p. s. th. Д/B); propose; suggest; order.
предло́|г *m* [1] pretext (on, under под T), pretense (under); *gr.* preposition; **~же́ние** *n* [12] offer; proposal, proposition, suggestion; *parl.* motion; ✝ supply; *gr.* sentence, clause (*cf.* пя́тый); **~жи́ть** *s.* предлага́ть; **~жный** [14] *gr.* prepositional (*case*).
предме́стье *n* [10] suburb.

предмéт *m* [1] object; subject (matter); ✝ article; на ~ (P) for the purpose of; **~ный** [14] subject...; [-тен, -тна] objective.
предназн|ачáть [1], ⟨**~áчить**⟩ [16] (-ся be) destine(d).
предна|мéренный [14 *sh.*] premeditated, deliberate; **~чертáть** [1] *pf.* predetermine.
прéдок *m* [1; -дка] ancestor.
предопредел|éние *n* [12] predestination; **~я́ть** [28], ⟨**~и́ть**⟩ [13] predetermine.
предост|авля́ть [28], ⟨**~áвить**⟩ [14] (Д) let (a p.) have; leave (to); give, render; grant; place (at a p.'s disposal).
предостер|егáть [1], ⟨**~éчь**⟩ [26 г/ж] warn (of от P); **~ежéние** *n* [12] warning.
предосторóжност|ь *f* [8] precaution(ary measure мéра **~и**).
предосуди́тельный [14; -лен, -льна] reprehensible, scandalous.
предотвра|щáть [1], ⟨**~ти́ть**⟩ [15 *е.*; -ащý, -ати́шь; -ащённый] avert, prevent; **~щéние** *n* [12] prevention.
предохран|éние *n* [12] protection (from, against от P); **~и́тельный** [14] precautionary; ⚕ preventive; ⊕ safety...; **~я́ть** [28], ⟨**~и́ть**⟩ [13] guard, preserve (from от P).
предпис|áние *n* [12] order, instruction, direction; **~ывать** [1], ⟨**~áть**⟩ [3] order, prescribe.
предпол|агáть [1], ⟨**~ожи́ть**⟩ [16] suppose, assume; *impf.* intend, plan; presuppose; **~ожи́тельный** [14; -лен, -льна] presumable; **~ожи́ть** *s.* **~агáть**.
предпо|слáть *s.* **~сылáть**; **~слéдний** [15] last but one; **~сылáть** [1], ⟨**~слáть**⟩ [-шлю, -шлёшь; *cf.* слать] premise; **~сы́лка** *f* [5; *g/pl.*: -лок] (pre)supposition; (pre-)condition, prerequisite.
предпоч|итáть [1], ⟨**~éсть**⟩ [25 -т-: -чтý, -чтёшь; -чёл, -члá; -чтённый] prefer; *pt.* + бы would rather; **~тéние** *n* [12] preference; favo(u)r; отдáть ~тéние (Д) prefer; **~ти́тельный** [14; -лен, -льна] preferable.
предпри|и́мчивость *f* [8] enterprise; **~и́мчивый** [14 *sh.*] enterprising; **~нимáтель** *m* [4] employer; industrialist, businessman; **~нимáть** [1], ⟨**~ня́ть**⟩ [-имý, -и́мешь; -и́нял, -á, -о; -и́нятый (-и́нят, -á, -о)] undertake; **~я́тие** *n* [12] undertaking, enterprise; business; plant, works, factory (at на П).
предраспол|агáть [1], ⟨**~ожи́ть**⟩ [16] predispose; **~ожéние** *n* [12] predisposition.
предрассýдок *m* [1; -дка] prejudice.
председáтель *m* [4] chairman, president; **~ство** *n* [9] presidency; **~ствовать** [7] preside (over на П), be in the chair.
предсказ|áние *n* [12] prediction; forecast; prophecy; **~ывать** [1], ⟨**~áть**⟩ [3] foretell, predict; forecast; prophesy.
предсмéртный [14] death..., dying.
представи́тель *m* [4] representative; *cf.* *a.* полпрéд; advocate; **~ный** [14; -лен, -льна] representative; stately, imposing; **~ство** *n* [9] representation; *cf.* *a.* полпрéдство.
предстáв|ить(ся) *s.* **~ля́ть(ся)**; **~лéние** *n* [12] presentation; performance; introduction; idea, notion; application (for на В); **~ля́ть** [28], ⟨**~ить**⟩ [14] present (o.s., occur, offer **-ся**); produce; introduce (o.s.); (*a.* собóй) represent, be; act (*a.* = feign -ся [T]); (*esp.* ~ля́ть себé) imagine; propose (for к Д); *refl.* *a.* appear; seem.
предст|авáть [5], ⟨**~áть**⟩ [-áну, -áнешь] appear; **~оя́ть** [-ои́т] be in store (of Д), expect; (will) have to; **~оя́щий** [17] (forth)coming.
преду|беждéние *n* [12] prejudice, bias; **~ведомля́ть** [28], ⟨**~вéдомить**⟩ [14] advise (of о П); **~гáдывать** [1], ⟨**~гадáть**⟩ [1] guess (beforehand), foresee; **~мы́шленный** [14] *s.* преднамéренный.
предупре|ди́тельный [14; -лен, -льна] preventive; obliging; **~ждáть** [1], ⟨**~ди́ть**⟩ [15 *е.*; -ежý, -еди́шь; -еждённый] forestall, anticipate (*p.*), prevent (*th.*); warn (of о П); give notice (of); **~ждéние** *n* [12] warning; notice; notification; prevention.
предусм|áтривать [1], ⟨**~отрéть**⟩ [9; -отрю́, -óтришь] foresee; provide (for), stipulate; **~отри́тельный** [14; -лен, -льна] prudent.
предчýвств|ие *n* [12] presentiment; **~овать** [7] have a presentiment (of).
предшéств|енник *m* [1] predecessor; **~овать** [7] (Д) precede.
предъяв|и́тель *m* [4] bearer; **~ля́ть** [28], ⟨**~и́ть**⟩ [14] present, produce, show; ⚖ bring (*action* against к Д); assert (*claim*).
пре|дыдýщий [17] preceding, previous; **~éмник** *m* [1] successor.
прéж|де formerly; (at) first; (P) before (*a.* ~де чем); **~деврéменный** [14; -енен, -енна] premature, early; **~ний** [15] former, previous.
презид|éнт *m* [1] president; **~иум** *m* [1] presidium (*Sov.*).
през|ирáть [1] despise; ⟨**~рéть**⟩ [9] scorn, disdain; **~рéние** *n* [12] contempt (for к Д); **~рéнный** [14 *sh.*] contemptible, despicable; **~рéть** *s.* **~ирáть**; **~ри́тельный** [14; -лен, -льна] contemptuous, scornful.
преимýществ|енно predominant-

ly, mainly; **~о** *n* [9] advantage; preference; privilege; по **~у** = **~**енно.
прейскура́нт *m* [1] price list.
преклон|е́ние *n* [12] inclination; admiration (of пе́ред Т); **~и́ться** *s.* **~я́ться**; **∠ный** [14] old, advanced; senile; **~я́ться** [28], ⟨**~и́ться**⟩ [13] bow (to, before пе́ред Т); admire.
прекосло́вить [14] contradict.
прекра́сный [14; -сен, -сна] beautiful; fine, splendid, excellent; *a.* very well.
прекра|ща́ть [1], ⟨**~ти́ть**⟩ [15 *e.*; -ащу́, -ати́шь; -ащённый] stop, cease, end (*v/i.* **-ся**); break off; **~ще́ние** *n* [12] cessation, stoppage.
преле́ст|ный [14; -тен, -тна] lovely, charming, delightful; **'~ь** *f* [8] charm; F *s.* **~ный**.
прелом|ле́ние *n* [12] refraction; **~ля́ть** [28], ⟨**~и́ть**⟩ [14; -млённый] (-ся be) refract(ed).
пре́лый [14 *sh.*] rotten, putrid.
прель|ща́ть [1], ⟨**~сти́ть**⟩ [15 *e.*; -льщу́, -льсти́шь; -льщённый] (-ся be) charm(ed), tempt(ed), entice(d), seduce(d).
прелю́дия *f* [7] prelude.
премя́|нуть [19] *pf.* fail; **~рова́ть** [7] (*im*)*pf.* award a prize (to В); **'~я** *f* [7] prize; bonus; premium; rate.
премье́р *m* [1] premier, (*usu.* **~**-мини́стр) prime minister; **~а** *f* [5] première, first night.
пренебр|ега́ть [1], ⟨**~е́чь**⟩ [26 г/ж], **~еже́ние** *n* [12] (Т) neglect, disregard, disdain, scorn, slight; **~ежи́тельный** [14; -лен, -льна] slighting, scornful, disparaging; **~е́чь** *s.* **~ега́ть**.
пре́ния *n/pl.* [12] debate, discussion.
преоблада́|ние *n* [12] predominance; **~ть** [1] prevail, predominate.
преобра|жа́ть [1], ⟨**~зи́ть**⟩ [15 *e.*; -ажу́, -ази́шь; -ажённый] change, transform (*v/i.* **-ся**); **~же́ние** *n* [12] transformation; *eccl.* Transfiguration; **~зи́ть(ся)** *s.* **~жа́ть(ся)**; **~зова́ние** *n* [12] transformation; reorganization; reform; **~зова́тель** *m* [4] reformer; **~зо́вывать** [1], ⟨**~зова́ть**⟩ [7] reform, reorganize; transform.
преодол|ева́ть [1], ⟨**~е́ть**⟩ [8] overcome, subdue; surmount.
препара́т *m* [1] preparation.
препира́тельство *n* [9] wrangle.
преподава́|ние *n* [12] teaching, instruction; **~тель** *m* [4], **~тельница** *f* [5] teacher, instructor; **~ть** [5] teach.
преподн|оси́ть [15], ⟨**~ести́**⟩ [24 -с-] present, offer.
препрово|жда́ть [1], ⟨**~ди́ть**⟩ [15 *e.*; -ожу́, -оди́шь; -ождённый] forward, send; spend, pass.
препя́тств|ие *n* [12] obstacle, hindrance; бег (*or* ска́чки) с **~и**ями steeplechase; **~овать** [7], ⟨вос-⟩ hinder, prevent (a p. from Д/в П).
прер|ва́ть(ся) *s.* **~ыва́ть(ся)**; **~ека́ние** *n* [12] squabble; **~ыва́ть** [1], ⟨**~ва́ть**⟩ [-ву́, -вёшь; -ал, -а́, -о; пре́рванный (-ан, -а́, -о)] interrupt; break (off), *v/i.* **-ся**; **~ы́вистый** [14 *sh.*] broken, faltering.
пресе|ка́ть [1], ⟨**∠чь**⟩ [26] cut short; suppress; **-ся** break; stop.
пресле́дов|ание *n* [12] pursuit; persecution; ⚖ prosecution; **~ать** [7] pursue; persecute; haunt; ⚖ prosecute.
пресловУ́тый [14] notorious.
пресмыка́|ться [1] creep, crawl; *fig.* cringe (to пе́ред Т); **~ющиеся** *n/pl.* [17] reptiles.
пре́сный [14; -сен, -сна́, -о] fresh (*water*); unleavened (*bread*); stale.
пресс *m* [1] ⊕ press; **∠а** *f* [5] press; **~-конфере́нция** *f* [7] press conference; **~-папье́** *n* [*ind.*] paperweight.
престаре́лый [14] aged.
престо́л *m* [1] throne; altar.
преступ|а́ть [1], ⟨**~и́ть**⟩ [14] break, infringe; **~ле́ние** *n* [12] crime; на ме́сте **~ле́ния** red-handed; **∠ник** *m* [1] criminal, delinquent; **∠ность** *f* [8] criminality, delinquency.
пресы|ща́ть [1], ⟨**∠тить**⟩ [15] surfeit (*v/i.* **-ся**), satiate; **~ще́ние** *n* [12] satiety.
претвор|я́ть [28], ⟨**~и́ть**⟩ [13] change, transform; **~я́ть** в жизнь put into practice, realize.
претен|дова́ть [7] (на В) (lay) claim (to); **∠зия** *f* [7] claim, pretension, title (to на В, к Д); быть в **∠зии** (на В [за В]) take (a p.'s [th.]) amiss *or* ill.
преувел|иче́ние *n* [12] exaggeration; **~и́чивать** [1], ⟨**~и́чить**⟩ [16] exaggerate.
преусп|ева́ть [1], ⟨**~е́ть**⟩ [8] succeed; thrive, prosper.
при (П) by, at, near; (*battle*) of; under, in the time of; in a p.'s presence; about (one **~** себе́), with; in (*health, weather, etc.*); for (all that **~** всём том); when, on (*-ing*); быть **~** have; be attached to; **~** э́том at that; ✝ **~** сём herewith; быть ни **~** чём F have nothing to do with (it тут), not be p.'s fault.
приба́в|ить(ся) *s.* **~ля́ть(ся)**; **~ка** *f* [5; *g/pl.*: -вок], **~ле́ние** *n* [12] increase, raise; addition; addendum; **~ля́ть** [28], ⟨**~ить**⟩ [14] (В *or* Р) add; increase; put on (*weight* в П); mend (one's pace **~ля́ть** ша́гу) **-ся** increase; be added; (a)rise; grow longer; **~очный** [14] additional; surplus...
прибалти́йский [16] Baltic.

прибаутка F *f* [5; *g/pl.:* -ток] byword, saying.
прибе|гать [1] **1.** ⟨~жать⟩ [4; -егу́, -ежишь, -егу́т] come running; **2.** ⟨ˏгнуть⟩ [20] resort, have recourse (to к Д); **~регать** [1], ⟨~речь⟩ [26 г/ж] save, reserve.
приби|вать [1], ⟨ˏть⟩ [-бью́, -бьёшь, *etc., cf.* бить] fasten, nail; beat (down); throw (*ashore*); **~рать** [1], ⟨прибрать⟩ [-беру́, -рёшь; -брал, -а́, -о; прибранный] tidy *or* clean (up); прибрать к рукам appropriate; **-ся** F make o.s. up; **ˏть** *s.* ~вать.
прибли|жать [1], ⟨ˏзить⟩ [15] approach, draw near (к Д; *v/i.* **-ся**); approximate; **~жение** *n* [12] approach(ing); approximation; **~жённый** [14] confidant; *a.* = **~зительный** [14; -лен, -льна] approximate; **ˏзить(ся)** *s.* ~жать(ся).
прибой *m* [3] surf.
прибор *m* [1] apparatus, instrument; set; cover; service; (*table*)ware; utensils *pl.*, (*shaving*) things *pl.*
прибрать *s.* прибирать.
прибрежный [14] littoral.
прибы|вать [1], ⟨ˏть⟩ [-бу́ду, -дешь; прибыл, -а́, -о] arrive (in, at в В); increase, rise; **'~ль** *f* [8] profit, gains *pl.*; rise; **'~льный** [14; -лен, -льна] profitable; **ˏтие** *n* [12] arrival (in, at в В; upon по П); **ˏть** *s.* ~вать.
привал *m* [1] halt, rest.
приве|дение *n* [12] putting (*in order* в В); ⚔ reduction; **~сти** *s.* привозить; **~редливый** [14 *sh.*] fastidious.
привержен|ец *m* [1; -нца] adherent; **~ный** [14 *sh.*] attached.
привести *s.* приводить.
привет *m* [1] greeting(s); *esp.* ⚔ salute; regards, compliments *pl.*; F hello!, hi!; **~ливый** [14 *sh.*] affable; **~ственный** [14] of welcome; **~ствие** *n* [12] greeting, welcome; **~ствовать** [7; *pt. a. pf.*] greet, salute; welcome.
приви|вать [1], ⟨ˏть⟩ [-вью́, -вьёшь, *etc., cf.* вить] inoculate, vaccinate; ⚘ (en)graft; **-ся** take; **ˏвка** *f* [5; *g/pl.:* -вок] inoculation, vaccination; grafting; **~дение** *n* [12] ghost, specter (*Brt.*-tre), apparition; **~легированный** [14] privileged; **~легия** *f* [7] privilege; **ˏнчивать** [1], ⟨~нтить⟩ [15 *e.*; -нчу́, -нтишь] screw on; **ˏть(ся)** *s.* ~вать(ся).
привкус *m* [1] smack (*a. fig.*).
привле|кательный [14; -лен, -льна] attractive; **~кать** [1], ⟨ˏчь⟩ [26] draw, attract; engage (in к Д); call (*to account*); bring (*to trial*); **~чение** *n* [12] attraction; calling.
привод *m* [1] bringing; ⊕ drive; **~ить** [15], ⟨привести⟩ [25] bring; lead; result (in к Д); quote, cite; ⚔ reduce; put, set; drive, throw; **-ся**, ⟨-сь⟩ Д + *vb.* F happen; have to; **~ной** [14] driving (*belt, etc.*).
привоз|ить [15], ⟨привезти⟩ [24] bring; import; **~ной** & **ˏный** [14] imported.
приволье *n* [10] open (space), expanse; freedom; ease, comfort; в ~ *a.* in clover.
привы|кать [1], ⟨ˏкнуть⟩ [21] get *or* be(come) accustomed *or* used (to к Д); **ˏчка** *f* [5; *g/pl.:* -чек] habit; custom; **ˏчный** [14; -чен, -чна] habitual.
привяз|анность *f* [8] attachment; **~ать(ся)** *s.* ~ывать(ся); **~чивый** F [14 *sh.*] affectionate; captious; obtrusive; **~ывать** [1], ⟨~ать⟩ [3] (к Д) tie, attach (to); **-ся** become attached; F run after; intrude (upon); cavil; **'~ь** *f* [8] leash.
пригла|сительный [14] invitation...; **~шать** [1], ⟨~сить⟩ [15 *e.*; -ашу́, -асишь; -ашённый] invite (to *mst* на В), ask; call (*doctor*); **~шение** *n* [12] invitation.
пригнать *s.* пригонять.
пригов|аривать [1], ⟨~орить⟩ [13] sentence; condemn; *impf.* F say (at the same time); **~ор** *m* [1] sentence; verdict (*a. fig.*); **~орить** *s.* ~аривать.
пригодный [14; -ден, -дна] *s.* годный.
пригонять [28], ⟨пригнать⟩ [-гоню́, -гонишь; -гнал, -а́, -о; пригнанный] drive; fit, adjust.
пригор|ать [1], ⟨~еть⟩ [9] burn; **'~од** *m* [1] suburb; **'~одный** [14] suburban; **'ˏшня** *f* [6; *g/pl.:* -ней & -шен] hand(ful).
пригот|авливать(ся) [1] *s.* ~овлять(ся); **~овительный** [14] preparatory; **~овить(ся)** *s.* ~овлять(-ся); **~овление** *n* [12] preparation (for к Д); **~овлять** [28], ⟨~овить⟩ [14] prepare (*v/i.*, o.s. **-ся**) (for к Д).
прида|вать [5], ⟨ˏть⟩ [-дам, -дашь, *etc., cf.* дать; придал, -а́, -о; приданный (-ан, -а́, -о)] add; give; attach; **ˏное** *n* [14] dowry; **ˏток** *m* [1; -тка] appendage; *anat.* appendix; **ˏточный** [14] *gr.* subordinate (*clause*); **ˏть** *s.* ~вать; **ˏча** *f* [5]: в ˏчу to boot.
придви|гать [1], ⟨ˏнуть⟩ [20] move up (*v/i.* **-ся**; draw near).
придворный [14] court(ier *su. m*).
придел|ывать, ⟨~ать⟩ [1] fasten, fix (to к Д).
придерж|ивать [1], ⟨~ать⟩ [4] hold (back); **-ся** *impf.* (P) adhere to; F hold (on [to]).
придир|аться [1], ⟨придраться⟩ [-деру́сь, -рёшься; -дрался, -ала́сь, -алось] (к Д) find fault (with), carp *or* cavil (at); seize; **~ка** *f* [5; *g/pl.:* -рок] cavil; **~чивый** [14 *sh.*] captious.

придра́ться *s.* придира́ться.
приду́м|ывать, ⟨~ать⟩ [1] think out, devise, contrive.
придыха́ние *n* [12] aspiration.
прие́з|д *m* [1] arrival (in в В; upon по П); **~жа́ть** [1], ⟨прие́хать⟩ [-е́ду, -е́дешь] arrive (in, at в В); **~жий** [17] visitant..., guest...
приём *m* [1] reception; acceptance, admission; consultation; engagement, ⚔ enlistment; taking; dose; movement (with в В); draught; sitting (at в В); device, trick; method, way; **~ник** *m* [1] receiver, receiving set; *s.* радиоприёмник; **~ный** [14] reception (*day*; *room: a.* waiting, *usu. su. f* ~ная), receiving, consultation..., office (*hours*); entrance (*examination*); foster (*father, etc.*; foster child *a.* **~ыш** *m* [1]).
при|е́хать *s.* ~езжа́ть; **~жа́ть(ся)** *s.* ~жима́ть(ся); **~жига́ть** [1], ⟨~же́чь⟩ [26 г/ж: -жгу́, -жжёшь; *cf.* жечь] cauterize; **~жима́ть** [1], ⟨~жа́ть⟩ [-жму́, -жмёшь; -а́тый] press (to, on к Д); **-ся** press; nestle; **~з** *m* [1] prize; **~заду́м(ыв)аться** *s.* заду́м(ыв)аться.
призва́|ние *n* [12] vocation, calling; **~ть** *s.* призыва́ть.
приземл|я́ться ✈ [28], ⟨~и́ться⟩ [13] land; **~е́ние** *n* [12] landing.
при́зма *f* [5] prism.
призна|ва́ть [5], ⟨*~ть*⟩ [1] (Т; *a.* за В) recognize, acknowledge (as); see, admit, own; find, consider, declare; **-ся** confess (s. th. в П), avow, admit; *~*ться *or* ~ю́сь to tell the truth, frankly speaking; **'~к** *m* [1] sign; feature, characteristic; **~ние** *n* [12] acknowledg(e)ment, recognition; confession; declaration (of love в любви́); **~тельность** *f* [8] gratitude; **~тельный** [14; -лен, -льна] grateful, thankful (for за В); **~ть(ся)** *s.* ~ва́ть(ся).
при́зра|к *m* [1] phantom, specter (*Brt.* -tre); **~чный** [14; -чен, -чна] ghostly; illusive.
призы́в *m* [1] appeal, call (for на В), summons; ⚔ draft, conscription; **~а́ть** [1], ⟨призва́ть⟩ [-зову́, -вёшь; -зва́л, -а́, -о; при́званный] call (for на В; to witness в свиде́тели), appeal; ⚔ draft, call out *or* up (for на В); **при́званный** *a.* qualified; **~ни́к** *m* [1 *e.*] draftee, conscript; **~но́й** [14] ⚔ draft(ee)...
при́иск *m* [1] mine, field.
прийти́(сь) *s.* приходи́ть(ся).
прика́з *m* [1] order, command; *hist.* office, board; **~а́ть** *s.* ~ывать; **~чик** *m* [1] † *s.* продаве́ц; steward; **~ывать** [1], ⟨~а́ть⟩ [3] order, command; tell; F should, ought; *s. a.* уго́дно.
при|ка́лывать [1], ⟨~коло́ть⟩ [17] pin, fasten; stab; **~каса́ться** [1], ⟨~косну́ться⟩ [20] (к Д, † Р) touch; **~ки́дывать** [1], ⟨~ки́нуть⟩ [20] weigh; calculate; estimate; **-ся** F pretend *or* feign to be, act (the Т).
прикла́д *m* [1] (*rifle*) butt; **~но́й** [14] applied; **~ывать** [1], ⟨приложи́ть⟩ [16] (к Д) apply (to), put (on); enclose (with); affix (*seal*); **-ся** kiss; F level; apply (s. th. to Т/к Д).
прикле́и|вать [1], ⟨~ть⟩ [13] paste.
приключ|а́ться F [1], ⟨~и́ться⟩ [16 *e.*; *3rd p. only*] happen, occur; **~е́ние** *n* [12] (**~е́нческий** [16] of) adventure.
прико́|вывать [1], ⟨~ва́ть⟩ [7 *e.*; -кую́, -куёшь] chain, fetter; arrest, captivate; **~ла́чивать** [1], ⟨~лоти́ть⟩ [15] nail (on, to к Д), fasten; **~ло́ть** *s.* прика́лывать; **~мандирова́ть** [7] *pf.* attach; **~снове́ние** *n* [12] touch, contact; **~сну́ться** *s.* прикаса́ться.
прикра́|са F *f* [5] embellishment; **~шивать** [1], ⟨~сить⟩ [15] embellish.
прикреп|и́ть(ся) *s.* ~ля́ть(ся); **~ле́ние** *n* [12] fastening; attaching; **~ля́ть** [28], ⟨~и́ть⟩ [14 *e.*; -плю́, -пи́шь; плённый] fasten; attach; **-ся** register (with к Д).
прикри́к|ивать [1], ⟨~нуть⟩ [20] shout (at на В).
прикры|ва́ть [1], ⟨*~*ть⟩ [22] cover; protect; **~тие** *n* [12] cover (*a.* ⚔); convoy; *fig.* cloak.
прила́вок *m* [1; -вка] counter.
прилага́|тельное *n* [14] adjective (*a.* и́мя ~тельное); **~ть** [1], ⟨приложи́ть⟩ [16] (к Д) enclose (with); apply (to); take (*pains*), make (*efforts*); ~емый enclosed.
прила́|живать [1], ⟨~дить⟩ [15] fit.
приле|га́ть [1] **1.** (к Д) (ad)join, border; **2.** ⟨*~*чь⟩ [26 г/ж: -ля́гу, -ля́жешь, -ля́гут; -лёг, -легла́; -ля́г(те)!] lie down (for a while); fit (closely); **~жа́ние** *n* [12] diligence; **~жный** [14; -жен, -жна] diligent, industrious; **~пля́ть** [28], ⟨~пи́ть⟩ [14] stick; **~та́ть** [1], ⟨~те́ть⟩ [11] arrive, fly; **~чь** *s.* ~га́ть 2.
прили́|в *m* [1] flood, flow; *fig.* rush; **~ва́ть** [1], ⟨~ть⟩ [-лью́, -льёшь; *cf.* лить] rush; add; **~па́ть** [1], ⟨~пнуть⟩ [21] stick; **~ть** *s.* ~ва́ть.
прили́ч|ие *n* [12] decency (for d.'s sake из *or* для Р), decorum; **~ный** [14; -чен, -чна] decent, proper; F respectable.
прилож|е́ние *n* [12] enclosure; supplement; application; *gr.* apposition; *seal*: affixture; **~и́ть** *s.* прикла́дывать & прилага́ть.
прима́нка *f* [5; *g/pl.*: -нок] bait, lure.
примен|е́ние *n* [12] application; use; adaptation; **~и́мый** [14 *sh.*] applicable; **~я́ть** [28], ⟨~и́ть⟩ [13;

-еню́, -е́нишь; -енённый] apply (to к Д); use, employ; -ся adapt o.s.

приме́р *m* [1] example (в ~ *cite* as an example); не в ~ F far + *comp.*; к ~у F = наприме́р; **~ивать** [1], ⟨~ить⟩ [13] try *or* fit on; **~ка** *f* [5; *g/pl.*: -рок] trying *or* fitting on; **~ный** [14; -рен, -рна] exemplary; approximate; **~я́ть** [28] = ~ивать.

при́месь *f* [8] admixture.

приме́|та *f* [5] mark, sign, token; omen; *pl.* signalment, description; на ~те in view; **~тить** *s.* ~ча́ть; **~тный** *s.* заме́тный; **~ча́ние** *n* [12] (foot)note; notice; **~ча́тельный** [14; -лен, -льна] notable, remarkable; **~ча́ть** F [1], ⟨~тить⟩ [15] notice; **~шивать** [1], ⟨~ша́ть⟩ [1] add, (ad)mix.

примир|е́ние *n* [12] reconciliation; **~и́тельный** [14; -лен, -льна] (re-) conciliatory; arbitration...; **~и́ть** (-ся) [28] *s.* мири́ть(ся).

примити́вный [14; -вен, -вна] primitive.

прим|кну́ть *s.* ~ыка́ть; **~о́рский** [16] coastal, seaside...; **~о́чка** *f* [5; *g/pl.*: -чек] lotion; **∠ула** *f* [5] primrose; **∠ус** *m* [1] kerosene stove; **~ча́ться** [4 *e.*; -мчу́сь, -чи́шься] *pf.* come in a great hurry; **~ыка́ть** [1], ⟨~кну́ть⟩ [20] join (*v/t.* к Д); *impf.* adjoin.

принадл|ежа́ть [4 *e.*; -жу́, -жи́шь] belong (to [к] Д), pertain; **~е́жность** *f* [8] accessory; material, implement; *pl.* *a.* equipment; membership.

принести́ *s.* приноси́ть.

принима́ть [1], ⟨приня́ть⟩ [приму́, -и́мешь; при́нял, -а́, -о; при́нятый (-ят, -а́, -о)] take (*a.* over; for за В; *measures*); accept; receive; admit ([in]to в, на В); pass (*law, etc.*); adopt; assume; ~ на себя́ take (up)on o.s., undertake; ~ на свой счёт feel hurt; ~ пара́д review troops; -ся [-ня́лся́, -ла́сь] (за В) set about *or* to, start; F take to task; ⚘, ⚕ take.

принорови́ть F [14 *e.*; -влю́, -ви́шь] *pf.* adapt; fit.

прин|оси́ть [15], ⟨~ести́⟩ [24 -с-: -есу́; -ёс, -есла́] bring (*a.* forth, in); yield (*a. profit, thanks*); make (*sacrifice* в В); ~оси́ть в дар *s.* дари́ть.

прину|ди́тельный [14; -лен, -льна] forced, compulsory, coercive; **~жда́ть** [1], ⟨∠дить⟩ [15] force, compel, constrain, oblige; **~жде́ние** *n* [12] compulsion, coercion, constraint (under по Д); **~ждённый** [14] forced, constrained, obliged.

при́нцип *m* [1] principle; (on в П, ~иа́льно); **~иа́льный** [14; -лен, -льна] of principle(s) (*a.* из ~а).

приня́|тие *n* [12] taking (over); acceptance; admission ([in]to в, на В); passing (*law, etc.*); adoption; assumption; **'~тый** [14] customary; *cf. a.* ~ть(ся) → принима́ть(ся).

приобре|та́ть [1], ⟨~сти́⟩ [25 -т-] acquire, obtain, get; buy; **~те́ние** *n* [12] acquisition.

приобщ|а́ть [1], ⟨~и́ть⟩ [16 *e.*; -щу́, -щи́шь; -щённый] (к Д) join, add; -ся join.

приостан|а́вливать [1], ⟨~ови́ть⟩ [14] stop (*v/i.* -ся); ⚖ suspend.

припа́док *m* [1; -дка] fit, attack.

припа́сы *m/pl.* [1] supplies, stores.

припая́ть [28] *pf.* solder (on to к Д).

припе́|в *m* [1] refrain; **~ва́ть** F [1] sing; ~ва́ючи F in clover; **~ка́ть** [1], ⟨~чь⟩ [26] burn, be hot.

припи́с|ка *f* [5; *g/pl.*: -сок] postscript; addition; **~ывать** [1], ⟨~а́ть⟩ [3] ascribe, attribute (to к Д); add.

припла́та *f* [5] extra payment.

припло́д *m* [1] increase, offspring.

приплы|ва́ть [1], ⟨∠ть⟩ [23] come, arrive, swim *or* sail (up to к Д).

приплю́снутый [14] flat (*nose*).

приподн|има́ть [1], ⟨~я́ть⟩ [-ниму́, -ни́мешь; -по́днял, -а́, -о; -по́днятый (-ят, -а́, -о)] lift *or* raise (-ся rise) (a little); **∠ятый** [14] high (*spirits*); elevated (*style*).

приполз|а́ть [1], ⟨~ти́⟩ [24] creep.

припом|ина́ть [1], ⟨∠нить⟩ [13] remember (*a. impers.* Д -ся И).

припра́в|а *f* [5] seasoning; **~ля́ть** [28], ⟨~ить⟩ [14] season, dress.

припух|а́ть [1], ⟨∠нуть⟩ [21] swell.

прира́вн|ивать [1], ⟨~я́ть⟩ [28] compare (to к Д); level.

прира|ста́ть [1], ⟨~сти́⟩ [24 -ст-: -стёт; -ро́с, -сла́] take; grow (to к Д); increase (by на В); **~ще́ние** *n* [12] increase; taking.

приро́|да *f* [5] nature (by, *a.* birth от Р [*a.* in]; по Д); **~дный** [14] natural; *a.* = **~ждённый** [14] (in)born; **~ст** *m* [1] increase.

прируч|а́ть [1], ⟨~и́ть⟩ [16 *e.*; -чу́, -чи́шь; -чённый] tame.

при|са́живаться [1], ⟨~се́сть⟩ [25; -ся́ду; -се́л] sit down (a while).

присв|а́ивать [1], ⟨~о́ить⟩ [13] appropriate; adopt; confer ([up]on Д); **~ое́ние** *n* [12] appropriation; adoption; conferment.

присе|да́ть [1], ⟨∠сть⟩ [25; -ся́ду; -се́л] squat; curts(e)y; **∠ст** *m* [1] sitting (at, in в В); **∠сть** *s.* ~да́ть & приса́живаться.

приска́к|ивать [1], ⟨~а́ть⟩ [3] come, arrive (at full gallop; leaping).

приско́рб|ие *n* [12] regret; **~ный** [14; -бен, -бна] deplorable, pitiable.

присла́ть *s.* присыла́ть.

прислон|я́ть [28], ⟨~и́ть⟩ [13] lean (*v/i.* -ся; against к Д).

прислу́|га *f* [5] servant(s); ⚔ crew, gunners *pl.*; **~живать** [1] wait

(up)on (Д), serve; **-ся** (Д) be subservient (to), ingratiate o. s. (with); **~шиваться**, ⟨**~шаться**⟩ [1] listen (to к Д).
присм|áтривать [1], ⟨**~отре́ть**⟩ [9; -отрю́, -о́тришь; -о́тренный] look after (за Т); F find; **-ся** (к Д) peer, look narrowly (at); examine (closely); familiarize o.s., get acquainted (with, *or* accustomed to); **~о́тр** *m* [1] care, supervision; **~отре́ть(ся)** *s.* **~а́тривать(ся)**.
присовокуп|ля́ть [28], ⟨**~и́ть**⟩ [14 *e.*; -плю́, -пи́шь; -плённый] add; enclose (with к Д).
присоедин|е́ние *n* [12] joining; connection; annexation; **~я́ть** [28], ⟨**~и́ть**⟩ [13] (к Д) join (*a.* **-ся**); connect, attach (to); annex, incorporate.
присп́ешник *m* [1] accomplice.
приспособ|ить(ся) *s.* **~ля́ть(ся)**; **~ле́ние** *n* [12] adaptation; device; **~ля́ть** [28], ⟨**~ить**⟩ [14] fit, adapt (o.s. **-ся**; to, for к Д, под В).
при́став *m* [1] (*form.*) police officer.
приста|ва́ть [5], ⟨**~ть**⟩ [-а́ну, -а́нешь] (к Д) stick (to); importune, pester; join; ⚓ land; F become; befit; ⚕ be taken (with); **~вить** *s.* **~вля́ть**; **~вка** *f* [5; *g*/*pl.*: -вок] prefix; **~вля́ть** [28], ⟨**~вить**⟩ [14] (к Д) set, put (to), lean (against); add, piece on; appoint (to look after); **'~льный** [14; -лен, -льна] steadfast; **'~нь** *f* [8; *from g*/*pl. e.*] quay, wharf, pier; **~ть** *s.* **~ва́ть**.
пристёгивать [1], ⟨**пристегну́ть**⟩ [20] button *or* fasten (to).
пристр|а́ивать [1], ⟨**~о́ить**⟩ [13] (к Д) add *or* attach (to); settle; place; provide; **-ся** F = устра́иваться; join.
пристра́ст|ие *n* [12] predilection (for к Д); bias; **~ный** [14; -тен, -тна] bias(s)ed, partial (to к Д).
пристре́ли|вать [1], ⟨**~ть**⟩ [13; -стрелю́, -е́лишь] shoot.
пристр|о́ить(ся) *s.* **~а́ивать(ся)**; **~о́йка** *f* [5; *g*/*pl.*: -о́ек] addition; annex.
при́ступ *m* [1] assault, onset, onslaught, storm (by Т); ⚕ & *fig.* fit, attack; F access; **~а́ть** [1], ⟨**~и́ть**⟩ [14] set about, start, begin; proceed (to); approach (*a.*, F, **-ся**).
прису|жда́ть [1], ⟨**~ди́ть**⟩ [15; -уждённый] (к Д) sentence, condemn (to); award; **~жде́ние** *n* [12] awarding.
прису́тств|ие *n* [12] presence (in в П; of mind ду́ха); † office (hours); **~овать** [7] be present (at на, в, при П); **~ующий** [17] present.
прису́щий [17 *sh.*] peculiar (to Д).
прис|ыла́ть [1], ⟨**~ла́ть**⟩ [-шлю́, -шлёшь; при́сланный] send (for за Т); **~ыпа́ть** [1], ⟨**~ы́пать**⟩ [2] (be)strew.
прися́|га *f* [5] oath (upon под Т); **~га́ть** [1], ⟨**~гну́ть**⟩ [20] swear; **~жный** [14] juror; суд **~жных** jury.
прита|и́ть [13] *pf.* F *s.* затаи́ть; **-ся** hold (*breath*); hide; keep quiet; **~скивать** [1], ⟨**~щи́ть**⟩ [16] drag (o.s. **-ся** F; [up] to к Д); F bring (come).
притвор|и́ть(ся) *s.* **~я́ть(ся)**; **~ный** [14; -рен, -рна] feigned, pretended, sham; **~ство** *n* [9] pretense, dissimulation; **~я́ть** [28], ⟨**~и́ть**⟩ [13; -орю́, -о́ришь; -о́ренный] close; leave ajar; **-ся** [13] feign, pretend (to be Т).
притесн|е́ние *n* [12] oppression; **~и́тель** *m* [4] oppressor; **~я́ть** [28], ⟨**~и́ть**⟩ [13] oppress; † press.
притих|а́ть [1], ⟨**~нуть**⟩ [21] become silent, stop; abate (*wind*).
прито́к *m* [1] tributary; afflux.
прито́м besides; to that *or* it.
прито́н *m* [1] den, nest.
при́торный [14; -рен, -рна] sugary, luscious.
притр|а́гиваться [1], ⟨**~о́нуться**⟩ [20] touch (slightly; *v*/*t.* к Д).
притуп|ля́ть [28], ⟨**~и́ть**⟩ [14] (**-ся** become) blunt, dull.
при́тча *f* [5] parable.
притя́|гивать [1], ⟨**~ну́ть**⟩ [19] draw, pull; attract; F *s.* привлека́ть; **~жа́тельный** [14] possessive; **~же́ние** *n* [12] attraction; **~за́ние** *n* [12] claim, pretension (to на В); **~ну́ть** *s.* **~гивать**.
приу|ро́чить [16] *pf.* time, date (for к Д); **~ча́ть** [1], ⟨**~чи́ть**⟩ [16] accustom, habituate; train.
при|хва́рывать F [1], ⟨**~хворну́ть**⟩ [20] be(come *pf.*) unwell *or* sickly.
прихо́д *m* [1] arrival, coming; † receipt(s), credit; parish; **~и́ть** [15], ⟨**прийти́**⟩ [приду́, -дёшь; пришёл, -шла́; -ше́дший; *g. pt.*: придя́] come (to), arrive (in, at в, на В; for за Т); *fig.* fall, get, fly (into в В); (Д) **~и́ть** в го́лову, на ум, *etc.* think of, hit on (the idea), take into one's head; *not: a.* dream; **~и́ть** в себя́ (*or* чу́вство) come to (o.s.); **-ся**, ⟨**~сь**⟩ suit, fit ([p.'s] s. th. [Д] по Д), be (to; Т p.'s *aunt, etc.*); fall (on в В; to на В); мне **~ится** I have to, must; придётся *a.* = попа́ло, *s.* попа́сть; **~ный** [14] receipt...; **~о-расхо́дный** [14] cash(*book*); **~ский** [16] parish...; **~я́щий** [17] day (*servant*); ⚕ ambulatory.
прихож|а́нин *m* [1; *pl.* -а́не, -а́н] parishioner; **~ая** *f* [17] *s.* пере́дняя.
прихот|ли́вый [14 *sh.*] freakish; fastidious; **'~ь** *f* [8] whim, freak.
прихра́мывать [1] limp slightly.
прице́л *m* [1] sight; *a.* = **~ивание** *n* [12] (taking) aim; **~иваться** [1], ⟨**~иться**⟩ [13] (take) aim (at в В).
прице́п *m* [1] trailer; **~ка** *f* [5; *g*/*pl.*:

-пок] coupling; ~ля́ть [28], ⟨~и́ть⟩ [14] hook (on; to к Д); couple; -ся stick, cling; *s. a.* приста́(ва́)ть; ~но́й [14]: ~но́й ваго́н *m* = ~.

прича́л *m* [1] mooring(s); **~ивать** [1], ⟨~ить⟩ [13] moor; land.

прича́|стие *n* [12] *gr.* participle; *eccl.* Eucharist; F = ~щение; **~стный** [14; -тен, -тна] participating *or* involved (in к Д); **~ща́ть** [1], ⟨~сти́ть⟩ [15 *e.*; -ащу́, -асти́шь; -ащённый] administer (-ся receive) the Lord's Supper *or* Sacraments; **~ще́ние** *n* [12] administration of the Lord's Supper.

причём: ... ~ изве́стно, что ... = ... it being known that ...

причёс|ка *f* [5; *g/pl.*: -сок] hairdo (*Brt.* -dress), coiffure; **~ывать** [1], ⟨причеса́ть⟩ [3] do, brush, comb (one's hair -ся).

причи́н|а *f* [5] cause; reason (for по Д); по ~е because of; **~ность** *f* [8] causality; **~ный** [14] causal; **~я́ть** [28], ⟨~и́ть⟩ [13] cause, do.

причи|сля́ть [28], ⟨~́слить⟩ [13] rank, number (among к Д); ⚔ assign; F add; **~та́ние** *n* [12] lamentation; **~та́ть** [1] lament; **~та́ться** [1] be due, (p.: с Р) have to pay.

причу́д|а *f* [5] whim, freak; **~ливый** [14 *sh.*] freakish; cranky.

при|ше́лец *m* [1; -льца] newcomer, arrival; **~шибленный** F [14] dejected; **~шива́ть** [1], ⟨~ши́ть⟩ [-шью́, -шьёшь, *etc.*, *cf.* шить] (к Д) sew ([on] to); F involve (in), impose ([up]on); **~шпо́рить** [13] *pf.* spur on; **~щемля́ть** [28], ⟨~щеми́ть⟩ [14 *e.*; -млю́, -ми́шь; -млённый] pinch, squeeze in; **~щу́ривать** [1], ⟨~щу́рить⟩ [13] *s.* жму́рить.

прию́т *m* [1] refuge, shelter; asylum, orphanage; **~и́ть** [15 *e.*; -ючу́, -юти́шь] *pf.* shelter (*v/i.* -ся).

прия́|тель *m* [4], **~тельница** *f* [5] friend; **~тельский** [16] friendly; **~тный** [14; -тен, -тна] pleasant, pleasing, agreeable.

про F (В) about, of; ~ себя́ to o.s., (*read*) silently.

про́ба *f* [5] trial (on [= probation] на В), test; ⊕ assay, sample; standard, hallmark.

пробе́|г *m* [1] run, race; **~га́ть** [1], ⟨~жа́ть⟩ [4 *e.*; -егу́, -ежи́шь, -гу́т] run (through, over), pass (by); cover; skim.

пробе́л *m* [1] blank, gap; defect.

проби|ва́ть [1], ⟨~́ть⟩ [-бью́, -бьёшь; -бе́й(те)!; проби́л, -а, -о] break through; pierce, punch; *s. a.* бить 2.; -ся fight (*or* make) one's way (through сквозь В); *fig.* F rough it; ⚘ come up; shine through; *pf.* toil (at над Т); **~ра́ть** [1], ⟨пробра́ть⟩ [-беру́, -рёшь; *cf.* брать] F scold; blow up, upbraid; -ся [-бра́лся, -ла́сь, -ло́сь] make one's way (through сквозь В); steal *or* slip; **~́рка** *f* [5; *g/pl.*: -рок] test tube; **~́ть(ся)** *s.* ~ва́ть(ся).

про́бк|а *f* [5; *g/pl.*: -бок] cork; stopper, plug; ⚡ fuse; *traffic*: jam; **~овый** [14] cork...

пробле́ма *f* [5] problem; **~ти́ческий** [16], **~ти́чный** [14; -чен, -чна] problematic(al).

про́блеск *m* [1] gleam; flash.

про́б|ный [14] trial..., test...; specimen..., sample...; touch(*stone*); pilot (*balloon*); **~овать** [7], ⟨по-⟩ try; taste.

пробо́ина *f* [5] hole; ⚓ leak.

пробо́р *m* [1] (hair) parting.

про́бочник *m* [1] corkscrew.

пробра́ться *s.* пробира́ть(ся).

пробу|жда́ть [1], ⟨~ди́ть⟩ [15; -уждённый] waken, rouse; -ся awake, wake up; **~жде́ние** *n* [12] awakening.

пробы́ть [-бу́ду, -бу́дешь; про́был, -а́, -о] *pf.* stay.

прова́л *m* [1] collapse; *fig.* failure; **~ивать** [1], ⟨~и́ть⟩ [13; -алю́, -а́лишь; -а́ленный] wreck; fail; reject; *thea.* damn; ~ивай(те)! F decamp; -ся break *or* fall in; fail, flunk; *thea.* be damned; disappear; ~и́сь! F the deuce take you!

прова́нский [16] olive (*oil*).

прове́|дать F [1] *pf.* visit; find out; **~де́ние** *n* [12] carrying out, realization; construction, installation; **~зти́** *s.* провози́ть; **~рить** *s.* ~ря́ть; **~рка** *f* [5; *g/pl.*: -рок] check(up), examination, control; **~ря́ть** [28], ⟨~́рить⟩ [13] examine, check (up), control; **~сти́** *s.* проводи́ть; **~трива́ть** [1], ⟨~три́ть⟩ [13] air, ventilate.

прови|а́нт *m* [1] *s.* ~́зия; **~́зия** *f* [7] provisions, foodstuffs, victuals *pl.*; **~ни́ться** [13] *pf.* commit offence, be guilty (of в П), offend (p. пе́ред Т; with в П); **~нциа́льный** [14; -лен, -льна] provincial; **~́нция** *f* [7] province.

про́во|д *m* [1; *pl.*: -да́, *etc. e.*] wire, line; cable; lead; **~ди́мость** *f* [8] conductivity; **~ди́ть** [15] **1.** ⟨провести́⟩ [25] lead, *a.* ⚡, *impf.* conduct, guide; carry out (*or* through), realize, put (*into practice*); put *or* get through; pass; spend (*time*; at за Т); draw (*line, etc.*); lay, construct; develop (*idea*); pursue (*policy*); hold (*meeting*); † enter, book; *pf.* F trick, cheat; **2.** *s.* ~жа́ть; **~́дка** *f* [5; *g/pl.*: -док] construction, installation; ⚡ lead; *tel.* line, wire(s); **~дни́к** *m* [1 *e.*] guide; 🚂, ⚡ conductor (*Brt.* 🚂 guard); **~жа́ть** [1], ⟨~ди́ть⟩ [15] see (off), accompany; follow; **~́з** *m* [1] transport(ation).

провозгла|ша́ть [1], ⟨~си́ть⟩ [15 *e.*; -ашу́, -аси́шь; -ашённый] proclaim; propose (*toast*).

провози́ть [15], ‹провезти́› [24] drive, convey; take, get, carry.
провока́|тор *m* [1] agent provocateur; **~ция** *f* [7] provocation.
про́вол|ока *f* [5] wire; **~о́чка** F *f* [5; *g/pl.*: -чек] delay (in с T), protraction.
прово́р|ный [14; -рен, -рна] quick, nimble, deft; **~ство** *n* [9] quickness, nimbleness, deftness.
провоци́ровать [7] (*im*)*pf.*, *a.* ‹с-› provoke (to на В).
прогада́ть F [1] *pf.* lose (by на П).
прога́лина *f* [5] glade; patch, spot.
прогл|а́тывать [1], ‹~оти́ть› [15] swallow, gulp; F lose (*tongue*); **~я́дывать** [1] **1.** ‹~ядеть› [11] overlook; look over (*or* through); **2.** ‹~яну́ть› [19] peep out, appear.
прогн|а́ть *s.* прогоня́ть; **~о́з** *m* [1] forecast; ⚕ prognosis.
прого|ва́ривать [1], ‹~вори́ть› [13] say; talk; **-ся** blab (*v/t.* о П); **~лода́ться** [1] *pf.* get *or* feel hungry; **~ня́ть** [28], ‹прогна́ть› [-гоню́, -го́нишь; -гна́л, -а́, -о; про́гнанный] drive (away); F *fig.* banish; F fire; run (the gantlet сквозь строй); **~ра́ть** [1], ‹~ре́ть› [9] burn through; F smash (up).
програ́мма *f* [5] program(me *Brt.*).
прогре́сс *m* [1] progress; **~и́вный** [14; -вен, -вна] progressive; **~и́ровать** [7] (make) progress.
прогрыз|а́ть [1], ‹~ть› [24; *pt. st.*] gnaw *or* bite through.
прогу́л *m* [1] truancy; **~ивать** [1], ‹~я́ть› [28] shirk (work), play truant; **-ся** take (*or* go for a) walk; **~ка** *f* [5; *g/pl.*: -лок] walk (for на В), stroll, ride; **~ьщик** *m* [1] shirker, truant; **~я́ть(ся)** *s.* ~ивать(ся).
прода|ва́ть [5], ‹~ть› [-да́м, -да́шь, *etc.*, *cf.* дать; про́дал, -а́, -о; про́данный (про́дан, -а́, -о)] sell (*v/i.* **-ся**; *a.* = be for *or* on sale); **~ве́ц** *m* [1; -вца́], **~вщи́ца** *f* [5] seller, sales(wo)man, (store) clerk, *Brt.* shop assistant; **~жа** *f* [5] sale (on в П; for в В); **~жный** [14] for sale; [-жен, -жна] venal, corrupt; **~ть** (**-ся**) *s.* ~ва́ть(ся).
продви|га́ть [1], ‹~нуть› [20] move, push (ahead); **-ся** advance; **~же́ние** *n* [12] advance(ment).
проде́л|ать *s.* ~ывать; **~ка** *f* [5; *g/pl.*: -лок] trick, prank; **~ывать**, ‹~ать› [1] break through, make; carry through *or* out, do; F play (*trick*).
проде́ть [-де́ну, -де́нешь; -де́нь (-те)!; -де́тый] *pf.* pass through, thread.
продл|ева́ть [1], ‹~и́ть› [13] prolong; **~е́ние** *n* [12] prolongation.
продово́льств|енный [14] food...; grocery...; **~ие** *n* [12] food(stuffs), provisions *pl.*
продол|гова́тый [14 *sh.*] oblong; **~жа́тель** *m* [4] continuator; **~жа́ть** [1], ‹~жить› [16] continue, go on; lengthen; prolong; **-ся** last; **~же́ние** *n* [12] continuation; sequel; course (in в В); ~же́ние сле́дует to be continued; **~жи́тельность** *f* [8] duration; **~жи́тельный** [14; -лен, -льна] long; **~жить** (**-ся**) *s.* ~жа́ть(ся); **~ьный** [14] longitudinal.
продро́гнуть [21] *pf.* be chilled (to the marrow).
проду́к|т *m* [1] product; material; *pl. a.* (food)stuffs; **~ти́вный** [14; -вен, -вна] productive; **~то́вый** [14] grocery (*store*); **~ция** *f* [7] production (= product[s]), output.
проду́м|ывать, ‹~ать› [1] think over.
про|еда́ть [1], ‹~е́сть› [-е́м, -е́шь, *etc.*, *cf.* есть[1]] eat away *or* through; F spend (on eating); eat.
прое́з|д *m* [1] passage, thoroughfare (no t.! ~а нет!); ~ом on the way, in passing; transient(ly); **~дить** *s.* ~жа́ть; **~дно́й** [14]: ~дно́й биле́т *m* ticket; ~дна́я пла́та *f* fare; **~жа́ть** [1] **1.** ‹прое́хать› [-е́ду, -е́дешь; -езжа́й(те)!] pass, drive *or* ride through (*or* past, by); travel; **-ся** F take a drive *or* ride; **2.** ‹~дить› [15] break in (*horse*); F spend (on fare *or* in driving, riding); **~жий** [17] (through) traveller, transient; **~жая доро́га** *f* highway.
прое́к|т *m* [1] project, plan, scheme; draft; **~ти́ровать** [7], ‹с-› project, plan; **~цио́нный** [14]: ~цио́нный аппара́т *m* projector.
прое́|сть *s.* ~да́ть; **~хать** *s.* ~зжа́ть.
проже́ктор *m* [1] searchlight.
прожи|ва́ть [1], ‹~ть› [-иву́, -иве́шь; про́жил, -а́, -о; про́житый (про́жит, -а́, -о)] live; F spend; **~га́ть** [1], ‹проже́чь› [26 г/ж: -жгу́, -жжёшь] burn (through); ~га́ть жизнь F live fast; **~точный** [14]: ~точный ми́нимум *m* living wage; **~ть** *s.* ~ва́ть.
прожо́рлив|ость *f* [8] gluttony, voracity; **~ый** [14 *sh.*] gluttonous.
про́за *f* [5] prose; **~ик** *m* [1] prose writer; **~и́ческий** [16] prosaic.
про́|звище *n* [11] nickname; по ~звищу nicknamed; **~зва́ть** *s.* ~зыва́ть; **~зева́ть** F [1] *pf.* miss; let slip; **~зорли́вый** [14 *sh.*] perspicacious; **~зра́чный** [14; -чен, -чна] transparent; **~зре́ть** [9] *pf.* recover one's sight: see, perceive; **~зыва́ть** [1], ‹~зва́ть› [-зову́, -вёшь; -зва́л, -а́, -о; про́званный] (T) nickname; **~зяба́ть** [1] vegetate; **~зя́бнуть** F [21] *s.* продро́гнуть.
прои́гр|ывать [1], ‹~а́ть› [1] lose (at play); F play; **-ся** lose all one's money; **'~ыш** *m* [1] loss (в П lose).

произв|еде́ние *n* [12] work, product(ion); **~ести́** *s.* ~одить; **~оди́тель** *m* [4] producer; **~оди́тельность** *f* [8] productivity; output; **~оди́тельный** [14; -лен, -льна] productive; **~оди́ть** [15], ‹~ести›[25] (-ся *impf.* be) make (made), carry (-ried) out, execute(d), effect (-ed); (⊕ *usu. impf.*) produce(d); bring forth; promote(d [to the rank of] [в И *pl.*]); *impf.* derive(d; from от Р); **~о́дный** [14] derivative (*a. su. f* ⅍); **~о́дственный** [14] production...; manufacturing; works...; industrial; **~о́дство** *n* [9] production, manufacture; plant, works, factory (at на П); execution; promotion.

произ|во́л *m* [1] arbitrariness; mercy; despotism, tyranny; **~во́льный** [14; -лен, -льна] arbitrary; **~носи́ть** [15], ‹~нести́› [24 -с-] pronounce; deliver, make (*speech*); utter; **~ноше́ние** *n* [12] pronunciation; **~ойти́** *s.* происходить.

про́ис|ки *m/pl.* [1] intrigues; **~ходи́ть** [15], ‹произойти› [-зойдёт; -зошёл, -шла; *g. pt.*: произойдя] take place, happen; arise, originate (from от Р); descend (from от, из Р); **~хожде́ние** *n* [12] origin (by [= birth] по Д), descent; **~ше́ствие** *n* [12] incident, occurrence, event.

про|йти́(сь) *s.* ~ходи́ть & ~ха́живаться).

прок F *m* [1] *s.* по́льза & впрок.

прока́з|а *f* [5] prank, mischief; ⚕ leprosy; **~ник** *m* [1], **~ница** *f* [5] F *s.* шалу́н(ья); **~ничать** [1] F *s.* шали́ть.

прока́|лывать [1], ‹проколо́ть› [17] pierce, stick, stab; **~пывать** [1], ‹прокопа́ть› [1] dig (through); **~рмливать** [1], ‹прокорми́ть› [14] support, nourish; feed; -ся F subsist (on, by Т).

прока́т *m* [1] hire (for на В), lease; (*film, etc.*) distribution; отда́ть в ~ hire out; **~а́ть(ся)** [15] *pf.* give (take) a drive *or* ride; **~ный** [14] rolled (*iron*); rolling (*mill*); for hire; lending; **~ывать**, ‹~а́ть› [1] mangle; ⊕ roll; ride; -ся F *s.* ~а́ться.

прокла́д|ка *f* [5; *g/pl.*: -док] laying; construction; packing; lining; **~ывать** [1], ‹проложи́ть› [16] lay (*a.* = build); *fig.* pave; force (one's *way* себе́), interlay; draw.

прокламáция *f* [7] leaflet.

прокл|ина́ть [1], ‹~я́сть› [-яну́, -янёшь; про́клял, -á, -o; про́клятый (про́клят, -á, -o)] curse, damn; **~я́тие** *n* [12] damnation; **~я́тый** [14] cursed, damned.

проко́|л *m* [1] perforation; **~ло́ть** *s.* прока́лывать; **~па́ть** *s.* прока́пывать; **~рми́ть(ся)** *s.* прока́рмливать(ся); **~рмле́ние** *n* [12] support.

прокра́|дываться [1], ‹~сться› [25; *pt. st.*] steal; go stealthily.

прокуро́р *m* [1] public prosecutor.

про|лага́ть *s.* ~кла́дывать; **~ла́мывать**, ‹~лома́ть› [1] & ‹~ломи́ть› [14] break (through; *v/i.* -ся); fracture; **~лега́ть** [1] run; **~леза́ть** [1], ‹~ле́зть› [24 *st.*] creep *or* get (in[to]); **~лёт** *m* [1] passage; flight; ⚠ span; well; **~летариа́т** *m* [1] proletariat; **~лета́рий** *m* [3], **~лета́рский** [16] proletarian; **~лета́ть** [1], ‹~лете́ть› [11] fly (past, by, over), pass (by, quickly); **~лётка** *f* [5; *g/pl.*: -ток] droshky.

проли́|в *m* [1] strait (*e.g.* Strait of Dover ~в Па-де-Кале́); **~ва́ть** [1], ‹~ть› [-лью́, -льёшь; -ле́й(те)!; про́ли́л, -á, -o; про́ли́тый (про́ли́т, -á, -o)] spill (*v/i.* -ся); shed; **~вно́й** [14]: ~вной дождь *m* downpour, cloudburst; **~ть** *s.* ~ва́ть.

проло́|г *m* [1] prologue; **~жи́ть** *s.* прокла́дывать; **~м** *m* [1] breach; fracture; **~ма́ть, ~ми́ть** *s.* прола́мывать.

про́мах *m* [1] miss; blunder (make дать *or* сде́лать; *a.* miss, fail; F fool); **∠иваться** [1], ‹~ну́ться› [20] miss; blunder.

промедле́ние *n* [12] delay.

промежу́то|к *m* [1; -тка] interval (at в П; ... of в В); period; **~чный** [14] intermediate.

проме|лькну́ть *s.* мелька́ть; **∠нивать** [1], ‹~ня́ть› [28] exchange (for на В); **~рза́ть** [1], ‹промёрзнуть› [21] freeze (through); F *s.* продро́гнуть.

промо|ка́тельный [14]: ~ка́тельная бума́га *f* blotting paper; **~ка́ть** [1], ‹∠кнуть› [21] get wet *or* drenched; **~лча́ть** [4 *e.*; -чу́, -чи́шь] *pf.* keep silent; **~чи́ть** [16] *pf.* wet, drench.

промтова́ры *m/pl.* [1] *s.* ширпотре́б.

промча́ться [4] *pf.* dash *or* fly (past, by).

промы|ва́ть [1], ‹∠ть› [22] wash (out, away); ⚕ irrigate.

про́мы|сел *m* [1; -сла] trade, (line of) business; (*oil, gold*) field; (*salt, etc.*) works; **~сло́вый** [14] trade(s) ...; **∠ть** *s.* ~ва́ть.

промы́шлен|ник *m* [1] industrialist; **~ность** *f* [8] industry; **~ный** [14] industrial.

пронести́(сь) *s.* проноси́ть(ся).

прон|за́ть [1], ‹~зи́ть› [15*e.*; -нжу́, -нзи́шь; -нзённый] pierce, stab; **~зи́тельный** [14; -лен, -льна] shrill, piercing, penetrating; **~и́зывать** [1], ‹~иза́ть› [3] penetrate, pierce.

прони|ка́ть [1], ‹∠кнуть› [21] penetrate; permeate; get (in); spread; -ся be imbued *or* inspired (with Т); **~кнове́ние** *n* [12] pene-

tration; fervo(u)r; **~кновéнный** [14; -éнен, -éнна] feeling, heartfelt, pathetic; **~цáемый** [14 *sh.*] permeable; **~цáтельный** [14; -лен, -льна] penetrating, searching; acute, shrewd; **~цáть** *s.* **~кáть**.
про|носи́ть [15] **1.** ⟨**~нести́**⟩ [24 -с-: -есу́; -ёс, -еслá] carry (through, by, away); speed; **-ся**, ⟨**-сь**⟩ fly (past, by), pass *or* spread (swiftly); **2.** *pf.* F wear out; **~ны́рливый** [14 *sh.*] crafty; **~ню́хать** P [1] smell out.
прообраз *m* [1] prototype.
пропагáнд|и́ровать [7] propagandize; **~и́стский** [16] propagandist...; propaganda...
пропа|дáть [1], ⟨**~сть**⟩ [25; *pt. st.*] get *or* be lost, be gone (wasted); be (missing; *a.* **~сть** бéз вести); lose, fail; vanish; perish, die; **~жа** *f* [5] loss; **~сть**[1] *s.* **~дáть**; **'~сть**[2] *f* [8] precipice, abyss; chasm, gap; disaster; F lots *or* a lot (of).
пропи|вáть [1], ⟨**~сть**⟩ [-пью́, -пьёшь; -пéй(те)!; прóпи́л, -á, -о; прóпи́тый (прóпи́т, -á, -о)] spend (on drinking); drink.
пропис|áть(ся) *s.* **~ывать(ся)**; **~ска** *f* [5; *g/pl.*: -сок] registration; **~нóй** [14] capital, *cf.* бу́ква; common; registration...; **~ывать** [1], ⟨**~áть**⟩ [3] prescribe (for Д), order; register (*v/i.* **-ся**); **'~ью** (*write*) in full.
пропи|тáние *n* [12] livelihood, living (*earn* one's себé на В); **~ты́вать**, ⟨**~тáть**⟩ [1] (**-ся** be[come]) impregnate(d), imbue(d; with Т); **~ть** *s.* **~вáть**.
проплы|вáть [1], ⟨**~сть**⟩ [23] swim *or* sail (by, under); pass; strut.
проповéд|ник *m* [1] preacher; **~овать** [1] preach; **~ь** ('prɔ-) *f* [8] *eccl.* sermon; propagation.
пропол|зáть [1], ⟨**~зти́**⟩ [24] creep (by, through, under); **~ка** *f* [5] weeding.
пропорционáльный [14; -лен, -льна] proportional, proportionate.
прóпус|к *m* [1] **1.** ommission, blank; absence; **2.** [*pl.*: -кá, *etc. e.*] pass(-age); ⚔ password; **~кáть** [1], ⟨**~ти́ть**⟩ [15] let pass (*or* through); pass; omit; miss; let slip; *impf.* leak; **~кнóй** [14] blotting (*paper*).
прорa|бáтывать, ⟨**~бóтать**⟩ F, [1] study; **~стáть** [1], ⟨**~сти́**⟩ [24 -ст-: -стёт; -рос, -рослá] grow (through); come up.
прорвáть(ся) *s.* прорывáть(ся).
прорез|áть [1], ⟨**~ать**⟩ [3] cut (through); **-ся** cut (*teeth*); **~и́ненный** [14] gummed.
прорéха *f* [5] slit, hole, tear.
прорó|к *m* [1] prophet; **~ни́ть** [13; -оню́, -óнишь; -óненный] *pf.* utter; **~ческий** [16] prophetic(al); **~чество** *n* [9] prophecy; **~чить** [16] prophesy.

проруб|áть [1], ⟨**~и́ть**⟩ [14] cut (through); **'~ь** *f* [8] ice-hole.
прор|ы́в *m* [1] break; breach; gap, arrear(s), hitch; **~ывáть** [1] **1.** ⟨**~вáть**⟩ [-ву́, -вёшь; -вáл, -á, -о; прóрванный (-ан, -á, -о)] tear; break through (*v/i.* **-ся**; burst open; force one's way); **2.** ⟨**~ы́ть**⟩ [22] dig (through).
про|сáчиваться [1], ⟨**~сочи́ться**⟩ [16 *e.*; *3rd p. only*] ooze (out), percolate; **~сверли́ть** [13] *pf.* bore (through).
просвé|т *m* [1] gleam, glimpse; chink; ⚠ bay, opening; *fig.* hope; **~ти́тельный** [14] of enlightenment; educational; **~ти́ть** *s.* **~щáть** & **~чивать 2.**; **~тлéть** [8] *pf.* clear up, brighten; **~чивать** [1] **1.** shine through, be seen; **2.** ⟨**~ти́ть**⟩ [15] radiograph, X-ray; test (*egg*); **~щáть** [1], ⟨**~ти́ть**⟩ [15 *e.*; -ещу́, -ети́шь; -ещённый] enlighten, educate, instruct; **~щéние** *n* [12] enlightenment, education, instruction.
прó|седь *f* [8] grayish (*Brt.* greyish), grizzly (hair); **~сéивать** [1], ⟨**~сéять**⟩ [27] sift; **~сека** *f* [5] glade; **~сёлок** *m* [1; -лка] = **~сёлочная** дорóга; **~сёлочный** [14]: **~сёлочная** дорóга *f* by-road, field path; **~сéять** *s.* **~сéивать**.
проси́|живать [1], ⟨**~дéть**⟩ [11] sit (up); stay, remain; spend; F wear out; **~тель** *m* [4], **~тельница** *f* [5] petitioner, applicant; **~ть** [15], ⟨по-⟩ ask (p. for В/о П; у Р/Р, *a.* beg p.'s), request; entreat; invite; intercede (for за В); прошу́, прóсят *a.* please; **-ся** (в, на В) ask (for; leave [to enter, go]; F suggest o. s.; **~я́ть** [28] *pf.* shine forth, brighten.
проск|ользну́ть [20] *pf.* slip (into в В); **~очи́ть** [16] *pf.* jump *or* slip (by, through, in[to]).
просл|авля́ть [28], ⟨**~áвить**⟩ [14] glorify, make (**-ся** become) famous; **~еди́ть** [15 *e.*; -ежу́, -еди́шь; -éженный] *pf.* follow up; **~ези́ться** [15 *e.*; -ежу́сь, -ези́шься] *pf.* shed tears.
прослóйка *f* [5; *g/pl.*: -óек] streak, layer.
про|слу́шать [1] *pf.* hear; ⚕ auscultate; F miss; **~смáтривать** [1], ⟨**~смотрéть**⟩ [9; -отрю́, -óтришь; -óтренный] look through *or* over; overlook; **~смóтр** *m* [1] examination, review, revision; oversight; **~сну́ться** *s.* **~сыпáться**; **~со** *n* [9] millet; **~сóвывать** [1], ⟨**~су́нуть**⟩ [20] pass *or* push (through); **~сóхнуть** *s.* **~сыхáть**; **~сочи́ться** *s.* **~сáчиваться**; **~спáть** *s.* **~сыпáть**.
проспéкт *m* [1] avenue; prospectus.
просрóч|ивать [1], ⟨**~ить**⟩ [16] let lapse, expire; exceed; **~ка** *f* [5; *g/pl.*: -чек] expiration; exceeding.
прост|áивать [1], ⟨**~оя́ть**⟩ [-ою́,

-ойшь] stand; stay; **~áк** *m* [1 *e.*] simpleton; **~ёнок** *m* [1; -нка] pier.
прост|ирáть [1], ⟨**~ерéть**⟩ [12] stretch (out; *v/i.* **-ся**), extend.
простúтельный [14; -лен, -льна] pardonable, excusable, venial.
проститýтка *f* [5; *g/pl.*: -ток] prostitute.
простúть(ся) *s.* прощáть(ся).
простодýш|ие *n* [12] naïveté; **~ный** [14; -шен, -шна] simple-minded, ingenuous, artless.
простóй 1. [14; прост, -á, -о; *comp.*: прóще] simple, plain; easy; artless, unsophisticated; ordinary, common; prime (*number*); **2.** *m* [3] stoppage, standstill.
простоквáша *f* [5] curdled milk.
простó|р *m* [1] open (space); freedom (in на П); scope; **~рéчие** *n* [12] language of the (uneducated) people; vernacular; **~рный** [14; -рен, -рна] spacious, roomy; **~сердéчный** [14; -чен, -чна] *s.* **~дýшный**; **~тá** *f* [5] simplicity; naïveté; silliness; **~фúля** *m/f* F [6] ninny; **~ять** *s.* простáивать.
простран|ный [14; -áнен, -áнна] vast; diffuse; **~ство** *n* [9] space; room; area.
прострéл *m* [1] lumbago; **~ивать** [1], ⟨**~úть**⟩ [13; -елю́, -éлишь; -éленный] shoot (through).
простý|да *f* [5] cold; **~живать** [1], ⟨**~дúть**⟩ [15] chill; **-ся** catch a cold.
простýпок *m* [1; -пка] offence.
простыня́ *f* [6; *pl.*: прóстыни, -ы́нь, *etc. e.*] (*bed*) sheet.
просý|нуть *s.* просóвывать; **~шивать** [1], ⟨**~шúть**⟩ [16] dry (up).
просфорá *f* [5; *pl.*: прóсфоры, -фóр, *etc. e.*] *eccl.* Host.
просчитáться [1] *pf.* miscalculate.
просыпáть [1], ⟨проспáть⟩ [-плю́, -пúшь; -спáл, -á, -о] oversleep; sleep; F miss (by sleeping); **~ся**, ⟨проснýться⟩ [20] awake, wake up.
прос|ыхáть [1], ⟨**~óхнуть**⟩ [21] dry.
прóсьба *f* [5] request (at по П; for о П); entreaty; † petition; please (don't не + *inf.*); (у Р/к Д) **~** (may p.) ask (p.) a favo(u)r.
про|тáлкивать [1], *once* ⟨**~толкнýть**⟩ [20], F ⟨**~толкáть**⟩ [1] push (through); **-ся** force one's way (through); **~тáптывать** [1], ⟨**~топтáть**⟩ [3] tread (out); F wear out *or* down; **~тáскивать** [1], ⟨**~тащúть**⟩ [16] carry *or* drag (past, by); F smuggle in.
протéз (-'tɛs) *m* [1] artificial limb.
протe|кáть [1], ⟨**~чь**⟩ [26] flow (by); leak; pass, elapse; take a ... course; **~кция** *f* [7] patronage; **~рéть** *s.* протирáть; **~ст** *m* [1], **~стовáть** [7], *v/t.* (*im*)*pf.* & ⟨о-⟩ protest; **~чь** *s.* **~кáть**.
прóтив (Р) against (*a.* as against); opposite; быть *or* имéть **~** (have) object(ion; to), mind; **~иться** [14], ⟨вос-⟩ (Д) oppose, object; **~ник** *m* [1] opponent, adversary; enemy; **~ный** [14; -вен, -вна] repugnant, disgusting, offensive, nasty; opposite, contrary; мне **~но** *a.* I hate; в **~ном** слýчае otherwise, failing which.
противо|вéс *m* [1] counterbalance; **~воздýшный** [14] anti-aircraft (*defense*), air-raid (*precautions, protection*); **~гáз** *m* [1] gas mask; **~дéйствие** *n* [12] counteraction; resistance; **~дéйствовать** [7] counteract; resist; **~естéственный** [14 *sh.*] unnatural; **~закóнный** [14; -óнен, -óнна] unlawful, illegal; **~общéственный** [14] antisocial; **~полóжность** *f* [8] contrast, opposition (in в В); antithesis; **~полóжный** [14; -жен, -жна] opposite; contrary, opposed; **~поставля́ть** [28], ⟨**~постáвить**⟩ [14] oppose; **~поставлéние** *n* [12] opposition; **~рéчие** *n* [12] contradiction; **~речúвый** [14 *sh.*] contradictory; **~рéчить** [16] (Д) contradict; **~стоя́ть** [-ою́, -оúшь] (Д) withstand; stand against; **~тáнковый** [14] antitank...; **~химúческий** [16] (anti)gas...; **~я́дие** *n* [12] antidote.
про|тирáть [1], ⟨**~терéть**⟩ [12] rub (through); wipe; **~ткнýть** *s.* **~тыкáть**; **~тóкол** *m* [1] (**~токолúровать** [7] [*im*]*pf.*, *a.* ⟨за-⟩ take down the) minutes *pl.*, record; *su. a.* protocol; **~толкáть**, **~толкнýть** *s.* **~тáлкивать**; **~топтáть** *s.* **~тáптывать**; **~торённый** [14] beaten (*path*), trodden; **~тóтип** *m* [1] prototype; **~тóчный** [14] flowing, running; **~трезвля́ться** [28], ⟨**~трезвúться**⟩ [14 *e.*; -влю́сь, -вúшься; -влённый] (become) sober; **~тыкáть** [1], *once* ⟨**~ткнýть**⟩ [20] pierce.
протя́|гивать [1], ⟨**~нуть**⟩ [19] stretch (out), extend, hold out; pass; drawl; P turn up (one's toes нóги); **~жéние** *n* [12] extent, stretch (at на П); course (in на П); **~жный** [14; -жен, -жна] drawling, lingering; **~нуть** *s.* **~гивать**.
проучúть F [16] *pf.* teach a lesson.
професс|ионáльный [14] professional; trade (*union, cf.* профсою́з); **~ия** *f* [7] profession (by по Д), calling, trade; **~ор** *m* [1; *pl.*: -рá, *etc. e.*] professor; **~ýра** *f* [5] professorship; professorate.
прóфиль *m* [4] profile.
профóрма F *f* [5] formality.
профсою́з *m* [1], **~ный** [14] trade union.
про|хáживаться [1], ⟨**~йтúсь**⟩ [-йдýсь, -йдёшься; -ошёлся, -шлáсь] (go for a) walk, stroll; F pass; mock (at насчёт Р); **~хвáты-**

вать F [1], ⟨**~хватить**⟩ [15] pierce; blow up; **~хвост** F *m* [1] scoundrel.
прохлáд|а *f* [5] cool(ness); **~и́тельный** [14; -лен, -льна] refreshing, cooling; **~ный** [14; -ден, -дна] cool (*a. fig.*), fresh.
прохó|д *m* [1] passage, pass; *anat.* duct (зáдний ~д anus); **~ди́мец** *m* [1; -мца] impostor, villain; **~ди́мость** *f* [8] passableness; maneuverability; **~ди́ть** [15], ⟨пройти́⟩ [пройду́, -дёшь; прошёл, -шлá; -шéдший; прóйденный; *g. pt.*: пройдя́] pass, go (by, through, over, along); take a ... course, be; spread; **~днóй** [14] (with a) through passage; **~ждéние** *n* [12] passing *or* going (through, over); **~жий** *m* [17] passer-by; traveller.
процветáть [1] prosper, thrive.
проце|дýра *f* [5] procedure; **∠жи́вать** [1], ⟨**~ди́ть**⟩ [15] filter; **∠нт** *m* [1] percent(age) (by на В); (*usu. pl.*) interest; **∠сс** *m* [1] process; ⚖ trial (at на П); **∠ссия** *f* [7] procession.
прочéсть *s.* прочи́тывать.
прóч|ий [17] other; *n & pl. a. su.* the rest; и ~ее and so on *or* forth, etc.; мéжду ~им by the way, incidentally; among other things.
прочи́|стить *s.* **~щáть**; **~тывать**, ⟨**~тáть**⟩ [1] & ⟨прочéсть⟩ [25 -т-: -чтý, -тёшь; -чёл, -члá; *g. pt.*: -чтя́; -чтённый] read (through); recite; **'~ть** [16] designate (to в В); **~щáть** [1], ⟨**~стить**⟩ [15] clean.
прóчн|ость *f* [8] durability; **~ый** [14; -чен, -чнá, -о] firm, solid, strong; lasting.
прочтéние *n* [12] reading, perusal.
прочь away, off (with you поди́[те] ~); *cf.* долóй; я не ~ + *inf.* F I wouldn't mind ...ing.
прош|éдший [17] past (*a. su. n* ~éдшее), *a. gr.*, last; **~éние** *n* [12] petition, application (for о П; on по Д); **~éствие** *n* [12] *s.* истечéние; **~логóдний** [15] last year's; **∠лый** [14] past (*a. su. n* ∠лое), last; **~мыгнýть** F [20] *pf.* slip, whisk.
прощ|áй(те)! farewell!, goodby(e)!, adieu!; **~áльный** [14] farewell...; parting; **~áние** *n* [12] parting (when, at при П; на В), leave-taking, farewell; **~áть** [1], ⟨прости́ть⟩ [15 *e.*; -ощý,ости́шь; -ощённый] forgive (p. Д), excuse, pardon; прости́(те) *a.* = **~áй(те)**, *s.*; **-ся** (с Т) take leave (of), say goodby (to); **~éние** *n* [12] forgiveness; pardon.
проявл|и́тель *m* [4] *phot.* developer; **~и́ть(ся)** *s.* **~я́ть(ся)**; **~éние** *n* [12] manifestation, display, demonstration; *phot.* development; **~я́ть** [28], ⟨**~и́ть**⟩ [14] show, display, evince, manifest; *phot.* develop.
проясн|я́ться [28], ⟨**~и́ться**⟩ [13] clear up, brighten.
пруд *m* [1 *e.*; в -ý] pond.
пружи́на *f* [5] spring; motive.
прусс|áк *m* [1*e.*], **∠кий** [16] Prussian.
прут *m* [1; *a. e.*; *pl.*: -ья, -ьев] rod, switch.
пры́|гать [1], *once* ⟨**~гнуть**⟩ [20] jump, spring, leap; **~гýн** *m* [1 *e.*] jumper; **~жóк** *m* [1; -жкá] jump, leap, bound; dive; **~ткий** [16; -ток, -ткá, -о] nimble, quick; **~ть** F *f* [8] agility; speed (at full во всю); **~щ** *m* [1 *e.*], **~щик** *m* [1] pimple.
пряди́ль|ный [14] spinning; **~щик** *m* [1], **~щица** *f* [5] spinner.
пря|дь *f* [8] lock, tress, strand; **∠жа** *f* [5] yarn; **∠жка** *f* [5; *g/pl.*: -жек] buckle **∠лка** *f* [*g/pl.*: -лок] spinning wheel.
прям|изнá *f* [5] straightness; **~одýшие** *n* [12] *s.* **~отá**; **~одýшный** [14; -шен, -шна] *s.* **~óй** *fig.*; **~óй** [14; прям, -á, -о] straight (*a.* [= bee] line **~áя** *su. f*); direct (*a. gr.*); 🚂 through...; ♪ right; *fig.* straight (-forward), downright, outspoken, frank; **~áя** кишкá *f* rectum; **~олинéйный** [14; -éен, -éйна] rectilinear; *fig. s.* **~óй** *fig.*; **~отá** *f* [5] straightforwardness, frankness; **~оугóльник** *m* [1] rectangle; **~оугóльный** [14] rectangular.
пря́н|ик *m* [1] gingerbread; **~ость** *f* [8] spice, *pl.* spicery; spiciness; **~ый** [14 *sh.*] spicy, piquant.
прясть [25; -ял, -á, -о], ⟨с-⟩ spin.
пря́т|ать [3], ⟨с-⟩ hide (*v/i.* **-ся**), conceal; **~ки** *f/pl.* [5; gen.: -ток] hide-and-seek.
пря́ха *f* [5] spinner.
псал|óм *m* [1; -лмá] psalm; **~óмщик** *m* [1] *s.* дьяк; **~ты́рь** *f* [8] Psalter.
псáрня *f* [6; *g/pl.*: -рен] kennel(s).
псевдони́м *m* [1] pseudonym.
псих|иáтр *m* [1] psychiatrist; **∠ика** *f* [5] mind, psyche; mentality; **~и́ческий** [16] mental, psychic(al); **~óлог** *m* [1] psychologist; **~олóгия** *f* [7] psychology.
птенéц [1; -нцá] nestling.
пти́|ца *f* [5] bird; домáшняя **~ца** poultry; **~чий** [18] bird('s); poultry...; вид с **~чьего** полёта bird's-eye view; **~чка** *f* [5; *g/pl.*: -чек] birdie.
пýбли|ка *f* [5] audience; public; **~кáция** *f* [7] publication; advertisement; **~ковáть** [7], ⟨о-⟩ publish; **~ци́ст** *m* [1] publicist; **∠чность** *f* [8] publicity; **∠чный** [14] public; **∠чная** жéнщина *f* prostitute.
пýг|ало *n* [9] scarecrow; **~áть** [1], ⟨ис-, на-⟩, *once* ⟨**~нýть**⟩ [20] (**-ся** be) frighten(ed; of Р), scare(d); **~ли́вый** [14 *sh.*] timid, fearful.
пýговица *f* [5] button.
пуд *m* [1; *pl. e.*] pood (= *36 lbs.*); **∠ель** *m* [4; *pl. a.* -ля́, *etc. e.*] poodle.

пу́др|а *f* [5] powder; са́харная ~а powdered sugar; **~еница** *f* [5] powder box; **~ить** [13], ‹на-› powder.
пуз|а́тый P [14 *sh.*] paunchy; **~о** P *n* [9] paunch.
пузыр|ёк [1; -рька́] vial; *a. dim. of* **~ь** *m* [4 *e.*] bubble; *anat.* bladder; F blister; kid.
пук *m* [1; *pl. e.*] wisp; bunch, bundle.
пулемёт *m* [1] machine gun; **~ный** [14] machine-gun; cartridge (*belt*); **~чик** *m* [1] machine gunner.
пуль|веризатор *m* [1] spray(er); **~с** *m* [1] pulse; **~си́ровать** [7] puls(at)e; **~т** *m* [1] desk, stand.
пу́ля *f* [6] bullet.
пункт *m* [1] point (at *all* по Д); station; place, spot; item, clause, article; **~и́р** *m* [1] dotted line; **~и́рный** [14] dotted; **~уа́льность** *f* [8] punctuality; accuracy; **~уа́льный** [14; -лен, -льна] punctual; accurate.
пунцо́вый [14] crimson.
пунш *m* [1] punch (*drink*).
пуп|о́к *m* [1; -пка́], F **~** *m* [1 *e.*] navel.
пурга́ *f* [5] blizzard, snowstorm.
пу́рпур *m* [1], **~ный**, **~овый** [14] purple.
пуск *m* [1] (*a.* ~ в ход) start(ing), setting in operation; **~а́й** F *s.* пусть; **~а́ть** [1], ‹пусти́ть› [15] let (go; in[to]), set (free; going, in motion *or* operation [*a.* ~а́ть в ход]); start; launch, throw; release; allow; put (forth); send; force; take (*root*); **~а́ть** под отко́с derail; **-ся** (+ *inf.*) start (...ing; *v/t.* в В), set out (on в В); enter *or* engage (into), begin, undertake.
пуст|е́ть [8], ‹о-, за-› become empty *or* deserted; **~и́ть** *s.* пуска́ть.
пуст|о́й [14; пуст, -а́, -о] empty; void; vain, idle (talk ~о́е *n su.*; *s. a.* **~я́к**); vacant; blank; dead (*rock*); F hollow; **~ота́** *f* [5; *pl. st.*: -о́ты] emptiness; void; *phys.* vacuum; vacancy.
пусты́|нный [14; -ы́нен, -ы́нна] desert, desolate; **~ня** *f* [6] desert, waste, wilderness; **~рь** *m* [4 *e.*] waste ground; **~шка** F *f* [5; *g/pl.*: -шек] blank; nonentity.
пусть let (him, *etc.*, + *vb.*; ~ [он] + *vb. 3rd. p.*), may; even (if).
пустя́|к F *m* [1 *e.*] trifle; *pl.* nonsense; (it's) nothing; **~ко́вый**, **~чный** (-ʃn-) F [14] trifling.
пу́та|ница *f* [5] confusion, muddle, mess; **~ть** [1], ‹за-, с-, пере-› (-ся get) confuse(d), muddle(d), mix(ed) up, entangle(d; interfere in в В).
путёвка *f* [5; *g/pl.*: -вок] pass (*Sov.*), permit.
путе|води́тель *m* [4] guide(book) (to по Д); **~во́дный** [14] lode..., pole(*star*); **~во́й** [14] travelling; traveller's; road...
путеше́ств|енник *m* [1] travel(l)er; **~ие** *n* [12] journey, travel, tour (on в В *or* П); voyage; **~овать** [7] travel (through по Д).
пу́т|ник *m* [1] travel(l)er; **~ный** F [14] *s.* де́льный; **~ы** *pl.* [9] shackles.
пут|ь *m* [8 *e.*; *instr/sg.*: -тём] way (*a. fig.*: [in] *that* way ~ём, *a.* by means of Р), road, path; 🚂 track (*a. fig.*), line; means; trip, journey (on в В *or* П); route; в *or* по ~и́ on the way; in passing; нам по ~и́ I (we) have the same way (as с Т); F *s.* толк.
пух *m* [1; в -ху́] down; в ~ (и прах) (*smash*) to pieces; (*defeat*) utterly, totally; F over(*dress*); **~ленький** F [16], **~лый** [14; пухл, -а́, -о] chubby, plump; **~нуть** [21], ‹рас-› swell; **~о́вка** *f* [5; *g/pl.*: -вок] powder puff; **~о́вый** [14] down...
пучи́на *f* [5] gulf, abyss; eddy.
пучо́к *m* [1; -чка́] *dim. of* пук, *s.*
пу́ш|ечный [14] gun..., cannon...; **~и́нка** *f* [5; *g/pl.*: -нок] down, fluff; **~и́стый** [14 *sh.*] downy, fluffy; **~ка** *f* [5; *g/pl.*: -шек] gun, cannon; F hoax; **~ни́на** *f* [5] furs *pl.*; **~но́й** [14] fur...; **~о́к** F *m* [1; -шка́] down.
пу́ще P more (than Р).
пчел|а́ *f* [5; *pl. st.*: пчёлы] bee; **~ово́д** *m* [1] beekeeper; **~ово́дство** *n* [9] beekeeping; **~ьник** *m* [1] apiary.
пшен|и́ца *f* [5] wheat; **~и́чный** [14] wheaten; **~ный** (ˈpʃɔ-) [14] millet...; **~о́** *n* [9] millet.
пыл *m* [1] ardo(u)r, zeal, blaze; в ~у́ in the thick (*of the fight*); **~а́ть** [1], ‹вос-, за-› blaze, flare (up), (in-) flame; glow, burn; (en)rage (with Т); **~есо́с** *m* [1] vacuum cleaner; **~и́нка** *f* [5; *g/pl.*: -нок] mote; **~и́ть** [13], ‹за-› dust; **-ся** be(come) dusty; **~кий** [16; -лок, -лка́, -о] ardent, fiery.
пыль *f* [8; в -ли́] dust; **~ный** [14; -лен, -льна́, -о] dusty (*a.* = в -ли́); **~ца́** *f* [5] pollen.
пыт|а́ть [1] torture; **~а́ться** [1], ‹по-› try, attempt; **~ка** *f* [5; *g/pl.*: -ток] torture; **~ли́вый** [14 *sh.*] inquisitive, searching.
пыхте́ть [11] puff, pant; F sweat.
пы́шн|ость *f* [8] splendo(u)r, pomp; **~ый** [14; -шен, -шна́, -о] magnificent, splendid, sumptuous; luxuriant, rich.
пьедеста́л *m* [1] pedestal.
пье́са *f* [5] *thea.* play; ♪ piece.
пьян|е́ть [8], ‹о-› get drunk (*a. fig.*; with от Р); **~ица** *m/f* [5] drunkard; **~ство** *n* [9] drunkenness; **~ствовать** [7] drink, F booze; **~ый** [14; пьян, -а́, -о] drunk(en), *a. fig.* (with от Р).
пюре́ (-ˈrɛ) *n* [*ind.*] mashed potatoes *pl.*
пяд|ь *f* [8; *from g/pl. e.*] span; *fig.* inch.
пят|а́ *f* [5; *nom/pl. st.*] heel (on по Д).
пят|а́к F *m* [1 *e.*], **~ачо́к** F *m* [1; -чка́]

five-kopeck coin; **~ёрка** *f* [5; *g/pl.*: -рок] five (*cf.* двóйка); F (*mark*) = отлично, *cf.*; five-ruble note; **~еро** [37] five (*cf.* двóе).
пяти|деся́тый [14] fiftieth; **~деся́тые** гóды *pl.* the fifties; *cf.* пя́тый; **~конéчный** [14] five-pointed (*star*); **~лéтка** *f* [5; *g/pl.*: -ток] five-year plan (*Sov.*); **~лéтний** [15] five-year (old), of five; **~сóтый** [14] five hundredth.
пя́титься [15], ⟨по-⟩ (move) back.
пя́тка *f* [5; *g/pl.*: -ток] heel (take to one's heels показáть **~и**).
пятнáдцат|ый [14] fifteenth; *cf.* пя́тый; **~ь** [35] fifteen; *cf.* пять.
пятни́стый [14 *sh.*] spotty, spotted.
пя́тн|ица *f* [5] Friday (on: в В, *pl.*: по Д); **~ó** *n* [9; *pl. st.*; *g/pl.*: -тен] spot, stain, blot(ch) (with *pl.* в П); роди́мое **~ó** birthmark, mole.
пя́т|ый [14] fifth; (*page, chapter, year, etc., sentence or lesson no.*) five; **~ая** *f su.* ⅍ fifth (*part*); **~ое** *n su.* fifth (*date*; on P: **~ого**; *cf.* числó); **~ь** (минýт) **~ого** five (minutes) past four; **~ь** [35] five; без **~и́** (минýт) час (два, *etc.*, [часá], **~ь**, *etc.* [часóв]) five (minutes) to one (two, *etc.* [o'clock]); **~ьдеся́т** [35] fifty; **~ьсóт** [36] five hundred; **~ью** five times.

Р

р. *abbr.*: **1.** рубль, -ля́, -лéй; **2.** рекá.
раб *m* [1 *e.*], **~á** *f* [5] slave; **~овладéлец** *m* [1; -льца] slaveholder; **~олéпство** *n* [9] servility, **~олéпствовать** [7] cringe (to пéред Т).
рабóт|а *f* [5] work (at за Т; на П); labo(u)r, toil; assignment, task; **~ать** [1] work (on th. над Т; for p. на В; as Т), function; labo(u)r, toil; be open; **~ник** *m* [1], **~ница** *f* [5] worker, working (wo)man; (day) labo(u)rer, (farm)hand; (*house*)maid; official, functionary; employee; member; clerk; **~одáтель** *m* [4] employer, F boss; **~оспосóбный** [14; -бен, -бна] able to work, able-bodied; hard-working, efficient.
рабóч|ий *m* [17] (*esp. industrial*) worker; *adj.*: working, work (*a. day*); workers', labo(u)r...; **~ая си́ла** *f* man power; labo(u)r.
рáб|ский [16] slave...; slavish, servile; **~ство** *n* [9] slavery; **~ы́ня** *f* [6] *s.* **~á**.
рáв|енство *n* [9] equality; **~нéние** *n* [12] ⚔ eyes (*right!*); **~ни́на** *f* [5] plain; **~нó** equal(ly); as well (as); всё **~нó** it's all the same, it doesn't matter; anyway, in any case.
равно|вéсие *n* [12] balance (*a. fig.*), equilibrium; **~дýшие** *n* [12] indifference (to к Д) **~дýшный** [14; -шен, -шна] indifferent (to к Д); **~знáчный** [14; -чен, -чна] equivalent; **~мéрный** [14; -рен, -рна] uniform, even, equal; **~прáвие** *n* [12] equality (of rights); **~прáвный** [14; -вен, -вна] (enjoying) equal (rights); **~си́льный** [14; -лен, -льна] equivalent; **~цéнный** [14; -éнен, -éнна] equal (in value).
рáвн|ый [14; рáвен, -внá] equal; (*a. su.*); **~ым** óбразом *s.* **~ó**; емý нет **~ого** he has no match; **~я́ть** [28], ⟨с-⟩ equalize; ⚔ dress (*ranks*); F compare; (*v/i.* **-ся**; *a.* be [equal to Д]).
рад [14; рáда] (be) glad (at, of Д; *a.* to see p.), pleased, delighted; would like; (be) willing; не ~ (be) sorry; ~ не ~ willy-nilly; **~áр** *m* [1] radar; **~и** (P) for the sake of (*or*... ['s] sake); for.
радиáтор *m* [1] radiator.
рáдий *m* [3] radium.
радикáл *m* [1], **~ьный** [14; -лен, льна] radical.
рáдио *n* [*ind.*] radio, *Brt. a.* wireless (on по Д); **~активность** *f* [8] radioactivity; **~акти́вный** [14; -вен, -вна] radioactive; **~аппарáт** *m* [1] *s.* **~приёмник**; **~вещáние** *n* [12] broadcasting (system); **~ла** *f* [5] radio-gramophone; **~люби́тель** *m* [4] radiofan; **~передáча** *f* [5] (radio)broadcast, transmission; **~приёмник** *m* [1] receiving set, radio, *Brt.* wireless (set); **~слýшатель** *m* [4] listener; **~стáнция** *f* [7] radio station; **~ýзел** [1; -злá] radio center (*Brt.*: -tre); **~установка** *f* [5; *g/pl.*: -вок] radio plant.
ради́|ст *m* [1] radio (wireless) operator; **'~ус** *m* [1] radius.
рáдо|вать [7], ⟨об-, по-⟩ (В) gladden, please, rejoice; **-ся** (Д) rejoice (at), be glad *or* pleased (of, at); look forward (to); **~стный** [14; -тен, -тна] joyful, glad; merry; **~сть** *f* [8] joy, gladness; pleasure.
рáду|га *f* [5] rainbow; **~жный** [14] iridescent, rainbow...; *fig.* rosy.
радýш|ие *n* [12] kindliness; hospitality; **~ный** [14; -шен, -шна] kindly, hearty; hospitable.
раз *m* [1; *pl. e., gen.* раз] time (*this, etc.* [в] В); one; (оди́н) ~ once; два **~а** twice; ни **~у** not once, never; не ~ repeatedly; как ~ just (in time F в сáмый ~; *s. a.* впóру), the very; вот тебé ~ F *s.* нá[2].
разба|вля́ть [28], ⟨**~вить**⟩ [14] dilute; **~лтывать** F, ⟨разболтáть⟩ [1] let out.

разбé|г *m* [1] start, run (with, at с Р); **~гáться** [1], ⟨**~жáться**⟩ [4; -егýсь, -ежúшься, -егýтся] take a run; scatter; disperse.

разби|вáть [1], ⟨**~ть**⟩ [разобью́, -бьёшь; разбе́й(те)!; -и́тый] break (to pieces), crash, crush; defeat; divide (into на В); lay out (*park*); pitch (*tent*); knock; **-ся** break; crash; split; come to nothing; **~рáтельство** *n* [9] trial; **~рáть** [1], ⟨разобрáть⟩ [разберý, -рёшь; разобрáл, -á, -о; -óбранный] take to pieces, dismantle, pull down; investigate, inquire into; review; analyze (*Brt.* -se), parse; make out, decipher, understand; sort out; ⚖ try; buy up; F take; *impf.* be particular; **-ся** F (в П) grasp, understand; unpack; **~тие** *n* [12] crash, defeat (*cf.* **~вáть**); **~тый** [14 *sh.*] broken; F jaded; **~ть(ся)** *s.* **~вáть(ся)**.

разбóй *m* [3] robbery; **~ник** *m* [1] robber; **~ничать** [1] rob; pirate; **~нический** [16], **~ничий** [18] predatory; of robbers *or* brigands.

разболтáть *s.* разбáлтывать.

разбóр *m* [1] analysis; review, critique; investigation, inquiry (into); ⚖ trial; без **~а**, **~у** F indiscriminately; **~ка** *f* [5] taking to pieces, dismantling; sorting (out); **~ный** [14] folding, collapsible; **~чивость** *f* [8] legibility; scrupulousness; **~чивый** [14 *sh.*] legible; discerning; scrupulous, fastidious.

разбр|áсывать, ⟨**~осáть**⟩ [1] scatter, throw about, strew; F squander; **~едáться** [1], ⟨**~естúсь**⟩ [25] disperse; **~óд** *m* [1] disorder, mess; **~óсанный** [14] scattered; **~осáть** *s.* **~áсывать**.

разбух|áть [1], ⟨**~нуть**⟩ [21] swell.

развáл *m* [1] collapse, breakdown; chaos; **~ивать** [1], ⟨**~и́ть**⟩ [13; -алю́, -áлишь] pull (*or* break) down; disorganize; **-ся** fall to pieces, collapse; F sprawl; **~ины** *f/pl.* ruins (F *a. sg* = *p.*).

рáзве really; perhaps; only; F unless.

развевáться [1] flutter; stream.

развéд|ать *s.* **~ывать**; **~éние** *n* [12] breeding; cultivation; **~ённый** [14] divorced, divorcé(e) *su.*; **~ка** *f* [5; *g/pl.*: -док] reconnaissance; intelligence service; **~очный** [14] reconnaissance...; **~чик** *m* [1] scout; intelligence officer; reconnaissance plane; **~ывательный** [14] *s.* **~очный**; **~ывать**, ⟨**~ать**⟩ [1] reconnoiter (*Brt.* -tre); F find out.

разве|стú *s.* развози́ть; **~нчáть** [1] *pf.* uncrown, dethrone; unmask.

развёр|нутый [14] large-scale; **~тывать** [1], ⟨развернýть⟩ [20] unfold, unroll, unwrap; open; ⚔ deploy; *fig.* develop; (**-ся** *v/i.*; *a.* turn).

разве|снóй [14] weighed out; **~сить** *s.* **~шивать**; **~стú(сь)** *s.* разводи́ть(ся); **~твлéние** *n* [12] ramification, branching; **~твля́ться** [28], ⟨**~тви́ться**⟩ [14 *e.*; *3rd p. only*] ramify, branch; **~шивать** [1], ⟨**~сить**⟩ [15] weigh (out); hang (out); **~ять** [27] *pf.* disperse, dispel.

разви|вáть [1], ⟨**~ть**⟩ [разовью́, -вьёшь; разве́й(те)!; разви́л, -á, -о; -ви́тый (рáзвит, -á, -о)] develop (*v/i.* **-ся**); evolve; untwist; **~нчивать** [1], ⟨**~нти́ть**⟩ [15 *e.*; -нчý, -нти́шь; -и́нченный] unscrew; **~тие** *n* [12] development; evolution; **~тóй** [14; рáзвит, -á, -о] developed; intelligent; advanced; **~ть(ся)** *s.* **~вáть(ся)**.

развле|кáть [1], ⟨**~чь**⟩ [26] entertain, amuse (o.s. **-ся**); divert; **~чéние** *n* [12] entertainment, amusement, diversion.

развóд *m* [1] divorce; ⚔ relief, mounting; **~и́ть** [15], ⟨развести́⟩ [25] take (along), bring; divorce (from с Т); separate; dilute; mix; rear, breed; plant, cultivate; light, make; ⚔ mount, relieve; **-ся**, ⟨**-сь**⟩ get divorced (from с Т); F multiply, grow *or* increase in number.

раз|вози́ть [15], ⟨**~везти́**⟩ [24] deliver, carry; **~ворáчивать** F *s.* **~вёртывать**.

разврá|т *m* [1] debauch; depravity; **~ти́ть(ся)** *s.* **~щáть(ся)**; **~тник** *m* [1] libertine, debauchee, rake; **~тничать** F [1] (indulge in) debauch; **~тный** [14; -тен, -тна] dissolute, licentious; **~щáть** [1], ⟨**~ти́ть**⟩ [15 *e.*; -ащý; -ати́шь; -щённый] (**-ся** become) deprave(d), debauch(ed), corrupt; **~щéние** *n* [12], **~щённость** *f* [8] depravity.

развяз|áть *s.* **~ывать**; **~ка** *f* [5; *g/pl.*: -зок] denouement; outcome, conclusion, head; **~ный** [14; -зен, -зна] forward, (free &) easy; **~ывать** [1], ⟨**~áть**⟩ [3] untie, undo; *fig.* unleash; F loosen; **-ся** come untied; F get rid (of с Т).

разгад|áть *s.* **~ывать**; **~ка** *f* [5; *g/pl.*: -док] solution; **~ывать**, ⟨**~áть**⟩ [1] solve, unriddle.

разгáр *m* [1] (в П *or* В) heat, thick (in), height (at), (in full) swing.

раз|гибáть [1], ⟨**~огнýть**⟩ [20] unbend, straighten (o.s. **-ся**).

разглá|живать [1], ⟨**~дить**⟩ [15] smooth; iron, press; **~шáть** [1], ⟨**~си́ть**⟩ [15 *e.*; -ашý, -аси́шь; -ашённый] divulge; trumpet.

разгляд|éть [11] *pf.* make out; **~ывать** [1] examine, view.

разгнéванный [14] angry.

разгов|áривать [1] talk (to, with с Т; about, of о П), converse, speak; **~óр** *m* [1] talk, conversation; *cf.* речь; **~óрный** [14] colloquial; **~óрчивый** [14 *sh.*] talkative.

разго́н *m* [1] dispersal; *a.* = разбе́г; в ~е out; **~я́ть** [28], ⟨разогна́ть⟩ [разгоню́, -о́нишь; разогна́л, -а́, -о; разо́гнанный] disperse, scatter; dispel; F drive away; **-ся** take a run.
разгор|а́ться [1], ⟨**~е́ться**⟩ [9] kindle (*a. fig.*), (in)flame, blaze up.
разгра|бля́ть [28], ⟨**~́бить**⟩ [14], **~бле́ние** *n* [12] plunder, pillage, loot; **~ниче́ние** *n* [12] delimitation; **~ни́чивать** [1], ⟨**~ни́чить**⟩ [16] demarcate, delimit.
разгро́м *m* [1] rout; debacle, destruction, ruin, chaos.
разгру|жа́ть [1], ⟨**~зи́ть**⟩ [15 & 15 *e.*; -ужу́, -у́зишь; -у́женный & -ужённый] (-ся be) unload(ed); F relieve(d); **~́зка** *f* [5; *g/pl.*: -зок] unloading.
разгу́л *m* [1] revelry, carouse; debauch(ery), licentiousness; **~ивать** F [1] stroll, saunter; **~я́ться**, ⟨**~я́ться**⟩ [28] clear up; F have a good walk *or* run, move without restraint; **~ьный** F [14; -лен, -льна] dissolute; loose, easy.
разда|ва́ть [5], ⟨**~́ть**⟩ [-да́м, -да́шь, *etc.*, *s.* дать; ро́здал, раздала́, ро́здало; ро́зданный (-ан, раздана́, ро́здано)] distribute; play (*cards:* deal) out; **-ся** (re)sound, be heard; give way; split, separate; F expand; **~́вливать** [1] *s.* дави́ть 2.; **~́ть(ся)** *s.* **~ва́ть(ся)**; **~́ча** *f* [5] distribution.
раздва́иваться *s.* двои́ться.
раздви|га́ть [1], ⟨**~́нуть**⟩ [20] part, separate, move apart; pull out; **~жно́й** [14] sash...; telescope, -pic.
раздвое́ние *n* [12] bifurcation.
раздева́|лка F *f* [5; *g/pl.*: -лок], F **~льня** *f* [6; *g/pl.*: -лен] checkroom, cloakroom; **~ть** [1], ⟨разде́ть⟩ [-де́ну, -де́нешь; -де́тый] undress (*v/i.* **-ся**), take off; F strip (of).
разде́л *m* [1] division; section; **~аться** F [1] *pf.* get rid *or* be quit (of с T); **~е́ние** *n* [12] division (into на B); *eccl.* schism; **~и́тельный** [14] dividing; *gr.* disjunctive; **~и́ть(ся)** *s.* **~я́ть(ся)** & дели́ть(ся); **~ьный** [14] separate; distinct; **~я́ть** [28], ⟨**~и́ть**⟩ [13; елю́, -е́лишь; -елённый] divide (into на B; *a.* [-ed] by); separate; share; **-ся** (be) divide(d), fall.
разде́ть(ся) *s.* раздева́ть(ся).
раз|дира́ть F [1], ⟨**~одра́ть**⟩ [раздеру́, -рёшь; разодра́л, -а́, -о; -о́дранный] *impf.* rend; *pf.* F tear; **~добы́ть** F [-бу́ду, -бу́дешь] *pf.* get, procure.
раздо́лье *n* [10] *s.* приво́лье.
раздо́р *m* [1] discord, contention.
раздоса́дованный F [14] angry.
раздраж|а́ть [1], ⟨**~и́ть**⟩ [16 *e.*; -жу́, -жи́шь; -жённый] irritate, provoke; vex, annoy; **-ся** lose one's temper; **~е́ние** *n* [12] irritation; temper; **~и́тельный** [14; -лен, -льна] irritable, touchy; **~и́ть(ся)** *s.* **~а́ть(ся)**.
раздробл|е́ние *n* [12] breaking; smashing; **~я́ть** [28] *s.* дроби́ть.
разду|ва́ть [1], ⟨**~́ть**⟩ [18] fan; blow (away); swell; puff up, exaggerate; **-ся** swell, inflate.
разду́м|ывать, ⟨**~ать**⟩ [1] change one's mind; *impf.* deliberate, consider; **~ье** *n* [10] thought(s), meditation; doubt(s).
разду́ть(ся) *s.* раздува́ть(ся).
раз|ева́ть F [1], ⟨**~и́нуть**⟩ [20] open wide; **~ева́ть** рот gape; **~жа́лобить** [14] *pf.* move to pity; **~жа́ловать** [7] *pf.* degrade (to в И *pl.*); **~жа́ть** *s.* **~жима́ть**; **~жёвывать** [1], ⟨**~жева́ть**⟩ [7 *e.*; -жую́, -жуёшь] chew; **~жига́ть** [1], ⟨**~же́чь**⟩ [г/ж: -зожгу́, -жжёшь, -жгу́т; разжёг, -зожгла́; разожжённый] kindle (*a. fig.*); heat; rouse; unleash; **~жима́ть** [1], ⟨**~жа́ть**⟩ [разожму́, -мёшь; разжа́тый] unclench, open; **~и́нуть** *s.* **~ева́ть**; **~и́ня** F *m/f* [6] gawk, gaper; **~и́тельный** [14; -лен, -льна] striking.
раз|лага́ть [1], ⟨**~ложи́ть**⟩ [16] analyze (*Brt.* -yse); decompose; (*v/i.* **-ся**); (become) demoralize(d), corrupt(ed; decay); **~ла́д** *m* [1] dissension, discord, dissonance; disturbance; **~ла́мывать** [1], ⟨**~лома́ть**⟩ [1], ⟨**~ломи́ть**⟩ [14] break; pull down; **~лета́ться** [1], ⟨**~лете́ться**⟩ [11] fly (away, asunder); F break (to pieces); come to naught; take a sweep.
разли́|в *m* [1] flood; **~ва́ть** [1], ⟨**~ть**⟩ [разолью́, -льёшь; *cf.* лить; -ле́й(те)!; -и́л, -а́, -о; -и́тый (-и́т, -а́, -о)] spill; pour out; bottle; ladle; flood, overflow; spread; bestow; (*v/i.* **-ся**).
различ|а́ть [1], ⟨**~и́ть**⟩ [16 *e.*; -чу́, -чи́шь; -чённый] distinguish; **-ся** *impf.* differ (in T, по Д); **~́ие** *n* [12] distinction, difference; **~и́тельный** [14] distinctive; **~и́ть** *s.* **~а́ть**; **~́ный** [14; -чен, -чна] different (from от P); different, various, diverse.
разлож|е́ние *n* [12] analysis; decomposition, decay; corruption, degeneration; **~и́ть(ся)** *s.* разлага́ть(ся) & раскла́дывать.
разлом|а́ть, **~и́ть** *s.* разла́мывать.
разлу́|ка *f* [5] separation (from с T), parting; **~ча́ть** [1], ⟨**~чи́ть**⟩ [16 *e.*; -чу́, -чи́шь; -чённый] separate (*v/i.* **-ся**; from с T), part.
разма́|зывать [1], ⟨**~зать**⟩ [3] smear, spread; **~тывать** [1], ⟨размота́ть⟩ unwind, wind off; **~х** *m* [1] swing, brandish (with [*a.* might] с **~ху**); span (✈ & *fig.*), sweep; amplitude; *fig.* vim, verve, élan; scope; **~хивать** [1], *once* ⟨**~хну́ть**⟩ [20] (T) swing, sway,

dangle; brandish; gesticulate; **-ся** lift (one's hand T); **~шистый** F [14 *sh.*] wide; diffuse.

разме|жевáть [7] *pf.* mark off, demarcate; **~льчáть** [1], ⟨**~льчи́ть**⟩ [16 *e.*; чý, -чи́шь; -чённый] pound, crush.

размéн *m* [1], **~ивать** [1], ⟨**~я́ть**⟩ [28] (ex)change (for на B); **~ный** [14]: ~ная монéта *f* change.

размéр *m* [1] size; dimension(s), measure(ment); rate (at в П), amount; scale; *poetic.*, ♪ meter (*Brt.* -tre; in T), ♪ *a.* time, measure (of в B); **~енный** [14 *sh.*] measured; **~я́ть** [28], ⟨**~ить**⟩ [13] measure (off).

разме|сти́ть *s.* ~щáть; **~чáть** [1], ⟨**~стить**⟩ [15] mark; **~шивать** [1], ⟨**~шáть**⟩ [1] stir (up); knead; **~щáть** [1], ⟨**~сти́ть**⟩ [15 *e.*; -ещý, -ести́шь; -ещённый] place; lodge, accommodate (in, at, with в П, по Д); distribute; **~щéние** *n* [12] distribution; accomodation; arrangement, order.

размин|áть [1], ⟨**размя́ть**⟩ [разомнý, -нёшь; размя́тый] knead; F stretch (*limbs*); **~ýться** F *pf.* [20] cross; miss o. a.

размнож|áть [1], ⟨**~ить**⟩ [16] multiply (*v/i.* **-ся**); mimeograph; **~éние** *n* [12] multiplication; propagation, reproduction; **~ить(ся)** *s.* ~áть(ся).

размо|зжи́ть [16 *e.*; -жý, -жи́шь; -жённый] *pf.* smash, crush; **~кáть** [1], ⟨**~кнуть**⟩ [21] soak, swell; **~лвка** *f* [5; *g/pl.*: -вок] tiff, quarrel; **~лóть** [17; -мелю́, -мéлешь] *pf.* grind, crush; **~тáть** *s.* размáтывать; **~чи́ть** [16] *pf.* soak.

размы|вáть [1], ⟨**~ть**⟩ [22] wash out *or* away; **~кáть** [1], ⟨разомкнýть⟩ [20] open (⚡, ⊕); **~ть** *s.* ~вáть.

размышл|éние *n* [12] reflection (for на B), thought; **~я́ть** [28] reflect, meditate (on о П).

размягч|áть (-xt∫-) [1], ⟨**~и́ть**⟩ [16 *e.*; -чý, -чи́шь; -чённый] soften, mollify.

раз|мя́ть *s.* ~минáть; **~нáшивать**, ⟨**~носи́ть**⟩ [15] tread out, wear to shape; **~нести** *s.* ~носи́ть 1.; **~нимáть** [1], ⟨**~ня́ть**⟩ [-нимý, -ни́мешь; -ня́л & рóзнял, -á, -о; -ня́тый (-ня́т, -á, -о)] part; take to pieces.

рáзница *f* [5] difference.

разно|ви́дность *f* [8] variety, sort; **~глáсие** *n* [12] discord, disagreement, difference, variance; discrepancy; **~кали́берный** F [14], **~мáстный** [14; -тен, -тна] *s.* ~шёрстный; **~обрáзие** *n* [12] variety, diversity, multiplicity; **~обрáзный** [14; -зен, -зна] manifold, multifarious, various; **~реч...** *s.* противореч...; **~рóдный** [14; -ден, -дна] heterogeneous.

разнóс *m* [1] delivery; peddlery; **~и́ть** [15] **1.** ⟨разнести́⟩ [25 -с-] deliver (to, at по Д), carry; hawk, peddle; F spread; smash, destroy; blow up; scatter; swell; **2.** *s.* разнáшивать; **~ка** *f* [5] *s.* ~; **~ный** [14] peddling.

разно|сторóнний [15; -óнен, -óння] many-sided; **'~сть** *f* [8] difference; **~счик** *m* [1] peddler, hawker; (*news*)boy, man; messenger; **~цвéтный** [14; -тен, -тна] multicolo(u)red; **~шёрстный** [14; -тен, -тна] variegated; F motley, mixed.

разнýзданный [14 *sh.*] unbridled.

рáзн|ый [14] various, different, diverse; **~я́ть** *s.* ~имáть.

разо|блачáть [1], ⟨**~блачи́ть**⟩ [16 *e.*; -чý, -чи́шь; -чённый] expose, disclose, unmask; **~блачéние** *n* [12] exposure, disclosure, unmasking; **~брáть(ся)** *s.* разбирáть(ся); **~гнáть(ся)** *s.* разгоня́ть(ся); **~гнýть(ся)** *s.* разгибáть(ся); **~гревáть** [1], ⟨**~грéть**⟩ [8; -éтый] warm (up); **~дéтый** F [14 *sh.*] dressed up; **~дрáть** *s.* раздирáть; **~йти́сь** *s.* расходи́ться; **~мкнýть** *s.* размыкáть; **~рвáть(ся)** *s.* разрывáть (-ся).

разор|éние *n* [12] ruin, destruction, devastation; **~и́тельный** [14; -лен, -льна] ruinous; **~и́ть(ся)** *s.* ~я́ть(ся); **~ужáть** [1], ⟨**~ужи́ть**⟩ [16 *e.*; -жý, -жи́шь; -жённый] disarm (*v/i.* **-ся**); **~ужéние** *n* [12] disarmament; **~я́ть** [28], ⟨**~и́ть**⟩ [13] (**-ся** be[come]) ruin(ed), destroy(ed), ravage(d).

разослáть *s.* рассылáть.

разостлáть *s.* расстилáть.

разочар|овáние *n* [12] disappointment; **~óвывать** [1], ⟨**~овáть**⟩ [7] (**-ся** be) disappoint(ed) (in в П).

разра|бáтывать, ⟨**~бóтать**⟩ [1] work up (into на B), process; work out, elaborate; ⚒ till; ⚒ exploit; **~бóтка** *f* [5; *g/pl.*: -ток] working (out); elaboration; ⚒ tillage; ⚒ exploitation; **~жáться** [1], ⟨**~зи́ться**⟩ [15 *e.*; -ажýсь, -ази́шься] burst out (into T); **~стáться** [1], ⟨**~сти́сь**⟩ [24; *3rd p. only*: -тётся; -рóсся, -слáсь] grow; enlarge, expand.

разрежённый [14] rarefied.

разрéз *m* [1] cut; section; angle (from в П); **~áть** [1], ⟨**~ать**⟩ [3] cut (up), slit; **~нóй** [14]: ~нóй нож *m* paper knife; **~ывать** [1] *s.* ~áть.

разреш|áть [1], ⟨**~и́ть**⟩ [16 *e.*; -шý, -ши́шь; -шённый] permit, allow; (re)solve; release (for к Д); absolve; settle; **-ся** be (re)solved; end, burst (in[to] T); be delivered (of T); **~éние** *n* [12] permission (with с Р); licence (for на B); (re)solution; settlement; absolution; delivery; **~и́ть(ся)** *s.* ~áть(ся).

раз|рисовáть [7] *pf.* ornament;

~ро́зненный [14] odd; isolated; **~руба́ть** [1], ⟨**~руби́ть**⟩ [14] split.

разру́|ха *f* [5] ruin; **~ша́ть** [1], ⟨**~шить**⟩ [16] destroy, demolish; ruin; frustrate; **-ся** (fall *or* come to) ruin; **~ше́ние** *n* [12] destruction, demolition, devastation; **~шить** (**-ся**) *s.* ~ша́ть(ся).

разры́|в *m* [1] breach, break, rupture; explosion; gap; ⊕ на ~в tensile; **~ва́ть** [1] 1. ⟨разорва́ть⟩ [-ву́, -вёшь; -ва́л, -а́, -о; -о́рванный] tear (to *pieces* на В); break (off); *impers.* burst, explode; (**-ся** *v/i.*); 2. ⟨~ть⟩ [22] dig up; **~вно́й** [14] explosive; **~да́ться** [1] *pf.* break into sobs; **~ть** *s.* ~ва́ть 2.; **~хля́ть** [28] *s.* рыхли́ть.

разря́|д *m* [1] category, class; discharge; unloading; **~ди́ть** *s.* ~жа́ть; **~дка** *f* [5; *g/pl.*: -док] spacing, space; slackening; disengagement; **~жа́ть** [1], ⟨~ди́ть⟩ [15 *e.* & 15; -яжу́, -я́дишь; -яжённый & -я́женный] unload; discharge; reduce, disengage (*tension*); *typ.* space; [15] F dress up.

разу|бежда́ть [1], ⟨**~беди́ть**⟩ [15 *e.*; -ежу́, -еди́шь; -еждённый] (в П) dissuade (from); **-ся** change one's mind (about); **~ва́ться** [1], ⟨**~́ться**⟩ [18] take off one's shoes; **~веря́ть** [28], ⟨**~ве́рить**⟩ [13] (в П) (**-ся** be) undeceive(d), disabuse(d) (of); disappoint(ed); **~знава́ть** F [5], ⟨**~зна́ть**⟩ [1] find out (about о П, В); **~кра́шивать** [1], ⟨**~кра́сить**⟩ [15] decorate; embellish; **~крупня́ть** [28], ⟨**~крупни́ть**⟩ [14] diminish; decentralize.

ра́зум *m* [1] reason; sense(s); **~́еть** [8] understand; know; mean, imply (by под Т); **-ся** be meant *or* understood; **~́ется** of course; **~́ный** [14; -мен, -мна] rational; reasonable, sensible; clever, wise.

разу́|ться *s.* ~ва́ться; **~чивать** [1], ⟨**~чи́ть**⟩ [16] study, learn; **-ся** forget, unlearn.

разъе|да́ть [1] *s.* есть[1] 2; **~диня́ть** [28], ⟨**~дини́ть**⟩ [13] separate; ⚡ disconnect; **~́зд** *m* [1] trip, journey (on в П); setting out, departure; ⚔ horse patrol; 🚂 siding; **~зжа́ть** [1] drive, ride, go about; be on a journey *or* trip; **-ся**, ⟨**~́хаться**⟩ [-е́дусь, -е́дешься; -езжа́йтесь!] leave (for по Д); separate; pass o. a. (с Т).

разъярённый [14] enraged, furious.

разъясн|е́ние *n* [12] explanation; clarification; **~я́ть** [28], ⟨**~и́ть**⟩ [13] explain, elucidate.

разы́|грывать, ⟨**~гра́ть**⟩ [1] play; raffle (off); **-ся** break out; run high; happen; **~скивать** [1], ⟨**~ска́ть**⟩ [3] seek, search (for; *pf.* out = find).

рай *m* [3; в раю́] paradise.

рай|ко́м *m* [1] (райо́нный комите́т) district committee (*Sov.*); **~о́н** *m* [1] district; region, area; **~о́нный** [14] district...; regional; **~сове́т** *m* [1] (райо́нный сове́т) district soviet (*or* council).

рак *m* [1] crawfish, *Brt.* crayfish; морско́й ~ lobster; ⚕, *ast.* (♋) cancer.

раке́т|а *f* [5] (*a.* sky) rocket; **~ка** *f* [5; *g/pl.*: -ток] racket (*sport*); **~ный** [14] rocket...

ра́ковина *f* [5] shell; sink; bowl.

ра́м|(к)а *f* [5; (*g/pl.*: -мок)] frame (-work, *a. fig.* = limits; within в П); **~па** *f* [5] footlights *pl.*; stage.

ра́н|а *f* [5] wound; **~г** *m* [1] rank; **~е́ние** *n* [12] wound(ing); **~еный** [14] wounded (*a. su.*); **~ец** *m* [1; -нца] satchel; ⚔ knapsack; **~ить** [13] (*im*)*pf.* wound, injure (in в В).

ра́н|ний [15] early (*adv.* ~о); morning...; spring...; ~о или по́здно sooner or later; **~ова́то** F rather early; **~ьше** earlier; formerly; first; (Р) before.

рап|и́ра *f* [5] rapier; **~́орт** *m* [1], **~ортова́ть** [7] (*im*)*pf.* report; **~с** *m* [1] ❀ rape; **~со́дия** *f* [7] rhapsody.

ра́са *f* [5] race.

раска́|иваться [1], ⟨**~яться**⟩ [27] repent (*v/t.*, of в П); **~лённый** [14], **~ли́ть(ся)** *s.* ~ля́ть(ся); **~лывать** [1], ⟨расколо́ть⟩ [17] split, cleave; crack; (*v/i.* **-ся**); **~ля́ть** [28], ⟨**~ли́ть**⟩ [13] make (**-ся** become) red-hot, white-hot; **~пывать** [1], ⟨раскопа́ть⟩ [1] dig out *or* up; **~т** *m* [1] roll, peal; **~тистый** [14 *sh.*] rolling; **~тывать**, ⟨**~та́ть**⟩ [1] (un-) roll; *v/i.* **-ся**; ⟨**~ти́ться**⟩ [15] gain speed; roll (off); **~чивать**, ⟨**~ча́ть**⟩ [1] swing; shake; F bestir; **~яние** *n* [12] repentance (of в П); **~яться** *s.* ~иваться.

расквартирова́ть [7] *pf.* quarter.

раски́|дывать [1], ⟨**~нуть**⟩ [20] spread (out); throw out; pitch (*tent*), set up.

раскла|дно́й [14] folding, collapsible; **~́дывать** [1], ⟨разложи́ть⟩ [16] lay *or* spread out, display; lay; set up; make, light; apportion, repartition; **~́ниваться** [1], ⟨**~́няться**⟩ [28] (с Т) bow (to), greet; take leave (of).

раско́|л *m* [1] split, schism; **~ло́ть** (**-ся**) *s.* раска́лывать(ся); **~па́ть** *s.* раска́пывать; **~пка** *f* [5; *g/pl.*: -пок] excavation.

раскр|а́шивать [1] *s.* кра́сить; **~епоща́ть** [1], ⟨**~епости́ть**⟩ [15 *e.*; -ощу́, -ости́шь; -ощённый] emancipate, liberate; **~епоще́ние** *n* [12] emancipation, liberation; **~итикова́ть** [7] *pf.* scarify; **~ича́ться** [4*e.*; -чу́сь, -чи́шься] *pf.* shout, bawl (at на В); **~ыва́ть** [1], ⟨**~ы́ть**⟩ [22] open (*v/i.* **-ся**); uncover; disclose, reveal; put *one's cards* on the table.

раску|ла́чить [16] *pf.* dispossess *or* oust (the kulak[s]) **~па́ть** [1],

⟨~пи́ть⟩ [14] buy up; **∠поривать** [1], ⟨∠порить⟩ [13] uncork; open; **∠сывать** [1], ⟨~си́ть⟩ [15] crack; F see through, get (the hang of); **∠тывать**, ⟨∠тать⟩ [1] unwind, unwrap.

ра́совый [14] racial.

распа́д *m* [1] disintegration; decay.

распа|да́ться [1], ⟨∠сться⟩ [25; -па́лся, -лась; -па́вшийся] fall to pieces; decay; disintegrate; break up (into на В), split; **~ко́вывать** [1], ⟨~кова́ть⟩ [7] unpack; **∠рывать** [1] *s.* поро́ть; **∠сться** *s.* ~да́ться; **∠хивать** [1] **1.** ⟨~ха́ть⟩ [3] plow (*Brt.* plough) up; **2.** ⟨~хну́ть⟩ [20] throw *or* fling open (*v/i.* **-ся**); **~я́ть** [24] *pf.* (**-ся** come) unsolder(ed).

распе|ва́ть [1] sing; **~ка́ть** F [1], ⟨∠чь⟩ [26] dress down, scold, call down, blow up; **~ча́тывать**, ⟨~ча́тать⟩ [1] unseal; open.

распи́|ливать [1], ⟨~ли́ть⟩ [13; -илю́, -и́лишь; -и́ленный] saw; **~на́ть** [1], ⟨распя́ть⟩ [-пну, -пнёшь; -пя́тый] crucify.

распис|а́ние *n* [12] timetable (🚂 ~а́ние поездо́в; *school:* ~а́ние уро́ков), schedule (on по Д); **~а́ть(ся)** *s.* ∠ывать(ся); **∠ка** *f* [5; *g/pl.*: -сок] receipt (against под В); **∠ывать** [1], ⟨~а́ть⟩ [3] write, enter; paint; ornament; **-ся** sign (one's name); (acknowledge) receipt (в П); F register one's marriage.

распл|авля́ть [28] *s.* пла́вить; **~а́каться** [3] *pf.* burst into tears; **~а́та** *f* [5] payment; requital; **~а́чиваться** [1], ⟨~ати́ться⟩ [15] (с Т) pay off, settle accounts (with); pay (for за В); **~еска́ть** [3] *pf.* spill.

распле|та́ть [1], ⟨~сти́⟩ [25 -т-] (**-ся**, ⟨-сь⟩ get) unbraid(ed); untwist.

расплы|ва́ться [1], ⟨∠ться⟩ [23] spread; run; swim about; blur; swell; F grow fat; **∠вчатый** [14 *sh.*] blurred, diffuse, vague.

расплю́щить [16] *pf.* flatten.

распозн|ава́ть [5], ⟨~а́ть⟩ [1] perceive, discern; find out.

распол|ага́ть [1], ⟨~ожи́ть⟩ [16] dispose (*a. fig.* = incline), arrange; place, lodge; *impf.* (Т) dispose (of), have (at one's disposal); **-ся** settle; encamp; *pf.* be situated; **~ага́ющий** [17] engaging; **~за́ться** [1], ⟨~зти́сь⟩ [24] creep *or* crawl (away); **~оже́ние** *n* [12] arrangement, order, (dis)position (toward[s] к Д); situation; inclination, favo(u)r; mind; ~оже́ние ду́ха mood; **~о́женный** [14 *sh.*] *a.* situated; (well-) disposed (toward[s] к Д); inclined; **~ожи́ть(ся)** *s.* ~ага́ть(ся).

распор|яди́тельность *f* [8] administrative ability, management; **~яди́тельный** [14; -лен, -льна] circumspect, efficient; **~яди́ться** *s.* ~яжа́ться; **~я́док** *m* [1; -дка] order, rule, (*office, etc.*) regulations *pl.*; **~яжа́ться** [1], ⟨~яди́ться⟩ [15 *e.*; -яжу́сь, -яди́шься] give orders; (Т) dispose (of); take charge *or* care (of); *impf.* manage, direct; **~яже́ние** *n* [12] order(s), instruction(s); decree; disposal (at в В; в П); charge, command (to в В).

распра́в|а *f* [5] punishment (of с Т); massacre; *short* work (of с Т); **~ля́ть** [28], ⟨~ить⟩ [14] straighten; smooth; spread, stretch; **-ся** (с Т) punish, avenge o.s. (on).

распредел|е́ние *n* [12] distribution; **~и́тельный** [14] distributing; ⊕ control...; ⚡ switch...; **~я́ть** [28], ⟨~и́ть⟩ [13] distribute; allot; assign (to по Д); arrange, classify.

распрод|ава́ть [5], ⟨~а́ть⟩ [-да́м, -да́шь, *etc.*, *s.* дать; -про́дал, -а́, -о; -про́данный] sell out (*or* off); **~а́жа** *f* [5] (clearance) sale.

распрост|ира́ть [1], ⟨~ере́ть⟩ [12] spread, stretch; extend; (*v/i.* **-ся**); **~ёртый** *a.* open (arms объя́тия *pl.*); **~и́ться** [15 *e.*; -ощу́сь, -ости́шься] (с Т) bid farewell (to); give up, abandon.

распростран|е́ние *n* [12] spread(-ing), expansion; dissemination, propagation; circulation; **~ённый** [14] widespread; **~я́ть** [28], ⟨~и́ть⟩ [13] spread, extend (*v/i.* **-ся**); propagate, disseminate; diffuse; **-ся** F enlarge upon.

распро|ща́ться [1] F = ~сти́ться.

ра́спря *f* [6; *g/pl.*: -рей] strife, contention, conflict; **~га́ть** [1], ⟨∠чь⟩ [26 г/ж: -ягу́, -яжёшь] unharness.

распу|ска́ть [1], ⟨~сти́ть⟩ [15] dismiss, disband, dissolve, break up; unfurl; undo; loosen; spread; melt; *fig.* spoil; **-ся** open; expand; loosen, untie; dissolve; F become spoiled; **∠тать** *s.* ∠тывать; **∠тица** *f* [5] impassability of roads; **∠тник** *s.* развра́тник; **∠тывать**, ⟨∠тать⟩ [1] untangle; **∠тье** *n* [10] crossroad(s); **~ха́ть** [1], ⟨∠хнуть⟩ [21] swell; **∠хший** [17] swollen; **∠щенный** [14 *sh.*] spoiled, undisciplined; dissolute.

распыл|и́тель *m* [4] spray(er), atomizer; **~я́ть** [28], ⟨~и́ть⟩ [13] spray, atomize; scatter.

распя́|тие *n* [12] crucifixion; **~ть** *s.* распина́ть.

расса́|да *f* [5] sprout(s); **~ди́ть** *s.* ~живать; **~дник** *m* [1] nursery; *fig.* hotbed; **~живать** [1], ⟨~ди́ть⟩ [15] transplant; seat; **-ся**, ⟨рассе́сться⟩ [рася́дусь, -дешься; -се́лся, -се́лась] sit down, take seats; F sit at ease.

рассве́|т *m* [1] dawn (at на П), daybreak; **~та́ть** [1], ⟨~сти́⟩ [25 -т-; -светёт; -свело́] dawn.

рассе|дла́ть [1] *pf.* unsaddle; **∠ивать** [1], ⟨∠ять⟩ [27] disseminate;

scatter, disperse (*v/i.* **-ся**); dissipate, dispel; divert (*usu.* **-ся** o.s.); **~ка́ть** [1], ‹**~чь**› [26] cut (up), dissect, hew, cleave; swish; **~ля́ть** [28], ‹**~ли́ть**› [13] settle (*v/i.* **-ся**); separate; **~сться** *s.* расса́живаться; **~янность** *f* [8] absent-mindedness; **~янный** [14 *sh.*] absent-minded; dissipated; scattered; *phys.* diffused; **~ять(ся)** *s.* **~ивать(ся)**.

расска́з *m* [1] story, tale, narrative; short novel (*or* story); **~а́ть** *s.* **~ывать**; **~чик** *m* [1] narrator; storyteller; **~ывать** [1], ‹**~а́ть**› [3] tell; relate, narrate.

расслаб|ля́ть [28], ‹**~ить**› [14] weaken, enervate (*v/i.* **~е́ть** [8] *pf.*).

рассл|е́дование *n* [12] investigation, inquiry into; **~е́довать** [7] (*im*)*pf.* investigate, inquire into; **~ое́ние** *n* [12] stratification; **~ы́шать** [16] *pf.* hear distinctly; не **~ы́шать** not (quite) catch.

рассм|а́тривать [1], ‹**~отре́ть**› [-отрю́, -о́тришь; -о́тренный] examine, view; consider; discern, distinguish; **~ея́ться** [27 *e.*; -ею́сь, -еёшься] *pf.* burst out laughing; **~отре́ние** *n* [12] examination (at при П); consideration; **~отре́ть** *s.* **~а́тривать**.

рассо́л *m* [1] brine, pickle.

расспр|а́шивать [1], ‹**~оси́ть**› [15] inquire, ask; **~о́сы** *pl.* [1] inquiries.

рассро́чка *f* [5] (payment by) instal(l)ments (by в В *sg.*).

расста|ва́ние *s.* проща́ние; **~ва́ться** [5], ‹**~ться**› [-а́нусь, -а́нешься] part, separate (from с Т); leave; **~вля́ть** [28], ‹**~вить**› [14] place; arrange; set (up); move apart; **~но́вка** *f* [5; *g/pl.*: -вок] arrangement; distribution; order; punctuation; drawing up; pause; **~ться** *s.* **~ва́ться**.

расст|ёгивать [1], ‹**~егну́ть**› [20] unbutton; unfasten (*v/i.* **-ся**); **~ила́ть** [1], ‹разостла́ть› [расстелю́, -е́лешь; разо́стланный] spread (*v/i.* **-ся**); **~оя́ние** *n* [12] distance (at на П).

расстр|а́ивать [1], ‹**~о́ить**› [13] upset, derange; disorganize; disturb, spoil; shatter; frustrate; ♪ put out of tune (*or* humo[u]r, *fig.*); **-ся** be(come) upset, *etc.*; fail.

расстре́л *m* [1] (death by) shooting, execution; **~ивать** [1], ‹**~я́ть**› [28] shoot, execute.

расстро́|ить(ся) *s.* расстра́ивать (-ся); **~йство** *n* [9] disorder, confusion; disturbance, derangement; frustration.

расступ|а́ться [1], ‹**~и́ться**› [14] give way, part; open, split.

рассу|ди́тельность *f* [8] judiciousness; **~ди́тельный** [14; -лен, -льна] judicious, wise; **~ди́ть** [15] *pf.* judge; decide (*a. issue*); consider; **~док** *m* [1; -дка] reason, sense(s); judg(e)ment, mind (of в П); **~дочный** [14; -чен, -чна] rational; **~жда́ть** [1] argue, reason; talk; **~жде́ние** *n* [12] reasoning, argument(ation); objection; treatise, essay (on о П).

рассчи́т|ывать [1], ‹**~а́ть**› [1] & ‹расче́сть› [25; разочту́, -тёшь; расчёл, разочла́; разочтённый; *g. pt.*: разочтя́]; (не mis)calculate, estimate; judge; dismiss, pay off; *impf.* count *or* reckon (on на В); expect; intend; **-ся** settle accounts, get even (with с Т), pay off; count off.

рассыл|а́ть [1], ‹разосла́ть› [-ошлю́, -ошлёшь; -о́сланный] send out (*or* round); **~ка** *f* [5] distribution, dispatch.

рассып|а́ть [1], ‹**~ать**› [2] scatter, spill; spread; (*v/i.* **-ся**; crumble, fall to pieces; break up; fail; shower [s. th. on в П/Д]; resound; burst out).

раста́|лкивать, ‹растолка́ть› [1] push aside; push; **~пливать** [1], ‹растопи́ть› [14] light, kindle; melt; (*v/i.* **-ся**); **~птывать** [1], ‹растопта́ть› [3] tread down; **~скивать** [1], ‹**~щи́ть**› [16], F ‹**~ска́ть**› [1] pilfer; take to pieces; F separate.

раство́р *m* [1] solution; mortar; **~и́мый** [14 *sh.*] soluble; **~я́ть** [28], ‹**~и́ть**› **1.** [13] dissolve; **2.** [13; -орю́, -о́ришь; -о́ренный] open.

расте́|ние *n* [12] plant; **~ре́ть** *s.* растира́ть; **~рза́ть** [1] *pf.* tear to pieces; lacerate; **~рянный** [14 *sh.*] confused, perplexed, bewildered; **~ря́ть** [28] *pf.* lose (one's head **-ся**; be[come] perplexed *or* puzzled).

расти́ [24 -ст-: -сту́, -стёшь; рос, -сла́; ро́сший], ‹вы́-› grow, increase.

раст|ира́ть [1], ‹**~ере́ть**› [12; разотру́, -трёшь] pound, pulverize; rub; smear.

расти́тельн|ость *f* [8] vegetation, flora; hair; **~ый** [14] vegetable; vegetative.

расти́ть [15 *e.*; ращу́, расти́шь] rear; F grow.

расто|лка́ть *s.* раста́лкивать; **~лкова́ть** [7] *pf.* expound, explain; **~пи́ть** *s.* раста́пливать; **~пта́ть** *s.* раста́птывать; **~пы́рить** F [13] *pf.* spread; **~рга́ть** [1], ‹**~ргнуть**› [21] break (off), annul; dissolve, sever; **~рже́ние** *n* [12] breaking off; annulment; dissolution; **~ро́пный** [14; -пен, -пна] deft, quick; **~ча́ть** [1], ‹**~чи́ть**› [16 *e.*; -чу́, -чи́шь; -чённый] squander, waste, dissipate; lavish (on Д); **~чи́тель** *m* [4], **~чи́тельный** [14; -лен, -льна] prodigal, spendthrift, extravagant.

растра|вля́ть [28], ‹**~ви́ть**› [14] irritate; fret, stir (up); **~та** *f* [5] waste; embezzlement; **∠тчик** *m* [1] embezzler; **∠чивать** [1], ⟨**∠тить**⟩ [15] spend, waste; embezzle.

растр|епать [2] *pf.* (-**ся** be[come]) tousle(d, **~ёпанный** [14]), dishevel (-[1]ed); tear (torn), thumb(ed).

растрогать [1] *pf.* move, touch.

растя|гивать [1], ⟨**~нуть**⟩ [19] stretch (*v/i.* -**ся**; F fall flat); ⚕ strain; drawl; extend, prolong; **~жение** *n* [12] stretching; strain(ing); **~жимый** [14 *sh.*] extensible, elastic; *fig.* vague; **~нутый** [14] long-drawn; **~нуть(ся)** *s.* **~гивать(ся)**.

рас|формировать [8] *pf.* disband; **~хаживать** [1] walk about *or* up & down, pace; **~хваливать** [1], ⟨**~хвалить**⟩ [13; -алю, -алишь; -аленный] extol(l *Brt.*), praise (highly); **~хватывать** F, ⟨**~хватать**⟩ [1] snatch away; buy up (quickly).

расхи|щать [1], ⟨**∠тить**⟩ [15] plunder; **~щение** *n* [12] plunder.

расхо|д *m* [1] expenditure (for на B), expense(s); ✝ *a.* debit; consumption; sale; **~иться** [15], ⟨**разойтись**⟩ [-ойдусь, -ойдёшься; -ошёлся, -ошлась; -ошедшийся; *g. pt.*: -ойдясь] disperse; break up; differ (from с T); diverge; part, separate, get divorced (from с T); pass *or* miss o.a., (*letters*) cross; be sold out, sell; be spent, (у P) run out of; melt, dissolve; ramify; radiate; F spread; become enraged; get excited *or* animated; **~довать** [7], ⟨из-⟩ spend, expend; *pf. a.* use up; **~ждение** *n* [12] divergence, difference (of в П); radiation.

расцарап|ывать, ⟨**~ать**⟩ [1] scratch.

расцве|т *m* [1] blossom, (*a. fig.*) bloom; prime; prosperity; **~тать** [1], ⟨**~сти**⟩ [25 -т-] blo(ss)om; flourish, thrive; **~тка** *f* [5; *g/pl.*: -ток] colo(u)ring.

расце|нивать [1], ⟨**~нить**⟩ [13; -еню, -енишь; -енённый] estimate, value, rate; **~нка** *f* [5; *g/pl.*: -нок] valuation; rate, tariff; **~плять** [28], ⟨**~пить**⟩ [14] uncouple, unhook.

рас|чесать *s.* **~чёсывать**; **~чёска** *f* [5; *g/pl.*: -сок] comb; **~честь** *s.* рассчитать; **~чёсывать** [1], ⟨**~чесать**⟩ [3] comb (one's hair -**ся** F).

расчёт *m* [1] calculation; estimation; settlement (of accounts); payment; dismissal, *Brt.* F *a.* sack; account, consideration; intention; providence; F use; ⚔ gunners *pl.*; из ~а on the basis (of); в ~е quits; **~ливый** [14 *sh.*] provident, thrifty; circumspect.

рас|чищать [1], ⟨**~чистить**⟩ [15] clear (away); **~членять** [28], ⟨**~членить**⟩ [13] dismember; **~шатывать,** ⟨**~шатать**⟩ [1] loosen (*v/i.* -**ся**); (be[come]) shatter(ed); **~шевелить** F [13] *pf.* stir (up).

расши|бать F *s.* ушибать; **~вать** [1], ⟨**∠ть**⟩ [разошью, -шьёшь; *cf.* шить] embroider; undo, rip; **~рение** *n* [12] widening, enlargement; expansion; **~рять** [28], ⟨**∠рить**⟩ [13] widen, enlarge; extend, expand; ⚕ dilate; **∠ть** *s.* **~вать**; **~фровывать** [1], ⟨**~фровать**⟩ [7] decipher, decode.

рас|шнуровать [7] *pf.* untie; **~щелина** *f* [5] crevice, cleft, crack; **~щепление** *n* [12] splitting; fission; **~щеплять** [28], ⟨**~щепить**⟩ [14 *e.*; -плю, -пишь; -плённый] split.

ратифи|кация *f* [7] ratification; **~цировать** [7] (*im*)*pf.* ratify.

ратовать [7] fight, struggle.

рафинад *m* [1] lump sugar.

рахит *m* [1] rickets.

рацион|ализировать [7] (*im*)*pf.* rationalize; **~альный** [14; -лен, -льна] rational (*a.* 𝔄, *no sh.*).

рвануть [20] *pf.* jerk; -**ся** dart.

рвать [рву, рвёшь; рвал, -а, -о] **1.** ⟨разо-, изо-⟩ [-орванный] tear (to, in *pieces* на, в B), *v/i.* -**ся**; **2.** ⟨со-⟩ pluck; **3.** ⟨вы-⟩ pull out; *impers.* (B) vomit, spew; **4.** ⟨пре-⟩ break off; **5.** ⟨взо-⟩ blow up; ~ и метать F be in a rage; -**ся** break; strive *or* long (eagerly).

рвение *n* [12] zeal; eagerness.

рвот|а *f* [5] vomit(ing); **~ный** [14] emetic (*a. n, su.*).

рдеть [8] redden, flush.

реа|билитировать [7] (*im*)*pf.* rehabilitate; **~гировать** [7] (на B) react (upon); respond (to); **~ктивный** [14] reactive; jet (*plane*); **~кционер** *m* [1], **~кционный** [14] reactionary.

реал|изм *m* [1] realism; **~изовать** [7] (*im*)*pf.* realize; ✝ *a.* sell; **~истический** [16] realistic; **∠ьность** *f* [8] reality; **∠ьный** [14; -лен, -льна] real; realistic.

ребёнок *m* [2; *pl. a.* дети, *s.*] child; baby, F kid; грудной ~ suckling.

ребро *n* [9; *pl.*: рёбра, рёбер, рёбрам] rib; edge (on ~м); ~м *fig.* point-blank.

ребя|та *pl. of* ребёнок; F boys; **~ческий** [16], **~чий** F [18] childish; **~чество** F [9] childishness; **~читься** F [16] behave childishly.

рёв *m* [1] roar; bellow; howl.

рев|анш *m* [1] revenge; return match; **~ень** *m* [4 *e.*] rhubarb; **~еть** [-ву, -вёшь] roar; bellow; howl; F cry.

ревиз|ия *f* [7] inspection; auditing; revision; **~ор** *m* [1] inspector; auditor.

ревмати|зм *m* [1] rheumatism; **~ческий** [16] rheumatic.

ревн|ивый [14 *sh.*] jealous; **~овать** [7], ⟨при-⟩ be jealous (of [p.'s] к Д [B]); **∠ость** *f* [8] jealousy; zeal, eagerness; **∠остный** [14; -тен, -тна] zealous, eager.

револ|ьвéр *m* [1] revolver; **~юционéр** *m* [1], **~юциóнный** [14] revolutionary; **~юция** *f* [7] revolution.
регистр *m* [1], **~и́ровать** [7], ⟨за-⟩ register (*v/i.* -ся; *a.* get married *in a civil ceremony*); index.
рег|лáмент *m* [1] order, regulations *pl.*; **~рéсс** *m* [1] retrogression.
регул|и́ровать [7], ⟨у-⟩ regulate; (*esp. pf.*) settle; **~я́рный** [14; -рен, -рна] regular; **~я́тор** *m* [1] regulator.
редак|ти́ровать [7], ⟨от-⟩ edit, redact; **∠тор** *m* [1] editor; **∠ция** *f* [7] editorial staff; editorship; editor's office; wording, text, version; redaction; (*radio*) desk.
ред|éть [8], ⟨по-⟩ (grow) thin; **~и́ска** *f* [5; *g/pl.*: -сок] (*red*) radish.
рéдк|ий [16; -док, -дкá, -о; *comp.*: рéже] rare; thin, sparse; scarce; *adv. a.* seldom; **~ость** *f* [8] rarity, curiosity; sparsity, thinness; uncommon (thing); на **~ость** F extremely, awfully.
рéдька *f* [5; *g/pl.*: -дек] radish.
режи́м *m* [1] regime(n); conditions *pl.*; regulations *pl.*, order.
режисс|ёр *m* [1] stage manager; director, producer; **~и́ровать** [7] stage.
рéзать [3] 1. ⟨раз-⟩ cut (up, open); carve (*meat*); 2. ⟨за-⟩ slaughter, kill; 3. ⟨вы́-⟩ carve, cut (in *wood* по Д, на П); 4. ⟨с-⟩ cut off; F fail; *impf.* hurt; F say; P talk; 5. -ся F cut (one's teeth); gamble.
резв|и́ться [14 *e.*; -влю́сь, -ви́шься] frolic, frisk, gambol; **∠ый** [14; резв, -á, -о] frisky, sportive, frolicsome; quick; lively.
резéрв *m* [1], reserve(s); **~и́ст** *m* [1] reservist; **~ный** [14] reserve...
резéц *m* [1; -зцá] incisor.
рези́н|а *f* [5] rubber; **~овый** [14] rubber...; **~ка** *f* [5; *g/pl.*: -нок] eraser, (india) rubber; elastic.
рéз|кий [16; -зок, -зкá, -о; *comp.*: рéзче] sharp, keen; biting, piercing; acute; harsh, shrill; glaring; rough, abrupt; **~кость** *f* [8] sharpness, *etc.*, *s.* **~кий**; harsh word; **~нóй** [14] carved; **~ня́** *f* [6] slaughter; **~олю́ция** *f* [7] resolution; decision; **~óн** *m* [1] reason; **~онáнс** *m* [1] resonance; **~óнный** F [14; -óнен, -óнна] reasonable; **~ультáт** *m* [1] result (as a в П); **~ьбá** *f* [5] carving.
резюм|é *n* [*ind.*] summary; **~и́ровать** [7] (*im*)*pf.* summarize.
рейд *m* [1] ⚓ road(stead); ⚔ raid.
Рейн *m* [1] Rhine.
рейс *m* [1] trip; voyage; flight.
рекá *f* [5; *ac/sg. a. st.*; *pl. st.*; *from dat/pl. a. e.*] river, stream.
реклáм|а *f* [5] advertising; advertisement; publicity; **~и́ровать** [7] (*im*)*pf.* advertise; boost; (re-)claim, complain; **~ный** [14] advertising.
реко|мендáтельный [14] of recommendation; **~мендáция** *f* [7] recommendation; reference; **~мендовáть** [7] (*im*)*pf.*, *a.* ⟨по-⟩ recommend, advise; † introduce; **~нструи́ровать** [7] (*im*)*pf.* reconstruct; **∠рд** *m* [1] record; **∠рдный** [14] record...; **~рдсмéн** *m* [1], **~рдсмéнка** *f* [5; *g/pl.*: -нок] champion.
рéктор *m* [1] president, (*Brt.* vice-)chancellor, rector (*univ.*).
рели|гиóзный [14; -зен, -зна] religious; **∠гия** *f* [7] religion; **∠квия** *f* [7] relic.
рельс *m* [1], **∠овый** [14] rail; track.
ремéнь *m* [4; -мня́] strap; belt.
ремéсл|енник *m* [1] (handi)craftsman, artisan; *fig.* bungler; **~енный** [14] trade...; handicraft...; home-made; bungling; **~ó** *n* [9; *pl.*: -мёсла, -мёсел, -мёслам] trade, (handi)craft; occupation.
ремóнт *m* [1] repair(s); remount (-ing); **~и́ровать** [7] (*im*)*pf.*, **~ный** [14] repair.
рéнта *f* [5] rent; revenue; (*life*) annuity; **∠бельный** [14; -лен, -льна] profitable.
рентгéновск|ий [16]: **~ий сни́мок** *m* roentgenogram; **~ие лучи́** *m/pl.* X-rays.
реорганизовáть [7] (*im*)*pf.* reorganize (*Brt.* -se).
рéпа *f* [5] turnip.
репа|рациóнный [14] reparation...; **~три́ировать** [7] (*im*)*pf.* repatriate.
репéйник *m* [1] bur(dock); agrimony.
репертуáр *m* [1] repertoire, repertory.
репети́|ровать [7], ⟨про-⟩ rehearse; **~ция** *f* [7] rehearsal.
рéплика *f* [5] retort; *thea.* cue.
репортáж *m* [1] report(ing).
репортёр *m* [1] reporter.
репрéсс(áл)ия *f* [7] reprisal.
репродýктор *m* [1] loud-speaker.
ресни́ца *f* [5] eyelash.
респýблик|а *f* [5] republic; **~áнец** *m* [1; -нца], **~áнский** [16] republican.
рессóра *f* [5] spring.
ресторáн *m* [1] restaurant (at в П).
ресýрсы *m/pl.* [1] resources.
рети́вый [14] zealous; mettlesome.
ре|туши́ровать [7] (*im*)*pf.*, ⟨от-⟩ retouch; **~ферáт** *m* [1] report, paper.
рефóрм|а *f* [5], **~и́ровать** [7] (*im*)*pf.* reform; **~áтор** *m* [1] reformer.
реценз|éнт *m* [1] reviewer; **~и́ровать** [7], ⟨про-⟩, **∠ия** *f* [7] review.
рецéпт *m* [1] recipe.
рецидив *m* [1] relapse.
речевóй [14] speech...
рéч|ка *f* [5; *g/pl.*: -чек] (small) river; **~нóй** [14] river...
реч|ь *f* [8; *from g/pl. e.*] speech;

discourse, talk, conversation; word; об э́том не мо́жет быть и ∠и that is out of the question; *cf.* идти́.
реш|а́ть [1], ⟨~и́ть⟩ [*e.*; -шу́, -ши́шь; -шённый] solve; decide, resolve (*a.* -ся [on, to на В]; make up one's mind); dare, risk; не ~а́ться hesitate; **~а́ющий** [17] decisive; **~е́ние** *n* [12] decision; (re)solution; **~ётка** *f* [5; *g/pl.*: -ток] grating; lattice; trellis; grate; **~ето́** *n* [9; *pl. st.*: -шёта] sieve; **~ётчатый** [14] trellis(ed); **~и́мость** *f* [8] determination; **~и́тельный** [14; -лен, -льна] resolute, firm; decisive; definite; absolute; **~и́ть(ся)** *s.* **~а́ть(ся)**.
ре́ять [27] soar, fly.
ржа́|веть [8], ⟨за-⟩, **~вчина** *f* [5] rust; **~вый** [14] rusty; **~но́й** [14] rye...; **~ть** [ржёт], ⟨за-⟩ neigh.
ри́за *f* [5] chasuble; robe.
Рим *m* [1] Rome; '**♀ля́нин** *m* [1; *pl.*: -яне, -ян], '**♀ля́нка** *f* [5; *g/pl.*: -нок], '**♀ский** [14] Roman.
ри́нуться [20] *pf.* rush; plunge.
рис *m* [1] rice.
риск *m* [1] risk (at на В); **~о́ванный** [14 *sh.*] risky; **~ова́ть** [7], ⟨~ну́ть⟩ [20] (*usu.* Т) risk, venture.
рисова́|ние *n* [12] drawing; designing; **~ть** [7], ⟨на-⟩ draw; design; -ся appear, loom; pose, mince.
ри́совый [14] rice...
рису́нок *m* [1; -нка] drawing, design; picture, illustration (in на П).
ритм *m* [1] rhythm; **~и́чный** [14; -чен, -чна] rhythmical.
риф *m* [1] reef; **∠ма** *f* [5] rhyme.
роб|е́ть [8], ⟨о-⟩ be timid, quail; не ~е́й! courage!; **∠кий** [16; -бок, -бка́, -о; *comp.*: ро́бче] shy, timid; **∠ость** *f* [8] shyness, timitidy.
ров *m* [1; рва; во рву] ditch.
рове́сник *m* [1] coeval, of the same age.
ро́вн|ый [14; -вен, -вна́, -о] even, level, flat; straight; equal; equable; **~о** precisely, exactly, *time a.* sharp; F absolutely; **∠я́** F *f* [5] equal.
рог *m* [1; *pl. e.*: -га́] horn; antler; bugle; **~а́тый** [14*sh.*] horned; **~ови́ца** *f* [5] cornea; **~ово́й** [14] horn ...
рого́жа *f* [5] (bast) mat.
род *m* [1; в, на -у́; *pl. e.*] genus; race; generation; kind; way; *gr.* gender; birth (by Т); F class; ∠ом из, с Р come *or* be from; о́т ~у (Д) *be* ... old; с ∠у in one's life.
роди́|льный [14] maternity (hospital дом *m*); **~мый** [14] *s.* родно́й & '~нка; **'~на** *f* [5] native land, home(land) (in на П); **'~нка** *f* [5; *g/pl.*: -нок] birthmark, mole; **~тели** *m/pl.* [4] parents; **~тельный** [14] genitive (*case*); **~тельский** [16] parental.
роди́ть [15 *e.*; рожу́, роди́шь; -и́л, -а (*pf.*: -а́), -о; рождённый] (*im-*) *pf.*, (*impf. a.* **рожда́ть**, F **рожа́ть** [1]) bear, give birth to; beget; *fig.* bring forth, produce; -ся [*pf.* -и́лся́] be born; arise; come up, grow.
родн|и́к *m* [1 *e.*] spring; **~о́й** [14] own; native; (my) dear; *pl.* = **~я́** *f* [6] relative(s), relation(s).
родо|во́й [14] patrimonial; generic; **~нача́льник** *m* [1] ancestor, (*a. fig.*) father; **~сло́вный** [14] genealogical; ~сло́вная *f* family tree.
ро́дствен|ник *m* [1], **~ница** *f* [5] relative, relation; **~ный** [14 *sh.*] related, kindred, cognate; of blood.
родств|о́ *n* [9] relationship; cognation; F relatives; в ~е́ related (to с Т).
ро́ды *pl.* [1] (child)birth.
ро́жа *f* [5] ⚕ erysipelas; P mug.
рожд|а́емость *f* [8] birth rate; **~а́ть(ся)** *s.* роди́ть(ся); **~е́ние** *n* [12] birth (by от Р); день ~е́ния birthday (on в В); **~е́ственский** [16] Christmas...; **~ество́** *n* [9] (*a.* ♀ество́ [Христо́во]) Christmas (at на В); поздра́вить с ♀ество́м Христо́вым wish a Merry Xmas; до (по́сле) Р.Хр. B.C. (A.D.).
рож|о́к *m* [1; -жка́] *dim. of* рог; ear trumpet; feeding bottle; (*gas*) burner; shoehorn; **~ь** *f* [8; ржи; *instr/sg.*: ро́жью] rye.
ро́за *f* [5] rose.
ро́зга *f* [5; *g/pl.*: -зог] rod.
розе́тка *f* [5; *g/pl.*: -ток] rosette; ⚡ (*plug*) socket.
ро́зн|ица *f* [5]: в ~ицу by retail; **~ичный** [14] retail...; **~ь** F *f* [8] discord; И/Д ~ь th. *or* p. & th/p. are not the same *or* different.
ро́зовый [14 *sh.*] pink, rosy.
ро́зыгрыш *m* [1] draw; drawn game; drawing of a lottery; ~ пе́рвенства play(s) for championship.
ро́зыск *m* [1] search (in/of в П *pl.*/Р); ⚖ preliminary trial; уголо́вный ~ criminal investigation department.
ро|и́ться [13], **~й** *m* [3; в рою́; *pl. e.*: рои́, роёв] swarm.
рок *m* [1] fate; **~ово́й** [14] fatal; **∠от** *m* [1], **~ота́ть** [3] roll.
ро́лик *m* [1] roller (skates *pl.*).
роль *f* [8; *from g/pl. e.*] part, role.
ром *m* [1] rum.
рома́н *m* [1] novel; F (love) affair, romance; **~и́ст** *m* [1] novelist; **~ти́зм** *m* [1] romanticism; **~ти́ческий** [16], **~ти́чный** [14; -чен, -чна] romantic.
ром|а́шка *f* [5; *g/pl.*: -шек] camomile; **~б** *m* [1] rhombus.
роня́ть [28], ⟨урони́ть⟩ [13; -оню́, -о́нишь; -о́ненный] drop; droop; lose; shed; *fig.* disparage, discredit.
ро́п|от *m* [1], **~та́ть** [3; -пщу́, ро́пщешь] murmur, grumble, growl (at на В).
роса́ *f* [5; *pl. st.*] dew.
роско́ш|ный [14; -шен, -шна] luxurious; magnificent, splendid,

sumptuous; F luxuriant, exuberant; ʼ~ь f [8] luxury; magnificence, sumptuousness; luxuriance.
рослый [14] big, tall.
роспись f [8] list; fresco.
роспуск m [1] dissolution; dismissal; disbandment; breaking up.
Росси́|я f [7] Russia; 2йский [16] Russian; cf. РСФСР.
рост m [1] growth; increase; stature, size; ... высокого ∠а tall ...
ростовщи́к m [1 e.] usurer.
рос|то́к m [1; -тка́] sprout, shoot; ∠черк m [1] flourish; stroke.
рот m [1; рта; во рту́] mouth; ∠а f [5] company; ∠ный [14] company (commander); ~озе́й F [3] gaper.
ро́ща f [5] grove.
роя́ль m [4] (grand) piano.
РСФСР (Российская Советская Федерати́вная Социалисти́ческая Респу́блика) Russian Soviet Federative Socialist Republic.
рту́ть f [8] mercury.
руба́|нок m [1; -нка] plane; ~шка f [5; g/pl.: -шек] shirt; chemise.
рубе́ж m [1 e.] boundary; border (line), frontier; за ~о́м abroad.
рубе́ц m [1; -бца́] hem; scar, wake.
руби́ть [14] 1. ‹на-› chop, cut, hew, hack; mince; 2. ‹с-› fell; F impf. speak bluntly; -ся fight (hand to hand).
ру́бка f [5] felling; ⚓ cabin.
ру́бленый [14] chopped, minced.
рубль m [e.] r(o)uble.
ру́б|рика f [5] heading; column; ~чатый [14] ribbed.
ру́га|нь f [8] abuse; ∠тельный [14] abusive; ∠тельство n [9] curse, oath; ∠ть [1], ‹вы́-› abuse, scold; -ся swear, curse; abuse o. a.
руд|а́ f [5; pl. st.] ore; ~ни́к m [1 e.] mine, pit; ~ни́чный [14] mine(r's); fire(damp); ~οко́п m [1] miner.
руж|е́йный [14] gun...; ~ьё n [10; pl. st.; g/pl.: -жей] gun, rifle.
рук|а́ f [5; ac/sg.: ру́ку; pl.: ру́ки, рук, -ка́м] hand; arm; ~а́ в ∠у (or об ~у) hand in hand (arm in arm; a. под ~у); из ~ вон (плохо) F quite wretched(ly); быть на́ ~у (Д) suit a p. (well); на́ ~у нечи́ст light-fingered; от ~и́ in handwriting; по ~а́м! it's bargain!; под ~о́й at hand, within reach; ~о́й пода́ть it's no distance (a stone's throw); (у Р) ∠и коротки́ F it's not in (p.'s) power; из пе́рвых ~ at first hand; приложи́ть ∠у sign.
рука́в m [1 e.; pl.: -ва́, -во́в] sleeve; branch; hose; ~и́ца f [5] mitten; gauntlet; ~чик m [1] cuff.
руковод|и́тель m [4] leader; chief; manager; teacher; ~и́ть [15] (Т) lead; direct, manage; -ся follow, conform (to); ∠ство n [9] leadership; guidance; instruction; text-book, guide; ∠ствовать(ся) [7] s. ~и́ть(ся); ~я́щий [17] leading.
руко|де́лие n [12] needlework; ~мо́йник m [1] washstand; ~па́шный [14] hand-to-hand; ʼ~пись f [8] manuscript; ~плеска́ние n [12] (mst pl.) applause; ~пожа́тие n [12] hand shake; ~я́тка f [5; g/pl.: -ток] handle, gripe; hilt.
рул|ево́й [14] steering; control...; su. steersman, helmsman; ~ь m [4 e.] rudder; helm; steering wheel; handle bar; ~ь высоты́ ✈ elevator.
румы́н m [1], ~ка f [5; g/pl.: -нок]; ~ский [16] R(o)umanian.
румя́н|а n/pl. [9] rouge; ~ец m [1; -нца] ruddiness; blush; ~ить [13] 1. ‹за-› redden; 2. ‹на-› rouge; ~ый [14 sh.] ruddy, rosy; red, scarlet.
ру|но́ n [9; pl. st.] fleece; ∠пор m [1] megaphone; mouthpiece.
руса́лка f [5; g/pl.: -лок] mermaid.
ру́сло n [9] bed, (a. fig.) channel.
ру́сский [16] Russian (a. su.); adv. по-ру́сски (in) Russian.
ру́сый [14sh.] fair(-haired), blond(e).
Русь f [8; -си́] hist., poet. Russia.
рути́н|а f [5], ~ный [14] routine.
ру́хлядь F f [8] lumber, stuff.
ру́хнуть [20] pf. crash down; fail.
руча́|тельство n [9] guarantee; ~ться [1], ‹поручи́ться› [16] (за В) warrant, guarantee, vouch for.
руче́й m [3 e.; -чья́] brook, stream.
ру́чка f [5; g/pl.: -чек] (small) hand; handle, knob; chair arm; lever; pen(holder).
ручно́й [14] hand...; manual; handmade; small; ⚔ a. light; tame; wrist (watch).
ру́шить(ся) [16] (im)pf. collapse, break down.
ры́б|а f [5] fish; ~а́к m [1 e.] fisherman; ~ий [18] fish...; cod-liver (oil); ~ный [14] fish(y); ~ный про́мысел m fishery.
рыболо́в m [1] angler; ~ный [14] fishing; fish...; ~ство n [9] fishery.
рыво́к m [1; -вка́] jerk.
рыг|а́ть [1], ‹~ну́ть› [20] belch.
рыда́|ние n [12] sob(bing); ~ть [1] sob.
ры́жий [17; рыж, -а́, -е] red; sorrel.
ры́ло n [9] snout; P mug.
ры́но|к m [1]; -нка] market (in на П); ~чный [14] market...
рыс|а́к m [1 e.] trotter; ∠кать [3] rove, run about; ~ь f [8] trot (at, in в В, на ~си́, Т); zo. lynx.
ры́твина f [5] rut, groove, hole.
рыть [22], ‹вы́-› dig; burrow, mine; ~ся rummage.
рыхл|и́ть [13], ‹вз-, раз-› loosen (soil); ∠ый [14; рыхл, -а́, -о] friable, crumbly, loose.

ры́цар|ский [16] knightly, chivalrous; knight's; **~ь** *m* [4] knight.
рыча́г *m* [1 *e.*] lever.
рыча́ть [4 *e.*; -чу́, -чи́шь] growl.
рья́ный [14 *sh.*] zealous; mettlesome.
рю́мка *f* [5; *g/pl.:* -мок] (wine-) glass.
ряби́на *f* [5] mountain ash; F pit.
ряби́ть [14 *e.*; -и́т] ripple; mottle; *impers.* flicker (before p.'s *eyes* в П/у Р).
рябо́й [14; ряб, -а́, -о] pockmarked; piebald, spotted; freckled.
ря́б|чик *m* [1] hazel grouse; **~ь** *f* ripples *pl.*; flicker.
ря́вк|ать F [1], *once* ⟨**~**нуть⟩ [20] bellow, bawl; snap (at на В).
ряд *m* [1; в -у́; *pl. e.*; *after* 2,3,4, ряда́] row; line; file; series; [в -е] number, several; *pl.* ranks; *thea. a.* tier; **~а́ми** in rows; из **~**а вон выходя́щий remarkable, outstanding; **~ово́й** [14] ordinary; *su.* ⚔ private; **~ом** side by side; (с Т) beside, next to; next door; close by.
ря́женый [14] disguised, masked; masker.
ря́са *f* [5] cassock.

С

с. *abbr.*: село́.
с, со: 1. (Р) from; since; with; for; 2. (В) about; 3. (Т) with; of; to.
са́бля *f* [6; *g/pl.*: -бель] saber (*Brt.* -bre).
сабот|а́ж *m* [1], sabotage; **~а́жник** *m* [1] saboteur; **~и́ровать** [7] (*im*)*pf.* sabotage.
са́ван *m* [1] shroud.
савра́сый [14] roan.
сад *m* [1; в -у́; *pl. e.*] garden.
сади́ть [15], ⟨по-⟩ *s.* сажа́ть; **~ся**, ⟨сесть⟩ [25; ся́ду, -дешь; сел, -а; се́вший] (на, в В) sit down; get in(to) *or* on, board; ⚓ embark, 🚂 entrain; mount (*horse*); alight (*bird*); ✈ land; set (*sun*); settle; sink; shrink (*fabric*); set (to *work* за В); run (aground на мель).
садо́в|ник *m* [1] gardener; **~о́дство** *n* [9] gardening, horticulture.
са́ж|а *f* [5] soot; в **~**е sooty.
сажа́ть [1] (*iter. of* сади́ть) seat; put; plant; ⚓ embark, 🚂 entrain.
са́жень *f* [8] *Russ.* fathom (= 7*ft.*).
саквоя́ж *m* [1] travel(l)ing bag.
сала́зки *f/pl.* [5; *gen.*: -зок] sled.
сала́т *m* [1] salad; lettuce.
са́ло *n* [9] bacon; suet, tallow.
салфе́тка *f* [5; *g/pl.*: -ток] napkin.
са́льдо *n* [*ind.*] ☨ balance.
са́льный [14; -лен, -льна] greasy; obscene.
салю́т *m* [1], **~ова́ть** [7] (*im*)*pf.* salute.
сам *m*, **~а́** *f*, **~о́** *n*, **~и** *pl.* [30] -self: я **~**(а) I ... myself; мы **~и** we ... ourselves; **~е́ц** *m* [1; -мца́] *zo.* male; **~ка** *f* [5; *g/pl.*: -мок] *zo.* female.
само|бы́тный [14; -тен, тна] original; **~ва́р** *m* [1] samovar; **~вла́стный** [14; -тен, -тна] autocratic; **~во́льный** [14; -лен, льна] arbitrary; **~го́н** *m* [1] home-brew; **~де́льный** [14] homemad, self-made.
самодержа́в|ие *n* [12] autocracy; **~ный** [14; -вен, -вна] autocratic.
само|де́ятельность *f* [8] amateur performance(s); **~дово́льный** [14; -лен, -льна] self-satisfied, self-complacent; **~ду́р** *m* [1] despot; **~защи́та** *f* [5] self-defense; **~зва́нец** *m* [1; -нца] impostor, usurper; pseudo...; **~ка́т** *m* [1] scooter; **~кри́тика** *f* [5] self-criticism.
самолёт *m* [1] airplane (*Brt.* aeroplane), aircraft; пассажи́рский **~** air liner; **~**-снаря́д *m* guided missile.
само|любя́вый [14 *sh.*] ambitious; vain, conceited; **~лю́бие** *n* [12] ambition; vanity; **~мне́ние** *n* [12] self-conceit; **~наде́янный** [14 *sh.*] self-confident, self-assertive; **~облада́ние** *n* [12] self-control; **~обма́н** *m* [1] self-deception; **~оборо́на** *f* [5] self-defense; **~обслу́живание** *n* [12] self-service; **~определе́ние** *n* [12] self-determination; **~отве́рженный** [14 *sh.*] self-denying, self-sacrificing; **~пи́шущий** [17] fountain (*pen*); **~поже́ртвование** *n* [12] self-sacrifice; **~ро́дный** [14; -ден, -дна] native, pure; original; **~сохране́ние** *n* [12] self-preservation.
самостоя́тельн|ость *f* [8] independence; **~ый** [14; -лен, -льна] independent.
само|су́д *m* [1] lynch law; **~уби́йство** *n* [9], **~уби́йца** *m/f* [5] suicide; **~уве́ренный** [14 *sh.*] self-confident; **~управле́ние** *n* [12] self-government; **~у́чка** *m/f* [5; *g/pl.*: -чек] self-taught p.; **~хва́льство** F *n* [9] boasting; **~хо́дный** [14] self-propelled; **~це́ль** *f* [8] end in itself; **~чу́вствие** *n* [12] (state of) health.
са́м|ый [14] the most, ...est; the very; the (self)same; just, right; early *or* late; **~**ое бо́льшее (ма́лое) F at (the) most (least).
сан *m* [1] dignity.
санато́рий *m* [3] sanatorium.
санда́лии *f/pl.* [7] sandals.
са́ни *f/pl.* [8; *from g/pl. e.*] sled(ge).
санита́р *m* [1], **~ка** *f* [5; *g/pl.*:

-рок] nurse; *m a.* hospital attendant, orderly; ~**ный** [14] sanitary.
сан|кционировать [7] *(im)pf.* sanction; ~**овник** *m* [1] dignitary.
сантиметр *m* [1] centimeter.
сапёр *m* [1] engineer, *Brt.* sapper.
сапог *m* [1 *e.*; *g/pl.:* сапог] boot.
сапожник *m* [1] shoemaker.
сарай *m* [3] shed; barn.
саранча *f* [5; *g/pl.:* -чей] locust.
сарафан *m* [1] sarafan (*long sleeveless gown of countrywomen*).
сард|елька *f* [5; *g/pl.*: -лек] wiener (thick variety); ~**ина** *f* [5] sardine.
сатана *m* [8] Satan.
сателлит *m* [1] satellite.
сатин *m* [1] sateen, glazed cotton.
сатир|а *f* [5] satire; ~**ик** *m* [1] satirist; ~**ический** [16] satirical.
сафьян *m* [1] morocco.
сахар *m* [1; *part. g.*: -у] sugar; ~**истый** [14 *sh.*] sugary; ~**ница** *f* [5] sugar bowl; ~**ный** [14] sugar...; ~ная болезнь *f* diabetes.
сачок *m* [1; -чка] butterfly net.
Саш([ень]к)а *m/f* [5] *dim. of* Александр, -а.
сбав|ить *s.* ~лять; ~**ка** *f* [5; *g/pl.:* -вок] reduction; ~**лять** [28], ⟨~ить⟩ [14] reduce.
сбе|гать[1] [1], ⟨~жать⟩ [4; -егу, -ежишь, -егут] run down; *pf.* run away, escape, flee; **-ся** come running; ∠гать[2] [1] *pf.* run (for за T).
сбере|гательный [14] savings (*bank*)...; ~**гать** [1], ⟨∠чь⟩ [26 г/ж: -регу, -режёшь, -регут] save; preserve; ~**жение** *n* [12] saving; preservation.
сберкасса *f* [5] savings bank.
сби|вать [1], ⟨~ть⟩ [собью, -бьёшь; сбей!; сбитый] knock down (*or* off); overthrow (*a.* с ног); shoot down; whip (*cream*), beat up (*eggs*), churn (*butter*); mix; lead (astray с пути; **-ся** lose one's way); (**-ся** be[come] confus(ed) *or* puzzl(ed) (с толку); *refl. a.* run o.s. off (one's legs с ног); flock; ∠**вчивый** [14 *sh.*] confused; uneven; ∠**ть(ся)** *s.* ~вать(ся).
сбли|жать [1], ⟨∠зить⟩ [15] bring *or* draw together; **-ся** become friends (with с T); ~**жение** *n* [12] (*a. pol.*) rapprochement; approach (-es).
сбоку sideways; next to it.
сбор *m* [1] collection; gathering; harvest; levy; tax; duty; receipts *pl.*; ⚔ muster; *pl.* preparations; в ∠е assembled; ∠**ище** *n* [11] concourse, crowd; ∠**ка** *f* [5; *g/pl.:* -рок] pleat, tuck; ⊕ assemblage; ∠**ник** *m* [1] collection; symposium; ∠**ный** [14] ⚔ assembly (*point*); *sport:* select (*team*); ∠**очный** [14] assembling.
сбр|асывать [1], ⟨~осить⟩ [15] throw off, drop, shed; discard; ~**од** *m* [1] rabble, riff-raff; ~**осить** *s.* ~асывать; ~**уя** *f* [6] harness.

сбы|вать [1], ⟨~ть⟩ [сбуду, -дешь; сбыл, -а, -о] sell, market; get rid of (*a.* с рук); fall; **-ся** come true; ~**т** *m* [1] sale; ~**ть(ся)** *s.* ~вать(ся).
свад|ебный [14], ~**ьба** *f* [5; *g/pl.:* -деб] wedding.
свал|ивать [1], ⟨~ить⟩ [13; -алю, -алишь] knock down, overthrow; fell; dump; heap up; shift (off) (to на B); **-ся** fall down; ~**ка** *f* [5; *g/pl.:* -лок] dump; brawl.
свар|ивать [1], ⟨~ить⟩ [13; сварю, сваришь; свареннный] weld; ~**ка** *f* [5], ~**очный** [14] welding.
сварливый [14 *sh.*] quarrelsome.
сва|т *m* [1] matchmaker; ∠**тать** [1], ⟨по-⟩ seek (**-ся** ask) in marriage (for за B); ∠**ха** *f* [5] matchmaker.
свая *f* [6; *g/pl.:* свай] pile.
свед|ение *n* [12] information; принять к ~ению take notice (of B); ~**ущий** [17 *sh.*] expert, versed.
свеж|есть *f* [8] freshness; ~**еть** [8], ⟨по-⟩ freshen, become fresh; ~**ий** [15; свеж, -а, -о, свежи] fresh; cool; latest; new.
свезти *s.* свозить.
свёкла *f* [5; *g/pl.:* -кол] beet.
свёкор *m* [1; -кра] (**свекровь** *f* [8]) father-(mother-)in-law (*husband's father or mother resp.*).
свер|гать [1], ⟨∠гнуть⟩ [21] overthrow; dethrone (с трона); shake off (*yoke*); ~**жение** *n* [12] overthrow; ∠**нуть** *s.* ~ять.
сверк|ать [1], *once* ⟨~нуть⟩ [20] sparkle, glitter; flash; молния ~ает it lightens.
сверл|ение *n* [12], ~**ильный** [14] drilling; ~**ить** [13], ⟨про-⟩, ~**о** *n* [9; *pl. st.*: свёрла] drill.
свер|нуть(ся) *s.* свёртывать(ся) & сворачивать; ∠**стник** *s.* ровесник.
свёрт|ок *m* [1; -тка] roll; parcel; ~**ывать** [1], ⟨свернуть⟩ [20] roll (up); turn; curtail; break up (*camp*); twist; **-ся** coil up; curdle; coagulate.
сверх (P) above, beyond; over; besides; ~ того moreover; ~**звуковой** [14] supersonic; ~**прибыль** *f* [8] surplus profit; ∠**у** from above; ~**урочный** [14] overtime; ~**штатный** [14] supernumerary; ~**ъестественный** [14 *sh.*] supernatural.
сверчок *m* [1; -чка] *zo.* cricket.
свер|ять [28], ⟨∠ить⟩ [13] compare, collate.
свесить *s.* свешивать.
свести(сь) *s.* сводить(ся).
свет *m* [1] light; world (in на П); day(light); (high) society; P dear, darling; чуть ~ at dawn; ~**ать** [1] dawn; ~**ило** *n* [9] star; (*celestial*) body; ~**ить(ся)** [15] shine.
светл|еть [8], ⟨по-⟩ brighten; grow light(er); ~**о...** light...; ∠**ый** [14; -тел, -тла, -о] light, bright; serene; ~**як** *m* [1 *e.*], ~**ячок** [1 *e.*; -чка] glowworm.

свето|во́й [14] light...; **~маскиро́вка** *f* [5; *g/pl.*: -вок] blackout; **~фо́р** *m* [1] traffic light.
све́тский [16] secular, worldly; of high society.
светя́щийся [17] luminous.
свеча́ *f* [5; *pl.*: све́чи, -е́й, -а́м] candle; ⚡ plug.
све́|шивать [1], ⟨**~сить**⟩ [15] hang down; dangle; **-ся** hang over.
сви|ва́ть [1], ⟨**~ть**⟩ [совью́, -вьёшь; *cf.* вить] braid, plait; build (*nest*).
свида́ни|е *n* [12] appointment, meeting (at на П); до **~я** good-by(e).
свиде́тель *m* [4], **~ница** *f* [5] witness; **~ство** *n* [9] evidence; certificate; licence; **~ствовать** [7], ⟨за-⟩ testify; *impf.* (о П) show.
свина́рник *m* [1] pigsty.
свине́ц *m* [1; -нца́] lead.
свин|и́на *f* [5] pork; **∠ка** *f* [5; *g/pl.*: -нок] mumps; морска́я **∠ка** guinea pig; **~о́й** [14] pig...; pork...; **∠ство** *n* [9] dirty *or* rotten act, smut; **~цо́вый** [14] lead(en).
сви́н|чивать [1], ⟨**~ти́ть**⟩ [15 *e.*; -нчу́, -нти́шь; сви́нченный] screw together, fasten with screws.
свинья́ *f* [6; *pl. st., gen.*: -не́й; *a.* -ньям] pig, hog, swine.
свире́ль *f* [8] pipe, reed.
свире́п|ствовать [7] rage; **~ый** [14 *sh.*] fierce, furious, grim.
свиса́ть [1] hang down; slouch.
свист *m* [1] whistle; hiss; **~а́ть** [3] & **~е́ть** [11], *once* ⟨**∠нуть**⟩ [20] whistle; *pf.* P pilfer; **~о́к** *m* [1; -тка́] whistle.
сви́т|а *f* [5] retinue, suite; **~ер** (-ter) *m* [1] sweater; **~ок** *m* [1; -тка] roll; **~ь** *s.* свива́ть.
свихну́ть F [20] *pf.* sprain; **-ся** go mad.
свищ *m* [1 *e.*] fistula; crack.
свобо́д|а *f* [5] freedom, liberty; на **~у** (*set*) free; **~ный** [14; -ден, -дна] free (from, of от Р); vacant (*seat, etc.*); spare (*time, etc.*); ready (*money*); easy; loose; fluent; exempt (from от Р); **~омы́слящий** [17] freethinking; *su.* freethinker, liberal.
свод *m* [1] 🏛 vault; ⚖ code.
своди́ть [15], ⟨свести́⟩ [25] lead, take (down); bring (together); close (*vault*); reduce (to в В); square (*accounts*); contract; remove; drive (mad с ума́); **~** на нет bring to nought; **-ся**, ⟨-сь⟩ (к Д) come *or* amount (to), result (in); turn (into на В).
сво́д|ка *f* [5; *g/pl.*: -док] summary; report, communiqué; *typ.* revise; **~ный** [14] summary; step...; **~ча́тый** [14] vaulted.
своє|во́льный [14; -лен, -льна] self-willed, wil(l)ful; **~вре́менный** [14; -менен, -менна] timely; **~нра́вный** [14; -вен, -вна] capricious; **~обра́зный** [14; -зен, -зна] original; peculiar.
свози́ть [15], ⟨свезти́⟩ [24] take.
сво|й *m*, **~я́** *f*, **~ё** *n*, **~и́** *pl.* [24] my, his, her, its, our, your, their (*refl.*); one's own; peculiar; *su. pl.* one's people, folks, relations; не **~й** frantic (*voice* in Т); **∠йственный** [14 *sh.*] peculiar (to Д); (р.'s Д) usual; **∠йство** *n* [9] property, quality; F kind.
сво́|лочь *f* [8] rabble, riff-raff; rascal; **~ра** *f* [5] pack; **~ра́чивать** [1], ⟨сверну́ть⟩ [20] &, P, ⟨**~роти́ть**⟩ [15] turn (off с Р); **~я́ченица** *f* [5] sister-in-law (*wife's sister*).
сві|ка́ться [1], ⟨**∠кнуться**⟩ [21] get used (to с Т); **~сока́** haughtily; **∠ше** from above; (Р) over; beyond.
связ|а́ть(ся) *s.* **∠ывать(ся)**; **~и́ст** *m* [1] signalman; **∠ка** *f* [5; *g/pl.*: -зок] bunch; *anat.* ligament; (*vocal*) cord; *gr.* copula; **∠ный** [16; -зен, -зна] coherent; **∠ывать** [1], ⟨**~а́ть**⟩ [3] tie (together), bind; connect, join; unite; associate; *teleph.* put through, connect; **-ся** get into touch, contact; associate (with с Т); **~ь** *f* [8; в -зи́] tie, bond; connection (*Brt.* connexion); relation; contact; liaison; ⚔ signal (*service, etc.*); communication; post(al system).
свят|и́ть [15 *e.*; -ячу́, -яти́шь], ⟨о-⟩ consecrate, hallow; **∠ки** *f/pl.* [5; *gen.*: -ток] Christmastide (at на П); **~о́й** [14; свят, -а́, -о] holy; sacred; godly; solemn; Easter (week *su. f*); *su.* saint; **∠ость** *f* [8] holiness, sanctity; **~ота́тство** *n* [9] sacrilege; **~о́ша** *m/f* [5] hypocrite; **~ы́ня** *f* [6] relic; sanctuary.
свяще́нн|ик *m* [1] priest; **~ый** [14 *sh.*] holy; sacred.
с. г. *abbr.*: сего́ го́да; *cf.* сей.
сгиб *m* [1], **~а́ть** [1], ⟨согну́ть⟩ [20] bend, curve, fold; *v/i.* **-ся**.
сгла́|живать [1], ⟨**~дить**⟩ [15] smooth; **-ся** be smoothed (out).
сгнива́ть [1] *s.* гнить.
сго́вор *m* [1] F *s.* уговор; **~и́ться** [13] *pf.* agree; come to terms; **∠чивый** [14 *sh.*] compliant, amenable.
сго|ня́ть [28], ⟨согна́ть⟩ [сгоню́, сго́нишь; согна́л, -а́, -о; со́гнанный] drive (off); **~ра́ние** *n* [12] combustion; **~ра́ть** [1], ⟨**~ре́ть**⟩ [9] burn down; perish; die (of от, с Р); **~ряча́** in a temper.
сгр|еба́ть [1], ⟨**~ести́**⟩ [24-б-: сгребу́; сгрёб, сгребла́] rake up; shovel (down); **~ужа́ть** [1], ⟨**~узи́ть**⟩ [15 & 15 *e.*; -ужу́, -у́зишь; -у́женный & -ужённый] unload.
сгу|сти́ть *s.* **~ща́ть**; **∠сток** *m* [1; -тка] clot; **~ща́ть** [1], ⟨**~сти́ть**⟩ [15 *e.*; -ущу́, -усти́шь; -ущённый] thicken; condense; **~ща́ть** кра́ски exaggerate.
сда|ва́ть [5], ⟨**~ть**⟩ [сдам, сдашь, *etc. s.* дать] deliver, hand in (*or* over); surrender; check, register; rent, let (out); deal (*cards*); return

(*change*); pass (*examination*); yield; P seem; -ся surrender; ~ётся ... ... for rent (*Brt.* to let); ∠вливать [1], ⟨~вить⟩ [14] squeeze; ~ть(ся) *s.* ~вать(ся); ∠ча *f* [5] surrender; delivery; deal; change; check, register.
сдвиг *m* [1] shift; (land)slide; ~**áть** [1], ⟨сдвинуть⟩ [20] move (*v/i.* -ся); join; knit (*brow*).
сдéл|ка *f* [5; *g/pl.*: -лок] bargain, transaction, deal; arrangement, settlement; ~**ьный** [14] piece(-*work*).
сдéрж|анный [14 *sh.*] reserved, (self-)restrained; ~**ивать** [1], ⟨~**áть**⟩ [4] check, restrain; suppress; keep (*word, etc.*); -ся control o.s.
сдирáть [1], ⟨содрáть⟩ [сдерý, -рёшь; содрáл, -á, -о; сóдранный] tear off (*or* down), strip; flay (*a. fig*).
сдóбн|ый [14]: ~ая бýл(оч)ка *f* bun.
сдружиться *s.* подружиться.
сду|вáть [1], ⟨~ть⟩ [16], *once* ⟨∠нуть⟩ [20] blow off (*or* away); ∠ру F foolishly.
сеáнс *m* [1] sitting; *cinema:* show.
себестóимость *f* [8] prime cost.
себ|я́ [21] myself, yourself, himself, herself, itself, ourselves, yourselves, themselves (*refl.*); oneself; к ~é home; into one's room; от ~я́ on p.'s behalf; тáк ~é so-so; ~**ялюби́вый** [14 *sh.*] selfish, self-loving.
сев *m* [1] sowing.
Севастóполь *m* [4] Sevastopol.
сéвер *m* [1] north; *cf.* востóк; ~**ный** [14] north(ern); northerly; arctic; 2ный Ледовитый океáн *m* Arctic Ocean; ~**о-востóк** *m* [1] northeast; ~**о-востóчный** [14] northeast...; ~**о-зáпад** *m* [1] northwest; ~**о-зáпадный** [14] northwest...
сегóдня today; ~ ýтром this morning; ~**шний** [15] today's; this (*day*).
сед|éть [8], ⟨по-⟩ turn gray (*Brt.* grey); ~**инá** *f* [5] gray hair; *pl. a. fig.* great age.
седл|áть [1], ⟨о-⟩, ~**ó** *n* [9; *pl. st.*: сёдла, сёдел, сёдлам] saddle.
седо|волóсый [14 *sh.*], ∠**й** [14; сед, -á, -о] gray(-haired, -headed), *Brt.* grey.
седóк *m* [1 *e.*] horseman; passenger.
седьмóй [14] seventh; *cf.* пя́тый.
сезóн *m* [1] season; ~**ный** [14] seasonal.
сей *m*, сия́ *f*, сиé *n*, сии́ *pl.* † [29] this; сим herewith, hereby; при сём enclosed; сегó гóда (мéсяца) of this year (month); *cf.* порá.
сейчáс now, at present; presently, (*a.* ~ же) immediately, at once; just (now).
секрéт *m* [1] secret (in по Д, под Т); ~**ариáт** *m* [1] secretariat; ~**áрь** *m* [4 *e.*] secretary; ~**ничать** F [1] be secretive, act secretely; whisper; ~**ный** [14; -тен, -тна] secret; confidential.
сек|суáльный [14; -лен, -льна] sexual; ∠**та** *f* [5] sect; ∠**тор** *m* [1] sector; sphere, branch.
секýнд|а *f* [5] second; ~**ный** [14] second...; ~**омéр** *m* [1] stop watch.
селёдка *f* [5; *g/pl.*: -док] herring.
селез|ёнка *f* [5; *g/pl.*: -нок] *anat.* spleen; ʹ~**ень** *m* [4; -зня] drake.
селéние *n* [12] settlement, colony.
сели́т|ра *f* [5] saltpeter, niter, *Brt.* nitre; ~**ь(ся)** [13] *s.* поселя́ть(ся).
сел|ó *n* [9; *pl. st.*: сёла] village (in в *or* на П); на ~é *a.* in the country; ни к ~ý ни к гóроду F without rhyme or reason.
сельд|ерéй *m* [3] celery; ~**ь** *f* [8; *from g/pl. e.*] herring.
сéль|ский [16] rural, country..., village...; ~ское хозя́йство *n* agriculture; ~**скохозя́йственный** [14] agricultural; farming; ~**совéт** *m* [1] village soviet.
сéльтерская *f* [16] Seltzer.
сёмга *f* [5] salmon.
семéй|ный [14] family...; married; ~**ство** *n* [9] family.
Семён *m* [1] Simeon.
семен|и́ть F [13] trip, mince; ~**нóй** [14] seed...; seminal.
семёрка *f* [5; *g/pl.*: -рок] seven; *cf.* двóйка.
сéмеро [37] seven; *cf.* двóе.
семé|стр *m* [1] term, semester; ʹ~**чко** *n* [9; *pl.*: -чки, -чек, -чкам] seed.
семи|деся́тый [14] seventieth; *cf.* пя́(тидеся́)тый; ~**лéтка** *f* [5; *g/pl.*: -ток] seven-year school (*or* plan); ~**лéтний** [15] seven-year (old), of seven.
семинáр *m* [1], ~**ий** *m* [3] seminar; ~**ия** *f* [7] seminary.
семисóтый [14] seven hundredth.
семнáдцат|ый [14] seventeenth; *cf.* пя́тый; ~**ь** [35] seventeen; *cf.* пять.
семь [35] seven; *cf.* пять & пя́тый; ∠**десят** [35] seventy; ~**сóт** [36] seven hundred; ∠**ю** seven times.
семья́ *f* [6; *pl.*: сéмьи, семéй, сéмьям] family; ~**ни́н** *m* [1] family man.
сéмя *n* [13; *pl.*: -менá, -мя́н, -менáм] seed (*a. fig.*).
сенáт *m* [1] senate; ~**ор** *m* [1] senator.
сéни *f/pl.* [8; *from gen. e.*] hall(way).
сéно *n* [9] hay; ~**вáл** *m* [1] hayloft; ~**кóс** *m* [1] haymaking; *cf.* коси́лка.
сен|сациóнный [14; -óнен, -óнна] sensational; ~**тиментáльный** [14; -лен, -льна] sentimental.
сентя́брь *m* [4 *e.*] September.
сень † *f* [8; в -ни́] shade; shelter.
сепарáтный [14] separate.
сéра *f* [5] sulfur; F earwax.
серб *m* [1], ∠(**ия́н**)**ка** *f* [5; *g/pl.*: -б(ия́н)ок] Serb(ian); ∠**ский** [16] Serbian.
серви́|з *m* [1] service, set; ~**ровáть** [7] (*im*)*pf.* serve.
Сергéй *m* [3] Sergius, Serge.

серде́чный [14; -чен, -чна] heart('s); hearty, cordial; intimate; dear; best.
серди́|тый [14 *sh.*] angry, mad (with, at на В), wrathful; irascible, fretful; spiteful, vicious; **~ть** [15], ⟨рас-⟩ annoy, vex, fret, anger; **-ся** be(come) angry (with на В).
се́рдц|е *n* [11; *pl. e.*: -дца́, -де́ц, -дца́м] heart; temper; anger; darling, love, sweetheart (*address*); от всего́ **~а** whole-heartedly; по́ **~у** (Д) to one's liking; положа́ ру́ку на́ **~е** F (quite) frankly; **~ебие́ние** *n* [12] palpitation; **~еви́на** *f* [5] core, heart.
серебр|и́стый [14 *sh.*] silvery; **~и́ть** [13], ⟨по-, вы́-⟩ silver; **-ся** glisten like silver; **~о́** *n* [9] silver; **~яный** [14] silver(y).
середи́на *f* [5] middle; center (*Brt.* -tre); mean.
Сер|ёж([ень]к)а *m* [5] *dim. of* Серге́й; **2е́ть** [8], ⟨по-⟩ turn (*impf.* show) gray (*Brt.* grey).
сержа́нт *m* [1] sergeant; мла́дший **~** corporal.
сери́|йный [14] serial; multiple; **'~я** *f* [7] series.
се́рна *f* [5] chamois.
се́р|ный [14] sulfuric; sulfur...; **~ова́тый** [14 *sh.*] grayish, Brt. greyish.
серп *m* [1 *e.*] sickle; crescent.
се́рый [14; сер, -а́, -о] gray, *Brt.* grey; dull (*a. fig.* = humdrum).
се́рьги *f/pl.* [5; серёг, серьга́м; *sg. e.*] earrings.
серьёзн|ый [14; -зен, -зна] serious, grave; earnest (in **~о**); **~о** *a.* indeed, really.
се́ссия *f* [7] session (in на П).
сестра́ *f* [5; *pl.*: сёстры, сестёр, сёстрам] sister; nurse; на́ша **~** F (such as) we.
сесть *s.* сади́ться.
се́т|ка *f* [5; *g/pl.*: -ток] net; ⚡ grid; scale; **~овать** [1] complain (about на В); **~ча́тка** *f* [5; *g/pl.*: -ток] retina; **~ь** *f* [8; в сети́; *from g/pl. e.*] net; network.
сече́ние *n* [12] section.
сечь[1] [26; *pt. e.*; сек, секла́] cut (up), chop, hew; cleave; **-ся** split; ravel; **~**[2] [26: *pt. st.*; сек, се́кла], ⟨вы́-⟩ whip, flog.
се́ялка *f* [5; *g/pl.*: -лок] seeder.
се́ять [27], ⟨по-⟩ sow (*a. fig.*).
сжа́литься [13] *pf.* (над Т) have *or* take pity (on), pity.
сжа́т|ие *n* [12] pressure; compression; **~ый** [14] compressed; compact, concise, terse; **~ь(ся)** *s.* сжима́ть(ся) & жать[1], жать[2].
сжига́ть [1], ⟨сжечь⟩ *cf.* жечь.
сжима́ть [1], ⟨сжать⟩ [сожму́, -мёшь; сжа́тый] (com)press, squeeze; clench; **-ся** contract; shrink; become clenched.
сза́ди (from) behind (*as prp.*: Р).
сзыва́ть *s.* созыва́ть.
Сиби́р|ь *f* [8] Siberia; **2ский** [16], **2я́к** *m* [1 *e.*], **2я́чка** *f* [5; *g/pl.*: -чек] Siberian.
си́вый [14; сив, -а́, -о] (ash) gray (grey).
сига́р(е́т)а *f* [5] cigar(ette).
сигна́л *m* [1], **~изи́ровать** [7] (*im*)*pf.*, **~ьный** [14] signal; alarm.
сиде́лка *f* [5; *g/pl.*: -лок] nurse.
сиде́|нье *n* [10] seat; **~ть** [11; си́дя] sit (at, over за Т); be, stay; fit (a p. на П); **-ся**: ему́ не сиди́тся he can't sit still.
сидр *m* [1] cider.
сидя́чий [17] sedentary; sitting.
си́зый [14; сиз, -а́, -о] (bluish) gray, *Brt.* grey; dove-colo(u)red.
си́л|а *f* [5] strength; force; power, might; vigo(u)r; intensity; efficacy; energy; volume; свои́ми **~ами** by o. s.; в **~у** (Р) by virtue (of); не в **~ах** unable; не по **~ам** above one's strength; **~** нет F awfully; изо всех **~** F with all one's might; **~а́ч** *m* [1 *e.*] athlete; **~иться** [13] try, endeavo(u)r; **~ово́й** [14] power...
сило́к *m* [1; -лка́] snare, noose.
си́льн|ый [14; си́лен & силён, -льна́, -о, си́льны́] strong; powerful, mighty; intense; heavy (*rain*); bad (*cold*); great; ⚡ power...; **~о** *a.* very much; hard.
си́мвол *m* [1] symbol; **~и́ческий** [16], **~и́чный** [14; -чен, -чна] symbolic(al).
симметри́|чный [14; -чен, -чна] symmetrical; **~я** *f* [7] symmetry.
симпат|изи́ровать [7] sympathize (with Д); **~и́чный** [14; -чен, -чна] nice, sympathetic; он мне **~и́чен** I like him; **~ия** *f* [7] sympathy.
симул|и́ровать [7] (*im*)*pf.* feign, sham; malinger; **~я́нт** *m* [1], **~я́нтка** *f* [5; *g/pl.*: -ток] simulator.
симфони́|ческий [16] symphonic, symphony...; **'~я** *f* [7] symphony.
синдика́т *m* [1] syndicate.
син|ева́ *f* [5] blue; **~ева́тый** [14 *sh.*] bluish; **~е́ть** [8], ⟨по-⟩ turn (*impf.* show) blue; **~ий** [15; синь, синя́, си́не] blue; **~и́льный** [14] hydrocyanic, prussic (*acid*); **~и́ть** [13], ⟨под-⟩ blue; **~и́ца** *f* [5] titmouse.
син|о́д *m* [1] synod; **~о́ним** *m* [1] synonym; **~таксис** *m* [1] syntax; **~тез** *m* [1] synthesis; **~тети́ческий** [16] synthetic(al); **~хронизи́ровать** [7] (*im*)*pf.* synchronize.
синь *f* [8], **~ка** *f* [5; *g/pl.*: -нек] blue.
синя́к *m* [1 *e.*] livid spot, bruise.
си́плый [14; сипл, -а́, -о] hoarse.
сире́на *f* [5] siren.
сире́н|евый [14], **~ь** *f* [8] lilac.
сиро́п *m* [1] syrup.
сирота́ *m/f* [5; *pl. st.*: сиро́ты] orphan.
систе́ма *f* [5] system; **~ти́ческий**

[16], **~тичный** [14; -чен, -чна] systematic(al).
ситец *m* [1; -тца] chintz, cotton.
сито *n* [9] sieve.
Сицилия *f* [7] Sicily.
сия|ние *n* [12] radiance; light, shine; halo; **~ть** [28] shine, beam; radiate.
сказ|ание *n* [12] legend; saga; story; **~ать** *s.* говорить; **∠ка** *f* [5; *g/pl.*: -зок] fairy tale; tale, fib; **∠очный** [14; -чен, -чна] fabulous, fantastic; fairy (tale)...
сказуемое *n* [14] *gr.* predicate.
скак|ать [3] skip, hop, leap; gallop; race; **~овой** [14] race...; racing.
скал|а *f* [5; *pl. st.*] rock, cliff, crag; **~истый** [14 *sh.*] rocky, cliffy; **∠ить** [13], ⟨о-⟩ show, bare (*one's teeth*); F *impf.* grin; jeer; **∠ка** *f* [5; *g/pl.*: -лок] rolling pin; **∠ывать** [1], ⟨сколоть⟩ [17] pin together; split (off); prick.
скам|еечка *f* [5; *g/pl.*: -чек] footstool; *a. dim. of* **~ейка** *f* [5; *g/pl.*: -еек], **~ья** *f* [6; *nom/pl. a. st.*] bench; **~ья** подсудимых dock.
скандал *m* [1] scandal; row; F shame; **~ить** [13], ⟨на-⟩ row; **~ьный** [14; -лен, -льна] scandalous; F wretched.
скандинавский [16] Scandinavian.
скапливать(ся) [1] *s.* скоплять (-ся).
скар|б F [1] belongings, things *pl.*; **∠едный** F [14; -ден, -дна] stingy; **~латина** *f* [5] scarlet fever.
скат *m* [1] slope, pitch.
скат|ать *s.* скатывать 2; **∠ерть** *f* [8; *from g/pl. e.*] tablecloth.
скат|ывать [1] **1.** ⟨**~ить**⟩ [15] roll (*or* slide) down (*v/i.* **-ся**); **2.** ⟨**~ать**⟩ [1] roll (up); P copy.
скач|ка *f* [5; *g/pl.*: -чек] gallop; *pl.* horse race(s); **~ок** *s.* прыжок.
скашивать [1], ⟨скосить⟩ [15] mow off *or* down; slope; bevel.
скважина *f* [5] chink, crack; pore; ⊕ hole; замочная ~ keyhole.
сквер *m* [1] square, park; **~нословить** [14] talk smut; **∠ный** [14; -рен, -рна, -о] nasty, foul.
сквоз|ить [15; -ит] shine through, appear; **~ит** there is a draft, *Brt.* draught; **~ной** [14] through...; thorough...; transparent; **~няк** *m* [1 *e.*] draft, *Brt.* draught; **~ь** (В) through.
скворе|ц *m* [1; -рца] starling; **~чница** (-ʃn-) *f* [5] nestling box.
скелет *m* [1] skeleton.
скептический [16] skeptic(al).
ски|дка *f* [5; *g/pl.*: -док] discount, rebate; **~дывать** [1], ⟨**~нуть**⟩ [20] throw off *or* down; take *or* put off; discount, reduce; **~петр** *m* [1] scepter, *Brt.* -tre; **~пидар** *m* [1] turpentine; **~рд** *m* [1 *e.*] haystack.
скис|ать [1], ⟨**∠нуть**⟩ [21] turn sour.
скита|лец *m* [1; -льца] wanderer; **~ться** [1] wander, rove.
склад *m* [1] warehouse, storehouse (in на П); ⚔ depot; constitution, disposition, turn; breed; way (*of life*); F harmony; sense; **∠ка** *f* [5; *g/pl.*: -док] pleat, fold; crease; wrinkle; **~ной** [14] fold(ing), collapsible; camp...; falt(*boat*); **∠ный** [14; -ден, -дна, -о] harmonious; coherent; fluent, smooth; P well-made (*or* -built); accommodating; **∠чина** *f* [5]: в **~чину** by clubbing (together); **∠ывать** [1], ⟨сложить⟩ [16] lay *or* put (together, up, down); pile up; pack (up); fold; add; compose; lay down (*arms; one's life*); сложа руки idle; **-ся** (be) form (-ed), develop; F club (together).
склеи|вать [1], ⟨**~ть**⟩ [13; **-ею**] stick together (*v/i.* **-ся**).
склеп *m* [1] crypt, vault.
склока *f* [5] squabble.
склон *m* [1] slope; **~ение** *n* [12] inclination; *gr.* declension; *ast.* declination; **~ить(ся)** *s.* **~ять(ся)**; **∠ность** *f* [8] inclination (*fig.*; to, for к Д), disposition; **∠ный** [14; -онен, -онна, -о] inclined (to к Д), disposed; **~ять** [28] **1.** ⟨**~ить**⟩ [13; -оню, -онишь; -онённый] bend, incline (*a. fig.*; *v/i.* **-ся**; sink); persuade; **2.** ⟨просклонять⟩ *gr.* (**-ся** be) decline(d).
скоб|а *f* [5; *pl.*: скобы, скоб, скобам] cramp (iron); **∠ка** *f* [5; *g/pl.*: -бок] cramp; *gr.*, *typ.* bracket, parenthesis; **~лить** [13; -облю, -облишь; -обленный] scrape; **~яной** [14] hard(*ware*).
сковать *s.* сковывать.
сковорода *f* [5; *pl.*: сковороды, -род, -дам] frying pan.
скова|ывать [1], ⟨**~ать**⟩ [7 *e.*; скую, скуёшь] forge (together); weld; fetter, chain; bind; arrest.
сколоть *s.* скалывать.
скольз|ить [15 *e.*; -льжу, -льзишь], *once* ⟨**~нуть**⟩ [20] slide, glide, slip; **∠кий** [16; -зок, -зка, -о] slippery.
сколько [32] how (*or* as) much, many; ~ лет, ~ зим *s.* вечность F.
скончаться [1] *pf.* die, expire.
скоп|лять [28], ⟨**~ить**⟩ [14] accumulate, gather (*v/i.* **-ся**), amass; save; **~ление** *n* [12] accumulation; gathering, crowd.
скорб|еть [10 *e.*; -блю, -бишь] grieve (over о П); **∠ный** [14; -бен, -бна] mournful, sorrowful; **~ь** *f* [8] grief, sorrow.
скорлупа *f* [5; *pl. st.*: -лупы] shell.
скорняк *m* [1 *e.*] furrier.
скоро|говорка *f* [5; *g/pl.*: -рок] tongue twister; rapid speech, sputter; **∠мный** [14; -мен, -мна] meat, milk (*food, forbidden in Lent*); **~постижный** [14; -жен, -жна] sudden; **~спелый** [14 *sh.*] early; pre-

cocious; **~стнóй** [14] (high-)speed-...; **'~сть** *f* [8; *from g/pl. e.*] speed; rate; *mot.* gear; груз большóй (мáлой) '~сти express (ordinary) freight; **~тéчный** [14; -чен, -чна] transient; ♧ galloping.

скóр|ый [14; скор, -á, -о] quick, fast, rapid, swift; speedy, prompt; first (*aid*); near (*future*); early (*reply*); **~о** *a.* soon; **~ée** всегó F most probably; на **~ую** рýку F in haste, offhand, anyhow.

скосúть *s.* скáшивать.

скот *m* [1 *e.*] cattle, livestock; **~úна** *f* [5] F cattle; P brute; dolt, boor; **∠ный** [14]: ∠ный двор cattle yard; **~обóйня** *f* [6; *g/pl.*: -óен] slaughterhouse; **~овóдство** *n* [9] cattle breeding; **~ский** [16] brutish, bestial, swinish.

скребóк *m* [1; -бкá] scraper.

скрéжет *m* [1], **~áть** [3] (T) gnash.

скрéп|а *f* [5] cramp, clamp; **~úть** *s.* **~лять**; **~ка** *f* [5; *g/pl.*: -пок] (paper) clip; **~лéние** *n* [12] fastening; **~лять** [28], ⟨**~úть**⟩ [14 *e.*; -плю, -пúшь; -плённый] fasten; tighten; corroborate; validate; countersign; **~я** сéрдце reluctantly.

скрестú [24 -б-: скребý; скрёб] scrape; scratch.

скрéщива|ть [1], ⟨скрестúть⟩ [15 *e.*; -ещý, -естúшь; -ещённый] cross (*v/i.* **-ся**); **~ние** *n* [12] crossing.

скрип *m* [1] creak; scratch; **~áч** *m* [1 *e.*] violinist; **~éть** [10 *e.*; -плю, -пúшь], ⟨про-⟩, *once* ⟨**∠нуть**⟩ [20] creak; scratch; grit, gnash; **∠ка** *f* [5; *g/pl.*: -пок] violin.

скрóмн|ость *f* [8] modesty; **~ый** [14; -мен, -мнá, -о] modest; frugal.

скрý|чивать [1], ⟨**~тúть**⟩ [15] braid; roll; bind; P bend.

скры|вáть [1], ⟨**~ть**⟩ [22] hide, conceal (from от Р); **-ся** disappear; hide; **∠тность** *f* [8] reserve; **∠тный** [14; -тен, -тна] reserved, reticent; **∠тый** [14] concealed; latent; secret; **∠ть(ся)** *s.* **~вáть(ся)**.

скрягá *m/f* [5] miser.

скýдный [14; -ден, -днá, -о] scanty, poor.

скýка *f* [5] boredom, ennui.

скулá *f* [5; *pl. st.*] cheekbone; **~стый** [14 *sh.*] with high cheekbones.

скулúть [13] whimper.

скульптýра *f* [5] sculpture.

скýмбрия *f* [7] mackerel.

скуп|áть [1], ⟨**~úть**⟩ [14] buy up.

скуп|úться [14], ⟨по-⟩ be stingy (*or* sparing), stint (in, of на В); **~óй** [14; скуп, -á, -о] avaricious, stingy; sparing (in на В); scanty, poor; taciturn (на словá); *su.* miser; **∠ость** *f* [8] avarice.

скуч|áть [1] be bored; (по П *or* Д) long (for), miss; **∠ный** (-ʃn-) [14; -чен, -чнá, -о] boring, tedious, dull; sad; (Д) **~но** feel bored.

слаб|éть [8], ⟨о-⟩ weaken, slacken; **~úтельный** [14] laxative (*n a. su.*); **~овóльный** [14; -лен, -льна] weak-willed (*or* -minded); **~осúльный** [14; -лен, -льна] *s.* **∠ый**; **∠ость** *f* [8] weakness (*a. fig.* = foible; for к Д); infirmity; **~oýмный** [14; -мен, -мна] feeble-minded; **~охарáктерный** [14; -рен, -рна] flabby; **∠ый** [14; слаб, -á, -о] weak (*a.* ♯), feeble; faint; infirm; delicate; flabby; poor.

слáв|а *f* [5] glory; fame, renown; reputation, repute; (Д) hail; long live; **~а** бóгу! God be praised!, thank goodness!; на **~у** F first-rate, A-one; **~ить** [14], ⟨про-⟩ glorify; praise, extol; **-ся** be famous (for T) **~ный** [14; -вен, -внá, -о] famous; glorious; F nice; capital, dandy.

славян|úн *m* [1; *pl.*: -яне, -ян], **∠ка** *f* [5; *g/pl.*: -нок] Slav; **∠ский** [16] Slavic, *Brt.* Slavonic.

слагáть [1], ⟨сложúть⟩ [16] compose; lay down; resign (from); exonerate; relieve o.s. (of); *cf.* склáдывать(ся); **-ся** *a.* be composed.

слáд|кий [16; -док, -дкá, -о; *comp.*: слáще] sweet; sugary; **~oe** *su.* dessert (for на В); **~остный** [14; -тен, -тна] sweet, delightful; **~острáстие** *n* [12] voluptuousness; **~острáстный** [14; -тен, -тна] voluptuous; **~ость** *f* [8] sweetness; delight; *cf.* слáсти.

слáженный [14 *sh.*] harmonious.

слáнец *m* [1; -нца] slate.

слáсти *f/pl.* [8; *from gen. e.*] candy *sg.*, *Brt. a.* sweets.

слать [шлю, шлёшь], ⟨по-⟩ send.

слащáвый [14 *sh.*] sugary.

слéва on, to (*or* from) the left.

слегкá (-хк-) slightly; in passing.

след *m* [1; *g/sg. e.* & -ду; на -дý; *pl. e.*] trace (*a. fig.*), track; footprint, footstep; print; scent; **∠ом** (right) behind; егó и **~** простыл F he was off and away; **~úть** [15 *e.*; -ежý, -едúшь] (за Т, † В) watch, follow; look after; shadow; trace.

слéдоват|ель *m* [4] examining magistrate; **~ельно** consequently, therefore; so; **~ь** [7] (за Т; Д) follow; ensue (from из Р); go, move; (Д) *impers.* should, ought to; be to be; как слéдует properly, duly; F downright, thoroughly; as it should be; комý *or* кудá слéдует to the proper p. *or* quarter; скóлько с меня слéдует? how much do I have to pay?

слéдствие *n* [12] consequence; inquest, trial.

слéдующий [17] following, next.

слéжка *f* [5; *g/pl.*: -жек] shadowing.

слез|á *f* [5; *pl.*: слёзы, слёз, слезáм] tear; **~áть** [1], ⟨**~ть**⟩ [24 *st.*] climb *or* get down; dismount, alight;

get out; F come off; **~иться** [15; -ится] water; **~ливый** [14 *h.*] tearful, lachrymose; **~оточивый** [14] tear (*gas*); watering; **~ть** *s.* **~ать**.

слеп|ень *m* [4; -пня] gadfly; **~ец** *m* [1; -пца] blind man; **~ить** 1. [14 *e.*; -плю, -пишь], ⟨о-⟩ [ослеплённый] blind; dazzle; 2. [14] *pf.*; *impf.*: **~лять** [28] stick together (*v/i.* -ся); *s. a.* лепить; **∠нуть** [21], ⟨о-⟩ grow (*or* become) blind; **~ой** [14; слеп, -а, -о] blind (in, *Brt.* of *one eye* на В); dull (*glass*); indistinct; *su.* blind man; **∠ок** *m* [1; -пка] mould, cast; **~ота** *f* [5] blindness.

слесар|ь *m* [4; *pl.*: -ря, *etc. e.*, & -ри] locksmith; fitter, mechanic.

слёт *m* [1] flight; rally, meeting (at на П).

слет|ать [1], ⟨**~еть**⟩ [11] fly (down, off); F fall (down, off); **-ся** fly together; F gather.

слечь F [26 г/ж: слягу, сляжешь; сляг(те)!] *pf.* fall ill.

слива *f* [5] plum.

сли|вать [1], ⟨**~ть**⟩ [солью, -льёшь; *cf.* лить] pour (off, out, together); fuse, merge, amalgamate (*v/i.* -ся).

слив|ки *f/pl.* [5; *gen.*: -вок] cream (*a. fig.* = elite); **~очный** [14] creamy; (*ice*) cream.

слиз|истый [14 *sh.*] mucous; slimy; **~ь** *f* [8] slime; mucus, phlegm.

слипаться [1] stick together; close.

слит|ный [14] conjoint; continuous; **~но** *a.* together; in one word; **~ок** *m* [1; -тка] ingot; **~ь(ся)** *s.* сливать(ся).

слич|ать [1], ⟨**~ить**⟩ [16 *e.*; -чу, -чишь; -чённый] compare, collate.

слишком too, too much; это (уж) ~ F that beats everything.

слияние *n* [12] confluence; fusion, amalgamation; blending.

словак *m* [1] Slovak.

словар|ный [14]: **~ный** состав *m* stock of words; **~ь** *m* [4 *e.*] dictionary; vocabulary, glossary; lexicon.

слов|ацкий [16], **~ачка** *f* [5; *g/pl.*: -чек] Slovak; **~енец** *m* [1; -нца], **~енка** *f* [5; *g/pl.*: -нок], **~енский** [16] Slovene.

словесн|ость *f* [8] literature; (*folk-*) lore; philology; **~ый** [14] verbal, oral; literary; philologic(al).

словно as if; like; F as it were.

слово *n* [9; *pl. e.*] word (in a T; ... for ... И/в В); term; speech; к слову сказать by the way; на словах by word of mouth, orally; по словам according to; просить (предоставить Д) ~ ask (give p.) permission to speak; **~изменение** *n* [12] inflection (*Brt.* -xion); **~охотливый** [14 *sh.*] talkative.

слог *m* [1; *from g/pl. e.*] syllable; [style.]

слоёный [14] puff (*paste*).

слож|ение *n* [12] addition; composition; constitution, build; laying down; resignation; **~ить(ся)** *s.* складывать(ся), слагать(ся) & класть 2.; **∠ность** *f* [8] complexity, complicacy, complication; **∠ный** [14; -жен, -жна, -о] complicated, complex, intricate; compound.

сло|истый [14 *sh.*] stratiform; flaky; **~й** *m* [3; *pl. e.*: слои, слоёв] layer, stratum (in T *pl.*); coat(ing).

слом *m* [1] demolition, destruction; **~ать** [14] *pf.* break, overcome; overpower; **~я** голову F headlong.

слон *m* [1 *e.*] elephant; bishop (*chess*); **~овый** [14]: **~овая** кость *f* ivory.

слоняться F [28] linger, loaf.

слу|га *m* [5; *pl. st.*] servant; **∠жащий** *m* [17] employee; **∠жба** *f* [5] (на П) service (in); employment, job; office, work (at); duty (on); **~жебный** [14] office...; official; secondary, subordinate, subservient; *gr.* relational; **~жение** *n* [12] service; **~жить** [16], ⟨по-⟩ serve (a p./th. Д); work (as T); be.

слух *m* [1] hearing; ear (by на В; по Д); rumo(u)r, hearsay; news, sign; **~овой** [14] of hearing; acoustic(al); ear...; dormer (*window*).

случа|й *m* [3] case; occurrence, event; occasion (on по Д; при П), opportunity, chance, (*a.* несчастный **~й**) accident; на всякий (пожарный F) **~й** to be on the safe side; по **~ю** second hand; (P) on account of; **∠йность** *f* [8] chance, fortuity; **∠йный** [14; -аен, -айна] accidental, casual, chance (by **∠йно**); **∠ться** [1], ⟨случиться⟩ [16 *e.*; *3rd p. or impers.*] happen (to с T); come; take place; F be.

слуша|тель *m* [4] listener, hearer; student; *pl.* audience; **~ть** [1], ⟨по-⟩ listen (to В), hear; attend; ⚕ auscultate; **~й!** *a.*, ⚔, attention!; **~ю!** *teleph.*: hullo!; **~ю(сь)!** yes (, sir); **-ся** obey (p. P); take (*advice*).

слыть [23], ⟨про-⟩ (T, за В) pass for, have the reputation of.

слыхать, ⟨у-⟩ *s.* слышать.

слы|шать [4] (F **~хать** [*no pr.*]), ⟨у-⟩ hear (of, about о П); F feel, notice; **~шаться** [4] be heard; **~шимость** *f* [8] audibility; **~шно** it can be heard (of о П); it is said; (мне) **~шно** one (I) can hear; что **~шно**? what is the news?; **~шный** [14; -шен, -шна, -о] audible.

слюда *f* [5] mica.

слюн|а *f* [5], **∠и** F *pl.* [8; *from gen. e.*] saliva, spittle; **∠ки** F *f/pl.*: **∠ки** текут mouth waters; **~явый** F [14 *sh.*] slobbery.

слякоть *f* [8] slush.

см. *abbr.*: смотри see, v(ide).

с. м. *abbr.*: сего месяца; *cf.* сей.

смаз|ать *s.* **~ывать**; **~ка** *f* [5 *g/pl.*: -зок] greasing, oiling, lubrication; **~очный** [14] lubricant; **~ывать**

[1], ⟨~ать⟩ [3] grease, oil, lubricate; F blur.
сма́|нивать [1], ⟨~ни́ть⟩ [13; сманю́, -а́нишь; -а́ненный & -анённый] lure away, entice; **~тывать**, ⟨смота́ть⟩ [1] reel on *or* off; **~хивать** [1], ⟨~хну́ть⟩ [20] brush off (*or* aside); *impf.* F have a likeness (with на В); **~чивать** [1], ⟨смочи́ть⟩ [16] moisten.
сме́жный [14; -жен, -жна] adjacent.
сме́л|ость *f* [8] boldness; courage; **~ый** [14; смел, -а́, -о] courageous, bold; **~о** *a.* F easily; offhand.
сме́н|а *f* [5] shift (in в В); ⚔ relief; change; supersession; successors *pl.*; прийти́ на **~у** *s.* **~и́ться**; **~я́ть** [28], ⟨~и́ть⟩ [13; -еню́, -е́нишь; -енённый] (-ся be) supersede(d; o. a.), ⚔ relieve(d), replace(d; by T), substitute(d; for); change.
смерк|а́ться [1], ⟨**~**нуться⟩ [20] grow dusky *or* dark.
смерт|е́льный [14; -лен, -льна] mortal, fatal, (*a. adv.*) deadly; **~ность** *f* [8] mortality, death rate; **~ный** [14; -тен, -тна] mortal (*a. su.*), deadly, fatal; (a. ⚖) death ...; ⚖ capital; **~ь** *f* [8; *from g/pl. e.*] death; F (*a.* **~ь** как, до́ **~и**, на́ **~ь**) deadly, utterly; при́ **~и** at death's door.
смерч *m* [1] waterspout; tornado.
смести́ *s.* смета́ть; **~ть** *s.* смеща́ть.
сме|сь *f* [8] mixture; blend; alloy; miscellanies *pl.*; **~та** *f* [5] estimate.
смета́на *f* [5] sour cream.
сме|та́ть [1], ⟨~сти́⟩ [25 -т-] sweep away; sweep together; wipe off.
сме́тливый [14 *sh.*] sharp(-witted).
сметь [8], ⟨по-⟩ dare, venture; beg.
смех *m* [1] laughter (with со́ **~у**); joke, fun (for ра́ди Р, в *or* на В); *cf.* шу́тка.
сме́ш|анный [14] mixed; **~а́ть(ся)** *s.* **~ивать(ся)**; **~е́ние** *n* [12] mixture; confusion; **~ивать**, ⟨~а́ть⟩ [1] mix (up), mingle, blend (*v/i.* -ся; get *or* be[come]) confuse(d).
смеш|и́ть [16 *e.*; -шу́, -ши́шь], ⟨рас-⟩ [-шённый] make laugh; **~но́й** [14; -шо́н, -шна́] laughable, ludicrous, ridiculous; funny; (Д) **~но́** amuse (p.).
сме|ща́ть [1], ⟨~сти́ть⟩ [15 *e.*; -ещу́, -ести́шь; -ещённый] displace, shift, dislocate; **~ще́ние** *n* [12] displacement.
смея́ться [27 *e.*; -ею́сь, -еёшься], ⟨за-⟩ laugh (at *impf.* над T); mock (at); deride; F joke.
смир|е́ние *n* [12], **~е́нность** *f* [8] humility; meekness; **~е́нный** [14 *sh.*] humble; meek; **~и́ть(ся)** *s.* **~я́ть(ся)**; **~ный** [14; -рен (F -рён), -рна́, -о] quiet, still; meek, gentle; **~но!** ⚔ (at) attention!; **~я́ть** [28], ⟨~и́ть⟩ [13] subdue; restrain, check; -ся humble o.s.
смо́кинг *m* [1] tuxedo, dinner jacket.
смол|а́ *f* [5; *pl. st.*] resin; pitch; tar; **~и́стый** [14 *sh.*] resinous; **~и́ть** [13], ⟨вы́-, за-⟩ pitch, tar; **~ка́ть** [1], ⟨**~**кнуть⟩ [21] grow silent; cease; **~оду** F from one's youth; **~яно́й** [14 pitch..., tar...
сморка́ться [1], ⟨вы́-⟩ blow one's nose.
сморо́дина *f* [5] currant(s *pl.*).
смота́ть *s.* сма́тывать.
смотр *m* [1; ⚔ на -у́ & *pl. e.*] review; parade, show; inspection; **~е́ть** [9; -отрю́, -о́тришь; -о́тренный], ⟨по-⟩ look (at на В; after за T), gaze; (re)view, see, watch; examine, inspect; mind (*v/t.* на В); look out; **~я́** it depends (on по Д), according (to); **~е́ть** в о́ба be all eyes; **~и́тель** *m* [4] inspector; (*post*)master.
смочи́ть *s.* сма́чивать.
смрад *m* [1] stench; **~ный** [14; -ден, -дна] stinking.
сму́глый [14; смугл, -а́, -о] swarthy.
смут|и́ть(ся) *s.* смуща́ть(ся); **~ный** [14; -тен, -тна́, -о] vague, dim; restless, uneasy; of unrest.
смущ|а́ть [1], ⟨смути́ть⟩ [15 *e.*; -ущу́, -ути́шь; -ущённый] (-ся be[come]) embarrass(ed), confuse(d), perplex(ed); **~е́ние** *n* [12] embarrassment, confusion; **~ённый** [14] embarrassed.
смы|ва́ть [1], ⟨**~**ть⟩ (22) wash off (*or* away); **~ка́ть** [1], ⟨сомкну́ть⟩ [20] close (*v/i.* -ся); **~сл** *m* [1] sense, meaning; respect; F use; **~слить** F [13] understand; **~ть** *s.* **~ва́ть**; **~чко́вый** [14] ♪ stringed; **~чо́к** *m* [1; -чка́] ♪ bow; **~шлёный** F [14 *sh.*] clever, bright.
смягч|а́ть (-xtʃ-) [1], ⟨~и́ть⟩ [16 *e.*; -чу́, -чи́шь; -чённый] soften (*v/i.* -ся); mitigate, alleviate; extenuate; *phon.* palatalize; -ся *a.* relent; **~а́ющий** ⚖ extenuating; **~е́ние** *n* [12] mitigation; extenuation; palatalization; **~и́ть(ся)** *s.* **~а́ть(ся)**.
смяте́ние *n* [12] confusion.
снаб|жа́ть [1], ⟨~ди́ть⟩ [15 *e.*; -бжу́, -бди́шь; -бжённый] supply, furnish, provide (with T); **~же́ние** *n* [12] supply, provision; purchasing (*dept.*).
сна́йпер *m* [1] sharpshooter.
снару́жи from (the) outside.
снаря́|д shell; missile, projectile; apparatus; tool, equipment; tackle; **~жа́ть** [1], ⟨~ди́ть⟩ [15 *e.*; -яжу́, -яди́шь; -яжённый] equip, fit out (with T); **~же́ние** *n* [12] equipment; munitions *pl.*
снасть *f* [8; *from g/pl. e.*] tackle; rigging.
снача́ла at first; first; over again.
снег *m* [1; в -у́; *pl. e.*: -а́] snow; **~** идёт it is snowing; **~и́рь** *m* [4 *e.*] bullfinch; **~опа́д** *m* [1] snowfall.

снеж|и́нка *f* [5; *g/pl.*: -нок] snowflake; **∠ный** [14; -жен, -жна] snow(y); **∼о́к** *m* [1; -жка́] *dim. of* снег; snowball.
снести́(сь) *s.* сноси́ть(ся).
сни|жа́ть [1], ⟨**∠зить**⟩ [15] lower; reduce, decrease; (**-ся** *v/i.*; *a.* fall; ✈ land); **∼же́ние** *n* [12] lowering; reduction, decrease; fall; landing; **∼зойти́** *s.* **∼сходи́ть**; **∠зу** from below.
сним|а́ть [1], ⟨**снять**⟩ [сниму́, сни́мешь; снял, -á, -o; сня́тый (снят, -á, -o)] take (off, away *or* down); remove, discard, dismiss; withdraw; cut (off); rent; (take a) photograph (of); reap, gather cancel, strike off; deprive (of); release (from с Р); raise (*siege*); strike (*camp*); make (*copy, etc.*); **∼а́ть** сли́вки skim; **-ся** take off; weigh (*anchor* с Р); have a picture of o.s. taken; be struck off (*a list*); **∠ок** *m* [1; -мка] photograph, picture (in на П).
сни́ск|ивать [1], ⟨**∼а́ть**⟩ [3] get, win.
снисхо|ди́тельный [14; -лен, -льна] indulgent; condescending; **∼ди́ть** [15], ⟨снизойти́⟩ [-ойду́, -ойдёшь; *cf.* идти́] condescend; **∼жде́ние** *n* [12] indulgence, leniency; condescension.
сни́ться [13], ⟨**при-**⟩ *impers.*: (Д) dream (of И).
сно́ва (over) again, anew.
сно|ва́ть [7 *e.*] scurry, whisk; **∼виде́ние** *n* [12] vision, dream.
сноп *m* [1 *e.*] sheaf.
сноро́вка *f* [5] knack, skill.
снос|и́ть [15], ⟨снести́⟩ [24 -с-: снесу́; снёс] carry (down, away *or* off, together), take; pull down, demolish; endure, bear, tolerate; *cf. a.* нести́; **-ся**, ⟨**-сь**⟩ communicate (with с Т); get in touch, contact; **∠ка** *f* [5; *g/pl.*: -сок] footnote; **∠ный** [14; -сен, -сна] tolerable.
сноха́ [5; *pl. st.*] daughter-in-law.
сноше́ние *n* [12] (*usu. pl.*) intercourse; relations.
сня́т|ие *n* [12] taking down; raising; removal; dismissal; **∼о́й** [14] skim (*milk*); **∼ь(ся)** *s.* снима́ть(ся).
соба́|ка *f* [5] dog; hound; **∼чий** [18] dog('s).
собесе́дник *m* [1] interlocutor.
собира́т|ель *m* [4] collector; **∼ельный** [14] *gr.* collective; **∼ь** [1], ⟨собра́ть⟩ [-беру́, -рёшь; -áл, -á, -o; со́бранный (-ан, -á, -o)] gather, collect; ⊕ assemble; prepare; **-ся** gather, assemble; prepare, make o.s. *or* be ready to start (*or* set out *or* go; on a journey в путь); be going, intend, collect (*one's thoughts* с Т); brace up (с си́лами).
собла́зн *m* [1] temptation; **∼и́тель** *m* [4] seducer, temper; **∼и́тельный** [14; -лен, -льна] tempting, seductive; **∼и́ть** [28], ⟨**∼и́ть**⟩ [13] (**-ся** be) tempt(ed); seduce(d).
соблю|да́ть [1], ⟨**∼сти́**⟩ [25] observe, obey, adhere (to); maintain (*order*); **∼де́ние** *n* [12] observance; maintenance; **∼сти́** *s.* **∼да́ть**.
соболе́знова|ние *n* [12] condolence; **∼ть** [7] condole (with Д).
со́бо|ль *m* [4; *pl. a.* -ля́, *etc. e.*] sable; **∠р** *m* [1] cathedral; council; diet; **∠ровать(ся)** [7] administer (receive) extreme unction.
собра́|ние *n* [12] meeting (at, in на П), assembly; collection; **∼ть(ся)** *s.* собира́ть(ся).
со́бственн|ик *m* [1] owner, proprietor; **∼ость** *f* [8] property; **∼ый** [14] own; proper; personal; dead (*weight*).
собы́тие *n* [12] event, occurrence.
сова́ *f* [5; *pl. st.*] owl.
сова́ть [7 *e.*; сую́, суёшь], ⟨су́нуть⟩ [20] put; F slip, give; poke (one's nose **-ся**; *a.* butt in).
соверш|а́ть [1], ⟨**∼и́ть**⟩ [16 *e.*; -шу́, -ши́шь; -шённый] accomplish; commit; make (*a. trip*); strike (*bargain*), effect; celebrate, do; **-ся** happen, take place; be effected, *etc.*; **∼еннолéтие** *n* [12] majority, full age; **∼еннолéтний** [15] (стать Т come) of age; **∼е́нный** [14; -е́нен, -е́нна] perfect(ive *gr.*); absolute, complete; *adv. a.* quite; **∼е́нство** *n* [9] perfection; в **∼е́нстве** *a.* perfectly; **∼е́нствовать** [7], ⟨**у-**⟩ perfect (o.s. **-ся**), improve, polish up; **∼и́ть(ся)** *s.* соверша́ть(ся).
со́вест|ливый [14 *sh.*] conscientious; **∼но** (р. Д) ashamed; **∼ь** *f* [8] conscience; по **∼и** honestly.
сове́т *m* [1] advice, counsel; council, board; *USSR a.* soviet; Верхо́вный ♀ Supreme Soviet; **∼ник** *m* [1] council(l)or; **∼овать** [7], ⟨**по-**⟩ advise (р. Д); **-ся** consult, deliberate (on о П); **∼ский** [16] Soviet; **∼чик** *m* [1] adviser.
совеща́|ние *n* [12] conference (at на П), meeting (*a.* in); deliberation, consultation (for на В); **∼тельный** [14] advisory, consultative; **∼ться** [1] confer, consult, deliberate.
совлада́ть F [1] *pf.* (с Т) master.
совме|сти́мый [14 *sh.*] compatible; **∼сти́ть** *s.* **∼ща́ть**; **∠стный** [14] joint, combined; co(*education*); **∠стно** together, conjointly; **∼ща́ть** [1], ⟨**∼сти́ть**⟩ [15 *e.*; -ещу́, ести́шь; -ещённый] combine; unite; reconcile.
сово́к *m* [1; -вка́] scoop.
совоку́пн|ость *f* [8] total(ity), aggregate, whole; **∼ый** [14] joint.
совпа|да́ть [1], ⟨**∠сть**⟩ [25; *pt. st.*] coincide; agree; ⊿ be congruent; **∼де́ние** *n* [12] coincidence, *etc. s. vb.*
совреме́нн|ик *m* [1] contemporary; **∼ый** [14; -е́нен, -е́нна] modern; present-day, up-to-date; *s. a.* **∼ик**.

совсе́м quite, entirely; at all.
совхо́з *m* [1] (сове́тское хозя́йство) state farm; *cf.* колхо́з.
согла́|сие *n* [12] consent (to на В; with с Р); agreement (by по Д); harmony, concord; accordance; **~си́ться** *s.* ~ша́ться; **~сно** (Д) according to, in accordance with; **~сный** [14; -сен, -сна] agreeable, accordant; harmonious; я ~сен (*f* ~сна) I agree (with с Т; to на В); (*a. su.*) consonant; **~сова́ние** *n* [12] coördination; *gr.* agreement, concord; **~сова́ть** *s.* ~со́вывать; **~сова́ться** [7] (*im*)*pf.* (с Т) conform (to); agree (with); **~со́вывать** [1], ‹~сова́ть› [7] coördinate; adjust; (*a. gr.*) make agree; **~ша́тельский** [16] conciliatory; **~ша́ться** [1], ‹~си́ться› [15 *e.*; -ашу́сь, -аси́шься] agree (with с Т; to на В), consent (to), assent; F admit; **~ше́ние** *n* [12] agreement, understanding; consent.
согна́ть *s.* сгоня́ть.
согну́ть(ся) *s.* сгиба́ть(ся).
согре|ва́ть [1], ‹~ть› [8] warm, heat.
соде́йств|ие *n* [12] assistance, help; **~овать** [7] (*im*)*pf.*, *a.* ‹по-› (Д) assist, help, coöperate; contribute (to), further, promote.
содерж|а́ние *n* [12] content(s); maintenance, support, upkeep; cost (at на П); salary; **~а́тель** *m* [4] holder, owner; **~а́тельный** [14; -лен, -льна] pithy, substantial; **~а́ть** [4] contain, hold; maintain, support; keep; **-ся** be contained, *etc.*; **~и́мое** *n* [14] contents *pl.*
содра́ть *s.* сдира́ть.
содрог|а́ние *n* [12], **~а́ться** [1], *once* ‹~ну́ться› [20] shudder.
содру́жество *n* [9] community.
соедин|е́ние *n* [12] union, junction, (at *a.* на П), connection; combination; ⚗ compound; ⚔ formation; **~и́тельный** [14] connective; *gr. a.* copulative; **~я́ть** [28], ‹~и́ть› [13] unite, join; (*a. teleph.*) connect; (*a.* ⚗) combine; (*v/i.* **-ся**); *cf.* США.
сожал|е́ние *n* [12] regret (for о П); pity (on к Д); к ~е́нию unfortunately, to (p.'s) regret; **~е́ть** [8] (о П) regret.
сожже́ние *n* [12] burning.
сожи́тельство *n* [9] cohabitation.
созв|а́ть *s.* созыва́ть; **~е́здие** *n* [12] constellation; **~они́ться** F [13] *pf.* (с Т) phone; **~у́чный** [14; -чен, -чна] conformable, accordant; concordant.
созда|ва́ть [5], ‹~ть› [-да́м, -да́шь *etc.*, *cf.* дать; со́здал, -а́, -о; со́зданный (-ан, -а́, -о)] create; produce; build up; prepare; **-ся** arise, form; **~ние** *n* [12] creation; creature; **~тель** *m* [4] creator; founder; **~ть** (**-ся**) *s.* ~ва́ть(ся).
созерца́т|ельный [14; -лен, -льна] contemplative; **~ь** [1] contemplate.
созида́тельный [14; -лен, -льна] creative.
созна|ва́ть [5], ‹~ть› [1] realize (*Brt.* realise), see; **-ся** (в П) confess, avow, own; **~ние** *n* [12] consciousness; realization, perception, awareness; confession (of в П); без ~ния unconscious; **~тельный** [14; -лен, -льна] conscious; class conscious; conscientious; **~ть(ся)** *s.* ~ва́ть(ся).
созы́в *m* [1] convocation; **~а́ть** [1], ‹созва́ть› [созову́, -вёшь; -зва́л, -а́, -о; со́званный] call, invite; convoke, convene, summon.
соизмери́мый [14 *sh.*] commensurable.
сойти́(сь) *s.* сходи́ть(ся).
сок *m* [1; в -у́] juice; sap.
со́кол *m* [1] falcon.
сокра|ща́ть [1], ‹~ти́ть› [15 *e.*; -ащу́, -ати́шь; -ащённый] shorten; abbreviate; abridge; reduce, curtail; *p. pt. p. a.* short, brief; **-ся** decrease, shorten; contract; **~ще́ние** *n* [12] abbreviation; reduction, curtailment; abridg(e)ment; contraction.
сокров|е́нный [14 *sh.*] secret; **~и́ще** *n* [11] treasure; F darling; **~и́щница** *f* [5] treasury, thesaurus.
сокруш|а́ть [1], ‹~и́ть› [16 *e.*; -шу́, -ши́шь; -шённый] smash, break; distress, afflict; **-ся** *impf.* grieve, be distressed; **~е́ние** *n* [12] destruction; distress, contrition; **~и́тельный** [14; -лен, -льна] shattering; **~и́ть** *s.* ~а́ть.
солда́т *m* [1; *g/pl.*: солда́т] soldier; **~ский** [16] soldier's.
сол|е́ние *n* [12] salting; **~ёный** [14; со́лон, -а́, -о] salt(y); saline; pickled; corned; *fig.* spicy.
солида́рн|ость *f* [8] solidarity; **~ый** [14; -рен, -рна] solidary; in sympathy with.
соли́дн|ость *f* [8] solidity; **~ый** [14; -ден, -дна] solid, firm, sound; respectable.
соли́ст *m* [1], **~ка** *f* [5; *g/pl.*: -ток] soloist.
солитёр *m* [1] tapeworm.
соли́ть [13; солю́, со́ли́шь; со́ленный] **1.** ‹по-› salt; **2.** ‹за-› pickle.
со́лн|ечный [14; -чен, -чна] sun(-ny); solar; **~це** ('sɔn-) *n* [11] sun (*lie* in на П).
со́лод *m* [1], **~о́вый** [14] malt.
солове́й *m* [3; -вья́] nightingale.
соло́м|а *f* [5] straw; thatch; **~енный** [14] straw...; thatched; grass (*widow*[*er*]); **~инка** *f* [5; *g/pl.*: -нок] straw.
солони́на *f* [5] corned beef.
соло́нка *f* [5; *g/pl.*: -нок] saltcellar.
сол|ь *f* [8; *from g/pl. e.*] salt (*a. fig.*); F point; **~яно́й** [14] salt...; hydrochloric (*acid*).
сом *m* [1 *e.*] catfish, sheatfish.

сомкну́ть(ся) *s.* смыка́ть(ся).

сомн|ева́ться [1], ⟨усомни́ться⟩ [13] (в П) doubt; **~е́ние** *n* [12] doubt (about в П); question (in под Т); **~и́тельный** [14; -лен, -льна] doubtful; dubious.

сон *m* [1; сна] sleep; dream (in во П); **~ли́вый** [14 *sh.*] sleepy; **~ный** [14] sleeping (*a.* ⚕); sleepy, drowsy; soporific; **~я** F *m/f* [6; *g/pl.*: -ней] sleepyhead; **'2я** *f* [6] *dim. of* Со́фья.

сообра|жа́ть [1], ⟨~зи́ть⟩ [15 *e.*; -ажу́, -ази́шь; -ажённый] consider, weigh, think (over); grasp, understand; **~же́ние** *n* [12] consideration; reason; grasp, understanding; **~зи́тельный** [14; -лен, -льна] sharp, quick-witted; **~зи́ть** *s.* ~жа́ть; **~зный** [14; -зен, -зна] conformable (to с Т); *adv. a.* according (to); **~зова́ть** [7] (*im*)*pf.* (make) conform, adapt (to с Т), coördinate (with); **-ся** conform (to с Т).

сообща́ together, conjointly.

сообщ|а́ть [1], ⟨~и́ть⟩ [16 *e.*; -щу́, -щи́шь; -щённый] communicate (*v/i.* **-ся** *impf.*), report; inform (p. of Д/о П); impart; **~е́ние** *n* [12] communication; report, statement, announcement, information; **~ество** *n* [9] community; company; **~и́ть** *s.* ~а́ть; **~ник** *m* [1], **~ница** *f* [5] accomplice.

сооору|жа́ть [1], ⟨~ди́ть⟩ [15 *e.*; -ужу́, -уди́шь; -ужённый] build, construct, erect, raise; **~же́ние** *n* [12] construction, building, structure.

соотве́тств|енный [14 *sh.*] corresponding; *adv. a.* according(ly) (to Д), in accordance (with); **~ие** *n* [12] conformity. accordance; **~овать** [7] (Д) correspond, conform (to), agree, comply (with); **~ующий** [17] corresponding, respective; suitable.

соотечественни|к *m* [1], **~ца** *f* [5] compatriot,fellow country(wo)man.

соотноше́ние *n* [12] correlation.

сопе́рни|к *m* [1] rival; **~чать** [1] compete, rival, vie; be a match (for с Т); **~чество** *n* [9] rivalry.

соп|е́ть [10 *e.*; соплю́, сопи́шь] wheeze; **~ли** P *pl.* [6; *gen.*: -ле́й, *etc. e.*] snot; **~ля́к** P *m* [1 *e.*] snot nose.

сопостав|ле́ние *n* [12] comparison; **~ля́ть** [28], ⟨~вить⟩ [14] compare.

сопри|каса́ться [1], ⟨~косну́ться⟩ [20] (с Т) adjoin; (get in) touch (with); **~коснове́ние** *n* [12] contact, touch.

сопрово|ди́тельный [14] covering (*letter*); **~жда́ть** [1] **1.** accompany; escort; **2.** ⟨~ди́ть⟩ [15 *e.*; -ожу́, -оди́шь; -ождённый] provide (with Т); **-ся** *impf.* be accompanied (by Т); entail; **~жде́ние** *n* [12] accompaniment; в **~жде́нии** (Р) accompanied (by).

сопротивл|е́ние *n* [12] resistance; **~я́ться** [28] (Д) resist, oppose.

сопряжённый [14; -жён, -жена́] connected.

сопу́тствовать [7] (Д) accompany.

сор *m* [1] rubbish, litter.

соразме́рно in proportion (to Д).

сора́тник *m* [1] brother-in-arms.

сорв|ане́ц F *m* [1; -нца́] madcap (fellow); **~а́ть(ся)** *s.* срыва́ть(ся); **~иголова́** F *m/f* [5; *ac/sg.*: сорвиголову́; *pl. s.* голова́] daredevil.

соревнова́|ние *n* [12] competition; contest; emulation; **~ться** [7] (с Т) compete (with); emulate.

сор|и́ть [13], ⟨на-⟩ litter; make dirty; **~ный** [14]: **~ная трава́** *f* = **~ня́к** *m* [1 *e.*] weed.

со́рок [35] forty; **~а** *f* [5] magpie.

сороко|во́й [14] fortieth; *cf.* пя́т(идеся́т)ый; **~но́жка** *f* [5; *g/pl.*: -жек] centipede.

соро́чка *f* [5; *g/pl.*: -чек] (under-) shirt.

сорт *m* [1; *pl.*: -та́, *etc. e.*] sort; quality; **~ирова́ть** [7], ⟨рас-⟩ (as-) sort; **~иро́вка** *f* [5] (as)sorting; **~иро́вочный** [14] 🚂 switching.

соса́ть [-су́, -сёшь; со́санный] suck.

сосе́д *m* [*sg.*: 1; *pl.*: 4], **~ка** *f* [5; *g/pl.*: -док] neighbo(u)r; **~ний** [15] neighbo(u)ring, adjoining; **~ский** [16] neighbo(u)r's; **~ство** *n* [9] neighbo(u)rhood.

соси́ска *f* [5; *g/pl.*: -сок] sausage.

со́ска *f* [5; *g/pl.*: -сок] (baby's) dummy.

соск|а́кивать [1], ⟨~очи́ть⟩ [16] jump *or* spring (off, down); **~а́льзывать** [1], ⟨~ользну́ть⟩ [20] slide (down, off); slip (off); **~у́читься** [16] *pf.* become bored; *s.* скуча́ть.

сосл|ага́тельный [14] *gr.* subjunctive; **~а́ть(ся)** *s.* ссыла́ть(ся); **~о́вие** *n* [12] estate, class; **~ужи́вец** *m* [1; -вца] colleague.

сосна́ *f* [5; *pl. st.*: со́сны, со́сен, со́снам] pine.

сосо́к *m* [1; -ска́] nipple, teat.

сосредото́ч|ение *n* [12] concentration; **~ивать** [1], ⟨~ить⟩ [16] concentrate (*v/i.* **-ся**); *p.pt.p. a.* intent.

соста́в *m* [1] composition, structure; body; (ли́чный ~) staff; рядово́й ~ rank & file; strength (of в П); *thea.* cast; 🚂 stock; ⚖ facts *pl.*; ⚗ solution, mixture; в ~е (Р) *a.* consisting of; **~и́тель** *m* [4] compiler, author; **~ить** *s.* ~ля́ть; **~ле́ние** *n* [12] composition; compilation; drawing up; **~ля́ть** [28], ⟨~ить⟩ [14] compose, make (up); put together, arrange; draw up, work out; compile; form, constitute; amount (*or* come) to; **~но́й** [14] composite, compound; component, constituent (*part*; **~на́я часть** *f a.* ingredient).

состоя́|ние *n* [12] state, condition; status, station; position; fortune;

быть в ~нии ... *a.* be able to ...; **~тельный** [14; -лен, -льна] well-to-do, well-off; solvent; valid, sound, well-founded; **~ть** [-ою́, -ои́шь] consist (of из P; in в П); be (*a.* T); occupy (*position* в П), work (with при П); **-ся** *pf.* take place; come about.
сострада́ние *n* [12] compassion.
состяза́|ние *n* [12] contest, competition; match; **~ться** [1] compete, vie, contend.
сосу́д *m* [1] vessel.
сосу́лька *f* [5; *g/pl.*: -лек] icicle.
сосуществова́|ние *n* [12] coexistence; **~ть** [7] coexist.
сотворе́ние *n* [12] creation.
со́тня *f* [6; *g/pl.*: -тен] a hundred.
сотру́дни|к *m* [1] collaborator; employee, member; *pl.* staff; contributor; colleague; **~чать** [1] collaborate, coöperate; **~чество** *n* [9] collaboration, coöperation.
сотрясе́ние *n* [12] concussion.
со́ты *m/pl.* [1] honeycomb(s); **~й** [14] hundredth; *cf.* пя́тый; две це́лых и два́дцать пять ~х 2.25.
со́ус *m* [1] sauce; gravy.
соуча́ст|ие *n* [12] complicity; **~ник** *m* [1] accomplice.
соучени́к *m* [1 *e.*] schoolmate.
Со́фья *f* [6] Sophia.
соха́ *f* [5; *pl. st.*] (wooden) plow, plough.
со́хнуть [21] **1.** ⟨вы́-⟩ dry; **2.** ⟨за-⟩ fade, wither; **3.** F *impf.* pine away.
сохран|е́ние *n* [12] preservation, conservation; charge (*give* into, *take* ... of на В); **~я́ть(ся)** *s.* **~я́ть** (-ся); **∠ность** *f* [8] safety; integrity; в ∠ности *a.* safe; **~я́ть** [28], ⟨**~и́ть**⟩ [13] keep; preserve; retain; maintain; reserve (to o.s. за собо́й); (*God*) forbid!; **-ся** be preserved; keep (safe, *etc.*).
социа́л|-демокра́т *m* [1] Social Democrat; **~-демократи́ческий** [16] Social Democrat(ic); **~и́зм** *m* [1] socialism; **~и́ст** *m* [1] socialist; **~исти́ческий** [16] socialist(ic); **~ьный** [14] social.
соц|соревнова́ние *n* [12] socialist competition (*Sov.*); **~стра́х** *m* [1] social insurance (*Sov.*).
соче́льник *m* [1] (Xmas) Eve.
сочета́|ние *n* [12] combination; union; **~ть** [1] combine (*v/i.* **-ся**); unite (in T).
сочин|е́ние *n* [12] composition; writing, work; thesis; *gr.* parataxis, coördination; **~и́тель** *m* [4] author; **~я́ть** [28], ⟨**~и́ть**⟩ [13] compose, write; invent; *gr.* coördinate.
соч|и́ться [16 *e.*; *3rd. p. only*] ooze (out); ~и́ться кро́вью bleed; **∠ный** [14; -чен, -чна́, -о] juicy; rich.
сочу́вств|енный [14 *sh.*] sympathetic, sympathizing; **~ие** *n* [12] sympathy (with, for к Д); **~овать** [7] (Д) sympathyze, feel with; approve (of); **~ующий** *m* [17] sympathizer.
сою́з *m* [1] union; alliance; confederacy; league; *gr.* conjunction; Сове́тский ♀ Soviet Union; *cf.* СССР; **~ник** *m* [1] ally; **~ный** [14] allied; (of the) Union (*Sov.*).
со́я *f* [6] soy(bean).
спа|да́ть [1], ⟨**~сть**⟩ [25; *pt. st.*] fall (down); **∠ивать 1.** ⟨**~я́ть**⟩ [28] solder; **2.** F ⟨спои́ть⟩ [13] make drunk; **∠йка** *f* [5] solder(ing); **∠лзывать** *s.* сполза́ть.
спа́льн|ый [14] sleeping; bed...; **~я** *f* [6; *g/pl.*: -лен] bedroom.
спа́ржа *f* [5] asparagus.
спас|а́тельный [14] life...; **~а́ть** [1], ⟨**~ти́**⟩ [24 -с-] save, rescue; redeem; **-ся**, ⟨-сь⟩ *a.* escape (*v/t.* от Р); **~е́ние** *n* [12] rescue; redemption.
спаси́бо (вам) thank you (very much большо́е ~), thanks (for за В, на П).
спаси́тель *m* [4] savio(u)r, rescuer; **~ный** [14] saving.
спас|ти́ *s.* **~а́ть**; **~ть** *s.* спада́ть.
спать [сплю, спишь; спал, -а́, -о] sleep; (*a.* идти́, ложи́ться ~) go to bed; мне не спи́тся F I can't sleep.
спая́ть *s.* спа́ивать 1.
спека́ться [1] F *s.* запека́ться; ⊕ conglomerate.
спекта́кль *m* [4] performance.
спекул|и́ровать [7] speculate (with T); **~я́нт** *m* [1] speculator.
спе́лый [14; спел, -а́, -о] ripe.
сперва́ F (at) first.
спе́реди in (from) front (*as prp.*: P).
спёртый F [14 *sh.*] stuffy, close.
спеси́вый [14 *sh.*] haughty.
спеть [8], ⟨по-⟩ ripen; *s. a.* петь.
спех F *m* [1] haste, hurry.
специ|ализи́роваться [7] (*im*)*pf.* specialize (in в П, по Д) **~али́ст** *m* [1] specialist, expert (in по Д); **~а́льность** *f* [8] special(i)ty, line, profession (by по Д); **~а́льный** [14; -лен, -льна] special; express; **~фи́ческий** [16] specific.
спецоде́жда *f* [5] overalls *pl.*
спеш|и́ть [16 *e.*; -шу́, -ши́шь] hurry (up), hasten; *clock*: be fast (5 min. на 5 мину́т); **∠иться** [16] *pf.* dismount; **∠ка** F *f* [5] haste, hurry; **∠ный** [14; -шен, -шна] urgent, pressing; special, express.
спин|а́ *f* [5; *ac/sg.*: спи́ну; *pl. st.*] back; **∠ка** *f* [5; *g/pl.*: -нок] back (*of chair, etc.*); **~но́й** [14] spinal (cord мозг *m*); vertebral (column хребе́т *m*), back(*bone*).
спира́ль *f* [8], **~ный** [14] spiral.
спирт *m* [1; *a.* в -у́; *pl. e.*] spirit(s *pl.*), alcohol; **~но́й** [14] alcoholic, strong (*drink*).
спис|а́ть *s.* **∠ывать**; **∠ок** *m* [1; -ска] list, register; copy; **∠ывать** [1],

⟨**~а́ть**⟩ [3] copy; write (off); plagiarize, crib; ♣ pay off.
спи́х|ивать [1], *once* ⟨**~ну́ть**⟩ F [20] push (down, aside).
спи́ца *f* [5] spoke; knitting needle.
спи́чка *f* [5; *g/pl.*: -чек] match.
сплав *m* [1] alloy; float(ing); **~ля́ть** [28], ⟨**~и́ть**⟩ [14] float; alloy.
спла́чивать [1], ⟨сплоти́ть⟩ [15 *e.*; -очу́, -оти́шь; -очённый] rally (*v/i.* -ся); fasten.
сплет|а́ть [1], ⟨сплести́⟩ [25 -т-] plait, braid; (inter)lace; F invent; **~е́ние** *n* [12] interlacement, texture; **~ник** *m* [1], **~ница** *f* [5] scandalmonger; **~ничать** [1], ⟨на-⟩ gossip; **~ня** *f* [6; *g/pl.*: -тен] gossip; *pl.* scandal.
спло|ти́ть(ся) *s.* **спла́чивать(ся)**; **~хова́ть** F [7] *pf.* blunder; **~че́ние** *n* [12] rallying; **~шно́й** [14] solid, compact; sheer, complete; continuous; **~шь** throughout, entirely, everywhere; quite often.
сплю́щить [16] *pf.* flatten.
сподви́жник *s.* сора́тник.
спои́ть *s.* спа́ивать 2.
споко́й|ный [14; -о́ен, -о́йна] calm, quiet, tranquil; composed; **~но** F *s.* сме́ло F; **~ной но́чи!** good night!; бу́дьте **~ны!** don't worry!; **~ствие** *n* [12] calm(ness), tranquility; composure; peace, order.
сполз|а́ть [1], ⟨**~ти́**⟩ [24] climb *or* slip (down, off).
сполна́ ... wholly, whole ..., total ...
сполосну́ть [20] *pf.* rinse.
спор *m* [1] dispute, controversy, argument; wrangle, quarrel; **~у** нет no doubt; **~ить** [13], ⟨по-⟩ dispute, argue, debate; quarrel; F bet; *poet.* fight; **~иться** F [13] succeed, get along; **~ный** [14; -рен, -рна] disputable, questionable.
спорт *m* [1] sport; лы́жный **~** skiing; **~и́вный** [14] sporting, athletic; sport(s)...; **~сме́н** *m* [1] sportsman; **~сме́нка** *f* [5; *g/pl.*: -нок] sportswoman.
спо́соб *m* [1] method, means; manner, way (in T); directions *pl.* (for *use* P); **~ность** *f* [8] (cap)ability (for к Д), talent; faculty; capacity; power; quality; **~ный** [14; -бен, -бна] (к Д) able, talented, clever (at); capable (of; *a.* на В); **~ствовать** [7], ⟨по-⟩ (Д) promote, further, contribute to.
спот|ыка́ться [1], ⟨**~кну́ться**⟩ [20] stumble (over о В).
спохва́т|ываться [1], ⟨**~и́ться**⟩ [15] bethink o.s.
спра́ва on, to (*or* from) the right.
справедли́в|ость *f* [8] justice; truth; по **~ости** by rights; **~ый** [14 *sh.*] just, fair; true, right.
спра́в|ить(ся) *s.* **~ля́ть(ся)**; **~ка** *f* [5; *g/pl.*: -вок] inquiry (make наводи́ть); information; certificate; **~ля́ть** [28], ⟨**~ить**⟩ [14] F celebrate; make (*holiday*); **-ся** inquire (after, about о П); consult (*v/t.* в П); (с Т) manage, cope with; **~очник** *m* [1] reference book, vade mecum; directory; guide; **~очный** [14] (of) information, inquiry; reference...
спра́шива|ть [1], ⟨спроси́ть⟩ [15] ask (р. *a.* у Р; for, s.th. *a.* Р), inquire; demand; (с Р) be taken to account; **-ся** *s.* проси́ться; **~ется** one may ask.
спрос *m* [1] demand (for на В); без **~а** *or* **~у** F without permission; **~и́ть(ся)** *s.* спра́шивать(ся).
спросо́нок F half asleep.
спроста́ F unintentionally, innocently.
спры́|гивать [1], *once* ⟨**~гнуть**⟩ [20] jump down (*or* off); **~скивать** [1], ⟨**~снуть**⟩ [20] sprinkle; F wet.
спря|га́ть [1], ⟨про-⟩ *gr.* (-ся *impf.* be) conjugate(d); **~же́ние** *n* [12] *gr.* conjugation.
спус|к *m* [1] lowering; descent; slope; launch(ing); drain(ing); *fig.* F quarter; **~ка́ть** [1], ⟨**~ти́ть**⟩ [15] lower, let down; launch; drain; unchain, set free; pull (*trigger*); slacken; F pardon; lose, gamble away; **-ся** go (*or* come) down(*stairs* по Д), descend; slip down, sink; **~тя́** (В) later, after.
спу́тни|к *m* [1], **~ца** *f* [5] fellow travel(l)er; (*life's*) companion; **~к** *ast.* satellite.
спя́чка *f* [5] hibernation; sleep.
ср. *abbr.*: сравни́ compare, cf.
сравн|е́ние *n* [12] comparison (in/with по Д/с Т); compare; simile; **~ивать** [1] 1. ⟨**~и́ть**⟩ [13] compare (to, with с Т; *v/i.* -ся); 2. ⟨**~я́ть**⟩ [28] level; equalize; **~и́тельный** [14] comparative; **~и́ть(ся)** *s.* **~ивать(ся)**; **~я́ть** *s.* **~ивать** 2.
сра|жа́ть [1], ⟨**~зи́ть**⟩ [15 *e.*; -ажу́, -ази́шь; -ажённый] smite; overwhelm; overtake; **-ся** fight, battle; F contend, play; **~же́ние** *n* [12] battle; **~зи́ть(ся)** *s.* **~жа́ть(ся)**.
сра́зу at once; at one stroke.
срам *m* [1] shame, disgrace; **~и́ть** [14 *e.*; -млю́, -ми́шь], ⟨о-⟩ [осрамлённый] disgrace, shame, compromise; **-ся** bring shame upon o.s.
сраст|а́ться [1], ⟨**~и́сь**⟩ [24 -ст-; сро́сся, сросла́сь] grow together, knit.
сред|а́ *f* 1. [5; *ac/sg.*: сре́ду; *nom/pl. st.*] Wednesday (on: в В, *pl.*: по Д); 2. [5; *ac/sg.*: -ду́; *pl. st.*] environment, surroundings *pl.*, sphere; medium; midst; **~и́** (Р) among; in the middle (of), amid(st); **~иземный** [14], **~иземномо́рский** [16] Mediterranean; **~невеко́вый** [14] medieval; **~ний** [15] middle; medium...; central; middling; average... (on в П); ⅋ mean; *gr.* neuter; secondary (*school*).

средото́чие *n* [12] center (*Brt.* -tre).
сре́дство *n* [9] means (within [beyond] one's [не] по Д *pl.*); remedy; ⚕ agent; *pl. a.* facilities.
срез|а́ть & **∠ывать** [1], ⟨∠ать⟩ [3] cut off; F cut short; fail (*v/i.* **-ся**).
сровня́ть *s.* сра́внивать 2.
сро́д|ный [14; -ден, -дна] related, cognate; **~ство́** *n* [9] affinity.
сро|к *m* [1] term (for/of T/на B), date, deadline; time (in, on в B, к Д), period; **∠чный** [14; -чен, -чна́, -о] urgent, pressing; timed.
сруб|а́ть [1], ⟨**~и́ть**⟩ [14] cut down, fell; carpenter, build.
сры|в *m* [1] frustration; failure, breakdown; breaking up; **~ва́ть** [1] **1.** ⟨сорва́ть⟩ [-ву́, -вёшь; сорва́л, -а́, -о; со́рванный] tear off; pluck, pick; F break up, disrupt, frustrate; vent; **-ся** (с Р) come off; break away (*or* loose); fall down; F dart off; escape; fail, go wrong; **2.** ⟨**~ть**⟩ [22] level, raze to the ground.
сса́дин|на *f* [5] graze, abrasion; **∠ть** [15] *pf.* graze; make alight; drop.
ссо́р|а *f* [5] quarrel; altercation; variance (at в П); **~иться** [13], ⟨по-⟩ quarrel, fall out.
СССР (Сою́з Сове́тских Социалисти́ческих Респу́блик) U.S.S.R. (Union of Soviet Socialist Republics).
ссу́д|а *f* [5] loan; **~и́ть** [15] *pf.* lend; **~ный** [14] loan...
ссыл|а́ть [1], ⟨сосла́ть⟩ [сошлю́, -лёшь; со́сланный] exile, banish; **-ся** (на B) refer to, cite; **∠ка** *f* [5; *g/pl.*: -лок] exile; deportation; reference (to на B); **∠ьный** [14] exiled (p.).
ссыпа́|ть [1], ⟨**'~ть**⟩ [2] pour, sack.
ст. *abbr.*: **1.** столе́тие; **2.** ста́нция; **3.** ста́рший.
стабил|из(и́р)ова́ть [7] (*im*)*pf.* stabilize; **∠ьный** [14; -лен, -льна] stable.
ста́вень *m* [4; -вня] shutter.
ста́в|ить [14], ⟨по-⟩ put, place, set, stand; (*clock, etc.*) set; put (*or* set) up; stake, (на B) back; *thea.* stage; ⚔ billet; make (*conditions, etc.*); drive; cite; impute (в B); bring (to p.'s *notice* B/в B); give; organize; value, esteem; F appoint, engage; **~ка** *f* [5; *g/pl.*: -вок] rate; wage, salary; stake; (head)quarters *pl.*; *fig.* hope; о́чная **~ка** confrontation; **~ленник** *m* [1] protegé; **~ня** *f* [6; *g/pl.*: -вен] *s.* **~ень.**
стадио́н *m* [1] stadium (in на П).
ста́дия *f* [7] stage.
ста́до *n* [9; *pl. e.*] herd; flock.
стаж *m* [1] length of service.
стака́н *m* [1] glass.
сталелите́йный [14] steel (*mill.*).
ста́лкивать [1], ⟨столкну́ть⟩ [20] push (off, down, together); **-ся** (с T) collide, run into; come across.
сталь *f* [8] steel; **~но́й** [14] steel...
стаме́ска *f* [5; *g/pl.*: -сок] chisel.
стан *m* [1] figure; camp; ⊕ mill.
станда́рт *m* [1] standard; **~ный** [14; -тен, -тна] standard...; prefabricated.
стани́ца *f* [5] Cossack village.
станови́ться [14], ⟨стать⟩ [ста́ну, -нешь] stand; (T) become, grow, get; step, place o. s., get, stop; ~ в о́чередь line, *Brt.* queue up; *pf.* begin; will; feel (*better*); во что́ бы то ни ста́ло at all costs, at any cost.
стано́к *m* [1; -нка́] machine; lathe; press; bench; тка́цкий ~ loom.
станци|о́нный [14] station...; waiting; post(*master*); **'~я** *f* [7] station (at на П); *teleph.* office, exchange; 🚂 *a.* yard; узлова́я **'~я** junction.
ста́птывать [1], ⟨стопта́ть⟩ [3] tread down; wear out.
стара́|ние *n* [12] pains *pl.*, care(ful effort); endeavo(u)r, trouble; **~тельный** [14; -лен, -льна] assiduous, diligent; careful; **~ться** [1], ⟨по-⟩ endeavo(u)r, try (hard); strive (for о П).
стар|е́ть [21] **1.** ⟨по-⟩ grow old, age; **2.** ⟨у-⟩ grow obsolete; **∠ец** *m* [1; -рца] (old) monk; *a.* = **~и́к** *m* [1 *e.*] old man; **~ина́** *f* [5] olden time *or* days (of yore) (in в B); F old man; **~и́нный** [14] ancient, antique; old; longstanding; **∠ить** [13], ⟨со-⟩ make (**-ся** grow) old.
старо|мо́дный [14; -ден, -дна] old-fashioned, out-of-date; **'~ста** *m* [5] (*village*) elder; (*church*) warden; (*class*) monitor; **'~сть** *f* [8] old age (in one's на П лет).
стартова́ть [7] (*im*)*pf.* start.
стар|у́ха *f* [5] old woman; **∠ческий** [16] senile; **∠ший** [17] elder, older, senior; eldest, oldest; higher, highest; fore(*man*); first (*lieutenant*); **~шина́** *m* [5] foreman; chairman, manager; ⚔ first sergeant (*or*, ⚓, mate); **~шинство́** *n* [9] seniority.
ста́р|ый [14; стар, -а́, -о] old; ancient, antique; olden; **~ьё** *n* [10] second-hand articles *pl.*; junk, *Brt.* lumber.
ста́|скивать [1], ⟨**~щи́ть**⟩ [16] pull (off, down); take, bring.
стати́ст *m* [1], **~ка** *f* [5; *g/pl.*: -ток] *thea.* supernumerary; *film*: extra; **~ика** *f* [5] statistics; **~и́ческий** [16] statistical.
ста́т|ный [14; -тен, -тна́, -о] stately, portly; **~уя** [6; *g/pl.*: -уй] statue; **~ь**[1] *f* [8] build; trait; F need, seemly; с како́й **~и**? F why (should I, *etc.*).
стать[2] *s.* станови́ться; **~ся** F (*impers.*) happen (to с T); (*may*)be.
статья́ *f* [6; *g/pl.*: -те́й] article; item, entry; F matter, business (another осо́бая).
стаха́новец *m* [1; -вца] Stakhanovite.

стационáрный [14] stationary.
стáчка *f* [5; *g/pl.*: -чек] strike.
стащúть *s.* стáскивать.
стáя *f* [6; *g/pl.*: стай] flight, flock; | shoal; pack, troop.
стáять [27] *pf.* thaw off, melt.
ствол *m* [1 *e.*] trunk; barrel.
створчатый [14] folding (*doors*).
стéбель *m* [4; -бля; *from g/pl. e.*] stalk, stem.
стёганый [14] quilted.
стегáть [1] 1. ⟨вы́-, про-⟩ quilt; 2. *once* ⟨стегнýть⟩ [20] whip.
сте|кáть [1], ⟨~чь⟩ [26] flow (down); -ся join; flock, gather.
стек|лó *n* [9; *pl.*: стёкла, стёкол, стёклам] glass; pane; (*lamp*) chimney; **~лянный** [14] glass...; glassy; **~óльщик** *m* [1] glazier.
стел|и́ть(ся) F *s.* стлать(ся); **~лáж** *m* [1 *e.*] shelf; **∠ька** *f* [5; *g/pl.*: -лек] inner sole; **∠ьный** [14]: **~ьная** корóва cow with calf.
стен|á *f* [5; *ac/sg.*: стéну; *pl.*: стéны, стен, стенáм] wall; **~газéта** *f* [5] (стеннáя газéта) wall newspaper; **∠ка** *f* [5; *g/pl.*: -нок] wall; **~нóй** [14] wall...
стеногрá|мма *f* [5] shorthand (verbatim) report *or* notes *pl.*; **~фи́ст** *m* [1], **~фи́стка** *f* [5; *g/pl.*: -ток] stenographer; **~фия** *f* [7] shorthand.
Степáн *m* [1] Stephen.
степéнный [14; -éнен, -éнна] sedate, staid, grave, dignified; mature.
стéпень *f* [8; *from g/pl. e.*] degree (to до Р), extent; ⅍ power.
степ|нóй [14] steppe...; **~ь** *f* [8; в -пи́; *from g/pl. e.*] steppe.
стéрва P *contp.* *f* [5] damned wretch.
стере|оти́пный [14; -пен, -пна] stereotyped; **∠ть** *s.* стирáть
стерéчь [26 г/ж: -егý, -ежёшь; -ёг, -еглá] guard, watch (over).
стéржень *m* [4; -жня] core (*a. fig.*); pivot.
стерил|изовáть [7] (*im*)*pf.* sterilize; **∠ьный** [14; -лен, -льна] sterile.
стерпéть [10] *pf.* endure, bear.
стесн|éние *n* [12] constraint, restraint; **~и́тельный** [14; -лен, -льна] constraining, embarrassing; **~я́ть** [28], ⟨~и́ть⟩ [13] constrain, restrain; embarrass, hamper; cramp; trouble, press; **~я́ться**, ⟨по-⟩ feel (*or* be) shy, self-conscious *or* embarrassed; (Р) be ashamed of; hesitate.
стеч|éние *n* [12] confluence; coincidence; **~ь(ся)** *s.* стекáть(ся).
стиль *m* [4] style; (*Old*, *New*) Style.
стипéндия *f* [7] scholarship.
стир|áльный [14] washing; **~áть** [1] 1. ⟨стерéть⟩ [12; сотрý, -трёшь; стёр(ла); стёрши & стерéв] wipe *or* rub off, out; erase, efface, blot out; clean; pulverize; 2. ⟨вы́-⟩ wash, launder; **∠ка** *f* [5] wash(ing), laundry; отдáть в **∠ку** send to the wash.
стáс|кивать [1], ⟨~нуть⟩ [20] clench; grasp, press.
стих (*a.* **~и́** *pl.*) *m* [1 *e.*] verse; *pl. a.* poem(s); **~áть** [1], ⟨∠нуть⟩ [21] abate; fall; cease; calm down, (become) quiet; **~и́йный** [14; -и́ен, -и́йна] elemental; spontaneous; natural; **~и́я** *f* [7] element(s); **∠нуть** *s.* **~áть**.
стихотворéние *n* [12] poem.
стлать & F **стели́ть** [стелю́, -стéлешь], ⟨по-⟩ [пóстланный] spread, lay; make (*bed*); -ся *impf.* (be) spread; drift; ♣ creep.
сто [35] hundred.
стог *m* [1; в стóге & в стогý; *pl.*: -á, *etc. e.*] stack, rick.
стóи|мость *f* [8] cost; value, worth (... Т/в В); **~ть** [13] cost; be worth; pay; take, require; (Д) need, if (*only*); matter; не **~т** F = нé за что.
стой! stop!, halt!; **∠ка** *f* [5; *g/pl.*: стóек] stand(ard); support; counter; **∠кий** [16; стóек, стойкá, -о; *comp.*: стóйче] firm, steadfast, steady; **∠кость** *f* [8] firmness; **∠ло** *n* [9] box (stall); **~мя́** upright.
сток *m* [1] flowing (off); drain.
Стокгóльм *m* [1] Stockholm.
стокрáтный [14] hundredfold.
стол *m* [1 *e.*] table (at за Т); board, fare; meal; office, bureau; *hist.* throne.
столб *m* [1 *e.*] post, pole; column; pillar; **~енéть** [8], ⟨о-⟩ petrify; **~éц** *m* [1; -бцá], **∠ик** *m* [1] column; **~ня́к** *m* [1 *e.*] stupor; tetanus; **~овóй** [14]: **~овáя** дорóга *f* highway.
столéтие *n* [12] century; centenary.
стóлик *m* [1] *dim. of* стол; F table.
столи́|ца *f* [5] capital; **~чный** [14] metropolitan.
столкн|овéние *n* [12] collision, clash; **~ýть(ся)** *s.* стáлкивать(ся).
столóв|ая *f* [14] dining room; restaurant; **~ый** [14] table(*spoon*); dinner (*service*).
столп *m* [1 *e.*] pillar; column.
столь so; **∠ко** [32] so much, so many; **∠ко** же as much *or* many.
столя́р *m* [1 *e.*] joiner; cabinetmaker; **~ный** [14] joiner's (*shop*, *etc.*).
стон *m* [1], **~áть** [-нý, стóнешь; стонáя], ⟨про-⟩ groan, moan.
стоп! stop!; **~á** *f* 1. [5 *e.*] foot; footstep (with Т; in по Д); 2. [5; *pl. st.*] foot (*verse*); pile; **∠ка** *f* [5; *g/pl.*: -пок] cup; roll, rouleau; **∠орить** [13], ⟨за-⟩ stop; **~тáть** *s.* стáптывать.
стóрож *m* [1; *pl.*: -á, *etc. e.*] guard, watchman; **~евóй** [14] watch...; on duty; sentry (*box*); observation (*post*); ⚓ patrol...; **~и́ть** [16 *e.*; -жý, -жи́шь] guard, watch (over).
сторон|á *f* [5; *ac/sg.*: стóрону; *pl.*: стóроны, сторóн, -нáм] side (on *a.* по Д; с Р); direction; part (on c[o]

P); place, region, country; party; distance (at в П; from с P); в '~у aside, apart (*a.* joking шутки); в ~é aloof, apart; нá ~у abroad; с однóй ~ы́ on the one hand; ... с вáшей ~ы́ *a.* ... of you; **~и́ться** [13; -онюсь, -óнишься], ⟨по-⟩ make way, step aside; (P) avoid, shun; ~и́сь! look out!; **∠ник** *m* [1] adherent, follower, supporter; partisan.
стóчный [14] waste..., soil...
стоя́|лый [14] stale; **~нка** *f* [5; *g/pl.*: -нок] stop (at на П); stand, station, (fixed) quarters *pl.*; parking place *or* lot; ⚓ anchorage.
стоя́|ть [стою́, стои́шь; стóя] stand; be; stop; lodge, quarter; stand up (for за В), defend; insist (on на П); стóй(те)! stop!; F wait!; **~чий** [17] standing; stagnant; stand-up (*collar*); standard (*lamp*).
стр. *abbr.*: страни́ца page, p.
страдá|лец *m* [1; -льца] martyr; **~ние** *n* [12] suffering; **~тельный** [14] *gr.* passive; **~ть** [1], ⟨по-⟩ suffer (from от Р, Т; for за В); F be poor.
страж *m* [1] guard; **∠а** *f* [5] guard(s); watch; custody (in[to] под Т [В]).
стран|á *f* [5; *pl. st.*] country; **~и́ца** *f* [5] page (*cf.* пя́тый); column (in на П); **∠ник** *m* [1] wanderer, travel(l)er; pilgrim; **∠ность** *f* [8] strangeness, oddity; **∠ный** [14; -áнен, -аннá, -о] strange, odd; **∠ств(ован)ие** *n* [12] wandering, travel; **∠ствовать** [7] wander, travel; ∠ствующий *a.* (*knight*-)errant.
страст|нóй (-sn-) [14] Holy; Good (*Friday*); **∠ный** (-sn-) [14; -тен, -тнá, -о] passionate, fervent; **~ь** *f* [8; *from g/pl. e.*] passion (for к Д); P awfully.
стратег|и́ческий [16] strategic(al); **∠ия** *f* [7] strategy.
стратосфéра *f* [5] stratosphere.
стрáус *m* [1] ostrich.
страх *m* [1] fear (for от, со Р); risk, peril (at на В); F awfully; **~кáсса** *f* [5] insurance office; **~овáние** *n* [12] insurance (*fire* ... от Р); **~овáть** [7], ⟨за-⟩ insure (against от Р); **~óвка** *f* [5; *g/pl.*: -вок] insurance (rate); **~овóй** [14] insurance...
страш|и́ть [16 *e.*; -шу́, -ши́шь], ⟨у-⟩ [-шённый] (**-ся** be) frighten (-ed; at P; fear, dread, be afraid of); **∠ный** [14; -шен, -шнá, -о] terrible, frightful, dreadful; Last (*Judg[e]ment*); F awful; мне ∠но I'm afraid, I fear.
стрекозá *f* [5; *pl. st.*: -óзы, -óз, -óзам] dragonfly.
стрел|á *f* [5; *pl. st.*] arrow(like T); ⚘ shaft; **∠ка** *f* [5; *g/pl.*: -лок] hand, pointer, indicator; needle; arrow (*drawing, etc.*); clock (*stocking*); tongue (*land*); 🚂 switch, *Brt.* point; **~кóвый** [14] shooting...; (of) rifles *pl.*; **~óк** *m* [1; -лкá] marksman, shot; ⚔ rifleman; **∠очник** 🚂 *m* [1] switchman, *Brt.* pointsman; **~ьбá** *f* [5; *pl. st.*] shooting, fire; **~я́ть** [28], ⟨вы́стрелить⟩ [13] shoot, fire (at в В, по Д; *gun* из Р); F *impers.* feel acute pains *pl.*; **-ся** *impf.* (fight a) duel.
стрем|гля́в headlong, headfirst; **~и́тельный** [14; -лен, -льна] impetuous, violent, rash; **~и́ться** [14 *e.*; -млю́сь, -ми́шься] (к Д) aspire (to, after), strive (for, after); rush; **~лéние** *n* [12] aspiration, striving, urge; tendency.
стрéмя *n* [13; *pl.*: -менá, -мя́н, -менáм] stirrup.
стриж *m* [1 *e.*] sand martin.
стри́|женый [14] bobbed, short-haired; shorn; trimmed; **~жка** *f* [5] haircut(ting); shearing; trimming; **~чь** [26 г/ж: -игу́, -ижёшь; *pt. st.*], ⟨по-, о(б)-⟩ cut; shear; clip, trim; **-ся** have one's hair cut.
строгáть [1], ⟨вы́-⟩ plane.
стрóг|ий [16; строг, -á, -о; *comp.*: стрóже] severe; strict; austere; stern; **~ость** *f* [8] severity, austerity, strictness.
строе|вóй [14] fighting, front(line); ~вóй лес *m* timber; **∠ние** *n* [12] construction, building; structure.
строи́тель *m* [4] builder, constructor; **~ный** [14] building...; **~ство** *n* [9] construction.
стрóить [13] **1.** ⟨по-⟩ build (up), construct; make, scheme; play *fig.* (из Р); **2.** ⟨вы́-⟩ ⚔ draw up, form; **-ся,** ⟨вы́-, по-⟩ be built; build a house; ⚔ fall in.
строй *m* **1.** [3; в строю́; *pl. e.*: строи́, строёв] order, array; line; **2.** [3] system, order, regime; ♪ tune; **∠ка** *f* [5; *g/pl.*: -óек] construction; **∠ность** *f* [8] harmony; slenderness; **∠ный** [14; -óен, -ойнá, -о] slender, slim; harmonious; symmetrical, well-shaped, well-disposed.
строкá *f* [5; *ac/sg.*: стрóку́; *pl.*: стрóки, строк, строкáм] line.
стропи́ло *n* [9] rafter.
строптúвый [14 *sh.*] obstinate, refractory.
строфá *f* [5; *nom/pl. st.*] stanza.
строч|и́ть [16 & 16 *e.*; -очу́, -óчишь; -óченный & -очённый] stitch, sew; F scribble, write; crackle; **∠ка** *f* [5; *g/pl.*: -чек] line; seam.
стру́|жка *f* [5; *g/pl.*: -жек] shaving; **~и́ться** [13] stream, flow, run; purl; **~йка** *f* [5; *g/pl.*: -у́ек] *dim. of* ~я́.
структу́ра *f* [5] structure.
струн|á ♪ *f* [5; *pl. st.*], **∠ный** [14] string.
струч|кóвый *s.* бобóвый; **~óк** *m* [1; -чкá] pod, husk.
струя́ *f* [6; *pl. st.*: -у́и] stream (in Т); jet; current; flood.
стря́|пать F [1], ⟨со-⟩ cook; **~хивать** [1], ⟨~хну́ть⟩ [20] shake off.

студе́н|т *m* [1], **~тка** *f* [5; *g/pl.*: -ток] student, undergraduate; **~ческий** [16] students'.
студёный F [14 *sh.*] (icy) cold.
сту́день *m* [4; -дня] jellied meat.
сту́дия *f* [7] studio, atelier.
стук *m* [1] knock; rattle, clatter, noise; **∠нуть** *s.* стучать.
стул *m* [1; *pl.*: сту́лья, -льев] chair; seat; ⚕ stool.
сту́па *f* [5] mortar (*vessel*).
ступ|а́ть [1], ⟨**~и́ть**⟩ [14] step, tread, go; **~е́нчатый** [14 *sh.*] (multi)graded; **~е́нь** *f* 1. [8; *pl.*: ступе́ни, ступе́ней] step; 2. [8; *pl.*: ступе́ни, -не́й, *etc. e.*] stage, grade; **~е́нька** *f* [5; *g/pl.*: -нек] step; rung; **~и́ть** *s.* **~а́ть**; **∠ка** *f* [5; *g/pl.*: -пок] (small) mortar; **~ня́** *f* [6; *g/pl.*: -не́й] foot; sole.
сту|ча́ть [4 *e.*; -чу́, -чи́шь] ⟨по-⟩, *once* ⟨**∠кнуть**⟩ [20] knock (at *door* в В; *a.* **-ся**); rap, tap; throb; chatter; clatter, rattle; **~ча́т** there's a knock at the door; **∠кнуть** F *s.* испо́лниться.
стыд *m* [1 *e.*] shame; **~и́ть** [15 *e.*; -ыжу́, -ыди́шь], ⟨при-⟩ [пристыжённый] shame, make ashamed; **-ся**, ⟨по-⟩ be ashamed (of P); **~ли́вый** [14 *sh.*] shy, bashful; **∠ный** F [14; -ден, -дна́, -о] shameful; **∠но!** (for) shame!; мне **∠но** I am ashamed (for p. за В).
стык *m* [1] joint, juncture (at на П).
сты́(ну)ть [21], ⟨о-⟩ (become) cool.
сты́чка *f* [5; *g/pl.*: -чек] skirmish.
стя́|гивать [1], ⟨**~ну́ть**⟩ [19] draw *or* pull together (off, down); tie up; ⚔ concentrate; F pilfer; **~жа́ть** [1] gain, acquire; **~ну́ть** *s.* **~гивать**.
суб|бо́та *f* [5] Saturday (on: в В, *pl.*: по Д); **~си́дия** *f* [7] subsidy.
субтропи́ческий [16] subtropical.
субъе́кт *m* [1] subject; F fellow; **~и́вный** [14; -вен, -вна] subjective.
суверен|ите́т *m* [1] sovereignty; **∠ный** [14; -е́нен, -е́нна] sovereign.
суг|ро́б *m* [1] snowdrift, bank; **~у́бый** [14 *sh.*] especial, exceptional.
суд *m* [1 *e.*] judg(e)ment (to на В); court (of justice); tribunal; trial (put on отда́ть под В; bring to преда́ть Д); justice; полево́й ~ court martial; **~а́к** *m* [1 *e.*] pike perch.
суда́р|ыня *f* [6] madam; **'~ь** *m* [4] sir.
суд|е́бный [14] judicial, legal; law-...; (of the) court; **~е́йский** [16] judicial, referee's; **~и́ть** [15; суждённый] 1. ⟨по-⟩ judge *fig.* (of о П; by по Д); 2. (*im*)*pf.* try, judge; destine; **∠я** по (Д) judging by; **-ся** be at law (with с Т).
су́д|но *n* 1. [9; *pl.*: суда́, -о́в] ⚓ ship, vessel; 2. [9; *pl.*: су́дна, -ден] vessel; **~омо́йка** *f* [5; *g/pl.*: -о́ек] scullery *or* kitchen maid.
су́доро|га *f* [5] cramp, spasm; **~жный** [14; -жен, -жна] convulsive.
судо|строе́ние *n* [12] shipbuilding; **~строи́тельный** [14] shipbuilding...; ship(*yard*); **~хо́дный** [14; -ден, -дна] navigable; **~хо́дство** *n* [9] navigation.
судьба́ *f* [5; *pl.*: су́дьбы, су́деб, су́дьбам] fate.
судья́ *m* [6; *pl.*: су́дьи, суде́й, су́дьям] judge; arbitrator, referee, umpire.
суеве́р|ие *n* [12] superstition; **~ный** [14; -рен, -рна] superstitious.
сует|а́ *f* [5] vanity; fuss; **~и́ться** [15 *e.*; суечу́сь, суети́шься] fuss; **~ли́вый** [14 *sh.*] fussy.
суж|де́ние *n* [12] judg(e)ment; **~е́ние** *n* [12] narrowing; ⚕ constriction; **∠ивать** [1], ⟨су́зить⟩ [15] narrow (*v/i.* **-ся**; taper).
сук *m* [1 *e.*; на -у́; *pl.*: су́чья, -ьев & -и́, -о́в] bough, branch; knot; **∠а** *f* [5] bitch; **∠ин** [19] of a bitch.
сукно́ *n* [9; *pl. st.*; су́кна, су́кон, су́кнам] cloth.
суко́нный [14] cloth...
сули́ть [13], ⟨по-⟩ promise.
султа́н *m* [1] sultan; plume.
сумасбро́д *m* [1] madman; crank; **~ный** [14; -ден, -дна] crazy, cranky, foolish; **~ство** *n* [9] folly, madness.
сумасше́|дший [17] mad, insane; *su.* madman; lunatic (asylum дом *m*); **~ствие** *n* [12] madness, insanity.
сумато́ха *f* [5] turmoil, fuss.
сум|бу́р *m* [1] *s.* пу́таница; **∠ерки** *f/pl.* [5; *gen.*: -рек] dusk, twilight; **∠ка** *f* [5; *g/pl.*: -мок] (hand)bag; pouch; satchel; wallet; **∠ма** *f* [5] sum (for/of на В/в В), amount; **~ма́рный** [14; -рен. -рна] summary; **~ми́ровать** [7] (*im*)*pf.* sum up.
су́мочка *f* [5; *g/pl.*: -чек] handbag.
су́мра|к *m* [1] twilight, dusk; gloom; **~чный** [14; -чен, -чна] gloomy.
сунду́к *m* [1 *e.*] trunk, chest.
су́нуть(ся) *s.* сова́ть(ся).
суп *m* [1; *pl. e.*], **~ово́й** [14] soup.
супру́|г *m* [1] husband; **~га** *f* [5] wife; **~жеский** [16] matrimonial, conjugal; married; **~жество** *n* [9] matrimony, wedlock.
сургу́ч *m* [1 *e.*] sealing wax.
суро́в|ость *f* [8] severity; **~ый** [14 *sh.*] harsh, rough; severe, austere; stern; rigorous.
суррога́т *m* [1] substitute.
сурьма́ *f* [5] antimony.
суста́в *m* [1] joint.
су́тки *f/pl.* [5; *gen.*: -ток] 24 hours, day (and night); кру́глые ~ round the clock.
су́толока *f* [5] turmoil.
су́точный [14] day's, daily, 24 hours'; *pl. su.* daily allowance.

сутýлый [14 *sh.*] round-shouldered.
сут|ь *f* [8] essence, core, main point; по **~**и (дéла) at bottom.
суфл|ёр *m* [1] prompter; **~úровать** [7] prompt (p. Д).
сух|áрь *m* [4 *e.*] cracker, zwieback, *Brt.* biscuit; **~ожúлие** *n* [12] sinew; **~óй** [14; сух, -á, -о; *comp.*: сýше] dry; arid; lean; land...; *fig.* cool, cold; boring, dull; **~опýтный** [14] land...; **~ость** *f* [8] dryness, *etc.*, *s.* **~óй**; **~ощáвый** [14 *sh.*] lean, meager.
сучúть [16] twist; roll.
сучóк *m* [1; -чкá] *dim. of* сук, *cf.*
сýш|а *f* [5] (main)land; **~éние** *n* [12] drying; **~ёный** [14] dried; **~úлка** *f* [5; *g/pl.*: -лок] drying apparatus; *a.* = **~úльня** *f* [6; *g/pl.*: -лен] drying room; **~úть** [16] **1.** ⟨вы́-⟩ dry; air; **2.** ⟨ис-⟩ wear out, emaciate; **~ка** *f* [5; *g/pl.*: -шек] drying; ring-shaped cracknel.
сущéств|енный [14 *sh.*] essential, substantial; **~úтельное** *n* [14] noun, substantive (*a.* úмя **~úтельное**); **~ó** *n* [9] creature, being; essence; по **~ý** at bottom; to the point; **~овáние** *n* [12] existence, being; subsistence; **~овáть** [7] exist, be; live.
сýщ|ий [17] existing; F plain (*truth*), quite (*true* or *right*), sheer, downright; **~ность** *f* [8] essence, substance; в **~ности** at bottom, properly.
суэ́цкий [16]: ♀ канáл Suez Canal.
сфéра *f* [5] sphere; field, realm.
с.-х. *abbr.*: сельскохозя́йственный.
схват|úть(ся) *s.* **~ывать(ся)**; **~ка** *f* [5; *g/pl.*: -ток] skirmish, fight, combat; scuffle; *pl. a.* (*childbirth*) labo(u)r; **~ывать** [1], ⟨**~úть**⟩ [15] seize (by за В), grasp (*a. fig.*), grab; snatch; catch; -ся seize, lay hold of; F grapple.
схéма *f* [5] diagram, scheme (in на П); **~тúческий** [16] schematic.
сход|úть [15], ⟨сойтú⟩ [сойдý, -дёшь; сошёл, -шлá; с(о)шéдший; *g. pt.*: сойдя́] go (*or* come) down, descend (from с Р); get off (out); come off (out); run off; leave; disappear; F pass (for за В); P do; pass off; **~úть** *pf.* go (& get, fetch за Т); *cf.* ум; -ся, ⟨-сь⟩ meet; gather; become friends; agree (upon в П); harmonize (in Т); coincide; approximate; F click; **~ка** *f* [5; *g/pl.*: -док] meeting (at на П); **~ни** *f/pl.* [6; *gen.*: -ней] gangplank, gangway; **~ный** [14; -ден, -днá, -о] similar (to с Т), like; F reasonable; **~ство** *n* [9] similarity (to с Т), likeness.
сцедúть [15] *pf.* draw off.
сцéн|а *f* [5] stage; scene (*a. fig.*); **~áрий** *m* [3] scenario, script; **~úческий** [16] stage..., scenic.
сцеп|úть(ся) *s.* **~ля́ть(ся)**; **~ка** *f* [5; *g/pl.*: -пок] coupling; **~лéние** *n* [12] *phys.* cohesion; ⊕ coupling; *fig.* concatenation; **~ля́ть** [28], ⟨**~úть**⟩ [14] link; ⊕ couple (*v/i.* -ся; concatenate; F grapple).
счаст|лúвец *m* [1; -вца] lucky man; **~лúвый** [14; счáстлив, -а, -о] happy; fortunate, lucky; **~лúвого путú** bon voyage!; **~лúво** F bye-bye, so long: **~лúво** отдéлаться have a narrow escape; **~ье** *n* [10] happiness; good luck; fortune; к, по **~ью** fortunately.
счесть(ся) *s.* считáть(ся).
счёт *m* [1; на -е & счетý; *pl.*: счетá, *etc. e.*] count, calculation; account (on в В; на В); bill; invoice; *sport* score; в конéчном **~е** ultimately; за **~** (Р) at the expense (of); на э́тот **~** in this respect, as for this; скáзано на мой **~** aimed at me; быть на хорóшем **~ý** (у Р) stand high (in p.'s) favo(u)r; у негó **~у** нет (Д) he has lots (of); **~ный** [14] calculating (*machine*, calculator); slide (*rule*).
счетовóд *m* [1] accountant.
счёт|чик *m* [1] meter; counter; **~ы** *pl.* [1] abacus *sg.*; accounts *fig.*
счислéние *n* [12] calculation.
считá|ть [1], ⟨со-⟩ & ⟨счесть⟩ [25; сочтý, -тёшь; счёл, сочлá; сочтённый; *g. pt.*: сочтя́] count; (*pf.* счесть) (Т, за В) consider, regard (*a.* as), hold, think; **~я** *a.* including; '**~нные** *pl.* very few; -ся count; settle accounts; (Т) be considered (*or* reputed) to be, pass for; (с Т) consider, regard.
США (Соединённые Штáты Амéрики) U.S.A. (United States of America).
сшиб|áть [1], ⟨**~úть**⟩ [-бý, -бёшь; *cf.* ушибúть] F *s.* сби(вá)ть; **~вáть** [1], ⟨**~ть**⟩ [сошью́, -шьёшь; сшéй(-те)!; сшúтый] sew (together).
съед|áть [1], ⟨съесть⟩ *s.* есть[1]; **~óбный** [14; -бен, -бна] edible.
съез|д *m* [1] congress (at на П); **~дить** [15] *pf.* go; (за Т) fetch; (к Д) visit; **~жáть** [1], ⟨съéхать⟩ [съéду, -дешь] go, drive (*or* slide) down; move; -ся meet; gather.
съёмка *f* [5; *g/pl.*: -мок] survey; shooting.
съестнóй [14] food...
съéхать(ся) *s.* съезжáть(ся).
сы́|воротка *f* [5; *g/pl.*: -ток] whey; serum; **~грáть** *s.* игрáть.
сы́знова F anew, (once) again.
сын *m* [1; *pl.*: сыновья́, -вéй, -вья́м; *fig. pl.*: сыны́] son; *fig. a.* child; **~óвний** [15] filial; **~óк** F *m* [1; -нкá] sonny.
сы́п|ать [2], ⟨по-⟩ strew, scatter; pour; F (Т, В) sputter, pelt, (*jokes*) crack, (*money*) squander; -ся pour; F spatter, hail, pelt; **~нóй** [14]: **~нóй** тиф spotted fever; **~ýчий** [17 *sh.*] dry; quick(*sand*); **~ь** *f* [8] rash.

сыр *m* [1; *pl. e.*] cheese; как ~ в масле (*live*) in clover; **~е́ть** [8], ⟨от-⟩ dampen; **~е́ц** *m* [1; -рца́]: шёлк-~е́ц raw silk; **∠ник** *m* [1] cheese cake; **∠ный** [14] cheese...; caseous; **~ова́тый** [14 *sh.*] dampish; rare, *Brt.* underdone; **~о́й** [14; сыр, -а́, -о] damp; moist; raw; crude; unbaked; **∠ость** *f* [8] dampness; moisture; **~ьё** *n* [10] *coll.* raw material.

сыск|а́ть F [3] *pf.* find; **-ся** be found; **~но́й** [14] detective.

сы́т|ный [14; сы́тен, -тна́, -о] substantial, rich; F fat; **~ый** [14; сыт, -а́, -о] satisfied; fat.

сыч *m* [1 *e.*] horned owl.

сы́щик *m* [1] detective, policeman.

сюда́ here, hither; this way.

сюже́т *m* [1] subject; plot.

сюрпри́з *m* [1] surprise.

сюрту́к *m* [1 *e.*] frock coat.

Т

т. *abbr.*: **1.** това́рищ; **2.** том; **3.** то́нна; **4.** ты́сяча.

таба́|к *m* [1 *e.*; *part. g.*: -у́] tobacco; **~ке́рка** *f* [5; *g/pl.*: -рок] snuffbox; **~чный** [14] tobacco...

та́бе|ль *m* [4] time sheet; **~ле́тка** *f* [5; *g/pl.*: -ток] tablet; **~ли́ца** *f* [5] table, schedule, list; scale; *gr.* paradigm; **~р** *m* [1] (*gipsy's*) camp; ⚔ party.

табу́н *m* [1 *e.*] herd, drove.

табуре́тка *f* [5; *g/pl.*: -ток] stool.

таджи́к *m* [1], **~ский** [16] Tajik.

таз *m* [1; в -у́; *pl. e.*] basin; *anat.* pelvis.

таи́нств|енный [14 *sh.*] mysterious; secret(ive); **′~о** *n* [9] sacrament.

таи́ть [13] conceal; **-ся** hide.

тайга́ *f* [5] taiga.

тай|ко́м secretly; behind (one's) back (от Р); **∠на** *f* [5] secret; mystery; **~ни́к** *m* [1 *e.*] hiding (place); (inmost) recess; **∠ный** [14] secret; stealthy; vague; privy.

так so, thus; like that; (~ же just) as; so much; just so; then; well; yes; one way ...; *s. a.* пра́вда; F properly; не ~ wrong(ly); ~ и (*both*...) and; F downright; ∠ как as, since; и ~ without that; **∠же** also, too; **∠же не** neither, nor; а **∠же** as well as; **~и́** F all the same; indeed; ~ **наз.** *abbr.*: ~ называ́емый so-called; alleged; **~ово́й** [14; -ко́в, -кова́] such; (a)like; same; был(а́) ~о́в(а́) disappeared, vanished; **~о́й** [16] such; so; **~о́е** *su.* such things; **~о́й** же the same; as ...; **~о́й-то** such-and-such; so-and-so; что (э́то) **~о́е**? F what's the matter?, what's on?; кто вы **~о́й** (**~а́я**)? = кто́ вы?

та́кса *f* [5] (fixed) rate.

такси́ *n* [*ind.*] taxi(cab).

таксирова́ть [7] (*im*)*pf.* rate.

такт *m* [1] ♪ time, measure, bar; *fig.* tact; **∠ика** *f* [5] tactics *pl.* & *sg.*; **~и́ческий** [16] tactical; **~и́чность** *f* [8] tactfulness; **~и́чный** [14; -чен, -чна] tactful.

тала́нт *m* [1] talent, gift (for к Д); **~ливый** [14 *sh.*] talented, gifted.

та́лия *f* [7] waist.

тало́н *m* [1] coupon.

та́лый [14] thawed; slushy.

там there; F then; ~ же in the same place; ibidem; ~ и сям F here and there.

тамо́ж|енный [14] custom(s)...; **~ня** *f* [6; *g/pl.*: -жен] custom house.

та́мошний [15] of that place, there.

та́н|ец *m* [1; -нца] dance (*go* dancing на В *pl.*); **~к** *m* [1] tank; **~ковый** [14] armo(u)red...; tank...

танц|ева́льный [14] dancing...; **~ева́ть** [7], ⟨с-⟩ dance; **~о́вщик** *m* [1], **~о́вщица** *f* [5] (ballet) dancer; **~о́р** *m* [1], **~о́рка** *f* [5; *g/pl.*: -рок] dancer.

Та́ня *f* [6] *dim. of* Татья́на.

та́почка *f* [5; *g/pl.*: -чек] sport slipper.

та́ра *f* [5] tare; packing.

тарака́н *m* [1] cockroach.

тара́нить [13], ⟨про-⟩ ram.

тарахте́ть F [11] rumble.

тара́щить [16], ⟨вы́-⟩: ~ глаза́ stare (at на В; with *surprise* от Р).

таре́лка *f* [5; *g/pl.*: -лок] plate.

тари́ф *m* [1] tariff; **~ный** [14] tariff...; standard (*wages*).

таска́ть [1] carry; drag, pull; F steal; P wear; **-ся** F roam; go; frequent; gad about.

тасова́ть [7], ⟨с-⟩ shuffle.

ТАСС (Телегра́фное Аге́нтство Сове́тского Сою́за) TASS (Telegraph Agency of the U.S.S.R.).

тата́р|ин *m* [1; *pl.*: -ры, -р, -рам], **~ка** *f* [5; *g/pl.*: -рок], **~ский** [16] Tartar.

Татья́на *f* [5] Tatyana.

тафта́ *f* [5] taffeta.

тача́ть [1], ⟨с-, вы́-⟩ seam, sew.

тащи́ть [16] **1.** ⟨по-⟩ drag, pull; carry, bring; **2.** F ⟨с-⟩ steal, pilfer; **~ся** F trudge, drag (o.s.) along.

та́ять [27], ⟨рас-⟩ thaw, melt; fade, die (away); languish, pine.

тварь *f* [8] creature; F wretch.

тверде́ть [8], ⟨за-, о-⟩ harden.

тверди́ть F [15 *e.*; -ржу́, -рди́шь] reiterate, repeat (over & over again); talk; practice; ⟨за-, вы́-⟩ learn.

твёрд|ость *f* [8] firmness; hardness; **~ый** [14; твёрд, тверда́, -о] hard;

solid; firm (*a. fig.*); (stead)fast, steady; fixed (*a. prices*); sound, good; F sure; ~o *a.* well, for sure.
тверды́ня *f* [6] stronghold.
тво|й *m*, **~я́** *f*, **~ё** *n*, **~и́** *pl.* [24] your; yours; *pl. su.* F your folks; *cf.* ваш.
твор|е́ние *n* [12] work; creature; **~е́ц** *m* [1; -рца́] creator; author; **~и́тельный** [14] *gr.* instrumental (*case*); **~и́ть** [13], ⟨со-⟩ create, do; perform; **-ся** F be (going) on; **~о́г** *m* [1 *e.*] curd(s).
тво́рче|ский [16] creative; **~ство** *n* [9] work(s), creation.
т. е. *abbr.*: то́ есть, *cf.*
теа́тр *m* [1] theater (*Brt.* -tre; at в П); house; stage; **~а́льный** [14; -лен, -льна] theatrical; theater...
тёзка *m/f* [5; *g/pl.*: -зок] namesake.
тексти́ль *m* [4] *coll.* textiles *pl.*; **~ный** [14] textile; cotton (*mill*).
теку́|чий [17 *sh.*] fluid; fluctuating; **~щий** [17] current; instant; present; miscellaneous.
телеви́|дение *n* [12] television (on по Д); **~зио́нный** [14] TV; **~зор** *m* [1] TV set.
теле́га *f* [5] cart, telega.
телегра́мма *f* [5] telegram, wire.
телегра́ф *m* [1] telegraph (office); wire (by по Д); **~и́ровать** [7] (*im*)*pf.* telegraph, wire, cable; **~ный** [14] telegraph(ic); telegram..., by wire.
теле́жка *f* [5; *g/pl.*: -жек] handcart.
телёнок *m* [2] calf.
телепереда́ча *f* [5] telecast.
телеско́п *m* [1] telescope.
теле́сный [14] corporal; corporeal; flesh-colo(u)red.
телефо́н *m* [1] telephone (by по Д); **~и́ровать** [7] (*im*)*pf.* (Д) telephone, F phone; **~и́ст** *m* [1], **~и́стка** *f* [5; *g/pl.*: -ток] operator; **~ный** [14] tele(phone)...; call (*box*).
тели́ться [13; те́лится], ⟨о-⟩ calve.
тёлка *f* [5; *g/pl.*: -лок] heifer.
те́ло *n* [9; *pl. e.*] body; *phys.* solid; иноро́дное ~ foreign matter; всем ~м all over; **~сложе́ние** *n* [12] build; constitution; **~храни́тель** *m* [4] bodyguard.
теля́|тина *f* [5], **~чий** [18] veal.
тем *s.* тот.
те́м(а́тик)а *f* [5] subject, theme(s).
тембр (tɛ-) *m* [1] timbre.
Те́мза *f* [5] Thames.
темн|е́ть [8] **1.** ⟨по-⟩ darken; **2.** ⟨с-⟩ grow *or* get dark; **3.** (*a.* **-ся**) appear *or* show dark; loom; **~и́ца** *f* [5] prison, dungeon.
тёмно... (*in compds.*) dark...
темнота́ *f* [5] darkness; obscurity.
тёмн|ый [14; тёмен, темна́] dark; *fig.* obscure; gloomy; shady, dubious; evil, malicious; ignorant, slow, backward.
темп (tɛ-) *m* [1] tempo; rate, pace.
темпера́мент *m* [1] temperament; spirits *pl.*; **~ный** [14; -тен, -тна] temperamental.
температу́ра *f* [5] temperature.
те́мя *n* [13] crown.
тенденци|о́зный (tɛndɛ-) [14; -зен, -зна] tendentious; **'~я** (tɛn'dɛ-) *f* [7] tendency.
те́ндер 🚂, ⚓ ('tɛnder) *m* [1] tender.
тени́стый [14 *sh.*] shady.
те́ннис ('tɛ-) *m* [1] tennis.
те́нор ♪ *m* [1; *pl.*: -ра́, *etc. e.*] tenor.
тень *f* [8; в тени́; *pl.*: те́ни, тене́й, *etc. e.*] shade; shadow.
теор|е́тик *m* [1] theorist; **~ети́ческий** [16] theoretical; **∠ия** *f* [7] theory; ∠ия позна́ния epistemology.
тепе́р|ешний [15] present, actual; **~ь** now, at present.
тепл|е́ть [8; *3rd p. only*], ⟨по-⟩ grow warm; **~и́ться** [13] burn; glimmer; **~и́ца** *f* [5], **~и́чный** [14] hothouse; **~о́ 1.** *n* [9] warmth; *phys.* heat; warm weather; **2.** *adv.*, *s.* тёплый; **~ово́й** [14] (of) heat, thermal; **~ота́** *f* [5] warmth; *phys.* heat; **~охо́д** *m* [1] motor ship; **~у́шка** *f* [5; *g/pl.*: -шек] heatable boxcar.
тёплый [14; тёпел, тепла́, -о́ & тёпло] warm (*a. fig.*); hot (*sun*); (мне) тепло́ it is (I am) warm.
терапи́я *f* [7] therapy.
тере|би́ть [14 *e.*; -блю́, -би́шь] pull; tousle; twitch; F pester; **'~м** *m* [1; *pl.*: -а́, *etc. e.*] attic; (tower-)chamber; **∠ть** [12] rub; grate; **-ся** F hang about.
терза́|ние *n* [12] torment, agony; **~ть** [1] **1.** ⟨ис-⟩ torment, torture; **2.** ⟨рас-⟩ tear to pieces.
тёрка *f* [5; *g/pl.*: -рок] grater.
те́рмин *m* [1] term; **~оло́гия** *f* [7] terminology.
термо́|метр *m* [1] thermometer; **'~с** ('tɛ-) *m* [1] vacuum *or* thermos bottle.
терни́стый [14 *sh.*] thorny.
терп|ели́вый [14 *sh.*] patient; **~е́ние** *n* [12] patience; **~е́ть** [10], ⟨по-⟩ suffer, endure; tolerate, bear, stand; not press, permit of delay; (Д) не **-ся** *impf.* be impatient *or* eager; **~и́мость** *f* [8] tolerance (toward[s] к Д); **~и́мый** [14 *sh.*] tolerant; bearable.
те́рпкий [16; -пок, -пка́, -о; *comp.*: те́рпче] tart.
терра́са *f* [5] terrace.
террит|ориа́льный [14] territorial; **~о́рия** *f* [7] territory.
терро́р *m* [1] terror; **~изи́ровать** & **~изова́ть** [7] *im*(*pf.*) terrorize.
тёртый F [14] cunning, sly.
теря́ть [28], ⟨по-⟩ lose; waste; shed (*leaves*); give up (*hope*); **-ся** be lost; disappear, vanish; become embarrassed, be at a loss.
теса́ть [3], ⟨об-⟩ hew, cut.
тесн|и́ть [13], ⟨с-⟩ press; oppress; **-ся** crowd, throng; jostle; **~ота́** *f* [5] narrowness; throng; **∠ый** [14;

те́сен, тесна́, -о] narrow; tight; clore; intimate.
те́ст|о *n* [9] dough, paste; **~ь** *m* [4] father-in-law (*wife's father*).
тесьма́ *f* [5; *g/pl.*: -сём] tape.
те́тер|ев *m* [1; *pl.*: -а́, *etc. e.*] black grouse, blackcock; **~я** P *f* [6]: глуха́я ~я deaf fellow; со́нная ~я sleepyhead.
тетива́ *f* [5] bowstring.
тётка *f* [5; *g/pl.*: -ток] aunt.
тетра́д|ь *f* [8], **~ка** *f* [5; *g/pl.*: -док] exercise book, notebook, copybook.
тётя F *f* [6; *g/pl.*: -тей] aunt.
те́хн|ик *m* [1] technician; **~ика** *f* [5] technics; technique; equipment; F skill; **~икум** *m* [1] technical school; **~и́ческий** [16] technical; **~ологи́ческий** [16] technological; **~оло́гия** *f* [7] technology.
теч|е́ние *n* [12] current; stream (up- [down-] вверх [вниз] по Д); course (in в В; in/of *time* с Т/Р); *fig.* trend; movement; **~ь** [26] **1.** flow, run; stream; move; leak; **2.** *f* [8] leak (spring дать).
те́шить [16], ⟨по-⟩ amuse; please; **-ся** amuse o. s.; take comfort; banter.
тёща *f* [5] mother-in-law (*wife's mother*).
тибе́тец *m* [1; -тца] Tibetan.
тигр *m* [1] tiger; **~и́ца** *f* [5] tigress.
ти́ка|нье *n* [10], **~ть** [1] tick.
Тимофе́й *m* [3] Timothy.
ти́н|а *f* [5] ooze; **~истый** [14 *sh.*] oozy.
тип *m* [1] type; F character; **~и́чный** [14; -чен, -чна] typical; **~огра́фия** *f* [7] printing plant *or* office; **~огра́фский** [16] printing (*press*); printer's (ink кра́ска *f*).
тир *m* [1] shooting gallery, rifle range.
тира́да *f* [5] tirade.
тира́ж *m* [1 *e.*] circulation; drawing (*of a lottery*).
тира́н *m* [1] tyrant; **~ить** [13] tyrannize; **~и́я** *f* [7], **~ство** *n* [9] tyranny.
тире́ *n* [*ind.*] dash.
ти́с|кать [1], ⟨**~нуть**⟩ [20] squeeze, press; print; **~ки́** *m/pl.* [1 *e.*] vice, grip; F fix; **~нёный** [14] (im-) printed.
ти́тул *m* [1], **~ьный** [14] title.
тиф *m* [1] typhus.
ти́|хий [16; тих, -а́, -о; *comp.*: ти́ше] quiet, still; calm; soft, gentle; slow; † dull, flat; *cap.* Pacific; **~хомо́лком** F on the quiet; **~ше!** silence!; **~шина́** *f* [5] silence, stillness, calm (-ness); **~шь** *f* [8; в тиши́] calm; silence.
т. к. *abbr.*: та́к как, *cf.* так.
тка|нь *f* [8] fabric, cloth; *biol.* tissue; **~ть** [тку, ткёшь; ткал, ткала́, -о], ⟨со-⟩ [со́тканный] weave; **~цкий** [16] weaver's; weaving; **~ч** *m* [1 *e.*], **~чи́ха** *f* [5] weaver.
ткнуть(ся) *s.* ты́кать(ся).
тле́|ние *n* [12] decay, putrefaction; smo(u)ldering; **~ть** [8], ⟨ис-⟩ (s)mo(u)lder, decay, rot, putrefy; glimmer.
то 1. [28] that; ~ же the same; к ~му́ (же) in addition (to that), moreover; add to this; ни ~ ни сё F neither fish nor flesh; ни с ~го́ ни с сего́ F all of a sudden, without any visible reason; до ~го́ so much; **2.** (*cj.*) then; ~ ... ~ now ... now; не ~ ... не ~ *or* ~ ли ... ~ ли either ... or, half ... half; не ~, чтобы not that; а не ~ (or) else; **3.** ~ -~ just, exactly; although; oh ...
тов. *abbr.*: това́рищ.
това́р *m* [1] commodity, article (of trade); *pl.* goods, wares.
това́рищ *m* [1] comrade, friend; mate, companion (in *arms* по Д); colleague; assistant; ~ по шко́ле schoolmate; ~ по университе́ту fellow student; **~еский** [16] friendly; companionable; **~ество** *n* [9] comradeship, fellowship; partnership; association, company.
това́р|ный [14] ware(*house*); goods-...; freight..., *Brt.* goods...; **~ообме́н** *m* [1] barter; **~ооборо́т** *m* [1] commodity circulation.
тогда́ then, at that time; ~ как whereas, while; **~шний** [15] of that (*or* the) time, then.
то́ есть that is (to say), i. e.
тожде́ств|енный [14 *sh.*] identical; **'~о** *n* [9] identity.
то́же also, too, as well; *cf.* та́кже.
ток *m* **1.** [1] current; **2.** [1; на -у́; *from g/pl. e.*] (threshing) floor.
тока́р|ный [14] turner's; turning (*lathe*); **'~ь** *m* [4] turner.
толк *m* [1; бе́з -у] sense; use; judg(e)ment; F talk, rumo(u)r; † doctrine; sect; знать ~ в (П) be a judge of; **~а́ть** [1], *once* ⟨**~нуть**⟩ [20] push, shove, thrust; *fig.* induce, prompt; F urge on, spur; **-ся** push (o. a.); F knock (at в В; about); **~ова́ть** [7] **1.** ⟨ис-⟩ interpret, expound, explain; comment; take (in ... part в ... сто́рону); **2.** ⟨по-⟩ F talk (to с Т); speak, tell, say; **~о́вый** [14] explanatory, commenting; F [*sh.*] sensible, smart, wise; **~ом** = **~о́во**; *a.* in earnest; **~отня́** F *f* [6] crush, crowd; **~у́чка** P *f* [5; *g/pl.*: -чек] second-hand market.
толо|кно́ *n* [9] oat flour; **~чь** [26; -лку́, -лчёшь, -лку́т; -ло́к, -лкла́; -лчённый], ⟨рас-, ис-⟩ pound; **~чься** P hang about.
толп|а́ *f* [5; *pl. st.*], **~и́ться** [14 *e.*; *no 1st. & 2nd p. sg.*], ⟨с-⟩ crowd, throng; mob; swarm.
толст|е́ть [8], ⟨по-, рас-⟩ grow stout; **~око́жий** [17 *sh.*] thick-skinned; **~ый** [14; толст, -а́, -о; *comp.*: то́лще] thick; large, big; stout, fat; **~я́к** F *m* [1 *e.*] fat man.
толч|ёный [14] pounded; **~ея́** F *f*

[6] crush, crowd; ~óк *m* [1; -чкá] push; shock; jolt; *fig.* impulse.
толщин|á *f* [5] thickness; stoutness; ~óй в (В), ... в ~ý ... thick.
толь *m* [4] roofing felt.
тóлько only, but; как ~ as soon as; лишь (*or* едвá) ~ no sooner ... than; ~ бы if only; ~ что just (now); ~-~ F barely.
том *m* [1; *pl.*: -á, *etc. e.*] volume.
том|и́тельный [14; -лен, -льна] painful, tormenting; oppressive; ~и́ть [14 *e.*; томлю́, томи́шь, томлённый], ‹ис-› torment, plague, harass, pester; pinch, oppress; -ся pine (for T), languish (with; be tormented, *etc.*, *s.* ~и́ть); ~лéние *n* [12], ∠ность *f* [8] languor; ∠ный [14; -мен, -мнá, -о] languishing.
тон *m* [1; *pl.*: -á, *etc. e.*] tone.
тóнк|ий [16; -нок, -нкá, -о; *comp.*: тóньше] thin; slim, slender; small; fine; delicate, subtle; keen; light (*sleep*); high (*voice*); F cunning; ~ость *f* [8] thinness, *etc. s.* ~ий; delicacy, subtlety; *pl.* details (go into вдавáться в В; F split hairs).
тóнна *f* [5] ton; ∠ж *m* [1] tonnage.
тонýть [19] *v/i.* **1.** ‹по-, за-› sink; submerge; **2.** ‹у-› drown.
Тóня *f* [6] *dim. of* Антони́на.
тóп|ать [1], *once* ‹~нуть› [20] stamp; ~и́ть [14] *v/t.* **1.** ‹за-, по-› sink; flood; **2.** ‹за-, ис-, на-› heat; light a fire; **3.** ‹рас-› melt; **4.** ‹у-› drown; ~ка *f* [5; *g/pl.*: -пок] heating; furnace; ~кий [16; -пок, -пкá, -о] boggy, marshy; ~лёный [14] melted; molten; ~ливо *n* [9] fuel; ~нуть *s.* ~ать.
топогрáфия *f* [7] topography.
тóполь *m* [4; *pl.*: -ля́, *etc. e.*] poplar.
топóр *m* [1 *e.*] ax(e); ~ный [14; -рен, -рна] coarse.
тóпот *m* [1] stamp(ing), tramp(ing).
топтáть [3], ‹по-, за-› trample, tread; ‹вы́-› press; ‹с-› wear out; ~ся tramp(le); F hang about; mark time (на мéсте).
топь *f* [8] marsh, mire, bog, fen.
торг *m* [1; на -ý; *pl.*: -и́, *etc. e.*] bargaining, chaffer; *pl.* auction (by с Р; at на П); ~áш *contp. m* [1 *e.*] dealer; ~овáть [8] trade, deal (in T); sell; be open; -ся, ‹с-› (strike a) bargain (for о П); ~óвец *m* [1; -вца] dealer, trader, merchant; ~óвка *f* [5; *g/pl.*: -вок] market woman; ~óвля *f* [6] trade, commerce; traffic; business; ~óвый [14] trade..., trading, commercial, of commerce; ⚓ mercantile, merchant...; ~прéд *m* [1] Soviet trade representative; ~прéдство *n* [9] trade agency of the U.S.S.R.
торжéств|енность *f* [8] solemnity; ~енный [14 *sh.*] solemn; festive; triumphant; ~ó *n* [9] triumph; festivity, celebration; ~овáть [7], ‹вос-› triumph (over над T); *impf.* celebrate.
тóрмо|з *m* **1.** [1; *pl.*: -á, *etc. e.*] brake; **2.** [1] *fig.* drag; ~зи́ть [15 *e.*; -ожý, -ози́шь; -ожённый], ‹за-› (put the) brake(s on); *fig.* hamper; *psych.* curb, restrain; ~ши́ть F [16 *e.*; -шý, -ши́шь] *s.* теребить.
тóрный [14] beaten (*road*, *a. fig.*).
тороп|и́ть [14], ‹по-› hasten, hurry up (*v/i.* -ся; *a.* be in a hurry); ~ли́вый [14 *sh.*] hasty, hurried.
торпéд|а *f* [5], ~и́ровать [7] (*im*)*pf.* torpedo; ~ный [14] torpedo...
торт *m* [1] pie; fancy cake.
торф *m* [1] peat; ~янóй [14] peat...
торчáть [4 *e.*; -чý, чи́шь] stick out; F hang about.
тоск|á *f* [5] melancholy; anxiety, grief; yearning; boredom, ennui; ~á по рóдине homesickness; ~ли́вый [14 *sh.*] melancholy; sad, dreary; ~овáть [7] grieve, feel sad (*or* lonely); feel bored; yearn *or* long (for по П *or* Д); be homesick (по рóдине).
тот *m*, та *f*, то *n*, те *pl.* [28] that, *pl.* those; the one; the other; не ~ wrong; (н)и тот (н)и другóй both (neither); тот же (сáмый) the same; тем бóлее the more so; тем лýчше so much the better; тем сáмым thereby; *cf. a.* то.
тóтчас (же) immediately, at once.
точи́|льный [14] grinding; ~льщик *m* [1] grinder; ~ть [16] **1.** ‹на-› whet, grind; sharpen; **2.** ‹вы́-› turn; **3.** ‹ис-› eat (*or* gnaw) away; gnaw at; perforate; wear; weather.
тóчк|а *f* [5; *g/pl.*: -чек] point; dot; *typ.*, *gr.* period, full stop; вы́сшая ~а zenith, climax (at на П); ~а с запятóй *gr.* semicolon; ~а! F enough!; *s. a.* точь.
тóчн|о *adv. of* ~ый; *a.* = слóвно; indeed; так ~о! ⚔ yes, sir!; ~ость *f* [8] accuracy, exactness, precision; в ~ости *s.* ~о; ~ый [14; -чен, -чнá, -о] exact, precise, accurate; punctual; (of) precision.
точь: ~ в ~ F exactly.
тошн|и́ть [13]; меня́ ~и́т I feel sick; I loathe; ~отá *f* [5] nausea; F loathing; ∠ый [14; -шен, -шнá, -о] loathsome, nauseous; мне ∠о *s.* ~и́ть.
тóщий [17; тощ, -á, -е] lean, lank, gaunt; F empty; scanty, poor.
травá *f* [5; *pl. st.*] grass; herb; weed.
трав|и́ть [14] **1.** ‹за-› bait, chase, course; *fig.* attack; **2.** ‹с-, вы́-› corrode, stain; exterminate; **3.** ⚓ ‹вы́-› loosen; ∠ля *f* [6; *g/pl.*: -лей] baiting; *fig.* defamation.
травян|и́стый [14 *sh.*], ~óй [14] grass(y).
траг|éдия *f* [7] tragedy; ∠ик *m* [1] tragedian; ~и́ческий [16], ~и́чный [14; -чен, -чна] tragic(al).

традицио́нный [14; -о́нен, -о́нна] traditional.
тракт *m* [1] highway; *anat.* tract; **~а́т** *m* [1] treatise; **~и́р** *m* [1] inn, tavern, *Brt.* public house, F pub; **~и́рщик** *m* [1] innkeeper; **~ова́ть** [7] treat; **~о́вка** *f* [5; *g/pl.*: -вок] treatment; **~ори́ст** *m* [1] tractor operator; **∠орный** [14] tractor...
тра́льщик *m* [1] trawler; ⚔ mine sweeper.
трамбова́ть [7], ⟨у-⟩ ram.
трамва́й *m* [3] streetcar, *Brt.* tramway, tram(car) (by T, на П).
трампли́н *m* [1] springboard.
транзи́т *m* [1], **~ный** [14] transit.
транс|криби́ровать [7] (*im*)*pf.* transcribe; **~ли́ровать** [7] (*im*)*pf.* transmit; relay; **~ля́ция** *f* [7] transmission; **~пара́нт** *m* [1] transparency.
тра́нспорт *m* [1] transport(ation; *a.* system [of]); **~и́ровать** [7] (*im*)*pf.* transport, convey; **~ный** [14] (of) transport(ation).
трансформа́тор *m* [1] transformer.
транше́я *f* [6; *g/pl.*: -е́й] trench.
трап *m* [1] gangway; **~е́ция** *f* [7] trapeze; ⩓ trapezium.
тра́сса *f* [5] route. line.
тра́т|а *f* [5] expenditure; expense; waste; **~ить** [15], ⟨ис-, по-⟩ spend; waste; **~та** † *f* [5] draft.
тра́ур *m* [1] mourning; **~ный** [14] mourning...; funeral...
трафаре́т *m* [1] cliché (*a. fig.*).
трах! crack!
тре́бова|ние *n* [12] demand (on по Д); requirement; claim; order; **~тельный** [14; -лен, -льна] exacting; particular; pretentious; **~ть** [7], ⟨по-⟩ (Р) demand; require; claim; cite, summon; call; **-ся** be required (*or* wanted); be necessary.
трево́|га *f* [5] alarm; warning, alert; anxiety; **~жить** [16] **1.** ⟨вс-, рас-⟩ alarm, disquiet; **2.** ⟨по-⟩ disturb, trouble; **-ся** be anxious; worry; **~жный** [14; -жен, -жна] restless, uneasy; alarm(ing), disturbing.
тре́зв|ость *f* [8] sobriety; **~ый** [14; трезв, -а́, -о] sober (*a. fig.*).
трель *f* [8] trill, shake; warble.
тре́нер *m* [1] trainer, coach.
тре́ние *n* [12] friction (*a. fig.*).
тренир|ова́ть [7], ⟨на-⟩ train, coach; *v/i.* **-ся**; **~о́вка** *f* [5] training.
трепа́ть [2] **1.** ⟨по-⟩ tousle; twitch; flutter; F tap (on по Д); wear out, fray; harass; prate; **2.** ⟨вы́-⟩ scutch.
тре́пет *m* [1] tremor; quiver; **~а́ть** [3], ⟨за-⟩ tremble (with от Р); quiver, shiver; flicker; palpitate; **~ный** [14; -тен, -тна] quivering; flickering.
треск *m* [1] crack, crash; **~а́** *f* [5] cod; **∠аться** [1], ⟨по-, тре́снуть⟩ [20] burst; crack, split; chap; **~отня́** *f* [6] crackle; rattle; chirp; gabble; **~у́чий** [17 *sh.*] hard, ringing (*frost*); *fig.* bombastic.
тре́снуть *s.* тре́скаться & треща́ть.
трест *m* [1] trust.
трет|е́йский [16] of arbitration; **∠ий** [18] third; **∠ьего дня** = позавчера́; *cf.* пя́тый; **~и́ровать** [7] (mal)treat; **~ь** *f* [8; *from g/pl. e.*] (one) third.
треуго́льн|ик *m* [1] triangle; **~ый** [14] triangular; three-cornered (*hat*).
тре́фы *f/pl.* [5] clubs (*cards*).
трёх|годи́чный [14] three years'; triennial; **~дне́вный** [14] three days'; **~колёсный** [14] three-wheeled; **~ле́тний** [15] three-years(-old)'; **~со́тый** [14] three hundredth; **~цве́тный** [14] three-colo(u)r; tricolor(ed); **~эта́жный** [14] three-storied (*Brt.* -reyed).
трещ|а́ть [4 *e.*; -щу́, -щи́шь] **1.** ⟨за-⟩ crack; **2.** ⟨про-⟩ crackle; rattle; chirp; F prattle; **3.** ⟨тре́снуть⟩ [20] burst; **∠ина** *f* [5] split (*a. fig.*), crack, cleft, crevice, fissure; chap; **~о́тка** *f* [5; *g/pl.*: -ток] rattle; F chatterbox.
три [34] three; *cf.* пять.
трибу́н|а *f* [5] tribune, platform; stand; **~а́л** *m* [1] tribunal.
тригономе́трия *f* [7] trigonometry.
тридца́|тый [14] thirtieth; *cf.* пятидеся́тый; **′~ть** [35 *e.*] thirty.
три́жды three times, thrice.
трико́ *n* [*ind.*] tights *pl.*; **~та́ж** *m* [1] hosiery; jersey.
трило́гия *f* [7] trilogy.
трина́дца|тый [14] thirteenth; *cf.* пя́тый; **~ть** [35] thirteen; *cf.* пять.
три́ста [36] three hundred.
триу́мф *m* [1] triumph; **~а́льный** [14] triumphal; triumphant.
тро́га|тельный [14; -лен, -льна] touching, moving; **~ть** [1], *once* ⟨тро́нуть⟩ [20] touch (*a. fig.* = move); F pester; **~й!** go!; **-ся** start; set out (on a journey в путь); move; be touched.
тро́е [37] three (*cf.* дво́е); **~кра́тный** [14; -тен, -тна] repeated three times.
тро́иц|а *f* [5] Trinity; Whitsunday.
тро́й|ка *f* [5; *g/pl.*: тро́ек] three (*cf.* дво́йка); troika (*team of 3 horses abreast* [+ *vehicle*]); triumvirate; F (*mark* =) посре́дственно, *cf.*; **~но́й** [14] threefold, triple, treble; **~ня** *f* [6; *g/pl.*: тро́ен] triplets *pl.*
тролле́йбус *m* [1] trolley bus.
трон *m* [1] throne; **∠ный** [14] *Brt.* King's (Queen's) (*speech*).
тро́нуть(ся) *s.* тро́гать(ся).
троп|а́ *f* [5; *pl.*: тро́пы, троп, -па́м] path, track; **~и́нка** [5; *g/pl.*: -нок] (small) path.
тропи́ческий [16] tropic(al).
трос *m* [1] hawser, cable.
трост|ни́к *m* [1 *e.*] reed; cane; **~ни-**

ко́вый [14] reed...; cane...; **∠очка** *f* [5; *g/pl.*: -чек], **~ь** *f* [8; *from g/pl. e.*] cane, *Brt. a.* walking stick.
тротуа́р *m* [1] sidewalk, *Brt.* pavement, footpath, footway.
трофе́й *m* [3], **~ный** [14] trophy.
тро|ю́родный [14] second (cousin брат *m*, сестра́ *f*); **~я́кий** [16 *sh.*] threefold, triple.
труб|а́ *f* [5; *pl. st.*] pipe, (*a. anat.*) tube; chimney; 🚂, ⚓ smokestack, funnel; (*fire*) engine; ♪ trumpet; **~а́ч** *m* [1 *e.*] trumpeter; **~и́ть** [14 *e.*; -блю́, -би́шь], ⟨про-⟩ blow (the в В); **∠ка** *f* [5; *g/pl.*: -бок] tube; pipe (*to smoke*); *teleph.* receiver; roll; **~опрово́д** *m* [1] pipe line; **~очи́ст** *m* [1] chimney sweep; **∠чатый** [14] tubular.
труд *m* [1 *e.*] labo(u)r, work; pains *pl.*, trouble; difficulty (with с Т; *a.* hard[ly]); *pl. a.* transactions; F service; **~и́ться** [15], ⟨по-⟩ work; toil, exert o.s.; trouble; **∠ность** *f* [8] difficulty; **∠ный** [14; -ден, -дна́, -о] difficult, hard; F heavy; **~ово́й** [14] labo(u)r...; working; workman's; earned; service...; **~олюби́вый** [14 *sh.*] industrious; **~оспосо́бный** [14; -бен, -бна] able-bodied, able to work; **~я́щийся** [17] working; *su.* worker.
тру́женик *m* [1] toiler, worker.
труни́ть [13] make fun (of над Т).
труп *m* [1] corpse, body.
тру́ппа *f* [5] company, troupe.
трус *m* [1] coward; **∠ики** *m/pl.* [1] trunks, shorts; **∠ить** [15], ⟨с-⟩ be afraid (of Р); **~и́ха** F *f* [5] *f of* ~; **~ли́вый** [14 *sh.*] cowardly; **∠ость** *f* [8] cowardice; **~ы́** *s.* **∠ики.**
трут *m* [1] tinder.
тру́тень *m* [4; -тня] drone.
трущо́ба *f* [5] slum, den, nest.
трюк *m* [1] trick, F stunt.
трюм ⚓ *m* [1] hold.
трюмо́ *n* [*ind.*] pier glass.
тряп|и́чник *m* [1] ragpicker; **∠ка** [5; *g/pl.*: -пок] rag; duster; patch; F milksop; **~ьё** *n* [10] rag(s).
трясина *f* [5] bog, fen, quagmire.
тря́с|ка *f* [5] jolting; **~кий** [16; -сок, -ска] shaky; jolty; **~ти́** [24 -с-], *once* ⟨тряхну́ть⟩ [20] shake (a p.'s Д *hand*; *head, etc.* Т; *a. fig.*); F (*impers.*) jolt; **~ти́сь** shake; shiver (with от Р).
тряхну́ть *s.* **трясти́.**
тсс! hush!
тт. *abbr.*: **1.** това́рищи; **2.** тома́.
туале́т *m* [1] toilet.
туберкулёз *m* [1] tuberculosis; **~ный** [14] tubercular; tuberculous (patient).
туго́|й [14; туг, -а́, -о; *comp.*: ту́же] tight, taut; stiff; crammed; F stingy; slow, hard (*a.* of hearing на́ ухо); *adv. a.* hard put to it; hard up; hard, with difficulty.
туда́ there, thither; that way.
тужи́ть F [16] grieve; long for (о П).
тужу́рка *f* [5; *g/pl.*: -рок] jacket.
туз *m* [1 *e.*] ace; F boss.
тузе́м|ец *m* [1; -мца] native; **~ный** [14] native.
ту́ловище *n* [11] trunk.
тулу́п *m* [1] sheepskin coat.
тума́н *m* [1] fog, mist; haze; smog; **~ный** [14; -а́нен, -а́нна] foggy, misty; *fig.* hazy, vague.
ту́мб|а *f* [5] curbstone (*Brt.* kerb-); pedestal; **~очка** *f* [5; *g/pl.*: -чек] bedside table.
тунея́дец *m* [1; -дца] parasite.
Туни́с *m* [1] Tunisia; Tunis.
тунне́ль (-ˈnɛ-) *m* [4] tunnel.
туп|е́ть [8], ⟨(п)о-⟩ grow blunt; **~и́к** *m* [1 *e.*] blind alley, dead end, (*a. fig.*) impasse; nonplus, tight corner; ста́вить в ~и́к baffle; стать в ~и́к be at one's wit's end; **~о́й** [14; туп, -а́, -о] blunt; ⩓ obtuse; *fig.* dull, stupid; apathetic; **∠ость** *f* [8] bluntness; dullness; **~оу́мный** [14; -мен, -мна] stupid.
тур *m* [1] round; tour; *zo.* aurochs.
тура́ *f* [5] rook, castle (*chess*).
турби́на *f* [5] turbine.
туре́цкий [16] Turkish.
тури́|зм *m* [1] tourism; **~ст** *m* [1] tourist.
туркме́н *m* [1] Turk(o)man; **~ский** [16] Turkmen(ian).
турне́ (-ˈnɛ) *n* [*ind.*] tour.
турни́к *m* [1 *e.*] horizontal bar.
турни́р *m* [1] tournament (in на П).
ту́р|ок *m* [1; -рка; *g/pl.*: ту́рок], **~ча́нка** *f* [5; *g/pl.*: -нок] Turk; **♀ция** *f* [7] Turkey.
ту́ск|лый [14; тускл, -а́, -о] dim; dull; dead (*gold, etc.*); **~не́ть** [8], ⟨по-⟩ & **~нуть** [20] grow dim *or* dull.
тут F here; there; then; **~!** present!; ~ же there & then, on the spot; ~ как ~ already there.
ту́тов|ый [14]: ~ое де́рево *n* mulberry.
ту́фля *f* [6; *g/pl.*: -фель] shoe; slip-[per.]
ту́х|лый [14; тухл, -а́, -о] bad (*egg*), rotten; **~нуть** [21] **1.** ⟨по-⟩ go *or* die out, expire; **2.** ⟨про-⟩ go bad.
ту́ч|а *f* [5] cloud; *dim.* **~ка** *f* [5; *g/pl.*: -чек]; **~ный** [14; -чен, -чна́, -о] corpulent, obese, stout, fat; fertile (*soil*).
туш ♪ *m* [1] flourish.
ту́ша *f* [5] carcass.
туш|ёный [14] stewed; **~и́ть** [16] ⟨по-, F за-⟩ put out, extinguish; *impf.* stew; *fig.* subdue.
тушь *f* [8] Indian ink.
тща́тельн|ость *f* [8] care(fulness); **~ый** [14; -лен, -льна] careful.
тще|ду́шный [14; -шен, -шна] sickly; **~сла́вие** *n* [12] vanity; **~сла́вный** [14; -вен, -вна] vain

(-glorious); ∠тный [14; -тен, -тна] vain, futile; ∠тно in vain.
ты [21] you, † thou; быть на ~ (с Т) thou (p.), be familiar (with).
тыкать [3], ⟨ткнуть⟩ [20] poke, jab, thrust (*v/i.* -ся); F (thee &) thou.
тыква *f* [5] pumpkin.
тыл *m* [1; в -у́; *pl. e.*] rear, base; глубо́кий ~ hinterland.
тысяч|а *f* [5] thousand; ~еле́тие *n* [12] millenium; ~ный [14] thousandth; of thousand(s).
тьма *f* [5] dark(ness); F lots of.
тьфу! F fie!, for shame!
тюбик *m* [1] tube.
тюк *m* [1 *e.*] bale, pack.
тюле́нь *m* [4] seal; F lout.
тюль *m* [4] tulle.
тюльпа́н *m* [1] tulip.
тюр|е́мный [14] prison ...; ~е́мщик *m* [1] jailer, *Brt.* gaoler, warder; ~ьма́ *f* [5; *pl.*: тю́рьмы, -рем, -рьмам] prison, jail, *Brt.* gaol.
тюфя́к *m* [1 *e.*] mattress.
тя́вкать F [1] yap, yelp.
тя́г|а *f* [5] draft, *Brt.* draught; traction; *fig.* bent (for к Д), desire (of); ~а́ться F [1] (с Т) be a match (for), cope, vie (with); be at law (with); ~остный [14; -тен, -тна] burdensome; painful; ~ость *f* [8] burden (*be* ... to в В/Д); ~оте́ние *n* [12] gravitation; *a.* = ∠а *fig.*; ~оте́ть [8] gravitate (toward[s] к Д); weigh (upon над Т); ~оти́ть [15 *e.*; -ощу́, -оти́шь] weigh upon, be a burden to; -ся feel the burden (of T); ~у́чий [17 *sh.*] viscous; ductile; drawling, lingering.
тя́ж|ба *f* [5] action, lawsuit; ~елове́с *m* [1] heavyweight; ~елове́сный [14; -сен -сна] heavy, ponderous; ~ёлый [14; -жёл, -жела́] heavy; difficult, hard; laborious; serious (*wound, etc.*); (*a.* ⚖) severe, grave; grievous, sad, oppressive, painful; close (*air*); (Д) ~ело́ feel sad; ~есть *f* [8] heaviness; weight; load; burden; gravity; seriousness; painfulness; ~кий [16; тя́жек, тяжка́, -о] heavy (*fig.*), *etc.*, *cf.* ~ёлый.
тян|у́ть [19] pull, draw; ⚓ tow; draw in (out = delay); protract; drawl (out); attract; gravitate; drive at; long; have a mind to; would like; waft; ∠ет there is a draft (*Brt.* draught) (of T); F drag (on); steal; take (from с Р); -ся stretch (*a.* = extend); last; drag, draw on; reach out (for к Д).

У

у (Р) at, by, near; with; (at) ...'s; at p.'s place; у меня́ (был, -а́ ...) I have (had); my; (*borrow, learn, etc.*) from; of; off (*coast*); in; у себя́ in (at) one's home *or* room, office.
убав|ля́ть [28], ⟨∠ить⟩ [14] lower, reduce, diminish, decrease; *v/i.* -ся.
убе|га́ть [1], ⟨~жа́ть⟩ [4; -гу́, -жи́шь, -гу́т] run away; escape.
убе|ди́тельный [14; -лен, -льна] convincing; urgent (*request*); ~жда́ть [1], ⟨~ди́ть⟩ [15 *e.*; *no 1st p. sg.*; -еди́шь; -еждённый] convince (of в П), persuade (*impf. a.* try to ...); ~жде́ние *n* [12] persuasion; conviction.
убеж|а́ть *s.* убега́ть; ∠ище *n* [11] shelter, refuge; asylum.
убер|ега́ть [1], ⟨~е́чь⟩ [26 г/ж] save, safeguard.
уби|ва́ть [1], ⟨∠ть⟩ [убью́, -ьёшь; уби́тый] kill; murder; beat (*card*); drive into despair; blight; F waste.
уби́й|ственный [14 *sh.*] killing; murderous; F deadly, terrible; ~ство *n* [9] murder; покуше́ние на ~ство murderous assault; ~ца *m/f* [5] murderer; assassin.
убира́|ть [1], ⟨убра́ть⟩ [уберу́, -рёшь; убра́л, -а́, -о; у́бранный] take (*or* put, clear) away (in); gather, harvest; tidy up; decorate, adorn, trim; dress up; -ся F clear off, away; ~йся (вон)! get out of here!
уби́ть *s.* убива́ть.
убо́|гий [16 *sh.*] needy, poor; wretched, miserable; scanty; crippled; ~жество *n* [9] poverty.
убо́й *m* [3] slaughter (for на В).
убо́р *m* [1] attire; (*head*)gear; ~истый [14 *sh.*] close: ~ка *f* [5; *g/pl.*: -рок] harvest, gathering; tidying up; ~ная *f* [14] lavatory, toilet, water closet; dressing room; ~очный [14] harvest(ing); ~щица *f* [5] charwoman.
убра́|нство *n* [9] attire; furniture; ~ть(ся) *s.* убира́ть(ся).
убы|ва́ть [1], ⟨∠ть⟩ [убу́ду, убу́дешь; у́был, -а́, -о] subside, fall; decrease; leave; fall out; '~ль *f* [8] decrease, fall; loss; ∠ток *m* [1; -тка] loss, damage; disadvantage (*be* at в П); ∠точный [14; -чен, -чна] unprofitable; ∠ть *s.* ~ва́ть.
уваж|а́емый [14] dear (*address*); ~а́ть [1], ~е́ние *n* [12] respect, esteem (*su.* for к Д); ~и́тельный [14; -лен, -льна] valid.
уведом|ля́ть [28], ⟨'~ить⟩ [14] inform, notify, advise (of о П); ~ле́ние *n* [12] notification, † advice.
увезти́ *s.* увози́ть.
увекове́чи|вать [1], ⟨~ть⟩ [16] immortalize.
увелич|е́ние *n* [12] increase; en-

largement; **∠ивать** [1], ⟨**∠ить**⟩ [16] increase; enlarge; magnify; *v/i.* -**ся**; **~ительный** [14] *opt.* magnifying; *gr.* augmentative.
увенчаться [1] *pf.* (Т) be crowned.
увер|ение *n* [12] assurance (of в П); **∠енность** *f* [8] firmness, assurance; certainty; confidence (in в П); **∠енный** [14 *sh.*] firm, steady; confident (of в П); positive, sure, certain; будьте ∠ены I assure you, you may depend on it; **∠ить** *s.* **~ять**.
увёрт|ка F *f* [5; *g/pl.*: -ток] subterfuge, dodge; **~ливый** [14 *sh.*] evasive.
увертюра *f* [5] overture.
увер|ять [28], ⟨**∠ить**⟩ [13] assure (of в П); make believe (sure -**ся**), persuade.
увесел|ение *n* [12] amusement; **~ительный** [14] pleasure...; **~ять** [[28] amuse.
увести *s.* уводить.
увеч|ить [16], ⟨из-⟩ mutilate; **~ный** [14] crippled; **~ье** *n* [10] mutilation.
увещ(ев)а|ние *n* [12] admonition; **~ть** [1] admonish.
увил|ивать [1], ⟨**~ьнуть**⟩ [20] shirk.
увлажн|ять [28], ⟨**~ить**⟩ [13] wet, dampen.
увле|кательный [14; -лен, -льна] fascinating; **~кать** [1], ⟨**∠чь**⟩ [26] carry (away; *a. fig.* = transport, captivate); -**ся** (Т) be carried away (by), be(come) enthusiastic (about); be(come) absorbed (in); take to; fall (*or* be) in love (with); **~чение** *n* [12] enthusiasm, passion (for Т).
уво|д *m* [1] ⚔ withdrawal; theft; **~дить** [15], ⟨увести⟩ [25] take, lead (away, off); steal; ⚔ withdraw; **~зить** [15], ⟨увезти⟩ [24] take, carry, drive (away, off); F steal, kidnap.
увол|ить *s.* **~ьнять**; **~ьнение** *n* [12] dismissal (from с Р); granting (of *leave* в В); **~ьнять** [28], ⟨**~ить**⟩ [13] dismiss (from с Р); give (leave of absence в отпуск); (от Р) dispense (with), spare.
увы! alas!
увя|дание *n* [12] withering; **~дать** [1], ⟨**∠нуть**⟩ [20] wither, fade; **∠дший** [17] withered.
увяз|ать [1] 1. ⟨**∠нуть**⟩ [21] stick, sink; 2. *s.* **∠ывать(ся)**; **∠ка** *f* [5] coördination; **∠ывать** [1], ⟨**~ать**⟩ [3] tie up; coördinate (*v/i.* -**ся**).
угад|ывать [1], ⟨**~ать**⟩ [1] guess.
угар *m* [1] coal gas; poisoning by coalgas; *fig.* frenzy, intoxication; **~ный** [14] full of coal gas; charcoal...
угас|ать [1], ⟨**∠нуть**⟩ [21] die (*or* fade) out, away, expire, become extinct.
угле|кислота *f* [5] carbonic acid; **~кислый** [14] carbon(ic); chokedamp...; **~коп** *m* [1] *s.* шахтёр; **~род** *m* [1] carbon.
угловой [14] corner...; angle...
углуб|ить(ся) *s.* **~лять(ся)**; **~ление** *n* [12] deepening; hollow, cavity; absorption; extension; **~лённый** [14 *sh.*] profound; *a. p.pt.p. of* **~ить(ся)**; **~лять** [28], ⟨**~ить**⟩ [14 *e.*; -блю, -бишь; блённый] deepen (*v/i.* -**ся**); make (become) more profound, extend; -**ся** *a.* go deep (into в В), be(come) absorbed (in).
угнать *s.* угонять.
угнет|атель *m* [4] oppressor; **~ать** [1] oppress; depress; **~ение** *n* [12] oppression; (*a.* **~ённость** *f* [8]) depression; **~ённый** [14; -тён, -тена] oppressed; depressed.
угов|аривать [1], ⟨**~орить**⟩ [13] (В) (*impf.* try to) persuade; -**ся** arrange, agree; **~ор** *m* [1] agreement, arrangement (by по Д); condition (on с Т); *pl.* persuasion(s); **~орить(ся)** *s.* **~аривать(ся)**.
угод|а *f* [5]: в **~у** (Д) for p.'s sake, to please s. o.; **~ить** *s.* угождать; **~ливый** [14 *sh.*] complaisant; obliging; ingratiating, toadyish; **~ник** *m* [1] saint; **~но** please; как (что) вам **~но** just as (whatever) you like; что вам **~но**? what can I do for you?; не **~но** ли вам ...? wouldn't you like ...; сколько (душе) **~но** *s.* вдоволь & всласть.
уго|ждать [1], ⟨**~дить**⟩ [15 *e.*; -ожу, -одишь] (Д, на В) please; *pf.* F get, come; (в В) hit.
угол *m* [1; угла; в, на углу] corner (at на П); ⊿ angle; nook; home; **~овный** [14] criminal.
уголок *m* [1; -лка] nook, corner.
уголь *m* [4; угля] coal; как на **∠ях** F on tenterhooks; **~ный**[1] [14] coal...; carbonic; **∠ный**[2] F [14] corner...
угомонить(ся) [13] *pf.* calm (down).
угонять [28], ⟨угнать⟩ [угоню, угонишь; угнал, -а, -о; угнанный] drive (away, off); steal; -**ся** F catch up (with за Т).
угор|ать [1], ⟨**~еть**⟩ [9] be poisoned by coal gas; F go mad.
угорь *m* [4 *e.*; угря] eel; blackhead.
уго|щать [1], ⟨**~стить**⟩ [15 *e.*; -ощу, -остишь; -ощённый] treat (with Т), entertain; **~щение** *n* [12] entertainment; food, drinks *pl.*
угро|жать [1] threaten (p. with Д/Т); **∠за** *f* [5] threat, menace.
угрызени|е *n* [12]; **~я** *pl.* совести remorse.
угрюмый [14 *sh.*] morose, gloomy.
удав *m* [1] boa.
уда|ваться [5], ⟨**∠ться**⟩ [удастся, -адутся; удался, -лась] succeed; мне **~ётся** (**~лось**) (+ *inf.*) I succeed (-ed) (in ...ing).
удал|ение *n* [12] removal; extraction; **~ить(ся)** *s.* **~ять(ся)**; **~ой**, **∠ый** [14; удал, -а, -о] bold, daring; **'~ь** *f* [8], F **~ьство** *n* [9] boldness, daring; **~ять** [28], ⟨**~ить**⟩

[13] remove; extract (*tooth*); **-ся** retire, withdraw; move away.
удáр *m* [1] blow (*a. fig.*); (*a.* ⚕) stroke; ⚡, *fig.* shock; impact; slash; (*thunder*)clap; F form; **~éние** *n* [12] stress, accent; **~ить(ся)** *s.* **~я́ть(ся)**; **~ник** *m* [1] shock worker, Stakhanovite (*Sov.*); **~ный** [14] shock...; impact...; foremost; **~я́ть** [28], ⟨**~ить**⟩ [13] strike (on по Д), hit; knock; beat, sound; punch (кулакóм); butt (головóй); kick (ногóй); set about, start (...ing в В *pl.*); attack (*v/t.* на В; with в В *pl.*); go (to *head* в В); F set in; stir; **-ся** strike *or* knock (with/against Т/о В); hit (в В); F fall into; throw o.s., plunge.
удáться *s.* удавáться.
удáч|а *f* [5] (good) luck; **~ник** F *m* [1] lucky man; **~ный** [14; -чен, -чна] successful; good.
удв|áивать [1], ⟨**~óить**⟩ [13] double (*v/i.* **-ся**).
удéл *m* [1] lot, destiny; appanage; **~и́ть** *s.* **~я́ть**; **~ьный** [14] specific (*gravity, a. fig.*); **~я́ть** [28], ⟨**~и́ть**⟩ [13] devote; spare; allot.
удéрж|ивать [1], ⟨**~áть**⟩ [4] withhold, restrain; keep, retain; suppress; deduct; **-ся** hold (on; to за В; *a.* out); refrain (from от Р).
удешев|ля́ть [28], ⟨**~и́ть**⟩ [14 *e.*; -влю́, -ви́шь; -влённый] cheapen.
удив|и́тельный [14; -лен, -льна] wonderful, marvel(l)ous; miraculous; amazing, strange; (не) **~и́тельно** it is a (no) wonder **~и́ть(ся)** *s.* **~ля́ть(ся)**; **~лéние** *n* [12] astonishment, surprise; **~ля́ть** [28], ⟨**~и́ть**⟩ [14 *e.*; -влю́, -ви́шь; -влённый] (**-ся** be) astonish(ed at Д), surprise(d, wonder).
удилá *n/pl.* [9; -и́л, -илáм] bit.
удирáть F [1], ⟨удрáть⟩ [удеру́, -рёшь; удрáл, -á, -о] run away.
уди́ть [15] angle (for *v/t.*), fish (ры́бу).
удлин|éние *n* [12] lengthening; **~я́ть** [28], ⟨**~и́ть**⟩ [13] lengthen.
удóб|ный [14; -бен, -бна] convenient; comfortable; **~о...** easily ...; **~овари́мый** [14 *sh.*] digestible; **~рéние** *n* [12] manure, fertilizer; fertilization; **~ря́ть** [28], ⟨**~рить**⟩ [13] fertilize, manure, dung; **~ство** *n* [9] convenience; comfort; *pl.* facilities.
удовлетвор|éние *n* [12] satisfaction; **~и́тельный** [14; -лен, -льна] satisfactory; *adv. a.* D (*mark*); **~я́ть** [28], ⟨**~и́ть**⟩ [13] satisfy; grant; (Д) meet; **-ся** content o.s. (with Т).
удо|вóльствие *n* [12] pleasure; **~рожáть** [1], ⟨**~рожи́ть**⟩ [16] raise the price of.
удост|áивать [1], ⟨**~óить**⟩ [13] (**-ся** be) hono(u)r(ed), (*a.* ✝) favo(u)r(ed) (with Р, Т); bestow, confer (on); award; deign (to look at p. взгля́да, -ом В); **~оверéние** *n* [12] certificate, certification; (*identity*) card; corroboration (in в В); **~оверя́ть** [28], ⟨**~овéрить**⟩ [13] certify, attest; prove (*one's identity*); convince (of в П; o.s. **-ся**; *a.* make sure); **~óить(ся)** *s.* **~áивать(ся)**.
удосу́житься F [16] find time.
у́дочк|а *f* [5; *g/pl.*: -чек] fishing tackle; *fig.* trap; заки́нуть **~у** F *fig.* drop a hint.
удрáть *s.* удирáть.
удружи́ть [16 *e.*; -жу́, -жи́шь] F *s.* услужи́ть.
удруч|áть [1], ⟨**~и́ть**⟩ [16 *e.*; -чу́, -чи́шь; -чённый] deject, depress.
удуш|éние *n* [12] suffocation; poisoning; **´ливый** [14 *sh.*] stifling, suffocating; oppressive (*heat*); poison (*gas*); **´ье** *n* [10] asthma.
уедин|éние *n* [12] solitude; **~ённый** [14 *sh.*] retired, secluded, lonely, solitary; **~я́ться** [28], ⟨**~и́ться**⟩ [13] retire, seclude o.s.
уéзд † *m* [1], **~ный** [14] district.
уезжáть [1], ⟨уéхать⟩ [уéду, -дешь] (в В) leave (for), go (away; to).
уж 1. *m* [1 *e.*] grass snake; **2.** = ужé; F indeed, well; *do, be* (+ *vb.*).
у́жас *m* [1] horror; terror, fright; F = **´ный**, **´но**; **~áть** [1], ⟨**~ну́ть**⟩ [20] horrify; **-ся** be horrified *or* terrified (at Р, Д); **~áющий** [17] horrifying; **´ный** [14; -сен, -сна] terrible, horrible, dreadful; F awful.
ужé already; as early as; **~** не not ... any more; (вóт) **~** for (*time*).
ужéние *n* [12] angling, fishing.
ужи|вáться [1], ⟨**´ться**⟩ [-иву́сь, -вёшься; -и́лся, -илáсь] get accustomed (to в П); live in harmony (with с Т); **´вчивый** [14 *sh.*] sociable, accomodating; **´мка** *f* [5; *g/pl.*: -мок] grimace; gesture.
у́жин *m* [1] supper (at за Т; for на В, к Д); **~ать** [1], ⟨по-⟩ have supper.
ужи́ться *s.* уживáться.
узакон|éние *n* [12] legalization; statute; **´ивать** & **~я́ть** [28], ⟨**´ить**⟩ [13] legalize.
узбéк *m* [1], **~ский** [16] Uzbek.
узд|á *f* [5; *pl. st.*], **~éчка** *f* [5; *g/pl.*: -чек] bridle.
у́зел *m* [1; узлá] knot; 🚉 junction; center, *Brt.* centre; *anat.* ganglion; bundle; **~óк** *m* [1; -лкá] knot; packet.
у́зк|ий [16; у́зок, узкá, -о; *comp.*: у́же] narrow (*a. fig.*); tight; **~ое мéсто** *n* bottleneck; weak point; **~околéйный** [14] narrow-gauge.
узлов|áтый [14 *sh.*] knotty; **~óй** [14] knot(ty); central, chief; 🚉 *s.* у́зел.
узна|вáть [5], ⟨**´ть**⟩ [1] recognize (by по Д); learn (from: p. от Р; th. из Р), find out, (get to) know, hear; позвóльте **´ть** tell me, please.

ýзник *m* [1] prisoner.
узóр *m* [1] pattern, design; с ~ами = **~чатый** [14 *sh.*] figured; pattern.
ýзость *f* [8] narrow(-minded)ness.
ýзы *f/pl.* [5] bonds, ties.
ýйма F *f* [5] a great lot.
уйтú *s.* уходúть.
укáз *m* [1] decree, edict, ukase; **~áние** *n* [12] instruction (by по Д), direction; indication (of P, на B); **~áтель** *m* [4] index; indicator; guide; **~áтельный** [14] indicatory; fore(*finger*), index; *gr.* demonstrative; **~áть** *s.* **∠ывать**; **~ка** *f* [5] pointer; F order (by по Д); **~ывать** [1], ⟨**~áть**⟩ [3] point out; point (to на B); show; indicate.
укáч|ивать, ⟨**~áть**⟩ [1] rock to sleep, lull; *impers.* make (sea)sick.
уклáд *m* [1] mode, way (*of life*); form; **~ка** *f* [5] packing; laying; **~ывать** [1], ⟨уложúть⟩ [16] put (to bed); lay; pack (up F -ся); place; cover; -ся *a.* find room; F manage.
уклóн *m* [1] slope, incline; slant (*a. fig.* = bias, bent, tendency); *pol.* deviation; **~éние** *n* [12] swerve, deviation; evasion; **~úться** *s.* **~ять-ся**; **~чивый** [14 *sh.*] evasive; **~ять-ся** [28], ⟨**~úться**⟩ [13; -онюсь, -óнишься] deviate; evade (*v/t.* от P); swerve; digress.
уклю́чина *f* [5] oarlock (*Brt.* row-).
укóл *m* [1] prick; ⚕ injection.
укомплектóв|ывать [1], ⟨**~áть**⟩ [7] complete, fill; supply (fully; with T).
укóр *m* [1] reproach; **~áчивать** [1], ⟨**~отúть**⟩ [15 *e.*; -очý, -отúшь; -óченный] shorten; **~енúть** [28], ⟨**~енúть**⟩ [13] implant; -ся take root; **~úзна** *f* [5] *s.* ~; **~úзненный** [14] reproachful; **~úть** *s.* **~ять**; **~отúть** *s.* **~áчивать**; **~ять** [28], ⟨**~úть**⟩ [13] reproach, blame (of в П, за B).
укрáдкой furtively.
Украúн|а *f* [5] Ukraine (in на П); **2ец** *m* [1; -нца], **2ка** *f* [5; *g/pl.*: -нок], **2ский** [16] Ukrainian.
укра|шáть [1], ⟨**∠сить**⟩ [15] adorn; (-ся be) decorate(d); trim; embellish; **~шéние** *n* [12] adornment; decoration; ornament; embellishment.
укреп|úть(ся) *s.* **~лять(ся)**; **~лéние** *n* [12] strengthening; consolidation; ⚔ fortification; **~лять** [28], ⟨**~úть**⟩ [14 *e.*; -плю́, -пúшь; -плённый] strengthen; fasten; consolidate; ⚔ fortify; **~ляющий** *a.* ⚕ restorative; -ся strengthen, become stronger; ⚔ entrench.
укрó|мный [14; -мен, -мна] secluded; **~п** *m* [1] fennel.
укро|тúтель *m* [4], **~тúтельница** [5] tamer; **~щáть** [1], ⟨**~тúть**⟩ [15 *e.*; -ощý, -отúшь; -ощённый] tame; break (*horse*); subdue, restrain; **~щéние** *n* [12] taming; subdual.
укрупн|ять [28], ⟨**~úть**⟩ [13] enlarge, extend; centralize.
укры|вáтель *m* [4] receiver; **~вáть** [1], ⟨**∠ть**⟩ [22] cover; shelter; conceal, harbo(u)r; -ся cover o.s.; hide; take shelter *or* cover; **∠тие** *n* [12] cover, shelter.
ýксус *m* [1] vinegar.
укýс *m* [1] bite; **~úть** *s.* кусáть.
укýт|ывать, ⟨**~ать**⟩ [1] wrap up.
ул. *abbr.*: ýлица.
улá|вливать [1], ⟨уловúть⟩ [14] catch, seize; grasp; **~живать** [1], ⟨**~дить**⟩ [15] settle, arrange; reconcile.
ýлей *m* [3; ýлья] beehive.
улет|áть [1], ⟨**~éть**⟩ [11] fly (away).
улетýчи|ваться [1], ⟨**~ться**⟩ [16] volatilize; F disappear, vanish.
улéчься [26 г/ж: улягусь, уля́жешься, уля́гутся] lie down, go (to bed); settle; calm down, abate.
улúка *f* [5] corpus delicti, proof.
улúтка *f* [5; *g/pl.*: -ток] snail; *anat.* cochlea.
ýлиц|а *f* [5] street (in, on на П); на **~е** *a.* outside, outdoors.
улич|áть [1], ⟨**~úть**⟩ [16 *e.*; -чý, -чúшь; -чённый] (в П) detect, catch (in the act [of]); convict (of); give (a p. *the lie*).
ýличный [14] street...
улóв *m* [1] catch; **~úмый** [14 *sh.*] perceptible; **~úть** *s.* улáвливать; **~ка** *f* [5; *g/pl.*: -вок] trick, ruse.
уложúть(ся) *s.* уклáдывать(ся).
улуч|áть F [1], ⟨**~úть**⟩ [16 *e.*; -чý, -чúшь; -чённый] find.
улучш|áть [1], ⟨**∠ить**⟩ [16] improve; *v/i.* -ся; **~éние** *n* [12] improvement; **∠ить(ся)** *s.* **~áть(ся)**.
улыб|áться [1], ⟨**~нýться**⟩ [20], **∠ка** *f* [5; *g/pl.*: -бок] smile (at Д).
ультракорóткий [16] very-high-frequency (*radio*).
ум *m* [1 *e.*] intellect; mind; sense(s); head (off не в П); без **~á** mad (about от P); зáдним **~óм** крéпок *be* wise after the event; быть на **~é** (у P) have in mind; не егó **~á** дéло beyond his reach; сойтú (F спя́тить) с **~á** go mad; сходúть с **~á** F *a.* be mad (about по П); (у P) ~ за рáзум захóдит F *be* crazy; (у P) ~ корóток F *be* dull *or* dense.
умал|éние *n* [12] belittling; **~úть (-ся)** *s.* **~ять(ся)**; **~ишённый** [14] *s.* сумасшéдший; **∠чивать** [1], ⟨умолчáть⟩ [4 *e.*; -чý, -чúшь] (о П) pass (th.) over in silence; **~ять** [28], ⟨**~úть**⟩ [13] belittle, derogate, disparage; curtail; -ся decrease, lessen.
умé|лый [14] skil(l)ful, skilled; **~ние** *n* [12] skill, faculty, knowhow.
уменьш|áть [1], ⟨**∠ить**⟩ [16 & 16 *e.*; -éньшý, -éньшúшь; -éньшенный & -шённый] reduce, diminish,

decrease (*v/i.* **-ся**); **~éние** *n* [12] decrease, reduction; **~ительный** [14] diminutive; **∠ить(ся)** *s.* **~áть** (-ся).
умéренн|ость *f* [8] moderation, moderateness; **~ый** [14 *sh.*] moderate, (*a. geogr.* [*no sh.*]) temperate.
умер|éть *s.* умирáть; **∠ить** *s.* **~я́ть**; **~тви́ть** *s.* **~щвля́ть**; **∠ший** [17] dead; **~щвля́ть** [28], ⟨**~тви́ть**⟩ [14 *e.*; -рщвлю́, -ртви́шь; -рщвлённый] kill, destroy; mortify; **~я́ть** [28], ⟨**∠ить**⟩ [13] moderate.
уме|сти́ть(ся) *s.* **~щáть(ся)**; **∠стный** (-ˈmesn-) [14; -тен, -тна] appropriate; **∠ть** [8], ⟨с-⟩ can; know how; **~щáть** [1], ⟨**~сти́ть**⟩ [15 *e.*; -ещу́, -ести́шь; -ещённый] get (into в В); **-ся** find room; sit down.
умил|éние *n* [12] deep emotion, affection; **~ённый** [14] affected; affectionate; **~я́ть** [28], ⟨**~и́ть**⟩ [13] (**-ся** be) move(d), touch(ed).
умирáть [1], ⟨умерéть⟩ [12; *pt.*: у́мер, умерлá, -о; умéрший] die (of, from от, с Р).
умн|éть [8], ⟨по-⟩ grow wiser; **∠ик** F *m* [1], **∠ица** *m/f* [5] clever (*or* good) boy, girl, (wo)man; **∠ичать** F [1] *s.* мудри́ть.
умнож|áть [1], ⟨**∠ить**⟩ [16] multiply (by на В); *v/i.* **-ся**; **~éние** *n* [12] multiplication.
у́м|ный [14; умён, умнá, у́мно́] clever, smart, wise; **~озаключéние** *n* [12] conclusion; **~озри́тельный** [14; -лен, -льна] speculative.
умол|и́ть *s* **~я́ть**; **ˈ~к**: без **ˈ~ку** incessantly; **~кáть** [1], ⟨**∠кнуть**⟩ [21] stop, become silent; subside; **~чáть** *s.* умáлчивать; **~я́ть** [28], ⟨**~и́ть**⟩ [13; -олю́, -о́лишь] implore (*v/t.*), beseech, entreat (for о П).
умопо|мешáтельство *n* [9], **~мрачéние** *n* [12] (mental) derangement.
умо́р|а F *f* [5], **~и́тельный** F [14; -лен, -льна] side-splitting, awfully funny; **~и́ть** F [13] *pf.* kill; exhaust, fatigue (*a.* with laughing со́ смеху).
у́мственный [14] intellectual, mental; brain (*work*[*er*]).
умудр|я́ть [28], ⟨**~и́ть**⟩ [13] make wise; **-ся** F contrive, manage.
умывá|льная *f* [14] washroom; **~льник** *m* [1] wash(ing) stand; washbowl, *Brt.* wash-basin; **~ние** *n* [12] washing; wash; **~ть** [1], ⟨умы́ть⟩ [22] (**-ся**) wash (*a.* o.s.).
у́мы|сел *m* [1; -сла] design, intent(ion); с **~слом** (без **~ла**) (un-) intentionally; **∠ть(ся)** *s.* **~вáть(ся)**; **∠шленный** [14] deliberate; intentional.
унаво́живать [1], *s.* наво́зить.
унести́(сь) *s.* уноси́ть(ся).
универ|мáг *m* [1] (**~сáльный** магази́н) department store, *Brt.* stores *pl.*; **~сáльный** [14; -лен, -льна] universal; *cf. a.* универмáг; **~ситéт** *m* [1] university (at, in в П).
уни|жáть [1], ⟨**∠зить**⟩ [15] humble, humiliate, abase; **~жéние** *n* [12] humiliation; **~жённый** [14 *sh.*] humble; **~зи́тельный** [14; -лен, -льна] humiliating; **∠зить** *s.* **~жáть**.
унимáть [1], ⟨уня́ть⟩ [уйму́, уймёшь; уня́л, -á, -о; -я́тый (-я́т, -á, -о)] appease, soothe; still (*pain*); stanch (*blood*); **-ся** calm *or* quiet down; subside.
уничижи́тельный [14] *ling.* pejorative.
уничт|ожáть [1], ⟨**~о́жить**⟩ [16] annihilate; destroy; abolish, annul; **~ожéние** *n* [12] annihilation; **~о́жить** *s.* **~ожáть**.
уноси́ть [15], ⟨унести́⟩ [24 -с-] carry, take (away, off); **-ся**, ⟨-сь⟩ speed away.
у́нтер-офицéр *m* [1] corporal.
уны|вáть [1] despond; **∠лый** [14 *sh.*] sad, dejected; **∠ние** *n* [12] despondency; ennui.
уня́ть(ся) *s.* унимáть(ся).
упáдо|к *m* [1; -дка] decay, decadence; **~к** ду́ха dejection; **~к** сил collapse; **~чный** [14; -чен, -чна] decadent; depressive.
упаков|áть *s.* **∠ывать**; **∠ка** *f* [5; *g/pl.*: -вок] packing; wrappings *pl.*; **∠щик** *m* [1] packer; **∠ывать** [1], ⟨**~áть**⟩ [7] pack (up).
упáсть *s.* пáдать.
упирáть [1], ⟨уперéть⟩ [12] prop, stay (against в В); rest (*a.*, F, *eyes* on в В); P steal; **-ся** lean, prop (s.th. Т; against в В); F rest (on в В); insist on; be obstinate.
упи́танный [14 *sh.*] well-fed, fat.
уплá|та *f* [5] payment (in в В); **~чивать** [1], ⟨**~ти́ть**⟩ [15] pay; meet (*bill*).
уплотн|я́ть [28], ⟨**~и́ть**⟩ [13] condense, compact; fill up (with work).
уплы|вáть [1], ⟨**∠ть**⟩ [23] swim *or* sail (away, off); pass (away), vanish.
уповáть [1] (на В) trust (in), hope (for).
упод|обля́ть [28], ⟨**~о́бить**⟩ [14] liken; assimilate (*v/i.* **-ся**).
упо|éние *n* [12] rapture, ecstasy; **~ённый** [14; -ён, -енá] enraptured; **~и́тельный** [14; -лен, -льна] rapturous, delightful; intoxicating.
уползти́ [24] *pf.* creep away.
уполномо́ч|енный *m* [14] plenipotentiary; **~ивать** [1], ⟨**~ить**⟩ [16] authorize, empower (to на В).
упоминá|ние *n* [12] mention (of о П); **~ть** [1], ⟨упомяну́ть⟩ [19] mention (*v/t.* В, о П).

упо́р *m* [1] rest; support, prop; 🚂 buffer stop; ⊕ stop, catch; де́лать ~ lay stress *or* emphasis (on на В); в ~ point-blank, straightforward (*a. look* at на В); **~ный** [14; -рен, -рна] pertinacious, persistent, persevering; stubborn, obstinate; **~ство** *n* [9] persistence, perseverance; obstinacy; **~ствовать** [7] persevere, persist (in в П).

употреб|и́тельный [14; -лен, -льна] common, customary; current; **~и́ть** *s.* **~ля́ть**; **~ле́ние** *n* [12] use; usage; **~ля́ть** [28], ‹~и́ть› [14 *e.*; -блю́, -би́шь; -блённый] (*impf.* -ся be) use(d), employ(ed); take (*medicine*); make (*efforts*); **~и́ть** во зло abuse.

управ|до́м *m* [1] (управля́ющий до́мом) manager of the house; **~иться** *s.* **~ля́ться**; **~ле́ние** *n* [12] administration (of P; T), management; direction; board; ⊕ control; *gr.* government; **~ля́ть** [28] (T) manage, operate; rule; govern (*a. gr.*); drive; ⚓ steer; ⊕ control; guide; ♪ conduct; **-ся**, ‹**~иться**› F [14] (с T) manage; finish; **~ля́ющий** *m* [17] manager; steward.

упражн|е́ние *n* [12] exercise; practice; **~я́ть** [28] exercise (*v/t.*, *v/refl.* -ся; в П: practise s.th.).

упраздн|е́ние *n* [12] abolition; **~и́ть** [28], ‹~и́ть› [13] abolish.

упра́шивать [1], ‹упроси́ть› [15] (*impf.* try to) persuade.

упрёк *m* [1] reproach, blame.

упрек|а́ть [1], ‹~ну́ть› [20] reproach, blame (with в П).

упро|си́ть *s.* упра́шивать; **~сти́ть** *s.* **~ща́ть**; **~че́ние** *n* [12] consolidation; **~чивать** [1], ‹~чить› [16] consolidate (*v/i.* -ся), stabilize; **~ща́ть** [1], ‹~сти́ть› [15 *e.*; -ощу́, -ости́шь; -ощённый] simplify; **~ще́ние** *n* [12] simplification.

упру́г|ий [16 *sh.*] elastic, resilient; **~ость** *f* [8] elasticity.

у́пряжь *f* [8] harness.

упря́м|иться [14] be obstinate; persist; **~ство** *n* [9] obstinacy, stubbornness; **~ый** [14 *sh.*] obstinate, stubborn.

упря́т|ывать [1], ‹~ать› [3] hide.

упу|ска́ть [1], ‹~сти́ть› [15] let go; let escape; miss; *cf.* вид); **~ще́ние** *n* [12] neglect, ommission.

ура́! hurrah!

уравн|е́ние *n* [12] equation; **~ивать** [1] **1.** ‹уровня́ть› [28] level; **2.** ‹~я́ть› [28] equalize, level *fig.*; **~и́тельный** [14] level(l)ing; **~ове́шивать** [1], ‹~ове́сить› [15] balance; *p.pt.p. a.* well-balanced, composed, calm; **~я́ть** *s.* **~ивать 2.**

урага́н *m* [1] hurricane.

Ура́л *m* [1], **2ьский** [16] Ural.

ура́н *m* [1], **~овый** [14] uranium.

урегули́рование *n* [12] settlement; regulation; *vb. cf.* регули́ровать.

урез|а́ть & **~ывать** F [1], ‹~ать› [3] cut (down), curtail; **~о́нить** F [13] *pf.* bring to reason.

у́рна *f* [5] urn; (*voting*) box.

у́ров|ень *m* [4; -вня] level (at, on на П; в В); standard; gauge; rate; **~ня́ть** *s.* ура́внивать 1.

уро́д *m* [1] monster; F ugly creature; **~и́ться** [15 *e.*; -и́тся; -ождённый] *pf.* grow, be born; F be like (р. в В); **~ливый** [14 *sh.*] deformed; ugly; abnormal; **~овать** [7], ‹из-› deform, disfigure; mutilate; spoil; **~ство** *n* [9] deformity; ugliness; abnormity.

урож|а́й *m* [3] harvest, (abundant) crop; **~а́йность** *f* [8] yield (heavy высо́кая), productivity; **~а́йный** [14] fruitful; **~дённая** [14] nee; **~е́нец** *m* [1; -нца], **~е́нка** *f* [5; *g/pl.*: -нок] native.

уро́|к *m* [1] lesson (in на П); task; **~н** *m* [1] loss(es); injury; **~ни́ть** *s.* роня́ть; **~чный** [14] set, fixed.

Уругва́й *m* [4] Uruguay.

урча́ть [4 *e.*; -чу́, -чи́шь] (g)rumble; murmur.

уры́вками F by fits (& starts).

ус *m* [1; *pl. e.*] (*mst pl.*) m(o)ustache; кито́вый ~ whalebone.

уса|ди́ть *s.* **~живать**; **~дьба** *f* [5; *g/pl.*: -деб] farm (land); manor; **~живать** [1], ‹~ди́ть› [15] seat; set; plant (with T); **-ся**, ‹усе́сться› [25; уся́дусь, -дешься; уся́дься, -дьтесь!; усе́лся, -лась] sit down, take a seat; settle down.

уса́тый [14] with a m(o)ustache.

усв|а́ивать [1], ‹~о́ить› [13] adopt; acquire, assimilate; master, learn; **~о́ение** *n* [12] adoption; acquirement, assimilation; mastering, learning.

усе́|ивать [1], ‹~ять› [27] stud.

усе́рд|ие *n* [12] zeal, eagerness (for к Д); assiduity; **~ный** [14; -ден, -дна] eager, zealous; assiduous.

усе́сться *s.* уса́живаться.

усе́ять *s.* усе́ивать.

усид|е́ть [11] *pf.* remain seated, sit still, (can) sit; hold out; **~чивый** [14 *sh.*] assiduous, persevering.

у́сик *m* [1] *dim. of* ус; *zo.* feeler.

усил|е́ние *n* [12] strengthening, reinforcement; intensification; amplification; **~енный** [14] intens(iv)e; substantial; pressing; **~ивать** [1], ‹~ить› [13] strengthen, reinforce; intensify; (*sound*) amplify; aggravate; -ся increase; **~ие** *n* [12] effort, strain, exertion; **~и́тель** *m* [4] amplifier (*radio*); **~ить(ся)** *s.* **~ивать(ся)**.

ускака́ть [3] *pf.* leap *or* gallop (away).

ускольз|а́ть [1], ⟨**~ну́ть**⟩ [20] slip (off, away), escape (from от P).
ускор|е́ние *n* [12] acceleration; **~я́ть** [28], ⟨**~́ить**⟩ [13] speed up, accelerate; *v/i.* **-ся**.
усла́|вливаться F *s.* усло́вливаться; **~жда́ть** [1], ⟨**~ди́ть**⟩ [15 *e.*; -ажу́, -ади́шь; -аждённый] sweeten, soften; delight, **~ть** *s.* усыла́ть.
усло́в|ие *n* [12] condition (on с T, при П; under на П), term; stipulation; proviso; agreement, contract; **~иться** *s.* **~ливаться**; **~ленный** [14 *sh.*] agreed upon, fixed; **~ливаться** [1], ⟨**~иться**⟩ [14] arrange, fix, agree (upon о П); **~ность** *f* [8] convention; **~ный** [14; -вен, -вна] conditional; conventional; relative; ⚖ probational; **~ные зна́ки** *pl.* conditional signes.
усложн|я́ть [28], ⟨**~и́ть**⟩ [13] (**-ся** become) complicate(d).
услу́|га *f* [5] service (at к Д *pl.*), favo(u)r; **~живать** [1], ⟨**~жи́ть**⟩ [16] do (p. Д) a service *or* favo(u)r; **~жливый** [14 *sh.*] obliging.
усм|а́тривать [1], ⟨**~отре́ть**⟩ [9; -отрю́, -о́тришь; -о́тренный] see (after за T); **~еха́ться** [1], ⟨**~ехну́ться**⟩ [20], **~е́шка** *f* [5; *g/pl.*: -шек] smile, grin; **~ире́ние** *n* [12] suppression; **~иря́ть** [28], ⟨**~ири́ть**⟩ [13] pacify; suppress; **~отре́ние** *n* [12] discretion (at по Д; to на В), judg(e)ment; **~отре́ть** *s.* **~а́тривать**
усну́ть [20] *pf.* fall asleep; sleep.
усоверше́нствован|ие *n* [12] improvement, perfection; **~ный** [14] improved, perfected.
усомни́ться *s.* сомнева́ться.
усо́пший [17] deceased.
успе|ва́емость *f* [8] progress; **~ва́ть** [1], ⟨**~́ть**⟩ [8] have (*or* find) time, manage, succeed; arrive, be in time (for к Д, на В); catch (*train* на В); *impf.* get on, make progress, learn; не **~́л(а)** (+ *inf.*), как no sooner + *pt.* than; **~ва́ющий** [17] advanced; **~́х** *m* [1] success; result; *pl. a.* progress; **~́шный** [14; -шен, -шна] successful; **~́шно** *a.* with success.
успок|а́ивать [1], ⟨**~о́ить**⟩ [13] calm, soothe; reassure; satisfy; **-ся** calm down; subside; become quiet; content o.s. (with на П); **~ое́ние** *n* [12] peace; calm; **~ои́тельный** [14; -лен, -льна] soothing, reassuring; **~о́ить(ся)** *s.* **~а́ивать(ся)**.
УССР (Украи́нская Сове́тская Социалисти́ческая Респу́блика) Ukrainian Soviet Socialist Republic.
уста́ † *n/pl.* [9] mouth, lips *pl.*
уста́в *m* [1] statute(s); regulations *pl.*; charter (*a. UNO*).
уста|ва́ть [5], ⟨**~́ть**⟩ [-а́ну, -а́нешь] get tired; **~вля́ть** [28], ⟨**~́вить**⟩ [14] place; cover (with T), fill; fix (*eyes* on на В); **-ся** stare (at, на *or* в В); **~́лость** *f* [8] weariness, fatigue; **~́лый** [14] tired, weary; **~на́вливать** [1], ⟨**~нови́ть**⟩ [14] set *or* put up; mount; arrange; fix; establish; find out, ascertain; adjust (to на В); **-ся** be established; form; set in; **~но́вка** *f* [5; *g/pl.*: -вок] mounting, installation; ⊕ plant; *fig.* orientation (toward[s] на В); **~новле́ние** *n* [12] establishment; **~ре́лый** [14] obsolete, out-of-date; **~́ть** *s.* **~ва́ть**.
устила́ть [1], ⟨устла́ть⟩ [-телю́, -те́лешь; у́стланный] cover, lay out (with T).
у́стный [14] oral, verbal.
усто́|и *m/pl.* [3] foundations; **~йчивость** *f* [8] stability; **~йчивый** [14 *sh.*] stable; **~я́ть** [-ою́, -ои́шь] keep one's balance; hold one's ground; resist (*v/t.* про́тив P, пе́ред T).
устр|а́ивать [1], ⟨**~о́ить**⟩ [13] arrange; organize, set up; furnish; construct; make (*scene, etc.*); provide (*job* на В, place in в В); F suit; **-ся** be settled; settle; get a job (*a.* на В); **~ане́ние** *n* [12] removal; elimination; **~аня́ть** [28], ⟨**~ани́ть**⟩ [13] remove; eliminate; **~аша́ть** (**-ся**) [1], *s.* страши́ть(ся); **~емля́ть** [28], ⟨**~еми́ть**⟩ [14 *e.*; -млю́, -ми́шь; -млённый] (на В) direct (to, at), fix (on); **-ся** rush; be directed; **~́ица** *f* [5] oyster; **~о́ить** (**-ся**) *s.* **~а́ивать(ся)**; **~о́йство** *n* [9] arrangement; establishment; equipment; installation; organization; system; mechanism.
усту́п *m* [1] ledge; projection; step; terrace; **~а́ть** [1], ⟨**~и́ть**⟩ [14] cede, let (p. Д) have; yield; be inferior to (Д); sell; abate (*v/t.* с P, в П); **~а́ть доро́гу** (Д) let p. pass, give way; **~и́тельный** [14] *gr.* concessive; **~ка** *f* [5; *g/pl.*: -пок] concession; cession; ✝ abatement, reduction; **~чивый** [14 *sh.*] compliant, pliant.
усты|жа́ть [1], ⟨**~ди́ть**⟩ [15 *e.*; -ыжу́, -ыди́шь; -ыжённый] (**-ся** be) ashame(d; of P).
у́стье *n* [10; *g/pl.*: -ьев] mouth (at в П).
усугуб|ля́ть [28], ⟨**~́ить**⟩ [14 & 14 *e.*; -гу́блю, -гу́би́шь; -гу́бленный & -гублённый] increase, redouble.
усы́ *s.* ус; **~ла́ть** [1], ⟨усла́ть⟩ [ушлю́, ушлёшь; у́сланный] send (away); **~новля́ть** [28], ⟨**~нови́ть**⟩ [14 *e.*; -влю́, -ви́шь; -влённый] adopt; **~па́ть** [1], ⟨**~пать**⟩ [2] (be)strew (with T); **~пи́тельный** [14; -лен, -льна] soporific; drowsy;

~пля́ть [28], ⟨~пи́ть⟩ [14 *e.*; -плю́, -пи́шь; -плённый] lull (to sleep); ⚕ narcotize.

ута́|ивать [1], ⟨~и́ть⟩ [13] conceal, hide; embezzle; **~йка** F: без ~йки frankly; **~птывать** [1], ⟨утопта́ть⟩ [3] tread *or* trample (down); **~скивать** [1], ⟨~щи́ть⟩ [16] carry, drag *or* take (off, away); F pilfer.

у́тварь *f* [8] implements, utensils *pl.*

утвер|ди́тельный [14; -лен, -льна] affirmative (in the -но); **~жда́ть** [1], ⟨~ди́ть⟩ [15 *e.*; -ржу́, -рди́шь; -рждённый] confirm; consolidate (*v/i.* -ся); *impf.* affirm, assert, maintain; **~жде́ние** *n* [12] confirmation; affirmation, assertion; consolidation.

уте|ка́ть [1], ⟨**´**чь⟩ [26] flow (away); F escape; **~ре́ть** *s.* утира́ть; **~рпе́ть** [10] *pf.*: не ~рпе́л, что́бы не (+ *inf. pf.*) could not help ...ing.

утёс *m* [1] cliff, rock.

уте́|чка *f* [5] leakage, escape; **~чь** *s.* ~ка́ть; **~ша́ть** [1], ⟨~шить⟩ [16] console, comfort; **-ся** *a.* take comfort (in T); **~ше́ние** *n* [12] comfort, consolation; **~ши́тельный** [14; -лен, -льна] comforting, consolatory.

ути́|ль *m* [4], **~льсырьё** *n* [10] scrap(s); **~ра́ть** [1], ⟨утере́ть⟩ [12] wipe; **~ха́ть** [1], ⟨~хнуть⟩ [21] subside, abate; cease; calm down.

у́тка *f* [5; *g/pl.*: у́ток] duck; canard.

уткну́ть(ся) F [20] *pf.* thrust; hide; put; be(come) engrossed.

утол|и́ть *s.* ~я́ть; **~ща́ть** [1], ⟨~сти́ть⟩ [15 *e.*; -лщу́, -лсти́шь; -лщённый] thicken; **~ще́ние** *n* [12] thickening; **~я́ть** [28], ⟨~и́ть⟩ [13] quench; appease; allay, still.

утом|и́тельный [14; -лен, -льна] wearisome, tiresome; **~и́ть(ся)** *s.* ~ля́ть(ся); **~ле́ние** *n* [12] fatigue, exhaustion; **~лённый** [14; -лён, -ена́] tired, weary; **~ля́ть** [28], ⟨~и́ть⟩ [14 *e.*; -млю́, -ми́шь; -млённый] tire, weary (*v/i.* -ся; *a.* get tired).

утонч|а́ть [1], ⟨~и́ть⟩ [16 *e.*; -чу́, -чи́шь; -чённый] thin; *fig.* refine; (*v/i.* -ся).

утоп|а́ть [1] **1.** ⟨утону́ть⟩ *s.* тону́ть 2.; **2.** overflow (with в П); wallow, revel; **´ленник** *m* [1] drowned man; **´ленница** *f* [5] drowned woman; **~та́ть** *s.* ута́птывать.

уточн|е́ние *n* [12] specification; **~я́ть** [28], ⟨~и́ть⟩ [13] specify.

утра́|ивать [1], ⟨утро́ить [13] treble; *v/i.* -ся; **~мбова́ть** [7] *pf.* ram; stamp; **~та** *f* [5] loss; **~чивать** [1], ⟨~тить⟩ [15] lose.

у́тренн|ий [15] morning; **~ик** *m* [1] matinee; morning frost.

у́тр|о *n* [9; с, до -а́; к -у́] morning (in the ~ом; по **´**ам);... ~а́ *a.* ... a.m. (*cf.* день); **~о́ба** *f* [5] womb; **~о́ить** (-ся) *s.* ~а́ивать(ся); **~ужда́ть** [1], ⟨~уди́ть⟩ [15 *e.*; -ужу́, -уди́шь; -уждённый] trouble, bother.

утю́|г *m* [1 *e.*] (flat)iron; **~жить** [16], ⟨вы́-, от-⟩ iron; stroke.

уха́ *f* [5] fish soup; **~б** *m* [1] hole; **~бистый** [14 *sh.*] bumpy.

уха́живать [1] (за T) nurse, look after; (pay) court (to), woo.

у́харский F [16] dashing.

у́хать [1], *once* ⟨у́хнуть⟩ [20] boom.

ухва́т|ывать [1], ⟨~и́ть⟩ [15] (за В) seize, grasp; **-ся** snatch; cling to.

ухи|тря́ться [28], ⟨~три́ться⟩ [13] contrive, manage; **~щре́ние** *n* [12], **~щря́ться** [28] shift.

ухмыл|я́ться F [28], ⟨~ьну́ться⟩ [20] grin, smile (contentedly).

у́хнуть *s.* у́хать.

у́хо *n* [9; *pl.*: у́ши, уше́й, *etc. e.*] ear (in на́ В); по́ уши over head and ears; пропуска́ть ми́мо уше́й turn a deaf ear (to В); держа́ть ~ востро́ *s.* насторо́же.

ухо́д *m* [1] departure; (за T) care, tendance; nursing; **~и́ть** [15], ⟨уйти́⟩ [уйду́, уйдёшь; ушёл, ушла́; уше́дший; *g.pt.*: уйдя́] leave (*v/t.* из, от P), depart (from), go (away); pass; escape; evade; resign; retire; be lost; fail; take; sink; plunge; F be spent (for на В).

ухудш|а́ть [1], ⟨**´**ить⟩ [16] deteriorate (*v/i.* -ся); **~е́ние** *n* [12] deterioration; change for the worse.

уцеле́ть [8] *pf.* escape; be spared.

уцепи́ться [14] F *s.* ухвати́ться.

уча́ст|вовать [7] participate, take part (in в П); **~вующий** [17] *s.* ~ник; **~ие** *n* [12] (в П) participation (in); interest (in), sympathy (with); **~и́ть(ся)** *s.* учаща́ть(ся); **~ливый** [14 *sh.*] sympathizing, sympathetic; **~ник** *m* [1], **~ница** *f* [5] participant, participator; competitor (*sports*); member; **~ок** *m* [1; -тка] (p)lot; section; region; district; site; *fig.* field, branch; † (police) station; **'~ь** *f* [8] fate, lot.

уча|ща́ть [1], ⟨~сти́ть⟩ [15 *e.*; -ащу́, -асти́шь; -ащённый] make (-ся become) more frequent; speed up.

уч|а́щийся *m* [17] schoolboy, pupil, student; **~ёба** *f* [5] studies *pl.*, study; training; drill; **~е́бник** *m* [1] textbook; **~е́бный** [14] school...; educational; text(*book*), exercise...; training; ⚔ drill...; ~е́бный план *m* curriculum.

уче́н|ие *n* [12] learning; instruction; apprenticeship; ⚔ drill; teaching, doctrine; **~и́к** *m* [1 *e.*] schoolboy (**~и́ца** *f* [5] schoolgirl), pupil;

student; apprentice; disciple; **~и́ческий** [16] pupils', students'.
учён|ость *f* [8] learning; **~ый** [14 *sh.*] learned; *su.* scholar.
уч|есть *s.* учитывать; **~ёт** *m* [1] calculation; registration; inventory; discount; list(s); *fig.* consideration, regard; вести́ ~ёт keep books *pl.*; взять на ~ёт register.
учи́лище *n* [11] school (at в П).
учиня́ть [28] *s.* чини́ть 2.
учи́тель *m* [4; *pl.*: -ля́, *etc. e.*; *fig. st.*], **~ница** *f* [5] teacher, instructor; **~ский** [16] (of) teachers(').
учи́тывать [1], ⟨уче́сть⟩ [25; учту́, -тёшь; учёл, учла́; *g. pt.*: учтя́; учтённый] take into account, consider; calculate; register; ☨ take late; stock; discount.
учи́ть [16] **1.** ⟨на-, об-, вы́-⟩ teach (p. s.th. В/Д), instruct; ⚔ drill; train; (*a.* **-ся** Д); **2.** ⟨вы́-⟩ learn, study.
учреди́тель *m* [4] founder; **~ный** [14] constituent.
учре|жда́ть [1], ⟨~ди́ть⟩ [15 *e.*; -ежу́, -еди́шь; -еждённый] found, constitute; establish, introduce; **~жде́ние** *n* [12] foundation, constitution; institution; institute, office (at в П).
учти́вый [14 *sh.*] polite; obliging.
уша́т *m* [1] tub, bucket.
ушио́ *m* [1] bruise; injury; **~а́ть** [1], ⟨~и́ть⟩ [-бу́, -бёшь; -и́б(ла); уши́бленный] hurt, bruise (o.s. **-ся**).
ушко́ *n* [9; *pl.*: -ки́, -ко́в] eye.
ушно́й [14] ear...
уще́лье *n* [10] gorge, ravine.
ущем|ля́ть [28], ⟨~и́ть⟩ [14 *e.*; -млю́, -ми́шь; -млённый] pinch, jam; *fig.* restrain; F wound, impair.
уще́рб *m* [1] damage; wane.
ущи́пнуть [20] *s.* щипа́ть.
Уэ́льс *m* [1] Wales.
ую́т *m* [1] coziness; **~ный** [14; -тен, -тна] snug, cozy, comfortable.
уязв|и́мый [14 *sh.*] vulnerable; **~ля́ть** [28], ⟨~и́ть⟩ [14 *e.*; -влю́, -ви́шь; -влённый] wound, sting; *fig.* hurt.
уясн|я́ть [28], ⟨~и́ть⟩ [13] comprehend; make clear, clear up.

Ф

фабзавко́м *m* [1] *s.* завко́м.
фа́бри|ка *f* [5] factory (in на П); mill; **~ка́нт** *m* [1] manufacturer; **~ка́т** *m* [1] product; **∠чный** [14] factory (*a.* worker); trade(*mark*).
фа́була *f* [5] plot.
фа́з|а *f* [5], **~ис** *m* [1] phase.
фаза́н *m* [1] pheasant.
фа́кел *m* [1] torch.
факт *m* [1] fact; ~ тот the matter is; **~и́ческий** [16] (f)actual, real; *adv. a.* in fact; **~у́ра** *f* [5] invoice.
факульте́т *m* [1] faculty (in на П).
фаль|сифици́ровать [7] (*im*)*pf.* falsify, forge; adulterate; **~ши́вить** [14], ⟨с-⟩ sing out of tune, play falsely; F cheat, be false; **~ши́вка** F *f* [5; *g/pl.*: -вок] forgery; **~ши́вый** [14 *sh.*] false; forged, counterfeit; base (*coin*); **~шь** *f* [8] falseness; hypocrisy; deceit(fulness).
фами́л|ия *f* [7] surname, family name; как ва́ша ~ия? what is your name?; **~ья́рный** [14; -рен, -рна] familiar.
фанати́|зм *m* [1] fanaticism; **~ческий** [16], **~чный** [14; -чен, -чна] fanatical.
фане́ра *f* [5] plywood; veneer.
фанта|зёр *m* [1] visionary; **~зи́ровать** [7] indulge in fancies, dream; ⟨с-⟩ invent; **∠зия** *f* [7] imagination; fancy; invention, fib; ♪ fantasia; F whim, freak; **~сти́ческий** [16], **~сти́чный** [14; -чен, -чна] fantastic.
фа́р|а *f* [5] headlight; **~ва́тер** *m* [1] waterway, fairway; *fig.* track; **~маце́вт** *m* [1] pharmac(eut)ist; **~тук** *m* [1] apron; **~фо́р** *m* [1], **~фо́ровый** [14] china, porcelain; **~ш** *m* [1] stuffing; forcemeat; **~широва́ть** [7] stuff.
фасо́|ль *f* [8] string (*Brt.* runner) bean(s); **~н** *m* [1] cut, style.
фат *m* [1] dandy, fop, dude.
фата́льный [14; -лен, -льна] fatal.
фаши́|зм *m* [1] fascism; **~ст** *m* [1] fascist; **~стский** [16] fascist...
фая́нс *m* [1], **~овый** [14] faïence.
февра́ль *m* [4 *e.*] February.
федера́|льный [14] federal; **~ти́вный** [14] federative, federal.
Фёдор *m* [1] Theodore; *dim.* **Фе́дя** [*m* [6].]
феери́ческий [16] fairylike.
фейерве́рк *m* [1] firework.
фельд|ма́ршал *m* [1] field marshal; **~фе́бель** *m* [4] sergeant; **∠шер** *m* [1] medical assistant.
фельето́н *m* [1] feuilleton.
фено́мен *m* [1] phenomenon.
феода́льный [14] feudal.
ферзь *m* [4 *e.*] queen (*chess*).
фе́рм|а *f* [5] farm; **~ер** *m* [1] farmer.
фестива́ль *m* [4] festival.
фетр *m* [1] felt; **∠овый** [14] felt...
фехтова́|льщик *m* [1] fencer; **~ние** *n* [12] fencing; **~ть** [7] fence.
фиа́лка *f* [5; *g/pl.*: -лок] violet.
фи́бра *f* [5] fiber, *Brt.* fibre.
фи́г|а *f* [5], **~овый** [14] fig.
фигу́р|а *f* [5] figure; (*chess*)man;

~а́льный [14; -лен, -льна] figurative; **~и́ровать** [7] figure, appear; **~ный** [14] figured; trick..., stunt...
фи́зи|к *m* [1] physicist; **~ка** *f* [5] physics; **~оло́гия** *f* [7] physiology; **~оно́мия** *f* [7] physiognomy; **∠ческий** [16] physical; manual.
физкульту́р|а *f* [5] physical culture; gymnastics; **~ник** *m* [1], **~ница** *f* [5] sports(wo)man, gymnast.
фик|са́ж *m* [1] fixative; **~си́ровать** [7], ⟨за-⟩ fix; **~ти́вный** [14; -вен, -вна] fictitious.
фила|нтро́п *m* [1] philanthropist; **~рмони́ческий** [16] philharmonic.
филе́ *n* [*ind.*] tenderloin, fillet.
филиа́л *m* [1] branch (office); **~ьный** [14] branch...
фи́лин *m* [1] eagle owl.
Филиппи́ны *f/pl.* [5] Philippines.
фило́л|ог *m* [1] philologist; **~оги́ческий** [16] philological; **~о́гия** *f* [7] philology.
фило́с|оф *m* [1] philosopher; **~о́фия** *f* [7] philosophy; **~о́фский** [16] philosophical; **~о́фствовать** [7] philosophize.
фильм *m* [1] film (*vb.*: снима́ть ~).
фильтр *m* [1], **~ова́ть** [7] filter.
фимиа́м *m* [1] incense.
фина́л *m* [1] final; ♪ finale.
финанс|и́ровать [7] (*im*)*pf.* finance; **∠овый** [14] financial; **∠ы** *m/pl.* [1] finance(s).
фи́ник *m* [1] date; **~овый** [14] date...
фин|ля́ндец *m* [1; -дца], **~н** *m* [1], **∠(ля́нд)ка** *f* [5; *g/pl.*: -н(ля́нд)ок] Finn; **♀ля́ндия** *f* [7] Finland; **∠(ля́нд)ский** [16] Finnish.
фиоле́товый [14] violet.
фи́рма *f* [5] firm.
фити́ль *m* [4 *e.*] wick; match.
флаг *m* [1] flag, colo(u)rs *pl.*; banner.
фланг *m* [1], **∠овый** [14] flank.
Фла́ндрия *f* [7] Flanders.
флане́л|евый [14], **~ь** *f* [8] flannel.
флегма *f* [5] phlegm; **~ти́чный** [14; -чен, -чна] phlegmatic(al).
флейта *f* [5] flute.
фли́|гель ⚠ *m* [4; *pl.*: -ля́, *etc. e.*] wing; **~рт** *m* [1] flirtation; **~ртова́ть** [7] flirt.
флот *m* [1] fleet; marine; navy; (*air*) force; **∠ский** [16] naval; *su.* F sailor.
флю|гер *m* [1] weathercock, weather vane; **~с** *m* [1] gumboil.
фля|га, ~жка *f* [5; *g/pl.*: -жек] flask; canteen, *Brt.* water bottle.
фойе́ *n* [*ind.*] *thea.* lobby, foyer.
фокстро́т *m* [1] fox trot.
фо́кус *m* [1] hocus-pocus, (juggler's) trick, sleight of hand; F trick; freak, whim; **~ник** *m* [1] juggler, conjurer; **~ничать** F [1] trick.
фо́льга *f* [5] foil.
фолькло́р *m* [1], **~ный** [14] folklore.
Фо|ма́ *m* [5] Thomas; **♀н** *m* [1] background (against на П).
фона́р|ик *m* [1] flashlight, *Brt.* (electric) torch; **~ь** *m* [4 *e.*] lantern; (street) lamp; (head)light; Fs. синя́к.
фонд *m* [1] fund.
фоне́т|ика *f* [5] phonetics; **~и́ческий** [16] phonetic(al).
фонта́н *m* [1] fountain.
форе́ль *f* [8] trout.
фо́рм|а *f* [5] form, shape; model; ⊕ mo(u)ld; ⚔ uniform; dress (*sports*); **~а́льность** *f* [8] formality; **~а́льный** [14; -лен, -льна] formal; **~а́т** *m* [1] size; form; **~енный** [14] formal; F downright; **~енная оде́жда** *f* uniform; **~ирова́ть** [7], ⟨с-⟩ (-ся be) form(ed); **~ова́ть** [7], ⟨с-, от-⟩ mo(u)ld, model; **~ули́ровать** [7] (*im*)*pf.* & ⟨с-⟩ formulate; **~ули-ро́вка** *f* [5; *g/pl.*: -вок] formulation; **~уля́р** *m* [1] form.
форпо́ст *m* [1] advanced post.
форси́ровать [7] (*im*)*pf.* force.
фо́|рточка *f* [5; *g/pl.*: -чек] window leaf; **~сфор** *m* [1] phosphorus.
фото|аппара́т *m* [1] camera; **∠граф** *m* [1] photographer; **~графи́ровать** [7], ⟨с-⟩ photograph; **~графи́ческий** [16] photographic; *cf.* ~аппара́т; **~гра́фия** *f* [7] photograph; photography; photographer's.
фра́за *f* [5] phrase; empty talk.
фрак *m* [1] dress coat.
фра́кция *f* [7] faction.
франки́ровать [7] (*im*)*pf.* stamp.
франт *m* [1] dandy, fop; **~и́ть** F [15 *e.*; -нчу́, -нти́шь] overdress; **~овско́й** [16] dandyish, dudish.
Фра́нц|ия *f* [7] France; **♀у́женка** *f* [5; *g/pl.*: -нок] Frenchwoman; **♀у́з** *m* [1] Frenchman; **♀у́зский** [16] French.
фрахт *m* [1], **~ова́ть** [7] freight.
ФРГ *cf.* Герма́ния.
фре́зер *m* [1] milling cutter.
френч *m* [1] (army-type) jacket.
фре́ска *f* [5] fresco.
фронт *m* [1] front; **~ово́й** [14] front...
фрукт *m* [1] (*mst pl.*) fruit; **~о́вый** [14] fruit...; **~о́вый сад** *m* orchard.
фу! fie!, ugh!
фуга́сный [14] demolition (*bomb*).
фунда́мент *m* [1] foundation; basis; **~а́льный** [14; -лен, -льна] fundamental.
функциони́ровать [7] function.
фунт *m* [1] pound (= *409.5 g*).
фур|а́ж *m* [1 *e.*] fodder; **~а́жка** *f* [5; *g/pl.*: -жек] (service) cap; **~го́н** *m* [1] van; **∠ия** *f* [7] fury; **~о́р** *m* [1] furor; **~у́нкул** *m* [1] furuncle, boil.
футбо́л *m* [1] soccer, *Brt. a.* association football; **~и́ст** *m* [1] soccer player; **~ьный** [14] soccer..., football...
футля́р *m* [1] case; sheath; box.
фуфа́йка *f* [5; *g/pl.*: -а́ек] jersey.
фы́рк|ать [1], ⟨~нуть⟩ [20] snort.

X

ха́ки [*ind.*] khaki.
хала́т *m* [1] dressing gown, bathrobe; smock; **~ный** F [14; -тен, -тна] careless, negligent; sluggish.
халту́ра F *f* [5] botch, bungle.
хам F *m* [1] cad, boor, churl.
хандр|а́ *f* [5] melancholy, blues *pl.*; **~и́ть** [13] be in the dumps.
ханж|а́ F *m/f* [5; *g/pl.*: -же́й] hypocrite; **~ество́** *n* [9] hypocrisy, bigotry.
хао́|с *m* [1] chaos; **~ти́ческий** [16], **~ти́чный** [14; -чен, -чна] chaotic.
хара́ктер *m* [1] character, nature; temper, disposition; principles *pl.*; **~изова́ть** [7] (*im*)*pf.* & ⟨o-⟩ characterize, mark; **~и́стика** *f* [5] character(istic); characterization; **~ный** [14; -рен, -рна] characteristic (of для P).
ха́рк|ать F [1], ⟨~нуть⟩ [20] spit.
харч|е́вня *f* [6; *g/pl.*: -вен] tavern; **~и́** P *m/pl.* [1 *e.*] food, grub; board.
ха́ря P *f* [6] mug, phiz.
ха́та *f* [5] (peasant's) hut.
хвал|а́ *f* [5] praise; **~е́бный** [14; -бен, -бна] laudatory; **~ли́ть** [13; хвалю́, хва́лишь] praise; **-ся** boast (of T).
хва́ст|аться &, F, **~ать** [1], ⟨по-⟩ boast, brag (of T); **~ли́вый** [14 *sh.*] boastful; **~овство́** *n* [9] boasting; **~у́н** *m* [1 *e.*] boaster, braggart.
хват|а́ть [1] **1.** ⟨(с)хвати́ть⟩ [15] (за B) snatch (at); grasp, seize (by); *a.*, F, (-ся за B; lay hold of); **2.** ⟨~и́ть⟩ (*impers.*) (P) suffice, be sufficient; (p. Д, у P) have enough; last (*v/t.* на B); (э́того мне) **~и́т** (that's) enough (for me); F hit, knock, strike; drink, eat; take; go.
хво́йный [14] coniferous.
хвора́ть F [1] be sick *or* ill.
хво́рост *m* [1] brushwood.
хвост *m* [1 *e.*] tail; brush (*fox*); F train; line, *Brt.* queue; в **~сте́** (*lag*) behind; поджа́ть **~** F come down a peg (or two).
хво́я *f* [6] (pine) needle(s *or* branches *pl.*).
хи́жина *f* [5] hut, cabin.
хи́лый [14; хил, -а́, -о] sickly.
хи́ми|к *m* [1] (*Brt.* analytical) chemist; **~ческий** [16] chemical; indelible *or* copying-ink (*pencil*); **~я** *f* [7] chemistry.
хини́н *m* [1] quinine.
хире́ть [8] weaken, grow sickly.
хиру́рг *m* [1] surgeon; **~и́ческий** [16] surgical; **~и́я** *f* [7] surgery.
хитр|е́ц *m* [1 *e.*] cunning fellow, dodger; **~и́ть** [13], ⟨c-⟩ dodge; fox; quibble; *cf.* мудри́ть; **~ость** *f* [8] craft(iness), cunning; artifice, ruse, trick; stratagem; **~ый** [14; -тёр, -тра́, хи́тро] cunning, crafty, sly, artful; ingenious.
хихи́кать [1] chuckle, giggle, titter.
хище́ние *n* [12] embezzlement.
хи́щн|ик *m* [1] beast (*or* bird) of prey; **~ый** [14; -щен, -щна] rapacious, predatory; of prey.
хладнокро́в|ие *n* [12] composure; **~ный** [14; -вен, -вна] cool(-headed), calm.
хлам *m* [1] trash, stuff, lumber.
хлеб *m* **1.** [1] bread; loaf; **2.** [1; *pl.*: -ба́, *etc. e.*] grain, *Brt.* corn; livelihood; *pl.* cereals; **~а́ть** [1], *once* ⟨~ну́ть⟩ [20] drink, sip; P eat; **~ный** [14] grain..., corn..., cereal; bread...; baker's; F profitable; **~опека́рня** *f* [6; *g/pl.*: -рен] bakery; **~осо́льный** [14; -лен, -льна] hospitable; **~осо́льство** *n* [9], F **~-со́ль** *f* [1/8] hospitality.
хлев *m* [1; в -е & -у́; *pl.*: -а́, *etc. e.*] shed; cote; sty.
хлест|а́ть [3], *once* ⟨~ну́ть⟩ [20] lash, whip, beat; splash; gush, spurt; pour.
хли́пать F [1] sob.
хлоп! crack!, plop!; *cf. a.* **~ать** [1], ⟨по-⟩, *once* ⟨~нуть⟩ [20] slap; clap; bang, slam (*v/t.* T); crack; pop (*cork*); detonate; resound; blink.
хло́пок *m* [1; -пка] cotton.
хлопот|а́ть [3], ⟨по-⟩ (о П) strive (for), endeavo(u)r; exert o. s. (on behalf of о П, за B); apply (for); *impf.* bustle (about); **~ли́вый** [14 *sh.*] troublesome; busy, fussy; **'~ы** *f/pl.* [5; *gen.*: -по́т] trouble(s), cares; business, commissions.
хлопу́шка *f* [5; *g/pl.*: -шек] fly flap; cracker.
хлопчатобума́жный [14] cotton...
хло́пья *n/pl.* [10; *gen.*: -ьев] flakes.
хлор *m* [1] chlorine; **~истый** [14] ... chloride; **~ный** [14] chloric; **~офо́рм** *m* [1], **~оформи́ровать** [7] (*im*)*pf.* chloroform.
хлы́нуть [20] *pf.* gush (forth); rush; (begin to) pour in torrents.
хлыст *m* [1 *e.*] horsewhip; switch.
хлю́пать F [1] squelch.
хмел|ь *m* [4] hop; intoxication; во **~ю́** drunk; **~ьно́й** F [14; -лён, -льна́] intoxicated; intoxicating.
хму́р|ить [13], ⟨на-⟩ knit (*the brow*); **-ся** frown, scowl; be(come) overcast; **~ый** [14; хмур, -а́, -о] gloomy, sullen; cloudy.
хны́кать F [3] whine, snivel.
хо́бот *m* [1] *zo.* trunk.
ход *m* [1; в (на) -у́ & -е; *pl.*: хо́ды́] motion; speed (at на П), pace; course; passage; walk; ⊕ *a.* action, movement; stroke (*piston*); entrance; access; lead (*cards*); move (*chess, etc.*); turn; vogue, currency;

в ~ý *a.* = ∠кий; на ~ý *a.* while walking, *etc.*; F in progress; пустить в ~ start, set going *or* on foot, circulate; все ~ы и выходы the ins and outs.

ходатай *m* [3] intercessor, advocate; **~ство** *n* [9] intercession; petition; **~ствовать** [7], ⟨по-⟩ intercede (with/for у Р/за В); petition (for о П).

ход|ить [15] go (to в, на В); walk; sail; run, ply; move; visit, attend (*v/t.* в, на В; р. к Д); circulate; (в П) wear; (за Т) look after, take care of, nurse; tend; (на В) hunt; lead (*cards*); F be current; ease o. s.; **∠кий** [16; ходок, -дка, -о; *comp.*: ходче] marketable, sal(e)able; current; F quick, easygoing; **~кая** книга *f* best seller; **~ульный** [14; -лен, -льна] stilted; **~ьба** *f* [5] walking; walk; **~ячий** [17] current; trivial; F walking. circulation.

хождение *n* [12] going, walking;

хозя|ин *m* [1; *pl.*: хозяева, хозяев] master, owner; boss, principal; landlord; host; innkeeper; manager; farmer; **~ева** = **~ин** & **~йка**; **~йка** *f* [5; *g/pl.*: -яек] mistress; landlady; hostess; housewife; **~йничать** [1] keep house; manage (at will); make o.s. at home; **~йственный** [14 *sh.*] economic(al); thrifty; **~йство** *n* [9] economy; household; farm.

хоккей *m* [3] hockey.

холера *f* [5] cholera.

холить [13] groom, care for, fondle.

хол|ка *f* [5; *g/pl.*: -лок] withers; **~м** *m* [1 *e.*] hill; **~мистый** [14 *sh.*] hilly.

холод *m* [1] cold (in на П); chill (*a. fig.*); *pl.* [-а, *etc. e.*] cold (weather) (in в В); **~еть** [8], ⟨по-⟩ grow cold, chill; **~ец** *m* [1; -дца] = студень; **~ильник** *m* [1] refrigerator; **∠ность** *f* [8] coldness; **∠ный** [14; холоден, -дна, -о] cold (*a. fig.*); *geogr.* & *fig.* frigid; (мне) **~но** it is (I am) cold.

холоп *m* [1] bondman; F toady.

холост|ой [14; холост] single, unmarried; bachelor('s); blank (*cartridge*); ⊕ idle (*motion*); **~як** *m* [1 *e.*] bachelor.

холст *m* [1 *e.*] linen; canvas.

холуй P *m* [3] cad; toady.

хомут *m* [1 *e.*] (horse) collar.

хомяк *m* [1 *e.*] hamster.

хор *m* [1] chorus; choir.

хорват *m* [1], **~ка** *f* [5; *g/pl.*: -ток] Croat; **~ский** [16] Croatian.

хорёк *m* [1; -рька] polecat, fitch.

хоровод *m* [1] round dance.

хоронить [13; -оню, -онишь], ⟨по-⟩ bury.

хорош|енький [16] pretty; **~енько** F properly; **~еть** [8], ⟨по-⟩ grow prettier; **~ий** [17; хорош, -а; *comp.*: лучше] good; fine, nice; (*a.* собой) pretty, good-looking, handsome; **~о** well; *mark*: good, В (*cf.* четвёрка); all right!, O.K.!, good!; мне **~о** I am well off; **~о** вам (+ *inf.*) it is very well for you to ...

хоте|ть [хочу, хочешь, хочет, хотим, хотите, хотят], ⟨за-⟩ (Р) want, wish; я **~л(а)** бы I would (*Brt.* should) like; я хочу, чтобы вы + *pt.* I want you to ...; хочешь не хочешь willy-nilly; **-ся** (*impers.*): мне хочется I'd like; *a.* = **~ть**.

хоть (*a.* ~ бы) at least; even (if *or* though); if only; ~ ... ~ whether ... whether, (either ...) or; if you please; so much, *etc.*, that; any ...; I wish I could (*or* you'd); ~ бы и так even if it be so; ~ убей for the life of me; *s. a.* хотя.

хотя although, though (*a.* ~ и); ~ бы even though; if; *s. a.* хоть.

хохол *m* [1; хохла] tuft; crest; forelock; *contp.* Ukrainian (*man*).

хохот *m* [1] (loud) laughter, roar; **~ать** [3], ⟨за-⟩ roar (with laughter).

храбр|ец *m* [1 *e.*] brave; **∠ость** *f* [8] valo(u)r, bravery; **∠ый** [14; храбр, -а, -о] brave, valient.

храм *m* [1] *eccl.* temple.

хран|ение *n* [12] keeping; storage; камера **~ения** ручного багажа 🚂 cloackroom, *Brt.* left-luggage office; **~илище** *n* [11] storehouse; archives *pl.*; **~итель** *m* [4] keeper, guardian; custodian; **~ить** [13], ⟨со-⟩ keep; store; preserve; observe; guard.

храп *m* [1], **~еть** [10 *e.*; -плю, -пишь] snore; snort.

хребет *m* [1; -бта] *anat.* spine; range.

хрен *m* [1] horse-radish.

хрип *m* [1], **~ение** *n* [12] rattle; **~еть** [10 *e.*; -плю, -пишь] rattle; be hoarse; F speak hoarsely; **∠лый** [14; хрипл, -а, -о] hoarse, husky; **∠нуть** [21], ⟨о-⟩ become hoarse; **~ота** *f* [5] hoarseness; husky voice.

христ|ианин *m* [1; *pl.*: -ане, -ан], **~ианка** *f* [5; *g/pl.*: -нок], **~ианский** [16] Christian; **~ианство** *n* [9] Christianity; **2ов** [19] Christ's; **2ос** *m* [Христа] Christ.

хром *m* [1] chromium; chrome.

хром|ать [1] limp; be lame; **~ой** [14; хром, -а, -о] lame; **~ота** *f* [5] lameness.

хрон|ика *f* [5] chronicle; current events; newsreel; **~ический** [16] chronic(al); **~ологический** [16] chronological; **~ология** *f* [7] chronology.

хру|пкий [16; -пок, -пка, -о; *comp.*: хрупче] brittle, fragile; frail, infirm; **~сталь** *m* [4 *e.*] crystal; **~стальный** [14] crystal...; **~стеть** [11] crunch; **~щ** *m* [1 *e.*] cockchafer.

хрюк|ать [1], *once* ⟨**~нуть**⟩ [20] grunt.

хрящ *m* [1 *e.*] cartilage.

худеть [8], ⟨по-⟩ grow thin.

ху́до *n* [9] evil; *s. a.* худо́й.
худо́ж|ественный [14 *sh.*] artistic; art(s)...; of art; belles(-*lettres*); applied (*arts*); **~ество** *n* [9] (applied) art; **~ник** *m* [1] artist; painter.
худ|о́й [14; худ, -á, -о; *comp.*: худе́е] thin, lean, scrawny (*a.* **~оща́вый** [14 *sh.*]); [*comp.*: ху́же] bad, evil; **~́ший** [16] worse, worst; *cf.* лу́чший.
ху́же worse; *cf.* лу́чше & тот.
хулига́н *m* [1] rowdy, hooligan.
ху́тор *m* [1] farm(stead); hamlet.

Ц

ца́п|ать F [1], *once* 〈**~нуть**〉 [20] snatch.
ца́пля *f* [6; *g/pl.*: -пель] heron.
цара́п|ать [1], 〈(п)о-〉, *once* 〈**~нуть**〉 [20], **~ина** *f* [5] scratch.
цар|е́вич *m* [1] czarevitch; prince; **~е́вна** *f* [5; *g/pl.*: -вен] princess; **~и́ть** [13] reign; prevail; **~и́ца** *f* [5] czarina; empress; *fig.* queen; **~́ский** [16] of the czar(s), czarist; imperial; **~́ство** *n* [9] empire; kingdom (*a. fig.*); rule; *a.* = **~́ствование** *n* [12] reign (in в В); **~́ствовать** [7] reign, rule; prevail; **~ь** *m* [4 *e.*] czar, (Russian) emperor; king.
цвести́ [25 -т-] bloom, blossom.
цвет *m* [1] **1.** [*pl.*: -á, *etc. e.*] colo(u)r; **~** лица́ complexion; защи́тного **~́а** khaki; **2.** [*only pl.*: -ы́, *etc. e.*] flowers; **3.** [*no pl.*; в -у́; *fig.* в(о) цве́те] blossom, bloom; *fig. a.* prime; **~е́ние** *n* [12] flowering; **~и́стый** [14 *sh.*] florid; **~ни́к** *m* [1 *e.*] flower bed; **~но́й** [14] colo(u)red; variegated; nonferrous (*metals*); technicolor (*film*); **~на́я** капу́ста *f* cauliflower; **~о́к** *m* [1; -тка́; *pl. usu.* = **~** 2] flower (*a. fig.*); **~о́чник** *m* [1] florist; **~о́чница** *f* [5] florist, *Brt.* flower girl; **~о́чный** [14] flower...; **~у́щий** [17 *sh.*] flowering; flourishing; prime (*of life*).
цеди́ть [15] **1.** 〈про-〉 strain, pass, filter; F murmur, utter (between one's teeth); **2.** 〈вы́-〉 draw (off).
Цейло́н *m* [1] Ceylon.
цейхга́уз (cɛjˈxa-) *m* [1] arsenal.
целе́|бный [14; -бен, -бна] curative, medicinal; **~во́й** [14] special, for a specified purpose, purposeful; principal; **~сообра́зный** [14; -зен, -зна] expedient; **~устремлённый** [14 *sh.*] purposeful.
цели|ко́м entirely, wholly; **~на́** *f* [5] virgin soil; **~́тельный** [14; -лен, -льна] salutary, curative; **ˈ~ть** (-ся) [13], 〈при-〉 aim (at в В).
целлюло́за *f* [5] cellulose.
целова́ть(ся) [7], 〈по-〉 kiss.
це́л|ое *n* [14] whole (on the в П; ✝ in the lump); **~ому́дренный** [14 *sh.*] chaste; **~ому́дрие** *n* [12] chastity; **~ость** *f* [8] integrity; в **~ости** intact; **~ый** [14; цел, -á, -о] whole; entire; safe, sound; intact; **~ое** число́ *n* integer; *cf.* деся́тый & со́тый.
цель *f* [8] aim, end, goal, object; target; purpose (for с Т, в П *pl.*); име́ть **~́ю** aim at; **~́ность** *f* [8] integrity; **~́ный** [14; це́лен, -льна́, -о] entire, whole; righteous; [*no sh.*] rich (*milk*).
цеме́нт *m* [1], **~и́ровать** [7] cement.
цен|á *f* [5; *ac/sg.*: це́ну; *pl. st.*] price (of Р, на В, Д; at/of по Д/в В), cost (at Т); value (of *or* one's Д); **~ы** нет (Д) be invaluable; любо́й **~о́й** at any price; **~зу́ра** *f* [5] censorship.
цен|и́тель *m* [4] judge, connoisseur; **~и́ть** [13; ценю́, це́нишь], 〈о-〉 value, estimate, appreciate; **~́ность** *f* [8] value; *pl.* valuables; **~́ный** [14; -е́нен, -е́нна] valuable; money (*letter*); **~́ные** бума́ги *pl.* securities.
це́нтнер *m* [1] centner (= *100 kg*).
центр *m* [1] center, *Brt.* centre; **~ализова́ть** [7] (*im*)*pf.* centralize; **~а́льный** [14] central; *cf.* ЦИК & ЦК; **~обе́жный** [14] centrifugal.
цеп *m* [1 *e.*] flail.
цеп|ене́ть [8], 〈о-〉 grow numb, stiffen; be transfixed; **~́кий** [16; -пок, -пка́, -о] clinging; tenacious; **~ля́ться** [28] cling (to за В); **~но́й** [14] chain(ed); **~о́чка** *f* [5; *g/pl.*: -чек] chain; **~ь** *f* [8; в, на -и́; *from g/pl. e.*] chain (*a. fig.*); ⚔ line; ⚡ circuit.
церемо́н|иться [13], 〈по-〉 stand on ceremony, be ceremonious; **~ия** *f* [7] ceremony; **~ный** [14] ceremonious.
церко́в|ный [14] church...; **ˈ~ь** *f* [8; -кви; *instr/sg.*: -ковью; *pl.*: -кви, -ве́й, -ва́м] church.
цех *m* [1] shop, section; † guild.
цивилиз|ова́ть [7] (*im*)*pf.* civilize; **~о́ванный** [14] civilized.
ЦИК (Центра́льный Исполни́тельный Комите́т) Central Executive Committee (*Sov.*); *cf.* ЦК.
цикл *m* [1] cycle; course, set; **~о́н** *m* [1] cyclone.
цико́рий *m* [3] chicory.
цили́ндр *m* [1] cylinder; top (*or* high) hat; **~и́ческий** [16] cylindrical.
цинга́ *f* [5] scurvy.
цини́|зм *m* [1] cynicism; **ˈ~к** *m* [1] cynic; **~чный** [14; -чен, -чна] cynical.
цинк *m* [1] zinc; **~́овый** [14] zinc ...
цино́вка *f* [5; *g/pl.*: -вок] mat.
цирк *m* [1], **~ово́й** [14] circus.
циркул|и́ровать [7] circulate; **ˈ~ь**

m [4] (один a pair of) compasses pl.; ~я́р m [1] circular.
цисте́рна f [5] cistern, tank.
цитаде́ль (-'dɛ-) f [8] citadel; stronghold.
цита́та f [5] quotation.
цити́ровать [7], ⟨про-⟩ quote.
циф|ербла́т m [1] dial, face (*watch, etc.*); ~ра f [5] figure.
ЦК (Центра́льный Комите́т) Central Committee (*Sov.*); cf. ЦИК.
цо́коль m [4] ⚠ socle; ⊕ socket.
цыга́н m [1; nom/pl.: -е & -ы; gen.: цыга́н], ~ка f [5; g/pl.: -нок], ~ский [16] Gypsy, Brt. Gipsy.
цыплёнок m [2] chicken.
цы́почк|и: на ~ах (or ~и) on tiptoe.

Ч

ч. abbr.: **1.** час; **2.** часть.
чад m [1; в -у́] smoke, fume(s); fig. daze; frenzy; ~и́ть [15 e.; чажу́, чади́шь], ⟨на-⟩ smoke.
ча́до † & iron. n [9] child.
чаевы́е pl. [14] tip.
чай[1] m [3; part. g.: -ю; в -е & -ю́; pl. e.: чаи́, чаёв] tea; tea party; дать на ~ tip; ~[2] P perhaps, I suppose.
ча́йка f [5; g/pl.: ча́ек] (sea) gull, mew.
ча́йн|ик m [1] teapot; teakettle; ~ый [14] tea(*spoon, etc.*).
чалма́ f [5] turban.
чан m [1; pl. e.] tub, vat.
ча́р|ка f [5; g/pl.: -рок] (*wine-etc.*) glass; ~ова́ть [20] charm; ~оде́й m [3] magician.
час m [1; в -е & -у́; after 2, 3, 4: -а́; pl. e.] hour (by the по ~а́м; for pl. ~а́ми); (one) o'clock (at в В); time, moment (at в В); an hour's ...; второ́й ~ (it is) past one; в пя́том ~у́ between four & five; (cf. пять & пя́тый); ~ о́т ~у or с ~у на ~ hourly; на ~а́х (*stand*) sentinel; ~о́вня f [6; g/pl.: -вен] chapel; ~ово́й [14] hour's; by the hour; watch..., clock-...; su. sentry, sentinel; ~ово́й ма́стер m = ~овщи́к [1 e.] watchmaker.
част|и́ца f [5] particle; ~и́чный [14; -чен, -чна] partial; ~ное n [14] quotient; ~ность f [8] particular; ~ный [14] private; particular; individual; ~око́л m [1] palisade; ~ота́ f [5; pl. st.: -о́ты] frequency; ~у́шка f [5; g/pl.: -шек] couplet; ~ый [14; част, -а́, -о; comp.: ча́ще] frequent (adv. a. often); thick(-set), dense; close; quick, rapid; ~ь f [8; from g/pl. e.] part (in Т; pl. a. по Д); share; piece; department, section (in a. по Д), F line, branch; ⚔ unit; † police station; бо́льшей ~ью, по бо́льшей ~и for the most part, mostly.
час|ы́ m/pl. [1] watch; clock; (*sun*)dial; на мои́х ~а́х by my watch.
ча́х|лый [14 sh.] sickly; stunted; ~нуть [21], ⟨за-⟩ wither, shrivel; grow stunted; ~о́тка f [5] consumption; ~о́точный [14; -чен, -чна] consumptive.
ча́ша f [5] cup, chalice; bowl.
ча́шка f [5; g/pl.: -шек] cup; pan; cap; надколе́нная ~ kneecap.
ча́ща f [5] thicket.
ча́ще more (~ всего́ most) often.
ча́я|ние n [12] expectation (contrary to па́че or сверх Р), hope, dream.
чва́н|иться F [13], ~ство n [9] brag, blow, swagger.
чей m, **чья** f, **чьё** n, **чьи** pl. [26] whose; ~ э́то дом? whose house is this?
чек m [1] check, Brt. cheque; ~а́нить [13], ⟨вы́-⟩ mint, coin; chase; ~а́нка f [5; g/pl.: -нок] minting, coinage; chase; ~и́ст m [1] member of ЧК, cf.; ~овый [14] check...
чёлн m [1 e.; челна́] boat; canoe.
челно́к m [1 e.] dim. of чёлн; a. shuttle.
чело́ † n [9; pl. st.] forehead, brow.
челове́|к m [1; pl.: лю́ди, cf.; 5, 6, etc. -е́к] man, human being; person, individual; one; † servant; waiter; ру́сский ~к Russian; ~колю́бие n [12] philanthropy; ~ческий [16] human(e); ~чество n [9] mankind, humanity; ~чный [14; -чен, -чна] humane.
че́люсть f [8] jaw; (full) denture.
че́лядь f [8] servants pl.
чем than; F instead of; ~ ..., тем ... the ... the ...; ~ода́н m [1] suitcase.
чемпио́н m [1] champion; ~а́т m [1] championship.
чепе́ц m [1; -пца́] cap.
чепуха́ F f [5] nonsense; trifle.
че́пчик m [1] cap.
че́рв|и f/pl. [4; from gen. e.] & ~ы f/pl. [5] hearts (*cards*).
черви́вый [14 sh.] worm-eaten.
черво́нец m [1; -нца] 10 rubles.
черв|ь m [4 e.; nom/pl. st.: че́рви, черве́й], ~я́к m [1 e.] worm.
черда́к m [1 e.] garret, attic, loft.
черёд F m [1 e.] turn; course.
чередова́|ние n [12] alternation; ~ть(ся) [7] alternate.
че́рез (В) through; across, over;

time: in, after; *go:* via; with (the help of); because of; ~ день *a.* every other day.
черёмуха *f* [5] bird cherry.
череп *m* [1; *pl.*: -á, *etc. e.*] skull.
черепá|ха *f* [5] tortoise; turtle; tortoise shell; **~ховый** [14] tortoise(-shell)...; **~ший** [18] tortoise's, snail's (pace шаг *m*; at T).
череп|úца *f* [5] tile (*of roof*); **~úчный** [14] tiled; **~óк** *m* [1; -пкá] fragment, piece.
чере|счýр too, too much; **∠шня** *f* [6; *g/pl.*: -шен] (sweet) cherry.
черкнýть F [20] *pf.*: ~ пáру (*or* нéсколько) слов drop a line.
черн|éть [8], ‹по-› blacken, grow black; *impf.* (*a.* **-ся**) show black; **~éц** *m* [1 *e.*] monk; **~úка** *f* [5] bilberry, -ries *pl.*; **~úла** *n/pl.* [9] ink; **~úльница** *f* [5] inkwell (*Brt.* inkpot), inkstand; **~úльный** [14] ink...; **~úть** [13] **1.** ‹на-› blacken; **2.** ‹о-› blacken (*fig.*), denigrate, slander.
черно|вúк *m* [1 *e.*] rough copy; draft; **~вóй** [14] draft...; rough; waste (*book*); **~волóсый** [14 *sh.*] black-haired; **~глáзый** [14 *sh.*] black-eyed; **~гóрец** *m* [1; -рца] Montenegrin; **~зём** *m* [1] chernozem, black earth; **~кóжий** [17 *sh.*] Negro; **~мáзый** [14 *sh.*] swarthy; **~мóрский** [16] Black Sea ...; **~рабóчий** *m* [17] unskilled worker; **~слúв** *m* [1] prune(s); **~тá** *f* [5] blackness.
чёрн|ый [14; чёрен, чернá] black (*a. fig.*); brown (*bread*); ferrous (*metals*); rough (*work*); back(*stairs, etc.*); leafy (*wood*); на ~ый день for a rainy day; ~ым по бéлому in black & white.
чернь *f* [8] mob, rabble.
чéрп|ать [1], ‹~нýть› [20] scoop, draw; gather (from из Р, в П).
черст|вéть [8], ‹за-, по-› grow stale; harden; **∠вый** (ˈtʃɔ-) [14; чёрств, -á, -о] stale, hard; callous.
чёрт *m* [1; *pl.* 4 чéрти, -тéй, *etc. e.*] devil; F the deuce (go: *a.* ступáй, убирáйся; take: возьмú, поберú, [по]дерú; *a.* confound; blast, damn it!); к ~у, на кой ~ F *a.* the deuce; ни чертá F nothing at all; never mind!
черт|á *f* [5] line; trait, feature (*a.* ~ы лицá); precincts *pl.* (within в П); term.
чертёж *m* [1 *e.*] (mechanical) drawing, draft (*Brt.* draught), design; **~ник** *m* [1] draftsman, *Brt.* draughtsman; **~ный** [14] drawing (*board, etc.*).
черт|úть [15], ‹на-› draw, design; **~óвский** [16] devilish.
чёрточка *f* [5; *g/pl.*: -чек] hyphen.
черчéние *n* [12] drawing.
чесáть [3] **1.** ‹по-› scratch; **2.** ‹при› F comb; **3.** *impf.* hackle, card; **-ся** *a.*, F, itch (му у меня́).
чеснóк *m* [1 *e.*] garlic.
чесóтка *f* [5] itch.
чéст|вование *n* [12] celebration; **~вовать** [7] celebrate, hono(u)r; **~ность** *f* [8] honesty; **~ный** [14; чéстен, -тнá, -о] honest, of hono(u)r; fair; **~олюбúвый** [14 *sh.*] ambitious; **~олюбие** *n* [12] ambition; **~ь** *f* [8] hono(u)r (in в В); credit; по ~и F honestly; ~ь ~ю F properly, well.
четá *f* [5] couple, pair; F match.
четвéр|г *m* [1 *e.*] Thursday (on: в В, *pl.*: по Д); **~éньки** F *f/pl.* [5] all fours (on на В, П); **~ка** (-ˈvɔr-) *f* [5; *g/pl.*: -рок] four (*cf.* трóйка); F (*mark*) = хорошó, *cf.*; **ʹ~о** [37] four (*cf.* двóе); **~онóгий** [16] four-footed; **~тый** (-ˈvɔr-) [14] fourth; *cf.* пя́тый; **ʹ~ть** *f* [8; *from g/pl. e.*] (one) fourth; quarter (to без Р; past one вторóго).
чёткий [16; чёток, четкá, -о] distinct, clear; legible; exact, accurate.
чётный [14] even.
четы́ре [34] four; *cf.* пять; **~жды** four times; **~ста** [36] four hundred.
четырёх|лéтний [15] four-years(-old)'; **~мéстный** [14] four-seated; **~сóтый** [14] four hundredth; **~угóльник** *m* [1] quadrangle; **~угóльный** [14] quadrangular; **~этáжный** [14] four-storied (*Brt.* -storeyed).
четы́рнадца|тый [14] fourteenth; *cf.* пя́тый; **~ть** [35] fourteen; *cf.* пять.
чех *m* [1] Czech.
чехардá *f* [5] leapfrog.
чехóл *m* [1; -хлá] case, cover.
Чехословá|кия *f* [7] Czechoslovakia; **2цкий** [16] Czechoslovak.
чечевúца *f* [5] lentil(s).
чéш|ка *f* [5; *g/pl.*: -шек] Czech (woman); **~ский** [16] Czech(ic).
чешуя́ *f* [6] scales *pl.*
чúбис *m* [1] lapwing.
чиж *m* [1 *e.*], F **∠ик** *m* [1] siskin.
Чи|кáго *n* [*ind.*] Chicago; **∠ли** *n* [*ind.*] Chile; **2лúец** *m* [1; -úйца] Chilean.
чин *m* [1; *pl. e.*] rank, grade; station; order, ceremony; official; **~úть** **1.** [13; чиню́, чúнишь] a) ‹по-› mend, repair; b) ‹о-› sharpen, point; **2.** [13], ‹у-› raise, cause; administer; **∠ный** [14; чúнен, чиннá, чúнно] proper; sedate; **~óвник** *m* [1] official; bureaucrat.
чирúк|ать [1], ‹~нуть› [20] chirp.
чúрк|ать [1], ‹~нуть› [20] strike.
числ|енность *f* [8] number; ⚔ strength (of/of T/в В); **~енный** [14] numerical; **~úтель** ⅔ *m* [4]

numerator; **~и́тельное** *n* [14] *gr.* numeral (*a.* и́мя ~и́тельное); **~иться** [13] be on the ... list (в П *or* по Д/Р); **~о́** *n* [9; *pl. st.*: чи́сла, чи́сел, чи́слам] number; date; day (in в П; on Р); кото́рое (како́е) сего́дня ~о́? what date is today? (*cf.* пя́тый); в ~е́ (Р), в том ~е́ including.
чи́стильщик *m* [1] (*boot*)black.
чи́ст|ить [15] **1.** ⟨по-, вы́-⟩ clean(se); brush; polish; **2.** ⟨о-⟩ peel; *pol.* purge; **~ка** *f* [5; *g/pl.*: -ток] clean(s)ing; polish(ing); *pol.* purge; **~окро́вный** [14; -вен, -вна] thoroughbred; *fig.* genuine; **~оплóтный** [14; -тен, -тна] cleanly; *fig.* clean; **~осерде́чный** [14; -чен, -чна] open-hearted, frank, sincere; **~ота́** *f* [5] clean(li)ness; purity; **~ый** [14; чист, -á, -o; *comp.*: чи́ще] clean; pure; neat, cleanly; clear; net; blank (*sheet*); fine, faultless; genuine; sheer; plain (*truth*); mere (*chance*); hard (*cash*); free, open (*field*).
чита́|льный [14]: ~льный зал *m*, **~льня** *f* [6; *g/pl.*: -лен] reading room; **~тель** *m* [4] reader; **~ть** [1], ⟨про-⟩ & ⟨проче́сть⟩ F [25; -чту́, -чтёшь; -чёл, -чла́; -чтённый] read, recite; give (*lecture* on о П), deliver, lecture; teach; ~ть по склада́м spell.
чи́тка *f* [5; *g/pl.*: -ток] reading.
чих|а́ть [1], *once* ⟨**~ну́ть**⟩ [20] sneeze.
ЧК (Чрезвыча́йная коми́ссия ...) Cheka (*predecessor, 1917—22, of the* ГПУ, *cf.*).
член *m* [1] member; limb; *gr.* article; part; **~ораздéльный** [14; -лен, -льна] articulate; **∠ский** [16] member(-ship)...; **∠ство** *n* [9] membership.
чмо́к|ать F [1], *once* ⟨**~нуть**⟩ [20] [smack.]
чо́к|аться [1], *once* ⟨**~нуться**⟩ [20] touch (glasses T) (with с T).
чо́|порный [14; -рен, -рна] prim, prudish; **~рт** *s.* чёрт.
чрев|а́тый [14 *sh.*] pregnant (*a. fig.*); **∠о** *n* [9] womb.
чрез *s.* че́рез; **~вычáйный** [14; -áен, -áйна] extraordinary; extreme; special; **~ме́рный** [14; -рен, -рна] excessive.
чте́|ние *n* [12] reading; recital; **~ц** *m* [1 *e.*] reader.
чтить *s.* почита́ть[1].
что [23] **1.** *pron.* what (*a.* ~ за); that, which; how; (*a.* а ~?) why (so?); (*a.* а ~) what about; what's the matter; F а ~? well?; how (*or* as) much, how many; во́т ~ the following; listen; that's it; ~ до меня́ as for me; ~ вы (ты)! you don't say!, what next!; не́ за ~ (you are) welcome, *Brt.* don't mention it; ни за ∠ not for the world; ну ~ же? what of that?; (уж) на ~ F however; с чего́? F why?, wherefore?; ~ и говори́ть F sure; *cf.* ни; F *s.* ∠-нибудь, ∠-то; **2.** *cj.* that; like, as if; ~ (ни) ..., то ... every ... (a)...
чтоб(ы) (in order) that *or* to (*a.* с тем, ~); ~ не lest, for fear that; вме́сто того́ ~ + *inf.* instead of ...ing; скажи́ ему́, ~ он + *pt.* tell him to *inf.*
что́|-либо, ~-нибудь, ~-то [23] something; anything; ~-то *a.* F somewhat; somehow, for some reason or other.
чу́вств|енный [14 *sh.*] sensuous; sensual; material; **~и́тельность** *f* [8] sensibility; **~и́тельный** [14; -лен, -льна] sensitive; sentimental; sensible (*a.* = considerable, great, strong); biting (*cold*); grievous (*loss*); **~о** *n* [9] sense; feeling; sensation; F love; без ~ unconscious, senseless; **~овать** [7], ⟨по-⟩ feel (*a.* себя́ [T s. th.]); -ся be felt.
чугу́н *m* [1 *e.*] cast iron; **~ный** [14] cast-iron; **~олите́йный** [14]: ~олите́йный заво́д *m* iron foundry.
чуд|а́к *m* [1 *e.*] crank, character; **~а́чество** *n* [9] eccentricity; **~е́сный** [14; -сен, -сна] wonderful, marvel(l)ous; miraculous; **~и́ть** [15 *e.*] F *s.* дури́ть; **∠иться** [15] F = мере́щиться; **~но́й** F [14; -дён, -дна́] queer, odd, strange; funny; **∠ный** [14; -ден, -дна] wonderful, marvel(l)ous; **∠о** *n* [9; *pl.*: чудеса́, -éс, -еса́м] miracle, marvel; wonder; *a.* = ∠но; **~о́вище** *n* [11] monster; **~о́вищный** [14; -щен, -щна] monstrous; **~отво́рец** *m* [1; -рца] wonderworker.
чуж|би́на *f* [5] foreign country (in на П; *a.* abroad); **~да́ться** [1] (Р) shun, avoid; **∠дый** [14; чужд, -á, -o] foreign; strange, alien; free (from Р); **~езе́мец** *m* [1; -мца] foreigner; **~о́й** [14] someone else's, alien; strange, foreign; *su. a.* stranger, outsider.
чул|а́н *m* [1] closet; pantry; **~о́к** *m* [1; -лка́; *g/pl.*: -ло́к] stocking.
чума́ *f* [5] plague, pestilence.
чума́зый F [14 *sh.*] dirty.
чурба́н *m* [1] block; blockhead.
чу́тк|ий [16; -ток, -тка́, -o; *comp.*: чу́тче] sensitive (to на В), keen; light (*sleep*); vigilant, watchful; wary; quick (of hearing); responsive; sympathetic; **~ость** *f* [8] keenness; delicacy (of feeling).
чу́точку F a bit.
чуть hardly, scarcely; a little; ~ не nearly, almost; ~ ли не F seem (-ingly); ~ что F on the least occasion; ~-~ *s.* ~; ~ё *n* [10] instinct (for на В); scent, flair.
чу́чело *n* [9] stuffed animal *or* bird; scarecrow; ~ горо́ховое F dolt.
чушь F *f* [8] bosh, baloney.
чу́ять [27], ⟨по-⟩ scent, feel.

Ш

шаба́ш F 1. *m* [1] (knocking-)off-time; 2. *int.* enough!, no more!; **~ить** F [16], ⟨по-⟩ knock off.

шабло́н *m* [1] stencil, pattern, cliché; **~ный** [14] trite, hackneyed.

шаг *m* [1; *after 2, 3, 4*: -á; в -ý; *pl. e.*] step (by step ~ за T) (*a. fig.*); pace (at T); stride; démarche; ни **∠у** (да́льше) no step further; на ка́ждом ~ý everywhere, on end; **~а́ть** [1], *once* ⟨**~ну́ть**⟩ [20] step, stride; march; walk; advance; (че́рез) cross; *pf. a.* take a step; далеко́ ~ну́ть *fig.* make great progress; **∠ом** at a slow pace, slowly.

ша́йба *f* [5] disk.

ша́йка *f* [5; *g/pl.*: ша́ек] gang.

шака́л *m* [1] jackal.

шала́ш *m* [1] hut; tent.

шал|и́ть [13] be naughty, frolic, romp; fool (about), play (pranks); be up to mischief; buck; **~и́шь!** P fiddlesticks!, on no account!; **~овли́вый** [14 *sh.*] frolicsome, playful; **~опа́й** F *m* [3] good-for-nothing; **∠ость** *f* [8] prank; **~ýн** *m* [1 *e.*] naughty boy; **~ýнья** *f* [6; *g/pl.*: -ний] tomboy, madcap.

шаль *f* [8] shawl.

шально́й [14] mad, crazy; stray...

ша́мкать [1] mumble.

шампа́нское *n* [16] champagne.

шампу́нь *m* [4] shampoo.

шанс *m* [1] chance, prospect (of на B).

шанта́ж *m* [1], **~и́ровать** [7] blackmail.

ша́пка *f* [5; *g/pl.*: -пок] cap; heading.

шар *m* [1; *after 2, 3, 4*: -á; *pl. e.*] sphere; ball; возду́шный ~ balloon; земно́й ~ globe.

шара́х|аться F [1], ⟨**~нуться**⟩ [20] rush (aside), recoil; shy; plop.

шарж *m* [1] cartoon, caricature.

ша́рик *m* [1] *dim. of* шар; corpuscle; **~овый** [14] ball (point *pen*); **~оподши́пник** *m* [1] ball bearing.

ша́рить [13], ⟨по-⟩ rummage.

ша́р|кать [1], *once* ⟨**~кнуть**⟩ [20] scrape; bow; **~ма́нка** *f* [5; *g/pl.*: -нок] hand organ.

шарни́р *m* [1] hinge, joint.

шаро|ва́ры *f/pl.* [5] baggy trousers; **~ви́дный** [14; -ден, -дна] **~обра́зный** [14; -зен, -зна] spherical, globular.

шарф *m* [1] scarf, neckerchief.

шасси́ *n* [*ind.*] chassis; ✈ undercarriage.

шат|а́ть [1], *once* ⟨(по)шатну́ть⟩ [20] (-ся be[come]) shake(n); rock; -ся *a.* stagger, reel, totter; F lounge *or* loaf, gad about.

шатёр *m* [1; -тра́] tent.

ша́т|кий [16; -ток, -тка] shaky, rickety, tottering; *fig.* unsteady, fickle; **~ну́ть(ся)** *s.* **~а́ть(ся)**.

ша́|фер *m* [1; *pl.*: -á, *etc. e.*] best man; **~х** *m* [1] shah; check (*chess*).

шахмат|и́ст *m* [1] chess player; **′~ный** [14] chess...; **′~ы** *f/pl.* [5] chess (*play v/t.* в B).

ша́хт|а *f* [5] mine, pit; **~ёр** *m* [1] miner, pitman; **~ёрский** [16] miner's.

ша́шка *f* [5; *g/pl.*: -шек] saber, *Brt.* sabre; checker, draughtsman; *pl.* checkers, *Brt.* draughts.

швед *m* [1], **∠ка** *f* [5; *g/pl.*: -док] Swede; **∠ский** [16] Swedish.

шве́йный [14] sewing (*machine*).

швейца́р *m* [1] doorman, doorkeeper, porter; **~ец** *m* [1; -рца], **~ка** *f* [5; *g/pl.*: -рок] Swiss; **⁀ия** *f* [7] Switzerland; **~ский** [16] Swiss; doorman's, porter's.

Шве́ция *f* [7] Sweden.

швея́ *f* [6] seamstress.

швыр|я́ть [28], *once* ⟨**~ну́ть**⟩ [20] hurl, fling (*a.* T); squander.

шеве|ли́ть [13; -елю́, -е́ли́шь], ⟨по-⟩, *once* ⟨(по)**~льну́ть**⟩ [20] stir, move (*v/i.* -ся); turn (*hay*).

шеде́вр (-'devr) *m* [1] masterpiece.

ше́йка *f* [5; *g/pl.*: ше́ек] neck.

ше́лест *m* [1], **~е́ть** [11] rustle.

шёлк *m* [1; *g/sg. a.* -у; в шелку́; *pl.*: шелка́, *etc. e.*] silk.

шелкови́|стый [14 *sh.*] silky; **~ца** *f* [5] mulberry (tree); **~чный** [14]: ~чный червь *m* silkworm.

шёлковый [14] silk(en).

шел|охну́ться [20] *pf.* stir; **~уха́** *f* [5], **~уши́ть** [16 *e.*; -шу́, -ши́шь] peel, husk; **∠ьма** F *f* [5] rascal, rogue.

шепеля́в|ить [14] lisp; **~ый** [14 *sh.*] lisping.

шёпот *m* [1] whisper (in a T).

шеп|та́ть [3], ⟨про-⟩, *once* ⟨**~ну́ть**⟩ [20] whisper (*v/i. a.* -ся).

шере́нга *f* [5] file, rank.

шерохова́тый [14 *sh.*] rough.

шерст|ь *f* [8; *from g/pl. e.*] wool; coat; fleece; **~яно́й** [14] wool([l]en).

шерша́вый [14 *sh.*] rough; shaggy.

шест *m* [1 *e.*] pole.

ше́ств|ие *n* [12] procession; **~овать** [7] step, stride, go, walk.

шест|ёрка [5; *g/pl.*: -рок] six (*cf.* тро́йка); **~ерня́** ⊕ *f* [6; *g/pl.*: -рён] pinion; cogwheel; **∠еро** [37] six (*cf.* дво́е); **~идеся́тый** [14] sixtieth; *cf.* пя́т(идеся́т)ый; **~име́сячный** [14] six-months(-old)'; **~исо́тый** [14] six hundredth; **~иуго́льник** *m* [1] hexagon; **~на́дцатый** [14] sixteenth; *cf.* пя́тый; **~на́дцать** [35] sixteen; *cf.* пять;

~ой [14] sixth; *cf.* пятый; **~ь** [35 *e.*] six; *cf.* пять; **~ьдесят** [35] sixty; **~ьсот** [36] six hundred; **´~ью** six times.
шеф *m* [1] chief, head, F boss; patron, sponsor; **´~ство** *n* [9] patronage, sponsorship.
шея *f* [6; *g/pl.*: шей] neck; back.
шиїбко P swiftly; very; **~ворот**: взять за ~ворот collar.
шик|арный [14; -рен, -рна] chic, smart; **´~ать** F [1], *once* ⟨**´~нуть**⟩ [20] hiss.
шило *n* [1; *pl.*: -лья, -льев] awl.
шина *f* [5] tire, *Brt.* tyre; ⚕ splint.
шинель *f* [8] greatcoat, overcoat.
шинковать [7] chop, shred.
шип *m* [1 *e.*] thorn; (dowel) pin.
шипе|ние *n* [12] hiss(ing); **~ть** [10], ⟨про-⟩ hiss; spit; whiz.
шиповник *m* [1] dogrose.
шип|учий [17 *sh.*] sparkling, fizzy; **~ящий** [17] sibilant.
шири|на *f* [5] width, breadth; **~ной** в (В) *or* ... в **~ну** ... wide; **'~ть** [13], (-ся) widen, spread.
ширма *f* [5] (*mst pl.*) screen.
широк|ий [16; широк, -ока, -око; *comp.*: шире] broad; wide; vast; (at) large; great; mass...; large-scale; *phon.* open; на **~ую** ногу in grand style; **~овещательный** [14] broadcasting; [-лен, -льна] promising; **~оплечий** [17 *sh.*] broad-shouldered.
шир|ота *f* [5; *pl. st.*: -оты] breadth; *geogr.* latitude; **~потреб** F *m* [1] consumers' goods; **~ь** *f* [8] breadth, width; open (space).
шить [шью, шьёшь; шей(те)!; шитый], ⟨с-⟩ [сошью, -ьёшь; сшитый] sew (*pf. a.* together); embroider; have made; **~ё** *n* [10] sewing; embroidery.
шифр *m* [1] cipher, code; pressmark; **~овать** [7], ⟨за-⟩ cipher, code.
шиш F *m* [1 *e.*] fig; **´~ка** *f* [5; *g/pl.*: -шек] bump, lump; ♣ cone; knot; F bigwig.
шка|ла *f* [5; *pl. st.*] scale; **~тулка** *f* [5; *g/pl.*: -лок] casket; **~ф** *m* [1; в -у; *pl. e.*] cupboard; wardrobe; (*book*)case; несгораемый **~ф** safe.
шквал *m* [1] squall, gust.
шкив ⊕ *m* [1] pulley.
школ|а *f* [5] school (*go* to в В; *be* at, in в П); высшая **~а** academy; university; **~ьник** *m* [1] schoolboy; **~ьница** *f* [5] schoolgirl; **~ьный** [14] school...
шкур|а *f* [5] skin (*a.* **~ка** *f* [5; *g/pl.*: -рок]), hide; **~ник** F *m* [1] self-seeker.
шлагбаум *m* [1] barrier, turnpike.
шлак *m* [1] slag, scoria; cinder.
шланг *m* [1] hose.
шлем *m* [1] helmet.
шлёп F crack!; **~ать** [1], *once* ⟨**~нуть**⟩ [20] slap; shuffle; plump (*v/i.* F -ся; plop).
шлифовать [7], ⟨от-⟩ grind; polish.
шлю|з *m* [1] sluice, lock; **´~пка** *f* [5; *g/pl.*: -пок] boat; launch.
шляп|а *f* [5] hat; F milksop; **~ка** *f* [5; *g/pl.*: -пок] *dim. of.* **~а**; (*lady's*) hat; head (*nail*); **~очник** *m* [1] hatter; **~ный** [14] hat...; hatter's; milliner's.
шляться P [1] *s.* шататься.
шмель *m* [4 *e.*] bumblebee.
шмыг quick!; **´~ать** F [1], *once* ⟨**~нуть**⟩ [20] whisk, scurry, slip.
шницель *m* [4] cutlet.
шнур *m* [1 *e.*] cord; **~овать** [7], ⟨за-⟩ lace (*or* tie) up; **~ок** *m* [1; -рка] shoestring, (shoe) lace.
шнырять F [28] poke about.
шов *m* [1; шва] seam; ⊕ *a.* joint.
шоколад *m* [1] chocolate.
шомпол *m* [1; *pl.*: -а, *etc. e.*] ramrod.
шопот *m* [1] *s.* шёпот.
шорник *m* [1] saddler.
шорох *m* [1] rustle.
шоссе (-'se) *n* [*ind.*] high road.
шотланд|ец *m* [1; -дца] Scotchman, *pl.* the Scotch; **~ка** *f* [5; *g/pl.*: -док] Scotchwoman; **ᴤия** *f* [7] Scotland; **~ский** [16] Scotch, Scottish.
шофёр *m* [1] driver, chauffeur.
шпага *f* [5] sword.
шпагат *m* [1] packthread, string.
шпал|а 🚂 *f* [5] cross tie, *Brt.* sleeper; **~ера** *f* [5] trellis; lane.
шпа|ргалка F *f* [5; *g/pl.*: -лок] pony, *Brt.* crib; **~т** *m* [1] *min.* spar.
шпиговать [7], ⟨на-⟩ lard.
шпик *m* [1] slab bacon, fat; F sleuth.
шпи|лька *f* [5; *g/pl.*: -лек] hairpin; hat pin; tack; *fig.* taunt, twit (*vb.*: пустить В); **~нат** *m* [1] spinach.
шпион *m* [1], **~ка** *f* [5; *g/pl.*: -нок] spy; **~аж** *m* [1] espionage; **~ить** [13] spy.
шпиц *m* [1] Pomeranian (*dog*).
шпор|а *f* [5], **~ить** [13] spur.
шприц *m* [1] syringe, squirt.
шпрот *m* [1] sprat, brisling.
шпулька *f* [5; *g/pl.*: -лек] spool, bobbin.
шрам *m* [1] scar.
шрифт *m* [1] type, print.
штаб ⚔ *m* [1] staff; headquarters.
штабель *m* [4; *pl.*: -ля, *etc. e.*] pile.
штабной ⚔ [14] staff...
штамп *m* [1], **~овать** [7], ⟨от-⟩ stamp.
штанга *f* [5] ⊕ pole; *sport*: weight.
штаны F *m/pl.* [1 *e.*] pants, trousers.
штат *m* [1] state; staff; *cf.* США; **~ив** *m* [1] support; *phot.* tripod; **´~ный** [14] (on the) staff; **´~ский** [16] civil; civilian; plain (*clothes*).
штемпел|евать (ʃte-) [6], **'~ь** *m* [4; *pl.*: -ля, *etc. e.*] stamp; postmark.
штепсель ('ʃte-) *m* [4; *pl.*: -ля, *etc. e.*] plug; jack.

шти|ль *m* [4] calm; **~фт** *m* [1 *e.*] pin.
штóп|ать [1], ⟨за-⟩ darn; **~ка** *f* [5] darning.
штóпор *m* [1] corkscrew; ✈ spin.
штó|ра *f* [5] blind; curtain; **~рм** *m* [1] storm; **~ф** *m* [1] quart, bottle; damask.
штраф *m* [1] fine, penalty, mulct; **~нóй** [14] fine...; penalty...; convict...; **~овáть** [7], ⟨о-⟩ fine.
штрейкбрéхер *m* [1] strikebreaker.
штрих *m* [1 *e.*] stroke; trait; touch; **~овáть** [7], ⟨за-⟩ hatch; shade.
штудúровать [7], ⟨про-⟩ study.
штýка *f* [5] piece; F thing; fish; trick; story; business; point.
штукатýр|ить [13], ⟨о-⟩, **~ка** *f* [5] plaster.
штурвáл *m* [1] steering wheel.
штурм *m* [1] storm, onslaught; **∠ан** *m* [1] navigator; **~овáть** [7] storm, assail; **~овúк** *m* [1 *e.*] battleplane.
штýчный [14] (by the) piece.
штык *m* [1 *e.*] bayonet.
шýба *f* [5] fur (coat).
шýлер *m* [1; *pl.*: -á, *etc. e.*] sharper.
шум *m* [1] noise; din; rush; bustle; buzz; F hubbub, row, ado; ~ и гам hullabaloo; надéлать ∠у cause a sensation; **~éть** [10 *e.*; шумлю́, шумúшь] make a noise; rustle; rush; roar; bustle; buzz; **~úха** F *f* [5] sensation, clamo(u)r; **~лúвый** [14 *sh.*] clamorous; **∠ный** [14; -мен, -мнá, -о] noisy, loud; sensational; **~овóй** [14] noise...; jazz...; **~óк** *m* [1; -мкá]: под ~óк F on the sly.
Шýра *m/f* [5] *dim. of* Алексáндр(а).
шýр|ин *m* [1] brother-in-law (*wife's brother*); **~шáть** [4 *e.*; -шý, шúшь], ⟨за-⟩ rustle.
шýстрый F [14; -тёр, -трá, -о] nimble.
шут *m* [1 *e.*] fool, jester, clown, buffoon; F deuce; **~úть** [15], ⟨по-⟩ joke, jest; make fun (of над Т); **∠ка** *f* [5; *g/pl.*: -ток] joke, jest (in в В); fun (for рáди Р); trick (*play:* on с Т); F trifle (it's no ∠ка ли); крóме ∠ок joking apart; are you in earnest?; не на ∠ку serious(ly); (Д) не до ∠ок be in no laughing mood; **~лúвый** F [14 *sh.*] jocose, playful; **~нúк** *m* [1 *e.*] joker, wag; **∠очный** [14] jocose, sportive, comic; laughing (*matter*); **~á** jokingly (не in earnest).
шушýкать(ся) F [1] whisper.
шхýна *f* [5] schooner.
ш-ш hush!

Щ

щавéль *m* [4 *e.*] ♣ sorrel.
щадúть [15 *e.*; щажý, щадúшь], ⟨по-⟩ [-щажённый], spare.
щéбень *m* [4; -бня] road metal.
щебетáть [3] chirp, twitter.
щегóл *m* [1; -глá] goldfinch; **~евáтый** [14 *sh.*] stylish, smart; **'~ь** ('ʃtʃɔ-) *m* [4] dandy, fop; **~ьскóй** [16] foppish; **~ять** [28] flaunt, parade.
щéдр|ость *f* [8] liberality; **~ый** [14; щедр, -á, -о] liberal, generous.
щекá *f* [5; *ac/sg.*: щéку; *pl.*: щёки, щёк, щекáм, *etc. e.*] cheek.
щекóлда *f* [5] latch.
щекот|áть [3], ⟨по-⟩, **∠ка** *f* [5] tickle; **~лúвый** [14 *sh.*] ticklish.
щёлк|ать [1], *once* ⟨~нуть⟩ [20] 1. *v/i.* click (*one's tongue* Т), snap (*one's fingers* Т), crack (*whip* Т); chatter (*one's teeth* Т); warble, sing (*birds*); 2. *v/t.* fillip (on по Д); crack (*nuts*).
щёло|к *m* [1] lye; **~чь** *f* [8; *from g/pl. e.*] alkali; **~чнóй** [14] alkaline.
щелчóк *m* [1; -чкá] fillip; crack.
щель *f* [8; *from g/pl. e.*] chink, crack, crevice; slit; голосовáя ~ glottis.
щемúть [14 *e.*; *3rd. p., a. impers.*] press; *fig.* oppress.
щенóк *m* [1; -нкá; *pl.*: -нкú & (2) -нята] puppy, whelp.
щеп|етúльный [14; -лен, -льна] scrupulous, punctilious, squeamish, fancy...; **∠ка** *f* [5; *g/pl.*: -пок] chip; *fig.* lath
щепóтка *f* [5; *g/pl.*: -ток] pinch.
щетúн|а *f* [5] bristle(s); **~истый** [14 *sh.*] bristly; **~иться** [13], ⟨о-⟩ bristle up.
щётка *f* [5; *g/pl.*: -ток] brush.
щи *f/pl.* [5; *gen.*: щей] cabbage soup.
щúколотка *f* [5; *g/pl.*: -ток] ankle.
щип|áть [2], *once* ⟨(у)~нýть⟩ [20] pinch, tweak (*v/t.* за В), (*a. cold*) nip; bite; twitch; pluck; browse; **~цы́** *m/pl.* [1 *e.*] tongs, pliers, pincers, nippers; ⚕ forceps; (nut)crackers; **∠чики** *m/pl.* [1] tweezers.
щит *m* [1 *e.*] shield; buckler; screen, guard, protection; (snow)shed; (⚡ switch)board; sluice gate; (tortoise) shell.
щитовúдный [14] thyroid (*gland*).
щýка *f* [5] pike (*fish*).
щýп|альце *n* [11; *g/pl.*: -лец] feeler, tentacle; **~ать** [1], ⟨по-⟩ feel; touch; *fig.* sound; **~лый** F [14; щупл, -á, -о] puny.
щýрить [13] screw up (one's eyes -ся).

Э

эвакуи́ровать [7] (*im*)*pf.* evacuate.
эволюцио́нный [14] evolution(ary).
эгои́|зм *m* [1] ego(t)ism, selfishness; **~ст** *m* [1], **~стка** *f* [5; *g/pl.*: -ток] egoist; **~сти́ческий** [16], **~сти́чный** [14; -чен, -чна] selfish.
Эдинбу́рг *m* [1] Edinburgh.
эй! halloo!, hullo!, hey!
эквивале́нт *m* [1], **~ный** [14; -тен, -тна] equivalent.
экза́м|ен *m* [1] examination (in ... на П; ... in по Д); **~ена́тор** *m* [1] examiner; **~енова́ть** [7], ⟨про-⟩ examine; **-ся** be examined (by у Р), have one's examination (with); *p. pr. p.* examinee.
экземпля́р *m* [1] copy; specimen.
экзоти́ческий [16] exotic.
э́кий F [16; *sh.*: no *m*, -а] what (a).
экип|а́ж *m* [1] carriage; ⚓, ✈ crew; **~ирова́ть** [7] (*im*)*pf.* fit out, equip.
эконо́м|ика *f* [5] economy; economics; **~ить** [14], ⟨с-⟩ save; economize; **~и́ческий** [16] economic; **~ия** *f* [7] economy; saving (of Р, в П); **~ный** [14; -мен, -мна] economical, thrifty.
экра́н *m* [1] screen.
экскава́тор *m* [1] dredge(r *Brt.*).
экскурс|а́нт *m* [1] excursionist; **∠ия** *f* [7] excursion, outing, trip; **~ово́д** *m* [1] guide.
экспеди́|тор *m* [1] forwarding agent(s); **~цио́нный** [14] forwarding...; expedition...; **~ция** *f* [7] dispatch (office); forwarding agency; expedition.
экспер|имента́льный [14] experimental; **∠т** *m* [1] expert (in по Д); **~ти́за** *f* [5] examination; (expert) opinion.
эксплуа|та́тор *m* [1] exploiter; **~та́ция** *f* [7] exploitation; ⊕ operation; **~ти́ровать** [7] exploit; sweat; ⊕ operate, run.
экспон|а́т *m* [1] exhibit; **~и́ровать** [7] (*im*)*pf.* exhibit; *phot.* expose.
э́кспорт *m* [1], **~и́ровать** [7] (*im*)*pf.* export; **~ный** [14] export...
экс|про́мт *m* [1] impromptu; **~про́мтом** *a.* extempore; **~та́з** *m* [1] ecstasy; **~тра́кт** *m* [1] extract; **∠тренный** [14 *sh.*] special; extra; urgent; **~центри́чный** [14; -чен, -чна] eccentric.
эласти́чн|ость *f* [8] elasticity; **~ый** [14; -чен, -чна] elastic.
элега́нтн|ость *f* [8] elegance; **~ый** [14; -тен, -тна] elegant, stylish.
эле́ктр|ик *m* [1] electrician; **~ифици́ровать** [7] (*im*)*pf.* electrify; **~и́ческий** [16] electric(al); **~и́чество** *n* [9] electricity; **~ово́з** *m* [1] electric locomotive; **~о́д** *m* [1] electrode; **~омонтёр** *s.* **~ик**; **~о́н** *m* [1], electron; **~оста́нция** *f* [7] power station; **~оте́хник** *m* [1] electrical engineer; **~оте́хника** *f* [5] electrical engineering.
элеме́нт *m* [1] element; **~а́рный** [14; -рен, -рна] elementary.
эма́л|евый [14], **~ирова́ть** [7], **~ь** *f* [8] enamel.
эмбле́ма *f* [5] emblem.
эмигр|а́нт *m* [1], **~а́нтка** *f* [5; *g/pl.*: -ток], **~а́нтский** [16] emigrant; emigre; **~и́ровать** [7] (*im*)*pf.* emigrate.
эмоциона́льный [14; -лен, -льна] emotional.
эмпири́зм *m* [1] empiricism.
энерг|и́чный [14; -чен, -чна] energetic; drastic; **∠ия** *f* [7] energy.
энтузиа́зм *m* [1] enthusiasm.
энциклопе́д|ия *f* [7] (*a.* **~и́ческий слова́рь** *m*) encyclop(a)edia.
эпи|гра́мма *f* [5] epigram; **~деми́ческий** [16], **~де́мия** *f* [7] epidemic; **~зо́д** *m* [1] episode; **~ле́псия** *f* [7] epilepsy; **~ло́г** *m* [1] epilogue; **∠тет** *m* [1] epithet.
э́по|с *m* [1] epic (poem), epos; **∠ха** *f* [5] epoch, era, period (in в В).
эроти́ческий [16] erotic.
эска́др|а *f* [5] ⚓ spuadron; **~и́лья** *f* [6; *g/pl.*: -лий] ✈ squadron.
эс|кала́тор *m* [1] escalator; **~ки́з** *m* [1] sketch; **~кимо́с** *m* [1] Eskimo; **~корти́ровать** [7] escort; **~ми́нец** *m* [1; -нца] ⚓ destroyer; **~се́нция** *f* [7] essence; **~тафе́та** *f* [5] relay race; **~тети́ческий** [16] aesthetic.
эсто́н|ец *m* [1; -нца], **~ка** *f* [5; *g/pl.*: -нок], **~ский** [16] Estonian.
эстра́да *f* [5] platform; *s.* варьете́.
эта́ж *m* [1 *e.*] floor, stor(e)y; дом в три **~а́** three-storied (*Brt.* -reyed) house; **~е́рка** *f* [5; *g/pl.*: -рок] whatnot; bookshelf.
э́так(ий) F *s.* так(о́й).
эта́п *m* [1] stage; base; transport(s).
э́тика *f* [5] ethics (*a. pl.*).
этике́тка *f* [5; *g/pl.*: -ток] label.
этимоло́гия *f* [7] etymology.
этногра́фия *f* [7] ethnography.
э́т|от *m*, **~а** *f*, **~о** *n*, **~и** *pl.* [27] this, *pl.* these; *su.* this one; that; it; there (-*in, etc.*); **~о** *a.* well, then, as a matter of fact.
этю́д *m* [1] study, étude; sketch.
эф|е́с *m* [1] (*sword*) hilt; **~и́р** *m* [1] ether; **~и́рный** [14; -рен, -рна] ethereal.
эффект|и́вность *f* [8] efficacy; **~и́вный** [14; -вен, -вна] efficacious; **∠ный** [14; -тен, -тна] effective.
эх ah!
эшафо́т *m* [1] scaffold.
эшело́н *m* [1] echelon; troop train.

Ю

юбил|éй *m* [3] jubilee; **~éйный** [14] jubilee...; **~я́р** *m* [1] p. celebrating his jubilee.
ю́бка *f* [5; *g/pl.*: ю́бок] skirt.
ювели́р *m* [1] jeweller('**~ный** [14]).
юг *m* [1] south; éхать на ~ travel south; *cf.* востóк; **~о-востóк** *m* [1] southeast; **~о-востóчный** [14] southeast...; **~о-зáпад** *m* [1] southwest; **~о-зáпадный** [14] southwest...; **⁀ослáвия** *f* [7] Yugoslavia.
югу́рт *m* [1] yogurt.
Ю́жно-Африкáнский Сою́з *m* [16/1] Union of South Africa.
ю́жный [14] south(ern); southerly.
юлá *f* [5] humming top; F fidgety p.
ю́мор *m* [1] humo(u)r; **~исти́ческий** [16] humorous; comic.
ю́нга *m* [5] cabin boy.
ю́ность *f* [8] youth (*age*).
ю́нош|а *m* [5; *g/pl.*: -шей] youth (*young man*); **~ество** *n* [9] youth.
ю́ный [14; юн, -á, -о] young, youthful.
юри|ди́ческий [16] juridical; of law; **~скóнсульт** *m* [1] legal adviser.
'Ю́рий *m* [3] George.
юри́ст *m* [1] lawyer; F law student.
ю́рк|ий [16; ю́рок, юркá, -о] nimble, quick; **~ну́ть** [20] *pf.* vanish (quickly).
юр|óдивый [14] fool(ish) „in Christ"; **⁀та** *f* [5] nomad's tent.
юсти́ция *f* [7] justice.
юти́ться [15 *e.*; ючу́сь, юти́шься] nestle; be cooped.
ю́фть *f* [8] Russia leather.

Я

я [20] I; э́то я it's me.
я́бед|а F *f* [5] slander, talebearing; **~ник** *m* [1] slanderer, informer; **~ничать** [1] slander (*v/t.* на В).
я́бло|ко *n* [9; *pl.*: -ки, -к] apple; (*eye*)ball; **~ня** *f* [6] apple tree.
яв|и́ть(ся) *s.* **~ля́ть(ся)**; **⁀ка** *f* [5] appearance; presence, attendance; submission, presentation; place of secret meeting; **~лéние** *n* [12] phenomenon; occurrence, event; *thea.* scene; appearance, apparition; **~ля́ть** [28], ⟨**~и́ть**⟩ [14] present, submit; do; show; **-ся** appear, turn up; come; (T) be; **⁀ный** [14; я́вен, я́вна] open; obvious, evident; avowed; **⁀ствовать** [7] follow.
ягнёнок *m* [2] lamb.
я́год|а *f* [5], **~ный** [14] berry.
я́годица *f* [5] buttock.
яд *m* [1] poison; *fig. a.* venom.
я́дерный [14] nuclear.
ядови́тый [14 *sh.*] poisonous; venomous.
ядр|ёный F [14 *sh.*] strong, stalwart, solid; pithy; fresh; **~ó** *n* [9; *pl. st.*; *g/pl.*: я́дер] kernel; *phys.*, ⚘ nucleus; cannon ball; *fig.* core, pith.
я́зв|а *f* [5] ulcer; plague; wound; **~и́тельный** [14; -лен, -льна] venomous; caustic.
язы́к *m* [1 *e.*] tongue; language (in на П); speech; на ру́сском **~é** *speak* (*text, etc.* in) Russian; держáть ~ за зубáми hold one's tongue; **~овéд** *m* [1] linguist; **~овóй** [14] language...; **~óвый** [14] tongue...; **~ознáние** *n* [12] linguistics.
язы́ч|еский [16] pagan; **~ество** *n* [9] paganism; **~ник** *m* [1] pagan.
язычóк *m* [1; -чкá] uvula; tongue.
яи́чн|ица (-ʃn-) *f* [5] (scrambled *or* fried) eggs *pl.*; **~ый** [14] egg...
яйцó *n* [9; *pl.*: я́йца, яи́ц, я́йцам] egg.
я́кобы allegedly; as it were.
'Я́ков *m* [1] Jakob.
я́кор|ь *m* [4; *pl.*: -ря́, *etc. e.*] anchor (at на П); стоя́ть на **~е** anchor.
я́лик *m* [1] jolly boat.
я́м|а *f* [5] hole, pit; F dungeon; **~(оч)ка** *f* [5; *g/pl.*: я́мо(че)к] dimple.
ямщи́к *m* [1 *e.*] coachman, driver.
янвáрь *m* [4 *e.*] January.
янтáрь *m* [4 *e.*] amber.
япóн|ец *m* [1; -нца], **~ка** *f* [5; *g/pl.*: -нок], **~ский** [16] Japanese; **⁀ия** *f* [7] Japan.
я́ркий [16; я́рок, яркá, -о; *comp.*: я́рче] bright; glaring; vivid, rich (*colo[u]r*); blazing; *fig.* striking, outstanding.
яр|лы́к *m* [1 *e.*] label; **⁀марка** *f* [5; *g/pl.*: -рок] fair (at на П).
ярмó *n* [9; *pl.*: я́рма, *etc. st.*] yoke.
яровóй [14] summer, spring (*crops*).
я́рост|ный [14; -тен, -тна] furious, fierce; **~ь** *f* [8] fury, rage.
я́рус *m* [1] circle (*thea.*); layer.
я́рый [14 *sh.*] fierce, violent; ardent.
я́сень *m* [4] ash (*tree*).
я́сли *m/pl.* [4; *gen.*: я́слей] crib, manger; day nursery, *Brt.* crèche.
ясн|ови́дец *m* [1; -дца] clairvoyant; **⁀ость** *f* [8] clarity; **⁀ый** [14; я́сен, яснá, -о] clear; bright; fine; limpid; distinct; evident; plain (*answer*).
я́стреб *m* [1; *pl.*: -бá & -бы] hawk.
я́хта *f* [5] yacht.
ячé|йка *f* [5; *g/pl.*: -éек], **~я́** *f* [6; *g/pl.*: ячéй] cell; mesh.
ячмéнь *m* [4 *e.*] barley; ⚕ sty.
'Я́ш(к)а *m* [5] *dim.* of 'Я́ков.
я́щерица *f* [5] lizard.
я́щик *m* [1] box, case, chest; drawer; откла́дывать в дóлгий ~ shelve; *cf.* для.

PART TWO

ENGLISH-RUSSIAN VOCABULARY

A

a [ei, ə] неопределённый арти́кль; как пра́вило, не перево́дится; ~ table стол; 10 roubles a dozen де́сять рубле́й дю́жина.
A 1 [ei'wʌn] **1.** F первокла́ссный; **2.** прекра́сно.
aback [ə'bæk] *adv.* наза́д.
abandon [ə'bændən] отка́зываться [-за́ться] от (Р); оставля́ть [-а́вить], покида́ть [-и́нуть]; **~ed** поки́нутый; распу́тный; **~ment** [-mənt] оставле́ние.
abase [ə'beis] унижа́ть [уни́зить]; **~ment** [-mənt] униже́ние.
abash [ə'bæʃ] смуща́ть [смути́ть]; **~ment** [-mənt] смуще́ние.
abate [ə'beit] *v/t.* уменьша́ть [-е́ньши́ть]; *v/i.* утиха́ть [ути́хнуть] (о бу́ре и т. п.); **~ment** [-mənt] уменьше́ние; ски́дка.
abattoir ['æbətwa:] скотобо́йня.
abb|ess ['æbis] настоя́тельница монастыря́; **~ey** ['æbi] монасты́рь *m*; **~ot** ['æbət] абба́т, настоя́тель *m.*
abbreviat|e [ə'bri:vieit] сокраща́ть [-рати́ть]; **~ion** [əbri:vi'eiʃən] сокраще́ние.
abdicat|e ['æbdikeit] отрека́ться от престо́ла; отка́зываться [-за́ться] от (Р); **~ion** [æbdi'keiʃən] отрече́ние от престо́ла.
abdomen [æb'doumen] живо́т; брюшна́я по́лость *f.*
abduct [æb'dʌkt] похища́ть [-и́тить] (же́нщину).
aberration [æbə'reiʃən] заблужде́ние; *ast.* аберра́ция.
abet [ə'bet] *v/t.* подстрека́ть [-кну́ть]; [по]соде́йствовать (дурно́му); **~tor** [-ə] подстрека́тель (-ница *f*) *m.*
abeyance [ə'beiəns] состоя́ние неизве́стности; in ~ без владе́льца; вре́менно отменённый (зако́н).
abhor [əb'hɔ:] ненави́деть; **~rence** [əb'hɔrəns] отвраще́ние; **~rent** [-ənt] □ отврати́тельный.
abide [ə'baid] [*irr.*] *v/i.* пребыва́ть; ~ by твёрдо держа́ться (Р); *v/t.* not ~ не терпе́ть.
ability [ə'biliti] спосо́бность *f.*
abject ['æbdʒekt] □ презре́нный, жа́лкий.
abjure [əb'dʒuə] отрека́ться [-е́чься] от (Р).
able ['eibl] □ спосо́бный; be ~ мочь, быть в состоя́нии; **~-bodied** ['bɔdid] здоро́вый; го́дный.
abnegat|e ['æbnigeit] отка́зывать [-за́ть] себе́ в (П); отрица́ть; **~ion** [æbni'geiʃən] отрица́ние; (само-) отрече́ние.
abnormal [æb'nɔ:məl] □ ненорма́льный.
aboard [ə'bɔ:d] ⚓ на кора́бль, на корабле́.
abode [ə'boud] **1.** *pt.* от abide; **2.** местопребыва́ние; жили́ще.
aboli|sh [ə'bɔliʃ] отменя́ть [-ни́ть]; упраздня́ть [-ни́ть]; **~tion** [æbo'liʃən] отме́на.
abomina|ble [ə'bɔminəbl] □ отврати́тельный; **~te** [-neit] *v/t.* пита́ть отвраще́ние к (Д); **~tion** [əbɔmi'neiʃən] отвраще́ние.
aboriginal [æbə'ridʒənəl] **1.** тузе́мный; **2.** тузе́мец.
abortion [ə'bɔ:ʃən] вы́кидыш, або́рт.
abound [ə'baund] изоби́ловать (in [Т]).
about [ə'baut] **1.** *prp.* вокру́г (Р); о́коло (Р); о (П), об (П), обо (П), насчёт (Р); у (Р); про (В); I had no money ~ me у меня́ не́ было с собо́й де́нег; **2.** *adv.* вокру́г, везде́; приблизи́тельно; be ~ to do собира́ться де́лать.
above [ə'bʌv] **1.** *prp.* над (Т); вы́ше (Р); свы́ше (Р); ~ all гла́вным о́бразом; **2.** *adv.* наверху́, наве́рх; вы́ше; **3.** *adj.* вышеска́занный.
abreast [ə'brest] в ряд.
abridg|e [ə'bridʒ] сокраща́ть [-рати́ть]; **~(e)ment** [-mənt] сокраще́ние.
abroad [ə'brɔ:d] за грани́цей, за грани́цу; there is a report ~ хо́дит слух.
abrogate ['æbrogeit] *v/t.* отменя́ть [-ни́ть]; аннули́ровать (*im*)*pf.*
abrupt [ə'brʌpt] □ обры́вистый; внеза́пный; ре́зкий.
abscond [əb'skɔnd] *v/i.* скры́(ва́)ться.
absence ['æbsns] отсу́тствие; отлу́чка; ~ of mind рассе́янность *f.*
absent 1. ['æbsnt] □ отсу́тсвующий; **2.** [æb'sent] ~ o. s. отлуча́ться [-чи́ться]; **~-minded** □ рассе́янный.
absolut|e ['æbsəlu:t] □ абсолю́тный; бесприме́рный; **~ion** [æbsə'lu:ʃən] отпуще́ние грехо́в.
absolve [əb'zɔlv] проща́ть [прости́ть]; освобожда́ть [-боди́ть] (from от Р).
absorb [əb'sɔ:b] впи́тывать [впита́ть]; абсорби́ровать (*im*)*pf.*
absorption [əb'sɔ:pʃən] вса́сывание, впи́тывание; *fig.* погружённость *f* (в ду́мы).
abstain [əbs'tein] возде́рживаться [-жа́ться] (from от Р).

abstemious [əbs'ti:miəs] □ воздéржанный, умéренный.
abstention [æbs'tenʃən] воздержáние.
abstinen|ce ['æbstinəns] умéренность *f*; трéзвость *f*; **~t** [-nənt] □ умéренный, воздéржанный; непьющий.
abstract 1. ['æbstrækt] □ отвлечённый, абстрáктный; 2. конспéкт; извлечéние; *gr.* отвлечённое имя существительное 3. [æbs'trækt] отвлекáть [-éчь]; резюмировать (*im*)*pf.*; **~ed** [-id] □ отвлечённый; **~ion** [-kʃən] абстрáкция.
abstruse [æbs'tru:s] □ *fig.* непонятный, тёмный.
abundan|ce [ə'bʌndəns] избыток, изобилие; **~t** [-dənt] □ обильный, богáтый.
abus|e 1. [ə'bju:s] злоупотреблéние; оскорблéние; брань *f*; 2. [ə'bju:z] злоупотреблять [-бить] (Т); [вы]ругáть; **~ive** [ə'bju:siv] □ оскорбительный.
abut [ə'bʌt] граничить (upon с Т).
abyss [ə'bis] бéздна.
academic|(al □) [ækə'demik(əl)] академический; **~ian** [əkædə'miʃən] акадéмик.
accede [æk'si:d]: ~ to вступáть [-пить] в (В).
accelerat|e [æk'seləreit] ускорять [-óрить]; **~or** [æk'seləreitə] ускоритель *m*.
accent 1. ['æksənt] ударéние; произношéние, акцéнт; 2. [æk'sent] *v/t.* дéлать или стáвить ударéние на (П); **~uate** [æk'sentjueit] дéлать или стáвить ударéние на (П); *fig.* подчёркивать [-черкнýть].
accept [ək'sept] принимáть [-нять]; соглашáться [-гласиться] с (Т); **~able** [ək'septəbl] □ приéмлемый; приятный; **~ance** [ək'septəns] приём, принятие; ✝ акцéпт.
access ['ækses] дóступ; прохóд; ⚕ приступ; easy of ~ достýпный; **~ary** [æk'sesəri] соучáстник (-ица); **~ible** [æk'sesəbl] □ достýпный, достижимый; **~ion** [æk'seʃən] вступлéние (to в В); дóступ (to к Д); ~ to the throne вступлéние на престóл.
accessory [æk'sesəri] □ 1. добáвочный, второстепéнный; 2. *pl.* принадлéжности *f/pl.*
accident ['æksidənt] случáйность *f*; катастрóфа, авáрия; **~al** [æksi'dentl] □ случáйный.
acclaim [ə'kleim] шýмно привéтствовать (В); аплодировать (Д).
acclamation [æklə'meiʃən] шýмное одобрéние.
acclimatize [ə'klaimətaiz] акклиматизировать(ся) (*im*)*pf.*
acclivity [ə'kliviti] подъём (дорóги).
accommodat|e [ə'kɔmədeit] приспособлять [-пособить]; давáть жильё (Д); **~ion** [əkɔmə'deiʃən] приют; помещéние.
accompan|iment [ə'kʌmpənimənt] аккомпанемéнт; сопровождéние; **~y** [-pəni] *v/t.* аккомпанировать (Д); сопровождáть [-водить].
accomplice [ə'kɔmplis] соучáстник (-ица).
accomplish [-pliʃ] выполнять [выполнить]; достигáть [-игнуть] (Р); **~ment** [-mənt] выполнéние; достижéние; **~s** *pl.* образóванность *f*.
accord [ə'kɔ:d] 1. соглашéние; гармóния; with one ~ единодýшно; 2. *v/i.* согласóвываться [-совáться] (с Т); гармонировать (с Т); *v/t.* предоставлять [-стáвить]; **~ance** [-əns] соглáсие; **~ant** [-ənt] □ соглáсный (с Т); **~ing** [-iŋ]: ~ to соглáсно (Д); **~ingly** [-iŋli] *adv.* соответственно; таким óбразом.
accost [ə'kɔst] заговáривать [-ворить] с (Т).
account [ə'kaunt] 1. счёт; отчёт; of no ~ незначительный; on no ~ ни в кóем слýчае; on ~ of из-за (Р); take into ~, take ~ of принимáть во внимáние; turn to ~ испóльзовать (*im*)*pf.*; call to ~ призывáть к отвéту; make ~ of придавáть значéние (Д); 2. *v/i.* ~ for отвечáть [-éтить] за (В); объяснять [-нить]; be much ~ed of имéть хорóшую репутáцию; *v/t.* считáть [счесть] (В/Т); **~able** [ə'kauntəbl] □ объяснимый; **~ant** [-ənt] счетовóд; (chartered, *Am.* certified public ~ присяжный) бухгáлтер; **~ing** [-iŋ] отчётность *f*; учёт.
accredit [ə'kredit] аккредитовáть (*im*)*pf.*; приписывать [-сáть].
accrue [ə'kru:] накопляться [-питься]; происходить [произойти] (from из Р).
accumulat|e [ə'kju:mjuleit] накáпливать(ся) [-копить(ся)]; скоплять(ся) [-пить(ся)]; **~ion** [əkju:mju'leiʃən] накоплéние; скоплéние.
accura|cy ['ækjurəsi] тóчность *f*; тщáтельность *f*; **~te** [-rit] □ тóчный; тщáтельный.
accurs|ed [ə'kə:sid], **~t** [-st] проклятый.
accus|ation [ækju'zeiʃən] обвинéние; **~e** [ə'kju:z] *v/t.* обвинять [-нить]; **~er** [-ə] обвинитель(ница *f*) *m*.
accustom [ə'kʌstəm] приучáть [-чить] (to к Д); get ~ed привыкáть [-выкнуть] (to к Д); **~ed** [-d] привычный; приýченный.
ace [eis] туз; *fig.* первоклáссный лётчик.
acerbity [ə'sə:biti] тéрпкость *f*.
acet|ic [ə'si:tik] ýксусный; **~ify** [ə'setifai] окислять(ся) [-лить(ся)].

ache [eik] 1. боль *f*; 2. *v/i.* болéть (о чáсти тéла).
achieve [ə'tʃi:v] достигáть [-и́гнуть] (Р); **~ment** [-mənt] достижéние.
acid ['æsid] ки́слый; éдкий; **~ity** [ə'siditi] кислотá; éдкость *f*.
acknowledg|e [ək'nɔlidʒ] *v/t.* подтверждáть [-erди́ть]; признá(вá)ть; **~(e)ment** [-mənt] признáние; распи́ска.
acme ['ækmi] вы́сшая тóчка (Р); кри́зис.
acorn ['eikɔ:n] ♣ жёлудь *m*.
acoustics [ə'kaustiks] акýстика.
acquaint [ə'kweint] *v/t.* [по]знакóмить; be **~ed** with быть знакóмым с (Т); **~ance** [-əns] знакóмство; знакóмый.
acquiesce [ækwi'es] мóлча и́ли неохóтно соглашáться (in на В); **~ment** [-mənt] молчали́вое и́ли неохóтное соглáсие.
acquire [ə'kwaiə] *v/t.* приобретáть [-ести́]; достигáть [-и́гнуть] (Р); **~ment** [-mənt] приобретéние.
acquisition [ækwi'ziʃən] приобретéние.
acquit [ə'kwit] *v/t.* оправдывать [-дáть]; **~** of освобождáть [-боди́ть] от (Р); выполня́ть [вы́полнить] (обя́занности); **~** o. s. well хорошó справля́ться с рабóтой; **~tal** [-l] оправдáние; **~tance** уплáта (дóлга и т. п.).
acre ['eikə] акр (0,4 га).
acrid ['ækrid] óстрый, éдкий.
across [ə'krɔs] 1. *adv.* поперёк; на ту стóрону; крестóм; 2. *prp.* сквозь (В), чéрез (В).
act [ækt] 1. *v/i.* дéйствовать; поступáть [-пи́ть]; *v/t. thea.* игрáть [сыгрáть] 2. дéло; постановлéние; акт; **~ing** [-iŋ] 1. исполня́ющий обя́занности; 2. дéйствия *n/pl.*; *thea.* игрá.
action ['ækʃən] постýпок; дéйствие (*a. thea.*); дéятельность *f*; ⚔ бой; иск; take **~** принимáть мéры.
activ|e ['æktiv] □ акти́вный; энерги́чный; дéятельный; **~ity** [æk'tiviti] дéятельность *f*; акти́вность *f*; энéргия.
act|or ['æktə] актёр; **~ress** [-tris] актри́са.
actual ['æktjuəl] □ действи́тельный.
actuate ['æktjueit] приводи́ть в дéйствие.
acute [ə'kju:t] □ óстрый; проницáтельный.
adamant ['ædəmənt] *fig.* несокруши́мый.
adapt [ə'dæpt] приспособля́ть [-посóбить] (to, for к Д); **~ation** [ædæp'teiʃən] приспособлéние; передéлка; аранжирóвка.
add [æd] *v/t.* прибавля́ть [-áвить]; ⅍ склáдывать [сложи́ть]; *v/i.* увели́чи(ва)ть (to В).
addict ['ædikt] наркомáн; **~ed** [ə'diktid] склóнный (to к Д).
addition [ə'diʃən] ⅍ сложéние; прибавлéние; in **~** крóме тогó, к томý же; in **~** to вдобáвок к (Д); **~al** [-l] □ добáвочный, дополни́тельный.
address [ə'dres] *v/t.* 1. адресовáть (*im*)*pf.*; обращáться [обрати́ться] к (Д); 2. áдрес; обращéние; речь *f*; **~ee** [ædre'si] адресáт.
adept ['ædept] адéпт.
adequa|cy ['ædikwəsi] соразмéрность *f*; **~te** [-kwit] □ достáточный; адеквáтный.
adhere [əd'hiə] прилипáть [-ли́пнуть] (to к Д); *fig.* придéрживаться (to Р); **~nce** [-rəns] привéрженность *f*; **~nt** [-rənt] привéрженец (-нка).
adhesive [əd'hi:siv] □ ли́пкий, клéйкий; **~** plaster, **~** tape ли́пкий плáстырь *m*.
adjacent [ə'dʒeisənt] □ смéжный (to с Т), сосéдний.
adjoin [ə'dʒɔin] примыкáть [-мкнýть] к (Д); грани́чить с (Т).
adjourn [ə'dʒə:n] *v/t.* отклáдывать [отложи́ть]; отсрóчи(ва)ть; *parl.* дéлать переры́в; **~ment** [-mənt] отсрóчка; переры́в.
adjudge [ə'dʒʌdʒ] выноси́ть приговóр (Д).
administ|er [əd'ministə] управля́ть (Т); **~** justice отправля́ть правосýдие; **~ration** [ədminis'treiʃən] администрáция; **~rative** [əd'ministrətiv] администрати́вный; исполни́тельный; **~rator** [əd'ministreitə] администрáтор.
admir|able ['ædmərəbl] □ превосхóдный; восхити́тельный; **~ation** [ædmi'reiʃən] восхищéние; **~e** [əd'maiə] восхищáться [-ити́ться] (Т); [по]любовáться (Т *or* на В).
admiss|ible [əd'misəbl] □ допусти́мый, приéмлемый; **~ion** [əd'miʃən] вход; допущéние; признáние.
admit [əd'mit] *v/t.* допускáть [-сти́ть]; **~tance** [-əns] дóступ, вход.
admixture [əd'mikstʃə] при́месь *f*.
admon|ish [əd'mɔniʃ] увещ(ев)áть *impf.*; предостерегáть [-рéчь] (of от Р); **~ition** [ædmo'niʃən] увещáние; предостережéние.
ado [ə'du:] суетá; хлóпоты *f/pl*.
adolescen|ce [ædo'lesns] ю́ность *f*; **~nt** [-snt] ю́ный, ю́ношеский.
adopt [ə'dɔpt] *v/t.* усыновля́ть [-ви́ть]; усвáивать [усвóить]; **~ion** [ə'dɔpʃən] усыновлéние; усвáивание.
ador|ation [ædo'reiʃən] обожáние; **~e** [ə'dɔ:] *v/t.* обожáть.
adorn [ə'dɔ:n] украшáть [укрáсить]; **~ment** [-mənt] украшéние.
adroit [ə'drɔit] □ лóвкий; находчи́вый.

adult ['ædʌlt] взрóслый, совершеннолéтний.
adulter|ate [ə'dʌltəreit] фальсифици́ровать (*im*)*pf*.; **~er** [ə'dʌltərə] наруша́ющий супру́жескую вéрность; **~ess** [-ris] наруша́ющая супру́жескую вéрность; **~y** [-ri] нарушéние супру́жеской вéрности.
advance [əd'vɑ:ns] **1.** *v/i.* подвига́ться вперёд; ⚔ наступа́ть [-пи́ть]; продвига́тся [-и́нуться]; дéлать успéхи; *v/t.* продвига́ть [-и́нуть]; выдвига́ть [вы́двинуть]; плати́ть ава́нсом; **2.** ⚔ наступлéние; успéх (в учéнии); прогрéсс; **~d** [-t] передовóй; **~ment** [-mənt] успéх; продвижéние.
advantage [əd'vɑ:ntidʒ] преиму́щество; вы́года; take **~** of [вос-]пóльзоваться (Т); **~ous** [ædvən'teidʒəs] □ вы́годный.
adventur|e [əd'ventʃə] приключéние; **~er** [-rə] иска́тель приключéний; авантюри́ст; **~ous** [-rəs] □ предприи́мчивый; авантю́рный.
advers|ary ['ædvəsəri] проти́вник (-ица); сопéрник (-ица); **~e** ['ædvə:s] □ враждéбный; **~ity** [əd'və:siti] бéдствие, несча́стье.
advertis|e ['ædvətaiz] реклами́ровать (*im*)*pf*.; объявля́ть [-ви́ть]; **~ement** [əd'və:tismənt] объявлéние; рекла́ма; **~ing** ['ædvətaiziŋ] рекла́мный.
advice [əd'vais] совéт.
advis|able □ [əd'vaizəbl] жела́тельный; **~e** [əd'vaiz] *v/t.* [по]совéтовать (Д); *v/i.* [по]совéтоваться (with с Т; on, about о П); **~er** [-ə] совéтник (-ица), совéтчик (-ица).
advocate **1.** ['ædvəkit] защи́тник (-ица); сторóнник (-ица); адвока́т; **2.** [-keit] отста́ивать [отстоя́ть].
aerial ['ɛəriəl] **1.** □ возду́шный; **2.** антéнна; outdoor **~** нару́жная антéнна.
aero... ['ɛərou] аэро...; **~drome** ['ɛərədroum] аэродрóм; **~naut** [-nɔ:t] аэрона́вт; **~nautics** [-'nɔ:tiks] аэрона́втика; **~plane** [-plein] самолёт, аэропла́н; **~stat** [-stæt] аэроста́т.
aesthetic [i:s'θetik] эстети́чный; **~s** [-s] эстéтика.
afar [ə'fɑ:] *adv.* вдалекé, вдали́; from **~** издалека́.
affable ['æfəbl] привéтливый.
affair [ə'fɛə] дéло.
affect [ə'fekt] *v/t.* [по]дéйствовать на (В); задé(ва́)ть; ⚕ поража́ть [-рази́ть]; **~ation** [æfek'teiʃən] жема́нство; **~ed** [ə'fektid] □ жема́нный; **~ion** [ə'fekʃən] привя́занность *f*; заболева́ние; **~ionate** □ нéжный.
affidavit [æfi'deivit] пи́сьменное показа́ние под прися́гой.
affiliate [ə'filieit] *v/t.* присоединя́ть [-ни́ть] (как филиа́л).
affinity [ə'finiti] сродствó.
affirm [ə'fə:m] утвержда́ть [-рди́ть]; **~ation** [æfə:'meiʃən] утверждéние; **~ative** [ə'fə:mətiv] □ утверди́тельный.
affix [ə'fiks] прикрепля́ть [-пи́ть] (to к Д).
afflict [ə'flikt] *v/t.* огорча́ть [-чи́ть]; be **~ed** страда́ть (with от Р); **~ion** [ə'flikʃən] гóре; болéзнь *f*.
affluen|ce ['æfluens] изоби́лие, бога́тство; **~t** [-ənt] **1.** □ оби́льный, бога́тый; **2.** притóк.
afford [ə'fɔ:d] позволя́ть [-вóлить] себé; I can **~** it я могу́ себé э́то позвóлить; предоставля́ть [-а́вить].
affront [ə'frʌnt] **1.** оскорбля́ть [-би́ть]; **2.** оскорблéние.
afield [ə'fi:ld] *adv.* вдалекé; в пóле; на войнé.
afloat [ə'flout] ⚓ на водé; в мóре; в ходу́.
afraid [ə'freid] испу́ганный; be **~** of боя́ться (Р).
afresh [ə'freʃ] *adv.* снóва, сы́знова.
African ['æfrikən] **1.** африка́нец (-нка); **2.** африка́нский.
after ['ɑ:ftə] **1.** *adv.* потóм, пóсле, затéм; позади́; **2.** *prp.* за (Т), позади́ (Р); чéрез (В); пóсле (Р); **3.** *cj.* с тех пор, как; пóсле тогó, как; **4.** *adj.* послéдующий; **~crop** вторóй урожа́й; **~math** [-mæθ] ота́ва; *fig.* послéдствия *n*/*pl*.; **~noon** [-'nu:n] врéмя пóсле полу́дня; **~-taste** (остаю́щийся) при́вкус; **~thought** мысль, пришéдшая пóздно; **~wards** [-wədz] *adv.* потóм.
again [ə'gein *Am.* ə'gen] *adv.* снóва, опя́ть; **~** and **~**, time and **~** то и дéло; as much **~** ещё стóлько же.
against [ə'geinst] *prp.* прóтив (Р); о, об (В); на (В); as **~** прóтив (Р); **~** the wall у стены́; к стенé.
age [eidʒ] вóзраст; года́ *m*/*pl*.; эпóха; of **~** совершеннолéтний; under **~** несовершеннолéтний; **~d** ['eidʒid] ста́рый, постарéвший; **~** twenty двадцати́ лет.
agency ['eidʒənsi] дéйствие; агéнтство.
agent ['eidʒənt] фа́ктор; агéнт; довéренное лицó.
agglomerate [ə'glɔməreit] *v/t.* соб(и)ра́ть; *v/i.* скопля́ться [-пи́ться].
agglutinate [ə'glu:tineit] склéи(ва)ть.
aggrandize ['ægrəndaiz) увели́чи(ва)ть; возвели́чи(ва)ть.
aggravate ['ægrəveit] усугубля́ть [-би́ть]; ухудша́ть [уху́дшить]; раздража́ть [-жи́ть].
aggregate **1.** ['ægrigeit] собира́ть (-ся) в однó цéлое; **2.** □ [-git] сову́пный; **3.** [-git] совоку́пность *f*; агрега́т.

aggress|ion [ə'greʃən] нападе́ние; агре́ссия; **~or** [ə'gresə] агре́ссор.
aghast [ə'gɑ:st] ошеломлённый, поражённый у́жасом.
agil|e ['ædʒail] □ прово́рный, живо́й; **~ity** [ə'dʒiliti] прово́рство, жи́вость *f*.
agitat|e ['ædʒiteit] *v/t*. [вз]волнова́ть, возбужда́ть [-уди́ть]; *v/i*. агити́ровать (for за В); **~ion** [ædʒi'teiʃən] волне́ние; агита́ция.
agnail ['ægneil] ⚕ заусе́ница.
ago [ə'gou]: a year ~ год тому́ наза́д.
agonize ['ægənaiz] быть в аго́нии; си́льно му́чить(ся).
agony ['ægəni] аго́ния; боль *f*.
agree [ə'gri:] *v/i*. соглаша́ться [-ласи́ться] (to с Т, на В); ~ [up]on усла́вливаться [усло́виться] о (П); **~able** [-əbl] согла́сный (to с Т, на В); прия́тный; **~ment** [-mənt] согла́сие; соглаше́ние, догово́р.
agricultur|al [ægri'kʌltʃərəl] сельскохозя́йственный; **~e** ['ægrikʌltʃə] се́льское хозя́йство; земледе́лие; агроно́мия; **~ist** [ægri'kʌltʃərist] агроно́м; земледе́лец.
ague ['eigju:] лихора́дочный озно́б.
ahead [ə'hed] вперёд, впереди́; straight ~ пря́мо, вперёд.
aid [eid] **1.** по́мощь *f*; помо́щник (-ица); **2.** помога́ть [помо́чь] (Д).
ail [eil]: what **~s** him? что его́ беспоко́ит?; **~ing** ['eiliŋ] больно́й, нездоро́вый; **~ment** ['eilmənt] нездоро́вье.
aim [eim] **1.** *v/i*. прице́ли(ва)ться (at в В); *fig*. ~ at име́ть в виду́; *v/t*. направля́ть [-ра́вить] (at на В); **2.** цель *f*, наме́рение; **~less** [eimlis] □ бесце́льный.
air¹ [ɛə] **1.** во́здух; by ~ самолётом; возду́шной по́чтой; *Am*. be on the ~ рабо́тать (о радиоста́нции); *Am*. put on the ~ передава́ть по ра́дио; *Am*. be off the ~ не рабо́тать (о радиоста́нции); **2.** прове́три(ва)ть.
air² [~] *mst pl*. аффекта́ция, ва́жничанье; give o.s. **~s** ва́жничать.
air³ [~] ♪ мело́дия; пе́сня; а́рия.
air|-base авиаба́за; **~-brake** возду́шный то́рмоз; **~conditioned** ‖ кондициони́рованным во́здухом; **~craft** самолёт; **~field** аэродро́м; **~force** вое́нно-возду́шный флот; **~-jacket** надувно́й спаса́тельный нагру́дник; **~-lift** «возду́шный мост», возду́шная перево́зка; **~-liner** ре́йсовый самолёт; **~-mail** возду́шная по́чта; **~man** лётчик, авиа́тор; **~plane** *Am*. самолёт; **~-port** аэропо́рт; **~-raid** возду́шный налёт; ~ precautions *pl*. противовозду́шная оборо́на; **~-route** возду́шная тра́сса; **~shelter** бомбоубе́жище; **~ship** дирижа́бль *m*; **~-tight** гермети́ческий; **~-tube** ка́мера ши́ны; *anat*. трахе́я; **~way** возду́шная тра́сса.
airy ['ɛəri] □ возду́шный; легкомы́сленный.
aisle [ail] ⛪ приде́л (хра́ма); прохо́д.
ajar [ə'dʒɑ:] приотво́ренный.
akin [ə'kin] ро́дственный, бли́зкий (to Д).
alarm [ə'lɑ:m] **1.** трево́га; страх; **2.** [вс]трево́жить], [вз]волнова́ть; **~-clock** буди́льник.
albuminous [æl'bju:minəs] содержа́щий бело́к; альбуми́нный.
alcohol ['ælkəhɔl] алкого́ль *m*; спирт; **~ic** [ælkə'hɔlik] **1.** алкого́льный; **2.** алкого́лик; **~ism** ['ælkəhɔlizm] алкоголи́зм.
alcove ['ælkouv] alько́в, ни́ша.
ale [eil] пи́во, эль *m*.
alert [ə'lə:t] **1.** □ живо́й, прово́рный; **2.** (возду́шная) трево́га; on the ~ настороже́.
alien ['eiliən] **1.** иностра́нный; чу́ждый; **2.** иностра́нец, чужестра́нец; **~able** [-əbl] отчужда́емый; **~ate** [-eit] отчужда́ть [-уди́ть]; **~ist** ['eiliənist] психиа́тр.
alight [ə'lait] **1.** сходи́ть [сойти́] (с Р); приземля́ться [-ли́ться]; **2.** *adj. predic*. зажжённый, в огне́; освещённый.
align [ə'lain] выра́внивать(ся) [вы́ровнять(ся)].
alike [ə'laik] **1.** *adj. pred*. одина́ковый; похо́жий; **2.** *adv*. то́чно так же; подо́бно.
aliment ['ælimənt] пита́ние; **~ary** [æli'mentəri] пищево́й; пита́тельный; ~ canal пищево́д.
alimony ['æliməni] алиме́нты *m/pl*.
alive [e'laiv] живо́й, бо́дрый; чу́ткий (to к Д); кише́щий (with Т); be ~ to я́сно понима́ть.
all [ɔ:l] **1.** *adj*. весь *m*, вся *f*, всё *n*, все *pl*; вся́кий; всевозмо́жный; for ~ that несмотря́ на то; **2.** всё, все; at ~ вообще́; not at ~ во́все не; for ~ (that) I care мне безразли́чно; for ~ I know поско́льку я зна́ю; **3.** *adv*. вполне́, всеце́ло, соверше́нно; ~ at once сра́зу; ~ the better тем лу́чше; ~ but почти́; ~ right хорошо́, ла́дно.
allay [ə'lei] успока́ивать [-ко́ить].
alleg|ation [æle'geiʃən] заявле́ние; голосло́вное утвержде́ние; **~e** [ə'ledʒ] ссыла́ться [сосла́ться] на (В); утвержда́ть (без основа́ния).
allegiance [ə'li:dʒəns] ве́рность *f*, пре́данность *f*.
alleviate [ə'li:vieit] облегча́ть [-чи́ть].
alley ['æli] алле́я; переу́лок.
alliance [ə'laiəns] сою́з.
allocat|e ['ælokeit] размеща́ть [-мести́ть]; распределя́ть [-ли́ть]; **~ion** [ælo'keiʃən] распределе́ние.

allot [ə'lɔt] *v/t.* распределя́ть [-ли́ть]; разда́(ва́)ть.
allow [ə'lau] позволя́ть [-о́лить]; допуска́ть [-сти́ть]; *Am.* утвержда́ть; **~able** [-əbl] □ позволи́тельный; **~ance** [-əns] (материа́льное) содержа́ние; ски́дка; разреше́ние; make ~ for принима́ть во внима́ние.
alloy [ə'lɔi] **1.** при́месь *f*; сплав; **2.** сплавля́ть [-а́вить].
all-round всесторо́нний.
allude [ə'lu:d] ссыла́ться [сосла́ться] (to на В); намека́ть [-кну́ть] (to на В).
allure [ə'ljuə] завлека́ть [-е́чь]; **~ment** [-mənt] обольще́ние.
allusion [ə'luʒən] намёк; ссы́лка.
ally 1. [ə'lai] соединя́ть [-ни́ть] (to, with с Т); **2.** ['ælɑi] сою́зник.
almanac ['ɔ:lmənæk] календа́рь *m*, альмана́х.
almighty [ɔ:l'maiti] всемогу́щий.
almond ['ɑ:mənd] **1.** минда́ль *m*; минда́лина (*a.* ⚕); **2.** минда́льный.
almost ['ɔ:lmoust] почти́, едва́ не.
alms [ɑ:mz] *sg. a. pl.* ми́лостыня; **~-house** богаде́льня.
aloft [ə'lɔft] наверху́, наве́рх.
alone ['loun] оди́н *m*, одна́ *f*, одно́ *n*, одни́ *pl.*; одино́кий (-кая); let (и́ли leave) ~ оста́вить в поко́е; let ~ ... не говоря́ уже́ о ... (П).
along [ə'lɔŋ] **1.** *adv.* вперёд; all ~ всё вре́мя; ~ with вме́сте с (Т); F get ~ with you! убира́йтесь!; **2.** *prp.* вдоль (Р), по (Д); **~side** [-said] бок-о́-бок, ря́дом.
aloof [ə'lu:f] по́одаль, в стороне́; stand ~ держа́ться в стороне́.
aloud [ə'laud] гро́мко, вслух.
alp [ælp] го́рное па́стбище; ♀s 'А́льпы *f/pl.*
already [ɔ:l'redi] уже́.
also ['ɔ:lsou] та́кже, то́же.
alter ['ɔ:ltə] изменя́ть(ся) [-ни́ть (-ся)]; **~ation** [ɔ:ltə'reiʃən] переме́на, измене́ние, переде́лка (to P).
alternat|e 1. ['ɔ:ltə:neit] чередова́ть(ся); **2.** □ [ɔ:l'tə:nit] переме́нный; ⚡ alternating current переме́нный ток; **~ion** [ɔ:ltə:'neiʃən] чередова́ние; **~ive** [ɔ:l'tə:nətiv] **1.** □ взаимоисключа́ющий, альтернати́вный; переме́нно де́йствующий; **2.** альтернати́ва; вы́бор, возмо́жность *f*.
although [ɔ:l'ðou] хотя́.
altitude ['æltitju:d] высота́; возвы́шенность *f*.
altogether [ɔ:ltə'geðə] вполне́, всеце́ло; в о́бщем.
alumin(i)um [ælju'minjəm] алюми́ний.
always ['ɔ:lwəz] всегда́.
am [æm; в предложе́нии: əm] [*irr.*] *1. pers. sg. prs.* от be.
amalgamate [ə'mælgəmeit] амальгами́ровать (*im*)*pf*.
amass [ə'mæs] соб(и)ра́ть; накопля́ть [-пи́ть].
amateur ['æmətə:, -tjuə] люби́тель(ница *f*) *m*; дилета́нт(ка).
amaz|e [ə'meiz] изумля́ть [-ми́ть], поража́ть [порази́ть]; **~ement** [-mənt] изумле́ние; **~ing** [ə'meiziŋ] удиви́тельный, изуми́тельный.
ambassador [æm'bæsədə] посо́л; посла́нец.
amber ['æmbə] янта́рь *m*.
ambigu|ity [æmbi'gjuiti] двусмы́сленность *f*; **~ous** [-'bigjuəs] □ двусмы́сленный; сомни́тельный.
ambitio|n [æm'biʃən] честолю́бие; **~us** [-ʃəs] □ честолюби́вый.
amble ['æmbl] **1.** и́ноходь *f*; **2.** идти́ и́ноходью.
ambulance ['æmbjuləns] каре́та ско́рой по́мощи.
ambuscade [æmbəs'keid], **ambush** ['æmbuʃ] заса́да.
ameliorate [ə'mi:liəreit] улучша́ть(ся) [улу́чшить(ся)].
amend [ə'mend] исправля́ть(ся) [-а́вить(ся)]; *parl.* вноси́ть попра́вки в (В); **~ment** [-mənt] исправле́ние; *parl.* попра́вка (к резолю́ции, законопрое́кту); **~s** [ə'mendz] компенса́ция.
amenity [ə'mi:niti] прия́тность *f*.
American [ə'merikən] **1.** америка́нец (-нка); **2.** америка́нский; **~ism** [-izm] американи́зм; **~ize** [-aiz] американизи́ровать (*im*)*pf*.
amiable ['eimjəbl] □ дружелю́бный; доброду́шный.
amicable ['æmikəbl] □ дру́жеский, дру́жественный.
amid(st) [ə'mid(st)] среди́ (Р), посреди́ (Р), ме́жду (Т *sometimes* Р).
amiss [ə'mis] *adv.* пло́хо, непра́вильно; некста́ти; несвоевре́менно; take ~ обижа́ться [оби́деться].
amity ['æmiti] дру́жба.
ammonia [ə'mounjə] ⚗ аммиа́к.
ammunition [æmju'niʃən] боеприпа́сы *m/pl.*
amnesty ['æmnesti] **1.** амни́стия; **2.** амнисти́ровать (*im*)*pf*.
among(st) [ə'mʌŋ(st)] среди́ (Р), ме́жду (Т *sometimes* Р).
amorous ['æmərəs] □ влюблённый (of в В); влю́бчивый.
amount [ə'maunt] **1.** ~ to равня́ться (Д); **2.** су́мма; коли́чество.
ample ['æmpl] □ доста́точный, оби́льный; просто́рный.
ampli|fication [æmplifi'keiʃən] расшире́ние; увеличе́ние; усиле́ние; **~fier** ['æmplifaiə] *phys.* усили́тель *m*; **~fy** ['æmplifai] уси́ли(ва)ть; распространя́ть(ся) [-ни́ть(ся)]; **~tude** [-tju:d] широта́, разма́х (мы́сли); *phys.*, *astr.* амплиту́да.
amputate ['æmpjuteit] ампути́ровать (*im*)*pf.*, отнима́ть [-ня́ть].

amuse [ə'mju:z] забавля́ть, позаба́вить *pf.*, развлека́ть [-е́чь]; **~ment** [-mənt] развлече́ние, заба́ва.
an [æn, ən] неопределённый член.
an(a)esthetic [æni:s'θetik] нарко́тик.
analog|ous [ə'næləgəs] □ аналоги́чный, схо́дный; **~y** [ə'nælədʒi] анало́гия, схо́дство.
analys|e ['ænəlaiz] анализи́ровать (*im*)*pf.*, *pf. a.* [про-]; **~is** [ə'næləsis] ана́лиз.
anarchy ['ænəki] ана́рхия.
anatom|ize [ə'nætəmaiz] анатоми́ровать (*im*)*pf.*; [про]анализи́ровать (*im*)*pf.*; **~y** анато́мия.
ancest|or ['ænsistə] пре́док; **~ral** [æn'sestrəl] насле́дственный, родово́й; **~ress** ['ænsistris] прароди́тельница; **~ry** ['ænsistri] происхожде́ние; пре́дки *m/pl.*
anchor ['æŋkə] **1.** я́корь *m*; at **~** на я́коре; **2.** ста́вить (стать) на я́корь.
anchovy [æn'tʃouvi] анчо́ус.
ancient ['einʃənt] **1.** дре́вний; анти́чный; **2.** the **~s** *pl. hist.* дре́вние наро́ды *m/pl.*
and [ænd, ənd, F ən] и; а.
anew [ə'nju:] *adv.* сно́ва, сы́знова; по-но́вому.
angel ['eindʒəl] а́нгел; **~ic(al** □) [æn'dʒelik(əl)] а́нгельский.
anger ['æŋgə] **1.** гнев; **2.** [рас]серди́ть.
angle ['æŋgl] **1.** у́гол; то́чка зре́ния; **2.** уди́ть (for В); уди́ть ры́бу; *fig.* заки́дывать у́дочку.
Anglican ['æŋglikən] **1.** член англика́нской це́ркви; **2.** англика́нский.
Anglo-Saxon ['æŋglou'sæksn] **1.** англоса́кс; **2.** англосаксо́нский.
angry ['æŋgri] серди́тый (with на В).
anguish ['æŋgwiʃ] му́ка.
angular ['æŋgjulə] углово́й, уго́льный; *fig.* углова́тый; нело́вкий.
animal ['æniməl] **1.** живо́тное; **2.** живо́тный; ско́тский.
animat|e ['ænimeit] оживля́ть [-ви́ть]; воодушевля́ть [-ви́ть]; **~ion** [æni'meiʃən] жи́вость *f*; оживле́ние.
animosity [æni'mɔsiti] вражде́бность *f.*
ankle ['æŋkl] лоды́жка.
annals ['ænlz] *pl.* ле́топись *f.*
annex **1.** [ə'neks] аннекси́ровать (*im*)*pf.*; присоединя́ть [-ни́ть]; **2.** ['æneks] пристро́йка, приложе́ние; **~ation** [ænek'seiʃən] анне́ксия.
annihilate [ə'naiəleit] уничтожа́ть [-о́жить], истребля́ть [-би́ть].
anniversary [æni'və:səri] годовщи́на.
annotat|e ['ænouteit] анноти́ровать (*im*)*pf.*; снабжа́ть примеча́ниями; **~ion** [ænou'teiʃən] примеча́ние.
announce [ə'nauns] объявля́ть [-ви́ть]; дава́ть знать; заявля́ть [-ви́ть]; **~ment** [-mənt] объявле́ние; **~r** [-ə] *radio* ди́ктор.
annoy [ə'nɔi] надоеда́ть [-е́сть] (Д); досажда́ть [досади́ть] (Д); **~ance** [-əns] доса́да; раздраже́ние; непри́ятность *f.*
annual ['ænjuəl] **1.** □ ежего́дный; годово́й; **2.** ежего́дник; однолё́тнее расте́ние.
annuity [ə'njuiti] годова́я ре́нта.
annul [ə'nʌl] аннули́ровать (*im*)*pf.*; отменя́ть [-ни́ть]; **~ment** [-mənt] аннули́рование.
anoint [ə'nɔint] нама́з(ыв)ать; *eccl.* пома́з(ыв)ать.
anomalous [ə'nɔmələs] □ анома́льный, непра́вильный.
anonymous [ə'nɔniməs] □ анони́мный.
another [ə'nʌðə] друго́й; ещё оди́н.
answer ['ɑ:nsə] **1.** *v/t.* отвеча́ть [-е́тить] (Д); удовлетворя́ть [-ри́ть]; **~** the bell *or* door открыва́ть дверь на звоно́к; *v/i.* отвеча́ть [-е́тить] (to a p. Д, to a question на вопро́с); **~** for отвеча́ть [-е́тить] за (В); **2.** отве́т (to на В); **~able** ['ɑ:nsərəbl] □ отве́тственный.
ant [ænt] мураве́й.
antagonis|m [æn'tægənizm] антагони́зм, вражда́; **~t** [-ist] антагони́ст, проти́вник.
antecedent [ænti'si:dənt] **1.** □ предше́ствующий, предыду́щий (to Д); **2.** **~s** *pl.* про́шлое (челове́ка).
anterior [æn'tiriə] предше́ствующий (to Д); пере́дний.
ante-room ['æntirum] пере́дняя.
anthem ['ænθəm] гимн.
anti... [ænti...] противо..., анти...; **~-aircraft** [ænti'εəkra:ft] противовозду́шный; **~** alarm возду́шная трево́га; **~** defence противовозду́шная оборо́на (ПВО).
antic ['æntik] **1.** □ шутовско́й; **2.** гроте́ск; **~s** *pl.* ужи́мки *f/pl.*; ша́лости *f/pl.*
anticipat|e [æn'tisipeit] предвкуша́ть [-уси́ть]; предчу́вствовать; предупрежда́ть [-реди́ть]; **~ion** [æntisi'peiʃən] ожида́ние; предчу́вствие; in **~** зара́нее.
antidote ['æntidout] противоя́дие.
antipathy [æn'tipəθi] антипа́тия.
antiqua|ry ['æntikwəri] антиква́р; **~ted** [-kweitid] устаре́лый; старомо́дный.
antiqu|e [æn'ti:k] **1.** □ анти́чный; стари́нный; **2.** анти́чное произведе́ние иску́сства; антиква́рная вещь *f*; **~ity** [æn'tikwiti] дре́вность *f*; старина́; анти́чность *f.*

antlers ['æntləz] *pl.* олéньи рогá *m/pl.*
anvil ['ænvil] наковáльня.
anxiety [æŋ'zaiəti] беспокóйство; стрáстное желáние; опасéние.
anxious ['æŋkʃəs] □ озабóченный; беспокóящийся (about, for о П).
any ['əni] 1. *pron.* какóй-нибудь; вся́кий, любóй; not ~ никакóй; 2. *adv.* скóлько-нибудь; нéсколько; **~body, ~one** ктó-нибудь; вся́кий; **~how** кáк-нибудь; так и́ли инáче, во вся́ком слу́чае; **~thing** чтó-нибудь; ~ but далéко не ..., совсéм не ...; **~where** гдé-нибудь, кудá-нибудь.
apart [ə'pɑ:t] отдéльно; пóрознь; ~ from крóме (Р); **~ment** [-mənt] кóмната (меблирóванная); **~s** *pl.* квартúра; *Am.* ~ house многоквартúрный дом.
ape [eip] 1. обезья́на; 2. подражáть (Д), [с]обезья́нничать.
aperient [ə'piəriənt] слабúтельное срéдство.
aperture ['æpətjuə] отвéрстие; проём.
apiculture ['eipikʌltʃə] пчеловóдство.
apiece [ə'pi:s] за штýку; за кáждого, с человéка.
apish ['eipiʃ] □ обезья́ний; глýпый.
apolog|etic [əpɔlə'dʒetik] (**~ally**) извинúтельный; извиня́ющийся; защитúтельный; **~ize** [ə'pɔlədʒaiz] извиня́ться [-нúться] (for за В; to пéред Т); **~y** [-dʒi] извинéние.
apoplexy ['æpopleksi] удáр, паралúч.
apostate [ə'pɔstit] отстýпник.
apostle [ə'pɔsl] апóстол.
apostroph|e [ə'pɔstrefi] апострóфа; апострóф; **~ize** [-faiz] обращáться [обратúться] к (Д).
appal [ə'pɔ:l] [ис]пугáть; устрашáть [-шúть].
apparatus [æpə'reitəs] прибóр; аппаратýра, аппарáт.
apparel [ə'pærəl] одéжда, плáтье.
appar|ent [ə'pærənt] □ очевúдный, несомнéнный; **~ition** [æpə'riʃən] появлéние; прúзрак.
appeal [ə'pi:l] 1. апеллúровать (*im*)*pf.*; подавáть жáлобу; обращáться [обратúться] (to к Д); привлекáть [-éчь] (to В); 2. воззвáние, призы́в; апелля́ция; привлекáтелность *f*; **~ing** [-iŋ] трóгательный; привлекáтельный.
appear [ə'piə] появля́ться [-вúться]; покáзываться [-зáться]; выступáть [вы́ступить] (на концéрте и т. п.); **~ance** [ə'piərəns] появлéние; внéшний вид, нарýжность *f*; **~s** *pl.* прилúчия *n/pl.*
appease [ə'pi:z] умиротворя́ть [-рúть]; успокáивать [-кóить].
appellant [ə'pelənt] апелля́нт.
append [ə'pend] прилагáть [-ложúть] (к Д), прибавля́ть [-áвить] (к Д); **~age** [-idʒ] придáток; **~ix** [ə'pendiks] приложéние.
appertain [æpə'tein] принадлежáть; относúться (to к Д).
appetite ['æpitait] аппетúт (for на В); *fig.* влечéние, склóнность *f* (for к Д).
appetizing ['æpitaiziŋ] аппетúтный.
applaud [ə'plɔ:d] *v/t.* аплодúровать (Д); одобря́ть [одóбрить].
applause [ə'plɔ:z] аплодисмéнты *m/pl.*; одобрéние.
apple [æpl] я́блоко; **~sauce** я́блочный мусс; *sl.* лесть *f*; ерундá.
appliance [ə'plaiəns] приспособлéние, прибóр.
applica|ble ['æplikəbl] применúмый, подходя́щий (to к Д); **~nt** [-kənt] просúтель(ница *f*) *m*; кандидáт (for на В); **~tion** [æpli'keiʃən] применéние; заявлéние; прóсьба (for о П).
apply [ə'plai] *v/t.* прилагáть [-ложúть] (to к Д); применя́ть [-нúть] (to к Д); ~ o. s. to занимáться [заня́ться] (Т); *v/i.* обращáться [обратúться] (for за Т; to к Д); относúться.
appoint [ə'pɔint] назначáть [-нáчить]; определя́ть [-лúть]; снаряжáть [-ядúть]; well **~ed** хорошó оборýдованный; **~ment** [-mənt] назначéние; свидáние; **~s** *pl.* оборýдование; обстанóвка.
apportion [ə'pɔ:ʃən] [по]делúть, разделя́ть [-лúть]; **~ment** [-mənt] пропорционáльное распределéние.
apprais|al [ə'preizəl] оцéнка; **~e** [ə'preiz] оцéнивать [-нúть], расцéнивать [-нúть].
apprecia|ble [ə'pri:ʃəbl] □ замéтный, ощутúмый; **~te** [-ieit] *v/t.* оцéнивать [-нúть]; [о]ценúть; понимáть [-ня́ть]; *v/i.* повышáться в цéнности; **~tion** [əpri:ʃi'eiʃən] оцéнка; понимáние.
apprehen|d [æpri'hend] предчýвствовать; боя́ться; задéрживать [-жáть], арестóвывать [-овáть]; **~sion** [-'henʃən] опасéние, предчýвствие; арéст; **~sive** [-'hensiv] □ озабóченный; поня́тливый.
apprentice [ə'prentis] 1. подмастéрье, ученúк; 2. отдавáть в учéние; **~ship** [-ʃip] учéние, ученúчество.
approach [ə'proutʃ] 1. приближáться [-блúзиться] к (Д); обращáться [обратúться] к (Д); 2. приближéние; пóдступ; *fig.* подхóд.
approbation [æpro'beiʃən] одобрéние; сáнкция.
appropriat|e 1. [ə'prouprieit] присвáивать [-свóить]; *parl.* пред-

назнача́ть [-зна́чить]; 2. [-it] □ подходя́щий; соотве́тствующий; **~ion** [əproupri'eiʃən] присвое́ние; *parl.* ассигнова́ние.
approv|al [ə'pru:vəl] одобре́ние; утвержде́ние; **~e** [ə'pru:v] одобря́ть [одо́брить]; утвержда́ть [-рди́ть]; санкциони́ровать *(im)pf.*
approximate 1. [ə'prɔksimeit] приближа́ть(ся) [-бли́зить(ся)] к (Д); 2. [-mit] □ приблизи́тельный.
apricot ['eiprikɔt] абрико́с.
April ['eiprəl] апре́ль *m.*
apron ['eiprən] пере́дник, фа́ртук.
apt [æpt] □ подходя́щий; спосо́бный; **~ to** скло́нный к (Д); **~itude** ['æptitju:d], **~ness** [-nis] спосо́бность *f*; скло́нность *f* (for, to к Д); уме́стность *f.*
aquatic [ə'kwætik] 1. водяно́й; во́дный; 2. **~s** *pl.* во́дный спорт.
aque|duct ['ækwidʌkt] акведу́к; **~ous** ['eikwiəs] водяни́стый.
Arab ['ærəb] ара́б(ка); **~ic** ['ærəbik] 1. ара́бский язы́к; 2. ара́бский.
arable ['ærəbl] па́хотный.
arbit|er ['ɑbitə] арби́тр, трете́йский судья́ *m*; *fig.* верши́тель су́деб; **~rariness** ['ɑ:bitrərinis] произво́л; **~rary** [-trəri] □ произво́льный; **~rate** ['ɑ:bitreit] реша́ть трете́йским судо́м; **~ration** [ɑ:bi'treiʃən] трете́йское реше́ние; **~rator** ['ɑ:bitreitə] ⚖ арби́тр, трете́йский судья́ *m.*
arbo(u)r ['ɑ:bə] бесе́дка.
arc [ɑ:k] *ast.*, ⩘, ⚡ дуга́; **~ade** [ɑ:'keid] пасса́ж; сво́дчатая галере́я.
arch[1] [ɑ:tʃ] 1. а́рка; свод; дуга́; 2. придава́ть фо́рму а́рки; изгиба́ть(ся) дуго́й.
arch[2] [~] 1. хи́трый, лука́вый; 2. *pref.* архи... (выраже́ние превосхо́дной сте́пени).
archaic [ɑ:'keiik] (**~ally**) устаре́лый.
archbishop ['ɑ:tʃbiʃəp] архиепи́скоп.
archery ['ɑ:tʃəri] стрельба́ из лу́ка.
architect ['ɑ:kitekt] архите́ктор; **~onic** [-'ɔnik] (**~ally**) архитекту́рный, конструкти́вный; **~ure** ['ɑ:kitektʃə] архитекту́ра.
archway ['ɑ:tʃwei] сво́дчатый прохо́д.
arc-lamp ['ɑ:klæmp] ⚡ дугова́я ла́мпа.
arctic ['ɑ:ktik] поля́рный, аркти́ческий.
arden|cy ['ɑ:dənsi] жар, пыл; рве́ние; **~t** ['ɑ:dənt] □ *mst fig.* горя́чий, пы́лкий; ре́вностный.
ardo(u)r ['ɑ:də] рве́ние; пыл.
arduous ['ɑ:djuəs] □ тру́дный.
are [ɑ:; в предложе́нии: ɑ] *s.* **be.**
area ['ɛəriə] пло́щадь *f*; о́бласть *f*, райо́н.
Argentine ['ɑ:dʒəntain] 1. аргенти́нский; 2. аргенти́нец (-и́нка).
argue ['ɑ:gju:] *v/t.* обсужда́ть [-уди́ть]; дока́зывать [-за́ть]; **~ a p. into** убежда́ть [убеди́ть] в (П); *v/i.* [по]спо́рить (с Т).
argument ['ɑ:gjumənt] до́вод, аргуме́нт; спор; **~ation** [ɑ:gjumen'teiʃən] аргумента́ция.
arid ['ærid] сухо́й (*a. fig.*), безво́дный.
arise [ə'raiz] [*irr.*] *fig.* возника́ть [-ни́кнуть] (from из Р); восст(ав)а́ть; **~n** [ə'rizn] *p. pt.* от arise.
aristocra|cy [æris'tɔkrəsi] аристокра́тия; **~t** ['æristəkræt] аристокра́т; **~tic(al** □) [æristə'krætik, -ikəl] аристократи́ческий.
arithmetic [ə'riθmətik] арифме́тика.
ark [ɑ:k] ковче́г.
arm[1] [ɑ:m] рука́; рука́в (реки́).
arm[2] [~] 1. ору́жие; род во́йск; 2. вооружа́ть(ся) [-жи́ть(ся)].
arma|ment ['ɑ:məmənt] вооруже́ние; **~ture** ['ɑ:mətjuə] броня́; ⊕ армату́ра.
armchair кре́сло.
armistice ['ɑ:mistis] переми́рие.
armo(u)r ['ɑ:mə] 1. доспе́хи *m/pl.*; броня́, па́нцирная обши́вка; 2. покрыва́ть броне́й; **~y** [-ri] арсена́л.
armpit [ɑ:mpit] подмы́шка.
army ['ɑ:mi] а́рмия; *fig.* мно́жество.
arose [ə'rouz] *pt.* от *arise.*
around [ə'raund] 1. *adv.* всю́ду, круго́м; 2. *prp.* вокру́г (Р).
arouse [ə'rauz] [раз]буди́ть; возбужда́ть [-уди́ть]; вызыва́ть [вы́звать].
arraign [ə'rein] привлека́ть к суду́; *fig.* находи́ть недоста́тки в (П).
arrange [ə'reindʒ] приводи́ть в поря́док; устра́ивать [-ро́ить]; классифици́ровать *(im)pf.*; усла́вливаться [усло́виться]; ♪ аранжи́ровать *(im)pf.*; **~ment** [-mənt] устро́йство; расположе́ние; соглаше́ние; мероприя́тие; ♪ аранжиро́вка.
array [ə'rei] 1. боево́й поря́док; *fig.* мно́жество, це́лый ряд; 2. оде́(ва́)ть; украша́ть [укра́сить]; выстра́ивать в ряд.
arrear [ə'riə] *mst. pl.* задо́лженность *f*, недои́мка.
arrest [ə'rest] 1. аре́ст, задержа́ние; 2. аресто́вывать [-ова́ть], заде́рживать [-жа́ть].
arriv|al [ə'raivəl] прибы́тие, прие́зд; **~s** *pl.* прибы́вшие *pl.*; **~e** [ə'raiv] прибы́(ва́)ть; приезжа́ть [-е́хать] (at в, на В).
arroga|nce ['ærəgəns] надме́н-

ность *f*, высокоме́рие; **~nt** □ надме́нный, высокоме́рный; **~te** [-geit] де́рзко тре́бовать (Р).
arrow ['ærou] стрела́.
arsenal ['ɑ:sinl] арсена́л.
arsenic ['ɑ:snik] мышья́к.
arson ['ɑ:sn] ⚖ поджо́г.
art [ɑ:t] иску́сство; *fig.* хи́трость *f*.
arter|ial [ɑ'tiəriəl]: ~ road магистра́ль *f*; **~y** ['ɑ:təri] арте́рия; гла́вная доро́га.
artful ['ɑ:tful] ло́вкий; хи́трый.
article ['ɑ:tikl] статья́; пара́граф; *gr.* арти́кль *m*, член; **~d** to о́тданный (в уче́ние) к (Д).
articulat|e 1. [ɑ:'tikjuleit] отчётливо, я́сно произноси́ть; **2.** [-lit] отчётливый; членоразде́льный; коле́нчатый; **~ion** [ɑ:tikju'leiʃən] артикуля́ция; членоразде́льное произноше́ние; *anat.* сочлене́ние.
artific|e ['ɑ:tifis] ло́вкость *f*; изобрете́ние, вы́думка; **~ial** [ɑ:ti'fiʃəl] □ иску́сственный.
artillery [ɑ:'tiləri] артилле́рия; **~man** [-mən] артиллери́ст.
artisan [ɑ:ti'zæn] реме́сленник.
artist ['ɑ:tist] худо́жник (-ица); актёр, актри́са; **~e** [ɑ:'tist] эстра́дный (-ная) арти́ст(ка); **~ic(al** □) [ɑ:'tistik, -tikəl] артисти́ческий, худо́жественный.
as [æz] *cj. a. adv.* когда́; в то вре́мя как; та́к как; хотя́; ~ it were ка́к бы; ~ well та́к же; в тако́й же ме́ре; such ~ тако́й как; как наприме́р; ~ well ~ и ... и ...; *prp.* ~ for, ~ to что каса́ется (Р); ~ from с (Р).
ascend [ə'send] поднима́ться [-ня́ться]; всходи́ть [взойти́] на (В); восходи́ть (to к Д); ✈ наб(и)ра́ть высоту́.
ascension [ə'senʃən] восхожде́ние; ♀ (Day) вознесе́ние.
ascent [ə'sent] подъём; крутизна́.
ascertain [æsə'tein] удостоверя́ться [-ве́риться] в (П).
ascribe [ə'skraib] припи́сывать [-са́ть] (Д/В).
aseptic [ei'septik] ⚕ стери́льный.
ash[1] [æʃ] ♣ я́сень *m*; mountain ~ ряби́на.
ash[2] [~], *mst pl.* **~es** [æʃiz] зола́, пе́пел.
ashamed [ə'ʃeimd] пристыжённый.
ash-can *Am.* ведро́ для му́сора.
ashen [æʃn] пе́пельный (цвет).
ashore [ə'ʃɔ:] на́ берег, на берегу́; run ~, be driven ~ наскочи́ть на мель.
ash-tray пе́пельница.
ashy ['æʃi] пе́пельный; бле́дный.
Asiatic [eiʃi'ætik] **1.** азиа́тский; **2.** азиа́т(ка).
aside [ə'said] в сто́рону, в стороне́; отде́льно.
ask [ɑ:sk] *v/t.* [по]проси́ть (a th. of, from a p. что́-нибудь у кого́-нибудь); ~ that проси́ть, что́бы ...; спра́шивать [спроси́ть]; ~ (a p.) a question задава́ть вопро́с (Д); *v/i.* ~ for [по]проси́ть (В *or* Р *or* о П).
askance [əs'kæns], **askew** [əs'kju:] и́скоса, ко́со; криво.
asleep [ə'sli:p] спя́щий; be ~ спать.
aslope [ə'sloup] *adv.* пока́то; на скло́не, на ска́те.
asparagus [əs'pærəgəs] ♣ спа́ржа.
aspect ['æspekt] вид (*a. gr.*); аспе́кт; сторона́.
asperity [æs'periti] стро́гость *f*; суро́вость *f*.
asphalt ['æsfælt] **1.** асфа́льт; **2.** покрыва́ть асфа́льтом.
aspir|ant [əs'paiərənt] кандида́т; **~ate** ['æspəreit] произноси́ть с придыха́нием; **~ation** [æspə'reiʃən] стремле́ние; *phon.* придыха́ние; **~e** [əs'paiə] стреми́ться (to, after, at к Д); домога́ться (Р).
ass [æs] осёл.
assail [ə'seil] напада́ть [-па́сть] на (В), атакова́ть (В) (*im*)*pf*.; *fig.* энерги́чно бра́ться за (де́ло); **~ant** [-ənt] проти́вник; напада́ющий.
assassin [ə'sæsin] уби́йца *m/f*; **~ate** [-ineit] уби́(ва́)ть; **~ation** [əsæsi'neiʃən] уби́йство.
assault [ə'sɔ:lt] **1.** нападе́ние, ата́ка; ⚖ слове́сное оскорбле́ние; физи́ческое наси́лие; **2.** напада́ть [напа́сть], набра́сываться [-ро́ситься] на (В).
assay [ə'sei] **1.** испыта́ние, опро́бование (мета́ллов); **2.** [ис]про́бовать, испы́тывать [испыта́ть].
assembl|age [ə'semblidʒ] собра́ние; скопле́ние; сбор; ⊕ монта́ж, сбо́рка; **~e** [ə'sembl] соз(ы)ва́ть; ⊕ [с]монти́ровать; **~y** [-i] собра́ние; ассамбле́я; ⊕ сбо́рка часте́й.
assent [ə'sent] **1.** согла́сие; **2.** соглаша́ться [-ласи́ться] (to на В; с Т).
assert [ə'sə:t] утвержда́ть [-рди́ть]; **~ion** [ə'sə:ʃən] утвержде́ние.
assess [ə'ses] облага́ть нало́гом; оце́нивать иму́щество (Р); **~able** [-əbl] □ подлежа́щий обложе́нию; **~ment** [-mənt] обложе́ние; оце́нка.
asset ['æset] це́нное ка́чество; ✝ статья́ дохо́да; **~s** *pl.* ✝ акти́в.
assiduous [ə'sidjuəs] □ приле́жный.
assign [ə'sain] определя́ть [-ли́ть]; назнача́ть [-на́чить]; ассигно́вывать, ассигнова́ть (*im*)*pf*; поруча́ть [-чи́ть]; **~ment** [ə'sainmənt] назначе́ние; ⚖ переда́ча; зада́ние.
assimilat|e [ə'simileit] ассимили́ровать(ся) (*im*)*pf*.; осва́ивать [осво́ить]; прира́внивать [-ня́ть];

~ion [əsimi'leiʃən] уподобле́ние; ассимиля́ция; усвое́ние.
assist [ə'sist] помога́ть [-мо́чь] (Д), [по]соде́йствовать (*im*)*pf.* (Д); **~ance** [-əns] по́мощь *f*; **~ant** [-ənt] ассисте́нт(ка); помо́щник (-ица).
associa|te 1. [ə'souʃieit] обща́ться (with с Т); ассоции́ровать(ся) (*im*)*pf.*; присоединя́ть(ся) [-ни́ть (-ся)] (with к Д); 2. [-ʃiit] a) свя́занный; объединённый; b) това́рищ, колле́га; соуча́стник; **~tion** [əsousi'eiʃən] ассоциа́ция; соедине́ние; о́бщество.
assort [ə'sɔ:t] [рас]сортирова́ть; подбира́ть [подобра́ть]; снабжа́ть ассортиме́нтом; **~ment** [-mənt] сортиро́вка.
assum|e [ə'sju:m] принима́ть [-ня́ть] (на себя́); предполага́ть [-ложи́ть]; **~ption** [ə'sʌmpʃən] предположе́ние; присвое́ние; *eccl.* ♀ успе́ние.
assur|ance [ə'ʃuərəns] увере́ние; уве́ренность *f*; страхо́вка; **~e** [ə'ʃuə] уверя́ть [уве́рить]; обеспе́чи(ва)ть; [за]страхова́ть; **~edly** [-ridli] *adv.* коне́чно, несомне́нно.
astir [əs'tə:] в движе́нии; на нога́х.
astonish [əs'tɔniʃ] удивля́ть [-ви́ть], изумля́ть [-ми́ть]; be **~ed** удивля́ться [-ви́ться] (at Д); **~ing** [-iʃiŋ] □ удиви́телный, изуми́тельный; **~ment** [əs'tɔniʃmənt] удивле́ние, изумле́ние.
astound [əs'taund] поража́ть [порази́ть].
astray [əs'trei]: go ~ заблуди́ться, сби́ться с пути́.
astride [əs'traid] верхо́м (of на П).
astringent [əs'trindʒənt] □ ⚕ вя́жущий (о сре́дстве).
astro|logy [əs'trɔlədʒi] астроло́гия; **~nomer** [əs'trɔnəmə] астроно́м; **~nomy** [əs'trɔnəmi] астроно́мия.
astute [əs'tju:t] □ хи́трый; проница́тельный; **~ness** [-nis] хи́трость *f*; проница́тельность *f*.
asunder [ə'sʌndə] по́рознь, отде́льно; в куски́, на ча́сти.
asylum [ə'sailəm] прию́т; убе́жище.
at [æt] *prp.* в (П, В); у (Р); при (П); на (П, В); о́коло (Р); за (Т); ~ school в шко́ле; ~ the age of в во́зрасте (Р).
ate [et, eit] *pt.* от eat.
atheism ['eiθiizm] атеи́зм.
athlet|e ['æθli:t] атле́т; **~ic(al** □) [æθ'letik(əl)] атлети́ческий; **~ics** *pl.* [æθ'letiks] атле́тика.
Atlantic [ət'læntik] 1. атланти́ческий; 2. (*a.* ~ Ocean) Атланти́ческий океа́н.
atmospher|e ['ætməsfiə] атмосфе́ра; **~ic(al** □) [ætməs'ferik(əl)] атмосфе́рный, атмосфери́ческий.
atom ['ætəm] ⚛ а́том; ~ (*a.* **~ic**) bomb а́томная бо́мба; **~ic** [ə'tɔmik] а́томный; ~ pile а́томный реа́ктор; ~ smashing расщепле́ние а́тома; **~izer** ['ætəmaizə] распыли́тель *m.*
atone [ə'toun]: ~ for загла́живать [-ла́дить], искупа́ть [-пи́ть]; **~ment** [-mənt] искупле́ние.
atroci|ous [ə'trouʃəs] □ зве́рский, ужа́сный; **~ty** [ə'trɔsiti] зве́рство.
attach [ə'tætʃ] *v/t.* *com.* прикрепля́ть [-пи́ть]; прикомандиро́вывать [-рова́ть] (к Д); прид(ав)а́ть; ⚖ налага́ть аре́ст на (В); аресто́вывать [-ова́ть]; ~ o. s. to привя́зываться [-за́ться] к (Д); **~ment** [-mənt] привя́занность *f*; прикрепле́ние; наложе́ние аре́ста.
attack [ə'tæk] 1. ата́ка, наступле́ние; припа́док; 2. *v/t.* атакова́ть (*im*)*pf.*; напада́ть [напа́сть] на (В); набра́сываться [-ро́ситься] на (В); ⚕ поража́ть [порази́ть] (о боле́зни).
attain [ə'tein] *v/t.* достига́ть [-и́гнуть] (Р), доби́(ва́)ться (Р); **~ment** [-mənt] приобрете́ние; достиже́ние; **~s** *pl.* зна́ния *n/pl.*; на́выки *m/pl.*
attempt [ə'tempt] 1. попы́тка; покуше́ние; 2. [по]пыта́ться; покуша́ться [-уси́ться] на (В).
attend [ə'tend] обслу́живать [-жи́ть]; посеща́ть [-ети́ть]; ⚕ ходи́ть, уха́живать за (Т); прислу́живать (to Д); прису́тствовать (at на П); быть внима́тельным; **~ance** [ə'tendəns] прису́тствие (at на П); обслу́живание; пу́блика; посеща́емость *f*; ⚕ ухо́д (за Т); **~ant** [-ənt] 1. сопровожда́ющий (on В); прису́тствующий (at на П); 2. посети́тель(ница *f*) *m*; спу́тник (-ица); ⚕ санита́р; служи́тель *m.*
attent|ion [ə'tenʃən] внима́ние; **~ive** [-tiv] □ внима́тельный.
attest [ə'test] [за]свиде́тельствовать; удостоверя́ть [-ве́рить]; *part.* ⚔ приводи́ть к прися́ге.
attic ['ætik] черда́к; манса́рда.
attire [ə'taiə] 1. наря́д; 2. оде́(ва́)ть, наряжа́ть [-яди́ть].
attitude ['ætitju:d] отноше́ние; пози́ция; по́за, оса́нка; *fig.* то́чка зре́ния.
attorney [ə'tə:ni] пове́ренный; power of ~ полномо́чие; ♀ General *Am.* мини́стр юсти́ции.
attract [ə'trækt] *v/t.* привлека́ть [-вле́чь] (*a. fig.*); притя́гивать [-яну́ть]; *fig.* прельща́ть [-льсти́ть]; **~ion** [ə'trækʃən] притяже́ние, тяготе́ние; *fig.* привлека́тельность *f*; *thea.* аттракцио́н; **~ive** [-tiv] привлека́тельный; зама́нчивый; **~iveness** [-tivnis] привлека́тельность *f*.
attribute 1. [ə'tribju:t] припи́сывать [-са́ть] (Д/В); относи́ть [от-

нести́] (к Д); 2. ['ætribju:t] сво́йство, при́знак; *gr.* определе́ние.
attune [ə'tju:n] приводи́ть в созву́чие.
auction ['ɔ:kʃən] 1. аукцио́н, торги́ *m/pl.*; sell by ~, put up for ~ продава́ть с аукцио́на; 2. продава́ть с аукцио́на (*mst* ~ off); **~eer** [ɔ:kʃə'niə] аукциони́ст.
audaci|ous [ɔ:'deiʃəs] □ сме́лый; де́рзкий; *b. s.* на́глый; **~ty** [ɔ:'dæsiti] сме́лость *f*; де́рзость *f*; *b.s.* на́глость *f*.
audible ['ɔ:debl] □ вня́тный, слы́шный.
audience ['ɔ:djəns] слу́шатели *m/pl.*, зри́тели *m/pl.*, пу́блика; аудие́нция (of, with у Р).
audit ['ɔ:dit] 1. прове́рка, реви́зия (бухга́лтерских книг); 2. проверя́ть [-е́рить] (отчётность); **~or** ['ɔ:ditə] слу́шатель *m*; ревизо́р, (фина́нсовый) контролёр.
auger ['ɔ:gə] ⊕ сверло́, бура́в.
augment [ɔ:g'ment] увели́чи(ва)ть; **~ation** [ɔ:gmen'teiʃən] увеличе́ние, приро́ст, прираще́ние.
augur ['ɔ:gə] 1. авгу́р, прорица́тель *m*; 2. предска́зывать [-за́ть] (well хоро́шее, ill плохо́е); **~y** предзнаменова́ние.
August ['ɔ:gəst] а́вгуст.
aunt [ɑ:nt] тётя, тётка.
auspic|e ['ɔ:spis] до́брое предзнаменова́ние; **~s** *pl.* покрови́тельство; **~ious** [ɔ:s'piʃəs] □ благоприя́тный.
auster|e [ɔ:s'tiə] □ стро́гий, суро́вый; **~ity** [ɔ:s'teriti] стро́гость *f*, суро́вость *f*.
Australian [ɔ:s'treiljən] 1. австрали́ец (-и́йка); 2. австрали́йский.
Austrian ['ɔ:striən] 1. австри́ец (-и́йка); 2. австри́йский.
authentic [ɔ:'θentik](**~ally**) по́длинный, достове́рный.
author ['ɔ:θə] а́втор; **~itative** [ɔ:'θɔriteitiv] □ авторите́тный; **~ity** [ɔ:'θɔriti] авторите́т; полномо́чие; власть *f* (over над Т); on the ~ of на основа́нии (Р); по утвержде́нию (Р); **~ize** ['ɔ:θəraiz] уполномо́чи(ва)ть; санкциони́ровать (*im*)*pf*.
autocar ['ɔ:təkɑ:] автомоби́ль *m*.
autocra|cy [ɔ:'tɔkrəsi] самодержа́вие, автокра́тия; **~tic(al** □) [ɔ:tə'krætik(əl)] самодержа́вный; деспоти́ческий.
autogyro ['ɔ:tou'dʒaiərou] ✈ автожи́р.
autograph ['ɔ:təgrɑ:f] авто́граф.
automat|ic [ɔ:tə'mætik] (**~ally**) автомати́ческий; ~ machine автома́т; **~on** [ɔ:'tɔmətən] автома́т.
automobile ['ɔtəməbi:l] *part. Am.* автомоби́ль *m*.
autonomy [ɔ:'tɔnəmi] автоно́мия, самоуправле́ние.
autumn ['ɔ:təm] о́сень *f*; **~al** [ɔ:'tʌmnəl] осе́нний.
auxiliary [ɔ:g'ziljəri] вспомога́тельный; доба́вочный.
avail [ə'veil] 1. помога́ть [помо́чь] (Д); ~ o. s. of [вос]по́льзоваться (Т); 2. по́льза, вы́года; of no ~ бесполе́зный; **~able** [ə'veiləbl] □ досту́пный; нали́чный.
avalanche ['ævəlɑ:nʃ] лави́на.
avaric|e ['ævəris] ску́пость *f*; жа́дность *f*; **~ious** [ævə'riʃəs] □ скупо́й; жа́дный.
aveng|e [ə'vendʒ] [ото]мсти́ть (Д за В); **~er** [-ə] мсти́тель(ница *f*) *m*.
avenue ['ævinju:] алле́я; *Am.* широ́кая у́лица, проспе́кт; *fig.* путь *m*.
aver [ə'və:] утвержда́ть.
average ['ævəridʒ] 1. сре́днее число́; at an ~ в сре́днем; 2. сре́дний; 3. выводи́ть сре́днее число́.
avers|e [ə'və:s] □ нерасполо́женный (to, from к Д); неохо́тный; **~ion** отвраще́ние, антипа́тия.
avert [ə'və:t] отвраща́ть [-рати́ть].
aviat|ion [eivi'eiʃən] авиа́ция; **~or** ['eivietə] лётчик, авиа́тор.
avoid [ə'vɔid] избега́ть [-ежа́ть] (Р); **~ance** [-əns] избежа́ние.
avow [ə'vau] призн(ав)а́ть; ~ oneself призн(ав)а́ться; **~al** [-əl] призна́ние.
await [ə'weit] ожида́ть (Р).
awake [ə'weik] 1. бо́дрствующий; be ~ to я́сно понима́ть; 2. [*irr.*] *v/t.* (*mst* **~n** [ə'weikən]) [раз]буди́ть; пробужда́ть [-уди́ть] (созна́ние, интере́с) (к Д); *v/i.* просыпа́ться [просну́ться]; ~ to a th. осозн(ав)а́ть (В).
aware [ə'weə]: be ~ of знать (В *or* о П), созн(ав)а́ть (В); become ~ of отдава́ть себе́ отчёт в (П).
away [ə'wei] прочь; далеко́.
awe [ɔ:] 1. благогове́ние, тре́пет (of пе́ред Т); 2. внуша́ть благогове́ние, страх (Д).
awful [ɔ:ful] □ внуша́ющий благогове́ние; стра́шный; F ужа́сный; чрезвыча́йный.
awhile [ə'wail] на не́которое вре́мя, ненадо́лго.
awkward ['ɔ:kwəd] неуклю́жий, нело́вкий; неудо́бный.
awl [ɔ:l] ши́ло.
awning ['ɔ:niŋ] наве́с, тент.
awoke [ə'wouk] *pt.* и *p. pt.* от awake.
awry [ə'rai] ко́со, на́бок; *fig.* непра́вильно.
ax(e) [æks] топо́р, колу́н.
axis ['æksis], *pl.* axes [-si:z] ось *f*.
axle ['æksl] ⊕ ось *f*; **~-tree** колёсный вал.
ay(e) [ai] да; *parl.* утверди́тельный го́лос (при голосова́нии).
azure ['æʒə] 1. лазу́рь *f*; 2. лазу́рный.

B

babble ['bæbl] 1. ле́пет; болтовня́; 2. [по]болта́ть; [за]лепета́ть.
baboon [bə'bu:n] *zo.* бабуи́н.
baby ['beibi] 1. младе́нец, ребёнок, дитя́ *n*; 2. небольшо́й, ма́лый; **~hood** ['beibihud] младе́нчество.
bachelor ['bætʃələ] холостя́к; *univ.* бакала́вр.
back [bæk] 1. спина́; спи́нка (сту́ла, пла́тья и т. п.); изна́нка (мате́рии); *football* защи́тник; 2. *adj.* за́дний; обра́тный; отдалённый; 3. *adv.* наза́д, обра́тно; тому́ наза́д; 4. *v/t.* подде́рживать [-жа́ть]; подкрепля́ть [-епи́ть]; [по]пя́тить; держа́ть пари́ на (В), [по]ста́вить на (ло́шадь); † индосси́ровать; *v/i.* отступа́ть [-пи́ть]; [по]пя́титься; **~bone** позвоно́чник, спинно́й хребе́т; *fig.* опо́ра; **~er** ['bækə] † индосса́нт; **~ground** за́дний план, фон; **~ing** подде́ржка; † индоссаме́нт; **~side** за́дняя, ты́льная сторона́; зад; **~slide** [*irr.* (slide)] отпада́ть [отпа́сть] (от ве́ры); **~stairs** чёрная ле́стница; **~stroke** пла́вание на спине́; **~-talk** *Am.* де́рзкий отве́т; **~ward** ['bækwəd] 1. *adj.* обра́тный; *fig.* отста́лый; 2. *adv.* (*a.* **~wards** [-z]) наза́д; за́дом; наоборо́т; обра́тно; **~water** за́водь *f*; **~wheel** за́днее колесо́.
bacon ['beikən] бeко́н, копчёная груди́нка.
bacteri|ologist [bæktiəri'ɔlədʒist] бактерио́лог; **~um** [bæk'tiəriəm], *pl.* **~a** [-riə] бакте́рия.
bad [bæd] □ плохо́й, дурно́й, скве́рный; he is **~ly** off его́ дела́ пло́хи́; **~ly** wounded тяжелора́неный; F want **~ly** о́чень хоте́ть.
bade [beid, bæd] *pt.* от bid.
badge [bædʒ] значо́к.
badger ['bædʒə] 1. *zo.* барсу́к; 2. [за]трави́ть; изводи́ть [извести́].
badness ['bædnis] него́дность *f*; вре́дность *f*.
baffle ['bæfl] расстра́ивать [-ро́ить]; сбива́ть с то́лку.
bag [bæg] 1. мешо́к; су́мка; 2. класть в мешо́к; *hunt.* уби́(ва́)ть.
baggage ['bægidʒ] бага́ж; **~-check** *Am.* бага́жная квита́нция.
bagpipe ['bægpaip] волы́нка.
bail [beil] 1. поручи́тельство; admit to ~ ⚖ выпуска́ть на пору́ки; 2. ~ out ⚖ брать на пору́ки.
bailiff ['beilif] суде́бный при́став; управля́ющий (име́нием).
bait [beit] 1. прима́нка, нажи́вка; *fig.* искуше́ние; 2. прима́нивать [-ни́ть]; *hunt.* трави́ть соба́ками; *fig.* пресле́довать насме́шками, изводи́ть [-вести́].
bak|e [beik] [ис]пе́чь(ся); обжига́ть [обже́чь] (кирпичи́); **~er** ['beikə] пе́карь *m*, бу́лочник; **~ery** [-ri] пека́рня; **~ing-powder** пека́рный порошо́к.
balance ['bæləns] 1. весы́ *m/pl.*; равнове́сие; противове́с; баланси́р; † бала́нс; са́льдо *n indecl.*; *sl.* оста́ток; ~ of power полити́ческое равнове́сие; ~ of trade акти́вный бала́нс; 2. [с]баланси́ровать (В); сохраня́ть равнове́сие; † подводи́ть бала́нс; взве́шивать [-е́сить] (в уме́); быть в равнове́сии.
balcony ['bælkəni] балко́н.
bald [bɔ:ld] лы́сый, плеши́вый; *fig.* просто́й; бесцве́тный (стиль).
bale [beil] † ки́па, тюк.
balk [bɔ:k] 1. межа́; брус; ба́лка; 2. *v/t.* [вос]препя́тствовать (Д), [по]меша́ть (Д); [за]арта́читься (*a. fig.*).
ball[1] [bɔ:l] 1. мяч; шар; клубо́к (ше́рсти); keep the ~ rolling подде́рживать разгово́р; 2. собира́ть(ся) в клубо́к; сви́(ва́)ть(ся).
ball[2] [~] бал, танцева́льный ве́чер.
ballad ['bæləd] балла́да.
ballast ['bæləst] 1. щёбень *m*; 🚂, ⚓ балла́ст; 2. грузи́ть балла́стом.
ball-bearing(s *pl.*) шарикоподши́пник.
ballet ['bælei] бале́т.
balloon [bə'lu:n] возду́шный шар, аэроста́т; **~ist** [-ist] аэрона́вт, пило́т аэроста́та.
ballot ['bælət] 1. баллотиро́вка, голосова́ние; 2. [про]голосова́ть; **~-box** избира́тельная у́рна.
ball-point (*a.* ~ **pen**) ша́риковая ру́чка.
ball-room ба́льный зал.
balm [bɑ:m] бальза́м; *fig.* утеше́ние.
balmy [bɑ:mi] □ арома́тный.
baloney [bə'louni] *Am. sl.* вздор.
balsam ['bɔ:lsəm] бальза́м; ⚘ бальзами́н.
balustrade ['bæləstreid] балюстра́да.
bamboo [bæm'bu:] бамбу́к.
bamboozle F [-zl] наду́(ва́)ть, обма́нывать [-ну́ть].
ban [bæn] 1. запреще́ние, запре́т; 2. налага́ть запреще́ние на (В).
banana [bə'nɑ:nə] бана́н.
band [bænd] 1. ле́нта, тесьма́; обо́д; ба́нда; отря́д; ♪ орке́стр; 2. свя́зывать [-за́ть]; ~ o. s. объединя́ться [-ни́ться].
bandage ['bændidʒ] 1. бинт, банда́ж; 2. [за]бинтова́ть, перевя́зывать [-за́ть].
bandbox ['bændbɔks] карто́нка (для шляп).

bandit ['bændit] бандит.
band-master ['bændma:stə] капельмейстер.
bandy ['bændi] обмениваться [-няться] (словами, мячом и т. п.).
bane [bein] *fig.* отрава.
bang [bæŋ] **1.** удар, стук; **2.** ударять(ся) [ударить(ся)]; стукать(ся) [-кнуть(ся)].
banish ['bæniʃ] изгонять [изгнать]; высылать [выслать]; **~ment** [-mənt] изгнание.
banisters ['bænistəz] *pl.* перила *n/pl.*
bank [bæŋk] **1.** берег; насыпь *f*; банк; ~ of issue эмиссионный банк; **2.** *v/t.* окружать валом; запруживать [-удить]; ✝ класть (деньги) в банк; *v/i.* быть банкиром; ✈ делать вираж, накреняться [-ниться]; ~ on полагаться [-ложиться] на (В); **~er** ['bæŋkə] банкир; **~ing** ['bæŋkiŋ] банковое дело; **~rupt** ['bæŋkrʌpt] **1.** банкрот; **2.** обанкротившийся; **3.** делать банкротом; **~ruptcy** ['bæŋkrʌptsi] банкротство.
banner ['bænə] знамя *n*, стяг.
banns [bænz] *pl.* оглашение (вступающих в брак).
banquet ['bæŋkwit] **1.** банкет, пир; **2.** давать банкет; пировать.
banter ['bæntə] подшучивать [-утить], поддразнивать [-нить].
baptism [bæp'tizm] крещение.
baptize [bæp'taiz] [о]крестить.
bar [ba:] **1.** брусок; засов; отмель *f*; бар; стойка; ♪ такт; *fig.* преграда, препятствие; ⚖ адвокатура; **2.** запирать на засов; преграждать [-радить]; исключать [-чить].
barb [ba:b] колючка; зубец; **~ed** wire колючая проволока.
barbar|ian [ba:'bɛəriən] **1.** варвар; **2.** варварский; **~ous** ['ba:bərəs] □ дикий; грубый, жестокий.
barbecue ['ba:bikju:] **1.** целиком жарить (тушу); **2.** целиком зажаренная туша.
barber ['ba:bə] парикмахер.
bare [bɛə] **1.** голый, обнажённый; пустой; **2.** обнажать [-жить], откры(ва)ть; **~faced** ['bɛəfeist] □ бесстыдный; **~-foot** босиком; **~-footed** босой; **~-headed** с непокрытой головой; **~ly** ['bɛəli] едва.
bargain ['ba:gin] **1.** сделка, выгодная покупка; **2.** [по]торговаться (о П, с Т).
barge [ba:dʒ] баржа; **~man** ['ba:dʒmən] лодочник с баржи.
bark¹ [ba:k] **1.** кора; **2.** сдирать кору с (Р).
bark² [~] **1.** лай; **2.** [за]лаять.
bar-keeper буфетчик.
barley ['ba:li] ячмень *m.*
barn [ba:n] амбар.
baron ['bærən] барон; **~ess** [-is] баронесса.
barrack(s *pl.*) ['bærək(s)] барак; казарма.
barrage ['bæra:ʒ] заграждение; ⚔ заградительный огонь *m.*
barrel ['bærəl] **1.** бочка, бочонок; ствол (ружья); ⊕ цилиндр; барабан; вал; **2.** разливать по бочкам.
barren ['bærən] □ неплодородный, бесплодный.
barricade [bæri'keid] **1.** баррикада; **2.** [за]баррикадировать.
barrier ['bæriə] барьер, застава; препятствие, помеха.
barrister ['bæristə] адвокат.
barrow ['bærou] тачка.
barter ['ba:tə] **1.** товарообмен, меновая торговля; **2.** [по]менять, обменивать [-нять] (for на В).
base¹ [beis] □ подлый, низкий.
base² [~] **1.** основа, базис, фундамент; 🏛 основание; **2.** основывать [-овать] (В на П), базировать.
base|-ball *Am.* бейсбол; **~less** ['beislis] без оснований; **~ment** [-mənt] подвал, подвальный этаж.
baseness ['beisnis] низость *f.*
bashful ['bæʃful] □ застенчивый, робкий.
basic ['beisik] (**~ally**) основной; 🏛 осно́вный.
basin [beisn] таз, миска; бассейн.
bas|is ['beisis], *pl.* **~es** [-i:z] основание, исходный пункт; ⚔, ⚓ база.
bask [ba:sk] греться (на солнце).
basket ['ba:skit] корзина; **~-ball** баскетбол.
bass [beis] ♪ **1.** бас; **2.** басовый.
basso ['bæsou] ♪ бас.
bastard ['bæstəd] **1.** □ внебрачный; поддельный; ломаный (о языке); **2.** внебрачный ребёнок.
baste¹ [beist] поливать жаркое соком (во время жарения).
baste² [~] намётывать [наметать].
bat¹ [bæt] летучая мышь *f.*
bat² [~] **1.** бита (в крикете); **2.** бить, ударять в мяч.
bath [ba:θ] **1.** ванна; купальня; **2.** [вы-, по]мыть, [вы]купать.
bathe [beið] [вы]купаться.
bathing ['beiðiŋ] купание; **~-hut** кабина; **~-suit** купальный костюм.
bath|-room ванная комната; **~-sheet** купальная простыня; **~-towel** купальное полотенце.
batiste [bæ'ti:st] ✝ батист.
baton ['bætən] жезл; дирижёрская палочка; полицейская дубинка.
battalion [bə'tæljən] батальон.
batter ['bætə] **1.** взбитое тесто; **2.** сильно бить, [по]колотить, [от-]дубасить; ~ down или in взламывать [взломать]; **~y** [-ri] батарея; assault and ~ оскорбление действием.
battle ['bætl] **1.** битва, сражение

(of под Т); **2.** сража́ться [срази́ться]; боро́ться; **~-ax(e)** *hist.* боево́й топо́р; *Am. fig.* бой-ба́ба.
battle|-field по́ле би́твы; **~-plane** ⚔ штурмови́к; **~-ship** ⚔ лине́йный кора́бль *m.*
bawdy ['bɔ:di] непристо́йный.
bawl [bɔ:l] крича́ть [кри́кнуть], [за]ора́ть; **~ out** выкри́кивать [вы́крикнуть].
bay¹ [bei] **1.** гнедо́й; **2.** гнеда́я ло́шадь *f.*
bay² [~] зали́в, бу́хта.
bay³ [~] ла́вровое де́рево.
bay⁴ [~] **1.** лай; **2.** [за]ла́ять; bring to ~ *fig.* припере́ть к стене́; загоня́ть [загна́ть] (зве́ря).
bayonet ['beiənit] ⚔ **1.** штык; **2.** коло́ть штыко́м.
bay-window ['bei'windou] ⚠ э́ркер; *Am.* брюшко́.
baza(a)r [bə'zɑ:] база́р.
be [bi:, bi] [*irr.*]: a) быть, быва́ть; жить; находи́ться; пожива́ть, чу́вствовать себя́; there is, are есть; ~ about соб(и)ра́ться (+ *inf.*); ~ at s. th. быть за́нятым (Т); ~ off отправля́ться [-а́виться]; ~ on быть в де́йствии; b) *v/aux.* (для образова́ния дли́тельной фо́рмы): ~ reading чита́ть; c) *v/aux.* (для образова́ния пасси́ва): ~ read чита́ться, быть чи́танным (чита́емым).
beach [bi:tʃ] **1.** пляж, взмо́рье; **2.** ⚓ вы́тащить на бе́рег; посади́ть на мель.
beacon ['bi:kən] сигна́льный ого́нь *m*; ба́кен; буй.
bead [bi:d] бу́сина, би́серина; ка́пля; **~s** *pl. a.* чётки *f/pl.*; бу́сы *f/pl.*; би́сер.
beak [bi:k] клюв; но́сик (сосу́да).
beam [bi:m] **1.** ба́лка, брус; луч; **2.** сия́ть; излуча́ть [-чи́ть].
bean [bi:n] боб.
bear¹ [bɛə] медве́дь *m* (-ве́дица *f*); † *sl.* спекуля́нт, игра́ющий на пониже́ние.
bear² [~] [*irr.*] *v/t.* носи́ть [нести́]; [вы́]терпе́ть, выде́рживать [вы́держать]; рожда́ть [роди́ть]; ~ down преодоле́(ва́)ть; ~ out подтвержда́ть [-рди́ть]; ~ o. s. держа́ться, вести́ себя́; ~ up подде́рживать [-жа́ть]; ~ (up)on каса́ться [косну́ться] (Р); име́ть отноше́ние к (Д); bring to ~ употребля́ть [-би́ть].
beard [biəd] **1.** борода́; зубе́ц; ♀ ость *f* (ко́лоса); **2.** *v/t.* сме́ло выступа́ть про́тив (Р).
bearer ['bɛərə] носи́льщик; пода́тель(ница *f*) *m*, предъяви́тель (-ница *f*) *m.*
bearing ['bɛəriŋ] ноше́ние; терпе́ние; мане́ра держа́ть себя́; деторожде́ние.
beast [bi:st] зверь *m*; скоти́на; **~ly** [-li] гру́бый, ужа́сный.
beat [bi:t] **1.** [*irr.*] *v/t.* [по]би́ть; ударя́ть [уда́рить]; [по]колоти́ть; ~ a retreat отступа́ть [-пи́ть]; ~ up изби́(ва́)ть; взби(ва́)ть; ~ about the bush подходи́ть к де́лу издалека́; *v/i.* бить; би́ться; [по]стуча́ться; **2.** уда́р; бой; бие́ние; ритм; **~en** [bi:tn] **1.** *p. pt.* от beat; **2.** би́тый, побеждённый; проторённый (путь).
beatitude [bi'ætitju:d] блаже́нство.
beau [bou] щёголь *m*; кавале́р.
beautiful ['bju:tiful] □ прекра́сный, краси́вый.
beautify ['bju:tifai] украша́ть [укра́сить].
beauty ['bju:ti] красота́; краса́вица.
beaver ['bi:və] бобр.
became [bi'keim] *pt.* от become.
because [bi'kɔz] потому́ что, та́к как; ~ of из-за (Р).
beckon ['bekən] [по]мани́ть.
becom|e [bi'kʌm] [*irr.* (come)] *v/i.* [с]де́латься; станови́ться [стать]; *v/t.* быть к лицу́, идти́ (об оде́жде) (Д); подоба́ть (Д); **~ing** [-iŋ] □ к лицу́ (оде́жда).
bed [bed] **1.** посте́ль *f*; крова́ть *f*; ✓ гря́дка, клу́мба; **2.** класть и́ли ложи́ться в посте́ль; выса́живать [вы́садить] (цветы́).
bed-clothes *pl.* посте́льное бельё.
bedding ['bediŋ] посте́льные принадле́жности *f/pl.*
bedevil [bi'devl] [ис]терза́ть, [из-]му́чить; околдо́вывать [-дова́ть].
bed|rid(den) прико́ванный к посте́ли (боле́знью); **~room** спа́льня; **~spread** покрыва́ло (на крова́ть); **~stead** крова́ть *f*; **~time** вре́мя ложи́ться спать.
bee [bi:] пчела́; have a ~ in one's bonnet F быть с причу́дой.
beech [bi:tʃ] ♀ бук, бу́ковое де́рево; **~nut** бу́ковый оре́шек.
beef [bi:f] говя́дина; **~-tea** кре́пкий бульо́н; **~y** [bi:fi] му́скулистый; мяси́стый.
bee|hive у́лей; **~-line** пряма́я ли́ния.
been [bi:n, bin] *p. pt.* от be.
beer [biə] пи́во; small ~ сла́бое пи́во.
beet [bit] ♀ свёкла.
beetle [bi:tl] жук.
befall [bi'fɔ:l] [*irr.* (fall)] *v/t.* постига́ть [-и́гнуть, -и́чь] (о судьбе́) (В); *v/i.* случа́ться [-чи́ться].
befit [bi'fit] прили́чествовать (Д), подходи́ть [подойти́] (Д).
before [bi'fɔ:] **1.** *adv.* впереди́, вперёд; ра́ньше; long ~ задо́лго; **2.** *cj.* пре́жде чем; скоре́е чем; **3.** *prp.* пе́ред (Т); впереди́ (Р); до (Р); **~hand** зара́нее, заблаговре́менно.
befriend [bi'frend] относи́ться по-дру́жески к (Д).
beg [beg] *v/t.* [по]проси́ть (Р);

умолять [-лить] (for о П); выпрашивать [выпросить] (of у Р); *v/i.* нищенствовать.
began [bi'gæn] *pt.* от begin.
beget [bi'get] [*irr.* (get)] рождать [родить], производить [-вести].
beggar ['begə] **1.** нищий, нищенка; **2.** разорять [-рить], доводить до нищеты; *fig.* превосходить [-взойти]; it ~s all description не поддаётся описанию.
begin [bi'gin] [*irr.*] нач(ин)ать (with с Р); **~ner** [-ə] начинающий, новичок; **~ning** [-iŋ] начало.
begot(ten) [bi'gɔt(n)] *pt.* от beget.
begrudge [bi'grʌdʒ] [по]завидовать (Д в П).
beguile [bi'gail] обманывать [-нуть]; [с]коротать (время).
begun [bi'gʌn] *pt.* от begin.
behalf [bi'hɑ:f] : on *or* in ~ of для (Р), ради (Р); от имени (Р).
behav|e [bi'heiv] вести себя; поступать [-пить]; **~iour** [-jə] поведение.
behead [bi'hed] обезглавливать [-главить].
behind [bi'haind] **1.** *adv.* после; позади, сзади; **2.** *prp.* за (Т); позади (Р), сзади (Р); после (Р).
behold [bi'hould] [*irr.* (hold)] **1.** замечать [-етить], [у]видеть; **2.** смотри!, вот!
behoof [bi'hu:f]: to (for, on) (the) ~ of в пользу (Р), за (В).
being ['bi:iŋ] бытие, существование.
belated [bi'leitid] запоздалый.
belch [beltʃ] **1.** отрыжка; столб (огня, дыма); **2.** рыгать [рыгнуть]; извергать [-ергнуть].
belfry ['belfri] колокольня.
Belgian ['beldʒən] **1.** бельгиец (-ийка); **2.** бельгийский.
belief [bi'li:f] вера (in в В); убеждение.
believable [bi'li:vəbl] правдоподобный.
believe [bi'li:v] [по]верить (in в В); **~r** [-ə] верующий.
belittle [bi'litl] *fig.* умалять [-лить]; принижать [-низить].
bell [bel] колокол; звонок.
belle [bel] красавица.
belles-lettres ['be'letr] *pl.* художественная литература, беллетристика.
belligerent [bi'lidʒərənt] **1.** воюющая сторона; **2.** воюющий.
bellow ['belou] **1.** мычание; рёв (бури); **2.** [за]мычать; [за]реветь, [за]бушевать; **~s** [-z] *pl.* кузнечные мехи *m/pl.*
belly ['beli] **1.** живот, брюхо; **2.** наду(ва)ть(ся).
belong [bi'lɔŋ] принадлежать (Д); относиться (к Д); **~ings** [-iŋz] *pl.* принадлежности *f/pl.*; пожитки *m/pl.*
beloved [bi'lʌvid, *pred.* bi'lʌvd] возлюбленный, любимый.
below [bi'lou] **1.** *adv.* внизу; ниже; **2.** *prp.* ниже (Р); под (В, Т).
belt [belt] **1.** пояс; зона; ⊕ приводной ремень *m*; ⚔ портупея; **2.** подпоясывать(ся); пороть ремнём.
bemoan [bi'moun] оплак(ив)ать.
bench [bentʃ] скамья; ⊕ верстак.
bend [bend] **1.** сгиб; изгиб (дороги); излучина (реки); ⚓ узел, шпангоут; **2.** [*irr.*] сгибать(ся) [согнуть(ся)]; направлять [-равить]; покорять [-рить].
beneath [bi'ni:θ] *s.* below.
benediction [beni'dikʃən] благословение.
benefact|ion [-'fækʃən] благодеяние; **~or** ['benifæktə] благодетель *m.*
beneficе|nce [bi'nefisns] благотворительность *f*; **~nt** □ благодетельный.
beneficial [beni'fiʃə] □ благотворный, полезный.
benefit ['benifit] **1.** выгода, польза; пособие; *thea.* бенефис; **2.** приносить пользу; извлекать пользу.
benevolen|ce [bi'nevələns] благожелательность *f*; **~t** [-ənt] □ благожелательный.
benign [bi'nain] □ добрый, милостивый; ⚕ доброкачественный.
bent [bent] **1.** *pt.* и *p. pt.* от bend; ~ on помешанный на (П); **2.** склонность *f.*
benz|ene [ben'zi:n] ⚗ бензол; **~ine** [~] бензин.
bequeath [bi'kwi:ð] завещать (*im*)*pf.*
bequest [bi'kwest] наследство.
bereave [bi'ri:v] [*irr.*] лишать [-шить] (Р); отнимать [-нять].
berry ['beri] ягода.
berth [bə:θ] ⚓ якорная стоянка; койка; *fig.* (выгодная) должность *f.*
beseech [bi'si:tʃ] [*irr.*] умолять [-лить], упрашивать [упросить] (+ *inf.*).
beset [bi'set] [*irr.* (set)] окружать [-жить]; осаждать [осадить].
beside [bi'said] *prp.* рядом с (Т), около (Р), близ (Р); мимо (Р); ~ o. s. вне себя (with от Р); ~ the question некстати, не по существу; **~s** [-z] **1.** *adv.* кроме того, сверх того; **2.** *prp.* кроме (Р).
besiege [bi'si:dʒ] осаждать [осадить].
besmear [bi'smiə] [за]пачкать, [за-] марать.
besom ['bi:zəm] метла, веник.
besought [bi'sɔ:t] *pt.* от beseech.
bespatter [bi'spætə] забрызг(ивать).
bespeak [bi'spi:k] [*irr.* (speak)] заказывать [-зать]; bespoke tailor портной, работающий по заказу.

best [best] 1. *adj.* лу́чший; ~ man ша́фер; 2. *adv.* лу́чше всего́, всех; 3. са́мое лу́чшее; to the ~ of ... наско́лько ...; по ме́ре ...; make the ~ of испо́льзовать наилу́чшим о́бразом; at ~ в лу́чшем слу́чае.
bestial ['bestjəl] □ ско́тский, живо́тный.
bestow [bi'stou] дарова́ть ([up]on Д/В *or* В/Т), награжда́ть [-ради́ть].
bet [bet] 1. пари́ *n indecl.*; 2. [*irr.*] держа́ть пари́; би́ться об закла́д.
betake [bi'teik] [*irr.* (take)]: ~ o. s. to отправля́ться [-а́виться] в (В); *fig* прибега́ть [-е́гнуть] к (Д).
bethink [bi'θiŋk] [*irr.* (think)]: ~ o. s. вспомина́ть [вспо́мнить]; ду́мать (of о П); ~ o. s. to *inf.* заду́м(ыв)ать.
betray [bi'trei] преда́(ва́)ть; вы́да(ва́)ть; **~er** [-ə] преда́тель(ница *f*) *m*.
betrothal [bi'trouðəl] помо́лвка, обруче́ние.
better ['betə] 1. *adj.* лу́чший; he is ~ ему́ лу́чше; 2. преиму́щество; **~s** *pl.* ли́ца стоя́щие вы́ше; get the ~ of взять верх над (Т); 3. *adv.* лу́чше; бо́льше; so much the ~ тем лу́чше; you had ~ go вам бы лу́чше пойти́; 4. *v/t.* улучша́ть [улу́чшить]; поправля́ть [-а́вить]; *v/i.* поправля́ться [-а́виться]; **~ment** [-mənt] улучше́ние.
between [bi'twi:n] 1. *adv.* ме́жду ни́ми; 2. *prp.* ме́жду (Т).
beverage ['bevəridʒ] напи́ток.
bevy ['bevi] стая́ (птиц); ста́до; гру́ппа, толпа́ (де́вушек).
bewail [bi'weil] скорбе́ть о (П), опла́к(ив)ать.
beware [bi'wɛə] оберега́ться [-ре́чься] (Р).
bewilder [bi'wildə] смуща́ть [смути́ть]; ста́вить в тупи́к; сбива́ть с то́лку; **~ment** [-mənt] смуще́ние, замеша́тельство; пу́таница.
bewitch [bi'witʃ] околдо́вывать [-дова́ть]; очаро́вывать [-рова́ть].
beyond [bi'jɔnd] 1. *adv.* вдали́, на расстоя́нии; 2. *prp.* за (В, Т); вне (Р); сверх (Р); по ту сто́рону (Р).
bias ['baiəs] предубежде́ние (про́тив Р); склон, укло́н; 2. склоня́ть [-ни́ть]; 3. ко́со.
bib [bib] де́тский нагру́дник.
Bible [baibl] би́блия.
biblical ['biblikəl] □ библе́йский.
bicarbonate [bai'kɑ:bənit] ⚗: ~ of soda двууглеки́слый на́трий.
bicker ['bikə] препира́ться (с Т).
bicycle ['baisikl] 1. велосипе́д; 2. е́здить на велосипе́де.
bid [bid] 1. [*irr.*] прика́зывать [-за́ть]; предлага́ть [-ложи́ть] (це́ну); ~ fair [по]сули́ть, [по]обеща́ть; ~ farewell [по]проща́ться [прости́ться]; 2. предложе́ние (цены́), зая́вка (на торга́х); *Am.* F приглаше́ние; **~den** [bidn] *p. pt.* от bid.
bide [baid]: ~ one's time ожида́ть благоприя́тного слу́чая.
biennial [bai'enjəl] двухле́тний.
bier [biə] похоро́нные дро́ги *f/pl.*
big [big] большо́й, кру́пный; взро́слый; F *fig.* ва́жный, ва́жничающий; F *fig.* ~ shot ва́жная «ши́шка»; talk ~ [по]хва́статься.
bigamy ['bigəmi] бига́мия, двоебра́чие.
bigot ['bigət] слепо́й приве́рженец; **~ry** [-ri] слепа́я приве́рженность *f*.
bigwig ['bigwig] F ва́жная «ши́шка».
bike [baik] F велосипе́д.
bile [bail] жёлчь *f*; *fig.* раздражи́тельность *f*.
bilious ['biljəs] □ жёлчный.
bill[1] [bil] клюв; носо́к я́коря.
bill[2] [~] 1. законопрое́кт, билль *m*; счёт; афи́ша; † ве́ксель *m*; ~ of fare меню́; ~ of lading коносаме́нт; ~ of sale ⚖ закладна́я; 2. объявля́ть [-ви́ть] (афи́шей).
billfold бума́жник.
billiards ['biljədz] *pl.* билья́рд.
billion ['biljən] биллио́н; *Am.* миллиа́рд.
billow ['bilou] больша́я волна́; 2. вздыма́ться (во́лнами), [вз]волнова́ться (о мо́ре); **~y** ['biloui] вздыма́ющийся (о во́лнах).
bin [bin] за́кром; ларь *m*; му́сорное ведро́.
bind [baind] [*irr.*] 1. *v/t.* [с]вяза́ть; свя́зывать [-за́ть]; обя́зывать [-за́ть]; переплета́ть [-плести́]; 2. *v/i.* затверде́(ва́)ть; **~er** ['baində] переплётчик; **~ing** [-iŋ] 1. переплёт; 2. связу́ющий.
binocular [bai'nɔkjulə] бино́кль *m*.
biography [bai'ɔgrəfi] биогра́фия.
biology [bai'ɔlədʒi] биоло́гия.
birch [bə:tʃ] 1. ⚘ (или ~-tree) берёза, берёзовое де́рево; ро́зга; 2. сечь ро́згой.
bird [bə:d] пти́ца; **~'s-eye** ['bə:dzai]: ~ view вид с пти́чьего полёта.
birth [bə:θ] рожде́ние; происхожде́ние; bring to ~ порожда́ть [-роди́ть]; **~day** день рожде́ния; **~-place** ме́сто рожде́ния.
biscuit ['biskit] пече́нье.
bishop ['biʃəp] епи́скоп; *chess* слон; **~ric** [-rik] епа́рхия.
bison ['baisn] *zo.* бизо́н, зубр.
bit [bit] 1. кусо́чек, части́ца; немно́го; удила́ *n/pl.*; боро́дка (ключа́); 2. *pt.* от ~e.
bitch [bitʃ] су́ка.
bite [bait] 1. уку́с; клёв (ры́бы); кусо́к; острота́; 2. [*irr.*] куса́ть [укуси́ть]; клева́ть [клю́нуть] (о ры́бе); жечь (о пе́рце); щипа́ть (о моро́зе); ⊕ брать [взять]; *fig.* [съ]язви́ть.

bitten ['bitn] *pt.* от bite.
bitter ['bitə] □ го́рький; ре́зкий; *fig.* го́рький, мучи́тельный; **~s** *pl.* [-z] го́рький лека́рственный напи́ток.
blab [blæb] F разба́лтывать [-болта́ть].
black [blæk] **1.** □ чёрный; тёмный, мра́чный; **2.** [по]черни́ть; *fig.* [о]позо́рить; **~ out** затемня́ть [-ни́ть]; **3.** чернота́; чёрный цвет; черноко́жий (негр); **~berry** ежеви́ка; **~bird** чёрный дрозд; **~board** кла́ссная доска́; **~en** ['blækn] *v/t.* [на]черни́ть; *fig.* [о]черни́ть; *v/i.* [по]черне́ть; **~-guard** ['blægɑ:d] **1.** негодя́й, подле́ц; **2.** □ по́длый; **~head** ⚕ угри́ *m/pl.*; **~ing** [blækiŋ] ва́кса; **~ish** ['blækiʃ] □ черنова́тый; **~leg** моше́нник; штрейкбре́хер; **~-letter** *typ.* стари́нный готи́ческий шрифт; **~mail 1.** вымога́тельство, шанта́ж; **2.** вымога́ть де́ньги у (Р); **~ness** [-nis] чернота́; **~out** затемне́ние; **~smith** кузне́ц.
bladder ['blædə] *anat.* пузы́рь *m.*
blade [bleid] ло́пасть *f; anat.* лопа́тка; ле́звие; клино́к; ♀ лист; сте́бель *m*, были́нка.
blame [bleim] **1.** упрёк; вина́; порица́ние; **2.** порица́ть; обвиня́ть [-ни́ть]; **be to ~ for** быть винова́тым в (П); **~ful** ['bleimful] заслу́живающий порица́ния; **~less** ['bleimlis] □ безупре́чный.
blanch [blɑ:ntʃ] [вы́]бели́ть; [вы́-] чи́стить (мета́лл); **~ over** обеля́ть [-ли́ть], опра́вдывать [-да́ть].
bland [blænd] □ ве́жливый; мя́гкий.
blank [blæŋk] **1.** □ пусто́й; бессодержа́тельный; невырази́тельный; ✝ незапо́лненный; **~ cartridge** ⚔ холосто́й патро́н; **2.** бланк; пробе́л; пустота́ (душе́вная).
blanket [blæŋkit] **1.** шерстяно́е одея́ло; **2.** покрыва́ть одея́лом.
blare [blɛə] [за]труби́ть.
blasphem|e [blæs'fi:m] богоху́льствовать; поноси́ть (against В); **~y** ['blæsfimi] богоху́льство.
blast [blɑ:st] **1.** си́льный поры́в ве́тра; звук (духово́го инструме́нта); взрывна́я волна́; подрывно́й заря́д; ♀ головня́; ⊕ дутьё; *fig.* па́губное влия́ние; **2.** взрыва́ть [взорва́ть]; проклина́ть [-кля́сть]; **~-furnace** ⊕ до́мна, до́менная печь *f.*
blaze [bleiz] **1.** я́ркое пла́мя *n*; вспы́шка (огня́, стра́сти); **2.** *v/i.* горе́ть; пыла́ть; сверка́ть [-кну́ть]; *v/t.* разглаша́ть [-гласи́ть]; **~r** ['bleizə] спорти́вная ку́ртка.
blazon ['bleizn] герб.
bleach [bli:tʃ] [вы́]бели́ть.
bleak [bli:k] □ го́лый, пусты́нный; суро́вый (по кли́мату).
blear [bliə] **1.** затума́ненный, нея́сный; **2.** затума́ни(ва)ть; **~-eyed** ['bliəraid] с затума́ненными глаза́ми.
bleat [bli:t] **1.** бле́яние; **2.** [за-] бле́ять.
bleb [bleb] волды́рь *m*; пузырёк во́здуха (в воде́).
bled [bled] *pt.* и *p. pt.* от bleed.
bleed [bli:d] [*irr.*] **1.** *v/i.* кровоточи́ть; истека́ть кро́вью; **2.** *v/t.* пуска́ть кровь (Д); **~ing** ['bli:diŋ] кровотече́ние; кровопуска́ние.
blemish ['blemiʃ] **1.** недоста́ток; пятно́; позо́р; **2.** [за]пятна́ть; [ис]по́ртить; [о]позо́рить.
blench [blentʃ] отступа́ть [-пи́ть] (пе́ред Т).
blend [blend] **1.** сме́шивать(ся) [-ша́ть(ся)]; разбавля́ть [-ба́вить]; сочета́ть(ся) (*im*)*pf.*; **2.** сме́шивание; смесь *f.*
bless [bles] благословля́ть [-ви́ть]; осчастли́вливать [-тли́вить]; **~ed** (*pt.* blest; *adj.* 'blesid) □ счастли́вый, бла́же́нный; **~ing** ['blesiŋ] благослове́ние.
blew [blu:] *pt.* от blow[2],[3].
blight [blait] **1.** ♀ ми́лдью *n indecl.* (и други́е боле́зни расте́ний); *fig.* ги́бель *f*; **2.** приноси́ть вред (расте́ниям); разби́(ва́)ть (наде́жды и т. п.).
blind [blaind] □ **1.** слепо́й (*fig.* **~ to** к Д); нечёткий, нея́сный; **~ alley** тупи́к; **~ly** *fig.* наугад, наобу́м; **2.** што́ра; марки́за; жалюзи́ *n indecl.*; **3.** ослепля́ть [-пи́ть]; **~-fold** ['blaindfould] завя́зывать глаза́ (Д).
blink [bliŋk] **1.** мерца́ние; морга́ние; миг; **2.** *v/i.* мига́ть [мигну́ть]; морга́ть [-гну́ть]; прищу́ри(ва)ться; *v/t.* закрыва́ть глаза́ на (В).
bliss [blis] блаже́нство.
blister ['blistə] **1.** волды́рь *m*; **2.** покрыва́ться пузыря́ми.
blizzard ['blizəd] бура́н, си́льная мете́ль *f.*
bloat [blout] распуха́ть [-пу́хнуть]; разду́(ва́)ться; **~er** ['bloutə] копчёная се́льдь *f.*
block [blɔk] **1.** коло́да, чурба́н; пла́ха; глы́ба; кварта́л (го́рода); **2. ~ in** набра́сывать вчерне́; (*mst* **~ up**) блоки́ровать (*im*)*pf.*
blockade [blɔ'keid] **1.** блока́да; **2.** блоки́ровать (*im*)*pf.*
blockhead ['blɔkhed] болва́н.
blond [blɔnd] **1.** белоку́рый; **~e** блонди́нка.
blood [blʌd] кровь *f*; **in cold ~** хладнокро́вно; **~-horse** чистокро́вная ло́шадь *f*; **~shed** кровопроли́тие; **~shot** нали́тый кро́вью (о глаза́х); **~thirsty** кровожа́дный; **~-vessel** кровено́сный сосу́д; **~y** ['blʌdi] □ окрова́вленный; крова́вый.

bloom [blu:m] 1. цвето́к; цвете́ние; расцве́т (*a. fig.*); 2. цвести́, быть в цвету́.
blossom ['blɔsəm] 1. цвето́к (фрукто́вого де́рева); расцве́т; 2. цвести́, расцвета́ть [-ести́].
blot [blɔt] 1. пятно́, кля́кса; *fig.* пятно́; 2. [за]па́чкать; промока́ть [-кну́ть]; вычёркивать [вы́черкнуть].
blotch [blɔtʃ] прыщ; пятно́; кля́кса.
blotter ['blɔtə] пресс-папье́ *n indecl.*
blotting-paper промока́тельная бума́га.
blouse [blauz] блу́за; блу́зка.
blow¹ [blou] уда́р.
blow² [~] [*irr.*] 1. цвести́; 2. цвете́ние.
blow³ [~] [*irr.*] 1. [по]ду́ть; ве́ять; [за]пыхте́ть; игра́ть на (духово́м инструме́нте); ~ up взрыва́ть (-ся) [взорва́ть(ся)]; разду́(ва́)ть (ого́нь); гнать (ту́чи); ~ one's nose [вы́]сморка́ться; 2. дунове́ние; ~er ['blouə] труба́ч; ~n [-n] *p. pt.* от blow²,³; ~-out *mot.* разры́в ши́ны; ~-pipe пая́льная тру́бка.
bludgeon ['blʌdʒən] дуби́на.
blue [blu:] 1. □ голубо́й; лазу́рный; си́ний; F уны́лый, пода́вленный; 2. си́няя кра́ска; си́ний цвет; голуба́я кра́ска; си́нька; ~s *pl.* меланхо́лия, хандра́; 3. окра́шивать в си́ний, голубо́й цвет; [по]сини́ть (бельё).
bluff [blʌf] 1. □ ре́зкий; грубова́тый; обры́вистый; 2. обма́н, блеф; 3. запу́гивать [-га́ть]; обма́нывать [-ну́ть].
bluish ['blu:iʃ] синева́тый, голубова́тый.
blunder ['blʌndə] 1. гру́бая оши́бка; 2. де́лать гру́бую оши́бку.
blunt [blʌnt] 1. □ тупо́й; ре́зкий; 2. притупля́ть [-пи́ть].
blur [blə:] 1. нея́сное очерта́ние; кля́кса, пятно́; 2. *v/t.* [за]мара́ть, [за]па́чкать, [за]пятна́ть (*a. fig.*); *fig.* затемня́ть [-ни́ть] (созна́ние).
blush [blʌʃ] 1. кра́ска стыда́; 2. [по]красне́ть.
bluster ['blʌstə] 1. хвастовство́, самохва́льство; пусты́е угро́зы *f/pl.*; 2. грози́ться; [по]хва́статься.
boar [bɔ:] бо́ров; *hunt.* каба́н.
board [bɔ:d] 1. доска́; стол (пита́ние); ⚓ борт; сце́на, подмо́стки *m/pl.*; правле́ние; ♀ of Trade министе́рство торго́вли; *Am.* торго́вая пала́та; 2. *v/t.* наст(и)ла́ть (пол); ⚓ брать на аборда́ж; *v/i.* столова́ться; сади́ться [сесть] на (по́езд, кора́бль); ~er [ˌbɔ:də] пансионе́р(ка); ~ing-house меблиро́ванные ко́мнаты со столо́м.
boast [boust] 1. хвастовство́; 2. (of, about) горди́ться (T); [по]хва́статься (T); ~ful ['boustful] □ хвастли́вый.
boat [bout] ло́дка; су́дно; ~ing ['boutiŋ] ката́ние на ло́дке.
bob [bɔb] 1. ги́ря (ма́ятника); рыво́к; ко́ротко подстри́женные во́лосы *m/pl.*; 2. *v/t.* стричь ко́ротко; *v/i.* подпры́гивать [-гнуть].
bobbin ['bɔbin] кату́шка; шпу́лька.
bode [boud] предвеща́ть [-ести́ть], предска́зывать [-за́ть].
bodice ['bɔdis] лиф, ли́фчик.
bodily ['bɔdili] теле́сный.
body ['bɔdi] те́ло; труп; *mot.* ку́зов; ⚔ войскова́я часть *f.*
bog [bɔg] 1. боло́то, тряси́на; 2. be ~ed увяза́ть [увя́знуть] (в тряси́не).
boggle ['bɔgl] [ис]пуга́ться (at P); неуме́ло рабо́тать.
bogus ['bougəs]подде́льный.
boil [bɔil] 1. кипе́ние; фуру́нкул, нары́в; 2. [с]вари́ть(ся); [вс]кипяти́ть(ся); кипе́ть; ~er ['bɔilə] котёл; куб, бак (для кипяче́ния).
boisterous ['bɔistərəs] □ бу́рный, шу́мный.
bold [bould] □ сме́лый; самоуве́ренный; на́глый; *typ.* жи́рный, отчётливый (шрифт); ~ness ['bouldnis] сме́лость *f*; на́глость *f.*
bolster ['boulstə] 1. (дива́нный) ва́лик; поду́шка; 2. подде́рживать [-жа́ть].
bolt [boult] 1. болт; засо́в, задви́жка; мо́лния; 2. *v/t.* запира́ть на засо́в; *v/i.* нести́сь стрело́й; убега́ть [убежа́ть]; понести́ *pf.* (о лошадя́х).
bomb [bɔm] 1. бо́мба; 2. бомби́ть.
bombard [bɔm'bɑ:d] бомбардирова́ть.
bombastic [bɔm'bæstik] напы́щенный.
bomb-proof непробива́емый бо́мбами.
bond [bɔnd] *pl.*: ~s у́зы *f/pl.*; око́вы *f/pl.*; ✝ долгово́е обяза́тельство; ~age ['bɔndidʒ] ра́бство; зави́симость *f*; ~(s)man ['bɔnd(z)mən] раб.
bone [boun] 1. кость *f*; ~ of contention я́блоко раздо́ра; make no ~s about F не церемо́ниться с (T); 2. вынима́ть, выреза́ть ко́сти.
bonfire ['bɔnfaiə] костёр.
bonnet ['bɔnit] че́пчик; ка́пор; шля́пка; *mot.* капо́т.
bonus ['bounəs] ✝ пре́мия; танттье́ма.
bony ['bouni] костля́вый; кости́стый.
booby ['bu:bi] болва́н, дура́к.
book [buk] 1. кни́га; 2. заноси́ть в кни́гу; регистри́ровать (*im*)*pf.*, *pf. a.* [за-]; зака́зывать и́ли брать (биле́т в теа́тр, на по́езд и т. п.); приглаша́ть [-ласи́ть] (арти́стов); ~-case кни́жный шкаф; ~ing-clerk ['bukiŋklɑ:k] касси́р; ~ing-office биле́тная ка́сса; ~-keeping

счетово́дство; ~**let** ['buklit] брошю́ра; ~**seller** книгопрода́вец; букини́ст.
boom[1] [bu:m] 1. ✝ бум; 2. производи́ть сенса́цию, шум вокру́г (Р).
boom[2] [~] 1. гул; гуде́ние; 2. [за-] гуде́ть; [за]жужжа́ть.
boon[1] [bu:n] благоде́яние.
boon[2] [~] благотво́рный; прия́тный.
boor [buə] гру́бый, невоспи́танный челове́к; ~**ish** ['buəriʃ] □ гру́бый, невоспи́танный.
boost [bu:st] поднима́ть [-ня́ть] (торго́влю).
boot[1] [bu:t]: to ~ в прида́чу, вдоба́вок *adv.*
boot[2] [~] сапо́г.
booth [bu:ð] пала́тка; кио́ск.
bootlegger ['bu:tlegə] *Am.* торго́вец контраба́ндными напи́тками.
booty ['bu:ti] добы́ча; награ́бленное добро́.
border ['bɔ:də] 1. грани́ца; край; кайма́ (на ска́терти и т. п.); 2. грани́чить (upon с Т); окаймля́ть [-ми́ть].
bore[1] [bɔ:] 1. вы́сверленное отве́рстие; кали́бр; *fig.* ску́чный челове́к; 2. [про]сверли́ть; [про-] бура́вить; надоеда́ть [-е́сть] (Д).
bore[2] [~] 1. *pt.* от bear[2].
born [bɔ:n] рождённый; прирождённый; ~**e** [~] *p. pt.* от bear[2].
borough ['bʌrə] небольшо́й го́род; municipal ~ го́род, име́ющий самоуправле́ние.
borrow ['bɔrou] занима́ть [-ня́ть] (from, of у Р).
bosom ['buzəm] грудь *f*; па́зуха; *fig.* ло́но; не́дра *n/pl.*
boss F [bɔs] 1. хозя́ин; предпринима́тель(ница *f*) *m*; *pol. Am.* руководи́тель полити́ческой па́ртии; 2. распоряжа́ться [-яди́ться] (Т), быть хозя́ином (Р); ~**y** *Am.* ['bɔsi] лю́бящий распоряжа́ться.
botany ['bɔtəni] бота́ника.
botch [bɔtʃ] 1. гру́бая запла́та; плоха́я почи́нка; 2. дела́ть гру́бые запла́ты на (П); пло́хо чини́ть.
both [bouθ] о́ба, о́бе; и тот и друго́й; ~ ... and ... как ... так и ...; и ... и ...
bother ['bɔðə] F 1. беспоко́йство; oh ~! кака́я доса́да!; 2. надоеда́ть [-е́сть] (Д); [по]беспоко́ить.
bottle [bɔtl] 1. буты́лка; 2. разлива́ть по буты́лкам.
bottom ['bɔtəm] 1. дно, дни́ще; ни́жняя часть *f*; грунт, по́чва; F зад; *fig.* осно́ва, суть *f*; at the ~ внизу́; *fig.* в су́щности; на дне (о́бщества); 2. са́мый ни́жний.
bough [bau] ве́тка, ветвь *f.*
bought [bɔ:t] *pt.* и *p. pt.* от buy.
boulder ['bouldə] валу́н.
bounce [bauns] 1. прыжо́к, скачо́к; 2. подпры́гивать [-гнуть]; отска́кивать [отскочи́ть] (о мяче́); F преувеличе́ние.
bound[1] [baund] 1. преде́л; ограниче́ние; 2. ограни́чи(ва)ть; сде́рживать [-жа́ть].
bound[2] [~] ⚓ гото́вый к отправле́нию, направля́ющийся (for в В).
bound[3] [~] 1. прыжо́к, скачо́к; 2. пры́гать [-гнуть], [по]скака́ть; отска́кивать [отскочи́ть].
bound[4] [~] 1. *pt.* и *p. pt.* от bind; 2. свя́занный; обя́занный; переплетённый.
boundary ['baundəri] грани́ца.
boundless [-lis] □ безграни́чный.
bounteous ['bauntiəs] □, **bountiful** ['bauntiful] □ ще́дрый (челове́к); оби́льный.
bounty ['baunti] ще́дрость *f*; ✝ прави́тельственная пре́мия.
bouquet ['bukei] буке́т; арома́т (вина́).
bout [baut] черёд; раз; ⚕ припа́док; *sport*: схва́тка.
bow[1] [bau] 1. покло́н; ⚓ нос; 2. *v/i.* [со]гну́ться; кла́няться [поклони́ться]; подчиня́ться [-ни́ться] (Д); *v/t.* [со]гну́ть.
bow[2] [bou] 1. лук; дуга́; бант; ♪ смычо́к; rain~ ра́дуга; 2. ♪ владе́ть смычко́м.
bowels ['bauəlz] *pl.* кишки́ *f/pl.*; вну́тренности *f/pl.*; не́дра *n/pl.* (земли́); *fig.* сострада́ние.
bower ['bauə] бесе́дка.
bowl[1] [boul] ку́бок, ча́ша; ва́за.
bowl[2] [~] 1. шар; 2. *v/t.* [по]кати́ть; *v/i.* игра́ть в шары́; ~ along кати́ться бы́стро.
box[1] [bɔks] 1. коро́бка; я́щик; сунду́к; ⊕ бу́кса; вту́лка; ⚘ букс; *thea.* ло́жа; 2. вкла́дывать в я́щик.
box[2] [~] 1. *sport* бокс; ~ on the ear пощёчина.
box|**-keeper** капельди́нер; ~**-office** театра́льная ка́сса.
boy [bɔi] ма́льчик; молодо́й челове́к; ~**hood** ['bɔihud] о́трочество; ~**ish** ['bɔiiʃ] □ мальчи́шеский, о́троческий.
brace [breis] 1. ⊕ связь *f*; ско́бка; па́ра (о дичи́); ~**s** *pl.* подтя́жки *f/pl.*; 2. свя́зывать [-за́ть]; подпира́ть [-пере́ть]; ~ up подба́дривать [-бодри́ть].
bracelet ['breislit] брасле́т.
bracket ['brækit] 1. ⚠ кронште́йн, консо́ль *f*; га́зовый рожо́к; *typ.* ско́бка; 2. заключа́ть в ско́бки; *fig.* ста́вить на одну́ до́ску с (Т).
brag [bræg] 1. [по]хва́статься; 2. хвастовство́.
braggart ['brægət] 1. хвасту́н; 2. □ хвастли́вый.
braid [breid] 1. коса́ (воло́с); тесьма́; галу́н; 2. заплета́ть [-ести́]; обшива́ть тесьмо́й.
brain [brein] 1. мозг; голова́; (*fig.*

mst ~s) рассýдок, ум; ýмственные спосóбности *f/pl.*; 2. размозжи́ть гóлову (Д).
brake [breik] 1. ⊕ тóрмоз; 2. [за-] тормози́ть.
bramble ['bræmbl] ♆ ежеви́ка.
bran [bræn] óтруби *f/pl.*
branch [brɑ:ntʃ] 1. ветвь *f*, вéтка, сук (*pl.*: сýчья); óтрасль *f* (наýки); филиáл; 2. разветвля́ть(ся) [-етви́ть(ся)]; расширя́ться [-ши́риться].
brand [brænd] 1. вы́жженное клеймó, таврó; ⊕ фабри́чное клеймó; сорт; 2. выжигáть клеймó; *fig.* [за]клейми́ть, [о]позóрить.
brandish ['brændiʃ] размáхивать [-хнýть] (Т).
bran(d)new ['brænd'nju:] F совершéнно нóвый, «с игóлочки».
brandy ['brændi] коньяк.
brass [brɑ:s] латýнь *f*, жёлтая медь *f*; F бессты́дство; ~ band духовóй оркéстр.
brassiere ['bræsiεə] бюстгáльтер.
brave [breiv] 1. хрáбрый, смéлый; 2. брави́ровать; хрáбро встречáть (опáсность и т. п.); ~ry ['breivəri] хрáбрость *f*, смéлость *f*.
brawl [brɔ:l] 1. шýмная ссóра, ýличный скандáл; 2. [по]ссóриться (с Т).
brawny ['brɔ:ni] си́льный; мýскулистый.
bray¹ [brei] 1. крик ослá; 2. [за-] кричáть (об ослé).
bray² [~] [ис]толóчь.
brazen ['breizn] □ мéдный, брóнзовый; бессты́дный, нáглый (*a.* ~-faced).
Brazilian [brə'ziljən] 1. брази́льский; 2. брази́лец, бразилья́нка.
breach [bri:tʃ] 1. пролóм; *fig.* разры́в (отношéний); нарушéние; ⚔ брешь *f*; 2. пробивáть брешь в (П).
bread [bred] хлеб.
breadth [bredθ] ширинá; широтá (кругозóра); ширóкий размáх.
break [breik] 1. переры́в; пáуза; рассвéт; трéщина; F a bad ~ неудáча; 2. [*irr.*] *v/t.* [с]ломáть; разби́(вá)ть; разрушáть [-рýшить]; прер(ы)вáть; взлáмывать [взломáть]; ~ up разлáмывать [-ломáть]; разби́(вá)ть; *v/i.* пор(ы)вáть (с Т); [по]ломáться, разби́(вá)ться; ~ away отделя́ться [-ли́ться] (от Р); ~ down потерпéть авáрию, неудáчу; ~able ['breikəbl] лóмкий, хрýпкий; ~age ['breikidʒ] полóмка; ~-down развáл, расстрóйство; *mot.* авáрия; ~fast ['breikfəst] 1. зáвтрак; 2. [по]зáвтракать; ~-up распáд, развáл; ~water мол; волнорéз.
breast [brest] грудь *f*; make a clean ~ of a th. чистосердéчно сознавáться в чём-либо; ~-stroke брасс.
breath [breθ] дыхáние; вздох; ~e [bri:ð] *v/i.* дышáть [дохнýть]; перевести́ дух; ~less ['breθlis] □ запыхáвшийся; безвéтренный.
bred [bred] 1. вскóрмленный; воспи́танный; 2. *pt.* и *p. pt.* от breed.
breeches ['bretʃiz] *pl.* бри́джи *pl.*, штаны́ *m/pl.*
breed [bri:d] 1. порóда; 2. [*irr.*] *v/t.* выводи́ть [вы́вести]; разводи́ть [-вести́]; выси́живать [вы́сидеть]; вскáрмливать [вскорми́ть]; *v/i.* размножáться [-óжиться]; [вы́]расти́; ~er ['bri:də] производи́тель *m*; скотовóд; ~ing [-diŋ] разведéние (живóтных); хорóшие манéры *f/pl.*; воспитáние.
breez|e [bri:z] лёгкий ветерóк, бриз; ~y ['bri:zi] свéжий, живóй, весёлый.
brethren ['breðrin] собрáтья *m/pl.*, брáтия.
brevity ['breviti] крáткость *f*.
brew [bru:] *v/t.* [с]вари́ть (пи́во); завáривать [-ри́ть] (чай); приготовля́ть [-тóвить]; *fig.* затевáть [затéять]; ~ery ['bruəri] пивовáренный завóд.
brib|e [braib] 1. взя́тка; пóдкуп; 2. подкупáть [-пи́ть]; давáть взя́тку (Д); ~ery ['braibəri] взя́точничество.
brick [brik] 1. кирпи́ч; *fig.* слáвный пáрень *m*; 2. класть кирпичи́; облицóвывать кирпичáми; ~layer кáменщик.
bridal ['braidl] □ свáдебный; ~ procession свáдебная процéссия.
bride [braid] невéста; новобрáчная; ~groom жени́х; новобрáчный; ~smaid подрýжка невéсты.
bridge [bridʒ] 1. мост; 2. соединя́ть мостóм; наводи́ть мост чéрез (В); *fig.* преодолé(вá)ть (препя́тствия).
bridle ['braidl] 1. уздá; пóвод; 2. *v/t.* взнýздывать [-дáть]; *v/i.* [за]артáчиться; задирáть нос (*a.* ~ up); ~-path верховáя тропá.
brief [bri:f] 1. □ корóткий, крáткий, сжáтый; 2. ⚖ резюмé дéла для защи́тника; hold a ~ for принимáть на себя́ ведéние дéла (Р); ~-case портфéль *m*.
brigade [bri'geid] ⚔ бригáда.
bright [brait] □ я́ркий; свéтлый, я́сный; ~en ['braitn] *v/t.* [на]полировáть; придавáть блеск (Д); *v/i.* проясня́ться [-ни́ться]; ~ness [-nis] я́ркость *f*; блеск.
brillian|ce, ~cy ['briljəns, -si] я́ркость *f*; блеск; великолéпие; ~t [-jənt] 1. □ блестя́щий (*a. fig.*); сверкáющий; 2. бриллиáнт.
brim [brim] 1. край; поля́ *n/pl.* (шля́пы); 2. наполня́ть(ся) до краёв.
brine [brain] рассóл; морскáя водá.
bring [briŋ] [*irr.*] приноси́ть [-нести́]; доставля́ть [-áвить];

привози́ть [-везти́]; приводи́ть [-вести́]; ~ about осуществля́ть [-ви́ть]; ~ down снижа́ть [сни́зить] (це́ны); ~ forth производи́ть [-вести́]; ~ home to дава́ть поня́ть (Д); ~ round приводи́ть [-вести́] в себя́ (по́сле о́бморока); ~ up воспи́тывать [-та́ть].

brink [briŋk] край (обры́ва); (круто́й) бе́рег.

brisk [brisk] □ живо́й, оживлённый.

bristl|e ['brisl] 1. щети́на; 2. [о]щети́ниться; [рас]серди́ться; ~ with изоби́ловать (Т); **~ed** [-d], **~y** [-i] щети́нистый, колю́чий.

British ['britiʃ] брита́нский; the ~ англича́не *m/pl.*

brittle ['britl] хру́пкий, ло́мкий.

broach [broutʃ] поч(ин)а́ть; поднима́ть [-ня́ть] (вопро́с); нач(ин)а́ть (разгово́р).

broad [brɔ:d] □ широ́кий; обши́рный; грубова́тый; **~cast** 1. разбра́сывать [-роса́ть] (семена́); распространя́ть [-ни́ть]; передава́ть по ра́дио, веща́ть; 2. радиопереда́ча; радиовеща́ние; **~cloth** то́нкое сукно́; бума́жная ткань *f.*

brocade [bro'keid] парча́.

broil [brɔil] 1. жа́реное мя́со; 2. жа́рить(ся) на огне́; F жа́риться на со́лнце.

broke [brouk] *pt.* от break.

broken ['broukən] 1. *p. pt.* от break; 2. разби́тый, расколо́тый; ~ health надло́мленное здоро́вье.

broker ['broukə] ма́клер.

bronc(h)o ['brɔŋkou] *Am.* полуди́кая ло́шадь *f.*

bronze [brɔnz] 1. бро́нза; 2. бро́нзовый; 3. бронзирова́ть *(im)pf.*; загора́ть на со́лнце.

brooch [broutʃ] бро́шка.

brood [bru:d] 1. вы́водок; стая́; 2. сиде́ть на я́йцах; *fig.* гру́стно размышля́ть.

brook [bruk] руче́й.

broom [bru:m, brum] метла́, ве́ник; **~stick** метлови́ще.

broth [brɔ:θ, brɔθ] бульо́н.

brothel ['brɔθl] публи́чный дом.

brother [brʌðə] брат; собра́т; **~hood** [-hud] бра́тство; **~-in-law** [-rinlɔ] шу́рин; зять *m*; де́верь *m*; своя́к; **~ly** [-li] бра́тский.

brought [brɔ:t] *pt.* и *pt.* от bring.

brow [brau] бровь *f*; вы́ступ (скалы́); **~beat** ['braubi:t] [*irr.* (beat)] запу́гивать [-га́ть].

brown [braun] 1. кори́чневый цвет; 2. кори́чневый; сму́глый; загоре́лый; 3. загора́ть [-ре́ть].

browse [brauz] 1.ощи́пывать, объеда́ть ли́стья; *fig.* чита́ть беспоря́дочно; 2. молоды́е побе́ги *m/pl.*

bruise [bru:z] 1. синя́к, кровоподтёк; 2. ушиба́ть [-би́ть]; подставля́ть синяки́.

brunt [brʌnt] гла́вный уда́р; вся тя́жесть *f.*

brush [brʌʃ] 1. щётка; кисть *f*; чи́стка щёткой; *Am.* ~wood; за́росль *f*; 2. *v/t.* чи́стить щёткой; причёсыва́ть щёткой (во́лосы); ~ up приводи́ть в поря́док; *fig.* освежа́ть в па́мяти; *v/i.* ~ by прошмы́гивать [-гну́ть]; ~ against a p. слегка́ заде́ть кого́-либо (проходя́ ми́мо); **~wood** [brʌʃwud] хво́рост, валёжник.

brusque [brusk] □ гру́бый; ре́зкий.

brut|al ['bru:tl] □ гру́бый; жесто́кий; **~ality** [bru:'tæliti] гру́бость *f*; жесто́кость *f*; **~e** [bru:t] 1. жесто́кий; бессозна́тельный; 2. живо́тное; F скоти́на (руга́тельство).

bubble ['bʌbl] 1. пузы́рь *m*; 2. пузы́риться; кипе́ть; бить ключо́м.

buccaneer [bʌkə'niə] пира́т.

buck [bʌk] 1. *zo.* саме́ц (оле́нь, за́яц и др.); 2. станови́ться на дыбы́; брыка́ться [-кну́ться]; ~ up F встряхну́ться *pf.*; оживля́ться, [-ви́ться].

bucket ['bʌkit] ведро́; бадья́.

buckle ['bʌkl] 1. пря́жка; 2. *v/t.* застёгивать [-тегну́ть] (пря́жкой); *v/i.* ⊕ сгиба́ться [согну́ться] (от давле́ния); ~ to *fig.* подтя́гиваться [-тяну́ться]; принима́ться энерги́чно за де́ло.

buckshot ['bʌkʃɔt] *hunt.* кру́пная дробь *f.*

bud [bʌd] 1. по́чка, буто́н; *fig.* заро́дыш; 2. *v/i.* ♂ дава́ть по́чки; пуска́ть ростки́; *fig.* разви́(ва́)ться.

budge ['bʌdʒ] шевели́ть(ся) [-льну́ть(ся)]; сдвига́ть с ме́ста.

budget ['bʌdʒit] бюдже́т; фина́нсовая сме́та; draft ~ прое́кт госуда́рственного бюдже́та.

buff [bʌf] 1. бу́йволовая ко́жа; 2. тёмно-жёлтый.

buffalo ['bʌfəlou] *zo.* бу́йвол.

buffer ['bʌfə] ⚙ бу́фер; амортиза́тор, де́мпфер.

buffet[1] ['bʌfit] 1. уда́р (руко́й), толчо́к; 2. наноси́ть уда́р (Д).

buffet[2] 1. [~] буфе́т; 2. ['bufei] буфе́тная сто́йка.

buffoon [bʌ'fu:n] шут, фигля́р.

bug [bʌg] клоп; *Am.* насеко́мое.

bugle ['bju:gl] рожо́к, горн.

build [bild] 1. [*irr.*] [по]стро́ить; сооружа́ть [-руди́ть]; [с]вить (гнездо́); ~ on полага́ться [положи́ться] на (В); 2. констру́кция; стиль *m*; телосложе́ние; **~er** ['bildə] строи́тель *m*; подря́дчик; пло́тник; **~ing** [-iŋ] зда́ние; постро́йка; строи́тельство.

built [bilt] *pt.* и *p. pt.* от build.

bulb [bʌlb] ♀ лу́ковица; ла́мпочка

bulge [bʌldʒ] **1.** вы́пуклость *f*; **2.** выпя́чиваться [вы́пятиться], выдава́ться [вы́даться].
bulk [bʌlk] объём; ⚓ вмести́мость *f*; in ~ в нава́лку; in the ~ в це́лом; **~y** [bʌlki] громо́здкий.
bull¹ [bul] бык; ✝ *sl.* спекуля́нт, игра́ющий на повыше́ние; *Am. sl.* неле́пость *f*; противоре́чие.
bull² [~] па́пская бу́лла.
bulldog ['buldɔg] бульдо́г.
bullet ['bulit] пу́ля; ядро́.
bulletin ['bulitin] бюллете́нь *m*.
bullion ['buljən] сли́ток зо́лота и́ли серебра́.
bully ['buli] **1.** задира *m*, забия́ка *m*; **2.** задира́ть; запу́гивать [-га́ть]; **3.** *Am.* F первокла́ссный, великоле́пный; хвастли́вый.
bulwark ['bulwək] ⚔ вал; *mst fig.* опло́т, защи́та.
bum [bʌm] *Am.* F **1.** за́д(ница); ло́дырь *m*, безде́льник, лентя́й; **2.** ло́дырничать.
bumble-bee ['bʌmblbi] шмель *m*.
bump [bʌmp] **1.** столкнове́ние; глухо́й уда́р; ши́шка; *fig.* спосо́бность *f* (of к Д); **2.** ударя́ть(ся) [уда́рить(ся)].
bumper ['bʌmpə] **1.** бока́л, по́лный до краёв; ~ crop F *sl.* небыва́лый урожа́й; **2.** *Am. mot.* амортиза́тор.
bun [bʌn] бу́лочка (с изю́мом).
bunch [bʌntʃ] **1.** свя́зка; пучо́к; па́чка; **2.** свя́зывать в пучо́к.
bundle ['bʌndl] **1.** у́зел; вяза́нка; **2.** *v/t.* собира́ть вме́сте (ве́щи); свя́зывать в у́зел (*a.* ~ up).
bungalow ['bʌŋgəlou] одноэта́жная да́ча, бу́нгало *n indecl.*
bungle ['bʌŋgl] **1.** (плоха́я) небре́жная рабо́та; оши́бка; пу́таница; **2.** неуме́ло, небре́жно рабо́тать; по́ртить рабо́ту.
bunk¹ [bʌŋk] *Am.* вздор.
bunk² [~] ложи́ться спать.
bunny ['bʌni] кро́лик.
buoy [bɔi] ⚓ **1.** ба́кен, буй; **2.** ста́вить ба́кены; подде́рживать на пове́рхности; (*mst* ~ up) *fig.* подде́рживать [-жа́ть]; **~ant** ['bɔiənt] □ плаву́чий; жизнера́достный; бо́дрый.
burden ['bə:dn] **1.** но́ша; тя́жесть *f*; бре́мя *n*; груз; **2.** нагружа́ть [-рузи́ть]; обременя́ть [-ни́ть]; **~some** [-səm] обремени́тельный.
bureau [bjuə'rou, 'bjuərou] конто́рка; конто́ра; бюро́ *n indecl.*; отде́л; **~cracy** [bjuə'rɔkrəsi] бюрокра́тия.
burglar ['bə:glə] вор-взло́мщик; **~y** [-ri] кра́жа со взло́мом.
burial ['beriəl] по́хороны *f/pl.*
burlesque [bə:'lesk] **1.** коми́чный; **2.** карикату́ра, паро́дия; **3.** пароди́ровать (*im*)*pf.*
burly ['bə:li] доро́дный.
burn [bə:n] **1.** ожо́г; клеймо́; **2.** [*irr.*] *v/i.* горе́ть; подгора́ть [-ре́ть] (о пи́ще); же́чь; *v/t.* [с]жечь; сжига́ть [сжечь]; **~er** ['bə:nə] горе́лка.
burnish ['bə:niʃ] **1.** полиро́вка; блеск (мета́лла); **2.** [от]полирова́ть (мета́лл); блесте́ть.
burnt [bə:nt] *pt.* и *p. pt.* от burn.
burrow ['bʌrou] **1.** нора́; **2.** рыть нору́; [по]ры́ться в (кни́гах и т. п.).
burst [bə:st] **1.** разры́в (снаря́да); взрыв *a. fig.*; вспы́шка (гне́ва, пла́мени); **2.** [*irr.*] *v/i.* взрыва́ться [взорва́ться] (о котле́, бо́мбе); прор(ы)ва́ться (о плоти́не); ло́паться [ло́пнуть] (with от Р); ~ forth и́ли out вспы́хивать [-хнуть] (о вражде́, войне́); ~ into tears залива́ться слеза́ми; *v/t.* взрыва́ть [взорва́ть]; разруша́ть [-ру́шить].
bury ['beri] [по]хорони́ть; зары́(ва́)ть.
bus [bʌs] F авто́бус.
bush ['buʃ] куст, куста́рник.
bushel ['buʃl] бу́шель *m* (ме́ра ёмкости сыпу́чих тел в 'Англии [= 36,3 л] и в США [=35,2 л]).
bushy ['buʃi] густо́й.
business ['biznis] де́ло, заня́тие; профе́ссия; ✝ фи́рма; торго́вое предприя́тие; ~ of the day пове́стка дня; ~ (*or* professional) discretion служе́бная обя́занность храни́ть молча́ние; have no ~ to *inf.* не име́ть пра́ва (+ *inf.*); **~-like** [-laik] делово́й; практи́чный.
bust [bʌst] бюст; же́нская грудь *f*.
bustle ['bʌsl] **1.** сумато́ха; суета́; **2.** *v/i.* [по]торопи́ться, [за]суети́ться; *v/t.* [по]торопи́ть.
busy ['bizi] **1.** □ де́ятельный; занято́й (at T); за́нятый; *Am. teleph.* за́нятая (ли́ния); **2.** (*mst* ~ o. s.) занима́ться [заня́ться] (with T).
but [bʌt] **1.** *cj.* но, а; одна́ко; тем не ме́нее; е́сли бы не (*a.* ~ that) **2.** *prp.* кро́ме (Р), за исключе́нием (Р); the last ~ one предпосле́дний; ~ for без (Р); **3.** *adv.* то́лько, лишь; ~ just то́лько что; ~ now лишь тепе́рь; all ~ едва́ не ...; nothing ~ ничего́ кро́ме, то́лько; I cannot ~ *inf.* не могу́ не (+ *inf.*).
butcher ['butʃə] **1.** мясни́к; *fig.* уби́йца *m*; **2.** бить (скот); уби́(ва́)ть; **~y** [-ri] скотобо́йня; резня́.
butler ['bʌtlə] дворе́цкий.
butt [bʌt] **1.** уда́р; прикла́д (ружья́); (*a.* ~ end) то́лстый коне́ц; **~s** *pl.* стре́льбище, полиго́н; *fig.* посме́шище; **2.** ударя́ть голово́й; бода́ть(ся) [бодну́ть]; наты́ка́ться [наткну́ться].
butter ['bʌtə] **1.** ма́сло; **2.** нама́зывать ма́слом; **~cup** ⚘ лю́тик; **~fly** ба́бочка; **~y** ['bʌtəri] **1.** кладова́я; **2.** ма́сляный.
buttocks ['bʌtəks] *pl.* я́годицы *f/pl.*

button ['bʌtn] **1.** пу́говица; кно́пка; буто́н (цветка́); **2.** застёгивать [-тегну́ть] (на пу́говицу).
buttress ['bʌtris] **1.** подпо́ра, усто́й; бык (моста́); *fig.* опо́ра, подде́ржка; **2.** подде́рживать [-жа́ть]; служи́ть опо́рой (Д).
buxom ['bʌksəm] здоро́вый; миловидный.
buy [bai] [*irr.*] *v/t.* покупа́ть [купи́ть] (from у Р); **~er** ['baiə] покупа́тель(ница *f*) *m.*
buzz [bʌz] **1.** жужжа́ние; гул; **2.** *v/i.* [за]жужжа́ть; [за]гуде́ть.
buzzard ['bʌzəd] сары́ч.
by [bai] **1.** *prp.* у (Р), при (П), о́коло (Р); вдоль (Р); ~ **the dozen** дю́жинами; ~ o. s. оди́н *m*, одна́ *f*; ~ land сухи́м путём; ~ rail по желе́зной доро́ге; day ~ day изо дня́ в де́нь; **2.** *adv.* бли́зко, ря́дом; ми́мо; ~ and ~ вско́ре; ~ the ~ ме́жду про́чим; ~ and large *Am.* вообще́ говоря́; **~-election** ['baii'lekʃən] дополни́тельные вы́боры *m/pl.*; **~-gone** про́шлый; **~-law** постановле́ние ме́стной вла́сти; **~-path** обхо́д, обхо́дная доро́га; **~-product** побо́чный проду́кт; **~-stander** свиде́тель(ница *f*) *m*; зри́тель(ница *f*) *m*; **~-street** глуха́я у́лица; переу́лок; **~-way** малопрое́зжая доро́га; **~-word** поговорка.

C

cab [kæb] экипа́ж; такси́ *n indecl.*; 🚂 бу́дка (на парово́зе).
cabbage ['kæbidʒ] капу́ста.
cabin ['kæbin] **1.** хи́жина; бу́дка; ⚓ каю́та; **2.** помеща́ть в те́сную ко́мнату и т. п.
cabinet ['kæbinit] кабине́т; го́рка; я́щик; ≈ Council сове́т мини́стров; **~-maker** столя́р.
cable ['keibl] **1.** ка́бель *m*; кана́т; **2.** *tel.* телеграфи́ровать (*im*)*pf.*; **~gram** [-græm] телегра́мма.
cabman ['kæbmən] изво́зчик.
cacao [kə'kɑ:ou] кака́овое де́рево; кака́о *n indecl.*
cackle ['kækl] **1.** куда́хтанье; гогота́нье; **2.** [за]куда́хтать; [за]гогота́ть.
cad [kæd] F невоспи́танный, гру́бый челове́к.
cadaverous [kə'dævərəs] □ исхуда́лый как труп; тру́пный.
cadence ['keidəns] ♪ каде́нция; модуля́ция.
cadet [kə'det] каде́т.
café ['kæfei] кафе́ *n indecl.*, кафе́-рестора́н.
cafeteria [kæfi'tiəriə] кафете́рий, кафе́-заку́сочная.
age [keidʒ] **1.** кле́тка; лифт; ⚒ склеть *f* (в ша́хтах); **2.** сажа́ть в кле́тку.
cajole [kə'dʒoul] [по]льсти́ть (Д).
cake [keik] **1.** торт; кекс; пиро́жное; **2.** спека́ться [спе́чься].
calami|tous [kə'læmitəs] □ па́губный; бе́дственный; **~ty** [-ti] бе́дствие.
calcify ['kælsifai] превраща́ться в и́звесть.
calculat|e ['kælkjuleit] *v/t.* вычисля́ть [вы́числить]; подсчи́тывать [-ита́ть]; [с]калькули́ровать; *v/i.* рассчи́тывать (on на В); **~ion** [kælkju'leiʃən] вычисле́ние; калькуля́ция; расчёт.
caldron ['kɔ:ldrən] котёл.
calendar ['kælində] **1.** календа́рь *m*; рее́стр; **2.** составля́ть и́ндекс (Р); [за]регистри́ровать.
calf[1] [kɑ:f], *pl.* calves [kɑ:vz] телёнок (*pl.*: теля́та); (или **~-skin**) теля́чья ко́жа, опо́ек.
calf[2] [~], *pl.* calves [~] икра́ (ноги́).
calibre ['kælibə] кали́бр.
calico ['kælikou] ✝ коленко́р; *Am.* си́тец.
call [kɔ:l] **1.** зов, о́клик; *teleph.* вы́зов; *fig.* предложе́ние (ме́ста, ка́федры и т. п.); призы́в; сигна́л; тре́бование; спрос (for на В); визи́т, посеще́ние; on ~ по тре́бованию; **2.** *v/t.* [по]зва́ть; соз(ы)ва́ть; вызыва́ть [вы́звать]; [раз]буди́ть; приз(ы)ва́ть; ~ in тре́бовать наза́д (долг); ~ over де́лать перекли́чку (Р); ~ up призыва́ть на вое́нную слу́жбу; *teleph.* вызыва́ть [вы́звать]; *v/i.* крича́ть [кри́кнуть]; *teleph.* [по]звони́ть; заходи́ть [зайти́] (at в В; on a p. к Д); ~ for [по-] тре́бовать; [по]зва́ть на (В); ~ for a p. заходи́ть [зайти́] за (Т); ~ in F забега́ть [-ежа́ть] (к Д); ~ on навеща́ть [-ести́ть] (В); взыва́ть [воззва́ть] к (Д) (for о П); приз(ы)ва́ть (to do *etc.* сде́лать и т. д.); **~-box** ['kɔ:lbɔks] телефо́нная бу́дка; **~er** ['kɔ:lə] го́сть(я *f*) *m*.
calling ['kɔ:liŋ] призва́ние; профе́ссия.
call-office ['kɔ:lɔfis] телефо́нная ста́нция.
callous ['kæləs] □ огрубе́лый, мозо́листый; *fig.* бессерде́чный.
calm [kɑ:m] **1.** □ споко́йный; безве́тренный; **2.** тишина́; штиль *m*; споко́йствие; **3.** ~ down успока́ивать(ся) [-ко́ить(ся)].
calori|c [kə'lɔrik] **1.** *phys.* теплота́ **2.** теплово́й; **~e** ['kæləri] *phys.* кало́рия.

calumn|iate [kə'lʌmnieit] [o]клеветать; **~iation** [kəlʌmni'eiʃən], **~y** ['kæləmni] клевета.
calve [kɑ:v] [o]телиться; **~s** *pl.* от calf.
cambric ['keimbrik] ✝ батист.
came [keim] *pt.* от come.
camera ['kæmərə] фотографический аппарат; in ~ ⚖ в кабинете судьи.
camomile ['kæməmail] ⚘ ромашка.
camouflage ['kæmu:flɑ:ʃ] ⚔ маскировка; **2.** [за]маскировать(ся).
camp [kæmp] **1.** лагерь *m*; ~ bed походная кровать *f*; **2.** располагаться лагерем; ~ out ночевать на открытом воздухе.
campaign [kæm'pein] **1.** ⚔ поход; кампания; **2** участвовать в походе; проводить кампанию.
camphor ['kæmfə] камфара.
can[1] [kæn] [*irr.*] могу и т. д.; *inf.*: be able = [с]мочь, быть в состоянии; [с]уметь.
can[2] [~] **1.** бидон; банка; **2.** *Am.* консервировать (*im*)*pf.*, *pf. a.* [за-].
canal [kə'næl] канал.
canard [kə'nɑ:] «утка», ложный слух.
canary [kə'nɛəri] канарейка.
cancel ['kænsəl] вычёркивать [вычеркнуть]; аннулировать (*im*)*pf.*; погашать [погасить] (марки); 𝔄 (*a.* ~ out) сокращать [-ратить].
cancer ['kænsə] *ast.* созвездие Рака; ⚕ рак; **~ous** [-rəs] раковый.
candid ['kændid] □ искренний, прямой.
candidate ['kændidit] кандидат(ка) (for на В).
candied ['kændid] засахаренный.
candle ['kændl] свеча; **~stick** [-stik] подсвечник.
cando(u)r ['kændə] искренность *f.*
candy ['kændi] **1.** леденец; *Am.* конфеты *f/pl.*, сласти *f/pl.*; **2.** *v/t.* засахари(ва)ть.
cane [kein] **1.** ⚘ камыш; тростник; трость *f*; **2.** бить палкой.
canker ['kæŋkə] ⚕ гангренозный стоматит; ⚘ рак.
canned [kænd] *Am.* консервированный (продукт).
cannibal ['kænibəl] каннибал.
cannon ['kænən] пушка; орудие.
cannot ['kænɔt] не в состоянии, *s.* can.
canoe [kə'nu:] челнок; байдарка.
canon ['kænən] ♪ канон; правило; критерий.
canopy ['kænəpi] полог; *fig.* небесный свод; ⌂ навес.
cant[1] [kænt] **1.** косяк, наклон; **2.** скашивать [скосить]; наклонять [-нить].
cant[2] [~] **1.** плаксивый тон; ханжество; **2.** говорить на распев; ханжить.
can't [kɑ:nt] F не в состоянии.
canteen [kæn'ti:n] ⚔ лавка; столовая; походная кухня.
canton **1.** ['kæntɔn] кантон; **2.** [kən'tu:n] ⚔ расквартировывать [-овать] (войска).
canvas ['kænvəs] холст; канва; *paint.* картина.
canvass [~] **1.** обсуждение; **2.** *v/t.* обсуждать [-удить]; *v/i.* собирать голоса; искать заказов.
caoutchouc ['kautʃuk] каучук.
cap [kæp] **1.** кепка, фуражка, шапка; ⊕ колпачок, головка; шляпка (гриба); пистон; set one's ~ at a p. заигрывать с кем-либо (о женщине); **2.** присуждать учёную степень (Д); *fig.* довершать [-шить]; F перещеголять.
capab|ility [keipə'biliti] способность *f*; **~le** ['keipəbl] □ способный (of на В), одарённый.
capaci|ous [kə'peiʃəs] □ просторный; объёмистый; **~ty** [kə'pæsiti] объём, вместительность *f*; способность *f*; in the ~ of в качестве (Р).
cape[1] [keip] плащ; пелерина.
cape[2] [~] мыс.
caper ['keipə] скачок; шалость *f*, проказа; cut **~s** дурачиться.
capital ['kæpitl] **1.** □ основной, капитальный; (*crime*) уголовный; (*sentence*, *punishment*) смертный; **2.** столица; капитал; (или ~ letter) прописная буква; **~ism** ['kæpitəlizm] капитализм; **~ize** [kə'pitəlaiz] капитализировать (*im*)*pf.*
capitulate [kə'pitjuleit] сд(ав)аться (to Д).
capric|e [kə'pri:s] каприз, причуда; **~ious** [kə'priʃəs] □ капризный.
capsize [kæp'saiz] *v/i.* ⚓ опрокидываться [-кинуться]; *v/t.* опрокидывать [-кинуть] (лодку и т.п.).
capsule ['kæpsju:l] капсюль *m*; ⚕ капсула.
captain ['kæptin] ⚔ капитан; руководитель(ница *f*) *m*; ⚓ капитан, командир.
caption ['kæpʃən] *part. Am.* заголовок (статьи, главы); (кино) надпись на экране.
captious ['kæpʃəs] □ придирчивый.
captiv|ate ['kæptiveit] пленять [-нить]; очаровывать [-овать]; **~e** ['kæptiv] **1.** пленник; пленный; **2.** взятый в плен; **~ity** [kæp'tiviti] плен.
capture ['kæptʃə] **1.** захватывать силой; брать в плен; **2.** поимка; захват; добыча; ⚓ приз.
car [kɑ:] вагон; автомобиль *m.*
caramel ['kærəmel] карамель *f.*
caravan [kærə'væn] караван; дом-автоприцеп.
caraway ['kærəwei] ⚘ тмин.
carbine ['kɑ:bain] карабин.
carbohydrate ['kɑ:bou'haidreit] ⚗ углевод.

carbon ['ka:bən] ⚗ углеро́д; (и́ли ~ paper) копи́рка.
carburet(t)or ['ka:bjuretə] *mot.* карбюра́тор.
carcas|e, *mst* **~s** ['ka:kəs] труп; ту́ша.
card ['ka:d] ка́рта; ка́рточка; **~board** [ka:dbɔ:d] карто́н.
cardigan ['ka:digən] шерстяно́й дже́мпер.
cardinal ['ka:dinl] **1.** □ гла́вный, основно́й; кардина́льный; ~ number коли́чественное числи́тельное; **2.** кардина́л.
card-index ['ka:dindeks] картоте́ка.
card-sharp(er) [ka:dʃa:pə] шу́лер.
care [kɛə] **1.** забо́та; попече́ние; внима́ние; ~ of (*abbr.* c/o) по а́дресу (Р); take ~ of [с]бере́чь (В); [по-] смотре́ть за (Т); with ~! осторо́жно!; **2.** име́ть жела́ние, [за-] хоте́ть (to: + *inf.*); ~ for: a) [по]забо́титься о (П); b) люби́ть (В); пита́ть интере́с к (Д); F I don't ~! мне всё равно́!; well **~d-for** вы́холенный; хорошо́ обеспе́ченный.
career [kə'riə] **1.** карье́р; *fig.* карье́ра, успе́х; **2.** бы́стро продвига́ться.
carefree ['kɛəfri:] беззабо́тный.
careful ['kɛəful] □ забо́тливый (for о П); аккура́тный; внима́тельный (к Д); **~ness** [-nis] забо́тливость *f.*
careless [-lis] □ легкомы́сленный; небре́жный; **~ness** [-nis] небре́жность *f.*
caress [kə'res] **1.** ла́ска; **2.** ласка́ть; [по]гла́дить.
caretaker ['kɛəteikə] дво́рник; сто́рож.
carfare ['ka:fɛə] *Am.* проездны́е (де́ньги).
cargo ['ka:gou] ⚓ груз.
caricature ['kærikə'tjuə] **1.** карикату́ра; **2.** изобража́ть в карикату́рном ви́де.
carn|al ['ka:nl] □ чу́вственный, пло́тский; **~ation** [ka:'neiʃən] ⚘ гвозди́ка.
carnival ['ka:nivəl] карнава́л.
carnivorous [ka:'nivərəs] плотоя́дный.
carol ['kærəl] **1.** рожде́ственский гимн; **2.** воспе́(ва́)ть, сла́вить.
carous|e [kə'rauz] **1.** *a.* **~al** [-əl] пиру́шка, попо́йка; **2.** пирова́ть.
carp[1] [ka:p] *zo.* карп.
carp[2] [~] прид(и)ра́ться (at к Д).
carpent|er ['ka:pintə] пло́тник; **~ry** [-tri] пло́тничное де́ло.
carpet [ka:pit] **1.** ковёр; **2.** устила́ть ковро́м.
carriage ['kæridʒ] экипа́ж; перево́зка; тра́нспорт; **~-drive** подъе́зд; ~ **free,** ~ **paid** пересы́лка беспла́тно.
carrier ['kæriə] посы́льный; носи́льщик; ⚔ транспортёр.
carrot ['kærət] морко́вь *f.*
carry ['kæri] **1.** *v/t.* носи́ть, [по-] нести́; вози́ть, [по]везти́; ~ o. s. держа́ться, вести́ себя́; be carried быть при́нятым; ✝ ~ forward и́ли over переноси́ть на другу́ю страни́цу; ~ on продолжа́ть [-до́лжить]; вести́ (де́ло, борьбу́ и т. п.); ~ out и́ли through доводи́ть до конца́; выполня́ть [вы́полнить]; *v/i.* доноси́ться [донести́сь]; ⚔ долета́ть [долете́ть] (о снаря́де); **2.** ⚔ дальнобо́йность *f*; да́льность полёта (снаря́да).
cart [ka:t] **1.** теле́га, пово́зка; **2.** везти́ в теле́ге; **~age** ['ka:tidʒ] перево́зка, сто́имость перево́зки.
carter ['ka:tə] во́зчик.
cartilage ['ka:tilidʒ] хрящ.
carton ['ka:tən] карто́н.
cartoon [ka:'tu:n] карикату́ра; ⊕ карто́н.
cartridge ['ka:tridʒ] патро́н; заря́д.
carve [ka:v] ре́зать (по де́реву); [вы́]гравирова́ть; нареза́ть [наре́зать] (мя́со); **~r** ['ka:və] ре́зчик (по де́реву); гравёр; нож для разде́лки мя́са.
carving ['ka:viŋ] резьба́ (по де́реву).
case[1] [keis] **1.** я́щик; футля́р; су́мка; витри́на; *typ.* набо́рная ка́сса; **2.** класть в я́щик.
case[2] [~] слу́чай; положе́ние; обстоя́тельство; ⚖ суде́бное де́ло.
case-harden ['keisha:dn] ⊕ цементи́ровать (сталь) (*im*)*pf.*; *fig.* де́лать нечувстви́тельным.
casement ['keismənt] ство́рный око́нный переплёт.
cash [kæʃ] **1.** де́ньги; нали́чные де́ньги *f/pl.*; ~ down, for ~ за нали́чный расчёт; ~ on delivery нало́женным платежо́м; ~ register ка́ссовый аппара́т; **2.** получа́ть де́ньги по (Д); **~-book** ка́ссовая кни́га; **~-ier** [kæ'ʃiə] касси́р(ша).
casing ['keisiŋ] опра́ва; ра́ма; обши́вка, оби́вка.
cask [ka:sk] бо́чка, бочо́нок.
casket ['ka:skit] шкату́лка; *Am.* гроб.
casserole ['kæsəroul] кастрю́ля.
cassock ['kæsək] ря́са, сута́на.
cast [ka:st] **1.** бросо́к, мета́ние; ги́псовый сле́пок; ⚓ броса́ние (я́коря); *thea.* распределе́ние роле́й; соста́в исполни́телей; **2.** [*irr.*] *v/t.* броса́ть [бро́сить]; кида́ть [ки́нуть]; мета́ть [-тну́ть]; ⊕ отли́(ва́)ть (мета́ллы); *thea.* распределя́ть [-ли́ть] (ро́ли); ~ iron чугу́н; ~ lots броса́ть жре́бий; be ~ down быть в уны́нии; *v/i.* ~ about for обду́м(ыв)ать (В).
castaway ['ka:stəwei] **1.** па́рия, отве́рженец; ⚓ потерпе́вший кораблекруше́ние; **2.** отве́рженный.
caste [ka:st] ка́ста.

castigate ['kæstigeit] нака́зывать [-за́ть]; *fig.* жесто́ко критикова́ть.
cast-iron чугу́нный.
castle ['kɑ:sl] за́мок; *chess* ладья́.
castor[1] ['kɑ:stə]: ~ oil касто́ровое ма́сло.
castor[2] [~] колёсико (на но́жке ме́бели).
castrate [kæs'treit] кастри́ровать (*im*)*pf*.
casual ['kæʒjuəl] □ случа́йный; небре́жный; **~ty** [-ti] несча́стный слу́чай; *pl.* ⚔ поте́ри (на войне́) *f/pl.*
cat [kæt] ко́шка.
catalog, *Brt.* **~ue** ['kætəlɔg] 1. катало́г; прейскура́нт; 2. каталогизи́ровать (*im*)*pf.*, вноси́ть в катало́г.
cataract ['kætərækt] водопа́д; ⚕ катара́кта.
catarrh [kə'tɑ:] ката́р.
catastrophe [kə'tæstrəfi] катастро́фа.
catch [kætʃ] 1. по́имка; захва́т; уло́в; добы́ча; лову́шка; ⊕ задви́жка; шпингале́т; 2. [*irr.*] *v/t.* лови́ть [пойма́ть]; схва́тывать [схвати́ть]; заража́ться [зарази́ться] (Т); поспе́(ва́)ть к (по́езду и т. п.); ~ cold простужа́ться [-уди́ться]; ~ a p.'s eye улавливать взгляд (Р); ~ up догоня́ть [догна́ть]; F поднима́ть [-ня́ть]; 3. *v/i.* зацепля́ться [-пи́ться]; F ~ on станови́ться мо́дным; ~ up with догоня́ть [догна́ть] (В); **~er** ['kætʃə] лове́ц; **~ing** ['kætʃiŋ] *fig.* зарази́тельный (смех); привлека́тельный; ⚕ зарази́тельный; **~word** мо́дное слове́чко; загла́вное сло́во.
catechism ['kætikizm] катехи́зис.
categor|ical [kæti'gɔrikəl] □ категори́ческий; реши́тельный; **~y** ['kætigəri] катего́рия, разря́д.
cater ['keitə]: ~ for поставля́ть прови́зию (Д); *fig.* [по]забо́титься о (П).
caterpillar *zo.*, ⊕ ['kætəpilə] гу́сеница.
catgut ['kætgʌt] кише́чная струна́.
cathedral [kə'θi:drəl] собо́р.
Catholic ['kæθəlik] 1. като́лик; 2. католи́ческий.
cattle [kætl] кру́пный рога́тый скот; **~-breeding** скотово́дство; **~-plague** чума́.
caught [kɔ:t] *pt.* и *pt.* от catch.
cauldron ['kɔ:ldrən] котёл.
cauliflower ['kɔliflauə] ♣ цветна́я капу́ста.
caulk [kɔ:k] ⚓ [про]конопа́тить.
caus|al ['kɔ:zəl] □ причи́нный; **~e** [kɔ:z] 1. причи́на, основа́ние; по́вод; ⚖ де́ло, проце́сс; 2. причиня́ть [-ни́ть]; вызыва́ть [вы́звать]; **~eless** ['kɔ:zlis] □ беспричи́нный, необосно́ванный.
caution ['kɔ:ʃən] 1. (пред)осторо́жность *f*; предостереже́ние; ~ money зало́г; 2. предостерега́ть [-ре́чь] (against от Р).
cautious ['kɔ:ʃəs] □ осторо́жный; предусмотри́тельный; **~ness** [-nis] осторо́жность *f*; предусмотри́тельность *f*.
cavalry ['kævəlri] ⚔ ко́нница.
cave ['keiv] 1. пеще́ра; 2. ~ in: *v/i.* оседа́ть [осе́сть], опуска́ться [-сти́ться].
cavil ['kævil] 1. приди́рка; 2. прид(и)ра́ться (at, about к Д, за В).
cavity ['kæviti] впа́дина; по́лость *f*.
caw [kɔ:] 1. ка́рканье; 2. [за]ка́ркать.
cease [si:s] *v/i.* перест(ав)а́ть; *v/t.* прекраща́ть [-крати́ть]; приоста́навливать [-нови́ть]; **~less** ['si:slis] □ непреры́вный, непреста́нный.
cede [si:d] уступа́ть [-пи́ть] (В).
ceiling ['si:liŋ] потоло́к; *attr.* максима́льный; ~ price преде́льная цена́.
celebrat|e ['selibreit] [от]пра́здновать; **~ed** [-id] знамени́тый; **~ion** [seli'breiʃən] торжества́ *n/pl.*; пра́зднование.
celebrity [si'lebriti] знамени́тость *f*.
celerity [-riti] быстрота́.
celery ['seləri] ♣ сельдере́й.
celestial [si'lestjəl] □ небе́сный.
celibacy ['selibəsi] целиба́т; обе́т безбра́чия.
cell [sel] яче́йка; тюре́мная ка́мера; ке́лья; ⚡ элеме́нт.
cellar ['selə] подва́л; ви́нный по́греб.
cement [si'ment] 1. цеме́нт; 2. цементи́ровать (*im*)*pf*.
cemetery ['semitri] кла́дбище.
censor ['sensə) 1. це́нзор; 2. подверга́ть цензу́ре; **~ious** [sen'sɔ:riəs] □ стро́гий, критику́ющий; **~ship** ['sensəʃip] цензу́ра.
censure [senʃə] 1. осужде́ние, порица́ние; 2. осужда́ть [осуди́ть], порица́ть.
census ['sensəs] пе́репись *f*.
cent [sent] со́тня *f*; *Am.* цент (0,01 до́ллара); per ~ проце́нт.
centennial [sen'tenjəl] столе́тний; происходя́щий раз в сто лет.
center *s.* centre.
centi|grade ['sentigreid] стогра́дусный; **~metre** [-mi:tə] сантиме́тр; **~pede** [-pi:d] *zo.* сороконо́жка.
central ['sentrəl] □ центра́льный; гла́вный; ~ office центра́льная конто́ра; ~ station гла́вный вокза́л; **~ize** [-laiz] централизова́ть (*im*)*pf*.
centre ['sentə] 1. центр; средото́чие; 2. [с]концентри́ровать(ся); сосредото́чи(ва)ть(ся).
century ['sentʃəri] столе́тие, век.
cereal ['siəriəl] хле́бный злак; *Am.* ка́ша.
ceremon|ial [seri'mounjəl] □ фор-

мáльный; церемониáльный; **~ious** [-njəs] церемóнный; жемáнный; **~y** ['seriməni] церемóния.

certain ['sə:tn] □ определённый; увéренный; нéкий; нéкоторый; **~ty** [-ti] увéренность *f*; определённость *f*.

certi|ficate **1.** [sə'tifikit] свидéтельство; сертификáт; ~ of birth свидéтельство о рождéнии, мéтрика; **2.** [-keit] вы́дать пи́сьменное удостоверéние (Д); **~fication** [sə:tifi'keiʃən] удостоверéние; **~fy** ['sə:tifai] удостоверя́ть [-éрить]; **~tude** [-tju:d] увéренность *f*.

cessation [se'seiʃən] прекращéние.

cession ['seʃən] устýпка, передáча.

cesspool ['sespu:l] вы́гребная я́ма; стóчный колóдец.

chafe [tʃeif] *v/t.* натирáть [натерéть]; нагрé(вá)ть; *v/i.* раздражáться [-жи́ться], нéрвничать.

chaff [tʃɑ:f] **1.** мяки́на; отбрóсы *m/pl.*; F подшýчивание, поддрáзнивание; **2.** мéлко нарéзать (солóму и т. п.); F подшýчивать [-шути́ть] над (Т), поддрáзнивать [-зни́ть].

chagrin ['ʃægrin] **1.** досáда, огорчéние; **2.** досаждáть [досади́ть] (Д); огорчáть [-чи́ть].

chain [tʃein] **1.** цепь *f*; **~s** *pl. fig.* окóвы *f/pl.*; ýзы *f/pl.*; **2.** скóвывать [скoвáть]; держáть в цепя́х; *fig.* прикóвывать [-овáть].

chair [tʃɛə] стул; кáфедра; председáтельское мéсто; be in the ~ председáтельствовать; **~man** ['tʃɛəmən] председáтель *m*.

chalk [tʃɔ:k] **1.** мел; **2.** писáть, рисовáть мéлом; (*mst* ~ up) запи́сывать [-исáть] (долг) ~ out набрáсывать [-бросáть]; намечáть [-éтить].

challenge ['tʃælindʒ] **1.** вы́зов; ⚔ óклик (часовóго); *part.* ⚖ отвóд (присяжных); **2.** вызывáть [вы́звать]; оспáривать [оспóрить]; [по]трéбовать (внимáния).

chamber ['tʃeimbə] кóмната; палáта; **~s** *pl.* контóра адвокáта; кáмера судьи́; **~maid** гóрничная.

chamois ['ʃæmwɑ:] **1.** сéрна; ['ʃæmi] зáмша; **2.** жёлто-кори́чневый.

champion ['tʃæmpjən] **1.** чемпиóн (-ка); победи́тель(ница) *f*) *m*; защи́тник (-ница); **2.** защищáть [-ити́ть]; борóться за (В).

chance [tʃɑ:ns] **1.** случáйность *f*; риск (в игрé); удáча; удóбный слýчай; шанс (of на В); by ~ случáйно; take a ~ рисковáть [-кнýть]; **2.** случáйный; **3.** *v/i.* случáться [-чи́ться]; ~ upon случáйно найти́ *pf.*; *v/t.* F прóбовать наудáчу.

chancellor ['tʃɑ:nsələ] кáнцлер.

chandelier [ʃændi'liə] люстра.

chandler ['tʃɑ:ndlə] лáвочник.

change ['tʃeindʒ] **1.** перемéна, изменéние; смéна (белья́); мéлочь *f*, сдáча (о дéньгáх); **2.** *v/t.* [по-] менять; изменя́ть [-ни́ть], переменя́ть[-ни́ть]; обмéнивать[-ня́ть]; размéнивать [-ня́ть] (дéньги); *v/i.* [по]меня́ться; изменя́ться [-ни́ться]; переменя́ться [-ни́ться]; переодé(вá)ться; обмéниваться [-ня́ться]; 🚂 пересáживаться [-сéсть]; **~able** ['tʃeindʒəbl] □ непостоя́нный, перемéнчивый; **~less** [-lis] □ неизмéнный, постоя́нный.

channel ['tʃænl] рýсло; фарвáтер; проли́в; *fig.* путь *m*; истóчник.

chant [tʃɑ:nt] **1.** песнь *f*; песнопéние; **2.** петь монотóнно; *fig.* вос[пé(вá)ть].

chaos ['keiɔs] хаóс.

chap¹ [tʃæp] **1.** щель *f*; трéщина; **2.** [по]трéскаться.

chap² [~] F мáлый, пáрень *m*.

chapel ['tʃæpəl] часóвня; капéлла.

chaplain ['tʃæplin] свящéнник.

chapter ['tʃæptə] главá.

char [tʃɑ:] обжигáть [обжéчь]; обýгли(ва)ть(ся).

character ['kæriktə] харáктер; ли́чность *f*; *thea.* дéйствующее лицó; бýква; **~istic** [kæriktə'ristik] **1.** (**~ally**) характéрный; типи́чный (of для Р); **2.** характéрная осóбенность *f*; **~ize** ['kæriktəraiz] характеризовáть (*im*)*pf.*; изображáть [-рази́ть].

charcoal ['tʃɑ:koul] древéсный ýголь *m*.

charge [tʃɑ:dʒ] **1.** заря́д; нагрýзка; поручéние; ценá; обвинéние; атáка; *fig.* попечéние, забóта; **~s** *pl.* ✝ расхóды *m/pl.*; издéржки *f/pl.*; be in ~ of завéдовать (Т); **2.** *v/t.* заряжáть [-яди́ть]; нагружáть [-узи́ть]; поручáть [-чи́ть] (Д); обвиня́ть [-ни́ть] (with в П); назначáть [-нáчить] (цéну) (to на В); *Am.* утверждáть [-рди́ть].

charitable ['tʃæritəbl] □ благотвори́тельный; милосéрдный.

charity ['tʃæriti] милосéрдие; благотвори́тельность *f*.

charlatan ['ʃɑ:lətən] шарлатáн.

charm [tʃɑ:m] **1.** амулéт; *fig.* чáры *f/pl.*; обая́ние, очаровáние; **2.** заколдóвывать [-довáть]; *fig.* очарóвывать [-овáть]; **~ing** ['tʃɑ:miŋ] □ очаровáтельный, обая́тельный.

chart [tʃɑ:t] **1.** ⚓ морскáя кáрта; **2.** наноси́ть на кáрту; черти́ть кáрту.

charter ['tʃɑ:tə] **1.** хáртия; прáво; привилéгия; **2.** даровáть привилéгию (Д); ⚓ [за]фрахтовáть (сýдно).

charwoman ['tʃɑ:wumən] подёнщица.

chary ['tʃɛəri] □ осторóжный; скупóй (на словá и т. п.).

chase [tʃeis] **1.** погóня *f*; охóта; **2.** охóтиться за (Т); преслéдовать; прогоня́ть [-гнáть].

chasm [kæzm] бéздна, прóпасть *f*.
chaste [tʃeist] □ целомýдренный.
chastity ['tʃæstiti] целомýдрие; дéвственность *f*.
chat [tʃæt] **1.** бесéда; **2.** [по]болтáть, [по]бесéдовать.
chattels ['tʃætlz] *pl.* (*mst* goods and ~) имýщество, вéщи *f/pl.*
chatter [tʃætə] **1.** болтовня́ *f*; щебетáние) **2.** [по]болтáть; **~er** [-rə] болтýн(ья).
chatty ['tʃæti] болтли́вый.
chauffeur ['ʃoufə] води́тель *m*, шофёр.
cheap [tʃi:p] □ дешёвый; *fig.* плохóй; **~en** ['tʃi:pən] [по]дешевéть; снижáть цéну (В); *fig.* унижáть [уни́зить].
cheat [tʃi:t] **1.** обмáнщик, плут; обмáн; **2.** обмáнывать [-нýть].
check [tʃek] **1.** *chess* шах; препя́тствие; останóвка; контрóль *m* (on над Т), провéрка (on P); *Am.* багáжная квитáнция; *Am.* † чек; клéтчатая ткань *f*; **2.** проверя́ть [-вéрить]; [про]контроли́ровать; останáвливать [-нови́ть]; препя́тствовать; **~er** ['tʃekə] контролёр; **~s** *pl. Am.* шáшки *f/pl.*; **~ing-room** *Am.* кáмера хранéния (багажá); **~mate 1.** шах и мат; **2.** дéлать мат; **~-up** *Am.* стрóгая провéрка.
cheek [tʃi:k] щекá (*pl.*: щёки); F нáглость *f*, дéрзость *f*.
cheer [tʃiə] **1.** весéлье; одобри́тельные вóзгласы *m/pl.*; **2.** *v/t.* ободря́ть [-ри́ть]; поощря́ть [-ри́ть]; привéтствовать грóмкими вóзгласами; *v/i.* ликовáть; **~ful** ['tʃiəful] □ бóдрый, весёлый; **~less** [-lis] □ уны́лый, мрáчный; **~y** [-ri] □ живóй, весёлый, рáдостный.
cheese [tʃi:z] сыр.
chemical ['kemikəl] **1.** □ хими́ческий; **2.** **~s** [-s] *pl.* хими́ческие препарáты *m/pl.*, химикáлии *f/pl.*
chemist ['kemist] хи́мик; аптéкарь *m*; **~ry** ['kemistri] хи́мия.
cheque [tʃek] † бáнковый чек.
chequer ['tʃekə] **1.** *mst* **~s** *pl.* клéтчатый узóр; **2.** графи́ть в клéтку.
cherish ['tʃeriʃ] лелéять (надéжду); храни́ть (в пáмяти); нéжно [люби́ть.]
cherry ['tʃeri] ви́шня.
chess [tʃes] шáхматы *f/pl.*; **~board** шáхматная доскá; **~man** шáхматная фигýра.
chest [tʃest] я́щик, сундýк; груднáя клéтка; ~ of drawers комóд.
chestnut ['tʃesnʌt] **1.** каштáн; F изби́тый анекдóт; **2.** каштáновый; гнедóй (о лóшади).
chevy ['tʃevi] *Brit.* F **1.** охóта; погóня; **2.** гнáться за (Т); уд(и)рáть.
chew [tʃu:] жевáть; размышля́ть; **~ing-gum** ['tʃu:iŋgʌm] жевáтельная рези́нка.
chicane [ʃi'kein] **1.** приди́рка; **2.** прид(и)рáться к (Д).
chick [tʃik], **~en** ['tʃikin] цыплёнок; птенéц; **~en-pox** ⚕ вéтряная óспа.
chief [tʃi:f] **1.** □ глáвный; руководя́щий; ~ clerk начáльник отдéла; **2.** главá, руководи́тель (-ница *f*) *m*; ...-in-~ глáвный ...; **~tain** ['tʃi:ftən] вождь *m* (клáна); атамáн.
chilblain ['tʃilblein] отморóженное мéсто.
child [tʃaild] ребёнок, дитя́ *n* (*pl.*: дéти); from a ~ с дéтства; with ~ берéменная; **~birth** рóды *m/pl.*; **~hood** [-hud] дéтство; **~ish** ['tʃaildiʃ] □ дéтский; **~like** [-laik] как ребёнок; неви́нный; **~ren** ['tʃildrən] *pl.* от child.
chill [tʃil] **1.** хóлод; хóлодность *f*; ⚕ простýда; **2.** холóдный; расхолáживающий; **3.** *v/t.* охлаждáть [- лади́ть]; [о]студи́ть; *v/i.* охлаждáться [-лади́ться]; **~y** ['tʃili] зя́бкий; холóдный.
chime [tʃaim] **1.** звон колоколóв; бой часóв; *fig.* гармони́чное сочетáние; **2.** [по]звони́ть (о колоколáх); [про]би́ть (о часáх); *fig.* соотвéтствовать; гармони́ровать.
chimney ['tʃimni] дымовáя трубá; лáмповое стеклó.
chin [tʃin] подбородóк.
china ['tʃainə] фарфóр.
Chinese ['tʃai'ni:z] **1.** китáец (-аянка); **2.** китáйский.
chink [tʃiŋk] щель *f*, сквáжина.
chip [tʃip] **1.** щéпка, лучи́на; стрýжка; оскóлок (стеклá); **2.** *v/t.* отбивáть края́ (посýды и т. д.); *v/i.* отлáмываться [отломáться].
chirp [tʃə:p] **1.** чири́канье; щебетáние; **2.** чири́кать [-кнуть]; [за-] щебетáть.
chisel ['tʃizl] **1.** долотó, стамéска; **2.** [из]вая́ть; *sl.* надý(вá)ть, обмáнывать [-нýть].
chit-chat ['tʃit-tʃæt] болтовня́.
chivalr|ous ['ʃivəlrəs] □ ры́царский; **~y** [-ri] ры́царство.
chlor|ine ['klɔ:ri:n] ⚗ хлор; **~oform** ['klɔrəfɔ:m] **1.** хлорофóрм; **2.** хлороформи́ровать (*im*)*pf*.
chocolate ['tʃɔkəlit] шоколáд.
choice [tʃɔis] **1.** вы́бор; отбóр; альтернати́ва; **2.** □ отбóрный.
choir ['kwaiə] хор.
choke [tʃouk] **1.** *v/t.* [за]души́ть; засоря́ть [-ри́ть]; ⚡ дросселировáть; (*mst* ~ down) глотáть с трудóм; дави́ться (with от Р); задыхáться [-дохнýться]; **2.** припáдок удýшья; ⊕ заслóнка.
choose [tʃu:z] [*irr.*] выбирáть [вы́брать]; предпочитáть [-чéсть]; ~ to *inf.* хотéть (+ *inf.*).
chop [tʃɔp] **1.** отбивнáя котлéта; **~s** *pl.* чéлюсть *f*; **2.** *v/t.* ⊕ стёсывать [стесáть]; долби́ть; [на]руби́ть; [на]кроши́ть; *v/i.* колебáть-

ся; меня́ться, перемени́ться *pf.* (о ве́тре); ~per ['tʃɔpə] коса́рь (нож) *m*; лесору́б; колу́н; ~py ['tʃɔpi] неспоко́йный (о мо́ре).
choral ['kɔrəl] □ хорово́й; ~(e) [kɔ'rɑ:l] ♪ хора́л.
chord [kɔ:d] струна́; ♪ акко́рд; созву́чие.
chore [tʃɔ:] *Am.* подённая рабо́та; рути́нная дома́шняя рабо́та.
chorus ['kɔ:rəs] 1. хор; му́зыка для хо́ра; 2. петь хо́ром.
chose [tʃouz] *pt.* от choose; ~n (~n) 1. *p. pt.* от choose; 2. и́збранный.
Christ [kraist] Христо́с.
christen ['krisn] [о]крести́ть; ~ing [-iŋ] крести́ны *f/pl.*; креще́ние.
Christian ['kristjən] 1. христиа́нский; ~ name и́мя (в отли́чие от фами́лии); 2. христиани́н (-а́нка); ~ity [kristi'æniti] христиа́нство.
Christmas ['krisməs] рождество́.
chromium ['kroumiəm] ⚗ хром; ~-plated покры́тый хро́мом.
chronic ['krɔnik] (~ally) хрони́ческий; ⚕ застаре́лый; P отврати́тельный; ~le [~l] 1. хро́ника, ле́топись *f*; 2. вести́ хро́нику (P).
chronolog|ical [krɔnə'lɔdʒikəl] □ хронологи́ческий; ~y [krə'nɔlədʒi] хроноло́гия.
chubby ['tʃʌbi] F по́лный, то́лстый.
chuck[1] [tʃʌk] 1. куда́хтанье; цыплёнок; my ~! голу́бчик !; 2. [за-] куда́хтать.
chuck[2] [~] 1. броса́ть [бро́сить]; F швыря́ть [-рну́ть]; 2. F увольне́ние.
chuckle ['tʃʌkl] посме́иваться.
chum [tʃʌm] F 1. това́рищ; закады́чный друг; 2. быть в дру́жбе.
chump [tʃʌmp] коло́да, чурба́н; F «башка́».
chunk [tʃʌŋk] F ломо́ть *m*; болва́н.
church [tʃə:rʃ] це́рковь *f*; ~ service богослуже́ние; ~yard кла́дбище.
churl [tʃə:l] гру́бый челове́к; ~ish ['tʃə:liʃ] □ скупо́й; гру́бый.
churn [tʃə:n] 1. маслобо́йка; 2. сбива́ть ма́сло; *fig.* взба́лтывать [взболта́ть]; вспе́ни(ва)ть.
cider ['saidə] сидр.
cigar [si'gɑ:] сига́ра.
cigarette [sigə'ret] папиро́са, сигаре́та; ~-case портсига́р.
cigar-holder мундшту́к.
cinch [sintʃ] *Am. sl.* не́что надёжное, ве́рное.
cincture ['siŋktʃə] по́яс; опоя́сывание.
cinder ['sində] шлак; ока́лина; ~s *pl.* зола́; ~-path *sport*: гарева́я доро́жка.
cinema ['sinimə] кинемато́граф, кино́ *n indecl.*
cinnamon ['sinəmən] кори́ца.
cipher ['saifə] 1. шифр; ци́фра; нуль *m or* ноль *m*; 2. зашифро́вывать [-ова́ть]; вычисля́ть [вы́числить]; высчи́тывать [вы́считать].
circle ['sə:kl] 1. круг; окру́жность *f*; орби́та; кружо́к; сфе́ра; *thea.* я́рус; 2. враща́ться вокру́г (P); соверша́ть круги́, кружи́ть(ся).
circuit ['sə:kit] кругооборо́т; объе́зд; о́круг (суде́бный); ⚡ цепь *f*, ко́нтур; ⚡ short ~ коро́ткое замыка́ние; ✈ кругово́й полёт.
circular ['sə:kjulə] 1. □ кру́глый, кругово́й; ~ letter циркуля́р, циркуля́рное письмо́; ~ note ✝ ба́нковый аккредити́в; 2. циркуля́р; проспе́кт.
circulat|e ['sə:kjuleit] *v/i.* распространя́ться [-ни́ться]; име́ть кругово́е движе́ние; циркули́ровать; ~ing [-iŋ]: ~ library библиоте́ка с вы́дачей книг на́ дом; ~ion [sə:kju'leiʃən] кровообраще́ние; циркуля́ция; тира́ж (газе́т и т. п.); *fig.* распростране́ние (слу́хов и т. п.).
circum... ['sə:kəm] *pref.* (в сло́жных слова́х) вокру́г, круго́м; ~ference [sə'kʌmfərəns] окру́жность *f*; перифери́я; ~jacent [sə:kəm'dʒeisnt] окружа́ющий; ~locution [-lə'kju:ʃən] многоречи́вость *f*; ~navigate [-'nævigeit] соверша́ть пла́вание вокру́г (P); ~scribe ['sə:kəmskraib] ⩓ опи́сывать [описа́ть] (круг); *fig.* ограни́чи(ва)ть (права́ и т. п.); ~spect [-spekt] □ осмотри́тельный, осторо́жный; ~stance ['sə:kəmstəns] обстоя́тельство; ~stantial [sə:kəm'stænʃəl] □ обстоя́тельный, подро́бный; ~vent [-'vent] обходи́ть [обойти́] (зако́н и т. п.).
cistern ['sistən] бак; водоём; цисте́рна.
cit|ation [sai'teiʃən] цита́та, ссы́лка; цити́рование; ~e [sait] ссыла́ться [сосла́ться] на (В).
citizen ['sitizn] граждани́н (-да́нка); ~ship [-ʃip] гражда́нство.
citron ['sitrən] цитро́н.
city ['siti] го́род; *attr.* городско́й; 2. the ♀ делово́й кварта́л в Ло́ндоне; ♀ article биржево́й бюллете́нь *m*; статья́ в газе́те по фина́нсовым и комме́рческим вопро́сам.
civic ['sivik] гражда́нский; ~s [-s] *pl.* ⚖ гражда́нские дела́ *n/pl.*; осно́вы гражда́нственности.
civil ['sivil] □ гражда́нский; шта́тский; ве́жливый; ⚖ гражда́нский (противополо́жный уголо́вному); ~ servant чино́вник; ~ service госуда́рственная слу́жба; ~ian [si'viljən] ⚔ шта́тский; ~ity [si'viliti] ве́жливость *f*; ~ization [sivilai'zeiʃən] цивилиза́ция; ~ize ['sivilaiz] цивилизова́ть (*im*)*pf.*
clad [klæd] *pt.* и *p. pt.* от clothe.
claim [kleim] 1. предъявля́ть прете́нзию на (В); [по]тре́бовать; заявля́ть права́; утвержда́ть [-рди́ть]; заявля́ть права́ на (В); 2. тре́бование; иск; прете́нзия; ~ to be

выдавáть себя́ за (В); **~ant** ['kleimənt] претендéнт; ⚖ истéц.
clairvoyant [klɛə'vɔiənt] яснови́дец.
clamber ['klæmbə] [вс]кара́бкаться.
clammy ['klæmi] □ клéйкий, ли́пкий; холóдный и влáжный.
clamo(u)r ['klæmə] **1.** шум, кри́ки *m/pl.*; протéсты *m/pl.* (шу́мные); **2.** шу́мно трéбовать (Р).
clamp [klæmp] ⊕ скобá; скрéпа; зажи́м; **2.** скрепля́ть [-пи́ть]; заж(им)áть; смыкáть [сомкну́ть].
clandestine [klæn'destin] □ тáйный.
clang [klæŋ] **1.** лязг, звон (ору́жия, колоколóв, мóлота); **2.** ля́згать [-гнуть].
clank [klæŋk] **1.** звон, лязг (цепéй, желéза и т. п.), бряцáние; **2.** бряцáть, [за]гремéть.
clap [klæp] **1.** хлопóк; хлóпанье; удáр (грóма); **2.** хлóпать (в ладóши); **~trap** погóня за эффéктом.
clarify ['klærifai] *v/t.* очищáть [очи́стить]; дéлать прозрáчным; *fig.* выясня́ть [вы́яснить]; *v/i.* дéлаться прозрáчным, я́сным.
clarity ['klæriti] я́сность *f.*
clash [klæʃ] **1.** столкновéние; противорéчие; конфли́кт; **2.** стáлкиваться [столкну́ться]; расходи́ться [разойти́сь] (о взгля́дах).
clasp [klɑ:sp] **1.** пря́жка, застёжка; *fig.* объя́тия *n/pl.*; **2.** *v/t.* застёгивать [застегну́ть]; сж(им)áть; *fig.* заключáть в объя́тия; *v/i.* обви́(вá)ться (о растéнии).
class [klɑ:s] **1.** класс (шкóлы); óбщественный класс; **2.** классифици́ровать *(im)pf.*
classic ['klæsik] **1.** клáссик; **2.** ~(al □) [~, -ikəl] класси́ческий.
classi|fication [klæsifi'keiʃən] классификáция; **~fy** [klæ'sifai] классифици́ровать *(im)pf.*
clatter ['klætə] **1.** звон (посу́ды); грóхот (маши́н); болтовня́; тóпот; **2.** [за]гремéть; [за]тóпать; *fig.* [по]болтáть.
clause [klɔ:z] пункт; статья́; клáузула (в договóре).
claw [klɔ:] **1.** кóготь *m*; клешня́ (рáка); **2.** разрывáть, терзáть когтя́ми.
clay [klei] гли́на; *fig.* прах.
clean [kli:n] **1.** *adj.* □ чи́стый; опря́тный; чистоплóтный; **2.** *adv.* нáчисто; совершéнно, пóлностью; **3.** [вы́]чи́стить; прочищáть [-чи́стить]; счищáть [счи́стить]; ~ up уб(и)рáть; приводи́ть в поря́док; **~ing** ['kli:niŋ] чи́стка; убóрка; очи́стка; **~liness** ['klenlinis] чистоплóтность *f*; **~ly** **1.** *adv.* ['kli:nli] чи́сто; целому́дренно; **2.** *adj.* ['klenli] чистоплóтный; **~se** [klenz] очищáть [очи́стить]; дезинфици́ровать *(im)pf.*
clear [kliə] **1.** □ я́сный, свéтлый; прозрáчный; *fig.* свобóдный (from, of от Р); † чи́стый (вес, дохóд и т. п.); **2.** *v/t.* очищáть [очи́стить] (from, of от Р); расчищáть [-и́стить]; распрод(ав)áть (товáр); ⚖ оправдывать [-дáть] (обвиня́емого); *v/i.* (*a.* ~ up) рассéиваться [-éяться] (о тумáне); проясня́ться [-ни́ться]; **~ance** ['kliərəns] очи́стка; устранéние препя́тствий; очи́стка от таможенных пóшлин; расчи́стка (под пáшню); **~ing** ['kliəriŋ] прояснéние; прóсека; кли́ринг (мéжду бáнками); ♀ House расчётная палáта.
cleave[1] [kli:v] [*irr.*] раскáлывать (-ся) [-колóть(ся)]; рассекáть [-éчь] (вóлны, вóздух).
cleave[2] [~] *fig.* оставáться вéрным (to Д).
cleaver ['kli:və] большóй нож мясникá.
clef [klef] 𝄞 ключ.
cleft [kleft] **1.** рассéлина; **2.** раскóлотый.
clemen|cy ['klemənsi] милосéрдие; снисходи́тельность *f*; **~t** ['klemənt] □ милосéрдный, ми́лостивый.
clench [klentʃ] заж(им)áть; сж(имáть) (кулаки́); сти́скивать [сти́снуть] (зу́бы); *s.* clinch.
clergy ['klə:dʒi] духовéнство; **~man** [-mən] свящéнник.
clerical ['klerikəl] **1.** □ клерикáльный; канцеля́рский; **2.** клерикáл.
clerk [klə:k] чинóвник; контóрский слу́жащий; *Am.* прикáзчик.
clever ['klevə] □ у́мный; дарови́тый, одарённый; лóвкий.
clew [klu:] **1.** клубóк; **2.** смáтывать в клубóк.
click [klik] **1.** щёлканье; ⊕ защёлка, собáчка; **2.** щёлкать [-кнуть] (замкóм); прищёлкивать [-кнуть] (языкóм); *Am.* имéть успéх.
client ['klaiənt] клиéнт(ка); постоя́нный (-ная) покупáтель(ница *f*) *m*; **~èle** [kli:ɑn'teil] клиенту́ра.
cliff [klif] утёс, скалá.
climate ['klaimit] кли́мат.
climax ['klaimæks] **1.** кульминациóнный пункт; **2.** достигáть кульминациóнного пу́нкта.
climb [klaim] [*irr.*] влез(á)ть на (В); поднимáться [-ня́ться] (нá гору); **~er** ['klaimə] альпини́ст; *fig.* честолю́бец; ♀ вью́щееся растéние.
clinch [klintʃ] **1.** ⊕ зажи́м; скобá; **2.** *v/t.* заклёпывать [-лепáть]; ~ a bargain заключáть сдéлку; *s.* clench.
cling [kliŋ] [*irr.*] (to) [при]льну́ть к (Д); ~ together держáться вмéсте.
clinic ['klinik] **1.** кли́ника; **2.** = **~al** [-ikəl] клини́ческий.

clink [kliŋk] 1. звон (металла, стекла); 2. [за]звенеть; [за]звучать.
clip[1] [klip] 1. стрижка; 2. обрезать [обрезать]; [о]стричь.
clip[2] [~] скрепка.
clipp|er ['klipə]: (a pair of) ~s *pl.* ножницы *f/pl.*; секатор; ⚓ клиппер (парусное судно); (flying ~) самолёт гражданской авиации; ~**ings** [-iŋz] *pl.* газетные вырезки *f/pl.*; обрезки *m/pl.*
cloak [klouk] 1. плащ; мантия; покров; *fig.* предлог; 2. покры(ва)ть (плащом и т. п.); *fig.* прикры(ва)ть; ~**-room** раздевальня; 🚂 камера хранения.
clock [klɔk] часы *m/pl.* (стенные, настольные, башенные).
clod [klɔd] ком (грязи); дурень *m*, олух.
clog [klɔg] 1. препятствие; путы *f/pl.*; деревянный башмак; 2. [вос]препятствовать (Д); засорять(ся) [-рить(ся)].
cloister ['klɔistə] монастырь *m*; крытая аркада.
close 1. [klous] □ закрытый; близкий; тесный; душный, спёртый (воздух); скупой; ~ by *adv.* рядом, поблизости; ~ to около (Р); ~ fight, ~ quarters *pl.* рукопашный бой; *hunt.* ~ season, ~ time запретное время охоты; 2. a) [klouz] конец; заключение; b) [klous] огороженное место; 3. [klouz] *v/t.* закры(ва)ть; заканчивать [-кончить]; кончать [кончить]; заключать [-чить] (речь); *v/i.* закры(ва)ться; кончаться [кончиться]; ~ in приближаться [-лизиться]; наступать [-пить]; ~ on (*prp.*) замыкаться вокруг (Р); ~**ness** ['klousnis] близость *f*; скупость *f*.
closet ['klɔzit] 1. чулан; уборная; стенной шкаф; 2. be ~ed with совещаться наедине с (Т).
closure ['klouʒə] закрытие; *parl.* прекращение прений.
clot [klɔt] 1. сгусток (крови); комок; 2. сгущаться [сгуститься], свёртываться [свернуться].
cloth [klɔ:θ, klɔθ], *pl.* ~s [klɔ:ðz, klɔθs] скатерть *f*; ткань *f*; сукно; F the ~ духовенство; ~ binding тканевый переплёт.
clothe [klouð] [*a. irr.*] оде(ва)ть; *fig.* облекать [-ечь].
clothes [klouðz] *pl.* одежда, платье; бельё; ~**-basket** бельевая корзина; ~**-line** верёвка для сушки белья; ~**-peg** зажимка для развешенного белья.
clothier ['klouðiə] фабрикант сукон.
clothing ['klouðiŋ] одежда, платье.
cloud [klaud] 1. облако, туча; 2. покрывать(ся) тучами, облаками; омрачать(ся) [-чить(ся)]; ~**-burst** ливень *m*; ~**less** ['klaudlis] □ безоблачный; ~**y** [-i] □ облачный; мутный (о жидкости); туманный (о мысли).
clove[1] [klouv] гвоздика (пряность).
clove[2] [~] *pt.* от cleave; ~**n** ['klouvn] *p. pt.* от cleave.
clover ['klouvə] ♣ клевер.
clown [klaun] клоун.
cloy [klɔi] пресыщать [-сытить].
club [klʌb] 1. клуб; дубина; *Am.* палка полицейского; ~s *pl.* трефы *f/pl.* (карточная масть); 2. *v/t.* [по]бить (палкой и т.п.); *v/i.* собираться вместе; устраивать складчину.
clue [klu:] ключ к разгадке; путеводная нить *f*.
clump [klʌmp] 1. комок; группа (деревьев); 2. тяжело ступать.
clumsy ['klʌmzi] □ неуклюжий; неловкий; бестактный.
clung [klʌŋ] *pt.* и *p. pt.* от cling.
cluster ['klʌstə] 1. кисть *f*; пучок; гроздь *f*; 2. расти гроздьями, пучками.
clutch [klʌtʃ] 1. сжатие; захват; ⊕ зажим; защёлка; муфта сцепления; 2. схватывать [-тить]; заж(им)ать.
clutter ['klʌtə] 1. суматоха; хаос; 2. приводить в беспорядок.
coach [koutʃ] 1. экипаж; тренер; инструктор; 🚂 пассажирский вагон; 2. ехать в карете; [на]тренировать; натаскивать к экзамену; ~**man** кучер.
coagulate [kou'ægjuleit] сгущаться [сгуститься].
coal [koul] 1. уголь *m* (каменный); 2. ⚓ грузить(ся) углем.
coalesce [kouə'les] срастаться [срастись].
coalition [kouə'liʃən] коалиция; союз.
coal-pit угольная шахта, копь *f*.
coarse [kɔ:s] □ грубый; крупный; неотёсанный.
coast [koust] 1. морской берег, побережье; 2. плыть вдоль побережья; ~**er** ['koustə] ⚓ каботажное судно.
coat [kout] 1. пиджак; пальто *n indecl.*; мех, шерсть *f* (у животных); слой; ~ of arms гербовый щит; 2. покры(ва)ть (краской, пылью и т. п.); облицовывать [-цевать]; ~**-hanger** вешалка; ~**ing** ['koutiŋ] слой (краски и т. п.).
coax [kouks] уговаривать [уговорить].
cob [kɔb] ком; *Am.* початок кукурузы.
cobbler ['kɔblə] сапожник; *fig.* халтурщик, плохой мастер.
cobweb ['kɔbweb] паутина.
cock [kɔk] 1. петух; кран; флюгер; курок; 2. (*a.* ~ up) настораживать [-рожить] (уши).
cockade [kɔ'keid] кокарда.

cockatoo [kɔkə'tu:] какаду́ *m indecl.*
cockboat ['kɔkbout] ⚓ судова́я шлю́пка.
cockchafer ['kɔktʃeifə] ма́йский жук.
cock-eyed ['kɔkaid] *sl.* косогла́зый; косо́й; *Am.* пья́ный.
cockpit ['kɔkpit] ме́сто петуши́ных боёв; ⚓ ку́брик; ✈ каби́на.
cockroach ['kɔkroutʃ] *zo.* тарака́н.
cock|sure F самоуве́ренный; **~tail** кокте́йль *m*; *fig.* вы́скочка; **~y** ['kɔki] □ F наха́льный; де́рзкий.
coco ['koukou] коко́совая па́льма.
cocoa ['koukou] кака́о (порошо́к, напи́ток) *n indecl.*
coco-nut ['koukənʌt] коко́совый оре́х.
cocoon [kɔ'ku:n] ко́кон.
cod [kɔd] треска́.
coddle ['kɔdl] изне́жи(ва)ть; [из-] балова́ть.
code [koud] **1.** ко́декс; *telegr.* код; **2.** коди́ровать (*im*)*pf.*
codger ['kɔdʒə] F чуда́к.
cod-liver: ~ oil ры́бий жир.
coerc|e [kou'ə:s] принужда́ть [-ну́дить]; **~ion** [-ʃən] принужде́ние.
coeval [kou'i:vəl] □ совреме́нный.
coexist ['kouig'zist] сосуществова́ть (с Т).
coffee ['kɔfi] ко́фе *m indecl.*; **~-pot** кофе́йник; **~-room** столо́вая в гости́нице; **~-set** кофе́йный серви́з.
coffer ['kɔfə] металли́ческий сунду́к.
coffin ['kɔfin] гроб.
cogent ['koudʒənt] □ неоспори́мый; убеди́тельный.
cogitate ['kɔdʒiteit] *v/i.* размышля́ть; *v/t.* обду́м(ыв)ать.
cognate ['kɔgneit] ро́дственный; схо́дный.
cognition [kɔg'niʃən] зна́ние; позна́ние.
coheir ['kou'ɛə] сонасле́дник.
coheren|ce [kou'hiərəns] связь *f*; свя́зность *f*; согласо́ванность *f*; **~t** [-rənt] □ свя́зный; согласо́ванный.
cohesi|on [kou'hi:ʒən] связь *f*; сплочённость *f*; **~ve** [-siv] связу́ющий; спосо́бный к сцепле́нию.
coiff|eur [kwɑ:'fə:] парикма́хер; **~ure** [-'fjuə] причёска.
coil [kɔil] **1.** кольцо́ (верёвки, змеи́ и т. п.); ⚡ кату́шка; ⊕ змееви́к; **2.** (*a.* ~ up) свёртываться кольцо́м (спира́лью).
coin [kɔin] **1.** моне́та; **2.** [вы́]чека́нить (моне́ты); вы́би(ва́)ть (меда́ли); **~age** ['kɔinidʒ] чека́нка (моне́т).
coincide [kouin'said] совпада́ть [-па́сть]; **~nce** [kou'insidəns] совпаде́ние; *fig.* случа́йное стече́ние обстоя́тельств.
coke [kouk] **1.** кокс; **2.** коксова́ть.

cold [kould] **1.** □ холо́дный; неприве́тливый; **2.** хо́лод; просту́да; **~ness** ['kouldnis] хо́лодность *f*; равноду́шие.
colic ['kɔlik] ⚕ ко́лики *f/pl.*
collaborat|e [kə'læbəreit] сотру́дничать; **~ion** [kəlæbə'reiʃən] сотру́дничество; in ~ в сотру́дничестве (с Т).
collapse [kə'læps] **1.** обва́л; разруше́ние; упа́док сил; **2.** обру́ши(ва)ться; обва́ливаться [-ли́ться]; си́льно слабе́ть.
collar ['kɔlə] **1.** воротни́к; оше́йник; хому́т; ⊕ вту́лка; о́бруч; ша́йба; **2.** схвати́ть за во́рот; *sl.* завладе́(ва́)ть (Т); захва́тывать [-ти́ть] (си́лой).
collate [kɔ'leit] слича́ть [-чи́ть]; сопоставля́ть [-ста́вить].
collateral [kɔ'lætərəl] **1.** □ побо́чный; ко́свенный; **2.** родство́ по боково́й ли́нии.
colleague ['kɔli:g] колле́га *f/m*, сослужи́вец (-вица).
collect **1.** ['kɔlekt] *eccl.* кра́ткая моли́тва; **2.** [kə'lekt] *v/t.* соб(и-)ра́ть; коллекциони́ровать; заходи́ть [зайти́] за (Т); *v/i.* соб(и)ра́ться; овладева́ть собо́й; **~ed** [kə'lektid] □ *fig.* хладнокро́вный; споко́йный; **~ion** [kə'lekʃən] колле́кция; собра́ние; **~ive** [-tiv] □ коллекти́вный; совоку́пный; **~or** [-tə] коллекционе́р; сбо́рщик.
college ['kɔlidʒ] колле́дж; сре́дняя шко́ла.
collide [kə'laid] ста́лкиваться [столкну́ться].
collie ['kɔli] ко́лли *m/f indecl.* (шотла́ндская овча́рка).
collier [kɔliə] шахтёр; ⚓ у́гольщик (су́дно); **~y** [kɔ'ljəri] каменноу́го́льный рудни́к.
collision ['kəliʒən] столкнове́ние.
colloquial [kə'loukwiəl] □ разгово́рный.
colloquy ['kɔləkwi] разгово́р, собесе́дование.
colon ['koulən] *typ.* двоето́чие.
colonel ['kə:nl] ⚔ полко́вник.
coloni|al [kə'lounjəl] **1.** колониа́льный; **2.** жи́тель(ница *f*) *m* коло́ний; **~ze** ['kɔlənaiz] колонизи́ровать (*im*)*pf.*; заселя́ть [-ли́ть].
colony ['kɔləni] коло́ния.
colo(u)r ['kʌlə] **1.** цвет; кра́ска; румя́нец (на лице́); *fig.* колори́т; **~s** *pl.* зна́мя *n*; **2.** *v/t.* [по]кра́сить; окра́шивать [окра́сить]; *fig.* прикра́шивать [-кра́сить]; *v/i.* [по-] красне́ть; [за]рде́ться (о лице́, плоде́ и т. п.); **~ed** [-d] окра́шенный; цветно́й; **~ful** [-ful] я́ркий; **~ing** [-riŋ] окра́ска, раскра́ска; *fig.* прикра́шивание; **~less** [-lis] □ бесцве́тный.
colt [koult] жеребёнок (*pl.* жереба́та); *fig.* нович́ок.

column ['kɔləm] ⚠, ⚔ коло́нна; столб; *typ.* столбе́ц.
comb [koum] 1. гре́бень *m*, гребёнка; со́ты *m/pl.*; ⊕ бёрдо, чеса́лка; 2. *v/t.* расчёсывать [-чеса́ть]; чеса́ть (*a.* ⊕); трепа́ть (лён и т. п.).
combat ['kɔmbət, 'kʌm-] 1. бой, сраже́ние; 2. сража́ться [срази́ться]; **~ant** [-ənt] бое́ц.
combin|ation [kɔmbi'neiʃən] соедине́ние; сочета́ние; *mst* **~s** *pl.* комбина́ция (бельё); **~e** [kəm'bain] объединя́ть(ся) [-ни́ть(ся)]; сочета́ть(ся) (*im*)*pf.*
combusti|ble [kəm'bʌstəbl] 1. горю́чий, воспламеня́емый; 2. **~s** *pl.* то́пливо; *mot.* горю́чее; **~on** [-tʃən] горе́ние, сгора́ние.
come [kʌm] [*irr.*] приходи́ть [прийти́]; приезжа́ть [прие́хать]; to ~ бу́дущий; ~ **about** случа́ться [-чи́ться], происходи́ть [произойти́]; ~ **across a p.** встреча́ться [-е́титься] с (Т), ната́лкиваться [натолкну́ться] на (В); ~ **at** доб(и)ра́ться до (Р); ~ **by** дост(ав)а́ть (случа́йно); ~ **off** отде́л(ыв)аться; сходи́ть [сойти́]; ~ **round** приходи́ть в себя́; F заходи́ть [зайти́] (к Д); *fig.* идти́ на усту́пки; ~ **to** доходи́ть [дойти́] до (Р); ⚓ останови́ть су́дно; равня́ться (Д), сто́ить (В *or* Р); ~ **up to** соотве́тствовать (Д).
comedian [kə'mi:diən] актёр-ко́мик; а́втор коме́дии.
comedy ['kɔmidi] коме́дия.
comeliness ['kʌmlinis] милови́дность *f.*
comfort ['kʌmfət] 1. комфо́рт, удо́бство; *fig.* утеше́ние; подде́ржка; 2. утеша́ть [уте́шить]; успока́ивать [-ко́ить]; **~able** [-əbl] □ удо́бный, комфорта́бельный; *Am.* F доста́точный; **~er** [-ə] утеши́тель *m*; *Am.* стёганое одея́ло; **~less** [-lis] □ неую́тный.
comic(al □) ['kɔmik(əl)] коми́ческий, смешно́й; юмористи́ческий.
coming ['kʌmiŋ] 1. прие́зд, прибы́тие; 2. бу́дущий; ожида́емый.
command [kə'mɑ:nd] 1. кома́нда, прика́з; кома́ндование; **have at** ~ име́ть в своём распоряже́нии; 2. прика́зывать [-за́ть] (Д); владе́ть (Т); ⚔ кома́ндовать; **~er** [kə'mɑ:ndə] ⚔ команди́р; ⚓ капита́н; **♀er-in-Chief** [-rin'tʃi:f] главнокома́ндующий; **~ment** [-mənt] прика́з; *eccl.* за́поведь *f.*
commemora|te [kə'meməreit] [от]пра́здновать (годовщи́ну); отмеча́ть [отме́тить] (собы́тие); **~tion** [kəmemə'reʃən] пра́зднование (годовщи́ны).
commence [kə'mens] нач(ин)а́ть (-ся); **~ment** [-mənt] нача́ло.
commend [kə'mend] рекомендова́ть (*im*)*pf.*
comment ['kɔment] 1. толкова́ние; коммента́рий; 2. (upon) комменти́ровать (*im*)*pf.*; объясня́ть [-ни́ть]; **~ary** ['kɔməntəri] коммента́рий; **~ator** ['kɔmenteitə] коммента́тор.
commerc|e ['kɔməs, -ə:s] торго́вля; обще́ние; **~ial** [kə'mə:ʃəl] □ торго́вый, комме́рческий.
commiseration [kəmizə'reiʃən] сочу́вствие, соболе́знование.
commissary ['kɔmisəri] комисса́р; уполномо́ченный; ⚔ интенда́нт.
commission [kə'miʃən] 1. коми́ссия; полномо́чие; поруче́ние; ⚔ пате́нт на офице́рский чин; 2. назнача́ть на до́лжность; уполномо́чи(ва)ть; ⚓ гото́вить (кора́бль) к пла́ванию; **~er** [kə'miʃənə] уполномо́ченный; комисса́р.
commit [kə'mit] поруча́ть [-чи́ть], вверя́ть [вве́рить]; преда́(ва́)ть (огню́, земле́, суду́ и т.п.); соверша́ть [-ши́ть] (преступле́ние); ~ (o. s.) [с]компромети́ровать (себя́); обя́зывать(ся) [-за́ть(ся)]; ~ (to prison) заключа́ть [-чи́ть] (в тюрьму́); **~ment** [-mənt], **~tal** [-l] переда́ча; обяза́тельство; **~tee** [-i] коми́ссия; комите́т.
commodity [kə'mɔditi] това́р, предме́т потребле́ния.
common ['kɔmən] 1. □ о́бщий; просто́й; гру́бый; обыкнове́нный; зауря́дный; ♀ Council муниципа́льный сове́т; ~ law обы́чное пра́во; ~ sense здра́вый смысл; in ~ совме́стно, сообща́; 2. общи́нная земля́; вы́гон; **~place** 1. бана́льность *f*; 2. бана́льный, F изби́тый; **~s** [-z] *pl.* о́бщий стол; (*mst* House of) ♀ пала́та о́бщин; **~wealth** [-welθ] содру́жество; федера́ция; the British ♀ of Nations Брита́нское Содру́жество На́ций.
commotion [kə'mouʃən] волне́ние; смяте́ние.
communal ['kɔmjunl] □ коммуна́льный; общи́нный; коллекти́вный.
communicat|e [kə'mju:nikeit] *v/t.* сообща́ть [-щи́ть]; перед(ав)а́ть; *v/i.* сообща́ться; **~ion** [kəmju:ni'keiʃən] сообще́ние; коммуника́ция; связь *f*; **~ive** [kə'mju:nikeitiv] □ общи́тельный, разгово́рчивый.
communion [kə'mju:njən] обще́ние; *eccl.* прича́стие.
communis|m ['kɔmjunizm] коммуни́зм; **~t** 1. коммуни́ст(ка); 2. коммунисти́ческий.
community [kə'mju:niti] общи́на; о́бщество.
commutation [kɔmju'teiʃən] заме́на; ⚖ смягче́ние наказа́ния; ⚡ коммута́ция; переключе́ние.
compact 1. ['kɔmpækt] догово́р; 2.

[kəm'pækt] *adj.* компа́ктный; пло́тный; сжа́тый (о сти́ле); 3. *v/t.* сж(им)а́ть; уплотня́ть [-ни́ть].
companion [kəm'pænjən] това́рищ; спу́тник; собесе́дник; **~ship** [-ʃip] компа́ния; това́рищеские отноше́ния *n/pl.*
company ['kʌmpəni] о́бщество; компа́ния, това́рищество; го́сти *pl.*; ⚓ экипа́ж (су́дна); *thea.* тру́ппа; have ~ име́ть госте́й; keep ~ with подде́рживать знако́мство с (Т).
compar|able ['kɔmpərəbl] □ сравни́мый; **~ative** [kəm'pærətiv] □ сравни́тельный; **~e** [kəm'pɛə] 1. beyond ~, without ~, past ~ вне вся́кого сравне́ния; 2. *v/t.* сра́внивать [-ни́ть], слича́ть [-чи́ть], (to с Т); уподобля́ть [-до́бить] (В/Д); *v/i.* сра́вниваться [-ни́ться]; **~ison** [kəm'pærisn] сравне́ние.
compartment [kəm'pa:tmənt] отделе́ние; перегоро́дка; 🚂 купе́ *n indecl.*
compass ['kʌmpəs] 1. ко́мпас; объём; окру́жность *f*; ♪ диапазо́н; (a pair of) **~es** *pl.* ци́ркуль *m*; 2. достига́ть [дости́гнуть] (Р); замышля́ть [-ы́слить] (дурно́е).
compassion [kəm'pæʃən] сострада́ние, жа́лость *f*; **~ate** [-it] □ сострада́тельный, жа́лостливый.
compatible [kəm'pætəbl] □ совмести́мый.
compatriot [-triət] сооте́чественник (-ица).
compel [kəm'pel] заставля́ть [-а́вить]; принужда́ть [-ну́дить].
compensat|e ['kɔmpenseit] *v/t.* вознагражда́ть [-ради́ть]; возмеща́ть [-ести́ть] (убы́тки); **~ion** [kɔmpen'seiʃən] вознагражде́ние; компенса́ция.
compete [kəm'pi:t] состяза́ться; конкури́ровать (with с Т, for ра́ди Р).
competen|ce, ~cy ['kɔmpitəns, -i] спосо́бность *f*; компете́нтность *f*; **~t** [-tənt] □ компете́нтный.
competit|ion [kɔmpi'tiʃən] состяза́ние; соревнова́ние; ✝ конкуре́нция; **~or** [kəm'petitə] конкуре́нт(ка); сопе́рник (-ица).
compile [kəm'pail] [с]компили́ровать; составля́ть [-а́вить] (from из Р).
complacen|ce, ~cy [kəm'pleisns, -snsi] самодово́льство.
complain [kəm'plein] [по]жа́ловаться (of на В); подава́ть жа́лобу; **~t** жа́лоба; ⚕ боле́знь *f*; **~ant** [-ənt] исте́ц.
complement ['kɔmplimənt] 1. дополне́ние; компле́кт; 2. дополня́ть [допо́лнить]; [у]комплектова́ть.
complet|e [kəm'pli:t] 1. □ по́лный; зако́нченный; 2. зака́нчивать [зако́нчить]; дополня́ть [-о́лнить]; **~ion** [-ʃən] оконча́ние.
complex ['kɔmpleks] 1. □ сло́жный; ко́мплексный, составно́й; *fig.* сло́жный, запу́танный; 2. ко́мплекс; **~ion** [kəm'plekʃən] цвет лица́; **~ity** [-siti] сло́жность *f*.
compliance [kəm'plaiəns] согла́сие; in ~ with в соотве́тствии с (Т).
complicate ['kɔmplikeit] усложня́ть(ся) [-ни́ть(ся)].
compliment 1. ['kɔmplimənt] комплиме́нт; приве́т; 2. [-'ment] *v/t.* говори́ть комплиме́нты (Д); поздравля́ть [-а́вить] (on с Т).
comply [kəm'plai] соглаша́ться [-ласи́ться] (with с Т); подчиня́ться [-ни́ться] (with Д).
component [kəm'pounənt] 1. компоне́нт; составна́я часть *f*; 2. составно́й.
compos|e [kəm'pouz] составля́ть [-а́вить]; сочиня́ть [-ни́ть]; писа́ть му́зыку; успока́иваться [-ко́иться]; *typ.* наб(и)ра́ть; **~ed** [-d] □ споко́йный, сде́ржанный; **~er** [-ə] компози́тор; **~ition** [kɔmpə'ziʃən] компози́ция; соста́в; сочине́ние; ✝ полюбо́вная сде́лка; **~ure** [kəm'pouʒə] самооблада́ние.
compound 1. ['kɔmpaund] соста́в, соедине́ние; 2. составно́й; сло́жный; ~ interest сло́жные проце́нты *m/pl.*; 3. [kəm'paund] *v/t.* сме́шивать [-ша́ть]; соединя́ть [-ни́ть]; ула́живать [ула́дить]; *v/i.* приходи́ть к компроми́ссу.
comprehend [kɔmpri'hend] постига́ть [пости́гнуть]; обхва́тывать [обхвати́ть].
comprehen|sible [kɔmpri'hensəbl] □ поня́тный, постижи́мый; **~sion** [-ʃən] понима́ние; поня́тливость *f*; **~sive** [-siv] □ объе́млющий; исче́рпывающий.
compress [kəm'pres] сж(им)а́ть; сда́вливать [сдави́ть]; ~ed air сжа́тый во́здух; **~ion** [kəm'preʃən] *phys.* сжа́тие; ⊕ компре́ссия; наби́вка; прокла́дка.
comprise [kəm'praiz] содержа́ть; заключа́ть в себе́.
compromise ['kɔmprəmaiz] 1. компроми́сс; 2. *v/t.* [с]компромети́ровать; подверга́ть ри́ску; *v/i.* пойти́ на компроми́сс.
compuls|ion [kəm'pʌlʃən] принужде́ние; **~ory** [-səri] принуди́тельный; обяза́тельный.
comput|ation [kɔmpju'teiʃən] вычисле́ние; вы́кладка; расчёт; **~e** [kəm'pju:t] вычисля́ть [вы́числить]; де́лать вы́кладки.
comrade ['kɔmrid] това́рищ.
con [kɔn] = contra про́тив.
conceal [kən'si:l] скры(ва́)ть;ута́ивать [-и́ть], ума́лчивать [умолча́ть].
concede [kən'si:d] уступа́ть [-пи́ть]; допуска́ть [-сти́ть].
conceit [kən'si:t] самомне́ние; тще-

сла́вие; **~ed** [-id] □ самодово́льный; тщесла́вный.
conceiv|able [kən'si:vəbl] мы́слимый; постижи́мый; **~e** [kən'si:v] *v/i.* представля́ть себе́; *v/t.* постига́ть [пости́гнуть]; понима́ть [-ня́ть]; заду́м(ыв)ать.
concentrate ['kɔnsentreit] сосредото́чи(ва)ть(ся).
conception [kən'sepʃən] поня́тие; конце́пция; за́мысел; *biol.* зача́тие; оплодотворе́ние.
concern [kən'sə:n] **1.** де́ло; уча́стие; интере́с; забо́та; ✝ предприя́тие; **2.** каса́ться [косну́ться] (Р); име́ть отноше́ние к (Д); ~ o. s. about, for [за]интересова́ться, занима́ться [заня́ться] (Т); **~ed** [-d] □ заинтересо́ванный; име́ющий отноше́ние; озабо́ченный; **~ing** [-iŋ] *prp.* относи́тельно (Р), каса́тельно (Р).
concert 1. ['kɔnsət] конце́рт; согла́сие, соглаше́ние; **2.** [kən'sə:t] сгова́риваться [сговори́ться]; **~ed** согласо́ванный.
concession [kən'seʃən] усту́пка; конце́ссия.
conciliat|e [kən'silieit] примиря́ть [-ри́ть]; **~or** [-ə] посре́дник.
concise [kən'sais] □ сжа́тый, кра́ткий; **~ness** [-nis] сжа́тость *f*, кра́ткость *f*.
conclude [kən'klu:d] заключа́ть [-чи́ть]; зака́нчивать [зако́нчить]; to be ~d оконча́ние сле́дует.
conclusi|on [kən'klu:ʒən] оконча́ние; заключе́ние; вы́вод; **~ve** [-siv] □ заключи́тельный; реша́ющий; убеди́тельный.
concoct [kən'kɔkt] [со]стря́пать (*a. fig.*); *fig.* приду́м(ыв)ать; **~ion** [kən'kɔkʃən] стряпня́; *fig.* небыли́ца.
concord ['kɔŋkɔ:d] согла́сие; соглаше́ние; догово́р, конве́нция; ♪ гармо́ния; **~ant** [kən'kɔ:dənt] □ согла́сный; согласу́ющийся; ♪ гармони́чный.
concrete ['kɔnkri:t] **1.** □ конкре́тный; **2.** бето́н; **3.** [за]бетони́ровать; [kən'kri:t] сгуща́ть(ся) [сгусти́ть(ся)]; [за]тверде́ть.
concur [kən'kə:] соглаша́ться [-ласи́ться]; совпада́ть [-па́сть]; [по]соде́йствовать; **~rence** [kən'kʌrəns] совпаде́ние; согла́сие.
condemn [kən'dem] осужда́ть [осуди́ть]; пригова́ривать [-вори́ть] (к Д); [за]бракова́ть; **~ation** ['kɔndem'neiʃən] осужде́ние.
condens|ation ['kɔnden''seiʃən] конденса́ция, уплотне́ние, сгуще́ние; **~e** [kən'dens] сгуща́ть(ся); ⊕ конденси́ровать (*im*)*pf.*; *fig.* сокраща́ть [-рати́ть].
condescen|d [kɔndi'send] снисходи́ть [снизойти́]; удоста́ивать [-сто́ить]; **~sion** [-'senʃən] снисхожде́ние; снисходи́тельность *f*.
condiment ['kɔndimənt] припра́ва.
condition [kən'diʃən] **1.** усло́вие; состоя́ние; **~s** *pl.* обстоя́тельства *n/pl.*; усло́вия *n/pl.*; **2.** ста́вить усло́вия; обусло́вливать [-о́вить]; **~al** [-l] □ усло́вный.
condol|e [kən'doul] соболе́зновать (with Д); **~ence** [-əns] соболе́знование.
conduc|e [kən'dju:s] спосо́бствовать (to Д); **~ive** [-iv] спосо́бствующий.
conduct 1. ['kɔndəkt] поведе́ние; **2.** [kən'dʌkt] вести́ себя́; руководи́ть (де́лом); ♪ дирижи́ровать; **~ion** [-kʃən] ⊕ проводи́мость *f*; **~or** [kən'dʌktə] конду́ктор (трамва́я и т. п.); *Am.* 🚂 вагоновожа́тый; ♪ дирижёр.
conduit ['kɔndjuit, 'kɔndit] трубопрово́д.
cone [koun] ко́нус; ♣ ши́шка.
confabulation [kənfæbju'leiʃən] болтовня́.
confection [kən'fekʃən] сла́сти *f/pl.*; **~er** [-ə] конди́тер; **~ery** [-əri] конди́терская; конди́терские изде́лия *n/pl.*
confedera|cy [kən'fedərəsi] конфедера́ция; сою́з; **~te 1.** [-rit] федерати́вный, сою́зный; **2.** [-rit] член конфедера́ции, сою́зник; **3.** [-reit] объединя́ться в сою́з; **~tion** [kənfedə'reiʃən] конфедера́ция; сою́з.
confer [kənfə:] *v/t.* дарова́ть; присужда́ть [-уди́ть]; *v/i.* совеща́ться; **~ence** ['kɔnfərəns] конфере́нция; съезд; совеща́ние.
confess [kən'fes] призн(ав)а́ться, созн(ав)а́ться в (П); испове́д(ов)ать(ся); **~ion** [-ʃən] призна́ние; и́споведь *f*; вероиспове́дание; **~ional** [-ʃənl] исповеда́льня *f*; **~or** [-sə] испове́дник.
confide [kən'faid] доверя́ть (in Д); вверя́ть [вве́рить]; полага́ться [положи́ться] (in на В); **~nce** ['kɔnfidəns] дове́рие; уве́ренность *f*; **~nt** ['kɔnfidənt] □ уве́ренный; **~ntial** [kɔnfi'denʃəl] □ конфиденциа́льный; секре́тный.
confine [kən'fain] ограни́чи(ва)ть; заключа́ть [-чи́ть] (в тюрьму́); be ~d рожа́ть [роди́ть] (of В); **~ment** [-mənt] ограниче́ние; заключе́ние; ро́ды *m/pl.*
confirm [kən'fə:m] подтвержда́ть [-рди́ть]; подде́рживать [-жа́ть]; **~ation** [kɔnfə'meiʃən] подтвержде́ние; *eccl.* конфирма́ция.
confiscat|e ['kɔnfiskeit] конфискова́ть (*im*)*pf.*; **~ion** [kɔnfis'keiʃən] конфиска́ция.
conflagration [kɔnflə'greiʃən] сожже́ние; бушу́ющий пожа́р.
conflict 1. ['kɔnflikt] конфли́кт; столкнове́ние; **2.** [kən'flikt] быть в конфли́кте.

conflu|ence ['kɔnfluəns] слия́ние (рек); стече́ние наро́да; **~ent** [-fluənt] 1. слива́ющийся; 2. прито́к (реки́).
conform [kən'fɔ:m] согласо́вываться [-сова́ться] (to с Т); подчиня́ться [-ни́ться] (to Д); **~able** [-əbl] □ (to) соотве́тствующий (Д); подчиня́ющийся (Д); **~ity** [-iti] соотве́тствие; подчине́ние.
confound [kən'faund] [с]пута́ть; поража́ть [порази́ть], приводи́ть в смуще́ние.
confront [kən'frʌnt] стоя́ть лицо́м к лицу́ с (Т); слича́ть [-чи́ть] (with с Т).
confus|e [kən'fju:z] сме́шивать [-ша́ть]; смуща́ть [-ути́ть]; **~ion** [kən'fju:ʒən] смуще́ние; беспоря́док.
confut|ation [kɔnfju:teiʃən] опроверже́ние; **~e** [kən'fju:t] опроверга́ть [-ве́ргнуть].
congeal [kən'dʒi:l] засты́(ва́)ть.
congenial [kən'dʒi:niəl] □ бли́зкий по ду́ху; благоприя́тный.
congestion [kən'dʒestʃən] перегру́женность *f*; перенаселённость *f*.
conglomeration [kɔn'glɔmə''reiʃən]накопле́ние, скопле́ние.
congratulat|e [kən'grætjuleit] поздравля́ть [-а́вить] (on с Т); **~ion** [kəngrætju'leiʃən] поздравле́ние.
congregat|e ['kɔŋgrigeit] соб(и)ра́ть(ся); **~ion** [kɔŋgri'geiʃən] собра́ние; *eccl.* прихожа́не *m/pl.*.
congress ['kɔŋgres] конгре́сс; съезд.
congruous ['kɔŋgruəs] □ соотве́тствующий; гармони́рующий (to с Т).
conifer ['kounifə] хво́йное де́рево.
conjecture [kən'dʒektʃə] 1. дога́дка, предположе́ние; 2. предполага́ть [-ложи́ть].
conjoin [kən'dʒɔin] соединя́ть(ся) [-ни́ть(ся)]; сочета́ть(ся) *(im)pf.*; **~t** [-t] о́бщий; объединённый.
conjugal ['kɔndʒugəl] □ супру́жеский, бра́чный.
conjunction [kən'dʒʌŋkʃən] соедине́ние, связь *f*.
conjur|e 1. ['kʌndʒə] *v/t.* вызыва́ть [вы́звать], заклина́ть [-ля́сть] (ду́хов); изгоня́ть ду́хов; ~ up *fig.* вызыва́ть в воображе́нии; *v/i.* занима́ться ма́гией; пока́зывать фо́кусы; 2. [kən'dʒuə] умоля́ть [-ли́ть], заклина́ть; **~er, ~or** [-rə] волше́бник; фо́кусник.
connect [kə'nekt] соединя́ть(ся) [-ни́ть(ся)]; свя́зывать(ся) [-за́ть (-ся)]; ⚡ соединя́ть [-ни́ть]; **~ed** [-id] □ свя́занный; свя́зный (о ре́чи); be ~ with име́ть свя́зи (с Т); **~ion** *s.* connexion.
connexion [kə'nekʃən] связь *f*; соедине́ние; родство́.
connive [kə'naiv]: ~ at потво́рствовать (Д), смотре́ть сквозь па́льцы на (В).
connoisseur [kɔni'sə:] знато́к.
connubial [kə'nju:biəl] □ бра́чный.
conquer ['kɔŋkə] завоёвывать [-оева́ть]; побежда́ть [победи́ть]; **~able** [-rəbl] победи́мый; **~or** [-rə] победи́тель(ница *f*) *m*; завоева́тель(ница *f*) *m*.
conquest ['kɔŋkwest] завоева́ние; побе́да.
conscience ['kɔnʃəns] со́весть *f*.
conscientious [kɔnʃi'enʃəs] □ добросо́вестный; **~ness** [-nis] добросо́вестность *f*.
conscious ['kɔnʃəs] □ сознательный; сознающий; **~ness** [-nis] созна́ние; созна́тельность *f*.
conscript ['kɔnskript] ⚔ призывни́к; **~ion** [kən'skripʃən] ⚔ во́инская пови́нность *f*.
consecrat|e ['kɔnsikreit] освяща́ть [-ята́ть]; посвяща́ть [-яти́ть]; **~ion** [kɔnsi'kreiʃən] освяще́ние; посвяще́ние.
consecutive [kən'sekjutiv] □ после́довательный.
consent [kən'sent] 1. согла́сие; 2. соглаша́ться [-ласи́ться].
consequen|ce ['kɔnsikwəns] (по-) сле́дствие; вы́вод, заключе́ние; **~t** [-kwənt] 1. после́довательный; 2. (по)сле́дствие; **~tial** [kɔnsi'kwenʃəl] □ логи́чески вытека́ющий; ва́жный; **~tly** ['kɔnsikwəntli] сле́довательно; поэ́тому.
conserv|ation [kɔnsə'veiʃən] сохране́ние; **~ative** [kən'sə:vətiv] 1. □ консервати́вный; охрани́тельный; 2. *pol.* консерва́тор; **~atory** [-tri] оранжере́я; ♪ консервато́рия; **~e** [kən'sə:v] сохраня́ть [-ни́ть].
consider [kən'sidə] *v/t.* обсужда́ть [-уди́ть]; обду́м(ыв)ать; полага́ть, счита́ть; счита́ться с (Т); *v/i.* сообража́ть [-рази́ть]; **~able** [-rəbl] □ значи́тельный; ва́жный; большо́й; **~ate** [-rit] □ внима́тельный (к Д); **~ation** [kənsidə'reiʃən] обсужде́ние; соображе́ние; внима́ние; on no ~ ни под каки́м ви́дом; **~ing** [kən'sidəriŋ] *prp.* учи́тывая (В), принима́я во внима́ние (В).
consign [kən'sain] перед(ав)а́ть; поруча́ть [-чи́ть]; ✝ посыла́ть (груз) на консигна́цию; **~ment** [-ment] па́ртия това́ров; коноса́мент.
consist [kən'sist] состоя́ть (of из Р); заключа́ться (in в П); **~ence, ~ency** [-əns, -ənsi] логи́чность *f*; пло́тность *f*; **~ent** [-ənt] □ пло́тный; после́довательный; согла́сующийся (with с Т).
consol|ation [kɔnsə'leiʃən] утеше́ние; **~e** [kən'soul] утеша́ть [уте́шить].
consolidate [kən'sɔlideit] под-

тверждáть [-рдить]; объединять (-ся) [-нить(ся)]; консолидировать (займы) (*im*)*pf*.
consonan|ce ['kɔnsənəns] созвучие; согласие; **~t** [-nənt] □ согласный (*a.* noun); совместимый.
consort ['kɔnsɔ:t] супруг(а).
conspicuous [kən'spikjuəs] □ заметный, бросающийся в глаза.
conspir|acy [kən'spirəsi] заговор; **~ator** [-tə] заговорщик (-ица); **~e** [kən'spaiə] устраивать заговор; сговариваться [-вориться].
constab|le ['kʌnstəbl] констебль *m*, полицейский; **~ulary** [kən'stæbjuləri] полиция.
constan|cy ['kɔnstənsi] постоянство; верность *f*; **~t** ['kɔnstənt] □ постоянный; верный.
consternation [kɔnstə'neiʃən] оцепенение (от страха).
constipation [kɔnsti'peiʃən] ⚕ запор.
constituen|cy [kən'stitjuənsi] избирательный округ; избиратели *m/pl.*; **~t** [-ənt] существенный; учредительный; **2.** избиратель *m*; составная часть *f*.
constitut|e ['kɔnstitju:t] составлять [-авить]; основывать [-новать]; **~ion** [kɔnsti'tju:ʃn] конституция; учреждение; телосложение; состав; **~ional** [-l] □ конституционный; органический.
constrain [kən'strein] принуждать [-нудить]; сдерживать [-жать]; **~t** [-t] принуждение; принуждённость *f*.
constrict [kən'strikt] стягивать [стянуть]; сж(им)ать; **~ion** [kən'strikʃən] сжатие; стягивание.
construct [kən'strʌkt] [по]строить; сооружать [-удить]; *fig.* созд(ав)ать; **~ion** [-kʃən] строительство, стройка; строение; **~ive** [-tiv] конструктивный; строительный; творческий; **~or** [-tə] строитель *m*.
construe [kən'stru:] истолковывать [-ковать]; *gr.* делать синтаксический разбор.
consul ['kɔnsəl] консул; **~ general** генеральный консул; **~ate** ['kɔnsjulit] консульство.
consult [kən'sʌlt] *v/t.* спрашивать совета у (Р); *v/i.* [по]советоваться, совещаться; **~ation** [kɔnsəl'teiʃən] консультация; консилиум (врачей); **~ative** [kən'sʌltətiv] совещательный.
consum|e [kən'sju:m] *v/t.* потреблять [-бить]; [из]расходовать; **~er** [-ə] потребитель *m*.
consummate **1.** [kən'sʌmit] □ совершенный, законченный; **2.** ['kɔnsʌmeit] доводить до конца; завершать [-шить].
consumpti|on [kən'sʌmpʃən] потребление, расход; ⚕ туберкулёз лёгких; **~ve** [-tiv] □ туберкулёзный, чахоточный.
contact ['kɔntækt] контакт; соприкосновение.
contagi|on [kən'teidʒən] ⚕ зараза, инфекция; **~ous** [-dʒəs] □ заразительный, инфекционный.
contain [kən'tein] содержать (в себе), вмещать [-естить]; **~ o. s.** сдерживаться [-жаться]; **~er** [-ə] вместилище; контейнер.
contaminate [kən'tæmineit] загрязнять [-нить]; *fig.* заражать [заразить]; осквернять [-нить].
contemplat|e ['kɔntempleit] созерцать; обдум(ыв)ать; **~ion** [kɔntem'pleiʃən] созерцание; размышление; **~ive** [kən'templətiv] □ созерцательный.
contempora|neous [kəntempə'reinjəs] □ современный; одновременный; **~ry** [kən'tempərəri] **1.** современный; одновременный; **2.** современник (-ица).
contempt [kən'tempt] презрение (for к Д); **~ible** [-əbl] □ презренный; **~uous** [-juəs] □ презрительный.
contend [kən'tend] *v/i.* бороться; соперничать; *v/t.* утверждать.
content [kən'tent] **1.** довольный; **2.** удовлетворять [-рить]; **3.** довольство; **4.** ['kɔntent] содержание; объём; **~ed** [kən'tentid] □ довольный, удовлетворённый.
contention [kən'tenʃən] спор, ссора.
contentment [kən'tentmənt] довольство.
contest **1.** ['kɔntest] соревнование; **2.** [kən'test] оспаривать [оспорить]; доби(ва)ться (места); отстаивать [отстоять] (территорию).
context ['kɔntekst] контекст.
contiguous [kən'tiguəs] □ смежный, соприкасающийся (to с Т).
continent ['kɔntinənt] **1.** □ сдержанный; целомудренный; **2.** материк, континент.
contingen|cy [kən'tindʒənsi] случайность *f*; непредвиденное обстоятельство; **~t** [-dʒənt] **1.** □ случайный, непредвиденный; **2.** ⚔, † контингент.
continu|al [kən'tinjuəl] □ беспрерывный, беспрестанный; **~ance** [-juəns] продолжительность *f*; **~ation** [kəntinju'eiʃən] продолжение; **~e** [kən'tinju:] *v/t.* продолжать [-должить]; to be **~d** продолжение следует; *v/i.* продолжаться [-должиться]; простираться; **~ity** [kɔntin'juiti] непрерывность *f*; **~ous** [kən'tinjuəs] □ непрерывный; сплошной.
contort [kən'tɔ:t] искажать [исказить] **~ion** [kən'tɔ:ʃən] искажение; искривление.
contour ['kɔntuə] контур, очертание.

contraband ['kɔntrəbænd] контрабанда.

contract 1. [kən'trækt] *v/t.* сокращать [-ратить]; сж(им)ать; заключать [-чить] (сделку, дружбу); заводить [-вести] (знакомство); вступать [-пить] в (брак); *v/i.* сокращаться [-ратиться]; сж(им)ать (-ся); 2. ['kɔntrækt] контракт, договор; **~ion** [kən'trækʃən] сжатие; сокращение; **~or** [-tə] подрядчик.

contradict [kɔntrə'dikt] противоречить (Д); **~ion** [kɔntrə'dikʃən] противоречие; **~ory** [-təri] □ противоречивый.

contrar|iety [kɔntrə'raiəti] разногласие, противоречие; **~y** ['kɔntrəri] 1. противоположный; ~ to *prp.* вопреки (Д), против (Р); 2. обратное; on the ~ наоборот.

contrast 1. ['kɔntræst] противоположность *f*, контраст; 2. [kən'træst] сопоставлять [-авить], противополагать [-ложить]; составлять контраст.

contribut|e [kən'tribju:t] содействовать, способствовать; [по]жертвовать; сотрудничать (to в П); **~ion** [kɔntri'bju:ʃən] вклад; взнос; статья; сотрудничество; **~or** [kən'tribjutə] сотрудник (-ица); **~ory** [-təri] содействующий; сотрудничающий.

contrit|e ['kɔntrait] □ сокрушающийся, кающийся; **~ion** [kən'triʃən] раскаяние.

contriv|ance [kən'traivəns] выдумка; изобретение; **~e** [kən'traiv] *v/t.* придум(ыв)ать; изобретать [-ести]; затевать [-еять]; *v/i.* ухитряться [-риться]; умудряться [-риться]; **~er** [-ə] изобретатель (ница *f*) *m.*

control [kən'troul] 1. руководство; надзор; контроль *m*; 2. управлять (Т); [про]контролировать, регулировать (*im*)*pf.*; сдерживать [-жать] (чувства, слёзы); **~ler** [-ə] контролёр, инспектор.

controver|sial [kɔntrə'və:ʃəl] □ спорный; **~sy** ['kɔntrəvə:si] спор, дискуссия, полемика; **~t** ['kɔntrəvə:t] оспаривать [оспорить].

contumacious [kɔntju'meiʃes] □ упорный; непокорный; ⚖ неподчиняющийся распоряжению суда.

contumely ['kɔntjum(i)li] оскорбление; дерзость *f*; бесчестье.

convalesce [kɔnvə'les] выздоравливать [выздороветь]; **~nce** [-ns] выздоровление; **~nt** [-nt] □ выздоравливающий.

convene [kən'vi:n] coз(ы)вать; соб(и)рать(ся); ⚖ вызывать [вызвать] (в суд).

convenien|ce [kən'vi:njəns] удобство; at your earliest как можно скорее; **~t** [-jənt] □ удобный.

convent ['kɔnvənt] монастырь *m*; **~ion** [kən'venʃən] собрание; съезд; соглашение; обычай.

converge [kən'və:dʒ] сходиться [сойтись]; сводить в одну точку.

convers|ant ['kɔnvəsnt] сведущий; **~ation** [kɔnvə'seiʃn] разговор, беседа; **~ational** [-l] разговорный; **~e** [kən'və:s] разговаривать, беседовать; **~ion** [kən'və:ʃən] превращение; изменение; ⊕ переработка, превращение; ⚡ трансформирование; *eccl.* обращение в другую веру; ✝ конверсия.

convert 1. ['kɔnvə:t] новообращённый; 2. [kən'və:t] превращать [-атить]; ⊕ перерабатывать [-ботать]; ⚡ трансформировать (*im*)*pf.*; *eccl.* обращать [-ратить] (в другую веру); ✝ конвертировать (*im*)*pf.*; **~er** [-ə] ⚡ конвертер; **~ible** [-əbl] □ изменяемый; обратимый; ✝ подлежащий конверсии.

convey [kən'vei] перевозить [-везти], переправлять [-править]; перед(ав)ать; **~ance** [-əns] перевозка; доставка; **~or** [-ə] ⊕ (или ~ belt) конвейер; транспортёр.

convict 1. ['kɔnvikt] осуждённый; каторжник; 2. [kən'vikt] признавать виновным; изобличать [-чить]; **~ion** [kən'vikʃən] ⚖ осуждение; убеждение.

convince [kən'vins] убеждать [убедить] (of в П).

convocation [kɔnvo'keiʃən] созыв; собрание.

convoke [kən'vouk] coз(ы)вать.

convoy 1. ['kɔnvɔi] конвой; сопровождение; 2. [kən'vɔi] сопровождать; конвоировать.

convuls|ion [kən'vʌlʃən] колебание (почвы); судорога; **~ive** [-siv] □ судорожный.

coo [ku:] ворковать.

cook [kuk] 1. кухарка, повар; 2. [со]стряпать, [при]готовить; **~ery** ['kukəri] кулинария; стряпня; **~ie, ~y** ['kuki] *Am.* печенье.

cool [ku:l] 1. прохладный; *fig.* хладнокровный; невозмутимый; *b. s.* дерзкий, нахальный; 2. прохлада; хладнокровие; 3. охлаждать(ся) [охладить(ся)]; осты(ва)ть.

coolness ['ku:lnis] холодок; прохлада; хладнокровие.

coop [ku:p] 1. курятник; 2. ~ up или in держать взаперти.

cooper ['ku:pə] бондарь *m.*

co-operat|e [kou'ɔpəreit] сотрудничать; **~ion** [kouɔpə'reiʃən] кооперация; сотрудничество; **~ive** [kou'ɔpərətiv] совместный, объединённый; ~ society кооперативное общество; **~or** [-eitə] сотрудник; кооператор.

co-ordinat|e 1. [kou'ɔ:dnit] □ неподчинённый; равный; 2. [-neit]

координи́ровать (*im*)*pf.*; согласо́вывать [-ова́ть]; **~ion** [kou'ɔ:di-'neiʃən] координа́ция.
cope [koup]: ~ with справля́ться [-а́виться] с (Т).
copious ['koupjəs] □ оби́льный; **~ness** [-nis] оби́лие.
copper ['kɔpə] **1.** медь *f*; ме́дная моне́та; **2.** ме́дный; **~y** [-ri] цве́та ме́ди.
coppice, copse ['kɔpis, kɔps] ро́ща.
copy ['kɔpi] **1.** ко́пия; ру́копись *f*; экземпля́р; **2.** перепи́сывать [-са́ть]; снима́ть ко́пию с (Р); **~-book** тетра́дь *f*; **~ing** ['kɔpiiŋ] перепи́сывание; **~ist** ['kɔpiist] перепи́счик; подража́тель *m*; **~right** [-rait] а́вторское пра́во.
coral ['kɔrəl] кора́лл.
cord [kɔ:d] **1.** верёвка, шнуро́к; *anat.* свя́зка; **2.** свя́зывать [-за́ть]; **~ed** ['kɔ:did] ру́бчатый (о мате́рии).
cordial ['kɔ:diəl] **1.** □ серде́чный, и́скренний; **2.** стимули́рующее (серде́чное) сре́дство; **~ity** [kɔ:-di'æliti] серде́чность *f*, раду́шие.
cordon ['kɔ:dən] **1.** кордо́н; **2.** ~ off отгора́живать [-роди́ть].
corduroy ['kɔ:dərɔi, -dju] ру́бчатый плис, вельве́т; **~s** *pl.* пли́совые (*or* вельве́товые) штаны́ *m/pl.*
core [kɔ:] **1.** сердцеви́на; вну́тренность *f*; ядро́; *fig.* суть *f*; **2.** выре́зывать сердцеви́ну из (Р).
cork [kɔ:k] **1.** про́бка; **2.** затыка́ть про́бкой; **~-jacket** спаса́тельный жиле́т; **~-screw** што́пор.
corn [kɔ:n] зерно́; хлеба́ *m/pl.*; *Am.* кукуру́за, маи́с; ⚕ мозо́ль *f*.
corner ['kɔ:nə] **1.** у́гол; **2.** ✝ ску́пка това́ра; **3.** *fig.* загна́ть в тупи́к; припере́ть к стене́; ✝ скупа́ть това́р.
cornet ['kɔ:nit] ♪ корне́т, корне́т-а-писто́н.
cornice ['kɔ:nis] ⚠ карни́з.
coron|ation [kɔrə'neiʃən] корона́ция; **~et** ['kɔrənit] коро́на, диаде́ма.
corpor|al ['kɔ:pərəl] **1.** □ теле́сный; **2.** ⚔ капра́л; **~ation** [kɔ:pə-'reiʃən] корпора́ция; муниципалите́т; *Am.* акционе́рное о́бщество.
corpse [kɔ:ps] труп.
corpulen|ce, ~cy ['kɔ:pjuləns] доро́дность *f*, ту́чность *f*; **~t** [-lənt] доро́дный, ту́чный.
corral *Am.* [kɔ'rɑ:l] **1.** заго́н (для скота́); **2.** загоня́ть [загна́ть].
correct [kə'rekt] **1.** □ пра́вильный, ве́рный, то́чный; **2.** *v/t.* исправля́ть [-а́вить], [про]корректи́ровать; **~ion** [kə'rekʃən] исправле́ние, попра́вка; house of ~ исправи́тельный дом.
correlate ['kɔrileit] устана́вливать соотноше́ние.
correspond [kɔris'pɔnd] соотве́тствовать (with, to Д); согласо́вываться [-сова́ться] (с Т); перепи́сываться (с Т); **~ence** [-əns] соотве́тствие, соотноше́ние; перепи́ска; **~ent** [-ənt] **1.** □ соотве́тствующий; **2.** корреспонде́нт(ка).
corridor ['kɔridɔ:] коридо́р; ~ train по́езд, состоя́щий из ваго́нов, соединённых та́мбурами.
corroborate [kə'rɔbəreit] подде́рживать [-жа́ть]; подтвержда́ть [-рди́ть].
corro|de [kə'roud] разъеда́ть [-е́сть]; [за]ржаве́ть; **~sion** [kə-'rouʒən] корро́зия; ржа́вчина; окисле́ние; **~sive** [-siv] **1.** □ е́дкий; **2.** е́дкое вещество́.
corrugate ['kɔrugeit] смо́рщи(ва)ть(ся); ⊕ де́лать рифлёным, волни́стым; **~d** iron рифлёное желе́зо.
corrupt [kə'rʌpt] **1.** □ испо́рченный; искажённый; развращённый; **2.** *v/t.* искажа́ть [-зи́ть]; развраща́ть [-рати́ть]; подкупа́ть [-пи́ть]; *v/i.* [ис]по́ртиться; искажа́ться [-зи́ться]; **~ible** [kə'rʌp-təbl] □ подкупно́й; **~ion** [-ʃən] по́рча; искаже́ние; прода́жность *f*.
corsage [kɔ:'sɑ:ʒ] корса́ж.
corset ['kɔ:sit] корсе́т.
co-signatory ['kou'signətəri] **1.** лицо́, подписа́вшее соглаше́ние совме́стно с други́ми; **2.** подпи́сывающий соглаше́ние совме́стно с други́ми.
cosmetic [kɔz'metik] **1.** космети́ческий; **2.** косме́тика.
cosmopolit|an [kɔzmo'pɔlitən] космополити́ческий; **~e** [kɔz'mɔpəlait] **1.** космополи́т(ка); **2.** космополити́ческий.
cost [kɔst] **1.** цена́, сто́имость *f*; first или prime ~ фабри́чная себесто́имость *f*; **2.** [*irr.*] сто́ить.
costl|iness ['kɔstlinis] дорогови́зна; **~y** [-li] дорого́й, це́нный.
costume ['kɔstju:m] (национа́льный или маскара́дный) костю́м.
cosy ['kouzi] **1.** □ ую́тный; **2.** стёганный чехо́л (для ча́йника).
cot [kɔt] де́тская крова́ть *f*; ⚓ ко́йка.
cottage ['kɔtidʒ] котте́дж; изба́; *Am.* ле́тняя да́ча; ~ piano небольшо́е пиани́но *n indecl.*
cotton ['kɔtn] **1.** хло́пок; хлопча́тая бума́га; ✝ си́тец; ни́тка; **2.** хлопчатобума́жный; ~ wool ва́та; **3.** F сдружи́ться (to с Т) *pf.*
couch [kautʃ] **1.** куше́тка; ло́говище; **2.** *v/t.* излага́ть [изложи́ть]; [с]формули́ровать; *v/i.* лежа́ть, притаи́ться *pf.* (о звеpя́х).
cough [kɔ:f, kɔf] **1.** ка́шель *m*; **2.** ка́шлять [кашляну́ть].
could [kud] *pt.* от can.

council ['kaunsl] сове́т; **~(l)or** [-silə] член сове́та; сове́тник.
counsel ['kaunsəl] **1.** обсужде́ние, совеща́ние; ⚖ адвока́т; ~ for the prosecution обвини́тель *m*; **2.** дава́ть сове́т (Д); **~(l)or** [-ə] сове́тник; *Am.* адвока́т.
count[1] [kaunt] **1.** счёт, подсчёт; ито́г; ⚖ статья́ в обвини́тельном а́кте; **2.** *v/t.* [со]счита́ть; подсчи́тывать [-ита́ть]; зачисля́ть [-и́слить]; *v/i.* счита́ться; име́ть значе́ние.
count[2] [~] граф (не англи́йский).
countenance ['kauntinəns] **1.** лицо́; самооблада́ние; подде́ржка; **2.** подде́рживать [-жа́ть], поощря́ть [-ри́ть].
counter[1] ['kauntə] прила́вок; сто́йка; таксо́метр; счётчик; фи́шка.
counter[2] [~] **1.** противополо́жный (to Д); встре́чный; **2.** *adv.* обра́тно; напро́тив; **3.** [вос]проти́виться (Д); (в бо́ксе) наноси́ть встре́чный уда́р.
counteract [kauntə'rækt] противоде́йствовать (Д); нейтрализова́ть (*im*)*pf*.
counterbalance 1. ['kauntəbæləns] противове́с; **2.** [kauntə'bæləns] уравнове́шивать [-ве́сить]; служи́ть противове́сом (Д).
counter-espionage ['kauntər'espiə'nɑ:ʒ] контрразве́дка.
counterfeit ['kauntəfit] **1.** подде́льный, подло́жный; **2.** подде́лка; **3.** подде́л(ыв)ать; обма́нывать [-ну́ть].
countermand 1. ['kauntə'mɑ:nd] контрприка́з; **2.** [kauntə'mɑ:nd] отменя́ть [-ни́ть] (зака́з, прика́з); отзыва́ть [отозва́ть] (лицо́, во́инскую часть).
counter-move ['kauntəmu:v] *fig.* отве́тная ме́ра.
counterpane [-pein] покрыва́ло; стёганое одея́ло.
counterpart [-pɑ:t] ко́пия; двойни́к; **~s** ли́ца и́ли ве́щи, взаи́мно дополня́ющие друг дру́га.
counterpoise [-pɔiz] **1.** противове́с; равнове́сие; **2.** держа́ть равнове́сие; (*a. fig.*) уравнове́шивать [-е́сить].
countersign [-sain] **1.** контрасигно́вка; ⚔ паро́ль *m*; **2.** скрепля́ть [-пи́ть] (по́дписью).
countervail [-veil] противостоя́ть (Д); уравнове́шивать [-е́сить].
countess ['kauntis] графи́ня.
counting-house ['kauntiŋhaus] конто́ра.
countless ['kauntlis] бесчи́сленный, несчётный.
country ['kʌntri] **1.** страна́; ме́стность *f*; дере́вня; **2.** дереве́нский; **~man** [-mən] крестья́нин; земля́к; **~side** [-'said] се́льская ме́стность *f*; се́льское населе́ние.
county ['kaunti] гра́фство; *Am.* о́круг.
coup [ku:] уда́чный ход (уда́р и [т. п.).]
couple [kʌpl] **1.** па́ра; сво́ра; **2.** соединя́ть [-ни́ть]; ассоции́ровать (*im*)*pf*.; ⊕ сцепля́ть [-пи́ть]; **~r** [-ə] *radio* устро́йство свя́зи.
coupling ['kʌpliŋ] совокупле́ние; ⊕ му́фта; сцепле́ние; *radio* связь *f*.
coupon ['ku:pɔn] купо́н, тало́н.
courage ['kʌridʒ] му́жество, сме́лость *f*, хра́брость *f*, отва́га; **~ous** [kə'reidʒəs] □ му́жественный, сме́лый, хра́брый.
courier ['kuriə] курье́р, наро́чный.
course [kɔ:s] **1.** направле́ние, курс; ход; тече́ние; блю́до (за обе́дом); of ~ коне́чно; **2.** *v/t.* гна́ться за (Т); охо́титься (с го́нчими) на (В) *or* за (Т); *v/i.* бе́гать, [по]бежа́ть.
court [kɔ:t] **1.** двор (*a. fig.*); суд; pay (one's) ~ уха́живать (to за Т); **2.** уха́живать за (Т); иска́ть расположе́ния (Р); **~eous** ['kə:tiəs] □ ве́жливый, учти́вый; **~esy** ['kə:tisi] учти́вость *f*, ве́жливость *f*; **~ier** ['kɔ:tjə] придво́рный; **~ly** [-ly] ве́жливый; **~-martial** ⚔ **1.** вое́нный трибуна́л; **2.** суди́ть вое́нным судо́м; **~ship** [-ʃip] уха́живание; **~yard** двор.
cousin ['kʌzn] двою́родный брат, двою́родная сестра́.
cove [kouv] (ма́ленькая) бу́хта; *fig.* убе́жище.
covenant ['kʌvinənt] **1.** ⚖ догово́р; заве́т; **2.** соглаша́ться [-ласи́ться].
cover ['kʌvə] **1.** кры́шка; обёртка; покрыва́ло; переплёт; конве́рт; ⚔ укры́тие; *fig.* покро́в; ⊕ кожу́х; *mot.* покры́шка; **2.** покры́(ва́)ть (*a.* ✝); прикры́(ва́)ть; скры(ва́)ть; **~ing** [-riŋ] (по)кры́шка; обши́вка; облицо́вка.
covert ['kʌvət] **1.** □ прикры́тый, та́йный; **2.** убе́жище для ди́чи.
covet ['kʌvit] жа́ждать (Р); **~ous** [-əs] □ жа́дный, а́лчный; скупо́й.
cow[1] [kau] коро́ва.
cow[2] [~] запу́гивать [-га́ть]; терроризова́ть (*im*)*pf*.
coward ['kauəd] **1.** □ трусли́вый; малоду́шный, ро́бкий; **2.** трус (-и́ха); **~ice** [-is] тру́сость *f*; малоду́шие; **~ly** [-li] трусли́вый.
cowboy ['kaubɔi] пасту́х; *Am.* ковбо́й.
cower ['kauə] съёжи(ва)ться.
cowl [kaul] капюшо́н.
coxcomb ['kɔkskoum] ♀ пету́ший гребешо́к; фат.
coxswain ['kɔkswein, *mst* 'kɔksn] рулево́й.
coy [kɔi] □ засте́нчивый, скро́мный.
crab [kræb] *zo.* краб; ⊕ лебёдка, во́рот; F ворчли́вый челове́к.
crab-louse ['kræblaus] площи́ца.

crack ['kræk] 1. треск; тре́щина; щель *f*; рассе́лина; F уда́р; *Am.* саркасти́ческое замеча́ние; *Am.* at ~ of day на заре́; 2. F перво-кла́ссный; 3. *v/t.* раска́лывать [-коло́ть], коло́ть; ~ a joke отпусти́ть шу́тку; *v/i.* производи́ть треск, шум; тре́скаться [тре́снуть], раска́лываться [-коло́ться]; лома́ться (о го́лосе); **~ed** [krækt] тре́снувший; F вы́живший из ума́; **~er** ['krækə] хлопу́шка-конфе́та; *Am.* то́нкое сухо́е пече́нье; **~le** ['krækl] потре́скивание; треск.
cradle ['kreidl] 1. колыбе́ль *f*; *fig.* нача́ло; младе́нчество; 2. убаю-к(ив)ать.
craft [krɑ:ft] ло́вкость; сноро́вка; ремесло́; су́дно (*pl.* суда́); **~sman** ['krɑ:ftsmən] ма́стер; реме́сленник; **~y** ['krɑ:fti] □ ло́вкий, иску́сный; хи́трый.
crag [kræg] скала́, утёс.
cram [kræm] впи́хивать [-хну́ть]; переполня́ть [-о́лнить]; [на]пи́чкать; F [за]зубри́ть.
cramp [kræmp] 1. су́дорога, спа́змы *f/pl.*; ⊕ зажи́м, скоба́; 2. вызыва́ть су́дорогу у (Р); стесня́ть [-ни́ть] (разви́тие); су́живать [су́зить] (по́ле де́йствия).
cranberry ['krænbəri] клю́ква.
crane [krein] 1. жура́вль *m*; ⊕ подъёмный кран; 2. поднима́ть кра́ном; вытя́гивать ше́ю.
crank [kræŋk] 1. рукоя́тка; причу́да; челове́к с причу́дами; 2. заводи́ть рукоя́тью (автомоби́ль и т. п.); **~-shaft** ⊕ коле́нчатый вал; **~y** [kræŋki] неиспра́вный (механи́зм); капри́зный; эксцентри́чный.
cranny ['kræni] щель *f*, тре́щина.
crape [kreip] креп; тра́ур.
crash [kræʃ] 1. гро́хот, треск; ✈ ава́рия; 🚂 круше́ние; † крах; 2. па́дать, ру́шиться с тре́ском; разби́(ва́)ть(ся); ✈ потерпе́ть ава́рию.
crater ['kreitə] кра́тер; ⚔ воро́нка.
crave [kreiv] *v/t.* настоя́тельно проси́ть; *v/i.* стра́стно жела́ть, жа́ждать (for P).
crawfish ['krɔ:fiʃ] речно́й рак.
crawl [krɔ:l] 1. по́лзание; *fig.* пресмыка́тельство; 2. пресмыка́ться; по́лзать, [по]ползти́.
crayfish ['kreifiʃ] речно́й рак.
crayon ['kreiən] цветно́й каранда́ш; пасте́ль *f* (каранда́ш); пасте́льный рису́нок.
craz|e [kreiz] 1. ма́ния; F мо́да, пова́льное увлече́ние; be the ~ быть в мо́де; 2. своди́ть с ума́; сходи́ть с ума́; **~y** ['kreizi] □ поме́шанный; ша́ткий.
creak [kri:k] 1. скрип; 2. [за]скрипе́ть.
cream [kri:m] 1. сли́вки *f/pl.*; крем; са́мое лу́чшее; 2. снима́ть сли́вки с (Р); **~ery** ['kri:məri] маслобо́йня; моло́чная; **~y** ['kri:mi] □ сли́вочный; кре́мовый.
crease [kri:s] 1. скла́дка; сгиб; 2. [с]мя́ть(ся); загиба́ть [загну́ть].
creat|e [kri'eit] [со]твори́ть; созд(ав)а́ть; **~ion** [-ʃən] созда́ние, (со)творе́ние; **~ive** [-tiv] тво́рческий; **~or** [-tə] созда́тель *m*, творе́ц; **~ure** ['kri:tʃə] созда́ние; существо́; тварь *f*.
creden|ce ['kri:dəns] ве́ра, дове́рие; **~tials** [kri:'denʃəlz] *pl.* вери́тельные гра́моты *f/pl.*, докуме́нты *m/pl.*
credible ['kredəbl] □ заслу́живающий дове́рие; вероя́тный.
credit ['kredit] 1. дове́рие; хоро́шая репута́ция; † креди́т; 2. ве́рить, доверя́ть (Д); † кредитова́ть (*im*)*pf.*; ~ a p. with a th. припи́сывать кому́-либо что-либо; **~able** ['kreditəbl] □ похва́льный; **~or** [-tə] кредито́р.
credulous ['kredjuləs] □ легкове́рный, дове́рчивый.
creed [kri:d] вероуче́ние; кре́до *indecl. n.*
creek [kri:k] бу́хта; зали́в; рука́в реки́; *Am.* прито́к; руче́й.
creep [kri:p] [*irr.*] по́лзать, [по-] ползти́; ви́ться (о расте́ниях); кра́сться; *fig.* ~ in вкра́дываться [вкра́сться]; **~er** ['kri:pə] вью́щееся расте́ние.
crept [krept] *pt.* и *p. pt.* от creep.
crescent ['kresnt] 1. расту́щий; ['kreznt] серпови́дный; 2. полуме́сяц.
crest [krest] гребешо́к (петуха́); хохоло́к (пти́цы); гре́бень *m* (волны́, горы́, шле́ма); **~-fallen** ['krestfɔ:lən] упа́вший ду́хом; уны́лый.
crevasse [kri'væs] рассе́лина (в леднике́); *Am.* проры́в плоти́ны.
crevice ['krevis] щель *f*, расще́лина, тре́щина.
crew¹ [kru:] брига́да, арте́ль рабо́чих; ⚓ судова́я кома́нда.
crew² [~] *pt.* от crow.
crib [krib] 1. я́сли *m/pl.*, корму́шка; де́тская крова́тка; *school*: шпарга́лка; 2. помеща́ть в те́сное помеще́ние; F спи́сывать тайко́м.
cricket ['krikit] *zo.* сверчо́к; кри́ке́т (игра́); F not ~ не по пра́вилам, нече́стно.
crime [kraim] преступле́ние.
crimina|l ['kriminəl] 1. престу́пник; 2. престу́пный; кримина́льный, уголо́вный; **~lity** [krimi'næliti] престу́пность *f*; вино́вность *f*.
crimp [krimp] гофрирова́ть (*im*)*pf.*
crimson ['krimzn] 1. багро́вый, мали́новый 2. [по]красне́ть.
cringe [krindʒ] раболе́пствовать.
crinkle ['kriŋkl] 1. скла́дка; мор-

щи́на; 2. [с]мо́рщиться; зави́(ва́)ться; [по]мя́ться.

cripple ['kripl] 1. кале́ка *m/f*, инвали́д; 2. [ис]кале́чить, [из]уро́довать; *fig.* парализова́ть (*im*)*pf.*

crisp [krisp] 1. кудря́вый; хрустя́щий; све́жий (о во́здухе); 2. зави́(ва́)ть(ся); хрусте́ть [хру́стнуть]; покрыва́ться ря́бью (о реке́ и т. п.).

criss-cross ['kriskrɔs] 1. *adv.* крест-на́крест; вкось; 2. перекре́щивать [-крести́ть].

criteri|on [krai'tiəriən], *pl.* **~a** [-riə] крите́рий, мери́ло.

criti|c ['kritik] кри́тик; **~cal** ['kritikəl] □ крити́ческий; разбо́рчивый; **~cism** [-sizm], **~que** [kri'ti:k] кри́тика; реце́нзия; **~cize** ['kritisaiz] [рас]критикова́ть; осужда́ть [осуди́ть].

croak [krouk] [за]ка́ркать; [за-] ква́кать.

crochet ['krouʃei] 1. вяза́ние (крючко́м); 2. вяза́ть (крючко́м).

crock [krɔk] гли́няный кувши́н; **~ery** ['krɔkəri] посу́да.

crone [kroun] F стару́ха; ста́рая карга́.

crony ['krouni] F закады́чный друг.

crook [kruk] 1. по́сох; крюк; поворо́т; заги́б; *sl.* обма́нщик, плут; 2. сгиба́ть(ся) [согну́ть(ся)]; искривля́ть(ся) [-ви́ть(ся)]; **~ed** ['krukid] изо́гнутый; криво́й; нече́стный.

croon [kru:n] 1. моното́нное пе́ние; 2. напева́ть.

crop [krɔp] 1. урожа́й; хлеба́ на корню́; кнутови́ще; зоб; 2. засева́ть [засе́ять]; собира́ть урожа́й; подстрига́ть [-ри́чь]; ~ **up** (внеза́пно) появля́ться [-ви́ться].

cross [krɔs, krɔ:s] 1. крест; распя́тие; 2. □ попере́чный; серди́тый; 3. *v/t.* [о]крести́ть; скре́щивать [-ести́ть] (ру́ки и т. п.); переходи́ть [перейти́], переезжа́ть [перее́хать]; *fig.* противоде́йствовать (Д); противоре́чить (Д); ~ **o. s.** [пере]крести́ться; *v/i.* ⚓ размину́ться *pf.*; **~-bar** попере́чина; **~-breed** по́месь *f*; гибри́д; **~-examination** перекрёстный допро́с; **~-eyed** косо́й, косогла́зый; **~ing** ['krɔsiŋ] перекрёсток; перепра́ва; перее́зд, перехо́д; **~-road** попере́чная доро́га; **~s** *pl.* или *sg.* перекрёсток; **~-section** попере́чное сече́ние; **~wise** крестообра́зно; кресто́м.

crotchet ['krɔtʃit] крючо́к; причу́да; ♪ четвертна́я но́та.

crouch [krautʃ] рабо́лепствовать; притаи́ться *pf.*

crow [krou] 1. воро́на; пе́ние петуха́; ра́достный крик (младе́нца); 2. [*irr.*] [про]пе́ть (о петухе́); ликова́ть; **~-bar** лом, ва́га.

crowd [kraud] 1. толпа́; мно́жество, ма́сса; толкотня́, да́вка; F компа́ния; 2. собира́ться толпо́й, толпи́ться; набива́ться битко́м.

crown [kraun] 1. вене́ц, коро́на; *fig.* заверше́ние; кро́на (де́рева); маку́шка (головы́); коро́нка (зу́ба); 2. [у]венча́ть; коронова́ть (*im*)*pf.*; *fig.* заверша́ть [-ши́ть]; поста́вить коро́нку (на зуб).

cruci|al ['kru:ʃiəl] □ крити́ческий; реша́ющий; **~ble** [-sibl] ти́гель *m*; **~fixion** [kru:si'fikʃən] распя́тие; **~fy** ['kru:sifai] распина́ть [-пя́ть].

crude [kru:d] □ сыро́й; необрабо́танный; незре́лый; гру́бый.

cruel ['kru:əl] □ жесто́кий; *fig.* мучи́тельный; **~ty** [-ti] жесто́кость *f*.

cruet-stand ['kruitstænd] судо́к.

cruise [kru:z] ⚓ 1. морско́е путеше́ствие; 2. крейси́ровать; соверша́ть ре́йсы; **~r** ['kru:zə] ⚓ кре́йсер.

crumb [krʌm] 1. кро́шка; 2. (= **~le** ['krʌmbl]) [рас-, ис]кроши́ть(ся).

crumple ['krʌmpl] [с]мя́ть(ся); [с]ко́мкать(ся).

crunch [krʌntʃ] разжёвывать [-жева́ть]; хрусте́ть [хру́стнуть].

crusade [kru:'seid] кресто́вый похо́д; кампа́ния; **~r** [-ə] кресторо́сец.

crush [krʌʃ] 1. да́вка; толкотня́; 2. *v/t.* [раз]дави́ть; выжима́ть [вы́жать]; уничтожа́ть [-о́жить].

crust [krʌst] 1. ко́рка; кора́; 2. покрыва́ть(ся) ко́ркой, коро́й; **~y** ['krʌsti] □ покры́тый ко́ркой, коро́й.

crutch [krʌtʃ] косты́ль *m*.

cry [krai] 1. крик; вопль *m*; плач; 2. [за]пла́кать; восклица́ть [-и́кнуть]; крича́ть [кри́кнуть]; ~ **for** [по]тре́бовать (Р).

crypt [kript] склеп; **~ic** ['kriptik] таи́нственный; сокрове́нный.

crystal ['kristl] хруста́ль *m*; криста́лл; *Am.* стекло́ для часо́в; **~line** [-təlain] хруста́льный; **~lize** [-təlaiz] кристаллизова́ть(ся) (*im*)*pf.*

cub [kʌb] 1. детёныш (зве́ря); *Am.* нович́ок; 2. [о]щени́ться.

cub|e [kju:b] ⅍ 1. куб; ~ **root** куби́ческий ко́рень *m*; 2. возводи́ть в куб; **~ic**(**al** □) ['kju:bik, -ikəl] куби́ческий.

cuckoo ['kuku:] куку́шка.

cucumber ['kju:kəmbə] огуре́ц.

cud [kʌd] жва́чка; **chew the** ~ жева́ть жва́чку.

cuddle ['kʌdl] *v/t.* прижима́ть к себе́; *v/i.* приж(им)а́ться (друг к дру́гу).

cudgel ['kʌdʒəl] 1. дуби́на; 2. дуба́сить дуби́ной.

cue [kju:] (билья́рдный) кий; намёк; *thea.* ре́плика.

cuff [kʌf] 1. манже́та, обшла́г; 2. [по]би́ть (руко́й), [по]колоти́ть.

culminate ['kʌlmineit] достига́ть вы́сшей то́чки (или сте́пени).
culpable ['kʌlpəbl] □ вино́вный; престу́пный.
culprit ['kʌlprit] престу́пник; вино́вный.
cultivat|e ['kʌltiveit] обраба́тывать [-бо́тать]; возде́л(ыв)ать; культиви́ровать; **~ion** [kʌlti'veiʃən] возде́лывание (земли́); разведе́ние, культу́ра (расте́ний); **~or** ['kʌltiveitə] культива́тор (⚒ ору́дие); земледе́лец.
cultural ['kʌltʃərəl] □ культу́рный.
culture ['kʌltʃə] культу́ра; разведе́ние, возде́лывание; **~d** [-d] культу́рный; культиви́рованный.
cumber ['kʌmbə] затрудня́ть [-ни́ть]; стесня́ть [-ни́ть]; **~some** [-səm], **cumbrous** ['kʌmbrəs] громо́здкий; обремени́тельный.
cumulative ['kju:mjulətiv] □ сово-ку́пный; кумуляти́вный; нако́пленный.
cunning ['kʌniŋ] **1.** ло́вкий; хи́трый; кова́рный; *Am.* изя́щный; преле́стный; **2.** ло́вкость *f*; хи́трость *f*; кова́рство.
cup [kʌp] ча́шка; ча́ша; ку́бок; **~board** ['kʌbəd] шкаф.
cupidity [kju'piditi] а́лчность *f*, жа́дность *f*, ска́редность *f*.
cupola ['kju:pələ] ку́пол.
cur [kə:] дворня́жка (соба́ка).
curate ['kjuərit] помо́щник прихо́дского свяще́нника.
curb [kə:b] **1.** мундшту́чная узде́чка; узда́ (*a. fig.*); (*a.* **~**-stone) обо́чина тротуа́ра; **2.** обу́здывать [-да́ть] (*a. fig.*).
curd [kə:d] **1.** творо́г; **2.** (*mst* **~le**, [kə:dl]) свёртываться [сверну́ться] (о молоке́, кро́ви).
cure [kjuə] **1.** лече́ние; сре́дство; **2.** [вы́]лечи́ть, исцеля́ть [-ли́ть]; заготовля́ть [-то́вить], консерви́ровать (*im*)*pf*.
curio ['kjuəriou] ре́дкая антиква́рная вещь *f*; **~sity** [kjuəri'ɔsiti] любопы́тство; ре́дкость *f*; **~us** ['kjuəriəs] □ любопы́тный; пытли́вый; стра́нный.
curl [kə:l] **1.** ло́кон; завито́к; спира́ль *f*; **2.** ви́ться; клуби́ться; **~y** ['kə:li] кудря́вый; курча́вый; вью́щийся.
currant ['kʌrənt] сморо́дина; (*a.* dried **~**) кори́нка.
curren|cy ['kʌrənsi] ✝ де́ньги *f/pl.*, валю́та; де́нежное обраще́ние; **~t** [-ənt] **1.** □ теку́щий; ходя́чий; ✝ находя́щийся в обраще́нии; **2.** пото́к; тече́ние; ⚡ ток.
curse [kə:s] **1.** прокля́тие; руга́тельство; бич, бе́дствие; **2.** проклина́ть [-кля́сть]; руга́ться; **~d** ['kə:sid] □ прокля́тый.
curt [kə:t] □ кра́ткий.
curtail [kə:'teil] укора́чивать [-роти́ть]; уре́з(ыв)ать; *fig.* сокраща́ть [сократи́ть].
curtain ['kə:tn] **1.** занаве́ска; за́навес; **2.** занаве́шивать [-ве́сить].
curts(e)y ['kə:tsi] **1.** ревера́нс; покло́н; **2.** де́лать ревера́нс (to Д).
curv|ature ['kə:vətʃə] искривле́ние; **~e** [kə:v] **1.** Ѧ крива́я; изги́б; кривизна́; **2.** [со]гну́ть; изгиба́ть (-ся) [изогну́ть(ся)].
cushion ['kuʃin] **1.** поду́шка; борт (билья́рдного стола́); **2.** подкла́дывать поду́шку под (В).
custody ['kʌstədi] опе́ка, попече́ние; заточе́ние.
custom ['kʌstəm] обы́чай; привы́чка; клиенту́ра; **~s** *pl.* тамо́женные по́шлины *f/pl.*; **~ary** [-əri] □ обы́чный; **~er** [-ə] постоя́нный (-ная) покупа́тель(ница *f*) *m*; клие́нт(ка); **~-house** тамо́жня; **~-made** *Am.* изгото́вленный на зака́з.
cut [kʌt] **1.** разре́з, поре́з; зару́бка, засе́чка; отре́з (мате́рии); покро́й (пла́тья); (*mst* short-**~**) сокращённый путь *m*; **2.** [*irr.*] *v/t.* ре́зать; разреза́ть [-ре́зать]; [по]стри́чь; [от]шлифова́ть; [с]коси́ть (траву́); проре́з(ыв)аться (о зуба́х); **~** short прер(ы)ва́ть; **~** down сокраща́ть [-рати́ть] (расхо́ды); **~** out выреза́ть [вы́резать]; [с]крои́ть; выключа́ть [вы́ключить]; *fig.* вытесня́ть [вы́теснить]; be **~** out for быть сло́вно со́зданным для (Р); *v/i.* ре́зать; **~** in вме́шиваться [-ша́ться].
cute [kju:t] □ F хи́трый; *Am.* ми́лый, привлека́тельный.
cutlery ['kʌtləri] ноже́вые изде́лия *n/pl.*
cutlet ['kʌtlit] котле́та.
cut|-out ⚡ автомати́ческий выключа́тель *m*, предохрани́тель *m*; **~ter** ['kʌtə] ре́зчик (по де́реву); закро́йщик; ⊕ ре́жущий инструме́нт; ⚓ ка́тер; **~-throat** головоре́з; уби́йца *m*; **~ting** ['kʌtiŋ] **1.** □ о́стрый, ре́зкий; язви́тельный; **2.** ре́зание; закро́йка; ⊕ фрезерова́ние; гране́ние; ❦ побе́г, черено́к; **~s** *pl.* обре́зки *m/pl.*; (газе́тные) вы́резки *f/pl.*; ⊕ стру́жки *f/pl.*
cycl|e ['saikl] **1.** цикл; круг; велосипе́д; ⊕ кругово́й проце́сс; **2.** е́здить на велосипе́де; **~ist** [-ist] велосипеди́ст(ка).
cyclone ['saikloun] цикло́н.
cylinder ['silində] цили́ндр (*geom.*); ⊕ бараба́н; ва́лик.
cymbal ['simbəl] ♪ таре́лки *f/pl.*
cynic ['sinik] **1.** (*a.* **~al** □, -ikəl) цини́чный; **2.** ци́ник.
cypress ['saipris] ❦ кипари́с.
Czech [tʃɛk] **1.** чех, че́шка; **2.** че́шский.
Czecho-Slovak ['tʃekou'slouvæk] **1.** жи́тель(ница) Чехослова́кии; **2.** чехослова́цкий.

D

dab [dæb] 1. шлепо́к; мазо́к; пятно́ (кра́ски); 2. слегка́ тро́гать (В); де́лать лёгкие мазки́ на (П).
dabble ['dæbl] плеска́ть(ся); бара́хтаться (в воде́ и т. п.); халту́рить, занима́ться че́м-либо пове́рхностно.
dad [dæd] F, **~dy** ['dædi] F па́па.
daffodil ['dæfədil] жёлтый нарци́сс.
dagger ['dægə] кинжа́л; be at ~s drawn быть на ножа́х (с Т).
daily ['deili] 1. *adv.* ежедне́вно; 2. ежедне́вный; 3. ежедне́вная газе́та.
dainty ['deinti] 1. □ ла́комый; изя́щный; изы́сканный; 2. ла́комство, деликате́с.
dairy ['dɛəri] моло́чная; масло-де́льня.
daisy ['deizi] маргари́тка.
dale [deil] доли́на, дол.
dall|iance ['dæliəns] несерьёзное заня́тие; флирт; **~y** ['dæli] зря теря́ть вре́мя; флиртова́ть.
dam [dæm] 1. ма́тка (живо́тных); да́мба, плоти́на; 2. запру́живать [-уди́ть].
damage ['dæmidʒ] 1. вред; поврежде́ние; убы́ток; **~s** *pl.* ⚖ убы́тки *m/pl.*; компенса́ция за убы́тки; 2. поврежда́ть [-еди́ть], [ис]по́ртить.
damask ['dæməsk] камка́.
damn [dæm] 1. проклина́ть [-ля́сть]; осужда́ть [осуди́ть]; руга́ться; 2. прокля́тие; руга́тельство; **~ation** [dæm'neiʃən] прокля́тие; осужде́ние.
damp [dæmp] 1. сы́рость *f*, вла́жность *f*; 2. вла́жный, за́тхлый; 3. *a.* **~en** ['dæmpən] [на]мочи́ть; [от-]сыре́ть; *fig.* обескура́жи(ва)ть.
danc|e [dɑ:ns] 1. та́нец; бал; 2. танцева́ть; **~er** ['dɑ:nsə] танцо́р, танцо́вщик (-ица); **~ing** [-iŋ] та́нцы *m/pl.*; пля́ска; *attr.* танцева́льный.
dandelion ['dændilaiən] ⚘ одува́нчик.
dandle ['dændl] [по]кача́ть (на рука́х).
dandruff ['dændrəf] пе́рхоть *f*.
dandy ['dændi] 1. щёголь *m*; *sl.* первокла́ссная вещь *f*; 2. *Am. sl.* первокла́ссный.
Dane [dein] датча́нин (-ча́нка).
danger ['deindʒə] опа́сность *f*; **~ous** ['deindʒrəs] □ опа́сный.
dangle ['dæŋgl] висе́ть, свиса́ть [сви́снуть]; болта́ть (Т).
Danish ['deiniʃ] да́тский.
dapple ['dæpl] испещря́ть [-ри́ть]; **~d** [-d] испещрённый, пёстрый; **~grey** се́рый в я́блоках (конь).
dar|e [dɛə] *v/i.* [по]сме́ть; отва́жи(ва)ться; *v/t.* вызыва́ть [вы́звать]; **~e-devil** смельча́к, сорвиголова́ *m*; **~ing** [dɛəriŋ] 1. □ сме́лый, отва́жный; де́рзкий; 2. сме́лость *f*, отва́жность *f*.
dark [dɑ:k] 1. тёмный; сму́глый; та́йный; мра́чный; ~ horse „тёмная лоша́дка“; ~ lantern потайно́й фона́рь *m*; 2. темнота́, тьма; неве́дение; **~en** ['dɑ:kən] затемня́ть(ся) [-ни́ть(ся)]; **~ness** ['dɑ:knis] темнота́, тьма; **~y** ['dɑ:ki] F черноко́жий, чёрный (о не́гре).
darling ['dɑ:liŋ] 1. люби́мец (-мица); ба́ловень *m*; 2. люби́мый.
darn [dɑ:n] [за]што́пать.
dart [dɑ:t] 1. стрела́; дро́тик; прыжо́к; 2. *v/t.* мета́ть [метну́ть] (стре́лы, взгля́ды и т. п.); *v/i. fig.* мча́ться стрело́й.
dash [dæʃ] 1. поры́в; уда́р; взмах; плеск (воды́); *fig.* при́месь *f*, чу́точка; набро́сок; штрих; тире́ *n indecl.* 2. *v/t.* броса́ть [бро́сить]; разби́(ва́)ть; разбавля́ть [-а́вить]; *v/i.* ри́нуться; броса́ться [бро́ситься]; **~-board** *mot.*, ✈ при́борная доска́; **~ing** ['dæʃiŋ] □ лихо́й.
data ['deitə] *pl.*, *Am. a. sg.* да́нные *n/pl.*; но́вости *f/pl.*; фа́кты *m/pl.*
date [deit] 1. да́та, число́; F свида́ние; out of ~ устаре́лый; up to ~ нове́йший; совреме́нный; 2. дати́ровать (*im*)*pf.*; *Am.* F усло́вливаться [-о́виться] с (Т) (о встре́че); име́ть свида́ние.
daub [dɔ:b] [по]ма́зать; [на]малева́ть.
daughter ['dɔ:tə] дочь *f*; **~-in-law** [-rinlɔ:] неве́стка, сноха́.
daunt [dɔ:nt] устраша́ть [-ши́ть], запу́гивать [-га́ть]; **~less** ['dɔ:ntlis] неустраши́мый, бесстра́шный.
dawdle ['dɔ:dl] F безде́льничать.
dawn [dɔ:n] 1. рассве́т, у́тренняя заря́; *fig.* зача́тки *m/pl.*; про́блески *m/pl.*; 2. света́ть.
day [dei] день *m*; (*mst* ~s *pl.*) жизнь *f*; ~ off выходно́й день *m*; the other ~ на дня́х; неда́вно; **~break** рассве́т; **~-labo(u)rer** подёнщик (-ица); **~-star** у́треняя звезда́.
daze [deiz] ошеломля́ть [-ми́ть]; ослепля́ть [-пи́ть].
dazzle ['dæzl] ослепля́ть [-пи́ть]; ⚓ маскирова́ть окра́ской.
dead [ded] 1. мёртвый; увя́дший (о цвета́х); онеме́вший (о па́льцах); неподви́жный; безразли́чный; ~ bargain дешёвка; ~ letter письмо́, недоста́вленное по а́дресу; a ~ shot стрело́к, не даю́щий про́маха; ~ wall глуха́я стена́; 2. *adv.* по́лно, соверше́нно; ~ against реши́тельно про́тив; 3. the ~ по-

ко́йники *m/pl.*; **~en** [dedn] лиша́ть (-ся) си́лы; заглуша́ть [-ши́ть]; **~-lock** *fig.* мёртвая то́чка; засто́й; **~ly** [-li] смерте́льный; смертоно́сный.

deaf [def] □ глухо́й; **~en** [defn] оглуша́ть [-ши́ть].

deal [di:l] 1. коли́чество; соглаше́ние; обхожде́ние; F сде́лка; a good ~ весьма́ мно́го; a great ~ о́чень мно́го; 2. [*irr.*] *v/t.* разд(ав)а́ть; распределя́ть [-ли́ть]; *v/i.* торгова́ть; ~ with обходи́ться [обойти́сь] *or* поступа́ть [-пи́ть] с (Т); име́ть де́ло с (Т); **~er** ['di:lə] торго́вец; **~ing** ['di:liŋ] (*mst* **~s** *pl.*) торго́вые дела́ *n/pl.*; **~t** [delt] *pt.* и *p. pt.* от ~.

dean [di:n] настоя́тель собо́ра; дека́н (факульте́та).

dear [diə] 1. □ дорого́й, ми́лый; 2. прекра́сный челове́к; 3. F o(h) ~!, ~ me! го́споди!

death [deθ] смерть *f*; **~-bed** сме́ртное ло́же; **~-duty** нало́г на насле́дство; **~less** ['deθlis] бессме́ртный; **~ly** [-li] смерте́льный; **~-rate** проце́нт сме́ртности; **~-warrant** сме́ртный пригово́р.

debar [di'bɑ:] исключа́ть [-чи́ть]; лиша́ть пра́ва.

debase [di'beis] унижа́ть [уни́зить]; понижа́ть ка́чество (Р).

debat|able [di'beitəbl] □ спо́рный, дискуссио́нный; **~e** [di'beit] 1. диску́ссия; пре́ния *n/pl.*, деба́ты *m/pl.*; 2. обсужда́ть [-уди́ть]; [по-] спо́рить; обду́м(ыв)ать.

debauch [di'bɔtʃ] 1. распу́тство; попо́йка; 2. развраща́ть [-рати́ть]; обольща́ть [-льсти́ть].

debilitate [di'biliteit] ослабля́ть [-а́бить]; расслабля́ть [-а́бить].

debit ['debit] ✝ 1. де́бет; 2. дебетова́ть (*im*)*pf.*, вноси́ть в де́бет.

debris ['debri:] разва́лины *f/pl.*; обло́мки *m/pl.*

debt [det] долг; **~or** ['dətə] должни́к (-и́ца).

decade ['dekəd] дека́да; десятиле́тие.

decadence ['dekədəns] упа́док; декаде́нтство.

decamp [di'kæmp] снима́ться с ла́геря; уд(и)ра́ть; **~ment** [-mənt] выступле́ние из ла́геря; бы́стрый ухо́д.

decant [di'kænt] [про]фильтрова́ть; сце́живать [сцеди́ть]; **~er** [-ə] графи́н.

decapitate [di'kæpiteit] обезгла́вливать [-ла́вить].

decay [di'kei] 1. гние́ние; разложе́ние; 2. [с]гнить; разлага́ться [-ложи́ться].

decease [di'si:s] *part.* ⚖ 1. смерть *f*, кончи́на; 2. умира́ть [умере́ть], сконча́ться *pf.*

deceit [di'si:t] обма́н; **~ful** [-ful] □ обма́нчивый.

deceiv|e [di'si:v] обма́нывать [-ну́ть]; **~er** [-ə] обма́нщик (-ица).

December [di'sembə] дека́брь *m.*

decen|cy ['di:snsi] прили́чие; благопристо́йность *f*; **~t** [-t] □ прили́чный; сла́вный.

deception [di'sepʃən] обма́н; ложь *f.*

decide [di'said] реша́ть(ся) [реши́ть(ся)]; принима́ть реше́ние; **~d** [-id] □ реши́тельный; определённый; бесспо́рный.

decimal ['desiməl] 1. десяти́чный; 2. десяти́чная дробь *f.*

decipher [di'saifə] расшифро́вывать [-ова́ть]; разбира́ть [разобра́ть].

decisi|on [di'siʒən] реше́ние; реши́тельность *f*; ⚖ пригово́р; **~ve** [di'saisiv] реша́ющий.

deck [dek] 1. ⚓ па́луба; *Am.* коло́да (карт); 2. украша́ть [укра́сить]; уб(и)ра́ть (цвета́ми и т. п.); **~-chair** складно́й стул.

declaim [di'kleim] произноси́ть [-нести́] (речь); [про]деклами́ровать.

declar|able [di'kleərəbl] подлежа́щий деклара́ции; **~ation** [deklə'reiʃən] заявле́ние; деклара́ция (*a.* ✝); **~e** [di'kleə] объявля́ть [-ви́ть]; заявля́ть [-ви́ть]; выска́зываться [вы́сказаться] (for за В, against про́тив Р); предъявля́ть [-ви́ть] (ве́щи в тамо́жне).

declin|ation [dekli'neiʃən] отклоне́ние; накло́н; **~e** [di'klain] 1. склон, укло́н; паде́ние; упа́док (сил); сниже́ние (цен); ухудше́ние (здоро́вья); зака́т (жи́зни); 2. *v/t.* отклоня́ть [-ни́ть] (предложе́ние); *gr.* [про]склоня́ть; *v/i.* приходи́ть в упа́док; ухудша́ться [уху́дшиться] (о здоро́вье и т. п.).

declivity [di'kliviti] пока́тость *f*; отло́гий спуск.

decode [di:'koud] *tel.* расшифро́вывать [-рова́ть].

decompose [di:kəm'pouz] разлага́ть(ся) [-ложи́ть(ся)]; [с]гнить.

decontrol ['di:kən'troul] освобожда́ть от контро́ля (торго́влю и т. п.).

decorat|e ['dekəreit] украша́ть [укра́сить]; награжда́ть зна́ком отли́чия; **~ion** [dekə'reiʃən] украше́ние; о́рден, знак отли́чия; **~ive** ['dekərətiv] декорати́вный.

decor|ous ['dekərəs] □ присто́йный; **~um** [di'kɔ:rəm] этике́т.

decoy [di'kɔi] 1. прима́нка, мано́к; 2. прима́нивать [-ни́ть]; завлека́ть [-е́чь].

decrease 1. ['di:kri:s] уменьше́ние, убыва́ние, пониже́ние; 2. [di:'kri:s] уменьша́ть(ся) [уме́ньшить (-ся)], убы́(ва́)ть.

decree [di'kri:] 1. ука́з, декре́т, прика́з; ⚖ постановле́ние 2. издава́ть декре́т.

decrepit [di'krepit] дряхлый; ветхий.
dedicat|e ['dedikeit] посвящать [-ятить]; **~ion** [dedi'keiʃən] посвящение.
deduce [di'dju:s] выводить [вывести] (заключение, формулу и т. п.).
deduct [di'dʌkt] вычитать [вычесть]; **~ion** [di'dʌkʃən] вычет; вывод, заключение; ✝ скидка.
deed [di:d] **1.** действие; поступок; подвиг; ⚖ документ; **2.** *Am.* передавать по акту.
deem [di:m] *v/t.* считать [счесть]; *v/i.* полагать; [по]думать (of о П).
deep [di:p] **1.** □ глубокий; хитрый; густой (о краске); **2.** бездна; *poet.* море, океан; **~en** ['di:pən] углублять(ся) [-бить(ся)]; сгущать(ся) [сгустить(ся)] (о красках, тенях); **~ness** [-nis] глубина.
deer [diə] *coll.* красный зверь *m*; олень *m*; лань *f*.
deface [di'feis] искажать [исказить]; стирать [стереть].
defam|ation [defə'meiʃən] диффамация; клевета; **~e** [di'feim] поносить; [о]клеветать.
default [di'fɔ:lt] **1.** невыполнение обязательств; неявка в суд; in **~** of за неимением (Р); **2.** не выполнять обязательств; прекращать платежи; не являться по вызову суда.
defeat [di'fi:t] **1.** поражение; расстройство (планов); **2.** ⚔ побеждать [-едить]; расстраивать [-роить] (планы).
defect [di'fekt] недостаток; неисправность *f*, дефект; изъян; **~ive** [-tiv] □ недостаточный; дефектный, повреждённый.
defence, *Am.* **defense** [di'fens] оборона, защита; **~less** [-lis] беззащитный.
defend [di'fend] оборонять(ся), [-нить(ся)], защищать(ся) [-итить(ся)]; ⚖ защищать на суде; **~ant** [-ənt] ⚖ подсудимый; **~er** [-ə] защитник.
defensive [di'fensiv] **1.** оборона; **2.** оборонный, оборонительный.
defer [di'fə] откладывать [отложить]; отсрочи(ва)ть; *Am.* ⚔ давать отсрочку от призыва.
defian|ce [di'faiəns] вызов; неповиновение; пренебрежение; **~t** [-ənt] □ вызывающий.
deficien|cy [di'fiʃənsi] недостаток; дефицит; **~t** [-ənt] недостаточный; несовершенный.
deficit ['defisit] недочёт, дефицит.
defile [di'fail] [про]дефилировать.
defin|e [di'fain] определять [-лить]; давать характеристику (Р); устанавливать значение (Р); **~ite** ['definit] □ определённый; точный; **~ition** [defi'niʃən] определение; **~itive** [di'finitiv] □ определительный.
deflect [di'flekt] отклонять(ся) [-нить(ся)].
deform [di'fɔ:m] [из]уродовать; искажать [исказить] (мысль); **~ed** изуродованный; искажённый (о мысли); **~ity** [di'fɔmiti] уродство.
defraud [di'frɔ:d] обманывать [-нуть]; выманивать [выманить] (of В).
defray [di'frei] оплачивать [оплатить].
deft [deft] □ ловкий, искусный.
defy [di'fai] вызывать [вызвать] (на спор, борьбу); пренебрегать [-бречь] (Т).
degenerate **1.** [di'dʒenəreit] вырождаться [выродиться]; **2.** [-rit] □ вырождающийся.
degrad|ation [degrə'deiʃən] понижение, деградация; **~e** [di'greid] *v/t.* понижать [понизить]; разжаловать *pf.*; унижать [унизить].
degree [di'gri:] градус; ступень *f*; уровень *m*; степень *f*; звание; by **~s** *adv.* постепенно; in no **~** *adv.* ничуть, нисколько.
deify ['di:ifai] боготворить.
deign [dein] соизволять [-олить]; удостаивать [-стоить].
deity ['di:iti] божество.
deject [di'dʒekt] удручать [-чить]; угнетать [-ести]; **~ed** [-id] □ удручённый; угнетённый; **~ion** [di'dʒekʃən] уныние.
delay [di'lei] **1.** задержка; отсрочка; замедление; **2.** *v/t.* задерживать [-жать]; откладывать [отложить]; медлить с (Т); *v/i.* медлить, мешкать.
delega|te **1.** ['deligit] делегат, представитель(ница *f*) *m*; **2.** [-geit] делегировать (*im*)*pf.*, поручать [-чить]; **~tion** [deli'geiʃən] делегация, депутация.
deliberat|e **1.** [di'libəreit] *v/t.* обдум(ыв)ать; взвешивать [-есить]; обсуждать [обсудить]; *v/i.* совещаться; **2.** [-rit] □ преднамеренный, умышленный; **~ion** [dilibə'reiʃən] размышление; обсуждение; осмотрительность *f*.
delica|cy ['delikəsi] деликатность *f*; лакомство; утончённость *f*; нежность *f*; чувствительность *f*; **~te** [-kit] □ деликатный; хрупкий; изящный; искусный (о работе); чувствительный; щепетильный; **~tessen** *Am.* [delikə'tesn] гастрономический магазин.
delicious [di'liʃəs] восхитительный; очень вкусный.
delight [di'lait] **1.** удовольствие; восторг; наслаждение; **2.** восхищать [-итить]; доставлять наслаждение (Д); наслаждаться (in Т); **~** to *inf.* иметь удовольствие (+*inf.*); **~ful** [-ful] □ очаровательный; восхитительный.

delineate [di'linieit] обрисóвывать [-ова́ть]; опи́сывать [-са́ть].
delinquent [di'liŋkwənt] 1. правонарушитель(ница *f*) *m*; престу́пник (-ица); 2. престу́пный.
deliri|ous [di'liriəs] находя́щийся в бреду́, вне себя́, в исступле́нии; **~um** [-əm] бред; исступле́ние.
deliver [di'livə] освобожда́ть [-боди́ть]; доставля́ть [-а́вить]; разноси́ть [-нести́] (газе́ты и т. п.); произноси́ть [-нести́] (речь); сда(ва́)ть (зака́з); наноси́ть [нанести́] (уда́р); be **~ed** ⚕ разреши́ться от бре́мени, роди́ть; **~ance** [-rəns] освобожде́ние; **~er** [-rə] освободи́тель *m*; поставщи́к; **~y** [-ri] ⚕ ро́ды *m/pl.*; ✉ разно́ска; † доста́вка.
dell [del] ле́систая доли́на.
delude [di'lu:d] вводи́ть в заблужде́ние; обма́нывать [-ну́ть].
deluge ['delju:dʒ] 1. наводне́ние; пото́п; 2. затопля́ть [-пи́ть]; наводня́ть [-ни́ть] *(a. fig.)*.
delus|ion [di'lu:ʒən] заблужде́ние; иллю́зия; **~ive** [-siv] □ обма́нчивый; иллюзо́рный.
demand [di'mɑ:nd] 1. тре́бование (*a.* ⚖); запро́с; потре́бность *f*; † спрос (на това́р); 2. [по]тре́бовать (Р).
demean [di'mi:n] вести́ себя́; ~ o. s. роня́ть своё досто́инство; **~o(u)r** [-ə] поведе́ние.
demented [di'mentid] сумасше́дший.
demilitarize [di:'militəraiz] демилитаризова́ть *(im)pf.*
demobilize [di:'moubilaiz] демобилизова́ть *(im)pf.*
democra|cy [di'mɔkrəsi] демокра́тия; **~tic(al** □) [demɔ'krætik(əl)] демократи́ческий.
demolish [di'mɔliʃ] разруша́ть [-ру́шить]; сноси́ть [снести́].
demon ['di:mən] де́мон, дья́вол.
demonstrat|e ['demənstreit] [про-] демонстри́ровать; дока́зывать [-за́ть]; **~ion** [deməns'treiʃən] демонстра́ция; демонстри́рование; доказа́тельство; **~ive** [di'mɔnstrətiv] □ убеди́тельный; демонстрати́вный; экспанси́вный; *gr.* указа́тельный.
demote [di:'mout] снижа́ть в до́лжности.
demur [di'mə:] 1. [по]колеба́ться; возража́ть [-рази́ть]; 2. колеба́ние; возраже́ние.
demure [di'mjuə] □ серьёзный; чо́порный.
den [den] ло́говище; берло́га; *sl.* прито́н.
denial [di'naiəl] отрица́ние; опроверже́ние; отка́з.
denominat|e [di'nɔmineit] наз(ы)ва́ть; дава́ть и́мя (Д); **~ion** [dinɔmi'neiʃn] наименова́ние; се́кта.
denote [di'nout] означа́ть [-на́чить], обознача́ть [-на́чить].
denounce [di'nauns] обвиня́ть [-ни́ть]; поноси́ть; денонси́ровать (догово́р) *(im)pf.*
dens|e [dens] □ густо́й; пло́тный; *fig.* глу́пый, тупо́й; **~ity** ['densiti] густота́; пло́тность *f*.
dent [dent] 1. вы́боина, вда́вленное ме́сто; 2. вда́вливать [вдави́ть].
dentist ['dentist] зубно́й врач.
denunciat|ion [dinʌnsi'eiʃən] доно́с; обличе́ние, обвине́ние; **~or** [di'nʌnsieitə] обвини́тель *m*; доно́счик (-ица).
deny [di'nai] отрица́ть; отка́зываться [-за́ться] от (Р); отка́зывать [-за́ть] в (П).
depart [di'pɑ:t] *v/i.* уходи́ть [уйти́], уезжа́ть [уе́хать]; отбы́(ва́)ть, отправля́ться [-а́виться]; отступа́ть [-пи́ть] (from от Р); **~ment** [-mənt] ве́домство; департа́мент; о́трасль *f* (нау́ки); отде́л, отделе́ние; о́бласть *f*; *Am.* министе́рство; State ♀ министе́рство иностра́нных дел; ~ store универма́г; **~ure** [di'pɑ:tʃə] отхо́д, отбы́тие, отъезд; ухо́д; отправле́ние; отклоне́ние.
depend [di'pend]: ~ (up)on зави́сеть от (Р); F it **~s** смотря́ по обстоя́тельствам; **~able** [-əbl] наде́жный; **~ant** [-ənt] подчинённый; иждиве́нец; **~ence** [-əns] зави́симость *f*; дове́рие; **~ency** [-ənsi] зави́симость *f*; коло́ния; **~ent** [-ənt] □ (on) зави́сящий (от Р); подчинённый (*a. gr.*).
depict [di'pikt] изобража́ть [-рази́ть]; *fig.* опи́сывать [-са́ть].
deplete [di'pli:t] опорожня́ть [-ни́ть]; *fig.* истоща́ть [-щи́ть].
deplor|able [di'plɔ:rəbl] □ плаче́вный; заслу́живающий сожале́ния; **~e** [di'plɔ:] оплак(ив)ать; сожале́ть о (П).
deport [di'pɔ:t] высыла́ть [вы́слать]; ссыла́ть [сосла́ть]; ~ o. s. вести́ себя́; **~ment** [-mənt] мане́ры *f/pl.*, уме́ние держа́ть себя́.
depose [di'pouz] смеща́ть [смести́ть]; сверга́ть [све́ргнуть] (с престо́ла); ⚖ дать показа́ния под прися́гой.
deposit [di'pɔzit] 1. отложе́ние; за́лежь *f*; † вклад (в банк); депози́т; зало́г; 2. класть [положи́ть]; депони́ровать *(im)pf.*; дава́ть оса́док; **~ion** [depə'ziʃən] сверже́ние (с престо́ла); показа́ние под прися́гой; оса́док; **~or** [di'pɔzitə] вкла́дчик (-ица).
depot 1. ['depou] 🚂 депо́ *n indecl.*; склад; сара́й; 2. ['di:po] *Am.* 🚂 ста́нция.
deprave [di'preiv] развраща́ть [[-рати́ть].
depreciate [di'pri:ʃieit] обесце́ни(ва)ть; недооце́нивать [-и́ть].

depress [di'pres] угнета́ть [-ести́]; подавля́ть [-ви́ть]; унижа́ть [-и́зить]; **~ed** [-t] *fig.* уны́лый; **~ion** [di'preʃən] сниже́ние; впа́дина; тоска́; ⚕ депре́ссия.
deprive [di'praiv] лиша́ть [лиши́ть] (of P).
depth [depθ] глубина́.
deput|ation [depju'teiʃən] депута́ция, делега́ция; **~e** [di'pju:t] делеги́ровать (*im*)*pf.*; **~y** ['depjuti] делега́т(ка); депута́т(ка); замести́тель(ница *f*) *m*.
derail [di'reil] 🚂 *v/i.* сходи́ть с ре́льсов; *v/t.* устро́ить круше́ние (по́езда).
derange [di'reindʒ] расстра́ивать [-ро́ить] (мы́сли, пла́ны); приводи́ть в беспоря́док.
derelict ['derilikt] поки́нутый (кора́бль, дом), (за)бро́шенный; **~ion** [deri'likʃən] забро́шенность *f*.
deri|de [di'raid] осме́ивать [-ся́ть], высме́ивать [вы́смеять]; **~sion** [di'riʒən] высме́ивание; **~sive** [di'raisiv] □ насме́шливый.
deriv|ation [deri'veiʃən] исто́чник; происхожде́ние; **~e** [di'raiv] происходи́ть [-изойти́]; извлека́ть [-вле́чь] (по́льзу) (from от P); устана́вливать происхожде́ние (P).
derogat|e ['derogeit] умаля́ть [-ли́ть] (from B); **~ion** [dero'geiʃən] умале́ние.
derrick ['derik] ⊕ де́ррик-кран; ⚒ бурова́я вы́шка; ⚓ подъёмная стрела́.
descend [di'send] спуска́ться [спусти́ться]; сходи́ть [сойти́]; ✈ снижа́ться [сни́зиться]; ~ (up)on обру́ши(ва)ться на (B); происходи́ть [-изойти́] (*from* из P); **~ant** [-ənt] пото́мок.
descent [di'sent] спуск; сниже́ние; склон; скат; происхожде́ние.
describe [dis'kraib] опи́сывать [-са́ть].
description [dis'kripʃən] описа́ние; изображе́ние.
desert 1. ['dezət] a) пусты́нный; забро́шенный; b) пусты́ня; 2. [di'zə:t] a) *v/t.* броса́ть [бро́сить]; покида́ть [-ки́нуть]; *v/i.* дезерти́ровать (*im*)*pf.*; b) заслу́га; **~er** [-ə] дезерти́р; **~ion** [-ʃən] дезерти́рство; оставле́ние.
deserv|e [di'zə:v] заслу́живать [-жи́ть]; име́ть заслу́ги (of пе́ред T); **~ing** [-iŋ] заслу́живающий; досто́йный (of P).
design [di'zain] 1. за́мысел; прое́кт; план; рису́нок; узо́р; наме́рение; 2. предназнача́ть [-зна́чить]; заду́м(ыв)ать; составля́ть план (P); [на]рисова́ть.
designat|e ['dezigneit] определя́ть [-ли́ть]; обознача́ть [-зна́чить]; предназнача́ть [-зна́чить]; **~ion** [dezig'neiʃən] указа́ние; назначе́ние.
designer [di'zainə] конструќтор; чертёжник; *fig.* интрига́н.
desir|able [di'zaiərəbl] □ жела́тельный; **~e** [di'zaiə] 1. жела́ние; тре́бование; 2. [по]жела́ть (P); [по]тре́бовать (P); **~ous** [-rəs] □ жела́ющий, жа́ждущий (of P).
desist [di'zist] отка́зываться [-за́ться] (from от P).
desk [desk] конто́рка; пи́сьменный стол.
desolat|e 1. ['desoleit] опустоша́ть [-ши́ть]; разоря́ть [-ри́ть]; 2. [-lit] □ опустошённый; несча́стный; одино́кий; **~ion** [deso'leiʃən] опустоше́ние; одино́чество.
despair [dis'pɛə] 1. отча́яние; безнадёжность *f*; 2. отча́иваться [-ча́яться]; теря́ть наде́жду (of на B); **~ing** [-riŋ] □ отча́ивающийся.
despatch *s.* dispatch.
desperat|e ['despərit] □ отча́янный; безнадёжный; отъя́вленный; *adv.* отча́янно; стра́шно; **~ion** [despə'reiʃən] отча́яние; безрассу́дство.
despise [dis'paiz] презира́ть.
despite [dis'pait] 1. зло́ба; in ~ of вопреки́ (Д); несмотря́ на (B); на́зло́ (Д); 2. *prp.* (*a.* ~ of) несмотря́ на (B).
despoil [dis'pɔil] [о]гра́бить; лиша́ть [лиши́ть] (of P).
despond [dis'pɔnd] уныва́ть; теря́ть наде́жду; па́дать ду́хом; **~ency** [-ənsi] уны́ние; упа́док ду́ха; **~ent** [-ənt] □ пода́вленный; уны́лый.
dessert [di:'zə:t] десе́рт.
destin|ation [desti'neiʃən] назначе́ние; ме́сто назначе́ния, цель *f* (путеше́ствия); **~e** ['destin] предназнача́ть [-зна́чить]; предопределя́ть [-ли́ть]; **~y** [-tini] судьба́; уде́л.
destitute ['destitju:t] □ нужда́ющийся; лишённый (of P).
destroy [dis'trɔi] уничтожа́ть [-о́жить]; истребля́ть [-би́ть]; разруша́ть [-у́шить].
destruct|ion [dis'trʌkʃən] разруше́ние; уничтоже́ние; разоре́ние; **~ive** [-tiv] □ разруши́тельный; па́губный; вре́дный.
detach [di'tætʃ] отделя́ть [-ли́ть]; отвя́зывать [-за́ть]; разъединя́ть [-ни́ть]; ⚔, ⚓ отряжа́ть [-яди́ть], пос(ы)ла́ть; **~ed** [-t] отде́льный; беспристра́стный; **~ment** [-mənt] разъедине́ние; ⚔ командирова́ние; ⚔ отря́д.
detail 1. ['di:teil] подро́бность *f*, дета́ль *f*; ⚔ наря́д, кома́нда; in ~ в подро́бностях, подро́бно; 2. [di'teil] входи́ть в подро́бности; ⚔ откомандиро́вывать [-рова́ть].
detain [di'tein] заде́рживать [-жа́ть]; содержа́ть под стра́жей.

detect [di'tekt] обнару́жи(ва)ть; ⚡ детекти́ровать; **~ion** [di'tekʃən] обнару́жение; ⚡ детекти́рование; **~ive** [-tiv] **1.** сы́щик, аге́нт сыскно́й поли́ции; **2.** сыскно́й, детекти́вный.

detention [di'tenʃən] задержа́ние, содержа́ние под аре́стом.

deter [di'tə:] отпу́гивать [-гну́ть] (from от P).

deteriorat|e [di'tiəriəreit] ухудша́ть(ся) [уху́дшить(ся)]; [ис]по́ртить(ся); **~ion** [ditiəriə'reiʃən] ухудше́ние; по́рча.

determin|ation [ditə:mi'neiʃən] определе́ние; установле́ние (грани́ц); калькуля́ция (цен); реши́тельность *f*; **~e** [di'tə:min] *v/t.* устана́вливать [-нови́ть]; определя́ть [-ли́ть]; реша́ть [реши́ть]; *v/i.* реша́ться [реши́ться]; **~ed** [-d] реши́тельный; твёрдый (хара́ктер).

detest [di'test] ненави́деть; пита́ть отвраще́ние к (Д); **~able** [-əbl] □ отврати́тельный; **~ation** [dites'teiʃən] отвраще́ние.

dethrone [di'θroun] сверга́ть с престо́ла.

detonate ['di:touneit] детони́ровать; взрыва́ть(ся) [взорва́ть(ся)].

detour [di'tuə] **1.** око́льный путь *m*; *Am.* объе́зд; make a ~ де́лать крюк.

detract [di'trækt] умаля́ть [-ли́ть], уменьша́ть [уме́ньшить]; **~ion** [di'trækʃən] умале́ние (досто́инства); клевета́.

detriment ['detrimənt] уще́рб, вред.

devaluate [di:'væljueit] обесце́ни(ва)ть.

devastat|e ['devəsteit] опустоша́ть [-ши́ть]; разоря́ть [-ри́ть]; **~ion** [devəs'teiʃən] опустоше́ние.

develop [di'veləp] разви́(ва́)ть(ся); излага́ть [изложи́ть] (пробле́му); *phot.* проявля́ть [-ви́ть]; *Am.* обнару́жи(ва)ть; **~ment** [-mənt] разви́тие; эволю́ция; рост; расшире́ние; собы́тие.

deviat|e ['di:vieit] отклоня́ться [-ни́ться]; уклоня́ться [-ни́ться]; **~ion** [di:vi'eiʃən] отклоне́ние; девиа́ция (ко́мпаса); *pol.* укло́н.

device [di'vais] приспособле́ние, изобрете́ние; деви́з, эмбле́ма; leave a p. to his own **~s** предоставля́ть челове́ка самому́ себе́.

devil [devl] **1.** дья́вол, чёрт, бес; **2.** *v/i.* исполня́ть черновую рабо́ту для како́го-либо литера́тора; **~ish** [-iʃ] □ дья́вольский; а́дский; **~(t)ry** чёрная ма́гия; чертовщи́на.

devious ['di:viəs] □ блужда́ющий.

devise [di'vaiz] **1.** ⚖ завеща́ние; **2.** приду́м(ыв)ать; изобрета́ть [-рести́]; ⚖ завеща́ть (*im*)*pf.*

devoid [di'vɔid] (of) лишённый (P).

devot|e [di'vout] посвяща́ть [-яти́ть] (В/Д); отд(ав)а́ть; **~ed** [-id] □ пре́данный; привя́занный; **~ion** [di'vouʃən] пре́данность *f*, привя́занность *f*; **~s** *pl.* религио́зные обря́ды *m/pl.*, моли́твы *f/pl.*

devour [di'vauə] пож(и)ра́ть.

devout [di'vaut] □ благогове́йный; на́божный, благочести́вый.

dew [dju:] **1.** роса́; *poet.* све́жесть *f*; **2.** ороша́ть [ороси́ть]; **~y** покры́тый росо́й; вла́жный.

dexter|ity [deks'teriti] прово́рство; ло́вкость *f*; **~ous** ['dekstərəs] □ ло́вкий; прово́рный.

diabolic(al □) [daiə'bɔlik(əl)] дья́вольский; *fig.* жесто́кий; злой.

diagram ['daiəgræm] диагра́мма; схе́ма.

dial ['daiəl] **1.** цифербла́т; со́лнечные часы́ *m/pl.*; *teleph.* диск; **2.** *teleph.* набира́ть но́мер.

dialect ['daiəlekt] диале́кт, наре́чие.

dialogue ['daiəlɔg] диало́г; разгово́р.

diameter [dai'æmitə] диа́метр.

diamond ['daiəmənd] алма́з; бриллиа́нт; ромб; **~s** *pl. cards*: бу́бны *f/pl.*

diaper ['daiəpə] пелёнка.

diaphragm ['daiəfræm] диафра́гма *a. opt.*; *teleph.* мембра́на.

diary ['daiəri] дневни́к.

dice [dais] **1.** (*pl.* от die[2]) ко́сти *f/pl.*; **2.** игра́ть в ко́сти; **~-box** стака́нчик для игра́льных косте́й.

dicker ['dikə] *Am.* торгова́ться по мелоча́м.

dictat|e **1.** ['dikteit] предписа́ние; веле́ние; *pol.* дикта́т; **2.** [dik'teit] [про]диктова́ть (*a. fig.*); предпи́сывать [-са́ть]; **~ion** [dik'teiʃən] дикто́вка, дикта́нт; предписа́ние; **~orship** [dik'teitəʃip] диктату́ра.

diction ['dikʃən] ди́кция; **~ary** [-ri] слова́рь *m.*

did [did] *pt.* от do.

die[1] [dai] умира́ть [умере́ть]; сконча́ться *pf.*; F томи́ться жела́нием; ~ away, ~ down замира́ть [-мере́ть] (о зву́ке); затиха́ть [-и́хнуть] (о ве́тре); увяда́ть [-я́нуть]; угаса́ть [уга́снуть].

die[2] [~] (*pl.* dice) игра́льная кость *f*; (*pl.* dies [daiz]) ⊕ штамп; чека́н; lower ~ ма́трица.

diet ['daiət] **1.** пи́ща, стол; дие́та; **2.** *v/t.* держа́ть на дие́те; *v/i.* быть на дие́те.

differ ['difə] различа́ться, отлича́ться; не соглаша́ться [-ласи́ться], расходи́ться [разойти́сь] (*from* с Т, in в П); **~ence** ['difrəns] ра́зница; разли́чие; разногла́сие; ⅍ ра́зность *f*; **~ent** [-t] □ ра́зный; друго́й, не тако́й (from как), ино́й; **~entiate** [difə'renʃieit] различа́ть (-ся) [-чи́ть(ся)], отлича́ть(ся) [-чи́ть(ся)].

difficult ['difikəlt] □ тру́дный; тре́бовательный; **~y** тру́дность *f*; затрудне́ние.
diffiden|ce ['difidəns] неуве́ренность *f*; засте́нчивость *f*; **~t** [-dənt] □ неуве́ренный; засте́нчивый.
diffus|e 1. [di'fju:z] *fig.* распространя́ть [-ни́ть]; разглаша́ть [-ласи́ть]; 2. [di'fju:s] □ распространённый; рассе́янный (о све́те); **~ion** [di'fju:ʒən] распростране́ние; рассе́ивание.
dig [dig] 1. [*irr.*] копа́ться; [вы́]копа́ть; ры́ться; [вы́]рыть; 2. F толчо́к, тычо́к.
digest 1. [di'dʒest] перева́ривать [-ри́ть] (пи́щу); усва́ивать [усво́ить]; *v/i.* перева́риваться [-ри́ться]; усва́иваться [усво́иться]; 2. ['daidʒest] о́черк, резюме́ *n indecl.*; ⚖ свод зако́нов; **~ible** [di'dʒestəbl] удобовари́мый; *fig.* легко́ усва́иваемый; **~ion** [-tʃən] пищеваре́ние.
dignif|ied ['dignifaid] досто́йный; вели́чественный; **~y** [-fai] возводи́ть в сан; *fig.* облагора́живать [-ро́дить].
dignit|ary ['dignitəri] сано́вник; **~y** [-ti] досто́инство; сан.
digress [dai'gres] отступа́ть [-пи́ть]; отклоня́ться [-ни́ться] (от те́мы).
dike [daik] 1. да́мба; плоти́на; гать *f*; 2. ока́пывать рвом; защища́ть да́мбой; осуша́ть кана́вами.
dilapidate [di'læpideit] приходи́ть в упа́док; приводи́ть в упа́док.
dilat|e [dai'leit] расширя́ть(ся) [-ши́рить(ся)]; **~ory** ['dilətəri] □ ме́дленный; запозда́лый.
diligen|ce ['dilidʒəns] прилежа́ние, усе́рдие; **~t** □ приле́жный, усе́рдный.
dilute [dai'lju:t] разбавля́ть [-ба́вить]; разводи́ть [-вести́].
dim [dim] 1. □ ту́склый, нея́сный (свет); сла́бый (о зре́нии); сму́тный (о воспомина́ниях); 2. [по-]тускне́ть; [за]тума́нить(ся).
dime [daim] *Am.* моне́та в 10 це́нтов (= 0,1 до́ллара).
dimin|ish [di'miniʃ] уменьша́ть(ся) [уме́ньши́ть(ся)]; убы́(ва́)ть; **~ution** [dimi'nju:ʃən] уменьше́ние; убавле́ние; **~utive** [di'minjutiv] □ миниатю́рный.
dimple ['dimpl] я́мочка (на щеке́).
din [din] шум; гро́хот.
dine [dain] [по]обе́дать; угоща́ть обе́дом; **~r** ['dainə] обе́дающий; 🚃 (*part. Am.*) ваго́н-ресторáн.
dingle ['diŋgl] глубо́кая лощи́на.
dingy ['dindʒi] □ гря́зный; ту́склый.
dining|-car 🚃 ваго́н-рестора́н; **~-room** столо́вая.
dinner ['dinə] обе́д; **~-party** го́сти на зва́ном обе́де.
dint [dint]: by ~ of посре́дством (Р).

dip [dip] 1. *v/t.* погружа́ть [-узи́ть]; окуна́ть [-ну́ть]; обма́кивать [-кну́ть]; *v/i.* погружа́ться [-узи́ться], окуна́ться [-ну́ться]; салютова́ть (фла́гом) (*im*)*pf.*; спуска́ться [-сти́ться]; 2. погруже́ние; отко́с; F карма́нник.
diploma [di'ploumə] дипло́м; свиде́тельство; **~cy** [-si] диплома́тия; **~t** *s.* **~tist**; **tic(al** □) [diplo'mætik, -ikəl] дипломати́ческий; **~tist** [di'ploumətist] диплома́т.
dipper ['dipə] ковш; черпа́к.
dire ['daiə] ужа́сный.
direct [di'rekt] 1. □ прямо́й; непосре́дственный; диаметра́льный; я́сный; откры́тый; ~ current ⚡ постоя́нный ток; ~ train беспереса́дочный по́езд; 2. *adv.* = **~ly**: непосре́дственно; пря́мо, неме́дленно; 3. руководи́ть (Т); управля́ть (Т); направля́ть [-а́вить]; ука́зывать доро́гу (Д); **~ion** [di'rekʃən] руково́дство; указа́ние; инстру́кция; направле́ние; **~ion-finder** радиопеленга́тор; **~ive** [di'rektiv] директи́вный; направля́ющий; **~ly** [-li] 1. *adv.* пря́мо, непосре́дственно; неме́дленно; 2. *cj.* как то́лько.
director [di'rektə] руководи́тель *m*, дире́ктор; *films* режиссёр; board of **~s** наблюда́тельный сове́т; **~ate** [-rit] дире́кция; правле́ние; дире́кторство; **~y** [-ri] а́дресная (и́ли телефо́нная) кни́га.
dirge [də:dʒ] погреба́льная песнь *f*.
dirigible ['diridʒəbl] дирижа́бль *m*.
dirt [də:t] грязь *f*; нечисто́ты *f/pl.*; **~-cheap** F деше́вле па́реной ре́пы; **~y** ['də:ti] 1. □ гря́зный; неприли́чный, скабрёзный; нена́стный (о пого́де); 2. загрязня́ть [-ни́ть].
disability [disə'biliti] неспосо́бность *f*, бесси́лие.
disable [dis'eibl] де́лать неприго́дным; [ис]калечи́ть; **~d** [-d] искале́ченный; ~ veteran инвали́д войны́.
disadvantage [disəd'vɑ:ntidʒ] невы́года; уще́рб; неудо́бство.
disagree [disə'gri:] расходи́ться во взгля́дах; противоре́чить друг дру́гу; быть вре́дным (with для Р); **~able** [-əbl] □ неприя́тный; **~ment** [-mənt] разла́д, разногла́сие.
disappear [disə'piə] исчеза́ть [-е́знуть]; скры́(ва́)ться; **~ance** [-rəns] исчезнове́ние.
disappoint [disə'pɔint] разочаро́вывать [-рова́ть]; обма́нывать [-ну́ть]; **~ment** разочарова́ние.
disapprov|al [disə'pru:vəl] неодобре́ние; **~e** ['disəpru:v] не одобря́ть [одо́брить] (Р); неодобри́тельно относи́ться (of к Д).
disarm [dis'ɑ:m] *v/t.* обезору́жи(ва)ть; разоружа́ть [-жи́ть];

v/i. разоружáться [-жи́ться]; **~ament** [dis'ɑːməmənt] разоружéние.

disarrange ['disə'reindʒ] расстрáивать [-рóить]; приводи́ть в беспоря́док.

disast|er [di'zɑːstə] бéдствие; катастрóфа; **~rous** [-rəs] □ бéдственный; катастрофи́ческий.

disband [dis'bænd] распускáть [-усти́ть].

disbelieve [disbi'liːv] не [по]вéрить; не доверя́ть (Д).

disburse [dis'bəːs] расплáчиваться [-лати́ться].

disc [disk] *s.* disk.

discard [dis'kɑːd] отбрáсывать [-рóсить] (за ненáдобностью); отвергáть [-éргнуть].

discern [di'səːn] различáть [-чи́ть]; распознавáть; разглядéть *pf.*; отличáть [-чи́ть]; **~ing** [-iŋ] □ проницáтельный; **~ment** [-mənt] распознавáние; проницáтельность *f.*

discharge [dis'tʃɑːdʒ] **1.** *v/t.* разгружáть [-узи́ть]; освобождáть [-боди́ть]; увольня́ть [увóлить]; уплáчивать [уплати́ть] (долги́); выполня́ть [вы́полнить] (обязáтельства); *v/i.* разряжáться [-яди́ться]; гнои́ться; **2.** разгру́зка; вы́стрел; освобождéние; увольнéние; разря́д; выполнéние.

disciple [di'saibl] учени́к (-и́ца); послéдователь(ница *f*) *m.*

discipline ['disiplin] **1.** дисципли́на, поря́док; **2.** дисциплини́ровать (*im*)*pf.*

disclose [dis'klouz] обнару́живать; разоблачáть [-чи́ть]; раскры́(вá)ть.

discolo(u)r [dis'kʌlə] обесцвéчивать(ся) [-éтить(ся)].

discomfort [dis'kʌmfət] **1.** неудóбство; беспокóйство; **2.** причиня́ть неудóбство (Д).

discompose [diskəm'pouz] расстрáивать [-рóить]; [вз]волновáть, [вс]тревóжить.

disconcert [diskən'səːt] смущáть [смути́ть]; приводи́ть в замешáтельство.

disconnect [diskə'nekt] разъединя́ть [-ни́ть] (*a.* ⚡); разобщáть [-щи́ть]; расцепля́ть [-пи́ть]; **~ed** [-id] □ бессвя́зный; отры́вистый.

disconsolate [dis'kɔnsəlit] □ неутéшный.

discontent ['diskən'tent] недовóльство; неудовлетворённость *f*; **~ed** [-id] □ недовóльный; неудовлетворённый.

discontinue ['diskən'tinjuː] прер(ы)вáть; прекращáть [-рати́ть].

discord ['diskɔːd], **~ance** [dis'kɔːdəns] разноглáсие; разлáд; ♪ диссонáнс.

discount 1. ['diskaunt] ✝ дискóнт, учёт векселéй; ски́дка; **2.** [dis'kaunt] ✝ дисконти́ровать (*im*)*pf.*, учи́тывать [учéсть] (векселя́); дéлать ски́дку.

discourage [dis'kʌridʒ] обескурáживать; отбивáть охóту (Д; from к Д); **~ment** [-mənt] обескурáженность *f*, упáдок ду́ха.

discourse [dis'kɔːs] **1.** рассуждéние; речь *f*; бесéда, разговóр; **2.** орáторствовать; вести́ бесéду.

discourte|ous [dis'kəːtiəs] □ невéжливый, неучти́вый; **~sy** [-tisi] невéжливость *f*, неучти́вость *f.*

discover [dis'kʌvə] дéлать откры́тие (Р); обнару́живать, раскры́(вá)ть; **~y** [-ri] откры́тие.

discredit [dis'kredit] **1.** дискредитáция; **2.** дискредити́ровать (*im*)*pf.*; [о]позóрить.

discreet [dis'kriːt] □ осторóжный; не болтли́вый.

discrepancy [dis'krepənsi] разноглáсие; рáзница; несхóдство.

discretion [dis'kreʃən] благоразу́мие; осторóжность *f*; усмотрéние.

discriminat|e [dis'krimineit] выделя́ть [вы́делить]; относи́ться по-рáзному; умéть распознавáть, различáть; **~ against** стáвить в неблагоприя́тные услóвия (В); **~ing** [-iŋ] □ умéющий различáть, распознавáть; **~ion** [-'neiʃən] проницáтельность *f*; дискриминáция.

discuss [dis'kʌs] обсуждáть [-уди́ть], дискути́ровать; **~ion** [-ʃən] обсуждéние, диску́ссия; прéния *n/pl.*

disdain [dis'dein] **1.** презирáть [-зрéть]; считáть ни́же своегó достóинства; **2.** презрéние; пренебрежéние.

disease [di'ziːz] болéзнь *f*; **~d** [-d] [больнóй.]

disembark ['disim'bɑːk] сходи́ть нá берег (с су́дна); выгружáть [вы́грузить] (товáры).

disengage ['disin'geidʒ] высвобождáть(ся) [вы́свободить(ся)]; разобщáть [-щи́ть]; ⊕ разъединя́ть [-ни́ть].

disentangle ['disin'tæŋgl] распу́т(ыв)ать(ся); *fig.* выпу́тываться [вы́путать(ся)] (из затруднéний).

disfavo(u)r ['dis'feivə] **1.** неми́лость *f*; **2.** не одобря́ть [одóбрить].

disfigure [dis'figə] обезобрáживать [-рáзить]; искажáть [исказúть].

disgorge [dis'gɔːdʒ] извергáть [-éргнуть] (лáву); изрыгáть [-гну́ть] (пи́щу).

disgrace [dis'greis] **1.** неми́лость *f*; позóр, бесчéстие; **2.** [о]позóрить; подвéргнуть неми́лости; **~ful** [-ful] □ посты́дный, позóрный.

disguise [dis'gaiz] **1.** маскирóвка; переодевáние; мáска; **2.** [за]маскировáть(ся); переодé(вá)ть(ся); скры(вá)ть.

disgust [dis'gʌst] **1.** отвращéние; **2.** внушáть отвращéние (Д); **~ing** [-iŋ] □ отвратúтельный.
dish [diʃ] **1.** блюдо, тарéлка, мúска; **~s** *pl.* посýда; блюдо, кýшанье; **2.** класть на блюдо; (*mst* **~ up**) подавáть на стол.
dishearten [dis'hɑ:tn] приводúть в уны́ние.
dishevel(l)ed [di'ʃevəld] растрёпанный, взъерóшенный.
dishonest [dis'ɔnist] □ нечéстный; недобросóвестный; **~y** [-i] недобросóвестность *f*; обмáн.
dishono(u)r [dis'ɔnə] **1.** бесчéстие, позóр; **2.** [о]бесчéстить, [о]позóрить; **~able** [-rəbl] □ бесчéстный; нúзкий.
disillusion [disi'lu:ʒən] **1.** разочаровáние; **2.** (*a.* **~ize** [-aiz]) разрушáть иллюзии (Р); открывáть прáвду (Д).
disinclined ['disin'klaind] нерасполóженный.
disinfect ['disin'fekt] дезинфицúровать (*im*)*pf.*; **~ant** [-ənt] дезинфицúрующее срéдство.
disintegrate [dis'intigreit] распадáться [-пáсться]; разрушáться [-ýшиться].
disinterested [dis'intristid] □ бескоры́стный; беспристрáстный.
disk [disk] диск.
dislike [dis'laik] **1.** не любúть; питáть отвращéние к (Д); **2.** нелюбóвь *f* (for к Д); антипáтия.
dislocate ['dislokeit] вывúхивать [вы́вихнуть]; нарушáть [нарýшить]; расстрáивать [-рóить].
dislodge [dis'lɔdʒ] смещáть [сместúть]; изгонять [изогнáть].
disloyal [dis'lɔiəl] □ нелоя́льный; верolóмный,
dismal ['dizməl] □ мрáчный; уны́лый; гнетýщий.
dismantl|e [dis'mæntl] ⚓ расснáщивать [-настúть]; ⊕ демонтúровать (*im*)*pf.*; **~ing** [-iŋ] демонтáж.
dismay [dis'mei] **1.** уны́ние; страх; **2.** *v/t.* приводúть в уны́ние.
dismiss [dis'mis] *v/t.* отпускáть [-стúть]; увольнять [увóлить]; освобождáть [-бодúть]; ⚖ прекращáть [-ратúть] (дéло); отклонять [-нúть] (иск); **~al** [-əl] рóспуск; увольнéние; освобождéние; ⚖ отклонéние.
dismount ['dis'maunt] *v/t.* разнимáть [-нять]; ⊕ разбирáть [разобрáть]; *v/i.* слезáть с лóшади, спéши(ва)ться.
disobedien|ce [diso'bi:djəns] непослушáние, неповиновéние; **~t** [-t] □ непослýшный, непокóрный.
disobey ['diso'bei] ослýшаться *pf.* (Р), не повиновáться (*im*)*pf.* (Д).
disorder [dis'ɔ:də] **1.** беспоря́док; ⚕ расстрóйство; **~s** *pl.* мáссовые волнéния *n/pl.*; **2.** приводúть в беспоря́док; расстрáивать [-рóить] (здорóвье); **~ly** [-li] беспоря́дочный; беспокóйный; распýщенный.
disorganize [dis'ɔ:gənaiz] дезорганизовáть (*im*)*pf.*, расстрáивать [-рóить].
disown [dis'oun] не призн(ав)áть; откáзываться [-зáться] от (Р).
dispassionate [dis'pæʃnit] □ беспристрáстный; бесстрáстный.
dispatch [dis'pætʃ] **1.** отпрáвка; отправлéние; депéша; донесéние; by **~** с курьéром **2.** пос(ы)лáть; отправлять [-áвить].
dispel [dis'pel] рассéивать [-сéять]; разгонять [разогнáть].
dispensa|ry [dis'pensəri] аптéка; амбулатóрия; **~tion** [dispen'seiʃən] раздáча; разделéние; велéние (судьбы́); освобождéние.
dispense [dis'pens] *v/t.* освобождáть [-бодúть]; приготовлять и распределять (лекáрства); отправлять [-áвить] (правосýдие).
disperse [dis'pə:s] разгонять [разогнáть]; рассéивать(ся) [-éять (-ся)]; распространять [-нúть].
dispirit [dis'pirit] удручáть [-чúть]; приводúть в уны́ние.
displace [dis'pleis] смещáть [сместúть]; переставлять [-áвить]; переклáдывать [переложúть]; вытеснять [вы́теснить].
display [dis'plei] **1.** выставлять [вы́ставить] (в витрúне); проявлять [-вúть]; выставлять напокáз; **2.** вы́ставка; проявлéние.
displeas|e [dis'pli:z] не [по]нрáвиться (Д); быть не по вкýсу (Д); **~ed** [-d] □ недовóльный; **~ure** [dis'pleʒə] недовóльство.
dispos|al [dis'pouzəl] расположéние; распоряжéние; употреблéние; удалéние (нечистóт и т. п.); **~e** [dis'pouz] *v/t.* располагáть [-ложúть] (В); склонять [-нúть]; *v/i.* **~ of** распоряжáться [-ядúться] (Т); отдéл(ыв)аться от (Р); **~ed** [-d] □ располóженный; настрóенный; **~ition** [dispə'ziʃən] расположéние; распоряжéние; предрасположéние (к Д), склóнность *f* (к Д).
disproof ['dis'pru:f] опровержéние.
disproportionate [disprə'pɔ:ʃənit] □ непропорционáльный, несоразмéрный.
disprove ['dis'pru:v] опровергáть [-вéргнуть].
dispute [dis'pju:t] **1.** оспáривать [оспóрить]; пререкáться; [по]спóрить; **2.** дúспут; дебáты *m/pl.*; полéмика.
disqualify [dis'kwɔlifai] дисквалифицúровать (*im*)*pf.*; лишáть прáва.

disregard ['disri'gɑ:d] 1. пренебреже́ние; игнори́рование; 2. игнори́ровать (*im*)*pf*.; пренебрега́ть [-бре́чь] (Т).
disreput|able [dis'repjutəbl] □ дискредити́рующий; по́льзующийся дурно́й репута́цией; **~e** ['disri'pju:t] дурна́я сла́ва.
disrespect ['disris'pekt] неуваже́ние, непочти́тельность *f*; **~ful** [-ful] □ непочти́тельный.
dissatis|faction ['dissætis'fækʃən] недово́льство; **~factory** [-təri] неудовлетвори́тельный; **~fy** ['dis'sætisfai] не удовлетворя́ть [-ри́ть].
dissect [di'sekt] рассека́ть [-е́чь]; вскры(ва́)ть (труп).
dissemble [di'sembl] *v/t.* скры(ва́)ть; *v/i.* притворя́ться [-ри́ться], лицеме́рить.
dissen|sion [di'senʃən] разногла́сие; ра́спря, разла́д; **~t** [-t] 1. несогла́сие; 2. расходи́ться во взгля́дах, мне́ниях.
dissimilar ['di'similə] □ непохо́жий, несхо́дный, разноро́дный.
dissimulation [disimju'leiʃən] симуля́ция; притво́рство, обма́н, лицеме́рие.
dissipat|e ['disipeit] рассе́ивать [-е́ять]; расточа́ть [-чи́ть], растра́чивать [-тра́тить]; **~ion** [disi'peiʃən] рассе́яние; расточе́ние; беспу́тный о́браз жи́зни.
dissoluble [di'sɔljubl] ⚗ раствори́мый; расторжи́мый (о бра́ке, догово́ре).
dissolut|e ['disəlu:t] □ распу́щенный; беспу́тный; **~ion** [disə'lu:ʃən] расторже́ние (бра́ка, догово́ра); ро́спуск (парла́мента).
dissolve [di'zɔlv] *v/t.* распуска́ть [-усти́ть] (парла́мент и т. п.); растopга́ть [-о́ргнуть]; аннули́ровать (*im*)*pf*.; *v/i.* растворя́ться [-ри́ться]; разлага́ться [-ложи́ться].
dissonant ['disonənt] ♪ нестро́йный, диссони́рующий.
dissuade [di'sweid] отгова́ривать [-вори́ть] (from от P).
distan|ce ['distəns] 1. расстоя́ние; даль *f*; промежу́ток, пери́од (вре́мени); at a ~ на изве́стном расстоя́нии; 2. оставля́ть далеко́ позади́ себя́; размеща́ть на ра́вном расстоя́нии; **~t** [-t] □ да́льний, далёкий; отдалённый; сде́ржанный; холо́дный.
distaste ['dis'teist] отвраще́ние; **~ful** [-ful] □ проти́вный, неприя́тный (на вкус, вид; to Д).
distemper [dis'tempə] нездоро́вье; соба́чья чума́.
distend [dis'tend] наду́(ва́)ть(ся).
distil [dis'til] сочи́ться, ка́пать; гнать (спирт и т. п.); ⚗ перегоня́ть [-гна́ть], дистилли́ровать (*im*)*pf*.; **~lery** [-əri] виноку́ренный заво́д.
distinct [dis'tiŋkt] □ осо́бый, индивидуа́льный; отчётливый; определённый; **~ion** [dis'tiŋkʃən] разли́чение; отли́чие; отличи́тельная осо́бенность *f*; знак отли́чия; **~ive** [-tiv] □ отличи́тельный, характе́рный.
distinguish [dis'tiŋgwiʃ] различа́ть [-чи́ть]; разгля́дывать [-де́ть]; выделя́ть [вы́делить]; **~ed** [-t] выдаю́щийся, изве́стный.
distort [-'tɔ:t] искажа́ть [искази́ть]; искривля́ть [-ви́ть]; извраща́ть [-рати́ть].
distract [dis'trækt] отвлека́ть [отвле́чь], рассе́ивать [-е́ять]; **~ion** [dis'trækʃən] развлече́ние; отвлече́ние (внима́ния).
distress [dis'tres] 1. го́ре; бе́дствие; страда́ние; нужда́, нищета́; 2. причиня́ть го́ре, страда́ние (Д); **~ed** [-t] нужда́ющийся; страда́ющий.
distribut|e [dis'tribju:t] распределя́ть [-ли́ть]; разд(ав)а́ть; распространя́ть [-ни́ть]; **~ion** [distri'bju:ʃən] распределе́ние; разда́ча; распростране́ние.
district ['distrikt] райо́н; о́круг; о́бласть *f*.
distrust [dis'trʌst] 1. недове́рие; подозре́ние; 2. не доверя́ть (Д); **~ful** [-ful] □ недове́рчивый; подозри́тельный; ~ (of o. s.) неуве́ренный в себе́.
disturb [dis'tə:b] [по]беспоко́ить; [по]меша́ть (Д); наруша́ть [-у́шить]; **~ance** [-əns] наруше́ние; трево́га, волне́ние.
disunite ['disju:'nait] разделя́ть [-ли́ть]; разъединя́ть(ся) [-ни́ть (-ся)].
disuse ['dis'ju:z] изъя́ть из употребле́ния.
ditch [ditʃ] кана́ва, ров.
ditto ['ditou] то же; сто́лько же.
dive [daiv] 1. ныря́ть [нырну́ть]; погружа́ться [-узи́ться]; броса́ться в во́ду; ✈ пики́ровать (*im*)*pf*.; 2. ныря́ние; погруже́ние; пики́рование; *Am.* прито́н; **~r** ['daivə] водола́з; ныря́льщик (-ица).
diverge [dai'və:dʒ] расходи́ться [разойти́сь]; отклоня́ться [-ни́ться], уклоня́ться [-ни́ться]; **~nce** [-əns] расхожде́ние; отклоне́ние, уклоне́ние; **~nt** [-ənt] □ расходя́щийся; отклоня́ющийся.
divers|e [dai'və:s] □ разли́чный, разнообра́зный; ино́й; **~ion** [dai'və:ʃən] развлече́ние; **~ity** [-siti] разнообра́зие; разли́чие.
divert [dai'və:t] отводи́ть в сто́рону (доро́гу и т. п.); отвлека́ть [-е́чь] (внима́ние); развлека́ть [-е́чь].
divest [dai'vest] разде́(ва́)ть; *fig.* лиша́ть [-ши́ть] (of P).
divid|e [di'vaid] *v/t.* [раз]дели́ть;

разделя́ть [-ли́ть]; *v/i.* [раз]дели́ться; разделя́ться [-ли́ться]; & дели́ться без оста́тка; **~end** ['dividend] дивиде́нд; & дели́мое.
divine [di'vain] 1. □ боже́ственный; ~ service богослуже́ние; 2. уга́дывать [-да́ть].
diving ['daiviŋ] ныря́ние; *sport* прыжки́ в во́ду.
divinity [di'viniti] богосло́вие; божество́; боже́ственность *f*.
divis|ible [di'vizəbl] □ дели́мый; **~ion** [di'viʃən] деле́ние; разделе́ние; перегоро́дка; ⚔ диви́зия; & деле́ние без оста́тка.
divorce [di'vɔ:s] 1. разво́д; разры́в; 2. расторга́ть брак (Р); разводи́ться [-вести́сь] с (Т).
divulge [dai'vʌldʒ] разглаша́ть [-ласи́ть] (та́йну).
dizz|iness ['dizinis] головокруже́ние; **~y** ['dizi] □ чу́вствующий головокруже́ние; головокружи́тельный.
do [du:] [*irr.*] (*s. a.* done) 1. *v/t.* [с]де́лать; выполня́ть [вы́полнить]; устра́ивать [-ро́ить]; приготовля́ть [-то́вить]; ~ London осма́тривать Ло́ндон; have done reading ко́нчить чита́ть; F ~ in обма́нывать [-ну́ть]; уби́(ва́)ть; ~ into переводи́ть [-вести́]; ~ over переде́л(ыв)ать; покры́(ва́)ть; обма́з(ыв)ать; ~ up завора́чивать [заверну́ть]; приводи́ть в поря́док; уб(и)ра́ть; 2. *v/i.* [с]де́лать; поступа́ть [-пи́ть], де́йствовать; ~ so as to ... устра́ивать так, что́бы ...; that will ~ доста́точно, дово́льно; сойдёт; how ~ you ~? здра́вствуй(те)!; как вы пожива́ете?; ~ well успева́ть; хорошо́ вести́ де́ло; ~ away with уничтожа́ть [-о́жить]; I could ~ with ... мне мог бы пригоди́ться (И); ~ without обходи́ться [обойти́сь] без (Р); ~ be quick поспеши́те!, скоре́й!; ~ you like London? — I do вам нра́вится Ло́ндон? — Да.
docil|e ['dousail] послу́шный; поня́тливый; **~ity** [dou'siliti] послуша́ние; поня́тливость *f*.
dock[1] [dɔk] обруба́ть [-уби́ть] (хвост); ко́ротко стричь (во́лосы); *fig.* сокраща́ть [сократи́ть].
dock[2] [~] 1. ⚓ док; ⚖ скамья́ подсуди́мых; 2. ⚓ ста́вить су́дно в док; входи́ть в док.
dockyard ['dɔkja:d] верфь *f*.
doctor ['dɔktə] 1. врач; до́ктор (учёная сте́пень); 2. F лечи́ть.
doctrine ['dɔktrin] уче́ние, доктри́на.
document 1. ['dɔkjumənt] докуме́нт; свиде́тельство; 2. [-'mənt] подтвержда́ть докуме́нтами.
dodge [dɔdʒ] 1. увёртка, уло́вка, хи́трость *f*; 2. увиливать [-льну́ть]; [с]хитри́ть; избега́ть [-ежа́ть] (Р).
doe [dou] са́мка (оле́ня, за́йца, кры́сы, кро́лика).
dog [dɔg] 1. соба́ка, пёс; 2. ходи́ть по пята́м (Р); высле́живать [вы́следить].
dogged ['dɔgid] □ упря́мый, упо́рный, насто́йчивый.
dogma ['dɔgmə] до́гма; до́гмат; **~tic(al** □) [dɔg'mætik, -ikəl] догмати́ческий; **~tism** ['dɔgmətizm] догмати́зм.
dog's-ear F заги́б (за́гнутый у́гол страни́цы).
dog-tired ['dɔg'taiəd] уста́лый как соба́ка.
doings ['du:iŋz] де́йствия *n/pl.*, посту́пки *m/pl.*
dole [doul] 1. *Brt.* посо́бие (безрабо́тным); 2. выдава́ть ску́по.
doleful ['doulful] □ ско́рбный, печа́льный.
doll [dɔl] ку́кла.
dollar ['dɔlə] до́ллар.
dolly ['dɔli] ку́колка.
dolt [doult] ду́рень *m*, болва́н.
domain [do'mein] владе́ние; име́ние; террито́рия; *fig.* о́бласть *f*, сфе́ра.
dome [doum] ку́пол; свод.
domestic [do'mestik] 1. (**~al**) дома́шний; семе́йный; домосе́дливый; 2. дома́шняя рабо́тница; слуга́ *m*; **~ate** [-tikeit] привя́зывать к семе́йной жи́зни; прируча́ть [-чи́ть] (живо́тное).
domicile ['dɔmisail] постоя́нное местожи́тельство; **~d** [-d] осе́длый; прожива́ющий.
domin|ant ['dɔminənt] госпо́дствующий, преоблада́ющий; **~ate** [-neit] госпо́дствовать, преоблада́ть; **~ation** [dɔmi'neiʃən] госпо́дство, преоблада́ние; **~eer** [dɔmi'niə] де́йствовать деспоти́чески; влады́чествовать; **~eering** [-riŋ] □ деспоти́ческий, вла́стный.
dominion [də'minjən] доминио́н; владе́ние.
don [dɔn] наде́(ва́)ть.
donat|e [dou'neit] *Am.* [по]же́ртвовать; **~ion** [-ʃən] поже́ртвование.
done [dʌn] 1. *p. pt.* от do; 2. *adj.* гото́вый; уста́лый; обма́нутый; well ~ хорошо́ пригото́вленный; прожа́ренный.
donkey ['dɔŋki] осёл.
donor ['dounɔ:] же́ртвователь(ница *f*) *m*; ⚕ до́нор.
doom [du:m] 1. рок, судьба́; 2. осужда́ть [осуди́ть]; обрека́ть [-е́чь] (to на В).
door [dɔ:] дверь *f*; next ~ ря́дом; (with)in **~s** внутри́, в до́ме; **~-handle** ру́чка две́ри; **~-keeper**, *Am.* **~man** швейца́р, привра́тник; **~way** вход; пролёт две́ри.
dope [doup] 1. нарко́тик; F дурма́н; 2. дава́ть нарко́тики (Д).
dormant ['dɔ:mənt] *mst fig.* безде́йствующий, спя́щий.

dormer(-**window**) ['dɔ:mə('windou)] слуховóе окнó.
dormitory ['dɔ:mitəri] дортуáр, óбщая спáльня; *Am.* общежи́тие.
dose [dous] 1. дóза, приём; 2. дози́ровать (*im*)*pf.*; давáть дóзами.
dot [dɔt] 1. тóчка; крóшечная вещь *f*; 2. стáвить тóчки над (Т); отмечáть пункти́ром.
dot|e [dout]: ~ (up)on люби́ть до безу́мия; **~ing** ['dɔutiŋ] безу́мно лю́бящий.
double ['dʌbl] □ двойнóй; двоя́кий; двули́чный; 2. двойни́к; двойнóе коли́чество; пáрная игрá; *thea.* дублёр; 3. *v/t.* удвáивать [удвóить]; склáдывать вдвóе; **~d up** скрю́чившийся; *v/i.* удвáиваться [удвóиться]; **~-breasted** двубóртный (пиджáк); **~-dealing** двуру́шничество; **~-edged** обоюдоóстрый; **~ entry** ✝ двойнáя бухгалтéрия.
doubt [daut] 1. *v/t.* сомневáться [усомни́ться] в (П); не доверя́ть (Д); подозревáть; *v/i.* имéть сомнéния; 2. сомнéние; по ~ без сомнéния; **~ful** ['dautful] □ сомни́тельный; **~fulness** [-nis] сомни́тельность *f*; **~less** ['dautlis] несомнéнно; вероя́тно.
douche [du:ʃ] 1. душ; обливáние; 2. принимáть душ; обливáть(ся) водóй.
dough [dou] тéсто; **~nut** ['dounʌt] [пóнчик.]
dove [dʌv] гóлубь *m*; *fig.* голу́бчик (-бушка).
dowel ['dauəl] ⊕ дю́бель *m*, штифт.
down[1] [daun] пух; холм; безлéсная возвы́шенность *f*.
down[2] [~] 1. *adv.* вниз, внизу́; ~ to вплоть до (Р); F be ~ upon нападáть [напáсть] на (В); 2. *prp.* вниз по (Д); вдоль по (Д); ~ the river вниз по рекé; 3. *adj.* напрáвленный вниз; ~ platform перрóн для поездóв, иду́щих из столи́цы (и́ли большóго гóрода); 4. *v/t.* опускáть [опусти́ть]; сби(вá)ть (самолёт); одолé(вá)ть; **~cast** ['daunkɑ:st] удручённый; **~fall** падéние; **~-hearted** пáвший ду́хом; **~hill** вниз; пóд гору; **~pour** ли́вень *m*; **~right** 1. *adv.* совершéнно; пря́мо; 2. *adj.* прямóй; откровéнный, чéстный; **~stairs** ['daun'stɛəz] вниз, внизу́; **~stream** вниз по течéнию; **~town** *part. Am.* в деловýю часть гóрода, в деловóй чáсти гóрода; **~ward(s)** [-wəd(z)] вниз, книзу.
downy ['dauni] пуши́стый, мя́гкий как пух; *sl.* хи́трый.
dowry ['dauəri] придáное.
doze [douz] 1. дремóта; 2. дремáть, «клевáть нóсом».
dozen ['dʌzn] дю́жина.
drab [dræb] желтовáто-сéрый; однообрáзный.
draft [drɑ:ft] 1. = draught; чек; су́мма, полу́ченная по чéку; ⚔ пополнéние, подкреплéние; 2. набрáсывать [-росáть].
drag [dræg] 1. обу́за, брéмя *n*; дрáга; боронá; 2. *v/t.* [по]тяну́ть, [по]волочи́ть; чи́стить дно (реки́ и т. п.); *v/i.* [по]волочи́ться; ~ on тяну́ться (о врéмени).
dragon ['drægən] дракóн; **~-fly** стрекозá.
drain [drein] 1. дренáж; канализáция; водостóк; 2. *v/t.* дрени́ровать (*im*)*pf.*; истощáть [-щи́ть]; осушáть [-ши́ть]; **~age** ['dreinidʒ] дренáж; сток; канализáция.
drake [dreik] сéлезень *m*.
drama|tic [drə'mætik] (~ally) драмати́ческий; драмати́чный; **~tist** ['dræmətist] драмату́рг; **~tize** [-taiz] драматизи́ровать (*im*)*pf.*
drank [dræŋk] *pt.* от drink.
drape [dreip] [за]драпировáть; располагáть склáдками; **~ry** ['dreipəri] драпирóвка; ткáни *f/pl.*
drastic ['dræstik] (~ally) реши́тельный, крутóй (о мéрах).
draught [drɑ:ft] тя́га; сквозня́к; глотóк; чернови́к, набрóсок; ⚓ водоизмещéние; **~s** *pl.* шáшки *f/pl.*; *s.* draft; ~ beer пи́во в бóчке; **~-horse** ломовáя лóшадь *f*; **~sman** [-smən] чертёжник.
draw [drɔ:] 1. [*irr.*] [на]рисовáть; [по]тяну́ть; [по]тащи́ть; вырывáть [вы́рвать]; чéрпать (вóду); привлекáть [-éчь] (внимáние); выводи́ть [вы́вести] (заключéние); кончáть (игру́) вничью́; ~ near приближáться [-ли́зиться]; ~ out вытя́гивать [вы́тянуть]; ~ up составля́ть [-áви́ть] (докумéнт) [останáвливаться [-нови́ться]; ~ (up)on ✝ вы́ставить вéксель на (В); 2. тя́га; жеребьёвка; F гвоздь *m* (сезóна, вéчера и т. п.); **~back** ['drɔ:bæk] помéха; недостáток; ✝ возврáтная пóшлина; **~er** 1. ['drɔ:ə] чертёжник; ✝ трассáнт; 2. [drɔ:] вы́движнóй я́щик; (a pair of) **~s** *pl.* кальсóны *f/pl.*
drawing ['drɔ:iŋ] рису́нок; рисовáние; чертёж; черчéние; **~-board** чертёжная доскá; **~-room** гости́ная.
drawn [drɔ:n] *p. pt.* от draw.
dread [dred] 1. боя́ться, страши́ться (Р); 2. страх, боя́знь *f*; **~ful** ['dredful] □ ужáсный, стрáшный.
dream [dri:m] 1. сон, сновидéние; мечтá; грёза; 2. [*a. irr.*] ви́деть во снé; мечтáть; грéзить; воображáть [-рази́ть]; **~er** ['dri:mə] мечтáтель(ница *f*) *m*, фантазёр(ка); **~y** [-i] □ мечтáтельный.
dreary ['driəri] □ тоскли́вый; ску́чный.
dredge [dredʒ] 1. землечерпáлка,

дра́га, экскава́тор; 2. драги́ровать (im)pf.; углубля́ть фарва́тер.
dregs [dregz] pl. оса́док; небольшо́й оста́ток; подо́нки m/pl.
drench [drentʃ] 1. промока́ние (под дождём); 2. прома́чивать на сквозь.
dress [dres] 1. оде́жда, пла́тье; одея́ние; thea. ~ rehearsal генера́льная репети́ция; 2. оде́(ва́)ть (-ся); украша́ть(ся) [укра́сить(ся)]; де́лать причёску; ⚔ равня́ться [вы́ровняться]; выра́внивать [вы́ровнять]; ⚕ перевя́зывать [-за́ть]; ~-circle thea. бельэта́ж; ~er ['dresə] ку́хонный шкаф; Am. туале́тный сто́лик.
dressing ['dresiŋ] перевя́зочный материа́л; перевя́зка; cook. припра́ва; ~ down вы́говор, головомо́йка; ~-gown хала́т; ~table туале́тный сто́лик.
dress|maker портни́ха; ~-parade вы́ставка мод.
drew ['dru:] pt. от draw.
dribble ['dribl] ка́пать; пуска́ть слю́ни.
dried [draid] сухо́й; вы́сохший.
drift [drift] 1. дрейф; сугро́б (сне́га); нано́с (песка́); fig. стремле́ние; тенде́нция; 2. v/t. относи́ть [отнести́]; наноси́ть [нанести́]; мести́ (сне́г, о ве́тре); v/i. дрейфова́ть (im)pf.; скопля́ться ку́чами (о ли́стьях и т. п.); fig. безде́йствовать, быть пасси́вным, не сопротивля́ться.
drill [dril] 1. сверло́; бура́в; коловоро́т; физи́ческое упражне́ние; ⚘ борозда́; ⚔ строево́е обуче́ние; 2. [на]тренирова́ть; ⚔ проводи́ть строево́е обуче́ние.
drink [driŋk] 1. питьё; напи́ток; 2. [irr.] [вы́]пить; пья́нствовать.
drip [drip] 1. ка́пание; 2. ка́пать.
drive [draiv] 1. ката́нье, езда́; подъездна́я алле́я (к до́му); ⚔ уда́р, ата́ка; ⊕ переда́ча, приво́д; fig. эне́ргия; си́ла; 2. [irr.] v/t. [по]гнать; вби(ва́)ть (гвоздь и т. п.); вози́ть, [по]везти́ (в автомоби́ле, экипа́же и т. п.); пра́вить (лошадьми́ и т. п.); управля́ть (маши́ной); v./i. е́здить, [по]е́хать; ката́ться; [по]нести́сь; ~ at [на-] ме́тить на (В).
drivel ['drivl] 1. распуска́ть слю́ни; нести́ вздор; 2. бессмы́слица, чепуха́.
driven ['drivn] p. pt. от drive.
driver ['draivə] пого́нщик (скота́); mot. шофёр, води́тель m; 🚂 машини́ст; ⊕ веду́щее колесо́.
drizzle ['drizl] 1. ме́лкий дождь m, и́зморось f; 2. мороси́ть.
drone [droun] 1. zo. тру́тень m; fig. безде́льник, лентя́й; 2. [за-] жужжа́ть; [за]гуде́ть.
droop [dru:p] v/t. склоня́ть [-ни́ть] (го́лову); v/i. свиса́ть [сви́снуть], поника́ть [-и́кнуть]; увяда́ть [увя́нуть] (о цвета́х).
drop [drɔp] 1. ка́пля; ледене́ц; паде́ние, пониже́ние; thea. за́навес; 2. v/t. роня́ть [урони́ть]; броса́ть [бро́сить] (привы́чку); ~ a p. a line черкну́ть кому́-либо слове́чко; v/i. ка́пать [ка́пнуть]; спада́ть [спасть]; па́дать [упа́сть]; понижа́ться [-и́зиться]; ~ in заходи́ть [зайти́], загля́дывать [загляну́ть].
drought [draut] за́суха.
drove [drouv] 1. гурт, ста́до; 2. pt. от drive.
drown [draun] v/t. затопля́ть [-пи́ть]; fig. заглуша́ть [-ши́ть] (звук); v/i. [у]тону́ть = be ~ed; ~ o. s. [у]топи́ться.
drows|e [drauz] [за]дрема́ть; ~y ['drauzi] со́нный.
drudge [drʌdʒ] исполня́ть ску́чную, тяжёлую рабо́ту, «тяну́ть ля́мку».
drug [drʌg] 1. лека́рство, медикаме́нт; нарко́тик; 2. употребля́ть нарко́тики; дава́ть нарко́тики (Д); ~gist ['drʌgist] апте́карь m.
drum [drʌm] 1. бараба́н; бараба́нный бой; anat. бараба́нная перепо́нка; 2. бить в бараба́н, бараба́нить.
drunk [drʌŋk] 1. p. pt. от drink; 2. пья́ный; get ~ напива́ться пья́ным; ~ard ['drʌŋkəd] пья́ница m/f; ~en ['drʌŋkən] пья́ный.
dry [drai] 1. □ сухо́й, вы́сохший; F жа́ждущий; F антиалкого́льный; ~ goods pl. Am. мануфакту́ра; галантере́я; 2. [вы́]суши́ть; [вы́]со́хнуть; ~ up высу́шивать [вы́сушить]; высыха́ть [вы́сохнуть], пересыха́ть [-со́хнуть] (о реке́ и т. п.); ~-clean чи́стить хими́чески; ~-nurse ня́ня.
dual ['dju:əl] □ дво́йственный; двойно́й.
dubious ['dju:biəs] □ сомни́тельный, подозри́тельный.
duchess ['dʌtʃis] герцоги́ня.
duck [dʌk] 1. у́тка; наклоне́ние головы́; ныря́ние; F ду́шка; 2. ныря́ть [нырну́ть]; окуна́ться [-ну́ться]; увёртываться [уверну́ться].
duckling ['dʌkliŋ] утёнок.
dudgeon ['dʌdʒən] оби́да.
due [dju:] 1. до́лжный, надлежа́щий; обя́занный; ожида́емый; in ~ time в своё вре́мя; it is his ~ ему́ э́то полага́ется; 2. adv. ⚓ то́чно, пря́мо (о стре́лке ко́мпаса); 3. до́лжное; то, что причита́ется; mst ~s pl. сбо́ры m/pl., нало́ги m/pl.; по́шлины f/pl.; чле́нский взнос.
duel ['dju:əl] 1. дуэ́ль f; 2. дра́ться на дуэ́ли.
dug [dʌg] pt. и p. pt. от dig.

duke [dju:k] гéрцог; **~dom** ['dju:kdəm] гéрцогство.
dull [dʌl] 1. □ тупóй (*a. fig.*); скýчный; ✝ вя́лый; пáсмурный (день); 2. притупля́ть(ся) [-пи́ть(-ся)]; *fig.* дéлать(ся) тупы́м, скýчным; **~ness** ['dʌlnis] скýка; вя́лость *f*; тýпость *f*.
duly ['dju:li] дóлжным óбразом.
dumb [dʌm] □ немóй; глýпый.
dummy ['dʌmi] манекéн, кýкла; ⚔ макéт; *fig.* фикти́вное лицó.
dump [dʌmp] 1. свáлка; ⚔ полевóй склад; 2. сбрáсывать [сбрóсить]; навáливать [-ли́ть]; свáливать [-ли́ть] (мýсор); **~s** *pl.* плохóе настроéние; **~ing** ✝ дéмпинг.
dun [dʌn] настóйчиво трéбовать уплáты дóлга.
dunce [dʌns] тупи́ца *m/f*.
dune [dʒu:n] дю́на.
dung [dʌŋ] 1. навóз; 2. унавáживать [унавóзить].
dungeon ['dʌndʒən] подзéмная тюрьмá.
duplic|ate 1. ['dju:plikit] a) двойнóй; запаснóй; b) дубликáт, кóпия; 2. [-keit] снимáть, дéлать кóпию с (Р); удвáивать [удвóить]; **~ity** [dju:'plisiti] двули́чность *f*.
dura|ble ['djuərəbl] □ прóчный; долговрéменный; **~tion** [djuə'reiʃən] продолжи́тельность *f*.
duress(e) [djuə'res] принуждéние.
during ['djuəriŋ] *prp.* в течéние (Р), во врéмя (Р).
dusk [dʌsk] сýмерки; **~y** ['dʌski] □ сýмеречный; смýглый.
dust [dʌst] 1. пыль *f*; 2. [за-, на-] пыли́ть; вытирáть пыль; **~-bin** мýсорный я́щик; **~er** ['dʌstə] пы́льная тря́пка; **~y** ['dʌsti] □ пы́льный.
Dutch [dʌtʃ] 1. голлáндец (-дка); 2. голлáндский; the ~ голлáндцы *pl.*
duty ['dju:ti] долг, обя́занность *f*; дежýрство; пóшлина; off ~ свобóдный от дежýрства; **~-free** *adv.* беспóшлинно.
dwarf [dwɔ:f] 1. кáрлик; 2. мешáть рóсту, останáвливать разви́тие (Р).
dwell [dwel] [*irr.*] жить, пребывáть; ~ (up)on задéрживаться [-жáться] на (П); **~ing** ['dweliŋ] жили́ще, дом.
dwelt [dwelt] *pt.* и *p. pt.* от dwell.
dwindle ['dwindl] уменьшáться [умéньши́ться], сокращáться [-рати́ться].
dye [dai] 1. крáска; окрáска; *fig.* of deepest ~ настоя́щий; 2. [по-] крáсить, окрáшивать [окрáсить].
dying ['daiiŋ] (*s.* die[1]) 1. □ умирáющий; предсмéртный; 2. умирáние.
dynam|ic [dai'næmik] динами́ческий; акти́вный; энерги́чный; **~ics** [-iks] *mst sg.* динáмика; **~ite** ['dainəmait] 1. динами́т; 2. взрывáть динами́том.

E

each [i:tʃ] кáждый; ~ other друг дрýга.
eager [i:gə] □ стремя́щийся; усéрдный; энерги́чный; **~ness** [-nis] пыл, рвéние.
eagle [i:gl] орёл, орли́ца.
ear [iə] ýхо (*pl.*: ýши); **~-drum** барабáнная перепóнка.
earl [ə:l] граф ((англи́йский).
early ['ə:li] 1. рáнний; преждеврéменный; 2. *adv.* рáно; заблаговрéммено; as ~ as ужé.
ear-mark ['iəma:k] отмечáть [-éтить].
earn [ə:n] зарабáтывать [-бóтать]; заслýживать [-жи́ть].
earnest ['ə:nist] 1. □ серьёзный; убеждённый; и́скренний; 2. серьёзность *f*.
earnings ['ə:niŋz] зáработок.
ear|piece рáковина телефóнной трýбки; **~-shot** предéлы слы́шимости.
earth [ə:θ] 1. земля́, земнóй шар; земля́, пóчва; 2. *v/t.* зары́(вá)ть; закáпывать [закопáть]; ⚡ заземля́ть [-ли́ть]; **~en** ['ə:θən] землянóй; **~enware** [-weə] гли́няная посýда; **~ing** ['ə:θiŋ] ⚡ заземлéние; **~ly** ['ə:θli] земнóй; *fig.* сýетный; **~quake** [-kweik] землетрясéние; **~worm** землянóй червь *m*.
ease [i:z] 1. покóй; лёгкость *f*; непринуждённость *f*; at ~ свобóдно, удóбно; 2. облегчáть [-чи́ть]; успокáивать [-кóить].
easel ['i:zl] мольбéрт.
easiness ['i:zinis] *s.* ease 1.
east [i:st] 1. востóк; 2. востóчный; 3. *adv.* на востóк; к востóку (of от Р).
Easter ['i:stə] пáсха.
easter|ly ['i:stəli], **~n** ['i:stən] востóчный.
eastward(s) ['i:stwəd(z)] на востóк.
easy [i:zi] лёгкий; спокóйный; непринуждённый; take it ~! не торопи́(те)сь!; спокóйнее!; **~-chair** крéсло; **~-going** *fig.* добродýшный; беззабóтный.
eat [i:t] 1. [*irr.*] [съ]есть; разъедáть [-éсть] 2. [et] *pt.* от eat 1; **~ables** ['i:təblz] *pl.* съестнóе; **~en** ['i:tn] *p. pt.* от eat 1.

eaves [i:vz] *pl.* карни́з; стреха́; **~drop** подслу́ш(ив)ать.
ebb [eb] 1. (*a.* ~-tide) отли́в; *fig.* переме́на к ху́дшему; 2. отли-(ва́)ть, убы́(ва́)ть (о воде́); *fig.* ослабе́(ва́)ть.
ebony ['ebəni] чёрное де́рево.
ebullition [ebə'liʃən] кипе́ние; вскипа́ние.
eccentric [ik'sentrik] 1. эксцентри́чный; ⚙ эксцентри́ческий; 2. чуда́к.
ecclesiastic [ikli:zi'æstik] 1. ✝, *mst* **~al** □ [-tikəl] духо́вный, церко́вный; 2. духо́вное лицо́.
echo ['ekou] 1. э́хо; *fig.* отголо́сок; 2. отдава́ться как э́хо.
eclipse [i'klips] 1. затме́ние; 2. затмева́ть [-ми́ть]; заслоня́ть [-ни́ть].
econom|ic(al □) [i:kə'nɔmik(əl)] экономи́ческий; эконо́мный, бережли́вый; **~ics** [-iks] *pl.* эконо́мика; наро́дное хозя́йство; **~ist** [i:'kɔnəmist] экономи́ст; **~ize** [-maiz] [с]эконо́мить; **~y** [-mi] хозя́йство; эконо́мия; бережли́вость *f*; political ~ полити́ческая эконо́мия.
ecsta|sy ['ekstəsi] экста́з; **~tic** [eks'tætik] (~ally) исступлённый.
eddy ['edi] 1. водоворо́т; 2. крути́ться в водоворо́те.
edge [edʒ] 1. край; ле́звие, остриё; кряж, хребе́т (гор); кро́мка (мате́рии); обре́з (кни́ги); be on ~ быть как на иго́лках; 2. обреза́ть края́; окаймля́ть [-ми́ть]; ната́чивать [наточи́ть]; **~ways**, **~wise** [-weiz, -waiz] кра́ем, бо́ком.
edging ['edʒiŋ] край, кайма́, бордю́р.
edible ['edibl] съедо́бный.
edifice ['edifis] зда́ние.
edit ['edit] изд(ав)а́ть; [от]редакти́ровать; **~ion** [i'diʃən] изда́ние; **~or** ['editə] изда́тель *m*; реда́ктор; **~orial** [edi'tɔ:riəl] 1. реда́кторский; редакцио́нный; 2. передова́я статья́; **~orship** ['editəʃip] реда́кторство.
educat|e ['edju:keit] дава́ть образова́ние (Д); воспи́тывать [-та́ть]; **~ion** [edju'keiʃən] образова́ние; воспита́ние; Board of ♀ министе́рство просвеще́ния; **~ional** [-ʃnl] □ педагоги́ческий; уче́бный; **~or** ['edjukeitə] педаго́г.
eel [i:l] у́горь *m*.
efface [i'feis] стира́ть [стере́ть]; вычёркивать [вы́черкнуть]; *fig.* ~ o. s. стушёвываться [-шева́ться].
effect [i'fekt] 1. сле́дствие; результа́т; ⊕ производи́тельность *f*; де́йствие; ~s *pl.* иму́щество; пожи́тки *m/pl.*; take ~, be of ~ вступа́ть в си́лу; in ~ в действи́тельности; to the ~ сле́дующего содержа́ния; 2. производи́ть [-вести́]; выполня́ть [вы́полнить]; соверша́ть [-ши́ть]; **~ive** [-iv] □ эффекти́вный, действи́тельный; име́ющий си́лу; ⊕ поле́зный; ~ date да́та вступле́ния в си́лу (P); **~ual** [juəl] □ действи́тельный; ⚖ име́ющий си́лу.
effeminate [i'feminit] □ женоподо́бный.
effervesce [efə'ves] [вс]пе́ниться; игра́ть (о вине́).
effete [e'fi:t] истощённый; беспло́дный.
efficacy ['efikəsi] действи́тельность *f*, си́ла.
efficien|cy [i'fiʃənsi] эффекти́вность *f*; уме́лость *f*; **~t** [-ənt] □ уме́лый, квалифици́рованный; эффекти́вный.
efflorescence [əflɔ:'resns] расцве́т.
effluence ['efluəns] истече́ние; эмана́ция.
effort ['efət] уси́лие; достиже́ние.
effrontery [e'frʌntəri] бессты́дство.
effulgent [e'fʌldʒənt] □ лучеза́рный.
effus|ion [i'fju:ʒən] излия́ние; **~ive** [i'fju:siv] □ экспанси́вный; несде́ржанный.
egg[1] [eg] подстрека́ть [-кну́ть] (*mst* ~ *on*).
egg[2] [~] яйцо́; buttered, scrambled ~s *pl.* я́ичница-болту́нья; fried ~s *pl.* я́ичница-глазу́нья.
egotism ['egoutizm] эготи́зм; самомне́ние.
egress ['i:gres] вы́ход; исто́к, истече́ние.
Egyptian [i'dʒipʃən] 1. египтя́нин (-я́нка); 2. еги́петский.
eight [eit] 1. во́семь; 2. восьмёрка; **~een** ['ei'ti:n] восемна́дцать; **~eenth** [-θ] восемна́дцатый; **~h** [eitθ] 1. восьмо́й; 2. восьма́я часть *f*; **~ieth** ['eitiiθ] восьмидеся́тый; **~y** ['eiti] во́семьдесят.
either ['aiðə] 1. *pron.* оди́н из двух; тот и́ли друго́й; и тот и друго́й, о́ба; 2. *cj.* ~ ... or ... и́ли ... и́ли ...; ли́бо ... ли́бо ...; not (...) ~ та́кже не.
ejaculate [i'dʒækjuleit] восклица́ть [-ли́кнуть]; изверга́ть [-е́ргнуть].
eject [i'dʒekt] изгоня́ть [изгна́ть]; выселя́ть [вы́селить]; изверга́ть [-е́ргнуть]; выпуска́ть [вы́пустить] (дым).
eke [i:k]: ~ out восполня́ть [-по́лнить]; ~ out one's existence перебива́ться кое-ка́к.
elaborat|e 1. [i'læbərit] □ сло́жный; тща́тельно вы́работанный; 2. [-reit] разраба́тывать [-бо́тать]; разви́(ва́)ть; **~eness** [-ritnis], **~ion** [ilæbə'reiʃən] разрабо́тка; разви́тие; уточне́ние.
elapse [i'læps] проходи́ть [пройти́], пролета́ть [-лете́ть] (о вре́мени).
elastic [i'læstik] 1. [~ally] эласти́ч-

ный; упру́гий; 2. рези́нка (шнур); **~ity** [elæs'tisiti] эласти́чность *f.*
elate [i'leit] 1. □ лику́ющий; 2. поднима́ть настрое́ние (P).
elbow ['elbou] 1. ло́коть *m*; ⊕ коле́но; уго́льник; at one's ~ под руко́й, ря́дом; 2. толка́ть локтя́ми; ~ out выта́лкивать [вы́толкнуть].
elder ['eldə] 1. ста́рший; 2. ⚘ бузина́; **~ly** ['eldəli] пожило́й.
eldest ['eldist] (са́мый) ста́рший.
elect [i'lekt] 1. изб(и)ра́ть; выбира́ть [вы́брать]; назнача́ть [-на́чить]; 2. и́збранный; **~ion** [i'lekʃən] вы́боры *m/pl.*; **~or** [-tə] избира́тель *m*; **~oral** [-tərəl] избира́тельный; **~orate** [-tərit] континге́нт избира́телей.
electri|c [i'lektrik] электри́ческий; ~ circuit электри́ческая цепь *f*; **~cal** [-trikəl] □ электри́ческий; ~ engineering электроте́хника; **~cian** [ilek'triʃən] электромонтёр.
electri|city [ilek'trisiti] электри́чество; **~fy** [i'lektrifai], **~ze** [i'lektraiz) электрифици́ровать (*im*)*pf.*; [на-] электризова́ть.
electro|cute [i'lektrəkju:t] казни́ть на электри́ческом сту́ле.
electron [i'lektrɔn] электро́н; **~-ray tube** опти́ческий индика́тор настро́йки, «маги́ческий глаз».
electro|plate гальванизи́ровать (*im*)*pf.*; **~type** гальванопла́стика.
elegan|ce ['eligəns] элега́нтность *f*, изя́щество; **~t** ['eligənt] □ элега́нтный, изя́щный.
element ['elimənt] элеме́нт; стихи́я; **~s** *pl.* осно́вы *f/pl.*; **~al** [eli'mentl] □ основно́й; стихи́йный; **~ary** [-təri] □ элемента́рный; elementaries *pl.* осно́вы *f/pl.* (како́й-либо нау́ки).
elephant ['elifənt] слон.
elevat|e ['eliveit] поднима́ть [-ня́ть], повыша́ть [-вы́сить]; *fig.* возвыша́ть [-вы́сить]; **~ion** [eli'veiʃən] возвыше́ние, возвы́шенность *f*; высота́ (над у́ровнем мо́ря); **~or** ['eliveitə] ⊕ элева́тор, грузоподъёмник; *Am.* лифт; ✈ руль высоты́.
eleven [i'levn] оди́ннадцать; **~th** [-θ] 1. оди́ннадцатый; 2. оди́ннадцатая часть *f*.
elf [elf] эльф; прока́зник.
elicit [i'lisit] извлека́ть [-éчь]; вызыва́ть [вы́звать].
eligible ['elidʒəbl] □ могу́щий быть и́збранным; подходя́щий.
eliminat|e [i'limineit] устраня́ть [-ни́ть]; уничтожа́ть [-то́жить]; **~ion** [ilimi'neiʃən] выключе́ние; уничтоже́ние.
elk [elk] *zo.* лось *m*.
elm [elm] ⚘ вяз.
elocution [elɔ'kju:ʃən] ора́торское иску́сство.
elope [i'loup] [у]бежа́ть (с возлю́бленным).
eloquen|ce ['elokwəns] красноре́чие; **~t** [-t] □ красноречи́вый.
else [els] ещё; кро́ме; и́наче; ино́й, друго́й; or ~ а то; и́ли же; **~where** ['els'wɛə] где́-нибудь в друго́м ме́сте.
elucidat|e [i'lu:sideit] разъясня́ть [-ни́ть]; **~ion** [ilu:si'deiʃən] разъясне́ние.
elude [i'lu:d] избега́ть [-ежа́ть] (P), уклоня́ться [-ни́ться] от (P).
elus|ive [i'lu:siv] неулови́мый; **~ory** [-səri] ускольза́ющий.
emaciate [i'meiʃieit] истоща́ть [-щи́ть], изнуря́ть [-ри́ть].
emanat|e ['eməneit] истека́ть [-е́чь]; происходи́ть [произойти́] (from от P); **~ion** [emə'neiʃən] эмана́ция; испуска́ние; *fig.* излуче́ние.
emancipat|e [i'mænsipeit] освободи́ть от ограниче́ний; **~ion** [imænsi'peiʃən] освобожде́ние.
embalm [im'bɑ:m] [на]бальзами́ровать.
embankment [im'bæŋkmənt] да́мба, на́сыпь *f*; на́бережная.
embargo [em'bɑ:gou] эмба́рго *n indecl.*; запреще́ние.
embark [im'bɑ:k] [по]грузи́ть(ся); сади́ться [сесть] (на кора́бль); *fig.* ~ in, (up)on нач(ин)а́ть (B).
embarras [im'bærəs] затрудня́ть [-ни́ть]; смуща́ть [смути́ть]; стесня́ть [-ни́ть]; **~ing** [-iŋ] □ затрудни́тельный; неудо́бный; стесни́тельный; **~ment** [-mənt] затрудне́ние; смуще́ние; замеша́тельство.
embassy ['embəsi] посо́льство.
embellish [im'beliʃ] украша́ть [укра́сить].
embers ['embəz] *pl.* после́дние тле́ющие уголькѝ *m/pl.*
embezzle [im'bezl] растра́чивать [-а́тить] (чужи́е де́ньги); **~ment** [-mənt] растра́та.
embitter [im'bitə] озлобля́ть [озло́бить].
emblem ['embləm] эмбле́ма, си́мвол.
embody [im'bɔdi] воплоща́ть [-лоти́ть]; олицетворя́ть [-ри́ть]; включа́ть [-чи́ть] (в соста́в).
embosom [im'buzəm] обнима́ть [обня́ть]; **~ed** with окружённый (T).
emboss [im'bɔs] выбива́ть вы́пуклый рису́нок на (П), [от-, вы́]чека́нить; лепи́ть релье́ф.
embrace [im'breis] 1. объя́тие; 2. обнима́ть(ся) [-ня́ть(ся)]; принима́ть [-ня́ть] (ве́ру и т. п.); обхва́тывать [обхвати́ть].
embroider [im'brɔidə] вы́ши(ва́)ть; **~y** [-ri] вышива́ние; вы́шивка.

embroil [im'brɔil] запу́т(ыв)ать (дела́); впу́т(ыв)ать (в неприя́тности).
emerald ['emərəld] изумру́д.
emerge [i'mə:dʒ] появля́ться [-ви́ться]; всплы(ва́)ть; **~ncy** [-ənsi] непредви́денный слу́чай; *attr.* запасно́й, вспомога́тельный; ~ call *teleph.* сро́чный вы́зов по телефо́ну; **~nt** [-ənt] непредви́денный; сро́чный.
emigra|nt ['emigrənt] **1.** эмигра́нт, переселе́нец; **2.** эмигри́рующий, переселе́нческий; **~te** [-greit] эмигри́ровать (*im*)*pf.*, переселя́ться [-ли́ться]; **~tion** [emi'greiʃən] эмигра́ция, переселе́ние.
eminen|ce ['eminəns] высота́; высо́кое положе́ние; **℈ce** высокопреосвяще́нство; **~t** [-ənt] □ *fig.* выдаю́щийся, замеча́тельный; *adv.* замеча́тельно.
emit [i'mit] изд(ав)а́ть, испуска́ть [-усти́ть] (за́пах, звук, крик); выделя́ть [вы́делить].
emoti|on [i'mouʃən] душе́вное волне́ние, возбужде́ние; эмо́ция; **~onal** [-l] □ взволно́ванный; волну́ющий (о му́зыке и т. п.).
emperor ['empərə] импера́тор.
empha|sis ['emfəsis] вырази́тельность *f*; ударе́ние, акце́нт; **~size** [-saiz] подчёркивать [-черкну́ть]; **~tic** [im'fætik] (~ally) вырази́тельный; подчёркнутый; насто́йчивый.
empire ['empaiə] импе́рия.
employ [im'plɔi] **1.** употребля́ть [-би́ть], применя́ть [-ни́ть], испо́льзовать (*im*)*pf.*; дава́ть рабо́ту (Д); **2.** in the ~ of на рабо́те у (Р), рабо́тающий у (Р); **~ee** [emplɔi'i:] слу́жащий (-щая), рабо́тник (-ица); **~er** [im'plɔiə] нанима́тель (-ница *f*) *m*, работода́тель(ница *f*) *m*; ☤ зака́зчик (-ица); **~ment** [-mənt] примене́ние; рабо́та, заня́тие; ℈ Exchange би́ржа труда́.
empower [im'pauə] уполномо́чи(ва)ть.
empress ['empris] императри́ца.
empt|iness ['emptinis] пустота́; **~y** [-ti] **1.** □ пусто́й, поро́жний; F голо́дный; **2.** опорожня́ть(ся) [-ни́ть(ся)]; [о]пусте́ть.
emul|ate ['emjuleit] соревнова́ться с (Т); **~ation** [emju'leiʃən] соревнова́ние.
enable [i'neibl] дава́ть возмо́жность и́ли пра́во (Д).
enact [i'nækt] предпи́сывать [-са́ть]; постановля́ть [-ви́ть]; *thea.* игра́ть роль; ста́вить на сце́не.
enamel [i'næml] **1.** эма́ль *f*; **2.** эмалирова́ть (*im*)*pf.*; покрыва́ть эма́лью.
enamo(u)red [i'næməd]: ~ of [влюблённый в (В).
encamp [in'kæmp] ⚔ располага́ться ла́герем.
enchain [in'tʃein] зако́вывать [-ова́ть]; прико́вывать [-ова́ть].
enchant [in'tʃɑ:nt] очаро́вывать [-ова́ть]; **~ment** [-ment] очарова́ние; **~ress** [-ris] чароде́йка.
encircle [in'sə:kl] окружа́ть [-жи́ть].
enclos|e [in'klouz] заключа́ть [-чи́ть]; огора́живать [-роди́ть]; прилага́ть [-ложи́ть]; **~ure** [-ʒə] огоро́женное ме́сто; вложе́ние, приложе́ние.
encompass [in'kʌmpəs] окружа́ть [-жи́ть].
encore [ɔŋ'kɔ:] *thea.* **1.** бис!; **2.** крича́ть «бис»; вызыва́ть [вы́звать].
encounter [in'kauntə] **1.** встре́ча; столкнове́ние; **2.** встреча́ть(ся) [-е́тить(ся)]; ната́лкиваться [натолкну́ться] на (тру́дности и т. п.).
encourage [in'kʌridʒ] ободря́ть [-ри́ть]; поощря́ть [-ри́ть]; **~ment** [-mənt] ободре́ние; поощре́ние.
encroach [in'kroutʃ]: ~ (up)on вторга́ться [вто́ргнуться] в (В); **~ment** [-mənt] вторже́ние.
encumb|er [in'kʌmbə] обременя́ть [-ни́ть]; загроможда́ть [-мозди́ть]; затрудня́ть [-ни́ть]; [вос]препя́тствовать (Д); **~rance** [-brəns] бре́мя *n*; обу́за; *fig.* препя́тствие.
encyclop(a)edia [ensaiklo'pi:diə] энциклопе́дия.
end [end] **1.** коне́ц, оконча́ние; цель *f*; результа́т; no ~ of безме́рно, бесконе́чно мно́го (Р); in the ~ в конце́ концо́в; on ~ сто́ймя́; ды́бом; беспреры́вно, подря́д; **2.** конча́ть(ся) [ко́нчить(ся)].
endanger [in'deindʒə] подверга́ть опа́сности.
endear [in'diə] внуша́ть любо́вь, заставля́ть полюби́ть; **~ment** [-mənt] ла́ска, выраже́ние не́жности.
endeavo(u)r [in'devə] **1.** [по]пыта́ться, прилага́ть уси́лия, [по-] стара́ться; **2.** попы́тка, стара́ние.
end|ing ['endiŋ] оконча́ние; **~less** ['endlis] □ бесконе́чный.
endorse [in'dɔ:s] ☤ индосси́ровать (*im*)*pf.*; одобря́ть [одо́брить]; **~ment** [in'dɔ:smənt] ☤ индоссаме́нт.
endow [in'dau] одаря́ть [-ри́ть] (умо́м и т. п.); наделя́ть [-ли́ть]; **~ment** [-mənt] наде́л.
endue [in'dju:] облека́ть [-е́чь].
endur|ance [in'djuərəns] выно́сливость *f*; про́чность *f*; **~e** [in'djuə] выноси́ть [вы́нести], терпе́ть.
enema ['enimə] кли́зма.
enemy ['enimi] враг; неприя́тель *m*; проти́вник.
energ|etic [enə'dʒetik] (~ally) энерги́чный; **~y** ['enədʒi] эне́ргия.
enervate ['enə:veit] обесси́ли(ва)ть, ослабля́ть [-а́бить].

enfold [in'fould] обнимáть [обнять], обхвáтывать [обхватить].
enforce [in'fɔ:s] навязывать [-зáть] (upon Д); настáивать [настоять] на (П); добивáться (Р) силой; усили(ва)ть; **~ment** [-mənt] принуждéние.
engage [in'geidʒ] *v/t.* нанимáть [нанять]; закáзывать [-зáть]; занимáть [занять]; привлекáть [-éчь]; завладé(вá)ть; *fig.* привязывать [-зáть]; вовлекáть [-éчь]; ⚔ вводить в бой; be **~d** быть зáнятым; быть помóлвленным; *v/i.* обязываться [-зáться]; занимáться [заняться] (in T); ⚔ вступáть в бой; **~ment** [-mənt] обязáтельство; свидáние; приглашéние; помóлвка; ⚔ бой.
engaging [-iŋ] □ очаровáтельный.
engender [in'dʒendə] *fig.* порождáть [породить].
engine ['endʒin] машина; ⊕ motóp; 🚂 паровóз; **~-driver** машинист.
engineer [endʒi'niə] **1.** инженéр; механик; машинист; **2.** сооружáть [-дить]; [за]проектировать; **~ing** [-riŋ] тéхника.
English ['iŋgliʃ] **1.** английский; **2.** английский язык; the **~** англичáне*pl.*; **~man** [-mən] англичáнин; **~woman** [-'wumən] англичáнка.
engrav|e [in'greiv] [вы]гравировáть; *fig.* запечатлé(вá)ть (в пáмяти); **~er** [-ə] гравёр; **~ing** [-iŋ] гравировáние; гравюра.
engross [in'grous] поглощáть [-лотить] (внимáние).
engulf [in'gʌlf] *fig.* поглощáть [-лотить] (о пучине).
enhance [in'hɑ:ns] повышáть [повысить]; усили(ва)ть.
enigma [i'nigmə] загáдка; **~tic(al** □) [enig'mætik, -ikəl] загáдочный.
enjoin [in'dʒɔin] втолкóвывать [-ковáть] (Д).
enjoy [in'dʒɔi] наслаждáться [насладиться] (T); **~** o. s. забавляться [забáвиться]; **~able** [-əbl] приятный; **~ment** [-mənt] наслаждéние, удовóльствие.
enlarge [in'lɑ:dʒ] увеличи(ва)ть (-ся); распространяться (on o П); **~ment** [-mənt] расширéние; увеличéние.
enlighten [in'laitn] *fig.* озарять [-рить]; просвещáть [-етить]; **~ment** просвещéние; просвещённость *f*.
enlist [in'list] *v/t.* ⚔ вербовáть на воéнную слýжбу; **~ed man** ⚔ рядовóй.
enliven [in'laivn] оживлять [-вить].
enmity ['enmiti] враждá, неприязнь *f*.
ennoble [i'noubl] облагорáживать [[-рóдить].
enorm|ity [i'nɔ:miti] чудóвищность *f*; **~ous** [-əs] □ огрóмный, громáдный; чудóвищный.
enough [i'nʌf] достáточно, довóльно.
enquire [in'kwaiə] *s.* inquire.
enrage [in'reidʒ] [вз]бесить, приводить в ярость.
enrapture [in'ræptʃə] восхищáть [-итить], очарóвывать [-овáть].
enrich [in'ritʃ] обогащáть [-гатить].
enrol(l) [in'roul] *v/t.* [за]регистрировать; ⚔ [за]вербовáть; *v/i.* поступáть на воéнную слýжбу; **~ment** [-mənt] регистрáция; вербóвка.
ensign ['ensain] значóк, эмблéма; знáмя, флаг; *Am.* ⚓ млáдший лейтенáнт.
enslave [in'sleiv] порабощáть [-ботить]; **~ment** [-mənt] порабощéние.
ensnare [in'snɛə] замáнивать [-нить].
ensue [in'sju:] [по]слéдовать; получáться в результáте.
entail [in'teil] влечь за собóй, вызывáть [вызвать] (чтó-либо).
entangle [in'tæŋgl] запýт(ыв)ать; **~ment** [-mənt] ⚔ (прóволочное) заграждéние.
enter ['entə] *v/t.* вступáть [-пить] в (B); поступáть [-пить] в (B); ✝ вносить [внести] (в книгу); входить [войти] в (B); проникáть [-никнуть] в (B); *v/i.* входить [войти], вступáть [-пить]; **~** (up)on ⚖ вступáть во владéние (T).
enterpris|e ['entəpraiz] предприятие; предприимчивость *f*; **~ing** [-iŋ] □ предприимчивый.
entertain [entə'tein] угощáть [угостить]; развлекáть [-лéчь], занимáть [занять]; **~ment** [-mənt] развлечéние; приём (гостéй).
enthrone [in'θroun] возводить на престóл.
enthusias|m [in'θju:ziæzm] востóрг; энтузиáзм; **~t** [-æst] энтузиáст(ка); **~tic** [inθju:zi'æstik] (**~ally**) востóрженный; пóлный энтузиáзма.
entic|e [in'tais] замáнивать [-нить]; соблазнять [-нить]; **~ement** [-mənt] соблáзн, примáнка.
entire [in'taiə] □ цéлый, цéльный; сплошнóй; **~ly** [-li] всецéло; совершéнно; **~ty** [-ti] полнотá, цéльность *f*; óбщая сýмма.
entitle [in'taitl] озаглáвливать [-лáвить]; давáть прáво (Д).
entity ['entiti] бытиé; сýщность *f*.
entrails ['entreilz] *pl.* внýтренности *f/pl.*; нéдра *n/pl.* (земли).
entrance ['entrəns] вход, въезд; выход (актёра на сцéну); дóступ.
entrap [in'træp] поймáть в ловýшку; запýт(ыв)ать.
entreat [in'tri:t] умолять; **~y** [-i] мольбá, прóсьба.
entrench [in'trentʃ] ⚔ окружáть окóпами.

entrust [in'trʌst] поручать [-чи́ть], вверя́ть [вве́рить].
entry ['entri] вход, вступле́ние, въезд; *thea.* вы́ход (на сце́ну); ⚖ вступле́ние во владе́ние; *sport:* зая́вка.
enumerate [i'nju:məreit] перечисля́ть [-и́слить].
enunciate [i'nʌnsieit] хорошо́ произноси́ть; [с]формули́ровать.
envelop [in'veləp] заку́т(ыв)ать; завора́чивать [заверну́ть]; ⚔ окружа́ть [-жи́ть]; **~e** ['enviloup] конве́рт; оболо́чка.
envi|able ['enviəbl] □ зави́дный; **~ous** □ зави́стливый.
environ [in'vaiərən] окружа́ть [-жи́ть]; **~ment** [-mənt] окружа́ющая обстано́вка; **~s** ['envirənz] *pl.* окре́стности *f/pl.*
envoy ['envɔi] посла́нник.
envy ['envi] 1. за́висть *f*; 2. [по]зави́довать (Д).
epic ['epik] 1. эпи́ческая поэ́ма; 2. эпи́ческий.
epicure ['epikjuə] эпикуре́ец.
epidemic [epi'demik] 🕮 1. (**~ally**) эпидеми́ческий; 2. эпиде́мия.
epilogue ['epilɔg] эпило́г.
episcopa|cy [i'piskəpəsi] епископа́льная систе́ма церко́вного управле́ния; **~l** [-pəl] епи́скопский.
epist|le [i'pisl] посла́ние; **~olary** [-tələri] эпистоля́рный.
epitaph ['epitɑ:f] эпита́фия.
epitome [i'pitəmi] конспе́кт, о́черк.
epoch ['i:pɔk] эпо́ха.
equable ['ekwəbl] □ равноме́рный, ро́вный; *fig.* уравнове́шенный.
equal ['i:kwəl] 1. □ ра́вный; одина́ковый; **~** to *fig.* спосо́бный на (В); 2. равня́ться (Д); **~ity** [i'kwɔliti] ра́венство; **~ization** [i:kwəlai'zeiʃən] ура́внивание; **~ize** [-aiz] ура́внивать [-ня́ть].
equat|ion [i'kweiʃən] 𝔄 уравне́ние; **~or** [-tə] эква́тор.
equestrian [i'kwestriən] 1. ко́нный; 2. вса́дник.
equilibrium [i:kwi'libriəm] равнове́сие.
equip [i'kwip] снаряжа́ть [-яди́ть]; снабжа́ть [-бди́ть]; **~ment** [-mənt] снаряже́ние; обмундирова́ние; обору́дование.
equipoise ['ekwipɔiz] равнове́сие; противове́с.
equity ['ekwiti] беспристра́стность [*f.*]
equivalent [i'kwivələnt] 1. эквивале́нт (to Д); 2. равноце́нный; равнозна́чащий.
equivoca|l [i'kwivəkəl] □ двусмы́сленный; сомни́тельный; **~te** [i'kwivəkeit] говори́ть двусмы́сленно.
era ['iərə] э́ра; эпо́ха.
eradicate [i'rædikeit] искореня́ть [-ни́ть].
eras|e [i'reiz] стира́ть [стере́ть]; подчища́ть [-и́стить]; **~er** [-ə] рези́нка; **~ure** [i'reiʒə] подчи́стка; стёртое рези́нкой.
ere [εə] 1. *cj.* пре́жде чем, скоре́е чем; 2. *prp.* до (Р); пе́ред (Т).
erect [i'rekt] 1. □ прямо́й; по́днятый; 2. сооружа́ть [-уди́ть], воздвига́ть [-и́гнуть]; **~ion** [i'rekʃən] сооруже́ние, строе́ние.
eremite ['erimait] отше́льник.
ermine ['ə:min] *zo.* горноста́й.
erosion [i'rouʒən] эро́зия; разъеда́ние.
erotic [i'rɔtik] эроти́ческий.
err [ə:] ошиба́ться [-би́ться], заблужда́ться.
errand ['erənd] поруче́ние; **~boy** ма́льчик на посы́лках.
errant ['erənt] □ стра́нствующий; блужда́ющий (о мы́слях).
errat|ic [i'rætik] (**~ally**) неусто́йчивый; **~um** [i'reitəm], *pl.* **~a** [-tə] опеча́тка, опи́ска.
erroneous [i'rounjəs] □ оши́бочный.
error ['erə] оши́бка, заблужде́ние; **~s** excepted исключа́я оши́бки.
erudit|e ['erudait] □ учёный; **~ion** [eru'diʃən] эруди́ция, учёность *f.*
eruption [i'rʌpʃən] изверже́ние; ⚕ высыпа́ние (сы́пи, прыще́й).
escalator ['eskəleitə] эскала́тор.
escap|ade [eskə'peid] сме́лая проде́лка; побе́г (из тюрьмы́); **~e** [is'keip] 1. *v/i.* бежа́ть (из тюрьмы́) (*im*)*pf.*; спаса́ться [спасти́сь]; *v/t.* избега́ть [-ежа́ть] (опа́сности и т. п.); ускольза́ть [-зну́ть] от (Р); 2. бе́гство; спасе́ние.
escort 1. ['eskɔ:t] эско́рт, конво́й; 2. [is'kɔ:t] конвои́ровать, сопровожда́ть.
escutcheon [is'kʌtʃən] щит герба́.
especial [is'peʃəl] осо́бенный; специа́льный; **~ly** [-i] осо́бенно.
espionage [espiə'nɑ:ʒ] шпиона́ж.
essay 1. ['esei] о́черк; попы́тка; сочине́ние; 2. [e'sei] подверга́ть испыта́нию; [по]пыта́ться.
essen|ce ['esns] су́щность *f*; существо́; эссе́нция; **~tial** [i'senʃəl] 1. □ суще́ственный (to для Р), ва́жный; 2. су́щность *f.*
establish [is'tæbliʃ] устана́вливать [-нови́ть]; учрежда́ть [-еди́ть], осно́вывать [-ова́ть]; **~** o. s. поселя́ться [-ли́ться], устра́иваться [-ро́иться] (в П); **2ed** Church госуда́рственная це́рковь *f*; **~ment** [-mənt] учрежде́ние, заведе́ние; хозя́йство.
estate [es'teit] *pol.* сосло́вие; иму́щество; име́ние; real **~** недви́жимость *f.*
esteem [is'ti:m] 1. уваже́ние; 2. уважа́ть.
estimable ['estiməbl] досто́йный уваже́ния.

estimat|e 1. [-meit] оце́нивать [-ни́ть]; 2. [-mit] сме́та, калькуля́ция; оце́нка; **~ion** [esti'meiʃən] оце́нка; мне́ние.
estrange [is'treindʒ] отчужда́ть [-уди́ть].
etch [etʃ] гравирова́ть травле́нием.
etern|al [i'tə:nəl] □ ве́чный; неизме́нный; **~ity** [-niti] ве́чность *f.*
ether ['i:θə] эфи́р; **~eal** [i'θiəriəl] □ эфи́рный; возду́шный.
ethic|al ['eθikəl] □ эти́чный, эти́ческий; **~s** ['eθiks] э́тика.
etiquette [eti'ket] этике́т.
etymology [eti'mɔlədʒi] этимоло́гия.
eucharist ['ju:kərist] евхари́стия.
European [juərə'piən] 1. европе́ец [-пе́йка]; 2. европе́йский.
evacuate [i'vækjueit] эвакуи́ровать (*im*)*pf.*
evade [i'veid] избега́ть [-ежа́ть] (P); ускольза́ть [-зну́ть] от (P); обходи́ть [обойти́] (зако́н и т. п.).
evaluate [i'væljueit] оце́нивать [-ни́ть]; выража́ть в чи́слах.
evangelic, ~al □ [ivæn'dʒelik, -ikəl] евангели́ческий; ева́нгельский.
evaporat|e [i'væpəreit] испаря́ть (-ся) [-ри́ть(ся)]; **~ion** [ivæpə'reiʃən] испаре́ние.
evasi|on [i'veiʒən] уклоне́ние, увёртка; **~ve** [-siv] □ укло́нчивый (of от P).
eve [i:v] кану́н; on the ~ of накану́не (P).
even ['i:vən] 1. *adj.* □ ро́вный, гла́дкий; ра́вный, одина́ковый; моното́нный; беспристра́стный; чётный (о числе́); 2. *adv.* ро́вно; как раз; да́же; not ~ да́же не; ~ though, ~ if хотя́ бы, да́же е́сли; 3. выра́внивать [вы́ровнять]; сгла́живать [сгла́дить]; **~-handed** ['hændid] беспристра́стный.
evening ['i:vniŋ] ве́чер; вечери́нка; ~ dress вече́рний туале́т, фрак.
evenness ['i:vənnis] ро́вность *f*; гла́дкость; равноме́рность *f.*
evensong вече́рня.
event [i'vent] собы́тие, происше́ствие; *fig.* исхо́д; но́мер (в програ́мме); at all ~s во вся́ком слу́чае; in the ~ of в слу́чае (P); **~ful** [-ful] по́лный собы́тий.
eventual [i'ventjuəl] □ возмо́жный; коне́чный; **~ly** в конце́ концо́в; со вре́менем.
ever ['evə] всегда́; когда́-нибудь, когда́-либо; ~ so о́чень; как бы ни; as soon as ~ I can как то́лько я смогу́; for ~ навсегда́; yours ~ ваш ... (в конце́ письма́); **~green** вечнозелёный; **~lasting** [evə'la:stiŋ] □ про́чный; постоя́нный; **~more** ['evəmɔ:] наве́ки, навсегда́.
every ['evri] ка́ждый; ~ now and then вре́мя от вре́мени; ~ other day че́рез день; **~body** все *pl.*; ка́ждый, вся́кий; **~day** ежедне́вный; **~one** ка́ждый, вся́кий; все *pl.*; **~thing** всё; **~where** везде́, всю́ду.
evict [i'vikt] выселя́ть [вы́селить]; оттяга́ть по суду́.
eviden|ce ['evidəns] 1. очеви́дность *f*; доказа́тельство; ⚖ ули́ка, свиде́тельское показа́ние; in ~ в доказа́тельство; 2. служи́ть доказа́тельством; **~t** [-t] □ очеви́дный.
evil ['i:vl] 1. □ злой; па́губный; дурно́й, плохо́й; the ♀ One дья́вол; 2. зло; бе́дствие.
evince [i'vins] проявля́ть [-ви́ть].
evoke [i'vouk] вызыва́ть [вы́звать] (воспомина́ния и т. п.).
evolution [i:və'lu:ʃən] эволю́ция; разви́тие; передвиже́ние.
evolve [i'vɔlv] разви́(ва́)ться; эволюциони́ровать (*im*)*pf.*
ewe [ju:] овца́.
exact [ig'zækt] 1. □ то́чный, аккура́тный; 2. [по]тре́бовать (P); взы́скивать [-ка́ть]; **~ing** [-iŋ] тре́бовательный, взыска́тельный; **~itude** [-titju:d], **~ness** [-nis] то́чность *f.*
exaggerate [ig'zædʒəreit] преувели́чи(ва)ть.
exalt [ig'zɔ:lt] возвыша́ть [-ы́сить]; превозноси́ть [-нести́]; **~ation** [egzɔ:l'teiʃən] возвыше́ние; восто́рг.
examin|ation [igzæmi'neiʃən] осмо́тр; иссле́дование; освиде́тельствование; эксперти́за; экза́мен; **~e** [ig'zæmin] осма́тривать [-мотре́ть]; иссле́довать (*im*)*pf.*; [про-] экзаменова́ть.
example [ig'za:mpl] приме́р; образе́ц; for ~ наприме́р.
exasperate [ig'za:spəreit] доводи́ть до бе́лого кале́ния; усили(ва)ть.
excavate ['ekskəveit] выка́пывать [вы́копать].
exceed [ik'si:d] превыша́ть [-вы́сить]; переходи́ть грани́цы (P); **~ing** [-iŋ] □ огро́мный; чрезвыча́йный.
excel [ik'sel] *v/t.* превосходи́ть [-взойти́] (in, at T); *v/i.* выделя́ться [вы́делиться]; **~lence** ['eksələns] превосхо́дство; **~lency** [-i] превосходи́тельство; **~lent** ['eksələnt] □ превосхо́дный.
except [ik'sept] 1. исключа́ть [-чи́ть]; 2. *prp.* исключа́я (P); кро́ме (P); ~ for за исключе́нием (P); **~ing** [-iŋ] *prp.* за исключе́нием (P); **~ion** [ik'sepʃən] исключе́ние; take ~ to возража́ть [-рази́ть] про́тив (P); **~ional** [~l] исключи́тельный; **~ionally** [-əli] исключи́тельно.
excess [ik'ses] избы́ток, изли́шек; эксце́сс; ~ fare допла́та, припла́та;

~ luggage бага́ж вы́ше но́рмы; ~ive [-iv] □ чрезме́рный.
exchange [iks'tʃeindʒ] **1.** обме́ниваться [-ня́ться] (Т); обме́нивать [-ня́ть], *by mistake*: [-ни́ть] (for на В); [по]меня́ться (Т); **2.** обме́н; разме́н; (*a.* ♀) би́ржа; foreign ~(s *pl.*) иностра́нная валю́та; ~ office меня́льная конто́ра.
exchequer [iks'tʃekə] казначе́йство; казна́; Chancellor of the ♀ мини́стр фина́нсов Великобрита́нии.
excit|able [ik'saitəbl] возбуди́мый; **~e** [ik'sait] возбужда́ть [-уди́ть], [вз]волнова́ть; **~ement** [-mənt] возбужде́ние, волне́ние.
exclaim [iks'kleim] восклица́ть [-и́кнуть].
exclamation [ekskl ə'meiʃən] восклица́ние.
exclude [iks'klu:d] исключа́ть [-чи́ть].
exclusi|on [iks'klu:ʒən] исключе́ние; **~ve** [-siv] □ исключи́тельный; еди́нственный; ~ of за исключе́нием (Р).
excommunicat|e [ekskə'mju:nikeit] отлуча́ть от це́ркви; **~ion** [ekskəmju:ni'keiʃən] отлуче́ние от це́ркви.
excrement ['ekskrimənt] экскреме́нты *m/pl.*, испражне́ния *n/pl.*
excrete [eks'kri:t] выделя́ть [вы́делить], изверга́ть [-е́ргнуть].
excruciate [iks'kru:ʃieit] [из-, за-] му́чить; терза́ть.
exculpate ['ekskʌlpeit] опра́вдывать [-да́ть].
excursion [iks'kə:ʃən] экску́рсия.
excursive [eks'kə:siv] □ отклоня́ющийся (от те́мы).
excus|able [iks'kju:zəbl] □ извини́тельный, прости́тельный; **~e** **1.** [iks'kju:z] извиня́ть [-ни́ть], проща́ть [прости́ть]; **2.** [iks'kju:s] извине́ние; оправда́ние; отгово́рка.
execra|ble ['eksikrəbl] □ отврати́тельный; **~te** ['eksikreit] пита́ть отвраще́ние к (Д); проклина́ть [-кля́сть].
execut|e ['eksikju:t] исполня́ть [-о́лнить]; выполня́ть [вы́полнить]; казни́ть (*im*)*pf.*; **~ion** [eksi'kju:ʃən] исполне́ние; выполне́ние; казнь *f*; **~ioner** [-ə] пала́ч; **~ive** [ig'zekjutiv] **1.** □ исполни́тельный; администрати́вный; ~ committee исполни́тельный комите́т; **2.** исполни́тельная власть *f*; ✝ администра́тор; **~or** [-tə] душеприка́зчик.
exemplary [ig'zempləri] образцо́вый, приме́рный.
exemplify [ig'zemplifai] поясня́ть приме́ром; служи́ть приме́ром (Р).
exempt [ig'zempt] **1.** освобожда́ть [-боди́ть] (от вое́нный слу́жбы и т. п.); **2.** освобождённый, свобо́дный (of от Р).
exercise ['eksəsaiz] **1.** упражне́ние; трениро́вка; моцио́н; take ~ де́лать моцио́н; **2.** упражня́ть(ся); разви́(ва́)ть; [на]тренирова́ть(ся); ⚔ обуча́ть(ся) [-чи́ть(ся)].
exert [ig'zə:t] напряга́ть [-ря́чь] (си́лы); ока́зывать [-за́ть] (влия́ние и т. п.); ~ o. s. [по]стара́ться; **~ion** [ig'zə:ʃən] напряже́ние и т. д.
exhale [eks'heil] выдыха́ть [вы́дохнуть]; испаря́ть(ся) [-ри́ть(ся)].
exhaust [ig'zɔ:st] **1.** изнуря́ть [-ри́ть], истоща́ть [-щи́ть]; **2.** ⊕ выхлопна́я труба́; вы́хлоп, вы́пуск; **~ion** [-ʃən] истоще́ние, изнуре́ние; **~ive** [-iv] □ истоща́ющий; исче́рпывающий.
exhibit [ig'zibit] **1.** пока́зывать [-за́ть], проявля́ть [-ви́ть]; выставля́ть [вы́ставить]; **2.** экспона́т; ⚖ веще́ственное доказа́тельство; **~ion** [eksi'biʃən] проявле́ние, пока́з; вы́ставка; **~or** [ig'zibitə] экспоне́нт.
exhilarate [ig'ziləreit] оживля́ть [-ви́ть]; развеселя́ть [-ли́ть].
exhort [ig'zɔ:t] увеща́ть, увещева́ть.
exigen|ce, ~cy ['eksidʒəns(i)] о́страя необходи́мость *f*, кра́йность *f*.
exile ['eksail] **1.** изгна́ние, ссы́лка; изгна́нник; **2.** изгоня́ть [изгна́ть], ссыла́ть [сосла́ть].
exist [ig'zist] существова́ть, жить; **~ence** [-əns] существова́ние, жизнь *f*; in ~ = **~ent** [-ənt] существу́ющий.
exit ['eksit] вы́ход; *fig.* смерть *f*; *thea.* ухо́д со сце́ны.
exodus ['eksədəs] ма́ссовый отъе́зд; исхо́д евре́ев из Еги́пта.
exonerate [ig'zɔnəreit] *fig.* реабилити́ровать (*im*)*pf.*; снять бре́мя (вины́ и т. п.) с (Р).
exorbitant [ig'zɔ:bitənt] □ непоме́рный, чрезме́рный.
exorci|se, ~ze ['eksɔ:saiz] изгоня́ть [изгна́ть] (ду́хов, нечи́стую си́лу); освобожда́ть [-боди́ть] (of от Р).
exotic [eg'zɔtik] экзоти́ческий.
expan|d [iks'pænd] расширя́ть(ся) [-и́рить(ся)], увели́чи(ва)ть(ся); разви́(ва́)ть(ся); **~se** [iks'pæns], **~sion** [-ʃən] простра́нство; протяже́ние; экспа́нсия; расшире́ние; **~sive** [-siv] □ спосо́бный расширя́ться; обши́рный; *fig.* экспанси́вный.
expatriate [eks'pætrieit] изгоня́ть [из оте́чества.]
expect [iks'pekt] ожида́ть (Р); рассчи́тывать, наде́яться; F полага́ть, [по]ду́мать; **~ant** [-ənt] **1.** ~ ожида́ющий; ~ mother бере́менная же́нщина; **2.** кандида́т; **~ation** [ekspek'teiʃən] ожида́ние; расчёт; наде́жда.

expectorate [eks'pektəreit] отхáркивать [-кнуть]; плевáть [плю́нуть].

expedi|ent [iks'pi:diənt] **1.** подходя́щий, целесообрáзный, соотвéтствующий (обстоя́тельствам); **2.** подру́чное срéдство; уло́вка; **~tion** [ekspi'diʃən] экспеди́ция; быстротá; поспéшность *f*.

expel [iks'pel] изгоня́ть [изгнáть] (из P), исключáть [-чи́ть] (из P).

expen|d [iks'pend] [ис]трáтить; [из]расхо́довать; **~diture** [-itʃə] расхо́д, трáта; **~se** [iks'pens] расхо́д, трáта; **~s** *pl.* расхо́ды *m/pl.*; **~sive** [-siv] □ дорого́й, до́рого сто́ящий.

experience [iks'piərəns] **1.** о́пыт (жи́зненный); переживáние; **2.** испы́тывать [испытáть]; пережи́(вá)ть; **~d** [-t] о́пытный.

experiment 1. [iks'perimənt] о́пыт, экспери́мéнт; **2.** [-'ment] производи́ть о́пыты; **~al** [eksperi'mentl] □ экспериментáльный, осно́ванный на о́пыте; про́бный.

expert ['ekspə:t] **1.** □ [*pred.* eks'pə:t] о́пытный, иску́сный; **2.** экспéрт, знато́к, специали́ст.

expir|ation [ekspai'reiʃən] вы́дыхáние; окончáние, истечéние (сро́ка); **~e** [iks'paiə] выдыхáть [вы́дохнуть]; умирáть [умерéть]; ✝ кончáться [ко́нчиться], истекáть [-éчь] (о сро́ке).

explain [iks'plein] объясня́ть [-ни́ть]; оправдывать [-дáть] (поведéние).

explanat|ion [eksplə'neiʃən] объяснéние; толковáние; **~ory** [iks'plænətəri] □ объясни́тельный.

explicable ['eksplikəbl] объясни́мый.

explicit [iks'plisit] □ я́сный, недвусмы́сленный.

explode [iks'ploud] взрывáть(ся) [взорвáть(ся)]; подрывáть [подорвáть]; разражáться [-рази́ться] (with T).

exploit 1. ['eksplɔit] по́двиг; **2.** [iks'plɔit] эксплуати́ровать; ⚒ разрабáтывать [-бо́тать]; **~ation** [eksplɔi'teiʃən] эксплуатáция; ⚒ разрабо́тка.

explor|ation [eksplɔ:'reiʃən] исслéдование; **~e** [iks'plɔ:] исслéдовать (*im*)*pf.*; развéд(ыв)ать **~er** [-rə] исслéдователь(ница *f*) *m*.

explosi|on [iks'plouʒən] взрыв; вспы́шка (гнéва); **~ve** [-siv] **1.** □ взры́вчатый; *fig.* вспы́льчивый; **2.** взры́вчатое веществó.

exponent [eks'pounənt] объясни́тель *m*; представи́тель *m*; образéц; ⅍ покáзатель стéпени.

export 1. ['ekspɔ:t] э́кспорт, вы́воз; **2.** [eks'pɔ:t] экспорти́ровать (*im*)*pf.*, вывози́ть [вы́везти] (товáры); **~ation** [ekspɔ:'teiʃən] вы́воз.

expos|e [iks'pouz] подвергáть [-éргнуть] (опáсности и т. п.); бросáть на произво́л судьбы́; выставля́ть [вы́ставить]; разоблачáть [-чи́ть]; *phot.* экспони́ровать (*im*)*pf.*; **~ition** [ekspo'ziʃən] вы́ставка; изложéние

exposure [iks'pouʒə] подвергáние; выставлéние; разоблачéние; *phot.* экспози́ция, вы́держка.

expound [iks'paund] излагáть [изложи́ть]; разъясня́ть [-ни́ть].

express [iks'pres] **1.** □ определённый, то́чно вы́раженный; специáльный; сро́чный; ~ company *Am.* трáнспортная контóра; **2.** курьéр, нарóчный; (*a.* ~ train) экспрéсс, курьéрский по́езд; **3.** *adv.* спéшно; с нарóчным; **4.** выражáть [вы́разить]; **~ion** [iks'preʃən] выражéние; вырази́тельность *f*; **~ive** [iks'presiv] □ вырази́тельный; выражáющий.

expropriate [eks'prouprieit] экспроприи́ровать (*im*)*pf.*; лишáть со́бственности.

expulsion [iks'pʌlʃən] изгнáние; исключéние (из шко́лы и т. п.).

exquisite ['ekskwizit] **1.** □ изы́сканный, утончённый; прелéстный; **2.** фат, щёголь *m*.

extant [eks'tænt] сохрани́вшийся.

extempor|aneous [ekstempə'reinjəs] □, **~ary** [iks'tempərəri] неподготóвленный; **~e** [-pəri] *adv.* экспрóмтом.

extend [iks'tend] *v/t.* протя́гивать [-тяну́ть]; распространя́ть [-ни́ть] (влия́ние); продлевáть [-ли́ть] (срок); ⚔ рассыпáть в цепь; *v/i.* простирáться [простерéться].

extensi|on [iks'tenʃən] вытя́гивание; расширéние; распространéние; протяжéние; продлéние; University ♀ популя́рные лéкции, организу́емые университéтом; **~ve** [-siv] □ обши́рный, прострáнный.

extent [iks'tent] протяжéние; размéр, стéпень *f*, мéра; to the ~ of в размéре (P); to some ~ до извéстной стéпени.

extenuate [eks'tenjueit] уменьшáть [умéньши́ть] (вину́); старáться найти́ извинéние; ослабля́ть [-áбить].

exterior [eks'tiəriə] **1.** □ внéшний, нару́жный; **2.** внéшность *f*, нару́жность *f*.

exterminate [eks'tə:mineit] искореня́ть [-ни́ть], истребля́ть [-би́ть].

external [eks'tə:nl] **1.** □ нару́жный, внéшний; **2. ~s** *pl.* внéшность *f*, нару́жность *f*; *fig.* внéшние обстоя́тельства.

extinct [iks'tiŋkt] угáсший; вы́мерший; поту́хший.

extinguish [iks'tiŋgwiʃ] [по]гаси́ть; [по]туши́ть; погашáть [погаси́ть] (долг).

extirpate ['ekstə:peit] искоренять [-нить], истреблять [-бить].
extol [iks'tɔl] превозносить [-нести].
extort [iks'tɔ:t] вымогать (деньги); выпытывать [выпытать] (тайну); **~ion** [iks'tɔ:ʃən] вымогательство.
extra ['ekstrə] **1.** добавочный, дополнительный; экстренный; **2.** *adv.* особо; особенно; дополнительно; **3.** приплата; *Am.* экстренный выпуск газеты; **~s** *pl.* побочные расходы (доходы).
extract 1. ['ekstrækt] экстракт; выдержка, извлечение; **2.** [iks'trækt] удалять [-лить]; извлекать [-ечь]; вырывать [вырвать]; **~ion** [-kʃən] извлечение; происхождение (человека).
extraordinary [iks'trɔ:dnri] необычайный; удивительный, странный.
extravagan|ce [iks'trævigəns] расточительность *f*; нелепость *f*; излишество; **~t** [-gənt] □ расточительный; сумасбродный, нелепый.
extrem|e [iks'tri:m] **1.** □ крайний; последний; чрезвычайный; **2.** крайность *f*; **~ity** [iks'tremiti] оконечность *f*; крайность *f*; крайняя нужда; крайняя мера; **~ities** [-z] *pl.* конечности *f/pl.*
extricate ['ekstrikeit] выводить [вывести] (из затруднительного положения).
exuberan|ce [ig'zju:bərəns] изобилие, избыток; **~t** [-t] обильный; пышный; цветистый, многословный.
exult [ig'zʌlt] ликовать; торжествовать.
eye [ai] **1.** глаз, око; взгляд; ушко; with an ~ to с целью (+ *inf.*); **2.** смотреть на (В), пристально разглядывать; **~ball** глазное яблоко; **~brow** бровь *f*; **...~d** [aid] ...глазый; **~-glass** линза; (a pair of) **~es** *pl.* очки *n/pl.*; лорнет; **~lash** ресница; **~lid** веко; **~sight** зрение.

F

fable ['feibl] басня.
fabric ['fæbrik] сооружение; структура; выделка; фабрикат; ткань *f*, материя; **~ate** ['fæbrikeit] (*mst fig.*) выдумывать [выдумать]; выделывать [выделать].
fabulous ['fæbjuləs] □ баснословный; неправдоподобный.
face [feis] **1.** лицо, физиономия; гримаса; лицевая сторона (ткани); фасад; on the ~ of it с первого взгляда; **2.** *v/t.* встречать смело; смотреть в лицо (Д); стоять лицом к (Д); выходить на (В) (об окне); ⚠ облицовывать [-цевать]; [на-, от]полировать; *v/i.* ~ about ⚔ поворачиваться кругом.
facetious [fə'si:ʃəs] □ шутливый.
facil|e ['fæsail] лёгкий; свободный (о речи и т. п.); **~itate** [fə'siliteit] облегчать [-чить]; **~ity** [fə'siliti] лёгкость *f*; способность *f*; плавность *f* (речи); облегчение.
facing ['feisiŋ] ⊕ облицовка; **~s** *pl.* отделка мундира.
fact [fækt] факт; дело; явление; истина; действительность *f*.
faction ['fækʃən] фракция; клика.
factitious [fæk'tiʃəs] □ искусственный.
factor ['fæktə] фактор; агент; ✝ комиссионер; **~y** [-ri] фабрика, завод.
faculty ['fækəlti] способность *f*; *fig.* дар; *univ.* факультет.
fad [fæd] F конёк; прихоть *f*, причуда.
fade [feid] увядать [увянуть]; постепенно исчезать.
fag [fæg] *v/i.* потрудиться; корпеть (над Т); *v/t.* утомлять [-мить].
fail [feil] **1.** *v/i.* ослабе(ва)ть; недост(ав)ать; потерпеть неудачу; проваливаться [-литься] (на экзамене); he ~ed to do ему не удалось сделать (P); забы(ва)ть; *v/t.* изменять [-нить] (Д), покидать [-инуть]; **2.** *su.*: without ~ наверняка; непременно; **~ing** ['feiliŋ] недостаток; слабость *f*; **~ure** [feiljə] неудача, неуспех; провал (на экзамене); банкротство; неудачник (-ица).
faint [feint] **1.** □ слабый; робкий (голос); тусклый; **2.** [о]слабеть; потерять сознание (with от P); **3.** обморок, потеря сознания; **~hearted** ['feint'hɑ:tid] малодушный.
fair[1] [fɛə] **1.** *adj* прекрасный, красивый; благоприятный; белокурый; ясный; попутный; справедливый; **2.** *adv.* честно; любезно; прямо, ясно; ~ copy чистовик; ~ play игра по правилам.
fair[2] [~] ярмарка.
fair|ly ['fɛəli] справедливо; довольно; сносно; **~ness** ['fɛənis] справедливость *f*; красота (*s.* fair[1]); **~way** ⚓ фарватер.
fairy ['fɛəri] фея; **~land** сказочная страна; **~-tale** сказка.
faith [feiθ] доверие, вера; вера (религия); **~ful** ['feiθful] □ верный, преданный; правдивый; yours **~ly** уважающий Вас; **~less** ['feiθlis] □ вероломный; неверующий.

fake [feik] *sl.* 1. подде́лка, фальши́вка; 2. подде́л(ыв)ать.
falcon ['fɔ:lkən] со́кол.
fall [fɔ:l] 1. паде́ние; упа́док; обры́в, склон; напо́р; *Am.* о́сень *f*; (*mst* ~s *pl.*) водопа́д; 2. [*irr.*] па́дать [упа́сть]; спада́ть [спасть]; убы́(ва́)ть (о воде́); обва́ливаться [-ли́ться] (о земле́); ~ back отступа́ть [-пи́ть]; ~ ill *или* sick заболе́(ва́)ть; ~ out [по]ссо́риться; ~ short of не оправда́ть (ожида́ний); не достига́ть [-и́чь] *a.* [-и́гнуть] (це́ли); ~ short не хвата́ть [-ти́ть], конча́ться [ко́нчиться]; ~ to принима́ться [-ня́ться] за (В).
fallacious [fə'leiʃəs] □ оши́бочный, ло́жный.
fallacy ['fæləsi] заблужде́ние, оши́бка.
fallen ['fɔ:lən] *p. pt.* от fall.
falling ['fɔ:liŋ] паде́ние; пониже́ние; ~-**sickness** эпиле́псия; ~-**star** метео́р, па́дающая звезда́.
fallow ['fælou] *adj.* вспа́ханный под па́р.
false [fɔ:ls] □ ло́жный, оши́бочный; фальши́вый; вероло́мный; иску́ственный (о зуба́х); ~**hood** ['fɔ:lshud], ~**ness** [-nis] ложь *f*; фальши́вость *f*; оши́бочность *f*.
falsi|fication [fɔ:lsifi'keiʃən] подде́лка; ~**fy** ['fɔ:lsifai] подде́л(ыв)ать; ~**ty** [-ti] ло́жность *f*, оши́бочность *f*; вероло́мство.
falter ['fɔ:ltə] спотыка́ться [-тькну́ться]; запина́ться [запну́ться]; *fig.* колеба́ться.
fame [feim] сла́ва; молва́; ~**d** [feimd] изве́стный, знамени́тый.
familiar [fə'miljə] 1. □ бли́зкий, хорошо́ знако́мый; обы́чный; 2. бли́зкий друг; ~**ity** [fəmili'æriti] бли́зость *f*; фамилия́рность *f*; осведомлённость *f*; ~**ize** [fə'miljəraiz] ознакомля́ть [-ко́мить].
family ['fæmili] семья́, семе́йство; in the ~ way в интере́сном положе́нии (бере́менна); ~ tree родосло́вное де́рево.
fami|ne ['fæmin] го́лод; голода́ние; ~**sh** голода́ть; мори́ть го́лодом.
famous ['feiməs] □ знамени́тый.
fan [fæn] 1. ве́ер; вентиля́тор; *sport* боле́льщик (-ица); покло́нник (-ица); 2. обма́хивать [-хну́ть].
fanatic [fə'nætik] 1. (*a.* ~**al** □ [-ikəl]) фанати́ческий; 2. фана́тик (-ти́чка).
fanciful ['fænsiful] □ прихотли́вый, капри́зный, причу́дливый.
fancy ['fænsi] 1. фанта́зия, воображе́ние; при́хоть *f*; пристра́стие; скло́нность *f*; 2. прихотли́вый; фантасти́ческий; орнамента́льный; ~ ball костюми́рованный бал; ~ goods *pl.* мо́дные това́ры *m/pl.*; 3. вообража́ть [-рази́ть]; представля́ть [-а́вить] себе́; [по-] люби́ть; [за]хоте́ть; just ~! предста́вьте себе́!
fang [fæŋ] клык; ядови́тый зуб (змеи́).
fantas|tic [fæn'tæstik] (~ally) причу́дливый, фантасти́чный; ~**y** ['fæntəsi] фанта́зия, воображе́ние.
far [fɑ:] *adj.* да́льний, далёкий, отдалённый; *adv.* далеко́; гора́здо; as ~ as до (Р); in so ~ as поско́льку; ~ away далеко́.
fare [fɛə] 1. проездны́е де́ньги *f/pl.*; пассажи́р; съестны́е припа́сы *m/pl.*; 2. быть, пожива́ть; пита́ться; ~**well** ['fɛə'wel] 1. проща́й(те)!; 2. проща́ние.
far-fetched ['fɑ:'fetʃt] *fig.* притя́нутый за́ волосы.
farm [fɑ:m] 1. фе́рма; 2. обраба́тывать зе́млю; ~**er** ['fɑ:mə] крестья́нин, фе́рмер; ~**house** жило́й дом на фе́рме; ~**ing** 1. заня́тие се́льским хозя́йством; 2. сельскохозя́йственный; ~**stead** ['fɑ:msted] уса́дьба.
far-off ['fɑ:rɔf] далёкий.
farthe|r ['fɑ:ðə] 1. *adv.* да́льше; 2. *adj.* отдалённый; ~**st** [-ðist] 1. *adj.* са́мый далёкий, са́мый да́льний; 2. *adv.* да́льше всего́.
fascinat|e ['fæsineit] очаро́вывать [-ова́ть], пленя́ть [-ни́ть]; ~**ion** [fæsi'neiʃən] очарова́ние, обая́ние.
fashion ['fæʃn] 1. мо́да; стиль *m*; фасо́н, покро́й; о́браз, мане́ра; in (out of) ~ (не)мо́дный; 2. придава́ть фо́рму, вид (Д into Р); ~**able** ['fæʃnəbl] □ мо́дный, фешене́бельный.
fast[1] [fɑ:st] про́чный, кре́пкий, твёрдый; бы́стрый; легкомы́сленный.
fast[2] [~] 1. *eccl.* пост; 2. пости́ться.
fasten ['fɑ:sn] *v/t.* прикрепля́ть [-пи́ть]; привя́зывать [-за́ть]; сви́нчивать [-нти́ть]; застёгивать [-тегну́ть]; *v/i.* запира́ться [запере́ться]; застёгивать(ся) [-тегну́ть (-ся)]; ~ upon *fig.* ухвати́ться за (В); ~**er** [-ə] запо́р, задви́жка; застёжка.
fastidious [fæs'tidiəs] □ привере́дливый.
fat [fæt] 1. □ жи́рный; са́льный; ту́чный; 2. жир; са́ло; 3. otка́рмливать [откорми́ть]; [раз-] жире́ть.
fatal ['feitl] □ рокова́й, фата́льный, неизбе́жный; смерте́льный; ~**ity** [fə'tæliti] обречённость *f*; фата́льность *f*; несча́стье; смерть *f* (от несча́стного слу́чая).
fate [feit] рок, судьба́.
father ['fɑ:ðə] оте́ц; ~**hood** [-hud] отцо́вство; ~-**in-law** ['fɑ:ðərinlɔ:] свёкор; тесть *m*; ~**less** [-lis] оста́вшийся без отца́; ~**ly** [-li] оте́ческий.

fathom ['fæðəm] **1.** ⚓ морска́я са́жень *f* (= 6 футам = 182 сантиме́трам); **2.** ⚓ измеря́ть глубину́ (Р); *fig.* вника́ть [вни́кнуть] в (В), понима́ть [поня́ть]; **~less** [-lis] неизмери́мый; бездо́нный.
fatigue [fə'ti:g] **1.** утомле́ние, уста́лость *f*; **2.** утомля́ть [-ми́ть], изнуря́ть [-ри́ть].
fat|ness ['fætnis] жи́рность *f*; **~ten** ['fætn] отка́рмливать [откорми́ть] (на убо́й); [раз]жире́ть.
fatuous ['fætjuəs] □ глу́пый, пусто́й.
faucet ['fɔ:sit] *Am.* (водопрово́дный) кран.
fault [fɔ:lt] недоста́ток, дефе́кт; просту́пок, вина́; find ~ with прид(и)ра́ться к (Д); be at ~ потеря́ть след; **~-finder** приди́ра *m/f*; **~less** ['fɔ:ltlis] □ безупре́чный; **~y** ['fɔ:lti] □ име́ющий недоста́ток, дефе́ктный.
favo(u)r ['feivə] **1.** благоскло́нность *f*, расположе́ние; одобре́ние; одолже́ние; your ~ ✝ Ва́ше письмо́; **2.** благоволи́ть к (Д); ока́зывать внима́ние (Д); покрови́тельствовать (Д); **~able** [-rəbl] □ благоприя́тный, удо́бный; **~ite** ['feivərit] **1.** люби́мец (-мица); фаворит(ка); **2.** люби́мый.
fawn [fɔ:n] **1.** молодо́й оле́нь *m*; кори́чневый цвет; **2.** подли́зываться [-за́ться] (upon к Д).
fear [fiə] **1.** страх, боя́знь *f*; опасе́ние; **2.** боя́ться (Р); **~ful** ['fiəful] □ стра́шный, ужа́сный; **~less** ['fiəlis] □ бесстра́шный, неустраши́мый.
feasible ['fi:zəbl] возмо́жный, вероя́тный; выполни́мый.
feast [fi:st] **1.** пир, пра́здество, банке́т; **2.** *v/t.* угоща́ть [угости́ть]; че́ствовать; *v/i.* пирова́ть.
feat [fi:t] по́двиг; трюк.
feather ['feðə] **1.** перо́; опере́ние; show the white ~ F прояви́ть тру́сость; in high ~ в отли́чном настрое́нии; **2.** украша́ть пе́рьями; **~-brained, ~-headed** пусто́й, ве́треный, глу́пый; **~ed** ['feðəd] перна́тый; **~y** [-ri] оперённый; пуши́стый.
feature ['fi:tʃə] **1.** осо́бенность *f*, сво́йство; *Am.* газе́тная статья́; **~s** *pl.* черты́ лица́; **2.** изобража́ть [-рази́ть]; пока́зывать [-за́ть] (на экра́не); выводи́ть в гла́вной ро́ли.
February ['februəri] февра́ль *m*.
fecund ['fekənd] плодоро́дный.
fed [fed] *pt.* и *p. pt.* от feed; I am ~ up with ... мне надое́л (-ла, -ло).
federa|l ['fedərəl] федера́льный; сою́зный; **~tion** [fedə'reiʃən] федера́ция.
fee [fi:] **1.** гонора́р; взнос; пла́та; чаевы́е *pl.* **2.** [за]плати́ть.
feeble ['fi:bl] □ сла́бый, хи́лый.
feed [fi:d] **1.** пита́ние, кормле́ние; пи́ща; ⊕ пода́ча (материа́ла); **2.** [*irr.*] *v/t.* пита́ть, [по]корми́ть; ⊕ снабжа́ть [-бди́ть] (материа́лом); *v/i.* пита́ться, корми́ться; пасти́сь; **~ing-bottle** де́тский рожо́к.
feel [fi:l] **1.** [*irr.*] [по]чу́вствовать (себя́); испы́тывать [-та́ть]; ощуща́ть [ощути́ть], осяза́ть; ~ like doing быть скло́нным сде́лать; **2.** ощуще́ние, осяза́ние; чутьё; **~er** ['fi:lə] щу́пальце; **~ing** ['fi:liŋ] **1.** □ чувстви́тельный; прочу́вствованный; **2.** чу́вство.
feet [fi:t] *pl.* от foot **1.**
feign [fein] притворя́ться [-ри́ться], симули́ровать (*im*)*pf.*
feint [feint] притво́рство; манёвр.
felicit|ate [fi'lisiteit] поздравля́ть [-а́вить]; **~ous** [-təs] □ уда́чный; счастли́вый.
fell [fel] **1.** *pt.* от fall; **2.** [с]руби́ть.
felloe ['felou] о́бод (колеса́).
fellow [~] това́рищ, собра́т; челове́к; the ~ of a glove па́рная перча́тка; **~-countryman** соотe̋чественник; **~ship** [-ʃip] това́рищество.
felly ['feli] о́бод (колеса́).
felon ['felən] ⚖ уголо́вный престу́пник; **~y** ['feləni] уголо́вное преступле́ние.
felt[1] [felt] *pt.* и *p. pt.* от feel.
felt[2] [~] **1.** во́йлок, фетр; **2.** сбива́ть (*or* сбива́ться в) во́йлок.
female ['fi:meil] **1.** же́нский; **2.** же́нщина.
feminine ['feminin] □ же́нский; же́нственный.
fen [fen] боло́то, топь *f*.
fence [fens] **1.** забо́р, и́згородь *f*, огра́да; sit on the ~ колеба́ться ме́жду двумя́ мне́ниями; занима́ть выжида́тельную пози́цию; **2.** *v/t.* огора́живать [-роди́ть]; защища́ть [-ити́ть]; *v/i.* фехтова́ть; укрыва́ть кра́деное.
fencing ['fensiŋ] **1.** и́згородь *f*, забо́р, огра́да; фехтова́ние; **2.** *attr.* фехтова́льный.
fender ['fendə] ками́нная решётка; *mot. Am.* крыло́.
ferment 1. ['fə:ment] заква́ска, ферме́нт; ⚗ броже́ние; *fig.* возбужде́ние, волне́ние; **2.** [fə'ment] вызыва́ть броже́ние; броди́ть; *fig.* волнова́ться; **~ation** [fə:men'teiʃən] броже́ние, фермента́ция.
fern [fə:n] ♀ па́поротник.
feroci|ous [fə'rouʃəs] □ жесто́кий, свире́пый; **~ty** [fə'rɔsiti] жесто́кость *f*, свире́пость *f*.
ferret ['ferit] **1.** *zo.* хорёк; **2.** [по-] ры́ться, [по]ша́рить; ~ out вы́искивать [вы́искать]; разве́д(ыв)ать.
ferry ['feri] **1.** перево́з, перепра́ва; паро́м; **2.** перевози́ть [-везти́]; **~man** перево́зчик.

fertil|e ['fə:tail] □ плодоро́дный; изоби́льный; изоби́лующий (T); **~ity** [fə:'tiliti] плодоро́дие; изоби́лие; **~ize** ['fə:tilaiz] удобря́ть [удо́брить]; оплодотворя́ть [-ри́ть]; **~izer** удобре́ние.
ferven|cy ['fə:vənsi] рве́ние, пыл; **~t** [-t] □ горя́чий, пы́лкий.
fervour ['fə:və] жар, пыл.
festal ['festl] □ пра́здничный.
fester [-tə] гнои́ться.
festiv|al ['festəvəl] пра́зднество; фестива́ль *m*; **~e** ['festiv] □ пра́здничный; **~ity** [fes'tiviti] пра́зднество; весе́лье.
fetch [fetʃ] сходи́ть, съе́здить за (T); приноси́ть [-нести́]; **~ing** F □ привлека́тельный.
fetid ['fetid] □ зловонный, воню́чий.
fetter ['fetə] **1.** *mst* **~s** *pl.* пу́ты *f/pl.*; кандалы́ *m/pl.*; *fig.* око́вы *f/pl.*, у́зы *f/pl.*; **2.** зако́вывать [-ова́ть].
feud [fju:d] вражда́; феода́льное поме́стье; **~al** ['fju:dəl] □ феода́льный; **~alism** [-delizm] феодали́зм.
fever ['fi:və] лихора́дка, жар; **~ish** [-riʃ] □ лихора́дочный.
few [fju:] немно́гие; немно́го, ма́ло (P); a **~** не́сколько (P).
fiancé(e) [fi'ɑ:ŋsei] жени́х (неве́ста).
fib [fib] **1.** вы́думка, непра́вда; **2.** прив(и)ра́ть.
fibr|e ['faibə] фи́бра, волокно́, нить *f*; **~ous** ['faibrəs] □ волокни́стый.
fickle ['fikl] непостоя́нный; **~ness** [-nis] непостоя́нство.
fiction ['fikʃən] вы́мысел, вы́думка; беллетри́стика; **~al** [-l] □ вы́мышленный; беллетристи́ческий.
fictitious [fik'tiʃəs] □ вы́мышленный; фикти́вный.
fiddle ['fidl] F **1.** скри́пка; **2.** игра́ть на скри́пке; **~stick** смычо́к.
fidelity [fi'deliti] ве́рность *f*, пре́данность *f*; то́чность *f*.
fidget ['fidʒit] F **1.** беспоко́йное состоя́ние; **2.** ёрзать, быть в волне́нии; приводи́ть в беспоко́йство; **~y** суетли́вый, беспоко́йный, не́рвный.
field [fi:ld] по́ле; луг; простра́нство; hold the **~** уде́рживать пози́ции; **~-glass** полево́й бино́кль *m*; **~-officer** штаб-офице́р; **~ of vision** по́ле зре́ния; **~-sports** *pl.* спорт на откры́том во́здухе.
fiend [fi:nd] дья́вол; злой дух; **~ish** ['fi:ndiʃ] □ дья́вольский; жесто́кий, злой.
fierce [fiəs] □ свире́пый, лю́тый; си́льный; **~ness** ['fiəsnis] свире́пость *f*, лю́тость *f*.
fif|teen ['fif'ti:n] пятна́дцать; **~teenth** [-θ] пятна́дцатый; **~th** [fifθ] **1.** пя́тый; **2.** пя́тая часть *f*; **~tieth** ['fiftiiθ] пятидеся́тый; **~ty** ['fifti] пятьдеся́т.
fig [fig] **1.** ви́нная я́года, инжи́р, смо́ква; **2.** F состоя́ние.
fight [fait] **1.** сраже́ние, бой; дра́ка; спор; борьба́; show **~** быть гото́вым к борьбе́; **2.** [*irr.*] *v/t.* боро́ться про́тив (P); отста́ивать [отстоя́ть]; *v/i.* сража́ться [срази́ться]; воева́ть; боро́ться; **~er** ['faitə] бое́ц; ✈ истреби́тель *m*; **~ing** ['faitiŋ] сраже́ние, бой; дра́ка; *attr.* боево́й.
figurative ['figjurətiv] □ перено́сный, метафори́ческий.
figure ['figə] **1.** фигу́ра; изображе́ние; ци́фра; диагра́мма; F цена́; **2.** *v/t.* изобража́ть [-рази́ть]; представля́ть себе́; вычисля́ть [вы́числить], рассчи́тывать [-ита́ть]; *v/i.* фигури́ровать.
filament ['filəmənt] ⚡ нить нака́ла; волокно́, волосо́к.
filbert ['filbət] ♀ лесно́й оре́х.
filch [filtʃ] [у]красть, [у-, с]тащи́ть (from у P).
file[1] [fail] **1.** ⊕ напи́льник; пи́лочка (для ногте́й); **2.** пили́ть, подпи́ливать [-ли́ть].
file[2] [~] **1.** регистра́тор; подши́тые бума́ги *f/pl.*; картоте́ка; **2.** регистри́ровать (докуме́нты) (*im*)*pf.*; подшива́ть к де́лу.
filial ['filjəl] □ сыно́вний, доче́рний.
filibuster ['filibʌstə] флибустье́р, пира́т.
fill [fil] **1.** наполня́ть(ся) [-о́лнить(-ся)]; [за]пломбирова́ть (зуб); удовлетворя́ть [-ри́ть]; *Am.* выполня́ть [вы́полнить] (зака́зы); **~** in заполня́ть [-о́лнить]; **2.** доста́ток; сы́тость *f*.
fillet ['filit] повя́зка (на го́лову); филе́(й) (мя́со) *n indecl.*
filling ['filiŋ] наполне́ние; погру́зка; (зубна́я) пло́мба; фарш, начи́нка; *mot.* **~** station бензи́новая коло́нка.
fillip ['filip] щелчо́к; толчо́к.
filly ['fili] молода́я кобы́ла.
film [film] **1.** плёнка; фильм; ды́мка; **~** cartridge кату́шка с плёнками; **2.** производи́ть киносъёмку (P); экранизи́ровать (*im*)*pf.*
filter ['filtə] **1.** фильтр, цеди́лка; **2.** [про]фильтрова́ть, проце́живать [-цеди́ть].
filth [filθ] грязь *f*; **~y** ['filθi] □ гря́зный, нечи́стый.
fin [fin] плавни́к (ры́бы); *sl.* рука́.
final ['fainl] **1.** □ заключи́тельный; оконча́тельный; **2.** *sport* фина́л.
financ|e [fi'næns] **1.** нау́ка о фина́нсах; **~s** *pl.* фина́нсы *m/pl.*; **2.** *v/t.* финанси́ровать (*im*)*pf.*; *v/i.* занима́ться фина́нсовыми опера́циями; **~ial** [fi'nænʃəl] □ фина́нсовый; **~ier** [-siə] финанси́ст.
finch [fintʃ] *zo.* зя́блик.

find [faind] [*irr.*] **1.** находи́ть [найти́]; счита́ть [счесть]; обрета́ть [обрести́]; заст(ав)ля́ть; all found на всём гото́вом; **2.** нахо́дка; **~ing** ['faindiŋ] ⚖ пригово́р; *pl.* вы́воды.

fine¹ [fain] □ то́нкий, изя́щный; прекра́сный; высокопро́бный.

fine² [~] **1.** штраф; in ~ в о́бщем, сло́вом; наконе́ц; **2.** [о]штрафова́ть.

fineness ['fainnis] то́нкость *f*, изя́щество; острота́ (чувств).

finery ['fainəri] пы́шный наря́д; украше́ние.

finger ['fiŋgə] **1.** па́лец; **2.** тро́гать, перебира́ть па́льцами; **~-language** язы́к глухонемы́х; **~-print** дактилоскопи́ческий отпеча́ток.

finish ['finiʃ] **1.** *v/t.* конча́ть [ко́нчить]; заверша́ть [-ши́ть]; отде́л(ыв)ать; доеда́ть [дое́сть], допи́(ва́)ть; *v/i.* конча́ть(ся) [ко́нчить(ся)]; **2.** коне́ц; зако́нченность *f*; отде́лка; *sport* фи́ниш.

finite ['fainait] □ ограни́ченный, име́ющий преде́л.

fir [fə:] ель *f*, пи́хта; **~-cone** ['fə:koun] ело́вая ши́шка.

fire ['faiə] **1.** ого́нь *m*; be on ~ горе́ть; **2.** *v/t.* зажига́ть [заже́чь], поджига́ть [-же́чь]; [за]топи́ть (пе́чку); обжига́ть [обже́чь] (кирпичи́ и т. п.); *fig.* воспламеня́ть [-ни́ть]; *Am.* F увольня́ть [уво́лить]; *v/i.* стреля́ть [вы́стрелить]; **~-alarm** пожа́рная трево́га; **~-brigade,** *Am.* **~-department** пожа́рная кома́нда; **~-engine** [''faiər'endʒin] пожа́рная маши́на; **~-escape** [''faiəris'keip] пожа́рная ле́стница; **~-extinguisher** [-riks'tiŋgwiʃə] огнетуши́тель *m*; **~man** пожа́рный; кочега́р; **~place** ками́н; **~plug** пожа́рный кран, гидра́нт; **~proof** огнеупо́рный; **~side** ме́сто о́коло ками́на; **~-station** пожа́рная ста́нция; **~wood** дрова́ *n/pl.*; **~works** *pl.* фейерве́рк.

firing ['faiəriŋ] стрельба́; отопле́ние.

firm [fə:m] **1.** □ кре́пкий, пло́тный, твёрдый; сто́йкий; насто́йчивый; **2.** фи́рма; **~ness** ['fə:mnis] твёрдость *f*.

first [fə:st] **1.** *adj.* пе́рвый; ра́нний; выдаю́щийся; ~ cost ✝ себесто́имость *f*; **2.** *adv.* сперва́, снача́ла; впервы́е; скоре́е; at ~ снача́ла; ~ of all пре́жде всего́; **3.** нача́ло; the ~ пе́рвое число́; from the ~ с са́мого нача́ла; **~-born** пе́рвенец; **~-class** первокла́ссный; **~ly** ['fə:stli] во-пе́рвых; **~-rate** первокла́ссный.

fish [fiʃ] **1.** ры́ба; F odd (или queer) ~ чуда́к; **2.** уди́ть ры́бу; выу́живать [вы́удить] (*a. fig.*); **~-bone** ры́бная кость *f*.

fisher|man ['fiʃəmən] рыба́к, рыболо́в; **~y** [-ri] рыболо́вство; ры́бный про́мысел.

fishing ['fiʃiŋ] ры́бная ло́вля; **~-line** ле́са́; **~-tackle** рыболо́вные принадле́жности *f/pl.*

fiss|ion ['fiʃən] ⚛ расщепле́ние; **~ure** ['fiʃə] тре́щина, рассе́лина.

fist [fist] кула́к; по́черк (шутли́во); **~icuffs** ['fistikʌfs] *pl.* кула́чный бой.

fit¹ [fit] **1.** □ го́дный, подходя́щий; здоро́вый; досто́йный; **2.** *v/t.* прила́живать [-ла́дить] (to к Д); подходи́ть [подойти́] к (Д); приспособля́ть [-спосо́бить] (for, to к Д); ~ out снаряжа́ть [-яди́ть]; снабжа́ть [-бди́ть]; ~ up соб(и)ра́ть, [с]монти́ровать; *v/i.* годи́ться; сиде́ть (о пла́тье); прила́живаться [-ла́диться]; приспособля́ться [-посо́биться]; **3.** ⊕ приго́нка; поса́дка.

fit² [fit] ⚕ припа́док, пароксі́зм, при́ступ; поры́в; by ~s and starts поры́вами, уры́вками; give a p. a ~ поража́ть [порази́ть] (В), возмуща́ть [-ути́ть] (В).

fit|ful ['fitful] □ су́дорожный, поры́вистый; **~ness** [-nis] приго́дность *f*; **~ter** [-ə] меха́ник, монтёр; **~ting** [-iŋ] **1.** □ подходя́щий, го́дный; **2.** устано́вка; сбо́рка, монта́ж; приме́рка (пла́тья); **~s** *pl.* армату́ра.

five [faiv] **1.** пять; **2.** пятёрка.

fix [fiks] **1.** устана́вливать [-нови́ть]; укрепля́ть [-пи́ть]; остана́вливать [-нови́ть] (взгляд, внима́ние) (на П); *Am.* приводи́ть в поря́док; ~ o. s. устра́иваться [-ро́иться]; ~ up реша́ть [реши́ть]; организова́ть (*im*)*pf.*; ула́живать [ула́дить]; устра́ивать [-ро́ить]; *v/i.* затверде́(ва)ть; остана́вливаться [-нови́ться] (on на П); **2.** F диле́мма, затрудни́тельное положе́ние; **~ed** [fikst] (*adv.* **~edly** ['fiksidli]) неподви́жный; **~ture** ['fikstʃə] армату́ра; прибо́р, приспособле́ние; устано́вленная величина́; lighting ~ освети́тельный прибо́р.

fizzle ['fizl] [за]шипе́ть.

flabby ['flæbi] □ вя́лый; *fig.* слабохара́ктерный.

flag [flæg] **1.** флаг, зна́мя *n*; плита́; плитня́к; **2.** сигнализи́ровать фла́гом; украша́ть фла́гами; мости́ть пли́тами.

flagitious [flə'dʒiʃəs] □ престу́пный, гну́сный, позо́рный.

flagrant ['fleigrənt] □ сканда́льный; очеви́дный.

flag|staff флагшто́к; **~-stone** плита́ (для моще́ния).

flair [flεə] чутьё, нюх.

flake [fleik] **1.** слой; **~s** *pl.* хло́пья *m/pl.*; **2.** па́дать хло́пьями; расслаиваться [-ло́иться].

flame [fleim] **1.** пла́мя *n*; ого́нь *m*; *fig.* пыл, страсть *f*; **2.** пламене́ть; пыла́ть.
flank [flæŋk] **1.** бок, сторона́; склон (горы́); ⚔ фланг; **2.** быть располо́женым сбо́ку, на фла́нге (P); ~ (on) грани́чить (с T), примыка́ть (к Д).
flannel ['flænl] флане́ль *f*; **~s** [-z] *pl.* флане́левые брю́ки *f/pl.*
flap [flæp] **1.** взмах (кры́льев); хлопо́к, шлепо́к; пола́; дли́нное у́хо (соба́ки и т. п.); **2.** *v/t.* маха́ть [махну́ть] (T); взма́хивать [-хну́ть] (кры́льями); шлёпать [-пнуть], ударя́ть легко́; *v/i.* свиса́ть; развева́ться [-ве́яться].
flare [flɛə] **1.** горе́ть я́рким пла́менем; расширя́ться [-ши́риться]; ~ up вспы́хивать [-хнуть]; *fig.* разрази́ться гне́вом, вспыли́ть *pf.*; **2.** вспы́шка; сигна́льная раке́та; вспы́хивание.
flash [flæʃ] **1.** показно́й, безвку́сный; крича́щий; **2.** вспы́шка; *fig.* про́блеск; in a ~ в мгнове́ние о́ка; **3.** сверка́ть [-кну́ть]; вспы́хивать [-хнуть]; бы́стро пронести́сь; сро́чно передава́ть (по телефо́ну, телегра́фу); **~-light** *phot.* вспы́шка ма́гния; *Am.* карма́нный электри́ческий фона́рь *m*; **~y** □ показно́й, безвку́сный.
flask [flɑ:sk] фля́жка; флако́н.
flat [flæt] **1.** □ пло́ский; ро́вный; ску́чный; † вя́лый (о ры́нке); ♪ бемо́льный, мино́рный; прямо́й; ~ price станда́ртная цена́; fall ~ не име́ть успе́ха; sing ~ детони́ровать; **2.** пло́скость *f*; равни́на, низи́на; ♪ бемо́ль *m*; **~-iron** утю́г; **~ness** ['flætnis] пло́скость *f*; безвку́сица; † вя́лость *f*; **~ten** ['flætn] де́лать(ся) пло́ским, ро́вным.
flatter ['flætə] [по]льсти́ть (Д); **~er** [-rə] льстец (льсти́ца); **~y** [-ri] лесть *f*.
flavo(u)r ['fleivə] **1.** прия́тный вкус; арома́т; *fig.* при́вкус; **2.** приправля́ть [-ра́вить] (пи́щу); придава́ть за́пах, вкус (Д); **~less** [-lis] безвку́сный.
flaw [flɔ:] **1.** тре́щина, щель *f*; недоста́ток; поро́к; брак (това́ра); ⚓ шквал, поры́в ве́тра; **2.** поврежда́ть [-еди́ть]; [по]тре́скаться; **~less** ['flɔ:lis] □ безупре́чный.
flax [flæks] ⚘ лён.
flay [flei] сдира́ть ко́жу с (P).
flea [fli:] блоха́.
fled [fled] *pt.* и *p. pt.* от flee.
flee [fli:] [*irr.*] [по]бежа́ть, спаса́ться бе́гством.
fleec|e [fli:s] **1.** руно́; ове́чья шерсть *f*; **2.** [о]стри́чь (овцу́); *fig.* обдира́ть [ободра́ть]; **~y** ['fli:si] покры́тый ше́рстью.
fleer [fliə] насмеха́ться [-ея́ться] (at над T).
fleet [fli:t] **1.** □ бы́стрый; неглубо́кий; **2.** флот.
flesh [fleʃ] **1.** сыро́е мя́со; плоть *f*; мя́коть *f* (плода́); *fig.* по́хоть *f*; **2.** приуча́ть вку́сом кро́ви (соба́ку к охо́те); **~ly** ['fleʃli] пло́тский, теле́сный; **~y** [-i] мяси́стый; то́лстый.
flew [flu:] *pt.* от fly.
flexib|ility [fleksə'biliti] ги́бкость *f*; **~le** ['fleksəbl] □ ги́бкий, гну́щийся; *fig.* пода́тливый.
flicker ['flikə] **1.** мерца́ние; трепета́ние; **2.** мерца́ть; мелька́ть [-кну́ть].
flier *s.* flyer лётчик.
flight [flait] полёт, перелёт; стая (птиц); ⚔, ✈ звено́; бе́гство; ряд ступе́ней; put to ~ обраща́ть в бе́гство; **~y** ['flaiti] □ ве́треный, капри́зный.
flimsy ['flimzi] непро́чный, то́нкий.
flinch [flintʃ] уклоня́ться [-ни́ться] (from от P).
fling ['fliŋ] **1.** бросо́к, швыро́к; жизнера́достность *f*; весе́лье; have one's ~ [по]весели́ться; **2.** [*irr.*] *v/i.* кида́ться [ки́нуться], броса́ться [бро́ситься]; *v/t.* кида́ть [ки́нуть], броса́ть [бро́сить]; распространя́ть [-ни́ть] (арома́т и т. п.); ~ open распа́хивать [-хну́ть] (окно́ и т. п.).
flint [flint] креме́нь *m*.
flip [flip] **1.** щелчо́к; **2.** щёлкать [щёлкнуть].
flippan|cy ['flipənsi] легкомы́слие, ве́треность *f*; **~t** □ легкомы́сленный, ве́треный.
flirt [flə:t] **1.** коке́тка; **2.** флиртова́ть; коке́тничать; **~ation** [flə:'teiʃən] флирт.
flit [flit] порха́ть [-хну́ть]; ю́ркать [юркну́ть]; (та́йно) переезжа́ть [перее́хать].
float [flout] **1.** поплаво́к; буй; паро́м; плот; пла́вательный по́яс; ломова́я теле́га; **2.** *v/t.* затопля́ть [-пи́ть]; наводня́ть [-ни́ть]; ⚓ снима́ть с ме́ли; † пуска́ть в ход (предприя́тие); *v/i.* пла́вать, [по-] плы́ть (о предме́те); держа́ться на воде́.
flock [flɔk] **1.** пуши́нка; клочо́к; ста́до (ове́ц); стая; **2.** стека́ться [сте́чься]; держа́ться вме́сте.
flog [flɔg] [вы́]поро́ть, [вы́]сечь.
flood [flʌd] **1.** (*a.* ~-tide) прили́в, подъём воды́; наводне́ние, полово́дье, разли́в; **2.** поднима́ться [-ня́ться] (об у́ровне реки́), выступа́ть из берего́в; затопля́ть [-пи́ть]; наводня́ть [-ни́ть]; **~-gate** шлюз.
floor [flɔ:] **1.** пол; эта́ж; ⚒ гумно́; have the ~ *parl.* взять сло́во; **2.** настила́ть пол; вали́ть на́ пол; *fig.*

смущáть [смутúть]; **~ing** ['flɔ:riŋ] настúлка полóв; пол.
flop [flɔp] 1. шлёпаться [-пнуться]; плю́хать(ся) [-хнуть(ся)]; бить (кры́льями); *Am.* потерпéть фиáско; 2. шлёпанье.
florid ['flɔrid] □ цветúстый (*a. fig.*).
florin [-in] флорúн (монéта).
florist ['flɔrist] торгóвец цветáми.
floss [flɔs] шёлк-сырéц.
flounce[1] [flauns] обóрка.
flounce[2] [~] бросáться [брóситься], рéзко двúгаться.
flounder[1] *zo.* ['flaundə] кáмбала.
flounder[2] [~] барáхтаться; [за]пýтаться (в словáх).
flour ['flauə] мукá.
flourish ['flʌriʃ] 1. рóсчерк; цветúстое выражéние; ♪ туш; 2. *v/i.* пы́шно растú; процветáть, преуспевáть; *v/t.* размáхивать (Т).
flout [flaut] насмехáться (at над Т).
flow [flou] 1. течéние, потóк; струя́; прилúв; изобúлие; плáвность *f* (рéчи); 2. течь; струúться; лúться.
flower [flauə] 1. цветóк; цветéние; расцвéт; 2. цвестú; **~y** [-ri] *fig.* цветúстый (стиль).
flown [floun] *p. pt.* от fly.
flu [flu:] = influenza F грипп.
fluctuat|e ['flʌktjueit] колебáться; быть неустóйчивым; **~ion** [flʌktju'eiʃən] колебáние; неустóйчивость *f*.
flue [flu:] дымохóд; ⊕ жаровáя трубá.
fluen|cy ['flu:ənsi] *fig.* плáвность *f*, бéглость *f* (рéчи); **~t** [-t] □ плáвный, бéглый; жúдкий; текýчий.
fluff [flʌf] пух, пушóк; **~y** ['flʌfi] пушúстый.
fluid ['flu:id] 1. жúдкость *f*; 2. жúдкий; текýчий.
flung [flʌŋ] *pt.* и *p. pt.* от fling.
flunk [flʌŋk] *Am.* F провалúться на экзáмене.
flunk(e)y ['flʌŋki] ливрéйный лакéй.
flurry ['flʌri] волнéние; суматóха.
flush [flʌʃ] 1. внезáпный притóк; прилúв крóви, крáска (на лицé); прилúв (чувст); 2. пóлный (до краёв); изобúлующий; 3. *v/t.* затопля́ть [-пúть]; спускáть вóду в (П); *v/i.* течь; хлы́нуть *pf.*; [по-] краснéть.
fluster ['flʌstə] 1. суетá, волнéние; 2. [вз]волновáть(ся); возбуждáть (-ся) [-дúть(ся)].
flute [flu:t] 1. ♪ флéйта; вы́емка (на колóнне); 2. игрáть на флéйте.
flutter ['flʌtə] 1. порхáние; трéпет, волнéние; 2. *v/i.* махáть кры́льями; развевáться (по вéтру); порхáть [-хнýть].
flux [flʌks] *fig.* течéние; потóк; ⚕ патологúческое истечéние.
fly [flai] 1. мýха; 2. [*irr.*] летáть, [по]летéть; пролетáть [-етéть]; [по]спешúть; поднимáть [-ня́ть] (флаг); ✈ управля́ть (самолётом); ~ at набрáсываться [-рóситься] (с брáнью) на (В); ~ into a passion вспылúть *pf.*
flyer ['flaiə] лётчик.
fly-flap ['flaiflæp] хлопýшка.
flying ['flaiiŋ] летáтельный; лётный; летýчий; ~ squad выезднáя полицéйская комáнда.
fly|-weight наилегчáйший вéс (о боксёре); **~-wheel** маховóе колесó.
foal [foul] 1. жеребёнок; ослёнок; 2. [о]жеребúться.
foam [foum] 1. пéна; мы́ло (на лóшади); 2. [вс]пéниться; взмы́ли(ва)ться (о лóшади); **~y** ['foumi] пéнящийся; взмы́ленный.
focus ['foukəs] 1. центр; *phys.*, ⚕ фóкус; 2. помещáть, быть в фóкусе; сосредотóчи(ва)ть (*a. fig.*).
fodder ['fɔdə] фурáж, корм (скотá).
foe [fou] враг.
fog [fɔg] 1. густóй тумáн; мглa; замешáтельство; *phot.* вуаль *f*; 2. [за]тумáнить; *fig.* напускáть (в глазá) тумáну; озадáчи(ва)ть; **~gy** ['fɔgi] □ тумáнный.
foible ['fɔibl] *fig.* слáбость *f*.
foil[1] [fɔil] фóльга; фон.
foil[2] [~] 1. стáвить в тупúк; расстрáивать плáны (Р); 2. рапúра.
fold[1] [fould] 1. (*mst* sheep-~) загóн, овчáрня; *fig.* пáства; 2. загоня́ть [загнáть] (овéц).
fold[2] [~] 1. склáдка, сгиб; 2. створ (двéри); ⊕ фальц; 3. *v/t.* склáдывать [сложúть]; сгибáть [согнýть]; скрéщивать [-естúть] (рýки); **~er** ['fouldə] фальцóвщик; *Am.* брошю́ра.
folding ['fouldiŋ] складнóй; створчатый; откиднóй; **~-camera** *phot.* складнóй аппарáт; **~-chair** складнóй стул; **~-door(s** *pl.*) двустворчатая дверь *f*; **~-screen** шúрма.
foliage ['fouliidʒ] листвá.
folk [fouk] нарóд, лю́ди *m/pl.*; **~lore** ['fouklɔ:] фольклóр; **~-song** нарóдная пéсня.
follow ['fɔlou] слéдовать (за Т *or* Д); следúть за (Т); [по]гнáться за (Т); занимáться [-ня́ться] (Т); ~ suit слéдовать примéру; **~er** ['fɔlouə] послéдователь(ница *f*) *m*; *pol.* попýтчик; поклóнник; **~ing** ['fɔlouiŋ] слéдующий; попýтный.
folly ['fɔli] безрассýдство, глýпость *f*, безýмие.
foment [fou'ment] класть припáрку (Д); подстрекáть [-кнýть].
fond [fɔnd] □ нéжный, любя́щий; be ~ of любúть (В).
fond|le ['fɔndl] [при]ласкáть; **~ness** [-nis] нéжность *f*, любóвь *f*.

font [fɔnt] купе́ль *f*; исто́чник.
food [fu:d] пи́ща; **~-stuffs** *pl.* съестны́е проду́кты *m/pl.*; **~-value** пита́тельность *f*.
fool [fu:l] **1.** дура́к, глупе́ц; make a ~ of a p. одура́чи(ва)ть кого́-либо; **2.** *v/t.* обма́нывать [-ну́ть]; ~ away упуска́ть [-сти́ть]; *v/i.* [по-] дура́читься; ~ about болта́ться зря.
fool|ery ['fu:ləri] дура́чество; **~-hardy** ['fu:lhɑ:di] □ безрассу́дно хра́брый; **~ish** ['fu:liʃ] □ глу́пый; **~ishness** [-nis] глу́пость *f*; **~-proof** несло́жный, безопа́сный.
foot [fut] **1.** (*pl.* feet) нога́, ступня́; фут (ме́ра); основа́ние; on ~ пешко́м; в ходу́; **2.** *v/t.* (*mst* ~ up) подсчи́тывать [-ита́ть]; ~ the bill заплати́ть по счёту; ~ it идти́ пешко́м; **~boy** паж; **~fall** по́ступь *f*; звук шаго́в; **~-gear** F *coll.* о́бувь *f*; чулки́ *m/pl.*; **~hold** *fig.* то́чка опо́ры.
footing ['futiŋ] опо́ра; основа́ние; ито́г столбца́ цифр; lose one's ~ оступа́ться [-пи́ться].
foot|lights *pl. thea.* ра́мпа; **~man** ['futmən] ливре́йный лаке́й; **~-path** тропи́нка; тротуа́р; **~print** след; **~-sore** со стёртыми нога́ми; **~step** стопа́; след; шаг; **~stool** скаме́ечка для ног; **~wear** *part. Am.* = ~-gear.
fop [fɔp] щёголь *m*, хлыщ.
for [fɔ:; fɔ:r; fə, fo, f] *prp. mst* для (Р); ра́ди (Р); за (В); в направле́нии (Р), к (Д); из-за (Р), по причи́не (Р), всле́дствие (Р); в тече́ние (Р), в продолже́ние (Р); ~ three days в тече́ние трёх дне́й; уже́ три дня; вме́сто (Р); в обме́н на (В); **2.** *cj.* так как, потому́ что, и́бо.
forage ['fɔridʒ] **1.** фура́ж; корм; **2.** фуражи́ровать.
foray ['fɔrei] набе́г, мародёрство.
forbad(e) [fə'beid] *pt.* от forbid.
forbear[1] [fɔ:'bɛə] [*irr.*] быть терпели́вым; возде́рживаться [-жа́ться] (from от Р).
forbear[2] ['fɔ:bɛə] пре́док; предше́ственник.
forbid [fə'bid] [*irr.*] запреща́ть [-ети́ть]; **~den** [-n] *p. pt.* от forbid; **~ding** [-iŋ] □ отта́лкивающий; угрожа́ющий.
forbor|e [fɔ:'bɔ:] *pt.* от forbear[1]; **~ne** [-n] *p. pt.* от forbear[1].
force [fɔ:s] **1.** си́ла; наси́лие, принужде́ние; смысл, значе́ние; armed ~s *pl.* вооружённые си́лы *f/pl.*; come in ~ вступа́ть в си́лу; **2.** заставля́ть [-а́вить], принужда́ть [-у́дить]; брать си́лой; ~ open взла́мывать [взлома́ть]; **~d** [-t]: ~ loan принуди́тельный заём; ~ landing вы́нужденная поса́дка; ~ march форси́рованный марш (похо́д); **~ful** □ си́льный, де́йственный.
forcible ['fɔ:səbl] □ наси́льственный; убеди́тельный; эффекти́вный.
ford [fɔ:d] **1.** брод; **2.** переходи́ть [вброд.]
fore [fɔ:] **1.** *adv.* впереди́; **2.** *adj.* пере́дний; **~bode** [fɔ:'boud] предвеща́ть; предчу́вствовать; **~boding** плохо́е предзнаменова́ние; предчу́вствие; **~cast 1.** ['fɔ:kɑ:st] предсказа́ние; **2.** [fɔ:'kɑ:st] [*irr.* (cast)] предска́зывать [-каза́ть]; **~father** пре́док; **~finger** указа́тельный па́лец; **~foot** пере́дняя нога́; **~go** [fɔ:'gou] [*irr.* (go)] предше́ствовать; **~gone** [fɔ:'gɔn, *attr.* 'fɔ:gɔn]: ~ conclusion зара́нее при́нятое реше́ние; **~ground** пере́дний план; **~head** ['fɔrid] лоб.
foreign ['fɔrin] иностра́нный; the ♀ Office министе́рство иностра́нных дел (в Ло́ндоне); ~ policy вне́шняя поли́тика; **~er** [-ə] иностра́нец (-нка).
fore|leg пере́дняя нога́; **~lock** чуб, прядь воло́с на лбу; **~man** ⚖ старшина́ прися́жных; деся́тник; про́раб; **~most** пере́дний, передово́й; **~noon** у́тро; **~runner** предве́стник (-ица); **~see** [fɔ:'si:] [*irr.* (see)] предви́деть; **~sight** ['fɔ:sait] предви́дение; предусмотри́тельность *f*.
forest ['fɔrist] **1.** лес; **2.** заса́живать ле́сом.
forestall [fɔ:'stɔ:l] предупрежда́ть [-упреди́ть]; предвосхища́ть [-хи́тить].
forest|er ['fɔristə] лесни́к, лесни́чий; **~ry** [-tri] лесни́чество; лесово́дство.
fore|taste ['fɔ:teist] **1.** предвкуше́ние; **2.** предвкуша́ть [-уси́ть]; **~tell** [fɔ:'tel] [*irr.* (*tell*)] предска́зывать [-за́ть].
forfeit ['fɔ:fit] **1.** штраф; конфиска́ция; утра́та (пра́ва); фант; **2.** [по]плати́ться (Т); утра́чивать [-а́тить] (пра́во).
forgave [fə'geiv] *pt.* от forgive.
forge[1] [fɔ:dʒ] (*mst* ~ ahead) насто́йчиво продвига́ться вперёд.
forge[2] [~] **1.** ку́зница; **2.** кова́ть; подде́л(ыв)ать; **~ry** ['fɔ:dʒəri] подде́лка, подло́г.
forget [fə'get] [*irr.*] забы́(ва́)ть; **~ful** [-ful] □ забы́вчивый; **~-me-not** [-minɔt] незабу́дка.
forgiv|e [fə:giv] [*irr.*] проща́ть [прости́ть]; **~en** [fa'givn] *p. pt.* от ~e; **~eness** [-nis] проще́ние; **~ing** □ всепроща́ющий, снисходи́тельный.
forgo [fɔ:'gou] [*irr.* (go)] возде́рживаться [-жа́ться] от (Р), отка́зываться [-за́ться] от (Р).
forgot, ~ten [fə'gɔt(n)] *pt. a. p. pt.* от forget.

fork [fɔ:k] ви́лка; ви́лы *f/pl.*; ♪ камерто́н; разветвле́ние (доро́ги).
forlorn [fəˈlɔ:n] забро́шенный, несча́стный.
form [fɔ:m] 1. фо́рма; фигу́ра; бланк; *school* па́рта; класс; 2. обрazо́вывать(ся) [-ова́ть(ся)]; составля́ть [-а́вить]; ⚔ [по]стро́ить (-ся); [с]формирова́ть.
formal [ˈfɔ:məl] □ форма́льный, официа́льный; **~ity** [fɔ:ˈmæliti] форма́льность *f*.
formation [fɔ:ˈmeiʃən] образова́ние; формирова́ние; ⚔ расположе́ние, строй; систе́ма; строе́ние.
former [ˈfɔ:mə] пре́жний, бы́вший; предше́ствующий; **~ly** [-li] пре́жде.
formidable [ˈfɔ:midəbl] □ стра́шный; грома́дный; тру́днопреодоли́мый (о зада́че).
formula [ˈfɔ:mjulə] фо́рмула; ⚕ реце́пт; **~te** [-leit] формули́ровать (*im*)*pf*., *pf*. *a*. [с-].
forsake [fəˈseik] [*irr*.] оставля́ть [-а́вить], покида́ть [-и́нуть].
forswear [fɔ:ˈswɛə] [*irr*. (swear)] отрека́ться [-е́чься] от (Р); ~ o. s. наруша́ть кля́тву.
fort [fɔ:t] ⚔ форт.
forth [fɔ:θ] *adv*. вперёд, да́льше; впредь; **~coming** предстоя́щий, гряду́щий; **~with** *adv*. тотча́с, неме́дленно.
fortieth [ˈfɔ:tiiθ] сороково́й; сорокова́я часть *f*.
forti|fication [fɔ:tifiˈkeiʃən] фортифика́ция; укрепле́ние; **~fy** [ˈfɔ:tifai] ⚔ укрепля́ть [-пи́ть], сооружа́ть укрепле́ние (Р); *fig*. подкрепля́ть [-пи́ть] (фа́ктами); **~tude** [-tju:d] си́ла ду́ха.
fortnight [ˈfɔ:tnait] две неде́ли *f/pl*.
fortress [ˈfɔ:tris] кре́пость *f*.
fortuitous [fɔ:ˈtjuitəs] □ случа́йный.
fortunate [ˈfɔ:tʃnit] счастли́вый, уда́чный; **~ly** *adv*. к сча́стью.
fortune [ˈfɔ:tʃən] судьба́; бога́тство, состоя́ние; **~-teller** гада́лка.
forty [ˈfɔ:ti] со́рок.
forward [ˈfɔ:wəd] 1. *adj*. пере́дний; передово́й; развя́зный, де́рзкий; ра́нний; 2. *adv*. вперёд, да́льше; впредь; 3. *sport* напада́ющий; 4. перес(ы)ла́ть; препровожда́ть [-води́ть].
forwarding-agent экспеди́тор.
forwent [fɔ:ˈwent] *pt*. от forego.
foster [ˈfɔstə] воспи́тывать [-ита́ть]; ходи́ть за (детьми́, больны́ми); *fig*. пита́ть (чу́вство), леле́ять (мысль); поощря́ть [-ри́ть]; благоприя́тствовать (Д).
fought [fɔ:t] *pt*. и *p*. *pt*. от fight.
foul [faul] 1. □ гря́зный, отврати́тельный; бу́рный (о пого́де); гно́йный; зара́зный; бесче́стный; run ~ of ста́лкиваться [столкну́ться] с (Т); 2. *sport* игра́ про́тив пра́вил; 3. [за]па́чкать(ся); нече́стно игра́ть.
found [faund] 1. *pt*. и *p*. *pt*. от find; 2. закла́дывать [заложи́ть] (фунда́мент); осно́вывать [основа́ть]; учрежда́ть [-еди́ть]; ⊕ пла́вить; отли́(ва́)ть.
foundation [faunˈdeiʃən] фунда́мент, осно́ва.
founder [ˈfaundə] 1. основа́тель(ница *f*) *m*, учреди́тель(ница *f*) *m*; 2. *v/i*. идти́ ко дну́.
foundry [ˈfaundri] ⊕ лите́йная; литьё.
fountain [ˈfauntin] исто́чник; фонта́н; **~-pen** автору́чка, ве́чное перо́.
four [fɔ:] 1. четы́ре; 2. четвёрка; **~-square** квадра́тный; *fig*. усто́йчивый; **~teen** [ˈfɔ:ˈti:n] четы́рнадцать; **~teenth** [-θ] четы́рнадцатый; **~th** [fɔ:θ] 1. четвёртый; 2. че́тверть *f*.
fowl [faul] дома́шняя пти́ца.
fox [fɔks] 1. лиси́ца, лиса́; 2. [с]хитри́ть; обма́нывать [-ну́ть]; **~y** [ˈfɔksi] хи́трый.
fraction [ˈfrækʃən] дробь *f*; части́ца.
fracture [ˈfræktʃə] 1. тре́щина, изло́м; ⚕ перело́м; 2. [с]лома́ть (*a*. ⚕); раздробля́ть [-би́ть].
fragile [ˈfrædʒail] хру́пкий, ло́мкий.
fragment [ˈfrægmənt] обло́мок, оско́лок; отры́вок.
fragran|ce [ˈfreigrəns] арома́т; **~t** [-t] □ арома́тный.
frail [freil] □ хру́пкий; хи́лый, боле́зненный; **~ty** *fig*. хру́пкость *f*.
frame [freim] 1. сооруже́ние; сруб, скеле́т; телосложе́ние; ра́мка, ра́ма; ~ of mind настрое́ние; 2. сооружа́ть [-уди́ть]; созд(ав)а́ть; вставля́ть в ра́му; **~work** ⊕ ра́ма; сруб, о́стов; *fig*. строй, ра́мки *f/pl*.
franchise [ˈfræntʃaiz] ⚖ пра́во уча́ствовать в вы́борах; привиле́гия.
frank [ˈfræŋk] □ и́скренний, открове́нный.
frankfurter [ˈfræŋkfətə] *Am*. соси́ска.
frankness [ˈfræŋknis] открове́нность *f*.
frantic [ˈfræntik] (**~ally**) неисто́вый.
fratern|al [frəˈtə:nl] □ бра́тский; *adv*. по-бра́тски; **~ity** [-niti] бра́тство; о́бщина; *Am*. *univ*. студе́нческая организа́ция.
fraud [frɔ:d] обма́н, моше́нничество; **~ulent** [ˈfrɔ:djulənt] □ обма́нный, моше́ннический.
fray [frei] 1. дра́ка, столкнове́ние; 2. изна́шивать(ся) [износи́ть(ся)].
freak [fri:k] капри́з, причу́да; уро́дец (в приро́де).

freckle ['frekl] веснушка.

free [fri:] **1.** □ *com.* свобо́дный, во́льный; незави́симый; неза́нятый; беспла́тный; he is ~ to он во́лен (+ *inf.*); make ~ to *inf.* позволя́ть себе́; set ~ выпуска́ть на свобо́ду; **2.** освобожда́ть [-боди́ть]; **~booter** ['fri:bu:tə] пира́т; **~dom** ['fri:dəm] свобо́да; ~ of a city зва́ние почётного граждани́на; **~holder** земе́льный со́бственник; **~mason** масо́н.

freez|e [fri:z] [*irr.*] *v/i.* замерза́ть [замёрзнуть]; засты́(ва́)ть; мёрзнуть; *v/t.* замора́живать [-ро́зить]; **~er** ['fri:zə] моро́женица; **~ing 1.** □ леденя́щий; **2.** замора́живание; замерза́ние; ~ point то́чка замерза́ния.

freight [freit] **1.** фрахт, груз; сто́имость перево́зки; **2.** [по]грузи́ть; [за]фрахтова́ть; **~-car** *Am.* 🚃 това́рный ваго́н.

French [frentʃ] **1.** францу́зский; take ~ leave уйти́ не прости́вшись; **2.** францу́зский язы́к; the ~ францу́зы *pl.*; **~man** ['frentʃmən] францу́з; **~woman** ['frentʃwumən] францу́женка.

frenz|ied ['frenzid] взбешённый; **~y** [-zi] безу́мие, бе́шенство.

frequen|cy ['fri:kwənsi] частота́ (*a. phys.*); ча́стое повторе́ние; **~t 1.** [-t] □ ча́стый; **2.** [fri'kwent] посеща́ть ча́сто.

fresh [freʃ] □ све́жий; но́вый; чи́стый; *Am.* F де́рзкий; ~ water пре́сная вода́; **~en** ['freʃn] освежа́ть [-жи́ть]; [по]свеже́ть; **~et** ['freʃit] полово́дье; *fig.* пото́к; **~man** [-mən] *univ. sl.* первоку́рсник; **~ness** [-nis] све́жесть *f.*

fret [fret] **1.** волне́ние, раздраже́ние; ♪ лад (в гита́ре); **2.** [о]беспоко́ить(ся), [вз]волнова́ть(ся); подта́чивать [-точи́ть], разъеда́ть [-е́сть]; **~ted** instrument стру́нный щипко́вый инструме́нт.

fretful ['fretful] □ раздражи́тельный, капри́зный.

friar ['fraiə] мона́х.

friction ['frikʃən] тре́ние (*a. fig.*).

Friday ['fraidi] пя́тница.

friend [frend] прия́тель(ница *f*) *m*, друг, подру́га; **~ly** [-li] дру́жеский; **~ship** [-ʃip] дру́жба.

frigate ['frigit] ⚓ фрега́т.

fright [frait] испу́г; *fig.* пу́гало, страши́лище; **~en** ['fraitn] [ис-]пуга́ть; вспу́гивать [-гну́ть]; **~ed** at или of испу́ганный (Т); **~ful** [-ful] □ стра́шный, ужа́сный.

frigid ['fridʒid] □ холо́дный.

frill [fril] обо́рка.

fringe [frindʒ] **1.** бахрома́; чёлка; кайма́; **2.** отде́лывать бахромо́й; окаймля́ть [-ми́ть].

frippery ['fripəri] безделу́шки *f/pl.*; мишу́рные украше́ния *n/pl.*

frisk [frisk] **1.** прыжо́к; **2.** резви́ться; **~y** ['friski] □ ре́звый, игри́вый.

fritter ['fritə] **1.** ола́дья; **2.** ~ away растра́чивать по мелоча́м.

frivol|ity [fri'vɔliti] легкомы́слие; фриво́льность *f*; **~ous** ['frivələs] □ легкомы́сленный, пове́рхностный; пустя́чный.

frizzle ['frizl] жа́рить(ся) с шипе́нием.

fro [frou]: to and ~ взад и вперёд.

frock [frɔk] да́мское или де́тское пла́тье; ря́са; (*mst* ~-coat) сюрту́к.

frog [frɔg] лягу́шка.

frolic ['frɔlik] **1.** ша́лость *f*, весе́лье, ре́звость *f*; **2.** резви́ться, [на]прока́зничать; **~some** [səm] □ игри́вый, ре́звый.

from [frɔm, frəm] *prp.* от (Р); из (Р); с (Р); по (Д); defend ~ защища́ть от (Р).

front [frʌnt] **1.** фаса́д; пере́дняя сторона́; ⚔ фронт; in ~ of пе́ред (Т); впереди́ (Р); **2.** пере́дний; **3.** выходи́ть на (В) (об окне́) (*a.* ~ on, towards); **~al** ['frʌntl] *anat.* ло́бный; ⚠ фаса́дный; фронта́льный; **~ier** ['frʌntjə] **1.** грани́ца; **2.** пограни́чный; **~ispiece** ['frʌntispi:s] *typ.* фронтиспи́с; ⚠ фаса́д.

frost [frɔst] **1.** моро́з; **2.** побива́ть моро́зом (расте́ния); **~-bite** ⚕ отморо́женное ме́сто; **~y** ['frɔsti] □ моро́зный; *fig.* ледяно́й.

froth [frɔθ] **1.** пе́на; **2.** [вс-, за]пе́нить(ся); **~y** ['frɔθi] □ пе́нистый; *fig.* пусто́й.

frown [fraun] **1.** хму́рый взгляд; нахму́ренные бро́ви *f/pl.*; **2.** *v/i.* [на]хму́риться; [на]су́питься.

frow|zy, ~sy ['frauzi] за́тхлый, спёртый; неря́шливый.

froze [frouz] *pt.* от freeze; **~n** [-n] **1.** *p. pt.* от freeze; **2.** замёрзший; заморо́женный.

frugal ['fru:gəl] □ уме́ренный, скро́мный.

fruit [fru:t] **1.** плод, фрукт; **2.** плодоноси́ть, дава́ть плоды́; **~erer** ['fru:tərə] торго́вец фру́ктами; **~ful** ['fru:tful] □ плодови́тый, плодоро́дный; *fig.* плодотво́рный; **~less** [-lis] □ беспло́дный.

frustrat|e [frʌs'treit] расстра́ивать [-ро́ить] (пла́ны), де́лать тще́тным; **~ion** [frʌs:'treiʃən] расстро́йство (пла́нов), круше́ние (наде́жд).

fry [frai] **1.** жа́реное (ку́шанье); **2.** [из]жа́рить(ся); **~ing-pan** ['fraiiŋpæn] сковорода́.

fudge [fʌdʒ] **1.** вы́думка; пома́дка; **2.** де́лать ко́е-ка́к.

fuel ['fjuəl] **1.** то́пливо; **2.** *mot.* горю́чее.

fugitive ['fju:dʒitiv] бегле́ц; бе́женец (-нка); **2.** бе́глый; мимолётный.

fulfil(l) [ful'fil] выполня́ть [вы́-

полнить], осуществля́ть [-ви́ть]; **~ment** [-mənt] осуществле́ние, выполне́ние.
full [ful] **1.** □ *com.* по́лный; це́лый; доро́дный; of ~ age совершенноле́тний; **2.** *adv.* вполне́; как раз; о́чень; **3.** по́лность *f*; in ~ по́лностью; to the ~ в по́лной ме́ре; **~-dress** пара́дная фо́рма; **~-fledged** вполне́ опери́вшийся, ра́звитый.
ful(l)ness ['fulnis] полнота́, оби́лие.
fulminate ['fʌlmineit] сверка́ть [-кну́ть]; [за]греме́ть; ~ against [раз]громи́ть (В).
fumble ['fʌmbl] нащу́п(ыв)ать; [про]мя́млить; верте́ть в рука́х.
fume [fju:m] **1.** пар, дым; испаре́ние; **2.** оку́ривать [-ри́ть]; испаря́ться [-ри́ться].
fumigate ['fju:migeit] оку́ривать [-ри́ть].
fun [fʌn] весе́лье; заба́ва; make ~ of высме́ивать [вы́смеять] (В).
function ['fʌŋkʃən] **1.** фу́нкция, назначе́ние; **2.** функциони́ровать, де́йствовать; **~ary** [-əri] должностно́е лицо́.
fund [fʌnd] **1.** запа́с; капита́л, фонд; **~s** *pl.* госуда́рственные проце́нтные бума́ги *f/pl.*; **2.** консолиди́ровать (*im*)*pf.*; фунди́ровать (*im*)*pf.*
fundament|al [fʌndə'mentl] □ основно́й, коренно́й, суще́ственный; **~als** *pl.* осно́вы *f/pl.*
funer|al ['fju:nərəl] **1.** по́хороны *f/pl.*; **2.** похоро́нный; **~eal** [fju:'niəriəl] □ тра́урный; мра́чный.
fun-fair ['fʌnfɛə] я́рмарка.
funnel ['fʌnl] воро́нка; ⚓, 🚂 дымова́я труба́.
funny ['fʌni] □ заба́вный, смешно́й; стра́нный.
fur [fə:] **1.** мех; шку́ра; **~s** *pl.* меха́ *m/pl.*, мехо́вые това́ры *m/pl.*, пушни́на; **2.** подбива́ть ме́хом.
furbish ['fə:biʃ] [от]полирова́ть; ~ up подновля́ть [-ви́ть].
furious ['fjuəriəs] □ взбешённый.
furl [fə:l] уб(и)ра́ть (паруса́); скла́дывать [сложи́ть] (зо́нтик).
furlough ['fə:lou] **1.** о́тпуск; **2.** увольня́ть в о́тпуск (*mst* о солда́тах).
furnace ['fə:nis] горн, печь *f*; то́пка.
furnish ['fə:niʃ] снабжа́ть [снабди́ть] (with Т); доставля́ть [-а́вить]; обставля́ть [-а́вить], меблирова́ть (*im*)*pf.*
furniture ['fə:nitʃə] ме́бель *f*, обстано́вка; обору́дование.
furrier ['fʌriə] мехо́вщи́к.
furrow ['fʌrou] борозда́; колея́; жёлоб; морщи́на.
further ['fə:ðə] **1.** да́льше, да́лее; зате́м; кро́ме того́; **2.** соде́йствовать, спосо́бствовать (Д); **~ance** [-rəns] продвиже́ние (of Р), соде́йствие (of Д); **~more** [-mɔ:] *adv.* к тому́ же, кро́ме того́.
furthest ['fə:ðist] са́мый да́льний.
furtive ['fə:tiv] □ скры́тый, та́йный.
fury ['fjuəri] неи́стовство, я́рость *f*.
fuse [fju:z] **1.** пла́вка; ⚔ взрыва́тель *m*; ⚡ пла́вкий предохрани́тель *m*; **2.** сплавля́ть(ся) [-а́вить(ся)]; ⚡ [рас]пла́вить(ся); ⚔ вставля́ть взрыва́тель в (В).
fusion ['fju:ʒən] пла́вка; *fig.* слия́ние.
fuss [fʌs] F **1.** суета́; возбуждённое состоя́ние; **2.** [за]суети́ться; [вз-]волнова́ться (about из-за Р); надоеда́ть с пустяка́ми (Д).
fusty ['fʌsti] за́тхлый, спёртый; *fig.* старомо́дный, устаре́вший.
futile ['fju:tail] бесполе́зный, тще́тный; пусто́й.
future ['fju:tʃə] **1.** бу́дущий; **2.** бу́дущее, бу́дущность *f*; **~s** *pl.* † това́ры, закупа́емые заблаговре́менно.
fuzz [fʌz] **1.** пух; пуши́нка; **2.** покры́(ва́)ться пу́хом; разлета́ться [-лете́ться] (о пу́хе).

G

gab [gæb] F болтовня́; the gift of the ~ хорошо́ подве́шенный язы́к.
gabble ['gæbl] **1.** бормота́ние, бессвя́зная речь *f*; **2.** [про]бормота́ть; [за]гогота́ть.
gaberdine ['gæbədi:n] габарди́н.
gable ['geibl] ⌂ фронто́н, щипе́ц.
gad [gæd]: ~ about шля́ться, шата́ться.
gad-fly ['gædflai] *zo.* о́вод, слепе́нь *m*.
gag [gæg] **1.** заты́чка, кляп; *parl.* прекраще́ние пре́ний; *Am.* острота́; **2.** затыка́ть рот (Д); заста́вить замолча́ть; *pol.* зажи(ма́)ть (кри́тику и т. п.).
gage [geidʒ] зало́г, закла́д; вы́зов.
gaiety ['geiəti] весёлость *f*.
gaily ['geili] *adv.* от gay ве́село; я́рко.
gain [gein] **1.** при́быль *f*; вы́игрыш; за́работок; приро́ст; **2.** выи́грывать [вы́играть]; приобрета́ть [-ести́]; **~ful** ['geinful] □ дохо́дный, вы́годный.
gait [geit] похо́дка.
gaiter ['geitə] гама́ша, ге́тра, кра́га.
gale [geil] шторм, си́льный ве́тер.

gall [gɔ:l] **1.** ⚕ жёлчь *f*; жёлчность *f*; ссáдина; **2.** раздражáть [-жи́ть]; [о]беспокóить.
gallant *mst* [gəˈlænt] **1.** □ галáнтный; внимáтельный; почти́тельный; **2.** [ˈgælənt] *adj.* □ хрáбрый, дóблестный; *su.* кавалéр; **~ry** [ˈgæləntri] хрáбрость *f*; галáнтность *f*.
gallery [ˈgæləri] галерéя.
galley [ˈgæli] ⚓ галéра; **~-proof** грáнка.
gallon [ˈgælən] галлóн (мéра жи́дких и сыпу́чих тел; англ. = 4,54 л; ам. = 3,78 л).
gallop [ˈgæləp] **1.** галóп; **2.** скакáть (пускáть) галóпом.
gallows [ˈgælouz] *sg.* ви́селица.
gamble [ˈgæmbl] **1.** азáртная игрá; рискóванное предприя́тие; **2.** игрáть в азáртные и́гры; спекули́ровать (на би́рже); **~r** [-ə] картёжник, игрóк.
gambol [ˈgæmbəl] **1.** прыжóк; **2.** пры́гать, скакáть.
game [geim] **1.** игрá; пáртия (игры́); дичь *f*; **~s** *pl.* состязáния *n/pl.*; и́гры *f/pl.*; **2.** F охóтно готóвый (сдéлать чтó-либо); **3.** игрáть на дéньги; **~ster** игрóк, картёжник.
gander [ˈgændə] гусáк.
gang [gæŋ] **1.** бригáда; артéль *f*; смéна (рабóчих); шáйка, бáнда; **2.** ~ up организовáть шáйку; **~-board** ⚓ схóдни *f/pl.*
gangway [-wei] прохóд мéжду рядáми (крéсел и т. п.); ⚓ схóдни *f/pl.*
gaol [dʒeil] тюрьмá; *s.* jail.
gap [gæp] пробéл; брешь *f*, щель *f*; *fig.* расхождéние (во взгля́дах).
gape [geip] разевáть рот; [по]глазéть; зия́ть.
garb [gɑ:b] наря́д, одея́ние.
garbage [ˈgɑ:bidʒ] (ку́хонные) отбрóсы *m/pl.*; му́сор.
garden [ˈgɑ:dn] **1.** сад; огорóд; **2.** занимáться садовóдством; **~er** садóвник, садовóд; **~ing** садовóдство.
gargle [ˈgɑ:gl] **1.** полоскáть гóрло; **2.** полоскáние для гóрла.
garish [ˈgɛəriʃ] □ кричáщий (о плáтье, крáсках); я́ркий.
garland [ˈgɑ:lənd] гирля́нда, венóк.
garlic [ˈgɑ:lik] ⚘ чеснóк.
garment [ˈgɑ:mənt] предмéт одéжды; *fig.* покрóв, одея́ние.
garnish [ˈgɑ:niʃ] **1.** гарни́р; украшéние; **2.** гарни́ровать (*im*)*pf.*; украшáть [укрáсить].
garret [ˈgærit] мансáрда.
garrison [ˈgærisn] ⚔ **1.** гарнизóн; **2.** стáвить (полк и т. п.) гарнизóном.
garrulous [ˈgæruləs] □ болтли́вый.
garter [ˈgɑ:tə] подвя́зка.
gas [gæs] **1.** газ; F болтовня́; *Am.* F бензи́н, горю́чее; **2.** выпускáть гáзы; отравля́ть гáзом; F болтáть, бахвáлиться; **~eous** [ˈgeiziəs] газообрáзный.
gash [gæʃ] **1.** глубóкая рáна, разрéз; **2.** наноси́ть глубóкую рáну (Д).
gas|-lighter гáзовая зажигáлка; **~-mantle** кали́льная сéтка; **~olene, ~oline** [ˈgæsoli:n] *mot.* газоли́н; *Am.* бензи́н.
gasp [gɑ:sp] задыхáться [задохну́ться]; ловить вóздух.
gas|sed [gæst] отрáвленный гáзом; **~-stove** гáзовая плитá; **~-works** *pl.* гáзовый завóд.
gate [geit] ворóта *n/pl.*; кали́тка; **~man** 🚂 стóрож; **~way** ворóта *n/pl.*, вход; подворóтня.
gather [ˈgæðə] **1.** *v/t.* соб(и)рáть; снимáть [снять] (урожáй); [на-, со]рвáть (о цветáх); *fig.* дéлать вы́вод; ~ speed набирáть скóрость; ускоря́ть ход; *v/i.* соб(и)рáться; **2.** **~s** *pl.* сбóрки *f/pl.*; **~ing** собирáние; сбóрище, собрáние.
gaudy [ˈgɔ:di] □ я́ркий, кричáщий, безвку́сный.
gauge [geidʒ] **1.** мéра; измери́тельный прибóр; масштáб; 🚂 ширинá колеи́; ⊕ шаблóн, лекáло; **2.** измеря́ть [-éрить]; градуи́ровать (*im*)*pf.*; выверя́ть [вы́верить]; *fig.* оцéнивать [-ни́ть] (человéка).
gaunt [gɔ:nt] □ исхудáлый, измождённый; мрáчный.
ga(u)ntlet [ˈgɔ:ntlit] **1.** *hist.* лáтная рукави́ца; рукави́ца (шофёра, фехтовáльная и т. п.); **2.** run the ~ пройти́ сквозь стрóй; подвергáться рéзкой кри́тике.
gauze [gɔ:z] газ (матéрия); мáрля.
gave [geiv] *pt.* от give.
gawk [gɔ:k] F остолóп, рази́ня *m/f*; **~y** [gɔ:ˈki] неуклю́жий.
gay [gei] □ весёлый; я́ркий, пёстрый.
gaze [geiz] **1.** внимáтельный взгляд; **2.** при́стально глядéть.
gazette [gəˈzet] **1.** официáльная газéта; **2.** опубликовáть в официáльной газéте.
gear [giə] **1.** механи́зм; приспособлéния *n/pl.*; ⊕ шестерня́; зубчáтая передáча; *mot.* передáча; скóрость *f*; in ~ включённый, дéйствующий; **2.** приводи́ть в движéние; включáть [-чи́ть]; **~ing** ⊕ зубчáтая передáча; привóд.
geese [gi:s] *pl.* от goose.
gem [dʒem] драгоцéнный кáмень *m*; *fig.* сокрóвище.
gender [ˈdʒendə] *gr.* род.
general [ˈdʒenərəl] **1.** □ óбщий; обы́чный; повсемéстный; глáвный; генерáльный; ~ election всеóбщие вы́боры *m/pl.*; **2.** ⚔ генерáл; **~ity** [dʒenəˈræliti] всеóбщность *f*; примени́мость ко

всему́; большинство́; **~ize** ['dʒenərəlaiz] обобща́ть [-щи́ть]; **~ly** [-li] вообще́; обы́чно.
generat|e ['dʒenəreit] порожда́ть [-роди́ть]; производи́ть [-вести́]; **~ion**; [dʒenə'reiʃən] поколе́ние; порожде́ние.
gener|osity [dʒenə'rɔsiti] великоду́шие; ще́дрость *f*; **~ous** ['dʒenərəs] □ великоду́шный; ще́дрый.
genial ['dʒi:njəl] □ тёплый, мя́гкий (кли́мат); до́брый, серде́чный.
genius ['dʒi:njəs] ге́ний; дух; одарённость *f*, гениа́льность *f*.
genteel [dʒen'ti:l] све́тский; элега́нтный.
gentle ['dʒentl] □ зна́тный; мя́гкий; кро́ткий; ти́хий; не́жный; сми́рный (о живо́тных); лёгкий (ве́тер); **~man** ['dʒentlmən] джентельме́н; господи́н; **~manlike**, **~manly** [-li] воспи́танный; **~ness** ['dʒentlnis] мя́гкость *f*; доброта́.
gentry ['dʒentri] мелкопоме́стное дворя́нство.
genuine ['dʒenjuin] □ по́длинный; и́скренний; неподде́льный.
geography [dʒi'ɔgrəfi] геогра́фия.
geology [dʒi'ɔlədʒi] геоло́гия.
geometry [dʒi'ɔmitri] геоме́трия.
germ [dʒə:m] **1.** микро́б; заро́дыш; **2.** *fig.* зарожда́ться [-оди́ться].
German[1] ['dʒə:mən] **1.** герма́нский, неме́цкий; ~ silver ⊕ нейзи́льбер; **2.** не́мец, не́мка; неме́цкий язы́к.
german[2] [~]: brother ~ родно́й брат; **~e** [dʒə:'mein] уме́стный, подходя́щий.
germinate ['dʒə:mineit] дава́ть ростки́, прораста́ть [-расти́].
gesticulat|e [dʒes'tikjuleit] жестикули́ровать; **~ion** [-'tikju''leiʃən] жестикуля́ция.
gesture ['dʒestʃə] жест; ми́мика.
get [get] [*irr.*] **1.** *v/t.* дост(ав)а́ть; получа́ть [-чи́ть]; зараба́тывать [-бо́тать]; добы́(ва́)ть; заставля́ть [заста́вить]; I have got я име́ю; ~ one's hair cut [по]стри́чься; ~ by heart учи́ть наизу́сть; **2.** *v/i.* [с]де́латься, станови́ться [стать]; ~ ready [при]гото́виться; ~ about начина́ть ходи́ть (по́сле боле́зни); ~abroad распростроня́ться [-ни́ться] (о слу́хах); ~ ahead продвига́ться вперёд; ~ at доб(и)ра́ться до (P); ~ away уд(и)ра́ть, уходи́ть [уйти́]; отправля́ться [-а́виться]; ~ in входи́ть [войти́]; ~ on with a p. ужи́(ва́)ться с ке́м-либо; ~ out выходи́ть [вы́йти]; ~ to hear (know, learn) узн(ав)а́ть; ~ up вст(ав)а́ть; **~-up** [get'ʌp] мане́ра одева́ться; оформле́ние; *Am.* предприи́мчивость *f*.
ghastly ['gɑ:stli] ужа́сный; мёртвенно-бле́дный.
ghost [goust] при́зрак, привиде́ние; дух (*a. eccl.*); *fig.* тень *f*, лёгкий след; **~like** ['goustlaik], **~ly** [-li] похо́жий на привиде́ние, при́зрачный.
giant ['dʒaiənt] **1.** велика́н, гига́нт, исполи́н; **2.** гига́нтский, исполи́нский.
gibber ['dʒibə] говори́ть невня́тно.
gibbet ['dʒibit] **1.** ви́селица; **2.** ве́шать [пове́сить].
gibe [dʒaib] *v/t.* смея́ться над (T); *v/i.* насмеха́ться (at над T).
gidd|iness ['gidinis] ⚕ головокруже́ние; легкомы́слие; **~y** ['gidi] □ испы́тывающий головокруже́ние; легкомы́сленный.
gift [gift] дар, пода́рок; спосо́бность *f*, тала́нт (of к Д); **~ed** ['giftid] одарённый, спосо́бный, тала́нтливый.
gigantic [dʒai'gæntik] (**~ally**) гига́нтский, грома́дный.
giggle ['gigl] **1.** хихи́канье; **2.** хихи́кать [-кнуть].
gild [gild] [*irr.*] [по]золоти́ть.
gill [gil] *zo.* жа́бра.
gilt [gilt] **1.** позоло́та; **2.** позоло́ченный.
gin [dʒin] джин (напи́ток); ⊕ подъёмная лебёдка.
ginger ['dʒindʒə] **1.** имби́рь *m*; F воодушевле́ние; **2.** F подстёгивать [-стегну́ть], оживля́ть [-ви́ть]; **~-bread** имби́рный пря́ник; **~ly** [-li] осторо́жный, ро́бкий.
Gipsy ['dʒipsi] цыга́н(ка).
gird [gə:d] [*irr.*] опоя́сывать(ся) [-сать(ся)]; окружа́ть [-жи́ть].
girder ['gə:də] ⊕ ба́лка, перекла́дина, подпо́рка.
girdle ['gə:dl] **1.** по́яс, куша́к; **2.** подпоя́сывать [-сать].
girl [gə:l] де́вочка, де́вушка; **~hood** ['gə:lhud] деви́чество; **~ish** □ деви́ческий.
girt [gə:t] *pt.* и *p. pt.* от gird.
girth [gə:θ] обхва́т, разме́р; подпру́га.
gist [dʒist] суть *f*, су́щность *f*.
give [giv] [*irr.*] **1.** *v/t.* да(ва́)ть; [по]дари́ть; причиня́ть [-ни́ть]; доставля́ть [-а́вить]; ~ birth to роди́ть; ~ away отд(ав)а́ть; F вы́да(ва́)ть, пред(ав)а́ть; ~ forth изд(ав)а́ть (за́пах и т. п.); объявля́ть [-ви́ть]; ~ in под(ав)а́ть; ~ up отка́зываться [-за́ться] от (P); **2.** *v/i.* ~ (in) уступа́ть [-пи́ть]; ~ into, ~ (up)on выходи́ть на (B) (об о́кнах и т. п.); ~ out конча́ться [ко́нчиться]; обесси́леть *pf.*; [ис]по́ртиться; **~n** [givn] **1.** *p. pt.* от give; **2.** *fig.* да́нный; скло́нный (to к Д); пре́данный (to Д).
glaci|al ['gleisiəl] □ леднико́вый; ледяно́й; леденя́щий; **~er** глё́тчер, ледни́к.
glad [glæd] □ дово́льный; ра́достный, весёлый; I am ~ я ра́д(а);

~ly охо́тно, ра́достно; ~den ['glædn] [об]ра́довать.
glade [gleid] прога́лина, про́сека.
gladness ['glædnis] ра́дость *f*.
glamo|rous ['glæmərəs] обая́тельный, очарова́тельный; ~(u)r ['glæmə] 1. очарова́ние; 2. очаро́вывать [-ровать].
glance [glɑ:ns] 1. бы́стрый взгляд; 2. скользи́ть [-зну́ть] (*mst* ~ aside, off); ~ at ме́льком взгляну́ть на (В).
gland [glænd] железа́.
glare [glɛə] 1. ослепи́тельно сверка́ть; при́стально смотре́ть; 2. при́стальный и́ли свире́пый взгляд; ослепи́тельный блеск.
glass [glɑ:s] 1. стекло́; стака́н, рю́мка; зе́ркало; (a pair of) ~es *pl*. очки́ *n/pl*.; 2. *attr*. стекля́нный; ~-shade (стекля́нный) колпа́к; абажу́р; ~y ['glɑ:si] □ зерка́льный; безжи́зненный; стекля́нный.
glaz|e [gleiz] 1. глазу́рь *f*, мурава́; 2. глазирова́ть (*im*)*pf*.; застекля́ть [-ли́ть]; ~ier ['gleiziə] стеко́льщик.
gleam [gli:m] 1. о́тблеск; сла́бый свет; *fig*. про́блеск; 2. мерца́ть, сла́бо свети́ться.
glean [gli:n] *v/t*. *fig*. тща́тельно собира́ть (фа́кты, све́дения); *v/i*. подбира́ть коло́сья (по́сле жа́твы).
glee [gli:] ликова́ние; ~ club клуб для хорово́го пе́ния.
glib [glib] □ гла́дкий; бо́йкий (о ре́чи).
glid|e [glaid] 1. скользи́ть, пла́вно дви́гаться; ✈ [с]плани́ровать; 2. пла́вное движе́ние; ~er ['glaidə] ✈ планёр.
glimmer ['glimə] 1. мерца́ние, ту́склый свет; *min*. слюда́; 2. мерца́ть, ту́скло свети́ть.
glimpse [glimps] 1. мимолётный взгляд; мимолётное впечатле́ние (of от P); 2. (у)ви́деть ме́льком.
glint [glint] 1. я́ркий блеск; 2. я́рко блесте́ть; отража́ть свет.
glisten ['glisn], **glitter** ['glitə] блесте́ть, сверка́ть, сия́ть.
gloat [glout]: ~ (up)on, over пожира́ть глаза́ми (В).
globe [gloub] шар; земно́й шар; гло́бус.
gloom [glu:m], ~iness ['glu:minis] мрак; мра́чность *f*; ~y ['glu:mi] □ мра́чный; угрю́мый.
glori|fy ['glɔ:rifai] прославля́ть [-а́вить]; восхваля́ть [-ли́ть]; ~ous ['glɔ:riəs] □ великоле́пный, чуде́сный.
glory ['glɔ:ri] 1. сла́ва; 2. торжествова́ть; горди́ться (in T)
gloss [glɔs] 1. вне́шний блеск; гло́сса; 2. наводи́ть гля́нец на (В); ~ over прикра́шивать [-кра́сить].
glossary ['glɔsəri] глосса́рий, слова́рь *m* (в конце́ кни́ги).
glossy ['glɔsi] □ глянцеви́тый, лощёный.
glove [glʌv] перча́тка.
glow [glou] 1. накаля́ться до́красна; горе́ть; тлеть; сия́ть; 2. зной; нака́л; за́рево; жар; румя́нец; ~-worm светля́к, светлячо́к.
glue [glu:] 1. клей; 2. [с]кле́ить.
glut [glʌt] пресыще́ние; затова́ривание (ры́нка).
glutton ['glʌtn] обжо́ра *m/f*; ~ous [-əs] □ обжо́рливый; ~y [-i] обжо́рство.
gnash [næʃ] [за]скрежета́ть (зуба́ми).
gnat [næt] кома́р.
gnaw [nɔ:] глода́ть.
gnome [noum] гном, ка́рлик.
go [gou] 1. [*irr*.] *com*. ходи́ть, идти́ [пойти́]; проходи́ть [пройти́]; уходи́ть [уйти́]; е́здить, [по]е́хать; [с]де́латься; рабо́тать (о маши́не, се́рдце); let ~ пуска́ть [пусти́ть]; выпуска́ть из рук; ~ shares дели́ться по́ровну; ~ to (*or* and) see заходи́ть [зайти́] к [Д], навеща́ть [-ести́ть]; ~ at набра́сываться [-ро́ситься] на (В); ~ between посре́дничать ме́жду (Т); ~ by проходи́ть [пройти́]; руководи́ться (Т); ~ for идти́ [пойти́] за (Т); ~ for a walk де́лать прогу́лку; ~ in for an examination [про]экзаменова́ться; ~ on продолжа́ть [-до́лжить]; идти́ да́льше; ~ through with доводи́ть до конца́ (В); ~ without обходи́ться [обойти́сь] без (Р); 2. ходьба́, движе́ние; F мо́да; эне́ргия; on the ~ на ходу́; на нога́х; it is no ~ ничего́ не поде́лаешь; in one ~ сра́зу; have a ~ at [по]про́бовать (В).
goad [goud] 1. побужда́ть [побуди́ть]; подстрека́ть [-кну́ть]; 2. стрека́ло; *fig*. сти́мул, возбуди́тель *m*.
goal [goul] цель *f*; ме́сто назначе́ния; *sport* воро́та *n/pl*.; гол; фи́ниш; ~-keeper врата́рь *m*.
goat [gout] козёл, коза́.
gobble [gɔbl] есть жа́дно, бы́стро; ~r [-ə] обжо́ра *m/f*; индю́к.
go-between ['goubitwi:n] посре́дник.
goblin ['gɔblin] гном, домово́й.
god бог (*eccl*.: ♀ Бог); божество́; *fig*. и́дол, куми́р; ~child кре́стник (-ица); ~dess ['godis] боги́ня; ~-father крёстный оте́ц; ~head божество́; ~less [-'lis] безбо́жный; ~like богоподо́бный; ~liness [-linis] на́божность *f*; благоче́стие; ~ly [-li] благочести́вый; ~mother крёстная мать *f*.
goggle [gɔgl] 1. тара́щить глаза́; 2. (a pair of) ~s *pl*. защи́тные очки́ *n/pl*.
going ['gouiŋ] 1. иду́щий; де́йствующий; be ~ to *inf*. намерева́ться, собира́ться (+ *inf*.); 2. ходьба́; ухо́д; отъе́зд.

gold [gould] 1. зо́лото; 2. золото́й; ~**en** ['gouldən] золото́й; ~**finch** *zo.* щего́л; ~**smith** золоты́х дел ма́стер.
golf [gɔlf] 1. гольф; 2. игра́ть в гольф.
gondola ['gɔndələ] гондо́ла.
gone [gɔn] *p. pt.* от go; уше́дший, уе́хавший; F безнадёжный, поте́рянный; уме́рший, поко́йный.
good [gud] 1. *com.* хоро́ший; до́брый; го́дный, поле́зный; ✝ кредитоспосо́бный; ♀ Friday *eccl.* вели́кая страстна́я пя́тница; be ~ at быть спосо́бным к (Д); 2. добро́, бла́го; по́льза; ~s *pl.* това́р; that's no ~ э́то бесполе́зно; for ~ навсегда́; ~**by**(e) [gud'bai] 1. до свида́ния!, проща́йте!; 2. проща́ние; ~**ly** ['gudli] милови́дный, прия́тный; значи́тельный, изря́дный; ~**natured** доброду́шный; ~**ness** [-nis] доброта́; *int.* го́споди!; ~**will** доброжела́тельность *f*.
goody ['gudi] конфе́та.
goose [gu:s], *pl.* geese [gi:s] гусь *m*, гусы́ня; портно́вский утю́г.
gooseberry ['gu:zbəri] крыжо́вник (*no pl.*).
goose|**-flesh**, *Am.* ~**-pimples** *pl. fig.* гуси́ная ко́жа (от хо́лода).
gore [gɔ:] 1. запёкшаяся кровь *f*; 2. забода́ть *pf*.
gorge [gɔ:dʒ] 1. пасть *f*, гло́тка; у́зкое уще́лье; пресыще́ние; 2. [со]жра́ть; ~ o. s. нажр(и)ра́ться.
gorgeous ['gɔ:dʒəs] □ пы́шный, великоле́пный.
gory ['gɔ:ri] □ окрова́вленный; кровопроли́тный.
gospel ['gɔspəl] ева́нгелие.
gossip ['gɔsip] 1. сплéтни *f/pl.*; спле́тник (-ица); 2. [на]спле́тничать.
got [gɔt] *pt.* и *p. pt.* от get.
Gothic ['gɔθik] готи́ческий; *fig.* ва́рварский.
gouge [gaudʒ] 1. ⊕ долото́, стаме́ска; 2. выда́лбливать [вы́долбить]; *Am.* F обма́нывать [-ну́ть].
gourd [guəd] ♀ ты́ква.
gout [gaut] ⚕ пода́гра.
govern ['gʌvən] *v/t.* пра́вить, управля́ть (Т); *v/i.* госпо́дствовать; ~**ess** [-is] гуверна́нтка; ~**ment** [-mənt] прави́тельство; управле́ние; губе́рния; *attr.* прави́тельственный; ~**mental** [gʌvən'mentl] прави́тельственный; ~**or** ['gʌvənə] прави́тель *m*; коменда́нт; губерна́тор; F оте́ц.
gown [gaun] 1. (же́нское) пла́тье; ма́нтия; 2. оде́(ва́)ть.
grab [græb] F 1. схва́тывать [-ати́ть]; 2. захва́т; ⊕ автомати́ческий ковш, черпа́к.
grace [greis] 1. гра́ция, изя́щество; любе́зность *f*; ми́лость *f*, милосе́рдие; Your ♀ Ва́ша Ми́лость *f*; 2. *fig.* украша́ть [укра́сить]; удоста́ивать [-сто́ить]; ~**ful** ['greisful] □ грацио́зный, изя́щный; ~**fulness** [-nis] грацио́зность *f*, изя́щность *f*.
gracious ['greiʃəs] □ снисходи́тельный; благоскло́нный; ми́лостивый.
gradation [grə'deiʃən] града́ция, постепе́нный перехо́д.
grade [greid] 1. сте́пень *f*; гра́дус; ранг; ка́чество; *Am.* класс (шко́лы); 🚂 укло́н; 2. [рас]сортирова́ть; ⊕ нивели́ровать (*im*)*pf*.
gradua|**l** ['grædjuəl] □ постепе́нный; после́довательный; ~**te** 1. [-eit] градуи́ровать (*im*)*pf*., наноси́ть деле́ния; конча́ть университе́т; *Am.* конча́ть (любо́е) уче́бное заведе́ние; 2. [-it] *univ.* око́нчивший университе́т с учёной сте́пенью; ~**tion** [grædju'eiʃən] градуиро́вка (сосу́да); *Am.* оконча́ние уче́бного заведе́ния; *univ.* получе́ние учёной сте́пени.
graft [gra:ft] 1. ✓ черено́к; приви́вка (расте́ния); *Am.* взя́тка; по́дкуп; 2. ✓ приви́(ва́)ть (расте́ние); ⚕ переса́живать ткань; *Am.* дава́ть (брать) взя́тки.
grain [grein] зерно́; хле́бные зла́ки *m/pl.*; крупи́нка; *fig.* склонность *f*, приро́да.
gramma|**r** ['græmə] грамма́тика; ~ school сре́дняя шко́ла; *Am.* ста́ршие кла́ссы сре́дней шко́лы; ~**tical** [grə'mætikəl] □ граммати́ческий.
gram(**me**) [græm] грамм.
granary ['grænəri] жи́тница; амба́р.
grand [grænd] 1. □ вели́чественный; грандио́зный; вели́кий; 2. ♪ (*a.* ~ piano) роя́ль *m*; ~**child** внук, вну́чка; ~**eur** ['grændʒə] грандио́зность *f*; вели́чие.
grandiose ['grændious] □ грандио́зный; напы́щенный.
grandparents *pl.* де́душка и ба́бушка.
grange [greindʒ] фе́рма.
grant [gra:nt] 1. предоставля́ть [-а́вить]; допуска́ть [-сти́ть]; дарова́ть (*im*)*pf*.; 2. дар; субси́дия; да́рственный акт; take for ~ed счита́ть дока́занным.
granul|**ate** ['grænjuleit] [раз]дробить; гранули́ровать(ся) (*im*)*pf*.; ~**e** ['grænju:l] зерно́, зёрнышко.
grape [greip] виногра́д; ~**-fruit** ♀ гре́йпфрут.
graph [græf] диагра́мма, гра́фик; ~**ic**(**al** □) ['græfik, -ikəl] графи́ческий; нагля́дный; ~ arts *pl.* изобрази́тельные иску́сства *n/pl.*; ~**ite** ['græfait] графи́т.
grapple ['græpl]: ~ with боро́ться с (Т); *fig.* пыта́ться преодоле́ть (затрудне́ние).

grasp [grɑ:sp] **1.** хвата́ть [схвати́ть] (by за В); заж(им)а́ть (в руке́); хвата́ться [схвати́ться] (at за В); понима́ть [поня́ть]; **2.** спосо́бность восприя́тия; схва́тывание, кре́пкое сжа́тие; власть *f*.
grass [grɑ:s] трава́; па́стбище; send to ~ выгоня́ть на подно́жный корм; **~hopper** кузне́чик; **~-widow** F «соло́менная» вдова́; **~y** травяни́стый; травяно́й.
grate [greit] **1.** решётка; ⊕ гро́хот; **2.** [на]тере́ть (тёркой); [за]скрежета́ть (зуба́ми); ~ on *fig.* раздража́ть [-жи́ть] (В).
grateful ['greitful] □ благода́рный.
grater ['greitə] тёрка.
grati|fication [grætifi'keiʃən] вознагражде́ние; удовлетворе́ние; **~fy** ['grætifai] удовлетворя́ть [-ри́ть].
grating ['greitiŋ] **1.** □ скрипу́чий, ре́зкий; **2.** решётка.
gratitude ['grætitju:d] благода́рность *f*.
gratuit|ous [grə'tju(:)itəs] □ дарово́й, безвозме́здный; **~y** [-i] де́нежный пода́рок; чаевы́е.
grave [greiv] **1.** □ серьёзный, ве́ский; ва́жный; тяжёлый; **2.** моги́ла; **3.** [*irr.*] *fig.* запечатле́(ва́)ть; **~-digger** моги́льщик.
gravel ['grævəl] **1.** гра́вий; ⚕ мочево́й песо́к; **2.** посыпа́ть гра́вием.
graveyard кла́дбище.
gravitation [grævi'teiʃən] притяже́ние; тяготе́ние (*a. fig.*).
gravity ['græviti] серьёзность *f*, ва́жность *f*; тя́жесть *f*, опа́сность (положе́ния).
gravy ['greivi] (мясна́я) подли́вка.
gray [grei] се́рый.
graze [greiz] пасти́(сь); щипа́ть траву́; заде́(ва́)ть.
grease [gri:s] **1.** са́ло; сма́зка, сма́зочное вещество́; **2.** [gri:z] сма́з(ыв)ать.
greasy ['gri:zi] □ са́льный, жи́рный; ско́льзкий (о гря́зной доро́ге).
great [greit] □ *com.* вели́кий; большо́й; огро́мный; F восхити́тельный; великоле́пный; ~ grandchild пра́внук (-учка); **~coat** ['greit'kout] пальто́ *n indecl.*; **~ly** ['greitli] о́чень, си́льно; **~ness** [-nis] вели́чие, си́ла.
greed [gri:d] жа́дность *f*, а́лчность *f*; **~y** ['gri:di] □ жа́дный, а́лчный (of, for к Д).
Greek [gri:k] **1.** грек, греча́нка; **2.** гре́ческий.
green [gri:n] **1.** □ зелёный; незре́лый; *fig.* нео́пытный; **2.** зелёный цвет, зелёная кра́ска; мо́лодость *f*; лужа́йка; **~s** *pl.* зе́лень *f*, о́вощи *m/pl.*; **~back** *Am.* банкно́та; **~grocer** зеленщи́к; **~house** тепли́ца, оранжере́я; **~ish** ['gri:niʃ] зеленова́тый; **~sickness** бле́дная не́мочь *f*.
greet [gri:t] приве́тствовать; кла́няться [поклони́ться] (Д); **~ing** ['gri:tiŋ] приве́тствие; приве́т.
grenade [gri'neid] ⚔ грана́та.
grew [gru:] *pt.* от grow.
grey [grei] **1.** □ се́рый; седо́й; **2.** се́рый цвет, се́рая кра́ска; **3.** де́лать(ся) се́рым; **~hound** борза́я (соба́ка).
grid [grid] решётка; се́тка; **~iron** [ра́шпер.]
grief [gri:f] го́ре, печа́ль *f*; come to ~ потерпе́ть неуда́чу, попа́сть в беду́.
griev|ance ['gri:vəns] оби́да; жа́лоба; **~e** [gri:v] горева́ть; огорча́ть [-чи́ть], опеча́ли(ва)ть; **~ous** ['gri:vəs] □ го́рестный, печа́льный.
grill [gril] **1.** ра́шпер; жа́реное на ра́шпере (мя́со и т. п.); **2.** жа́рить на ра́шпере; **~-room** ко́мната рестора́на, где мя́со жа́рится при пу́блике.
grim [grim] □ жесто́кий; мра́чный, злове́щий.
grimace [gri'meis] **1.** грима́са, ужи́мка; **2.** грима́сничать.
grim|e [graim] грязь *f*, са́жа (на ко́же); **~y** ['graimi] □ запа́чканный, гря́зный.
grin [grin] **1.** усме́шка; **2.** усмеха́ться [-хну́ться].
grind [graind] [*irr.*] **1.** [с]моло́ть; разма́лывать [-моло́ть]; растира́ть [растере́ть] (в порошо́к); [на]точи́ть; *fig.* зубри́ть; **2.** разма́лывание; тяжёлая, ску́чная рабо́та; **~stone** точи́льный ка́мень *m.*; жёрнов.
grip [grip] **1.** схва́тывание, зажа́тие, пожа́тие; руко́ять *f*; *fig.* тиски́ *m/pl.*; **2.** схва́тывать [схвати́ть] (*a. fig.*); овладева́ть внима́нием (Р).
gripe [graip] зажи́м; руко́ятка; **~s** *pl.* ко́лики *f/pl.*
grisly ['grizli] ужа́сный.
gristle ['grisl] хрящ.
grit [grit] **1.** песо́к, гра́вий; F твёрдость хара́ктера, вы́держка; **~s** *pl.* овся́ная крупа́; **2.** [за]скрежета́ть (Т).
grizzly ['grizli] **1.** се́рый; с про́седью; **2.** североамерика́нский се́рый медве́дь *m*, гри́зли *m indecl.*
groan [groun] о́хать [о́хнуть]; [за-] стона́ть.
grocer ['grousə] бакале́йщик; **~ies** [-riz] *pl.* бакале́я; **~y** [-ri] бакале́йная ла́вка; торго́вля бакале́йными това́рами.
groggy ['grɔgi] нетвёрдый на нога́х; ша́ткий.
groin [grɔin] *anat.* пах.
groom [grum] **1.** грум, ко́нюх; жени́х; **2.** ходи́ть за (ло́шадью); хо́лить; well- **~ed** вы́холенный.

groove [gru:v] **1.** желобóк, паз; *fig.* рутúна, привы́чка, колея́; **2.** дéлать вы́емку на (П).
grope [group] идтú óщупью; нащу́п(ыв)ать (*a. fig.*).
gross [grous] **1.** □ большóй; ту́чный; гру́бый; ✝ валовóй, брýтто; **2.** мáсса; гросс; in the ~ óптом, гуртóм.
grotto ['grɔtou] пещéра, грот.
grouch [grautʃ] *Am.* F **1.** дурнóе настроéние; **2.** быть не в дýхе; **~y** ['grautʃi] ворчлúвый.
ground[1] [graund] *pt.* и *p. pt.* от grind; ~ glass мáтовое стеклó.
ground[2] [graund] **1.** *mst* земля́, пóчва; учáсток земли́; площáдка; основáние; дно; **~s** *pl.* сад, парк (при дóме); (кофéйная) гу́ща; on the ~(s) of на основáнии (P); stand one's ~ удержáть свои́ позúции, прояви́ть твёрдость; **2.** класть на зéмлю; обоснóвывать [-новáть]; ⚡ заземля́ть [-ли́ть]; обучáть оснóвам предмéта; **~-floor** ни́жний этáж; **~less** [-lis] □ беспричи́нный, необоснóванный; **~-staff** ✈ нелётный состáв; **~work** фундáмент, оснóва.
group [gru:p] **1.** грýппа; фрáкция; **2.** (с)группировáть(ся); классифици́ровать (*im*)*pf*.
grove [grouv] рóща, лесóк.
grovel ['grɔvl] *mst fig.* пóлзать, пресмыкáться.
grow [grou] [*irr.*] *v/i.* расти́; вырастáть [вы́расти]; [с]дéлаться, станови́ться [стáть]; *v/t.* ⚘ вырáщивать [вы́растить]; культиви́ровать (*im*)*pf.*; **~er** ['grouə] садовóд, плодовóд.
growl [graul] [за]рычáть; [за]ворчáть.
grow|n [groun] *p. pt.* от grow; **~n-up** ['groun'ʌp] взрóслый; **~th** [grouθ] рост.
grub [grʌb] **1.** личи́нка; гу́сеница; **2.** вскáпывать [вскопáть]; выкорчёвывать [вы́корчевать]; **~by** ['grʌbi] чумáзый, неря́шливый.
grudge [grʌdʒ] **1.** недовóльство; зáвисть *f*; **2.** [по]зави́довать в (П); неохóтно давáть; [по]жалéть.
gruff [grʌf] □ грýбый.
grumble ['grʌmbl] [за]ворчáть; [по]жáловаться; [за]грохотáть; **~r** [-ə] *fig.* ворчу́н(ья).
grunt [grʌnt] хрю́кать [-кнуть].
guarant|ee [gærən'ti:] **1.** поручи́тель(ница *f*) *m*; гарáнтия; поручи́тельство; **2.** гаранти́ровать (*im*)*pf.*, ручáться за (В); **~or** [gærən'tɔ] поручи́тель *m*; **~y** ['gærənti] гарáнтия.
guard [gɑ:d] **1.** стрáжа; ⚔ караýл; 🚂 кондýктор; *Am.* тюрéмщик; **~s** *pl.* гвáрдия; be off ~ быть недостáточно бди́тельным; **2.** *v/t.* охраня́ть [-ни́ть]; сторожи́ть; защищáть [защити́ть] (from от P); *v/i.* [по]берéчься, остерегáться [-рéчься] (against P); **~ian** ['gɑ:djən] храни́тель *m*; ⚖ опекýн; **~ianship** [-ʃip] охрáна; ⚖ опекýнство.
guess [ges] **1.** догáдка, предположéние; **2.** отгáдывать [-дáть], угáдывать [-дáть]; *Am.* считáть, полагáть.
guest [gest] гóсть(я *f*) *m*.
guffaw [gʌ'fɔ:] хóхот.
guidance ['gaidəns] руководство.
guide [gaid] **1.** проводни́к, гид; ⊕ передáточный рычáг; Girl ♀s *pl.* скáутки *f/pl.*; **2.** направля́ть [-рáвить]; руководи́ть (T); **~-book** путеводи́тель *m*; **~-post** указáтельный столб.
guild [gild] цех, ги́льдия; организáция.
guile [gail] хи́трость *f*, ковáрство; **~ful** ['gailful] □ ковáрный; **~less** [-lis] □ простодýшный.
guilt [gilt] винá, винóвность *f*; **~less** ['giltlis] □ невинóвный; **~y** ['gilti] □ винóвный, виновáтый.
guise [gaiz] нарýжность *f*; мáска.
guitar [gi'tɑ:] ♪ гитáра.
gulf [gʌlf] зали́в; прóпасть *f*.
gull [gʌl] **1.** чáйка; глупéц; **2.** обмáнывать [-нýть]; [о]дурáчить.
gullet ['gʌlit] пищевóд; глóтка.
gulp [gʌlp] **1.** жáдно глотáть; **2.** глотóк.
gum [gʌm] деснá; гýмми *n indecl.*; клей; **~s** *pl. Am.* галóши *f/pl.*; **2.** склéи(ва)ть; гумми́ровать (*im*)*pf*.
gun [gʌn] **1.** орýдие, пýшка; ружьё; *Am.* револьвéр; F big ~ *fig.* вáжная персóна, «ши́шка»; **2.** *Am.* охóтиться; **~boat** канонéрка; **~man** *Am.* бандит; **~ner** ⚔, ⚓ ['gʌnə] артиллери́ст, пулемётчик; **~powder** пóрох; **~smith** оружéйный мáстер.
gurgle ['gə:gl] [за]журчáть, [за]бýлькать.
gush [gʌʃ] **1.** си́льный потóк; ли́вень *m*; *fig.* излия́ние; **2.** хлы́нуть *pf.*; ли́ться потóком; *fig.* изливáть чýвства; **~er** ['gʌʃə] *fig.* человéк, изливáющий свои́ чýвства; *Am.* нефтянóй фонтáн.
gust [gʌst] поры́в (вéтра).
gut [gʌt] кишкá; **~s** *pl.* внýтренности *f/pl.*; F си́ла вóли.
gutter ['gʌtə] водостóчный жёлоб; стóчная канáва.
guy [gai] **1.** пýгало, чýчело; *Am.* F пáрень *m*, мáлый; **2.** издевáться над (T), осмéивать [-еять].
guzzle ['gʌzl] жáдно пить; есть с жáдностью.
gymnas|ium [dʒim'neizjəm] гимнасти́ческий зал; **~tics** [dzim'næstiks] *pl.* гимнáстика.
gyrate [dʒaiə'reit] вращáться по крýгу, двигаться по спирáли.
gyroplane ['dʒaiərəplein] автожи́р.

H

haberdashery ['hæbədæʃəri] галантерéя; *Am.* мужскóе бельё.
habit ['hæbit] 1. привы́чка; сложéние; свóйство; 2. одé(вá)ть; **~able** ['hæbitəbl] гóдный для жилья́; **~ation** [hæbi'teiʃən] жили́ще.
habitual [hə'bitjuəl] □ обы́чный, привы́чный.
hack [hæk] 1. тесáть; руби́ть [руб(а)нýть]; разбивáть на куски́; 2. наёмная лóшадь *f*; моты́га.
hackneyed ['hæknid] *fig.* изби́тый, банáльный.
had [hæd] *pt.* и *p. pt.* от **have**.
hag [hæg] (*mst fig.* old ~) вéдьма.
haggard ['hægəd] □ измождённый, осýнувшийся.
haggle [hægl] [с]торговáться.
hail [heil] 1. град; óклик; 2. it **~s** град идёт; *fig.* сы́паться грáдом; привéтствовать; ~ from происходи́ть из (Р); **~stone** грáдина.
hair [hɛə] вóлос; **~-breadth** минимáльное расстоя́ние; **~-cut** стри́жка; **~-do** причёска; **~dresser** парикмáхер; **~less** ['hɛəlis] лы́сый, безволóсый; **~pin** шпи́лька; **~-raising** стрáшный; **~splitting** крохобóрство; **~y** [-ri] волосáтый.
hale [heil] здорóвый, крéпкий.
half [hɑ:f] 1. полови́на; ~ a crown полкрóны; by halves кóе-кáк; go halves дели́ть попoлáм; 2. полу...; полови́нный; 3. почти́; наполови́ну; **~-back** полузащи́тник; **~-breed** мети́с; гибри́д; **~-caste** человéк смéшанной рáсы; **~-hearted** □ равнодýшный, вя́лый; **~-length** (*a.* ~ portrait) пояснóй портрéт; **~penny** ['heipni] полпéнни *n indecl.*; **~-time** *sport* тайм, полови́на игры́; **~-way** на полпути́; **~witted** слабоýмный.
halibut ['hælibət] пáлтус (ры́ба).
hall [hɔ:l] зал; холл, вестибю́ль *m*; *Am.* коридóр; *univ.* общежи́тие для студéнтов.
halloo [hə'lu:] кричáть атý; наýськ(ив)ать.
hallow ['hælou] освящáть [-яти́ть]; **~mas** [-mæs] *eccl.* день «всех святы́х».
halo ['heilou] *ast.* венéц; ореóл.
halt [hɔ:lt] 1. привáл; останóвка; 2. останáвливать(ся) [-нови́ть(ся)]; дéлать привáл; *mst fig.* колебáться; запинáться [запнýться].
halter ['hɔ:ltə] пóвод, недоýздок.
halve [hɑ:v] 1. дели́ть попoлáм; 2. **~s** [hɑ:vz] *pl.* от half.
ham [hæm] óкорок, ветчинá.
hamburger ['hæmbə:gə] *Am.* (рýбленая) котлéта.
hamlet ['hæmlit] деревýшка.
hammer ['hæmə] 1. молотóк, мóлот; ♪ молотóчек; 2. ковáть мóлотом; бить молоткóм; [по]стучáть; выкóвывать [вы́ковать].
hammock ['hæmək] гамáк, подвеснáя кóйка.
hamper ['hæmpə] 1. корзи́на с кры́шкой; 2. [вос]препя́тствовать, [по]мешáть (Д).
hand [hænd] 1. рукá; пóчерк; стрéлка (часóв); рабóчий; at ~ под рукóй; a good (poor) ~ at (не-) искýсный в (П); ~ and glove в тéсной свя́зи; lend a ~ помогáть [-мóчь]; off ~ экспрóмтом; on ~ † имéющийся в продáже, в распоряжéнии; on the one ~ с однóй стороны́; on the other ~ с другóй стороны́; **~-to-~** рукопáшный; come to ~ получáться [-чи́ться]; прибы́(вá)ть; 2. ~ down оставля́ть потóмству; ~ in вручáть [-чи́ть]; ~ over перед(ав)áть; **~-bag** дáмская сýмочка; **~bill** реклáмный листóк; **~-brake** ⊕ ручнóй тóрмоз; **~cuff** нарýчник; **~ful** ['hændful] горсть *f*; F «наказáние»; **~-glass** ручнóе зéркало.
handicap ['hændikæp] 1. помéха; *sport* гандикáп; 2. стáвить в невы́годное положéние.
handi|craft [-krɑ:ft] ручнáя рабóта, ремеслó; **~craftsman** кустáрь *m*; ремéсленник; **~work** рукодéлие; ручнáя рабóта.
handkerchief ['hæŋkətʃi(:)f] носовóй платóк; косы́нка.
handle [hændl] 1. рýчка, рукоя́тка; 2. держáть в рукáх, трóгать и́ли брать рукáми; обходи́тся [обойти́сь] с (Т).
hand|made ручнóй рабóты; **~-set** *Am.* телефóнная трýбка; **~shake** рукопожáтие; **~some** ['hænsəm] □ краси́вый; поря́дочный; **~work** ручнáя рабóта; **~writing** пóчерк; **~y** ['hændi] □ удóбный; бли́зкий.
hang [hæŋ] 1. [*irr.*] *v/t.* вéшать [повéсить]; подвéшивать [-вéсить]; (*pt.* и *p. pt.* **~ed**) вéшать [повéсить]; *v/i.* висéть; ~ about (*Am.* around) слоня́ться, околáчиваться, шля́ться; ~ on прицепля́ться -[пи́ться] к (Д); *fig.* упóрствовать; 2. смысл, сýщность *f*.
hangar ['hæŋə] ангáр.
hang-dog пристыжённый, винoвáтый (вид).
hanger ['hæŋə] вéшалка (плáтья); крючóк, крюк; **~-on** *fig.* прихлебáтель *m*.
hanging ['hæŋiŋ] вéшание; повéшение (казнь); **~s** [-s] *pl.* драпирóвки *f/pl.*
hangman ['hæŋmən] палáч.

hang-over F похмéлье.
hap|hazard ['hæp'hæzəd] 1. случáйность *f*; at ~ наудáчу; 2. случáйный; **~less** [-lis] □ злополýчный.
happen ['hæpən] случáться [-чи́ться], происходи́ть [произойти́]; окáзываться [-зáться]; he **~ed** to be at home он случáйно оказáлся дóма; ~ (up)on, *Am.* ~ in with случáйно встрéтить; **~ing** ['hæpniŋ] слýчай, собы́тие.
happi|ly ['hæpili] счастли́во; к счáстью; **~ness** [-nis] счáстье.
happy ['hæpi] □ *com.* счастли́вый; удáчный.
harangue [hə'ræŋ] 1. речь *f*; 2. произноси́ть речь.
harass ['hærəs] [вс]тревóжить; изводи́ть [-вести́].
harbo(u)r ['hɑːbə] 1. гáвань *f*, порт; 2. стать на я́корь; дать убéжище (Д); *fig.* затáивать [-и́ть]; **~age** [-ridʒ] убéжище, прию́т.
hard [hɑːd] 1. *adj. com.* твёрдый, жёсткий; крéпкий; трýдный; тяжёлый; *Am.* спиртнóй; ~ cash нали́чные *pl.* (дéньги); ~ currency устóйчивая валю́та; ~ of hearing тугóй нá ухо; 2. *adv.* твёрдо; крéпко; си́льно; упóрно; с трудóм; ~ by бли́зко, ря́дом; ~ up в затрудни́тельном финáнсовом положéнии; **~-boiled** свáренный вкрутýю; бесчýвственный, чёрствый; *Am.* хладнокрóвный; **~en** ['hɑːdn] дéлать(ся) твёрдым; [за-]твердéть; *fig.* закаля́ть(ся) [-ли́ть (-ся)]; **~-headed** практи́чный, трéзвый; **~-hearted** □ бесчýвственный; **~iness** выносливость *f*; **~ly** ['hɑːdli] с трудóм; едвá; едвá ли; **~ness** [-nis] твёрдость *f* и т. д.; **~ship** [-ʃip] лишéние, нуждá; **~ware** скобянóй товáр; **~y** ['hɑːdi] □ смéлый, отвáжный; выносливый.
hare [hɛə] зáяц; **~-brained** рассéянный.
hark [hɑːk] прислýш(ив)аться (to к Д); ~! чу!
harlot ['hɑːlət] проститýтка.
harm [hɑːm] 1. вред, зло; оби́да; 2. [по]вреди́ть (Д); **~ful** ['hɑːmful] □ врéдный, пáгубный; **~less** [-lis] □ безврéдный, безоби́дный.
harmon|ic [hɑː'mɔnik] (**~ally**, **~ious** □ [hɑː'mounjəs]) гармони́чный, стрóйный; **~ize** ['hɑːmənaiz] *v/t.* гармонизи́ровать *(im)pf.*; приводи́ть в гармóнию; *v/i.* гармони́ровать; **~y** [-ni] гармóния, созвýчие; соглáсие.
harness ['hɑːnis] 1. ýпряжь *f*, сбрýя; 2. запрягáть [запря́чь].
harp [hɑːp] 1. áрфа; 2. игрáть на áрфе; ~ (up)on завести́ волы́нку о (П).
harpoon [hɑː'puːn] гарпýн, острогá.
harrow ⚒ ['hærou] 1. боронá; 2. [вз]борони́ть; *fig.* [из]мýчить, [ис]терзáть.
harry ['hæri] разоря́ть [-ри́ть], опустошáть [-ши́ть].
harsh [hɑːʃ] □ рéзкий; жёсткий; стрóгий, сурóвый; тéрпкий.
hart [hɑːt] *zo.* олéнь *m*.
harvest ['hɑːvist] 1. жáтва, убóрка (хлéба), сбор (я́блок и т. п.); урожáй; 2. собирáть урожáй.
has [hæz] 3. *p. sg. pres.* от have.
hash [hæʃ] 1. рýбленое мя́со; *fig.* пýтаница; 2. [по]руби́ть, [по]кроши́ть (о мя́се).
hast|e [heist] поспéшность *f*, торопли́вость *f*; make ~ [по]спеши́ть; **~en** ['heisn] [по]торопи́ть(ся); **~y** ['heisti] □ поспéшный; вспы́льчивый; необдýманный.
hat [hæt] шля́па.
hatch [hætʃ] 1. вы́водок; ⚓, ✈ люк; 2. выси́живать [вы́сидеть] (цыпля́т и т. п.) (*a. fig.*); вылупля́ться из яйцá.
hatchet ['hætʃit] топóрик.
hatchway ['hætʃwei] ⚓ люк.
hat|e [heit] 1. нéнависть *f*; 2. ненави́деть; **~eful** ['heitful] □ ненави́стный; **~red** ['heitrid] нéнависть *f*.
haught|iness ['hɔːtinis] надмéнность *f*, высокомéрие; **~y** [-ti] □ надмéнный, высокомéрный.
haul [hɔːl] 1. перевóзка; тя́га; 2. [по]тянýть; таскáть, [по]тащи́ть; перевози́ть [-везти́].
haunch [hɔːntʃ] бедрó, ля́жка; зáдняя ногá.
haunt [hɔːnt] 1. появля́ться [-ви́ться] в (П) (о при́зраке); чáсто посещáть (мéсто); 2. люби́мое мéсто; притóн; **~ed** house дом с привидéнием.
have [hæv] 1. [*irr.*] *v/t.* имéть; I ~ to do я дóлжен сдéлать; ~ one's hair cut стри́чься; he will ~ it that ... он настáивает на том, чтóбы (+ *inf.*); I had better go мне бы лýчше пойти́; I had rather go я предпочёл бы пойти́; ~ about one имéть при себé; 2. *v/aux.* вспомогáтельный глагóл для образовáния перфéктной фóрмы: I ~ come я пришёл.
haven ['heivn] гáвань *f*; убéжище.
havoc ['hævək] опустошéние.
hawk [hɔːk] 1. я́стреб; 2. торговáть вразнóс.
hawthorn ['hɔːθɔːn] ♀ боя́рышник.
hay [hei] сéно; ~ fever сеннáя лихорáдка; **~cock**, **~stack** копнá сéна; **~loft** сеновáл.
hazard ['hæzəd] 1. шанс; риск; 2. рисковáть [-кнýть]; **~ous** ['hæzədəs] □ рискóванный.
haze [heiz] 1. лёгкий турмáн, ды́мка; 2. *Am.* зло подшýчивать над (Т)

hazel ['heizl] **1.** ♀ орéшник; **2.** кáрий (цвет); **~-nut** леснóй орéх.
hazy ['heizi] □ тумáнный; *fig.* смýтный.
he [hi:] **1.** *pron. pers.* он; ~ who ... тот, кто ...; **2.** ~-... пéред названием живóтного обозначáет самцá.
head [hed] **1.** *com.* головá; главá; начáльник; вождь *m*; изголóвье; лицевáя сторонá (монéты); come to a ~ назрé(вá)ть (о нарыве); *fig.* достúгнуть критúческой стáдии; get it into one's ~ that ... забрáть себé в гóлову, что ...; **2.** глáвный; **3.** *v/t.* возглавлять; ~ off отклонять [-нúть]; *v/i.* направлятъся [-áвиться]; ~ for держáть курс на (В); **~ache** ['hedeik] головнáя боль *f*; **~-dress** головнóй убóр; причёска; **~ing** [-iŋ] заголóвок; **~land** мыс; **~light** ⛭ головнóй фонáрь *m*; *mot.* фáра; **~-line** заголóвок; **~long** *adj.* опромéтчивый; *adv.* опромéтчиво; очертя гóлову; **~master** дирéктор шкóлы; **~-phone** наýшник; **~quarters** *pl.* ⚔ штаб-квартúра; **~strong** своевóльный, упрямый; **~waters** *pl.* истóки *m/pl.*; **~way**: make ~ дéлать успéхи; **~y** ['hedi] □ стремúтельный; опьяняющий.
heal [hi:l] излéчивать [-чúть], исцелять [-лúть]; (*a.* ~ up) зажи(вá)ть.
health [helθ] здорóвье; **~ful** ['helθful] □ целéбный; **~-resort** курóрт; **~y** ['helθi] □ здорóвый; полéзный.
heap [hi:p] **1.** кýча, мáсса; грýда; **2.** нагромождáть [-моздúть]; нагружáть [-узúть]; накоплять [-пúть] (*a* ~ up).
hear [hiə] [*irr.*] [у]слы́шать; [по-]слýшать; **~d** [hə:d] *pt.* и *p. pt.* от hear; **~er** ['hiərə] слýшатель(ница *f*) *m*; **~ing** [-iŋ] слух; ⚖ слýшание, разбóр дéла; **~say** ['hiəsei] слух, молвá.
hearse [hə:s] катафáлк.
heart [hɑ:t] *com.* сéрдце; мýжество; суть *f*; сердцевúна; **~s** *pl.* чéрви *f/pl.* (кáрточная масть); *fig.* сéрдце, душá; by ~ наизýсть; out of ~ в уны́нии; lay to ~ принимáть блúзко к сéрдцу; lose ~ терять мýжество; take ~ собрáться с дýхом; **~ache** ['hɑ:teik] душéвная боль *f*; **~-break** сúльная печáль *f*; **~-broken** убúтый гóрем; **~burn** изжóга; **~en** ['hɑ:tən] ободрять [-рúть]; **~felt** úскренний.
hearth [hɑ:θ] очáг (*a. fig.*).
heart|less ['hɑ:tlis] □ бессердéчный; **~rending** душераздирáющий; **~y** ['hɑ:ti] □ дрýжеский, сердéчный; здорóвый.
heat [hi:t] **1.** *com.* жарá, жар; пыл; *sport* забéг, заплы́в, заéзд; **2.** нагрé(вá)ть(ся); топúть; [раз]горячúть; **~er** ['hi:tə] ⊕ нагревáтель *m*; калорúфер, радиáтор.
heath [hi:θ] мéстность, порóсшая вéреском; ♀ вéреск.
heathen ['hi:ðən] **1.** язы́чник; **2.** язы́ческий.
heating ['hi:tiŋ] нагревáние; отоплéние; накáливание.
heave [hi:v] **1.** подъём; волнéние (мóря); **2.** [*irr.*] *v/t.* поднимáть [-нять]; [по]тянýть (якорь); *v/i.* вздымáться; напрягáться [-ячься].
heaven ['hevn] небесá *n/pl.*, нéбо; **~ly** [-li] небéсный.
heaviness ['hevinis] тяжесть *f*; инéртность *f*; депрéссия.
heavy ['hevi] □ *com.* тяжёлый; обúльный (урожáй); сúльный (вéтер и т. п.); бýрный (о мóре); мрáчный; неуклюжий; ⚡ ~ current ток высóкого напряжéния; **~-weight** *sport* тяжеловéс.
heckle ['hekl] прерывáть замечáниями (орáтора).
hectic ['hektik] ⚕ чахóточный; лихорáдочный, возбуждённый.
hedge [hedʒ] **1.** úзгородь *f*; **2.** *v/t.* огорáживать úзгородью; ограничи(ва)ть; *fig.* окружáть [-жúть] (with T); *v/i.* уклоняться от прямóго отвéта; **~hog** *zo.* ёж.
heed [hi:d] **1.** внимáние, осторóжность *f*; take no ~ of не обращáть внимáния на (В); **2.** обращáть внимáние на (В); **~less** [-lis] □ небрéжный; необдýманный.
heel [hi:l] **1.** пятка; каблýк; *Am. sl.* хам, подлéц; head over ~s, ~s over head вверх тормáшками; down at ~ *fig.* неряшливый; **2.** прибивáть каблýк к (Д); слéдовать по пятáм за (Т).
heifer ['hefə] тёлка.
height [hait] высотá; вышинá; возвы́шенность *f*; верх; **~en** ['haitn] повышáть [повы́сить]; усили(ва)ть.
heinous ['heinəs] □ отвратúтельный, ужáсный.
heir [ɛə] наслéдник; ~ apparent закóнный наслéдник; **~ess** ['ɛəris] наслéдница; **~loom** [-lu:m] наслéдство.
held [held] *pt.* и *p. pt.* от hold.
helicopter ['helikɔptə] вертолёт.
hell [hel] ад; *attr.* áдский; raise ~ скандáлить, безобрáзничать; **~ish** ['heliʃ] □ áдский.
hello ['hʌ'lou, hə'lou] аллó!
helm [helm] ⚓ руль *m*, рулевóе колесó, штурвáл; *fig.* кормúло.
helmet ['helmit] шлем.
helmsman ['helmzmən] ⚓ рулевóй; кóрмчий.
help [help] **1.** *com.* пóмощь *f*; спасéние; mother's ~ бóнна **2.** *v/t.* помогáть [помóчь] (Д); угощáть [уго-

сти́ть] (to Т); ~ o. s. не церемо́ниться, брать (за столо́м); I could not ~ laughing я не мог не смея́ться; *v/i.* помога́ть [-мо́чь]; годи́ться; **~er** ['helpə] помо́щник (-ица); **~ful** ['helpful] □ поле́зный; **~ing** ['helpiŋ] по́рция; **~less** ['helplis] □ беспо́мощный; **~lessness** [-nis] беспо́мощность *f*; **~-mate** ['helpmeit], **~meet** [-mi:t] помо́щник (-ица); това́рищ, подру́га; супру́г(а).
helve [helv] ру́чка, рукоя́ть *f*.
hem [hem] **1.** рубе́ц, кро́мка; **2.** подруба́ть [-би́ть]; ~ in окружа́ть [-жи́ть].
hemisphere ['hemisfiə] полуша́рие.
hemlock ['hemlɔk] ⚘ болиголо́в.
hemp [hemp] конопля́, пенька́.
hemstitch ['hemstitʃ] ажу́рная стро́чка.
hen [hen] ку́рица; са́мка (пти́ца).
hence [hens] отсю́да; сле́довательно; a year ~ че́рез год; **~forth** ['hens'fɔ:θ], **~forward** ['hens'fɔ:wəd] с э́того вре́мени, впредь.
henpecked находя́щийся под башмако́м у жены́.
her [hə:, hə] её; ей.
herald ['herəld] **1.** ве́стник; **2.** возвеща́ть [-вести́ть], объявля́ть [-ви́ть]; ~ in вводи́ть [ввести́].
herb [hə:b] (целе́бная) трава́; (пря́ное) расте́ние; **~ivorous** [hə:'bivərəs] травоя́дный.
herd [hə:d] **1.** ста́до, гурт; *fig.* толпа́; **2.** *v/t.* пасти́ (скот); *v/i.* (*a.* ~ together) ходи́ть ста́дом; [с]толпи́ться; **~sman** ['hə:dzmən] пасту́х.
here [hiə] здесь, тут; сюда́; вот; ~'s to you! за ва́ше здоро́вье!
here|after [hiər'ɑ:ftə] **1.** в бу́дущем; **2.** бу́дущее; **~by** э́тим, настоя́щим; при сём; таки́м о́бразом.
heredit|ary [hi'reditəri] . насле́дственный; **~y** [-ti] насле́дственность *f*.
here|in ['hiər'in] в э́том; здесь; при сём; **~of** э́того, об э́том; отсю́да, из э́того.
heresy ['herisi] е́ресь *f*.
heretic ['heritik] ерети́к (-и́чка).
here|tofore ['hiətu'fɔ:] пре́жде, до э́того; **~upon** вслед за э́тим, по́сле э́того; вследствие э́того; **~with** настоя́щим, при сём.
heritage ['heritidʒ] насле́дство; насле́дие (*mst fig.*).
hermit ['hə:mit] отше́льник, пусты́нник.
hero ['hiərou] геро́й; **~ic** [-'rouik] (**~ally**) герои́ческий, геро́йский; **~ine** ['herouin] герои́ня; **~ism** [-izm] герои́зм.
heron ['herən] *zo.* ца́пля.
herring ['heriŋ] сельдь *f*, селёдка.
hers [hə:z] *pron. poss.* её.
herself [hə:'self] сама́; себя́, -ся, -сь.
hesitat|e ['heziteit] [по]колеба́ться; запина́ться [запну́ться]; **~ion** [hezi'teiʃən] колеба́ние; запи́нка.
hew [hju:] [*irr.*] руби́ть; разруба́ть [-би́ть]; прокла́дывать [проложи́ть] (доро́гу); высека́ть [вы́сечь].
hey [hei] эй!
heyday ['heidei] *fig.* зени́т, расцве́т.
hicc|up, ['hikʌp] *a.* **~ough 1.** ико́та; **2.** ика́ть [икну́ть].
hid [hid], **hidden** ['hidn] *pt* и *p. pt.* от **hide**.
hide [haid] [*irr.*] [с]пря́тать(ся); скры́(ва́)ть(ся); **~-and-seek** игра́ в пря́тки.
hidebound ['heidbaund] *fig.* у́зкий, ограни́ченный.
hideous ['hidiəs] □ отврати́тельный, ужа́сный.
hiding-place потаённое ме́сто, убе́жище.
high [hai] **1.** *adj.* □ *com.* высо́кий; возвы́шенный; си́льный; вы́сший, верхо́вный; дорого́й (о цене́); с душко́м (мя́со); with a ~ hand своево́льно, вла́стно; ~ spirits *pl.* припо́днятое настрое́ние; ~ life вы́сшее о́бщество; ~ light основно́й моме́нт; ~ words гне́вные слова́ *n/pl.*; **2.** *adv.* высоко́; си́льно; **~-bred** поро́дистый; **~-brow** *Am. sl.* претенцио́зный интеллиге́нт; **~-class** первокла́ссный; **~-day** пра́здник; **~-grade** высокопроце́нтный; высокосо́ртный; **~-handed** своево́льный; повели́тельный; **~lands** *pl.* го́рная страна́; **~ly** ['haili] о́чень, весьма́; speak ~ of положи́тельно отзыва́ться о (П); **~-minded** возвы́шенный, благоро́дный; **~ness** ['hainis] возвы́шенность *f*; *fig.* высо́чество; **~-power**: ~ station мо́щная электроста́нция; **~-road** шоссе́ *n*, *indecl.*; гла́вная доро́га; **~-strung** о́чень чувстви́тельный; **~way** больша́я доро́га, шоссе́; *fig.* прямо́й путь *m*; **~wayman** разбо́йник.
hike [haik] F **1.** пешехо́дная экску́рсия; **2.** путеше́ствовать пешко́м; **~r** ['heikə] пешехо́дный путеше́ственник; стра́нник (-ица).
hilarious [hi'lɛəriəs] □ (шу́мно) весёлый.
hill [hil] холм, возвыше́ние; **~billy** *Am.* ['hilbili] челове́к из глухо́й стороны́; **~ock** ['hilək] хо́лмик; **~y** [-i] холми́стый.
hilt [hilt] рукоя́тка (са́бли и т. п.).
him [him] *pron. pers.* (ко́свенный паде́ж от he) его́, ему́; **~self** [him'self] сам; себя́, -ся, -сь.
hind [haind] **1.** лань *f*; **2.** ~ leg за́дняя нога́; **~er 1.** ['haində] *adj.* за́дний; **2.** ['hində] *v/t.* [по]ме-

ша́ть, препя́тствовать (Д); **~most** са́мый за́дний.
hindrance ['hindrəns] поме́ха, препя́тствие.
hinge [hindʒ] **1.** пе́тля; крюк; шарни́р; *fig.* сте́ржень *m*, суть *f*; **2.** ~ upon *fig.* зави́сеть от (Р).
hint [hint] **1.** намёк; **2.** намека́ть [-кну́ть] (at на В).
hip [hip] бедро́; ⚘ я́года шипо́вника.
hippopotamus [hipə'pɔtəməs] гиппопота́м.
hire [haiə] **1.** наём, прока́т; **2.** нанима́ть [наня́ть]; ~ out сдава́ть в наём, дава́ть напрока́т.
his [hiz] *pron. poss.* его́, свой.
hiss [his] *v/i.* [про]шипе́ть; *v/t.* осви́стывать [-ста́ть].
histor|ian [his'tɔ:riən] исто́рик; **~ic(al** □) [his'tɔrik, -rikəl] истори́ческий; **~y** ['histəri] исто́рия.
hit [hit] **1.** уда́р, толчо́к; попада́ние (в цель); *thea.*, ♪ успе́х, боеви́к; **2.** [*irr.*] ударя́ть [уда́рить]; поража́ть [порази́ть]; попада́ть [попа́сть] в (цель и т. п.); *Am.* F прибы́(ва́)ть в (В); ~ a p. a blow наноси́ть уда́р (Д); F ~ it off with [по-]ла́дить с (Т); ~ (up)on находи́ть [найти́] (В); напада́ть [напа́сть] на (В).
hitch [hitʃ] **1.** толчо́к, рыво́к; ⚓ пе́тля, у́зел; *fig.* препя́тствие; **2.** подта́лкивать [-толкну́ть]; зацепля́ть(ся) [-пи́ть(ся)], прицепля́ть (-ся) [-пи́ть(ся)]; **~-hike** *Am.* F *mot.* путеше́ствовать, по́льзуясь попу́тными автомоби́лями.
hither ['hiðə] *lit.* сюда́; **~to** [-'tu:] *lit.* до сих по́р.
hive [haiv] **1.** у́лей; рой пчёл; *fig.* людско́й мураве́йник; **2.** ~ up запаса́ть [-сти́]; жить вме́сте.
hoard [hɔ:d] **1.** запа́с, склад; **2.** накопля́ть [-пи́ть]; запаса́ть [-сти́] (В); припря́т(ыв)ать.
hoarfrost ['hɔ:'frɔst] и́ней.
hoarse [hɔ:s] □ хри́плый, охри́пший.
hoary ['hɔ:ry] седо́й; покры́тый и́неем.
hoax [houks] **1.** обма́н, мистифика́ция; **2.** подшу́чивать [-ути́ть] над (Т), мистифици́ровать (*im*)*pf.*
hobble ['hɔbl] **1.** прихра́мывающая похо́дка; **2.** *v/i.* прихра́мывать; *v/t.* [с]трено́жить (ло́шадь).
hobby ['hɔbi] *fig.* конёк, люби́мое заня́тие.
hobgoblin ['hɔbgɔblin] домово́й.
hobo ['houbou] *Am.* F бродя́га *m.*
hod [hɔd] лото́к (для подно́са кирпиче́й); коры́то (для и́звести).
hoe [hou] ⚒ **1.** моты́га; **2.** моты́жить; разрыхля́ть [-ли́ть] (моты́гой).
hog [hɔg] **1.** свинья́ (*a. fig.*); бо́ров; **2.** выгиба́ть спи́ну; ко́ротко подстрига́ть (гри́ву); **~gish** ['hɔgiʃ] □ сви́нский; обжо́рливый.
hoist [hɔist] **1.** лебёдка; лифт; **2.** поднима́ть [-ня́ть].
hold [hould] **1.** владе́ние; захва́т; власть *f*, влия́ние; ⚓ трюм; catch (*or* get, lay, take) ~ of схва́тывать [схвати́ть] (В); keep ~ of уде́рживать [-жа́ть] (В); **2.** [*irr.*] *v/t.* держа́ть; выде́рживать [вы́держать]; остана́вливать [-нови́ть]; проводи́ть [-вести́] (собра́ние и т. п.); завладе́(ва́)ть (внима́нием); занима́ть [-ня́ть]; вмеща́ть [вмести́ть]; ~ one's own отста́ивать свою́ пози́цию; ~ the line! *teleph.* не ве́шайте тру́бку; ~ over откла́дывать [отложи́ть]; ~ up подде́рживать [-жа́ть]; заде́рживать [-жа́ть]; останови́ть с це́лью грабежа́; **3.** *v/i.* остана́вливаться [-нови́ться]; держа́ться (о пого́де); ~ forth рассужда́ть; разглаго́льствовать; ~ good (*or* true) име́ть си́лу; ~ off держа́ться поо́даль; ~ on держа́ться за (В); ~ to приде́рживаться (Р); ~ up держа́ться пря́мо; **~er** ['houldə] аренда́тор; владе́лец; **~ing** [-iŋ] уча́сток земли́; владе́ние; **~-over** *Am.* пережи́ток; **~-up** *Am.* налёт, ограбле́ние.
hole [houl] дыра́, отве́рстие; я́ма; нора́; F *fig.* затрудни́тельное положе́ние; pick **~s** in находи́ть недоста́тки в (П).
holiday ['hɔlədi] пра́здник; день о́тдыха; о́тпуск; **~s** *pl.* кани́кулы *f/pl.*
hollow ['hɔlou] **1.** □ пусто́й, по́лый; впа́лый, ввали́вшийся; **2.** пустота́; дупло́; лощи́на; **3.** выда́лбливать [вы́долбить].
holly ['hɔli] ⚘ остроли́ст, па́дуб.
holster ['houlstə] кобура́.
holy ['houli] свято́й, свяще́нный; ~ water свята́я вода́; ♀ Week страстна́я неде́ля.
homage ['hɔmidʒ] почте́ние, уваже́ние; do (*or* pay, render) ~ ока́зывать почте́ние (to Д).
home [houm] **1.** дом, жили́ще; ро́дина; at ~ до́ма; **2.** *adj.* дома́шний; вну́тренний; ♀ Office, *Am.* ♀ Departement министе́рство вну́тренних дел; ♀ Secretary мини́стр вну́тренних дел; **3.** *adv.* домо́й; hit (*or* strike) ~ попа́сть в цель; **~-felt** прочу́вствованный, серде́чный; **~less** ['houmlis] бездо́мный; **~like** ую́тный; **~ly** [-li] *fig.* просто́й, обы́денный; дома́шний; некраси́вый; **~-made** дома́шнего изготовле́ния; **~sickness** тоска́ по ро́дине; **~stead** дом с уча́стком земли́; уса́дьба; **~ward(s)** [-wəd(s)] домо́й.
homicide ['hɔmisaid] уби́йство; уби́йца *m/f.*

homogeneous [hɔmo'dʒi:niəs] □ однорóдный.
hone [houn] **1.** оселóк, точи́льный кáмень *m*; **2.** [на]точи́ть.
honest ['ɔnist] □ чéстный; **~y** [-i] чéстность *f*.
honey ['hʌni] мёд; my **~**! дýшенька!; **~comb** ['hʌnikoum] сóты *m/pl.*; **~ed** ['hʌnid] медóвый; **~moon 1.** медóвый мéсяц; **2.** проводи́ть медóвый мéсяц.
honorary ['ɔnərəri] почётный.
hono(u)r ['ɔnə] **1.** честь *f*; чéстность *f*; почёт; пóчесть *f*; Your **~** вáша честь *f*; **2.** почитáть [-чти́ть]; удостáивать [-стóить]; † плати́ть в срок (по вéкселю); **~able** ['ɔnərəbl] □ почётный; благорóдный; почтéнный.
hood [hud] **1.** капюшóн; *mot.* капóт; **2.** покрывáть капюшóном.
hoodwink ['hudwiŋk] обмáнывать [пýть].
hoof [hu:f] копы́то.
hook [hu:k] **1.** крюк, крючóк; багóр; серп; by **~** or by crook прáвдами и непрáвдами, так и́ли инáче; **2.** зацепля́ть [-пи́ть]; застёгивать(ся) [-стегнýть(ся)].
hoop [hu:p] **1.** óбруч; ⊕ обóйма, бýгель *m*, кольцó; **2.** набивáть óбручи на (В); скрепля́ть óбручем.
hooping-cough коклю́ш.
hoot [hu:t] **1.** крик совы́; ги́канье; **2.** *v/i.* [за]улюлю́кать, [за]ги́кать; *mot.* [за]гудéть; *v/t.* осви́стывать [-истáть].
hop [hɔp] **1.** ⚘ хмель *m*; прыжóк; *sl.* танцевáльный вéчер; **2.** собирáть хмель; скакáть, пры́гать на однóй ногé.
hope [houp] **1.** надéжда; **2.** надéяться (for на В); **~** in полагáться [положи́ться] на (В); **~ful** ['houpful] □ подаю́щий надéжды; надéющийся; **~less** [-lis] □ безнадёжный.
horde [hɔ:d] ордá; ватáга, шáйка.
horizon [ho'raizn] горизóнт; *fig.* кругозóр.
horn [hɔ:n] рог; *mot.* гудóк; ♪ рожóк; **~** of plenty рог изоби́лия.
hornet ['hɔ:nit] *zo.* шéршень *m*.
horny ['hɔ:ni] □ мозóлистый.
horr|ible ['hɔrəbl] □ стрáшный, ужáсный, **~id** ['hɔrid] □ ужáсный; проти́вный; **~ify** ['hɔrifai] ужасáть [-снýть]; шоки́ровать; **~or** ['hɔrə] ýжас; отвращéние.
horse [hɔ:s] лóшадь *f*, конь *m*; кóзлы *f/pl.*; *sport* конь *m*; take **~** сесть на лóшадь; **~back**: on **~** верхóм; **~hair** кóнский вóлос; **~-laugh** F грýбый, грóмкий хóхот; **~man** [-mən] всáдник, верховóй; **~power** лошади́ная си́ла; **~-radish** ⚘ хрен; **~shoe** подковá.
horticulture ['hɔ:tikʌltʃə] садовóдство.
hose [houz] † *coll.* чулки́ *m/pl.* (как назвáние товáра); шланг.
hosiery ['houʒəri] † чулóчные издéлия *n/pl.*, трикотáж.
hospitable ['hɔspitəbl] □ гостеприи́мный.
hospital ['hɔspitl] больни́ца, гóспиталь *m*; **~ity** [hɔspi'tæliti] гостеприи́мство.
host [houst] хозя́ин; содержáтель гости́ницы; *fig.* мнóжество; **~s** of heaven *eccl.* áнгелы, си́лы небéсные.
hostage ['hɔstidʒ] залóжник (-ица).
hostel ['hɔstəl] общежи́тие; турбáза.
hostess ['houstis] хозя́йка (*s.* host).
hostil|e ['hɔstail] враждéбный; **~ity** [hɔs'tiliti] враждéбность *f*; враждéбный акт.
hot [hɔt] горячий; жаркий; пылкий; **~** dogs горя́чие соси́ски *f/pl.*; **~bed** парни́к; *fig.* очáг.
hotchpotch ['hɔtʃpɔtʃ] овощнóй суп; *fig.* вся́кая вся́чина.
hotel [ho(u)'tel] отéль *m*, гости́ница.
hot|headed опромéтчивый; **~-house** оранжерéя, тепли́ца; **~spur** вспы́лчивый человéк.
hound [haund] **1.** гóнчая собáка; *fig.* негодя́й, подлéц; **2.** трави́ть собáками.
hour [auə] час; врéмя; **~ly** ['auəli] [ежечáсный.]
house 1. [haus] *com.* дом; здáние; *parl.* палáта; *univ.* коллéдж; **2.** [hauz] *v/t.* поселя́ть [-ли́ть]; помещáть [-ести́ть]; приюти́ть *pf.*; *v/i.* помещáться [-ести́ться]; жить; **~breaker** взлóмщик, грома́ла *m*; **~-check** *Am.* óбыск; **~hold** домáшнее хозя́йство; домочáдцы *m/pl.*; **~holder** главá семьи́; **~keeper** экономка; **~keeping** домáшнее хозя́йство, домоводство; **~warming** новосéлье; **~wife** хозя́йка; **~wifery** ['hauswifəri] домáшнее хозя́йство; домовóдство.
housing ['hauziŋ] снабжéние жили́щем; жили́щное строи́тельство.
hove [houv] *pt.* и *p. pt.* от heave.
hovel ['hɔvəl] навéс; лачýга, хибáрка.
hover ['hɔvə] пари́ть (о пти́це); *fig.* колебáться, не решáться.
how [hau] как?, каки́м óбразом?; **~** about ...? как обстои́т дéло с (Т)?; **~ever** [hau'evə] **1.** *adv.* как бы ни; **2.** *cj.* однáко, тем не мéнее.
howl [haul] **1.** вой, завывáние; **2.** [за]вы́ть; **~er** ['haulə] *sl.* грýбая оши́бка.
hub [hʌb] ступи́ца (колесá), втýлка; *fig.* центр (внимáния).
hubbub ['hʌbʌb] шум, гам.
huckster ['hʌkstə] мелочнóй торгóвец; бары́шник.

huddle ['hʌdl] **1.** сва́ливать в ку́чу, укла́дывать кое-ка́к; сверну́ться «кала́чиком»; ~ on надева́ть на́спех; **2.** ку́ча; су́толока, сумато́ха.
hue [hju:] отте́нок; ~ and cry пого́ня с кри́ками.
huff [hʌf] **1.** раздраже́ние; **2.** *v/t.* задира́ть; запу́гивать [-га́ть]; *v/i.* оскорбля́ться [-би́ться], обижа́ться [оби́деться].
hug [hʌg] **1.** объя́тие; **2.** обнима́ть [-ня́ть]; *fig.* быть приве́рженным, скло́нным к (Д).
huge [hju:dʒ] □ огро́мный, гига́нтский; **~ness** ['hju:dʒnis] огро́мность *f.*
hulk [hʌlk] *fig.* большо́й, неуклю́жий челове́к.
hull [hʌl] **1.** ⚘ шелуха́, скорлупа́; ко́рпус (корабля́); **2.** [на]шелуши́ть, [об]лущи́ть.
hum [hʌm] [за]жужжа́ть; напева́ть; F make things ~ вноси́ть оживле́ние в рабо́ту.
human ['hju:mən] **1.** □ челове́ческий; **~ly** по-челове́чески; **2.** F челове́к; **~e** [hju:'mein] □ гума́нный, челове́чный; **~itarian** [hjumæni'tɛəriən] филантро́п; **2.** гуманита́рный; гума́нный; **~ity** [hju'mæniti] челове́чество; гума́нность *f*; **~kind** ['hju:mən'kaind] людско́й род.
humble ['hʌmbl] **1.** □ скро́мный; поко́рный, смире́нный; **2.** унижа́ть [уни́зить]; смиря́ть [-ри́ть].
humble-bee ['hʌmblbi:] шмель *m.*
humbleness [-nis] скро́мность *f*; поко́рность *f.*
humbug ['hʌmbʌg] чепуха́; хвасту́н.
humdrum ['hʌmdrʌm] бана́льный, ску́чный.
humid ['hju:mid] сыро́й, вла́жный; **~ity** [hju'miditi] сы́рость *f*, вла́га.
humiliat|e [hju'milieit] унижа́ть [уни́зить]; **~ion** [hjumili'eiʃən] униже́ние.
humility [hju'militi] смире́ние; поко́рность *f.*
humming ['hʌmiŋ] F мо́щный; **~bird** *zo.* коли́бри *m/f indecl.*
humorous ['hju:mərəs] □ юмористи́ческий; коми́ческий.
humo(u)r ['hju:mə] **1.** ю́мор; шутли́вость *f*; настрое́ние; out of ~ не в ду́хе; **2.** потака́ть (Д); ублажа́ть [-жи́ть].
hump [hʌmp] **1.** горб; **2.** [с]го́рбить(ся).
hunch [hʌntʃ] **1.** горб; *Am.* подозре́ние; ломо́ть *m*; **2.** [с]го́рбить(-ся) (*a.* ~ out, up); **~back** горбу́н(ья).
hundred ['hʌndrəd] **1.** сто; **2.** со́тня; **~th** [-θ] со́тый; со́тая часть *f*; **~weight** це́нтнер.
hung [hʌŋ] *pt.* и *p.pt.* от hang.
Hungarian [hʌŋ'gɛəriən] **1.** венге́рец (-рка); **2.** венге́рский.
hunger ['hʌŋgə] **1.** го́лод; *fig.* жа́жда; **2.** *v/i.* голода́ть; быть голо́дным; *fig.* жа́ждать (for P).
hungry ['hʌŋgri] □ голо́дный.
hunk [hʌŋk] то́лстый кусо́к.
hunt [hʌnt] **1.** охо́та; по́иски *m/pl.* (for P); **2.** охо́титься на (В) *or* за (Т); трави́ть; ~ out *or* up оты́скивать [-ка́ть]; ~ for *fig.* охо́титься за (Т), иска́ть (P *or* B); **~er** ['hʌntə] охо́тник; охо́тничья ло́шадь *f*; **~ing-ground** райо́н охо́ты.
hurdle ['hə:dl] препя́тствие, барье́р; **~-race** ска́чки с препя́тствиями; барье́рный бег.
hurl [hə:l] **1.** си́льный бросо́к; **2.** швыря́ть [-рну́ть], мета́ть [метну́ть].
hurricane ['hʌrikən] урага́н.
hurried ['hʌrid] □ торопли́вый.
hurry ['hʌri] **1.** торопли́вость *f*, поспе́шность *f*; **2.** *v/t.* [по]торопи́ть; поспе́шно посыла́ть; *v/i.* [по]спеши́ть (*a.* ~ up).
hurt [hə:t] **1.** поврежде́ние; **2.** [*irr.*] (*a. fig.*) причиня́ть боль; поврежда́ть [-еди́ть]; боле́ть (о ча́сти те́ла).
husband ['hʌzbənd] **1.** муж, супру́г; **2.** [с]эконо́мить, эконо́мно расхо́довать.
hush [hʌʃ] **1.** тишина́, молча́ние; **2.** ти́ше!; **3.** водворя́ть тишину́; ~ up зама́лчивать [замолча́ть]; *v/i.* успока́иваться [-ко́иться]; утиха́ть [ути́хнуть].
husk [hʌsk] **1.** ⚘ шелуха́; **2.** очища́ть от шелухи́, [на]шелуши́ть; **~y** ['hʌski] □ си́плый, охри́пший (го́лос); *Am.* ро́слый.
hustle ['hʌsl] **1.** *v/t.* толка́ть [-кну́ть]; [по]торопи́ть; понужда́ть [-ну́дить]; *v/i.* толка́ться [-кну́ться]; [по]торопи́ться; *part. Am.* бы́стро де́йствовать; **2.** толкотня́; *Am.* F энерги́чная де́ятельность *f*; ~ and bustle толкотня́ и шум.
hut [hʌt] хи́жина, хиба́рка; бара́к.
hutch [hʌtʃ] кле́тка (для кро́ликов и т. п.).
hybrid ['haibrid] 🕮 гибри́д, по́месь *f*; **~ize** ['haibridaiz] скре́щивать [-ести́ть] (расте́ния, живо́тных).
hydro... ['haidro...] 🕮 водо...; **~chloric** [-'klɔrik]: ~ acid соля́ная кислота́; **~gen** ['haidridʒən] ⚗ водоро́д; **~pathy** [hai'drɔpəθi] водолече́ние; **~phobia** ['haidrə'foubiə] водобоя́знь *f*; **~plane** ['haidroplein] гидропла́н.
hygiene ['haidʒi:n] гигие́на.
hymn [him] **1.** церко́вный гимн; **2.** петь ги́мны.
hyphen ['haifən] **1.** дефи́с, соеди-

ни́тельная чёрточка; 2. писа́ть че́рез чёрточку.
hypnotize ['hipnətaiz] [за]гипнотизи́ровать.
hypo|chondriac [haipo'kɔndriæk] ипохо́ндрик; **~crisy** [hi'pɔkrəsi] лицеме́рие; **~crite** ['hipokrit] лицеме́р; **~critical** [hipo'kritikəl] □ лицеме́рный; **~thesis** [hai'pɔθisis] гипо́теза, предположе́ние.
hyster|ical [his'terikəl] □ истери́чный; **~ics** [his'teriks] *pl.* исте́рика.

I

I [ai] *pers. pron.* я.
ice [ais] 1. лёд; моро́женое; 2. замора́живать [-ро́зить]; покрыва́ть льдом; глазирова́ть (*im*)*pf*.; **~-age** ледниковый пери́од; **~-bound** затёртый льда́ми; **~-box**, **~-chest** холоди́льник, ле́дник; **~-cream** моро́женое.
icicle ['aissikl] (ледяна́я) сосу́лька.
icing ['aisiŋ] са́харная глазу́рь *f*; ✈ обледене́ние.
icy ['aisi] □ ледяно́й.
idea [ai'diə] иде́я; поня́тие, представле́ние; мысль *f*; **~l** [-l] 1. □ идеа́льный; вообража́емый; 2. идеа́л.
identi|cal [ai'dentikəl] □ тожде́ственный; одина́ковый; **~fication** [ai'dentifi'keiʃən] отождествле́ние; установле́ние ли́чности; **~fy** [-fai] отождествля́ть [-ви́ть]; устана́вливать ли́чность (то́ждество) (Р); **~ty** [-ti] тожде́ственность *f*; ~ card удостовере́ние ли́чности.
idiom ['idiəm] идио́ма; го́вор.
idiot ['idiət] идио́т(ка); **~ic** [idi'ɔtik] (-ally) идио́тский.
idle ['aidl] 1. □ неза́нятый; безрабо́тный; лени́вый; пра́здный; тще́тный; ⊕ безде́йствующий, холосто́й; ~ hours *pl.* часы́ досу́га; 2. *v/t.* проводи́ть (вре́мя) без де́ла (*mst* ~ away); *v/i.* лени́ться, безде́льничать; **~ness** [-nis] пра́здность *f*, безде́лье; **~r** [-ə] безде́льник (-ица), лентя́й(ка).
idol ['aidl] и́дол; *fig.* куми́р; **~atry** [ai'dɔlətri] идолопокло́нство; обожа́ние; **~ize** ['aidəlaiz] боготвори́ть.
idyl(l) ['aidil] иди́ллия.
if [if] *cj.* е́сли; е́сли бы; (= whether) ли: ~ he knows зна́ет ли он.
ignit|e [ig'nait] зажига́ть [-же́чь]; загора́ться [-ре́ться], воспламеня́ться [-ни́ться]; **~ion** [ig'niʃən] *mot.* зажига́ние; запа́л; *attr.* запа́льный.
ignoble [ig'noubl] □ ни́зкий, позо́рный.
ignor|ance ['ignərəns] неве́жество; неве́дение; **~ant** [-rənt] неве́жественный; несве́дущий; **~e** [ig'nɔ:] игнори́ровать (*im*)*pf*.; ⚖ отверга́ть [-е́ргнуть].
ill [il] 1. *adj.* больно́й, нездоро́вый; дурно́й; 2. *adv.* едва́ ли; пло́хо, ду́рно; 3. зло, вред.
ill|-advised неблагоразу́мный; **~-bred** невоспи́танный.
illegal [i'li:gəl] □ незако́нный.
illegible [i'ledʒəbl] □ неразбо́рчивый.
illegitimate [ili'dʒitimit] □ незако́нный; незаконнорождённый.
ill|-favo(u)red некраси́вый; неприя́тный; **~-humo(u)red** в дурно́м настрое́нии, не в ду́хе.
illiberal [i'libərəl] □ ограни́ченный (о взгля́дах); скупо́й.
illicit [i'lisit] □ запрещённый (зако́ном).
illiterate [i'litərit] □ 1. негра́мотный; 2. необразо́ванный челове́к; не́уч.
ill|-mannered невоспи́танный, гру́бый; **~-natured** □ дурно́го нра́ва, зло́бный.
illness ['ilnis] боле́знь *f*.
ill|-timed несвоевре́менный, неподходя́щий; **~-treat** пло́хо обраща́ться с (Т).
illumin|ate [i'lju:mineit] освеща́ть [-ети́ть], озаря́ть [-ри́ть]; просвеща́ть [-ети́ть]; пролива́ть свет на (В); **~ating** [-neitiŋ] освеща́ющий, освети́тельный; **~ation** [ilju:mi'neiʃən] освеще́ние; иллюмина́ция.
illus|ion [i'lu:ʒən] иллю́зия, обма́н чувств; **~ive** [-siv], □ **~ory** □ обма́нчивый, иллюзо́рный.
illustrat|e ['iləstreit] иллюстри́ровать (*im*)*pf*.; поясня́ть [-ни́ть]; **~ion** [iləs'treiʃən] иллюстра́ция; **~ive** ['iləstreitiv] □ иллюстрати́вный.
illustrious [i'lʌstriəs] □ знамени́тый.
ill-will недоброжела́тельность *f*.
image ['imidʒ] о́браз; изображе́ние; отраже́ние; подо́бие.
imagin|able [i'mædʒinəbl] □ вообрази́мый; **~ary** [-nəri] вообража́емый; мни́мый; **~ation** [imædʒi'neiʃən] воображе́ние, фанта́зия; **~ative** [i'mæddʒinətiv] □ одарённый воображе́нием; **~e** [i'mædʒin] вообража́ть [-рази́ть]; представля́ть [-а́вить] себе́.
imbecile ['imbisail] 1. □ слабоу́мный; 2. глупе́ц.
imbibe [im'baib] впи́тывать [впита́ть], вдыха́ть [вдохну́ть]; *fig.* усва́ивать [усво́ить] (иде́и).

imbue [im'bju:] насыщáть [-ы́тить]; окрáшивать [окрáсить]; *fig.* наполня́ть [-óлнить].

imita|te ['imiteit] подражáть (Д); передрáзнивать [-ни́ть]; поддé-л(ыв)ать; **~tion** [imi'teiʃən] подражáние; поддéлка, суррогáт; *attr.* поддéльный, искýсственный.

immaculate [i'mækjulit] □ безукори́зненный; незапя́тнанный (*a. fig.*).

immaterial [imə'tiəriəl] □ несущéственный, невáжный; невещéственный.

immature [imə'tjuə] незрéлый; недорáзвитый.

immediate [i'mi:djət] □ непосрéдственный; ближáйший; безотлагáтельный; **~ly** [-li] *adv.* непосрéдственно; немéдленно.

immense [i'mens] □ огрóмный.

immerse [i'mə:s] погружáть [-узи́ть], окунáть [-нýть]; *fig.* ~ o. s. in погружáться [-узи́ться] в (В).

immigra|nt ['imigrənt] иммигрáнт(ка); **~te** [greit] иммигри́ровать (*im*)*pf.*; **~tion** [imi'greiʃən] иммигрáция.

imminent ['iminənt] □ грозя́щий, нави́сший.

immobile [i'moubail] неподви́жный.

immoderate [i'mɔdərit] неумéренный, чрезмéрный.

immodest [i'mɔdist] □ нескрóмный.

immoral [i'mɔrəl] □ безнрáвственный.

immortal [i'mɔ:tl] □ бессмéртный.

immovable [i'mu:vəbl] □ недви́жимый, неподви́жный; непоколеби́мый.

immun|e [i'mju:n] невосприи́мчивый (from к Д); иммýнный; **~ity** [-iti] освобождéние (от платежá); ⚕ иммунитéт, невосприи́мчивость *f* (from к Д); *pol.* иммунитéт.

imp [imp] бесёнок; шалуни́шка *m/f.*

impair [im'pɛə] ослабля́ть [-áбить]; [ис]пóртить; повреждáть [-еди́ть].

impart [im'pɑ:t] прид(ав)áть; перед(ав)áть (нóвости т. п.).

impartial [im'pɑ:ʃəl] □ беспристрáстный, непредвзя́тый; **~ity** ['impɑ:ʃi'æliti] беспристрáстность *f.*

impassable [im'pɑ:səbl] □ непроходи́мый, непроéзжий.

impassioned [im'pæʃənd] стрáстный, пы́лкий.

impassive [im'pæsiv] □ спокóйный, безмятéжный.

impatien|ce [im'peiʃəns] нетерпéние; **~t** [-t] □ нетерпели́вый.

impeach [im'pi:tʃ] порицáть; набрáсывать тень на (В).

impeccable [im'pekəbl] □ безупрéчный; непогреши́мый.

impede [im'pi:d] [вос]препя́тствовать (Д); [по]мешáть (Д).

impediment [im'pedimənt] помéха; задéржка.

impel [im'pel] принуждáть [-ýдить].

impend [im'pend] нависáть [-и́снуть]; надвигáться [-и́нуться].

impenetrable [im'penitrəbl] □ непроходи́мый; непроницáемый; *fig.* непостижи́мый.

imperative [im'perətiv] □ повели́тельный, влáстный; крáйне необходи́мый.

imperceptible [impə'septəbl] □ незамéтный.

imperfect [im'pə:fikt] □ непóлный; несовершéнный, дефéктный.

imperial [im'piəriəl] □ импéрский; императóрский; государственный.

imperil [im'peril] подвергáть опáсности.

imperious [im'piəriəs] □ влáстный; настоя́тельный; высокомéрный.

impermeable [im'pə:miəbl] непроницáемый.

impersonal [im'pə:snl] □ безли́чный.

impersonate [im'pə:səneit] олицетворя́ть [-ри́ть]; исполня́ть роль (Р).

impertinen|ce [im'pə:tinəns] дéрзость *f*; **~t** [-nənt] □ дéрзкий.

impervious [im'pə:viəs] □ непроницáемый, непроходи́мый; глухóй (to к Д).

impetu|ous [im'petjuəs] □ стреми́тельный; **~s** ['impitəs] дви́жущая си́ла.

impiety [im'paiəti] невéрие; неуважéние.

impinge [im'pindʒ] *v/i.* ударя́ться [удáриться] (on о В); покушáться [-уси́ться] (on на В).

impious ['impiəs] □ нечести́вый.

implacable [im'pleikəbl] □ неумоли́мый; непримири́мый.

implant [im'plɑ:nt] насаждáть [насади́ть]; внушáть [-ши́ть].

implement ['implimənt] 1. инструмéнт; орýдие; принадлéжность *f*; 2. выполня́ть [вы́полнить].

implicat|e ['implikeit] вовлекáть [-éчь], впýт(ыв)ать; заключáть в себé; **~ion** [impli'keiʃən] вовлечéние; вы́вод.

implicit [im'plisit] □ безоговóрочный; подразумевáемый.

implore [im'plɔ:] умоля́ть [-ли́ть].

imply [im'plai] подразумевáть; намекáть [-кнýть] на (В); значи́ть.

impolite [impo'lait] □ невéжливый, неучти́вый.

impolitic [im'pɔlitik] □ нецелесообрáзный.

import 1. ['impɔ:t] ввоз, и́мпорт; **~s** *pl.* ввози́мые това́ры *m/pl.*; **2.** [im'pɔ:t] ввози́ть [ввезти́], импорти́ровать (*im*)*pf.*; име́ть значе́ние; **~ance** [im'pɔ:təns] значи́тельность *f*, ва́жность *f*; **~ant** [-tənt] □ ва́жный, значи́тельный; **~ation** [impɔ:'teiʃən] ввоз, и́мпорт.
importun|ate [im'pɔ:tjunit] □ назо́йливый; **~e** [im'pɔ:tju:n] докуча́ть (Д), надоеда́ть [-е́сть] (Д).
impos|e [im'pouz] *v/t.* навя́зывать [-за́ть]; облага́ть [обложи́ть]; *v/i.* ~ upon производи́ть впечатле́ние на (В), импони́ровать (Д); **~ition** [impə'ziʃən] наложе́ние; обложе́ние.
impossib|ility [im'pɔsə'biliti] невозмо́жность *f*; невероя́тность *f*; **~le** [im'pɔsəbl] □ невозмо́жный; невероя́тный.
impost|or [im'pɔstə] обма́нщик; самозва́нец; **~ure** [im'pɔstʃə] обма́н, плутовство́.
impoten|ce ['impotəns] басси́лие, сла́бость *f*; **~t** [-tənt] бесси́льный, сла́бый.
impoverish [im'pɔvəriʃ] доводи́ть до бе́дности; обедня́ть [-ни́ть].
impracticable [im'præktikəbl] □ неисполни́мый, неосуществи́мый.
impregnate ['impregneit] оплодотворя́ть [-ри́ть]; ⚗ насыща́ть [-ы́тить], пропи́тывать [-пита́ть].
impress 1. ['impres] отпеча́ток (*a. fig.*); *typ.* о́ттиск; **2.** [im'pres] отпеча́т(ыв)ать; запечатле́(ва́)ть; внуша́ть [-ши́ть] (on Д); производи́ть впечатле́ние на (В); **~ion** [im'preʃən] впечатле́ние; *typ.* о́ттиск; печа́тание; I am under the ~ that у меня́ впечатле́ние, что ...; **~ive** [im'presive] □ внуши́тельный, производя́щий впечатле́ние.
imprint 1. [im'print] запечатле́(ва́)ть; отпеча́т(ыв)ать; **2.** ['imprint] отпеча́ток; *typ.* выходны́е све́дения *n/pl.*
imprison [im'prizn] заключа́ть в тюрьму́, заточа́ть [-чи́ть]; **~ment** [-mənt] заточе́ние, заключе́ние (в тюрьму́).
improbable [im'prɔbəbl] □ невероя́тный, неправдоподо́бный.
improper [im'prɔpə] □ неуме́стный; непристо́йный; непра́вильный.
improve [im'pru:v] *v/t.* улучша́ть [улу́чшить]; [у]соверше́нствовать; повыша́ть це́нность (Р); *v/i.* улучша́ться [улу́чшиться]; [у]соверше́нствоваться; ~ upon улучша́ть [улу́чшить] (В); **~ment** [-mənt] усоверше́нствование; улучше́ние.
improvise ['improvaiz] импровизи́ровать (*im*)*pf.*
imprudent [im'pru:dənt] □ неблагоразу́мный; неосторо́жный.
impuden|ce ['impjudəns] бессты́дство; де́рзость *f*; **~t** [-dənt] □ наха́льный; бессты́дный.
impuls|e ['impʌls], **~ion** [im'pʌlʃən] толчо́к; поры́в; ⚡ возбужде́ние.
impunity [im'pju:niti] безнака́занность *f*; with ~ безнака́занно.
impure [im'pjuə] □ нечи́стый; с при́месью.
imput|ation [impju'teiʃən] обвине́ние; **~e** [im'pju:t] вменя́ть [-ни́ть] (в вину́); припи́сывать [-са́ть] (Д/В).
in [in] **1.** *prp. com.* в, во (П or В); ~ number в коли́честве (Р), число́м в (В); ~ itself само́ по себе́; ~ 1949 в 1949-ом (в ты́сяча девятьсо́т со́рок девя́том) году́; cry out ~ alarm закрича́ть в испу́ге (*or* от стра́ха); ~ the street на у́лице; ~ my opinion по моему́ мне́нию, по-мо́ему; ~ English по-англи́йски; a novel ~ English рома́н на англи́йском языке́; ~ tens по десяти́; ~ the circumstances при да́нных усло́виях; a coat ~ velvet ба́рхатное пальто́ (*or* из ба́рхата); ~ this manner таки́м о́бразом; ~ a word одни́м сло́вом; ~ crossing the road переходя́ че́рез у́лицу; be ~ power быть у вла́сти; be engaged ~ reading занима́ться чте́нием; **2.** *adv.* внутри́; внутрь; be ~ for: a) быть обречённым на (что́-либо неприя́тное); b) I am ~ for an examination мне предстои́т экза́мен; F be ~ with быть в хоро́ших отноше́ниях с (Т).
inability [inə'biliti] неспосо́бность [*f.*]
inaccessible [inæk'sesəbl] □ недосту́пный; недосяга́емый.
inaccurate [in'ækjurit] □ нето́чный; неаккура́тный.
inactiv|e [in'æktiv] □ безде́ятельный; неде́йствующий; **~ity** [inæk'tiviti] безде́ятельность *f*; ине́ртность *f*.
inadequate [in'ædikwit] □ несоразме́рный; недоста́точный.
inadmissible [inəd'misəbl] недопусти́мый, неприе́млемый.
inadvertent [inəd'və:tənt] □ невнима́тельный; ненаме́ренный.
inalienable [in'eiliənəbl] □ неотъе́млемый.
inane [i'nein] □ бессмы́сленный; пусто́й.
inanimate [in'ænimit] □ неодушевлённый; безжи́зненный.
inapproachable [inə'proutʃəbl] недосту́пный, непристу́пный.
inappropriate [-priit] □ неуме́стный, несоотве́тствующий.
inapt [in'æpt] □ неспосо́бный; неподходя́щий.
inarticulate [inɑ:'tikjulit] □ нечленоразде́льный, невня́тный.
inasmuch [inəz'mʌtʃ]: ~ as *adv.* так как; ввиду́ того́, что.

inattentive [inə'tentiv] □ невнимательный.
inaugura|te [i'nɔ:gjureit] откры́(ва́)ть (вы́ставку и т. п.); вводи́ть в до́лжность; **~tion** [inɔgju'reiʃən] вступле́ние в до́лжность; (торже́ственное) откры́тие.
inborn ['in'bɔ:n] врождённый; приро́дный.
incalculable [in'kælkjuləbl] □ неисчисли́мый, несчётный; ненадёжный (о челове́ке).
incandescent [inkæn'desnt] раскалённый; кали́льный.
incapa|ble [in'keipəbl] □ неспосо́бный (of к Д *or* на В); **~citate** [inkə'pæsiteit] де́лать неспосо́бным, неприго́дным.
incarnate [in'ka:nit] воплощённый; олицетворённый.
incautious [in'kɔ:ʃəs] □ неосторо́жный, опроме́тчивый.
incendiary [in'sendjəri] **1.** поджига́тель *m*; *fig.* подстрека́тель *m*; **2.** зажига́тельный (*a.* ⚔); *fig.* подстрека́ющий.
incense[1] ['insens] ла́дан, фимиа́м.
incense[2] [in'sens] [рас]серди́ть, приводи́ть в я́рость.
incentive [in'sentiv] побуди́тельный моти́в, побужде́ние.
incessant [in'sesnt] □ непреры́вный.
incest ['insest] кровосмеше́ние.
inch [intʃ] дюйм (= 2,54 см); *fig.* пядь *f*; by ~es ма́ло-пома́лу.
inciden|ce ['insidəns] сфе́ра де́йствия; **~t** [-t] **1.** слу́чай, случа́йность *f*; происше́ствие; **2.** случа́йный; прису́щий (to Д); **~tal** [insi'dentl] □ случа́йный; побо́чный; прису́щий (Д); **~ly** случа́йно; ме́жду про́чим.
incinerate [in'sinəreit] сжига́ть [сжечь]; испепеля́ть [-ли́ть].
incis|e [in'saiz] надре́з(ыв)ать; де́лать надре́з на (П); **~ion** [in'siʒən] разре́з, надре́з; насе́чка; **~ive** [in'saisiv] □ ре́жущий; о́стрый.
incite [in'sait] подстрека́ть [-кну́ть]; побужда́ть [-уди́ть]; **~ment** [-mənt] подстрека́тельство; побужде́ние, сти́мул.
inclement [in'klemənt] суро́вый, холо́дный.
inclin|ation [inkli'neiʃən] накло́н, отко́с; отклоне́ние; накло́нность *f*, скло́нность *f*; **~e** [in'klain] **1.** *v/i.* склоня́ться [-ни́ться]; ~ to *fig.* быть скло́нным к (Д); *v/t.* склоня́ть [-ни́ть] (*a fig.*); располага́ть [-ложи́ть]; **2.** накло́н; скло́нность *f*.
inclose [in'klouz] *s.* enclose.
inclu|de [in'klu:d] заключа́ть [-чи́ть], содержа́ть (в себе́); включа́ть [-чи́ть]; **~sive** [-siv] □ включа́ющий в себя́, содержа́щий.
incoheren|ce [inko'hiərəns] несвя́зность *f*, непосле́довательность *f*; **~t** [-t] □ несвя́зный, непосле́довательный.
income ['inkəm] дохо́д.
incommode [inkə'moud] [по]беспоко́ить.
incomparable [in'kɔmpərəbl] □ несравни́мый; несравне́нный.
incompatible [inkəm'pætəbl] □ несовмести́мый.
incompetent [in'kɔmpitənt] □ несве́дущий, неуме́лый; ⚖ неправоспосо́бный.
incomplete [inkəm'pli:t] □ непо́лный; незако́нченный.
incomprehensible [in'kɔmpri''hensəbl] □ непоня́тный, непостижи́мый.
inconceivable [inkən'si:vəbl] □ невообрази́мый.
incongruous [in'kɔŋgruəs] □ неуме́стный, неле́пый; несовмести́мый.
inconsequent(ial) [in'kɔnsikwənt, -'kwenʃəl] □ непосле́довательный.
inconsidera|ble [inkən'sidərəbl] □ незначи́тельный, нева́жный; **~te** [-rit] □ неосмотри́тельный; необду́манный; невнима́тельный (к други́м).
inconsisten|cy [inkən'sistənsi] несовмести́мость *f*; **~t** [-tənt] □ несовмести́мый.
inconstant [in'kɔnstənt] □ непостоя́нный, неусто́йчивый.
incontinent [in'kɔntinənt] □ несде́ржанный; невозде́ржанный.
inconvenien|ce [inkən'vi:njəns] **1.** неудо́бство; беспоко́йство; **2.** [по-] беспоко́ить; **~t** [-njənt] □ неудо́бный, затрудни́тельный.
incorporat|e **1.** [in'kɔ:pəreit] объединя́ть(ся) [-ни́ть(ся)]; включа́ть [-чи́ть] (into в В); **2.** [-rit] соединённый, объединённый; **~ed** [-reitid] зарегистри́рованный (об о́бществе; **~ion** [in'kɔ:pə''reiʃən] объедине́ние; регистра́ция.
incorrect [inkə'rekt] □ непра́вильный; неспра́вный.
incorrigible [in'kɔridʒəbl] □ неисправи́мый.
increase **1.** [in'kri:s] увели́чи(ва)ть(ся); уси́ли(ва)ть(ся); **2.** ['inkri:s] рост; увеличе́ние; приро́ст.
incredible [in'kredəbl] □ невероя́тный.
incredul|ity [inkri'dju:liti] недове́рчивость *f*; **~ous** [in'kredjuləs] □ недове́рчивый, скепти́ческий.
incriminate [in'krimineit] ⚖ инкримини́ровать (*im*)*pf*., обвиня́ть в преступле́нии.
incrustation [inkrʌs'teiʃən] кора́, ко́рка; ⊕ на́кипь *f*.
incub|ate ['inkjubeit] выводи́ть [вы́вести] (цыпля́т); **~ator** [-beitə] инкуба́тор.
inculcate ['inkʌlkeit] внедря́ть [-ри́ть], вселя́ть [-ли́ть] (upon Д).

incumbent [in'kʌmbənt] возло́женный, (воз)лежа́щий.
incur [in'kə:] подверга́ться [-е́ргнуться] (Д); наде́лать *pf.* (долго́в).
incurable [in'kjuərəbl] **1.** неизлечи́мый; **2.** страда́ющий неизлечи́мой боле́знью.
incurious [in'kjuəriəs] □ нелюбопы́тный; невнима́тельный.
incursion [in'kə:ʃən] вторже́ние.
indebted [in'detid] в долгу́; *fig.* обя́занный.
indecen|cy [in'di:snsi] непристо́йность *f*, неприли́чие; **~t** [-snt] □ неприли́чный.
indecisi|on [indi'siʒən] нереши́тельность *f*; колеба́ние; **~ve** [-saisiv] □ нереши́тельный; не реша́ющий.
indecorous [in'dekərəs] □ некорре́ктный; неприли́чный.
indeed [in'di:d] в са́мом де́ле, действи́тельно; неуже́ли!
indefensible [indi'fensəbl] □ неприго́дный для оборо́ны; *fig.* несостоя́тельный.
indefinite [in'definit] □ неопределённый; неограни́ченный.
indelible [in'delibl] □ неизглади́мый; несмыва́емый.
indelicate [in'delikit] □ неделика́тный, нескро́мный.
indemni|fy [in'demnifai] возмеща́ть убы́тки (Р); обезопа́сить *pf.*; компенси́ровать *(im)pf.*; **~ty** [-ti] гара́нтия от убы́тков; возмеще́ние, компенса́ция.
indent [in'dent] **1.** зазу́бривать [-ри́ть]; выреза́ть [вы́резать]; предъявля́ть тре́бование; ✝ зака́зывать това́ры; **2.** тре́бование; ✝ зака́з на това́ры; о́рдер; **~ation** [inden'teiʃən] зубе́ц; вы́резка; **~ure** [in'dentʃə] **1.** докуме́нт, контра́кт, догово́р; **2.** обя́зывать догово́ром.
independen|ce [indi'pendəns] незави́симость *f*, самостоя́тельность *f*; **~t** [-t] □ незави́симый, самостоя́тельный.
indescribable [indis'kraibəbl] □ неопису́емый.
indestructible [-'strʌktəbl] □ неразруши́мый.
indeterminate [indi'tə:minit] □ неопределённый; нея́сный.
index ['indeks] **1.** и́ндекс, указа́тель *m*; показа́тель *m*; указа́тельный па́лец; **2.** заноси́ть в и́ндекс.
India ['indjə] 'Индия; **~** rubber каучу́к; рези́на; **~n** [-n] **1.** инди́йский; инде́йский; **~** corn маи́с, кукуру́за; **2.** инди́ец, индиа́нка; (Red **~**) инде́ец, индиа́нка.
indicat|e ['indikeit] ука́зывать [-за́ть]; предпи́сывать [-са́ть]; **~ion** [indi'keiʃən] указа́ние.
indict [in'dait] предъявля́ть обвине́ние (for в П); **~ment** [-mənt] обвини́тельный акт.
indifferen|ce [in'difrəns] равноду́шие, безразли́чие; **~t** [-t] □ равноду́шный, беспристра́стный; незначи́тельный.
indigenous [in'didʒinəs] ме́стный, тузе́мный.
indigent ['indidʒənt] □ нужда́ющийся.
indigest|ible [indi'dʒestəbl] □ неудобовари́мый; **~ion** [-tʃən] расстро́йство желу́дка.
indign|ant [in'dignənt] □ негоду́ющий; **~ation** [indig'neiʃən] негодова́ние; **~ity** [in'digniti] пренебреже́ние, оскорбле́ние.
indirect [indi'rekt] □ непрямо́й; око́льный; укло́нчивый.
indiscre|et [indis'kri:t] □ нескро́мный; неблагоразу́мный; болтли́вый; **~tion** [-'kreʃən] нескро́мность *f*; неосмотри́тельность *f*; болтли́вость *f*.
indiscriminate [indis'kriminit] □ неразбо́рчивый.
indispensable [indis'pensəbl] □ необходи́мый, обяза́тельный.
indispos|ed [indis'pouzd] нездоро́вый; **~ition** ['indispə''ziʃən] недомога́ние, нездоро́вье; нерасположе́ние (to к Д).
indistinct [indis'tiŋkt] □ нея́сный, неотчётливый; невня́тный.
indite [in'dait] выража́ть в слова́х; сочиня́ть [-ни́ть].
individual [indi'vidjuəl] **1.** □ ли́чный, индивидуа́льный; характе́рный; отде́льный; **2.** индиви́дуум; ли́чность *f*; **~ity** [-vidju'æliti] индивидуа́льность *f*.
indivisible [indi'vizəbl] недели́мый.
indolen|ce ['indoləns] пра́здность *f*; вя́лость *f*; **~t** [-t] □ пра́здный; вя́лый.
indomitable [in'dɔmitəbl] □ упо́рный; неукроти́мый.
indoor ['indɔ:] вну́тренний; ко́мнатный; **~s** ['in'dɔ:z] в до́ме, внутри́ до́ма.
indorse *s.* endorse.
induce [in'dju:s] побужда́ть [-уди́ть]; вызыва́ть [вы́звать]; **~ment** [-mənt] побужде́ние.
induct [in'dʌkt] водворя́ть [-ри́ть]; вводи́ть в до́лжность; **~ion** [in'dʌkʃən] вступле́ние, введе́ние.
indulge [in'dʌldʒ] *v/t.* доставля́ть удово́льствие (Д with Т); балова́ть; потво́рствовать (Д); *v/i.* **~** in a th. увлека́ться [-е́чься] (Т); пред(ав)а́ться (Д); **~nce** [-əns] снисхожде́ние; потво́рство; **~nt** [-ənt] □ снисходи́тельный; потво́рствующий.
industri|al [in'dʌstriəl] □ промы́шленный; производи́тельный; **~alist** [-ist] промы́шленник; **~ous**

[in'dʌstriəs] □ трудолюби́вый, приле́жный.
industry ['indəstri] промы́шленность *f*, инду́стрия; прилежа́ние.
inebriate 1. [in'i:briit] пья́ный; опьяне́вший; **2.** [-ieeit] опьяня́ть [-ни́ть].
ineffable [in'efəbl] □ невырази́мый.
ineffect|ive [ini'fektiv], **~ual** [-tjuəl] □ безрезульта́тный; недействи́тельный.
inefficient [ini'fiʃənt] □ неспосо́бный, неуме́лый; непроизводи́тельный.
inelegant [in'eligənt] □ грубова́тый, безвку́сный.
inept [i'nept] □ неуме́стный, неподходя́щий; глу́пый.
inequality [ini'kwɔliti] нера́венство; неодина́ковость *f*.
inequitable [in'ekwitəbl] пристра́стный.
inert [i'nə:t] □ ине́ртный; вя́лый; ко́сный; **~ia** [i'nə:ʃiə], **~ness** [i'nə:tnis] ине́рция; вя́лость *f*.
inestimable [in'estiməbl] □ неоцени́мый.
inevitable [in'evitəbl] □ неизбе́жный, немину́емый.
inexact [inig'zækt] □ нето́чный.
inexhaustible [inig'zɔ:stəbl] □ неистощи́мый, неисчерпа́емый.
inexorable [in'eksərəbl] □ неумоли́мый, непрекло́нный.
inexpedient [iniks'pi:diənt] □ нецелесообра́зный.
inexpensive [iniks'pensiv] □ недорого́й, дешёвый.
inexperience [iniks'piəriəns] нео́пытность *f*; **~d** [-t] нео́пытный.
inexpert [ineks'pə:t] □ нео́пытный; неиску́сный, неуме́лый.
inexplicable [in'eksplikəbl] □ необъясни́мый, непоня́тный.
inexpressi|ble [iniks'presəbl] □ невырази́мый, неопису́емый; **~ve** [-siv] □ невырази́тельный.
inextinguishable [iniks'tiŋgwiʃəbl] □ неугаси́мый.
inextricable [in'ekstrikəbl] □ запу́танный; безвы́ходный.
infallible [in'fæləbl] □ безоши́бочный, непогреши́мый.
infam|ous ['infəməs] □ посты́дный, позо́рный, бесче́стный; **~y** [-mi] бесче́стье, позо́р; ни́зость *f*, по́длость *f*.
infan|cy ['infənsi] младе́нчество; **~t** [-t] младе́нец.
infanti|le ['infəntail], **~ne** [-tain] младе́нческий; инфанти́льный.
infantry ['infəntri] ⚔ пехо́та, инфанте́рия.
infatuate [in'fætjueit] вскружи́ть го́лову (Д); увлека́ть [-е́чь].
infect [in'fekt] заража́ть [-рази́ть]; **~ion** [in'fekʃən] инфе́кция, зара́за; зарази́тельность *f*; **~ious** [-ʃəs] □, **~ive** [-tiv] инфекцио́нный, зара́зный; зарази́тельный.
infer [in'fə:] де́лать вы́вод; подразумева́ть; **~ence** ['infərəns] вы́вод, заключе́ние; подразумева́емое.
inferior [in'fiəriə] **1.** ни́зший (по чи́ну); ху́дший, неполноце́нный; **2.** подчинённый; **~ity** [in'fiəri'ɔriti] бо́лее ни́зкое ка́чество (положе́ние, досто́инство); неполноценность *f*.
infernal [in'fə:nl] □ а́дский.
infertile [in'fə:tail] беспло́дный, неплодоро́дный.
infest [in'fest] *fig.* наводня́ть [-ни́ть]; be **~ed** with кише́ть (Т).
infidelity [infi'deliti] неве́рие; неве́рность *f* (to Д).
infiltrate [in'filtreit] *v/t.* пропуска́ть сквозь фильтр; *v/i.* проника́ть [-и́кнуть]; проса́чиваться [-сочи́ться].
infinit|e ['infinit] □ бесконе́чный, безграни́чный; **~y** [in'finiti] бесконе́чность *f*, безграни́чность *f*.
infirm [in'fə:m] □ не́мощный, дря́хлый; слабохара́ктерный; **~ary** [-əri] больни́ца; **~ity** [-iti] не́мощь *f*; недоста́ток.
inflame [in'fleim] воспламеня́ть (-ся) [-ни́ть(ся)]; ⚕ воспаля́ть(ся) [-ли́ть(ся)]; **~ed** [-d] воспалённый.
inflamma|ble [in'flæməbl] □ воспламеня́ющийся; огнеопа́сный; **~tion** [inflə'meiʃən] воспламене́ние; ⚕ воспале́ние; **~tory** [in'flæmətəri] поджига́тельский; воспали́тельный.
inflat|e [in'fleit] наду́(ва́)ть (га́зом, во́здухом); ✝ взду(ва́)ть; **~ion** [-ʃən] надува́ние; *fig.* напы́щенность *f*; инфля́ция.
inflexi|ble [in'fleksəbl] □ неги́бкий, негну́щийся; *fig.* непрекло́нный, непоколеби́мый; **~on** [-ʃən] изги́б; модуля́ция.
inflict [in'flikt] налага́ть [-ложи́ть]; наноси́ть [-нести́] (ра́ну и т. п.); причиня́ть [-ни́ть] (боль); **~ion** [infli'kʃən] наложе́ние и т. д.
influen|ce ['influəns] **1.** влия́ние, возде́йствие; **2.** возде́йствовать на (В) (*im*)*pf.*, [по]влия́ть на (В); **~tial** [influ'enʃəl] □ влия́тельный.
influx ['inflʌks] впаде́ние (прито́ка); *fig.* наплы́в, прили́в.
inform [in'fɔ:m] *v/t.* информи́ровать (*im*)*pf.*, уведомля́ть [уве́домить] (of о П); *v/i.* доноси́ть [-нести́] (against a p. на В); **~al** [-l] □ неофициа́льный; непринуждённый; **~ality** [infɔ:'mæliti] несоблюде́ние форма́льностей; отсу́тствие церемо́ний; **~ation** [infə'meiʃən] информа́ция, све́дения *n/pl.*; спра́вка; осведомле́ние;

~ative [in'fɔːmətiv] информацио́нный.
infrequent [in'friːkwənt] □ ре́дкий.
infringe [in'frindʒ] наруша́ть [-ру́шить] (*a.* ~ upon).
infuriate [in'fjuərieit] [вз]беси́ть.
infuse [in'fjuːz] ⚕ вли(ва́)ть; *fig.* вселя́ть [-ли́ть]; наста́ивать [насто́ять] (тра́вы и т. п.).
ingen|ious [in'dʒiːnjəs] □ изобрета́тельный; **~uity** [indʒi'njuiti] изобрета́тельность *f*; **~uous** [in'dʒenjuəs] □ чистосерде́чный; просто́й, бесхи́тростный.
ingot ['iŋgət] сли́ток, брусо́к (мета́лла).
ingratitude [in'grætitjuːd] неблаго́дарность *f*.
ingredient [in'griːdiənt] составна́я часть *f*, ингредие́нт.
inhabit [in'hæbit] обита́ть, жить в (П); **~ant** [-itənt] жи́тель(ница *f*) *m*, обита́тель(ница *f*) *m*.
inhal|ation [inhə'leiʃən] вдыха́ние; ⚕ ингаля́ция; **~e** [in'heil] вдыха́ть [вдохну́ть].
inherent [in'hiərənt] □ прису́щий; прирождённый.
inherit [in'herit] насле́довать (*im*)*pf*.; унасле́довать *pf*.; **~ance** [-itəns] насле́дство; *biol.* насле́дственность *f*.
inhibit [in'hibit] [вос]препя́тствовать (Д); *biol.* [за]тормози́ть; **~ion** [inhi'biʃən] сде́рживание; *biol.* торможе́ние.
inhospitable [in'hɔspitəbl] □ негостеприи́мный.
inhuman [in'hjuːmən] □ бесчелове́чный, нечелове́ческий.
inimitable [i'nimitəbl] □ неподража́емый; несравне́нный.
iniquity [i'nikwiti] несправедли́вость *f*; беззако́ние.
initia|l [i'niʃəl] **1.** □ нача́льный, первонача́льный; **2.** нача́льная бу́ква; **~s** *pl.* инициа́лы *m/pl.*; **~te** **1.** [-iit] при́нятый (в о́бщество), посвящённый (в та́йну); **2.** [-ieit] вводи́ть [ввести́]; посвяща́ть [-вяти́ть]; положи́ть нача́ло (Д); **~tive** [i'niʃiətiv] инициати́ва, почи́н; **~tor** [-ieitə] инициа́тор.
inject [in'dʒekt] впры́скивать [-снуть].
injunction [in'dʒʌŋkʃən] прика́з; постановле́ние суда́.
injur|e ['indʒə] [по]вреди́ть по-; врежда́ть [-еди́ть]; ра́нить (*im*)*pf*.; **~ious** [in'dʒuəriəs] □ вре́дный; оскорби́тельный; **~y** ['indʒəri] оскорбле́ние; поврежде́ние, ра́на.
injustice [in'dʒʌstis] несправедли́вость *f*.
ink [ink] **1.** черни́ла *n/pl.*; (*mst* printer's ~) типогра́фская кра́ска; **2.** ме́тить черни́лами; сади́ть кля́ксы на (В).
inkling ['iŋkliŋ] намёк (of на В); подозре́ние.
ink|pot черни́льница; **~stand** пи́сьменный прибо́р; **~y** ['iŋki] черни́льный.
inland ['inlənd] **1.** вну́тренняя террито́рия страны́; **2.** вну́тренний; **3.** [in'lænd] внутрь, внутри́ (страны́).
inlay [in'lei] **1.** [*irr.* (lay)] вкла́дывать [вложи́ть]; выстила́ть [вы́стлать]; покрыва́ть моза́икой; **2.** ['in'lei] моза́ика, инкруста́ция.
inlet ['inlet] у́зкий зали́в, бу́хта; входно́е (*or* вво́дное) отве́рстие.
inmate ['inmeit] сожи́тель(ница *f*) *m* (по ко́мнате).
inmost ['inmoust] глубоча́йший, сокрове́нный.
inn [in] гости́ница.
innate ['in'neit] □ врождённый, приро́дный.
inner ['inə] вну́тренний; **~most** [-moust] *s.* inmost.
innings ['iniŋz] о́чередь пода́чи мяча́.
innkeeper хозя́ин гости́ницы.
innocen|ce ['inosns] ⚖ невино́вность *f*; неви́нность *f*; простота́; **~t** [-snt] **1.** □ неви́нный; ⚖ невино́вный; **2.** проста́к, наи́вный челове́к.
innocuous [i'nɔkjuəs] □ безвре́дный, безоби́дный.
innovation [ino'veiʃən] нововведе́ние, но́вшество; нова́торство.
innuendo [inju'endou] ко́свенный намёк, инсинуа́ция.
innumerable [in'juːmərəbl] □ бесчётный, бесчи́сленный.
inoculate [i'nɔkjuleit] де́лать приви́вку (Д), приви́(ва́)ть; *fig.* внуша́ть [-ши́ть].
inoffensive [inə'fensiv] безоби́дный, безвре́дный.
inoperative [in'ɔpərətiv] безде́йствующий; неде́йствующий.
inopportune [in'ɔpətjuːn] □ несвоевре́менный, неподходя́щий.
inordinate [i'nɔːdinit] □ неуме́ренный, чрезме́рный.
inquest ['inkwest] ⚖ сле́дствие, дозна́ние; coroner's ~ суде́бный осмо́тр тру́па.
inquir|e [in'kwaiə] узн(ав)а́ть; наводи́ть спра́вки (about, after, for о П; of у Р); ~ into иссле́довать (*im*)*pf*; **~ing** [-riŋ] □ пытли́вый; **~y** [-ri] спра́вка; рассле́дование, сле́дствие.
inquisit|ion [inkwi'ziʃən] рассле́дование; **~ive** [in'kwizitiv] □ любозна́тельный; лыбопы́тный.
inroad ['inroud] набе́г, наше́ствие; *fig.* посяга́тельство.
insan|e [in'sein] □ душевнобольно́й; безу́мный; **~ity** [in'sæniti] умопомеша́тельство; безу́мие.

insatia|ble [in'seiʃiəbl] □, **~te** [-ʃiət] ненасы́тный, жа́дный.
inscribe [in'skraib] впи́сывать [-са́ть]; надпи́сывать [-са́ть] (in, on В/Т *or* В на П); посвяща́ть [-яти́ть] (кни́гу).
inscription [in'skripʃən] на́дпись *f*; посвяще́ние (кни́ги).
inscrutable [ins'kru:təbl] □ непостижи́мый, зага́дочный.
insect ['insekt] насеко́мое; **~icide** [in'sektisaid] сре́дство для истребле́ния насеко́мых.
insecure [insi'kjuə] □ ненадёжный; небезопа́сный.
insens|ate [in'senseit] бесчу́вственный; бессмы́сленный; **~ible** [-əbl] □ нечувстви́тельный; потеря́вший созна́ние; незаме́тный; **~itive** [-itiv] нечувстви́тельный.
inseparable [in'sepərəbl] □ неразлу́чный; неотдели́мый.
insert 1. [in'sə:t] вставля́ть [-а́вить]; помеща́ть [-ести́ть] (в газе́те); **2.** ['insə:t] вста́вка, вкла́дыш; **~ion** [in'sə:ʃən] вста́вка; объявле́ние.
inside ['in'said] **1.** вну́тренняя сторона́; вну́тренность *f*; изна́нка (оде́жды); **2.** *adj.* вну́тренний; **3.** *adv.* внутрь, внутри́; **4.** *prp.* внутри́ (Р).
insidious [in'sidiəs] □ хи́трый, кова́рный.
insight ['insait] проница́тельность *f*; интуи́ция.
insignia [in'signiə] *pl.* зна́ки отли́чия; значки́ *m/pl.*
insignificant [insig'nifikənt] незначи́тельный.
insincere [insin'siə] неи́скренний.
insinuat|e [in'sinjueit] инсинуи́ровать (*im*)*pf.*; намека́ть [-кну́ть] на (В); **~** o. s. *fig.* вкра́дываться [вкра́сться]; **~ion** [in'sinju'eiʃən] инсинуа́ция; вкра́дчивость *f*.
insipid [in'sipid] безвку́сный, пре́сный.
insist [in'sist] **~** (up)on: наста́ивать [-стоя́ть] на (П), утвержда́ть (В); **~ence** [-əns] насто́йчивость *f*; **~ent** [-ənt] □ насто́йчивый.
insolent ['insələnt] □ на́глый.
insoluble [in'sɔljubl] нераствори́мый; неразреши́мый.
insolvent [in'sɔlvənt] несостоя́тельный (должни́к).
inspect [in'spekt] осма́тривать [осмотре́ть]; инспекти́ровать; **~ion** [in'spekʃən] осмо́тр; инспе́кция.
inspir|ation [inspə'reiʃən] вдыха́ние; вдохнове́ние; воодушевле́ние; **~e** [in'spaiə] вдыха́ть [вдохну́ть]; *fig.* вдохновля́ть [-ви́ть].
install [in'stɔ:l] устана́вливать [-нови́ть]; вводи́ть в до́лжность; ⊕ [с]монти́ровать; **~ation** [instɔ:'leiʃən] устано́вка; устро́йство.
instalment [in'stɔ:lmənt] очередно́й взнос (при рассро́чке); отде́льный вы́пуск (кни́ги).
instance ['instəns] слу́чай; приме́р; тре́бование; ⚖ инста́нция; for **~** наприме́р.
instant ['instənt] □ **1.** неме́дленный, безотлага́тельный; on the 10th **~** 10-го теку́щего ме́сяца; **2.** мгнове́ние, моме́нт; **~aneous** [instən'teinjəs] □ мгнове́нный; **~ly** ['instəntli] неме́дленно, то́тчас.
instead [in'sted] взаме́н, вме́сто; **~** of вме́сто (Р).
instep ['instep] подъём (ноги́).
instigat|e ['instigeit] побужда́ть [-уди́ть]; подстрека́ть [-кну́ть]; **~or** [-ə] подстрека́тель(ница *f*) *m.*
instil(l) [in'stil] влива́ть по ка́пле; *fig.* внуша́ть [-ши́ть] (into Д).
instinct ['instiŋkt] инсти́нкт; **~ive** [in'stiŋktiv] □ инстинкти́вный.
institut|e ['institju:t] нау́чное учрежде́ние, институ́т; **2.** учрежда́ть [-еди́ть]; устана́вливать [-нови́ть]; **~ion** [insti'tju:ʃən] установле́ние; учрежде́ние, заведе́ние.
instruct [in'strʌkt] [на]учи́ть, обуча́ть [-чи́ть]; инструкти́ровать (*im*)*pf.*; **~ion** [in'strʌkʃən] обуче́ние; предписа́ние; инстру́кция; **~ive** [-tiv] □ поучи́тельный; **~or** [-tə] руководи́тель *m*, инстру́ктор; преподава́тель *m.*
instrument ['instrumənt] инструме́нт; ору́дие (*a. fig.*); прибо́р, аппара́т; ⚖ докуме́нт; **~al** [instru'mentl] □ слу́жащий сре́дством; инструмента́льный; **~ality** [-men'tæliti] сре́дство, спо́соб.
insubordinate [insə'bɔ:dnit] неподчиня́ющийся дисципли́не.
insufferable [in'sʌfərəbl] □ невыноси́мый, нестерпи́мый.
insufficient [insə'fiʃənt] недоста́точный.
insula|r ['insjulə] □ островно́й; *fig.* за́мкнутый; **~te** [-leit] ⚡ изоли́ровать (*im*)*pf.*; **~tion** [insju'leiʃən] ⚡ изоля́ция.
insult 1. ['insʌlt] оскорбле́ние; **2.** [in'sʌlt] оскорбля́ть [-би́ть].
insur|ance [in'ʃuərəns] страхова́ние; *attr.* страхово́й; **~e** [in'ʃuə] [за]страхова́ть(ся).
insurgent [in'sə:dʒənt] **1.** мяте́жный; **2.** повста́нец; мяте́жник.
insurmountable [insə'mauntabl] □ непреодоли́мый.
insurrection [insə'rekʃən] восста́ние; мяте́ж.
intact [in'tækt] нетро́нутый; неповреждённый.
intangible [in'tændʒəbl] □ неосяза́емый; *fig.* неуловимый.
integ|ral ['intigrəl] □ неотъе́млемый; це́лый; це́лостный; **~rate** [-greit] объединя́ть [-ни́ть]; интегри́ровать (*im*)*pf.*; **~rity** [in'tegriti] че́стность *f*; це́лостность *f*.

intellect ['intilekt] ум, рассу́док; **~ual** [inti'lektjuəl] 1. □ интеллектуа́льный, у́мственный; 2. интеллиге́нт(ка); **~s** *pl.* интеллиге́нция.
intelligence [in'telidʒəns] ум, рассу́док, интелле́кт; Intelligence service разве́дывательная слу́жба, разве́дка.
intellig|ent [in'telidʒənt] □ у́мный; смышлёный; **~ible** [-dʒəbl] □ поня́тный.
intemperance [in'tempərəns] неуме́ренность *f*; невозде́рж(ан)ность *f*; пристра́стие к спиртны́м напи́ткам.
intend [in'tend] намерева́ться; име́ть в виду́; ~ for предназнача́ть [-зна́чить] для (Р).
intense [in'tens] □ си́льный; интенси́вный, напряжённый.
intensify [in'tensifai] уси́ли(ва)ть (-ся); интенсифици́ровать (*im*)*pf*.
intensity [in'tensiti] интенси́вность *f*, си́ла; я́ркость *f* (кра́ски).
intent [in'tent] 1. □ стремя́щийся, скло́нный (on к Д); внима́тельный, при́стальный; 2. наме́рение, цель *f*; to all ~s and purposes в су́щности; во всех отноше́ниях; **~ion** [in'tenʃən] наме́рение; **~ional** [-l] □ наме́ренный, умы́шленный.
inter [in'tə:] предава́ть земле́, [по-] хорони́ть.
inter... ['intə] *pref.* меж..., между...; пере...; взаимо...
interact [intər'ækt] де́йствовать друг на дру́га, взаимоде́йствовать.
intercede [intə'si:d] хода́тайствовать.
intercept [-'sept] перехва́тывать [-хвати́ть]; прер(ы)ва́ть; преграждáть путь (Д); **~ion** [-pʃən] перехва́т(ывание); пересече́ние.
intercess|ion [intə'seʃən] хода́тайство, засту́пничество; **~or** [-sə] хода́тай, засту́пник.
interchange 1. [intə'tʃeindʒ] *v/t.* чередова́ть; обме́ниваться [-ня́ться] (Т); *v/i.* чередова́ться; 2. ['intə'tʃeindʒ] обме́н; чередова́ние, сме́на.
intercourse ['intəkɔ:s] обще́ние, связь *f*; отноше́ния *n/pl.*; сноше́ния *n/pl.*
interdict 1. [intə'dikt] запреща́ть [-рети́ть]; лиша́ть пра́ва по́льзования; 2. ['intədikt], **~ion** [intə'dikʃən] запреще́ние.
interest ['intrist] 1. *com.* интере́с; заинтересо́ванность *f* (in в П); вы́года; проце́нты *m/pl.* (на капита́л); 2. *com.* интересова́ть; заинтересо́вывать [-сова́ть]; **~ing** [-iŋ] □ интере́сный.
interfere [intə'fiə] вме́шиваться [-ша́ться]; [по]меша́ть, надоеда́ть [-е́сть] (with Д); **~nce** [-rəns] вмеша́тельство; поме́ха.
interim ['intərim] 1. промежу́ток вре́мени; 2. вре́менный, промежу́точный.
interior [in'tiəriə] 1. □ вну́тренний; 2. вну́тренность *f*; вну́тренние о́бласти страны́; *pol.* вну́тренние дела́ *n/pl.*
interjection [intə'dʒekʃən] восклица́ние; *gr.* междоме́тие.
interlace [intəl'eis] переплета́ть(ся) [-плести́(сь)].
interlock [intə'lɔk] сцепля́ть(ся) [-пи́ть(ся)].
interlocut|ion [intəlo'kju:ʃən] бесе́да, диало́г; **~or** [intə'lɔkjutə] собесе́дник.
interlope [intə'loup] вме́шиваться [-ша́ться]; **~r** [-ə] вме́шивающийся в чужи́е дела́.
interlude ['intəlu:d] антра́кт; промежу́точный эпизо́д.
intermeddle [intə'medl] вме́шиваться [-ша́ться] (with, in в В); сова́ться не в своё де́ло.
intermedia|ry [-'mi:diəri] 1. = intermediate; посре́днический; 2. посре́дник; **~te** [-'mi:djət] □ промежу́точный; сре́дний.
interment [in'tə:mənt] погребе́ние.
interminable [in'tə:minəbl] □ бесконе́чный.
intermingle [intə'miŋgl] сме́шивать(ся) [-ша́ть(ся)]; обща́ться.
intermission [-'miʃən] переры́в, па́уза, переме́на (в шко́ле).
intermit [intə'mit] прер(ы)ва́ть (-ся); **~tent** [-ənt] □ преры́вистый; перемежа́ющийся.
intermix [intə'miks] переме́шивать(ся) [-ша́ть(ся)].
intern [in'tə:n] интерни́ровать (*im*)*pf*.
internal [in'tə:nl] □ вну́тренний.
international [intə'næʃnl] □ междунаро́дный, интернациона́льный; ~ law междунаро́дное пра́во.
interpolate [in'tə:poleit] интерполи́ровать (*im*)*pf*.
interpose [intə'pouz] *v/t.* вставля́ть [-а́вить], вводи́ть [ввести́]; *v/i.* станови́ться [стать] (between ме́жду Т); вме́шиваться [-ша́ться] (в В).
interpret [in'tə:prit] объясня́ть [-ни́ть], растолко́вывать [-кова́ть]; переводи́ть [-вести́] (у́стно); **~ation** [-''eiʃən] толкова́ние, интерпрета́ция, объясне́ние; **~er** [-ə] перево́дчик (-ица).
interrogat|e [in'terogeit] допра́шивать [-роси́ть]; спра́шивать [спроси́ть]; **~ion** [-''geiʃən] допро́с; вопро́с; **~ive** [intə'rɔgətiv] □ вопроси́тельный.
interrupt [intə'rʌpt] прер(ы)ва́ть; **~ion** [-'rʌpʃən] переры́в.
intersect [intə'sekt] пересека́ть(ся) [-се́чь(ся)]; скре́щивать(ся) [-ести́ть(ся)]; **~ion** [-kʃən] пересече́ние.

intersperse [intə'spə:s] разбра́сывать [-броса́ть], рассыпа́ть [-ы́пать]; усе́ивать [усе́ять].
intertwine [intə'twain] сплета́ть (-ся) [-ести́(сь)].
interval ['intəvəl] промежу́ток, расстоя́ние, интерва́л; па́уза, переме́на.
interven|e [intə'vi:n] вме́шиваться [-ша́ться]; вступа́ться [-пи́ться]; **~tion** [-'venʃən] интерве́нция; вмеша́тельство.
interview ['intəvju:] **1.** свида́ние, встре́ча; интервью́ *n indecl.*; **2.** интервьюи́ровать *(im)pf.*, име́ть бесе́ду с (Т).
intestine [in'testin] **1.** вну́тренний; **2.** кишка́; **~s** *pl.* кишки́ *f/pl.*, кише́чник.
intima|cy ['intiməsi] инти́мность *f*, бли́зость *f*; **~te 1.** [-meit] сообща́ть [-щи́ть]; намека́ть [-кну́ть] на (В); **2.** [-mit] a) □ инти́мный, ли́чный; бли́зкий; b) бли́зкий друг; **~tion** [inti'meiʃən] сообще́ние; намёк.
intimidate [in'timideit] [ис]пуга́ть; запу́гивать [-га́ть].
into ['intu, intə] *prp.* в, во (В).
intolera|ble [in'tɔlərəbl] □ невыноси́мый, нестерпи́мый; **~nt** [-rənt] □ нетерпи́мый.
intonation [intou'neiʃən] интона́ция.
intoxica|nt [in'tɔksikənt] опьяня́ющий (напи́ток); **~te** [-keit] опьяня́ть [-ни́ть]; **~tion** [-''keiʃən] опьяне́ние.
intractable [in'træktəbl] □ непода́тливый.
intrepid [in'trepid] неустраши́мый, бесстра́шный, отва́жный.
intricate ['intrikit] □ сло́жный, затрудни́тельный.
intrigue [in'tri:g] **1.** интри́га; любо́вная связь *f*; **2.** интригова́ть; [за]интригова́ть, [за]интересова́ть; **~r** [-ə] интрига́н(ка).
intrinsic(**al** □) [in'trinsik, -sikəl] вну́тренний; сво́йственный; суще́ственный.
introduc|e [intrə'dju:s] вводи́ть [ввести́]; представля́ть [-а́вить]; **~tion** [-'dʌkʃən] введе́ние; представле́ние; ♪ интроду́кция; **~tory** [-'dʌktəri] вступи́тельный, вво́дный.
intru|de [in'tru:d] вторга́ться [вто́ргнуться]; навя́зываться [-за́ться]; **~der** [-ə] проны́ра *m/f*; незва́ный гость *m*; **~sion** [-ʒən] вторже́ние; появле́ние без приглаше́ния; **~sive** [-siv] □ назо́йливый, навя́зчивый.
intrust [in'trʌst] *s.* entrust.
intuition [intju'iʃən] интуи́ция.
inundate ['inʌndeit] затопля́ть [-пи́ть], наводня́ть [-ни́ть].
inure [i'njuə] приуча́ть [-чи́ть] (to к Д).
invade [in'veid] вторга́ться [вто́ргнуться]; *fig.* овладе́(ва́)ть (Т); **~r** [-ə] захва́тчик, интерве́нт.
invalid 1. [in'vælid] недействи́тельный, не име́ющий зако́нной си́лы; **2.** ['invəli:d] a) нетрудоспосо́бный; b) инвали́д; **~ate** [in'vælideit] лиша́ть зако́нной си́лы, сде́лать недействи́тельным.
invaluable [in'væljuəbl] □ неоцени́мый.
invariable [in'veəriəbl] □ неизме́нный; неизменя́емый.
invasion [in'veiʒən] вторже́ние, набе́г; ⚖ посяга́тельство; ⚕ инва́зия.
inveigh [in'vei]: **~ against** поноси́ть, [об]руга́ть (В).
invent [in'vent] изобрета́ть [-брести́]; выду́мывать [вы́думать]; **~ion** [in'venʃən] изобрете́ние; изобрета́тельность *f*; **~ive** [-tiv] □ изобрета́тельный; **~or** [-tə] изобрета́тель *m*; **~ory** ['invəntri] **1.** о́пись *f*, инвента́рь *m*; *Am.* переучёт това́ра, инвентариза́ция; **2.** составля́ть о́пись (Р); вноси́ть в инвента́рь.
inverse ['invə:s] □ перевёрнутый, обра́тный.
invert [in'və:t] перевёртывать [переверну́ть], переставля́ть [-а́вить].
invest [in'vest] вкла́дывать [вложи́ть] (капита́л); *fig.* облека́ть [обле́чь] (with Т); ⚔ обложи́ть *pf.* (кре́пость).
investigat|e [in'vestigeit] рассле́довать *(im)pf.*; разузн(ав)а́ть; иссле́довать *(im)pf.* **~ion** [investi'geiʃən] ⚖ сле́дствие; иссле́дование; **~or** [in'vestigeitə] иссле́дователь *m.*; ⚖ сле́дователь *m.*
invest|ment [in'vestmənt] вложе́ние де́нег, инвести́рование; вклад; **~or** [-ə] вкла́дчик.
inveterate [in'vetərit] закорене́лый; F зая́длый; застаре́лый.
invidious [in'vidiəs] □ вызыва́ющий вражде́бное чу́вство; ненави́стный; зави́дный.
invigorate [in'vigəreit] дава́ть си́лы (Д); воодушевля́ть [-ви́ть].
invincible [in'vinsəbl] □ непобеди́мый.
inviola|ble [in'vaiələbl] □ неруши́мый; неприкоснове́нный; **~te** [-lit] нару́шенный.
invisible [in'vizəbl] неви́димый.
invit|ation [invi'teiʃən] приглаше́ние; **~e** [in'vait] приглаша́ть [-ласи́ть].
invoice ['invɔis] ✝ накладна́я, факту́ра.
invoke [in'vouk] вызыва́ть [вы́звать] (ду́ха); взыва́ть [воззва́ть] о (П); приз(ы)ва́ть.
involuntary [in'vɔləntəri] □ нево́льный; непроизво́льный.

involve [in'vɔlv] включáть в себя́; вовлекáть [-éчь]; впу́т(ыв)ать.
invulnerable [in'vʌlnərəbl] □ неуязвúмый.
inward ['inwəd] **1.** внýтренний; ýмственный; **2.** *adv.* (*mst* ~s [-z]) внутрь; внýтренне; **3.** ~s *pl.* внýтренности *f/pl.*
inwrought ['in'rɔ:t] вóтканный в матéрию (об узóре); *fig.* тéсно свя́занный (with с T).
iodine ['aiədi:n] йод.
IOU ['aiou'ju:] (= I owe you) долговáя распúска.
irascible [i'ræsibl] □ раздражúтельный.
irate [ai'reit] гнéвный.
iridescent [iri'desnt] рáдужный, перелúвчатый.
iris ['aiəris] *anat.* рáдужная оболóчка (глáза); ♀ úрис, касáтик.
Irish ['aiəriʃ] **1.** ирлáндский; **2.** the ~ ирлáндцы *m/pl.*
irksome ['ə:ksəm] утомúтельный, скýчный.
iron ['aiən] **1.** желéзо; (*mst* flat-~) утю́г; ~s *pl.* окóвы *f/pl.*, кандалы́ *m/pl.*; **2.** желéзный; **3.** [вы́]утю́жить, [вы́]глáдить; ~**clad 1.** покры́тый бронёй, бронирóванный; **2.** броненóсец; ~**-hearted** *fig.* жестокосéрдный.
ironic(**al** □) [aiə'rɔnik, -nikəl] ирони́ческий.
iron|ing ['aiəniŋ] **1.** глáженье; вéщи для глáженья; **2.** гладúльный; ~**mongery** скобянóй товáр; ~**mould** ржáвое пятнó; ~**works** *mst sg.* чугуноплавúльный úли железодéлательный завóд.
irony ['aiərəni] ирóния.
irradiate [i'reidieit] озаря́ть [-рúть]; ⚕ облучáть [-чúть]; *phys.* испускáть лучú; *fig.* распространя́ть [-нúть] (знáния и т. п.); проливáть свет на (B).
irrational [i'ræʃnl] неразýмный; ⅄ иррационáльный.
irreconcilable [i'rekənsailəbl] □ непримирúмый; несовместúмый.
irrecoverable [iri'kʌvərəbl] □ непоправúмый, невозврáтный.
irredeemable [iri'di:məbl] □ невозврáтимый; безысхóдный; не подлежáщий вы́купу.
irrefutable [i'refjutəbl] □ неопровержúмый.
irregular [i'regjulə] □ непрáвильный (*a. gr.*); беспоря́дочный; нерегуля́рный.
irrelevant [i'relivənt] □ не относя́щийся к дéлу; неумéстный.
irreligious [iri'lidʒəs] □ нерелигиóзный; невéрующий.
irremediable [iri'mi:diəbl] □ непоправúмый; неизлечúмый.
irreparable [i'repərəbl] □ непоправúмый.
irreproachable [iri'proutʃəbl] □ безукорúзненный, безупрéчный.
irresistible [iri'zistəbl] □ неотразúмый; непреодолúмый (о желáнии и т. п.).
irresolute [i'rezəlu:t] □ нерешúтельный.
irrespective [iris'pektiv] □ безотносúтельный (of к Д); независúмый (of от P).
irresponsible [iris'pɔnsəbl] □ безотвéтственный; невменя́емый.
irreverent [i'revərənt] □ непочтúтельный.
irrevocable [i'revəkəbl] □ безвозврáтный.
irrigate ['irigeit] орошáть [оросúть].
irrita|ble ['iritəbl] □ раздражúтельный; болéзненно чувствúтельный; ~**nt** [-tənt] раздражáющее срéдство; ~**te** [-teit] раздражáть [-жúть]; ~**tion** [iri'teiʃən] раздражéние.
irruption [i'rʌpʃən] набéг, нашéствие.
is [iz] 3. *p. sg. pres.* от be.
island ['ailənd] óстров; ~**er** [-ə] островитя́нин (-тя́нка).
isle [ail] óстров; ~**t** [ai'lit] островóк.
isolat|e ['aisəleit] изолúровать; (*im*)*pf.*, отделя́ть [-лúть]; ~**ion** [aisə'leiʃən] изолúрование.
issue ['isju:] **1.** вытекáние, излия́ние; вы́ход; потóмство; спóрный вопрóс; вы́пуск, издáние; исхóд, результáт; ~ in law разноглáсие о прáвильности применéния закóна; be at ~ быть в разноглáсии; быть предмéтом спóра; point at ~ предмéт обсуждéния; **2.** *v/i.* исходúть [изойтú] (from из P); вытекáть [вы́течь] (from из P); происходúть [произойтú] (from от P); *v/t.* выпускáть [вы́пустить], изд(ав)áть.
isthmus ['isməs] перешéек.
it [it] *pron. pers.* он, онá, онó; э́то.
Italian [i'tæljən] **1.** итальянский; **2.** итальянец (-нка); **3.** итальянский язы́к.
italics [i'tæliks] *typ.* курсúв.
itch [itʃ] **1.** ⚕ чесóтка; зуд; **2.** чесáться, зудéть; be ~ing to *inf.* горéть желáнием (+ *inf.*).
item ['aitem] **1.** пункт, парáграф; вопрóс (на повéстке); нóмер (прогрáммы); **2.** *adv.* тáкже, тóже; ~**ize** ['aitəmaiz] *part. Am.* перечисля́ть по пу́нктам.
iterate ['itəreit] повторя́ть [-рúть].
itinerary [i'tinərəri, ai't-] маршру́т, путь *m*; путеводúтель *m.*
its [its] *pron. poss.* от it егó, её, свой.
itself [it'self] (сам *m*, самá *f*,) самó *n*; себя́, -ся, -сь; себé; in ~ самó по себé; by ~ самó собóй; отдéльно.
ivory ['aivəri] слонóвая кость *f.*
ivy ['aivi] ♀ плющ.

J

jab [dʒæb] F **1.** толкáть [-кнýть]; тыкать [ткнуть]; пырять [-рнýть]; **2.** толчóк, пинóк, (кóлющий) удáр.
jabber ['dʒæbə] болтáть, таратóрить.
jack [dʒæk] **1.** пáрень *m*; валéт (кáрта); ⊕ домкрáт; ⚓ матрóс; флаг, гюйс; **2.** поднимáть домкрáтом; *Am. sl.* повышáть [-ысить] (цéны); **~ass** осёл; дурáк.
jacket ['dʒækit] жакéт; кýртка; ⊕ чехóл, кожýх.
jack|-knife складнóй нож; **~-of-all-trades** на все рýки мáстер.
jade [dʒeid] кляча; *contp.* шлюха; неряха.
jag [dʒæg] зубéц; зазýбрина; дырá, прорéха; **~ged** ['dʒægid], **~gy** [-i] зубчáтый; зазýбренный.
jail [dʒeil] тюрьмá; тюрéмное заключéние; **~er** ['dʒeilə] тюрéмщик.
jam[1] [dzæm] варéнье.
jam[2] [~] **1.** сжáтие, сжимáние; ⊕ перебóй; traffic ~ затóр в ýличном движéнии; *Am.* be in a ~ быть в затруднúтельном положéнии; **2.** заж(им)áть; защемлять [-мить]; набивáть биткóм; загромождáть [-моздить]; глушить (радиопередáчи).
jangle ['dʒæŋgl] издавáть рéзкие звýки; нестрóйно звучáть.
janitor ['dʒænitə] швейцáр; двóрник.
January ['dʒænjuəri] январь *m*.
Japanese [dʒæpə'ni:z] **1.** япóнский; **2.** япóнец (-нка); the ~ *pl.* япóнцы *pl.*
jar [dʒɑ:] **1.** кувшин; бáнка; ссóра; неприятный, рéзкий звук; дребезжáние; **2.** [за]дребезжáть; [по-] корóбить; дисгармонúровать.
jaundice ['dʒɔ:ndis] ⚕ желтýха; жёлчность *f*; *fig.* зáвисть *f*; **~d** [-t] желтýшный; *fig.* завистливый.
jaunt [dʒɔ:nt] **1.** увеселúтельная поéздка, прогýлка; **2.** предпринимáть увеселúтельную поéздку и т. п.; **~y** ['dʒɔ:nti] □ весёлый, бóйкий.
javelin ['dʒævlin] копьё.
jaw [dʒɔ:] чéлюсть *f*; **~s** *pl.* рот, пасть *f*; ⊕ *mst pl.* губá (клещéй); **~-bone** челюстнáя кость *f*.
jealous ['dʒeləs] □ ревнúвый; завúстливый; **~y** [-i] рéвность *f*; зáвисть *f*.
jeep [dʒi:p] *Am.* ⚔ джип.
jeer [dʒiə] **1.** насмéшка, глумлéние; **2.** насмехáться [-еяться], [по]глумиться (at над Т).
jejune [dʒi'dʒu:n] □ прéсный; пустóй, неинтерéсный.
jelly ['dʒeli] **1.** желé *n indecl.*; стýдень *m*; **2.** засты(вá)ть; **~-fish** медýза.
jeopardize ['dʒepədaiz] подвергáть опáсности.
jerk [dʒə:k] **1.** рывóк; толчóк; подёргивание (мýскула); **2.** рéзко толкáть или дёргать; двигаться толчкáми; **~y** ['dʒə:ki] □ отрывистый; **~ily** *adv.* рывкáми.
jersey ['dʒə:zi] фуфáйка; вязаный жакéт.
jest [dʒest] **1.** шýтка; насмéшка; **2.** [по]шутить; насмéшничать; **~er** ['dʒestə] шутник (-ица); шут.
jet [dʒet] **1.** струя (воды, гáза и т. п.); ⊕ жиклёр, форсýнка; *attr.* реактúвный; **2.** бить струёй; выпускáть струёй.
jetty ['dʒeti] ⚓ прúстань *f*; мол; дáмба.
Jew [dʒu:] еврéй; *attr.* еврéйский.
jewel ['dʒu:əl] драгоцéнный кáмень *m*; **~(l)er** [-ə] ювелúр; **~(le)ry** [-ri] драгоцéнности *f/pl.*
Jew|ess ['dʒu:is] еврéйка; **~ish** [-iʃ] еврéйский.
jib [dʒib] ⚓ клúвер.
jiffy ['dʒifi] F миг, мгновéние.
jig-saw *Am.* машúнная ножóвка; ~ puzzle составнáя картúнка-загáдка.
jilt [dʒilt] **1.** кокéтка, обмáнщица; **2.** увлéчь и обманýть (о жéнщине).
jingle ['dʒiŋgl] **1.** звон, звяканье; **2.** [за]звенéть, звякать [-кнуть].
job [dʒɔb] **1.** рабóта, труд; дéло; задáние; by the ~ сдéльно, поурóчно; ~ lot вéщи кýпленные гуртóм по дешёвке; ~ work сдéльная рабóта; **2.** *v/t.* брать (давáть) внаём; *v/i.* рабóтать поштýчно, сдéльно; быть мáклером; **~ber** ['dʒɔbə] занимáющийся случáйной рабóтой; сдéльщик; мáклер; спекулянт.
jockey ['dʒɔki] **1.** жокéй; **2.** обмáнывать [-нýть], надý(вá)ть.
jocose [dʒə'kous] шутлúвый, игрúвый.
jocular ['dʒɔkjulə] шутлúвый, юмористúческий.
jocund ['dʒɔkənd] □ весёлый, живóй; приятный.
jog [dʒɔg] **1.** толчóк; тряская ездá; мéдленная ходьбá; **2.** *v/t.* толкáть [-кнýть]; *v/i.* (*mst* ~ along,) éхать подпрыгивая, трястись.
join [dʒɔin] **1.** *v/t.* соединять [-нить], присоединять [-нить]; присоединяться [-нúться] к (Д); войтú в компáнию (Р); вступить в члéны (Р); ~ battle вступáть в бой; ~ hands объединяться [-нúться]; брáться зá руки; *v/i.*

соединя́ться [-ни́ться]; объединя́ться [-ни́ться]; ~ in with присоединя́ться [-ни́ться] к (Д); ~ up вступа́ть в а́рмию; 2. соедине́ние; то́чка (ли́ния, пло́скость) соедине́ния.

joiner ['dʒɔinə] столя́р; **~y** [-ri] столя́рничество.

joint [dʒɔint] 1. ме́сто соедине́ния; *anat.* суста́в; ⚘ у́зел; кусо́к мя́са для жа́рения; put out of ~ выви́хивать [вы́вихнуть]; 2. □ соединённый; о́бщий; ~ heir сонасле́дник; 3. соединя́ть [-ни́ть]; расчленя́ть [-ни́ть]; **~-stock** акционе́рый капита́л; ~ company акционе́рное о́бщество.

jok|e [dʒouk] 1. шу́тка, острота́; 2. *v/i.* [по]шути́ть; *v/t.* поддра́знивать [-ни́ть], **~er** ['dʒoukə] шутни́к (-и́ца); **~y** [-ki] □ шутли́вый; шу́точный.

jolly ['dʒɔli] весёлый, ра́достный; F преле́стный, сла́вный.

jolt [dʒoult] 1. трясти́ [тряхну́ть], встря́хивать [-хну́ть]; 2. толчо́к; тря́ска.

jostle ['dʒɔsl] 1. толка́ть(ся) [-кну́ть(ся)]; тесни́ть(ся); 2. толчо́к; толкотня́, да́вка (в толпе́).

jot [dʒɔt] 1. ничто́жное коли́чество, йо́та; 2. ~ down бе́гло наброса́ть, кра́тко записа́ть.

journal ['dʒə:nl] дневни́к; журна́л; *parl.* протоко́л заседа́ния; ⊕ ше́йка (ва́ла), ца́пфа; **~ism** ['dʒə:nlizm] журнали́стика.

journey ['dʒə:ni] 1. пое́здка, путеше́ствие; 2. путеше́ствовать; **~man** подмасте́рье; наёмник.

jovial ['dʒouviəl] весёлый, общи́тельный.

joy [dʒɔi] ра́дость *f*, удово́льствие; **~ful** ['dʒɔiful] □ ра́достный, весёлый; **~less** [-lis] □ безра́достный; **~ous** [-əs] □ ра́достный, весёлый.

jubil|ant ['dʒu:bilənt] лику́ющий; **~ate** [-leit] ликова́ть, торжествова́ть; **~ee** ['dʒu:bili:] юбиле́й.

judge [dʒʌdʒ] 1. судья́ *m*; арби́тр; знато́к, цени́тель; 2. *v/i.* суди́ть, посуди́ть *pf.*; быть арби́тром; *v/t.* суди́ть о (П); оце́нивать [-ни́ть]; осужда́ть [осуди́ть], порица́ть.

judg(e)ment ['dʒʌdʒmənt] пригово́р, реше́ние суда́; сужде́ние; рассуди́тельность *f*; мне́ние, взгляд.

judicature ['dʒu:dikətʃə] суде́йская корпора́ция; судоустро́йство; отправле́ние правосу́дия.

judicial [dʒu:'diʃəl] □ суде́бный; суде́йский; рассуди́тельный.

judicious [dʒu:'diʃəs] □ здравомы́слящий, рассуди́тельный; **~ness** [-nis] рассуди́тельность *f*.

jug [dʒʌg] кувши́н; F тюрьма́.

juggle ['dʒʌgl] 1. фо́кус, трюк; 2. жонгли́ровать; обма́нывать [-ну́ть]; **~r** [-ə] жонглёр; фо́кусник (-ица).

juic|e [dʒu:s] сок; **~y** ['dʒu:si] □ со́чный; F колори́тный; интере́сный.

July [dʒu'lai] ию́ль *m*.

jumble ['dʒʌmbl] 1. пу́таница, беспоря́док; 2. толка́ться; сме́шивать(ся) [-ша́ть(ся)]; дви́гаться в беспоря́дке; **~-sale** прода́жа вся́ких сбо́рных веще́й с благотвори́тельной це́лью.

jump [dʒʌmp] 1. прыжо́к; скачо́к; вздра́гивание (от испу́га); 2. *v/i.* пры́гать [-гнуть]; скака́ть [-кну́ть]; ~ at охо́тно приня́ть (предложе́ние, пода́рок), ухва́тываться [ухвати́ться] за (В); ~ to conclusions де́лать поспе́шные вы́воды; *v/t.* перепры́гивать [-гнуть]; **~er** ['dʒʌmpə] прыгу́н; скаку́н; дже́мпер; **~y** [-pi] не́рвный, легко́ вздра́гивающий.

junct|ion ['dʒʌŋkʃən] соедине́ние; 🚂 железнодоро́жный у́зел; **~ure** [-ktʃə] соедине́ние; стече́ние обстоя́тельств, положе́ние дел; (крити́ческий) моме́нт; at this ~ of things при подо́бном положе́нии дел.

June [dʒu:n] ию́нь *m*.

jungle ['dʒʌŋgl] джу́нгли *f/pl.*; густы́е за́росли *f/pl.*

junior ['dʒu:njə] 1. мла́дший; моло́же (to P *or* чем И); 2. мла́дший.

junk [dʒʌŋk] □ джо́нка; *Am.* старьё; *sl.* хлам, отбро́сы *m/pl.*

juris|diction [dʒuəris'dikʃən] отправле́ние правосу́дия; юрисди́кция; **~prudence** ['dʒuərispru:dəns] юриспруде́нция, законове́дение.

juror ['dʒuərə] ⚖ прися́жный; член жюри́.

jury [-ri] ⚖ прися́жные *m/pl.*; жюри́ *n indecl.*; **~man** прися́жный; член жюри́.

just [dʒʌst] 1. □ *adj.* справедли́вый; пра́ведный; ве́рный, то́чный; 2. *adv.* то́чно, как раз, и́менно; то́лько что; пря́мо; ~ now сейча́с, сию́ мину́ту; то́лько что.

justice ['dʒʌstis] справедли́вость *f*; правосу́дие; судья́ *m*; court of ~ суд.

justification [dʒʌstifi'keiʃən] оправда́ние; реабилита́ция.

justify ['dʒʌstifai] опра́вдывать [-да́ть], извиня́ть [-ни́ть].

justly ['dʒʌstli] справедли́во.

justness [-nis] справедли́вость *f*.

jut [dʒʌt] (*a.* ~ out) выступа́ть; вы́да(ва́)ться.

juvenile ['dʒu:vinail] 1. ю́ный, ю́ношеский; 2. ю́ноша *m*, подро́сток.

K

kangaroo [kæŋgə'ru:] кенгуру́ *m/f. indecl.*
keel [ki:l] **1.** киль *m*; **2.** ~ over опроки́дывать(ся) [-и́нуть(ся)].
keen [ki:n] □ о́стрый; ре́зкий; проница́тельный; си́льный; be ~ on о́чень люби́ть (В), стра́стно увлека́ться (Т); **~ness** ['ki:nnis] острота́; проница́тельность *f*.
keep [ki:p] **1.** содержа́ние; пропита́ние; for ~s F *part. Am.* навсегда́; **2.** [*irr.*] *v/t. com.* держа́ть; сохраня́ть [-ни́ть], храни́ть; содержа́ть; вести́ (кни́ги и т. п.); [с]держа́ть (сло́во и т. п.); ~ company with подде́рживать знако́мство с (Т); ~ waiting заставля́ть ждать; ~ away не подпуска́ть (from к Д); ~ a th. from a p. уде́рживать что́-либо от (Р); ~ in не выпуска́ть; оставля́ть (шко́льника) по́сле уро́ков; ~ on не снима́ть (шля́пы и т. п.); ~ up подде́рживать [-жа́ть]; **3.** *v/i.* держа́ться; уде́рживаться [-жа́ться] (from от Р); ост(ав)а́ться; не по́ртиться (о пи́ще); F и́ли *Am.* жить, обрета́ться; ~ doing продолжа́ть де́лать; ~ away держа́ться в отдале́нии; ~ from возде́рживаться [-жа́ться] от (Р); ~ off держа́ться в отдале́нии от (Р); ~ on (talking) продолжа́ть (говори́ть); ~ to приде́рживаться (Р); ~ up держа́ться бо́дро; ~ up with держа́ться наравне́ с (Т), идти́ в но́гу с (Т).
keep|er ['ki:pə] храни́тель *m*; сто́рож; **~ing** ['ki:piŋ] хране́ние; содержа́ние; be in (out of) ~ with ... (не) согласова́ться с (Т); **~sake** ['ki:pseik] пода́рок на па́мять.
keg [keg] бочо́нок.
kennel ['kenl] конура́.
kept [kept] *pt.* и *p. pt.* от keep.
kerb(stone) ['kə:b(stoun)] край тротуа́ра; бордю́рный ка́мень *m*.
kerchief ['kə:tʃif] (головно́й) плато́к; косы́нка.
kernel ['kə:nl] зерно́, зёрнышко; ядро́; *fig.* суть *f*.
kettle ['ketl] ча́йник (для кипяче́ния воды́); котёл; **~drum** ♪ лита́вра; F зва́ный вече́рний чай.
key [ki:] **1.** ключ; код; ⊕ клин; шпо́нка; кла́виш(а); ♪ ключ, тона́льность *f*; *fig.* тон; **2.** запира́ть [запере́ть] (на ключ); ♪ настра́ивать [-ро́ить]; ~ up *fig.* придава́ть реши́мость (Д); be ~ed up *Am.* быть в взви́нченном состоя́нии; **~board** клавиату́ра; **~hole** замо́чная сква́жина; **~-note** тона́льность *f*; *fig.* основна́я мысль *f*; **~stone** ⚠ ключево́й ка́мень *m*.
kick [kik] **1.** уда́р (ного́й, копы́том); пино́к; F си́ла сопротивле́ния; **2.** *v/t.* ударя́ть [уда́рить] (ного́й); брыка́ть [-кну́ть]; ~ out *Am. sl.* вышвы́ривать [вы́швырнуть], выгоня́ть [вы́гнать]; *v/i.* брыка́ться [-кну́ться], ляга́ться [лягну́ться]; [вос]проти́виться; **~er** ['kikə] брыкли́вая ло́шадь *f*; футболи́ст.
kid [kid] **1.** козлёнок; ла́йка (ко́жа); F ребёнок; **2.** *sl.* поддра́знивать [-ни́ть].
kidnap ['kidnæp] похища́ть [-хи́тить] (люде́й); **~(p)er** [-ə] похити́тель-вымога́тель *m*.
kidney ['kidni] *anat.* по́чка; F тип, хара́ктер.
kill [kil] уби́(ва́)ть; бить (скот); *fig.* [по]губи́ть; *parl.* прова́ливать [-ли́ть] (законопрое́кт и т. п.); ~ off уничтожа́ть [-о́жить]; ~ time убива́ть вре́мя; **~er** ['kilə] уби́йца *m/f*.
kiln [kiln] обжига́тельная печь *f*.
kin [kin] семья́; родня́.
kind [kaind] **1.** □ до́брый, серде́чный, любе́зный; **2.** сорт, разнови́дность *f*; род; pay in ~ плати́ть нату́рой; **~-hearted** мягкосерде́чный, до́брый.
kindle ['kindl] зажига́ть(ся) [заже́чь(ся)]; воспламеня́ть [-ни́ть].
kindling ['kindliŋ] расто́пка.
kind|ly ['kaindli] до́брый; **~ness** [-nis] доброта́; до́брый посту́пок.
kindred ['kindrid] **1.** ро́дственный; **2.** кро́вное родство́.
king [kiŋ] коро́ль *m*; **~dom** ['kiŋdəm] короле́вство; ♀, *zo.* (расти́тельное, живо́тное) ца́рство; **~like** [-laik], **~ly** [-li] короле́вский; вели́чественный.
kink [kiŋk] изги́б; пе́тля; у́зел; *fig.* стра́нность *f*, причу́да.
kin|ship ['kinʃip] родство́; **~sman** ['kinzmən] ро́дственник.
kiss [kis] **1.** поцелу́й; **2.** [по]целова́ть(ся).
kit [kit] ка́дка; ра́нец; ⚔ ли́чное обмундирова́ние; **~-bag** ⚔ вещево́й мешо́к; ⊕ набо́р инструме́нтов.
kitchen ['kitʃin] ку́хня.
kite [kait] (бума́жный) змей.
kitten ['kitn] котёнок.
knack [næk] уда́чный приём; уме́ние, сноро́вка.
knapsack ['næpsæk] ра́нец, рюкза́к.
knave [neiv] моше́нник; вале́т (ка́рта).
knead [ni:d] [с]меси́ть.
knee [ni:] коле́но; **~-cap** *anat.* коле́нная ча́шечка; **~l** [ni:l] [*irr.*]

становиться на колени; стоять на коленях (to перед T).
knell [nel] похоронный звон.
knelt [nelt] *pt.* и *p. pt.* от kneel.
knew [nju:] *pt.* и *p. pt.* от know.
knickknack ['niknæk] безделушка.
knife [naif] 1. (*pl.* knives) нож; 2. резать, колоть ножом.
knight [nait] 1. рыцарь *m*; *chess* конь *m*; 2. возводить в рыцари; **~-errant** странствующий рыцарь *m*; **~hood** ['naithud] рыцарство; **~ly** [-li] рыцарский.
knit [nit] [*irr.*] [с]вязать; связывать [-зать]; срастаться [срастись]; ~ the brows хмурить брови; **~ting** ['nitiŋ] 1. вязание; 2. вязальный.
knives [naivz] *pl.* от knife.
knob [nɔb] шишка; набалдашник; ручка; кнопка; головка.
knock [nɔk] 1. удар, стук; 2. ударять(ся) [ударить(ся)]; [по]стучать(ся); F ~ about рыскать по свету; ~ down сбивать с ног; ⊕ разбирать [-зобрать]; be ~ed down попадать под автомобиль и т. п.; ~ off work прекращать работу; ~ off стряхивать [-хнуть], смахивать [-хнуть]; ~ out выби(ва)ть, выколачивать [выколотить]; *sport.* нокаутировать (*im*)*pf.*; **~-kneed** с вывернутыми внутрь коленями; *fig.* слабый; **~-out** нокаут (*a.* ~ blow).
knoll [noul] холм, бугор.
knot [nɔt] 1. узел; союз, узы *f/pl.*; 2. завязывать узел (или узлом); спут(ыв)ать; **~ty** ['nɔti] узловатый; сучковатый; *fig.* затруднительный.
know [nou] [*irr.*] знать; быть знакомым с (T); узн(ав)ать; [с]уметь; ~ French говорить по-французски; come to ~ узн(ав)ать; **~ing** ['nouiŋ] □ ловкий, хитрый; проницательный; **~ledge** ['nɔlidʒ] знание; to my ~ по моим сведениям; **~n** [noun] *p. pt.* от know; come to be ~ сделаться известным; make ~ объявлять [-вить].
knuckle ['nʌkl] 1. сустав пальца; 2. ~ down, ~ under уступать [-пить]; подчиняться [-ниться].

L

label ['leibl] 1. ярлык, этикетка; 2. наклеивать ярлык на (B); *fig.* относить к категории (as P).
laboratory [lə'bɔrətəri] лаборатория; ~ assistant лабораторный (-ная) ассистент(ка).
laborious [lə'bɔ:riəs] □ трудный; старательный.
labo(u)r ['leibə] 1. труд; работа; родовые муки *f/pl.*; hard ~ принудительный труд; ♀ Exchange биржа труда; 2. рабочий; трудовой; 3. *v/i.* трудиться, работать; прилагать усилия; *v/t.* вырабатывать [выработать]; **~-creation** предоставление работы; **~ed** вымученный; трудный; **~er** [-rə] рабочий.
lace [leis] 1. кружево; шнурок; 2. [за]шнуровать; окаймлять [-мить] (кружевом и т. п.); хлестать [-тнуть], [вы]пороть (*a.* ~ into *a p.*).
lacerate ['læsəreit] разрывать [разорвать], раздирать [разодрать].
lack [læk] 1. недостаток, нужда; отсутствие (P); 2. испытывать недостаток, нужду в (П) he ~s money у него недостаток денег; be ~ing недост(ав)ать: water is ~ing недостаёт воды; **~-lustre** тусклый.
lacquer ['lækə] 1. лак, политура; 2. [от]лакировать.
lad [læd] парень *m*, юноша *m*.
ladder ['lædə] лестница; ⚓ трап.
laden ['leidn] нагружённый; *fig.* обременённый.
lading ['leidiŋ] погрузка; груз, фрахт.
ladle ['leidl] 1. ковш; черпак; половник; 2. вычерпывать [вычерпнуть]; разли(ва)ть (суп) (*a.* ~ out).
lady ['leidi] дама; леди *f. indecl.* (титул); **~like** имеющая манеры леди; **~love** возлюбленная; **~ship** [-ʃip]: your ~ ваша милость *f*.
lag [læg] 1. запаздывать; отст(авать) (*a.* ~ behind); 2. запаздывание; отставание.
laggard ['lægəd] медленный, вялый человек.
lagoon [lə'gu:n] лагуна.
laid [leid] *pt.* и *p. pt.* от lay; **~-up** лежачий (больной).
lain [lein] *p. pt.* от lie[2].
lair [lɛə] логовище, берлога.
laity ['leiiti] миряне *pl.*; профаны *m/pl.*
lake [leik] озеро.
lamb [læm] 1. ягнёнок; 2. [о]ягниться.
lambent ['læmbənt] играющий, колыхающийся (о пламени).
lambkin ['læmkin] ягнёночек.
lame [leim] 1. □ хромой; *fig.* неубедительный; 2. [из]увечить, [ис]калечить.
lament [lə'ment] 1. стенание, жалоба; 2. стенать; оплак(ив)ать; [по]жаловаться; **~able** ['læməntəbl] жалкий; печальный; **~ation** [læmən'teiʃən] жалоба, плач.

lamp [læmp] ла́мпа; фона́рь *m*; *fig.* све́точ, свети́ло.
lampoon [læm'pu:n] **1.** памфле́т, па́сквиль *m*; **2.** писа́ть па́сквиль на (В).
lamp-post фона́рный столб.
lampshade абажу́р.
lance [lɑ:ns] **1.** пи́ка; острога́; **2.** пронза́ть пи́кой; вскрыва́ть ланце́том; **~-corporal** *Brit.* ⚔ ефре́йтор.
land [lænd] **1.** земля́, су́ша; страна́; **~s** *pl.* поме́стья *n/pl.*; **~** register поземе́льная кни́га; **2.** ⚓ выса́живать(ся) [вы́садить(ся)]; выта́скивать на бе́рег; ⚓ пристава́ть к бе́регу, прича́ли(ва)ть; ✈ приземля́ться [-ли́ться]; **~ed** ['lændid] земе́льный; **~holder** владе́лец земе́льного уча́стка.
landing ['lændiŋ] вы́садка; ✈ приземле́ние, поса́дка; **~** ground поса́дочная площа́дка; **~-stage** при́стань *f*.
land|lady хозя́йка (меблиро́ванных ко́мнат); поме́щица; **~lord** поме́щик; хозя́ин (кварти́ры, гости́ницы); **~mark** межево́й знак, ве́ха; ориенти́р; **~-owner** землевладе́лец; **~scape** ['lænskeip] ландша́фт, пейза́ж; **~slide** о́ползень *m*; *pol.* ре́зкое измене́ние (в распределе́нии голосо́в ме́жду па́ртиями).
lane [lein] тропи́нка; переу́лок.
language ['læŋgwidʒ] язы́к (речь); strong **~** си́льные выраже́ния *n/pl.*, брань *f*.
languid ['læŋgwid] □ то́мный.
languish ['læŋgwiʃ] [за]ча́хнуть; тоскова́ть, томи́ться.
languor ['læŋgə] апати́чность *f*; томле́ние; то́мность *f*.
lank ['læŋk] □ высо́кий и худо́й; прямо́й (о волоса́х); **~y** ['læŋki] □ долговя́зый.
lantern ['læntən] фона́рь *m*; **~-slide** диапозити́в.
lap [læp] **1.** пола́; коле́ни *n/pl.*; *fig.* ло́но; ⊕ накла́дка; перекры́тие; *sport.* круг; **2.** перекры́(ва́)ть; [вы́]лака́ть; жа́дно пить; плеска́ться.
lapel [lə'pel] отворо́т (пальто́ и т. п.).
lapse [læps] **1.** ход (вре́мени); оши́бка, опи́ска; (мора́льное) паде́ние; **2.** па́дать [упа́сть] (мора́льно); приня́ться за ста́рое; теря́ть си́лу (о пра́ве).
larceny ['lɑ:sni] ⚖ воровство́.
lard [lɑ:d] **1.** свино́е са́ло; **2.** [на-] шпигова́ть; **~er** ['lɑ:də] кладова́я.
large [lɑ:dʒ] □ большо́й, кру́пный; оби́льный; ще́дрый; at **~** на свобо́де; простра́нно, подро́бно; **~ly** ['lɑ:dʒli] в значи́тельной сте́пени; оби́льно, ще́дро; на широ́кую но́гу, в широ́ком масшта́бе; **~ness** [-nis] большо́й разме́р; широта́ (взгля́дов).
lark [lɑ:k] жа́воронок; *fig.* шу́тка, прока́за, заба́ва.
larva ['lɑ:və] *zo.* личи́нка.
larynx ['læ:riŋks] горта́нь *f*.
lascivious [lə'siviəs] □ похотли́вый.
lash [læʃ] **1.** плеть *f*; бич; реме́нь *m* (часть кнута́); уда́р (пле́тью и т. п.); ресни́ца; **2.** хлеста́ть [-тну́ть]; привя́зывать [-за́ть]; *fig.* бичева́ть.
lass, ~ie [læs, 'læsi] де́вушка, де́вочка.
lassitude ['læsitju:d] уста́лость *f*.
last[1] [lɑ:st] **1.** *adj.* после́дний; про́шлый; кра́йний; **~** but one предпосле́дний; **~** night вчера́ ве́чером; **2.** коне́ц; at **~** наконе́ц; **3.** *adv.* в после́дний раз; по́сле всех; в конце́.
last[2] [~] продолжа́ться [-до́лжиться]; [про]дли́ться; хвата́ть [-ти́ть]; сохраня́ться [-ни́ться].
last[3] [~] коло́дка.
lasting ['lɑ:stiŋ] □ дли́тельный, постоя́нный; про́чный.
lastly ['lɑ:stli] наконе́ц.
latch [lætʃ] **1.** щеко́лда, задви́жка; америка́нский замо́к; **2.** запира́ть [запере́ть].
late [leit] по́здний; запозда́лый; неда́вний; уме́рший, поко́йный; *adv.* по́здно; at (the) **~st** не поздне́е; of **~** за после́днее вре́мя; be **~** опа́здывать [опозда́ть]; **~ly** ['leitli] неда́вно; за после́днее вре́мя.
latent ['leitənt] □ скры́тый; 📖 [лате́нтный.]
lateral ['lætərəl] □ боково́й; побо́чный, втори́чный.
lath [lɑ:θ] **1.** дра́нка; пла́нка; **2.** прибива́ть пла́нки к (Д).
lathe [leið] тока́рный стано́к.
lather ['lɑ:ðə] **1.** мы́льная пе́на; **2.** *v/t.* намы́ли(ва)ть; *v/i.* мы́литься, намы́ли(ва)ться; взмы́ли(ва)ться (о ло́шади).
Latin ['lætin] **1.** лати́нский язы́к; **2.** лати́нский.
latitude ['lætitju:d] *geogr.*, *ast.* широта́; *fig.* свобо́да де́йствий.
latter ['lætə] неда́вний; после́дний; **~ly** [-li] неда́вно; к концу́.
lattice ['lætis] решётка (*a.* **~-work**).
laud [lɔ:d] **1.** хвала́; **2.** [по]хвали́ть; **~able** ['lɔ:dəbl] □ похва́льный.
laugh [lɑ:f] **1.** смех; **2.** смея́ться; **~** at a p. высме́ивать [вы́смеять] (В), смея́ться над (Т); **~able** ['lɑ:fəbl] □ смешно́й; **~ter** ['lɑ:ftə] смех.
launch [lɔ:ntʃ] **1.** барка́с; мото́рная ло́дка; **2.** запуска́ть [-сти́ть]; спуска́ть [-сти́ть] (су́дно на́ воду); *fig.* пуска́ть в ход.
laund|ress ['lɔ:ndris] пра́чка; **~ry** [-ri] пра́чечная; бельё для сти́р[ки.]
laurel ['lɔrəl] ⚘ лавр.

lavatory ['lævətəri] убо́рная.
lavender ['lævində] ⚘ лава́нда.
lavish ['læviʃ] 1. □ ще́дрый, расточи́тельный; 2. расточа́ть [-чи́ть].
law [lɔ:] зако́н; пра́вило; ⚖ пра́во; ⚖ юриспруде́нция; go to ~ нача́ть суде́бный проце́сс; lay down the ~ задава́ть тон; **~-abiding** ⚖ законопослу́шный, соблюда́ющий зако́н; **~-court** суд; **~ful** ['lɔ:ful] □ зако́нный; **~less** ['lɔ:lis] □ беззако́нный.
lawn [lɔ:n] лужа́йка, газо́н; бати́ст (ткань).
law|suit ['lɔ:sju:t] суде́бный проце́сс; **~yer** ['lɔ:jə] юри́ст; адвока́т.
lax [læks] □ вя́лый; ры́хлый; небре́жный; нера́шливый; **~ative** ['læksətiv] слаби́тельное.
lay[1] [lei] 1. *pt.* от lie[2]; 2. све́тский, мирско́й (не духо́вный).
lay[2] [~] 1. положе́ние, направле́ние; 2. [*irr.*] *v/t.* класть [положи́ть]; возлага́ть [-ложи́ть; успока́ивать [-ко́ить]; накры́(ва́)ть (на стол); ~ before a p. предъявля́ть [-ви́ть] (Д); ~ in stocks запаса́ться [запасти́сь] (of T); ~ low опроки́дывать [-и́нуть]; ~ open излага́ть [изложи́ть]; откры́(ва́)ть; ~ out выкла́дывать [вы́ложить]; разби́(ва́)ть (сад, парк и т. п.); ~ up [на]копи́ть; прико́вывать к посте́ли; ~ with обкла́дывать [обложи́ть] (T); *v/i.* [с]нести́сь (о пти́цах); держа́ть пари́ (*a.* ~ a wager).
layer ['leiə] слой, пласт, наслое́ние.
layman ['leimən] миря́нин; неспециали́ст, люби́тель *m.*
lay|off приостано́вка произво́дства; **~-out** план; разби́вка.
lazy ['leizi] □ лени́вый.
lead[1] [led] свине́ц; ⚓ лот; грузи́ло; *typ.* шпо́ны *m/f pl.*
lead[2] [li:d] 1. руково́дство; инициати́ва; *sport.* ли́дерство; *thea.* гла́вная роль *f*; ⚡ вво́дный про́вод; 2. [*irr.*] *v/t.* води́ть, [по-] вести́; приводи́ть [-вести́]; склоня́ть [-ни́ть] (to к Д); руководи́ть (T); ходи́ть [пойти́] с (P *pl.*) (о ка́рточной игре́); ~ on соблазня́ть [-ни́ть]; *v/t.* вести́; быть пе́рвым ~ off нач(ин)а́ть, класть нача́ло.
leaden ['ledn] свинцо́вый (*a. fig.*).
leader ['li:də] руководи́тель(ница *f*) *m*; вождь *m*; передова́я статья́.
leading ['li:diŋ] 1. руководя́щий; веду́щий; передово́й; выдаю́щийся; 2. руково́дство; веде́ние.
leaf [li:f] (*pl.*: leaves) лист (⚘ *pl.*: ли́стья); листва́; **~let** ['li:flit] листо́вка; **~y** ['li:fi] покры́тый ли́стьями.
league [li:g] 1. ли́га, сою́з; 2. вступа́ть в сою́з; объединя́ть(ся) [-ни́ть(ся)].
leak [li:k] 1. течь *f*; уте́чка, 2. дава́ть течь, пропуска́ть во́ду; ~ out проса́чиваться [-сочи́ться]; *fig.* обнару́жи(ва)ться; **~age** ['li:kidʒ] проса́чивание; *fig.* обнару́жение (та́йны и т. п.); **~y** ['li:ki] с те́чью.
lean [li:n] 1. [*irr.*] прислоня́ть(ся) [-ни́ть(ся)] (against к Д); опира́ться [опере́ться] (on на В) (*a. fig.*); наклоня́ть(ся) [-ни́ть(ся)]; 2. то́щий, худо́й.
leant [lent] *pt.* и *p. pt.* от lean.
leap [li:p] 1. прыжо́к, скачо́к; 2. [*a. irr.*] пры́гать [-гнуть], скака́ть [скакну́ть]; **~t** [lept] *pt.* и *p. pt.* от leap; **~-year** високо́сный год.
learn [lə:n] [*a. irr.*] изуча́ть [-чи́ть], [на]учи́ться (Д); ~ from узн(ав)а́ть от (P); **~ed** [lə:nid] □ учёный; **~ing** ['lə:niŋ] уче́ние; учёность *f*, эруди́ция; **~t** [lə:nt] *pt.* и *p. pt.* от learn.
lease [li:s] 1. аре́нда; наём; 2. сдава́ть внаём, в аре́нду; брать внаём, в аре́нду.
least [li:st] *adj.* мале́йший; наиме́ньший; *adv.* ме́нее всего́, в наиме́ньшей сте́пени; at (the) ~ по кра́йней ме́ре.
leather ['leðə] 1. ко́жа; реме́нь *m*; 2. (*a.* ~n) ко́жаный.
leave [li:v] 1. разреше́ние, позволе́ние; о́тпуск; 2. [*irr.*] *v/t.* оставля́ть [-а́вить]; покида́ть [поки́нуть]; предоставля́ть [-а́вить]; *Am.* позволя́ть [-о́лить]; ~ off броса́ть [бро́сить] (де́лать что́-либо); *v/i.* уезжа́ть [уе́хать]; уходи́ть [уйти́].
leaves [li:vz] *pl.* от leaf.
leavings ['li:viŋz] оста́тки *m/pl.*; отбро́сы *m/pl.*
lecture ['lektʃə] 1. докла́д; ле́кция; наставле́ние; 2. *v/i.* чита́ть ле́кции; *v/t.* отчи́тывать [-ита́ть]; **~r** [-rə] докла́дчик (-ица); ле́ктор; *univ.* преподава́тель *m.*
led [led] *pt.* и *p. pt.* от lead.
ledge [ledʒ] вы́ступ, усту́п; риф.
ledger ['ledʒə] † гроссбу́х, гла́вная кни́га.
leech [li:tʃ] *zo.* пия́вка.
leer [liə] 1. взгляд и́скоса; 2. смотре́ть, гляде́ть и́скоса (at на B).
leeway ['li:wei] ⚓ дрейф; *fig.* make up for ~ навёрстывать упу́щенное.
left[1] [left] *pt.* и *p. pt.* от leave; be ~ ост(ав)а́ться.
left[2] [~] 1. ле́вый; 2. ле́вая сторона́; **~-hander** левша́ *m/f.*
leg [leg] нога́ (от бедра́ до ступни́); но́жка (стола́ и т. п.); штани́на.
legacy ['legəsi] насле́дство.
legal ['li:gəl] □ зако́нный, лега́льный; правово́й; **~ize** [-aiz] узако́ни(ва)ть, легализова́ть (*im*)*pf.*
legation [li'geiʃən] дипломати́ческая ми́ссия.
legend ['ledʒənd] леге́нда; на́дпись *f*; **~ary** [-əri] легенда́рный.

leggings ['legiŋz] гама́ши *f/pl.*, кра́ги *f/pl.*
legible ['ledʒəbl] □ разбо́рчивый.
legionary ['li:dʒənəri] легионе́р.
legislat|ion [ledʒis'leiʃən] законода́тельство; **~ive** ['ledʒisleitiv] законода́тельный; **~or** законода́тель *m.*
legitima|cy [li'dʒitiməsi] зако́нность *f*; **~te 1.** [-meit] узако́ни(ва)ть; **2.** [-mit] зако́нный.
leisure ['leʒə] досу́г; at your ~ когда́ вам удо́бно; **~ly** не спеша́, споко́йно.
lemon ['lemən] лимо́н; **~ade** [lemə'neid] лимона́д.
lend [lend] [*irr.*] ода́лживать [одолжи́ть]; дава́ть взаймы́; *fig.* д(ав)а́ть, прид(ав)а́ть.
length [leŋð] длина́; расстоя́ние; продолжи́тельность *f*; отре́з (мате́рии); at ~ подро́бно; go all **~s** пойти́ на всё; **~en** ['leŋθən] удлиня́ть(ся) [-ни́ть(ся)]; **~wise** [-waiz] в длину́; вдоль; **~y** [-i] растя́нутый; многосло́вный.
lenient ['li:niənt] □ мя́гкий; снисходи́тельный.
lens [lenz] ли́нза.
lent[1] [lent] *pt.* и *p. pt.* от lend.
Lent[2] [~] вели́кий пост.
less [les] **1.** (*comp.* от little) ме́ньший; **2.** *adv.* ме́ньше, ме́нее; **3.** *prp.* без (Р).
lessen ['lesn] *v/t.* уменьша́ть [уме́ньши́ть]; недооце́нивать [-ни́ть]; *v/i.* уменьша́ться [уме́ньши́ться].
lesser ['lesə] ме́ньший.
lesson ['lesn] уро́к; *fig.* give a ~ to a p. проучи́ть (В) *pf.*; предостереже́ние.
lest [lest] что́бы не, как бы не.
let [let] [*irr.*] оставля́ть [-а́вить]; сдава́ть внаём; позволя́ть [-во́лить] (Д), пуска́ть [пусти́ть]; ~ alone оста́вить в поко́е; *adv.* не говоря́ уже́ о ... (П); ~ down опуска́ть [-сти́ть]; *fig.* подводи́ть [-вести́]; ~ go выпуска́ть из рук; вы́кинуть из головы́ (мысль); ~ into посвяща́ть [-яти́ть] в (та́йну и т. п.); ~ off стреля́ть [вы́стрелить] из (Р); *fig.* выпа́ливать [вы́палить] (шу́тку); ~ out выпуска́ть [вы́пустить]; ~ up *Am.* ослабе́(ва́)ть.
lethargy ['leθədʒi] летарги́я; апати́чность *f.*
letter ['letə] **1.** бу́ква; ли́тера; письмо́; **~s** *pl.* литерату́ра; учёность *f*; *attr.* пи́сьменный; to the ~ буква́льно; **2.** помеча́ть бу́квами; де́лать на́дпись на (П); **~-case** бума́жник; **~-cover** конве́рт; **~ed** [-d] начи́танный, образо́ванный; **~-file** регистра́тор (па́пка); **~ing** [-riŋ] на́дпись *f*; тисне́ние; **~press** текст в кни́ге (в отли́чие от иллюстра́ций).
lettuce ['letis] сала́т.
level ['levl] **1.** горизонта́льный; ро́вный; одина́ковый, ра́вный, равноме́рный; my ~ best всё, что в мои́х си́лах; **2.** у́ровень *m*; ватерпа́с, нивели́р; *fig.* масшта́б; ~ of the sea у́ровень мо́ря; on the ~ *Am.* че́стно, правди́во; **3.** *v/t.* выра́внивать [вы́ровнять]; ура́внивать [-вня́ть]; сгла́живать [сгла́дить]; сра́внивать, [с]ровня́ть (с землёй); ~ up повыша́ть ура́внивая; *v/i.* ~ at прице́ли(ва)ться в (В); **~-headed** уравнове́шенный.
lever ['li:və] рыча́г, ва́га; **~age** [-ridʒ] подъёмная си́ла.
levity ['leviti] легкомы́слие, ве́тренность *f.*
levy ['levi] **1.** сбор, взима́ние (нало́гов); ⚔ набо́р (ре́крутов); **2.** взима́ть (нало́г); ⚔ наб(и)ра́ть.
lewd [lju:d] □ похотли́вый.
liability [laiə'biliti] отве́тственность *f* (*a.* ⚖); обяза́тельство; задо́лженность *f*; *fig.* подве́рженность *f*, скло́нность *f*; liabilities *pl.* обяза́тельства *n/pl.*; † долги́ *m/pl.*
liable ['laiəbl] □ отве́тственный (за В); обя́занный; подве́рженный; be ~ to быть предрасполо́женным к (Д).
liar ['laiə] лгу́н(ья).
libel ['laibəl] **1.** клевета́; **2.** [на-] клевета́ть на (В).
liberal ['libərəl] **1.** □ ще́дрый, оби́льный; *pol.* либера́льный; **2.** либера́л(ка); **~ity** [libə'ræliti] ще́дрость *f*; либера́льность *f.*
liberat|e ['libəreit] освобожда́ть [-боди́ть]; **~ion** [libə'reiʃən] освобожде́ние; **~or** ['libəreitə] освободи́тель *m.*
libertine ['libətain] распу́тник; вольноду́мец.
liberty [-ti] свобо́да; во́льность *f*; бесцеремо́нность *f*; be at ~ быть свобо́дным.
librar|ian [lai'breəriən] библиоте́карь *m*; **~y** ['laibrəri] библиоте́ка.
lice [lais] *pl.* от louse.
licen|ce, *Am.* **~se** ['laisəns] **1.** разреше́ние, † лице́нзия; во́льность *f*; driving ~ води́тельские права́ *n/pl.*; **2.** разреша́ть [-ши́ть]; дава́ть пра́во, пате́нт на (В).
licentious [lai'senʃəs] □ распу́щенный, безнра́вственный.
lick [lik] **1.** obли́зывание; **2.** лиза́ть [лизну́ть]; обли́зывать [-за́ть]; F [по]би́ть, [по]колоти́ть; ~ the dust быть пове́рженным на́земь; быть уби́тым; ~ into shape привести́ в поря́док.
lid [lid] кры́шка; ве́ко.
lie[1] [lai] **1.** ложь *f*, обма́н; give the ~ облича́ть во лжи; **2.** [со]лга́ть.
lie[2] [~] **1.** положе́ние; направле́ние; **2.** [*irr.*] лежа́ть; быть рас-

положенным, находиться; заключаться; ~ by оставаться без употребления; ~ down ложиться [лечь]; ~ in wait for поджидать (В).
lien ['liən] ⚖ право наложения ареста на имущество должника.
lieu [lju:]: in ~ of вместо (Р).
lieutenant [lef'tenənt, ⚓ and *Am.* lut-] лейтенант; **~-commander** капитан-лейтенант.
life [laif] жизнь *f*; образ жизни; биография; живость *f*; for ~ пожизненный; на всю жизнь; ~ sentence пожизненное заключение; **~-assurance** страхование жизни; **~-boat** спасательная лодка; **~-guard** лейб-гвардия; **~less** □ бездыханный, безжизненный; **~-like** словно живой; **~-long** пожизненный; **~-preserver** спасательный пояс; трость, налитая свинцом; **~-time** вся жизнь *f*, целая жизнь *f*.
lift [lift] **1.** лифт; подъёмная машина; *phys.*, ✈ подъёмная сила; *fig.* возвышение; give a p. a ~ подвозить [-везти] кого-либо; **2.** *v/t.* поднимать [-нять]; возвышать [-высить]; *sl.* [у]красть; *v/i.* возвышаться [-выситься]; подниматься [-няться].
light[1] [lait] **1.** свет, освещение; огонь *m*; *fig.* светило; аспект; will you give me a ~ позвольте прикурить; put a ~ to зажигать [зажечь]; **2.** светлый, ясный; **3.** [*a. irr.*] *v/t.* зажигать [зажечь]; освещать [-етить]; *v/i.* (*mst* ~ up) загораться [-реться]; освещаться [-етиться].
light[2] [~] **1.** *adj.* □ лёгкий, легковесный; незначительный; пустой, легкомысленный; ~ current ⚡ ток слабого напряжения; make ~ of относиться несерьёзно к (Д); **2.** ~ on неожиданно натолкнуться на (В), случайно напасть на (В).
lighten ['laitn] освещать [-етить]; [по]светлеть; сверкать [-кнуть] (о молнии); делать(ся) более лёгким.
lighter ['laitə] зажигалка; запал; ⚓ лихтер.
light|headed легкомысленный; в бреду; **~-hearted** □ беззаботный; весёлый; **~house** маяк.
lighting ['laitiŋ] освещение.
light|-minded легкомысленный; **~ness** лёгкость *f*.
lightning [-niŋ] молния; **~-conductor, ~-rod** громоотвод.
light-weight *sport* легковес.
like [laik] **1.** похожий, подобный; равный; such ~ подобный тому, такой; F feel ~ хотеть (+ *inf.*); what is he ~? что он за человек?; **2.** нечто подобное; **~s** *pl.* склонности *f/pl.*, влечения *n/pl.*; his ~ ему подобные; **3.** любить; [за-] хотеть; how do you ~ London? как вам нравится Лондон? I should ~ to know я хотел бы знать.
like|lihood ['laiklihud] вероятность *f*; **~ly** ['laikli] вероятный; подходящий; he is ~ to die он вероятно умрёт.
like|n ['laikən] уподоблять [-обить]; сравнивать [-нить]; **~ness** ['laiknis] сходство, подобие; **~wise** [-waiz] тоже, также; подобно.
liking ['laikiŋ] расположение (for к Д).
lilac ['lailək] **1.** сирень *f*; **2.** лиловый.
lily ['lili] лилия; ~ **of the valley** ландыш.
limb [lim] член, конечность *f*; ветка.
limber ['limbə] гибкий, мягкий.
lime [laim] известь *f*; ♀ лиметта (разновидность лимона); **~light** свет рампы; *fig.* центр общего внимания.
limit ['limit] граница, предел; off ~s вход воспрещён (надпись); be ~ed to ограничи(ва)ться (Т); **~ation** [limi'teiʃən] ограничение; ⚖ предельный срок; **~ed** ['limitid]: ~ (liability) company общество с ограниченной ответственностью; **~less** ['limitlis] □ безграничный.
limp [limp] **1.** [за]хромать; **2.** прихрамывание, хромота; **3.** мягкий, нетвёрдый; слабый.
limpid ['limpid] прозрачный.
line [lain] **1.** линия (*a.* 🚂, *tel.*); строка; черта, штрих; шнурок; леса (удочки); специальность *f*, занятие; ⚔ развёрнутый строй; ⚔ рубеж; **~s** *pl.* стихи; ~ of conduct образ действия; hard ~s *pl.* неудача; in ~ with в согласии с (Т); stand in ~ *Am.* стоять в очереди; **2.** *v/t.* разлиновывать [-новать]; класть на подкладку; ~ out набрасывать [-росать]; тянуться вдоль (Р).; *v/i.* ~ up выстраиваться [выстроиться] (в ряд).
linea|ge ['liniidʒ] родословная, происхождение; **~ment** [-mənt] черты (лица); очертание (гор); **~r** ['liniə] линейный.
linen ['linin] **1.** полотно; *coll.* бельё; **2.** полотняный.
liner ['lainə] пассажирский пароход или самолёт.
linger ['liŋgə] [по]медлить, [про-] мешкать; ~ over задерживаться [-жаться] на (П).
lingerie ['læ:nʒəri:] † дамское бельё.
lining ['lainiŋ] подкладка; ⊕ обивка, облицовка, футеровка.
link [liŋk] **1.** звено; связь *f*; соеди-

нéние; *fig.* ýзы *f/pl.*; **2.** соединя́ть [-ни́ть]; смыкáть [сомкнýть]; примыкáть [-мкнýть].

linseed ['linsi:d] льнянóе сéмя *n*; ~ oil льнянóе мáсло.

lion ['laiən] лев; **~ess** [-is] льви́ца.

lip [lip] губá; край; F дéрзкая болтовня́; **~-stick** губнáя помáда.

liquefy ['likwifai] превращáть(ся) в жи́дкость.

liquid ['likwid] **1.** жи́дкий; прозрáчный; ⚕ легкó реализýемый; **2.** жи́дкость *f*.

liquidat|e ['likwideit] ликвиди́ровать *im(pf.)*; выплáчивать [вы́платить] (долг); **~ion** [likwi'deiʃən] ликвидáция; вы́плата дóлга.

liquor ['likə] жи́дкость *f*; (*a.* strong ~) спиртнóй напи́ток.

lisp [lisp] **1.** шепеля́вость *f*; лéпет; **2.** шепеля́вить, сюсю́кать.

list [list] **1.** спи́сок, реéстр, пéречень *m*; крен (сýдна); **2.** вноси́ть в спи́сок; составля́ть спи́сок (Р); [на]крени́ться.

listen ['lisn] [по]слýшать; прислýш(ив)аться; (to к Д); ~ in подслýш(ив)ать (to В); слýшать рáдио; **~er, ~er-in** [-ə'rin] слýшатель(ница *f*) *m*.

listless ['listlis] апати́чный.

lit [lit] *pt.и p. pt.* от light¹.

literal ['litərəl] □ буквáльный, дослóвный.

litera|ry ['litərəri] □ литератýрный; **~ture** ['litəritʃə] литератýра.

lithe [laið] ги́бкий.

lithography [li'θɔgrəfi] литогрáфия.

litigation [liti'geiʃən] тя́жба; спор.

litter ['litə] **1.** носи́лки *f/pl.*; подсти́лка (для скотá); помёт (приплóд); беспоря́док; **2.** подстилáть [подостлáть] (солóму и т. п.); [о]щени́ться, [о]пороси́ться и т. п.; разбрáсывать в беспоря́дке.

little ['litl] **1.** *adj.* мáленький, небольшóй; корóткий (о врéмени); a ~ one малы́ш; **2.** *adv.* немнóго, мáло; **3.** пустя́к, мéлочь *f*; a ~ немнóго; ~ by ~ мáло-помáлу, постепéнно; not a ~ немáло.

live 1. [liv] *com.* жить; существовáть; ~ to see дожи́(вá)ть до (Р); ~ down заглáживать [-лáдить]; ~ out пережи́(вá)ть; ~ up to a standard жить соглáсно трéбованиям; **2.** [laiv] живóй; жи́зненный; горя́щий; ⚔ боевóй, дéйствующий (снаря́д); ⚡ под напряжéнием; **~lihood** ['laivlihud] срéдства к жи́зни; **~liness** [-nis] жи́вость *f*; оживлéние; **~ly** ['laivli] живóй; оживлённый.

liver ['livə] *anat.* пéчень *f*; *cook.* печёнка.

livery ['livəri] ливрéя.

live|s [laivz] *pl.* от life; **~-stock** ['laivstɔk] живóй инвентáрь *m*.

livid ['livid] мéртвенно блéдный.

living ['liviŋ] **1.** □ живóй; живýщий, существýющий; **2.** срéдства к жи́зни; жизнь *f*, óбраз жи́зни; **~-room** жилáя кóмната.

lizard ['lizəd] я́щерица.

load [loud] **1.** груз; тя́жесть *f*, брéмя *n*; заря́д; **2.** [на]грузи́ть; отягощáть [-готи́ть]; заряжáть [-яди́ть] (об орýжии); *fig.* обременя́ть [-ни́ть]; **~ing** ['loudiŋ] погрýзка; груз; заря́дка.

loaf [loaf] **1.** (*pl.* loaves) хлеб, каравáй; **2.** бездéльничать; шатáться, слоня́ться без дéла.

loafer ['loufə] бездéльник; бродя́га *m*.

loam [loum] жи́рная гли́на; плодорóдная земля́.

loan [loun] **1.** заём; on ~ взаймы́; **2.** давáть взаймы́, ссужáть [ссуди́ть].

lo(a)th [louθ] □ несклóнный; **~e** [louð] питáть отвращéние к (Д); **~some** ['louðsəm] □ отврати́тельный.

loaves [louvz] *pl.* хлéбы *m/pl.*

lobby ['lɔbi] **1.** прихóжая; *parl.* кулуáры *m/pl.*; *thea.* фойé *n indecl.*; **2.** *part. Am. parl.* пытáться воздéйствовать на члéнов конгрéсса.

lobe [loub] ⚘ *anat.* дóля; мóчка (ýха).

lobster ['lɔbstə] омáр.

local ['loukəl] **1.** □ мéстный; ~ government мéстное самоуправлéние; **2.** мéстное извéстие; (*a.* ~ train) при́городный пóезд; **~ity** [lou'kæliti] мéстность *f*, райóн; окрéстность *f*; **~ize** ['loukəlaiz] локализовáть *(im)pf.*; ограни́чивать распространéние (Р).

locat|e [lou'keit] *v/t.* определя́ть мéсто (Р); располагáть в определённом мéсте; назначáть мéсто для (Р); *Am.* отмечáть грани́цу (Р); be ~d быть располóженным; *v/i.* поселя́ться [-ли́ться]; **~ion** [-ʃən] размещéние; определéние мéста; *Am.* местонахождéние.

lock [lɔk] **1.** замóк; запóр; затóр; шлюз; лóкон; пучóк; **2.** *v/t.* запирáть [заперéть]; ⊕ [за]тормози́ть; ~ in запирáть [заперéть]; ~ up вложи́ть (капитáл) в трýдно реализýемые бумáги; *v/i.* запирáться [заперéться]; замыкáться [замкнýться].

lock|er ['lɔkə] запирáющийся шкáфчик; **~et** ['lɔkit] медальóн; **~-out** локáут; **~smith** слéсарь *m*; **~-up** врéмя закры́тия (школ, магази́нов и т. п.); арестáнтская кáмера.

locomotive ['loukəmoutiv] **1.** дви́жущий(ся); **2.** (и́ли ~ engine) локо-

мотив, паровоз, тепловоз, электровоз.
locust ['loukəst] саранча.
lodestar путеводная звезда.
lodg|e [lɔdʒ] 1. сторожка; (*mst* охотничий) домик; (масонская) ложа; 2. *v/t.* дать помещение (Д); депонировать (*im*)*pf.* (деньги); под(ав)ать (жалобу); *v/i.* квартировать; застревать [-рять] (о пуле и т. п.); **~er** ['lɔdʒə] жилец, жилица; **~ing** ['lɔdʒiŋ] жилище; **~s** *pl.* квартира; комната (снимаемая).
loft [lɔft] чердак; галерея; **~y** ['lɔfti] □ высокомерный; величественный.
log [lɔg] колода; бревно; ⚓ лаг; **~-cabin** бревенчатая хижина; **~gerhead** ['lɔgəhed]: be at **~s** быть в ссоре, ссориться (with с Т).
logic ['lɔdʒik] логика; **~al** ['lɔdʒikəl] □ логический.
loin [lɔin] филейная часть *f*; **~s** *pl.* поясница.
loiter ['lɔitə] слоняться без дела; мешкать.
loll [lɔl] сидеть развалясь; стоять облокотясь.
lone|liness ['lounlinis] одиночество; **~ly** [-li] □, **~some** [-səm] □ одинокий.
long[1] [lɔŋ] 1. долгий срок, долгое время *n*; before ~ вскоре; for ~ надолго; 2. *adj.* длинный; долгий; медленный; in the ~ run в конце концов; be ~ медлить; долго длиться; 3. *adv.* долго; ~ ago давно; so ~! пока (до свидания)!; **~er** дольше; больше.
long[2] [~] страстно желать, жаждать (for Р), тосковать (по Д).
long|-distance *attr.* дальний; *sport* на длинные дистанции; **~evity** [lɔn'dʒeviti] долговечность *f*.
longing ['lɔŋiŋ] 1. □ тоскующий; 2. сильное желание, стремление (к Д), тоска (по Д).
longitude ['lɔndʒitju:d] *geogr.* долгота.
long|shoreman ['lɔŋʃɔ:mən] портовый грузчик; **~sighted** дальнозоркий; **~-suffering** 1. многострадальный; долготерпеливый; 2. долготерпение; **~-term** долгосрочный; **~-winded** □ могущий долго бежать, не задыхаясь; многоречивый.
look [luk] 1. взгляд; выражение (глаз, лица); вид, наружность *f* (*a.* **~s** *pl.*); have a ~ at a th. посмотреть на (В); ознакомляться [-комиться] с (Т); 2. *v/i.* [по-] смотреть (at на В); выглядеть; ~ for искать (В *or* Р); ~ forward to предвкушать [-усить] (В); с радостью ожидать (Р); ~ into исследовать (*im*)*pf.*; ~ out! берегись!, смотри!; ~ (up)on *fig.* смотреть как на (В), считать за (В); *v/t.* ~ disdain смотреть с презрением; ~ over не замечать [-етить]; просматривать [-мотреть]; ~ up [по]искать (в словаре и т. п.); навещать [-естить].
looker-on ['lukər'ɔn] зритель(ница *f*) *m*; наблюдатель(ница *f*) *m*.
looking-glass зеркало.
look-out ['luk'aut] вид (на море и т. п.); виды *m/pl.*, шансы *m/pl.*; that is my ~ это моё дело.
loom [lu:m] 1. ткацкий станок; 2. маячить, неясно вырисовываться.
loop [lu:p] 1. (✈ мёртвая) петля; 2. делать (✈ мёртвую) петлю; закреплять петлей; **~hole** лазейка (*a. fig.*); *fig.* увёртка; ⚔ бойница, амбразура.
loose [lu:s] 1. □ *com.* свободный; неопределённый; просторный; болтающийся, шатающийся; распущенный (о нравах); несвязанный; рыхлый; 2. освобождать [-бодить]; развязывать [-язать]; **~n** ['lu:sn] ослаблять(ся) [-абить (-ся)]; развязывать [-язать]; разрыхлять [-лить]; расшатывать [-шатать].
loot [lu:t] 1. [о]грабить; 2. добыча, награбленное добро.
lop [lɔp] обрубать [-бить] (ветки); **~-sided** кривобокий; накренённый.
loquacious [lo'kweiʃəs] болтливый.
lord [lɔ:d] господин, барин; лорд; повелитель *m*; the ♀ господь *m*; my ~ [mi'lɔ:d] милорд (обращение); the ♀'s prayer отче наш (молитва); the ♀'s Supper тайная вечеря; **~ly** ['lɔ:dli] высокомерный; **~ship** ['lɔ:dʃip]: your ~ ваша светлость *f*.
lorry ['lɔri] 🚗 грузовик; вагон-платформа; подвода; полок.
lose [lu:z] [*irr.*] *v/t.* [по]терять; упускать [-стить]; проигрывать [-рать]; ~ o. s. заблудиться *pf.*; *v/i.* [по]терять; проигрывать(ся) [-рать(ся)]; отст(ав)ать (о часах).
loss [lɔs] потеря, утрата; урон; убыток; проигрыш; at a ~ в затруднении.
lost [lɔst] *pt.* и *p. pt.* от lose; be ~ пропадать [-пасть]; погибать [-гибнуть]; *fig.* растеряться *pf.*
lot [lɔt] жребий; † вещи продаваемые партией на аукционе; участь *f*, доля; *Am.* участок земли; F масса, уйма; draw **~s** бросать жребий; fall to a p.'s ~ выпасть на долю кого-нибудь.
lotion ['louʃən] жидкое косметическое средство, жидкий крем.
lottery ['lɔtəri] лотерея.
loud [laud] □ громкий, звучный; шумный, крикливый; *fig.* кричащий (о красках).
lounge [laundʒ] 1. сидеть разва-

ля́сь; стоя́ть опира́ясь; **2.** пра́здное времяпрепровожде́ние; дива́н; *thea.* фойе́ *n indecl.*
lour ['lauə] смотре́ть угрю́мо; [на]хму́риться.
lous|e [laus] (*pl.*: lice) вошь *f* (*pl.*: вши); **~y** ['lauzi] вши́вый; *fig.* парши́вый.
lout [laut] неуклю́жий, неотёсанный челове́к.
lovable ['lʌvəbl] □ привлека́тельный, ми́лый.
love [lʌv] **1.** любо́вь *f*; влюблённость *f*; предме́т любви́; give (*or* send) one's ~ to a p. передава́ть, посыла́ть приве́т (Д); in ~ with влюблённый в (В); make ~ to уха́живать за (Т); **2.** люби́ть; ~ to do де́лать с удово́льствием; **~-affair** любо́вная интри́га; **~ly** ['lʌvli] прекра́сный, чу́дный; **~r** ['lʌvə] любо́вник; возлю́бленный; люби́тель(ница *f*) *m.*
loving ['lʌviŋ] □ лю́бящий.
low[1] [lou] ни́зкий, невысо́кий; *fig.* сла́бый; ти́хий (о го́лосе); ни́зкий, непристо́йный; ~est bid са́мая ни́зкая цена́, предло́женная на аукцио́не.
low[2] [~] **1.** мыча́ние; **2.** [за]мыча́ть.
lower[1] ['louə] **1.** *compr.* от low[1]; ни́зший; ни́жний; **2.** *v/t.* спуска́ть [-сти́ть] (ло́дку, па́рус); опуска́ть [-сти́ть] (глаза́); снижа́ть [-и́зить]; *v/i.* снижа́ться [-и́зиться] (о це́нах, звуке и т. п.); уменьша́ться [уме́ньшиться].
lower[2] ['lauə] *s.* lour.
low|land ни́зменная ме́стность *f*, ни́зменность *f*; **~liness** ['loulinis] скро́мность *f*; **~ly** скро́мный; **~-necked** с ни́зким вы́резом; **~-spirited** пода́вленный, уны́лый.
loyal ['lɔiəl] □ ве́рный, лоя́льный; **~ty** [-ti] ве́рность *f*, лоя́льность *f*.
lozenge ['lɔzindʒ] табле́тка; ромб.
lubber ['lʌbə] у́валень *m.*
lubric|ant ['lu:brikənt] сма́зка; **~ate** [-keit] сма́з(ыв)ать (маши́ну); **~ation** [lu:bri'keiʃən] сма́зка.
lucid ['lu:sid] □ я́сный; прозра́чный.
luck [lʌk] уда́ча, сча́стье; good ~ счастли́вый слу́чай, уда́ча; bad ~, hard ~, ill ~ неуда́ча; **~ily** ['lʌkili] к сча́стью; **~y** ['lʌki] □ счастли́вый, уда́чный; принося́щий уда́чу.
lucr|ative ['lu:krətiv] □ при́быльный, вы́годный; **~e** ['lu:kə] бары́ш, при́быль *f*.
ludicrous ['lu:dikrəs] □ неле́пый, смешно́й.
lug [lʌg] [по]тащи́ть, [по]волочи́ть.
luggage ['lʌgidʒ] бага́ж; **~-office** 🚂 ка́мера хране́ния багажа́.
lugubrious [lu:gju:briəs] □ мра́чный.
lukewarm ['lu:kwɔ:m] теплова́тый; *fig.* равноду́шный.
lull [lʌl] **1.** убаю́к(ив)ать; усыпля́ть [-пи́ть]; **2.** вре́менное зати́шье; вре́менное успокое́ние.
lullaby ['lʌləbai] колыбе́льная пе́сня.
lumber ['lʌmbə] нену́жные громо́здкие ве́щи *f/pl.*; *Am.* пиломатериа́лы *m/pl.*; **~man** *Am.* лесопромы́шленник; лесору́б.
lumin|ary ['lu:minəri] свети́ло; **~ous** [-əs] □ светя́щийся, све́тлый; *fig.* пролива́ющий свет.
lump [lʌmp] **1.** глы́ба, ком; *fig* чурба́н; кусо́к (са́хара и т. п.); in the ~ о́птом, гурто́м; ~ sum о́бщая су́мма; **2.** *v/t.* брать огу́лом; сме́шивать в ку́чу; *v/i.* свёртываться в ко́мья; **~ish** ['lʌmpiʃ] неуклю́жий; тупоу́мный; **~y** ['lʌmpi] □ комкова́тый.
lunatic ['lu:nətik] **1.** сумасше́дший, безу́мный; **2.** психи́чески больно́й; ~ asylum психиатри́ческая больница.
lunch(eon) ['lʌntʃ(ən)] **1.** второ́й за́втрак; **2.** [по]за́втракать.
lung [lʌŋ] лёгкое; (a pair of) **~s** *pl.* лёгкие *n/pl.*
lunge [lʌndʒ] **1.** вы́пад, уда́р (рапи́рой, шпа́гой) **2.** *v/i.* наноси́ть уда́р (at Д).
lurch [lə:tʃ] **1.** [на]крени́ться; идти́ шата́ясь; **2.** leave a. p. in the ~ поки́нуть кого́-нибудь в беде́, в тяжёлом положе́нии.
lure [ljuə] **1.** прима́нка; *fig.* собла́зн; **2.** прима́нивать [-ни́ть]; *fig.* соблазня́ть [-ни́ть].
lurid ['ljuərid] мра́чный.
lurk [lə:k] скрыва́ться в заса́де; таи́ться.
luscious ['lʌʃəs] □ со́чный; при́торный.
lustr|e ['lʌstə] гля́нец; лю́стра; **~ous** ['lʌstrəs] □ глянцеви́тый.
lute[1] [lu:t, lju:t] ♪ лю́тня.
lute[2] [~] **1.** зама́зка, масти́ка; **2.** зама́зывать зама́зкой.
Lutheran ['lu:θərən] лютера́нский.
luxur|iant [lʌg'zjuəriənt] □ пы́шный; **~ious** [-riəs] □ роско́шный, пы́шный; **~y** ['lʌkʃəri] ро́скошь *f*; предме́т ро́скоши.
lye [lai] щёлок.
lying ['laiiŋ] **1.** *p. pr.* от lie[1] и lie[2]; **2.** *adj.* лжи́вый, ло́жный; лежа́щий; **~-in** [-'in] ро́ды *m/pl.*; ~ hospital роди́льный дом.
lymph [limf] ли́мфа.
lynch [lintʃ] расправля́ться самосу́дом с (Т); **~-law** ['lintʃlɔ:] самосу́д; зако́н Ли́нча.
lynx [links] *zo.* рысь *f*.
lyric ['lirik], **~al** [-ikəl] □ лири́ческий; **~s** *pl.* ли́рика.

M

macaroni [mækə'rouni] макаро́ны *f/pl.*
macaroon [mækə'ru:n] минда́льное пече́нье.
machin|ation [mæki'neiʃən] махина́ция, интри́га; **~s** *pl.* ко́зни *f/pl.*; **~e** [mə'ʃi:n] **1.** маши́на; механи́зм; *attr.* маши́нный; ~ fitter сле́сарь-монта́жник; **2.** подверга́ть маши́нной обрабо́тке; **~e-made** сде́ланный механи́ческим спо́собом; **~ery** [-əri] маши́нное обору́дование; **~ist** [-ist] меха́ник; маши́ни́ст.
mackerel ['mækrəl] *zo.* макре́ль *f.*
mackintosh ['mækintɔʃ] макинто́ш, плащ.
mad [mæd] □ сумасше́дший, поме́шанный; бе́шеный; *fig.* ди́кий; *Am.* взбешённый; go ~ сходи́ть с ума́; drive ~ своди́ть с ума́.
madam ['mædəm] мада́м *f indecl.*; суда́рыня.
mad|cap **1.** сорвиголова́ *m/f*; **2.** сумасбро́дный; **~den** ['mædn] [вз]беси́ть; своди́ть с ума́.
made [meid] *pt.* и *p. pt.* от make.
made-up прихоро́шенный; гото́вый (об оде́жде); ~ of состоя́щий из (P).
mad|house дом умалишённых; **~man** сумасше́дший; **~ness** ['mædnis] сумасше́ствие.
magazine [mægə'zi:n] склад боеприпа́сов; журна́л; ⊕, ⚔ магази́н.
maggot ['mægət] личи́нка.
magic ['mædʒik] **1.** (*a.* **~al** ['mædʒikəl] □) волше́бный; **2.** волшебство́; **~ian** [mə'dʒiʃən] волше́бник.
magistra|cy ['mædʒistrəsi] до́лжность судьи́; магистра́т; **~te** [-trit] мирово́й судья́ *m.*
magnanimous [mæg'næniməs] □ великоду́шный.
magnet ['mægnit] магни́т; **~ic** [mæg'netik] (**~ally**) магни́тный; магнети́ческий.
magni|ficence [mæg'nifisns] великоле́пие; **~ficent** [-snt] великоле́пный; **~fy** ['mægnifai] увели́чи(ва)ть; **~tude** ['mægnitju:d] величина́; разме́ры *m/pl.*; ва́жность *f.*
mahogany [mə'hɔgəni] кра́сное де́рево.
maid [meid] деви́ца, де́вушка; го́рничная, служа́нка; old ~ ста́рая де́ва; ~ of honour фре́йлина; *Am.* подру́жка неве́сты.
maiden ['meidn] **1.** деви́ца, де́вушка; **2.** незаму́жняя; *fig.* де́вственный; *fig.* пе́рвый; ~ name де́вичья фами́лия; **~head**, **~hood** деви́чество; де́вственность *f*; **~ly** [-li] деви́чий.
mail¹ [meil] кольчу́га.
mail² [~] **1.** по́чта; *attr.* почто́вый; **2.** *Am.* сдава́ть на по́чту; посыла́ть по́чтой; **~-bag** почто́вая су́мка; **~man** *Am.* почтальо́н.
maim [meim] [ис]кале́чить, [из-]уве́чить.
main [mein] **1.** гла́вная часть *f*; **~s** *pl.* ⚡ магистра́ль *f*; ⚡ сеть си́льного то́ка; *f.*; in the ~ в основно́м; **2.** гла́вный, основно́й; **~land** ['meinlənd] матери́к; **~ly** ['meinli] гла́вным о́бразом; бо́льшей ча́стью; **~spring** *fig.* гла́вная дви́жущая си́ла; **~stay** *fig.* гла́вная подде́ржка, опо́ра.
maintain [men'tein] подде́рживать [-жа́ть]; утвержда́ть [-рди́ть]; сохраня́ть [-ни́ть].
maintenance ['meintinəns] содержа́ние, сре́дства к существова́нию; подде́ржка; сохране́ние.
maize [meiz] ♀ маис, кукуру́за.
majest|ic [mə'dʒestik] (**~ally**) вели́чественный; **~y** ['mædʒisti] вели́чество; вели́чественность *f.*
major ['meidʒə] **1.** ста́рший, бо́льший; ♪ мажо́рный; ~ key мажо́р; совершенноле́тний; **2.** майо́р; *Am. univ.* гла́вный предме́т; **~-general** генера́л-майо́р; **~ity** [mə'dʒɔriti] совершенноле́тие; большинство́; чин майо́ра.
make [meik] **1.** [*irr.*] *v/t. com.* [с]де́лать, производи́ть [-вести́]; [при-]гото́вить; составля́ть [-а́вить]; заключа́ть [-чи́ть] (мир и т. п.); заставля́ть [-ста́вить]; ~ good исправля́ть [-а́вить; [с]держа́ть (сло́во); do you ~ one of us? вы с на́ми? ~ a port входи́ть в порт, га́вань; ~ sure of удостоверя́ться [-ве́риться] в (П); ~ way уступа́ть доро́гу (for Д); ~ into превраща́ть [-рати́ть], переде́л(ыв)ать в (В); ~ out разбира́ть [разобра́ть]; выпи́сывать [вы́писать]; ~ over переда(ва́)ть; ~ up составля́ть [-а́вить] ула́живать [ула́дить] (о ссо́ре); [за]гримирова́ть; навёрстывать [наверста́ть] (вре́мя); = ~ up for (*v/i.*); ~ up one's mind реша́ться [-ши́ться]; **2.** *v/i.* направля́ться [-а́виться] (for к Д); ~ away with отде́л(ыв)аться от (P); ~ off уезжа́ть [уе́хать]; уходи́ть [уйти́]; ~ up for возмеща́ть [-мести́ть]; **3.** тип, моде́ль *f*; изде́лие; ма́рка (фи́рмы); **~-believe** притво́рство; предло́г; **~-shift** заме́на; подру́чное сре́дство; **~-up** соста́в; грим, косме́тика.
maladjustment ['mæləd'dʒʌstmənt] неуда́чное приспособле́ние.
maladministration ['mæladminis'treiʃən] плохо́е управле́ние.

malady ['mælədi] боле́знь *f.*
malcontent ['mælkəntent] **1.** недово́льный; **2.** недово́льный (челове́к).
male [meil] **1.** мужско́й; **2.** мужчи́на; саме́ц.
malediction [mæli'dikʃən] прокля́тие.
malefactor ['mælifæktə] злоде́й.
malevolen|ce [mə'levələns] злора́дство; недоброжела́тельность *f*; **~t** [-lənt] □ злора́дный; недоброжела́тельный.
malice ['mælis] зло́ба.
malicious [mə'liʃəs] □ зло́бный; **~ness** [-nis] зло́бность *f*.
malign [mə'lain] **1.** □ па́губный, вре́дный; **2.** [на]клевета́ть на (В); злосло́вить; **~ant** [mə'lignənt] □ зловре́дный; зло́бный, зло́стный; ⚕ злока́чественный; **~ity** [-niti] зло́бность *f*; па́губность *f*; ⚕ злока́чественность *f*.
malleable ['mæliəbl] ко́вкий; *fig.* пода́тливый.
mallet ['mælit] колоту́шка.
malnutrition ['mælnju:'triʃən] недоста́точное пита́ние.
malodorous ['mæ'loudərəs] □ злово́нный, воню́чий.
malt [mɔ:lt] со́лод; F пи́во.
maltreat [mæl'tri:t] ду́рно обраща́ться с (T).
mammal ['mæməl] млекопита́ющее (живо́тное).
mammoth ['mæməθ] **1.** грома́дный; **2.** ма́монт.
man [mæn] **1.** (*pl.* **men**) челове́к; мужчи́на *m*; челове́чество; слуга́ *m*; фигу́ра (игры́); **2.** ⚔ ⚓ укомплекто́вывать соста́вом; ~ o. s. мужа́ться.
manage ['mænidʒ] *v/t.* управля́ть (T), заве́довать (T); стоя́ть во главе́ (P); справля́ться [-а́виться] с (T); обходи́ться [обойти́сь] (with (T, without без P); ~ to (+ *inf.*) [с]уме́ть ...; **~able** [-əbl] □ послу́шный, сми́рный; сгово́рчивый; **~ment** [-mənt] управле́ние, заве́дование; уме́ние спра́виться; **~r** [-ə] заве́дующий; дире́ктор; **~ress** [-əres] заве́дующая.
managing ['mænidʒiŋ] руководя́щий; делово́й.
mandat|e ['mændeit] манда́т; нака́з; **~ory** ['mændətəri] манда́тный; повели́тельный.
mane [mein] гри́ва; *fig.* ко́смы *f/pl.*
manful ['mænful] □ му́жественный.
mange [meindʒ] *vet.* чесо́тка.
manger ['meindʒə] я́сли *m/pl.*, корму́шка.
mangle ['mæŋgl] **1.** като́к (для белья́); **2.** [вы́]ката́ть (бельё); *fig.* искажа́ть [искази́ть].
mangy ['meindʒi] чесо́точный; парши́вый.
manhood ['mænhud] возмужа́лость *f*; му́жественность *f*.
mania ['meiniə] ма́ния; **~c** ['meiniæk] **1.** манья́к (-я́чка); **2.** поме́шанный.
manicure ['mænikjuə] **1.** маникю́р; **2.** де́лать маникю́р (Д).
manifest ['mænifest] **1.** □ очеви́дный, я́вный; **2.** ⚓ деклара́ция судово́го гру́за; **3.** *v/t.* обнару́живать; обнаро́довать *pf.*; проявля́ть [-ви́ть]; **~ation** ['mænifes'teiʃən] проявле́ние; манифеста́ция; **~o** [-'festou] манифе́ст.
manifold ['mænifould] □ **1.** разнообра́зный, разноро́дный; **2.** размножа́ть [-о́жить] (докуме́нты).
manipulat|e [mə'nipjuleit] манипули́ровать; **~ion** [mənipju'leiʃən] манипуля́ция; подтасо́вка.
man|kind [mæn'kaind] **1.** челове́чество; **2.** ['mænkaind] мужско́й род; **~ly** [-li] му́жественный.
manner ['mænə] спо́соб, ме́тод; мане́ра; о́браз де́йствий; **~s** *pl.* уме́ние держа́ть себя́; мане́ры *f/pl.*; обы́чаи *m/pl.*; in a ~ в не́которой сте́пени; **~ed** [-d] вы́чурный; **~ly** [-li] ве́жливый.
manoeuvre [mə'nu:və] **1.** манёвр; **2.** проводи́ть манёвры; маневри́ровать.
man-of-war вое́нный кора́бль *f.*
manor ['mænə] поме́стье.
mansion ['mænʃən] большо́й поме́щичий дом.
manslaughter ['mænslɔ:tə] непредумы́шленное уби́йство.
mantel [mæntl] облицо́вка ками́на; **~piece**, **~shelf** по́лка ками́на.
mantle [mæntl] **1.** ма́нтия; *fig.* покро́в; **2.** *v/t.* оку́т(ыв)ать; покры́(ва́)ть; *v/i.* [по]красне́ть.
manual [-juəl] **1.** ручно́й; **2.** руково́дство (кни́га), уче́бник, спра́вочник.
manufactory [mænju'fæktəri] фа́брика.
manufactur|e [mænju'fæktʃə] **1.** произво́дство; изде́лие; **2.** выде́лывать [вы́делать], [с]фабрикова́ть; **~er** [-rə] фабрика́нт; заво́дчик; **~ing** [-riŋ] произво́дство, вы́делка; *attr.* фабри́чный, промы́шленный.
manure [mən'juə] **1.** удобре́ние; **2.** удобря́ть [-о́брить].
many ['meni] **1.** мно́гие, многочи́сленные; мно́го; ~ a ино́й; **2.** мно́жество; a good ~ поря́дочное коли́чество; a great ~ грома́дное коли́чество.
map [mæp] **1.** ка́рта; **2.** наноси́ть на ка́рту; ~ out [с]плани́ровать.
mar [mɑ:] искажа́ть [искази́ть]; [ис]по́ртить.
marble [mɑ:bl] **1.** мра́мор; **2.** распи́сывать под мра́мор.
March[1] [mɑ:tʃ] март.

march² [~] 1. ⚔ марш; похо́д; *fig.* разви́тие (собы́тий); 2. марширова́ть; *fig.* идти́ вперёд (*a.* ~ on).
marchioness ['mɑːʃənis] марки́за (ти́тул).
mare [mɛə] кобы́ла; ~'s nest иллю́зия; газе́тная у́тка.
margin ['mɑːdʒin] край; поля́ *n/pl.* (страни́цы); опу́шка (ле́са); **~al** [-l] □ находя́щийся на краю́; ~ note заме́тка на поля́х страни́цы.
marine [mə'riːn] 1. морско́й; 2. солда́т морско́й пехо́ты; *paint.* морско́й вид (карти́на); **~r** ['mærinə] моря́к, матро́с.
marital [mə'raitl] □ супру́жеский.
maritime ['mæritaim] примо́рский; морско́й.
mark¹ [mɑːk] ма́рка (де́нежная едини́ца).
mark² [~] 1. ме́тка, знак; балл, отме́тка (оце́нка зна́ний); фабри́чная ма́рка; мише́нь *f*; но́рма; a man of ~ выдаю́щийся челове́к; up to the ~ *fig.* на до́лжной высоте́; 2. *v/t.* отмеча́ть [-е́тить]; ста́вить расце́нку на (това́р); ста́вить отме́тку в (П); ~ off отделя́ть [-ли́ть]; ~ out расставля́ть указа́тельные зна́ки на (П); ~ time ⚔ отбива́ть шаг на ме́сте; **~ed** [mɑːkt] □ отме́ченный; заме́тный.
market ['mɑːkit] 1. ры́нок, база́р; ✝ сбыт; in the ~ в прода́же; 2. привози́ть на ры́нок (для прода́жи); покупа́ть на ры́нке; продá(ва́)ть; go ~ing ходи́ть на ры́нок; **~able** [-əbl] □ хо́дкий.
marksman ['mɑːksmən] ме́ткий стрело́к.
marmalade ['mɑːməleid] (апельси́нное) варе́нье; мармела́д.
maroon [mə'ruːn] выса́живать на необита́емом о́строве.
marquee [mɑː'kiː] шатёр.
marquis ['mɑːkwis] марки́з.
marriage ['mæridʒ] брак; сва́дьба; civil ~ гражда́нский брак; **~able** [-əbl] дости́гший (-шая) бра́чного во́зраста; **~-lines** *pl.* свиде́тельство о бра́ке.
married ['mærid] жена́тый; заму́жняя; ~ couple супру́ги *pl.*
marrow ['mærou] ко́стный мозг; *fig.* су́щность *f*; **~y** [-i] костномозгово́й; *fig.* кре́пкий.
marry ['mæri] *v/t.* жени́ть; выдава́ть за́муж; *eccl.* сочета́ть бра́ком; жени́ться на (П), вы́йти за́муж за (В); *v/i.* жени́ться; вы́йти за́муж.
marsh [mɑːʃ] боло́то.
marshal ['mɑːʃəl] 1. ма́ршал; церемонийме́йстер; *Am.* нача́льник поли́ции; 2. выстра́ивать [вы́строить] (войска́ и т. п.); торже́ственно вести́.
marshy ['mɑːʃi] боло́тистый, боло́тный.
mart [mɑːt] ры́нок; аукцио́нный зал.
marten ['mɑːtin] *zo.* куни́ца.
martial ['mɑːʃl] □ вое́нный; вои́нственный; ~ law вое́нное положе́ние.
martyr ['mɑːtə] 1. му́ченик (-ица); 2. за]му́чить (до́ смерти).
marvel ['mɑːvel] 1. ди́во, чу́до; 2. удивля́ться [-ви́ться]; **~lous** ['mɑːvələs] □ изуми́тельный, удиви́тельный.
mascot ['mæskət] талисма́н.
masculine ['mɑːskjulin] мужско́й; му́жественный.
mash [mæʃ] 1. мешани́на; су́сло; 2. размина́ть [-мя́ть]; разда́вливать [-дави́ть]; ~ed potatoes *pl.* карто́фельное пюре́ *n indecl.*
mask [mɑːsk] 1. ма́ска; 2. [за]маскирова́ть; скры(ва́)ть; **~ed** [-t]: ~ ball маскара́д.
mason ['meisn] ка́менщик; масо́н; **~ry** [-ri] ка́менная (и́ли кирпи́чная) кла́дка; масо́нство.
masquerade [mæskə'reid] 1. маскара́д; 2. *fig.* притворя́ться [-ри́ться].
mass [mæs] 1. ма́сса; *eccl.* ме́сса; ~ meeting ма́ссовое собра́ние; 2. собира́ться толпо́й, собира́ть(ся) в ку́чу; ⚔ масси́ровать (*im*)*pf.*
massacre ['mæsəkə] 1. резня́, избие́ние; 2. выреза́ть [вы́резать] (люде́й).
massage ['mæsɑːʒ] 1. масса́ж; 2. масси́ровать.
massive ['mæsiv] масси́вный; кру́пный.
mast [mɑːst] ⚓ ма́чта.
master ['mɑːstə] 1. хозя́ин; господи́н; капита́н (су́дна); учи́тель *m*; ма́стер; *univ.* глава́ колле́джа; ♀ of Arts маги́стр иску́сств; 2. одоле́(ва́)ть; справля́ться [-а́виться] с (Т); овладе́(ва́)ть (Т); владе́ть (языко́м); 3. *attr.* мастерско́й; веду́щий; **~-builder** строи́тель *m*; **~ful** ['mɑːstəful] □ вла́стный; мастерско́й; **~key** отмы́чка; **~ly** [-li] мастерско́й; **~piece** шеде́вр; **~ship** [-ʃip] мастерство́; до́лжность учи́теля; **~y** ['mɑːstəri] госпо́дство, власть *f*; мастерство́.
masticate ['mæstikeit] [с]жева́ть.
mastiff ['mæstif] англи́йский дог.
mat [mæt] 1. цино́вка, рого́жа; 2. *fig.* спу́т(ыв)ать.
match¹ [mætʃ] спи́чка; ⚔ фити́ль *m.*
match² [~] 1. ро́вня́ *m/f*; матч, состяза́ние; вы́годный брак, па́ртия; be a ~ for быть ро́вней (Д); 2. *v/t.* [с]равня́ться с (Т); подбира́ть под па́ру; well ~ed couple хоро́шая па́ра; *v/i.* соотве́тствовать; сочета́ться; to ~ подходя́щий (по цве́ту, то́ну и т. п.); **~less** ['mætʃlis] □ несравне́нный, бесподо́бный.
mate [meit] 1. това́рищ; сожи́тель

(-ница *f*) *m*; супру́г(а); саме́ц (са́мка); ⚓ помо́щник капита́на; 2. сочета́ть(ся) бра́ком.

material [mə'tiəriəl] 1. □ материа́льный; суще́ственный; 2. материа́л (*a. fig.*); мате́рия; вещество́.

matern|al [mə'tə:nl] □ матери́нский; **~ity** [-niti] матери́нство; (*mst* ~ hospital) роди́льный дом.

mathematic|ian [mæθimə'tiʃən] матема́тик; **~s** [-mæ'tiks] (*mst sg.*) матема́тика.

matriculate [mə'trikjuleit] приня́ть и́ли быть при́нятым в университе́т.

matrimon|ial [mætri'mounjəl] □ бра́чный; супру́жеский; **~y** ['mætriməni] супру́жество, брак.

matrix ['meitriks] ма́трица.

matron ['meitrən] заму́жняя же́нщина; эконо́мка; сестра́-хозя́йка (в больни́це).

matter ['mætə] 1. вещество́; материа́л; предме́т; де́ло; по́вод; what's the ~? что случи́лось?, в чём де́ло?; no ~ who ... всё равно́, кто ...; ~ of course само́ собо́й разуме́ющееся де́ло; for that ~ что каса́ется э́того; ~ of fact факт; 2. име́ть значе́ние; it does not ~ ничего́; **~-of-fact** факти́ческий; делово́й.

mattress ['mætris] матра́ц, тюфя́к.

matur|e [mə'tjuə] 1. □ зре́лый; вы́держанный; ✝ подлежа́щий упла́те; 2. созре́(ва́)ть; вполне́ развива́ться; ✝ наступа́ть [-пи́ть] (о сро́ке); **~ity** [-riti] зре́лость *f*; ✝ срок платежа́ по ве́кселю.

maudlin ['mɔ:dlin] □ плакси́вый.

maul [mɔ:l] [рас]терза́ть; *fig.* жесто́ко критикова́ть.

mawkish ['mɔ:kiʃ] □ сентимента́льный; неприя́тный на вкус.

maxim ['mæksim] афори́зм; при́нцип; **~um** [-siməm] 1. ма́ксимум; вы́сшая сте́пень *f*; 2. максима́льный.

May[1] [mei] май.

may[2] [~] [*irr.*] (мода́льный глаго́л без инфинити́ва и прича́стий) [с]мочь; име́ть разреше́ние.

maybe ['meibi:] *Am.* мо́жет быть.

May-day ['meidei] пра́здник пе́рвого ма́я.

mayor [mεə] мэр.

maz|e [meiz] лабири́нт; *fig.* пу́таница; be ~d и́ли in a ~ быть расте́рянным; **~y** ['meizi] □ запу́танный.

me [mi:, mi] ко́свенный паде́ж от I: мне, меня́; F я.

meadow ['medou] луг.

meagre ['mi:gə] худо́й, то́щий; ску́дный.

meal [mi:l] еда́ (за́втрак, обе́д, у́жин); мука́.

mean[1] [mi:n] □ по́длый, ни́зкий; ска́редный.

mean[2] [~] 1. сре́дний; in the ~ time тем вре́менем; 2. середи́на; ~s *pl.* состоя́ние, бога́тство; (*a. sg.*) сре́дство; спо́соб; by all ~s любо́й цено́й; коне́чно; by no ~s нисколько; отню́дь не ...; by ~s of посре́дством (P).

mean[3] [~] [*irr.*] намерева́ться; име́ть в виду́; хоте́ть сказа́ть, подразумева́ть; предназнача́ть [-зна́чить]; зна́чить; ~ well (ill) име́ть до́брые (плохи́е) наме́рения.

meaning ['mi:niŋ] 1. □ зна́чащий; 2. значе́ние; смысл; **~less** [-lis] бессмы́сленный.

meant [ment] *pt.* и *p. pt.* от **mean**.

mean|time, ~while тем вре́менем.

measles ['mi:zlz] *pl.* ⚕ корь *f*.

measure ['meʒə] 1. ме́ра; ме́рка; мероприя́тие; масшта́б; ♪ такт; ~ of capacity ме́ра объёма; beyond ~ непоме́рно; in a great ~ в большо́й сте́пени; made to ~ сде́ланный по ме́рке; 2. измеря́ть [-е́рить]; [с]ме́рить; снима́ть ме́рку с (P); **~less** [-lis] □ неизмери́мый; **~ment** [-mənt] разме́р; измере́ние.

meat [mi:t] мя́со; *fig.* содержа́ние; **~y** ['mi:ti] мяси́стый; *fig.* содержа́тельный.

mechanic [mi'kænik] меха́ник; реме́сленник; **~al** [-nikəl] □ маши́нный; механи́ческий; машина́льный; **~ian** [mekə'niʃən] меха́ник; **~s** (*mst sg.*) меха́ника.

mechanize ['mekənaiz] механизи́ровать (*im*)*pf.*; ⚔ моторизова́ть (*im*)*pf.*

medal [medl] меда́ль *f*.

meddle [medl] (with, in) вме́шиваться [-ша́ться] (в В); **~some** [-səm] □ надое́дливый.

media|l ['mi:diəl] □, **~n** [-ən] сре́дний; среди́нный.

mediat|e ['mi:dieit] посре́дничать; **~ion** [mi:di'eiʃən] посре́дничество; **~or** ['mi:dieitə] посре́дник.

medical ['medikəl] □ медици́нский; враче́бный; ~ certificate больни́чный листо́к; медици́нское свиде́тельство; ~ man вра́ч, ме́дик.

medicin|al [me'disinl] □ лека́рственный; целе́бный; **~e** ['med(i)sin] медици́на; лека́рство.

medi(a)eval [medi'i:vəl] □ средневеко́вый.

mediocre ['mi:dioukə] посре́дственный.

meditat|e ['mediteit] *v/i.* размышля́ть [-ы́слить]; *v/t.* обду́м(ыв)ать (В); **~ion** [medi'teiʃən] размышле́ние; созерца́ние; **~ive** ['mediteitiv] □ созерца́тельный.

Mediterranean [meditə'reinjən] (и́ли ~ Sea) Средизе́мное мо́ре.

medium ['mi:diəm] 1. середи́на; сре́дство, спо́соб; ме́диум (у спири́тов); аге́нт; 2. сре́дний; уме́ренный.

medley ['medli] смесь *f*; ♪ попурри́ *n indecl.*
meek [mi:k] □ кро́ткий, мя́гкий; **~ness** ['miknis] кро́тость *f*, мя́гкость *f*.
meet [mi:t] [*irr.*] *v/t.* встреча́ть [-е́тить]; [по]знако́миться с (Т); удовлетворя́ть [-ри́ть] (тре́бования и т. п.); опла́чивать [-лати́ть] (долги́); go to ~ a p. идти́ навстре́чу (Д); *v/i.* [по]знако́миться; сходи́ться [сойти́сь], соб(и)ра́ться; ~ with испы́тывать [-пыта́ть] (В), подверга́ться [-ве́ргнуться] (Д); **~ing** ['mi:tiŋ] заседа́ние; встре́ча; ми́тинг, собра́ние.
melancholy ['melənkəli] **1.** уны́ние; грусть *f*; **2.** пода́вленный; уны́лый.
mellow ['melou] **1.** □ спе́лый; прия́тный на вкус; **2.** смягча́ть (-ся) [-чи́ть(ся)]; созре́(ва́)ть.
melo|dious [mi'loudjəs] □ мелоди́чный; **~dy** ['melədi] мело́дия.
melon ['melən] ♣ ды́ня.
melt [melt] [рас]та́ять; [рас]плави́ть(ся); *fig.* смягча́ть(ся) [-чи́ть (-ся)].
member ['membə] член (*a. parl.*); **~ship** [-ʃip] чле́нство.
membrane ['membrein] плева́, оболо́чка; перепо́нка; ⊕ мембра́на.
memento [me'mentou] напомина́ние.
memoir ['memwɑ:] мемориа́лная статья́; **~s** *pl.* мемуа́ры *m/pl.*
memorable ['memərəbl] □ незабве́нный.
memorandum [memə'rændəm] заме́тка; *pol.* мемора́ндум.
memorial [mi'mɔ:riəl] **1.** па́мятник; **~s** *pl.* хро́ника; **2.** мемориа́льный.
memorize ['meməraiz] *part. Am.* зау́чивать наизу́сть.
memory ['meməri] па́мять *f*; воспомина́ние.
men [men] (*pl.* от man) лю́ди *m/pl.*; мужчи́ны *m/pl.*
menace ['menəs] **1.** угрожа́ть [-ози́ть], [по]грози́ть (Д; with Т); **2.** угро́за; опа́сность *f*.
mend [mend] **1.** *v/t.* исправля́ть [-а́вить]; [по]чини́ть; ~ one's ways исправля́ться [-а́виться]; *v/i.* улучша́ться [улу́чшиться]; поправля́ться [-а́виться]; **2.** почи́нка; on the ~ на попра́вку (о здоро́вье).
mendacious [men'deiʃəs] □ лжи́вый.
mendicant ['mendikənt] ни́щий; ни́щенствующий мона́х.
menial ['mi:niəl] *contp.* **1.** □ рабо-ле́пный, лаке́йский; **2.** слуга́ *m*, лаке́й.
mental [mentl] □ у́мственный; психи́ческий; ~ arithmetic счёт в уме́; **~ity** [men'tæliti] спосо́бность мышле́ния; склад ума́.
mention ['menʃən] **1.** упомина́ние; **2.** упомина́ть [-мяну́ть] (В *or* о П); don't ~ it! не сто́ит!, не́ за что!
mercantile ['mə:kəntail] торго́вый, комме́рческий.
mercenary ['mə:sinəri] **1.** □ коры́стный; наёмный; **2.** наёмник.
mercer ['mə:sə] торго́вец шёлком и ба́рхатом.
merchandise ['mə:tʃəndaiz] това́р (-ы *pl.*).
merchant ['mə:tʃənt] торго́вец, купе́ц; law ~ торго́вое пра́во; **~man** [-mən] торго́вое су́дно.
merci|ful ['mə:siful] □ милосе́рдный; **~less** [-lis] □ немилосе́рдный.
mercury ['mə:kjuri] ртуть *f*.
mercy [-si] милосе́рдие; сострада́ние; проще́ние; be at a p.'s ~ быть во вла́сти кого́-либо.
mere [miə] □ просто́й; сплошно́й; **~ly** то́лько, про́сто.
meretricious [meri'triʃəs] □ показно́й; мишу́рный; распу́тный.
merge [mə:dʒ] сли́(ва́)ть(ся) (in с Т); **~r** ['mə:dʒə] слия́ние, объедине́ние.
meridian [mə'ridiən] **1.** полу́денный; *fig.* вы́сший; **2.** по́лдень *m*; *geogr.* меридиа́н; *fig.* вы́сшая то́чка; расцве́т.
merit ['merit] **1.** заслу́га; досто́инство; make a ~ of a th. ста́вить что́-либо себе́ в заслу́гу; **2.** заслу́живать [-ужи́ть]; **~orious** [meri'tɔ:riəs] □ досто́йный награ́ды; похва́льный.
mermaid ['mə:meid] руса́лка, ная́да.
merriment ['merimənt] весе́лье.
merry ['meri] □ весёлый, ра́достный; make ~ весели́ться; **~-go-round** карусе́ль *f*; **~-making** весе́лье; пра́здество.
mesh [meʃ] **1.** пе́тля; ~(es *pl.*) се́ти *f/pl.*; ⊕ be in ~ сцепля́ться [-пи́ться]; **2.** *fig.* опу́тывать сетя́ми; запу́таться в сетя́х.
mess[1] [mes] **1.** беспоря́док, пу́таница; неприя́тность *f*; каварда́к; make a ~ of a th. прова́ливать де́ло; **2.** *v/t.* приводи́ть в беспоря́док; *v/i.* F ~ about рабо́тать кое-ка́к.
mess[2] [~] ⚔ о́бщий стол; столо́вая.
message ['mesidʒ] сообще́ние; посла́ние; поруче́ние.
messenger ['mesindʒə] посы́льный; предве́стник.
met [met] *pt.* и *p. pt.* от meet.
metal ['metl] **1.** мета́лл; ще́бень *m*; **2.** мости́ть ще́бнем; **~lic** [mi'tælik] (**~ally**) металли́ческий; **~lurgy** ['metələ:dʒi] металлурги́я.
meteor ['mi:tjə] метео́р; **~ology** [mi:tjə'rɔlədʒi] метеороло́гия.
meter ['mi:tə] счётчик; измери́тель *m*.

method ['meθəd] ме́тод, спо́соб; систе́ма, поря́док; **~ic**, *mst.* **~ical** □ [mi'θɔdik, -dikəl] системати́ческий; методи́ческий, методи́чный.
meticulous [mi'tikjuləs] □ дото́шный; щепети́льный.
metre ['mi:tə] метр.
metric ['metrik] (~ally) метри́ческий; ~ system метри́ческая систе́ма.
metropoli|s [mi'trɔpəlis] столи́ца; метропо́лия; **~tan** [metrə'pɔlitən] столи́чный.
mettle [metl] темпера́мент; пыл.
Mexican ['meksikən] **1.** мексика́нский; **2.** мексика́нец (-нка).
miauw [mi'au] [за]мяу́кать.
mice [mais] *pl.* мы́ши *f/pl.*
Michaelmas ['miklməs] Миха́йлов день *m* (29 сентября́).
micro... ['maikro] микро...
micro|phone ['maikrəfoun] микрофо́н; **~scope** микроско́п.
mid [mid] сре́дний; среди́нный; **~air**: in ~ высоко́ в во́здухе; **~day** **1.** по́лдень *m*; **2.** полу́денный.
middle [midl] **1.** середи́на; **2.** сре́дний; ♀ Ages *pl.* сре́дние века́ *m/pl.*, средневеко́вье; **~-aged** сре́дних лет; **~-class** сре́дняя буржуази́я; **~man** посре́дник; **~-sized** сре́дней величины́; **~-weight** сре́дний ве́с (о бо́ксе); (боксёр) сре́днего ве́са.
middling ['midliŋ] посре́дственный.
middy ['midi] F = midshipman.
midge [midʒ] мо́шка; **~t** ['midʒit] ка́рлик; *attr.* миниатю́рный.
mid|land ['midlənd] вну́тренняя часть страны́; **~most** центра́льный; **~night** по́лночь *f*; **~riff** ['midrif] *anat.* диафра́гма; **~ship** ми́дель *m*; **~shipman** корабе́льный гардемари́н; **~st** [midst] середи́на; среда́; in the ~ of среди́ (Р); in our ~ в на́шей среде́; **~summer** середи́на ле́та; **~way** на полпути́; **~wife** акуше́рка; **~wifery** ['midwifəri] акуше́рство; **~winter** середи́на зимы́.
mien [mi:n] ми́на (выраже́ние лица́).
might [mait] **1.** мощь *f*; могу́щество; with ~ and main изо всех си́л; **2.** *pt.* и *p.pt.* от may; **~y** ['maiti] могу́щественный; грома́дный.
migrat|e [mai'greit] мигри́ровать; **~ion** [-ʃən] мигра́ция; перелёт; **~ory** ['maigrətəri] кочу́ющий; перелётный.
mild [maild] □ мя́гкий; кро́ткий; сла́бый (о напи́тке, табаке́ и т. п.).
mildew ['mildju:] ⚘ ми́лдью *n indecl.*; пле́сень *f.*
mildness ['maildnis] мя́гкость *f*; кро́ткость *f.*; уме́ренность *f.*
mile [mail] ми́ля (= 1609,33 м).
mil(e)age ['mailidʒ] расстоя́ние в ми́лях.
milit|ary ['militəri] **1.** □ вое́нный; во́инский; ♀ Government вое́нное прави́тельство; **2.** вое́нные; вое́нные вла́сти *f/pl.*; **~ia** [mi'liʃə] мили́ция; ополче́ние.
milk [milk] **1.** молоко́; powdered ~ моло́чный порошо́к; whole ~ це́льное молоко́; **2.** [вы́]доить; **~maid** доя́рка; **~man** моло́чник; **~sop** бесхара́ктерный челове́к, «тря́пка»; **~y** ['milki] моло́чный; ♀ Way Мле́чный путь *m.*
mill[1] [mil] **1.** ме́льница; фа́брика, заво́д; **2.** [с]моло́ть; ⊕ [от]фрезерова́ть (*im*)*pf.*
mill[2] [~] *Am.* (= 1/10 *cent*) милл (ты́сячная часть до́ллара).
millepede ['milipi:d] *zo.* многоно́жка.
miller ['milə] ме́льник; ⊕ фре́зерный стано́к; фрезеро́вщик.
millet ['milit] ⚘ про́со.
milliner ['milinə] моди́стка; **~y** [-ri] магази́н да́мских шляп.
million ['miljən] миллио́н; **~aire** [miljə'nɛə] миллионе́р; **~th** ['miljənθ] **1.** миллио́нный; **2.** миллио́нная часть *f.*
mill-pond ме́льничный пруд; **~stone** жёрнов.
milt [milt] моло́ки *f/pl.*
mimic ['mimik] **1.** подража́тельный; **2.** имита́тор; **3.** пароди́ровать (*im*)*pf.*; подража́ть (Д); **~ry** [-ri] подража́ние; *zo.* мимикри́я.
mince [mins] **1.** *v/t.* [из]руби́ть (мя́со); he does not ~ matters он говори́т без обиняко́в; *v/i.* говори́ть жема́нно; **2.** ру́бленое мя́со (*mst* ~d meat); **~meat** фарш из изю́ма, я́блок и т. п.; **~-pie** пиро́г (*s.* mincemeat).
mincing-machine мясору́бка.
mind [maind] **1.** ум, ра́зум; мне́ние; наме́рение; охо́та; па́мять *f*; to my ~ по моему́ мне́нию; out of one's ~ без ума́; change one's ~ переду́м(ыв)ать; bear in ~ по́мнить, не забы́(ва́)ть; have a ~ to име́ть жела́ние (+ *inf.*); have a th. on one's ~ беспоко́иться о чём-либо; make up one's ~ реша́ться [-ши́ться]; **2.** по́мнить; [по]забо́титься о (П); остерега́ться [-ре́чься] (Р); never ~! ничего́!; I don't ~ (it) я ничего́ не име́ю про́тив; would you ~ taking off your hat? бу́дьте добры́, снять шля́пу; **~ful** ['maindful] □ (of) внима́тельный (к Д); забо́тливый.
mine[1] [main] *pred.* мой *m*, моя́ *f*, моё *n*, мои́ *pl.*; **2.** мои́ (родны́е) моя́ семья́.
mine[2] [~] **1.** рудни́к, копь *f*, ша́хта; *fig.* исто́чник; ⚔ ми́на; **2.** добы́(ва́)ть; рыть; производи́ть го́рные рабо́ты; ⚔ мини́ровать

(*im*)*pf*.; подры́(ва́)ть; *fig*. подрыва́ть [подорва́ть]; ~r ['mainə] горня́к, шахтёр.
mineral ['minərəl] **1.** минера́л; ~s *pl*. минера́льные во́ды *f/pl*.; **2.** минера́льный.
mingle ['miŋgl] сме́шивать(ся) [-ша́ть(ся)].
miniature ['minjətʃə] **1.** миниатю́ра; **2.** миниатю́рный.
minim|ize ['minimaiz] доводи́ть до ми́нимума; *fig*. преуменьша́ть [-е́ньши́ть]; ~um [-iməm] **1.** ми́нимум; **2.** минима́льный.
mining ['mainiŋ] го́рная промы́шленность *f*.
minister ['ministə] **1.** мини́стр; посла́нник; свяще́нник; **2.** *v/i*. соверша́ть богослуже́ние; [по-] служи́ть.
ministry ['ministri] служе́ние; министе́рство.
mink [miŋk] *zo*. но́рка.
minor ['mainə] **1.** мла́дший; ме́ньший; второстепе́нный; ♪ мино́рный; A ~ ля мино́р; **2.** несовершенноле́тний; *Am. univ*. второстепе́нный предме́т; ~ity [mai'nɔriti] несовершенноле́тие; меньшинство́.
minstrel ['minstrəl] менестре́ль *m*; ~s *pl*. исполни́тели негритя́нских пе́сен.
mint [mint] ♆ мя́та; моне́та; моне́тный двор; *fig*. «золото́е дно»; a ~ of money больша́я су́мма; **2.** [вы́-, от]чека́нить.
minuet [minju'et] ♪ менуэ́т.
minus ['mainəs] **1.** *prp*. без (Р), ми́нус; **2.** *adj*. отрица́тельный.
minute **1.** [mai'nju:t] □ ме́лкий; незначи́тельный; подро́бный, дета́льный; **2.** ['minit] мину́та; моме́нт; ~s *pl*. протоко́л; ~ness [mai'nju:tnis] ма́лость *f*; то́чность *f*.
mirac|le ['mirəkl] чу́до; ~ulous [mi'rækjuləs] □ чуде́сный.
mirage ['mira:ʒ] мира́ж.
mire ['maiə] **1.** трясина; грязь *f*; **2.** завя́знуть в трясине.
mirror ['mirə] **1.** зе́ркало; **2.** отража́ть [отрази́ть].
mirth [mə:θ] весе́лье, ра́дость *f*; ~ful ['mə:θful] □ весёлый, ра́достный; ~less [-lis] □ безра́достный.
miry ['maiəri] то́пкий.
mis... [mis] *pref*. означа́ет непра́вильность и́ли недоста́ток, напр.: misadvise дать непра́вильный сове́т.
misadventure ['misəd'ventʃə] несча́стье; несча́стный слу́чай.
misanthrop|e ['mizənθroup], ~ist [mi'zænθropist] мизантро́п, человеконенави́стник.
misapply ['misə'plai] злоупотребля́ть [-би́ть] (Т); непра́вильно испо́льзовать.
misapprehend ['misæpri'hend] понима́ть оши́бочно.
misbehave ['misbi'heiv] ду́рно вести́ себя́.
misbelief ['misbi'li:f] заблужде́ние; е́ресь *f*.
miscalculate ['mis'kælkjuleit] ошиба́ться в расчёте; непра́вильно рассчи́тывать.
miscarr|iage ['mis'kæridʒ] неуда́ча; недоста́вка по а́дресу; вы́кидыш, або́рт; ~ of justice суде́бная оши́бка; ~y [-ri] терпе́ть неуда́чу; сде́лать вы́кидыш.
miscellaneous [misi'leinjəs] □ сме́шанный; разносторо́нний.
mischief ['mistʃif] озорство́; прока́зы *f/pl*; вред; зло.
mischievous ['mistʃivəs] □ вре́дный; озорно́й, шаловли́вый.
misconceive ['miskən'si:v] непра́вильно понима́ть.
misconduct **1.** ['mis'kɔndəkt] дурно́е поведе́ние; плохо́е управле́ние; **2.** [-kən'dʌkt] пло́хо управля́ть (Т); ~ o. s. ду́рно вести́ себя́.
misconstrue ['miskən'stru:] непра́вильно истолко́вывать.
miscreant ['miskriənt] негодя́й, злоде́й.
misdeed ['mis'di:d] злодея́ние.
misdemeano(u)r ['misdi'mi:nə] ⚖ суде́бно наказу́емый просту́пок.
misdirect ['misdi'rekt] неве́рно напра́вить; непра́вильно адресова́ть.
miser ['maizə] скупе́ц, скря́га *m/f*.
miserable ['mizərəbl] □ жа́лкий, несча́стный; убо́гий, ску́дный.
miserly ['maizəli] скупо́й.
misery ['mizəri] невзго́да, несча́стье, страда́ние; нищета́.
misfortune [mis'fɔ:tʃən] неуда́ча, несча́стье.
misgiving [mis'giviŋ] опасе́ние, предчу́вствие дурно́го.
misguide [mis'gaid] вводи́ть в заблужде́ние; непра́вильно напра́вить.
mishap ['mishæp] неуда́ча.
misinform ['misin'fɔ:m] непра́вильно информи́ровать.
misinterpret ['misin'tə:prit] неве́рно истолко́вывать.
mislay [mis'lei] [*irr*. (lay)] положи́ть не на ме́сто.
mislead [mis'li:d] [*irr*. (lead)] вводи́ть в заблужде́ние.
mismanage ['mis'mænidʒ] пло́хо управля́ть (Т); [ис]по́ртить.
misplace ['mis'pleis] положи́ть не на ме́сто; *p.pt*. ~d *fig*. неуме́стный.
misprint ['mis'print] **1.** непра́вильно печа́тать; сде́лать опеча́тку; **2.** опеча́тка.
misread ['mis'ri:d] [*irr*. (read)] чита́ть непра́вильно; непра́вильно истолко́вывать.
misrepresent ['misrepri'zent] представля́ть в ло́жном све́те.
miss[1] [mis] мисс, ба́рышня.

miss² [~] 1. про́мах; отсу́тствие; поте́ря; 2. *v/t.* упуска́ть [-сти́ть]; опа́здывать [-да́ть] на (В); прогляде́ть *pf.*, не заме́тить; не заста́ть до́ма; чу́вствовать отсу́тствие (кого́-либо); *v/i.* прома́хиваться [-хну́ться]; не попада́ть в цель.
missile ['misail] мета́тельный снаря́д; раке́та.
missing ['misiŋ] отсутствующий, недостающий; ⚔ бе́з вести пропа́вший; be ~ отсу́тствовать.
mission ['miʃən] ми́ссия, делега́ция; призва́ние; поруче́ние; *eccl.* миссионе́рская де́ятельность *f*; **~ary** ['miʃnəri] миссионе́р.
mis-spell ['mis'spel] [*a. irr.* (spell)] орфографи́чески непра́вильно писа́ть.
mist [mist] лёгкий тума́н; ды́мка.
mistake [mis'teik] 1. [*irr.* (take)] ошиба́ться [-би́ться]; непра́вильно понима́ть; принима́ть [-ня́ть] (for за (В); be **~n** ошиба́ться [-би́ться]; 2. оши́бка; заблужде́ние; **~n** [ən] □ оши́бочный, непра́вильно по́нятый; неуме́стный.
mister ['mistə] ми́стер, господи́н (ста́вится перед фами́лией).
mistletoe ['misltou] ⚘ оме́ла.
mistress ['mistris] хозя́йка до́ма; учи́тельница; мастери́ца; любо́вница; сокращённо: Mrs. ['misiz] ми́ссис, госпожа́ (ста́вится пе́ред фами́лией заму́жней же́нщины).
mistrust ['mis'trʌst] 1. не доверя́ть (Д); 2. недове́рие; **~ful** [-ful] □ недове́рчивый.
misty ['misti] □ тума́нный; нея́сный.
misunderstand ['misʌndə'stænd] [*irr.* (stand)] непра́вильно понима́ть; **~ing** [-iŋ] недоразуме́ние; размо́лвка.
misuse 1. ['mis'ju:z] злоупотребля́ть [-би́ть](Т); ду́рно обраща́ться с (Т); 2. [-'ju:s] злоупотребле́ние.
mite [mait] *zo.* клещ; ле́пта; малю́тка *m/f.*
mitigate ['mitigeit] смягча́ть [-чи́ть]; уменьша́ть [уме́ньши́ть].
mitre ['maitə] ми́тра.
mitten ['mitn] рукави́ца.
mix [miks] [с]меша́ть(ся); переме́шивать [-ша́ть]; враща́ться (в о́бществе); **~ed** переме́шанный, сме́шанный; разноро́дный; ~ up перепу́т(ыв)ать; be **~ed** up with быть заме́шанным в (П); **~ture** ['mikstʃə] смесь *f.*
moan [moun] 1. стон; 2. [за]стона́ть.
moat [mout] крепостно́й ров.
mob [mɔb] 1. толпа́; чернь *f.* 2. [с]толпи́ться; напада́ть толпо́й на (В).
mobil|e ['moubail] подвижно́й; ⚔ моби́льный, подвижно́й; **~ization** [moubilai'zeiʃən] ⚔ мобилиза́ция; **~ize** ['moubilaiz] ⚔ мобилизова́ть (*im*)*pf.*;
moccasin ['mɔkəsin] мокаси́н (о́бувь инде́йцев).
mock [mɔk] 1. насме́шка; 2. подде́льный; мни́мый; 3. *v/t.* осме́ивать [-ея́ть]; *v/i.* ~ at насмеха́ться [-ея́ться] над (Т); **~ery** [-ri] насме́шка.
mode [moud] ме́тод, спо́соб; обы́чай; фо́рма; мо́да.
model [mɔdl] 1. моде́ль *f*; манеке́н; нату́рщик (-ица); *fig.* приме́р, образе́ц; *attr.* образцо́вый, приме́рный; 2. модели́ровать (*im*)*pf.*; [вы́]лепи́ть; оформля́ть [офо́рмить].
moderat|e 1. ['mɔdərit] □ уме́ренный; возде́ржанный; вы́держанный; 2. ['mɔdəreit] умеря́ть [уме́рить]; смягча́ть(ся) [-чи́ть(ся)]; **~ion** [mɔdə'reiʃən] уме́ренность *f*; воздержа́ние.
modern ['mɔdən] совреме́нный; **ize** [-aiz] модернизи́ровать (*im*)*pf.*
modest ['mɔdist] □ скро́мный; благопристо́йный; **~y** [-i] скро́мность *f.*
modi|fication [mɔdifi'keiʃən] видоизмене́ние; модифика́ция; **~fy** ['mɔdifai] видоизменя́ть [-ни́ть]; смягча́ть [-чи́ть].
modulate ['mɔdjuleit] модули́ровать.
moist [mɔist] вла́жный; **~en** ['mɔisn] увлажня́ть(ся) [-ни́ть(ся)]; **~ure** ['mɔistʃə] вла́жность; вла́га.
molar ['moulə] коренно́й зуб.
molasses [mə'læsiz] чёрная па́тока.
mole [moul] *zo.* крот; ро́динка; мол, да́мба.
molecule ['mɔlikju:l] моле́кула.
molest [mo'lest] приста́(ва́)ть к (Д).
mollify ['mɔlifai] успока́ивать [-ко́ить], смягча́ть [-чи́ть].
mollycoddle ['mɔlikɔdl] 1. не́женка *m/f.*; 2. изне́жи(ват)ь.
molten ['moultən] распла́вленный; лито́й.
moment ['moumənt] моме́нт, миг, мгнове́ние; = **~um**; **~ary** [-əri] □ момента́льный; кратковре́менный; **~ous** [mou'mentəs] □ ва́жный; **~um** [-təm] дви́жущая си́ла; *phys.* моме́нт.
monarch ['mɔnək] мона́рх; **~y** ['mɔnəki] мона́рхия.
monastery ['mɔnəstri] монасты́рь *m.*
Monday ['mʌndi] понеде́льник.
monetary ['mʌnitəri] моне́тный; валю́тный; де́нежный.
money ['mʌni] де́ньги *f/pl.*; readv ~ нали́чные де́ньги *f/pl*; **~-box** копи́лка; **~-changer** меня́ла *m*; **~-order** почто́вый де́нежный перево́д.
mongrel ['mʌŋgrəl] 1. *biol.* мети́с;

по́месь *f*; дворня́жка; **2.** нечистокро́вный.
monitor ['mɔnitə] наста́вник; ⚓ монито́р.
monk [mʌŋk] мона́х.
monkey ['mʌŋki] **1.** обезья́на; ⊕ копро́вая ба́ба; **2.** F [по]дура́читься; ~ with вози́ться с (Т); **~-wrench** ⊕ раздвижно́й га́ечный ключ.
monkish ['mʌŋkiʃ] мона́шеский.
mono|cle ['mɔnɔkl] моно́кль *m*; **~gamy** [mɔ'nɔgəmi] единобра́чие; **~logue** [-lɔg] моноло́г; **~polist** [mə'nɔpəlist] монополи́ст; **~polize** [-laiz] монополизи́ровать (*im*)*pf*.; *fig*. присва́ивать себе́ (В); **~poly** [-li] монопо́лия (Р); **~tonous** [mə'nɔtənəs] □ моното́нный; однозву́чный; **~tony** [-təni] моното́нность *f*.
monsoon [mɔn'su:n] муссо́н.
monster ['mɔnstə] чудо́вище; уро́д; *fig*. и́зверг; *attr*. исполи́нский.
monstro|sity [mɔns'trɔsiti] чудо́вищность *f*; уро́дство; **~us** ['mɔnstrəs] □ уро́дливый; чудо́вищный.
month [mʌnθ] ме́сяц; **~ly** ['mʌnθli] **1.** (еже)ме́сячный; **2.** ежеме́сячный журна́л.
monument ['mɔnjumənt] па́мятник; **~al** [mɔnju'mentl] □ монумента́льный.
mood [mu:d] настрое́ние, расположе́ние ду́ха.
moody [mu:di] □ капри́зный; угрю́мый, уны́лый; не в ду́хе.
moon [mu:n] **1.** луна́, ме́сяц; **2.** F проводи́ть вре́мя в мечта́ниях; **~light** лу́нный свет; **~lit** зали́тый лу́нным све́том; **~struck** лунати́ческий.
Moor[1] [muə] марокка́нец (-нка); мавр(ита́нка).
moor[2] [~] торфяни́стая ме́стность, поро́сшая ве́реском.
moor[3] [~] ⚓ прича́ли(ва)ть; **~ings** ['muəriŋz] *pl*. ⚓ шварто́вы *m/pl*.
moot [mu:t] : ~ point спо́рный вопро́с.
mop [mɔp] **1.** шва́бра; **2.** чи́стить шва́брой.
mope [moup] хандри́ть.
moral ['mɔrəl] **1.** □ мора́льный, нра́вственный; **2.** нравоуче́ние, мора́ль *f*; **~s** *pl*. нра́вы *m/pl*.; **~e** [mɔ'ra:l] *part*. ⚔ мора́льное состоя́ние; **~ity** [mə'ræliti] мора́ль *f*, э́тика; **~ize** ['mɔrəlaiz] морализи́ровать.
morass [mə'ræs] боло́то, тряси́на.
morbid ['mɔ:bid] □ боле́зненный.
more [mɔ:] бо́льше; бо́лее; ещё; once ~ ещё раз; so much the ~ тем бо́лее; no ~ бо́льше не ...; **~over** [mɔ:'rouvə] сверх того́, кро́ме того́.
moribund ['mɔribʌnd] умира́ющий.
morning ['mɔ:niŋ] у́тро; tomorrow ~ за́втра у́тром; ~ **coat** визи́тка.
morose [mə'rous] □ угрю́мый.
morphia ['mɔ:fiə], **morphine** ['mɔ:fi:n] мо́рфий.
morsel ['mɔ:səl] кусо́чек.
mortal ['mɔ:tl] **1.** □ сме́ртный; смерте́льный; **2.** сме́ртный, челове́к; **~ity** [mɔ:'tæliti] смерте́льность *f*; сме́ртность *f*.
mortar ['mɔ:tə] сту́пка; известко́вый раство́р; ⚔ морти́ра; миномёт.
mortgage ['mɔ:gidʒ] **1.** закла́д; ипоте́ка; закладна́я; **2.** закла́дывать [заложи́ть]; **~e** [mɔ:gə'dʒi:] кредито́р по закладно́й.
mortgag|er, ~or ['mɔ:gədʒə] должни́к по закладно́й.
morti|fication [mɔ:tifi'keiʃən] умерщвле́ние (пло́ти); униже́ние; **~fy** ['mɔ:tifai] умерщвля́ть [-рти́ть] (плоть); огорча́ть [-чи́ть], унижа́ть [уни́зить].
morti|ce, ~se ['mɔ:tis] ⊕ гнездо́ шипа́.
mortuary ['mɔ:tjuəri] мертве́цкая.
mosaic [mə'zeiik] моза́ика.
moss [mɔs] мох; **~y** мши́стый.
most [moust] **1.** *adj*. □ наибо́льший; **2.** *adv*. бо́льше всего́; ~ beautiful са́мый краси́вый; **3.** наибо́льшее коли́чество; бо́льшая часть *f*; at (the) ~ са́мое бо́льшее, не бо́льше чем; **~ly** ['moustli] по бо́льшей ча́сти; гла́вным о́бразом; ча́ще всего́.
moth [mɔθ] моль *f*; мотылёк; **~-eaten** изъе́денный мо́лью.
mother ['mʌðə] **1.** мать *f*; **2.** относи́ться по-матери́нски к (Д); **~hood** ['mʌðəhud] матери́нство; **~-in-law** [-rinlɔ:] тёща; свекро́вь *f*; **~ly** [-li] матери́нский; **~-of-pearl** [-rev'pə:l] перламу́тровый; **~-tongue** родно́й язы́к.
motif [mou'ti:f] моти́в.
motion ['mouʃən] **1.** движе́ние; ход; *parl*. предложе́ние; **2.** *v/t*. пока́зывать же́стом; *v/i*. кива́ть [кивну́ть] (to на В); **~less** [-lis] неподви́жный; **~-picture** *Am*. кино...; **~s** *pl*. фильм; кино́ *n indecl*.
motive ['moutiv] **1.** дви́жущий; двигательный; **2.** по́вод, моти́в; **3.** побужда́ть [-уди́ть]; мотиви́ровать (*im*)*pf*.; **~less** беспричи́нный.
motley ['mɔtli] разноцве́тный; пёстрый.
motor ['moutə] **1.** дви́гатель *m*, мото́р; = **~-car**; **2.** мото́рный; авто..., автомоби́льный; ~ mechanic, **~fitter** авторемо́нтный меха́ник; **3.** е́хать (*или* везти́) на автомоби́ле; **~-bicycle** мотоци́кл; **~-bus** авто́бус; **~-car** автомоби́ль

m, F маши́на; ~-**cycle** мотоци́кл; ~**ing** ['moutəriŋ] автомоби́льное де́ло; автомоби́льный спорт; ~**ist** [-rist] автомобили́ст(ка); ~**lorry**, *Am.* ~**truck** грузово́й автомоби́ль *m*, грузови́к.
mottled [mɔtld] кра́пчатый.
mould [mould] **1.** садо́вая земля́; по́чва; пле́сень *f*; фо́рма (лите́йная); шабло́н; склад, хара́ктер; **2.** отлива́ть в фо́рму; *fig.* [с]формирова́ть.
moulder ['mouldə] рассыпа́ться [-ы́паться].
moulding ['mouldiŋ] ⚠ карни́з.
mouldy ['mouldi] запле́сневелый.
moult [moult] *zo.* [по]линя́ть.
mound [maund] на́сыпь *f*; холм; курга́н.
mount [maunt] **1.** гора́; ло́шадь под седло́м; **2.** *v/i.* восходи́ть [взойти́]; поднима́ться [-ня́ться]; сади́ться на ло́шадь; *v/t.* устана́вливать [-нови́ть] (ра́дио и т. п.), [с]монти́ровать; вставля́ть в ра́му (в опра́ву).
mountain ['mauntin] **1.** гора́; **2.** го́рный, наго́рный; ~**eer** [maunti'niə] альпини́ст(ка); ~**ous** ['mauntinəs] гори́стый.
mourn [mɔ:n] горева́ть; опла́к(ив)ать; ~**er** ['mɔ:nə] скорбя́щий; ~**ful** ['mɔ:nful] □ тра́урный; ~**ing** ['mɔ:niŋ] тра́ур; плач; *attr.* тра́урный.
mouse [maus] (*pl.* mice) мышь *f*.
m(o)ustache [məs'tɑ:ʃ] усы́ *m/pl*.
mouth [mauθ], *pl.* ~**s** [-z] рот, уста́ *n/pl.*; у́стье (реки́); вход (в га́вань); ~-**organ** губна́я гармо́ника; ~**piece** мундшту́к; *fig.* ру́пор.
move [mu:v] **1.** *v/t. com.* дви́гать [дви́нуть]; передвига́ть [-и́нуть]; тро́гать [тро́нуть]; вноси́ть [внести́] (предложе́ние); *v/i.* дви́гаться [дви́нуться]; переезжа́ть [перее́хать]; разви́(ва́)ться (о собы́тиях); идти́ [пойти́] (о дела́х); *fig.* враща́ться (в о́бществе и т. п.); ~ for a th. предлага́ть [-ложи́ть] что́-либо; ~ in въезжа́ть [въе́хать]; ~ on дви́гаться вперёд; **2.** движе́ние; перее́зд; ход (в игре́); *fig.* шаг; on the ~ на ходу́; make a ~ встать из-за стола́; предпринима́ть что́-либо; ~**ment** ['mu:vmənt] движе́ние; ♪ темп, ритм; ♪ часть *f* (симфо́нии и т. п.); ⊕ ход (маши́ны).
movies ['mu:viz] *s. pl.* кино́ *n indecl.*
moving ['mu:viŋ] □ дви́жущийся; ~ staircase эскала́тор.
mow [mou] [*irr.*] [с]коси́ть; ~**n** [-n] *p. pt.* от mow.
Mr ['mistə] *s.* mister.
Mrs ['misiz] *s.* mistress.
much [mʌtʃ] *adj.* мно́го; *adv.* мно́го, о́чень; I thought as ~ я так и ду́мал; make ~ of высоко́ цени́ть (В); I am not ~ of a dancer я нева́жно танцу́ю.
muck [mʌk] наво́з; *fig.* дрянь *f*.
mucus ['mju:kəs] слизь *f*.
mud [mʌd] грязь *f*; ~**dle** [mʌdl] **1.** *v/t.* запу́тывать [-тать]; [с]пу́тать (*a.* ~ up, together); F опьяня́ть [-ни́ть]; *v/i.* халту́рить; де́йствовать без пла́на; **2.** F пу́таница, неразбери́ха; ~**dy** ['mʌdi] гря́зный; ~-**guard** крыло́.
muff [mʌf] му́фта; ~**etee** [mʌfi'ti:] напу́льсник.
muffin ['mʌfin] сдо́бная бу́лка.
muffle ['mʌfl] глуши́ть, заглуша́ть [-ши́ть] (го́лос и т. п.); заку́т(ыв)ать; ~**r** [-ə] кашне́ *n indecl.*; *mot.* глуши́тель *m*.
mug [mʌg] кру́жка.
muggy ['mʌgi] ду́шный, вла́жный.
mulatto [mju'lætou] мула́т(ка).
mulberry ['mʌlbəri] ту́товое де́рево, шелкови́ца; ту́товая я́года.
mule [mju:l] мул; упря́мый челове́к; ~**teer** [mju:li'tiə] пого́нщик мулов.
mull[1] [mʌl] мусли́н.
mull[2] [~] *Am.*: ~ over обду́м(ыв)ать; размышля́ть [-мы́слить].
mulled [mʌld]: ~ wine глинтве́йн.
multi|farious [mʌlti'fɛəriəs] □ разнообра́зный; ~**form** ['mʌltifɔ:m] многообра́зный; ~**ple** ['mʌltipl] **1.** ⅍ кра́тный; **2.** ⅍ кра́тное число́; многокра́тный; разнообра́зный; ~**plication** [mʌltipli'keiʃən] умноже́ние; увеличе́ние; ~ table табли́ца умноже́ния; ~**plicity** [-'plisiti] многочи́сленность *f*; разнообра́зие; ~**ply** ['mʌltiplai] увели́чи(ва)ть(-ся); ⅍ умножа́ть [-о́жить]; ~**tude** [-tju:d] мно́жество; ма́сса; толпа́; ~**tudinous** [mʌlti'tju:dinəs] многочи́сленный.
mum [mʌm] ти́ше!
mumble [mʌmbl] [про]бормота́ть; с трудо́м жева́ть.
mummery ['mʌməri] пантоми́ма, маскара́д; *contp.* «представле́ние».
mumm|ify ['mʌmifai] мумифици́ровать; (*im*)*pf.*; ~**y** ['mʌmi] му́мия.
mumps [mʌmps] *sg.* ⚕ сви́нка.
mundane ['mʌndein] □ мирско́й; све́тский.
municipal [mju'nisipəl] □ муниципа́льный; ~**ity** [-nisi'pæliti] муниципалите́т.
munificen|ce [mju:'nifisns] ще́дрость *f*; ~**t** [-t] ще́дрый.
murder ['mə:də] **1.** уби́йство; **2.** уби́(ва́)ть; *fig.* прова́ливать [-ли́ть] (пье́су и т. п.); ~**er** [-rə] уби́йца; ~**ess** [-ris] же́нщина-уби́йца; ~**ous** [-rəs] □ уби́йственный.
murky ['mə:ki] □ тёмный; па́смурный.
murmur ['mə:mə] **1.** журча́ние; шо́рох (ли́стьев); ро́пот; **2.** [за]журча́ть; ропта́ть.
murrain ['mʌrin] чума́ (рога́того скота́).

muscle [mʌsl] му́скул, мы́шца; **~ular** ['mʌskjulə] му́скулистый; му́скульный.
Muse[1] [mju:z] му́за.
muse[2] [~] заду́м(ыв)аться (on над [Т).
museum [mju:'ziəm] музе́й.
mushroom ['mʌʃrum] 1. гриб; 2. расплю́щи(ва)ть(ся); *Am.* ~ up расти́ как грибы́.
music ['mju:zik] му́зыка; музыка́льное произведе́ние; но́ты *f/pl.*; set to ~ положи́ть на му́зыку; **~al** ['mju:zikəl] □ музыка́льный; мелоди́чный; ~ box шарма́нка; **~-hall** мю́зик-холл, эстра́дный теа́тр; **~ian** [mju:'ziʃən] музыка́нт (-ша); **~stand** пюпи́тр для нот; **~-stool** табуре́т для роя́ля.
musketry ['mʌskitri] руже́йный ого́нь *m*; стрелко́вая подгото́вка.
muslin ['mʌzlin] мусли́н (ткань).
mussel [mʌsl] ми́дия.
must [mʌst]: I ~ я до́лжен (+ *inf.*); I ~ not мне нельзя́; 2. виногра́дное су́сло; пле́сень *f*.
mustache *Am.* усы́ *m/pl.*
mustard ['mʌstəd] горчи́ца.
muster ['mʌstə] 1. смотр, осмо́тр; ⚔ сбор; 2. проверя́ть [-е́рить].
musty ['mʌsti] за́тхлый.
muta|ble ['mju:təbl] □ изме́нчивый, непостоя́нный; **~tion** [mju:'teiʃən] измене́ние, переме́на.
mute [mju:t] 1. □ немо́й; 2. немо́й; стати́ст; 3. надева́ть сурди́нку на (В).
mutilat|e ['mju:tileit] [из]уве́чить; **~ion** [-'eiʃən] уве́чье.
mutin|eer [mju:ti'niə] мяте́жник; **~ous** ['mju:tinəs] □ мяте́жный; **~y** [-ni] 1. мяте́ж; 2. поднима́ть мяте́ж.
mutter ['mʌtə] 1. бормота́нье; ворча́ние; 2. [про]бормота́ть; [за-] ворча́ть.
mutton [mʌtn] бара́нина; leg of ~ бара́нья но́жка; ~ chop бара́нья котле́та.
mutual ['mju:tjuəl] □ обою́дный, взаи́мный; о́бщий.
muzzle ['mʌzl] 1. мо́рда, ры́ло; ду́ло, жерло́; намо́рдник; 2. надева́ть намо́рдник (Д); *fig.* заста́вить молча́ть.
my [mai, *a.* mi] *pron. poss.* мой *m*, моя́ *f*, моё *n*; мои́ *pl.*
myrtle [mə:tl] ⚘ мирт.
myself [mai'self, mi-] *pron. refl.* 1. себя́, меня́ самого́; -ся, -сь; 2. (для усиле́ния) сам.
myster|ious [mis'tiəriəs] □ таи́нственный; **~y** [-ri] та́йна; таи́нство.
mysti|c ['mistik] (*a.* **~al** [-ikəl] □) мисти́ческий; **~fy** [-tifai] мистифици́ровать (*im*)*pf.*; озада́чи(ва)ть.
myth [miθ] миф; мифи́ческое ли- [цо.

N

nab [næb] *sl.* схвати́ть на ме́сте преступле́ния.
nacre ['neikə] перламу́тр.
nag [næg] F 1. кля́ча; 2. прид(и)ра́ться к (Д).
nail [neil] 1. *anat.* но́готь *m*; гвоздь *m*; 2. заби́(ва́)ть гвоздя́ми, пригвожда́ть [-озди́ть], приби́(ва́)ть; *fig.* прико́вывать [-ова́ть].
naïve [nai'i:v, nɑ:'iv] □, **naive** [neiv] □ наи́вный; безыску́сственный.
naked ['neikid] □ наго́й, го́лый; я́вный; **~ness** [-nis] нагота́; обнажённость *f*.
name [neim] 1. и́мя *n*; фами́лия; назва́ние; of (F by) the ~ of под и́менем (Р), по и́мени (И); in the ~ of во и́мя (Р); от и́мени (Р); call a p. **~s** [об]руга́ть (В); 2. наз(ы)ва́ть; дава́ть и́мя (Д); **~less** ['neimlis] □ безымя́нный; **~ly** [-li] и́менно; **~-plate** доще́чка с фами́лией; **~sake** тёзка *m/f*.
nap [næp] 1. ворс; лёгкий сон; 2. дрема́ть [вздремну́ть].
nape [neip] заты́лок.
napkin ['næpkin] салфе́тка; подгу́зник.
narcotic [nɑ:'kɔtik] 1. (**~ally**) наркоти́ческий; 2. нарко́тик.
narrat|e [næ'reit] расска́зывать [-за́ть]; **~ion** [-ʃən] расска́з; **~ive** ['nærətiv] 1. □ повествова́тельный; 2. расска́з.
narrow ['nærou] 1. □ у́зкий; те́сный; ограни́ченный (об интелле́кте); 2. **~s** *pl.* проли́в; 3. су́живать(ся) [су́зить(ся)]; уменьша́ть (-ся) [уме́ньши́ть(ся)]; ограни́чи(ва)ть; **~-chested** узкогру́дый; **~-minded** □ ограни́ченный, у́зкий; недалёкий; **~ness** [-nis] у́зость *f*.
nasal ['neizəl] □ носово́й; гнуса́вый.
nasty ['nɑ:sti] □ проти́вный; неприя́тный; гря́зный; зло́бный.
natal ['neitl]: ~ day день рожде́ния.
nation ['neiʃən] на́ция.
national ['næʃnl] 1. □ национа́льный, наро́дный; госуда́рственный; 2. сооте́чественник; по́дданный; **~ity** [næʃə'næliti] национа́льность *f*; по́дданство; **~ize** ['næʃnəlaiz] национализи́ровать (*im*)*pf.*; натурализова́ть (*im*)*pf.*
native ['neitiv] 1. □ родно́й; ту-

зе́мный; ~ language родно́й язы́к; 2. уроже́нец (-нка); тузе́мец (-мка).
natural ['nætʃrəl] □ есте́ственный; ~ sciences есте́ственные нау́ки *f/pl.*; **~ist** [-ist] натурали́ст (в иску́сстве); естествоиспыта́тель *m*; **~ize** [-aiz] натурализова́ть (*im*)*pf.*; **~ness** [-nis] есте́ственность *f*.
nature ['neitʃə] приро́да; хара́ктер.
naught [nɔ:t] ничто́; ноль *m*; set at ~ пренебрега́ть [-бре́чь] (Т); **~y** ['nɔ:ti] □ непослу́шный, капри́зный.
nause|a ['nɔ:siə] тошнота́; отвраще́ние; **~ate** [-eit] *v/t.* тошни́ть; it ~s me меня́ тошни́т от э́того; внуша́ть отвраще́ние (Д); be ~d испы́тывать тошноту́; *v/i.* чу́вствовать тошноту́; **~ous** [-əs] □ тошнотво́рный. [хо́дный.]
nautical ['nɔ:tikəl] морско́й; море-
naval ['neivəl] (вое́нно-)морско́й.
nave [neiv] △ неф (це́ркви).
navel ['neivəl] пуп, пупо́к.
naviga|ble ['nævigəbl] □ судохо́дный; **~te** [-geit] *v/i.* управля́ть (су́дном, аэропла́ном); пла́вать (на су́дне); лета́ть (на аэропла́не); *v/t.* управля́ть (су́дном и т. д.); пла́вать по (Д); **~tion** [nævi'geiʃən] морехо́дство; навига́ция; **~tor** ['nævigeitə] мореплаватель *m*; шту́рман.
navy ['neivi] вое́нный флот.
nay [nei] нет; да́же; бо́лее того́.
near [niə] 1. *adj.* бли́зкий; бли́жний; скупо́й; ~ at hand под руко́й; ~ silk полушёлк; 2. *adv.* по́дле; бли́зко, недалеко́; почти́; 3. *prp.* о́коло (Р), у (Р); 4. приближа́ться [-ли́зиться] к (Д); **~by** ['niə'bai] ря́дом; **~ly** ['niəli] почти́; **~ness** [-nis] бли́зость *f*.
neat [ni:t] □ чи́стый, опря́тный; стро́йный; иску́сный; кра́ткий; **~ness** ['ni:tnis] опря́тность *f* и т. д.
nebulous ['nebjuləs] □ о́блачный; тума́нный.
necess|ary ['nesisəri] 1. □ необходи́мый, ну́жный; 2. необходи́мое; **~itate** [ni'sesiteit] де́лать необходи́мым; **~ity** [-ti] необходи́мость *f*, нужда́.
neck [nek] ше́я; го́рлышко (буты́лки и т. п.); вы́рез (в пла́тье); ~ of land переше́ек; ~ and ~ голова́ в го́лову; **~band** во́рот (руба́шки); **~erchief** ['nekətʃif] ше́йный плато́к; **~lace** [-lis] ожере́лье; **~tie** [га́лстук.]
née [nei] урождённая.
need [ni:d] 1. на́добность *f*; потре́бность *f*; нужда́; недоста́ток; be in ~ of нужда́ться в (П); 2. бе́дствовать; нужда́ться в (П); I ~ it мне э́то ну́жно; **~ful** ['ni:dful] □ ну́жный.
needle ['ni:dl] игла́, иго́лка; спи́ца (вяза́льная).
needless ['ni:dlis] □ нену́жный.
needlewoman швея́.
needy ['ni:di] □ нужда́ющийся; бе́дствующий.
nefarious [ni'fɛəriəs] бесче́стный.
negat|ion [ni'geiʃən] отрица́ние; **~ive** ['negətiv] 1. □ отрица́тельный; негати́вный *f*; 2. отрица́ние; *phot.* негати́в; 3. отрица́ть.
neglect [ni'glekt] 1. пренебреже́ние; небре́жность *f*; 2. пренебрега́ть [-бре́чь] (Т); **~ful** [-ful] □ небре́жный.
negligen|ce ['neglidʒəns] небре́жность *f*; **~t** [-t] □ небре́жный.
negotia|te [ni'gouʃieit] вести́ перегово́ры; догова́риваться [-вори́ться] о (П); F преодоле́(ва́)ть; **~tion** [nigouʃi'eiʃən] перегово́ры *m/pl.*; преодоле́ние (затрудне́ний); **~tor** [ni'gouʃieitə] лицо́, веду́щее перегово́ры.
negr|ess ['ni:gris] негритя́нка; **~o** ['ni:grou], *pl.* ~es [-z] негр.
neigh [nei] 1. ржа́ние; 2. [за]ржа́ть.
neighbo(u)r ['neibə] сосе́д(ка); **~hood** [-hud] сосе́дство; **~ing** [-riŋ] сосе́дний, сме́жный.
neither ['neiðə] 1. ни тот, ни друго́й; 2. *adv.* та́кже не; ~ ... nor ... ни ... ни...
nephew ['nevju:] племя́нник.
nerve [nə:v] 1. нерв; му́жество, хладнокро́вие; на́глость *f*; 2. придава́ть си́лы (хра́брости) (Д); **~less** ['nə:vlis] □ беcси́льный, вя́лый.
nervous ['nə:vəs] □ не́рвный; нерво́зный; си́льный; **~ness** [-nis] не́рвность *f*, нерво́зность *f*; эне́ргия.
nest [nest] 1. гнездо́ (*a. fig.*); 2. вить гнездо́; **~le** [nesl] *v/i.* удо́бно устро́иться; приж(им)а́ться (to, on, against к Д); *v/t.* приж(им)а́ть (го́лову).
net[1] [net] 1. сеть *f*; 2. расставля́ть се́ти; пойма́ть и́ли покры́ть се́тью.
net[2] [~] 1. не́тто *adj. indecl.*, чи́стый (вес, дохо́д); 2. приноси́ть (и́ли получа́ть) чи́стого дохо́да.
nettle [netl] 1. ♀ крапи́ва; 2. обжига́ть крапи́вой; *fig.* уязвля́ть [-ви́ть].
network ['netwə:k] плетёнка; сеть *f* (желе́зных доро́г, радиоста́нций и т. п.).
neuter ['nju:tə] 1. *gr.* сре́дний; ♀ беспо́лый; 2. сре́дний род; кастри́рованное живо́тное.
neutral ['nju:trəl] 1. □ нейтра́льный; сре́дний, неопределённый; 2. нейтра́льное госуда́рство; граждани́н нейтра́льного госуда́рства; **~ity** [nju'træliti] нейтралите́т; **~ize** ['nju:trəlaiz] нейтрализова́ть (*im*)*pf*.
never ['nevə] никогда́; совсе́м не; **~more** никогда́ бо́льше; **~theless** [nevəðə'les] тем не ме́нее; несмотря́ на э́то.

new [nju:] но́вый; молодо́й (об овоща́х); све́жий; **~-comer** новоприбы́вший; **~ly** ['nju:li] за́ново, вновь; неда́вно.
news [nju:z] но́вости *f/pl.*, изве́стия *n/pl.*; **~-agent** газе́тчик; **~-boy** газе́тчик-разно́счик; **~-monger** спле́тник (-ица); **~-paper** газе́та; **~-print** газе́тная бума́га; **~-reel** киножурна́л; **~stall**, *Am.* **~-stand** газе́тный кио́ск.
New Year Но́вый год; **~'s Eve** кану́н Но́вого го́да.
next [nekst] **1.** *adj.* сле́дующий; ближа́йший; ~ door to *fig.* чуть (ли) не, почти́; ~ to во́зле (Р); вслед за (Т); **2.** *adv.* пото́м, по́сле; в сле́дующий раз.
nibble [nibl] *v/t.* обгры́з(а́)ть; [о]щипа́ть (*a. v/i.* ~ at); *v/i.* ~ at *fig.* прид(и)ра́ться к (Д).
nice [nais] □ прия́тный, ми́лый, сла́вный; хоро́шенький; то́нкий; привере́дливый; **~ty** ['naisiti] то́чность *f*; разбо́рчивость *f*; *pl.* то́нкости *f/pl.*, дета́ли *f/pl.*
niche [nitʃ] ни́ша.
nick [nik] **1.** зару́бка; in the ~ of time как раз во́-время; **2.** сде́лать зару́бку в (П); поспе́ть во́-время на (В).
nickel [nikl] **1.** *min.* ни́кель *m*; *Am.* моне́та в 5 це́нтов; **2.** [от]никелирова́ть.
nickname ['nikneim] **1.** про́звище; **2.** да(ва́)ть про́звище (Д).
niece [ni:s] племя́нница.
niggard ['nigəd] скупе́ц; **~ly** [-li] скупо́й, ска́редный.
night [nait] ночь *f*, ве́чер; by ~, at ~ но́чью, ве́чером; **~-club** ночно́й клуб; **~fall** су́мерки *f/pl.*; **~-dress**, **~gown** (же́нская) ночна́я соро́чка; **~ingale** ['naitiŋgeil] солове́й; **~ly** ['naitli] ночно́й; *adv.* но́чью; ежено́щно; **~mare** кошма́р; **~-shirt** ночна́я руба́шка.
nil [nil] *particul. sport* ноль *m or* нуль *m*; ничего́.
nimble [nimbl] □ прово́рный, ло́вкий; живо́й.
nimbus ['nimbəs] сия́ние, орео́л.
nine [nain] де́вять; **~pins** *pl.* ке́гли *f/pl.*; **~teen** ['nain'ti:n] девятна́дцать; **~ty** ['nainti] девяно́сто.
ninny ['nini] F простофи́ля *m/f.*
ninth [nainθ] **1.** девя́тый; **2.** девя́тая часть *f*; **~ly** ['nainθli] в-девя́тых.
nip [nip] **1.** щипо́к; уку́с; си́льный моро́з; **2.** щипа́ть [щипну́ть]; прищемля́ть [-ми́ть]; поби́ть моро́зом; ~ in the bud пресека́ть в заро́дыше.
nipper ['nipə] клешня́; (a pair of) **~s** *pl.* щипцы́ *m/pl.*
nipple [nipl] сосо́к.
nitre ['naitə] ⚗ сели́тра.
nitrogen ['naitridʒən] азо́т.
no [nou] **1.** *adj.* никако́й; in ~ time в мгнове́ние о́ка; ~ one никто́; **2.** *adv.* нет; **3.** отрица́ние.
nobility [nou'biliti] дворя́нство; благоро́дство.
noble ['noubl] **1.** □ благоро́дный; зна́тный; **2.** = **~man** титуло́ванное лицо́, дворяни́н; **~ness** ['noublnis] благоро́дство.
nobody ['noubədi] никто́.
nocturnal [nɔk'tə:nl] ночно́й.
nod [nɔd] **1.** кива́ть голово́й; дрема́ть, «клева́ть но́сом»; **2.** киво́к голово́й.
node [noud] ♣ у́зел; ⚕ наро́ст, утолще́ние.
noise [nɔiz] **1.** шум, гам; гро́хот; **2.** ~ abroad разглаша́ть [-ласи́ть]; **~less** ['nɔizlis] □ бесшу́мный.
noisome ['nɔisəm] вре́дный; нездоро́вый; злово́нный.
noisy ['nɔizi] □ шу́мный; шумли́вый; *fig.* крича́щий (о кра́сках).
nomin|al ['nɔminl] □ номина́льный; именно́й; ~ value номина́льная цена́; **~ate** ['nɔmineit] назнача́ть [-зна́чить]; выставля́ть [вы́ставить] (кандида́та); **~ation** [nɔmi'neiʃən] выставле́ние (кандида́та); назначе́ние.
non [nɔn] *prf.* не..., бес..., без...
nonage ['nounidʒ] несовершенноле́тие.
non-alcoholic безалкого́льный.
nonce [nɔns]: for the ~ то́лько для да́нного слу́чая.
non-commissioned ['nɔnkə'miʃənd]: ~ officer сержа́нт, у́нтер-офице́р.
non-committal уклы́нчивый.
non-conductor ⚡ непроводни́к.
nonconformist ['nɔnkən'fɔ:mist] челове́к не подчиня́ющийся о́бщим пра́вилам.
nondescript ['nɔndiskript] неопределённый; неопредели́мый.
none [nʌn] **1.** ничто́, никто́; ни оди́н; никако́й; **2.** нисколько, совсе́м не ...; ~ the less тем не ме́нее.
nonentity [nɔ'nentiti] небытие́; ничто́жество (о челове́ке); фи́кция.
non-existence небытие́.
non-party ['nɔn'pa:ti] беспарти́йный.
non-performance неисполне́ние.
nonplus [-'plʌs] **1.** замеша́тельство; **2.** приводи́ть в замеша́тельство.
non-resident не прожива́ющий в да́нном ме́сте.
nonsens|e ['nɔnsəns] вздор, бессмы́слица; **~ical** [nɔn'sensikəl] □ бессмы́сленный.
non-skid ['nɔn'skid] приспособле́ние про́тив буксова́ния колёс.
non-stop безостано́вочный; ✈ беспоса́дочный.
non-union не состоя́щий чле́ном профсою́за.
noodle ['nu:dl]: **~s** *pl.* лапша́.

nook [nuk] укромный уголок; закоулок.

noon [nu:n] полдень *m* (*a.* ~day, ~tide, ~time).

noose [nu:s] **1.** петля; аркан; **2.** ловить арканом; вешать [повесить].

nor [nɔ:] и не; также не; ни.

norm [nɔ:m] норма; стандарт, образец; **~al** ['nɔ:məl] □ нормальный; **~alize** [-aiz] нормировать (*im*)*pf*.; нормализовать (*im*)*pf*.

north [nɔ:θ] **1.** север; **2.** северный; **3.** *adv.* ~ of к северу от (Р); **~-east** **1.** северо-восток; **2.** северо-восточный (*a.* **~-eastern** [-ən]); **~erly** ['nɔ:ðəli], **~ern** ['nɔ:ðən] северный; **~ward(s)** ['nɔ:θwəd(z)] *adv.* на север; к северу; **~-west** **1.** северо-запад; ⚓ норд-вест; **2.** северо-западный (*a.* **~-western** [-ən]).

nose [nouz] **1.** нос; носик (чайника и т. п.); чутьё; нос (лодки и т. п.); **2.** *v/t.* [по]нюхать; разнюх(ив)ать; **~-dive** ✈ пикировка; **~gay** букет цветов.

nostril ['nɔstril] ноздря.

nosy ['nouzi] F любопытный.

not [nɔt] не.

notable ['noutəbl] **1.** □ достопримечательный; **2.** выдающийся человек.

notary ['noutəri] нотариус (*a.* ~ public).

notation [nou'teiʃən] нотация; запись *f*.

notch [nɔtʃ] **1.** зарубка; зазубрина; **2.** зарубать [-бить]; зазубри(ва)ть.

note [nout] **1.** заметка; запись *f*; примечание; долговая расписка; (дипломатическая) нота; ♪ нота; репутация; внимание; **2.** замечать [-етить]; упоминать [-мянуть]; (*a* ~ down) делать заметки, записывать [-сать]; отмечать [-етить]; **~book** записная книжка; **~d** ['noutid] хорошо известный; **~worthy** достопримечательный.

nothing ['nʌθiŋ] ничто, ничего; for ~ зря, даром; bring (come) to ~ свести (сойти) на нет.

notice ['noutis] **1.** внимание; извещение, уведомление; предупреждение; at short ~ без предупреждения; give ~ предупреждать об увольнении (или об уходе); извещать [-естить]; **2.** замечать [-етить]; обращать внимание на (В); **~able** ['noutisəbl] □ достойный внимания; заметный.

noti|fication [noutifi'keiʃən] извещение, сообщение; объявление; **~fy** ['noutifai] извещать [-естить], уведомлять [уведомить].

notion ['nouʃən] понятие, представление; **~s** *pl. Am.* галантерея.

notorious [nou'tɔ:riəs] □ пресловутый.

notwithstanding [nɔtwiθ'stændiŋ] несмотря на (В), вопреки (Д).

nought [nɔ:t] ничто; ⅍ ноль *m* or нуль *m*.

nourish ['nʌriʃ] питать (*a. fig.*); [на-, по]кормить; *fig.* [вз]лелеять (надежду и т. п.); **~ing** [-iŋ] питательный; **~ment** [-mənt] питание; пища (*a. fig.*).

novel ['nɔvəl] **1.** новый; необычный; **2.** роман; **~ist** [-ist] романист (автор); **~ty** ['nɔvəlti] новинка; новизна.

November [no'vembə] ноябрь *m*.

novice ['nɔvis] начинающий; новичок; *eccl.* послушник (-ица).

now [nau] **1.** теперь, сейчас; тотчас; just ~ только что; ~ and again (или then) от времени до времени; **2.** *cj.* когда, раз.

nowadays ['nauədeiz] в наше время.

nowhere ['nouwɛə] нигде, никуда.

noxious ['nɔkʃəs] □ вредный.

nozzle [nɔzl] носик (чайника и т.п.); ⊕ сопло.

nucle|ar ['nju:kliə] ядерный; ~ pile ядерный реактор; **~us** [-s] ядро.

nude [nju:d] нагой; *paint.* обнажённая фигура.

nudge [nʌdʒ] F **1.** подталкивать локтем; **2.** лёгкий толчок локтем.

nuisance [nju:sns] неприятность *f*; досада; *fig.* надоедливый человек.

null [nʌl] невыразительный; недействительный; ~ and void потерявший законную силу (о договоре); **~ify** ['nʌlifai] аннулировать (*im*)*pf*.; **~ity** [-ti] ничтожность *f*; ничтожество (о человеке); ⚖ недействительность *f*.

numb [nʌm] **1.** онемелый, оцепенелый; окоченелый; **2.** вызывать онемение (или окоченение) (Р).

number ['nʌmbə] **1.** число; номер; **2.** [за]нумеровать; насчитывать; **~less** [-lis] бесчисленный.

numera|l ['nju:mərəl] **1.** имя числительное; цифра; **2.** числовой; **~tion** [nju:mə'reiʃən] исчисление; нумерация.

numerical [nju:'merikəl] □ числовой; цифровой.

numerous ['nju:mərəs] □ многочисленный.

nun [nʌn] монахиня; *zo.* синица-лазоревка.

nunnery ['nʌnəri] женский монастырь *m*.

nuptial ['nʌpʃəl] **1.** брачный, свадебный; **2.** **~s** [-z] *pl.* свадьба.

nurse [nə:s] **1.** кормилица (*mst* wet-~); няня (*a.* ~-maid); сиделка (в больнице); медицинская сестра; at ~ на попечении няни; **2.** кормить, вскармливать грудью; нянчить; ухаживать за (Т); **~ry** ['nə:sri] детская (комната); ⚘ питомник, рассадник; ~ school детский сад.

nurs(e)ling ['nə:sliŋ] питомец (-мица).

nurture ['nə:tʃə] **1.** пита́ние; воспита́ние; **2.** пита́ть; воспи́тывать [-та́ть].
nut [nʌt] opéх; ⊕ га́йка; ~s *pl.* ме́лкий у́голь *m*; **~cracker** щипцы́ для оре́хов; щелку́нчик; **~meg** ['nʌtmeg] муска́тный opéх.
nutri|tion [nju:'triʃən] пита́ние; пи́ща; **~tious** [-ʃəs], **~tive** ['nju:tritiv] □ пита́тельный.
nut|shell оре́ховая скорлупа́; **in a ~** кра́тко, в двух слова́х; **~ty** ['nʌti] име́ющий вкус оре́ха; щегольско́й.
nymph [nimf] ни́мфа.

O

oaf [ouf] дурачо́к; неуклю́жий челове́к.
oak [ouk] дуб.
oar [ɔ:] **1.** весло́; **2.** *poet.* грести́; **~sman** ['ɔ:zmən] гребе́ц.
oasis [ou'eisis] оа́зис.
oat [out] овёс (*mst* ~s *pl.*).
oath [ouθ] кля́тва; ⚔, ⚖ прися́га; руга́тельство.
oatmeal ['outmi:l] овся́нка (крупа́).
obdurate ['ɔbdjurit] □ закосне́лый.
obedien|ce [o'bi:djəns] послуша́ние, повинове́ние; **~t** [-t] □ послу́шный, поко́рный.
obeisance [o'beisəns] ни́зкий покло́н, рева́ранс; почте́ние; **do ~** выража́ть почте́ние.
obesity [ou'bi:siti] ту́чность *f*, полнота́.
obey [o'bei] повинова́ться (*im*)*pf.* (Д); [по]слу́шаться (Р).
obituary [o'bitjuəri] некроло́г; спи́сок уме́рших.
object 1. ['ɔbdʒikt] предме́т, вещь *f*; объе́кт; *fig.* цель *f*, наме́рение; **2.** [əb'dʒekt] не люби́ть, не одобря́ть (Р); возража́ть [-рази́ть] (to про́тив Р).
objection [əb'dʒekʃən] возраже́ние; **~able** [-əbl] □ нежела́тельный; неприя́тный.
objective [ɔb'dʒektiv] **1.** □ объекти́вный; целево́й; **2.** ⚔ объе́кт, цель *f*.
object-lens *opt.* ли́нза объекти́ва.
obligat|ion [ɔbli'geiʃən] обяза́тельство; обя́занность *f*; **~ory** [ɔ'bligətəri] □ обяза́тельный.
oblig|e [ə'blaidʒ] обя́зывать [-за́ть]; принужда́ть [-у́дить]; ~ **a p.** де́лать одолже́ние кому́-либо; **much ~d** о́чень благода́рен (-рна); **~ing** [-iŋ] □ услу́жливый, любе́зный.
oblique [o'bli:k] □ косо́й; око́льный; *gr.* ко́свенный.
obliterate [o'blitəreit] изгла́живать(ся) [-ла́дить(ся)]; вычёркивать [вы́черкнуть].
oblivi|on [o'bliviən] забве́ние; **~ous** [-əs] □ забы́вчивый.
obnoxious [əb'nɔkʃəs] □ неприя́тный, проти́вный, несно́сный.
obscene [ɔb'si:n] □ непристо́йный.
obscur|e [əb'skjuə] **1.** □ тёмный; мра́чный; нея́сный; неизве́стный; непоня́тный; **2.** затемня́ть [-ни́ть]; **~ity** [-riti] мрак, темнота́ и т. д.
obsequies ['ɔbsikwiz] *pl.* погребе́ние.
obsequious [əb'si:kwiəs] □ раболе́пный, подобостра́стный.
observ|able [əb'zə:vəbl] □ заме́тный; **~ance** [-vəns] соблюде́ние (зако́на, обря́да и т. п.); обря́д; **~ant** [-vənt] □ наблюда́тельный; **~ation** [ɔbzə'veiʃən] наблюде́ние; наблюда́тельность *f*; замеча́ние; **~atory** [əb'zə:vətri] обсервато́рия; **~e** [əb'zə:v] *v/t.* наблюда́ть; *fig.* соблюда́ть [-юсти́]; замеча́ть [-е́тить] (В); *v/i.* замеча́ть [-е́тить].
obsess [əb'ses] завладе́(ва́)ть (Т); **~ed by,** *a.* **with** одержи́мый (Т); пресле́дуемый (Т).
obsolete ['ɔbsoli:t, -səl-] устаре́лый.
obstacle ['ɔbstəkl] препя́тствие.
obstinate ['ɔbstinit] □ упря́мый.
obstruct [əb'strʌkt] [по]меша́ть (Д), затрудня́ть [-ни́ть]; загражда́ть [-ради́ть]; **~ion** [əb'strʌkʃən] препя́тствие, поме́ха; загражде́ние; обстру́кция; **~ive** [-tiv] меша́ющий; обструкцио́нный.
obtain [əb'tein] *v/t.* добы́(ва́)ть, доста́(ва́)ть; *v/i.* быть в обы́чае; **~able** [-əbl] † получа́емый; достижи́мый.
obtru|de [əb'tru:d] навя́зывать(ся) [-за́ть(ся)] (on Д); **~sive** [-siv] навя́зчивый.
obtuse [əb'tju:s] □ тупо́й (*a. fig.*).
obviate ['ɔbvieit] избега́ть [-ежа́ть] (Р).
obvious ['ɔbviəs] □ очеви́дный, я́сный.
occasion [ə'keiʒən] **1.** слу́чай; возмо́жность *f*; по́вод; причи́на; F собы́тие; **on the ~ of** по слу́чаю (Р); **2.** причиня́ть [-ни́ть]; дава́ть по́вод к (Д); **~al** [-ʒnl] □ случа́йный; ре́дкий.
Occident ['ɔksidənt] За́пад, стра́ны За́пада; **♀al** [ɔksi'dentl] □ за́падный.
occult [ɔ'kʌlt] □ окку́льтный, та́йный.
occup|ant ['ɔkjupənt] жи́тель(ница *f*) *m*; владе́лец (-лица); **~ation** [ɔkju'peiʃən] завладе́ние; ⚔ оккупа́ция; заня́тие, профе́ссия; **~y** ['ɔkjupai] занима́ть [заня́ть]; завладе́(ва́)ть (Т); оккупи́ровать (*im*)*pf*.
occur [ə'kə:] случа́ться [-чи́ться];

встречáться [-éтиться]; ~ to a p. приходи́ть в гóлову комý; **~rence** [ə'kʌrəns] происшéствие, слýчай.

ocean ['ouʃən] океáн.

o'clock [ə'klɔk]: five ~ пять часóв.

ocul|ar ['ɔkjulə] □ глазнóй; **~ist** ['ɔkjulist] окули́ст, глазнóй врач.

odd [ɔd] □ нечётный; непáрный; ли́шний; разрóзненный; чуднóй, стрáнный; **~ity** ['ɔditi] чудаковáтость *f*; **~s** [ɔdz] *pl.* нерáвенство; разноглáсие; рáзница; преимýщество; гандикáп; шáнсы *m/pl.*; be at ~ with не лáдить с (Т); ~ and ends остáтки *m/pl.*; то да сё.

odious ['oudiəs] ненави́стный; отврати́тельный.

odo(u)r ['oudə] зáпах; аромáт.

of [ov; *mst* əv, v] *prp.* о, об (П); из (Р); от (Р); укáзывает на причи́ну, принадлéжность, объéкт дéйствия, кáчество, истóчник; чáсто соотвéтствует рýсскому роди́тельному падежý; think ~ a th. дýмать о (П); ~ charity из милосéрдия; die ~ умерéть от (Р); cheat ~ обсчи́тывать на (В); the battle ~ Quebec би́тва под Квéбеком; proud ~ гóрдый (Т); the roof ~ the house кры́ша дóма.

off [ɔ:f, ɔf] **1.** *adv.* прочь; far ~ далекó; чáще всегó переводится вербáльными приставками: go ~ уходи́ть [уйти́]; switch ~ выключáть [вы́ключить]; take ~ снимáть [снять]; ~ and on от врéмени до врéмени; be well (badly) ~ быть зажи́точным (бéдным), быть в хорóшем (плохóм) положéнии; **2.** *prp.* с (Р), со (Р) (выражáет удалéние предмéта с повéрхности); от (Р) (укáзывает на расстоя́ние); **3.** *adj.* свобóдный от слýжбы (рабóты); дáльний, бóлее удалённый; боковóй; прáвый (о сторонé).

offal ['ɔfəl] отбрóсы *m/pl.*; пáдаль *f*; **~s** *pl.* потрохá *m/pl.*

offen|ce, *Am.* **~se** [ə'fens] простýпок; оби́да, оскорблéние; наступлéние.

offend [ə'fend] *v/t.* обижáть [оби́деть], оскорбля́ть [-би́ть]; *v/i.* нарушáть [-ýшить] (against В); **~er** оби́дчик; правонаруши́тель(ница *f*) *m*; first ~ престýпник, суди́мый впервы́е.

offensive [ə'fensiv] **1.** □ оскорби́тельный, оби́дный; агресси́вный, наступáтельный; проти́вный; **2.** наступлéние.

offer ['ɔfə] **1.** предложéние; **2.** *v/t.* предлагáть [-ложи́ть]; приноси́ть в жéртву; *v/i.* выражáть готóвность (+ *inf.*); [по]пытáться; явля́ться [яви́ться]; **~ing** [-riŋ] жéртва; предложéние.

off-hand ['ɔ:f'hænd] *adv.* F бесцеремóнно; без подготóвки.

office ['ɔfis] слýжба, дóлжность *f*; контóра, канцеля́рия; *eccl.* богослужéние; ♀ министéрство; **~r** ['ɔfisə] дóлжностное лицó, чинóвник (-ица); ⚔ офицéр.

official [ə'fiʃəl] **1.** □ официáльный; служéбный; ~ channel служéбный поря́док; ~ hours *pl.* служéбные часы́ *m/pl.*; **2.** служéбное лицó, слýжащий; чинóвник.

officiate [ə'fiʃieit] исполня́ть обя́занности (as Р).

officious [ə'fiʃəs] □ назóйливый; официóзный.

off|set возмещáть [-ести́ть]; **~shoot** побéг; óтпрыск; ответвлéние; **~spring** óтпрыск, потóмок.

often ['ɔ:fn; *a.* 'ɔ:ftən] чáсто, мнóго раз.

ogle [ougl] **1.** стрóить глáзки (Д); **2.** влюблённый взгля́д.

ogre ['ougə] людоéд.

oil [ɔil] **1.** мáсло (расти́тельное, минерáльное); нефть *f*; **2.** смáз(ыв)ать; *fig.* подмáз(ыв)ать; **~cloth** клеёнка; **~skin** дождеви́к; **~y** ['ɔili] □ масляни́стый, мáсляный; *fig.* елéйный.

ointment ['ɔintmənt] мазь *f*.

O. K., okay ['ou'kei] F **1.** *pred.* всё в поря́дке, хорошó; **2.** *int.* хорошó!, лáдно!, есть!

old [ould] *com.* стáрый; (in times) of ~ в старинý; ~ age стáрость *f*; **~-fashioned** ['ould'fæʃənd] старомóдный; **~ish** ['ouldiʃ] старовáтый.

olfactory [ɔl'fæktəri] *anat.* обоня́тельный.

olive ['ɔliv] ♀ оли́ва; оли́вковый [цвет.]

ominous ['ɔminəs] □ злovéщий.

omission [o'miʃən] упущéние; прóпуск.

omit [o'mit] пропускáть [-сти́ть]; упускáть [-сти́ть].

omnipoten|ce [ɔm'nipotəns] всемогýщество; **~t** [-tənt] □ всемогýщий.

on [ɔn] **1.** *prp. mst* на (П *or* В); ~ the wall на стенé; march ~ London марш на Лóндон; ~ good authority из достовéрного истóчника; ~ the 1st of April пéрвого апрéля; ~ his arrival по егó прибы́тии; talk ~ a subject говори́ть на тéму; ~ this model по э́тому образцý; ~ hearing it услы́шав э́то; **2.** *adv.* дáльше; вперёд; дáлее; keep one's hat ~ оставáться в шля́пе; have a coat ~ быть в пальтó; and so ~ и так дáлее (и т. д.); be ~ быть пýщенным в ход, вклю́чённым (и т. п.).

once [wʌns] **1.** *adv.* раз; нéкогда, когдá-то; at ~ сейчáс же; ~ for all раз навсегдá; ~ in a while и́зредка; this ~ на э́тот раз; **2.** *cj.* как тóлько.

one [wʌn] **1.** оди́н; еди́ный; еди́нственный; какóй-то; ~ day однáжды; ~ never knows никогдá не знáешь; **2.** (числó) оди́н; едини́ца;

the little ~s малыши́ *m/pl.*; ~ another друг дру́га; at ~ заодно́, сра́зу; ~ by ~ оди́н за други́м; I for ~ я со свое́й стороны́.
onerous ['ɔnərəs] □ обремени́тельный.
one|self [wʌn'self] *pron. refl.* -ся, -сь, (самого́) себя́; **~-sided** □ односторо́нний; **~-way**: ~ street у́лица односторо́ннего движе́ния.
onion ['ʌnjən] лук, лу́ковица.
onlooker ['ɔnlukə] зри́тель(ница *f*) *m*; наблюда́тель(ница *f*) *m*.
only ['ounli] **1.** *adj.* еди́нственный; **2.** *adv.* еди́нственно; то́лько; исключи́тельно; ~ yesterday то́лько вчера́; **3.** *cj.* но; ~ that ... е́сли бы не то, что ...
onset ['ɔnset], **onslaught** [-slɔːt] ата́ка, на́тиск, нападе́ние.
onward ['ɔnwəd] **1.** *adj.* продвига́ющийся вперёд; **2.** *adv.* вперёд; впереди́.
ooze [uːz] **1.** ил, ти́на; **2.** проса́чиваться [-сочи́ться]; ~ away убы́(ва́)ть.
opaque [ou'peik] □ непрозра́чный.
open ['oupən] **1.** □ *com.* откры́тый; открове́нный; я́вный; ~ to досту́пный (Д); in the ~ air на откры́том во́здухе; **2.** bring into the ~ обнару́жи(ва)ть; **3.** *v/t.* откры́(ва́)ть; нач(ин)а́ть; *v/i.* откры́(ва́)ться; нач(ин)а́ться; ~ into откры́(ва́)ться в (В) (о две́ри); ~ on to выходи́ть на *or* в (В); **~-handed** ще́дрый; **~ing** ['oupniŋ] отве́рстие; нача́ло; откры́тие; **~-minded** *fig.* непредубеждённый.
opera ['ɔpərə] о́пера; **~-glass(es** *pl.***)** бино́кль *m*.
operat|e ['ɔpəreit] *v/t.* управля́ть (Т); *part. Am.* приводи́ть в де́йствие; *v/i.* опери́ровать (*im*)*pf.*; ока́зывать влия́ние; рабо́тать; де́йствовать; **~ion** [ɔpə'reiʃən] де́йствие; ⚕, ⚔, ✝ опера́ция; проце́сс; be in ~ быть в де́йствии; **~ive** **1.** ['ɔpəreitiv] □ де́йствующий; действи́тельный; операти́вный (*a.* ⚕); **2.** ['ɔpərətiv] (фабри́чный) рабо́чий; **~or** ['ɔpəreitə] опера́тор; телеграфи́ст(ка).
opinion [ə'pinjən] мне́ние; взгляд; in my ~ по-мо́ему.
opponent [ə'pounənt] оппоне́нт, проти́вник.
opportun|e ['ɔpətjuːn] □ благоприя́тный; подходя́щий; своевре́менный; **~ity** [ɔpə'tjuːniti] удо́бный слу́чай, возмо́жность *f*.
oppos|e [ə'pouz] противопоставля́ть [-ста́вить]; [вос]проти́виться (Д); **~ed** [-d] противопоста́вленный; be ~ to быть про́тив (Р); **~ite** ['ɔpəzit] **1.** □ противополо́жный; **2.** *prp., adv.* напро́тив, про́тив (Р); **3.** противополо́жность *f*; **~ition** [ɔpə'ziʃən] сопротивле́ние; оппози́ция; контра́ст.
oppress [ə'pres] притесня́ть [-ни́ть], угнета́ть; **~ion** [-ʃən] притесне́ние, угнете́ние; угнетённость *f*; **~ive** [-siv] □ гнету́щий, угнета́ющий; ду́шный.
optic ['ɔptik] глазно́й, зри́тельный; **~al** [-tikəl] □ опти́ческий; **~ian** [ɔp'tiʃən] о́птик.
option ['ɔpʃən] вы́бор, пра́во вы́бора; ~ right пра́во преиму́щественной поку́пки; **~al** ['ɔpʃənl] □ необяза́тельный, факультати́вный.
opulence ['ɔpjuləns] бога́тство.
or [ɔː] и́ли; ~ else и́наче; и́ли же.
oracular [ɔ'rækjulə] □ проро́ческий.
oral ['ɔːrəl] □ у́стный; слове́сный.
orange ['ɔrindʒ] **1.** апельси́н; ора́нжевый цвет; **2.** ора́нжевый.
orat|ion [o'reiʃən] речь *f*; **~or** ['ɔrətə] ора́тор; **~ory** [-ri] красноре́чие; часо́вня.
orb [ɔːb] шар; орби́та; *fig.* небе́сное свети́ло; держа́ва.
orchard ['ɔːtʃəd] фрукто́вый сад.
orchestra ['ɔːkistrə] ♪ орке́стр.
ordain [ɔː'dein] посвяща́ть в духо́вный сан; предпи́сывать [-са́ть].
ordeal [ɔː'diːl] *fig.* испыта́ние.
order ['ɔːdə] **1.** поря́док; знак отли́чия; прика́з; ✝ зака́з; ранг; ⚔ строй; take (holy) ~s принима́ть духо́вный сан; in ~ to что́бы; in ~ that с тем, что́бы; make to ~ де́лать на зака́з; *parl.* standing ~s *pl.* пра́вила процеду́ры; **2.** прика́зывать [-за́ть]; назнача́ть [-на́чить]; ✝ зака́зывать [-за́ть]; **~ly** [-li] **1.** акку ра́тный; споко́йный; регуля́рный; **2.** ⚔ вестово́й, ордина́рец.
ordinance ['ɔːdinəns] ука́з, декре́т.
ordinary ['ɔːdnri] □ обыкнове́нный; зауря́дный.
ordnance ['ɔːdnəns] ⚔, ⚓ артиллери́йские ору́дия *n/pl.*; артиллери́йское и техни́ческое снабже́ние.
ordure ['ɔːdjuə] наво́з; отбро́сы *m/pl*; грязь *f*.
ore ['ɔː] руда́.
organ ['ɔːgən] о́рган; го́лос; ♪ орга́н; **~grinder** шарма́нщик; **~ic** [ɔː'gænik] (**~ally**) органи́ческий; **~ization** [ɔːgənai'zeiʃən] организа́ция; **~ize** ['ɔːgənaiz] организова́ть (*im*)*pf.*; **~izer** [-ə] организа́тор.
orgy ['ɔːdʒi] о́ргия.
orient ['ɔːrient] **1.** восто́к; Восто́к, восто́чные стра́ны *f/pl.*; **2.** ориенти́ровать (*im*)*pf.*; **~al** [ɔːri'entl] **1.** □ восто́чный, азиа́тский; **2.** жи́тель Восто́ка; **~ate** ['ɔːrienteit] ориенти́ровать (*im*)*pf.*
orifice ['ɔrifis] отве́рстие; у́стье.
origin ['ɔridʒin] исто́чник; происхожде́ние; нача́ло.

original [ə'ridʒənl] 1. □ первонача́льный; оригина́льный; по́длинный; 2. оригина́л, по́длинник; чуда́к; **~ity** [əridʒi'næliti] оригина́льность *f*.
originat|e [ə'ridʒineit] *v/t.* дава́ть нача́ло (Д), порожда́ть [породи́ть]; *v/i.* происходи́ть [-изойти́] (from от Р); **~or** [-ə] созда́тель *m*; инициа́тор.
ornament 1. ['ɔ:nəmənt] украше́ние, орна́мент; *fig.* краса́; 2. [-ment] украша́ть [укра́сить]; **~al** [ɔ:nə'mentl] □ декорати́вный.
ornate [ɔ:'neit] □ разукра́шенный; витиева́тый (стиль).
orphan ['ɔ:fən] 1. сирота́ *m/f*.; 2. осироте́лый (*a*. **~ed**); **~age** [-idʒ], **~-asylum** прию́т для сиро́т.
orthodox ['ɔ:θədɔks] □ правове́рный; *eccl.* правосла́вный.
oscillate ['ɔsileit] вибри́ровать; *fig.* колеба́ться.
ossify ['ɔsifai] [о]костене́ть.
ostensible [ɔs'tensəbl] □ очеви́дный.
ostentatio|n [ɔstən'teiʃən] хвастовство́; выставле́ние напока́з; **~us** [-ʃəs] □ показно́й.
ostler ['ɔslə] ко́нюх.
ostrich ['ɔstritʃ] *zo.* стра́ус.
other ['ʌðə] друго́й; ино́й; **the ~ day** на дня́х; **the ~ morning** неда́вно у́тром; **every ~ day** че́рез день; **~wise** [waiz] и́на́че; и́ли же.
otter ['ɔtə] *zo.* вы́дра.
ought [ɔ:t]: **I ~ to** мне сле́довало бы; **you ~ to have done it** вам сле́довало э́то сде́лать.
ounce [auns] у́нция (= 28,3 г).
our ['auə] *pron. poss.* **~s** ['auəz] *pron. poss. pred.* наш, на́ша, на́ше; на́ши *pl*.; **~selves** [auə'selvz] *pron.* 1. *refl.* себя́, -ся, -сь; 2. (для усиле́ния) (мы) са́ми.
oust [aust] выгоня́ть [вы́гнать], вытесня́ть [вы́теснить].
out [aut] 1. *adv.* нару́жу; вон; до конца́; ча́сто перево́дится приста́вкой вы- : **take ~** вынима́ть [вы́нуть]; **be ~ with** быть в ссо́ре с (Т); **~ and ~** соверше́нно; **way ~** вы́ход; 2. *parl.* **the ~s** *pl.* оппози́ция; 3. ✝ **~ size** разме́р бо́льше норма́льного; 4. *prp.* **~ of**: из (Р); вне (Р); из-за (Р).
out... [~] пере...; вы...; рас...; про...; воз..., вз...; из...; **~balance** [aut'bæləns] переве́шивать [-ве́сить]; **~bid** [-'bid] [*irr.* (bid)] перебива́ть це́ну; **~-break** ['autbreik] взрыв, вспы́шка (гне́ва); (внеза́пное) нача́ло (войны́, эпиде́мии и т. п.); **~building** ['autbildiŋ] надво́рное строе́ние; **~burst** [-'bə:st] взрыв, вспы́шка; **~cast** [-kɑ:st] 1. изгна́нник (-ица); па́рия *m/f*; 2. и́згнанный; **~come** [-'kʌm] результа́т; **~cry** [-krai] вы́крик; проте́ст; **~do** [aut'du:] [*irr.* (do)] превосходи́ть [-взойти́]; **~door** ['autdɔ:] *adj.* (находя́щийся) вне до́ма и́ли на откры́том во́здухе; нару́жный; **~doors** ['aut'dɔ:z] *adv.* на откры́том во́здухе, вне до́ма.
outer ['autə] вне́шний, нару́жный; **~most** ['autəmoust] кра́йний.
out|fit [-fit] снаряже́ние; обмундиро́вка; обору́дование; **~going** [-gouiŋ] 1. уходя́щий; исходя́щий (о бума́гах, пи́сьмах и т. п.); 2. **~s** *pl.* расхо́ды *m/pl.*; **~grow** [aut'grou] [*irr.* (grow)] выраста́ть [вы́расти] из (пла́тья и т. п.); **~-house** [-haus] надво́рное строе́ние; фли́гель *m*.
outing ['autiŋ] (за́городная) прогу́лка.
out|last [aut'lɑ:st] продолжа́ться до́льше, чем ...; пережи́(ва́)ть; **~law** ['autlɔ:] 1. челове́к вне зако́на; 2. объявля́ть вне зако́на; **~lay** [-lei] изде́ржки *f/pl.*; **~let** [-let] выпускно́е отве́рстие; вы́ход; **~line** [-lain] 1. (*a. pl.*) очерта́ние, ко́нтур; 2. рисова́ть ко́нтур (Р); де́лать набро́сок (Р); **~live** [aut'liv] пережи́(ва́)ть; **~look** ['autluk] вид, перспекти́ва; то́чка зре́ния, взгляд; **~lying** [-laiiŋ] отдалённый; **~number** [aut'nʌmbə] превосходи́ть чи́сленностью; **~-post** [-poust] аванпо́ст; **~pouring** [-pɔ:riŋ] *mst pl.* излия́ние (чувств); **~put** [-put] вы́пуск; производи́тельность *f*; проду́кция.
outrage ['autreidʒ] 1. гру́бое наруше́ние (on Р); 2. гру́бо наруша́ть (зако́н); **~ous** [aut'reidʒəs] □ неи́стовый; возмути́тельный.
out|right ['aut'rait] откры́то; сра́зу; вполне́; **~run** [aut'rʌn] [*irr.* (run)] перегоня́ть [-гна́ть], опережа́ть [-реди́ть]; *fig.* преступа́ть преде́лы (Р); **~set** ['autset] нача́ло; отправле́ние; **~shine** [aut'ʃain] [*irr.* (shine)] затмева́ть [-ми́ть]; **~side** ['aut'said] нару́жная сторона́; вне́шняя пове́рхность *f*; вне́шность *f*; кра́йность *f*; **at the ~** в кра́йнем слу́чае; 2. нару́жный, вне́шний; кра́йний; 3. *adv.* нару́жу; снару́жи; на (откры́том) во́здухе; 4. *prp.* вне (Р); **~sider** ['aut'saidə] посторо́нний (челове́к); **~skirts** ['autskə:ts] *pl.* окра́ина; **~spoken** [aut'spoukən] □ открове́нный; **~standing** ['autstændiŋ] выступа́ющий; *fig.* выдаю́щийся; неупла́ченный (счёт); **~stretch** [aut'stretʃ] протя́гивать [-тяну́ть]; **~strip** [-'strip] опережа́ть [-реди́ть]; превосходи́ть [-взойти́].
outward ['autwəd] 1. вне́шний, пове́рхностный; 2. *adv.* (*mst* **~s** [-z]) нару́жу; за преде́лы.

outweigh [aut'wei] превосходи́ть ве́сом; *fig.* переве́шивать [переве́сить].
oven ['ʌvn] (хле́бная) печь *f*; духо́вка.
over ['ouvə] **1.** *adv.* ча́ще всего́ перево́дится приста́вками глаго́лов: пере..., вы..., про...; сно́ва; вдоба́вок; сли́шком; ~ and above кро́ме того́; (all) ~ again сно́ва, ещё раз; ~ against напро́тив; ~ and ~ (again) то и де́ло; read ~ перечи́тывать [-чита́ть]; **2.** *prp.* над (Т); по (Д); за (В); свы́ше (Р); сверх (Р); че́рез (В); о(б) (П); all ~ the town по всему́ го́роду.
over ... ['ouvə] *pref.* как приста́вка, означа́ет: сверх...; над...; пере...; чрезме́рно; **~act** ['ouver'ækt] переи́грывать [-гра́ть] (роль); **~all** ['ouvərɔ:l] спецоде́жда; **~awe** [ouvər'ɔ:] держа́ть в благогове́йном стра́хе; **~balance** [ouvə'bæləns] теря́ть равнове́сие; переве́шивать [-ве́сить]; **~bearing** [-'bɛəriŋ] □ вла́стный; **~board** ['ouvəbɔ:d] ⚓ за́ борт, за бо́ртом; **~cast** ['ouvə'kɑ:st] па́смурный; **~-charge** [ouvə'tʃɑ:dʒ] **1.** сли́шком высо́кая цена́; **2.** перегружа́ть [-узи́ть]; запра́шивать сли́шком высо́кую це́ну с (Р) (for за В); **~coat** [-kout] пальто́ *n indecl.*; **~come** [-'kʌm] [*irr.* (come)] преодоле́(ва́)ть, побежда́ть [-еди́ть]; **~crowd** [ouvə'kraud] переполня́ть [-о́лнить] (за́л и т. п.); **~do** [-'du:] [*irr.* (do)] пережа́ри(ва)ть (мя́со и т. п.); де́лать сли́шком усе́рдно, утри́ровать (*im*)*pf*.; **~draw** ['ouvə'drɔ:] [*irr.* (draw)] ✝ превыша́ть [-вы́сить] (креди́т); **~dress** [-'dres] одева́ться сли́шком пы́шно; **~due** [-'dju:] просро́ченный; **~eat** [ouvər'i:t] [*irr.* (eat)]: ~ o. s. объеда́ться [объе́сться]; **~flow 1.** [ouvə'flou] [*irr.* (flow)] *v/t.* затопля́ть [-пи́ть]; *v/i.* перели́(ва́)ться; **2.** ['ouvəflou] наводне́ние; разли́в; **~grow** ['ouvə'grou] [*irr.* (grow)] заглуша́ть [-ши́ть] (о расте́ниях); расти́ сли́шком бы́стро; **~hang 1.** ['ouvə'hæŋ] [*irr.* (hang)] *v/i.* нависа́ть [-и́снуть]; **2.** ['ouvəhæŋ] свес; вы́ступ; **~haul** [ouvə'hɔ:l] [от]ремонти́ровать; **~head 1.** ['ouvə'hed] *adv.* над голово́й, наверху́; **2.** ['ouvəhed] *adj.* ве́рхний; ✝ накладно́й; **3.** **~s** *pl.* ✝ накладны́е расхо́ды *m/pl.*; **~hear** [ouvə'hiə] [*irr.* (hear)] подслу́ш(ив)ать; нечая́нно слы́шать; **~lap** [ouvə'læp] *v/t.* части́чно покрыва́ть; *v/i.* заходи́ть оди́н за друго́й; **~lay** [ouvə'lei] [*irr.* (lay)] ⊕ покры́(ва́)ть; **~load** [ouvə'loud] перегружа́ть [-узи́ть]; **~look** [ouvə'luk] обозре́(ва́)ть; прогля́дывать [-де́ть]; **~master** [ouvə'mɑ:stə] подчиня́ть себе́; **~much** ['ouvə'mʌtʃ] чрезме́рно; **~pay** [-'pei] [*irr.* (pay)] перепла́чивать [-лати́ть]; **~power** [ouvə'pauə] переси́ли(ва)ть; **~reach** [ouvə'ri:tʃ] перехитри́ть *pf.*; ~ o. s. брать сли́шком мно́го на себя́, сли́шком напряга́ть си́лы; **~ride** [-'raid] [*irr.* (ride)] перее́хать ло́шадью; *fig.* отверга́ть [-е́ргнуть]; **~run** [-'rʌn] [*irr.* (run)] перелива́ться че́рез край; **~sea** ['ouvə'si:] **1.** замо́рский; заграни́чный; **2.** (*a.* **~seas**) за́ морем, за́ море; **~see** [-'si:] [*irr.* (see)] надзира́ть за (Т); **~seer** ['ouvəsiə] надзира́тель(ница *f*) *m*; **~shadow** [ouvə'ʃædou] броса́ть тень на (В); омрача́ть [-чи́ть]; **~sight** [-sait] недосмо́тр; **~sleep** ['ouvəsli:p] [*irr.* (sleep)] прос(ы)па́ть; **~spread** [ouvə'spred] [*irr.* (spread)] покры́(ва́)ть; **~state** ['ouvə'steit] преувеличи(ва)ть; **~strain** [-'strein] **1.** переутомле́ние; **2.** переутомля́ть [-ми́ть]; **~take** [ouvə'teik] [*irr.* (take)] догоня́ть [догна́ть]; застигну́ть враспло́х; **~tax** ['ouvə'tæks] обременя́ть чрезме́рным нало́гом; *fig.* сли́шком напряга́ть (си́лы и т. п.) **~throw 1.** [ouvə'θrou] [*irr.* (throw)] сверга́ть [све́ргнуть]; опроки́дывать [-и́нуть]; **2.** ['ouvəθrou] сверже́ние; ниспроверже́ние; **~time** ['ouvətaim] **1.** сверхуро́чные часы́ *m/pl.*; **2.** *adv.* сверхуро́чно.
overture ['ouvətjuə] ♪ увертю́ра; нача́ло (перегово́ров и т. п.); форма́льное предложе́ние.
over|turn [ouvə'tə:n] опроки́дывать [-и́нуть]; **~weening** [ouvə'wi:niŋ] высокоме́рный; **~whelm** [ouvə'welm] подавля́ть [-ви́ть]; переси́ли(ва)ть; **~work** [-wə:k] **1.** перегру́зка; переутомле́ние; **2.** [*irr.* (work)] переутомля́ть(ся) [-ми́ть(ся)]; **~wrought** ['ouvə'rɔ:t] переутомлённый; возбуждённый (о не́рвах).
owe [ouv] быть до́лжным (Д/В); быть обя́занным (Д/Т).
owing ['ouiŋ] до́лжный; неупла́ченный; ~ to *prp.* благодаря́ (Д).
owl [aul] сова́.
own [oun] **1.** свой, со́бственный; родно́й; **2.** my ~ моя́ со́бственность *f*; a house of one's ~ со́бственный дом; hold one's ~ сохраня́ть свои́ пози́ции; **3.** владе́ть (Т); призна́(ва́)ть (В); призна́(ва́)ться в (П).
owner ['ounə] владе́лец (-лица *f*); **~ship** [-ʃip] со́бственность *f*; пра́во со́бственности.
ox [ɔks], *pl.* **oxen** вол, бык.
oxid|e ['ɔksaid] 🜍 о́кись *f*; **~ize** ['ɔksidaiz] окисля́ть(ся) [-ли́ть(ся)].
oxygen ['ɔksidʒən] 🜍 кислоро́д.
oyster ['ɔistə] у́стрица.

P

pace [peis] **1.** шаг; походка, поступь *f*; темп; **2.** *v/t.* измерять шагами; *v/i.* [за]шагать.
pacific [pə'sifik] (~ally) миролюбивый; ♀ Ocean Тихий океан; **~ation** ['pæsifi'keiʃən] умиротворение; усмирение.
pacify ['pæsifai] умиротворять [-рить]; усмирять [-рить].
pack [pæk] **1.** пачка; вьюк; связка; кипа; колода (карт); свора (собак); стая (волков); **2.** *v/t.* (*often* ~ up) упаковывать [-ковать]; заполнять [заполнить], наби(ва)ть; (*a.* ~ off) выпроваживать [выпроводить]; ⊕ уплотнять [-нить]; *v/i.* упаковываться [-оваться]; (*often* ~ up) укладываться [уложиться]; **~age** ['pækidʒ] тюк; кипа; упаковка; место (багажа); **~er** ['pækə] упаковщик (-ица); **~et** ['pækit] пакет; почтовый пароход; **~thread** бечёвка, шпагат.
pact [pækt] пакт, договор.
pad [pæd] **1.** мягкая прокладка; блокнот; **2.** подби(ва)ть, наби(ва)ть (ватой и т. п.); **~ding** ['pædiŋ] набивочный материал; *fig.* многословие.
paddle [pædl] **1.** весло, гребок; ⚓ лопасть *f* (гребного колеса); **2.** грести гребком; плыть на байдарке; **~-wheel** гребное колесо.
paddock ['pædək] выгон, загон.
padlock ['pædlɔk] висячий замок.
pagan ['peigən] **1.** язычник; **2.** языческий.
page [peidʒ] **1.** паж; страница; **2.** нумеровать страницы (P).
pageant ['pædʒənt] пышное (историческое) зрелище; карнавальное шествие.
paid [peid] *pt.* и *p. pt.* от **pay.**
pail [peil] ведро, бадья.
pain [pein] **1.** боль *f*; страдание; наказание; ~s *pl.* (*often sg.*) старания *n/pl.*; on ~ of под страхом (P); be in ~ испытывать боль; take ~s [по]стараться; **2.** причинять боль (Д); **~ful** ['peinful] □ болезненный; мучительный; **~less** [-lis] □ безболезненный; **~staking** ['peinzteikiŋ] усердный, старательный.
paint [peint] **1.** краска; румяна *n/pl.*; **2.** [по]красить; [на]румянить(ся); **~-brush** кисть *f*; **~er** ['peintə] художник; маляр; **~ing** ['peintiŋ] живопись *f*; картина; **~ress** [-tris] художница.
pair [pɛə] **1.** пара; чета; a ~ of scissors ножницы *f/pl.*; **2.** соединять(ся) по двое; спаривать(ся).
pal [pæl] *sl.* приятель(ница *f*) *m.*
palace ['pælis] дворец.
palatable ['pælətəbl] вкусный.
palate [-it] нёбо; вкус.
pale[1] [peil] **1.** □ бледный; тусклый; ~ ale светлое пиво; **2.** [по]бледнеть.
pale[2] [~] кол; *fig.* пределы *m/pl.*
paleness ['peilnis] бледность *f.*
pall [pɔ:l] окутывать покровом.
pallet ['pælit] соломенный тюфяк.
palliat|e ['pælieit] облегчать [-чить] (болезнь); *fig.* покры(ва)ть; **~ive** ['pælietiv] паллиативный; смягчающий.
pall|id ['pælid] □ бледный; **~idness** [-nis], **~or** [-lə] бледность *f.*
palm [pɑ:m] **1.** ладонь *f*; ⚘ пальма; **2.** трогать, гладить ладонью; прятать в руке; ~ off on a p. всучивать [-чить] (Д); **~tree** пальмовое дерево.
palpable ['pælpəbl] □ осязаемый; *fig.* очевидный, явный.
palpitat|e ['pælpiteit] трепетать; биться (о сердце); **~ion** [-ʃən] сердцебиение.
palsy ['pɔ:lzi] **1.** паралич; *fig.* слабость *f*; **2.** парализовать (*im*)*pf.*
palter ['pɔ:ltə] [с]плутовать; кривить душой.
paltry ['pɔ:ltri] □ пустяковый, ничтожный.
pamper ['pæmpə] [из]баловать, изнежи(ва)ть.
pamphlet ['pæmflit] брошюра.
pan [pæn] кастрюля; сковорода.
pan... [~] *pref.* пан...; обще...
panacea [pænə'siə] панацея, универсальное средство.
pancake ['pænkeik] блин; оладья.
pandemonium [pændi'mounjəm] 🕮 *fig.* «ад кромешный».
pander ['pændə] **1.** потворствовать (to Д); сводничать; **2.** сводник (-ица).
pane [pein] (оконное) стекло.
panegyric [pæni'dʒirik] панегирик, похвала.
panel [pænl] **1.** ⚠ панель *f*; филёнка; ⚖ список присяжных заседателей; **2.** обшивать панелями (стены).
pang [pæŋ] внезапная острая боль *f*; ~s *pl. fig.* угрызения (совести).
panic ['pænik] **1.** панический; **2.** паника.
pansy ['pænzi] ⚘ анютины глазки *m/pl.*
pant [pænt] задыхаться [задохнуться]; тяжело дышать; страстно желать (for, after P).
panties ['pæntiz] *Am.* F (a pair of ~) (дамские) панталоны *m/pl.*
pantry ['pæntri] кладовая; буфетная (для посуды).
pants [pænts] *pl. Am.* или F (a pair of ~) подштанники *m/pl.*; штаны *m/pl.*

pap [pæp] кашка (для детей).
papal ['peipəl] □ папский.
paper ['peipə] 1. бумага; газета; обои *m/pl.*; научный доклад; документ; 2. о(б)клеивать обоями; ~-**bag** кулёк; ~-**clip**, ~-**fastener** скрепка; ~-**hanger** обойщик; ~-**weight** пресс-папье *n indecl.*
pappy ['pæpi] кашицеобразный.
par [pɑ:] равенство; † номинальная стоимость *f*; at ~ альпари; be on a ~ with быть наравне, на одном уровне с (Т).
parable ['pærəbl] притча.
parachut|e ['pærəʃu:t] парашют; ~**ist** [-ist] парашютист.
parade [pə'reid] 1. выставление напоказ; ⚔ парад; ⚔ плац (= ~-ground); место для гулянья; make a ~ of выставлять напоказ; 2. выставлять напоказ; ⚔ выстраивать(ся) на парад.
paradise ['pærədais] рай.
paragon [-gən] образец (совершенства, добродетели).
paragraph ['pærəgra:f] абзац; параграф; газетная заметка.
parallel ['pærəlel] 1. параллельный; 2. параллель *f* (*a. fig.*); *geogr.* параллель *f*; without ~ несравнимый; 3. быть параллельным с (Т), проходить параллельно (Д); сравнивать [-нить].
paraly|se ['pærəlaiz] парализовать (*im*)*pf.*; ~**sis** [pə'rælisis] ⚕ паралич.
paramount ['pærəmaunt] верховный, высший; первостепенный.
parapet ['pærəpit] ⚔ бруствер; парапет, перила *n/pl.*
paraphernalia [pærəfə'nei'ljə] *pl.* принадлежности *f/pl.*
parasite ['pærəsait] паразит (*a. fig.*); *fig.* тунеядец (-дка).
parasol [pærə'sɔl] зонтик (от солнца).
paratroops ['pærətru:ps] *pl.* ⚔ парашютно-десантные войска *n/pl.*
parboil ['pɑ:bɔil] слегка проваривать.
parcel [pɑ:sl] 1. пакет; посылка; 2. (*mst* ~ out) делить на участки; выделять [выделить].
parch [pɑ:tʃ] иссушать [-шить]; опалять [-лить] (о солнце).
parchment [-mənt] пергамент.
pardon [pɑ:dn] 1. прощение; ⚖ помилование; 2. прощать [простить]; помиловать *pf.*; ~**able** [-əbl] □ простительный.
pare [pɛə] [по]чистить (овощи и т. п.); обрезать [-резать]; *fig.* уре-з(ыв)ать.
parent ['pɛərənt] родитель(ница *f*) *m*; *fig.* источник; ~**s** *pl.* родители *m/pl.*; ~**age** [-idʒ] происхождение; ~**al** [pə'rentl] □ родительский.
parenthe|sis [pə'renθisis], *pl.* ~**ses** [-si:z] вводное слово, вводное предложение; *pl. typ.* (круглые) скобки *f/pl.*
paring ['pɛəriŋ] кожура, корка, шелуха; ~**s** *pl.* обрезки *m/pl.*; очистки *f/pl.*
parish ['pæriʃ] 1. церковный приход; прихожане *pl.*; (*a.* civil ~) гражданский округ; 2. приходский.
parity ['pæriti] равенство; равноценность *f.*
park [pɑ:k] 1. парк; *mot.* стоянка; 2. *mot.* ставить на стоянку; ~**ing** ['pɑ:kiŋ] *mot.* стоянка; *attr.* стояночный.
parlance ['pɑ:ləns] способ выражения, язык.
parley [pɑ:li] 1. переговоры *m/pl.*; 2. вести переговоры.
parliament ['pɑ:ləmənt] парламент; ~**ary** [-'mentəri] парламентарный, парламентский.
parlo(u)r ['pɑ:lə] приёмная; жилая комната; гостиная; *Am.* зал, ателье *n indecl.*; ~-**maid** горничная.
parochial [pə'roukjəl] □ приходский; *fig.* местный; узкий, ограниченный.
parole [pə'roul] ⚔ пароль *m*; честное слово.
parquet ['pɑ:kei] паркет; *thea.* передние ряды партера.
parrot ['pærət] 1. попугай; 2. повторять как попугай.
parry ['pæri] отражать [отразить], [от]парировать (удар).
parsimonious [pɑ:si'mounjəs] □ бережливый, экономный; скупой.
parsley ['pɑ:sli] ⚘ петрушка.
parson [pɑ:sn] приходский священник, пастор.
part [pɑ:t] 1. часть *f*, доля; участие; *thea. a. fig.* роль *f*; местность *f*; ♪ партия; a man of ~s способный человек; take in good (bad) ~ хорошо (плохо) принимать (слова и т. п.); for my (own) ~ с моей стороны; in ~ частично; on the ~ of со стороны (Р); 2. *adv.* частью, отчасти; 3. *v/t.* разделять [-лить]; ~ the hair делать пробор; *v/i.* разлучаться [-читься], расст(ав)аться (with, from с Т).
partake [pɑ:'teik] [*irr.* (take)] принимать участие; разделять [-лить].
partial ['pɑ:ʃəl] □ частичный; пристрастный; неравнодушный (to к Д); ~**ity** [pɑ:ʃi'æliti] пристрастие; склонность *f*.
particip|ant [pɑ:'tisipənt] участник (-ица); ~**ate** [-peit] участвовать (in в П); ~**ation** [-peiʃən] участие.
particle ['pɑ:tikl] частица; крупица.
particular [pə'tikjulə] 1. □ особенный; особый; частный; разборчивый; 2. подробность *f*, де-

та́ль *f*; in ~ в осо́бенности; **~ity** [pətikju'læriti] осо́бенность *f*; тща́тельность *f*; **~ly** [pə'tikjuləli] осо́бенно; чрезвыча́йно.

parting ['pɑːtiŋ] **1.** разлу́ка; пробо́р; ~ of the ways *part. fig.* перепу́тье; **2.** проща́льный.

partisan [pɑːti'zæn] **1.** сторо́нник (-ица); ⚔ партиза́н; **2.** партиза́нский.

partition [pɑː'tiʃən] **1.** разде́л; перегоро́дка; **2.** ~ off отделя́ть перегоро́дкой.

partly ['pɑːtli] ча́стью, отча́сти.

partner['pɑːtnə] **1.** уча́стник (-ица); † компаньо́н(ка); партнёр(ша); **2.** ста́вить в па́ру; де́лать партнёром; быть партнёром; **~ship** [-ʃip] уча́стие; † това́рищество, компа́ния.

part-owner совладе́лец.

part-time непо́лная за́нятость *f*; *attr.* не по́лностью за́нятый; ~ worker рабо́чий, за́нятый не по́лный рабо́чий день.

party ['pɑːti] па́ртия; отря́д; уча́стник (to в П); компа́ния; вечери́нка; ~ line *parl.* парти́йные директи́вы *f/pl.*; ~ ticket *Am.* парти́йная програ́мма.

pass ['pɑːs] **1.** прохо́д; перева́л; па́спорт; про́пуск; беспла́тный биле́т; *univ.* посре́дственная сда́ча экза́мена; **2.** *v/i.* проходи́ть [пройти́]; прекраща́ться [-крати́ться]; умира́ть [умере́ть]; происходи́ть [-изойти́], случа́ться [-чи́ться]; переходи́ть [перейти́] (from ... to ... из [Р] ... в [В] ...); име́ть хожде́ние; *cards* [с]пасова́ть; come to ~ случа́ться [-чи́ться]; ~ as, for счита́ться (Т), слыть (Т); ~ away исчеза́ть [-е́знуть]; умира́ть [умере́ть]; ~ by проходи́ть ми́мо; ~ into переходи́ть [перейти́] в (В); ~ off проходи́ть [пройти́] (о бо́ли и т. п.); ~ on идти́ да́льше; ~ out выходи́ть [вы́йти]; **3.** *v/t.* проходи́ть [пройти́]; проезжа́ть [-е́хать]; минова́ть (*im*)*pf.*; выде́рживать [вы́держать] (экза́мен); обгоня́ть [обогна́ть], опережа́ть [-реди́ть]; переправля́ть(ся) [-а́вить(ся)] че́рез (В); (*a.* ~ on) перед(ав)а́ть; выноси́ть [вы́нести] (пригово́р); проводи́ть [-вести́] (вре́мя); принима́ть [-ня́ть] (зако́н); **~able** ['pɑːsəbl] □ проходи́мый; ходя́чий (о деньга́х); посре́дственный, сно́сный.

passage ['pæsidʒ] прохо́д; тече́ние (вре́мени); перее́зд, перепра́ва; коридо́р; отры́вок (из кни́ги).

passenger ['pæsindʒə] пассажи́р; седо́к; **~-train** пассажи́рский по́езд.

passer-by ['pɑːsə'bai] прохо́жий.

passion ['pæʃən] страсть *f*; гнев; ♀ *eccl.* кре́стные му́ки *f/pl.*; ♀ Week страстна́я неде́ля; **~ate** [-it] □ стра́стный.

passive ['pæsiv] □ пасси́вный; поко́рный.

passport ['pɑːspɔːt] па́спорт.

password [-wəːd] ⚔ паро́ль *m*.

past [pɑːst] **1.** *adj.* про́шлый; мину́вший; for some time ~ за после́днее вре́мя; **2.** *adv.* ми́мо; **3.** *prp.* за (Т); по́сле (Р); ми́мо (Р); свы́ше (Р); half ~ two полови́на тре́тьего; ~ endurance нестерпи́мый; ~ hope безнадёжный; **4.** про́шлое.

paste [peist] **1.** те́сто; па́ста; клей; **2.** кле́ить, прикле́и(ва)ть; **~board** карто́н; *attr.* карто́нный.

pastel ['pæstel] пасте́ль *f*.

pasteurize ['pæstəraiz] пастеризова́ть (*im*)*pf.*

pastime ['pɑːstaim] времяпрепровожде́ние.

pastor ['pɑːstə] па́стор; па́стырь *m*; **~al** [-rəl] пастора́льный; пасту́шеский.

pastry ['peistri] пиро́жное, пече́нье; **~-cook** конди́тер.

pasture ['pɑːstʃə] **1.** па́стбище; вы́гон; **2.** пасти́(сь).

pat [pæt] **1.** похло́пывание; кружо́чек (ма́сла); **2.** похло́п(ыв)ать; **3.** кста́ти; во́-время.

patch [pætʃ] **1.** запла́та; клочо́к земли́; обры́вок; лоску́т; **2.** [за-] лата́ть, [по]чини́ть.

pate [peit] F башка́, голова́.

patent ['peitənt] **1.** я́вный; откры́тый; патенто́ванный; ~ fastener кно́пка (застёжка); ~ leather лакиро́ванная ко́жа; **2.** (*a.* letters ~ *pl.*) пате́нт; дипло́м; **3.** [за]патентова́ть; **~ee** [peitən'tiː] владе́лец пате́нта.

patern|al [pə'təːnl] □ отцо́вский; оте́ческий; **~ity** [-niti] отцо́вство.

path [pɑːθ], *pl.* **~s** [pɑːðz] тропи́нка, доро́жка.

pathetic [pə'θetik] (~ally) патети́ческий; тро́гательный.

patien|ce ['peiʃəns] терпе́ние; насто́йчивость *f*; **~t** [-t] **1.** □ терпели́вый; **2.** пацие́нт(ка).

patrimony ['pætriməni] родово́е поме́стье, во́тчина.

patrol [pə'troul] ⚔ **1.** патру́ль *m*; дозо́р; **2.** патрули́ровать.

patron ['peitrən] патро́н; покрови́тель *m*; клие́нт; **~age** ['pætrənidʒ] покрови́тельство; клиенту́ра; **~ize** [-naiz] покрови́тельствовать; снисходи́тельно относи́ться к (Д); постоя́нно покупа́ть у (Р).

patter ['pætə] говори́ть скорогово́ркой; [про]бормота́ть; бараба́нить (о дожде́); топота́ть, семени́ть.

pattern ['pætən] **1.** образе́ц; моде́ль *f*; узо́р; **2.** де́лать по образцу́ (on Р).

paunch [pɔ:ntʃ] брюшко́, пу́зо.
pauper ['pɔ:pə] ни́щий (-щая); **~ize** [-raiz] доводи́ть до нищеты́.
pause [pɔ:z] **1.** па́уза, переры́в, остано́вка; **2.** де́лать па́узу.
pave [peiv] [на]мости́ть; *fig.* прокла́дывать [проложи́ть] (путь); **~ment** ['peivmənt] тротуа́р, пане́ль *f*; мостова́я.
paw [pɔ:] **1.** ла́па; F рука́; **2.** тро́гать ла́пой; бить копы́том.
pawn [pɔ:n] **1.** зало́г, закла́д; *chess* пе́шка; in, at ~ в закла́де; **2.** закла́дывать [заложи́ть]; **~broker** ростовщи́к; **~shop** ломба́рд, ссу́дная ка́сса.
pay [pei] **1.** пла́та, упла́та; зарпла́та, жа́лованье; **2.** [*irr.*] *v/t.* [за]плати́ть; опла́чивать [оплати́ть]; вознагражда́ть [-ради́ть]; [с]де́лать (визи́т); ~ **attention to** обраща́ть внима́ние на (В); ~ down плати́ть нали́чными; *v/i.* окупа́ться [-пи́ться] (*a. fig.*); ~ for [у-, за]плати́ть за (В), опла́чивать [оплати́ть] (В); *fig.* [по]плати́ться за (В); **~able** ['peiəbl] подлежа́щий упла́те; **~-day** день вы́платы жа́лованья; **~ing** ['peiiŋ] вы́годный; **~master** казначе́й, касси́р; **~ment** [mənt] упла́та, платёж; **~roll** платёжная ве́домость *f*.
pea [pi:] ⚘ горо́х; горо́шина; **~s** *pl.* горох; *attr.* горо́ховый.
peace [pi:s] мир; споко́йствие; **~able** ['pi:səbl] □ миролюби́вый, ми́рный; **~ful** [-ful] □ ми́рный, споко́йный; **~maker** миротво́рец.
peach [pi:tʃ] пе́рсик; пе́рсиковое де́рево.
pea|cock ['pi:kɔk] павли́н; **~hen** [-hen] па́ва.
peak [pi:k] верши́на (горы́); козырёк (ке́пки); *attr.* максима́льный; вы́сший.
peal [pi:l] **1.** звон колоколо́в; раска́т (гро́ма); ~ of laughter взрыв сме́ха; 2. разда́(ва́)ться; греме́ть; трезвони́ть.
peanut ['pi:nʌt] земляно́й оре́х.
pear [pɛə] ⚘ гру́ша; гру́шевое де́рево.
pearl [pə:l] *coll.* же́мчуг; жемчу́жина *a. fig.*; *attr.* жемчу́жный; **~y** ['pə:li] как же́мчуг.
peasant ['pezənt] **1.** крестья́нин; **2.** крестья́нский; **~ry** [-ri] крестья́нство.
peat [pi:t] торф.
pebble ['pebl] голы́ш, га́лька.
peck [pek] **1.** пек, ме́ра сыпу́чих тел (= 9,087 ли́тра); *fig.* мно́жество; **2.** клева́ть [клю́нуть].
peculate ['pekjuleit] (незако́нно) растра́чивать [-ра́тить].
peculiar [pi'kju:ljə] □ своеобра́зный; осо́бенный; стра́нный; **~ity** [pikju:li'æriti] осо́бенность *f*; стра́нность *f*.
pecuniary [pi'kju:njəri] де́нежный.
pedagogue ['pedəgɔg] педаго́г, учи́тель(ница *f*) *m*.
pedal [pedl] **1.** педа́ль *f*; **2.** ножно́й; **3.** е́хать на велосипе́де; рабо́тать педа́лями.
peddle [pedl] торгова́ть вразно́с.
pedest|al ['pedistl] пьедеста́л (*a. fig.*); **~rian** [pi'destriən] **1.** пешехо́д; **2.** пешехо́дный.
pedigree ['pedigri:] родосло́вная.
pedlar ['pedlə] разно́счик, коробе́йник.
peek [pi:k] *Am.* **1.** ~ in загля́дывать [-яну́ть]; **2.** бе́глый взгляд.
peel [pi:l] **1.** ко́рка, ко́жица, шелуха́; **2.** (*a.* ~ off) *v/t.* снима́ть ко́жицу, ко́рку, шелуху́ с (Р); [по-] чи́стить (фру́кты, о́вощи); *v/i.* [об]лупи́ться, сходи́ть [сойти́] (о ко́же).
peep [pi:p] **1.** взгляд укра́дкой; **2.** взгля́дывать укра́дкой; *fig.* проявля́ться [-ви́ться]; [про]пища́ть; **~-hole** глазо́к (око́шечко).
peer [piə] **1.** [с]равня́ться с (Т); ~ at вгля́дываться [-де́ться] в (В); **2.** ро́вня́ *m/f.*; пэр; **~less** ['piəlis] □ несравне́нный.
peevish ['pi:viʃ] □ брюзгли́вый.
peg [pəg] **1.** ко́лышек; ве́шалка; ♪ коло́к; зажи́мка для белья́; *fig.* take a p. down a ~ сбива́ть спесь с кого́-либо; **2.** прикрепля́ть ко́лышком; отмеча́ть ко́лышками; ~ away, along F упо́рно рабо́тать; **~-top** юла́ (игру́шка).
pellet ['pelit] ша́рик; пилю́ля; дроби́нка.
pell-mell ['pel'mel] вперемё́шку.
pelt [pelt] **1.** ко́жа, шку́ра; **2.** *v/t.* обстре́ливать [-ля́ть]; забра́сывать [-роса́ть]; *v/i.* бараба́нить (о дожде́ и т. п.).
pen [pen] **1.** перо́; заго́н; **2.** [на-] писа́ть; [*irr.*] загоня́ть в заго́н.
penal [pi:nl] □ уголо́вный; кара́тельный; ~ servitude ка́торжные рабо́ты *f/pl.*; **~ize** ['pi:nəlaiz] нака́зывать [-за́ть]; **~ty** ['penlti] наказа́ние; ✝, *sport.* штраф; *attr.* штрафно́й.
penance ['penəns] эпитими́я.
pence [pens] *pl.* от penny.
pencil [pensl] **1.** каранда́ш; кисть *f* (живопи́сца); **2.** [на]рисова́ть; писа́ть карандашо́м; вычё́рчивать [вы́чертить].
pendant ['pendənt] куло́н, брело́к.
pending ['pendiŋ] **1.** ⚖ ожида́ющий реше́ния; **2.** *prp.* в продолже́ние (Р); (вплоть) до (Р).
pendulum ['pendjuləm] ма́ятник.
penetra|ble ['penitrəbl] □ проница́емый; **~te** [-treit] проника́ть [-ни́кнуть] в (В), глубоко́ тро́гать; прони́зывать [-за́ть]; *fig.* вника́ть [вни́кнуть] в (В); **~tion** [peni'treiʃən] проника́ние; проница́тель-

ность *f*; **~tive** ['penitreitiv] □ проникающий; проницательный.
penholder ручка (для пера).
peninsula [pi'ninsjulə] полуостров.
peniten|ce ['penitəns] раскаяние; покаяние; **~t 1.** □ раскаивающийся; **2.** кающийся грешник; **~tiary** [peni'tenʃəri] исправительный дом; *Am.* каторжная тюрьма.
penman ['penmən] писатель *m*; }
pen-name псевдоним. [писец.}
pennant ['penənt] ⚓ вымпел.
penniless ['penilis] □ без копейки.
penny ['peni] пенни *n indecl.*, пенс; *Am.* монета в 1 цент; **~weight** 24 грана (= 1,5552 гр).
pension 1. ['penʃən] пенсия; **2.** увольнять на пенсию; давать пенсию (Д); **~ary, ~er** ['penʃənəri, -ʃənə] пенсионер(ка).
pensive ['pensiv] □ задумчивый.
pent [pent] заключённый; **~-up** накопленный (о гневе и т. п.).
penthouse ['penthaus] навес.
penu|rious [pi'njuəriəs] скудный; скупой; **~ry** ['penjuri] нужда; недостаток.
people [pi:pl] **1.** народ; *coll.* люди *m/pl.*; население; **2.** заселять [-лить]; населять [-лить].
pepper ['pepə] **1.** перец; **2.** [по-, на-] перчить; **~mint** ⚘ мята; **~y** [-ri] □ наперченный; *fig.* вспыльчивый.
per [pə:] по (Д), через (В), посредством (Р); за (В), на (В), в (В); ~ cent процент.
perambulat|e [pə'ræmbjuleit] обходить [обойти], объезжать [-ехать]; **~or** ['præmbjuleitə] детская коляска.
perceive [pə'si:v] воспринимать [-нять]; ощущать [ощутить]; понимать [-нять].
percentage [pə'sentidʒ] процент; процентное отношение или содержание.
percepti|ble [pə'septəbl] □ ощутимый; **~on** [-ʃən] ощущение; восприятие.
perch [pə:tʃ] **1.** *zo.* окунь *m*; перч, мера длины (= 5.029 м); насест; **2.** садиться [сесть]; усаживаться [усесться]; сажать на насест.
percolate ['pə:kəleit] [про]фильтровать; процеживать [-цедить].
percussion [pə:'kʌʃən] удар.
perdition [pə:'diʃən] гибель *f*.
peregrination [perigri'neiʃən] странствование; путешествие.
peremptory [pə'remptəri] безапелляционный; повелительный, властный.
perennial [pə'renjəl] □ вечный, неувядаемый; ⚘ многолетний.
perfect 1. ['pə:fikt] □ совершенный; законченный; **2.** [pə'fekt] [у]совершенствовать; завершать [-шить]; **~ion** [-ʃən] совершенство; *fig.* высшая степень *f*.
perfidious [pə'fidiəs] □ вероломный.
perfidy ['pə:fidi] вероломство.
perforate ['pə:fəreit] перфорировать (*im*)*pf*..
perform [pə'fɔ:m] исполнять [-олнить] (*a. thea.*); *thea.*, ♪ играть [сыграть] (роль, пьесу и т. п.), представлять [-авить]; **~ance** [əns] исполнение (*a. thea.*); *thea.* представление; *sport* достижение; **~er** [-ə] исполнитель(ница *f*) *m*.
perfume 1. ['pə:fju:m] духи *m/pl.*; благоухание; **2.** [pə'fju:m] [на-] душить; **~ry** [-əri] парфюмерия.
perfunctory [pə'fʌŋktəri] □ *fig.* механический; поверхностный.
perhaps [pə'hæps, præps] может быть.
peril ['peril] **1.** опасность *f*; **2.** подвергать опасности; **~ous** [-əs] □ опасный.
period ['piəriəd] период; абзац; **~ic** [piəri'ɔdik] периодический; **~ical** [-dikəl] **1.** □ периодический; **2.** периодическое издание.
perish ['periʃ] погибать [-ибнуть]; [по]губить; **~able** ['periʃəbl] □ скоропортящийся; тленный.
periwig ['periwig] парик.
perjur|e ['pə:dʒə]: ~ o. s. лжесвидетельствовать; нарушать клятву; **~y** [-ri] лжесвидетельство; клятвопреступление.
perk [pə:k] F: *mst* ~ up *v/i.* задирать нос; *v/t.* ~ o. s. прихорашиваться.
perky ['pə:ki] □ дерзкий; самоуверенный.
permanen|ce ['pə:mənəns] постоянство; **~t** [-t] □ постоянный, неизменный.
permea|ble ['pə:miəbl] проницаемый; **~te** [-mieit] проникать [-икнуть], пропитывать [-итать].
permissi|ble [pə'misəbl] □ позволительный; **~on** [-ʃən] позволение, разрешение.
permit 1. [pə'mit] разрешать [-шить], позволять [-волить]; допускать [-устить]; **2.** ['pə:mit] разрешение; пропуск.
pernicious [pə:'niʃəs] пагубный.
perpendicular [pə:pən'dikjulə] □ перпендикулярный.
perpetrate ['pə:pitreit] совершать [-шить] (преступление и т. п.).
perpetu|al [pə'petjuəl] постоянный, вечный; **~ate** [-jueit] увековечи(ва)ть.
perplex [pə'pleks] озадачи(ва)ть, сбивать с толку; **~ity** [-iti] озадаченность *f*; недоумение; затруднение.
perquisites ['pə:kwizits] *pl.* случайные доходы *m/pl.*
persecut|e ['pə:sikju:t] преследовать; **~ion** [pə:si'kju:ʃən] преследование.

persever|ance [pə:si'viərəns] настойчивость *f*, упорство; **~e** [-'viə] *v/i.* выдерживать [выдержать]; упорно продолжать (in B).
persist [pə'sist] упорствовать (in в П); **~ence** [-əns] настойчивость *f*; **~ent** [-ənt] □ настойчивый.
person ['pə:sn] лицо, личность *f*, особа, человек; **~age** [-idʒ] важная персона; персонаж; **~al** [-l] □ личный; **~ality** [pə:sə'næliti] личность *f*; колкость *f*; **~ate** ['pə:səneit] играть роль (P); выдавать себя за (B); **~ify** [pə:'sɔnifai] олицетворять [-рить], воплощать [-лотить]; **~nel** [pə:sə'nel] персонал, личный состав.
perspective [pə'spektiv] перспектива; вид.
perspicuous [pə'spikjuəs] □ ясный.
perspir|ation [pə:spə'reiʃən] потение; пот; **~e** [pəs'paiə] [вс]потеть.
persua|de [pə'sweid] убеждать [убедить]; склонять [-нить] (into к Д); **~sion** [-ʒən] убеждение; убедительность *f*; **~sive** [-siv] □ убедительный.
pert [pə:t] □ дерзкий; развязный.
pertain [pə:'tein] (to) принадлежать (Д); относиться [отнестись] (к Д).
pertinacious [pə:ti'neiʃəs] □ упрямый, неуступчивый.
pertinent ['pə:tinənt] □ уместный; относящийся к делу.
perturb [pə'tə:b] нарушать [-ушить] (спокойствие); [о]беспокоить.
perus|al [pə'ru:zəl] внимательное прочтение; **~e** [pə'ru:z] [про]читать; внимательно прочитывать.
pervade [pə:'veid] распространяться [-ниться] по (Д) (о запахе и т. п.).
pervers|e [pə'və:s] □ превратный, ошибочный; ⚕ извращённый; **~ion** [-ʃən] ⚕ извращение.
pervert 1. [pə'və:t] извращать [-ратить]; совращать [-ратить]; 2. ['pə:və:t] отступник (-ица).
pest [pest] *fig.* язва, бич; паразит; **~er** ['pestə] докучать (Д), надоедать [-есть] (Д).
pesti|ferous [pes'tifərəs] □ заразный; **~lence** ['pestiləns] чума; **~lent** [-t] смертоносный; **~lential** [pesti'lenʃəl] □ чумной; зловонный.
pet [pet] 1. комнатное животное; любимец, баловень *m*; 2. любимый; ~ dog комнатная собачка, болонка; ~ name ласкательное имя; 3. баловать; ласкать.
petition [pi'tiʃən] 1. прошение, петиция; просьба; 2. [по]просить; подавать прошение.
petrify ['petrifai] превращать(ся) в камень; приводить в оцепенение.
petrol ['petrəl] *Brit. mot.* бензин.
petticoat ['petikout] нижняя юбка.
pettish ['petiʃ] □ обидчивый.
petty ['peti] □ мелкий; мелочный.
petulant ['petjulənt] раздражительный.
pew [pju:] церковная скамья.
pewter ['pju:tə] оловянная посуда.
phantasm ['fæntæzm] фантом; иллюзия.
phantom ['fæntəm] фантом, призрак; иллюзия.
Pharisee ['færisi:] фарисей.
pharmacy ['fɑ:məsi] фармация; аптека.
phase [feiz] фаза; период.
phenomen|on [fi'nɔminən], *pl.* **~a** [-nə] явление; феномен.
phial ['faiəl] склянка, пузырёк.
philander ['fi'lændə] флиртовать.
philanthropist [fi'lænθrəpist] филантроп.
philologist [fi'lɔlədʒist] филолог.
philosoph|er [fi'lɔsəfə] философ; **~ize** [-faiz] философствовать; **~y** [-fi] философия.
phlegm [flem] мокрота; флегматичность *f*.
phone [foun] F *s.* telephone.
phonetics [fo'netiks] *pl.* фонетика.
phosphorus ['fɔsfərəs] фосфор.
photograph ['foutəgrɑ:f] 1. фотография, снимок; 2. [с]фотографировать; **~er** [fə'tɔgrəfə] фотограф; **~y** [-fi] фотография (дело).
phrase [freiz] 1. фраза, выражение; слог; 2. выражать [выразить].
physic|al ['fizikəl] □ физический; телесный; **~ian** [fi'ziʃən] врач; **~ist** ['fizisist] физик; **~s** ['fiziks] *sg.* физика.
physique [fi'zi:k] телосложение.
pick [pik] 1. удар (острым); выбор; кирка; 2. выбирать [выбрать]; ковырять [-рнуть] в (П); соб(и)рать (цветы, плоды); обгладывать [обглодать]; [по]клевать; срывать [сорвать] (цветок, фрукт); ~ out выбирать [выбрать]; ~ up соб(и)рать; подбирать [подобрать]; поднимать [-нять]; заезжать [заехать] за (Т); **~-a-back** ['pikəbæk] (о детях) на спине (отца и т. п.); **~axe** кирка.
picket ['pikit] 1. кол; ⚔ сторожевая застава; стачечный пикет; 2. выставлять пикеты вокруг (Р); обносить частоколом.
picking ['pikiŋ] собирание, отбор и т. д. (*s. verb*); **~s** *pl.* остатки *m/pl.*, объедки *m/pl.*; *mst* **~s** *pl.* мелкая пожива.
pickle [pikl] 1. рассол; *pl.* пикули *f/pl.*; F неприятности *f/pl.*; 2. [по-]солить; **~d** herring солёная селёдка.

pick|lock ['piklɔk] отмы́чка; **~pocket** карма́нный вор.
pictorial [pik'tɔ:riəl] **1.** иллюстри́рованный; изобрази́тельный; **2.** иллюстри́рованный журна́л.
picture ['piktʃə] **1.** карти́на; the **~s** *pl.* кино́ *indecl.*; **~-gallery** карти́нная галере́я; **~ (post)card** откры́тка с ви́дом; **2.** изобража́ть [-рази́ть]; опи́сывать [-са́ть]; вообража́ть [-рази́ть]; **~sque** [piktʃə'resk] живопи́сный.
pie [pai] паште́т; пиро́г; торт.
piebald ['paibɔ:ld] пе́гий (о ло́шади).
piece [pi:s] **1.** кусо́к, часть *f*; обры́вок, обло́мок; шту́ка; **~ of advice** сове́т; **~ of news** но́вость *f*; **by the ~** пошту́чно; **give a ~ of one's mind** выска́зывать своё мне́ние; **take to ~s** разбира́ть на ча́сти; **2.** [по]чини́ть; соединя́ть в одно́ це́лое, собира́ть из кусо́чков; **~meal** по частя́м, постепе́нно; **~work** сде́льная рабо́та.
pier [piə] усто́й; бык (моста́); мол; волноло́м; при́стань *f*.
pierce [piəs] пронза́ть [-зи́ть]; просве́рливать [-ли́ть]; прони́зывать [-за́ть].
piety ['paiəti] благоче́стие, на́божность *f*.
pig [pig] свинья́.
pigeon ['pidʒin] го́лубь *m*; **~-hole** **1.** отделе́ние (пи́сьменного стола́ и т. п.); **2.** раскла́дывать по я́щикам; откла́дывать в до́лгий я́щик.
pig|headed ['pig'hedid] упря́мый; **~-iron** чугу́н в болва́нках; **~skin** свина́я ко́жа; **~sty** свина́рник; **~tail** коси́чка, коса́.
pike [paik] ⚔ копьё; пи́ка; *zo.* щу́ка.
pile [pail] **1.** ку́ча, гру́да; ⚡ батаре́я; костёр; шта́бель *m*; **~s** *pl.* геморро́й; **2.** скла́дывать [сложи́ть]; сва́ливать в ку́чу.
pilfer ['pilfə] [у]ворова́ть.
pilgrim ['pilgrim] пало́мник; **~age** ['pilgrimidʒ] пало́мничество.
pill [pil] пилю́ля.
pillage ['pilidʒ] **1.** грабёж; **2.** [о]гра́бить.
pillar ['pilə] столб, коло́нна; **~-box** почто́вый я́щик.
pillion ['piljən] *mot.* за́днее сиде́нье.
pillory ['piləri] **1.** позо́рный столб; **2.** поста́вить к позо́рному столбу́.
pillow ['pilou] поду́шка; **~-case, ~-slip** на́волочка.
pilot ['pailət] **1.** ✈ пило́т; ⚓ ло́цман; **2.** ⚓ проводи́ть [-вести́]; ✈ пилоти́ровать; **~-balloon** шар-пило́т.
pimp [pimp] **1.** сво́дник (-ица); **2.** сво́дничать.
pimple [pimpl] пры́щик.
pin [pin] **1.** була́вка; шпи́лька; кно́пка; ке́гля; ♪ ко́лок; **2.** прика́лывать [-коло́ть]; *fig.* пригвожда́ть [-озди́ть].
pinafore ['pinəfɔ:] пере́дник.
pincers ['pinsəz] *pl.* клещи́ *f/pl.*; щипцы́ *m/pl.*
pinch [pintʃ] **1.** щипо́к; щепо́тка (со́ли и т. п.); стеснённое положе́ние, кра́йность *f*; **2.** *v/t.* щипа́ть [щипну́ть]; прищемля́ть [-ми́ть]; *v/i.* [по]скупи́ться; жать (об о́буви).
pine [pain] **1.** ⚘ сосна́; **2.** [за]ча́хнуть; изны́(ва́)ть; **~-apple** анана́с; **~-cone** сосно́вая ши́шка.
pinion ['pinjən] **1.** оконе́чность пти́чьего крыла́; перо́ (крыла́); ⊕ шестерня́; **2.** подреза́ть кры́лья (Д); *fig.* свя́зывать ру́ки (Д).
pink [piŋk] **1.** ⚘ гвозди́ка; *fig.* вы́сшая сте́пень *f*; **2.** ро́зовый.
pinnacle ['pinəkl] △ остроконе́чная ба́шенка; верши́на (горы́); *fig.* верх.
pint [paint] пи́нта (= 0,47 ли́тра).
pioneer [paiə'niə] **1.** пионе́р; ⚔ сапёр; **2.** прокла́дывать путь (for Д); руководи́ть (ке́м-либо).
pious ['paiəs] □ на́божный.
pip [pip] *vet.* типу́н; ко́сточка, зёрнышко (плода́); очко́ (на ка́ртах); звёздочка (на пого́не).
pipe [paip] **1.** труба́; тру́бка; ♪ свире́ль *f*, ду́дка; бо́чка (для вина́); **2.** игра́ть на свире́ли и т. п.; [за-] пища́ть; **~-layer** прокла́дчик труб; **~-line** трубопрово́д; нефтепрово́д; **~r** ['paipə] ду́дочник; волы́нщик.
piping ['paipiŋ]: **1.** **~ hot** о́чень горя́чий; **2.** кант (на пла́тье).
pique [pi:k] **1.** доса́да; **2.** возбужда́ть [-уди́ть] (любопы́тство); коло́ть [кольну́ть], заде́(ва́)ть (самолю́бие); **~ o. s. on** чва́ниться (Т).
pira|cy ['paiərəsi] пира́тство; наруше́ние а́вторского пра́ва; **~te** [-rit] **1.** пира́т; наруши́тель а́вторского пра́ва; **2.** самово́льно переиздава́ть.
pistol [pistl] пистоле́т.
piston ['pistən] ⊕ по́ршень *m*; **~-rod** шату́н; **~-stroke** ход по́ршня.
pit [pit] **1.** я́ма; ша́хта; о́спина; *thea.* парте́р; *Am.* отде́л това́рной би́ржи; **2.** скла́дывать в я́му (на́ зиму).
pitch [pitʃ] **1.** смола́; дёготь *m*; бросо́к; сте́пень *f*; ♪ высота́ то́на; ⚓ килева́я ка́чка; ⊕ накло́н; **2.** *v/t.* разби́(ва́)ть (пала́тку); мета́ть [метну́ть], броса́ть [бро́сить]; ♪ дава́ть основно́й тон (Д); *v/i.* ⚔ располага́ться ла́герем; подверга́ться ка́чке; F **~ into** набра́сываться [-ро́ситься] на (В).
pitcher ['pitʃə] кувши́н.
pitchfork ['pitʃfɔ:k] ви́лы *f/pl.*; ♪ камерто́н.
pitfall ['pitfɔ:l] *fig.* лову́шка.
pith [piθ] спинно́й мозг; сердцеви́на; *fig.* су́щность *f*, суть *f*; **~y**

['piθi] с сердцеви́ной; энерги́чный.

pitiable ['pitiəbl] □ жа́лкий.

pitiful ['pitiful] □ жа́лостливый; жа́лостный; (*a. contp.*) жа́лкий.

pitiless ['pitilis] □ безжа́лостный.

pittance ['pitəns] ску́дное жа́лование.

pity ['piti] **1.** жа́лость *f* (for к Д); it is a ~ жаль; **2.** [по]жале́ть.

pivot ['pivət] **1.** то́чка враще́ния; ⊕ сте́ржень *m* (*a. fig.*); штифт; **2.** враща́ться ([up]on вокру́г Р).

placable ['pleikəbl] □ кро́ткий, незлопа́мятный.

placard ['plækɑ:d] **1.** плака́т; **2.** расклеи́(ва)ть (объявле́ния); реклами́ровать плака́тами.

place [pleis] **1.** ме́сто; месте́чко, селе́ние; пло́щадь *f*; жили́ще; уса́дьба; до́лжность *f*, слу́жба; ~ of delivery ме́сто доста́вки; give ~ to уступа́ть ме́сто (Д); in ~ of вме́сто (Р); out of ~ неуме́стный; **2.** [по]ста́вить, класть [положи́ть]; размеща́ть [-ести́ть], помеща́ть [-ести́ть].

placid ['plæsid] □ споко́йный, безмяте́жный.

plagiar|ism ['pleidʒiərizm] плагиа́т; **~ize** [-raiz] незако́нно заи́мствовать (мы́сли и т. п.).

plague [pleig] **1.** бе́дствие, бич; чума́; **2.** [из]му́чить; F надоеда́ть [-е́сть] (Д).

plaid [plæd] шотла́ндка; плед.

plain [plein] **1.** □ просто́й; поня́тный; я́сный, я́вный; очеви́дный; обыкнове́нный; гла́дкий, ро́вный; **2.** *adv.* я́сно; разбо́рчиво; открове́нно; **3.** равни́на; пло́скость *f*; **~-clothes man** сы́щик; **~dealing** прямота́.

plaint|iff ['pleintif] исте́ц, исти́ца; **~ive** ['pleintiv] □ жа́лобный, зауны́вный.

plait [plæt, *Am.* pleit] **1.** коса́ (воло́с); **2.** заплета́ть [-ести́].

plan [plæn] **1.** план; **2.** составля́ть план; *fig.* намеча́ть [-е́тить]; намерева́ться.

plane [plein] **1.** пло́ский; **2.** пло́скость *f*; прое́кция; ✈ несу́щая пове́рхность *f*; самолёт; *fig.* у́ровень *m*; ⊕ руба́нок; **3.** [вы́]строга́ть; ✈ [с]плани́ровать.

plank [plæŋk] **1.** доска́, пла́нка; *Am. pol.* пункт парти́йной програ́ммы; **2.** настила́ть и́ли обшива́ть до́сками; *sl.* ~ down выкла́дывать [вы́ложить] (де́ньги).

plant [plɑ:nt] **1.** расте́ние; ⊕ заво́д, фа́брика; **2.** сажа́ть [посади́ть] (расте́ние); устана́вливать [-нови́ть]; **~ation** [plæn'teiʃən] планта́ция; насажде́ние; **~er** ['plɑ:ntə] планта́тор.

plaque [plɑ:k] таре́лка (как стенно́е украше́ние); доще́чка.

plash [plæʃ] плеска́ть(ся) [-сну́ть].

plaster ['plɑ:stə] **1.** *pharm.* пла́стырь *m*; ⊕ штукату́рка; (*mst* ~ of Paris) гипс; **2.** [о]штукату́рить; накла́дывать пла́стырь на (В).

plastic ['plæstik] (~ally) пласти́ческий; ~ material пластма́сса.

plat [plæt] план, съёмка; уча́сток.

plate [pleit] **1.** пласти́нка; плита́; полоса́ (мета́лла); доще́чка с на́дписью; столо́вое серебро́; таре́лка; ⊕ листово́е желе́зо; **2.** покрыва́ть мета́ллом.

plat(t)en [plætn] ва́лик (пи́шущей маши́нки).

platform ['plætfɔ:m] перро́н, платфо́рма; трибу́на; площа́дка (ваго́на); полити́ческая програ́мма.

platinum ['plætinəm] *min.* пла́тина.

platitude [-titju:d] бана́льность *f*.

platoon [plə'tu:n] ⚔ взвод.

platter ['plætə] деревя́нная таре́лка.

plaudit ['plɔ:dit] рукоплеска́ния [*n/pl.*]

plausible ['plɔ:zəbl] □ правдоподо́бный.

play [plei] **1.** игра́; пье́са; ⊕ зазо́р; мёртвый ход; **2.** игра́ть [сыгра́ть] (в В, ♪ на П); свобо́дно дви́гаться (о механи́зме); ~ off *fig.* разы́грывать [-ра́ть]; стра́вливать [страви́ть] (against с Т); **~ed out** вы́дохшийся; **~bill** театра́льная афи́ша; **~er** ['pleiə] игро́к; актёр; **~er-piano** пиано́ла; **~fellow, ~mate** това́рищ игр, друг де́тства; партнёр; **~ful** ['pleiful] □ игри́вый; **~goer** театра́л; **~-ground** площа́дка для игр; **~-house** теа́тр; **~thing** игру́шка; **~wright** драмату́рг.

plea [pli:] оправда́ние, до́вод; мольба́; on the ~ (of и́ли that ...) под предло́гом (Р *or* что ...).

plead [pli:d] *v/i.* обраща́ться к суду́; ~ for вступа́ться [-пи́ться] за (В); говори́ть за (В); ~ guilty признава́ть себя́ вино́вным; *v/t.* защища́ть [-ити́ть] (в суде́); приводи́ть в оправда́ние; **~er** ['pli:də] ⚖ защи́тник; **~ing** ['pli:diŋ] ⚖ защи́та.

pleasant [pleznt] □ прия́тный; **~ry** [-ri] шу́тка.

please [pli:z] [по]нра́виться (Д); угожда́ть [угоди́ть] (Д); if you ~ с ва́шего позволе́ния; изво́льте! ~ come in! войди́те пожа́луйста!; доставля́ть удово́льствие (Д); be ~d to do де́лать с удово́льствием; be ~d with быть дово́льным (Т); ~d [pli:zd] дово́льный.

pleasing ['pli:ziŋ] □ прия́тный.

pleasure ['pleʒə] удово́льствие, наслажде́ние; *attr.* увесели́тельный; at ~ по жела́нию.

pleat [pli:t] **1.** скла́дка; **2.** де́лать скла́дки на (П).

pledge [pledʒ] **1.** зало́г, закла́д; обе́т, обеща́ние; **2.** закла́дывать [заложи́ть]; руча́ться [поручи́ться] (T); he ~d himself он связа́л себя́ обеща́нием.
plenary [pli:nəri] по́лный, плена́рный.
plenipotentiary [plenipə'tenʃəri] полномо́чный представи́тель *m*.
plentiful ['plentiful] □ оби́льный.
plenty [-ti] **1.** изоби́лие; доста́ток; избы́ток; ~ of мно́го (P); **2.** F чрезвы́чайно; вполне́.
pliable ['plaiəbl] □ ги́бкий; *fig.* пода́тливый, мя́гкий.
pliancy ['plaiənsi] ги́бкость *f*.
pliers ['pleiəz] *pl.* плоскогу́бцы *m/pl.*
plight [plait] **1.** свя́зывать обеща́нием; помо́лвить *pf.*; **2.** (плохо́е) положе́ние.
plod [plɔd] (*a.* ~ along, on) таска́ться, [по]тащи́ться; корпе́ть (at над T).
plot [plɔt] **1.** уча́сток земли́. деля́нка; за́говор; план; фа́була, сюже́т; **2.** *v/i.* составля́ть за́говор; [за]интригова́ть; *v/t.* наноси́ть [нанести́] (на ка́рту); *b. s.* замышля́ть [-ы́слить].
plough, *Am. a.* plow [plau] **1.** плуг; **2.** [вс]паха́ть; *fig.* [из]борозди́ть; ~**share** ле́ме́х.
pluck [plʌk] **1.** дёрганье; F сме́лость *f*, му́жество; потроха́ *m/pl.*; **2.** срыва́ть [сорва́ть] (цвето́к); ощи́пывать [-па́ть] (пти́цу); ~ at дёргать [дёрнуть] (B); хвата́ть(ся) [схвати́ть(ся)] за (B); ~ up courage собра́ться с ду́хом; ~**y** ['plʌki] сме́лый, отва́жный.
plug [plʌg] **1.** вту́лка; заты́чка; ⚡ ште́псель *m*; ~ socket ште́псельная розе́тка; **2.** *v/t.* затыка́ть [заткну́ть]; [за]пломбирова́ть (зуб).
plum [plʌm] сли́ва.
plumage ['plu:midʒ] опере́ние.
plumb [plʌm] **1.** вертика́льный; отве́сный; **2.** отве́с; лот; **3.** *v/t.* ста́вить по отве́су; измеря́ть ло́том; проника́ть вглубь (P); *v/i.* рабо́тать водопрово́дчиком; ~**er** ['plʌmə] водопрово́дчик; ~**ing** [-iŋ] водопрово́д(ное де́ло).
plume [plu:m] **1.** перо́; плюма́ж; **2.** украша́ть плюма́жем; ~ o. s. on кичи́ться (T).
plummet ['plʌmit] свинцо́вый отве́с; грузи́ло.
plump [plʌmp] **1.** *adj.* пу́хлый, по́лный; F □ реши́тельный; **2.** [по]толсте́ть; бу́хать(ся) [-хнуть (-ся)]; **3.** тяжёлое паде́ние; **4.** F *adv.* пря́мо, без обиняко́в.
plunder ['plʌndə] **1.** грабёж; награ́бленные ве́щи *f/pl.*; **2.** [о]гра́бить.
plunge [plʌndʒ] **1.** ныря́ть [нырну́ть]; окуна́ть(ся) [-ну́ть(ся)]; **2.** ныря́ние; погруже́ние; take the ~ де́лать реши́тельный шаг.
plurality [pluə'ræliti] мно́жество; большинство́; мно́жественность *f*.
plush [plʌʃ] плюш, плис.
ply [plai] **1.** слой; скла́дка; оборо́т; three-~ трёхсло́йный; **2.** *v/t.* засыпа́ть [засы́пать], забра́сывать [-роса́ть] (вопро́сами); *v/i.* курси́ровать; ~**-wood** фане́ра.
pneumatic [nju:'mætik] **1.** (~ally) пневмати́ческий; ~ post пневмати́ческая по́чта; **2.** пневмати́ческая ши́на.
pneumonia [nju:'mounjə] ⚕ воспале́ние лёгких.
poach [poutʃ] браконье́рствовать; ~ed egg яйцо́-пашо́т.
poacher ['poutʃə] браконье́р.
pocket ['pɔkit] **1.** карма́н; ✈ возду́шная я́ма; **2.** класть в карма́н; прикарма́ни(ва)ть; присва́ивать [-сво́ить]; подавля́ть [-ви́ть] (чу́вство); прогла́тывать [-лоти́ть] (оби́ду); **3.** карма́нный.
pod [pɔd] ⚘ стручо́к; шелуха́.
poem ['pouim] поэ́ма; стихотворе́ние.
poet ['pouit] поэ́т; ~**ess** [-is] поэте́сса; ~**ic**(**al** □) [pou'etik, -tikəl] поэти́ческий; поэти́чный; ~**ics** [-tiks] *pl.* поэ́тика; ~**ry** ['pouitri] поэ́зия.
poignan|cy ['pɔi(g)nənsi] острота́; ~**t** [-t] о́стрый; *fig.* мучи́тельный.
point [pɔint] **1.** то́чка; пункт, смысл; суть де́ла; очко́; деле́ние (шкалы́); остриё, о́стрый коне́ц; 🚂 стре́лка; ~ of view то́чка зре́ния; the ~ is that ... де́ло в том, что ...; make a ~ of *ger.* поста́вить себе́ зада́чей (+ *inf.*); in ~ of в отноше́нии (P); off the ~ не (относя́щийся) к де́лу; be on the ~ of *ger.* соб(и)ра́ться (+ *inf.*); win on ~s выи́грывать по пу́нктам; to the ~ к де́лу (относя́щийся); **2.** *v/t.* ~ one's finger пока́зывать па́льцем (at на B); заостря́ть [-ри́ть]; (*often* ~ out) ука́зывать [-за́ть]; ~ at направля́ть [-ра́вить] (ору́жие) на (B); *v/i.* ~ at ука́зывать [-за́ть] на (B); ~ to быть напра́вленным на (B); ~**ed** ['pɔintid] □ остроконе́чный; о́стрый; *fig.* ко́лкий; ~**er** ['pɔintə] указа́тель *m*; ука́зка; по́йнтер; ~**less** [-lis] пло́ский; бессмы́сленный.
poise [pɔiz] **1.** равнове́сие; оса́нка; **2.** *v/t.* уравнове́шивать [-е́сить]; держа́ть (го́лову и т. п.); *v/i.* находи́ться в равнове́сии; пари́ть.
poison ['pɔizn] **1.** яд, отра́ва; **2.** отравля́ть [-ви́ть]; ~**ous** [-əs] (*fig.* *a.*) ядови́тый.
poke [pouk] **1.** толчо́к, тычо́к; **2.** *v/t.* ты́кать [ткнуть]; толка́ть [-кну́ть]; сова́ть [су́нуть]; меша́ть кочерго́й; ~ fun at подшу́чивать [-шути́ть] над (T); *v/i.* сова́ть нос

(into в В); искáть óщупью (for В) [*or* Р).

poker ['poukə] кочергá.

poky ['pouki] тéсный; убóгий.

polar ['poulə] полярный; ~ bear бéлый медвéдь *m*.

pole [poul] пóлюс; шест; жердь *f*; кол; 2 поля́к, пóлька; **~cat** *zo.* хорёк.

polemic [po'lemik] (*a.* **~al** [-mikəl] □) полеми́ческий.

pole-star Поля́рная звездá; *fig.* путевóдная звездá.

police [pə'li:s] **1.** поли́ция; **2.** поддéрживать поря́док в (П); **~-man** полицéйский; **~-station** полицéйский учáсток.

policy ['pɔlisi] поли́тика; ли́ния поведéния; страховóй пóлис.

Polish[1] ['pouliʃ] пóльский.

polish[2] ['pɔliʃ] **1.** полирóвка; *fig.* лоск; **2.** [на]полировáть; *fig.* утончáть [-чи́ть].

polite [pə'lait] □ вéжливый, благовоспи́танный; **~ness** [-nis] вéжливость *f*.

politic ['pɔlitik] □ полити́чный; расчётливый; **~al** [pə'litikəl] □ полити́ческий; госудáрственный; **~ian** [pɔli'tiʃən] поли́тик; **~s** ['pɔlitiks] *pl.* поли́тика.

poll [poul] **1.** голосовáние; подсчёт голосóв; спи́сок избирáтелей; **2.** *v/t.* получáть [-чи́ть] (голосá); *v/i.* [про]голосовáть; **~-book** спи́сок избирáтелей.

pollen ['pɔlin] ⚘ пыльцá.

poll-tax ['pɔltæks] подýшный налóг.

pollute [pə'lu:t] загрязня́ть [-ни́ть]; осквернять [-ни́ть].

polyp(e) ['pɔlip] *zo.*, **~us** [-lipəs] ⚕ поли́п.

pommel ['pʌml] **1.** головка (эфéса шпáги); лукá (седлá), **2.** [по]би́ть; [по]колоти́ть.

pomp [pɔmp] пóмпа; великолéпие.

pompous ['pɔmpəs] □ напы́щенный.

pond [pɔnd] пруд.

ponder ['pɔndə] *v/t.* обдýм(ыв)ать; *v/i.* задýм(ыв)аться; **~able** [-rəbl] весóмый; **~ous** [-rəs] □ *fig.* тяжеловéсный.

pontiff ['pɔntif] первосвящéнник.

pontoon [pɔn'tu:n] ⚔ понтóн; **~-bridge** понтóнный мост.

pony ['pouni] пóни *m indecl.* (лошáдка).

poodle [pu:dl] пýдель *m*.

pool [pu:l] **1.** лýжа; бассéйн; óмут; *cards* пýлька; † пул; **2.** † объединя́ть в óбщий фонд; склáдываться [сложи́ться] (with с Т).

poop [pu:p] ⚓ кормá.

poor [puə] □ бéдный, неимýщий; несчáстный; скýдный; плохóй; **~-house** богадéльня; **~-law** закóн о бéдных; **~ly** ['puəli] *adj.* нездорóвый; **~ness** ['puənis] бéдность *f*.

pop [pɔp] **1.** хлóпанье; F шипýчий напи́ток; **2.** *v/t.* совáть [сýнуть]; *v/i.* хлóпать [-пнуть] (о прóбке); [по]трéскаться (о каштáнах и т.п.); ~ in внезáпно появи́ться.

popcorn ['pɔpkɔ:n] *Am.* калёные зёрна кукурýзы.

pope [poup] (ри́мский) пáпа *m*.

poplar ['pɔplə] ⚘ тóполь *m*.

poppy ['pɔpi] ⚘ мак.

popula|ce ['pɔpjuləs] простонарóдье; **~r** [-lə] □ нарóдный; популя́рный; **~rity** [-'læriti] популя́рность *f*.

populat|e ['pɔpjuleit] населя́ть [-ли́ть]; **~ion** [pɔpju'leiʃən] населéние.

populous ['pɔpjuləs] □ многолю́дный.

porcelain ['pɔ:slin] фарфóр.

porch [pɔ:tʃ] подъéзд; пóртик; *Am.* верáнда.

pore [pɔ:] **1.** пóра; **2.** погружáться [-узи́ться] (over в В).

pork [pɔ:k] свини́на.

porous ['pɔ:rəs] □ пóристый.

porridge ['pɔridʒ] овся́ная кáша.

port [pɔ:t] **1.** гáвань *f*, порт; ⚓ лéвый борт; портвéйн; **2.** ⚓ брать налéво.

portable ['pɔ:təbl] портати́вный.

portal [pɔ:tl] портáл; тáмбур (двéрей).

portend [pɔ:'tend] предвещáть.

portent ['pɔ:tent] предвéстник, знáмение (плохóго); чýдо; **~ous** [pɔ:'tentəs] □ зловéщий; знаменáтельный.

porter ['pɔ:tə] привра́тник, швейцáр; носи́льщик; пóртер (пи́во).

portion ['pɔ:ʃən] **1.** часть *f*; пóрция; *fig.* удéл, ýчасть *f*; **2.** дели́ть (на чáсти); наделя́ть [-ли́ть].

portly ['pɔ:tli] дорóдный; представи́тельный.

portmanteau [pɔ:t'mæntou] чемодáн.

portrait ['pɔ:trit] портрéт.

portray [pɔ:'trei] рисовáть портрéт с (Р); изображáть [-рази́ть]; опи́сывать [-сáть]; **~al** [-əl] рисовáние портрéта; изображéние; описáние.

pose [pouz] **1.** пóза; **2.** пози́ровать; стáвить в пóзу; [по]стáвить (вопрóс); ~ as выдавáть себя́ за (В).

position [pə'ziʃən] мéсто; положéние; пози́ция; состоя́ние; тóчка зрéния.

positive ['pɔzətiv] **1.** □ положи́тельный; позити́вный; увéренный; самоувéренный; абсолю́тный; **2.** *gr.* положи́тельная стéпень *f*; *phot.* позити́в.

possess [pə'zes] обладáть (Т); владéть (Т); *fig.* овладé(вá)ть (Т); be **~ed** быть одержи́мым; ~ o. s. of завладé(вá)ть (Т); **~ion** [-ʃən] владéние; обладáние; *fig.* одержи́мость *f*; **~or** [-sə] владéлец.

possib|ility [pɔsə'biliti] возмóжность *f*; **~le** ['pɔsəbl] □ возмóж-

ный; **~ly** [-i] возмо́жно; if I ~ can е́сли у меня́ бу́дет возмо́жность *f*.
post [poust] **1.** по́чта; столб; до́лжность *f*; пост; *Am.* ~ exchange гарнизо́нный магази́н; **2.** *v/t.* отправля́ть по по́чте; раскле́и(ва)ть (афи́ши); расставля́ть [-а́вить]; well ~ed хорошо́ осведомлённый; *v/i.* [по]спеши́ть.
postage [-tidʒ] почто́вая опла́та; ~**-stamp** почто́вая ма́рка.
postal ['poustəl] □ почто́вый; ~ order де́нежный почто́вый перево́д.
post-card откры́тка.
poster ['poustə] афи́ша, плака́т.
posterior [pɔs'tiəriə] **1.** □ после́дующий; за́дний; **2.** зад.
posterity [pɔs'teriti] пото́мство.
post-free без почто́вой опла́ты.
post-haste ['poust'heist] поспе́шно.
posthumous ['pɔstjuməs] □ посме́ртный; рождённый по́сле сме́рти отца́.
post|man почтальо́н; ~**mark** **1.** почто́вый ште́мпель *m*; **2.** [за-] штемпелева́ть; ~**master** почтме́йстер.
post-mortem ['poust'mɔːtem] **1.** посме́ртный; **2.** вскры́тие тру́па.
post|(-)office по́чта, почто́вая конто́ра; ~ box абонеме́нтный почто́вый я́щик; ~**-paid** франки́рованный.
postpone [poust'poun] отсро́чи(ва)ть; откла́дывать [отложи́ть]; ~**ment** [-mənt] отсро́чка.
postscript ['pous(s)kript] постскри́птум.
postulate **1.** ['pɔstjulit] постула́т; **2.** [-leit] ста́вить усло́вием; постули́ровать (*im*)*pf.*; [по]тре́бовать.
posture ['pɔstʃə] **1.** по́за; положе́ние; **2.** пози́ровать; ста́вить в по́зу.
post-war ['poust'wɔː] послевое́нный.
posy ['pouzi] буке́т цвето́в.
pot [pɔt] **1.** горшо́к; котело́к; **2.** класть и́ли сажа́ть в горшо́к; заготовля́ть впрок.
potation [pou'teiʃən] питьё, напи́ток; (*part.* ~s *pl.*) попо́йка.
potato [pə'teitou] карто́фелина; ~**es** *pl.* карто́фель *m*; F карто́шка.
pot-belly пу́зо; пуза́тый челове́к.
poten|cy ['poutənsi] си́ла, могу́щество; ~**t** [-tənt] □ могу́щественный; кре́пкий; ~**tial** [pə'tenʃəl] **1.** потенциа́льный, возмо́жный; **2.** потенциа́л.
pother ['pɔðə] сумато́ха; шум.
pot|-herb пря́ное расте́ние; ~**house** каба́к.
potion ['pouʃən] ⚕ миксту́ра; зе́лье.
potter ['pɔtə] гонча́р; ~**y** [-ri] гли́няные изде́лия *n/pl.*; гонча́рня.
pouch [pautʃ] **1.** су́мка (*a. biol.*); мешо́чек; **2.** прикарма́ни(ва)ть; класть в су́мку.
poultry ['poultri] дома́шняя пти́ца.
pounce [pauns] **1.** прыжо́к, наско́к; **2.** набра́сываться [-ро́ситься] ([up]on на В).
pound [paund] **1.** фунт; заго́н; ~ (sterling) фунт сте́рлингов (сокр. £ = 20 ш.); **2.** [ис]толо́чь; колоти́ть(ся); ~ at бомбардирова́ть.
pour [pɔː] *v/t.* лить; ~ out нали́(ва́)ть; сы́пать, насыпа́ть [насы́пать]; *v/i.* ли́ться; [по]сы́паться.
pout [paut] **1.** наду́тые гу́бы *f/pl.*; **2.** *v/t.* наду́(ва́)ть (гу́бы); *v/i.* [на-] ду́ться.
poverty ['pɔvəti] бе́дность *f*.
powder ['paudə] **1.** порошо́к; пу́дра; по́рох; **2.** [ис]толо́чь; [на-] пу́дрить(ся); посыпа́ть [посы́пать]; ~**-box** пу́дреница.
power ['pauə] си́ла; мо́щность *f*; *pol.* держа́ва; власть *f*; ⚖ полномо́чие; ⅍ сте́пень *f*; ~**-current** ток высо́кого напряже́ния; ~**ful** [-ful] □ мо́щный, могу́щественный; си́льный; ~**less** [-lis] бесси́льный; ~ **plant** силова́я устано́вка; ~**-station** электроста́нция.
pow-wow ['pau'wau] зна́харь (у инде́йцев) *m*; *Am.* шу́мное собра́ние.
practica|ble ['præktikəbl] □ осуществи́мый; проходи́мый (о доро́ге); ~**l** [-kəl] □ практи́ческий; практи́чный; факти́ческий; ~ joke (гру́бая) шу́тка, прока́за.
practice ['præktis] пра́ктика; упражне́ние, трениро́вка; привы́чка; обы́чай; put into ~ осуществля́ть [-ви́ть].
practise [~] *v/t.* применя́ть [-ни́ть]; занима́ться [-ня́ться] (Т); упражня́ться в (П); практикова́ть; *v/i.* упражня́ться; ~ (up)on злоупотребля́ть [-би́ть] (Т); ~**d** [-t] о́пытный.
practitioner [præk'tiʃnə] практику́ющий врач.
praise [preiz] **1.** хвала́; **2.** [по]хвали́ть.
praiseworthy ['preizwəːði] досто́йный похвалы́.
prance [prɑːns] станови́ться на дыбы́; гарцева́ть.
prank [præŋk] вы́ходка, прока́за.
prate [preit] **1.** пустосло́вие; **2.** пустосло́вить, болта́ть.
pray [prei] [по]моли́ться; [по]проси́ть; ~! прошу́ вас!
prayer [prɛə] моли́тва; про́сьба; Lord's ~ о́тче наш; ~**-book** моли́твенник; ~**ful** [-ful] □ богомо́льный.
pre... [priː, pri] до...; пред...
preach [priːtʃ] пропове́довать; ~**er** ['priːtʃə] пропове́дник.
preamble [priː'æmbl] преа́мбула; вступле́ние.
precarious [pri'kɛəriəs] ненадёжный.
precaution [pri'kɔːʃən] предосторо́жность *f*.
precede [pri'siːd] предше́ствовать

(Д); **~nce, ~ncy** [-əns(i)] пéрвенство,; преимýщественное значéние; **~nt** ['presidənt] прецедéнт.

precept ['pri:sept] наставлéние; зáповедь *f*; **~or** [pri'septə] настáвник.

precinct ['pri:siŋkt] предéл; (полицéйский) учáсток; (избирáтельный óкруг; **~s** *pl.* окрéстности *f/pl.*

precious ['preʃəs] 1. ☐ драгоцéнный; 2. F *adv.* óчень; **~!** здóрово!

precipi|ce ['presipis] прóпасть *f*; **~tate** 1. [pri'sipiteit] низвергáть [-éргнуть]; [по]торопи́ть; ⚗ осаждáть [осади́ть]; 2. [-tit] a) ☐ опромéтчивый; стреми́тельный; b) ⚗ осáдок; **~tation** [prisipi'teiʃən] низвержéние; стреми́тельность *f*; осáдки *m/pl.*; ⚗ осаждéние; **~tous** [pri'sipitəs] ☐ крутóй; обры́вистый.

precis|e [pri'sais] ☐ тóчный; **~ion** [-'siʒən] тóчность *f*.

preclude [pri'klu:d] исключáть зарáнее; предотвращáть [-рати́ть] (В); [по]мешáть (Д).

precocious [pri'kouʃəs] ☐ преждеврéменно развитóй.

preconceive ['pri:kən'si:v] представля́ть себé зарáнее; **~d** предвзя́тый. [предвзя́тое мнéние.]

preconception ['pri:kən'sepʃən]

precursor [pri'kə:sə] предтéча *m/f*; предшéственник (-ица).

predatory ['predətəri] хи́щный.

predecessor ['pri:disesə] предшéственник (-ица).

predestin|ate [pri:'destineit] предопределя́ть [-ли́ть]; **~ed** [-tind] предопределённый.

predicament [pri'dikəmənt] серьёзное затруднéние.

predicate ['predikit] предикáт.

predict [pri'dikt] предскáзывать [-зáть]; **~ion** [-kʃən] предсказáние.

predilection [pri:di'lekʃən] склóнность *f*, пристрáстие (for к Д).

predispos|e ['pri:dis'pouz] предрасполагáть [-ложи́ть].

predomina|nce [pri'dɔminəns] госпóдство, преобладáние; **~nt** [-nənt] ☐ преобладáющий; домини́рующий; **~te** [-neit] госпóдствовать, преобладáть (over над Т).

pre-eminent [pri:'eminənt] ☐ выдаю́щийся.

pre-emption [pri:'emʃən] (*a.* right of **~**) преимýщественное прáво на покýпку.

prefabricate ['pri:'fæbrikeit] изготовля́ть зарáнее (чáсти стандáртного дóма и т. п.).

preface ['prefis] 1. предисло́вие; 2. предпос(ы)лáть (Д with В); снабжáть предисло́вием.

prefect ['pri:fekt] префéкт.

prefer [pri'fə:] предпочитáть [-почéсть]; повышáть [-ы́сить] (в чи́не); под(ав)áть (прошéние); выдвигáть [вы́двинуть] (трéбование); **~able** ['prefərəbl] ☐ предпочти́тельный; **~ence** [rəns] предпочтéние; **~ential** [prefə'renʃəl] ☐ предпочти́тельный; льгóтный.

prefix ['pri:fiks] прéфикс, пристáвка.

pregnan|cy ['pregnənsi] берéменность *f*; богáтство (воображéния и т. п.); **~t** [-nənt] ☐ берéменная; *fig.* чревáтый; богáтый.

prejud|ge ['pri:'dʒʌdʒ] осуждáть, не вы́слушав; **~ice** ['predʒudis] 1. предрассýдок; предубеждéние; 2. предубеждáть [-беди́ть] (прóтив Р); наноси́ть ущéрб (Д); **~icial** [predʒu'diʃəl] пáгубный.

prelate ['prelit] прелáт.

preliminar|y [pri'liminəri] 1. ☐ предвари́тельный; вступи́тельный; 2. подготови́тельное мероприя́тие.

prelude ['prelju:d] ♪ прелю́дия.

prematur|e [premə'tjuə] преждеврéменный.

premeditation [primedi'teiʃən] преднамéренность *f*.

premier ['premjə] 1. пéрвый; 2. премьéр-мини́стр.

premises ['premisiz] *pl.* помещéние; дом (с пристрóйками).

premium ['pri:mjəm] наградá, прéмия; † лаж; страховáя прéмия; at a **~** вы́ше номинáльной стóимости; в большóм спрóсе.

premonit|ion [pri:mo'niʃən] предчýвствие; предупреждéние.

preoccup|ied [pri'ɔkjupaid] озабóченный; **~y** [-pai] поглощáть внимáние (Р); занимáть рáньше (чем ктó-либо).

preparat|ion [prepə'reiʃən] приготовлéние; подготóвка; **~ory** [pri:pærətəri] ☐ предвари́тельный; подготови́тельный, приготови́тельный.

prepare [pri'pɛə] *v/t.* приготовля́ть [-тóвить]; [при]готóвить; подготовля́ть [-тóвить]; *v/i.* [при]готóвиться; подготовля́ться [-тóвиться] (for к Д); **~d** [-d] ☐ подготóвленный; готóвый.

prepondera|nce [pri'pɔndərəns] преобладáние; **~nt** [-rənt] ☐ преобладáющий; **~te** [-reit] имéть перевéс; **~** over превосходи́ть [-взойти́] (В).

prepossess [pri:pə'zes] располагáть к себé; **~ing** [-iŋ] ☐ располагáющий.

preposterous [pri'pɔstərəs] несообрáзный, нелéпый, абсýрдный.

prerequisite ['pri:'rekwizit] предпосы́лка.

presage ['presidʒ] 1. предзнаменовáние; предчýвствие; 2. (*a.* [pri'seidʒ])предзнаменовáть,предвещáть; предчýвствовать.

prescribe [pris'kraib] предпи́сы-

вать [-писа́ть]; ⚕ пропи́сывать [-писа́ть].
prescription [pris'kripʃən] предписа́ние; ⚕ реце́пт.
presence [prezns] прису́тствие; ~ of mind прису́тствие ду́ха.
present[1] [preznt] 1. □ прису́тствующий; тепе́решний, настоя́щий; да́нный; 2. настоя́щее вре́мя; пода́рок; at ~ в да́нное вре́мя; for the ~ на э́тот раз.
present[2] [pri'zent] представля́ть [-а́вить]; преподноси́ть [-нести́]; под(ав)а́ть (проше́ние); [по]ста́вить (пье́су); одаря́ть [-ри́ть]; под(ав)а́ть.
presentation [prezen'teiʃən] представле́ние; подноше́ние; пода́ча.
presentiment [pri'zentimənt] предчу́вствие.
presently ['prezntli] вско́ре; сейча́с.
preservati|on [prezə'veiʃən] сохране́ние; сохра́нность *f*; **~ve** [pri'zə:vətiv] 1. предохрани́тельный; 2. предохрани́тельное сре́дство.
preserve [pri'zə:v] 1. сохраня́ть [-ни́ть]; предохраня́ть [-ни́ть]; заготовля́ть впрок (о́вощи и т. п.); 2. (*mst pl.*) консе́рвы *m/pl.* (*a. opt.*); варе́нье; запове́дник.
preside [pri'zaid] председа́тельствовать (over на П).
presiden|cy ['prezidənsi] президе́нтство; председа́тельство; **~t** [-dənt] президе́нт; председа́тель *m*.
press [pres] 1. печа́ть *f*, пре́сса; да́вка; ⊕ пресс; 2. *v/t.* жать; дави́ть; наж(им)а́ть; навя́зывать [-за́ть] (on Д); *Am.* [вы́]гла́дить; be **~ed** for time спеши́ть; *v/i.* дави́ть (on на В); ~ for наста́ивать [настоя́ть] на (П); ~ on [по]спеши́ть; ~ (up)on наседа́ть [-е́сть] на (В); **~ing** ['presiŋ] □ неотло́жный; **~ure** ['preʃə] давле́ние (*a. fig.*); сжа́тие.
presum|able [pri'zju:məbl] □ предположи́тельный; **~e** [pri'zju:m] *v/t.* предполага́ть [-ложи́ть]; *v/i.* полага́ть; осме́ли(ва)ться; ~ (up)on злоупотребля́ть [-би́ть] (Т); кичи́ться (Т).
presumpt|ion [pri'zʌmpʃən] самонаде́янность *f*; предположе́ние; **~ive** [-tiv] □ предполага́емый; **~uous** [-tjuəs] □ самонаде́янный.
presuppos|e [pri:sə'pouz] предполага́ть [-ложи́ть]; **~ition** ['pri:sʌpə'ziʃən] предположе́ние.
pretence [pri'tens] прете́нзия, тре́бование; притво́рство; предло́г.
pretend [pri'tend] притворя́ться [-ри́ться]; симули́ровать (*im*)*pf.*; претендова́ть (to на В).
pretension [pri'tenʃən] прете́нзия, притяза́ние (to на В).
pretentious [-ʃəs] претенцио́зный.
pretext ['pri:tekst] предло́г.
pretty ['priti] 1. □ хоро́шенький; прия́тный; 2. *adv.* дово́льно.
prevail [pri'veil] превозмога́ть [-мо́чь] (over В); преоблада́ть (over над Т *or* среди́ Р); ~ (up)on a p. to do убеди́ть кого́-нибудь что́-либо сде́лать; **~ing** [-iŋ] □ преоблада́ющий.
prevalent ['prevələnt] □ преоблада́ющий; широко́ распространённый.
prevaricat|e [pri'værikeit] отклоня́ться от прямо́го отве́та, увиливать [-льну́ть].
prevent [pri'vent] предотвраща́ть [-ати́ть]; [по]меша́ть (Д); предупрежда́ть [-упреди́ть]; **~ion** [pri'venʃən] предупрежде́ние; предотвраще́ние; **~ive** [-tiv] 1. □ предупреди́тельный; профилакти́ческий; 2. ⚕ профилакти́ческое сре́дство.
pre|view ['pri:vju:] предвари́тельный осмо́тр (фи́льма, мод и т. п.).
previous ['pri:vjəs] □ предыду́щий; преждевре́менный; предвари́тельный; ~ to до (Р); **~ly** пре́жде.
pre-war ['pri:wɔ:] довое́нный.
prey [prei] 1. добы́ча; же́ртва; beast (bird) of ~ хи́щный зверь *m* (хи́щная пти́ца); 2. ~ (up)on: (о)гра́бить; терза́ть; подта́чивать [-точи́ть].
price [prais] 1. цена́; 2. оце́нивать [-ни́ть]; назнача́ть це́ну (Д); **~less** ['praislis] бесце́нный.
prick [prik] 1. проко́л; уко́л; шип; 2. *v/t.* коло́ть [кольну́ть]; ~ up one's ears навостри́ть у́ши; *v/i.* коло́ться; **~le** [prikl] шип, колю́чка; **~ly** ['prikli] колю́чий.
pride [praid] 1. го́рдость *f*; take ~ in горди́ться (Т); 2. ~ o. s. горди́ться ([up]on Т).
priest [pri:st] свяще́нник.
prim [prim] □ чо́порный; натя́нутый.
prima|cy ['praiməsi] пе́рвенство; **~ry** [-ri] □ первонача́льный; основно́й; нача́льный; перви́чный.
prime [praim] 1. □ гла́вный; первонача́льный; перви́чный; основно́й; превосхо́дный; ~ cost ✝ себесто́имость *f*; ♀ Minister премье́р-мини́стр; 2. *fig.* расцве́т; 3. *v/t.* снабжа́ть информа́цией; учи́ть гото́вым отве́там.
primer ['primə] буква́рь *m*; нача́льный уче́бник.
primeval [prai'mi:vəl] первобы́тный.
primitive ['primitiv] □ первобы́тный; примити́вный; основно́й.
primrose ['primrouz] ⚘ при́мула.
prince [prins] принц; князь *m*; **~ss** [prin'ses] принце́сса; княги́ня; княжна́.
principal ['prinsəpəl] 1. □ гла́вный, основно́й; 2. принципа́л,

главá; рéктор университéта; дирéктор шкóлы; основнóй капитáл.
principle ['prinsəpl] при́нцип; прáвило; причи́на, истóчник; on ~ из при́нципа.
print [print] 1. *typ.* печáть *f*; óттиск; шрифт; след; отпечáток; штамп; гравю́ра; произведéние печáти; ✝ набивнáя ткань *f*; out of ~ распрóданный (о печáтном); 2. [на]печáтать; *phot.* отпечáт(ыв)ать; *fig.* запечатлé(вá)ть (on на П); **~er** ['printə] печáтник.
printing ['printiŋ] печáтание; печáтное издáние; *attr.* печáтный; **~-ink** типогрáфская крáска; **~-office** типогрáфия.
prior ['praiə] 1. предшéствующий (to Д); 2. *adv.* ~ to до (Р); 3. *eccl.* настоя́тель *m*; **~ity** [prai'ɔriti] приоритéт; очерёдность *f*.
prism [prizm] при́зма.
prison ['prizn] тюрьмá; **~er** [-ə] заключённый; плéнный.
privacy ['praivəsi] уединéние; сохранéние в тáйне.
private ['praivit] 1. □ чáстный; ли́чный; уединённый; конфиденциáльный; 2. ⚔ рядовóй; in ~ конфиденциáльно.
privation [prai'veiʃən] лишéние, нуждá.
privilege ['privilidʒ] 1. привилéгия; 2. давáть привилéгию (Д).
privy ['privi]: ~ to посвящённый в (В); ♀ Council тáйный совéт; ♀ Councillor член тáйного совéта; ♀ Seal мáлая государственная печáть *f*.
prize [praiz] 1. прéмия, приз; ⚓ приз; трофéй; вы́игрыш; 2. удостóенный прéмии; 3. высокó ценить; взлáмывать [взломáть]; **~-fighter** боксёр-профессионáл.
probab|ility [prɔbə'biliti] вероя́тность *f*; **~le** ['prɔbəbl] □ вероя́тный.
probation [prə'beiʃən] испытáние; испытáтельный стаж; ⚖ услóвное освобождéние.
probe [proub] ⚕ 1. зонд; 2. зонди́ровать.
probity ['proubiti] чéстность *f*.
problem ['prɔbləm] проблéма; ♗ задáча; **~atic(al** □) [prɔbli'mætik, -tikəl] проблемати́чный.
procedure [prə'si:dʒə] процеду́ра; óбраз дéйствия.
proceed [prə'si:d] отправля́ться дáльше; приступáть [-пи́ть] (to к Д); поступáть [-пи́ть]; продолжáть [-дóлжить] (with В); ~ from исходи́ть (от Р); **~ing** [-iŋ] посту́пок; **~s** *pl.* ⚖ судопроизвóдство; протокóлы *m/pl.*, труды́ *m/pl.*; **~s** ['prousi:dz] дохóд; вы́ручка, вы́рученная су́мма.
process 1. ['prouses] процéсс; движéние, течéние; ход; спóсоб; in ~ на ходу́; in ~ of construction стрóящийся; 2. [prə'ses] привлекáть к суду́; ⊕ обрабáтывать [-бóтать]; **~ion** [-ʃən] процéссия.
proclaim [prə'kleim] провозглашáть [-ласи́ть]; объявля́ть [-ви́ть] (войну́ и т. п.).
proclamation [prɔklə'meiʃən] воззвáние; объявлéние; проклáмация.
proclivity [prə'kliviti] склóнность *f*.
procurat|ion [prɔkjuə'reiʃən] полномóчие, довéренность *f*; **~or** ['prɔkjuəreitə] повéренный.
procure [prə'kjuə] *v/t.* дост(ав)áть; *v/i.* свóдничать.
prod [prɔd] 1. тычóк, толчóк; 2. ты́кать [ткнуть]; толкáть [-кну́ть]; *fig.* подстрекáть [-кну́ть].
prodigal ['prɔdigəl] 1. расточи́тельный; ~ son блу́дный сын; 2. мот(óвка).
prodig|ious [prə'didʒəs] □ удиви́тельный; громáдный; **~y** ['prɔdidʒi] чу́до.
produc|e 1. [prə'dju:s] предъявля́ть [-ви́ть]; представля́ть [-áвить]; производи́ть [-вести́]; [по]стáвить (фильм и т. п.); из-д(ав)áть; 2. ['prɔdju:s] проду́кция; проду́кт; **~er** [prə'dju:sə] производи́тель *m*; режиссёр *m*.
product ['prɔdəkt] проду́кт, издéлие; **~ion** [prə'dʌkʃən] произвóдство; проду́кция; постанóвка; (худóжественное) произведéние; **~ive** [prə'dʌktiv] □ производи́тельный, продукти́вный; плодорóдный; **~iveness** [-nis], **~ivity** [prɔdʌk'tiviti] продукти́вность *f*, производи́тельность *f*.
profan|e [prə'fein] 1. □ мирскóй, свéтский; богоху́льный; 2. осквернять [-ни́ть]; профани́ровать (*im*)*pf.*; **~ity** [prə'fæniti] богоху́льство.
profess [prə'fes] исповéдовать (вéру); откры́то признавáть; заявля́ть [-ви́ть]; претендовáть на (В); *univ.* преподавáть; **~ion** [prə'feʃən] профéссия; заявлéние; вероисповéдание; **~ional** [-l] 1. □ профессионáльный; 2. специали́ст; профессионáл (*a. sport*); **~or** [-sə] профéссор.
proffer ['prɔfə] 1. предлагáть [-ложи́ть]; 2. предложéние.
proficien|cy [prə'fiʃənsi] óпытность *f*; умéние; **~t** [-ʃənt] 1. □ умéлый; иску́сный; 2. мáстер, знатóк.
profile ['proufi:l] прóфиль *m*.
profit ['prɔfit] 1. при́быль *f*; вы́года, пóльза; 2. *v/t.* приноси́ть пóльзу (Д); *v/i.* ~ by [вос]пóльзоваться (Т); извлекáть пóльзу из (Р); **~able** ['prɔfitəbl] □ при́быльный; вы́годный; полéзный; **~eer** [prɔfi'tiə] 1. спекуля́нт; 2. спеку-

ли́ровать; **~-sharing** уча́стие в при́были.
profligate ['prɔfligit] **1.** □ распу́тный; **2.** распу́тник.
profound [prə'faund] □ глубо́кий; основа́тельный; проникнове́нный.
profundity [prə'fʌnditi] глубина́.
profus|e [prə'fju:s] □ изоби́льный; ще́дрый; **~ion** [prə'fju:ʒən] изоби́лие.
progen|itor [prou'dʒenitə] прароди́тель(ница *f*) *m*; **~y** ['prɔdʒini] пото́мство.
program, ~me ['prougræm] програ́мма.
progress 1. ['prougres] прогре́сс; продвиже́ние; успе́хи *m/pl.*; be in ~ развива́ться; вести́сь; **2.** [prə'gres] продвига́ться вперёд; де́лать успе́хи; **~ion** [prə'greʃən] движе́ние вперёд; ♆ прогре́ссия; **~ive** [-siv] **1.** □ передово́й, прогресси́вный; прогресси́рующий; **2.** *pol.* член прогресси́вной па́ртии.
prohibit [prə'hibit] запреща́ть [-ети́ть]; препя́тствовать (Д); **~ion** [proui'biʃən] запреще́ние; **~ive** [prə'hibitiv] □ запрети́тельный.
project 1. ['prɔdʒekt] прое́кт; план; **2.** [prə'dʒekt] *v/t.* броса́ть [бро́сить]; [с-, за]проекти́ровать; *v/i.* обду́мывать план; вы́да(ва́)ться; **~ile** [prə'dʒektail] снаря́д; **~ion** [prə'dʒekʃən] мета́ние; проекти́рование; прое́кт; вы́ступ; прое́кция; **~or** [-tə] ✝ проектиро́вщик; *opt.* проже́ктор; волше́бный фона́рь *m.*
proletarian [proule'teəriən] **1.** пролета́рий; **2.** пролета́рский.
prolific [prə'lifik] (**~ally**) плодоро́дный; плодови́тый.
prolix ['prouliks] □ многосло́вный.
prologue ['proulɔg] проло́г.
prolong [prə'lɔŋ] продлева́ть [-ли́ть]; продолжа́ть [-до́лжить].
promenade [prɔmi'nɑ:d] **1.** прогу́лка; ме́сто для прогу́лки; **2.** прогу́ливаться [-ля́ться].
prominent ['prɔminənt] □ выступа́ющий; релье́фный; *fig.* выдаю́щийся.
promiscuous [prə'miskjuəs] □ разноро́дный; сме́шанный; неразбо́рчивый.
promis|e ['prɔmis] **1.** обеща́ние; **2.** обеща́ть (*im*)*pf.*, *pf. a.* [по-]; **~ing** [-iŋ] □ *fig.* подаю́щий наде́жды; **~sory** [-əri] заключа́ющий в себе́ обеща́ние; ~ note ✝ долгово́е обяза́тельство.
promontory ['prɔməntri] мыс.
promot|e [prə'mout] спосо́бствовать (*im*)*pf.*, *pf. a.* [по-] (Д); соде́йствовать (*im*)*pf.*, *pf. a.* [по-] (Д); выдвига́ть [вы́двинуть]; продвига́ть [-и́нуть]; повыша́ть по слу́жбе; ⚔ присво́ить зва́ние (Р); **~ion** [prə'mouʃən] повыше́ние (в чи́не и т. п.); продвиже́ние.
prompt [prɔmpt] **1.** □ бы́стрый; прово́рный; **2.** побужда́ть [-уди́ть]; внуша́ть [-ши́ть]; подска́зывать [-за́ть] (Д); суфли́ровать (Д); **~er** ['prɔmptə] суфлёр; **~ness** ['prɔmptnis] быстрота́; прово́рство.
promulgate ['prɔməlgeit] провозглаша́ть [-ласи́ть].
prone [proun] □ (лежа́щий) ничко́м; распростёртый; ~ to скло́нный к (Д).
prong [prɔŋ] зубе́ц (ви́лки); шпенёк.
pronounce [prə'nauns] произноси́ть [-нести́]; объявля́ть [-ви́ть].
pronunciation [-nʌnsi'eiʃən] произноше́ние.
proof [pru:f] **1.** доказа́тельство; про́ба. испыта́ние; *typ.* корректу́ра, про́бный о́ттиск; **2.** непроница́емый; недосту́пный; **~-reader** корре́ктор.
prop [prɔp] подпо́рка; опо́ра.
propaga|te ['prɔpəgeit] размножа́ть(ся) [-о́жить(ся)]; распространя́ть(ся) [-ни́ть(ся)]; **~tion** [prɔpə'geiʃən] размноже́ние; распростране́ние.
propel [prə'pel] продвига́ть вперёд; **~ler** [-ə] пропе́ллер, возду́шный винт; гребно́й винт.
propensity [prə'pensiti] скло́нность *f.*
proper ['prɔpə] □ сво́йственный, прису́щий; подходя́щий; пра́вильный; со́бственный; прили́чный; **~ty** [-ti] иму́щество, со́бственность *f*; сво́йство.
prophe|cy ['prɔfisi] проро́чество; **~sy** [-sai] [на]проро́чить.
prophet ['prɔfit] проро́к.
propi|tiate [prə'piʃieit] умилостивля́ть [уми́лостивить]; **~tious** [prə'piʃəs] □ благоскло́нный; благоприя́тный.
proportion [prə'pɔ:ʃən] **1.** пропо́рция; соразме́рность *f*; часть *f*; **~s** *pl.* разме́ры *m/pl.*; **2.** соразмеря́ть [-ме́рить]; **~al** [-l] □ пропорциона́льный.
propos|al [prə'pouzəl] предложе́ние; план; **~e** [prə'pouz] *v/t.* предлага́ть [-ложи́ть]; ~ to o. s. ста́вить себе́ це́лью; *v/i.* де́лать предложе́ние (бра́ка); наме́реваться, предполага́ть; **~ition** [prɔpə'ziʃən] предложе́ние.
propound [prə'paund] предлага́ть на обсужде́ние.
propriet|ary [prə'praiətəri] со́бственнический; ча́стный; *pharm.* патенто́ванный; **~or** [-tə] владе́лец (-лица); **~y** [-ti] уме́стность *f*, присто́йность *f*; the proprieties *pl.* прили́чия *n/pl.*
propulsion [prə'pʌlʃən] ⊕ приво́д; движе́ние вперёд.
pro-rate [prou'reit] распределя́ть пропорциона́льно.

prosaic [prou'zeiik] (~ally) *fig.* прозаи́чный.
proscribe [pros'kraib] объявля́ть вне зако́на; запреща́ть [-ети́ть].
prose [prouz] 1. про́за; 2. прозаи́ческий; *fig.* прозаи́чный.
prosecut|e ['prɔsikju:t] проводи́ть [-вести́], [по]вести́; пресле́довать суде́бным поря́дком; **~ion** [prɔsi'kju:ʃən] суде́бное пресле́дование; **~or** ['prɔsikju:tə] ⚖ обвини́тель *m*; public ~ прокуро́р.
prospect 1. ['prɔspekt] перспекти́ва, вид (*a. fig.*); † предполага́емый покупа́тель *m* (клие́нт и т. п.); 2. [prəs'pekt] ⚒ разве́д(ыв)ать (for на В); **~ive** [prəs'pektiv] □ бу́дущий, ожида́емый; **~us** [-təs] проспе́кт.
prosper ['prɔspə] *v/t.* благоприя́тствова́ть (Д); *v/i.* процвета́ть; преуспева́ть; **~ity** [prɔs'periti] процвета́ние; благосостоя́ние; *fig.* расцве́т; **~ous** ['prɔspərəs] □ благоприя́тный; состоя́тельный; процвета́ющий.
prostitute ['prɔstitju:t] 1. проститу́тка; 2. проституи́ровать (*im*) *pf.*; [о]бесче́стить.
prostrat|e 1. ['prɔstreit] распростёртый; пове́рженный; обесси́ленный; 2. [prɔs'treit] поверга́ть ниц; унижа́ть [уни́зить]; истоща́ть [-щи́ть]; ~ o. s. па́дать ниц; **~ion** [-ʃən] распростёртое положе́ние; изнеможе́ние.
prosy ['prouzi] □ *fig.* проза́ичный; бана́льный.
protect [prə'tekt] защища́ть [-ити́ть]; (пред)охраня́ть [-ни́ть] (from от Р); **~ion** [prə'tekʃən] защи́та; **~ive** [-tiv] защи́тный; предохрани́тельный; ~ duty покрови́тельственная по́шлина; **~or** [-tə] защи́тник; **~orate** [-tərit] протекторáт.
protest 1. ['proutest] проте́ст; опротестова́ние (ве́кселя); 2. [prə'test] [за]протестова́ть; опроте́стовывать [-стова́ть] (ве́ксель).
Protestant ['prɔtistənt] 1. протеста́нт(ка); 2. протеста́нтский.
protestation [proutes'teiʃən] торже́ственное заявле́ние.
protocol ['proutəkɔl] протоко́л.
prototype [-taip] прототи́п.
protract [prə'trækt] тяну́ть (В *or* с Т); продолжа́ть [-до́лжить].
protru|de [prə'tru:d] выдава́ться нару́жу, торча́ть; **~sion** [-ʒən] вы́ступ.
protuberance [prə'tju:bərəns] вы́пуклость *f*; опу́холь *f*.
proud [praud] □ го́рдый (of Т).
prove [pru:v] *v/t.* дока́зывать [-за́ть]; удостоверя́ть [-ве́рить]; испы́тывать [-пыта́ть]; *v/i.* ока́зываться [-за́ться].
provender ['prɔvində] корм.
proverb ['prɔvəb] посло́вица.
provide [prə'vaid] *v/t.* заготовля́ть [-то́вить]; снабжа́ть [-бди́ть]; обеспе́чи(ва)ть; ⚖ ста́вить усло́вием; *v/i.* запаса́ться [-сти́сь]; **~d** (that) при усло́вии (что).
providen|ce ['prɔvidəns] провиде́ние; предусмотри́тельность *f*; **~t** [-dənt] □ предусмотри́тельный; **~tial** [prɔvi'denʃəl] □ провиденциа́льный.
provider [prə'vaidə] поставщи́к [(-и́ца).
provin|ce ['prɔvins] о́бласть *f*; прови́нция; *fig.* сфе́ра де́ятельности; **~cial** [prə'vinʃəl] 1. провинциа́льный; 2. провинциа́л(ка).
provision [prə'viʒən] снабже́ние; обеспе́чение; ⚖ положе́ние (догово́ра и т. п.); ~s *pl.* прови́зия; **~al** [-l] □ предвари́тельный; вре́менный.
proviso [prə'vaizou] усло́вие.
provocat|ion [prɔvə'keiʃən] вы́зов; провока́ция; раздраже́ние; **~ive** [prə'vɔkətiv] вызыва́ющий (о поведе́нии и т. п.); провокацио́нный.
provoke [prə'vouk] [с]провоци́ровать; возбужда́ть [-буди́ть]; вызыва́ть [вы́звать]; [рас]серди́ть.
provost 1. ['prɔvest] ре́ктор; дека́н; 2. [prə'vou] ⚔ офице́р вое́нной поли́ции.
prow [prau] ⚓ нос (су́дна).
prowess ['prauis] до́блесть *f*.
prowl [praul] кра́сться; броди́ть.
proximity [prɔk'simiti] бли́зость *f*.
proxy ['prɔksi] замести́тель *m*; полномо́чие; переда́ча го́лоса; дове́ренность *f*.
prude [pru:d] щепети́льная, стыдли́вая же́нщина.
pruden|ce ['pru:dəns] благоразу́мие; предусмотри́тельность *f*; осторо́жность *f*; **~t** [-t] □ благоразу́мный; осторо́жный.
prud|ery ['pru:dəri] чрезме́рная стыдли́вость *f*; **~ish** [-diʃ] □ чрезме́рно стыдли́вый.
prune [pru:n] 1. чернос́лив; 2. ✂ подреза́ть [-ре́зать], обреза́ть [обре́зать]; *fig.* сокраща́ть [-рати́ть].
prurient ['pruəriənt] □ похотли́вый.
pry [prai] 1. подгля́дывать [-яде́ть]; ~ into сова́ть нос в (В); *Am.* ~ open вскры́(ва́)ть, взла́мывать [взлома́ть]; ~ up поднима́ть [-ня́ть]; 2. рыча́г.
psalm [sɑ:m] псало́м. [дони́м.]
pseudonym ['(p)sju:dənim] псев-
psychiatrist [sai'kaiətrist] психиа́тр.
psychic ['saikik], **~al** [-kikəl] □ психи́ческий.
psycholog|ical [saikə'lɔdʒikəl] □ психологи́ческий; **~ist** [sai'kɔlədʒist] психо́лог; **~y** [-dʒi] психоло́-[гия.]
pub [pʌb] F тракти́р, каба́к.

puberty ['pju:bəti] половáя зрéлость *f*.
public ['pʌblik] 1. □ публи́чный, общéственный; госудáрственный; коммунáльный; ~ house трактúр; ~ law междунарóдное прáво; ~ spirit дух солидáрности, патриоти́зма; 2. пýблика; общéственность *f*; ~**an** ['pʌblikən] трактирщик; ~**ation** [pʌbli'keiʃən] опубликовáние; издáние; monthly ~ ежемéсячник; ~**ity** [pʌ'blisiti] глáсность *f*; реклáма.
publish ['pʌbliʃ] [о]публиковáть, изд(ав)áть; опубликóвывать [-ковáть]; оглашáть [-ласи́ть]; ~**ing house** издáтельство; ~**er** [-ə] издáтель *m*; ~**s** *pl*. издáтельство.
pucker ['pʌkə] 1. [с]мóрщить(ся); 2. морщи́на.
pudding ['pudiŋ] пýдинг; black ~ кровянáя колбасá.
puddle ['pʌdl] лýжа.
puerile ['pjuərail] □ ребя́ческий.
puff [pʌf] 1. дуновéние (вéтра); клуб (ды́ма); пухóвка; 2. *v/t*. надý(вá)ть; выпя́чивать [вы́пятить]; расхвáливать [-ли́ть], преувели́ченно реклами́ровать; ~**ed eyes** распýхшие глазá *m/pl*.; *v/i*. дуть поры́вами; пыхтéть; ~ **away at** попы́хивать (Т); ~ **out** надý(вá)ться; ~**-paste** слоёное тéсто; ~**y** ['pʌfi] запыхáвшийся; отёкший; одутловáтый.
pug [pʌg], ~**-dog** мопс.
pugnacious [pʌg'neiʃəs] драчли́вый.
pug-nosed ['pʌgnouz] курнóсый.
puke [pju:k] рвóта.
pull [pul] 1. тя́га; рýчка (звонкá и т. п.); затя́жка (ды́мом); 2. [по-] тянýть; таскáть, [по]тащи́ть; выдёргивать [вы́дернуть]; дёргать [-рнуть]; ~ **down** сноси́ть [снести́] (здáние и т. п.); ~ **out** 🚂 отходи́ть [отойти́] (от стáнции); ⚕ ~ **through** выхáживать [вы́ходить]; поправля́ться [-áвиться] (от болéзни); ~ **o. s. together** взять себя́ в рýки; ~ **up** подтя́гивать [-янýть]; осáживать [осади́ть] (лошадéй); останáвливать(ся) [-нови́ть(ся)].
pulley ['puli] ⊕ блок; вóрот; ремённый шкив.
pulp [pʌlp] мя́коть плодá; пýльпа (зýба); ⊕ бумáжная мáсса.
pulpit ['pulpit] кáфедра (проповéдника).
pulpy ['pʌlpi] □ мя́гкий; мяси́стый.
puls|ate [pʌl'seit] пульси́ровать; би́ться; ~**e** [pʌls] пульс.
pulverize ['pʌlvəraiz] *v/t*. распыля́ть [-ли́ть]; размельчáть в порошóк; *v/i*. распыля́ться [-ли́ться].
pumice ['pʌmis] пéмза.
pump [pʌmp] 1. насóс; лёгкая бáльная тýфля; 2. качáть[качнýть] (насóсом); ~ **up** накáчивать [-чáть].
pumpkin ['pʌmpkin] ⚘ ты́ква.
pun [pʌn] 1. каламбýр; 2. каламбýрить.
Punch[1] [pʌntʃ] полишинéль *m*.
punch[2] [~] 1. ⊕ кéрнер, пробóйник; компóстер; удáр кулакóм; 2. проби́(вá)ть (отвéрстия); [от-] штамповáть; бить кулакóм.
punctilious [pʌŋk'tiliəs] педанти́чный; щепети́льный до мелочéй.
punctual ['pʌŋktjuəl] □ пунктуáльный; ~**ity** [pʌŋktju'æliti] пунктуáльность *f*.
punctuat|e ['pʌŋktjueit] стáвить знáки препинáния; *fig*. перемежáть; ~**ion** [pʌŋktju'eiʃən] пунктуáция.
puncture ['pʌŋktʃə] 1. прокóл; ⚡ пробóй; 2. прокáлывать [-колóть]; получáть прокóл.
pungen|cy ['pʌndʒənsi] остротá, éдкость *f*; ~**t** [-t] óстрый, éдкий.
punish ['pʌniʃ] накáзывать [-зáть]; ~**able** [-əbl] □ наказýемый; ~**ment** [-mənt] наказáние.
puny ['pju:ni] □ крóхотный; тщеду́шный.
pupil [pju:pl] *anat*. зрачóк; учени́к (-и́ца).
puppet ['pʌpit] марионéтка (*a. fig*.); ~**show** кýкольный теáтр.
puppy ['pʌpi] щенóк; *fig*. молокосóс; фат.
purchase ['pə:tʃəs] 1. покýпка, закýпка; приобретéние; ⊕ механи́зм для поднятия грýзов (рычáг; лебёдка и т. п.); *fig*. тóчка опóры; 2. покупáть [купи́ть]; приобретáть [-рести́]; ~**r** [-ə] покупáтель(ница *f*) *m*.
pure [pjuə] □ *com*. чи́стый; беспорóчный; беспри́месный; ~**-bred** ['pjuəbred] *Am*. чистокрóвный.
purgat|ive ['pə:gətiv] слаби́тельное; ~**ory** [-t(ə)ri] чисти́лище.
purge [pə:dʒ] 1. ⚕ слаби́тельное; *pol*. чи́стка; 2. очищáть [очи́стить]; *pol*. проводи́ть чи́стку в (П).
purify ['pjuərifai] очищáть [очи́стить].
purity ['pjuəriti] чистотá; непорóчность *f*.
purl [pə:l] журчáть.
purlieus ['pə:lju:z] *pl*. окрéстности *f/pl*.
purloin [pə:'lɔin] [у]воровáть.
purple [pə:pl] 1. пурпýрный; багрóвый; 2. пýрпур; 3. turn ~ [по-] багровéть.
purport ['pə:pət] смысл, содержáние.
purpose ['pə:pəs] 1. намéрение, цель *f*; ýмысел; **on** ~ нарóчно; **to the** ~ кстáти; к дéлу; **to no** ~ напрáсно; 2. имéть цéлью; намеревáться [намéриться]; ~**ful** [-ful] □ умы́шленный; целеустремлённый; ~**less** [-lis] □ бесцéльный; ~**ly** [-li] нарóчно.
purr [pə:] [за]мурлы́кать.
purse [pə:s] 1. кошелёк; дéнежный приз; public ~ казнá; 2. подж(им)áть (гýбы); зажмýри(ва)ть (глазá).

pursuan|ce [pə'sju(:)əns]: in ~ of согла́сно (Д); **~t** [-ənt]: ~ to согла́сно (Д).
pursu|e [pə'sju:] пресле́довать (В); занима́ться [заня́ться] (Т); продолжа́ть [-до́лжить]; **~er** [-ə] пресле́дователь(ница *f*) *m*; **~it** [pə'sju:t] пого́ня *f*; *mst* **~s** *pl.* заня́тие.
purvey [pə:'vei] поставля́ть [-а́вить] (проду́кты); снабжа́ть [-бди́ть] (Т); **~or** [-ə] поставщи́к.
pus [pʌs] ⚕ гной.
push [puʃ] 1. толчо́к; уда́р; давле́ние; напо́р; уси́лие; 2. толка́ть [-кну́ть]; наж(им)а́ть (на В); продвига́ть(ся) [-ви́нуть(ся)] (*a.* ~ on); притесня́ть [-ни́ть]; [по]торопи́ть; ~ one's way прота́лкиваться [протолка́ться]; **~-button** ⚡ кно́пка (звонка́ и т. п.).
pussillanimous [pju:si'lænimәs] □ малоду́шный.
puss(y) ['pus(i)] ко́шечка, ки́ска.
put [put] [*irr.*] 1. класть [положи́ть]; [по]ста́вить; сажа́ть [посади́ть]; зад(ав)а́ть (вопро́с, зада́чу и т. п.); сова́ть [су́нуть]; ~ across успе́шно проводи́ть (ме́ру); перевози́ть [-везти́]; ~ back ста́вить на ме́сто (обра́тно); ста́вить наза́д; ~ by откла́дывать [отложи́ть] (де́ньги); ~ down подавля́ть [-ви́ть] (восста́ние); запи́сывать [-са́ть]; заставля́ть замолча́ть; припи́сывать [-са́ть] (to Д); ~ forth проявля́ть [-ви́ть]; пуска́ть [пусти́ть] (побе́ги); пуска́ть в обраще́ние; ~ in вставля́ть [-а́вить]; всо́вывать [всу́нуть]; ~ off снима́ть [снять] (оде́жду); отде́л(ыв)аться от (P with T); отта́лкивать [оттолкну́ть]; откла́дывать [отложи́ть]; ~ on наде́(ва́)ть (пла́тье и т. п.); *fig.* принима́ть [-ня́ть] (вид); прибавля́ть [-а́вить]; ~ out выкла́дывать [вы́ложить]; протя́гивать [-тяну́ть]; выгоня́ть [вы́гнать]; [по]туши́ть (ого́нь); ~ through *teleph.* соединя́ть [-ни́ть] (to с Т); ~ to прибавля́ть [-ба́вить]; ~ to death казни́ть (*im*)*pf.*; ~ to the rack пыта́ть; ~ up [по-]стро́ить, возводи́ть [-вести́] (зда́ние); [по]ста́вить (пье́су); дава́ть прию́т (Д); 2. *v/i.*: ⚓ ~ off, ~ to sea уходи́ть в мо́ре; ~ in ⚓ заходи́ть в порт; ~ up at остана́вливаться [останови́ться] в (П); ~ up with [по]мири́ться с (Т).
putrefy ['pju:trifai] (с)гнить.
putrid ['pju:trid] □ гнило́й; воню́чий; **~ity** [pju:'triditi] гниль *f*.
putty ['pʌti] 1. (око́нная) зама́зка; 2. зама́з(ыв)ать (о́кна).
puzzle [pʌzl] 1. недоуме́ние; затрудне́ние; зага́дка; головоло́мка; 2. *v/t.* озада́чи(ва)ть; ста́вить в тупи́к; ~ out распу́т(ыв)ать; *v/i.* би́ться (over над Т); **~-headed** ['pʌzl'hedid] бестолко́вый; сумбу́рный.
pygm|ean [pig'mi:ən] ка́рликовый; **~y** ['pigmi] ка́рлик, пигме́й.
pyjamas [pə'dʒɑ:məz] *pl.* пижа́ма.
pyramid ['pirəmid] пирами́да; **~al** [pi'ræmidl] □ пирамида́льный.
pyre ['paiə] погреба́лный костёр.
pyrotechnic [pairo'teknik] пироте́хни́ческий; ~ display фейерве́рк.
Pythagorean [pai'θægə'ri:ən] пифаго́ре́йский.
pyx [piks] *eccl.* дарохрани́тельница.

Q

quack [kwæk] 1. зна́харь *m* (-рка); шарлата́н; кря́канье (у́ток); 2. шарлата́нский; 3. кря́кать [-кнуть]; **~ery** ['kwækəri] шарлата́нство.
quadrangle [kwɔ'dræŋgl] четырёхуго́льник; шко́льный двор.
quadrennial [kwɔ'dreniəl] □ четырёхле́тний; происходя́щий раз в четы́ре го́да.
quadru|ped ['kwɔdruped] четвероно́гое живо́тное; **~ple** ['kwɔdrupl] □ учетверённый; четверно́й.
quagmire ['kwægmaie] тряси́на, боло́то.
quail [kweil] дро́гнуть *pf.*; [с]тру́сить.
quaint [kweint] □ стра́нный, необы́чный.
quake [kweik] [за]трясти́сь; [за-]дрожа́ть; дро́гнуть *pf.*
Quaker ['kweikə]ква́кер.
quali|fication [kwɔlifi'keiʃən] квалифика́ция; сво́йство; ограниче́ние; **~fy** ['kwɔlifai] *v/t.* квалифици́ровать (*im*)*pf.*; ограни́чи(ва)ть; смягча́ть [-чи́ть]; наз(ы)ва́ть (as T); *v/i.* подгота́вливаться [-гото́виться] (for к Д); **~ty** [-ti] ка́чество; сво́йство; досто́инство.
qualm [kwɔ:m, kwɑ:m] тошнота́; сомне́ние; при́ступ малоду́шия.
quantity ['kwɔntiti] коли́чество; 𝔄 величина́; мно́жество.
quarantine ['kwɔrənti:n] 1. каранти́н; 2. подверга́ть каранти́ну.
quarrel ['kwɔrəl] 1. ссо́ра, перебра́нка; 2. [по]ссо́риться; **~some** [-səm] □ вздо́рный; приди́рчивый.
quarry ['kwɔri] 1. каменоло́мня; добы́ча (на охо́те) 2. добы́(ва́)ть (ка́мни); *fig.* [по]ры́ться.
quart [kwɔ:t] ква́рта (=1,14 ли́тра).
quarter ['kwɔ:tə] 1. че́тверть *f*; че́тверть часа́; кварта́л; ме́сто, сторона́; поща́да; **~s** *pl.* кварти́ра; ⚔ каза́рмы *f/pl.*; *fig.* исто́чники

m/pl.; from all ~s со всех сторо́н; **2.** дели́ть на четы́ре ча́сти; ⚔ расквартиро́вывать [-ирова́ть]; четвертова́ть (*im*)*pf.*; **~-day** день, начина́ющий кварта́л го́да; **~-deck** шка́нцы *m/pl.*; **~ly** [-li] **1.** кварта́льный; **2.** журна́л, выходя́щий ка́ждый кварта́л го́да; **~master** ⚔ квартирме́йстер.
quartet(te) [kwɔ:'tet] ♪ кварте́т.
quash [kwɔʃ] ⚖ аннули́ровать (*im*)*pf.*
quaver ['kweivə] **1.** дрожь *f*; ♪ трель *f*; **2.** вибри́ровать; говори́ть дрожа́щим го́лосом.
quay [ki:] на́бережная.
queasy ['kwi:zi] □ сла́бый (о желу́дке); тошнотво́рный.
queen [kwi:n] короле́ва; *chess* ферзь *m*; **~like, ~ly** ['kwi:nli] подоба́ющий короле́ве; ца́рственный.
queer [kwiə] стра́нный, эксцентри́чный.
quench [kwentʃ] утоля́ть [-ли́ть] (жа́жду); [по]туши́ть; охлажда́ть [охлади́ть].
querulous ['kweruləs] □ ворчли́вый.
query ['kwiəri] **1.** вопро́с; **2.** спра́шивать [спроси́ть]; подверга́ть сомне́нию.
quest [kwest] **1.** по́иски *m/pl.*; **2.** оты́скивать [-ка́ть], разы́скивать [-ка́ть].
question ['kwestʃən] **1.** вопро́с; сомне́ние; пробле́ма; beyond (all) ~ вне вся́кого сомне́ния; in ~ (лицо́, вопро́с,) о кото́ром идёт речь; call in ~ подверга́ть сомне́нию; that is out of the ~ об э́том не мо́жет быть и ре́чи; **2.** расспра́шивать [-роси́ть]; задава́ть вопро́с (Д); допра́шивать [-роси́ть]; подверга́ть сомне́нию; **~able** [-əbl] □ сомни́тельный; **~naire** [kestiə'nɛə, kwestʃə'nɛə] анке́та.
queue [kju:] **1.** о́чередь *f*, «хвост»; коса́ (воло́с); **2.** заплета́ть в ко́су; (*mst* ~ up) стоя́ть в о́череди.
quibble [kwibl] **1.** игра́ слов, каламбу́р; увёртка; **2.** [с]остри́ть; уклоня́ться [-ни́ться].
quick [kwik] **1.** живо́й; бы́стрый, ско́рый; прово́рный; о́стрый (слух и т. п.); **2.** чувстви́тельное ме́сто; to the ~ *fig.* за живо́е; до мо́зга косте́й; cut to the ~ заде́ва́ть за живо́е; **~en** ['kwikən] *v/t.* ускоря́ть [-о́рить]; оживля́ть [-ви́ть]; *v/i.* ускоря́ться [-о́риться]; оживля́ться [-ви́ться]; **~ness** ['kwiknis] быстрота́; оживлённость *f*; сообрази́тельность *f*; **~sand** плыву́н, сыпу́чие пески́ *m/pl.*; **~silver** ртуть *f*; **~-witted** нахо́дчивый.
quiescen|ce [kwai'esns] поко́й; неподви́жность *f*; **~t** [-t] неподви́жный; *fig.* споко́йный.
quiet ['kwaiət] **1.** □ споко́йный, ти́хий; бесшу́мный; сми́рный; **2.** поко́й; тишина́; **3.** успока́ивать(ся), [-ко́ить(ся)]; **~ness** [-nis], **~ude** [-ju:d] тишина́; поко́й; споко́йствие.
quill [kwil] пти́чье перо́; ствол пера́; *fig.* перо́ (для письма́); игла́ (ежа́ и т. п.); **~ing** ['kwiliŋ] рюш (на пла́тье).
quilt [kwilt] **1.** стёганое одея́ло; **2.** [вы́]стега́ть.
quince [kwins] ♀ айва́.
quinine [kwi'ni:n, *Am.* 'kwainain] *pharm.* хини́н.
quintuple ['kwintjupl] пятикра́тный.
quip [kwip] сарка́зм; острота́; ко́лкость *f*.
quirk [kwə:k] = quibble, quip; причу́да; ро́счерк пера́; завито́к (рису́нка).
quit [kwit] **1.** покида́ть [-и́нуть]; оставля́ть [-а́вить]; give notice to ~ заявля́ть об ухо́де (с рабо́ты); **2.** свобо́дный, отде́лавшийся (of от Р).
quite [kwait] вполне́, соверше́нно, совсе́м; дово́льно; ~ a hero настоя́щий геро́й; ~ (so)!, ~ that! так!, соверше́нно ве́рно!
quittance ['kwitəns] квита́нция.
quiver ['kwivə] [за]дрожа́ть; [за-]трепета́ть.
quiz [kwiz] **1.** шу́тка; мистифика́ция; насме́шка; *part. Am.* опро́с, прове́рка зна́ний; **2.** подшу́чивать [-ути́ть] над (Т); *part. Am.* опра́шивать [опроси́ть].
quorum ['kwɔ:rəm] *parl.* кво́рум.
quota ['kwoutə] до́ля, часть *f*, кво́та.
quotation [kwou'teiʃən] цита́та; цити́рование; ✝ котиро́вка, курс.
quote [kwout] [про]цити́ровать; ✝ коти́ровать (*im*)*pf.*; дава́ть расце́нку на (В).

R

rabbi ['ræbai] равви́н.
rabbit ['ræbit] кро́лик.
rabble [ræbl] сброд; толпа́.
rabid ['ræbid] □ не́истовый, я́ростный; бе́шеный.
rabies ['reibii:z] бе́шенство.
race [reis] **1.** ра́са; род; поро́да; состяза́ние в ско́рости; бег; го́нки *f/pl.*; (*mst* ~s *pl.*) ска́чки *f/pl.*; бега́ *m/pl.*; **2.** [по]мча́ться; состяза́ться в ско́рости; уча́ствовать в ска́чках и т. п.; **~-course** доро́жка; трек; **~r** ['reisə] уча́стник го́нок и́ли ска́чек (ло́шадь, автомоби́ль и т. п.).
racial ['reiʃəl] ра́совый.

rack [ræk] 1. вéшалка; подстáвка; пóлка; стóйка; кормýшка; 🚂 luggage ~ сéтка для вещéй; 2. класть в сéтку или на пóлку; пытáть; ~ one's brains ломáть себé гóлову; go to ~ and ruin погибáть [-и́бнуть]; разоря́ться [-ри́ться].
racket ['rækit] тéннисная ракéтка; шум, гам; *Am.* шантáж; ~**eer** [ræki'tiə] *Am.* вымогáтель *m*.
racy ['reisi] □ характéрный; крéпкий; пикáнтный; колори́тный.
radar ['reidɑ:] радáр; ~ set радиолокáтор.
radian|ce ['reidiəns] сия́ние; ~**t** [-t] □ лучи́стый; сия́ющий, лучезáрный.
radiat|e ['reidieit] излучáть [-чи́ть] (свет, теплó); ~**ion** [reidi'eiʃən] излучéние; ~**or** ['reidieitə] излучáтель *m*; △, *mot.* радиáтор.
radical ['rædikəl] 1. □ основнóй, коренно́й; фундаментáльный; радикáльный; 2. *pol.* радикáл.
radio ['reidiou] 1. рáдио *n indecl.*; ~ drama, ~ play радиопостанóвка; ~ set радиоприёмник; 2. передавáть по рáдио; ~**graph** [-grɑ:f] 1. рентгéновский сни́мок; 2. дéлать рентгéновский сни́мок с (Р); ~**scopy** [reidi'ɔskəpi] исслéдование рентгéновскими лучáми; ~**-telegram** радио(теле)грáмма.
radish ['rædiʃ] рéдька; (red) ~ реди́ска.
raffle [ræfl] 1. *v/t.* разы́грывать в лотерéю; *v/i.* учáствовать в лотерéе; 2. лотерéя.
raft [rɑ:ft] 1. плот; парóм 2. сплавля́ть [-áвить] (лес); ~**er** ['rɑ:ftə] ⊕ стропи́ло.
rag [ræg] тря́пка; ~s *pl.* тряпьё, вéтошь *f*; лохмóтья *m/pl.*
ragamuffin ['rægəmʌfin] оборвáнец; ýличный мáльчик.
rage [reidʒ] 1. я́рость *f*, гнев; повáльное увлечéние; предмéт увлечéния; it is all the ~ э́то послéдний крик мóды; 2. [вз]беси́ться; бушевáть.
ragged ['rægid] □ нерóвный; рвáный, понóшенный.
raid [reid] 1. налёт; набéг; облáва; 2. дéлать набéг, налёт на (В); вторгáться [втóргнуться] в (В).
rail [reil] 1. пери́ла *n/pl.*; огрáда; 🚂 рельс; поперéчина; (main) ~ ⚓ пóручень *m*; run off the ~s сойти́ с рéльсов; 2. éхать по желéзной дорóге; [вы́]ругáть, [вы́]брани́ть (at, against В).
railing ['reiliŋ] огрáда; пери́ла *n/pl.*
raillery ['reiləri] беззлóбная насмéшка, подшýчивание.
railroad ['reilroud] *part. Am.*, **railway** [-wei] желéзная дорóга.
rain [rein] 1. дождь *m*; 2. идти́ (о дождé); *fig.* [по]сы́паться; ~**bow** рáдуга; ~**coat** *Am.* дождеви́к, непромокáемое пальтó *n indecl.*; ~**fall** коли́чество осáдков; ~**-proof** непромокáемый; ~**y** ['reini] □ дождли́вый.
raise [reiz] (*often* ~ up) поднимáть [-ня́ть]; воздвигáть [-ви́гнуть] (пáмятник и т. п.); возвышáть [-ы́сить]; воспи́тывать [-итáть]; вызывáть [вы́звать] (смех, гнев и т. п.); возбуждáть [-уди́ть] (чýвство); добы́(вá)ть (дéньги).
raisin [reizn] изю́минка; *pl.* изю́м.
rake [reik] 1. грáбли *f/pl.*; кочергá; повéса *m*; распýтник; 2. *v/t.* сгребáть [-ести́]; разгребáть [-ести́]; *fig.* ~ for тщáтельно искáть (В *or* Р).
rally ['ræli] 1. вновь собирáть(ся); овладé(вá)ть собóй; 2. *Am.* мáссовый ми́тинг; объединéние; съезд.
ram [ræm] 1. барáн; тарáн; 2. [про-] тарáнить; заби́(вá)ть.
rambl|e ['ræmbl] 1. прогýлка (без цéли); 2. броди́ть без цéли; говори́ть бессвя́зно; ~**er** [-ə] праздношатáющийся; ползýчее растéние; ~**ing** [-iŋ] бродя́чий; бессвя́зный; разбрóсанный; ползýчий.
ramify ['ræmifai] разветвля́ться [-етви́ться].
ramp [ræmp] скат, уклóн; ~**ant** ['ræmpənt] стоя́щий на зáдних лáпах (о геральди́ческом живóтном); *fig.* необýзданный.
rampart ['ræmpɑ:t] вал.
ramshackle ['ræmʃækl] вéтхий.
ran [ræn] *pt.* от run.
ranch [ræntʃ] *Am.* скотовóдная фéрма.
rancid ['rænsid] □ прогóрклый.
ranco(u)r ['ræŋkə] злóба, затаённая враждá.
random ['rændəm] 1. at ~ наугáд, наобýм; 2. сдéланный (вы́бранный и т. д.) наугáд; случáйный.
rang [ræŋ] *pt.* от ring.
range [reindʒ] 1. ряд; ли́ния (домóв); цепь *f* (гор); óбласть распространéния (растéний и т. п.); предéл, амплитýда; диапазóн (гóлоса); ⚔ дáльность дéйствия; стрéльбище; 2. *v/t.* выстрáивать в ряд; стáвить в поря́дке; классифици́ровать (*im*)*pf.*; ⚓ плáвать, [по]плы́ть вдоль (Р); *v/i.* выстрáиваться в ряд; простирáться; броди́ть, ры́скать.
rank [ræŋk] 1. ряд; ⚔ шерéнга; звáние, чин; категóрия; ~ and file рядовóй состáв; *fig.* людскáя мáсса; 2. *v/t.* стрóить в шерéнгу; выстрáивать в ряд; классифици́ровать (*im*)*pf.*; *v/i.* стрóиться в шерéнгу; равня́ться (with Д); 3. бýйный (о расти́тельности); прогóрклый (о мáсле); отъя́вленный.
rankle [ræŋkl] *fig.* мýчить, терзáть (об оби́де и т. п.); ~ in терзáть (В).
ransack ['rænsæk] [по]ры́ться в (П); [о]грáбить.
ransom ['rænsəm] 1. вы́куп; 2. выкупáть [вы́купить].

rant [rænt] **1.** деклама́ция; высокопа́рная речь *f*; **2.** говори́ть напы́щенно; [про]деклами́ровать; шу́мно весели́ться.
rap [ræp] **1.** лёгкий уда́р; стук (в дверь и т. п.); *fig.* not a ~ ни гроша́; **2.** ударя́ть [уда́рить]; [по-] стуча́ть.
rapaci|ous [rə'peiʃəs] □ жа́дный; хи́щный; **~ty** [rə'pæsiti] жа́дность *f*; хи́щность *f*.
rape [reip] **1.** похище́ние; изнаси́лование; **2.** похища́ть [-и́тить]; [из]наси́ловать.
rapid ['ræpid] **1.** □ бы́стрый, ско́рый; круто́й; **2. ~s** *pl.* поро́ги *m/pl.*, стремни́ны *f/pl.*; **~ity** [rə'piditi] ско́рость *f*.
rapt [ræpt] восхищённый; увлечённый; **~ure** ['ræptʃə] восто́рг, экста́з; **go into ~s** приходи́ть в восто́рг.
rare [rɛə] □ ре́дкий; *phys.* разреже́нный.
rarefy ['rɛərifai] разрежа́ть(ся) [-еди́ть(ся)].
rarity [-riti] ре́дкость *f*.
rascal ['rɑ:skəl] моше́нник; **~ity** [rɑ:s'kæliti] моше́нничество; **~ly** ['rɑ:skəli] моше́ннический.
rash[1] [ræʃ] □ стреми́тельный; опроме́тчивый; необду́манный.
rash[2] [~] сыпь *f*.
rasp [rɑ:sp] **1.** ра́шпиль *m*; скре́жет; **2.** подпи́ливать ра́шпилем; соскреба́ть [-ести́]; раздража́ть [-жи́ть].
raspberry ['rɑ:zbəri] мали́на.
rat [ræt] кры́са; *sl.* изме́нник; smell a ~ чу́five недо́брое.
rate [reit] **1.** но́рма; ста́вка; пропо́рция; сте́пень *f*; ме́стный нало́г; разря́д; ско́рость *f*; at any ~ во вся́ком слу́чае; ~ of exchange (валю́тный) курс; **2.** оце́нивать [-ни́ть], расце́нивать [-ни́ть]; [вы́-] брани́ть; ~ among счита́ться среди́ (P).
rather [rɑ:ðə] скоре́е; предпочти́тельно; верне́е; дово́льно; I had ~ ... я предпочёл бы ...
ratify ['rætifai] ратифици́ровать (*im*)*pf.*; утвержда́ть [-рди́ть].
rating ['reitiŋ] оце́нка; су́мма нало́га; ранг; класс.
ratio ['reiʃiou] 🕮 отноше́ние.
ration ['ræʃən] **1.** рацио́н; паёк; **2.** снабжа́ть продово́льствием; нормирова́ть вы́дачу (P).
rational [ræʃnl] □ рациона́льный; разу́мный; **~ity** [ræʃ'næliti] рациона́льность *f*; разу́мность *f*; **~ize** ['ræʃnəlaiz] рационализи́ровать (*im*)*pf*.
ratten [rætn] саботи́ровать (*im*)*pf*.
rattle [rætl] **1.** треск; дребезжа́ние; трещо́тка (*a. fig.*); погрему́шка; **2.** [про]треща́ть; [за]дребезжа́ть; [за]греме́ть (T); говори́ть без у́молку; ~ off отбараба́нить *pf.*; **~snake** грему́чая змея́; **~trap** *fig.* ве́тхий экипа́ж, автомоби́ль и т. п.
rattling ['rætliŋ] *fig.* бы́стрый; великоле́пный.
raucous ['rɔkəs] □ хри́плый.
ravage ['rævidʒ] **1.** опустоше́ние; **2.** опустоша́ть [-ши́ть]; разоря́ть [-ри́ть].
rave [reiv] бре́дить (*a. fig.*), говори́ть бессвя́зно; неи́стовствовать.
ravel [rævl] *v/t.* запу́т(ыв)ать; распу́т(ыв)ать; *v/i.* запу́т(ыв)аться; (*a.* ~ out) располза́ться по швам.
raven [reivn] во́рон.
raven|ing ['rævniŋ], **~ous** [-əs] прожо́рливый; хи́щный.
ravine [rə'vi:n] овра́г, лощи́на.
ravish ['ræviʃ] приводи́ть в восто́рг; [из]наси́ловать; похища́ть [-и́тить]; **~ment** [-mənt] похище́ние; восхище́ние; изнаси́лование.
raw [rɔ:] □ сыро́й; необрабо́танный; нео́пытный; обо́дранный; **~-boned** худо́й, костля́вый.
ray [rei] **1.** луч; *fig.* про́блеск; ⚕ ~ treatment облуче́ние.
raze [reiz] разруша́ть до основа́ния; сноси́ть [снести́] (зда́ние и т. п.); вычёркивать [вы́черкнуть].
razor ['reizə] бри́тва; **~-blade** ле́звие безопа́сной бри́твы.
re... [ri:] *pref.* (придаёт сло́ву значе́ния:) сно́ва, за́ново, ещё раз, обра́тно.
reach [ri:tʃ] **1.** преде́л досяга́емости; круг понима́ния, кругозо́р; о́бласть влия́ния; beyond ~ вне преде́лов досяга́емости; within easy ~ побли́зости; под руко́й; **2.** *v/t.* достига́ть [-и́гнуть] (P); доезжа́ть [дое́хать], доходи́ть [дойти́] до (P); простира́ться [-стере́ться] до (P); протя́гивать [-яну́ть]; дост(ав)а́ть до (P); *v/i.* протя́гивать ру́ку (for за T).
react [ri'ækt] реаги́ровать; ~ upon each other взаимоде́йствовать; противоде́йствовать (against Д).
reaction [ri'ækʃən] реа́кция; **~ary** [-ʃənəri] **1.** реакцио́нный; **2.** реакционе́р(ка).
read 1. [ri:d] [*irr.*] [про]чита́ть; изуча́ть [-чи́ть]; истолко́вывать [-кова́ть]; пока́зывать [-за́ть] (о прибо́ре); гласи́ть; ~ to a p. чита́ть кому́-нибудь вслух; **2.** [red] a) *pt.* и *p. pt.* от read 1.; b) *adj.* начи́танный; **~able** ['ri:dəbl] □ интере́сный; чёткий; **~er** ['ri:də] чита́тель(ница *f*) *m*; чтец; ле́ктор; хрестома́тия.
readi|ly ['redili] *adv.* охо́тно; бы́стро; легко́; **~ness** [-nis] гото́вность *f*; подгото́вленность *f*.
reading ['ri:diŋ] чте́ние; ле́кция; толкова́ние, понима́ние; *parl.* чте́ние (законопрое́кта).
readjust ['ri:ə'dʒʌst] сно́ва приводи́ть в поря́док; переде́л(ыв)ать;

~ment [-mənt] приведéние в порядок; передéлка.
ready ['redi] □ готóвый; склóнный; ⚕ налúчный; make (или get) ~ [при]готóвить(ся); **~-made** готóвый (о плáтье).
reagent [ri'eidʒənt] ⚗ реактúв.
real [riəl] □ действúтельный; реáльный; настоящий; ~ estate недвижимость *f*; **~ity** [ri'æliti] действúтельность *f*; **~ization** [riəlai'zeiʃən] понимáние, осознáние; осуществлéние; ⚕ реализáция; **~ize** ['riəlaiz] представлять себé; осуществлять [-вúть]; осозн(ав)áть; реализовáть (*im*)*pf*.
realm [relm] королéвство; цáрство; сфéра.
realty ['riəlti] недвúжимое имýщество.
reap [ri:p] [с]жать (рожь и т. п.); *fig.* пож(ин)áть; **~er** ['ri:pə] жнец, жнúца.
reappear ['ri:ə'piə] появляться снóва.
rear [riə] **1.** *v/t.* воспúтывать [-тáть]; вырáщивать [вы́растить]; *v/i.* становúться на дыбы́; **2.** зáдняя сторонá; ⚔ тыл; at the ~ of, in (the) ~ of позадú (Р); **3.** зáдний; ты́льный; ⚔ тыловóй; **~-admiral** ⚓ контр-адмирáл; **~-guard** ⚔ арьергáрд.
re-arm ['ri:ɑ:m] перевооружáть (-ся) [-жúть(ся)].
reason [ri:zn] **1.** рáзум; рассýдок; основáние; причúна; by ~ of по причúне (Р); for this ~ поэ́тому; it stands to ~ that ... ясно, что ..., очевúдно, что ...; **2.** *v/i.* рассуждáть [-удúть]; заключáть [-чúть]; резюмúровать (*im*)*pf*.; *v/t.* ~ out продýмать до концá; ~ out of разубеждáть [-едúть] в (П); **~able** ['ri:znəbl] □ (благо)разýмный; умéренный; недорогóй.
reassure ['ri:ə'ʃuə] снóва уверять; успокáивать [-кóить].
rebate ['ri:beit] ⚕ скúдка; устýпка.
rebel **1.** [rebl] бунтовщúк (-úца); повстáнец; **2.** [~] (*a.* **~lious** [ri'beljəs]) мятéжный; **3.** [ri'bel] восст(ав)áть; бунтовáть [вз-ся]; **~lion** [ri'beljən] мятéж, восстáние; бунт.
rebirth ['ribə:θ] возрождéние.
rebound [ri'baund] **1.** отскáкивать [-скочúть]; **2.** рикошéт; отскóк.
rebuff [ri'bʌf] **1.** отпóр; рéзкий откáз; **2.** давáть отпóр (Д).
rebuild ['ri:'bild] [*irr.* (build)] восстанáвливать [-новúть] (здáние и т. п.).
rebuke [ri'bju:k] **1.** упрёк; вы́говор; **2.** упрекáть [-кнýть]; дéлать вы́говор (Д).
rebut [ri'bʌt] давáть отпóр (Д).
recall [ri'kɔ:l] **1.** отозвáние (депутáта, послá и т. п.); ⚕ отмéна; **2.** отзывáть [отозвáть]; призывáть обрáтно; отменять [-нúть]; напоминáть [-óмнить]; вспоминáть [-óмнить] (В); ⚕ брать (или трéбовать) обрáтно (капитáл); отменять [-нúть].
recapitulate [ri:kə'pitjuleit] резюмúровать (*im*)*pf*.
recast ['ri:'kɑ:st] [*irr.* (cast)] придавáть нóвую фóрму (Д); ⊕ отливáть зáново.
recede [ri'si:d] отступáть [-пúть]; удаляться [-лúться].
receipt [ri'si:t] **1.** распúска, квитáнция; получéние; рецéпт (кулинáрный); **~s** *pl.* прихóд; **2.** распúсываться [-сáться] на (П).
receiv|able [ri'si:vəbl] ⚕ неоплáченный (счёт); **~e** [ri'si:v] получáть [-чúть]; принимáть [-нять]; воспринимáть [-нять]; **~ed** [-d] общепрúзнанный; **~er** [-ə] получáтель(ница *f*) *m*; *teleph.* телефóнная трýбка; ⚖ судéбный исполнúтель *m*.
recent [ri:snt] □ недáвний; свéжий; нóвый; **~ly** [-li] недáвно.
receptacle [ri'septəkl] вместúлище.
reception [ri'sepʃən] получéние; приём; принятие.
receptive [ri'septiv] □ восприúмчивый (к Д).
recess [ri'ses] канúкулы *f/pl.*; перерыв; нúша; уединённое мéсто; **~es** *pl. fig.* тайникú *m/pl.*; **~ion** [-ʃən] удалéние; углублéние; ⚕ спад.
recipe ['resipi] рецéпт.
recipient [ri'sipiənt] получáтель (-ница *f*) *m*.
reciproc|al [ri'siprəkəl] взаúмный; обоюдный; эквивалéнтный; **~ate** [-keit] ⊕ двúгать(ся) взад и вперёд; обмéниваться [-няться] (услýгами и т. п.); **~ity** [resi'prɔsiti] взаúмность *f*.
recit|al [ri'saitl] чтéние, декламáция; повествовáние; ♪ концéрт (солúста); **~ation** [resi'teiʃən] декламáция; **~e** [ri'sait] [про]декламúровать; расскáзывать [-зáть].
reckless ['reklis] □ безрассýдный; опромéтчивый; беспéчный.
reckon ['rekən] *v/t.* исчислять [-чúслить]; причислять [-чúслить] (among к Д); считáть [счесть] за (В); *v/i.* предполагáть [-ложúть]; ~ (up)on *fig.* рассчúтывать на (В); **~ing** [-iŋ] подсчёт; счёт; расплáта.
reclaim [ri'kleim] исправлять [-áвить]; поднимáть [-нять] (целинý).
recline [ri'klain] откúдывать(ся) [-úнуть(ся)]; полулежáть.
recluse [ri'klu:s] отшéльник (-ица).
recogni|tion [rekəg'niʃən] опознáние; узнавáние; признáние (Р); **~ze** ['rekəgnaiz] узн(ав)áть; призн(ав)áть.

recoil [ri'kɔil] **1.** отско́к; ⚔ отда́ча, отка́т; **2.** отска́кивать [-скочи́ть]; отка́тываться [-кати́ться].
recollect [rekə'lekt] вспомина́ть [вспо́мнить] (В); **~ion** [rekə'lekʃən] воспомина́ние, па́мять *f* (of о П).
recommend [rekə'mend] рекомендова́ть (*im*)*pf.*, *pf. a.* [по-]; **~ation** [rekəmen'deiʃən] рекоменда́ция.
recompense ['rekəmpəns] **1.** вознагражде́ние; компенса́ция; **2.** вознагражда́ть [-ради́ть]; отпла́чивать [отплати́ть] (Д).
reconcil|e ['rekənsail] примиря́ть [-ри́ть] (to с Т); ула́живать [ула́дить]; **~e** o. s. примиря́ться [-ри́ться]; **~iation** ['rekənsili'eiʃən] примире́ние.
recondition ['ri:kən'diʃən] [от]ремонти́ровать; переобору́довать.
reconn|aissance [ri'kɔnisəns] ⚔ разве́дка; **~oitre** [rekə'nɔitə] производи́ть разве́дку; разве́д(ыв)ать.
reconsider ['ri:kən'sidə] пересма́тривать [-мотре́ть].
reconstitute ['ri:kɔnstitju:t] восстана́вливать [-нови́ть].
reconstruct ['ri:kəns'trʌkt] восстана́вливать [-нови́ть]; перестра́ивать [-стро́ить]; **~ion** [-s'trʌkʃən] реконстру́кция; восстановле́ние.
reconvert ['ri:kən'və:t] перестра́ивать на ми́рный лад.
record **1.** ['rekɔ:d] за́пись *f*; *sport* реко́рд; ⚖ протоко́л (заседа́ния и т. п.); place on ~ запи́сывать [-са́ть]; граммофо́нная пласти́нка; репута́ция; ♀ Office госуда́рственный архи́в; off the ~ *Am.* неофициа́льно; on ~ зарегистри́рованный; **2.** [ri'kɔ:d] запи́сывать [-са́ть]; [за]регистри́ровать; **~er** [ri'kɔ:də] регистра́тор; регистри́рующий прибо́р.
recount [ri'kaunt] излага́ть [изложи́ть] (подро́бно).
recoup [ri'ku:p] компенси́ровать (*im*)*pf.*, возмеща́ть [-ести́ть] (Д for В).
recourse [ri'kɔ:s] обраще́ние за по́мощью; прибе́жище; have ~ to прибега́ть к по́мощи (Р).
recover [ri'kʌvə] *v/t.* получа́ть обра́тно; верну́ть (себе́) *pf.*; навёрстывать [-верста́ть] (вре́мя); *v/i.* оправля́ться [-а́виться] (*a.* ~ o. s.); **~y** [-ri] восстановле́ние; выздоровле́ние; возмеще́ние; ⚖ взыска́ние.
recreat|e ['rekrieit] *v/t.* освежа́ть [-жи́ть]; развлека́ть [-е́чь]; *v/i.* освежа́ться [-жи́ться] (по́сле рабо́ты и т. п.) (*a.* ~ o. s.); развлека́ться [-е́чься]; **~ion** [rekri'eiʃən] о́тдых; развлече́ние.
recrimination [rikrimi'neiʃən] взаи́мное (и́ли встре́чное) обвине́ние.
recruit [ri'kru:t] **1.** ре́крут, новобра́нец; *fig.* новичо́к; **2.** [у]комплектова́ть; [за]вербова́ть (новобра́нцев).
rectangle ['rektæŋgl] прямоуго́льник.
recti|fy ['rektifai] исправля́ть [-а́вить]; выверя́ть [вы́верить]; ⚡ выпрямля́ть [вы́прямить]; **~tude** ['rektitju:d] прямота́, че́стность *f*.
rector ['rektə] ре́ктор; па́стор, свяще́нник; **~y** [-ri] дом свяще́нника.
recumbent [ri'kʌmbənt] □ лежа́чий.
recuperate [ri'kju:pəreit] восстана́вливать си́лы; оправля́ться [опра́виться].
recur [ri'kə:] возвраща́ться [-рати́ться] (to к Д); приходи́ть сно́ва на у́м; происходи́ть вновь; **~rence** [ri'kʌrəns] повторе́ние; **~rent** [-rənt] □ повторя́ющийся; периоди́ческий; ⚕ возвра́тный.
red [red] **1.** кра́сный; ~ heat кра́сное кале́ние; ~ herring *fig.* отвлече́ние внима́ния; ~ tape канцеля́рщина; **2.** кра́сный цве́т; **~s** *pl.* (*part. pol.*) кра́сные *pl.*
red|breast ['redbrest] мали́новка; **~den** [redn] [по]красне́ть; **~dish** ['rediʃ] красновáтый.
redeem [ri'di:m] искупа́ть [-пи́ть]; выкупа́ть [вы́купить]; спаса́ть [-сти́]; **~er** [-ə] спаси́тель *m*.
redemption [ri'dempʃən] искупле́ние; вы́куп; спасе́ние.
red-handed ['red'hændid]: take a p. ~ пойма́ть кого́-либо на ме́сте преступле́ния.
red-hot накалённый до́красна́; *fig.* взбешённый; горя́чий.
red-letter: ~ day пра́здничный день *m.*
redness ['rednis] краснота́.
redolent ['redolənt] благоуха́ющий.
redouble [ri'dʌbl] удва́ивать(ся) [удво́ить(ся)].
redound [ri'daund]: ~ to спосо́бствовать (Д), помога́ть [помо́чь] (Д).
redress [ri'dres] **1.** исправле́ние; ⚖ возмеще́ние; **2.** исправля́ть [-а́вить]; загла́живать [-ла́дить] (вину́); возмеща́ть [-ести́ть].
reduc|e [ri'dju:s] понижа́ть [-и́зить]; снижа́ть [-и́зить]; доводи́ть [довести́] (to до Р); уменьша́ть [уме́ньши́ть]; сокраща́ть [-рати́ть]; уре́з(ыв)ать; ~ to writing излага́ть пи́сьменно; **~tion** [ri'dʌkʃən] сниже́ние (цен), ски́дка; уменьше́ние; сокраще́ние; уме́ньшенная ко́пия (карти́ны и т. п.).
redundant [ri'dʌndənt] □ изли́шний; чрезме́рный.
reed [ri:d] тростни́к; свире́ль *f*.
reef [ri:f] риф, подво́дная скала́.
reek [ri:k] **1.** вонь *f*, за́тхлый за́пах; дым; пар; **2.** *v/i.* дыми́ться; (неприя́тно) па́хнуть (of Т); испуска́ть пар.

reel [ri:l] **1.** катýшка; бобúна; барабáн, вóрот; **2.** *v/i.* [за]кружúться, [за]вертéться; шатáться [шатнýться]; *v/t.* [на]мотáть; ~ off размáтывать [-мотáть]; *fig.* отбарабáнить *pf.*; ~ up намáтывать на катýшку.

re-elect ['ri:i'lekt] переизб(и)рáть.

re-enter ['ri:'entə] входúть снóва в (В).

re-establish ['ri:is'tæbliʃ] восстанáвливать [-новúть].

refection [ri'fekʃən] закýска.

refer [ri'fə:]: ~ to *v/t.* припúсывать [-сáть] (Д); относúть [отнестú] (к Д); направлять [-рáвить] (к Д); передавáть на рассмотрéние (Д); *v/i.* ссылáться [сослáться] на (В); относúться [отнестúсь] к (Д); **~ee** [refə'ri:] *sport* судья́ *m*; **~ence** ['refrəns] спрáвка; ссы́лка; рекомендáция; упоминáние; отношéние; лицó, дáвшее рекомендáцию; in ~ to относúтельно (Р); ~ book спрáвочник; ~ library спрáвочная библиотéка; make ~ to ссылáться [сослáться] на (В).

referendum [refə'rendəm] референдум.

refill ['ri:'fil] наполня́ть снóва; пополня́ть(ся) [-пóлнить(ся)].

refine [ri'fain] ⊕ очищáть [очúстить] рафинúровать (*im*)*pf.*; дéлать(ся) бóлее утончённым; ~ (up)on [у]совершéнствовать; **~ment** [-mənt] очищéние, рафинúрование; отдéлка; усовершéнствование; утончённость *f*; **~ry** [-əri] ⊕ очистúтельный завóд.

reflect [ri'flekt] *v/t.* отражáть [отразúть]; *v/i.* ~ (up)on: бросáть тень на (В); размышля́ть [-ы́слить] о (П); отражáться [-разиться] на (В); **~ion** [ri'flekʃən] отражéние; óтсвéт; размышлéние, обдýмывание; *fig.* тень *f*; рефлéксия.

reflex ['ri:fleks] **1.** отражéние; óтсвéт, óтблеск; рефлéкс; **2.** рефлектóрный.

reforest ['ri:fɔrist] снóва засаждáть лéсом.

reform [ri'fɔ:m] **1.** реформа; улучшéние; **2.** улучшáть(ся) [улýчшить(ся)]; реформúровать (*im*)*pf.*; исправля́ть(ся); **~ation** [refə'meiʃən] преобразовáние; исправлéние (морáльное); *eccl.* ♀ Реформáция; **~atory** [ri'fɔ:mətəri] исправúтельное заведéние; **~er** [-mə] реформáтор.

refract|ion [ri'frækʃən] рефрáкция, преломлéние; **~ory** [-təri] □ упря́мый; непокóрный; ⊕ огнеупóрный.

refrain [ri'frein] **1.** *v/t.* сдéрживать [-жáть]; *v/i.* воздéрживаться [-жáться] (from от Р); **2.** припéв, рефрéн.

refresh [ri'freʃ] освежáт- [-жúть]; подкрепля́ть(ся) [-пúть(ся)]; подновля́ть [-вúть]; **~ment** [-mənt] подкреплéние; закýска.

refrigerat|e [ri'fridʒəreit] заморáживать [-рóзить]; охлаждáть(ся) [охладúть(ся)]; **~ion** [rifridʒə'reiʃən] заморáживание; охлаждéние.

refuel ['ri:'fjuəl] *mot.* заправля́ться горю́чим.

refuge ['refju:dʒ] убéжище; **~e** [refju'dʒi:] бéженец (-нка).

refulgent [ri'fʌldʒənt] лучезáрный.

refund [ri'fʌnd] возмещáть расхóды (Д); возвращáть [-ратúть].

refusal [ri'fju:zəl] откáз.

refuse 1. [ri'fju:z] *v/t.* откáзываться [-зáться] от (Р); откáзывать [-зáть] в (П); отвергáть [отвéргнуть]; *v/i.* откáзываться [-зáться]; [за]артáчиться (о лóшади); **2.** ['refju:s] брак ⊕; отбрóсы *m/pl.*; мýсор.

refute [ri'fju:t] опровергáть [-вéргнуть].

regain [ri'gein] получáть обрáтно; снóва достигáть.

regal [ri:gəl] □ королéвский; цáрственный.

regale [ri'geil] *v/t.* угощáть [угостúть]; *v/i.* пировáть; угощáться [угостúться] (on Т).

regard [ri'gɑ:d] **1.** взгляд, взор; внимáние; уважéние; with ~ to по отношéнию к (Д); kind **~s** сердéчный привéт; **2.** [по]смотрéть на (В); рассмáтривать (as как); [по]считáться с (Т); относúться [отнестúсь] к (Д); as **~s** ... что касáется (Р); **~ing** [-iŋ] относúтельно (Р); **~less** [-lis] *adv.* ~ of не обращáя внимáния на (В); не считáясь с (Т).

regenerate 1. [ri'dʒenəreit] перерождáть(ся) [-одúть(ся)]; возрождáться [-родúться]; ⊕ регенерúровать; **2.** [-rit] возрождённый.

regent ['ri:dʒənt] рéгент.

regiment ['redʒimənt] **1.** полк; **2.** формировáть полк(ú) из (Р); организовáть (*im*)*pf.*; **~als** [redʒi'mentlz] *pl.* полковáя фóрма.

region ['ri:dʒən] óбласть *f*; райóн; **~al** [-l] □ областнóй; мéстный.

register ['redʒistə] **1.** журнáл (зáписей); реéстр; официáльный спúсок; ♪ регúстр; ⊕ заслóнка; **2.** регистрúровать(ся) (*im*)*pf.*, *pf. a.* [за-]; заносúть в спúсок; ✉ посылáть заказны́м.

registr|ar [redʒis'trɑ:] регистрáтор; слýжащий зáгса; **~ation** [redʒis'treiʃən] регистрáция; **~y** ['redʒistri] регистратýра; регистрáция; регистрациóнная зáпись *f*; реéстр.

regret [ri'gret] **1.** сожалéние; раскáяние; **2.** [по]жалéть (that ... что ...); сожалéть о (П); горевáть

о (П); раска́иваться [-ка́яться] в (П); **~ful** [-ful] □ по́лный сожале́ния; **~table** [-əbl] □ прискорбный.
regular ['regjulə] □ пра́вильный; регуля́рный (*a.* ⚔); форма́льный; **~ity** [regju'læriti] регуля́рность *f*.
regulat|e ['regjuleit] [у]регули́ровать, упоря́дочи(ва)ть; ⊕ [от]регули́ровать; **~ion** [regju'leiʃən] **1.** регули́рование; предписа́ние; **~s** *pl.* уста́в; **2.** *attr.* устано́вленный.
rehears|al [ri'hə:səl] *thea.*, ♪ репети́ция; **~e** [ri'hə:s] *thea.* [про]репети́ровать.
reign [rein] **1.** ца́рствование; *fig.* власть *f*; **2.** ца́рствовать; госпо́дствовать (*a. fig.*); *fig.* цари́ть.
reimburse [ri:im'bə:s] возвраща́ть [-рати́ть]; возмеща́ть расхо́ды (Д).
rein [rein] **1.** вожжа́; **2.** пра́вить (лошадьми́); сде́рживать [-жа́ть].
reinforce [ri:in'fɔ:s] подкрепля́ть [-пи́ть]; уси́ли(ва)ть; **~ment** [-mənt] подкрепле́ние.
reinstate ['ri:in'steit] восстана́вливать [-нови́ть] (в права́х и т. п.).
reinsure ['ri:in'ʃuə] перестрахо́вывать [-ова́ть].
reiterate [ri:'itəreit] повторя́ть [-ри́ть] (*mst* многокра́тно).
reject [ri'dʒekt] отверга́ть [отве́ргнуть]; отка́зываться [-за́ться] от (Р); отклоня́ть [-ни́ть]; **~ion** [ri'dʒekʃən] отклоне́ние; отка́з.
rejoic|e [ri'dʒɔis] *v/t.* [об]ра́довать *v/i.* [об]ра́доваться (at, in Д); **~ing** [-iŋ] (ча́сто **~s** *pl.*) весе́лье; пра́зднование.
rejoin 1. ['ri:'dʒɔin] сно́ва соединя́ться [-ни́ться] с (Т); сно́ва примыка́ть [-мкну́ть] к (Д); **2.** [ri'dʒɔin] возража́ть [-рази́ть].
rejuvenate [ri'dʒu:vineit] омола́живать(ся) [омолоди́ть(ся)].
relapse [ri'læps] **1.** рециди́в (⚖, ⚕); **2.** сно́ва впада́ть (в е́ресь, заблужде́ние и т. п.); сно́ва заболева́ть.
relate [ri'leit] *v/t.* расска́зывать [-за́ть]; приводи́ть в связь; *v/i.* относи́ться [отнести́сь]; **~d** [-id] ро́дственный (to с Т).
relation [ri'leiʃən] отноше́ние; связь *f*; родство́; ро́дственник (-ица); in **~** to по отноше́нию к (Д); **~ship** [-ʃip] родство́.
relative ['relətiv] **1.** □ относи́тельный; сравни́тельный (to с Т); усло́вный; **2.** ро́дственник (-ица).
relax [ri'læks] уменьша́ть напряже́ние (Р); смягча́ть(ся) [-чи́ть (-ся)]; де́лать(ся) ме́нее стро́гим; **~ation** [ri:læk'seiʃən] ослабле́ние; смягче́ние; о́тдых от рабо́т; развлече́ние.
relay [ri'lei] **1.** сме́на; *sport* эстафе́та; *attr.* эстафе́тный; **2.** *radio* трансли́ровать (*im*)*pf*.
release [ri'li:s] **1.** освобожде́ние; высвобожде́ние; избавле́ние; вы́пуск (фи́льма на прока́т и т. п.); **2.** освобожда́ть [-боди́ть]; высвобожда́ть [вы́свободить]; избавля́ть [-а́вить]; выпуска́ть [вы́пустить]; отпуска́ть [-сти́ть]; проща́ть [прости́ть] (долг).
relegate ['religeit] отсыла́ть [отосла́ть]; направля́ть [-ра́вить] (to к Д); ссыла́ть [сосла́ть].
relent [ri'lent] смягча́ться [-чи́ться]; **~less** [-lis] □ безжа́лостный.
relevant ['relivənt] уме́стный; относя́щийся к де́лу.
reliab|ility [rilaiə'biliti] надёжность *f*; про́чность *f*; **~le** [ri'laiəbl] □ надёжный; достове́рный.
reliance [ri'laiəns] дове́рие; уве́ренность *f*.
relic ['relik] пережи́ток; рели́квия; рели́кт; **~s** *pl.* оста́нки *m/pl.*
relief [ri'li:f] облегче́ние; по́мощь *f*; посо́бие; подкрепле́ние; сме́на (*a.* ⚔); ⚔ сня́тие оса́ды; релье́ф; **~** works *pl.* обще́ственные рабо́ты для безрабо́тных.
relieve [ri'li:v] облегча́ть [-чи́ть]; освобожда́ть [-боди́ть]; ока́зывать по́мощь (Д); выруча́ть [вы́ручить]; ⚔ снять оса́ду с (Р); сменя́ть [-ни́ть].
religion [ri'lidʒən] рели́гия.
religious [ri'lidʒəs] □ религио́зный; благогове́йный; добросо́вестный; *eccl.* мона́шеский.
relinquish [ri'liŋkwiʃ] оставля́ть [-а́вить] (наде́жду и т. п.); броса́ть [бро́сить] (привы́чку).
relish ['reliʃ] **1.** вкус; при́вкус; припра́ва; **2.** наслажда́ться [-ла-ди́ться] (Т); получа́ть удово́льствие от (Р); придава́ть вкус (Д).
reluctan|ce [ri'lʌktəns] нежела́ние; нерасположе́ние; **~t** [-t] □ сопротивля́ющийся; неохо́тный.
rely [ri'lai]: **~** (up)on полага́ться [-ложи́ться] на (В), наде́яться на (В).
remain [ri'mein] ост(ав)а́ться; **~der** [-də] оста́ток.
remark [ri'ma:k] **1.** замеча́ние; заме́тка; **2.** замеча́ть [-е́тить]; выска́зываться [вы́сказаться] (on о П); **~able** [ri'ma:kəbl] □ замеча́тельный.
remedy ['remidi] **1.** сре́дство, лека́рство; ме́ра (for про́тив Р); **2.** исправля́ть [-а́вить]; выле́чивать [вы́лечить].
rememb|er [ri'membə] по́мнить; вспомина́ть [-о́мнить]; **~** me to ... переда́й(те) приве́т (Д); **~rance** [-brəns] воспомина́ние; па́мять *f*; суве́нир; **~s** *pl.* приве́т.
remind [ri'maind] напомина́ть [-о́мнить] (Д; of о П *or* В); **~er** [-ə] напомина́ние.
reminiscence [remi'nisns] воспомина́ние.
remiss [ri'mis] □ неради́вый;

невнима́тельный; вя́лый; **~ion** [ri'miʃən] проще́ние; отпуще́ние (грехо́в); освобожде́ние от упла́ты; уменьше́ние.
remit [ri'mit] отпуска́ть [-сти́ть] (грехи́); пере́с(ы)ла́ть (това́ры); уменьша́ть(ся) [уме́ньши́ть(ся)]; **~tance** [-əns] де́нежный перево́д.
remnant ['remnənt] оста́ток; пережи́ток.
remodel ['ri:mɔdl] перестра́ивать [-стро́ить].
remonstra|nce [ri'mɔnstrəns] проте́ст; увеща́ние; **~te** [-treit] протестова́ть; увещева́ть, увеща́ть (with В).
remorse [ri'mɔ:s] угрызе́ния (*n/pl.*) со́вести; раска́яние; **~less** [-lis] □ безжа́лостный.
remote [ri'mout] □ отдалённый; да́льний; уединённый; **~ness** [-nis] отдалённость *f.*
remov|al [ri'mu:vəl] перее́зд; устране́ние; смеще́ние; ~ van фурго́н для перево́за ме́бели; **~e** [ri'mu:v] *v/t.* удаля́ть [-ли́ть]; уноси́ть [унести́]; передвига́ть [-и́нуть]; смеща́ть [смести́ть]; *v/i.* переезжа́ть [перее́хать]; **~er** [-ə] перево́зчик ме́бели.
remunerat|e [ri'mju:nəreit] вознагражда́ть [-ради́ть]; опла́чивать [оплати́ть]; **~ive** [ri'mju:nərətiv] □ хорошо́ опла́чиваемый, вы́годный.
renascence [ri'næsns] возрожде́ние; возобновле́ние.
rend [rend] [*irr.*] разрыва́ть(ся) [разорва́ть(ся)]; раздира́ть(ся) [разодра́ть(ся)].
render ['rendə] возд(ав)а́ть; ока́зывать [оказа́ть] (услу́гу и т. п.); представля́ть [-а́вить]; изобража́ть [-рази́ть]; [за]плати́ть (Т for за В); ♪ исполня́ть [-о́лнить]; переводи́ть [-вести́] (на друго́й язы́к); раста́пливать [-топи́ть] (са́ло).
renew [ri'nju:] возобновля́ть [-нови́ть]; **~al** [-əl] возобновле́ние.
renounce [ri'nauns] отка́зываться [-за́ться] от (Р); отрека́ться [-ре́чься] от (Р).
renovate ['renoveit] восстана́вливать [-нови́ть]; освежа́ть [-жи́ть].
renown [ri'naun] *rhet.* изве́стность *f*; **~ed** [-d] *rhet.* знамени́тый.
rent[1] [rent] 1. *pt.* и *p. pt.* от rend; 2. проре́ха; дыра́.
rent[2] [~] 1. аре́ндная пла́та; кварти́рная пла́та; ре́нта; 2. нанима́ть [наня́ть] и́ли сда(ва́)ть (дом и т. п.); **~al** [rentl] аре́ндная пла́та.
renunciation [rinʌnsi'eiʃən] отрече́ние; отка́з (of от Р).
repair[1] [ri'pɛə] 1. почи́нка, ремо́нт; in (good) ~ в испра́вном состоя́нии; 2. [по]чини́ть, [от]ремонти́ровать; исправля́ть [-а́вить].
repair[2]: ~ to отправля́ться [-а́виться] в (В).
reparation [repə'reiʃən] возмеще́ние; исправле́ние; *pol.* make **~s** *pl.* плати́ть репара́ции.
repartee [repɑ:'ti:] нахо́дчивость *f*; остроу́мный отве́т.
repast [ri'pɑ:st] тра́пеза.
repay [*irr.* (pay)] [ri'pei] отпла́чивать [-лати́ть]; отдава́ть до́лг (Д); возвраща́ть [-рати́ть] (де́ньги); возмеща́ть [-ести́ть]; **~ment** [-mənt] возвра́т (де́нег); возмеще́ние.
repeal [ri'pi:l] 1. аннули́рование; 2. аннули́ровать (*im*)*pf.*; отменя́ть [-ни́ть].
repeat [ri'pi:t] 1. повторя́ть(ся) [-ри́ть(ся)]; говори́ть наизу́сть; 2. ♪ повторе́ние; знак повторе́ния; ✝ повто́рный зака́з.
repel [ri'pel] отта́лкивать [оттолкну́ть]; ⚔ отража́ть [-рази́ть]; отверга́ть [-е́ргнуть].
repent [ri'pent] раска́иваться [-ка́яться] (of в П); **~ance** [-əns] раска́яние; **~ant** [-ənt] ка́ющийся.
repetition [repi'tiʃən] повторе́ние; повторе́ние наизу́сть.
replace [ri:'pleis] ста́вить, класть обра́тно; заменя́ть [-ни́ть]; замеща́ть [-ести́ть] (кого́-либо); **~ment** [-mənt] замеще́ние.
replenish [ri'pleniʃ] пополня́ть [-о́лнить]; **~ment** [-mənt] пополне́ние (*a.* ⚔).
replete [ri'pli:t] напо́лненный; насы́щенный.
replica ['replikə] то́чная ко́пия.
reply [ri'plai] 1. отве́т (to на В); 2. отвеча́ть [-е́тить]; возража́ть [-рази́ть].
report [ri'pɔ:t] 1. отчёт; сообще́ние; донесе́ние; докла́д; молва́, слух; свиде́тельство; звук (взры́ва и т. п.); 2. сообща́ть [-щи́ть] (В *or* о П); доноси́ть [-нести́] о (П); докла́дывать [доложи́ть]; рапортова́ть (*im*)*pf.* о (П); **~er** [-ə] докла́дчик (-ица); репортёр(ша F).
repos|e [ri'pouz] 1. о́тдых; поко́й; 2. *v/t.* дава́ть о́тдых (Д); *v/i.* отдыха́ть [отдохну́ть] (*a.* ~ o. s.); поко́иться; быть осно́ванным (на П); **~itory** [ri'pɔzitəri] склад; храни́лище.
reprehend [repri'hend] де́лать вы́говор (Д).
represent [repri'zent] представля́ть [-а́вить]; изобража́ть [-рази́ть]; *thea.* исполня́ть роль (Р); **~ation** [-zən'teiʃən] изображе́ние; представи́тельство; *thea.* представле́ние; **~ative** □ [repri'zentətiv] 1. характе́рный; показа́тельный; представля́ющий (of В); *parl.* представи́тельный; 2. представи́тель(ница *f*) *m*; House of ♀s *pl. Am. parl.* пала́та представи́телей.
repress [ri'pres] подавля́ть [-ви́ть]; **~ion** [ri'preʃən] подавле́ние.
reprimand ['reprimɑ:nd] 1. вы́говор; 2. де́лать вы́говор (Д).

reprisal [ri'praizəl] репресса́лия.

reproach [ri'proutʃ] 1. упрёк; укóр; 2. (~ a p. with a th.) упрека́ть [-кну́ть], укоря́ть [-ри́ть] (когó-либо в чём-либо).

reprobate ['reprobeit] распу́тник; подле́ц.

reproduc|e [ri:prə'dju:s] воспроизводи́ть [-извести́]; размножа́ться [-óжиться]; **~tion** [-'dʌkʃən] воспроизведе́ние; размноже́ние; репроду́кция

reproof [ri'pru:f] порица́ние; вы́говор.

reprove [ri'pru:v] порица́ть; де́лать вы́говор (Д).

reptile ['reptail] пресмыка́ющееся (живóтное).

republic [ri'pʌblik] респу́блика; **~an** [-likən] 1. республика́нский; 2. республика́нец (-нка).

repudiate [ri'pju:dieit] отрека́ться [-е́чься] от (Р); отверга́ть [-ве́ргнуть].

repugnan|ce [ri'pʌgnəns] отвраще́ние; нерасположе́ние; противоре́чие; **~t** [-nənt] □ проти́вный, отта́лкивающий.

repuls|e [ri'pʌls] 1. отка́з; отпóр; 2. ⚔ отража́ть [отрази́ть]; отта́лкивать [оттолкну́ть]; **~ive** [-iv] □ отта́лкивающий.

reput|able ['repjutəbl] □ почте́нный; **~ation** [repju:'teiʃən] репута́ция; **~e** [ri'pju:t] óбщее мне́ние; репута́ция; **~ed** [ri'pju:tid] изве́стный; предполага́емый; **be ~ed** (to be ...) слыть (за В).

request [ri'kwest] 1. тре́бование; прóсьба; ✝ спрос; in (great) ~ в (большóм) спрóсе; (*a. radio*) зая́вка; 2. [по]проси́ть (В or Р or о П).

require [ri'kwaiə] нужда́ться в (П); [по]тре́бовать (Р); **~d** [-d] потре́бный; обяза́тельный; тре́буемый; **~ment** [-mənt] тре́бование; потре́бность *f*.

requisite ['rekwizit] 1. необходи́мый; 2. **~s** *pl.* всё необходи́мое, ну́жное; **~ion** [rekwi'ziʃən] 1. официа́льное предписа́ние; тре́бование; ⚔ реквизи́ция; 2. де́лать зая́вку на (В); ⚔ реквизи́ровать (*im*)*pf*.

requital [ri'kwaitl] вознагражде́ние; возме́здие.

requite [ri'kwait] отпла́чивать [-лати́ть] (Д for за В); вознагражда́ть [-ради́ть]; [ото]мсти́ть за (В).

rescind [ri'sind] аннули́ровать (*im*)*pf*.

rescission [ri'siʒən] аннули́рование, отме́на.

rescue ['reskju:] 1. освобожде́ние; спасе́ние; ⚖ незакóнное освобожде́ние; 2. освобожда́ть [-боди́ть]; спаса́ть [-сти́]; ⚖ незакóнно освобожда́ть.

research [ri'sə:tʃ] изыска́ние (*mst pl.*); иссле́дование (нау́чное).

resembl|ance [ri'zembləns] схóдство (to с Т); **~e** [ri'zembl] походи́ть на (В), име́ть схóдство с (Т).

resent [ri'zent] обижа́ться [оби́деться] за (В); **~ful** [-ful] □ оби́женный; злопа́мятный; **~ment** [-mənt] негодова́ние; чу́вство оби́ды.

reservation [rezə'veiʃən] оговóрка; скрыва́ние; *Am.* резерва́ция; запове́дник; резерви́рование; предвари́тельный зака́з.

reserve [ri'zə:v] 1. запа́с; ✝ резе́рвный фонд; ⚔ резе́рв; сде́ржанность *f*; скры́тность *f*; 2. сберега́ть [-ре́чь]; приберега́ть [-ре́чь]; откла́дывать [отложи́ть]; резерви́ровать (*im*)*pf.*; оставля́ть за собóй; **~d** [-d] □ скры́тный; зака́занный зара́нее.

reside [ri'zaid] прожива́ть; ~ in быть прису́щим (Д); **~nce** ['rezidəns] местожи́тельство; резиде́нция; **~nt** [-dənt] 1. прожива́ющий; живу́щий; 2. постоя́нный жи́тель *m*; резиде́нт.

residu|al [ri'zidjuəl] оста́точный; **~e** ['rezidju:] оста́ток; оса́док.

resign [ri'zain] *v/t.* отка́зываться [-за́ться] от (дóлжности, пра́ва); оставля́ть [-а́вить] (наде́жду); слага́ть [сложи́ть] (обя́занности); уступа́ть [-пи́ть] (права́); ~ o. s. to покоря́ться [-ри́ться] (Д); *v/i.* уходи́ть в отста́вку; **~ation** [rezig'neiʃən] отста́вка; отка́з от дóлжности; **~ed** [ri'zaind] □ покóрный, безрóпотный.

resilien|ce [ri'ziliəns] упру́гость *f*, эласти́чность *f*; **~t** [-t] упру́гий, эласти́чный.

resin ['rezin] 1. смола́; 2. [вы́]смоли́ть.

resist [ri'zist] сопротивля́ться (Д); противостоя́ть (Д); **~ance** [-əns] сопротивле́ние; **~ant** [-ent] сопротивля́ющийся.

resolut|e ['rezəlu:t] □ реши́тельный; **~ion** [rezə'lu:ʃən] резолю́ция; реши́тельность *f*, реши́мость *f*.

resolve [ri'zɔlv] 1. *v/t.* растворя́ть [-ори́ть]; *fig.* реша́ть [реши́ть]; разреша́ть [-ши́ть]; *v/i.* реша́ть(ся) [реши́ть(ся)]; ~ (up)on реша́ться [-ши́ться] на (В); 2. реше́ние; **~d** [-d] □ пóлный реши́мости.

resonant ['reznənt] □ зву́чный; резони́рующий.

resort [ri'zɔ:t] 1. прибе́жище; курóрт; summer ~ да́чное ме́сто; 2. ~ to: прибега́ть [-е́гнуть] к (Д); ча́сто посеща́ть (В).

resound [ri'zaund] [про]звуча́ть; оглаша́ть(ся) [огласи́ть(ся)]; отража́ть [-рази́ть] (звук).

resource [ri'sɔ:s] ресу́рс; сре́дство; возмóжность *f*; нахóдчивость *f*; **~ful** [-ful] □ нахóдчивый.

respect [ri'spekt] **1.** уважéние; отношéние; почтéние (of к Д); ~s *pl.* привéт, поклóн; **2.** *v/t.* уважáть, почитáть; **~able** [-əbl] □ почтéнный; представительный; *part.* ✝ солидный; **~ful** [-ful] □ почтительный; **~ing** [-iŋ] относительно (Р); **~ive** [-iv] □ соответствeнный; we went to our ~ places мы пошли по местáм; **~ively** [-ivli] *или*; соответственно.

respirat|ion [respə'reiʃən] дыхáние; вдох и вы́дох; **~or** ['respəreitə] респирáтор; противогáз.

respire [ris'paiə] дышáть; переводить дыхáние.

respite ['respait] передышка; отсрóчка.

respond [ris'pɔnd] отвечáть [-éтить]; ~ to реагировать на; отзывáться [отозвáться] на (В).

response [ris'pɔns] отвéт; *fig.* óтклик; óтзыв.

responsi|bility [rispɔnsə'biliti] ответственность *f*; **~ble** [ris'pɔnsəbl] ответственный (to пéред Т).

rest [rest] **1.** óтдых; покóй; лóже; опóра; **2.** *v/i.* отдыхáть [отдохнýть]; [по]лежáть; опирáться [оперéться] (on на В); *fig.* ~ (up)on основываться [-овáться] на (П); *v/t.* давáть óтдых (Д).

restaurant ['restərɔ:ŋ] рестoрáн.

restitution [resti'tju:ʃən] возврáт (об имýществе); восстановлéние; возмещéние убы́тков.

restive ['restiv] □ норовистый (о лóшади); упрямый.

restless ['restlis] непосéдливый; беспокóйный, неугомóнный; **~ness** [-nis] непосéдливость *f*; неугомóнность *f*.

restorat|ion [resto'reiʃən] реставрáция; восстановлéние; **~ive** [ris'tɔrətiv] укрепляющий, тонический.

restore [ris'tɔ:] восстанáвливать [-новить]; возвращáть [-ратить]; *paint.* реставрировать (*im*)*pf.*; ~ to health вылéчивать [вы́лечить].

restrain [ris'trein] сдéрживать [-жáть]; задéрживать [-жáть]; подавлять [-вить] (чýвства); **~t** [-t] сдéржанность *f*; ограничéние; обуздáние.

restrict [ris'trikt] ограничи(ва)ть; **~ion** [ris'trikʃən] ограничéние.

result [ri'zʌlt] **1.** результáт; исхóд; **2.** происткáть [-éчь] (from от, из Р); ~ in приводить [-вести] к (Д).

resum|e [ri'zju:m] возобновлять [-вить]; получáть обрáтно; резюмировать (*im*)*pf.*; **~ption** [ri'zʌmpʃən] возобновлéние; продолжéние.

resurrection [rezə'rekʃən] воскресéние; воскрешéние (обы́чая и т. п.).

resuscitate [ri'sʌsiteit] воскрешáть [-есить]; оживлять [-вить].

retail 1. ['ri:teil] рóзничная продáжа; by ~ в рóзницу; *attr.* рóзничный; **2.** [ri:'teil] продавáть(ся) в рóзницу; **~er** [-ə] рóзничный торгóвец.

retain [ri'tein] удéрживать [-жáть]; сохранять [-нить].

retaliat|e [ri'tælieit] отплáчивать [-латить] (тем же); **~ion** [ritæli'eiʃən] отплáта, возмéздие.

retard [ri'tɑ:d] задéрживать [-жáть]; замедлять [-éдлить]; запáздывать [запоздáть].

retention [ri'tenʃən] удержáние; сохранéние.

reticent ['retisənt] сдéржанный; молчаливый.

retinue ['retinju:] свита.

retir|e [ri'taiə] *v/t.* увольнять в отстáвку; изымáть из обращéния; *v/i.* выходить в отстáвку; удаляться [-литься]; уединяться [-ниться]; **~ed** [-d] □ уединённый; отставнóй, в отстáвке; ~ pay пéнсия; **~ement** [-mənt] отстáвка; уединéние; **~ing** [-riŋ] скрóмный, застéнчивый.

retort [ri'tɔ:t] **1.** рéзкий (*или* нахóдчивый) отвéт; ⚗ ретóрта; **2.** отпарировать *pf.* (кóлкость); возражáть [-разить].

retouch ['ri:tʌtʃ] дéлать попрáвки в (П); *phot.* ретушировать (*im*)*pf.*

retrace [ri'treis] прослéживать до истóчника; ~ one's steps возвращáться по своим следáм (*a. fig.*).

retract [ri'trækt] отрекáться [отрéчься] от (Р); брать назáд (словá и т. п.); втягивать [втянýть].

retreat [ri'tri:t] **1.** отступлéние (*part.* ⚔); уединéние; пристáнище; ⚔ отбóй; ⚔ вечéрняя заря; **2.** уходить [уйти]; удаляться [-литься]; (*part.* ⚔) отступáть [-пить].

retrench [ri'trentʃ] урéз(ыв)ать, сокращáть [-ратить] (расхóды).

retrieve [ri'tri:v] (снóва) находить [найти]; восстанáвливать [-новить].

retro... ['retro(u), 'ri:tro(u)] обрáтно...; **~active** [retrou'æktiv] имéющий обрáтную силу; **~grade** ['retrougreid] **1.** ретрогрáдный; реакциóнный; **2.** регрессировать; **~gression** [retrou'greʃən] регрéсс, упáдок; **~spect** ['retrouspekt] взгляд на прóшлое; **~spective** [retrou'spektiv] □ ретроспективный; имéющий обрáтную силу.

return [ri'tə:n] **1.** возвращéние; возврáт; ✝ оборóт; дохóд, прибыль *f*; отдáча; результáт вы́боров; *attr.* обрáтный (билéт и т. п.); many happy ~s of the day поздравляю с днём рождéния; in ~ в обмéн (for на В); в отвéт; by ~ (of post) с обрáтной пóчтой; ~ ticket обрáтный билéт; **2.** *v/i.* возвращáться [-ратиться]; вернýться *pf.*;

v/t. возвращáть [-ратúть]; вернýть *pf.*; отплáчивать [-латúть]; приносúть [-нестú] (дохóд); присылáть назáд; отвечáть [-éтить]; *parl.* изб(и)рáть. [воссоединéние.]
reunion ['ri:'ju:njən] собрáние;
revalorization [ri:vælərai'zeiʃən] переоцéнка.
reveal [ri'vi:l] обнарýживать(ва)ть; откры́(вá)ть; **~ing** [-iŋ] обнарýживающий; показáтельный.
revel [revl] **1.** пировáть; упú(вá)ться (in T); **2.** пирýшка.
revelation [revi'leiʃən] откровéние; обнарýжéние; откры́тие.
revel|(l)er ['revlə] гуля́ка *m*; **~ry** [-ri] разгýл, кутёж.
revenge [ri'vendʒ] **1.** месть *f*; ревáнш; отмéстка; **2.** [ото]мстúть за (B); **~ful** [-ful] □ мстúтельный.
revenue ['revinju:] (годовóй) дохóд; *pl.* дохóдные статьú *f/pl.*; ~ board, ~ office департáмент госудáрственных сбóров.
reverberate [re'və:bəreit] отражáть(ся) [отразúть(ся)].
revere [ri'viə] уважáть, почитáть; **~nce** ['revərəns] **1.** почтéние; **2.** уважáть; благоговéть пéред (T); **~nd** [-d] **1.** почтéнный; **2.** *eccl.* преподóбие.
reverent(ial) ['revərənt, revə'renʃəl] почтúтельный; пóлный благоговéния.
reverie ['revəri] мечты́ *f/pl.*; мечтáтельность *f*.
revers|al [ri'və:səl] перемéна; обрáтный ход; отмéна; изменéние; **~e** [ri'və:s] **1.** обрáтная сторонá; перемéна; противополóжное; **~s** *pl.* преврáтности *f/pl.*; **2.** □ обрáтный; противополóжный; **3.** поворáчивать назáд; ⊕ давáть обрáтный ход; ⚖ отменя́ть [-нúть]; **~ion** [ri'və:ʃən] возвращéние; *biol.* атавúзм.
revert [ri'və:t] возвращáться [-ратúться] (в прéжнее состоя́ние úли к вопрóсу).
review [ri'vju:] **1.** обзóр; провéрка; ⚖ пересмóтр; ⚔, ⚓ смотр; обозрéние (журнáл); рецéнзия; **2.** пересмáтривать [-смотрéть]; писáть рецéнзию о (П); обозрé(вá)ть (B); ⚔, ⚓ производúть смотр (P).
revile [ri'vail] оскорбля́ть [-бúть].
revis|e [ri'vaiz] пересмáтривать [-смотрéть]; исправля́ть [-áвить]; **~ion** [ri'viʒən] пересмóтр; ревúзия; испрáвленное издáние.
reviv|al [ri'vaivəl] возрождéние; оживлéние; **~e** [ri'vaiv] приходúть úли приводúть в чýвство; оживля́ть [-вúть]; ожú(вá)ть.
revocation [revə'keiʃən] отмéна, аннулúрование (закóна и т. п.).
revoke [ri'vouk] *v/t.* отменя́ть [-нúть] (закóн и т. п.); *v/i.* дéлать ренóнс.
revolt [ri'voult] **1.** восстáние; мятéж; **2.** *v/i.* восст(ав)áть; *fig.* отпадáть [отпáсть] (from от P); *v/t.* *fig.* оттáлкивать [оттолкнýть].
revolution [revə'lu:ʃən] кругóвое вращéние; ⊕ оборóт; *pol.* революция; **~ary** [-əri] **1.** революциóнный; **2.** революционéр(ка); **~ize** [-aiz] революционизúровать (*im*)*pf.*
revolv|e [ri'vɔlv] *v/i.* вращáться; периодúчески возвращáться; *v/t.* вращáть; обдýм(ыв)ать; **~ing** [-iŋ] вращáющийся; поворóтный.
revulsion [ri'vʌlʃən] внезáпное изменéние (чувств и т. п.).
reward [ri'wɔ:d] **1.** нагрáда; вознаграждéние; **2.** вознаграждáть [-радúть]; награждáть [-радúть].
rewrite ['ri:'rait] [*irr.* (write)] переписывать [-сáть].
rhapsody ['ræpsədi] рапсóдия.
rheumatism ['ru:mətizm] ревматúзм.
rhubarb ['ru:bɑ:b] ⚘ ревéнь *m*.
rhyme [raim] **1.** рúфма; (рифмóванный) стих; without ~ or reason без смы́сла; **2.** рифмовáть(ся) (with, to с T).
rhythm [riðm] ритм; **~ic(al)** [-mik, -mikəl] ритмúчный, ритмúческий.
rib [rib] **1.** ребрó; **2.** ⊕ укрепля́ть рёбрами.
ribald ['ribəld] грýбый, непристóйный.
ribbon ['ribən] лéнта; **~s** *pl.* клóчья *m/pl.*
rice [rais] рис.
rich [ritʃ] □ богáтый (in T); роскóшный; плодорóдный (о пóчве); жúрный (о пúще); пóлный (тон); густóй (о крáсках); ~ milk цéльное молокó; **~es** ['ritʃiz] *pl.* богáтство; сокрóвища *n/pl.*
rick [rik] ⚒ стог, скирд(á).
ricket|s ['rikits] рахúт; **~y** [-i] рахитúчный; шáткий.
rid [rid] [*irr.*] избавля́ть [-áвить] (of от P); get ~ of отдéл(ыв)аться от (P), избавля́ться [-áвиться] от (P).
ridden [ridn] **1.** *p. pt.* от ride; **2.** (в слóжных словáх) одержúмый (стрáхом, предрассýдками и т. п.), под влáстью (чегó-либо).
riddle [ridl] **1.** загáдка; решетó; **2.** изрешéчивать [-шетúть].
ride [raid] **1.** ездá верхóм; катáние; прогýлка; **2.** [*irr.*] *v/i.* éздить, [по]éхать (на лóшади, автомобúле и т. п.); катáться верхóм; *v/t.* éздить, [по]éхать на (П); катáть (на спинé); **~r** ['raidə] верховóй; наéздник (-ица) (в цúрке); всáдник (-ица).
ridge [ridʒ] гóрный кряж, хребéт; ⚠ конёк (кры́ши); ⚒ гря́дка.
ridicul|e ['ridikju:l] **1.** осмеяние, насмéшка; **2.** высмéивать [вы́-

смеять]; **~ous** ['ri'dikjuləs] □ нелепый, смешной.
riding ['raidiŋ] верховая езда; *attr.* верховой.
rife [raif] □: ~ with изобилующий (T).
riff-raff ['rifræf] подонки (общества) *m/pl.*
rifle [raifl] **1.** винтовка; **2.** [о]грабить; **~man** ⚔ стрелок.
rift [rift] трещина, расселина.
rig [rig] **1.** ⚓ оснастка; F наряд; **2.** оснащать [оснастить]; F наряжать [-ядить]; **~ging** ['rigiŋ] ⚓ такелаж, снасти *f/pl.*
right [rait] **1.** □ правильный, верный; правый; be ~ быть правым; put ~ приводить в порядок; **2.** *adv.* прямо; правильно; справедливо; как раз; ~ away сразу; ~ on прямо вперёд; **3.** право; справедливость *f*; the ~s *pl.* (of a story) настоящие факты *m/pl.*; by ~ of на основании (P); on (*or* to) the ~ направо; **4.** приводить в порядок; выпрямлять(ся) [выпрямить(ся)]; **~eous** ['raitʃəs] □ праведный; **~ful** ['raitful] □ справедливый; законный.
rigid ['ridʒid] □ негнущийся, негибкий, жёсткий; *fig.* суровый; непреклонный; **~ity** [ri'dʒiditi] жёсткость *f*; непреклонность *f.*
rigo(u)r ['rigə] суровость *f*; строгость *f.*
rigorous [-rəs] □ суровый; строгий.
rim [rim] ободок; край; обод; оправа (очков).
rime [raim] иней; изморозь *f*; = rhyme.
rind [raind] кора, кожура; корка.
ring [riŋ] **1.** кольцо; круг; звон (колоколов); звонок; ✝, *sport* ринг; **2.** надевать кольцо на (B); (*mst* ~ in, round, about) окружать [-жить]; [*irr.*] [за]звучать; ~ the bell [по]звонить (у двери); звонить в колокол; ~ a p. up позвонить кому-нибудь по телефону; **~-leader** зачинщик (-ица); **~let** ['riŋlit] колечко; локон.
rink [riŋk] каток, скетинг-ринк.
rinse [rins] [вы]полоскать.
riot ['raiət] **1.** бунт; буйство; разгул; run ~ вести себя буйно; разгуливаться [-ляться]; **2.** принимать участие в бунте; предаваться разгулу; **~er** [-ə] бунтарь *m*; **~ous** [-əs] □ буйный, разгульный.
rip [rip] [рас]пороть(ся).
ripe [raip] □ зрелый (*a. fig.*); спелый; готовый; **~n** [raipn] созре(ва)ть, [по]спеть; **~ness** ['raipnis] спелость *f*; зрелость *f.*
ripple [ripl] **1.** рябь *f*, зыбь *f*; журчание; **2.** покрывать(ся) рябью; журчать.
rise [raiz] **1.** повышение; восход; подъём; выход (на поверхность); возвышенность *f*; происхождение; take (one's) ~ происходить [произойти]; **2.** [*irr.*] подниматься [-няться]; всходить [взойти]; вст(ав)ать; восст(ав)ать; нач(ин)аться; ~ to быть в состоянии справиться с (T); **~n** [rizn] *p. pt.* от rise.
rising ['raiziŋ] вставание; возвышение; восстание; восход.
risk [risk] **1.** риск; run a (*or* the) ~ рисковать [-кнуть]; **2.** отважи(ва)ться на (B); рисковать [-кнуть] (T); **~y** ['riski] □ рискованный.
rit|e [rait] обряд, церемония; **~ual** ['ritjuəl] **1.** ритуальный; **2.** ритуал.
rival ['raivəl] **1.** соперник (-ица); ✝ конкурент; **2.** соперничающий; **3.** соперничать с (T); **~ry** [-ri] соперничество; соревнование.
rive [raiv] [*irr.*] раскалывать(ся) [расколоть(ся)].
river ['rivə] река; поток (*a. fig.*); **~side** берег реки; *attr.* прибрежный.
rivet ['rivit] **1.** заклёпка; **2.** заклёпывать [-лепать]; *fig.* приковывать [-овать] (B к Д).
rivulet ['rivjulit] ручей; речушка.
road [roud] дорога; путь *m*; *mst* ~s *pl.* ⚓ рейд (*a.* ~stead); **~ster** ['roudstə] дорожный велосипед; родстер (двухместный открытый автомобиль *m*); **~way** мостовая.
roam [roum] *v/t.* бродить по (Д); *v/i.* странствовать; скитаться.
roar [rɔ:] **1.** [за]реветь; [за]грохотать; ~ with laughter хохотать во всё горло; **2.** рёв; грохот; громкий хохот.
roast [roust] **1.** [из]жарить(ся); калить (орехи и т. п.); **2.** жареный; ~ meat жареное, жаркое.
rob [rɔb] [о]грабить; *fig.* лишать [-шить] (of P); **~ber** ['rɔbə] грабитель *m*; **~bery** [-ri] грабёж.
robe [roub] мантия (судьи); ряса; халат.
robust [ro'bʌst] □ крепкий, здоровый.
rock [rɔk] **1.** скала; утёс; горная порода; ~ crystal горный хрусталь *m*; **2.** качать(ся) [качнуть (-ся)]; убаюк(ив)ать.
rocket ['rɔkit] ракета; *attr.* ракетный; **~-powered** с ракетным двигателем.
rocking-chair кресло-качалка.
rocky ['rɔki] каменистый; скалистый.
rod [rɔd] жезл; прут (*a.* ⊕); розга, розги; удочка; ⊕ шток; стержень *m*; род (мера длины, около 5-ти метров).
rode [roud] *pt.* от ride.
rodent ['roudənt] грызун.
rodeo [rou'deiou] *Am.* загон для клеймения скота; состязание ковбоев.

roe [rou] косу́ля; икра́; soft ~ моло́ки *n/pl.*
rogu|e [roug] жу́лик, моше́нник; **~ish** ['rougiʃ] жуликова́тый, моше́ннический.
roister ['rɔistə] бесчи́нствовать.
rôle [roul] *thea.* роль *f* (*a. fig.*).
roll [roul] 1. свёрток (мате́рии и т. п.); руло́н; кату́шка; рее́стр, спи́сок; раска́т (гро́ма); бу́лочка; 2. *v/t.* ката́ть, [по]кати́ть; враща́ть; раска́тывать [-ката́ть] (те́сто); прока́тывать [-ката́ть] (мета́лл); ~ up свёртывать [сверну́ть]; ска́тывать [скатать]; *v/i.* ката́ться, [по]кати́ться; валя́ться (in в П); (о гро́ме) грохота́ть; ⚓ име́ть бокову́ю ка́чку; **~-call** ⚔ перекли́чка; **~er** ['roulə] ро́лик; вал; ~ skate конёк на ро́ликах.
rollick ['rɔlik] шу́мно весели́ться.
rolling ['rouliŋ] прока́тный; холми́стый; ~ mill ⊕ прока́тный стан.
Roman ['roumən] 1. □ ри́мский; 2. ри́млянин (-янка); *typ.* прямо́й све́тлый шрифт.
romance [rə'mæns] 1. ♪ рома́нс; рома́н; 2. *fig.* прикра́шивать действи́тельность; 3. ♀ рома́нский; **~r** [-ə] романи́ст (а́втор).
romantic [ro'mæntik] (**~ally**) романти́чный; **~ism** [-tisizm] романти́зм, рома́нтика; **~ist** [-tisist] рома́нтик.
romp [rɔmp] 1. возня́; сорвиголова́ *m/f*; 2. вози́ться, шу́мно игра́ть.
röntgenogram [rɔnt'genəgræm] рентгеногра́мма.
rood [ru:d] че́тверть а́кра = 0,1 гекта́ра; распя́тие.
roof [ru:f] 1. кры́ша; ~ of the mouth нёбо; 2. [по]кры́ть (дом); **~ing** ['ru:fiŋ] 1. кро́вельный материа́л; 2. кро́вля; ~ felt кро́вельный толь *m.*
rook [ruk] 1. грач; *chess* ладья́; *fig.* моше́нник; 2. обма́нывать [-ну́ть].
room [ru:m] 1. ко́мната; ме́сто; помеще́ние; простра́нство; **~s** *pl.* кварти́ра; ко́мнаты *f/pl.*; 2. *Am.* жить квартира́нтом (-тко́й); **~er** ['rumə] квартира́нт(ка), жиле́ц, жили́ца; **~mate** сожи́тель(ница *f*) *m*; **~y** ['rumi] □ просто́рный.
roost [ru:st] 1. насе́ст; 2. уса́живаться на насе́ст; *fig.* устра́иваться на́ ночь; **~er** ['ru:stə] пету́х.
root [ru:t] ко́рень *m*; strike ~ пуска́ть ко́рни; укореня́ться [-ни́ться]; ~ out вырыва́ть с ко́рнем (*a. fig.*); вы́искивать [вы́искать] (*a.* ~ up); **~ed** ['ru:tid] укорени́вшийся.
rope [roup] 1. кана́т; верёвка; трос; ни́тка (же́мчуга, бус); F come to the end of one's ~ дойти́ до то́чки; know the ~s *pl.* знать все ходы́ и вы́ходы; 2. свя́зывать верёвкой привя́зывать кана́том; (*mst* ~ off) оцепля́ть кана́том.
rosary ['rouzəri] *eccl.* чётки *f/pl.*
rose [rouz] 1. ро́за; се́тка (на ле́йке); ро́зовый цвет; 2. *pt.* от rise.
rosin ['rɔzin] канифо́ль *f.*
rostrum ['rɔstrəm] ка́федра; трибу́на.
rosy ['rouzi] □ ро́зовый; румя́ный; *fig.* ра́дужный.
rot [rɔt] 1. гние́ние; гниль *f*; 2. *v/t.* [с]гнои́ть; *v/i.* сгни(ва́)ть, [с]гнить.
rota|ry ['routəri] враща́тельный; ротацио́нный; **~te** [rou'teit] враща́ть(ся); чередова́ть(ся); **~tion** [rou'teiʃən] враще́ние; чередова́ние; **~tory** [rou'teitəri]: *s.* rotary; ⚡ многофа́зный.
rote [rout]: by ~ *fig.* механи́чески.
rotten [rɔtn] □ гнило́й; испо́рченный; F отврати́тельный.
rouge [ru:ʒ] 1. румя́на *n/pl.*; 2. [на-] румя́нить(ся).
rough [rʌf] 1. □ гру́бый; шерша́вый; шерохова́тый; косма́тый; бу́рный; неделика́тный; ~ and ready сде́ланный ко́е-ка́к, на́спех; грубова́тый; 2. буя́н; 3. ~ it перебива́ться с трудо́м; **~cast** 1. ⊕ штукату́рка намётом; 2. на́черно разрабо́танный; 3. ⊕ штукату́рить намётом; **~en** ['rʌfən] де́лать(ся) гру́бым, шерохова́тым; **~ness** ['rʌfnis] шерохова́тость *f*; гру́бость *f*; **~shod**: ride ~ over обходи́ться гру́бо, суро́во с (Т).
round [raund] 1. □ кру́глый; кругово́й; прямо́й, и́скренний; ~ trip *Am.* пое́здка ту́да и обра́тно; 2. *adv.* круго́м, вокру́г; обра́тно; (*often* ~ about) вокру́г да о́коло; all the year ~ кру́глый год; 3. *prp.* вокру́г, круго́м (Р); за (В *or* Т); по (Д); 4. круг; цикл; тур (в та́нце); *sport* ра́унд; обхо́д; объе́зд; 100 **~s** ⚔ сто патро́нов; 5. *v/t.* закругля́ть [-ли́ть]; огиба́ть [обогну́ть]; ~ up окружа́ть [-жи́ть]; *v/i.* закругля́ться [-ли́ться]; **~about** ['raundəbaut] 1. око́льный; 2. око́льный путь *m*; карусе́ль *f*; **~ish** ['raundiʃ] круглова́тый; **~-up** обла́ва.
rous|e [rauz] *v/t.* [раз]буди́ть; возбужда́ть [-уди́ть]; воодушевля́ть [-ви́ть]; ~ o. s. стряхну́ть лень; *v/i.* просыпа́ться [-сну́ться]; **~ing** ['rauziŋ] возбужда́ющий; бу́рный.
rout [raut] 1. разгро́м; бе́гство; put to ~ разгроми́ть на́голову; обраща́ть в бе́гство; 2. = put to ~; рыть ры́лом.
route [ru:t, ⚔ raut] путь *m*; ⚔ маршру́т.
routine [ru:'ti:n] 1. заведённый поря́док; рути́на; 2. рути́нный.
rove [rouv] скита́ться; броди́ть.
row[1] [rou] 1. ряд; прогу́лка в ло́дке; 2. грести́ (весло́м); пра́вить (ло́дкой).

row² [rau] F 1. галдёж, гвалт; драка; ссора; 2. задавать нагоняй (Д).
row-boat ['roubout] гребная лодка.
rower ['rouə] гребец (*wo*)*man*.
royal ['rɔiəl] □ королевский; великолепный; **~ty** [-ti] член королевской семьи; королевская власть *f*; **~s** *pl.* авторский гонорар.
rub [rʌb] 1. трение; растирание; *fig.* препятствие; 2. *v/t.* тереть; протирать [-тереть]; натирать [натереть]; ~ out стирать [стереть]; ~ up [от]полировать; освежать [-жить] (в памяти); *v/i.* тереться (against о В); *fig.* ~ along, on проби(ва)ться с трудом.
rubber ['rʌbə] каучук; резина; резинка; *cards* роббер; **~s** *pl. Am.* галоши *f/pl.*; *attr.* резиновый.
rubbish ['rʌbiʃ] мусор; хлам; *fig.* вздор; глупости *f/pl.*
rubble [rʌbl] щебень *m*; ⚠ бут.
ruby ['ru:bi] рубин; рубиновый цвет.
rudder ['rʌdə] ⚓ руль *m*; ✈ руль поворота.
rudd|iness ['rʌdinis] краснота; румянец; **~y** ['rʌdi] ярко-красный; румяный.
rude [ru:d] □ неотёсанный; грубый; невежливый; *fig.* крепкий (о здоровье).
rudiment ['ru:diment] *biol.* рудимент, зачаток; **~s** *pl.* начатки *m/pl.*
rueful ['ru:ful] □ унылый, печальный.
ruff [rʌf] брыжи *f/pl.*; *zo.* ёрш.
ruffian ['rʌfjən] грубиян; хулиган.
ruffle [rʌfl] 1. манжетка; рюш; суматоха; рябь *f*; 2. [взъ]ерошить (волосы); рябить (воду); *fig.* нарушать спокойствие (Р), [вс]тревожить.
rug [rʌg] плед; ковёр, коврик; **~ged** ['rʌgid] □ неровный; шероховатый; суровый; пересечённый; резкий.
ruin ['ruin] 1. гибель *f*; разорение; крушение (надежд и т. п.); *mst* **~s** *pl.* развалины *f/pl.*; 2. [по]губить; разорять [-рить]; разрушать [-рушить]; [о]бесчестить; **~ous** ['ruinəs] □ разорительный; губительный.
rul|e [ru:l] 1. правило; устав; правление; власть *f*; линейка; as a ~ обычно; 2. *v/t.* управлять (Т); постановлять [-вить]; [на]линовать; [раз]графить; ~ out исключать [-чить]; *v/i.* господствовать; **~er** ['ru:lə] правитель(ница *f*) *m*; линейка.
rum [rʌm] ром; *Am.* спиртной напиток.
Rumanian [ru(:)'meinjən] 1. румынский; 2. румын(ка).
rumble ['rʌmbl] 1. громыхание; грохот; (*Am.* ~-seat) откидное сиденье; 2. [за]громыхать; [за-] грохотать; [за]греметь (о громе).
rumina|nt ['ru:minənt] жвачное животное; **~te** [-neit] жевать жвачку; *fig.* размышлять [-мыслить].
rummage ['rʌmidʒ] 1. распродажа мелочей (с благотворительной целью); 2. *v/t.* вытаскивать [вытащить]; переры(ва)ть; *v/i.* рыться.
rumo(u)r ['ru:mə] 1. слух; молва; 2. it is ~ed ... ходят слухи ...
rump [rʌmp] огузок.
rumple [rʌmpl] [с]мять; [взъ]ерошить (волосы, перья и т. п.).
run [rʌn] 1. [*irr.*] *v/i. com.* бегать, [по]бежать; [по]течь; расплы(ва)ться (о красках и т. п.); вращаться, работать (о машине); гласить; ~ across a p. наталкиваться [натолкнуться] на (В); ~ away убегать [убежать]; понести *pf.* (о лошади); ~ down сбегать [сбежать]; останавливаться [-новиться (о часах и т. п.); истощаться [-щиться]; ~ dry иссякать [-якнуть]; ~ for *parl.* выставлять свою кандидатуру на (В); ~ into впадать [впасть] в (В); доходить [дойти] до (Р); встречать [-етить]; ~ on продолжаться [-должиться]; говорить без умолку; ~ out, short кончаться [кончиться]; ~ through прочитать бегло; проматывать]-мотать]; ~ to достигать [-игнуть] (суммы); ~ up to доходить [дойти] до (Р); 2. *v/t.* пробегать [-бежать] (расстояние); нали(ва)ть (воду и т. п.); вести (дела); выгонять в поле (скот); вонзать [-зить]; управлять (конторой и т. п.); проводить [-вести] (Т, over по Д); ~ the blockade прорвать блокаду; ~ down задавлять [-вить]; *fig.* говорить плохо о (П); унижать [унизить]; переутомлять [-мить]; ~ over переезжать [-ехать], задавлять [-вить]; прочитать бегло; ~ up взду(ва)ть (цены); возводить [-вести] (здание); ~ up a bill at [за]должать (Д); 3. бег; пробег; ход, работа, действие (машины); течение, ход (времени); ряд; поездка, прогулка; ✝ спрос; управление; *Am.* ручей, поток; загон; пастбище; разрешение пользоваться (of Т); the common ~ обыкновенные люди *m/pl.*; *thea.* have a ~ of 20 nights идти двадцать вечеров подряд (о пьесе); in the long ~ со временем; в конце концов.
run|about ['rʌnəbaut] лёгкий автомобиль *m*; **~away** беглец; дезертир.
rung¹ [rʌŋ] *p. pt.* от ring.
rung² [~] ступенька.
run|let ['rʌnlit], **~nel** ['rʌnl] ручеёк; канава.
runner ['rʌnə] бегун; полоз (у саней); побег (растения); **~-up** [-'rʌp] занимающий второе место (в состязании).

running ['rʌniŋ] **1.** бегу́щий; беговóй; теку́щий; two days ~ два дня подря́д; ~ fire ⚔ бéглый огóнь *m*; ~ hand бéглый пóчерк; **2.** бéганье; бег; бегá *m/pl.*; дéйствие; **~-board** поднóжка.
runway ['rʌnwei] ✈ взлётно-посáдочная полосá.
rupture ['rʌptʃə] **1.** перелóм; разры́в; ⚕ гры́жа; **2.** разрывáть [разорвáть] (*a. fig.*); прор(ы)вáть.
rural ['ruərəl] □ сéльский, деревéнский
rush [rʌʃ] **1.** ♀ тростни́к, камы́ш; нáтиск; † напли́в (покупáтелей); ~ hours *pl.* часы́-пик; ⚔ перебéжка; **2.** *v/i.* мчáться; бросáться [брóситься]; носи́ться, [по]нести́сь; ~ into бросáться необду́манно в (В); ~ into print сли́шком поспéшно выступáть в печáти; *v/t.* мчать; увлекáть [увлéчь]; [по]торопи́ть; *fig.* ⚔ брать стреми́тельным нáтиском.
russet ['rʌsit] крáсно-кори́чневый.
Russia ['rʌʃə] Росси́я; **~n** [-n] **1.** ру́сский; **2.** ру́сский, ру́сская; ру́сский язы́к.
rust [rʌst] **1.** ржáвчина; **2.** [за]ржа-[вéть.]
rustic ['rʌstik] **1.** (~ally) деревéнский; простóй; гру́бый; **2.** сéльский жи́тель *m*.
rustle [rʌsl] **1.** [за]шелестéть; **2.** шéлест, шóрох.
rust|less ['rʌstlis] нержавéющий; **~y** ['rʌsti] заржáвленный, ржáвый; порыжéвший.
rut [rʌt] колея́ (*a. fig.*); ⊕ фальц, жёлоб; *zo.* тéчка.
ruthless ['ru:θlis] □ безжáлостный.
rutted ['rʌtid], **rutty** ['rʌti] изрéзанный колея́ми.
rye [rai] ♀ рожь *f*.

S

sabotage ['sæbotɑ:ʒ] **1.** саботáж; **2.** саботи́ровать (В) (*a.* ~ on *a th.*) (*im*)*pf*.
sabre ['seibə] сáбля, шáшка.
sack [sæk] **1.** грабёж; мешóк, куль *m*; сак (пальтó); **2.** класть, ссыпáть в мешóк; [о]грáбить; F увольня́ть [уво́лить] (В); **~cloth, ~ing** ['sækiŋ] дерю́га, холст.
sacrament ['sækrəmənt] *eccl.* таи́нство, причáстие.
sacred ['seikrid] □ святóй; священный; ♪ духóвный.
sacrifice ['sækrifais] **1.** жéртва; жертвоприношéние; at a ~ † себé в убы́ток; **2.** [по]жéртвовать.
sacrileg|e ['sækrilidʒ] святотáтство, кощу́нство; **~ious** [sækri'lidʒəs] □ святотáтственный.
sad [sæd] □ печáльный, гру́стный; досáдный; ту́склый.
sadden [sædn] [о]печáлить(ся).
saddle [sædl] **1.** седлó; **2.** [о]седлáть; *fig.* взвáливать [-ли́ть] (upon на В); обременя́ть [-ни́ть]; **~r** шóрник.
sadism ['sɑ:dizm] сади́зм.
sadness ['sædnis] печáль *f*, грусть *f*.
safe [seif] **1.** □ невреди́мый; надёжный; безопáсный; (бу́дучи) в безопáсности; **2.** сейф, несгорáемый шкаф; шкаф для прови́зии; **~-conduct** охрáнное свидéтельство; **~guard 1.** охрáна; предосторóжность *f*; защи́та; **2.** охраня́ть [-ни́ть]; защищáть [-ити́ть].
safety ['seifti] **1.** безопáсность *f*; надёжность *f*; **2.** безопáсный; **~-pin** англи́йская булáвка; **~-razor** безопáсная бри́тва.
saffron ['sæfrən] шафрáн.
sag [sæg] оседáть [осéсть]; прогибáться [-гну́ться]; обвисáть [-и́снуть]; ⚓ отклоня́ться от ку́рса.
sagacious [sə'geiʃəs] проницáтельный, прозорли́вый; **~ty** [sə'gæsiti] проницáтельность *f*, прозорли́вость *f*.
sage [seidʒ] **1.** □ му́дрый; разу́мный; **2.** мудрéц; ♀ шалфéй.
said [sed] *pt.* и *p. pt.* от say.
sail [seil] **1.** пáрус; плáвание под парусáми; пáрусное су́дно; **2.** *v/i.* идти́ под парусáми; плáвать, [по-] плы́ть; отплы́(вá)ть; носи́ться, [по]нести́сь (об облакáх); *v/t.* управля́ть (су́дном); плáвать по (Д); **~-boat** *Am.* пáрусная лóдка; **~or** ['seilə] моря́к, матрóс; be a (good) bad ~ (не) страдáть морскóй болéзнью; **~-plane** планёр.
saint [seint] **1.** святóй; **2.** причисля́ть к ли́ку святы́х; **~ly** ['seintli] *adj.* святóй.
sake [seik]: for the ~ of рáди (Р); for my ~ рáди меня́.
sal(e)able ['seiləbl] хóдкий (товáр).
salad ['sæləd] салáт.
salary ['lsæləri] **1.** жáлованье; **2.** плати́ть жáлованье (Д).
sale [seil] продáжа; распродáжа; аукциóн; be for ~, be on ~ продавáться.
sales|man продавéц; *Am.* коммивояжёр; **~woman** продавщи́ца.
salient ['seiljənt] выдаю́щийся, выступáющий; вы́пуклый.
saline ['seilain] солянóй; солёный.
saliva [sə'laivə] ⚕ слюнá.
sallow ['sælou] болéзненный, желтовáтый (о цвéте лицá).
sally ['sæli] **1.** ⚔ вы́лазка; рéплика,

острота́; 2. ⚔ де́лать вы́лазку; ~ forth, ~ out отправля́ться [-а́виться].
salmon ['sæmən] сёмга; ло́сось *m*.
saloon [sə'lu:n] зал; сало́н (на парохо́де); сало́н-ваго́н; *Am.* бар, пивна́я.
salt [sɔ:lt] 1. соль *f*; *fig.* остроу́мие; old ~ быва́лый моря́к; 2. солёный; жгу́чий; е́дкий; 3. [по]соли́ть; заса́ливать [-соли́ть]; **~-cellar** соло́нка; **~petre** ['sɔ:ltpitə] сели́тра; **~y** ['sɔ:lti] солёный.
salubrious [sə'lu:briəs] □, **salutary** ['sæljutəri] □ благотво́рный; поле́зный для здоро́вья.
salut|ation [sælju'teiʃən] приве́тствие; **~e** [sə'lu:t] 1. приве́тствие; ⚔ салю́т; ⚔ отда́ние че́сти; 2. приве́тствовать; ⚔ салютова́ть (*im*)*pf.* (Д); ⚔ отдава́ть честь (Д).
salvage ['sælvidʒ] 1. спасе́ние (иму́щества и́ли су́дна); спасённое иму́щество; подъём (затону́вших судо́в); 2. спаса́ть [спасти́] (иму́щество от огня́, су́дно на мо́ре и т. п.).
salvation [sæl'veiʃən] спасе́ние; ♀ Army 'А́рмия спасе́ния.
salve[1] [sælv] = salvage.
salve[2] [sɑ:v] 1. сре́дство для успоко́ения; 2. успока́ивать [-ко́ить] (со́весть); сгла́живать [сгла́дить] (тру́дность).
salvo ['sælvou] (оруди́йный) залп; *fig.* взрыв аплодисме́нтов.
same [seim]: the ~ тот же са́мый; та же са́мая; то же са́мое; it is all the ~ to me мне всё равно́.
sample [sɑ:mpl] 1. про́ба; обра́зчик, образе́ц; 2. [по]про́бовать; отбира́ть образцы́ (Р).
sanct|ify ['sæŋktifai] освяща́ть [-яти́ть]; **~imonious** [sæŋkti'mounjəs] □ ха́нжеский; **~ion** ['sæŋkʃən] 1. са́нкция; утвержде́ние; принуди́тельная ме́ра; 2. санкциони́ровать (*im*)*pf.*; утвержда́ть [-рди́ть]; **~ity** [-titi] свя́тость *f*; **~uary** [-tjuəri] святи́лище; убе́жище.
sand [sænd] 1. песо́к; **~s** *pl.* песча́ный пляж; о́тмель *f*; пески́ *m/pl.* (пусты́ни); 2. посыпа́ть песко́м.
sandal [sændl] санда́лия.
sandwich ['sænwidʒ, -witʃ] 1. бутербро́д, са́ндвич; 2. просла́ивать [-сло́ить].
sandy ['sændi] песча́ный; песо́чный; песо́чного цве́та.
sane [sein] норма́льный; здра́вый; здравомы́слящий.
sang [sæŋ] *pt.* от sing.
sanguin|ary ['sæŋgwinəri] □ крова́вый; кровожа́дный; **~e** [-gwin] сангвини́ческий; оптимисти́ческий.
sanitary ['sænitəri] □ санита́рный; гигиени́ческий.
sanit|ation [sæni'teiʃən] оздоровле́ние; улучше́ние санита́рных усло́вий; санитари́я; **~y** ['sæniti] здра́вый ум.
sank [sæŋk] *pt.* от sink.
sap [sæp] 1. сок (расте́ний); *fig.* жи́зненные си́лы *f/pl.*; ⚔ са́па; 2. истоща́ть [-щи́ть]; подка́пывать [-копа́ть]; **~less** ['sæplis] худосо́чный; истощённый; **~ling** ['sæpliŋ] молодо́е деревцо́.
sapphire ['sæfaiə] *min.* сапфи́р.
sappy ['sæpi] со́чный; *fig.* си́льный.
sarcasm ['sɑ:kæzm] сарка́зм.
sardine [sɑ:'di:n] сарди́н(к)а.
sardonic [sɑ:'dɔnik] (**~ally**) сардони́ческий.
sash [sæʃ] куша́к, по́яс.
sash-window подъёмное окно́.
sat [sæt] *pt.* и *p. pt.* от sit.
satchel ['sætʃəl] (шко́льный) ра́нец.
sate [seit] насыща́ть [-ы́тить]; пресыща́ть [-ы́тить].
sateen [sæ'ti:n] сати́н.
satellite ['sætəlait] сателли́т (*a. astr.*); приспе́шник; *astr.* спу́тник.
satiate ['seiʃieit] пресыща́ть [-ы́тить]; насыща́ть [-ы́тить].
satin ['sætin] атла́с.
satir|e ['sætaiə] сати́ра; **~ist** ['sætərist] сати́рик; **~ize** [-raiz] высме́ивать [вы́смеять].
satisfaction [sætis'fækʃən] удовлетворе́ние.
satisfactory [sætis'fæktəri] удовлетвори́тельный.
satisfy ['sætisfai] удовлетворя́ть [-ри́ть]; утоля́ть [-ли́ть] (го́лод, любопы́тство и т. п.); выполня́ть [вы́полнить] (обяза́тельства); убежда́ть [убеди́ть].
saturate ['sætʃəreit] ⚗ насыща́ть [-ы́тить]; пропи́тывать [-ита́ть].
Saturday ['sætədi] суббо́та.
sauce [sɔ:s] 1. со́ус; *fig.* припра́ва; F де́рзость *f*; 2. приправля́ть со́усом; F [на]дерзи́ть (Д); **~pan** кастрю́ля; **~r** ['sɔ:sə] блю́дце.
saucy ['sɔ:si] □ F де́рзкий.
saunter ['sɔ:ntə] 1. прогу́ливаться; фланирова́ть; шата́ться; 2. прогу́лка.
sausage ['sɔsidʒ] соси́ска, колбаса́.
savage ['sævidʒ] 1. □ ди́кий; жесто́кий; свире́пый; 2. дика́рь *m* (-а́рка); *fig.* ва́рвар(ка *f*); **~ry** [-ri] ди́кость *f*; жесто́кость *f*.
save [seiv] спаса́ть [спасти́]; избавля́ть [-а́вить] (from от Р); сберега́ть [-ре́чь]; откла́дывать [отложи́ть].
saving ['seiviŋ] 1. □ спаси́тельный; сберега́тельный; 2. спасе́ние; **~s** *pl.* сбереже́ния *n/pl.*
savings-bank сберега́тельная касса.
saviour ['seivjə] спаси́тель *m*; ♀ Спаси́тель *m*.
savo(u)r ['seivə] 1. вкус; F смак; *fig.* пика́нтность *f*; при́вкус; 2. F смакова́ть; ~ of: отзыва́ться (Т); па́хнуть (Т); **~y** [-ri] □ вку́сный; пика́нтный; F сма́чный.

saw [sɔ:] 1. *pt.* от see; 2. погово́рка; пила́; 3. [*irr.*] пили́ть; **~dust** опи́лки *f/pl.*; **~-mill** лесопи́льный заво́д; **~n** [sɔ:n] *p. pt.* от saw.
Saxon ['sæksn] 1. саксо́нский; 2. саксо́нец (-нка).
say [sei] 1. [*irr.*] говори́ть [сказа́ть]; ~ grace чита́ть моли́тву (пе́ред едо́й); that is to ~ то́ есть, т. е.; you don't ~ so! неуже́ли!; I ~! послу́шай(те)!; he is said to be ... говоря́т, что он ...; 2. речь *f*; сло́во; it is my ~ now о́чередь за мной тепе́рь говори́ть; **~ing** ['seiiŋ] погово́рка.
scab [skæb] струп (на я́зве); чесо́тка; *sl.* штрейкбре́хер.
scabbard ['skæbəd] но́жны *f/pl.*
scabrous ['skeibrəs] скабрёзный.
scaffold ['skæfəld] ⚠ леса́ *m/pl.*; подмо́стки *pl.*; эшафо́т; **~ing** [-iŋ] ⚠ леса́ *m/pl.*
scald [skɔ:ld] 1. ожо́г (кипя́щей жи́дкостью); 2. [о]шпа́рить; обва́ривать [-ри́ть].
scale[1] [skeil] 1. чешу́йка (*coll.*: чешуя́); ви́нный ка́мень *m* (на зуба́х); на́кипь *f*, ока́лина (в котле́ и т. п.); (a pair of) **~s** *pl.* весы́ *m/pl.*; 2. соскобля́ть чешую́ с (P); ⊕ снима́ть ока́лину с (P); шелуши́ться; чи́стить от ви́нного ка́мня; взве́шивать [-е́сить].
scale[2] [~] 1. ле́стница; масшта́б; разме́р; шкала́; ♪ га́мма; *fig.* разме́р; 2. взбира́ться [взобра́ться] (по ле́стнице и т. п.); ~ up увели́чивать по масшта́бу; ~ down уменьша́ть по масшта́бу.
scallop ['skɔləp] 1. *zo.* гребешо́к (моллю́ск); **~s** *pl.* фесто́ны *m/pl.*; 2. украша́ть фесто́нами.
scalp [skælp] 1. скальп; 2. скальпи́ровать (*im*)*pf.*, *pf. a.* [о-].
scaly ['skeili] чешу́йчатый; покры́тый на́кипью.
scamp [skæmp] 1. безде́льник; 2. рабо́тать кое-ка́к; **~er** [-ə] 1. бежа́ть стремгла́в; уд(и)ра́ть; 2. поспе́шное бе́гство; гало́п; *fig.* бе́глое чте́ние.
scandal ['skændl] сканда́л; позо́р; спле́тни *f/pl.*; **~ize** ['skændəlaiz] скандализи́ровать (*im*)*pf.*; **~ous** [-ləs] □ сканда́льный; клеветни́ческий.
scant, ~y [skænt, 'skænti] ску́дный; [ограни́ченный.]
scapegoat ['skeipgout] козёл отпуще́ния.
scapegrace [-greis] пове́са *m*, шалопа́й.
scar [skɑ:] 1. шрам; рубе́ц; 2. *v/t.* покрыва́ть рубца́ми; *v/i.* [за]рубцева́ться.
scarc|e [skɛəs] недоста́точный; ску́дный; ре́дкий; **~ely** ['skɛəsli] едва́ ли; как то́лько, едва́; **~ity** [-siti] недоста́ток; дорогови́зна.
scare [skɛə] 1. [на-, ис]пуга́ть; отпу́гивать [-гну́ть] (*a.* ~ away); па́ника; **~crow** пу́гало, чу́чело (*a. fig.*).
scarf [skɑ:f] шарф; шаль *f*; га́лстук.
scarlet ['skɑ:lit] 1. а́лый цвет; 2. а́лый; ~ fever ⚕ скарлати́на.
scarred [skɑ:d] в рубца́х.
scathing ['skeiðiŋ] е́дкий; ре́зкий; *fig.* уничтожа́ющий.
scatter ['skætə] разбра́сывать [-броса́ть]; рассыпа́ть(ся) [-ы́пать (-ся)]; рассе́ивать(ся) [-е́ять(ся)].
scavenger ['skævindʒə] му́сорщик.
scenario [si'nɑ:riou] сцена́рий.
scene [si:n] сце́на; ме́сто де́йствия; декора́ция; **~s** *pl.* кули́сы *f/pl.*; **~ry** ['si:nəri] декора́ции *f/pl.*; пейза́ж.
scent [sent] 1. арома́т, за́пах; духи́ *m/pl.*; *hunt.* чутьё, нюх; 2. [по-] чу́ять; [на]души́ть; **~less** ['sentlis] без арома́та, за́паха.
sceptic ['skeptik] ске́птик; **~al** [-tikəl] □ скепти́ческий.
scept|er, ~re ['septə] ски́петр.
schedule ['ʃedju:l, *Am.* 'skedju:l] 1. табли́ца; гра́фик, пла́н; *Am.* расписа́ние поездо́в; 2. составля́ть расписа́ние (P); назнача́ть [назна́чить, намеча́ть [-е́тить].
scheme [ski:m] 1. схе́ма; план; прое́кт; 2. *v/t.* [за]проекти́ровать; *v/i.* интригова́ть.
schism ['sizm] схи́зма, раско́л.
scholar ['skɔlə] учёный; учени́к (-и́ца); **~ly** [-li] *adj.* учёный; **~ship** [-ʃip] учёность *f*, эруди́ция; *univ.* стипе́ндия.
scholastic [skə'læstik] (**~ally**) схоласти́ческий; шко́льный.
school [sku:l] 1. шко́ла; класс (помеще́ние); at ~ в шко́ле; primary ~ нача́льная шко́ла; secondary ~ сре́дняя шко́ла; 2. дисциплини́ровать (*im*)*pf.*; [вы́]шко́лить]; **~boy** шко́льник; **~fellow** шко́льный това́рищ; **~girl** шко́льница; **~ing** ['sku:liŋ] обуче́ние в шко́ле; **~master** учи́тель *m*; **~mate** *s.* schoolfellow; **~mistress** учи́тельница; **~room** кла́ссная ко́мната.
science ['saiəns] нау́ка; есте́ственные нау́ки *f/pl.*
scientific [saiən'tifik] [**~ally**] нау́чный; уме́лый.
scientist ['saiəntist] учёный; естествове́д.
scintillate ['sintileit] сверка́ть [-кну́ть]; мерца́ть.
scion ['saiən] побе́г (расте́ния); о́тпрыск, пото́мок.
scissors ['sizəz] *pl.* (a pair of ~) но́жницы *f/pl.*
scoff [skɔf] 1. насме́шка; 2. [по-] глуми́ться (at над T).
scold [skould] 1. сварли́вая же́нщина; 2. [вы́]брани́ть.
scon(e) [skɔn, skoun] лепёшка.
scoop [sku:p] 1. сово́к; черпа́к;

ковш; углубле́ние; сенсацио́нная но́вость (одно́й определённой газе́ты); 2. заче́рпывать [-пну́ть].

scooter ['sku:tə] *mot.* моторо́ллер; ⚓ ску́тер; самока́т (игру́шка).

scope [skoup] кругозо́р; разма́х; охва́т; просто́р.

scorch [skɔ:tʃ] *v/t.* обжига́ть [обже́чь]; опаля́ть [-ли́ть]; *v/i.* пали́ть; F бе́шено нести́сь.

score [skɔ:] 1. зару́бка; ме́тка; счёт (в игре́); два деся́тка; ♪ партиту́ра; ~s *pl.* мно́жество; run up ~s *pl.* де́лать долги́; on the ~ of по причи́не (P); what's the ~? како́в счёт? (в игре́); 2. отмеча́ть [-е́тить]; засчи́тывать [-ита́ть]; выи́грывать [вы́играть]; заби́ва́ть гол; оркестрова́ть *(im)pf.*; *Am.* [вы́]брани́ть.

scorn [skɔ:n] 1. презре́ние; 2. презира́ть [-зре́ть]; **~ful** ['skɔ:nful] □ презри́тельный.

Scotch [skɔtʃ] 1. шотла́ндский; 2. шотла́ндский диале́кт; the ~ шотла́ндцы *m/pl.*; **~man** ['skɔtʃmən] шотла́ндец.

scot-free ['skɔt'fri:] невреди́мый; ненака́занный.

scoundrel ['skaundrəl] негодя́й, подле́ц.

scour ['skauə] *v/t.* [по]чи́стить; отчища́ть [отчи́стить]; [вы́]мыть; смы(ва́)ть; ры́скать по (Д); *v/i.* ры́скать (*a.* ~ about).

scourge [skə:dʒ] 1. бич; бе́дствие; 2. бичева́ть; [по]кара́ть.

scout [skaut] 1. разве́дчик (*a.* ✈); Boy ♀s *pl.* бойска́уты *m/pl.*; ~ party ⚔ разве́дочный отря́д; 2. производи́ть разве́дку; отверга́ть с презре́нием.

scowl [skaul] 1. хму́рый вид; 2. [на]хму́риться.

scrabble ['skræbl] цара́пать; [вс]кара́бкаться; сгреба́ть [сгрести́].

scramble ['skræmbl] 1. [вс]кара́бкаться; [по]дра́ться (for за В); ~d eggs *pl.* яи́чница-болту́нья; 2. сва́лка, борьба́; кара́бканье.

scrap [skræp] 1. клочо́к; кусо́чек; лоскуто́к; вы́резка (из газе́ты); ⊕ лом; утильсырьё; ~s *pl.* оста́тки *m/pl.*; объе́дки *m/pl.*; 2. отдава́ть на слом; выбра́сывать [вы́бросить]; **~-book** альбо́м для газе́тных вы́резок.

scrap|e [skreip] 1. скобле́ние; цара́пина; затрудне́ние; 2. скобли́ть; скрести́(сь); соскреба́ть [-ести́] (*mst* ~ off); отчища́ть [-и́стить]; заде́(ва́)ть; ша́ркать [-кнуть] (Т); скаре́дничать; **~er** ['skreipə] скоба́ для чи́стки о́буви.

scrap|-heap сва́лка отбро́сов (и́ли ло́ма); **~-iron** желе́зный лом.

scratch [skrætʃ] 1. цара́пина; *sport* черта́ ста́рта; 2. случа́йный; разноше́рстный; *sport* без гандика́па; 3. [о]цара́пать; [по]чеса́ть; ~ out вычёркивать [вы́черкнуть].

scrawl [skrɔ:l] 1. кара́кули *f/pl.*; 2. писа́ть кара́кулями.

scream [skri:m] 1. вопль *m*; крик; 2. пронзи́тельно крича́ть; **~y** [-i] крикли́вый; крича́щий (о кра́сках).

screech [skri:tʃ] пронзи́тельно крича́ть; взви́згивать [-гнуть].

screen [skri:n] 1. ши́рма; экра́н; щит; перегоро́дка; плете́нь *m*; ⚠ та́мбур; гро́хот, си́то; ⚔ прикры́тие; the ~ кино́ *n indecl.*; 2. прикры́(ва́)ть; заслоня́ть [-ни́ть]; *opt.* пока́зывать на экра́не; просе́ивать [-е́ять].

screw [skru:] 1. га́йка; винт; = screw-propeller; 2. приви́нчивать [-нти́ть] (*mst* ~ on); скрепля́ть винта́ми; *fig.* притесня́ть [-ни́ть]; ~ up [с]мо́рщить (лицо́); **~driver** отвёртка; **~-propeller** гребно́й винт.

scribble ['skribl] 1. кара́кули *f/pl.*; 2. [на]цара́пать.

scrimp [skrimp] *v/t.* уре́з(ыв)ать; *v/i.* [по]скупи́ться.

scrip [skrip] † квита́нция о подпи́ске на а́кции.

script [skript] рукопи́сный шрифт; *film* сцена́рий.

Scripture ['skriptʃə] свяще́нное писа́ние.

scroll [skroul] сви́ток (перга́мента); спи́сок; ⚠ завито́к (украше́ние).

scrub [skrʌb] 1. куст; ~s *pl.* куста́рник; по́росль *f*; 2. скрести́; чи́стить щёткой.

scrubby ['skrʌbi] низкоро́слый; захуда́лый.

scrup|le ['skru:pl] 1. сомне́ния *n/pl.*, колеба́ния *n/pl.*; 2. [по]стесня́ться; **~ulous** ['skru:pjuləs] □ щепети́льный; добросо́вестный.

scrutin|ize ['skru:tinaiz] рассма́тривать [-мотре́ть]; тща́тельно проверя́ть; **~y** ['skru:tini] испыту́ющий взгляд; то́чная прове́рка.

scud [skʌd] 1. гони́мые ве́тром облака́ *n/pl.*; стреми́тельный бег; 2. носи́ться, [по]нести́сь; скользи́ть [-зну́ть[.

scuff [skʌf] идти́, волоча́ но́ги.

scuffle ['skʌfl] 1. дра́ка; 2. [по-] дра́ться.

scullery ['skʌləri] помеще́ние при ку́хне для мытья́ посу́ды.

sculptor ['skʌlptə] ску́льптор, ва́ятель *m*.

sculptur|e ['skʌlptʃə] 1. скульпту́ра; 2. [из]ва́ять; высека́ть [вы́сечь].

scum [skʌm] пе́на; на́кипь *f*; *fig.* подо́нки *m/pl.*

scurf [skə:f] пе́рхоть *f*.

scurrilous ['skʌriləs] гру́бый, непристо́йный.

scurry ['skʌri] бы́стро бе́гать; снова́ть (туда́ и сюда́).
scurvy ['skə:vi] ⚕ цинга́.
scuttle ['skʌtl] **1.** ведёрко для у́гля; **2.** уд(и)ра́ть; дезерти́ровать (*im*)*pf*.
scythe [saið] ⚒ коса́.
sea [si:] мо́ре; *attr.* морско́й; be at ~ *fig.* не знать, что де́лать; недоумева́ть; **~board** бе́рег мо́ря; **~faring** ['si:fɛəriŋ] мореплава́ние; **~-going** да́льнего пла́вания (о су́дне).
seal [si:l] **1.** *zo.* тюле́нь *m*; печа́ть *f*; пло́мба; клеймо́; **2.** запеча́т(ыв)ать; скрепля́ть печа́тью; опеча́т(ыв)ать; ~ up ⊕ гермети́чески уку́поривать; зама́з(ыв)ать; ~ (with lead) [за]пломби́ровать.
sea-level ['levl] у́ровень мо́ря.
sealing-wax сургу́ч.
seam [si:m] **1.** шов (*a.* ⊕); рубе́ц; *geol.* просло́йка; **2.** сши(ва́)ть; [из]борозди́ть.
seaman ['si:mən] моря́к; матро́с.
seamstress ['semstris] швея́.
sea-plane гидропла́н.
sear [siə] иссуша́ть [-ши́ть]; опаля́ть [-ли́ть]; ⚕ прижига́ть [-же́чь]; *fig.* притупля́ть [-пи́ть].
search [sə:tʃ] **1.** по́иски *m/pl.*; о́быск; ро́зыск; in ~ of в по́исках (Р); **2.** *v/t.* обы́скивать [-ка́ть]; зонди́ровать (ра́ну); прони́зывать [-за́ть]; *v/i.* разы́скивать [-ка́ть] (for В); ~ into проника́ть [-и́кнуть] в (В); **~ing** [-iŋ] тща́тельный; испыту́ющий; **~-light** проже́ктор; **~-warrant** докуме́нт на пра́во о́быска.
sea|-shore морско́й бе́рег; **~sick** страда́ющий морско́й боле́знью; **~side** побере́жье; взмо́рье; *attr.* примо́рский; ~ place, ~ resort морско́й куро́рт.
season ['si:zn] **1.** вре́мя го́да; пери́од; сезо́н; out of ~ не во́время; with the compliments of the ~ с лу́чшими пожела́ниями к пра́зднику; **2.** *v/t.* приправля́ть [-а́вить] (пи́щу); выде́рживать [вы́держать] (вино́, лес и т. п.); закаля́ть [-ли́ть] (to про́тив Р); **~able** [-əbl] □ своевре́менный; по сезо́ну; **~al** ['si:zənl] □ сезо́нный; **~ing** ['si:zniŋ] припра́ва; **~-ticket** сезо́нный биле́т.
seat [si:t] **1.** сиде́нье; стул; скамья́; ме́сто (в теа́тре и т. п.); поса́дка (на ло́шади); уса́дьба; подста́вка; **2.** уса́живать [усади́ть]; снабжа́ть сту́льями; вмеща́ть [вмести́ть]; **~ed** сидя́щий; be **~ed** сиде́ть, сади́ться [сесть].
sea|-urchin морско́й ёж; **~ward** ['si:wəd] *adj.* напра́вленный к мо́рю; *adv.* (*a.* ~s) к мо́рю; **~weed** морска́я во́доросль *f*; **~worthy** го́дный для морепла́вания.
secede [si'si:d] отка́лываться [отколо́ться], отпада́ть [отпа́сть] (от сою́за и т. п.).
secession [si'seʃən] раско́л; отпаде́ние; *hist.* вы́ход из сою́за (США); **~ist** [-ist] отсту́пник (-ица).
seclu|de [si'klu:d] уединя́ть [-ни́ть]; **~sion** [si'klu:ʒən] уедине́ние.
second ['sekənd] **1.** □ второ́й; втори́чный; уступа́ющий (to Д); on ~ thoughts по зре́лом размышле́нии; **2.** секу́нда; помо́щник; секунда́нт; **~s** *pl.* † това́р второ́го со́рта; **3.** подде́рживать [-жа́ть]; подкрепля́ть [-пи́ть]; **~ary** [-əri] □ втори́чный; второстепе́нный; побо́чный; **~-hand** поде́ржанный; из вторы́х рук; **~ly** [-li] во-вторы́х; **~-rate** второсо́ртный; второразря́дный.
secre|cy ['si:krisi] скры́тность *f*; секре́тность *f*; **~t** ['sikrit] **1.** □ та́йный, секре́тный; скры́тный; **2.** та́йна, секре́т; in ~ секре́тно, тайко́м; be in the ~ быть посвящённым в секре́т.
secretary ['sekrətri] секрета́рь *m*, секрета́рша; мини́стр.
secret|e [si'kri:t] (с)пря́тать; выделя́ть [вы́делить]; **~ion** [-ʃən] секре́ция, выделе́ние; **~ive** [-iv] скры́тный.
section ['sekʃən] сече́ние; разре́з; отре́зок; ⚕ вскры́тие, се́кция; отде́л; разде́л (кни́ги); ⚔ отделе́ние.
secular ['sekjulə] □ мирско́й, све́тский; веково́й.
secur|e [si'kjuə] **1.** □ безопа́сный; надёжный; уве́ренный; **2.** закрепля́ть [-пи́ть]; обеспе́чи(ва)ть; обезопа́сить *pf*; дост(ав)а́ть; **~ity** [-riti] безопа́сность *f*; надёжность *f*; обеспе́чение; зало́г; **~ities** *pl.* це́нные бума́ги *f/pl.*
sedate [si'deit] □ степе́нный; уравнове́шенный.
sedative ['sedətiv] *mst* ⚕ успока́ивающее сре́дство.
sedentary ['sedntəri] □ сидя́чий.
sediment ['sedimənt] оса́док.
sedition [si'diʃən] призы́в к бу́нту.
seditious [-ʃəs] □ бунта́рский.
seduc|e [si'dju:s] соблазня́ть [-ни́ть]; **~tion** [si'dʌkʃən] собла́зн; **~tive** [-tiv] □ соблазни́тельный.
sedulous ['sedjuləs] □ приле́жный.
see [si:] [*irr.*] *v/i.* [у]ви́деть; I ~ я понима́ю; ~ about a th. [по]забо́титься о (П); ~ through a p. ви́деть насквозь кого́-либо; ~ to присма́тривать [-смотре́ть] за (Т); *v/t.* [у]ви́деть; [по]смотре́ть (фильм, и т. п.); замеча́ть [-е́тить]; понима́ть [-ня́ть]; посеща́ть [-ети́ть]; ~ a p. home провожа́ть кого́-нибудь домо́й; ~ off провожа́ть [-води́ть]; ~ a th. through доводи́ть [довести́] что́-нибудь до конца́; ~ a p. through

помога́ть [помо́чь] (Д); live to ~ дожи́(ва́т)ь до (Р).
seed [si:d] **1.** се́мя *n*; зерно́; *coll.* семена́ *n/pl.*; засе́в; зёрнышко (я́блока и т. п.); пото́мство; go to ~ пойти́ в семена́; *fig.* опуска́ться [-сти́ться]; **2.** *v/t.* засева́ть [засе́ять]; [по]се́ять; *v/i.* пойти́ в се́мя; **~ling** ['si:dliŋ] ⚘ се́янец; **~s** *pl.* расса́да; **~y** ['si:di] напо́лненный семена́ми; потрёпанный, обноси́вшийся; F нездоро́вый.
seek [si:k] [*irr.*] *mst fig.* [по]иска́ть (Р); [по]пыта́ться; [по]стара́ться; ~ after добива́ться (Р).
seem [si:m] [по]каза́ться; **~ing** ['si:miŋ] □ ка́жущийся; мни́мый; **~ly** [-li] подоба́ющий; присто́йный.
seen [si:n] *p. pt.* от see.
seep [si:p] проса́чиваться [-сочи́ться]; протека́ть [-е́чь].
seer ['si(:)ə] прови́дец.
seesaw ['si:'sɔ:] **1.** каче́ли *f/pl.*; кача́ние на доске́; **2.** кача́ться на доске́.
seethe [si:ð] кипе́ть, бурли́ть.
segment ['segmənt] сегме́нт, отре́зок; до́ля, до́лька.
segregate ['segrigeit] отделя́ть [-ли́ть].
seiz|e [si:z] хвата́ть [схвати́ть]; захва́тывать [захвати́ть]; ухвати́ться за (В) *pf.* (*a. fig.*); конфискова́ть (*im*)*pf.*; *fig.* охва́тывать [-ти́ть] (о чу́встве); **~ure** ['si:ʒə] конфиска́ция; захва́т; ⚕ апоплекси́ческий уда́р.
seldom ['seldəm] *adv.* ре́дко, и́зредка.
select [si'lekt] **1.** отбира́ть [отобра́ть]; подбира́ть [подобра́ть]; **2.** отбо́рный; и́збранный; **~ion** [si'lekʃən] вы́бор; подбо́р; отбо́р.
self [self] **1.** *pron.* сам; себя́; ✝ или F = myself etc. я сам и т. д.; **2.** *adj.* одноцве́тный; **3.** *su.* (*pl.* **selves**, selvz) ли́чность *f*; **~-centred** эгоцентри́чный; **~-command** самооблада́ние; **~-conceit** самомне́ние; **~-conceited** чванли́вый; **~-conscious** засте́нчивый; **~-contained** самостоя́тельный; *fig.* за́мкнутый; **~-control** самооблада́ние; **~-defence**: in ~ при самозащи́те; **~-denial** самоотрече́ние; **~-evident** очеви́дный; **~interest** своекоры́стие; **~ish** ['selfiʃ] □ эгоисти́чный; **~-possession** самооблада́ние; **~-reliant** самоуве́ренный; **~-seeking** своекоры́стный; **~-willed** своево́льный.
sell [sel] [*irr.*] прод(ав)а́ть; торгова́ть; ~ off, ~ out ✝ распрод(ав)а́ть; **~er** ['selə] продаве́ц (-вщи́ца); good ~ ✝ хо́дкий това́р.
semblance ['sembləns] подо́бие; нару́жность *f*; вид.
semi... ['semi...] полу...; **~-final** полуфина́л.
seminary ['seminəri] духо́вная семина́рия; расса́дник (*fig.*).
sempstress [-stris] швея́.
senate ['senit] сена́т; *univ.* сове́т.
senator ['senətə] сена́тор.
send [send] [*irr.*] пос(ы)ла́ть; отправля́ть [-а́вить]; ~ for пос(ы)ла́ть за (Т); ~ forth испуска́ть [-усти́ть]; изд(ав)а́ть; ~ up вызыва́ть повыше́ние (Р); ~ word сообща́ть [-щи́ть].
senil|e ['si:nail] ста́рческий; **~ity** [si'niliti] ста́рость *f*; дря́хлость *f*.
senior ['si:njə] **1.** ста́рший; ~ partner ✝ глава́ фи́рмы; **2.** пожило́й челове́к; ста́рший; he is my ~ by a year он ста́рше меня́ на́ год; **~ity** [si:ni'ɔriti] старшинство́.
sensation [sen'seiʃən] ощуще́ние; чу́вство; сенса́ция; **~al** [-ʃnl] □ сенсацио́нный; сенсуа́льный.
sense [sens] **1.** чу́вство; ощуще́ние; смысл; значе́ние; in (out of) one's ~s *pl.* (не) в своём уме́; bring one to his ~s *pl.* привести́ кого́-либо в себя́; make ~ име́ть смысл; быть поня́тным; **2.** ощуща́ть [ощути́ть]; [по]чу́вствовать.
senseless ['senslis] □ бесчу́вственный; бессмы́сленный; бессодержа́тельный; **~ness** [-nis] бесчу́вственность *f* и т. д.
sensibility [-i'biliti] чувстви́тельность *f*; то́чность *f* (прибо́ра).
sensible ['sensəbl] □ (благо)разу́мный; здравомы́слящий; ощути́мый, заме́тный; be ~ of созн(ав)а́ть (В).
sensitiv|e ['sensitiv] □ чувстви́тельный (to к Д); **~ity** [-'tiviti] чувстви́тельность *f* (to к Д).
sensual ['sensjuəl] □ чу́вственный.
sensuous ['sensjuəs] □ чу́вственный; эстети́чный.
sent [sent] *pt.* и *p. pt.* от send.
sentence ['sentəns] **1.** ⚖ пригово́р; *gr.* предложе́ние; serve one's ~ отбыва́ть наказа́ние; **2.** пригова́ривать [-говори́ть].
sententious [sen'tenʃəs] нравоучи́тельный; сентенцио́зный.
sentient ['senʃənt] чу́вствующий.
sentiment ['sentimənt] чу́вство; настрое́ние; мне́ние; мысль *f*; *s.* **~ality**; **~al** [senti'mentl] сентимента́льный; **~ality** [sentimen'tæliti] сентимента́льность *f*.
sentinel ['sentinl], **sentry** ['sentri] ⚔ часово́й; карау́льный.
separa|ble ['sepərəbl] □ отдели́мый; **~te 1.** ['seprit] □ отде́льный, осо́бый; сепара́тный; **2.** ['sepəreit] отделя́ть(ся) [-ли́ть(ся)]; разлуча́ть(ся) [-чи́ть(ся)]; расходи́ться [разойти́сь]; **~tion** [sepə'reiʃən] отделе́ние; разлуче́ние; разобще́ние.
September [sep'tembə] сентя́брь *m*.

sepul|chre ['sepəlkə] *rhet.* гробница; **~ture** ['sepəltʃə] погребе́ние.
sequel ['si:kwəl] продолже́ние; после́дствие.
sequen|ce ['si:kwəns] после́довательность *f*; **~t** [-kwənt] сле́дующий.
sequestrate [si'kwestreit] ⚖ секвестрова́ть (*im*)*pf.*; конфискова́ть (*im*)*pf.*
serenade [seri'neid] **1.** ♪ серена́да; **2.** петь серена́ду (Д).
seren|e [si'ri:n] □ безо́блачный (*a. fig.*); я́сный; безмяте́жный; Your ♀ Highness ва́ша све́тлость *f*; **~ity** [si'reniti] **1.** безмяте́жность *f*; безо́блачность *f*; **2.** ♀ све́тлость *f.*
serf [sə:f] крепостно́й; раб.
sergeant ['sɑ:dʒənt] ⚔ сержа́нт.
serial ['siəriəl] **1.** □ сери́йный; после́довательный; **2.** рома́н и́ли фильм в не́скольких частя́х.
series ['siəri:z] *pl.* се́рия; ряд.
serious ['siəriəs] □ серьёзный; be ~ серьёзно говори́ть; **~ness** [-nis] серьёзность *f.*
sermon ['sə:mən] про́поведь *f.*
serpent ['sə:pənt] змея́; **~ine** [-ain] изви́листый; змееви́дный.
servant ['sə:vənt] слуга́ *m*/*f*; служа́нка; служи́тель *m*; прислу́га.
serve [sə:v] **1.** *v*/*t.* [по]служи́ть (Д); под(ав)а́ть (обе́д, мяч в те́ннисе и т. п.); обслу́живать [-жи́ть]; вруча́ть [-чи́ть] (on Д); отбы́(ва́)ть (срок и т. п.); удовлетворя́ть [-ри́ть]; (it) ~s him right так ему́ и на́до; ~ out вы́да(ва́)ть, разд(ав)а́ть; *v*/*i.* [по]служи́ть (*a.* ⚔) (as Т); ~ at table прислу́живать за столо́м; **2.** *tennis*: пода́ча.
service ['sə:vis] **1.** слу́жба; обслу́живание; услу́га; (*a.* divine ~) богослуже́ние; сообще́ние; *tennis*: пода́ча (мяча́); the ~s *pl.* ⚔ а́рмия, флот и вое́нная авиа́ция; be at a p.'s ~ быть к чьи́м-либо услу́гам; **2.** *Am.* ⊕ [от]ремонти́ровать; **~able** ['se:visəbl] □ поле́зный; про́чный.
servil|e ['sə:vail] □ ра́бский; раболе́пный; холо́пский; **~ity** [sə:viliti] ра́бство; раболе́пство.
servitude ['sə:vitju:d] ра́бство; penal ~ ка́торга.
session ['seʃən] се́ссия; заседа́ние.
set [set] **1.** [*irr.*] *v*/*t.* [по]ста́вить; класть [положи́ть]; помеща́ть [-ести́ть]; размеща́ть [-ести́ть]; сажа́ть [посади́ть] (насе́дку на я́йца); зад(ав)а́ть (уро́ки и т. п.); вставля́ть в ра́му (карти́ну и т. п.); уса́живать [усади́ть] (to за В); ⚕ вправля́ть [-а́вить] (ру́ку, но́гу); ~ a p. laughing [рас]смеши́ть кого́-нибудь; ~ sail пуска́ться в пла́вание; ~ one's teeth сти́снуть зу́бы; ~ aside откла́дывать [отложи́ть]; ~ store by высоко́ цени́ть (В); счита́ть ва́жным (В); ~ forth излага́ть [изложи́ть]; ~ off оттеня́ть [-ни́ть]; ~ up учрежда́ть [-еди́ть]; устра́ивать [-ро́ить]; **2.** *v*/*i. ast.* заходи́ть [зайти́], сади́ться [сесть]; засты́(ва́)ть; ~ about a th. принима́ться [-ня́ться] за что́-нибудь; ~ forth отправля́ться [-а́виться]; ~ (up)on нач(ин)а́ть (В); ~ out отправля́ться [-а́виться]; ~ to вступа́ть в бой; бра́ться [взя́ться] за (рабо́ту, еду́); ~ up for выдава́ть себя́ за (В); **3.** неподви́жный; устано́вленный; засты́вший (взгляд); твёрдый; ~ (up)on поглощённый (Т); ~ with опра́вленный (Т); hard ~ нужда́ющийся; ~ speech пригото́вленная ре́чь *f*; **4.** набо́р; компле́кт; прибо́р; се́рия; ряд; систе́ма; гарниту́р; серви́з (обе́денный и т. п.); (ра́дио)приёмник; круг (о́бщества); *tennis*: сет; покро́й (пла́тья); *thea.* обстано́вка.
set|back ['set'bæk] неуда́ча; **~-down** отпо́р; **~-off** контра́ст; украше́ние.
setting ['setiŋ] опра́ва (камне́й); декора́ции и костю́мы; *fig.* окружа́ющая обстано́вка; захо́д (со́лнца); ♪ му́зыка на слова́.
settle ['setl] *v*/*t.* водворя́ть [-ри́ть]; приводи́ть в поря́док; успока́ивать [-ко́ить]; реша́ть [-и́ть] (вопро́с); ула́живать [-а́дить]; заселя́ть [-ли́ть]; опла́чивать [-ати́ть] (счёт); устра́ивать [-ро́ить] (дела́); *v*/*i.* (*often* ~ down) поселя́ться [-ли́ться]; водворя́ться [-ри́ться]; устра́иваться [-ро́иться]; уса́живаться [усе́сться]; приходи́ть к реше́нию; отста́иваться [-тоя́ться]; оседа́ть [осе́сть]; устана́вливаться [-нови́ться] (о пого́де); **~d** ['setld] постоя́нный; усто́йчивый; **~ment** ['setlmənt] реше́ние; урегули́рование; поселе́ние; ⚖ да́рственная за́пись *f*; **~r** ['setlə] поселе́нец.
set-to (кула́чный) бой; схва́тка.
seven ['sevn] семь; **~teen(th)** [-ti:n(θ)] семна́дцать(-тый); **~th** ['sevnθ] **1.** □ седьмо́й; **2.** седьма́я часть *f*; **~tieth** ['sevntiiθ] семидеся́тый; **~ty** ['sevnti] се́мьдесят.
sever ['sevə] разъединя́ть [-ни́ть]; разлуча́ть [-чи́ть]; [по]рва́ть(ся).
several ['sevrəl] не́сколько (Р); □ отде́льный; **~ly** в отде́льности.
severance ['sevərəns] разры́в; отделе́ние.
sever|e [si'viə] □ стро́гий, суро́вый; ре́зкий; си́льный; жесто́кий; е́дкий; кру́пный (убы́ток); **~ity** [si'veriti] стро́гость *f*; суро́вость *f*; жесто́кость *f.*
sew [sou] [*irr.*] [с]шить.
sewer ['sjuə] сто́чная труба́; **~age** ['sjuəridʒ] канализа́ция.

sew|ing ['souiŋ] шитьё; *attr.* швейный; **~n** [soun] *p. pt.* от sew.
sex [seks] пол.
sexton ['sekstən] церковный сторож, пономарь *m*; могильщик.
sexual ['seksjuəl] □ половой; сексуальный.
shabby ['ʃæbi] □ потёртый; жалкий; захудалый; подлый.
shack [ʃæk] *Am.* лачуга, хижина.
shackle ['ʃækl] 1. **~s** *pl.* кандалы *m/pl.*; оковы *f/pl.*; 2. заковывать в кандалы.
shade [ʃeid] 1. тень *f*; оттенок; абажур (для лампы); нюанс; тени *f/pl.* (в живописи); 2. затенять [-нить]; омрачать [-чить]; [за-] штриховать; ♪ нюансировать (*im*)*pf.*; **~ off** незаметно переходить (into в В).
shadow ['ʃædou] 1. тень *f*; призрак; 2. осенять [-нить]; (*mst* **~ forth**) излагать туманно; следить тайно за (Т); **~y** [-i] тенистый; призрачный; смутный.
shady ['ʃeidi] тенистый; F тёмный, сомнительный; теневой.
shaft [ʃɑ:ft] древко; рукоятка; оглобля; *fig.* стрела (*a.* ♀); ⊕ вал.
shaggy ['ʃægi] косматый; волосатый.
shake [ʃeik] 1. [*irr.*] *v/t.* трясти (В *or* Т); тряхнуть (Т) *pf.*; встряхивать [-хнуть]; потрясать [-сти]; [по-] колебать; **~ hands** пожать руку друг другу, обменяться рукопожатием; *v/i.* [за]трястись; [за]дрожать (with, at от Р); ♪ пускать трель; 2. встряска; дрожь *f*; потрясение; ♪ трель *f*; **~-hands** *pl.* рукопожатие; **~n** ['ʃeikən] 1. *p. pt.* от shake; 2. *adj.* потрясённый.
shaky ['ʃeiki] □ нетвёрдый (на ногах); трясущийся; шаткий.
shall [ʃæl] [*irr.*] *v/aux.* вспом. глагол, образующий будущее (1-ое лицо единственного и множественного числа:) I shall do я буду делать, я сделаю.
shallow ['ʃælou] 1. мелкий; *fig.* поверхностный; 2. отмель *f*.
sham [ʃæm] 1. притворный; поддельный; 2. притворство; подделка; притворщик (-ица); 3. *v/t.* симулировать (*im*)*pf.*; *v/i.* притворяться [-риться].
shamble ['ʃæmbl] волочить ноги; **~s** [-z] бойня.
shame [ʃeim] 1. стыд; позор; for **~!** стыдно!; put to **~** [при]стыдить; 2. [при]стыдить; [о]срамить; **~-faced** ['ʃeimfeist] □ застенчивый; **~ful** ['ʃeimful] □ стыдный; позорный; **~less** ['ʃeimlis] □ бесстыдный.
shampoo [ʃæm'pu:] 1. шампунь *m*; мытьё головы; 2. мыть шампунем.
shamrock ['ʃæmrɔk] ♀ трилистник.
shank [ʃæŋk] голень *f*; ствол.
shanty ['ʃænti] хибарка, хижина.
shape [ʃeip] 1. форма; образ; очертание; 2. *v/t.* созд(ав)ать; придавать форму, вид (Д); *v/i.* [с]формироваться; **~less** ['ʃeiplis] бесформенный; **~ly** [-li] хорошо сложённый; приятной формы.
share [ʃɛə] 1. доля, часть *f*; участие; акция; лемех, сошник (плуга); go **~s** *pl.* делиться поровну; 2. *v/t.* [по]делиться (Т); *v/i.* участвовать (in в П); **~holder** ✝ пайщик (-ица).
shark [ʃɑ:k] акула; *fig.* мошенник.
sharp [ʃɑ:p] 1. □ *com.* острый (*a. fig.*); *fig.* отчётливый; крутой; едкий; кислый; резкий; пронзительный; колкий; F продувной; 2. *adv.* круто; точно; look **~**! живо!; 3. ♪ диез; **~en** ['ʃɑ:pən] [на-] точить; заострять [-рить]; **~er** ['ʃɑ:pə] шулер; **~ness** ['ʃɑ:pnis] острота; резкость *f* (и т. д.); **~-sighted** зоркий; **~-witted** остроумный.
shatter ['ʃætə] разбивать вдребезги; разрушать [-рушить] (надежды); расстраивать [-роить] (нервы, здоровье).
shave [ʃeiv] 1. [*irr.*] [по]брить(ся); [вы]строгать (доску и т. п.); едва не задеть (В); 2. бритьё; have a **~** [по]бриться; have a close **~** едва избежать опасности; **~n** ['ʃeivn] бритый.
shaving ['ʃeiviŋ] 1. бритьё; **~s** *pl.* стружки *f/pl.*
shawl [ʃɔ:l] шаль *f*; большой платок (на плечи).
she [ʃi:] 1. она; 2. женщина; **she-...** самка (животного): she-wolf волчица.
sheaf [ʃi:f] сноп; связка; пучок.
shear [ʃiə] 1. [*irr.*] [о]стричь (овец); *fig.* обдирать как липку; 2. **~s** *pl.* (большие) ножницы *f/pl.*
sheath [ʃi:θ] ножны *f/pl.*; **~e** [ʃi:ð] вкладывать в ножны; ⊕ общи(ва)ть.
sheaves [ʃi:vz] *pl.* от sheaf.
shed[1] [ʃed] [*irr.*] [по]терять (волосы, зубы); проли(ва)ть (слёзы, кровь); сбрасывать [сбросить] (одежду, кожу).
shed[2] [~] навес, сарай; ангар.
sheen [ʃi:n] блеск; отблеск.
sheep [ʃi:p] овца; **~-dog** овчарка; **~-fold** овчарня; **~ish** ['ʃi:piʃ] □ глуповатый; робкий; **~skin** овчина; баранья кожа.
sheer [ʃiə] явный; полнейший; *Am.* прозрачный (о ткани); отвесный.
sheet [ʃi:t] простыня; лист (бумаги, железа); широкая полоса; ✝ таблица; **~ iron** листовое железо; **~ lightning** зарница.
shelf [ʃelf] полка; уступ; риф; on the **~** *fig.* сданный в архив.

shell [ʃel] **1.** скорлупа́; ра́ковина; щит (черепа́хи); ⚔ снаря́д; ги́льза; **2.** снима́ть скорлупу́ с (Р); [об]лущи́ть; обстре́ливать [-ля́ть]; **~-fish** моллю́ск; **~-proof** непробива́емый снаря́дами.

shelter ['ʃeltə] **1.** прию́т, *fig.* кров; убе́жище (*a.* ⚔); **2.** *v/t.* дава́ть прию́т (Д), приюти́ть *pf.*; *v/i.* (*a.* take ~) укры́(ва́)ться; приюти́ться *pf.*

shelve [ʃelv] ста́вить на по́лку; *fig.* откла́дывать в до́лгий я́щик; увольня́ть [уво́лить].

shelves [ʃelvz] *pl.* от shelf.

shepherd ['ʃepəd] **1.** пасту́х; па́стырь *m*; **2.** пасти́; направля́ть [-а́вить] (люде́й как ста́до).

sherbet ['ʃə:bət] шербе́т.

shield [ʃi:ld] **1.** щит; защи́та; **2.** заслоня́ть [-ни́ть] (from от Р).

shift [ʃift] **1.** сме́на (на заво́де и т. п.); измене́ние; сдвиг; переме́на; уло́вка; make ~ ухитря́ться [-ри́ться]; [у]дово́льствоваться (with Т); **2.** *v/t.* [по]меня́ть; перемеща́ть [-мести́ть]; *v/i.* извора́чиваться [изверну́ться]; перемеща́ться [-мести́ться]; ~ for o. s. обходи́ться без по́мощи; **~less** ['ʃiftlis] □ беспо́мощный; **~y** ['ʃifti] □ *fig.* изворо́тливый, ло́вкий.

shilling ['ʃiliŋ] ши́ллинг.

shin [ʃin] **1.** (или ~-bone) го́лень *f*; **2.** ~ up вскара́бк(ив)аться.

shine [ʃain] **1.** сия́ние; свет; блеск, гля́нец, лоск; **2.** [*irr.*] сия́ть; свети́ть; блесте́ть; [от]полирова́ть; [по]чи́стить (о́бувь); *fig.* блиста́ть.

shingle ['ʃiŋgl] га́лька; кро́вельная дра́нка; *Am.* вы́веска; **~s** *pl.* ⚕ опоя́сывающий лиша́й.

shiny ['ʃaini] □ со́лнечный; лосня́щийся; блестя́щий.

ship [ʃip] **1.** су́дно, кора́бль *m*; **2.** грузи́ть на су́дно; перевози́ть [-везти́]; производи́ть поса́дку, нагру́зку (Р на су́дно); **~board**: ⚓ on ~ на корабле́; **~ment** ['ʃipmənt] нагру́зка; погру́зка; **~-owner** владе́лец су́дна; **~ping** ['ʃipiŋ] погру́зка; торго́вый флот, суда́ *n/pl.*; судохо́дство; *attr.* судохо́дный; **~wreck** **1.** кораблекруше́ние; **2.** потерпе́ть кораблекруше́ние; **~-wrecked** потерпе́вший кораблекруше́ние; **~yard** верфь *f*.

shire ['ʃaiə, ...ʃiə] гра́фство.

shirk [ʃə:k] увиливать [-льну́ть] от (Р); **~er** ['ʃə:kə] прогу́льщик.

shirt [ʃə:t] мужска́я руба́шка, соро́чка; (*a.* ~-blouse) блу́за.

shiver ['ʃivə] **1.** дрожь *f*; **2.** [за]дрожа́ть; вздра́гивать [-ро́гнуть]; **~y** [-ri] дрожа́щий.

shoal [ʃoul] **1.** мелково́дье; мель *f*; ста́я, công ся́к (ры́бы); **2.** ме́лкий; **3.** [об]меле́ть.

shock [ʃɔk] **1.** уда́р, толчо́к; потрясе́ние; копна́; ⚕ шок; **2.** *fig.* потряса́ть [-ясти́]; шоки́ровать; **~ing** ['ʃɔkiŋ] □ потряса́ющий; сканда́льный; ужа́сный.

shod [ʃɔd] *pt.* и *p. pt.* от shoe.

shoddy ['ʃɔdi] **1.** волокно́ из шерстяны́х тря́пок; *fig.* хлам; **2.** подде́льный; дрянно́й.

shoe [ʃu:] **1.** ту́фля; башма́к; полуботи́нок; подко́ва; **2.** [*irr.*] обу́(ва́)ть; подко́вывать [-кова́ть]; **~black** чи́стильщик сапо́г; **~blacking** ва́кса; **~horn** рожо́к (для о́буви); **~-lace,** *Am.* **~-string** шнуро́к для боти́нок; **~maker** сапо́жник; **~polish** *s.* shoeblacking.

shone [ʃɔn] *pt.* и *p. pt.* от shine.

shook [ʃuk] *pt.* от shake.

shoot [ʃu:t] **1.** стрельба́; ♀ росто́к, побе́г; **2.** [*irr.*] *v/t.* стреля́ть; застрели́ть *pf.*; расстре́ливать [-ля́ть]; снима́ть [снять], засня́ть *pf.* (фильм); *v/i.* стреля́ть [вы́стрелить]; дёргать (о бо́ли); (*a.* ~ along, past) проноси́ться [-нести́сь]; промелькну́ть *pf.*; промча́ться *pf.*; ♀ расти́ (бы́стро); ~ ahead ри́нуться вперёд; **~er** ['ʃu:tə] стрело́к.

shooting ['ʃu:tiŋ] стрельба́; охо́та; ~ star па́дающая звезда́.

shop [ʃɔp] **1.** ла́вка, магази́н; мастерска́я; talk ~ говори́ть в о́бществе о свое́й профе́ссии; **2.** де́лать поку́пки (*mst* go ~ping); **~keeper** ла́вочник (-ица); **~man** ла́вочник; продаве́ц; **~-steward** цехово́й ста́роста *m*; **~-window** витри́на.

shore [ʃɔ:] **1.** бе́рег; взмо́рье, побере́жье; on ~ на́ берег, на берегу́; подпо́рка; **2.** ~ up подпира́ть [-пере́ть].

shorn [ʃɔ:n] *p. pt.* от shear.

short [ʃɔ:t] коро́ткий; кра́ткий; невысо́кий (рост); недоста́точный; непо́лный; отры́вистый, сухо́й (отве́т); песо́чный (о пече́нье); in ~ вкра́тце; come (или fall) ~ of име́ть недоста́ток в (П); не достига́ть [-и́чь] *or* [-и́гнуть] (Р); не опра́вдывать [-да́ть] (ожида́ний); cut ~ прер(ы)ва́ть; fall (или run) ~ истоща́ться [-щи́ться], иссяка́ть [-я́кнуть]; stop ~ of не доезжа́ть [дое́хать], не доходи́ть [дойти́] до (Р); **~age** ['ʃɔ:tidʒ] нехва́тка; **~coming** недоста́ток; изъя́н; **~cut** сокраще́ние доро́ги; **~-dated** ✝ краткосро́чный; **~en** ['ʃɔ:tn] *v/t.* сокраща́ть [-рати́ть]; укора́чивать [-роти́ть]; *v/i.* сокраща́ться [-рати́ться]; укора́чиваться [-роти́ться];**~ ening** [-iŋ] жир для те́ста; **~hand** стеногра́фия; **~ly** ['ʃɔ:tli] *adv.* вско́ре; ко́ротко; **~ness** [-nis] коро́ткость *f*; кра́ткость *f*; **~-sighted** близору́кий; **~-term** краткосро́чный; **~-winded** страда́ющий оды́шкой.

shot [ʃɔt] **1.** *pt.* и *p. pt.* от shoot; **2.** вы́стрел; ядро́ (пу́шки); дробь *f*, дроби́нка (*mst* small ~); стрело́к; *sport* ядро́ (для толка́ния); уда́р; *phot.* сни́мок; ⚕ инъе́кция; have a ~ сде́лать попы́тку; F not by a long ~ отню́дь не; **~-gun** дробови́к.
should [ʃud, ʃəd] *pt.* от shall.
shoulder ['ʃouldə] **1.** плечо́; усту́п, вы́ступ; **2.** взва́ливать на пле́чи; *fig.* брать на себя́; ⚔ брать к плечу́ (ружьё); **~-blade** лопа́тка (*anat.*).
shout [ʃaut] **1.** крик; во́зглас; **2.** [за]крича́ть [кри́кнуть]; [на]крича́ть (at на В).
shove [ʃʌv] **1.** толчо́к; **2.** пиха́ть [пихну́ть]; толка́ть [-кну́ть].
shovel ['ʃʌvl] **1.** лопа́та, сово́к; **2.** копа́ть [копну́ть]; сгреба́ть лопа́той.
show [ʃou] **1.** [*irr.*] *v/t.* пока́зывать [-за́ть]; выставля́ть [вы́ставить]; проявля́ть [-ви́ть]; дока́зывать [-за́ть]; ~ in вводи́ть [ввести́]; ~ up изоблича́ть [-чи́ть]; *v/i.* пока́зываться [-за́ться]; проявля́ться [-ви́ться]; ~ off пуска́ть пыль в глаза́; **2.** зре́лище; вы́ставка; ви́димость *f*; пока́зывание; **~-case** витри́на.
shower ['ʃauə] **1.** ли́вень *m*; душ; **2.** ли́ться ли́внем; ороша́ть [ороси́ть]; поли́(ва́)ть; *fig.* осыпа́ть [осы́пать]; **~y** ['ʃauəri] дождли́вый.
show|n [ʃoun] *p. pt.* от show; **~-room** вы́ставочный зал; **~-window** *Am.* витри́на; **~y** ['ʃoui] □ роско́шный; эффе́ктный.
shrank [ʃræŋk] *pt.* от shrink.
shred [ʃred] **1.** лоскуто́к, клочо́к; кусо́к; **2.** [*irr.*] ре́зать, рвать на клочки́; F [ис]кромса́ть.
shrew [ʃru:] сварли́вая же́нщина.
shrewd [ʃru:d] проница́тельный; хи́трый.
shriek [ʃri:k] **1.** пронзи́тельный крик, вопль *m*; **2.** [за]вопи́ть.
shrill [ʃril] **1.** □ пронзи́тельный; **2.** пронзи́тельно крича́ть, [за]визжа́ть.
shrimp [ʃrimp] *zo.* креве́тка; *fig.* сморчо́к.
shrine [ʃrain] ра́ка; святы́ня.
shrink [ʃriŋk] [*irr.*] сокраща́ться [-рати́ться]; усыха́ть [усо́хнуть]; сади́ться [сесть] (о мате́рии, ше́рсти); устраша́ться [-ши́ться] (from, at P); **~age** ['ʃriŋkidʒ] сокраще́ние; уса́дка; усу́шка.
shrivel ['ʃrivl] смо́рщи(ва)ть(ся); съёжи(ва)ться.
shroud [ʃraud] **1.** са́ван; *fig.* покро́в; **2.** завёртывать в са́ван; оку́т(ыв)ать (*a. fig.*).
shrub [ʃrʌb] куст; **~s** *pl.* кусте́рник.
shrug [ʃrʌg] **1.** пожи(м)а́ть (плеча́ми); **2.** пожима́ние (плеча́ми).
shrunk [ʃrʌŋk] *pt.* и *p. pt.* от shrink (*a.* **~en**).
shudder ['ʃʌdə] **1.** вздра́гивать [-ро́гнуть]; содрога́ться [-гну́ться]; **2.** дрожь *f*; содрога́ние.
shuffle ['ʃʌfl] **1.** ша́ркать [-кнуть] (при ходьбе́); волочи́ть (но́ги); [с]тасова́ть (ка́рты); виля́ть (лука́вить); ~ off свали́ть с себя́ (отве́тственность); **2.** ша́рканье; тасова́ние (карт); увёртка.
shun [ʃʌn] избега́ть [-ежа́ть] (P); остерега́ться [-ре́чься] (P).
shunt [ʃʌnt] **1.** 🚂 маневри́ровать; ⚡ шунти́ровать; *fig.* откла́дывать [отложи́ть]; **2.** 🚂 стре́лка; перево́д на запа́сный путь; ⚡ шунт.
shut [ʃʌt] [*irr.*] **1.** закры́(ва́)ть(ся), затворя́ть(ся) [-ри́ть(ся)]; ~ down прекраща́ть рабо́ту; ~ up! замолчи́!; **2.** закры́тый; **~ter** ['ʃʌtə] ста́вень *m*; *phot.* затво́р.
shuttle ['ʃʌtl] ⊕ челно́к; ~ train при́городный по́езд.
shy [ʃai] **1.** пугли́вый; засте́нчивый; **2.** [ис]пуга́ться (at P).
shyness ['ʃainis] засте́нчивость *f*.
Siberian [sai'biəriən] **1.** сиби́рский; **2.** сибиря́к (-я́чка).
sick [sik] **1.** больно́й (of T); чу́вствующий тошноту́; уста́вший (of от P); be ~ for тоскова́ть по (Д *or* П); **~en** ['sikn] *v/i.* заболе́(ва́)ть; [за]ча́хнуть; ~ at чу́вствовать отвраще́ние к (Д); *v/t.* де́лать больны́м; вызыва́ть тошноту́ у (P); **~fund** больни́чная ка́сса.
sickle ['sikl] серп.
sick|-leave о́тпуск по боле́зни; **~ly** ['sikli] боле́зненный; тошнотво́рный; нездоро́вый (кли́мат); **~ness** (-nis) боле́знь *f*; тошнота́.
side [said] **1.** *com.* сторона́; бок; край; ~ by ~ бок о́ бок; take ~ with примыка́ть к стороне́ (P); **2.** *attr.* боково́й; побо́чный; **3.** ~ with стать на сто́рону (P); **~board** буфе́т; **~-car** *mot.* коля́ска мотоци́кла; **~-light** боково́й фона́рь *m*; **~long** *adv.* вкось; *adj.* косо́й; боково́й; **~-path** тротуа́р; **~-stroke** пла́вание на боку́; **~-track 1.** 🚂 запасно́й путь *m*; **2.** переводи́ть (по́езд) на запа́сный путь; **~walk** *Am.* тротуа́р; **~ward** (**-s**) ['saidwədz], **~ways** в сто́рону; вкось; бо́ком.
siding ['saidiŋ] 🚂 ве́тка.
sidle ['saidl] подходи́ть (и́ли ходи́ть) бочко́м.
siege [si:dʒ] оса́да; lay ~ to осажда́ть [осади́ть].
sieve [si:v] си́то.
sift [sift] просе́ивать [-е́ять]; *fig.* [про]анализи́ровать.
sigh [sai] **1.** вздох; **2.** вздыха́ть [вздохну́ть].

sight [sait] **1.** зре́ние; вид; взгляд; зре́лище; прице́л; ~s *pl.* достопримеча́тельности *f/pl.*; catch ~ of уви́деть *pf.*, заме́тить *pf.*; lose ~ of потеря́ть из ви́ду; **2.** уви́деть *pf.*; вы́смотреть *pf.*; прице́ли(ва)ться (at в В); **~ly** ['saitli] краси́вый; прия́тный на вид; **~-seeing** ['sait-si:iŋ] осмо́тр достопримеча́тельностей.
sign [sain] **1.** знак; при́знак; симпто́м; вы́веска; in ~ of в знак (Р); **2.** *v/i.* подава́ть зна́к (Д); *v/t.* подпи́сывать [-са́ть].
signal ['signl] **1.** сигна́л; **2.** □ выдаю́щийся, замеча́тельный; **3.** [про]сигнализи́ровать; **~ize** ['signəlaiz] отмеча́ть [-е́тить].
signat|ory ['signətəri] **1.** подписа́вший; **2.** сторона́, подписа́вшая (догово́р); ~ powers *pl.* держа́вы-уча́стницы (догово́ра); **~ure** ['signitʃə] по́дпись *f.*
sign|board вы́веска; **~er** ['sainə] лицо́, подписа́вшее како́й-либо докуме́нт.
signet ['signit] печа́тка.
signific|ance [sig'nifikəns] значе́ние; **~ant** [-kənt] □ значи́тельный, многозначи́тельный; характе́рный (of для Р); **~ation** [signifi'keiʃən] значе́ние; смысл.
signify ['signifai] зна́чить, означа́ть; выка́зывать [вы́казать].
signpost указа́тельный столб.
silence ['sailəns] **1,** молча́ние; безмо́лвие; ~! молча́ть!; **2.** заста́вить молча́ть; заглуша́ть [-ши́ть]; **~r** [-ə] глуши́тель *m.*
silent ['sailənt] □ безмо́лвный; молчали́вый; бесшу́мный.
silk [silk] **1.** шёлк; **2.** шёлковый; **~en** ['silkən] □ шелкови́стый; **~worm** шелкови́чный червь *m*; **~y** ['silki] шелкови́стый.
sill [sil] подоко́нник; поро́г.
silly ['sili] □ глу́пый, дура́шливый.
silt [silt] **1.** ил; **2.** засоря́ть(ся) и́лом (*mst* ~ up).
silver ['silvə] **1.** серебро́; **2.** сере́бряный; **3.** [по]серебри́ть; **~y** [-ri] серебри́стый.
similar ['similə] □ схо́дный (с Т), похо́жий (на В); подо́бный; **~ity** [simi'læriti] схо́дство; подо́бие.
simile ['simili] сравне́ние (как ритори́ческая фигу́ра).
similitude [si'militju:d] подо́бие; о́браз; схо́дство.
simmer ['simə] ме́дленно кипе́ть (и́ли кипяти́ть).
simper ['simpə] **1.** жема́нная улы́бка; **2.** жема́нно улыба́ться.
simple ['simpl] □ просто́й; несло́жный; простоду́шный; **~-hearted** наи́вный; **~ton** [-tən] простаќ.
simpli|city [sim'plisiti] простота́; простоду́шие; **~fy** [-fai] упроща́ть [-ости́ть].
simply ['simpli] про́сто; несло́жно.
simulate ['simjuleit] симули́ровать (*im*)*pf.*, притворя́ться [-ори́ться].
simultaneous [siməl'teinjəs] □ одновре́ме́нный.
sin [sin] **1.** грех; **2.** согреша́ть [-ши́ть], греши́ть.
since [sins] **1.** *prp.* с (Р); **2.** *adv.* с тех пор; ... тому́ наза́д; **3.** *cj.* с тех пор, как; так как; поско́льку.
sincer|e [sin'siə] □ и́скренний; **~ity** [sin'seriti] и́скренность *f.*
sinew ['sinju:] сухожи́лие; *fig. mst* **~s** *pl.* физи́ческая си́ла; **~y** [-jui] му́скулистый; си́льный.
sinful ['sinful] □ гре́шный.
sing [siŋ] [*irr.*] [с]петь; воспе́(ва́)ть; **~ing bird** пе́вчая пти́ца.
singe [sindʒ] опаля́ть [-ли́ть].
singer ['siŋə] певе́ц, певи́ца.
single ['siŋgl] **1.** □ еди́нственный; одино́чный; одино́кий; холосто́й, незаму́жняя; ~ entry проста́я бухгалте́рия; in ~ file гусько́м; **2.** одино́чная игра́ (в те́ннисе); **3.** ~ out отбира́ть [отобра́ть]; **~-breasted** однобо́ртный (пиджа́к); **~-handed** самостоя́тельно, без посторо́нней по́мощи; **~t** ['siŋglit] те́льная фуфа́йка; **~-track** одноколе́йный.
singular ['siŋgjulə] необыча́йный; стра́нный; еди́нственный; **~ity** [siŋgju'læriti] необыча́йность *f.*
sinister ['sinistə] злове́щий.
sink [siŋk] **1.** [*irr.*] *v/i.* опуска́ться [-сти́ться]; [по-, у]тону́ть; погружа́ться [-узи́ться]; *v/t.* затопля́ть [-пи́ть]; [вы́]рыть (коло́дец); прокла́дывать [проложи́ть] (тру́бы); помеща́ть невы́годно (капита́л); зама́лчивать [замолча́ть] (фа́кты); **2.** ра́ковина (водопрово́дная); **~ing** [-iŋ] ⚕ внеза́пная сла́бость *f*; ~ fund амортизацио́нный фонд.
sinless ['sinlis] безгре́шный.
sinner ['sinə] гре́шник (-ица).
sinuous ['sinjuəs] □ изви́листый.
sip [sip] **1.** ма́ленький глото́к; **2.** пить ма́ленькими глотка́ми.
sir [sə:] су́дарь *m* (обраще́ние); ♀ сэр (ти́тул).
siren ['saiərin] сире́на.
sirloin ['sə:lɔin] филе́й.
sister ['sistə] сестра́; **~hood** [-hud] се́стринская общи́на; **~-in-law** [-rinlɔ:] неве́стка; золо́вка; своя́ченица; **~ly** [-li] се́стринский.
sit [sit] [*irr.*] *v/i.* сиде́ть; заседа́ть; *fig.* быть располо́женным; ~ down сади́ться [сесть]; *v/t.* сажа́ть [посади́ть] (на я́йца).
site [sait] местоположе́ние; уча́сток (для строи́тельства).
sitting ['sitiŋ] заседа́ние; **~-room** гости́ная.
situat|ed ['sitjueitid] располо́женный; **~ion** [sitju'eiʃən] положе́ние; ситуа́ция; до́лжность *f.*

six [siks] 1. шесть; 2. шестёрка; **~teen** ['siks'ti:n] шестнáдцать; **~teenth** [-θ] шестнáдцатый; **~th** [siksθ] 1. шестóй; 2. шестáя часть *f*; **~tieth** ['sikstiiθ] шестидесятый; **~ty** ['siksti] шестьдесят.

size [saiz] 1. размéр, величинá; формáт; нóмер (óбуви и т. п.); 2. сортировáть по размéрам; ~ **up** определять величинý (Р); ... **~d** [-d] ... размéра.

siz(e)able ['saizəbl] порядочного размéра.

sizzle ['sizl] [за]шипéть.

skat|e [skeit] 1. конёк (*pl.*: коньки́); (= roller-~) конёк на рóликах; 2. катáться на конькáх; **~er** ['skeitə] конькобéжец (-жка).

skein [skein] мотóк пряжи.

skeleton ['skelitn] скелéт, óстов; каркáс; *attr.* ⚔ недоукомплектóванный (полк и т. д.); ~ **key** отмы́чка.

sketch [sketʃ] 1. эскиз, набрóсок; 2. дéлать набрóсок (Р); рисовáть эскизы.

ski [ʃi:, *Am.* ski:] 1. (*pl.* ~ или ~s) лы́жа; 2. ходить на лы́жах.

skid [skid] 1. тормознóй башмáк; буксовáние; ✈ хвостовóй костыль *m*; 2. *v/t.* [за]тормозить; *v/i.* буксовáть.

skilful ['skilful] □ искýсный, умéлый.

skill [skil] мастерствó, умéние; **~ed** квалифици́рованный; искýсный.

skim [skim] 1. снимáть [снять] (нáкипь, сли́вки и т. п.); [по-] нестись по (Д), скользить [-знýть] по (Д); просмáтривать [-смотрéть]; ~ **over** бéгло прочи́тывать; 2. ~ **milk** снятóе молокó.

skimp [skimp] скýдно снабжáть; урéз(ыв)ать; [по]скупи́ться (**in** на В); **~y** ['skimpi] □ скýдный; ýзкий.

skin [skin] 1. кóжа; шкýра; кожурá; оболóчка; 2. *v/t.* сдирáть кóжу, шкýру, корý с (Р); ~ **off** *F* снимáть [снять] (перчáтки, чулки́ и т. п.); *v/i.* зажи́(вá)ть (о рáне) (*a.* ~ **over**); **~-deep** поверхностный; **~flint** скряга *m*; **~ny** ['skini] тóщий.

skip [skip] 1. прыжóк; ⚒ бадья; 2. *v/i.* [по]скакáть; *fig.* перескáкивать [-скочи́ть] (**from** с [Р]), **to** на [В]); *v/t.* пропускáть [-сти́ть] (страни́цу и т. п.).

skipper ['skipə] шки́пер, капитáн.

skirmish ['skə:miʃ] 1. ⚔ перестрéлка; сты́чка; 2. перестрéливаться.

skirt [skə:t] 1. ю́бка; полá; край, окрáина; 2. окаймлять [-ми́ть]; идти́ вдоль крáя (Р); быть располóженным на окрáине (Р).

skit [skit] сати́ра, парóдия; **~tish** ['skitiʃ] □ игри́вый, кокéтливый.

skittle ['skitl] кéгля; **play (at) ~s** *pl.* игрáть в кéгли; **~-alley** кегельбáн.

skulk [skʌlk] скрывáться; прятаться; крáсться; **~er** ['skʌlkə] скрывáющийся; прогýльщик.

skull [skʌl] чéреп.

sky [skai] нéбо (*eccl.*: небесá); **~lark** 1. жáворонок; 2. выки́дывать штýки; **~light** вéрхний свет; свéтлый люк; **~line** горизóнт; очертáние (на фóне нéба); **~-scraper** небоскрёб; **~ward(s)** ['skaiwəd(z)] к нéбу.

slab [slæb] плитá; пласти́на.

slack [slæk] 1. нерадивый; расхлябанный; слáбый; мéдленный; ненатянутый (о повóдьях и т. п.); (*a.* ✝) вялый; 2. ⚓ слабинá (канáта); ✝ застóй; **~s** *pl.* свобóдные (рабóчие) брю́ки *f/pl.*; 3. = **~en**; = **slake**; **~en** ['slækn] ослаблять [-áбить]; [о]слáбнуть; замедлять [-éдлить]; лóдырничать.

slag [slæg] шлак, окáлина.

slain [slein] *p. pt.* от **slay**.

slake [sleik] утолять [-ли́ть] (жáжду); гаси́ть (и́звесть).

slam [slæm] 1. хлóпанье; (в кáрточной игрé) шлем; 2. хлóпать [-пнуть] (Т); захлóпывать(ся) [-пнуть(ся)].

slander ['slɑ:ndə] 1. клеветá; 2. [на]клеветáть; **~ous** [-rəs] □ клеветни́ческий.

slang [slæŋ] слэнг; жаргóн.

slant [slɑ:nt] 1. склон, уклóн; *Am.* тóчка зрéния; 2. *v/t.* класть кóсо; направлять вкось; *v/i.* лежáть кóсо; **~ing** ['slɑ:ntiŋ] *adj.* □ косóй; **~wise** [-waiz] *adv.* кóсо.

slap [slæp] 1. шлепóк; ~ **in the face** пощёчина; 2. шлёпать [-пнуть].

slash [slæʃ] 1. удáр сплечá; разрéз; вы́рубка; 2. руби́ть [рубанýть] (сáблей); [по]рáнить (ножóм); [ис]полосовáть [полоснýть] (кнутóм и т. п.).

slate [sleit] 1. слáнец, ши́фер; гри́фельная доскá; 2. крыть ши́ферными пли́тами; **~-pencil** гри́фель *m*.

slattern [slætən] неряха (жéнщина).

slaughter ['slɔ:tə] 1. убóй (скотá); резня, кровопроли́тие; 2. [за]рéзать (домáшнее живóтное); **~-house** бóйня.

Slav [slɑ:v] 1. славяни́н (-янка); 2. славянский.

slave [sleiv] 1. раб(ы́ня); *attr.* рáбский; 2. рабóтать как кáторжник.

slaver ['slævə] 1. слю́ни *f/pl.*; 2. [за]слюнявить; пускáть слю́ни.

slav|ery ['sleivəri] рáбство; **~ish** [-viʃ] □ рáбский.

slay [slei] [*irr.*] уби́(вá)ть.

sled [sled], **~ge**[1] [sledʒ] сáни *f/pl.*; салáзки *f/pl.*

sledge[2] [~] кузнéчный мóлот.

sleek [sli:k] 1. □ глáдкий, прили́-

занный; хо́леный; **2.** пригла́живать [-гла́дить]; **~ness** [sli:knis] гла́дкость *f.*
sleep [sli:p] **1.** [*irr.*] *v/i.* спать; ~ (up-) on отложи́ть до за́втра; *v/t.* дава́ть (кому́-нибудь) ночле́г; ~ away прос(ы)па́ть; **2.** сон; **~er** [-ə] спя́щий; 🚂 шпа́ла; F спа́льный ваго́н; **~ing** [-iŋ]: ~ partner компаньо́н, не уча́ствующий акти́вно в дела́х; **~ing-car(riage)** 🚂 спа́льный ваго́н; **~less** [-lis] □ бессо́нный; **~-walker** луна́тик; **~y** [-i] □ со́нный, за́спанный.
sleet [sli:t] **1.** дождь со сне́гом и́ли гра́дом; **2.** it ~s идёт дождь со сне́гом; **~y** ['sli:ti] сля́котный.
sleeve [sli:v] рука́в; ⊕ му́фта; вту́лка.
sleigh [slei] са́ни *f/pl.*; сала́зки *f/pl.*
sleight [slait] (*mst* ~ of hand) ло́вкость *f* (рук); фо́кусничество.
slender ['slendə] □ стро́йный; то́нкий; ску́дный.
slept [slept] *pt.* и *p. pt.* от sleep.
sleuth [slu:θ] соба́ка-ище́йка; *fig.* сы́щик.
slew [slu:] *pt.* от slay.
slice [slais] **1.** ло́мтик; то́нкий слой; часть *f*; **2.** ре́зать ло́мтиками.
slick [slik] F гла́дкий; *Am.* хи́трый; **~er** *Am.* ['slikə] жу́лик.
slid [slid] *pt.* и *p. pt.* от slide.
slide [slaid] **1.** [*irr.*] скользи́ть [-зну́ть]; ката́ться по льду; вдвига́ть [-и́нуть], всо́вывать [всу́нуть] (into в В); let things ~ относи́ться ко всему́ спустя́ рукава́; **2.** скольже́ние; ледяна́я гора́ и́ли доро́жка; о́ползень *m*; накло́нная пло́скость *f*; ⊕ сала́зки *f/pl.*; диапозити́в; **~-rule** логарифми́ческая лине́йка.
slight [slait] **1.** □ то́нкий, хру́пкий; незначи́тельный; сла́бый; **2.** пренебреже́ние; **3.** пренебрега́ть [-бре́чь] (T); трети́ровать.
slim|e [slaim] слизь *f*; ли́пкий ил; **~y** ['slaimi] слизи́стый; вя́зкий.
sling [sliŋ] **1.** (руже́йный) реме́нь *m*; рога́тка; праща́; ⚕ повя́зка; **2.** [*irr.*] швыря́ть [швырну́ть]; ве́шать через плечо́; подве́шивать [-е́сить].
slink [sliŋk] [*irr.*] кра́сться.
slip [slip] **1.** [*irr.*] *v/i.* скользи́ть [-зну́ть]; поскользну́ться *pf.*; выскольза́ть [вы́скользнуть] (*a.* ~ away); буксова́ть (о колёсах); ошиба́ться [-би́ться]; *v/t.* сова́ть [су́нуть]; спуска́ть [спусти́ть] (соба́ку); выпуска́ть [вы́пустить] (стрелу́); ~ a p.'s memory ускольза́ть из па́мяти (P); ~ on (off) наде́(ва́)ть (сбра́сывать [сбро́сить]); **2.** скольже́ние; полоса́; про́мах; оши́бка; опи́ска; опеча́тка; комбина́ция (бельё); ⚓ э́аллинг, ста́пель *m*; на́волочка; give a p. the ~ ускольза́ть [-зну́ть] от (P); **~per** ['slipə] ко́мнатная ту́фля, **~s** *pl.* шлёпанцы *m/pl.*; **~pery** ['slipəri] □ ско́льзкий; ненадёжный; **~shod** ['slipʃɔd] неря́шливый; небре́жный; **~t** [slipt] *pt.* и *p. pt.* от slip.
slit [slit] **1.** разре́з; щель *f*; **2.** [*irr.*] разреза́ть в длину́.
sliver ['slivə] ще́пка, лучи́на.
slogan [slougən] ло́зунг, деви́з.
sloop [slu:p] ⚓ шлюп.
slop [slɔp]: **1.** лу́жа; **~s** *pl.* жи́дкая пи́ща; **~s** *pl.* помо́и *m/pl.*; **2.** проли́(ва́)ть; расплёскивать(ся) [-еска́ть(ся)].
slope [sloup] **1.** накло́н, склон, скат; **2.** клони́ться; име́ть накло́н.
sloppy ['slɔpi] □ мо́крый (о доро́ге); жи́дкий (о пи́ще); неря́шливый.
slot [slɔt] щель *f*; паз.
sloth [slouθ] лень *f*, ле́ность *f*; *zo.* лени́вец.
slot-machine автома́т (для прода́жи папиро́с и т. п.).
slouch [slautʃ] **1.** [с]суту́литься; неуклю́же держа́ться; свиса́ть [сви́снуть]; **2.** суту́лость *f*; ~ hat мя́гкая шля́па.
slough[1] [slau] боло́то; топь *f*.
slough[2] [slʌf] сбро́шенная ко́жа (змей).
sloven ['slʌvn] неря́ха *m/f*; **~ly** [-li] неря́шливый.
slow [slou] **1.** □ ме́дленный; медли́тельный; тупо́й; вя́лый; be ~ отст(ав)а́ть (о часа́х); **2.** (*a.* ~ down, up, off) замедля́ть(ся) [заме́длить (-ся)]; **~coach** тугоду́м; отста́лый челове́к; **~-worm** *zo.* медяни́ца.
sludge [slʌdʒ] *f*; отсто́й; ти́на.
slug [slʌg] **1.** слизня́к; *Am.* F жето́н для телефо́нных автома́тов; **2.** *Am.* F [от]тузи́ть.
slugg|ard ['slʌgəd] лежебо́ка *m/f.*; **~ish** ['slʌgiʃ] □ ме́дленный, вя́лый.
sluice [slu:s] **1.** шлюз; **2.** отводи́ть шлю́зом; шлюзова́ть (*im*)*pf.*; обли́(ва́)ть (over B).
slum [slʌm] *mst* ~s *pl.* трущо́ба.
slumber ['slʌmbə] **1.** (*a.* ~s *pl.*) сон; **2.** дрема́ть; спа́ть.
slump [slʌmp] **1.** ре́зкое паде́ние (цен, спро́са); **2.** ре́зко па́дать; тяжело́ опуска́ться (на стул и т. п.).
slung [slʌŋ] *pt.* и *p. pt.* от sling.
slunk [slʌŋk] *pt.* и *p. pt.* от slink.
slur [slə:] **1.** слия́ние (зву́ков); *fig.* пятно́ (на репута́ции); ♪ ли́га; **2.** *v/t.* сли(ва́)ть (слова́); ~ over зама́зы(ва)ть; ♪ игра́ть лега́то.
slush [slʌʃ] сля́коть *f*; та́лый снег.
sly [slai] □ хи́трый; лука́вый; on the ~ тайко́м.
smack [smæk] **1.** (при́)вкус; за́пах; чмо́канье; зво́нкий поцелу́й; *fig.*

отте́нок; 2. отзыва́ться [отозва́ться] (of T); па́хнуть (of T); име́ть при́вкус (of P); чмо́кать [-кнуть] (губа́ми); хло́пать [-пнуть] (T); шлёпать [-пнуть].

small [smɔ:l] *com.* ма́ленький, небольшо́й; ме́лкий; незначи́тельный; ~ change ме́лочь *f*; ~ fry ме́лкая рыбёшка; мелюзга́; ~ of the back *anat.* поясни́ца; **~-arms** *pl.* ручно́е огнестре́льное ору́жие; **~ish** [smɔ:liʃ] дово́льно ма́ленький; **~pox** *pl.* ⚕ о́спа; **~-talk** лёгкий, бессодержа́тельный разгово́р.

smart [smɑ:t] 1. □ ре́зкий, си́льный (уда́р); суро́вый (о наказа́нии); ло́вкий; остроу́мный; щеголева́тый; наря́дный; 2. боль *f*; 3. боле́ть (о ча́сти те́ла); страда́ть; **~-money** компенса́ция за уве́чье; отступны́е де́ньги *f/pl.*; **~ness** ['smɑ:tnis] наря́дность *f*; элега́нтность *f*; ло́вкость *f*.

smash [smæʃ] 1. *v/t.* сокруша́ть [-ши́ть] *a. fig.*; разбива́ть вдре́безги; *v/i.* разби́(ва́)ться; ста́лкиваться [столкну́ться] (into с T); ✝ [о]банкро́титься; 2. битьё вдре́безги; столкнове́ние (поездо́в и т. п.); **~-up** катастро́фа; банкро́тство.

smattering ['smætəriŋ] пове́рхностное зна́ние.

smear [smiə] 1. пятно́; мазо́к; 2. [на]ма́зать, изма́з(ыв)ать.

smell [smel] 1. за́пах; обоня́ние; 2. [*irr.*] обоня́ть (B); [по]чу́ять (B); (*a.* ~ at) [по]ню́хать (B); ~ of па́хнуть (T).

smelt[1] [smelt] *pt.* и *p. pt.* от smell.

smelt[2] [~] выплавля́ть [вы́плавить] (мета́лл).

smile [smail] 1. улы́бка; 2. улыба́ться [-бну́ться].

smirch [smə:tʃ] *rhet.* [за]пятна́ть.

smirk [smə:k] ухмыля́ться [-льну́ться].

smite [smait] [*irr.*] поража́ть [порази́ть]; ударя́ть [уда́рить]; разби́(ва́)ть (непри́ятеля); разруша́ть [-ру́шить].

smith [smiθ] кузне́ц.

smithereens ['smiðə'ri:nz] *pl.* оско́лки *m/pl.*; черепки́ *m/pl.*; (in)to ~ вдре́безги.

smithy ['smiði] ку́зница.

smitten ['smitn] 1. *p.pt.* от smite; 2. поражённый (with T); очаро́ванный (with T).

smock [smɔk] 1. украша́ть обо́рками; 2. **~-frock** рабо́чий хала́т.

smoke [smouk] 1. дым; have a ~ покури́ть *pf.*; 2. кури́ть; [на-] дыми́ть; [за]дыми́ться; выку́ривать [вы́курить] (*a.* ~ out); **~-dried** копчёный; **~r** ['smoukə] куря́щий; 🚃 F ваго́н для куря́щих; отделе́ние для куря́щих; **~-stack** 🚃 ⚓ дымова́я труба́.

smoking ['smoukiŋ] куря́щий; кури́тельный (о ко́мнате); **~ compartment** отделе́ние для куря́щих.

smoky [-ki] ды́мный; закопте́лый.

smooth [smu:ð] 1. □ гла́дкий; *fig.* пла́вный; споко́йный; вкра́дчивый, льсти́вый; 2. пригла́живать [-ла́дить]; разгла́живать [-ла́дить]; *fig.* (*a.* ~ over) смягча́ть [-чи́ть], сма́з(ыв)ать; **~ness** ['smu:ðnis] гла́дкость *f* и т. д.

smote [smout] *pt.* от smite.

smother ['smʌðə] [за]души́ть.

smoulder ['smouldə] тлеть.

smudge [smʌdʒ] 1. [за]па́чкать(ся); 2. гря́зное пятно́.

smug [smʌg] самодово́льный.

smuggle ['smʌgl] занима́ться контраба́ндой; протаскивать контраба́ндой; **~r** [-ə] контрабанди́ст(ка).

smut [smʌt] 1. са́жа, у́гольная пыль *f* и т. п.; гря́зное пятно́; непристо́йности *f/pl.*; ⚘ головня́; 2. [за-] па́чкать.

smutty ['smʌti] □ гря́зный.

snack [snæk] лёгкая заку́ска; **~-bar** заку́сочная.

snaffle ['snæfl] тре́нзель *m*.

snag [snæg] коря́га; сучо́к; обло́манный зуб; *fig.* препя́тствие.

snail [sneil] *zo.* ули́тка.

snake [sneik] *zo.* змея́.

snap [snæp] 1. щёлк, треск; застёжка; хрустя́щее пече́нье; де́тская ка́рточная игра́; *fig.* энерги́чность *f*; cold ~ внеза́пное похолода́ние; 2. *v/i.* [с]лома́ться; щёлкать [-кнуть]; ухва́тываться [ухвати́ться] (at за B); огрыза́ться [-зну́ться] (at на B); [по]рва́ться; ца́пать [ца́пнуть] (at B); *v/t.* защёлкивать [защелкну́ть]; *phot.* де́лать момента́льный сни́мок (P); ~ out отре́зать *pf.*; ~ up подхва́тывать [-хвати́ть]; **~fastener** кно́пка (застёжка); **~pish** ['snæpiʃ] □ раздражи́тельный; **~py** ['snæpi] F энерги́чный; живо́й; **~shot** *phot.* момента́льный сни́мок.

snare [snɛə] 1. сило́к; *fig.* лову́шка; западня́; 2. пойма́ть в лову́шку.

snarl [snɑ:l] 1. рыча́ние; 2. [про-] рыча́ть; *fig.* огрыза́ться [-зну́ться].

snatch [snætʃ] 1. рыво́к; хвата́ние; обры́вок; кусо́чек; 2. хвата́ть [схвати́ть]; ~ at хвата́ться [схвати́ться] за (B); ~ up подхва́тывать [-хвати́ть].

sneak [sni:k] 1. *v/i.* кра́сться; *v/t.* F стащи́ть *pf.*, укра́сть *pf.*; 2. трус; я́бедник (-ица); **~ers** ['sni:kəz] *pl.* те́ннисные ту́фли *f/pl*; та́почки *f/pl.*

sneer [sniə] 1. усме́шка; насме́шка; 2. насме́шливо улыба́ться; [по-] глуми́ться (at над T).

sneeze [sni:z] 1. чиха́нье; 2. чиха́ть [чихну́ть].

snicker ['snikə] тихо ржать; хихикать [-кнуть].
sniff [snif] фыркать [-кнуть] (в знак презрения); [за]сопеть; [по-] нюхать.
snigger ['snigə] подавленный смешок.
snip [snip] 1. обрезок; надрез; 2. резать ножницами.
snipe [snaip] стрелять из укрытия.
snippy ['snipi] F отрывисто-грубый; надменный.
snivel ['snivl] [за]хныкать; F распускать сопли.
snob [snɔb] сноб; **~bery** ['snɔbəri] снобизм.
snoop [snu:p] *Am.* 1. совать нос в чужие дела; 2. проныра *m/f*.
snooze [snu:z] F 1. лёгкий, короткий сон; 2. дремать, вздремнуть *pf*.
snore [snɔ:] [за]храпеть.
snort [snɔ:t] фыркать [-кнуть]; [за]храпеть (о лошади).
snout [snaut] рыло; морда.
snow [snou] 1. снег; 2. it **~s** снег идёт; be **~ed under** быть занесённым снегом; **~-drift** снежный сугроб; **~y** ['snoui] □ снежный; белоснежный.
snub [snʌb] 1. *fig.* осаживать [осадить]; 2. выговор; **~-nosed** курносый.
snuff [snʌf] 1. нюхательный табак; 2. снимать нагар (со свечи); (*a.* take **~**) нюхать табак; **~le** ['snʌfl] гнусавить, говорить в нос.
snug [snʌg] □ уютный; достаточный; **~gle** ['snʌgl] (ласково) приж(им)ать(ся) (to к Д).
so [sou] так; итак; таким образом; I hope **~** я надеюсь; are you tired? **~** I am вы устали? — да; you are tired, **~** am I вы устали и я тоже; **~** far до сих пор.
soak [souk] *v/t.* [на]мочить; впитывать [впитать]; *v/i.* промокать; пропитываться [-питаться]; просачиваться [-сочиться].
soap [soup] 1. мыло; soft **~** жидкое мыло; 2. намыли(ва)ть; **~-box** мыльница; импровизированная трибуна; **~y** ['soupi] □ мыльный.
soar [sɔ:] высоко летать; парить; ✈ [с]планировать.
sob [sɔb] 1. рыдание; 2. [за]рыдать, разрыдаться *pf*.
sober ['soubə] 1. □ трезвый; умеренный; 2. вытрезвлять [вытрезвить]; **~ness** [-nis], **~sobriety** [sou'braiəti] трезвость *f*.
so-called ['soukɔ:ld] так называемый.
sociable ['souʃəbl] 1. □ общительный; дружеский; 2. *Am.* вечеринка.
social ['souʃəl] 1. □ общественный; социальный; светский; **~** service социальное учреждение; 2. вечеринка; **~ize** [-aiz] социализировать (*im*)*pf*.
society [sə'saiəti] общество; компания (торговая); общественность *f*; объединение.
sociology [sousi'ɔlədʒi] социология.
sock [sɔk] носок; стелька.
socket ['sɔkit] впадина (глазная); углубление; ⚡ патрон (электрической лампочки); ⊕ муфта.
soda ['soudə] сода; содовая вода; **~-fountain** сифон.
sodden ['sɔdn] промокший.
soft [sɔft] □ *com.* мягкий; нежный; тихий; неяркий; кроткий; изнеженный; придурковатый; **~ drink** *Am.* F безалкогольный напиток; **~en** ['sɔfn] смягчать(ся) [-чить(ся)].
soggy ['sɔgi] сырой; пропитанный водой.
soil [sɔil] 1. почва, земля; грязь *f*; пятно; 2. [за]пачкать(ся).
sojourn ['sɔdʒə:n, 'sʌdʒ-] 1. пребывание; 2. (временно) проживать.
solace ['sɔləs] 1. утешение; 2. утешать [утешить].
sold [sould] *pt.* и *p. pt.* от sell.
solder ['sɔ(l)də] 1. спайка; 2. паять, запаивать [запаять].
soldier ['souldʒə] солдат; **~like, ~ly** [-li] воинский; воинственный; **~y** [-ri] солдаты *m/pl*.
sole[1] [soul] □ единственный; исключительный.
sole[2] [~] 1. подошва; подмётка; 2. ставить подмётку к (Д).
solemn ['sɔləm] □ торжественный; важный; **~ity** [sə'lemniti] торжественность *f*; **~ize** ['sɔləmnaiz] [от]праздновать; торжественно отмечать.
solicit [sə'lisit] [по]ходатайствовать; выпрашивать [выпросить]; прист(ав)ать (к мужчине на улице); **~ation** [səlisi'teiʃən] ходатайство; настойчивая просьба; **~or** [sə'lisitə] ⚖ стряпчий; поверенный; *Am.* агент фирмы; **~ous** [-əs] □ заботливый; **~** of стремящийся к (Д); **~ude** [-ju:d] заботливость *f*, забота.
solid ['sɔlid] 1. □ твёрдый; прочный; сплошной; массивный; △ пространственный, кубический; *fig.* солидный; надёжный; единогласный; сплочённый; a **~** hour целый час; **~** tire массивная шина; 2. твёрдое тело; **~arity** [sɔli'dæriti] солидарность *f*; **~ify** [sə'lidifai] [за]твердеть; делать твёрдым; **~ity** [-ti] твёрдость *f*; прочность *f*.
soliloquy [sə'liləkwi] монолог; разговор с самим собой.
solit|ary ['sɔlitəri] □ одинокий; уединённый; отдельный; **~ude** [-tju:d] одиночество; уединённое место.

solo ['soulou] со́ло *n indecl.*; ✈ одино́чный полёт; **~ist** ['soulouist] соли́ст(ка).
solu|ble ['sɔljubl] раствори́мый; разреши́мый; **~tion** [sə'lu:ʃən] растворе́ние; реше́ние; ⊕ раство́р; рези́новый клей.
solv|e [sɔlv] реша́ть [реши́ть], разреша́ть [-ши́ть]; **~ent** [-vənt] 1. растворя́ющий; † платёжеспосо́бный; 2. раствори́тель *m*.
somb|er, ~re ['sɔmbə] □ мра́чный.
some [sʌm, səm] не́кий; како́й-то; како́й-нибудь; не́сколько; не́которые; о́коло (P); ~ 20 miles миль два́дцать; in ~ degree, to ~ extent до изве́стной сте́пени; **~body** ['sʌmbədi] кто́-то; кто́-нибудь; **~how** [-hau] ка́к-то; ка́к-нибудь; ~ or other так и́ли ина́че; **~one** [~wʌn] *s.* somebody.
somer|sault ['sʌməsɔ:lt], **~set** [-set] кувырка́ние; turn ~s *pl.* кувырка́ться, turn a ~ кувыркну́ться *pf*.
some|thing ['sʌmθiŋ] что́-то; что́-нибудь; кое-что́; ~ like приблизи́тельно; что-то вро́де (P): **~time** [-taim] 1. когда́-то; не́когда; 2. бы́вший, пре́жний; **~times** иногда́; **~what** [-wɔt] слегка́, немно́го; до не́которой сте́пени; **~where** [-wɛə] где́-то, куда́-то; где́-нибудь, куда́-нибудь.
son [sʌn] сын (*pl.*: сыновья́; *fig.* *pl.*: сыны́).
song [sɔŋ] пе́сня; рома́нс; F for a mere ~ за бесце́нок; **~-bird** пе́вчая пти́ца; **~ster** ['sɔŋstə] певе́ц; пе́вчая пти́ца.
son-in-law зять *m*.
sonorous [sə'nɔ:rəs] □ зву́чный.
soon [su:n] ско́ро, вско́ре; ра́но; охо́тно; as (*or* so) ~ as как то́лько; **~er** ['su:nə] скоре́е; no ~ ... than едва́ ..., как; no ~ said than done ска́зано — сде́лано.
soot [su:t] 1. са́жа; ко́поть *f*; 2. покрыва́ть са́жей.
sooth|e [su:ð] успока́ивать [-ко́ить]; утеша́ть [уте́шить]; **~sayer** ['su:θseiə] предсказа́тель(ница *f*) *m*.
sooty ['su:ti] □ закопчённый; чёрный как са́жа.
sop [sɔp] 1. обмакну́тый (в подли́вку и т. п.) кусо́к хле́ба и т. п.; *fig.* взя́тка; 2. обма́кивать [-макну́ть]; нама́чивать [-мочи́ть].
sophist|icate [so'fistikeit] извраща́ть [-рати́ть]; подде́л(ыв)ать; лиша́ть на́ивности; **~icated** [-id] извращённый, искажённый; лишённый наи́вности; искушённый; **~ry** ['sɔfistri] софи́стика.
soporific [soupə'rifik] усыпля́ющее, снотво́рное сре́дство.
sorcer|er ['sɔ:sərə] волше́бник; **~ess** [-ris] волше́бница; ве́дьма; **~y** [-ri] волшебство́.
sordid ['sɔ:did] □ гря́зный; убо́гий.
sore [sɔ:] 1. □ чувстви́тельный; боле́зненный; больно́й, воспалённый; оби́женный; ~ throat боль в го́рле; 2. боля́чка; я́зва (*a. fig.*).
sorrel ['sɔ:rəl] 1. гнедо́й (о ло́шади); 2. гнеда́я ло́шадь *f*.
sorrow ['sɔrou] 1. го́ре, печа́ль *f*; 2. горева́ть, печа́литься; **~ful** ['sɔrouful] □ печа́льный, ско́рбный.
sorry ['sɔri] □ по́лный сожале́ния; (I am) (so) ~! мне о́чень жаль!; винова́т!; I am ~ for you мне вас жаль.
sort [sɔ:t] 1. род, сорт; people of all ~s *pl.* всевозмо́жные лю́ди *m/pl.*; ~ of F как бу́дто; be out of ~s *pl.* быть не в ду́хе; пло́хо чу́вствовать себя́; 2. сортирова́ть; ~ out рассортиро́вывать [-ирова́ть].
sot [sɔt] го́рький пья́ница *m*.
sough [sau] 1. ше́лест; 2. [за-] шелесте́ть.
sought [sɔ:t] *pt.* и *p. pt.* от seek.
soul [soul] душа́.
sound [saund] 1. □ здоро́вый, кре́пкий, про́чный; здра́вый; норма́льный; † платёжеспосо́бный; ⚖ зако́нный; 2. звук, шум; звон; зонд; проли́в; пла́вательный пузы́рь *m* (у ры́бы); 3. звуча́ть (*a. fig.*); разд(ав)а́ться; зонди́ровать (*a. fig.*); измеря́ть глубину́ (P); выслу́шивать [вы́слушать] (больно́го); **~ing** ['saundiŋ] ⚓ проме́р глубины́ ло́том; зонди́рование; **~less** [-lis] □ беззву́чный; **~ness** [-nis] здоро́вье и т. д.; **~-proof** звуконепроница́емый.
soup [su:p] суп.
sour ['sauə] 1. □ ки́слый; *fig.* угрю́мый; раздражи́тельный; 2. *v/t.* [за]ква́сить; *fig.* озлобля́ть [озло́бить]; *v/i.* закиса́ть [-и́снуть]; прокиса́ть [-и́снуть].
source [sɔ:s] исто́к; исто́чник (*mst fig.*), ключ, родни́к.
sour|ish ['sauəriʃ] □ кислова́тый; **~ness** [-nis] кислота́; *fig.* го́речь *f*; раздражи́тельность *f*.
souse [saus] [за]соли́ть; [за]маринова́ть; ока́чивать [окати́ть].
south [sauθ] 1. юг; 2. ю́жный; **~-east** 1. юго-восто́к; 2. юго-восто́чный (*a.* ~-eastern).
souther|ly ['sʌðəli], **~n** ['sʌðən] ю́жный; **~ner** [-ə] южа́нин, южа́нка; *Am.* жи́тель(ница) ю́жных шта́тов.
southernmost [-moust] са́мый ю́жный.
southward, ~ly ['sauθwəd, -li], **~s** [-dz] *adv.* к ю́гу, на юг.
south|-west 1. юго-за́пад; 2. юго-за́падный (*a.* ~-westerly, ~-western); **~-wester** юго-за́падный ве́тер; ⚓ зюйдве́стка.

souvenir ['su:vəniə] сувени́р.
sovereign ['sɔvrin] 1. □ верхо́вный; сувере́нный; превосхо́дный; 2. мона́рх; совере́н (моне́та в оди́н фунт сте́рлингов); **~ty** [-ti] верхо́вная власть *f*; суверените́т.
soviet ['souviet] 1. сове́т; 2. сове́тский.
sow[1] [sau] *zo.* свинья́, свинома́тка; ⊕ чу́шка.
sow[2] [sou] [*irr.*] [по]се́ять; засева́ть [засе́ять]; **~n** [soun] *p. pt.* от sow[2].
spa [spɑ:] куро́рт (с минера́льными во́дами); целе́бные во́ды *f/pl.*
space [speis] 1. простра́нство; ме́сто; промежу́ток; срок; *attr.* косми́ческий; 2. *typ.* набира́ть в разря́дку.
spacious ['speiʃəs] □ просто́рный; обши́рный; вмести́тельный.
spade [speid] лопа́та; **~s** пи́ки *f/pl.* (ка́рточная масть).
span [spæn] 1. пролёт (мо́ста́); коро́ткое расстоя́ние или вре́мя; *Am.* па́ра лошаде́й (воло́в и т. п.); 2. стро́ить мост че́рез (В); измеря́ть [-е́рить].
spangle ['spæŋgl] 1. блёстка; 2. украша́ть блёстками; *fig.* усе́ивать [усе́ять].
Spaniard ['spænjəd] испа́нец (-нка).
Spanish ['spæniʃ] испа́нский.
spank [spæŋk] F 1. шлёпать [-пнуть]; отшлёп(ыв)ать; 2. шлепо́к; **~ing** ['spæŋkiŋ] све́жий (ве́тер).
spar [spɑ:] 1. ⚓ рангóутное де́рево; ✈ лонжеро́н; 2. бокси́ровать (в трениро́вке); *fig.* [по]спо́рить, препира́ться.
spare [speə] 1. □ запасно́й; ли́шний, свобо́дный; ску́дный; худоща́вый; скро́мный; ~ time свобо́дное вре́мя *n*; 2. ⊕ запасна́я часть *f*; 3. [по]щади́ть; [по]жале́ть; [с]бере́чь; уделя́ть [-ли́ть] (вре́мя); избавля́ть [-а́вить] от (Р).
sparing ['speəriŋ] □ уме́ренный; бережли́вый; ску́дный.
spark [spɑ:k] 1. и́скра; щёголь *m*; 2. [за]и́скриться; **~(ing)-plug** *mot.* запа́льная свеча́.
sparkle ['spɑ:kl] 1. и́скра; сверка́ние; 2. [за]и́скриться, [за]сверка́ть; sparkling wine шипу́чее вино́.
sparrow ['spærou] воробе́й.
sparse [spɑ:s] □ ре́дкий; разбро́санный.
spasm [spæzm] спа́зма, су́дорога; **~odic(al** □) [spæz'mɔdik, -dikəl] су́дорожный.
spat [spæt] 1. ге́тра; 2. *pt.* и *p.pt.* от spit.
spatter ['spætə] бры́згать [-знуть]; расплёскивать [-плеска́ть].
spawn [spɔ:n] 1. икра́; *fig. contp.* отро́дье; 2. мета́ть икру́; *contp.* [рас]плоди́ться.
speak [spi:k] [*irr.*] *v/i.* говори́ть; [по]говори́ть (with, to с Т); разгова́ривать; ~ out, ~ up выска́зываться [вы́сказаться]; говори́ть гро́мко; *v/t.* выска́зывать [вы́сказать]; говори́ть [сказа́ть] (пра́вду и т. п.); **~er** ['spi:kə] ора́тор; *parl.* спи́кер (председа́тель пала́ты); **~ing-trumpet** ру́пор.
spear [spiə] 1. копьё; дро́тик; острога́; 2. пронза́ть копьём; бить острого́й (ры́бу).
special ['speʃəl] 1. □ специа́льный; осо́бенный; осо́бый; э́кстренный; 2. специа́льный корреспонде́нт; э́кстренный по́езд; **~ist** [-ist] специали́ст; **~ity** [speʃi'æliti] осо́бенность *f*; специа́льность *f*; **~ize** ['speʃəlaiz] специализи́ровать(ся) (*im*)*pf.* (в П *or* по Д); **~ty** ['speʃəlti] *s.* speciality.
specie ['spi:ʃi:] зво́нкая моне́та; **~s** ['spi:ʃi:z] вид; разнови́дность *f*.
speci|fic [spi'sifik] (**~ally**) характе́рный; осо́бенный; определённый; **~fy** [-fai] специфици́ровать (*im*)*pf.*; то́чно определя́ть; **~men** [-min] образе́ц; обра́зчик; экземпля́р.
specious ['spi:ʃəs] □ благови́дный; показно́й.
speck [spek] 1. пя́тнышко; крапи́нка; 2. [за]пятна́ть; **~le** ['spekl] 1. пя́тнышко; 2. испещря́ть [-ри́ть]; [за]пятна́ть.
spectacle ['spektəkl] зре́лище; **~s** *pl.* очки́ *n/pl.*
spectacular [spek'tækjulə] □ эффе́ктный, импоза́нтный.
spectator [spek'teitə] зри́тель(ница *f*) *m*.
spect|er ['spektə] при́зрак; **~ral** ['spektrəl] □ при́зрачный; **~re** *s.* **~er**.
speculat|e ['spekjuleit] размышля́ть [-ы́слить]; ✝ спекули́ровать (in T); **~ion** [spekju'leiʃən] размышле́ние; предположе́ние; ✝ спекуля́ция; **~ive** ['spekjulətiv] □ умозри́тельный; спекуляти́вный; **~or** [-leitə] ✝ спекуля́нт.
sped [sped] *pt.* и *p. pt.* от speed.
speech [spi:tʃ] речь *f*; го́вор; **~less** ['spi:tʃlis] □ безмо́лвный.
speed [spi:d] 1. ско́рость *f*, быстрота́; *mot.* ход, ско́рость *f*; good ~! всего́ хоро́шего!; 2. [*irr.*] *v/i.* [по]спеши́ть; идти́ поспе́шно; успева́ть (в заня́тиях); *v/t.* ~ up ускоря́ть [-о́рить]; **~-limit** допуска́емая ско́рость *f* (езды́); **~ometer** [spi:'dɔmitə] *mot.* спидо́метр; **~y** ['spi:di] □ бы́стрый.
spell [spel] 1. (коро́ткий) пери́од; промежу́ток вре́мени; рабо́чее вре́мя *n*; ча́ры *f/pl.*; обая́ние; 2. [*a. irr.*] писа́ть, чита́ть по бу́квам; писа́ть пра́вильно; означа́ть [озна́чить]; **~bound** *fig.* очаро́ванный;

~**er** ['spelə] *part. Am.* буква́рь *m*; ~**ing** [-iŋ] правописа́ние; ~**ing-book** буква́рь *m*.
spelt [spelt] *pt.* и *p. pt.* от spell.
spend [spend] [*irr.*] [по]тра́тить, [из]расхо́довать (де́ньги); проводи́ть [-вести́] (вре́мя); истоща́ть [-щи́ть]; ~**thrift** ['spendθrift] мот (-о́вка), расточи́тель(ница *f*) *m*.
spent [spent] **1.** *pt.* и *p. pt.* от spend. **2.** *adj.* истощённый.
sperm [spə:m] спе́рма; кашало́т.
spher|e [sfiə] шар; земно́й шар; небе́сная сфе́ра; гло́бус; *fig.* сфе́ра; круг, по́ле де́ятельности; среда́; ~**ical** ['sferikəl] □ сфери́ческий.
spice [spais] **1.** спе́ция, пря́ность *f*; *fig.* соль *f*; при́вкус; **2.** приправля́ть [-а́вить].
spick and span ['spikən'spæn] щегольско́й, с иго́лочки.
spicy ['spaisi] □ пря́ный; пика́нтный.
spider ['spaidə] *zo.* пау́к.
spigot ['spigət] *Am.* кран (бо́чки).
spike [spaik] **1.** остриё; шип, гвоздь *m* (на подо́шве); ⚘ ко́лос; **2.** прибива́ть гвоздя́ми; снабжа́ть шипа́ми; пронза́ть [-зи́ть].
spill [spil] **1.** [*irr.*] *v/t.* проли́(ва́)ть; рассыпа́ть [-ы́пать]; F выва́ливать [вы́валить] (седока́); *v/i.* проли́(ва́)ться; **2.** F паде́ние.
spilt [spilt] *pt.* и *p. pt.* от spill.
spin [spin] **1.** [*irr.*] [с]прясть; [с]сучи́ть (кана́т и т. п.); крути́ться; [за]кружи́ть(ся); ~ a yarn расска́зывать небыли́цы; ~ along ката́ться, [по]кати́ться; **2.** круже́ние; бы́страя езда́.
spinach ['spinidʒ] ⚘ шпина́т.
spinal ['spainl] спинно́й; ~ column спинно́й хребе́т; ~ cord, ~ marrow спинно́й мозг.
spindle ['spindl] веретено́.
spine [spain] *anat.* спинно́й хребе́т, позвоно́чный столб; колю́чка.
spinning|-mill пряди́льная фа́брика; ~**-wheel** пря́лка.
spinster ['spinstə] ста́рая де́ва; ⚖ незаму́жняя (же́нщина).
spiny ['spaini] колю́чий.
spiral ['spaiərəl] **1.** □ спира́льный; ~ staircase винтова́я ле́стница; **2.** спира́ль *f*.
spire ['spaiə] шпиль *m*; шпиц; остроконе́чная верши́на.
spirit ['spirit] **1.** *com.* дух; привиде́ние; смысл; воодушевле́ние; спирт; ~s *pl.* (high припо́днятое, low пода́вленное) настрое́ние; спиртны́е напи́тки *m/pl.*; **2.** ~ away, off таи́нственно похища́ть; ~**ed** [-id] □ живо́й; сме́лый; энерги́чный; ~**less** [-lis] □ вя́лый; ро́бкий; безжи́зненный.
spiritual ['spiritjuəl] □ духо́вный; одухотворённый; религио́зный; ~**ism** [-izm] спирит(уал)и́зм.
spirituous ['spiritjuəs] спиртно́й, алкого́льный.
spirt [spə:t] *s.* spurt.
spit [spit] **1.** ве́ртел; слюна́; плево́к; *fig.* подо́бие; **2.** [*irr.*] плева́ть [плю́нуть]; треща́ть (об огне́); шипе́ть (о ко́шке); мороси́ть.
spite [spait] **1.** зло́ба, злость *f*; in ~ of не смотря́ на (B); **2.** досажда́ть [досади́ть]; ~**ful** ['spaitful] зло́бный.
spitfire ['spitfaiə] вспы́льчивый челове́к.
spittle ['spitl] слюна́; плево́к.
spittoon [spi'tu:n] плева́тельница.
splash [splæʃ] **1.** бры́зги *f/pl.* (*mst* ~es *pl.*); плеск; **2.** бры́згать [-знуть]; плеска́ть(ся) [-сну́ть].
splayfoot ['spleifut] косола́пый.
spleen [spli:n] *anat.* селезёнка; хандра́.
splend|id ['splendid] □ блестя́щий; великоле́пный, роско́шный; ~**o(u)r** [-də] блеск; великоле́пие, ро́скошь *f*; пы́шность *f*.
splice [splais] ⚓ сплета́ть [-ести́] (кана́ты), сплёсни(ва)ть.
splint [splint] **1.** ⚕ лубо́к; **2.** накла́дывать лубо́к на (B); ~**er** ['splintə] **1.** оско́лок; лучи́на; зано́за; **2.** расщепля́ть(ся) [-пи́ть(ся)].
split [split] **1.** тре́щина; щель *f*; *fig.* раско́л; **2.** расщеплённый; раско́лотый; **3.** [*irr.*] *v/t.* раска́лывать [-коло́ть]; расщепля́ть [-пи́ть]; ~ hairs вдава́ться в то́нкости; ~ one's sides with laughing надрыва́ться от сме́ха; *v/i.* раска́лываться [-коло́ться]; ло́паться [ло́пнуть]; ~**ting** ['splitiŋ] ужа́сный (о головно́й бо́ли); оглуши́тельный.
splutter ['splʌtə] *s.* sputter.
spoil [spɔil] **1.** (*a.* ~s *pl.*) награ́бленное добро́, добы́ча; *pol. part. Am.* ~s system распределе́ние госуда́рственных должносте́й за услу́ги; **2.** [*irr.*] [ис]по́ртить; [по]губи́ть; [ис]по́ртиться (о пи́ще); [из]балова́ть (ребёнка).
spoke [spouk] **1.** *pt.* от speak; **2.** спи́ца (колеса́); ступе́нька, перекла́дина; ~**n** ['spoukən] *p. pt.* от speak; ~**sman** ['spouksmən] представи́тель *m*.
sponge [spʌndʒ] **1.** гу́бка; **2.** *v/t.* вытира́ть и́ли мыть гу́бкой; ~ up впи́тывать гу́бкой; *v/i.* жить на чужо́й счёт; ~**-cake** бисквит; ~**r** ['spʌndʒə] прижива́льщик (-лка).
spongy ['spʌndʒi] гу́бчатый.
sponsor ['spɔnsə] **1.** покрови́тель (-ница *f*) *m*; поручи́тель(ница *f*) *m*; крёстный оте́ц, крёстная мать *f*; *Am.* абоне́нт радиореклáмы; **2.** руча́ться [поручи́ться] за (B); быть крёстным отцо́м (крёстной ма́терью) у (P).
spontane|ity [spɔntə'ni:iti] непо-

сре́дственность *f*; самопроизво́льность *f*; **~ous** [spɔn'teinjəs] □ непосре́дственный; непринуждённый; самопроизво́льный.
spook [spu:k] привиде́ние.
spool [spu:l] 1. шпу́лька; 2. нама́тывать на шпу́льку.
spoon [spu:n] 1. ло́жка; 2. че́рпать ло́жкой; **~ful** ['spu:nful] ло́жка (ме́ра).
sport [spɔ:t] 1. спорт; **~s** *pl.* спорти́вные и́гры *f/pl.*; *attr.* спорти́вный; *fig.* игру́шка; развлече́ние, заба́ва; *sl.* молоде́ц; 2. *v/i.* игра́ть, весели́ться, резви́ться; *v/t.* F щеголя́ть [-льну́ть] (T); **~ive** ['spɔ:tiv] □ игри́вый; весёлый; **~sman** ['spɔ:tsmən] спортсме́н.
spot [spɔt] 1. *com.* пятно́; кра́пинка; ме́сто; on the ~ на ме́сте; сра́зу, неме́дленно; 2. нали́чный; подлежа́щий неме́дленной упла́те; 3. [за]пятна́ть; ⚔ обнару́жи(ва)ть; F опозн(ав)а́ть; **~less** ['spɔtlis] □ безупре́чный; незапя́тнанный; **~-light** проже́ктор; *fig.* центр внима́ния; **~ty** ['spɔti] пятни́стый; кра́пчатый; прыщева́тый.
spouse [spauz] супру́г(а).
spout [spaut] 1. струя́; но́сик (ча́йника и т. п.); водосто́чная труба́; 2. выпуска́ть струёй (В); би́ть струёй; F ора́торствовать.
sprain [sprein] 1. растяже́ние (свя́зок); 2. растя́гивать [-тяну́ть]; вы́вихнуть *pf.*
sprang [spræŋ] *pt.* от **spring**.
sprawl [sprɔ:l] растя́гивать(ся) [-яну́ть(ся)]; разва́ливаться [-ли́ться] (в кре́сле); ⚘ бу́йно разраста́ться.
spray [sprei] 1. водяна́я пыль *f*; бры́зги *f/pl.*; пульвериза́тор, распыли́тель *m* (*a.* ~er); 2. распыля́ть [-ли́ть]; обры́зг(ив)ать.
spread [spred] 1. [*irr.*] *v/t.* (*a.* ~ out) расстила́ть [разостла́ть]; распространя́ть [-ни́ть]; нама́з(ыв)ать (T); ~ the table накры́(ва́)ть на стол; *v/i.* простира́ться [простере́ться]; распространя́ться [-ни́ться]; 2. *pt.* и *p. pt.* от **spread** 1.; 3. распростране́ние; протяже́ние.
spree [spri:] весе́лье; ша́лость *f*; кутёж.
sprig [sprig] ве́точка, побе́г; *fig.* о́тпрыск; ⊕ шти́фтик; гво́здик.
sprightly ['spraitli] оживлённый, весёлый.
spring [spriŋ] 1. прыжо́к, скачо́к; родни́к, ключ; (*a.* ~*time*) весна́; ⊕ пружи́на, рессо́ра; *fig.* моти́в; 2. [*irr.*] *v/t.* взрыва́ть [взорва́ть]; вспу́гивать [-гну́ть] (дичь); ~ a leak ⚓ дава́ть течь (о корабле́); ~ a th. (up)on a p. неожи́данно сообщи́ть (В/Д); *v/i.* пры́гать [-гнуть]; вска́кивать [вскочи́ть]; ⚘ появля́ться [-ви́ться] (о по́чках); ~ up возника́ть [-и́кнуть]; **~-board** трампли́н; **~tide** весна́; ~ tide сизиги́йный прили́в; **~y** ['spriŋi] □ упру́гий.
sprinkl|e ['spriŋkl) бры́згать [-знуть]; [о]крopи́ть; **~ing** [-iŋ] лёгкий дождь *m*; а ~ немно́го.
sprint [sprint] *sport* 1. спринт (бег на коро́ткую диста́нцию); 2. бе́гать на ско́рость.
sprite [sprait] эльф.
sprout [spraut] 1. пуска́ть ростки́; всходи́ть [взойти́] (о семена́х); отра́щивать [отрасти́ть]; 2. ⚘ росто́к, побе́г.
spruce[1] [spru:s] □ щеголева́тый; наря́дный.
spruce[2] [~] ⚘ ель *f*.
sprung [sprʌŋ] *pt.* и *p. pt.* от **spring**.
spry [sprai] *part. Am.* живо́й; сообрази́тельный; прово́рный.
spun [spʌn] *pt.* и *p. pt.* от **spin**.
spur [spə:] 1. шпо́ра; *fig.* побужде́ние; act on the ~ of the moment де́йствовать под влия́нием мину́ты; 2. пришпо́ри(ва)ть; побужда́ть [-уди́ть].
spurious ['spuəriəs] □ подде́льный, подло́жный.
spurn [spə:n] отверга́ть с презре́нием; отта́лкивать [оттолкну́ть] (ного́й).
spurt [spə:t] 1. наддава́ть хо́ду; бить струёй; выбра́сывать [вы́бросить] (пла́мя); 2. струя́; поры́в ве́тра; рыво́к; *sport* спурт.
sputter ['spʌtə] 1. бры́зги *f/pl.*; шипе́ние; 2. [за]шипе́ть (об огне́); бры́згать слюно́й; говори́ть бессвя́зно.
spy [spai] 1. шпио́н(ка); та́йный аге́нт; 2. шпио́нить, следи́ть (on за T); **~-glass** подзо́рная труба́.
squabble ['skwɔbl] 1. перебра́нка, ссо́ра; 2. [по]вздо́рить.
squad [skwɔd] брига́да; отря́д; ⚔ отделе́ние; гру́ппа, кома́нда; **~ron** ['skwɔdrən] ⚔ эскадро́н; ✈ эскадри́лья; ⚓ эска́дра.
squalid ['skwɔlid] □ убо́гий.
squall [skwɔ:l] 1. шквал; вопль *m*; крик; 2. [за]вопи́ть.
squander ['skwɔndə] прома́тывать [-мота́ть]; расточа́ть [-чи́ть].
square [skwεə] 1. □ квадра́тный; прямоуго́льный; пра́вильный; ро́вный; то́чный; прямо́й, че́стный; недвусмы́сленный; ~ measure квадра́тная ме́ра; 2 feet ~ 2 фу́та в квадра́те; 2. квадра́т; прямоуго́льник; пло́щадь *f*; 3. *v/t.* де́лать прямоуго́льным; опла́чивать [оплати́ть] (счёт); согласо́вывать [-сова́ть]; *v/i.* согласо́вываться [-сова́ться]; сходи́ться [сойти́сь]; **~-toes** F педа́нт.
squash [skwɔʃ] 1. фрукто́вый напи́ток; разда́вленная ма́сса; F толчея́; 2. разда́вливать [-дави́ть].
squat [skwɔt] 1. приземи́стый;

2. сидеть на корточках; **~ter** ['skwɔːtə] *Am.* поселившийся самовольно в незанятом доме, на незанятой земле.

squawk [skwɔːk] **1.** пронзительный крик (птицы); **2.** пронзительно кричать.

squeak [skwiːk] [про]пищать; *sl.* доносить [донести].

squeal [skwiːl] [за]визжать; *s.* squeak.

squeamish ['skwiːmiʃ] □ щепетильный; обидчивый; привередливый; брезгливый.

squeeze [skwiːz] **1.** сж(им)ать; стискивать [-снуть]; выжимать [выжать]; *fig.* вымогать (from у Р); **2.** сжатие; пожатие; давление; давка; **~r** ['skwiːzə] выжималка.

squelch [skweltʃ] F хлюпать; раздавливать ногой; *fig.* подавлять [-вить].

squint [skwint] косить (глазами); [со]щуриться.

squire ['skwaiə] **1.** сквайр (титул); **2.** сопровождать (даму).

squirm [skwəːm] F изви(ва)ться, [с]корчиться.

squirrel [skwirəl, *Am.* 'skwəːrəl] белка.

squirt [skwəːt] **1.** струя; шприц; F выскочка *m/f*; **2.** пускать струю (Р); бить струёй.

stab [stæb] **1.** удар (чем-либо острым); **2.** *v/t.* закалывать [заколоть]; *v/i.* наносить удар (at Д).

stabili|ty [stə'biliti] устойчивость *f*; прочность *f*; **~ze** ['stæbilaiz] стабилизировать (*im*)*pf.*

stable[1] ['steibl] □ стойкий; устойчивый.

stable[2] [~] **1.** конюшня; хлев; **2.** ставить в конюшню (или в хлев).

stack [stæk] **1.** стог (сена и т. п.); штабель *m*; труба (парохода); куча; **2.** складывать в стог и т. д.; нагромождать [-моздить].

stadium ['steidiəm] *sport* стадион; ⚕ стадия.

staff [stɑːf] **1.** посох; жезл; древко; ⚔ штаб; *attr.* штабной; ♪ нотная линейка; служебный персонал; **2.** снабжать персоналом.

stag [stæg] *zo.* олень-самец.

stage [steidʒ] **1.** подмостки *m/pl.*; сцена; эстрада; стадия; перегон; этап; **2.** [по]ставить (пьесу), инсценировать (*im*)*pf.*; **~-coach** дилижанс; **~-manager** режиссёр.

stagger ['stægə] **1.** *v/i.* шататься [(по)шатнуться]; *v/t.* потрясать [-ясти]; поражать [поразить]; **2.** шатание.

stagna|nt ['stægnənt] □ стоячий (о воде); *fig.* косный; **~te** [-neit] застаиваться [застояться]; *fig.* [за-]коснеть.

staid [steid] □ солидный, уравновешенный.

stain [stein] **1.** пятно; ⊕ протрава; **2.** [за]пачкать; [за]пятнать; ⊕ протравливать [-равить] (дерево); [по]красить; **~ed glass** цветное стекло; **~less** ['steinlis] незапятнанный; нержавеющий (о стали); *fig.* безупречный.

stair [stɛə] ступенька; **~s** *pl.* лестница; **~case,** *Am.* **~way** лестница; лестничная клетка.

stake [steik] **1.** кол; ставка, заклад (в пари); **~s** *pl.* приз; be at ~ быть поставленным на карту (*a. fig.*); **2.** подпирать (или огораживать) кольями; ставить на карту; ~ out, off отмечать вехами.

stale [steil] □ несвежий; выдохшийся; спёртый (воздух); избитый.

stalk [stɔːk] **1.** стебель *m*, черенок; *hunt.* подкрадывание; **2.** *v/i.* важно шествовать, гордо выступать; *v/t.* подкрадываться [-расться] к (Д).

stall [stɔːl] **1.** стойло; прилавок; киоск, ларёк; *thea.* место в партере; **2.** ставить в стойло; застревать [-рять] (в снегу и т. п.); ✈ терять скорость.

stallion ['stæljən] жеребец.

stalwart ['stɔːlwət] рослый, дюжий; стойкий.

stamina ['stæminə] выносливость *f*.

stammer ['stæmə] **1.** заикаться [-кнуться]; запинаться [запнуться]; **2.** заикание.

stamp [stæmp] **1.** штамп, штемпель *m*; печать *f* (*a. fig.*); клеймо; (почтовая, гербовая) марка; топанье; **2.** [от]штамповать; [за]штемпелевать; [за]клеймить; топать ногой.

stampede [stæm'piːd] **1.** паническое бегство; **2.** обращать(ся) в паническое бегство.

stanch [stɑːntʃ] **1.** останавливать кровотечение из (Р); **2.** верный, лояльный.

stand [stænd] **1.** [*irr.*] *v/i. com.* стоять; постоять *pf.*; простаивать [-стоять]; останавливаться [-новиться]; держаться; устоять *pf.*; ~ against [вос]противиться, сопротивляться (Д); ~ aside [по]сторониться; ~ back отступать [-пить]; ~ by присутствовать; *fig.* быть наготове; поддерживать [-жать] (В); ~ for быть кандидатом (Р); стоять за (В); значить; ~ off отодвигаться [-инуться] от (Р); ~ out выделяться [выделиться] (against на П); ~ over оставаться нерешённым; ~ to держаться (Р); ~ up вст(ав)ать, подниматься [-няться]; ~ up for защищать [-итить]; **2.** *v/t.* [по]ставить; выдерживать [выдержать], выносить [вынести]; F угощать [угостить] (Т); **3.** остановка; сопротивление; точка зрения; ки-

о́ск; пози́ция; ме́сто; подста́вка; трибу́на; make a ~ against сопротивля́ться (Д).
standard ['stændəd] 1. зна́мя *n*, флаг, штанда́рт; но́рма, станда́рт; образе́ц; у́ровень *m*; 2. станда́ртный; образцо́вый; **~ize** [-aiz] нормирова́ть (*im*)*pf*.
stand-by ['stænd'bai] опо́ра.
standing ['stændiŋ] 1. □ стоя́щий; стоя́чий; постоя́нный; ~ orders *pl.* уста́в; *parl.* пра́вила процеду́ры; 2. стоя́ние; положе́ние; продолжи́тельность *f*; **~-room** ме́сто для стоя́щих (пассажи́ров, зри́телей).
stand|-offish сде́ржанный; **~point** то́чка зре́ния; **~still** безде́йствие; мёртвая то́чка; **~-up**: ~ collar стоя́чий воротничо́к.
stank [stæŋk] *pt.* от stink.
stanza ['stænzə] строфа́, станс.
staple ['steipl] 1. гла́вный проду́кт; гла́вная те́ма; 2. основно́й.
star [stɑ:] 1. звезда́ (*a. fig.*); *fig.* судьба́; ~s and stripes *pl. Am.* национа́льный флаг США; 2. украша́ть звёздами; игра́ть гла́вную роль; предоставля́ть гла́вную роль (Д).
starboard ['stɑ:bəd] ⚓ 1. пра́вый борт; 2. класть руль напра́во.
starch [stɑ:tʃ] 1. крахма́л; *fig.* чо́порность *f*; 2. [на]крахма́лить.
stare [stɛə] 1. при́стальный взгляд; 2. смотре́ть при́стально; тара́щить глаза́ (at на В).
stark [stɑ:k] окочене́лый; соверше́нный; *adv.* соверше́нно.
star|ry ['stɑ:ri] звёздный; как звёзды; **~-spangled** [-'spæŋgld] усе́янный звёздами; ~ banner *Am.* национа́льный флаг США.
start [stɑ:t] 1. вздра́гивание; отправле́ние; ✈ взлёт; *sport* старт; нача́ло; *fig.* преиму́щество; get the ~ of a p. получи́ть преиму́щество пе́ред ке́м-либо; 2. *v/i.* вздра́гивать [-ро́гнуть]; вска́кивать [вскочи́ть]; отправля́ться в путь; *sport* стартова́ть (*im*)*pf*.; нач(ин)а́ться; ✈ взлета́ть [-ете́ть]; *v/t.* пуска́ть [пусти́ть] (в ход); *sport* дава́ть старт (Д); *fig.* нач(ин)а́ть; учрежда́ть [-еди́ть]; вспу́гивать [-гну́ть]; побужда́ть [-уди́ть] (a p. doing кого́-либо де́лать); **~er** ['stɑ:tə] *mot.* ста́ртер; *sport* ста́ртер, F стартёр; *fig.* инициа́тор.
startl|e [stɑ:tl] поража́ть [порази́ть]; вздра́гивать [-ро́гнуть]; **~ing** ['stɑ:tliŋ] порази́тельный.
starv|ation [stɑ:'veiʃən] го́лод; голода́ние; **~e** [stɑ:v] голода́ть; умира́ть с го́лоду; мори́ть го́лодом; ~ for *fig.* жа́ждать (Р).
state [steit] 1. состоя́ние; положе́ние; госуда́рство (*pol. a.* ♎); штат; *attr.* госуда́рственный; in ~ с по́мпой; 2. заявля́ть [-ви́ть]; констати́ровать (*im*)*pf*.; [с]формули́ровать; излага́ть [изложи́ть]; **~ly** велича́вый, вели́чественный; **~ment** утвержде́ние; заявле́ние; официа́льный отчёт; † ~ of account извлече́ние (или вы́писка) из счёта; **~room** пара́дный зал; ⚓ отде́льная каю́та (на парохо́де); **~sman** ['steitsmən] госуда́рственный (*Am. a.* полити́ческий) де́ятель *m*.
static ['stætik] стати́ческий; стациона́рный.
station ['steiʃən] 1. ме́сто, пост; ста́нция; вокза́л; остано́вка; ⚓ вое́нно-морска́я ба́за; 2. [по]ста́вить, помеща́ть [-ести́ть]; ⚔ размеща́ть [-ести́ть]; **~ary** ['steiʃnəri] □ неподви́жный; стациона́рный; **~ery** [~] канцеля́рские принадле́жности *f/pl.*; **~-master** 🚂 нача́льник ста́нции.
statistics [stə'tistiks] стати́стика.
statu|ary ['stætjuəri] скульпту́рный; **~e** [-ju:] ста́туя, изва́яние.
stature ['stætʃə] рост, стан, фигу́ра.
status ['steitəs] положе́ние, состоя́ние; ста́тус.
statute ['stætju:t] стату́т; зако́н; законода́тельный акт; уста́в.
staunch [stɔ:ntʃ] *s.* stanch.
stave [steiv] 1. клёпка (боча́рная); перекла́дина; строфа́; 2. [*irr.*] (*mst* ~ in) прола́мывать [-ломи́ть], разби́(ва́)ть (бо́чку и т. п.); ~ off предотвраща́ть [-врати́ть].
stay [stei] 1. ⚓ штаг; опо́ра, подде́ржка; остано́вка; пребыва́ние; ~s *pl.* корсе́т; 2. *v/t.* подде́рживать [-жа́ть]; заде́рживать [-жа́ть]; *v/i.* ост(ав)а́ться; остана́вливаться [-нови́ться], жить (at в П); *sport* проявля́ть выно́сливость; **~er** ['steiə] выно́сливый челове́к; *sport* ста́йер; ~ race велосипе́дная го́нка за ли́дером.
stead [sted]: in ~ of вме́сто (Р); **~fast** ['stedfəst] сто́йкий, непоколеби́мый.
steady ['stedi] 1. □ усто́йчивый; установи́вшийся; твёрдый; равноме́рный; степе́нный; 2. де́лать (-ся) усто́йчивым; приходи́ть в равнове́сие.
steal [sti:l] [*irr.*] *v/t.* [у]воровáть, [у]кра́сть; *v/i.* кра́сться, прокра́дываться [-ра́сться].
stealth [stelθ]: by ~ укра́дкой, тайко́м; **~y** ['stelθi] □ та́йный; бесшу́мный.
steam [sti:m] 1. пар; испаре́ние; 2. *attr.* парово́й; 3. *v/i.* выпуска́ть пар; пла́вать [по]плы́ть, (о парохо́де); *v/t.* вари́ть на пару́; па́рить; выпа́ривать [вы́парить]; **~er** ['sti:mə] ⚓ парохо́д; **~y** ['sti:mi] □ парообра́зный; насы́щенный пара́ми.
steel [sti:l] 1. сталь *f*; 2. стально́й

(*a.* ~у); *fig.* жесто́кий; **3.** покрыва́ть ста́лью; *fig.* закаля́ть [-ли́ть].
steep [sti:p] **1.** круто́й; F невероя́тный; **2.** погружа́ть [-узи́ть] (в жи́дкость); пропи́тывать [-ита́ть]; *fig.* погружа́ться [-узи́ться] (in в В).
steeple ['sti:pl] шпиль *m*; колоко́льня; **~-chase** ска́чки с препя́тствиями.
steer[1] [stiə] кастри́рованный бычо́к.
steer[2] [~] пра́вить рулём; управля́ть (Т); води́ть, [по]вести́ ((су́дно); **~age** ['stiəridʒ] ⚓ управле́ние рулём; сре́дняя па́луба; **~sman** ['stiəzmən] рулево́й.
stem [stem] **1.** ствол; сте́бель *m*; *gr.* осно́ва; ⚓ нос; **2.** заде́рживать [-жа́ть]; сопротивля́ться (Д).
stench [stentʃ] злово́ние.
stencil ['stensl] трафаре́т.
stenographer [ste'nɔgrəfə] стенографи́ст(ка).
step[1] [step] **1.** шаг; похо́дка; ступе́нька; подно́жка; *fig.* ме́ра; посту́пок; tread in the ~s of *fig.* идти́ по стопа́м (Р); ~s *pl.* стремя́нка; **2.** *v/i.* шага́ть [шагну́ть]; ступа́ть [-пну́ть]; ходи́ть, идти́ [пойти́]; ~ out бо́дро шага́ть; *v/t.* измеря́ть шага́ми (*a.* ~ out); ~ up продвига́ть [-и́нуть].
step[2] [~]: **~daughter** па́дчерица; **~-father** ['stepfɑ:ðə] о́тчим; **~-mother** ма́чеха; **~son** па́сынок.
steppe [step] степь *f*.
stepping-stone *fig.* трампли́н.
steril|e ['sterail] беспло́дный; стери́льный; **~ity** [ste'riliti] беспло́дие; стери́льность *f*; **~ize** ['sterilaiz] стерилизова́ть (*im*)*pf*.
sterling ['stə:liŋ] полнове́сный; полноце́нный; † сте́рлинговый.
stern [stə:n] **1.** □ стро́гий, суро́вый; неумоли́мый; **2.** ⚓ корма́; **~ness** ['stə:nnis] стро́гость *f*, суро́вость *f*; **~-post** ⚓ ахтерште́вень *m*.
stevedore ['sti:vidɔ:] ⚓ гру́зчик.
stew [stju:] **1.** [с]туши́ть(ся); **2.** туше́ное мя́со; F беспоко́йство.
steward [stjuəd] эконо́м; управля́ющий; ⚓, ✈ стю́ард, бортпроводни́к; распоряди́тель *m*; **~ess** ['stjuədis] ⚓, ✈ стюарде́сса, бортпроводни́ца.
stick [stik] **1.** па́лка; трость *f*; прут; по́сох; **2.** [*irr.*] *v/i.* прикле́и(ва)ться, прилипа́ть [-ли́пнуть]; застрева́ть [-ря́ть]; завяза́ть [-я́знуть]; торча́ть (до́ма и т. п.); ~ to приде́рживаться [-жа́ться] (Р); ~ at nothing не остана́вливаться ни перед че́м; ~ out, ~ up торча́ть; стоя́ть торчко́м; *v/t.* вка́лывать [вколо́ть]; втыка́ть [воткну́ть]; прикле́и(ва)ть; раскле́и(ва)ть; F терпе́ть, вы́терпеть *pf*.
sticky ['stiki] □ ли́пкий, кле́йкий.
stiff [stif] □ жёсткий, неги́бкий; туго́й; тру́дный; окостене́лый; натя́нутый; **~en** ['stifn] де́лать (-ся) жёстким и т. д.; окостене́(ва́)ть; **~necked** ['stif'nekt] упря́мый.
stifle ['staifl] [за]души́ть; задыха́ться [задохну́ться].
stigma ['stigmə] *eccl.* стигма́т; *fig.* пятно́, клеймо́; **~tize** [-taiz] [за-] клейми́ть.
still [stil] **1.** *adj.* ти́хий; неподви́жный; **2.** *adv.* ещё, всё ещё; **3.** *cj.* всё же, одна́ко; **4.** успока́ивать [-ко́ить]; **5.** дистилля́тор; **~-born** мертворождённый; **~-life** натюрмо́рт; **~ness** ['stilnis] тишина́.
stilt [stilt] ходу́ля; **~ed** ['stiltid] ходу́льный, высокопа́рный.
stimul|ant ['stimjulənt] **1.** ⚕ возбужда́ющее сре́дство; **2.** ⚕ стимули́рующий, возбужда́ющий; **~ate** [-leit] возбужда́ть [-уди́ть]; поощря́ть [-ри́ть]; **~ation** [stimju'leiʃən] возбужде́ние; поощре́ние; **~us** ['stimjuləs] сти́мул.
sting [stiŋ] **1.** жа́ло; уку́с (насеко́мого); о́страя боль *f*; *fig.* ко́лкость *f*; **2.** [*irr.*] [у]жа́лить; же́чь (-ся) (о крапи́ве); уязвля́ть [-ви́ть]; **~iness** ['stindʒinis] ска́редность *f*; **~y** ['stindʒi] ска́редный, скупо́й.
stink [stiŋk] **1.** вонь *f*; **2.** [*irr.*] воня́ть.
stint [stint] **1.** ограниче́ние; преде́л; **2.** уре́з(ыв)ать; ограни́чи(ва)ть; [по]скупи́ться на (В).
stipend ['staipend] жа́лованье, окла́д (*mst* свяще́нника).
stipulat|e ['stipjuleit] ста́вить усло́вием; обусло́вливать [-вить]; **~ion** [stipju'leiʃən] усло́вие; кла́узула, огово́рка.
stir [stə:] **1.** шевеле́ние; суета́, сумато́ха; движе́ние; *fig.* оживле́ние; **2.** шевели́ть(ся) [-льну́ть (-ся)]; [по]меша́ть (чай и т. п.); [вз]волнова́ть; ~ up возбужда́ть [-уди́ть]; разме́шивать [-ша́ть].
stirrup ['stirəp] стре́мя *n* (*pl.*: стремена́).
stitch [stitʃ] **1.** стежо́к (о шитье́); пе́тля (о вяза́нии); ⚕ шов; **2.** [с]шить, проши́(ва́)ть.
stock [stɔk] **1.** ствол; опо́ра; ру́чка; ло́жа (винто́вки); инвента́рь *m*; запа́с; † сырьё; live ~ живо́й инвента́рь *m*; скот; † основно́й капита́л; фо́нды *m/pl.*; *Am.* а́кция, а́кции; ~s *pl.* госуда́рственный долг; ~s *pl.* ⚓ ста́пель *m*; † take ~ of де́лать переучёт (Р); *fig.* крити́чески оце́нивать; **2.** име́ющийся в запа́се (и́ли нагото́ве); изби́тый, шабло́нный; **3.** обору́довать (хозя́йство); снабжа́ть [-бди́ть]; † име́ть на скла́де.
stockade [stɔ'keid] частоко́л.
stock|-breeder животново́д; **~-**

broker биржевóй мáклер; ~ exchange фóндовая бúржа; **~holder** *Am.* акционéр.
stockinet ['stɔkinet] трикотáж.
stocking ['stɔkiŋ] чулóк.
stock|-jobber биржевóй спекулянт, мáклер; **~-taking** переучёт товáра; провéрка инвентарá; *fig.* обзóр результáтов; **~y** ['stɔki] коренáстый.
stoic ['stouik] **1.** стóик; **2.** стоúческий.
stoker ['stoukə] кочегáр; истопнúк.
stole [stoul] *pt.* от steal; **~n** ['stoulən] *p. pt.* от steal.
stolid ['stɔlid] □ флегматúчный; бесстрáстный; тупóй.
stomach ['stʌmək] **1.** желýдок; живóт; *fig.* охóта (for к Д); **2.** перевáривать [-варúть] (*a. fig.*); *fig.* сносúть [снестú].
stone [stoun] **1.** кáмень *m*; кóсточка (плодá); **2.** кáменный; **3.** облицóвывать камнямú; забрáсывать камнямú; вынимáть кóсточки из (Р); **~-blind** совсéм слепóй; **~ware** гончáрные издéлия *n/pl.*
stony ['stouni] кáменный; каменúстый; *fig.* кáменный.
stood [stud] *pt.* и *p. pt.* от stand.
stool [stu:l] табурéтка; ⚕ стул; **~-pigeon** *Am.* провокáтор.
stoop [stu:p] **1.** *v/i.* наклонáться [-нúться], нагибáться [нагнýться]; [с]сутýлиться; унижáться [унúзиться] (to до Р); снисходúть [снизойтú]; *v/t.* [с]сутýлить; **2.** сутýлость *f*; *Am.* верáнда.
stop [stɔp] **1.** *v/t.* затыкáть [заткнýть] (*a.* ~ up); задéл(ыв)ать; [за]пломбировáть (зуб); преграждáть [-градúть]; удéрживать [-жáть]; прекращáть [-кратúть]; останáвливать [-новúть]; ~ it! брось!; *v/i.* перест(ав)áть; останáвливаться [-новúться]; прекращáться [-кратúться]; кончáться [кóнчиться]; **2.** останóвка; пáуза; задéржка; ⊕ стóпор; упóр; ♪ клáпан; ♪ лад (стрýнного инструмéнта); ♪ педáль *f* (оргáна); *gr.* (*a.* full~) тóчка; **~-gap** затычка; подрýчное срéдство; **~page** ['stɔpidʒ] задéржка, останóвка; прекращéние рабóты; ⊕ засорéние; **~per** ['stɔpə] прóбка; **~ping** ['stɔpiŋ] (зубнáя) плóмба.
storage ['stɔ:ridʒ] хранéние; склад.
store [stɔ:] **1.** запáс; склад; амбáр; *fig.* изобúлие; *Am.* лáвка; **~s** *pl.* припáсы *m/pl.*; универмáг; in ~ наготóве; про запáс; **2.** снабжáть [снабдúть]; запасáть [-стú]; хранúть на склáде; **~house** склад; *fig.* сокрóвищница; **~-keeper** кладовщúк; *Am.* лáвочник.
stor(e)y ['stɔ:ri] этáж.
stork [stɔ:k] áист.
storm [stɔ:m] **1.** бýря; ⚓ *a.* шторм; ⚔ штурм; **2.** бушевáть, свирéпствовать (*a. fig.*); it **~s** бýря бушýет; ⚔ штурмовáть; **~y** □ бýрный; штормовóй; áростный.
story ['stɔ:ri] расскáз; пóвесть *f*; *thea.* фáбула; F ложь *f*.
stout [staut] **1.** □ крéпкий, прóчный, плóтный; тýчный; отвáжный; **2.** крéпкое пúво.
stove [stouv] печь *f*, пéчка; (кýхонная) плитá.
stow [stou] уклáдывать [уложúть] (о грýзе и т. п.); **~away** ⚓ безбилéтный пассажúр, «зáяц».
straddle ['strædl] расставлáть [-áвить] (нóги); ходúть, расставлáя нóги; стоáть, расстáвив нóги; сидéть верхóм на (П).
straggl|e ['strægl] отст(ав)áть; идтú вразбрóд; быть разбрóсанным; **~ing** [-iŋ] разбрóсанный (о домáх и т. п.); беспорáдочный.
straight [streit] **1.** *adj.* прямóй; прáвильный; чéстный; *Am.* неразбáвленный; put ~ приводúть в порáдок; **2.** *adv.* прáмо; срáзу; **~en** ['streitn] выпрямлáть(ся) [вы́прямить(ся)]; ~ out приводúть в порáдок; **~forward** ['fɔ:wəd] □ чéстный, прямóй, откровéнный.
strain [strein] **1.** порóда; плéмя *n*; ⊕ деформáция; напряжéние; растяжéние (*a.* ⚕); ♪ *mst* **~s** *pl.* напéв, мелóдия; влечéние (of к Д); **2.** *v/t.* натáгивать [натянýть]; (*a.* ⊕) напрягáть [-áчь]; процéживать [-едúть]; переутомлáть [-мúть]; ⊕ деформúровать (*im*)*pf.*, сгибáть [согнýть]; ⚕ растáгивать [-янýть]; *v/i.* напрягáться [-áчься]; тянýться (after за Т); тянýть изо всех сил (at В); [по]старáться; **~er** ['streinə] дуршлáг; сúто; фильтр.
strait [streit] пролúв; **~s** *pl.* затруднúтельное положéние; ~ waistcoat смирúтельная рубáшка; **~ened** ['streitnd] стеснённый.
strand [strænd] **1.** бéрег (морскóй); прядь *f*; **2.** сесть на мель; be **~ed** *fig.* быть без срéдств.
strange [streindʒ] □ чужóй; чýждый; стрáнный; **~r** ['streindʒə] чужезéмец (-мка); чужóй (человéк); посторóнний (человéк).
strangle ['stræŋgl] [у]давúть.
strap [stræp] **1.** ремéнь *m*; лáмка; штрúпка; ⊕ крепúтельная плáнка; **2.** стáгивать ремнём; порóть ремнём.
stratagem ['strætidʒəm] стратагéма, (воéнная) хúтрость *f*.
strateg|ic [strə'ti:dʒik] (**~ally**) стратегúческий; **~y** ['strætidʒi] стратéгия.
strat|um ['streitəm], *pl.* **~a** [-tə] *geol.* пласт; слой (óбщества).
straw [strɔ:] **1.** солóма; солóминка; **2.** солóменный; ~ vote *Am.*

неофициа́льное про́бное голосова́ние; **~berry** клубни́ка; (*a.* wild ~) земляни́ка.
stray [strei] 1. сбива́ться с пути́; заблуди́ться *pf.*; отби́(ва́)ться (from от Р); блужда́ть; 2. (*a.* ~ed) заблуди́вшийся; бездо́мный; случа́йный; 3. отби́вшееся живо́тное; беспризо́рник (-ница).
streak [stri:k] 1. прослойка; поло́ска; *fig.* черта́; 2. проводи́ть по́лосы на (П).
stream [stri:m] 1. пото́к; руче́й; струя́; 2. *v/i.* [по]те́чь; струи́ться; развева́ться; **~er** ['stri:mə] вы́мпел; дли́нная ле́нта; транспара́нт; столб (се́верного сия́ния); *typ.* кру́пный газе́тный заголо́вок.
street [stri:t] у́лица; *attr.* у́личный; **~-car** *Am.* трамва́й.
strength [streŋθ] си́ла; кре́пость *f* (материа́ла); on the ~ of в си́лу (Р); на основа́нии (Р); **~en** ['streŋθən] *v/t.* уси́ли(ва)ть; укрепля́ть [-пи́ть]; *v/i.* уси́ли(ва)ться.
strenuous ['strenjuəs] □ си́льный; энерги́чный; напряжённый.
stress [stres] 1. давле́ние; напряже́ние; ударе́ние; 2. подчёркивать [-черкну́ть]; ста́вить ударе́ние на (П).
stretch [stretʃ] 1. *v/t.* натя́гивать [-яну́ть]; растя́гивать [-яну́ть]; вытя́гивать [вы́тянуть]; раски́дывать [-ки́нуть]; протя́гивать [-яну́ть] (*mst* ~ out); *fig.* преувели́чи(ва)ть; *v/i.* тяну́ться; растя́гиваться [-яну́ться]; натя́гиваться [-яну́ться]; 2. растя́гивание; напряже́ние; протяже́ние; натя́жка; преувеличе́ние; простра́нство; промежу́ток вре́мени; **~er** ['stretʃə] носи́лки *f/pl.*
strew [stru:] [*irr.*] посыпа́ть [посы́пать]; разбра́сывать [-роса́ть].
stricken ['strikən] *p. pt.* от strike.
strict [strikt] то́чный; стро́гий; **~ness** ['striktnis] то́чность *f*; стро́гость *f*.
stridden ['stridn] *p. pt.* от stride.
stride [straid] 1. [*irr.*] шага́ть [шагну́ть]; ~ over перешагивать [-гну́ть]; 2. большо́й шаг.
strident ['straidnt] □ скрипу́чий.
strike [straik] 1. ста́чка; забасто́вка; be on ~ бастова́ть; 2. [*irr.*] *v/t.* ударя́ть [уда́рить]; высека́ть [вы́сечь] (огонь); [от]чека́нить; спуска́ть [-сти́ть] (флаг); поража́ть [порази́ть]; находи́ть [найти́]; подводи́ть [-вести́] (бала́нс); заключа́ть [-чи́ть] (сде́лку); принима́ть [-ня́ть] (по́зу); наноси́ть [нанести́] (уда́р); ~ up завя́зывать [-за́ть] (знако́мство); *v/i.* [про]би́ть (о часа́х); [за]бастова́ть; ⚓ сесть на мель; ~ home *fig.* попада́ть в са́мую то́чку; **~r** ['straikə] забасто́вщик (-ица).
striking ['straikiŋ] □ порази́тельный; замеча́тельный; уда́рный.
string [striŋ] 1. верёвка; бечёвка; тетива́ (лу́ка); ♪ струна́; ни́тка (бус); **~s** *pl.* ♪ стру́нные инструме́нты *m/pl.*; pull the ~s быть закули́сным руководи́телем; 2. [*irr.*] натя́гивать стру́ны на (В); напряга́ть [-ря́чь]; *Am.* завя́зывать [завяза́ть]; нани́зывать [-за́ть]; *Am. sl.* води́ть за́ нос; **~-band** стру́нный орке́стр.
stringent ['strindʒənt] стро́гий; то́чный; обяза́тельный; стеснённый (в деньга́х).
strip [strip] 1. сдира́ть [содра́ть] (*a.* ~ off); обдира́ть [ободра́ть]; разде́(ва́)ть(ся); *fig.* лиша́ть [-ши́ть] (of Р); [о]гра́бить; ⊕ разбира́ть [разобра́ть] (на ча́сти); ⚓ разоружа́ть [-жи́ть] (су́дно); 2. полоса́; ле́нта.
stripe [straip] полоса́; ⚔ наши́вка.
strive [straiv] [*irr.*] [по]стара́ться; стреми́ться (for к Д); **~n** [-n] *p. pt.* от strive.
strode [stroud] *pt.* от stride.
stroke [strouk] 1. уда́р (*a.* ⚕); взмах; штрих, черта́; ⊕ ход (по́ршня); ~ of luck уда́ча; 2. [по]гла́дить; приласка́ть *pf.*
stroll [stroul] 1. прогу́ливаться [-ля́ться]; 2. прогу́лка.
strong [strɔŋ] □ *com.* си́льный; про́чный; кре́пкий; о́стрый; твёрдый; **~hold** кре́пость *f*; *fig.* опло́т; **~-willed** реши́тельный; упря́мый.
strop [strɔp] 1. реме́нь для пра́вки бритв; 2. пра́вить (бри́тву).
strove [strouv] *pt.* от strive.
struck [strʌk] *pt.* и *p. pt.* от strike.
structure ['strʌktʃə] структу́ра, строй; устро́йство; ⚠ строе́ние, сооруже́ние.
struggle ['strʌgl] 1. боро́ться; вся́чески стара́ться; би́ться (with над Т); ~ through с трудо́м пробива́ться; 2. борьба́.
strung [strʌŋ] *pt.* и *p. pt.* от string.
strut [strʌt] 1. *v/i.* ходи́ть го́голем; *v/t.* ⊕ подпира́ть [-пере́ть]; 2. ва́жная похо́дка; ⊕ подпо́рка.
stub [stʌb] 1. пень *m*; оку́рок; огры́зок; 2. выкорчёвывать [вы́корчевать]; ударя́ться [уда́риться] (ного́й) (against о В).
stubble ['stʌbl] жнивьё.
stubborn ['stʌbən] □ упря́мый; неподатливый; упо́рный.
stuck [stʌk] *pt.* и *p. pt.* от stick; **~-up** F высокоме́рный.
stud [stʌd] 1. гвоздь *m* (для украше́ния); за́понка; ко́нный заво́д; 2. оби́(ва́)ть (гвоздя́ми); усе́ивать [усе́ять] (with Т); **~-horse** племенно́й жеребе́ц.
student ['stju:dənt] студе́нт(ка).
studied ['stʌdid] обду́манный;

преднамéренный; изы́сканный; дéланный.
studio ['stju:diou] стýдия; ателье́ *n indecl.*; мастерская.
studious ['stju:djəs] □ прилéжный, старáтельный, усéрдный.
study ['stʌdi] **1.** изучéние; наýчное занятие; наýка; задýмчивость *f*; кабинéт; *paint.* этю́д, эски́з; **2.** учи́ться (Д); изучáть [-чи́ть]; исслéдовать (*im*)*pf*.
stuff [stʌf] **1.** материáл; веществó; матéрия; F дрянь *f*; чепухá; **2.** *v/t.* наби́(вá)ть; заби́(вá)ть; начинять [-ни́ть]; засóвывать [засýнуть]; *v/i.* объедáться [объéсться]; **~ing** ['stʌfiŋ] наби́вка (подýшки и т. п.); начи́нка; **~y** ['stʌfi] □ спёртый, дýшный.
stultify ['stʌltifai] выставлять в смешнóм ви́де; своди́ть на нéт.
stumble ['stʌmbl] **1.** спотыкáние; запи́нка; **2.** спотыкáться [-ткнýться]; запинáться [запнýться]; **~** upon натыкáться [наткнýться] на (В).
stump [stʌmp] **1.** пень *m*; обрýбок; окýрок; **2.** *v/t.* F стáвить в тупи́к; **~** the country агити́ровать по странé; *v/i.* тяжелó ступáть; **~y** ['stʌmpi] □ призéмистый.
stun [stʌn] оглушáть [-ши́ть] (*a. fig.*); *fig.* ошеломлять [-ми́ть].
stung [stʌŋ] *pt.* и *p. pt.* от sting.
stunk [stʌŋk] *pt.* и *p. pt.* от stink.
stunning ['stʌniŋ] F сногсшибáтельный.
stunt[1] [stʌnt] *Am.* F трюк; ✈ фигýра вы́сшего пилотáжа.
stunt[2] [~] задéрживать рост (Р); **~ed** ['stʌntid] чáхлый.
stup|efy ['stju:pifai] изумлять [-ми́ть]; поражáть [порази́ть]; **~endous** [stju:'pendəs] □ изуми́тельный; **~id** ['stju:pid] □ глýпый, тупóй; **~idity** [stju'piditi] глýпость *f*; **~or** ['stju:pə] оцепенéние.
sturdy ['stə:di] си́льный, крéпкий; здорóвый.
stutter ['stʌtə] заикáться [-кнýться]; запинáться [запнýться].
sty [stai] свинáрник; ячмéнь *m* (на глазý).
style [stail] **1.** стиль *m*; слог; мóда; фасóн; ти́тул; **2.** титуловáть (*im*)*pf*.
stylish ['stailiʃ] □ мóдный; элегáнтный; **~ness** [-nis] элегáнтность *f*.
suave [sweiv] учти́вый; мягкий.
sub... [sʌb] *mst* под...; суб...
subdivision ['sʌbdi'viʒən] подразделéние.
subdue [səb'dju:] подчинять [-ни́ть]; покорять [-ри́ть]; подавлять [-ви́ть].
subject ['sʌbdʒikt] **1.** подчинённый; подвлáстный; *fig.* **~** to подлежáщий (Д); **2.** *adv.* **~** to при услóвии (Р); **3.** пóдданный; предмéт; сюжéт; (*a.* **~** matter) тéма; **4.** [səb'dʒekt] подчинять [-ни́ть]; *fig.* подвергáть [-éргнуть]; **~ion** [səb'dʒekʃən] покорéние; подчинéние.
subjugate ['sʌbdʒugeit] порабощáть [-боти́ть].
sublease ['sʌb'li:s], **sublet** ['sʌb'let] [*irr.* (let)] сдать на правáх субарéнды
sublime [[sə'blaim] □ возвы́шенный.
submachine ['sʌbmə'ʃi:n]: **~** gun автомáт.
submarine ['sʌbməri:n] **1.** подвóдный; **2.** ⚓ подвóдная лóдка.
submerge [sʌb'mə:dʒ] погружáть (-ся) [-узи́ть(ся)]; затоплять [-пи́ть].
submiss|ion [səb'miʃən] подчинéние; покóрность *f*; представлéние (докумéнта и т. п.); **~ive** [səb'misiv] □ покóрный.
submit [səb'mit] подчинять(ся) [-ни́ть(ся)] (Д); представлять [-áвить] (на рассмотрéние).
subordinate **1.** [sə'bɔ:dnit] подчинённый; *gr.* придáточный; **2.** [~] подчинённый (-ённая); **3.** [sə'bɔ:dineit] подчинять [-ни́ть].
suborn [sʌ'bɔ:n] подкупáть [-пи́ть].
subscribe [səb'skraib] *v/t.* подпи́сывать [-сáть]; [по]жéртвовать; *v/i.* присоединяться [-ни́ться] (to к Д); подпи́сываться [-сáться] (to на В; † for на В); абони́роваться (to на В); **~r** [-ə] подпи́счик (-чица); абонéнт(ка).
subscription [səb'skripʃən] подпи́ска (на журнáл и́ли на заём); абонемéнт.
subsequent ['sʌbsikwənt] □ послéдующий; **~ly** впослéдствии.
subservient [səb'sə:vient] раболéпный; содéйствующий (to Д).
subsid|e [səb'said] спадáть [спáсть] (о температýре); убы́(вá)ть (о водé); утихáть [ути́хнуть], улéчься *pf.*; **~iary** [səb'sidjəri] **1.** □ вспомогáтельный; **2.** филиáл; **~ize** ['sʌbsidaiz] субсиди́ровать (*im*)*pf.*; **~y** [-di] субси́дия.
subsist [səb'sist] существовáть; жить (on, by Т); **~ence** [-əns] существовáние; срéдства к существовáнию.
substance ['sʌbstəns] сýщность *f*, суть *f*; содержáние; веществó; имýщество.
substantial [səb'stænʃəl] □ сущéственный, вáжный; прóчный; вещéственный; состоятельный; питáтельный.
substantiate [səb'stænʃieit] докáзывать справедли́вость (Р); подтверждáть [-рди́ть].
substitut|e ['sʌbstitju:t] **1.** заменять [-ни́ть]; замещáть [-ести́ть] (for В); **2.** замести́тель(ница *f*) *m*; за-

ме́на; суррога́т; ~**ion** [sʌbsti'tju:ʃən] заме́на; замеще́ние.
subterfuge ['sʌbtəfju:dʒ] увёртка, отгово́рка.
subterranean [sʌbtə'reinjən] ☐ [подзе́мный.]
subtle ['sʌtl] ☐ то́нкий; неулови́мый; утончённый; ~**ty** [-ti] то́нкость *f*; неулови́мость *f*.
subtract [səb'trækt] ⩘ вычита́ть [вы́честь].
suburb ['sʌbə:b] при́город; предме́стье; ~**an** [sə'bə:bən] при́городный.
subver|sion [sʌb'və:ʃən] ниспроверже́ние; ~**sive** [-siv] *fig.* подрывно́й; разруши́тельный; ~**t** [sʌb'və:t] ниспроверга́ть [-е́ргнуть]; разруша́ть [-у́шить].
subway ['sʌbwei] тонне́ль *m* (*a.* тунне́ль); *Am.* метро́(полите́н) *n indecl.*
succeed [sək'si:d] [по]сле́довать за (Т); быть прее́мником (Р); достига́ть це́ли; преуспе́(ва́)ть.
success [sək'ses] успе́х; уда́ча; ~**ful** [sək'sesful] ☐ успе́шный; уда́чный; уда́чливый; ~**ion** [-'seʃən] после́довательность *f*; непреры́вный ряд; прее́мственность *f*; in ~ оди́н за други́м; подря́д; ~**ive** [-'sesiv] ☐ после́дующий; после́довательный; ~**or** [-'sesə] прее́мник (-ица); насле́дник (-ица).
succo(u)r ['sʌkə] **1.** по́мощь *f*; **2.** приходи́ть на по́мощь (Д).
succulent ['sʌkjulənt] со́чный.
succumb [sə'kʌm] уступа́ть [-пи́ть] (to Д); не выде́рживать [вы́держать] (to Р); быть побеждённым.
such [sʌtʃ] тако́й; *pred.* тако́в, -а́ и т. д.; ~ a man тако́й челове́к; ~ as тако́й, как ...; как наприме́р.
suck [sʌk] **1.** соса́ть; выса́сывать [вы́сосать] (*a.* ~ out); вса́сывать [всоса́ть] (*a.* ~ in); **2.** соса́ние; ~**er** ['sʌkə] сосуно́к; ⚘, *zo.* присо́ска, присо́сок; *Am.* проста́к; ~**le** ['sʌkl] корми́ть гру́дью; ~**ling** ['sʌkliŋ] грудно́й ребёнок; сосу́н(о́к).
suction ['sʌkʃən] **1.** вса́сывание; **2.** *attr.* вса́сывающий.
sudden ['sʌdn] ☐ внеза́пный; all of a ~ внеза́пно, вдруг.
suds [sʌdz] *pl.* мы́льная вода́.
sue [sju:] *v/t.* пресле́довать суде́бным поря́дком; ~ out выхлопа́тывать [вы́хлопота́ть]; *v/i.* возбужда́ть иск (for о П).
suéde [sweid] за́мша.
suet [sjuit] по́чечное са́ло.
suffer ['sʌfə] *v/i.* [по]страда́ть (from от Р *or* Т); *v/t.* [по]терпе́ть; сноси́ть [снести́]; ~**ance** [-rəns] попусти́тельство; ~**er** [-rə] страда́лец (-лица); ~**ing** [-riŋ] страда́ние.
suffice [sə'fais] хвата́ть [-ти́ть], быть доста́точным.
sufficien|cy [sə'fiʃənsi] доста́точность *f*; доста́ток; ~**t** [-ənt] ☐ доста́точный.
suffocate ['sʌfəkeit] души́ть, удуша́ть [-ши́ть]; задыха́ться [задохну́ться].
suffrage ['sʌfridʒ] избира́тельное [пра́во.]
suffuse [sə'fju:z] зали́(ва́)ть (слеза́ми); покры́(ва́)ть (кра́ской).
sugar ['ʃugə] **1.** са́хар; **2.** са́харный; ~**y** [-ri] са́харный (*a. fig.*); *fig.* при́торный, слаща́вый.
suggest [sə'dʒest] внуша́ть [-ши́ть]; подска́зывать [-за́ть]; наводи́ть на мысль о (П); [по]сове́товать; предлага́ть [-ложи́ть]; ~**ion** [-ʃən] внуше́ние; сове́т, предложе́ние; намёк; ~**ive** [-iv] ☐ наводя́щий на размышле́ние; соблазни́тельный; двусмы́сленный.
suicide ['sjuisaid] самоуби́йца *m/f*; самоуби́йство.
suit [sju:t] **1.** проше́ние; набо́р; (*a.* ~ of clothes) костю́м; (ка́рточная) масть *f*; ⚖ тя́жба; иск; **2.** *v/t.* приспоса́бливать [-осо́бить] (to, with к Д); соотве́тствовать (Д); удовлетворя́ть [-ри́ть]; быть (кому́-либо) к лицу́ (*a.* with a p.); устра́ивать [-ро́ить]; подходи́ть [подойти́] (Д); ~**ed** подходя́щий; *v/i.* годи́ться; ~**able** ['sju:təbl] ☐ подходя́щий; соотве́тствующий; ~**-case** чемода́н; ~**e** [swi:t] сви́та; набо́р; ♪ сю́ита; (и́ли ~ of rooms) анфила́да ко́мнат; гарниту́р (ме́бели); ~**or** ['sju:tə] уха́живатель *m*; ⚖ исте́ц; проси́тель(ница *f*) *m*.
sulk [sʌlk] **1.** [на]ду́ться; быть не в ду́хе; **2.** ~**s** [-s] *pl.* плохо́е настрое́ние; ~**y** ['sʌlki] ☐ наду́тый, угрю́мый.
sullen ['sʌlən] угрю́мый, мра́чный; серди́тый.
sully ['sʌli] *mst fig.* [за]пятна́ть.
sulphur ['sʌlfə] ⚗ се́ра; ~**ic** [sʌl'fjuərik] се́рный.
sultriness ['sʌltrinis] духота́, зно́й.
sultry ['sʌltri] ☐ ду́шный, зно́йный.
sum [sʌm] **1.** су́мма; ито́г; *fig.* содержа́ние; су́щность; ~**s** *pl.* арифме́тика; **2.** (*a.* ~ up) ⩘ скла́дывать [сложи́ть]; *fig.* подводи́ть ито́г.
summar|ize ['sʌməraiz] сумми́ровать (*im*)*pf.*; резюми́ровать (*im*-)*pf.*; ~**y** [-ri] **1.** ☐ кра́ткий; сокращённый; ⚖ дисциплина́рный; **2.** (кра́ткое) изложе́ние, резюме́ *n indecl.*
summer ['sʌmə] ле́то; ~**(l)y** [-ri, -li] ле́тний.
summit ['sʌmit] верши́на (*a. fig.*); преде́л; верх.
summon ['sʌmən] соз(ы)ва́ть (собра́ние и т. п.); ⚖ вызыва́ть [вы́звать] (в суд); приз(ы)ва́ть; ~**s** [-z] вы́зов (в суд); суде́бная пове́стка; ⚔ предложе́ние сда́ться.

sumptuous ['sʌmptjuəs] роско́шный; пы́шный.
sun [sʌn] 1. со́лнце; 2. со́лнечный; 3. гре́ть(ся) на со́лнце; **~burn** ['sʌnbə:n] зага́р.
Sunday ['sʌndi] воскресе́нье.
sun|-dial со́лнечные часы́ *m/pl.*; **~-down** *Am.* зака́т, захо́д со́лнца.
sundries ['sʌndriz] *pl.* вся́кая вся́чина; ✝ разные расхо́ды *m/pl.*
sung [sʌŋ] *p. pt.* от sing.
sun-glasses *pl.* тёмные очки́ *n/pl.*
sunk [sʌŋk] *p. pt.* от sink.
sunken [sʌŋkən] *fig.* впа́лый.
sun|ny ['sʌni] □ со́лнечный; **~rise** восхо́д со́лнца; **~set** захо́д со́лнца, зака́т; **~shade** зо́нт(ик) от со́лнца; **~shine** со́лнечный свет; in the **~** на со́лнце; **~stroke** ⚕ со́лнечный уда́р; **~up** ['sʌnʌp] *Am.* восхо́д со́лнца.
sup [sʌp] [по]у́жинать.
super... ['sju:pə] *pref.*: пере..., пре...; сверх...; над...; супер...; **~abundant** [sju:pərə'bʌndənt] □ изоби́льный; **~annuate** [sju:pə'rænjueit] переводи́ть на пе́нсию; *fig.* сдава́ть в архи́в; **~d** преста́релый; устаре́лый. [прекра́сный.]
superb [sju'pə:b] роско́шный,
super|charger ['sju:pətʃɑ:dʒə] ⊕ нагнета́тель *m*; **~cilious** [sju:pə'siliəs] □ высокоме́рный; **~ficial** [sju:pə'fiʃəl] □ пове́рхностный; **~fine** ['sju:pə'fain] чрезме́рно утончённый; вы́сшего со́рта; **~fluity** [sju:pə'fluiti] изоби́лие, изли́шек; изли́шество; **~fluous** [sju'pə:fluəs] □ изли́шний; **~heat** [sju:pə'hi:t] ⊕ перегре́(ва́)ть; **~intend** [sju:prin'tend] надзира́ть за (Т); заве́довать (Т); **~intendent** [-ənt] надзира́тель *m*; заве́дующий; управдо́м.
superior [sju'piəriə] 1. □ вы́сший; ста́рший (по чи́ну); лу́чший; превосхо́дный; превосходя́щий (to В); 2. ста́рший, нача́льник; *eccl.* настоя́тель *m*, (*mst* lady **~**) настоя́тельница; **~ity** [sjupiəri'ɔriti] превосхо́дство.
super|lative [sju'pə:lətiv] 1. □ высоча́йший; велича́йший; 2. превосхо́дная сте́пень *f*; **~numerary** [sju:pə'nju:mərəri] 1. сверхшта́тный; 2. сверхшта́тный рабо́тник; *thea.* стати́ст; **~scription** [sju:pə'skripʃən] на́дпись *f*; **~sede** [-si:d] заменя́ть [-ни́ть]; вытесня́ть [вы́теснить]; *fig.* обгоня́ть [обогна́ть]; **~stition** [-'stiʃən] суеве́рие; **~stitious** [-'stiʃəs] суеве́рный; **~vene** [sju:pə'vi:n] добавля́ться [-а́виться]; неожи́данно возника́ть; **~vise** ['sju:pəvaiz] надзира́ть за (Т); **~vision** [sju:pə'viʒən] надзо́р; **~visor** ['sju:pəvaizə] надзира́тель *m*. [♀ та́йная ве́черя.]
supper ['sʌpə] у́жин; the (Lord's)
supplant [sə'plɑ:nt] вытесня́ть [вы́теснить] (В).
supple ['sʌpl] ги́бкий; пода́тливый.
supplement 1. ['sʌplimənt] добавле́ние, дополне́ние; приложе́ние; 2. [-'ment] дополня́ть [допо́лнить]; **~al** [sʌpli'mentl] □, **~ary** [-təri] дополни́тельный, доба́вочный.
suppliant ['sʌpliənt] проси́тель (-ница *f*) *m*.
supplicat|e ['sʌplikeit] умоля́ть (for о П); **~ion** [sʌpli'keiʃən] мольба́; про́сьба.
supplier [sə'plaiə] поставщи́к (-и́ца).
supply [sə'plai] 1. снабжа́ть [-бди́ть] (with Т); поставля́ть [-а́вить]; доставля́ть [-а́вить]; возмеща́ть [-ести́ть]; замеща́ть [-ести́ть]; 2. снабже́ние; поста́вка; запа́с; вре́менный замести́тель *m*; *pl.* продово́льствие; припа́сы *m/pl.*; ✝ предложе́ние; *mst pl. parl.* ассигнова́ния *n/pl.* (утверждённые парла́ментом).
support [sə'pɔ:t] 1. подде́ржка; опо́ра; 2. подпира́ть [-пере́ть]; подде́рживать [-жа́ть]; содержа́ть (семью́ и т. п.).
suppose [sə'pouz] предполага́ть [-ложи́ть]; полага́ть; F **~** we do so? а е́сли мы э́то сде́лаем?
supposed [sə'pouzd] □ предполага́емый; **~ly** [-zidli] предположи́тельно; я́кобы.
supposition [sʌpə'ziʃən] предположе́ние.
suppress [sə'pres] подавля́ть [-ви́ть]; запреща́ть [-ети́ть] (газе́ту); сде́рживать [-жа́ть] (смех, гнев и т. п.); **~ion** [sə'preʃən] подавле́ние и т. д.
suppurate ['sʌpjuəreit] гнои́ться.
suprem|acy [sju'preməsi] превосхо́дство; верхо́вная власть *f*; **~e** [sju'pri:m] □ верхо́вный; вы́сший; кра́йний.
surcharge [sə:'tʃɑ:dʒ] 1. перегружа́ть [-узи́ть]; 2. ['sə:tʃɑ:dʒ] перегру́зка; припла́та, допла́та (за письмо́ и т. п.); надпеча́тка.
sure [ʃuə] □ *com.* ве́рный; уве́ренный; безопа́сный; надёжный; to be **~**! *Am.* **~**! безусло́вно, коне́чно; **~ly** ['ʃuəli] несомне́нно; наве́рно; **~ty** [-ti] пору́ка; поручи́тель *m*.
surf [sə:f] прибо́й.
surface ['sə:fis] 1. пове́рхность *f*; 2. пове́рхностный.
surfeit ['sə:fit] 1. изли́шество; пресыще́ние; 2. пресыща́ть(ся) [-ы́тить(ся)] (on Т); переедать [перее́сть] (on P).
surge [sə:dʒ] 1. волна́; 2. вздыма́ться (о волна́х); *fig.* [вз]волнова́ться.

surg|eon ['sə:dʒən] хиру́рг; **~ery** ['sə:dʒəri] хирурги́я; хирурги́ческий кабине́т.
surgical ['sə:dʒikəl] □ хирурги́ческий.
surly [sə:li] □ угрю́мый; гру́бый.
surmise ['sə:maiz] **1.** предположе́ние, дога́дка; **2.** [sə:'maiz] предполага́ть [-ложи́ть].
surmount [sə:'maunt] преодоле́(ва́)ть, превозмога́ть [-мо́чь].
surname ['sə:neim] фами́лия; про́звище.
surpass [sə:'pɑ:s] перегоня́ть [-гна́ть]; превосходи́ть [-взойти́]; **~ing** [-iŋ] превосхо́дный.
surplus ['sə:pləs] **1.** изли́шек; оста́ток; **2.** изли́шний; доба́вочный, приба́вочный.
surprise [sə'praiz] **1.** удивле́ние; неожи́данность *f*, сюрпри́з; *attr.* неожи́данный; ⚔ внеза́пный; **2.** удивля́ть [-ви́ть]; застава́ть врасплох.
surrender [sə'rendə] **1.** сда́ча; капитуля́ция; **2.** *v/t.* сда(ва́)ть; отка́зываться [-за́ться] от (Р); *v/i.* сд(ав)а́ться (*a.* ~ o. s.).
surround [sə'raund] окружа́ть [-жи́ть]; **~ing** [-iŋ] окружа́ющий; **~ings** [-iŋz] *pl.* окре́стности *f/pl.*
surtax ['sə:tæks] доба́вочный нало́г.
survey **1.** [sə:'vei] обозре́(ва́)ть; осма́тривать [осмотре́ть]; *surv.* межева́ть; **2.** ['sə:vei] осмо́тр; обзо́р; *fig.* обсле́дование; *surv.* межева́ние; *attr.* обзо́рный; **~or** [sə:'veiə] землеме́р; *Am.* инспе́ктор.
surviv|al [sə'vaivəl] выжива́ние; пережи́ток; **~e** [sə'vaiv] *v/t.* пережи́(ва́)ть; выжива́ть по́сле (Р); *v/i.* остава́ться в живы́х, выжи(ва́)ть; **~or** [-ə] оста́вшийся в живы́х.
susceptible [sə'septəbl] □ восприи́мчивый (to к Д); оби́дчивый; be ~ of допуска́ть [-сти́ть] (В).
suspect [səs'pekt] **1.** подозрева́ть, заподо́зривать [-до́зрить] (of в П); сомнева́ться [усомни́ться] в (по́длинности и т. п.); полага́ть; **2.** подозри́тельный; подозрева́емый.
suspend [səs'pend] ве́шать [пове́сить]; приостана́вливать [-нови́ть]; откла́дывать [отложи́ть]; вре́менно прекраща́ть; **~ed** подвесно́й; **~ers** [-əz] *pl. Am.* подтя́жки *f/pl.*; подвя́зки *f/pl.*
suspens|e [səs'pens] напряжённое внима́ние; состоя́ние неизве́стности; be in ~ быть нерешённым; **~ion** [səs'penʃən] подве́шивание; прекраще́ние; вре́менная отста́вка; ~ bridge вися́чий мост.
suspici|on [səs'piʃən] подозре́ние; *fig.* чу́точка; **~ous** [-əs] □ подозри́тельный.
sustain [səs'tein] подпира́ть [-пере́ть]; подде́рживать [-жа́ть]; подтвержда́ть [-рди́ть]; выде́рживать [вы́держать]; выноси́ть [вы́нести], испы́тывать [испыта́ть].
sustenance ['sʌstinəns] пи́ща; сре́дства к существова́нию.
svelte [svelt] стро́йный.
swab [swɔb] **1.** шва́бра; ⚕ мазо́к; **2.** (*a.* ~ down) мыть шва́брой.
swaddle ['swɔdl] [c-, за]пелена́ть; swaddling clothes *pl.* пелёнки *f/pl.*
swagger ['swægə] ва́жничать; чва́ниться; [по]хва́стать (*a.* -ся).
swallow ['swɔlou] **1.** *zo.* ла́сточка; глото́к; **2.** глота́ть; прогла́тывать [-лоти́ть].
swam [swæm] *pt.* от swim.
swamp [swɔmp] **1.** боло́то, топь *f*; **2.** затопля́ть [-пи́ть], зали́(ва́)ть; **~y** ['swɔmpi] боло́тистый.
swan [swɔn] ле́бедь *m.* (*poet. a. f.*).
swap [swɔp] F **1.** обме́нивать(ся) [-ня́ть(ся)]; [по]меня́ть; **2.** обме́н.
sward [swɔ:d] газо́н; дёрн.
swarm [swɔ:m] **1.** рой (пчёл); стая (птиц); толпа́; **2.** рои́ться (о пчёлах); кише́ть (with T).
swarthy ['swɔ:ði] сму́глый.
swash [swɔʃ] плеска́ть [-сну́ть]; плеска́ться.
swath [swɔ:θ] ⚒ проко́с.
swathe [sweið] [за]бинтова́ть; заку́т(ыв)ать.
sway [swei] **1.** колеба́ние; кача́ние; влия́ние; **2.** кача́ть(ся) [качну́ть (-ся)]; [по]колеба́ться; име́ть влия́ние на (В); властвова́ть над (Т).
swear [sweə] [*irr.*] [по]кля́сться (by T); заставля́ть покля́сться (to в П); *b. s.* [вы́]руга́ться.
sweat [swet] **1.** пот; поте́ние; **2.** [*irr.*] *v/i.* [вс]поте́ть; исполня́ть тяжёлую рабо́ту; *v/t.* заставля́ть поте́ть; эксплуати́ровать; выделя́ть [вы́делить] (вла́гу); **~y** ['sweti] по́тный.
Swede [swi:d] шве́д(ка).
Swedish ['swi:diʃ] шве́дский.
sweep [swi:p] **1.** [*irr.*] мести́, подмета́ть [-ести́]; [по]чи́стить; проноси́ться [-нести́сь] (*a.* ~ past, along); *fig.* увлека́ть [-е́чь] (*a.* ~ along); ⚔ обстре́ливать [-ля́ть]; **2.** подмета́ние; разма́х; взмах; трубочи́ст; make a clean ~ (of) отде́л(ыв)аться (от Р); **~er** ['swi:pə] мете́льщик; **~ing** ['swi:piŋ] □ стреми́тельный; широ́кий, разма́шистый; огу́льный; **~ings** [-z] *pl.* му́сор.
sweet [swi:t] **1.** □ сла́дкий; све́жий; души́стый; ми́лый; have a ~ tooth быть сластёной; **2.** конфе́та; **~s** *pl.* сла́дости *f/pl.*, сласти *f/pl.*; **~en** ['swi:tn] подсла́щивать [-ласти́ть]; **~heart** возлю́бленный (-енная); **~ish** ['swi:tiʃ] сладкова́тый; **~meat** конфе́та; **~ness** ['swi:tnis] сла́дость *f*.
swell [swel] **1.** [*irr.*] *v/i.* [о]пу́хнуть; разду́(ва́)ться; набуха́ть [-у́хнуть];

нарастáть [-стú] (о звýке); *v/t.* раздý(вá)ть; увелúчи(ва)ть; **2.** F щегольскóй; шикáрный; великолéпный; **3.** вы́пуклость *f*; óпухоль *f*; ⚓ мёртвая зыбь *f*; F щёголь *m*; свéтский человéк; **~ing** ['sweliŋ] óпухоль *f*.
swelter ['sweltə] томúться от жары́.
swept [swept] *pt.* и *p. pt.* от sweep.
swerve [swə:v] **1.** отклоня́ться от прямóго путú; (вдруг) сворáчивать в стóрону; **2.** отклонéние.
swift [swift] □ бы́стрый, скóрый; **~ness** ['swiftnis] быстротá.
swill [swil] **1.** помóи *m/pl.*; пóйло; **2.** [про]полоскáть; [вы́]лакáть.
swim [swim] **1.** [*irr.*] плáвать, [по-] плы́ть; переплы́(вá)ть; my head ~s у меня́ головá кружúтся; **2.** плáвание; be in the ~ быть в кýрсе дéла.
swindle ['swindl] **1.** обмáнывать [-нýть], надý(вá)ть; **2.** обмáн, надувáтельство.
swine [swain] (*sg. mst fig.*) свинья́; свúньи *f/pl.*
swing [swiŋ] **1.** [*irr.*] качáть(ся) [качнýть(ся)]; [по]колебáть(ся); размáхивать (рукáми); болтáть (ногáми); висéть; F быть повéшенным; **2.** качáние, колебáние; размáх; взмах; ритм; качéли *f/pl.*; in full ~ в пóлном разгáре; **~-door** дверь, открывáющаяся в любýю стóрону.
swinish ['swainiʃ] □ свúнский.
swipe [swaip] **1.** ударя́ть сплечá; **2.** удáр сплечá.
swirl [swə:l] **1.** кружúть(ся) в водоворóте; клубúться; **2.** водоворóт; кружéние; вúхрь *m.*
Swiss [swis] **1.** швейцáрский; **2.** швейцáрец (-рка); the ~ *pl.* швейцáрцы *m/pl.*
switch [switʃ] **1.** прут; 🚂 стрéлка; ⚡ выключáтель *m*; фальшúвая косá; **2.** хлестáть [-стнýть]; 🚂 маневрúровать; ⚡ переключáть [-чúть] (*often* ~ over) (*a. fig.*); *fig.* переменя́ть направлéние (P); ~ on ⚡ включáть [-чúть]; ~ off выключáть [вы́ключить]; **~-board** ⚡ коммутáтор.

swollen ['swoulən] *p. pt.* от swell.
swoon [swu:n] **1.** óбморок; **2.** пáдать в óбморок.
swoop [swu:p] **1.** (*a.* ~ down), устремля́ться вниз (на добы́чу и т. п.); налетáть [-етéть] (on на B); **2.** налёт, внезáпное нападéние.
sword [sɔ:d] шпáга; меч.
swordsman ['sɔdzmən] фехтовáльщик.
swore [swɔ:] *pt.* от swear.
sworn [swɔ:n] *p. pt.* от swear.
swum [swʌm] *p. pt.* от swim.
swung [swʌŋ] *pt.* и *p. pt.* от swing.
sycophant ['sikofənt] льстец.
syllable ['siləbl] слог.
symbol ['simbəl] сúмвол, эмблéма; знак; **~ic(al** □) [sim'bɔlik, -əl] символúческий; **~ism** ['simbəlizm] символúзм.
symmetr|ical [si'metrikəl] □ симметрúчный; **~y** ['simitri] симметрúя.
sympath|etic [simpə'θetik] (~ally) сочýвственный; симпатúчный; ~ strike забастóвка солидáрности; **~ize** ['simpəθaiz] [по]сочýвствовать (with Д); симпатизúровать (with Д); **~y** [-θi] сочýвствие (with к Д); симпáтия (for к Д).
symphony ['simfəni] симфóния.
symptom ['simptəm] симптóм.
synchron|ize ['siŋkrənaiz] *v/i.* совпадáть по врéмени; *v/t.* синхронизúровать (*im*)*pf.*; устанáвливать одноврéмéнность (собы́тий); сверя́ть [свéрить] (часы́); **~ous** [-nəs] □ синхрóнный.
syndicate **1.** ['sindikit] синдикáт; **2.** [-keit] синдицúровать (*im*)*pf.*
synonym ['sinənim] синóним; **~ous** [si'nɔniməs] синонимúческий.
synopsis [si'nɔpsis] конспéкт; синóпсис.
synthe|sis ['sinθisis] сúнтез; **~tic(al** □) [sin'θetik, -tikəl] синтетúческий.
syringe ['sirindʒ] **1.** шприц; **2.** спринцевáть.
syrup ['sirəp] сирóп; пáтока.
system ['sistim] систéма; **~atic** [sistə'mætik] (~ally) систематúческий.

T

tab [tæb] вéшалка; пéтелька; ⚔ петлúца (на воротникé).
table ['teibl] **1.** стол; óбщество за столóм; плитá; дощéчка; таблúца; тáбель *m*; ~ of contents оглавлéние; **2.** класть на стол; представля́ть [-áвить] (предложéние и т. п.); **~-cloth** скáтерть *f*; **~-spoon** столóвая лóжка.
tablet ['tæblit] дощéчка; блокнóт; таблéтка; кусóк (мы́ла и т. п.).

taboo [tə'bu:] **1.** табý *n indecl.*; запрещéние, запрéт; **2.** подвергáть табý; запрещáть [-етúть]; **3.** запрещённый.
tabulate ['tæbjuleit] располагáть в вúде таблúц.
tacit ['tæsit] □ молчалúвый (о соглáсии и т. п.); подразумевáемый; **~urn** ['tæsitə:n] □ молчалúвый, неразговóрчивый.
tack [tæk] **1.** гвóздик с ширóкой

шля́пкой; кно́пка (канцеля́рская); стежо́к; ⚓ галс; *fig.* полити́ческая ли́ния; **2.** *v/t.* прикрепля́ть гво́здиками и́ли кно́пками; смётывать [смета́ть]; присоединя́ть [-ни́ть], добавля́ть [-а́вить] (to, on к Д); *v/i.* ⚓ повора́чивать на друго́й галс; *fig.* меня́ть полити́ческий курс.

tackle ['tækl] **1.** принадле́жности *f/pl.*; снасть *f*; ⊕, ⚓ та́ли *f/pl.*; **2.** энерги́чно бра́ться за (В); би́ться над (Т).

tact [tækt] такт, такти́чность *f*; **~ful** ['tæktful] □ такти́чный.

tactics ['tæktiks] та́ктика.

tactless ['tæktlis] □ беста́ктный.

taffeta ['tæfitə] тафта́.

tag [tæg] **1.** ярлычо́к, этике́тка; ушко́ (сапога́); *fig.* изби́тая фра́за; **2.** прикрепля́ть ярлы́к, ушко́ к (Д).

tail [teil] **1.** хвост; коса́ (воло́с); пола́, фа́лда; обра́тная сторона́ (моне́ты); **2.** *v/t.* снабжа́ть хвосто́м; отруба́ть хвост (щеня́т); высле́живать [вы́следить]; *v/i.* тяну́ться дли́нной верени́цей; ~ off отст(ав)а́ть; **~-coat** фрак; **~-light** *mot.*, 🚃 за́дний фона́рь *m*; ✈ хвостово́й ого́нь *m*.

tailor ['teilə] **1.** портно́й; **2.** портня́жничать; [с]шить; **~-made** сши́тый на зака́з.

taint [teint] **1.** поро́к; пятно́ позо́ра; зара́за; испо́рченность *f*; **2.** [за]пятна́ть; [ис]по́ртить(ся); ⚕ заража́ть(ся) [зарази́ть(ся)].

take [teik] **1.** [*irr.*] *v/t.* брать [взять]; принима́ть [-ня́ть]; [съ]есть, [вы́-]пить; занима́ть [заня́ть] (ме́сто); *phot.* снима́ть [снять]; отнима́ть [-ня́ть] (вре́мя); I ~ it that я полага́ю, что ...; ~ the air выходи́ть на во́здух; ✈ отлета́ть [-ете́ть]; ~ fire загора́ться [-ре́ться]; ~ in hand бра́ться [взя́ться] за (В), предпринима́ть [-ня́ть]; ~ pity on сжа́литься *pf.* над (Т); ~ place случа́ться [-чи́ться], происходи́ть [произойти́]; ~ rest отдыха́ть [отдохну́ть]; ~ a seat сади́ться [сесть]; ~ a view выска́зывать свою́ то́чку зре́ния; ~ a walk [по]гуля́ть, прогу́ливаться [-ля́ться]; ~ down снима́ть [снять]; запи́сывать [-са́ть]; ~ for принима́ть [-ня́ть] за (В); ~ from брать [взять] у (Р); отнима́ть [отня́ть] у (Р) *or* от (Р); ~ in обма́нывать [-ну́ть]; принима́ть [-ня́ть] (го́стя); получа́ть (газе́ту и т. п.); ~ off снима́ть [снять] (оде́жду); ~ out вынима́ть [вы́нуть]; ~ to pieces разбира́ть [разобра́ть] (на ча́сти); ~ up бра́ться [взя́ться] за (В); занима́ть [заня́ть], отнима́ть [отня́ть] (ме́сто, вре́мя); **2.** *v/i.* [по]де́йствовать; име́ть успе́х; ~ after походи́ть на (В); ~ off уменьша́ться [уме́ньши́ться]; ✈ взлета́ть [-ете́ть]; оторва́ться от земли́; ~ over принима́ть до́лжность (from от Р); ~ to пристрасти́ться к (Д) *pf.*; привяза́ться к (Д) *pf.*; that won't ~ with me э́тим меня́ не возьмёшь; **3.** уло́в (ры́бы); (театра́льный) сбор; **~s** *pl.* бары́ши́ *m/pl.*; **~n** ['teikən] *p. pt.* от take; be ~ ill заболе́(ва́)ть; **~-off** ['tei'kɔf] карикату́ра; подража́ние; ✈ взлёт.

taking ['teikiŋ] **1.** □ привлека́тельный; зара́зный; **2.** **~s** [-z] *pl.* ✝ бары́ши́ *m/pl.*

tale [teil] расска́з, по́весть *f*; вы́думка; спле́тня.

talent ['tælənt] тала́нт; **~ed** [-id] тала́нтливый.

talk [tɔ:k] **1.** разгово́р; бесе́да; слух; **2.** [по]говори́ть; разгова́ривать; [по]бесе́довать; [на]спле́тничать; **~ative** ['tɔ:kətiv] болтли́вый; **~er** ['tɔ:kə] **1.** говору́н(ья), болту́н(ья); собесе́дник (-ница).

tall [tɔ:l] высо́кий; F невероя́тный; ~ order чрезме́рное тре́бование; ~ story *Am.* F неправдоподо́бный расска́з, небыли́ца.

tallow ['tælou] топлёное са́ло (для свече́й).

tally ['tæli] **1.** би́рка; ко́пия, дублика́т; опознава́тельный ярлы́к; **2.** отмеча́ть [-е́тить]; подсчи́тывать [-ита́ть]; соотве́тствовать (with Д).

tame [teim] **1.** □ ручно́й, приручённый; поко́рный; пасси́вный; ску́чный; **2.** прируча́ть [-чи́ть]; смиря́ть [-ри́ть].

tamper ['tæmpə]: ~ with вме́шиваться [-ша́ться] в (В); неуме́ло вози́ться с (Т); подде́л(ыв)ать (В); стара́ться подкупи́ть (В).

tan [tæn] **1.** зага́р; корьё, толчёная дубо́вая кора́; **2.** рыжева́то-кори́чневый; **3.** [вы́]дуби́ть (ко́жу); загора́ть.

tang [tæŋ] ре́зкий при́вкус; налёт.

tangent ['tændʒənt] ⩓ та́нгенс; go (*a.* fly) off at a ~ внеза́пно отклоня́ться (от те́мы и т. п.).

tangible ['tændʒəbl] □ осяза́емый, ощути́мый.

tangle ['tæŋgl] **1.** пу́таница, неразбери́ха; **2.** запу́т(ыв)ать(ся).

tank [tæŋk] **1.** цисте́рна; бак; ⚔ танк, *attr.* та́нковый; **2.** налива́ть в бак.

tankard ['tæŋkəd] высо́кая кру́жка.

tannery ['tænəri] коже́венный заво́д.

tantalize ['tæntəlaiz] [за-, из]му́чить.

tantrum ['tæntrəm] F вспы́шка гне́ва и́ли раздраже́ния.

tap[1] [tæp] **1.** вту́лка; кран; F сорт, ма́рка (напи́тка); **2.** вставля́ть кран в (бо́чку); де́лать проко́л (для выпуска́ния жи́дкости) у

(больно́го); де́лать надре́з на (де́реве для получе́ния со́ка); выпра́шивать де́ньги у (Р).
tap[2] [~] 1. [по]стуча́ть; хло́пать [-пнуть]; 2. лёгкий стук; шлепо́к; ~**-dance** чечётка.
tape [teip] тесьма́; *sport* фи́нишная ле́нточка; телегра́фная ле́нта; red ~ бюрократи́зм, канцеля́рщина; ~**-measure** ['teipmeʒə] руле́тка.
taper ['teipə] 1. то́нкая восково́я свеча́; 2. *adj.* су́живающийся к концу́; кони́ческий; 3. *v/i.* су́живаться к концу́; *v/t.* заостря́ть [-ри́ть].
tape-recorder магнитофо́н.
tapestry ['tæpistri] гобеле́н.
tape-worm ⚕ солитёр.
tap-room ['tæprum] пивна́я.
tar [tɑ:] 1. дёготь *m*; смола́; 2. обма́зывать дёгтем; [вы́]смоли́ть.
tardy ['tɑ:di] □ медли́тельный; запозда́лый, по́здний.
tare[1] [tɛə] та́ра; ски́дка на та́ру.
tare[2] [~] ⚘ посевна́я ви́ка.
target ['tɑ:git] цель *f*; мише́нь (*a. fig.*); ~ practice стрельба́ по мише́ням.
tariff ['tærif] тари́ф.
tarnish ['tɑ:niʃ] 1. *v/t.* лиша́ть бле́ска (мета́лл); *fig.* [о]поро́чить; *v/i.* [по]тускне́ть (о мета́лле); 2. ту́склость *f*; *fig.* пятно́.
tarry[1] ['tæri] ме́длить, ме́шкать; ~ for ждать (В *or* Р), дожида́ться (Р).
tarry[2] ['tɑ:ri] вы́мазанный дёгтем.
tart [tɑ:t] 1. сла́дкая ватру́шка; 2. ки́слый, те́рпкий; е́дкий; *fig.* ко́лкий.
task [tɑ:sk] 1. зада́ча; уро́к; take to ~ призыва́ть к отве́ту; отчи́тывать [-ита́ть]; 2. дава́ть зада́ние (Д); обременя́ть [-ни́ть], перегружа́ть [-узи́ть].
tassel ['tæsl] ки́сточка (украше́ние).
taste [teist] 1. вкус; скло́нность *f* (for к Д); про́ба; 2. [по]про́бовать (на вкус), отве́д(ыв)ать; *fig.* испы́тывать [-пыта́ть]; ~ sweet быть сла́дким на вкус; ~**ful** ['teistful] □ (сде́ланный) со вку́сом; ~**less** [-lis] □ безвку́сный.
tasty ['teisti] □ F вку́сный; прия́тный.
tatter ['tætə] 1. изна́шивать(ся) в лохмо́тья; рва́ть(ся) в кло́чья; 2. ~s *pl.* лохмо́тья *n/pl.*; кло́чья *m/pl.* (*sg.* клок).
tattle ['tætl] 1. болтовня́; 2. [по-]болта́ть; [по]суда́чить.
tattoo [tə'tu:] 1. ⚔ сигна́л вече́рней зари́; татуиро́вка; 2. татуи́ровать (*im*)*pf*.
taught [tɔ:t] *pt.* и *p. pt.* от teach.
taunt [tɔ:nt] 1. насме́шка, «шпи́лька»; 2. говори́ть ко́лкости (Д); [съ]язви́ть.
taut [tɔ:t] ⚓ ту́го натя́нутый; вполне́ испра́вный (о корабле́).
tavern ['tævən] таве́рна.
tawdry ['tɔ:dri] □ мишу́рный, безвку́сный.
tawny ['tɔ:ni] рыжева́то-кори́чневый.
tax [tæks] 1. нало́г (on на В); *fig.* напряже́ние; бре́мя *n*; испыта́ние; 2. облага́ть нало́гом; ⚖ такси́ровать (*im*)*pf.*; определя́ть разме́р (изде́ржек, штра́фа и т. п.); чрезме́рно напряга́ть (си́лы); подверга́ть испыта́нию; ~ a p. with a th. обвиня́ть [-ни́ть] кого́-либо в чём-либо; ~**ation** [tæk'seiʃən] обложе́ние нало́гом; взима́ние нало́га; ⚖ такса́ция.
taxi ['tæksi] 1. = ~**-cab** такси́ *n indecl.*; 2. е́хать в такси́; ✈ рули́ть.
taxpayer ['tækspeiə] налогоплате́льщик.
tea [ti:] чай.
teach [ti:tʃ] [*irr.*] [на]учи́ть, обуча́ть [-чи́ть]; преподава́ть; ~**able** ['ti:tʃəbl] □ спосо́бный к уче́нию; подлежа́щий обуче́нию; ~**er** ['ti:tʃə] учи́тель(ница *f*) *m*, преподава́тель (-ница *f*) *m*.
team [ti:m] упря́жка (лошаде́й и т. п.); *sport* кома́нда; брига́да, арте́ль *f* (рабо́чих); ~**ster** ['ti:mstə] возни́ца *m*; ~**-work** совме́стная рабо́та; согласо́ванная рабо́та.
teapot ['ti:pɔt] ча́йник (для зава́рки).
tear[1] [tɛə] 1. [*irr.*] дыра́, проре́ха; 2. [по]рва́ть(ся); разрыва́ть(ся) [разорва́ть(ся)]; *fig.* раздира́ть (-ся); [по]мча́ться.
tear[2] [tiə] слеза́ (*pl.* слёзы).
tearful ['tiəful] □ слезли́вый; по́лный слёз (о глаза́х).
tease [ti:z] 1. зади́ра *m/f*; челове́к, лю́бящий дразни́ть; 2. F дразни́ть; задира́ть (В); прист(ав)а́ть к (Д).
teat [ti:t] сосо́к.
technic|al ['teknikəl] □ техни́ческий; ~**ality** [tekni'kæliti] техни́ческая сторона́ де́ла; техни́ческая дета́ль *f*; ~**ian** [tek'niʃən] те́хник.
technique [tek'ni:k] те́хника.
technology [tek'nɔlədʒi] техноло́гия; техни́ческие нау́ки *f/pl.*
tedious ['ti:diəs] □ ску́чный, утоми́тельный.
tedium ['ti:diəm] ску́ка.
tee [ti:] мише́нь *f* (в и́грах); ме́тка для мяча́ (в го́льфе).
teem [ti:m] изоби́ловать, кише́ть (with Т).
teens [ti:nz] *pl.* во́зраст от трина́дцати до девятна́дцати лет.
teeth [ti:θ] *pl.* от tooth; ~**e** [ti:ð]: the child is teething у ребёнка прореза́ются зу́бы.
teetotal(l)er [ti:'toutlə] тре́звенник.
telegram ['teligræm] телегра́мма.
telegraph ['teligrɑ:f] 1. телегра́ф; 2. телеграфи́ровать (*im*)*pf.*; 3. *attr.*

телегра́фный; ~ic [teli'græfik] (~ally) телегра́фный; ~y [ti'legrəfi] телеграфи́я.
telephon|e ['telifoun] **1.** телефо́н; **2.** телефони́ровать (*im*)*pf*.; ~ic [teli'fɔnik] (~ally) телефо́нный; ~y [ti'lefəni] телефони́я; телефони́рование.
telephoto ['teli'foutou] *phot.* телефотогра́фия.
telescope ['teliskoup] **1.** телеско́п; **2.** скла́дывать(ся) [сложи́ть(ся)] (подо́бно телеско́пу); вреза́ться друг в дру́га (о ваго́нах при круше́нии).
televis|ion ['teli'viʒən] телеви́дение; ~or [-vaizə] телеви́зор.
tell [tel] [*irr.*] *v/t.* говори́ть [сказа́ть]; расска́зывать [-за́ть]; уверя́ть [уве́рить]; отлича́ть [-чи́ть]; ~ a p. to do a th. веле́ть кому́-либо что́-либо де́лать; ~ off F [вы́]брани́ть, «отде́л(ыв)ать»; *v/i.* ска́зываться [сказа́ться]; выделя́ться [вы́делиться]; расска́зывать [-за́ть] (about о П); ~er ['telə] расска́зчик; касси́р (в ба́нке); ~ing ['teliŋ] □ многоговоря́щий, многозначи́тельный; ~tale ['telteil] спле́тник (-ица); болту́н(ья); доно́счик (-ица); ⊕ предупреди́тельное сигна́льное приспособле́ние.
temper ['tempə] **1.** умеря́ть [уме́рить]; смягча́ть [-чи́ть]; ⊕ отпуска́ть [-сти́ть]; закаля́ть [-ли́ть] (*a fig.*); **2.** хара́ктер; настрое́ние; раздраже́ние, гнев; ⊕ о́тпуск (мета́лла); ~ament [-rəmənt] темпера́мент; ~amental [tempərə'mentl] □ темпера́ментный; ~ance ['tempərəns] уме́ренность *f*; ~ate [-rit] □ уме́ренный, возде́ржанный; ~ature ['tempritʃə] температу́ра.
tempest ['tempist] бу́ря; ~uous [tem'pestjuəs] □ бу́рный, бу́йный.
temple ['templ] храм; *anat.* висо́к.
tempor|al ['tempərəl] □ вре́менный; мирско́й, све́тский; ~ary [-rəri] □ вре́менный; ~ize [-raiz] стара́ться вы́играть вре́мя; приспособля́ться к обстоя́тельствам.
tempt [tempt] искуша́ть [-уси́ть], соблазня́ть [-ни́ть]; привлека́ть [-е́чь]; ~ation [temp'teiʃən] искуше́ние, собла́зн; ~ing [-tiŋ] □ зама́нчивый, соблазни́тельный.
ten [ten] **1.** де́сять; **2.** деся́ток.
tenable ['tenəbl] про́чный; ⚔ обороноспосо́бный.
tenaci|ous [ti'neiʃəs] □ упо́рный; це́пкий; вя́зкий; ~ty [ti'næsiti] це́пкость *f*; сто́йкость *f*, упо́рство.
tenant ['tenənt] education нанима́тель(ница *f*) *m*; арендáтор; жи́тель(ница *f*) *m*.
tend [tend] *v/i.* име́ть скло́нность (to к Д); клони́ться; направля́ться [-ра́виться]; *v/t.* [по]забо́титься о (П); уха́живать, [по]смотре́ть за (Т); ⊕ обслу́живать [-и́ть]; ~ance ['tendəns] уха́живание (of за Т); присмо́тр (of за Т); ~ency [-si] тенде́нция; накло́нность *f*.
tender ['tendə] **1.** □ *com.* не́жный; мя́гкий; сла́бый (о здоро́вье); чувстви́тельный; ла́сковый; чу́ткий; **2.** (официа́льное) предложе́ние; зая́вка (*part.* ✝); 🚂 те́ндер; ⚓ посы́льное су́дно; плаву́чая ба́за; legal ~ зако́нное платёжное сре́дство; **3.** предлага́ть [-ложи́ть]; представля́ть [-а́вить] (докуме́нты); приноси́ть [-нести́] (извине́ние, благода́рность); ~foot F новичо́к; ~ness [-nis] не́жность *f*.
tendon ['tendən] *anat.* сухожи́лие.
tendril ['tendril] ⚘ у́сик.
tenement ['tenimənt] снима́емая кварти́ра; ~ house многокварти́рный дом.
tenor ['tenə] ♪ те́нор; тече́ние, направле́ние; укла́д (жи́зни); о́бщий смысл (ре́чи и т. п.).
tens|e [tens] **1.** *gr.* вре́мя *n*; **2.** □ натя́нутый; возбуждённый; напряжённый; ~ion ['tenʃən] напряже́ние (*a.* ⚡); натяже́ние; *pol.* напряжённость *f*; натя́нутость *f*.
tent¹ [tent] **1.** пала́тка, тент; **2.** размеща́ть в пала́тках; жить в пала́тках.
tent² [~] **1.** тампо́н; **2.** вставля́ть тампо́н в (В).
tentacle ['tentəkl] *zo.* щу́пальце.
tentative ['tentətiv] □ про́бный; эксперимента́льный; ~ly в ви́де о́пыта.
tenth [tenθ] **1.** деся́тый; **2.** деся́тая часть *f*.
tenure ['tenjuə] владе́ние; пребыва́ние (в до́лжности); срок владе́ния.
tepid ['tepid] □ теплова́тый.
term [tə:m] **1.** преде́л; срок; семе́стр; те́рмин; ⅍ член; ⚖ се́ссия; день упла́ты аре́нды и т. п.; ~s *pl.* усло́вия; be on good (bad) ~s быть в хоро́ших (плохи́х) отноше́ниях; come to ~s прийти́ к соглаше́нию; **2.** выража́ть [вы́разить]; наз(ы)ва́ть; [на]именова́ть.
termina|l ['tə:minl] **1.** □ заключи́тельный; коне́чный; семестро́вый; **2.** коне́чный пункт; коне́чный слог; экза́мен в конце́ семе́стра; ⚡ зажи́м; *Am.* 🚂 коне́чная ста́нция; ~te [-neit] конча́ть(ся) [ко́нчить(ся)]; ~tion [tə:mi'neiʃən] оконча́ние; коне́ц.
terminus ['tə:minəs] 🚂 коне́чная ста́нция.
terrace ['terəs] терра́са; на́сыпь *f*; ряд домо́в; ~d [-t] располо́женный терра́сами.
terrestrial [ti'restriəl] □ земно́й; *zo.* сухопу́тный.
terrible ['terəbl] □ ужа́сный, стра́шный.

terri|fic [təˈrifik] (~ally) ужаса́ющий; F великоле́пный; **~fy** [ˈterifai] *v/t.* ужаса́ть [-сну́ть].
territor|ial [teriˈtɔːriəl] **1.** □ территориа́льный; земе́льный; ♀ Army, Force территориа́льная а́рмия; **2.** ⚔ солда́т территориа́льной а́рмии; **~y** [ˈteritəri] террито́рия; о́бласть *f*; сфе́ра.
terror [ˈterə] у́жас; терро́р; **~ize** [-raiz] терроризова́ть *(im)pf.*
terse [təːs] □ сжа́тый, вырази́тельный (стиль).
test [test] **1.** испыта́ние; крите́рий; про́ба; ана́лиз; ⚗ реакти́в; *attr.* испыта́тельный; про́бный; **2.** подверга́ть испыта́нию, прове́рке, (⚗) де́йствию реакти́ва.
testify [ˈtestifai] дава́ть показа́ние, свиде́тельствовать (to в по́льзу Р, against про́тив Р, on о П).
testimon|ial [testiˈmounjəl] аттеста́т; рекоменда́тельное письмо́; **~y** [ˈtestimeni] у́стное показа́ние; пи́сьменное свиде́тельство.
test-tube ⚗ проби́рка.
testy [ˈtesti] □ вспы́льчивый, раздражи́тельный.
tether [ˈteðə] **1.** при́вязь *f* (живо́тного); come to the end of one's ~ дойти́ до то́чки; **2.** привя́зывать [-за́ть] (живо́тное).
text [tekst] текст; те́ма (про́поведи); **~book** уче́бник, руково́дство.
textile [ˈtekstail] **1.** тексти́льный; **2.** ~s *pl.* тексти́льные изде́лия *n/pl.*; тка́ни *f/pl.*
texture [ˈtekstʃə] ткань *f*; ка́чество тка́ни; строе́ние, структу́ра (ко́жи и т. п.).
than [ðæn, ðən] чем, не́жели.
thank [θæŋk] **1.** [по]благодари́ть (В); ~ you благодарю́ вас; **2.** ~s *pl.* спаси́бо!; ~s to благодаря́ (Д); **~ful** [ˈθæŋkful] □ благода́рный; **~less** [-lis] □ неблагода́рный; **~sgiving** [θæŋksgiviŋ] благода́рственный моле́бен.
that [ðæt, ðət] **1.** *pron.* тот, та, то; те *pl.*; (*a.* э́тот и т. д.); кото́рый и т. д.; **2.** *cj.* что; что́бы.
thatch (θætʃ] **1.** соло́менная и́ли тростнико́вая кры́ша; **2.** крыть соло́мой и́ли тростнико́м.
thaw [θɔː] **1.** о́ттепель *f*; та́яние; **2.** *v/i.* [рас]та́ять; отта́ивать [отта́ять]; *v/t.* раста́пливать [растопи́ть] (снег и т. п.).
the [ðiː; пе́ред гла́сными ði; пе́ред согла́сными ðə] **1.** определённый член, арти́кль; **2.** *adv.* ~ ... ~ ... чем ..., тем ...
theatr|e [ˈθiətə] теа́тр; *fig.* аре́на; ~ of war теа́тр вое́нных де́йствий; **~ic(al** □) [θiˈætrik, -trikəl] театра́льный (*a. fig.*); сцени́ческий.
theft [θeft] воровство́, кра́жа.
their [ðɛə] *pron. poss.* (от they) их; свой, своя́, своё, свои́ *pl.*; **~s** [ðɛəz] *pron. poss. pred.* их, свой и т. д.
them [ðem, ðəm] *pron. pers.* (ко́свенный паде́ж от they) их, им.
theme [θiːm] те́ма, предме́т (разгово́ра и т. п.); шко́льное сочине́ние.
themselves [ðemˈselvz] *pron. refl.* себя́, -ся; *emphasis* са́ми.
then [ðen] **1.** *adv.* тогда́; пото́м, зате́м; **2.** *cj.* тогда́, в тако́м слу́чае; зна́чит; **3.** *adj.* тогда́шний.
thence *lit.* [ðens] отту́да; с того́ вре́мени; *fig.* отсю́да, из э́того.
theolog|ian [θiəˈloudʒiən] богосло́в; **~y** [θiˈɔlədʒi] богосло́вие.
theor|etic(al □) [θiəˈretik, -tikəl] теорети́ческий; **~ist** [ˈθiərist] теоре́тик; **~y** [ˈθiəri] тео́рия.
there [ðɛə] там, туда́; ~! вот!, ну!; ~ is, ~ are [ðəˈriz, ðəˈrɑː] есть, име́ется, име́ются; **~about(s)** [ˈðɛərəbaut(s)] побли́зости; о́коло э́того, приблизи́тельно; **~after** [ðɛərˈɑːftə] с э́того вре́мени; **~by** [ˈðɛəˈbai] посре́дством э́того; таки́м о́бразом; **~fore** [ˈðɛəfɔː] поэ́тому; сле́довательно; **~upon** [ˈðɛərəˈpɔn] по́сле того́, вслед за те́м; вследствие того́.
thermo|meter [θəˈmɔmitə] термо́метр, гра́дусник; **~s** [ˈθəːmɔs] (*or* ~ flask, ~ bottle) те́рмос.
these [ðiːz] *pl.* от this.
thes|is [ˈθiːsis], *pl.* **~es** [-siːz] те́зис; диссерта́ция.
they [ðei] *pron. pers.* они́.
thick [θik] **1.** □ *com.* то́лстый; густо́й; пло́тный; хри́плый (го́лос); F глу́пый; ~ with гу́сто покры́тый (Т); **2.** ча́ща; *fig.* гу́ща; in the ~ of в са́мой гу́ще (Р); в разга́ре (Р); **~en** [ˈθikən] [по]толсте́ть; сгуща́ть(ся) [сгусти́ть(ся)]; учаща́ться [участи́ться]; **~et** [ˈθikit] ча́ща; за́росли *f/pl.*; **~-headed** тупоголо́вый, тупоу́мный; **~ness** [ˈθiknis] толщина́; пло́тность *f*; сгущённость *f*; **~-set** [ˈθikˈset] гу́сто наса́женный; корена́стый; **~-skinned** (*a. fig.*) толстоко́жий.
thie|f [θiːf], *pl.* **~ves** [θiːvz] вор; **~ve** [θiːv] *v/t.* [у]красть; *v/i.* ворова́ть.
thigh [θai] бедро́.
thimble [ˈθimbl] напёрсток.
thin [θin] **1.** □ *com.* то́нкий; худо́й, худоща́вый; ре́дкий; жи́дкий; in a ~ house в полупусто́м за́ле (теа́тра); **2.** де́лать(ся) то́нким, утонча́ть(ся) [-чи́ть(ся)]; [по]реде́ть; [по]худе́ть.
thing [θiŋ] вещь *f*; предме́т; де́ло; ~s *pl.* ли́чные ве́щи *f/pl.*; бага́ж; оде́жда; принадле́жности *f/pl.*; the ~ (не́что) са́мое ва́жное, ну́жное; ~s are going better положе́ние улучша́ется.

think [θiŋk] [*irr.*] *v/i.* [по]ду́мать (of, about о П); мы́слить; полага́ть; вспомина́ть [вспо́мнить] (of о П); намерева́ться (+ *inf.*); приду́м(ыв)ать (of В); *v/t.* счита́ть [счесть]; ~ much of быть высо́кого мне́ния о (П).
third [θɔ:d] 1. тре́тий; 2. треть *f.*
thirst [θɔ:st] 1. жа́жда; 2. жа́ждать (for, after Р) (*part. fig.*); **~y** ['θəsti] □ томи́мый жа́ждой; I am ~ я хочу́ пить.
thirt|een ['θɔ:ti:n] трина́дцать; **~eenth** ['θɔ:'ti:nθ] трина́дцатый; **~ieth** ['θɔ:tiiθ] тридца́тый; **~y** ['θɔ:ti] три́дцать.
this [ðis] *pron. demonstr.* (*pl.* these) э́тот, э́та, э́то; э́ти *pl.*; ~ morning сего́дня у́тром.
thistle ['θisl] ♀ чертополо́х.
thong [θɔŋ] реме́нь *m*; плеть *f.*
thorn [θɔ:n] ♀ шип; колю́чка; *fig.* ~s *pl.* те́рния *n/pl.*; **~y** ['θɔ:ni] колю́чий; *fig.* тяжёлый, терни́стый.
thorough ['θʌrə] □ основа́тельный; соверше́нный; **~ly** *adv.* основа́тельно, доскона́льно; соверше́нно; **~bred** 1. чистокро́вный; 2. чистокро́вное живо́тное; **~fare** прохо́д; прое́зд; гла́вная арте́рия (го́рода); **~going** радика́льный.
those [ðouz] *pl.* от that.
though [ðou] *conj.* хотя́; да́же е́сли бы, хотя́ бы; *adv.* тем не ме́нее; одна́ко; всё-таки; as ~ как бу́дто, сло́вно.
thought [θɔ:t] 1. *pt.* и *p. pt.* от think; 2. мысль *f*; мышле́ние; размышле́ние; забо́та; внима́тельность *f*; **~ful** ['θɔ:tful] □ заду́мчивый; глубокомы́сленный; забо́тливый; внима́тельный (of к Д); **~less** ['θɔ:tlis] □ беспе́чный; необду́манный; невнима́тельный (of к Д).
thousand ['θauzənd] ты́сяча; **~th** ['θauzən(t)θ] 1. ты́сячный; 2. ты́сячная часть *f.*
thrash [θræʃ] [с]молоти́ть; [по]би́ть; F побежда́ть [-еди́ть] (в состяза́нии); ~ out тща́тельно обсужда́ть (вопро́с и т. п.); *s.* thresh; **~ing** ['θræʃiŋ] молотьба́; побо́и *m/pl.*, F взбу́чка.
thread [θred] 1. ни́тка, нить *f*; *fig.* нить *f*; ⊕ (винтова́я) резьба́, наре́зка; 2. продева́ть ни́тку в (иго́лку); нани́зывать [-за́ть] (бу́сы); ⊕ нареза́ть [-е́зать]; **~bare** ['θredbɛə] потёртый, изно́шенный; *fig.* изби́тый.
threat [θret] угро́за; **~en** ['θretn] *v/t.* [при]грози́ть, угрожа́ть (Д with Т); *v/i.* грози́ть.
three [θri:] 1. три; 2. тро́йка; **~fold** ['θri:fould] тройно́й; *adv.* втройне́; **~pence** ['θrepəns] три пе́нса (моне́та); **~-score** ['θri:'skɔ:] шестьдеся́т.
thresh [θreʃ] ✓ [с]молоти́ть; *s.* thrash; ~ out *fig.* = thrash out.
threshold ['θreʃ(h)ould] поро́г.
threw [θru:] *pt.* от throw.
thrice [θrais] три́жды.
thrift [θrift] бережли́вость *f*, эконо́мность *f*; **~less** ['θriftlis] □ расточи́тельный; **~y** ['θrifti] □ эконо́мный, бережли́вый.
thrill [θril] 1. *v/t.* [вз]волнова́ть; приводи́ть в тре́пет, [вз]будора́жить; *v/i.* [за]трепета́ть (with от Р); [вз]волнова́ться; 2. тре́пет; глубо́кое волне́ние; не́рвная дрожь *f*; **~er** ['θrilə] сенсацио́нный рома́н (*mst* детекти́вный).
thrive [θraiv] [*irr.*] процвета́ть; преуспева́ть; разраста́ться; **~n** ['θrivn] *p. pt.* от thrive.
throat [θrout] го́рло, гло́тка; clear one's ~ отка́шливаться [-ляться].
throb [θrɔb] 1. пульси́ровать; си́льно би́ться; 2. пульса́ция; бие́ние; *fig.* тре́пет.
throes [θrouz] *pl.* му́ки *f/pl.*; аго́ния; родовы́е му́ки *f/pl.*
throne [θroun] трон, престо́л.
throng [θrɔŋ] 1. толпа́, толчея́; 2. [с]толпи́ться; заполня́ть [-о́лнить] (о толпе́).
throttle ['θrɔtl] 1. [за]души́ть (за го́рло); ⊕ дроссели́ровать; 2. ⊕ дро́ссель *m.*
through [θru:] 1. че́рез (В); сквозь (В); по (Д); *adv.* насквозь; от нача́ла до конца́; 2. прямо́й, беспереса́дочный (по́езд и т. п.); сквозно́й (биле́т); **~out** [θru:'aut] 1. *prp.* че́рез (В); по всему́, всей ...; 2. повсю́ду; во всех отноше́ниях.
throve [θrouv] *pt.* от thrive.
throw [θrou] 1. [*irr.*] броса́ть [бро́сить], кида́ть [ки́нуть], мета́ть [метну́ть]; ~ over перебра́сывать [-бро́сить]; покида́ть [-и́нуть] (друзе́й); ~ up изверга́ть [-е́ргнуть]; вски́дывать [вски́нуть]; 2. бросо́к; броса́ние; **~n** [-n] *p. pt.* от throw.
thru *Am.* = through.
thrum [θrʌm] бренча́ть, тре́нькать.
thrush [θrʌʃ] дрозд.
thrust [θrʌst] 1. толчо́к; уда́р; ⊕ распо́р; end ~ осево́е давле́ние; 2. [*irr.*] толка́ть [-кну́ть]; ты́кать [ткнуть]; ~ o.s. into *fig.* втира́ться [втере́ться] в (В); ~ upon a p. навя́зывать [-за́ть] (Д).
thud [θʌd] 1. глухо́й звук; 2. па́дать с глухи́м зву́ком.
thug *Am.* [θʌg] уби́йца *m*, головоре́з.
thumb [θʌm] 1. большо́й па́лец (руки́); 2. захва́тывать [захвата́ть], загрязня́ть [-ни́ть] (па́льцами); **~tack** *Am.* чертёжная кно́пка.
thump [θʌmp] 1. глухо́й стук; тяжёлый уда́р; 2. наноси́ть тяжёлый уда́р (Д).

thunder ['θʌndə] 1. гром; 2. [за-] греме́ть; it ~s гром греми́т; *fig.* мета́ть гро́мы и мо́лнии; **~bolt** уда́р мо́лнии; **~clap** уда́р гро́ма; **~ous** ['θʌndərəs] □ грозово́й; громово́й, оглуша́ющий; **~-storm** гроза́; **~-struck** сражённый уда́ром мо́лнии; *fig.* как гро́мом поражённый.

Thursday ['θə:zdi] четве́рг.

thus [ðʌs] так, таки́м о́бразом.

thwart [θwɔ:t] 1. ба́нка (скамья́ для гребца́); 2. меша́ть исполне́нию (жела́ний и т. п.), расстра́ивать [-ро́ить].

tick [tik] 1. *zo.* клещ; креди́т, счёт; ти́канье; тик (мате́рия); 2. *v/i.* ти́кать; *v/t.* брать и́ли отпуска́ть в креди́т; ~ off отмеча́ть «пти́чкой»; F проб(и)ра́ть, отде́л(ыв)ать.

ticket ['tikit] 1. биле́т; ярлы́к; удостовере́ние; квита́нция; *Am.* спи́сок кандида́тов па́ртии; 2. прикрепля́ть ярлы́к к (Д); **~office**, *Am.* **~-window** биле́тная ка́сса.

tickl|e ['tikl] [по]щекота́ть; **~ish** [-iʃ] □ щекотли́вый.

tidal ['taidl]: ~ wave прили́вная волна́.

tide [taid] 1. low ~ отли́в; high ~ прили́в; *fig.* тече́ние; 2. *fig.* ~ over преодоле́(ва́)ть.

tidings ['taidiŋz] *pl.* но́вости *f/pl.*, изве́стия *n/pl.*

tidy ['taidi] 1. опря́тный, аккура́тный; значи́тельный; 2. приб(и)ра́ть; приводи́ть в поря́док.

tie [tai] 1. связь *f*; га́лстук; ра́вный счёт (голосо́в и́ли очко́в); ничья́; ⊕ скре́па; *pl.* у́зы *f/pl.*; 2. *v/t.* завя́зывать [-за́ть]; свя́зывать [-за́ть]; *v/i.* игра́ть вничью́; сравня́ть счёт.

tier [tiə] ряд; я́рус.

tie-up связь *f*; сою́з; *Am.* прекраще́ние рабо́ты и́ли у́личного движе́ния.

tiger ['taigə] тигр.

tight [tait] □ пло́тный, компа́ктный; непроница́емый; туго́й; ту́го натя́нутый; те́сный; F подвы́пивший; F ~ place *fig.* затрудни́тельное положе́ние; **~en** ['taitn] стя́гивать(ся) [стяну́ть(ся)] (*a.* ~ up); затя́гивать [-яну́ть]; подтя́гивать [-яну́ть]; **~-fisted** скупо́й; **~ness** ['taitnis] пло́тность *f* и т. д.; **~s** [taits] *pl.* трико́ *n indecl.*

tigress ['taigris] тигри́ца.

tile [tail] 1. черепи́ца; ка́фель *m*, изразе́ц; 2. крыть черепи́цей и т. д.

till [til] 1. де́нежный я́щик, ка́сса (в прила́вке); 2. *prp.* до (Р); 3. *cj.* пока́; 4. ⚒ возде́л(ыв)ать (В); [вс]паха́ть; **~age** ['tilidʒ] па́шня; обрабо́тка земли́.

tilt [tilt] 1. накло́нное положе́ние, накло́н; уда́р копьём; 2. наклоня́ть(ся) [-ни́ть(ся)]; опроки́дывать(ся) [-и́нуть(ся)]; би́ться на ко́пьях; ~ against боро́ться с (Т).

timber ['timbə] 1. лесоматериа́л, строево́й лес; ба́лка; 2. пло́тничать; столя́рничать; стро́ить из де́рева.

time [taim] 1. вре́мя *n*; пери́од; пора́; раз; такт; темп; at the same ~ в то же вре́мя; for the ~ being пока́, на вре́мя; in (*or* on) ~ во́время; 2. (уда́чно) выбира́ть вре́мя для (Р); назнача́ть вре́мя для (Р); хронометри́ровать (*im*)*pf.*; **~ly** ['taimli] своевре́менный; **~-piece** часы́ *m/pl.*; **~-table** 🚂 расписа́ние.

timid ['timid] □, **timorous** ['timərəs] □ ро́бкий.

tin [tin] 1. о́лово; (*a.* **~-plate**) жесть *f*; жестя́нка; 2. [по]луди́ть; [за-] консерви́ровать (в жестя́нках).

tincture ['tiŋktʃə] 1. ⚕ тинкту́ра; *fig.* отте́нок; 2. окра́шивать [окра́сить].

tinfoil ['tin'fɔil] фо́льга.

tinge [tindʒ] 1. слегка́ окра́шивать; *fig.* придава́ть отте́нок (Д); 2. лёгкая окра́ска; *fig.* отте́нок.

tingle ['tiŋgl] испы́тывать и́ли вызыва́ть пока́лывание (в онеме́вших чле́нах), пощи́пывание (на моро́зе), зуд, звон в уша́х и т. п.

tinker ['tiŋkə] 1. луди́льщик; 2. неуме́ло чини́ть (at В); вози́ться (at с Т).

tinkle ['tiŋkl] звя́кать [-кнуть].

tin-plate ['tin'pleit] (бе́лая) жесть *f*.

tinsel ['tinsəl] блёстки *f/pl.*; мишура́.

tinsmith ['tinsmiθ] жестя́н(щ)ик.

tint [tint] 1. кра́ска; отте́нок, тон; 2. слегка́ окра́шивать.

tiny ['taini] □ о́чень ма́ленький, кро́шечный.

tip [tip] 1. (то́нкий) коне́ц; наконе́чник; ко́нчик; чаевы́е *pl.*; ча́стная информа́ция; намёк; лёгкий толчо́к; 2. снабжа́ть наконе́чником; опроки́дывать [-и́нуть]; дава́ть на чай (Д); дава́ть ча́стную информа́цию (Д).

tipple ['tipl] пья́нствовать; выпи(ва́)ть, пить.

tipsy ['tipsi] подвы́пивший.

tiptoe ['tip(')tou]: on ~ на цы́почках.

tire [taiə] 1. о́бод колеса́; *mot.* ши́на; 2. утомля́ть [-ми́ть]; уст(ав)а́ть; **~d** [-d] уста́лый; **~less** ['taiəlis] неутоми́мый; **~some** [-səm] утоми́тельный; надое́дливый; ску́чный.

tiro ['taiərou] новичо́к.

tissue ['tisju:] ткань *f* (*a. biol.*); *fig.* сплете́ние (лжи и т. п.); **~-paper** [-'peipə] шёлковая бума́га; папиро́сная бума́га.

titbit ['titbit] ла́комый кусо́чек; *fig.* пика́нтная но́вость *f.*
titillate ['titileit] [по]щекота́ть.
title ['taitl] загла́вие; ти́тул; зва́ние; ⚖ пра́во со́бственности (to на В); ~d титуло́ванный.
titter ['titə] **1.** хихи́канье; **2.** хихи́кать [-кнуть].
tittle ['titl] мале́йшая части́ца; to a ~ тю́телька в тю́тельку; **~-tattle** [-tætl] спле́тни *f/pl.*, болтовня́.
to [tu:, tu, tə] *prp.* (ука́зывает на направле́ние движе́ния, цель): к (Д); в (В); на (В); (ука́зывает на лицо́, по отноше́нию к кото́рому что́-либо происхо́дит, и соотве́тствует ру́сскому да́тельному падежу́): ~ me *etc.* мне и т. д.; ~ and fro *adv.* взад и вперёд; (части́ца, слу́жащая показа́телем инфинити́ва): ~ work рабо́тать; I weep ~ think of it я пла́чу, ду́мая об э́том.
toad [toud] жа́ба; **~stool** пога́нка (гриб); **~y** ['toudi] **1.** подхали́м; **2.** подхали́мничать пе́ред (Т).
toast [toust] **1.** грено́к; тост; **2.** приготовля́ть гренки́; поджа́ри(ва)ть; *fig.* гре́ть(ся) (у огня́); пить за чьё-либо здоро́вье, пить за (В).
tobacco [tə'bækou] таба́к; **~nist** [tə'bækənist] торго́вец таба́чными изде́лиями.
toboggan [tə'bɔgən] **1.** сала́зки *f/pl.*; **2.** ката́ться на сала́зках (с горы́).
today [tə'dei] сего́дня; в на́ше вре́мя.
toe [tou] **1.** па́лец (на ноге́); носо́к (чулка́, башмака́); **2.** каса́ться носко́м (Р).
together [tə'geðə] вме́сте; друг с дру́гом; подря́д, непреры́вно.
toil [tɔil] **1.** тяжёлый труд; **2.** уси́ленно труди́ться; идти́ с трудо́м.
toilet ['tɔilit] туале́т (одева́ние и костю́м); убо́рная; **~-table** туале́тный сто́лик.
toilsome ['tɔilsəm] □ тру́дный, утоми́тельный.
token ['toukən] знак; приме́та; пода́рок на па́мять; ~ money билло́нные де́ньги *f/pl.*
told [tould] *pt.* и *p. pt.* от tell.
tolera|ble ['tɔlərəbl] □ терпи́мый; сно́сный; **~nce** [-rəns] терпи́мость *f*; **~nt** [-rənt] □ терпи́мый; **~te** [-reit] [по]терпе́ть, допуска́ть [-сти́ть]; **~tion** [tɔlə'reiʃən] терпи́мость *f*; допуще́ние.
toll [toul] по́шлина; *fig.* дань *f*; **~-bar, ~-gate** заста́ва (где взима́ется по́шлина).
tom [tɔm]: ~ cat кот.
tomato [tə'mɑ:tou, *Am.* tə'meitou], *pl.* **~es** [-z] помидо́р, тома́т.
tomb [tu:m] моги́ла; надгро́бный па́мятник.
tomboy ['tɔmbɔi] сорване́ц (о де́вочке).
tomfool ['tɔm'fu:l] шут; дура́к.
tomorrow [tə'mɔrou] за́втра.
ton [tʌn] (metric) то́нна (= 1000 кг).
tone [toun] **1.** тон (♪, *paint.*, *fig.*); интона́ция; **2.** придава́ть жела́тельный тон (зву́ку, кра́ске); настра́ивать [-ро́ить] (инструме́нт).
tongs [tɔŋz] *pl.* щипцы́ *m/pl.*, кле́щи́ *f/pl.*
tongue [tʌŋ] язы́к; hold one's ~ держа́ть язы́к за зуба́ми; **~-tied** ['tʌŋtaid] косноязы́чный; молчали́вый.
tonic ['tɔnik] **1.** (**~ally**) тони́ческий (*a.* ♪); укрепля́ющий; **2.** ♪ основно́й тон; ⚕ укрепля́ющее сре́дство.
tonight [tə'nait] сего́дня ве́чером.
tonnage ['tʌnidʒ] ⚓ тонна́ж; грузоподъёмность *f*; грузова́я по́шлина.
tonsil ['tɔnsl] *anat.* гла́нда, минда́лина.
too [tu:] та́кже, то́же; сли́шком; о́чень.
took [tuk] *pt.* от take.
tool [tu:l] (рабо́чий) инструме́нт; ору́дие (*a. fig.*)
toot [tu:t] **1.** звук рожка́, гудо́к; **2.** труби́ть в рожо́к.
tooth [tu:θ] (*pl.* teeth) зуб; **~ache** зубна́я боль *f*; **~-brush** зубна́я щётка; **~less** ['tu:θlis] □ беззу́бый; **~pick** зубочи́стка; **~some** ['tu:θsəm] вку́сный.
top [tɔp] **1.** ве́рхняя часть *f*; верху́шка, верши́на (горы́); маку́шка (головы́, де́рева); верх (автомоби́ля, ле́стницы, страни́цы); волчо́к; at the ~ of one's voice во весь го́лос; on ~ наверху́; **2.** вы́сший, пе́рвый; максима́льный (о ско́рости и т. п.); **3.** покры́(ва́)ть (све́рху); *fig.* превыша́ть [-ы́сить]; быть во главе́ (Р).
toper ['toupə] пья́ница *m/f.*
top-hat F цили́ндр (шля́па).
topic ['tɔpik] те́ма, предме́т; **~al** ['tɔpikəl] ме́стный; злободне́вный.
topmost ['tɔpmoust] са́мый ве́рхний; са́мый ва́жный.
topple ['tɔpl] опроки́дывать(ся) [-и́нуть(ся)] (*a.* ~ over).
topsyturvy ['tɔpsi'tə:vi] □ вверх дном; ши́ворот-навы́ворот.
torch [tɔtʃ] фа́кел; electric ~ карма́нный электри́ческий фона́рь *m*; **~-light** свет фа́кела; ~ procession фа́кельное ше́ствие.
tore [tɔ:] *pt.* от tear.
torment **1.** ['tɔ:ment] муче́ние, му́ка; **2.** [tɔ:'ment] [из-, за]му́чить; изводи́ть [извести́].
torn [tɔ:n] *p. pt.* от tear.
tornado [tɔ:'neidou] торна́до *m indecl.*, смерч; урага́н *a. fig.*
torpedo [tɔ:'pi:dou] **1.** торпе́да; **2.**

торпеди́ровать (*im*)*pf.*; *fig.* взрыва́ть [взорва́ть].
torpid ['tɔ:pid] □ онеме́лый, оцепене́лый; вя́лый, апати́чный; **~ity** [tɔ:'piditi], **torpor** ['tɔ:pə] оцепене́ние; апа́тия.
torrent ['tɔrənt] пото́к (*a. fig.*).
torrid ['tɔrid] жа́ркий, зно́йный.
tortoise ['tɔ:təs] *zo.* черепа́ха.
tortuous ['tɔ:tjuəs] □ изви́листый; *fig.* укло́нчивый, нейскренний.
torture ['tɔ:tʃə] **1.** пы́тка; **2.** пыта́ть, [из-, за]му́чить.
toss [tɔs] **1.** мета́ние, броса́ние; толчо́к, сотрясе́ние; (*a.* ~-up) броса́ние моне́ты (в орля́нке); **2.** броса́ть [бро́сить]; беспоко́йно мета́ться (о больно́м); вски́дывать [-и́нуть] (го́лову); подбра́сывать [-ро́сить] (*mst* ~ up); ~ (up) игра́ть в орля́нку; *sport* разы́грывать воро́та.
tot [tɔt] F ма́ленький ребёнок, малы́ш.
total ['toutl] **1.** □ по́лный, абсолю́тный; тота́льный; о́бщий; **2.** це́лое, су́мма; ито́г; **3.** подводи́ть ито́г, подсчи́тывать [-ита́ть]; составля́ть в ито́ге; равня́ться (Д); **~itarian** [toutæli'tɛəriən] тоталита́рный; **~ity** [tou'tæliti] вся су́мма, всё коли́чество.
totter ['tɔtə] идти́ неве́рной похо́дкой; шата́ться [(по)шатну́ться].
touch [tʌtʃ] **1.** осяза́ние; прикоснове́ние; *fig.* соприкоснове́ние, обще́ние; чу́точка; при́месь *f*; лёгкий при́ступ (боле́зни); ♪ туше́ *n indecl.*; штрих; **2.** тро́гать [тро́нуть] (В) (*a. fig.*); прикаса́ться [-косну́ться], притра́гиваться [-тро́нуться] к (Д); *fig.* каса́ться [косну́ться] (Р), затра́гивать [-ро́нуть] (В) (те́му и т. п.); be ~ed *fig.* быть тро́нутым; быть слегка́ поме́шанным; ~ up отде́л(ыв)ать, поправля́ть [-а́вить] (не́сколькими штриха́ми); ~ at ⚓ заходи́ть [зайти́] в (порт); **~ing** ['tʌtʃiŋ] тро́гательный; **~stone** пробі́рный ка́мень *m*, осело́к; *fig.* про́бный ка́мень *m*; **~y** ['tʌtʃi] □ оби́дчивый; сли́шком чувстви́тельный.
tough [tʌf] **1.** жёсткий; вя́зкий; упру́гий; выно́сливый; тру́дный; **2.** *Am.* хулига́н; **~en** ['tʌfn] де́лать(ся) жёстким, пло́тным и т. д.; **~ness** ['tʌfnis] жёсткость *f* и т. д.
tour [tuə] **1.** кругово́е путеше́ствие; турне́ *n indecl.*; тур, объе́зд; **2.** соверша́ть путеше́ствие и́ли турне́ по (Д); путеше́ствовать (through по Д); **~ist** ['tuərist] тури́ст(ка); ~ agency бюро́ путеше́ствий.
tournament [-nəmənt] турни́р.
tousle ['tauzl] взъеро́ши(ва)ть, растрёпывать [-репа́ть].
tow [tou] ⚓ **1.** букси́рный кана́т, трос; буксиро́вка; take in ~ брать на букси́р; **2.** букси́ровать; тяну́ть (ба́ржу) на бечеве́.
towards [tə'wɔ:dz, tɔ:dʒ] *prp.* (ука́зывает на направле́ние к предме́ту, отноше́ние к чему́-либо) по направле́нию к (Д); к (Д), по отноше́нию к (Д); для (Р).
towel ['tauəl] полоте́нце.
tower ['tauə] **1.** ба́шня; вы́шка; *fig.* опо́ра; **2.** возвыша́ться [-ы́ситься] (above, over над Т) (*a. fig.*).
town [taun] **1.** го́род; **2.** *attr.* городско́й; ~ council городско́й сове́т; ~ hall ра́туша; **~sfolk** ['taunzfouk], **~speople** [-pi:pl] горожа́не *m/pl.*; **~sman** ['taunzmən] горожа́нин; сограждани́н.
toxi|c(al □) ['tɔksik, -sikəl] ядови́тый; **~n** ['tɔksin] токси́н.
toy [tɔi] **1.** игру́шка; заба́ва; безделу́шка; **2.** *attr.* игру́шечный; **3.** игра́ть; забавля́ться; флиртова́ть; **~book** де́тская кни́га с карти́нками.
trace [treis] **1.** след; черта́; постро́мка; **2.** [на]черти́ть; высле́живать [вы́следить] (В); просле́живать [-еди́ть] (В); *a. fig.* [с]кальки́ровать.
tracing [treisiŋ] чертёж на ка́льке.
track [træk] **1.** след; просёлочная доро́га; тропи́нка; бегова́я доро́жка; 🚂 колея́, ре́льсовый путь *m*; **2.** следи́ть за (Т); просле́живать [-еди́ть] (В); ~ down, ~ out высле́живать [вы́следить] (В).
tract [trækt] тракта́т; брошю́ра; простра́нство, полоса́ (земли́, воды́).
tractable ['træktəbl] сгово́рчивый; поддаю́щийся обрабо́тке.
tract|ion ['trækʃən] тя́га; волоче́ние; ~ engine тяга́ч; **~or** [træ'ktə] ⊕ тра́ктор.
trade [treid] **1.** профе́ссия; ремесло́; торго́вля; **2.** торгова́ть (in Т; with с Т); обме́нивать [-ня́ть] (for на В); ~ on испо́льзовать (*im*)*pf.*; **~-mark** фабри́чная ма́рка; **~-price** опто́вая цена́; **~r** ['treidə] торго́вец; торго́вое су́дно; **~sman** ['treidzmən] торго́вец, ла́вочник; реме́сленник; **~(s)-union** ['treid(z)'ju:njən] профсою́з; **~wind** ⚓ пасса́тный ве́тер.
tradition [trə'diʃən] тради́ция; преда́ние; ста́рый обы́чай; **~al** □ традицио́нный.
traffic [træfik] **1.** движе́ние (у́личное, железнодоро́жное и т. п.); торго́вля; ~ jam зато́р у́личного движе́ния; **2.** торгова́ть.
traged|ian (trə'dʒi:diən] а́втор траге́дии; тра́гик; **~y** ['trædʒidi] траге́дия.
tragic(al □) ['trædʒik, -dʒikəl] траги́ческий, траги́чный.

trail [treil] **1.** след; тропá; **2.** *v/t.* таскáть, [по]тащи́ть, [по]волочи́ть; идти́ по слéду (P); *v/i.* таскáться, [по]тащи́ться; ⚘ свисáть [сви́снуть]; **~er** ['treilə] *mot.* прицéп.

train [trein] **1.** пóезд; шлейф (плáтья); цепь *f*, верени́ца; хвост (комéты, павли́на); сви́та, толпá (поклóнников); by ~ пóездом; **2.** воспи́тывать [-тáть]; приучáть [-чи́ть]; [на]тренировáть(ся); ⚔ обучáть [-чи́ть]; [вы́]дрессировáть.

trait [treit] чертá (лицá, харáктера).

traitor ['treitə] предáтель *m*, измéнник.

tram [træm] *s.* ~-car, ~way; **~-car** ['træmkɑ:] вагóн трамвáя.

tramp [træmp] **1.** бродя́га *m*; (дóлгое) путешéствие пешкóм; звук тяжёлых шагóв; **2.** тяжелó ступáть; тащи́ться с трудóм; F тóпать; бродя́жничать; **~le** ['træmpl] топтáть; тяжелó ступáть; поп(и)рáть (B); ~ down затáптывать [-топтáть].

tramway ['træmwei] трамвáй.

trance [trɑ:ns] ⚕ транс; экстáз.

tranquil ['træŋkwil] □ спокóйный; **~lity** [træŋ'kwiliti] спокóйствие; **~lize** ['træŋkwilaiz] успокáивать (-ся) [-кóить(ся)].

transact [træn'zækt] проводи́ть [-вести́] (дéло), совершáть [-ши́ть]; **~ion** [-'zækʃən] дéло, сдéлка; ведéние, отправлéние (дéла); **~s** *pl.* труды́ *m/pl.*, протокóлы *m/pl.* (наýчного óбщества).

transatlantic ['trænzət'læntik] трансатланти́ческий.

transcend [træn'send] переступáть предéлы (P); превосходи́ть [-взойти́], превышáть [-вы́сить].

transcribe [træns'kraib] переписывать [-сáть]; *gr.*, ♪ транскриби́ровать *(im)pf.*

transcript ['trænskript] кóпия; **~ion** [træn'skripʃən] перепи́сывание; кóпия; *gr.*, ♪ транскри́пция.

transfer 1. [træns'fə:] *v/t.* переноси́ть [-нести́], перемещáть [-мести́ть]; перед(ав)áть; переводи́ть [-вести́] (в другóй гóрод, на другýю рабóту); *v/i. Am.* пересáживаться [-сéсть]; **2.** ['trænsfə:] перенóс; передáча; трансфéрт; перевóд; *Am.* пересáдка; **~able** [træns'fə:rəbl] предостáвленный с прáвом передáчи; допускáющий передáчу.

transfigure [træns'figə] видоизменя́ть [-ни́ть]; преображáть [-рази́ть].

transfix [-'fiks] пронзáть [-зи́ть]; прокáлывать [-колóть]; **~ed** *fig.* прикóванный к мéсту (with от P).

transform (-'fɔ:m] превращáть [-врати́ть]; преобразóвывать [-зовáть]; **~ation** [-fə'meiʃən] преобразовáние; превращéние; ⚡ трансформáция.

transfuse [-'fu:z] перели́(вá)ть; ⚕ дéлать переливáние (крóви); *fig.* перед(ав)áть (свой энтузиáзм и т. п.).

transgress (-'gres] *v/t.* преступáть [-пи́ть], нарушáть [-ýшить] (закóн и т. п.); *v/i.* [со]греши́ть; **~ion** [-'greʃən] проступок; нарушéние (закóна и т. п.); **~or** [-'gresə] (право)наруши́тель(ница *f*) *m*; грéшник (-ица).

transient ['trænʃənt] **1.** *s.* transitory; **2.** *Am.* проéзжий (-жая).

transition [træn'siʒən] перехóд; перехóдный пери́од.

transitory ['trænsitəri] □ мимолётный, скоротéчный, скоропреходя́щий.

translat|e [trɑ:ns'leit] переводи́ть [-вести́] (from с P, into на B); *fig.* перемещáть [-мести́ть]; **~ion** [trɑ:ns'leiʃən] перевóд.

translucent [trænz'lu:snt] просвéчивающий; полупрозрáчный.

transmigration [trænzmai'greiʃən] переселéние.

transmission [trænz'miʃən] передáча (*a.* ⊕); пересы́лка; ⊕ трансми́ссия; *radio* передáча; трансля́ция; *opt.* пропускáние.

transmit [trænz'mit] отправля́ть [-áвить]; пос(ы)лáть; перед(ав)áть (*a. radio*); *opt.* пропускáть [-сти́ть]; **~ter** [-ə] передáтчик (*a. radio*); *tel.* микрофóн.

transmute [trænz'mju:t] превращáть [-врати́ть].

transparent [træns'pɛərənt] □ прозрáчный.

transpire [-'paiə] испаря́ться [-ри́ться]; просáчиваться [-сочи́ться]; *fig.* обнарýжи(ва)ться.

transplant [-'plɑ:nt] пересáживать [-сади́ть]; *fig.* переселя́ть [-ли́ть].

transport 1. [træns'pɔ:t] перевози́ть [-везти́]; перемещáть [-мести́ть]; *fig.* увлекáть [-éчь], восхищáть [-ити́ть]; **2.** ['trænspɔ:t] трáнспорт; перевóзка; трáнспортное (-ные) срéдство (-ства *n/pl.*); be in ~s быть вне себя́ (of от P); **~ation** [trænspɔ:'teiʃən] перевóзка.

transpose [træns'pouz] перемещáть [-мести́ть]; переставля́ть [-áвить] (словá и т. п.); ♪ транспони́ровать *(im)pf.*

transverse ['trænzvə:s] □ поперéчный.

trap [træp] **1.** ловýшка, западня́; капкáн; **2.** расставля́ть ловýшки; лови́ть в ловýшку; *fig.* замани́ть в ловýшку; **~-door** ['træpdɔ:] люк; опускнáя дверь *f*.

trapeze [trə'pi:z] трапéция.

trapper ['træpə] охóтник, стáвящий капкáны.

trappings ['træpiŋz] *pl.* ко́нская (пара́дная) сбру́я; пара́дный мунди́р.

traps [træps] *pl.* F ли́чные ве́щи *f/pl.*; бага́ж.

trash [træʃ] хлам; отбро́сы *m/pl.*; *fig.* дрянь *f*; макулату́ра (о кни́ге); вздор, ерунда́; **~y** ['træʃi] □ дрянно́й.

travel ['trævl] **1.** *v/i.* путеше́ствовать; е́здить, [по]е́хать; передвига́ться [-и́нуться]; распространя́ться [-ни́ться] (о све́те, зву́ке); *v/t.* объезжа́ть [-е́здить, -е́хать]; проезжа́ть [-е́хать] (... км в час и т. п.); **2.** путеше́ствие; ⊕ ход; (пере)движе́ние; **~(l)er** [-ə] путеше́ственник (-ица).

traverse ['trævə:s] **1.** пересека́ть [-се́чь]; проходи́ть [пройти́] (В); **2.** попере́чина; ⚓, ⚔ тра́верс.

travesty ['trævisti] **1.** паро́дия; искаже́ние; **2.** пароди́ровать; искажа́ть [искази́ть].

trawler ['trɔ:lə] тра́льщик.

tray [trei] подно́с; лото́к.

treacher|ous ['tretʃərəs] □ преда́тельский, вероло́мный; ненадёжный; **~y** [-ri] преда́тельство, вероло́мство.

treacle ['tri:kl] па́тока.

tread [tred] **1.** [*irr.*] ступа́ть [-пи́ть]; **~ down** зата́птывать [затопта́ть]; **2.** по́ступь *f*, похо́дка; ступе́нька; *mot.* проте́ктор; **~le** ['tredl] педа́ль *f* (велосипе́да); подно́жка (шве́йной маши́ны).

treason ['tri:zn] изме́на; **~able** [-əbl] □ изме́ннический.

treasure ['treʒə] **1.** сокро́вище; **2.** храни́ть; высо́ко́ цени́ть; **~r** [-rə] казначе́й.

treasury ['treʒəri] казначе́йство; сокро́вищница.

treat [tri:t] **1.** *v/t.* обраба́тывать [-бо́тать]; ⚕ лечи́ть; угоща́ть [угости́ть] (to Т); обраща́ться [обрати́ться] с (Т), обходи́ться [обойти́сь] с (Т); *v/i.* **~ of** име́ть предме́том, обсужда́ть [-уди́ть] (В); **~ with** вести́ перегово́ры с (Т); **2.** удово́льствие, наслажде́ние; угоще́ние; **~ise** ['tri:tiz] тракта́т; **~-ment** ['tri:tmənt]; обрабо́тка (Т); лече́ние; обраще́ние (of с Т); **~y** ['tri:ti] догово́р.

treble ['trebl] **1.** □ тройно́й, утро́енный; **2.** тройно́е коли́чество; ♪ ди́скант; **3.** утра́ивать(ся) [утро́ить(ся)].

tree [tri:] де́рево; родосло́вное де́рево; (сапо́жная) коло́дка.

trefoil ['trefɔil] трили́стник.

trellis ['trelis] **1.** решётка; ✐ шпале́ра; **2.** обноси́ть решёткой; сажа́ть (расте́ния) шпале́рой.

tremble ['trembl] [за]дрожа́ть, [за-] трясти́сь (with от Р).

tremendous [tri'mendəs] □ стра́шный, ужа́сный; F грома́дный.

tremor ['tremə] дрожа́ние.

tremulous ['tremjuləs] □ дрожа́щий; тре́петный, ро́бкий.

trench [trentʃ] **1.** кана́ва; ⚔ транше́я, око́п; **2.** рыть рвы, транше́и и т. п.; вска́пывать [вскопа́ть]; **~ (up)on** посяга́ть [-гну́ть] на (В); **~ant** ['tren(t)ʃənt] □ ре́зкий, ко́лкий.

trend [trend] **1.** направле́ние (*a. fig.*); *fig.* тече́ние; напра́вленность *f*; **2.** отклоня́ться [-ни́ться] (to к Д) (о грани́це и т. п.); име́ть тенде́нцию (towards к Д).

trespass ['trespəs] **1.** наруша́ть грани́цы (on Р); соверша́ть просту́пок; злоупотребля́ть [-би́ть] (on Т); **2.** наруше́ние грани́ц; злоупотребле́ние ([up]on Т); **~er** [-ə] наруши́тель грани́ц; правонаруши́тель *m*.

tress [tres] ло́кон; коса́.

trestle ['tresl] ко́злы *f/pl.*; подста́вка.

trial ['traiəl] испыта́ние; о́пыт, про́ба; ⚖ суде́бное разбира́тельство; суд; **on ~** на испыта́нии, на испыта́ние; под судо́м; **give a. p. a ~** нанима́ть кого́-либо на испыта́тельный срок; **~ ...** *attr.* про́бный, испыта́тельный.

triang|le ['traiæŋgl] треуго́льник; **~ular** [trai'æŋgjulə] □ треуго́льный.

tribe [traib] пле́мя *n*; *contp.* компа́ния.

tribun|al [trai'bju:nl] суд; трибуна́л; **~e** ['tribju:n] трибу́на; трибу́н.

tribut|ary ['tribjutəri] **1.** □ платя́щий дань; *fig.* подчинённый; спосо́бствующий; **2.** да́нник (-ица); *geogr.* прито́к; **~e** ['tribju:t] дань *f*; подноше́ние.

trice [trais]: **in a ~** мгнове́нно.

trick [trik] **1.** шту́ка, ша́лость *f*; фо́кус, трюк; уло́вка; сноро́вка; **2.** обма́нывать [-ну́ть]; наду́(ва́)ть; иску́сно украша́ть; **~ery** ['trikəri] надува́тельство; проде́лка.

trickle ['trikl] те́чь стру́йкой; сочи́ться.

trick|ster ['trikstə] обма́нщик; **~y** ['triki] □ хи́трий; мудрёный, сло́жный, тру́дный.

tricycle ['traisikl] трёхколёсный велосипе́д.

trifl|e ['traifl] **1.** пустя́к; ме́лочь *f*; **a ~** *fig.* немно́жко; **2.** *v/i.* [по]шути́ть; занима́ться пустяка́ми; *v/t.* **~ away** зря тра́тить; **~ing** ['traifliŋ] пустя́чный, пустяко́вый.

trig [trig] **1.** опря́тный; наря́дный; **2.** наряжа́ть [-яди́ть]; [за]тормози́ть.

trigger ['trigə] ⚔ спусково́й крючо́к; ⊕ соба́чка, защёлка.

trill [tril] **1.** трель *f*; **2.** выводи́ть трель.

trim [trim] **1.** □ наря́дный; приведённый в поря́док; **2.** наря́д;

порядок; состояние готовности; ⚓ (правильное) размещение груза; 3. приводить в порядок; (~ up) подрезать [-езать], подстригать [-ичь]; отдел(ыв)ать (платье); ⚓ уравновешивать [-есить] (судно); **~ming** ['trimiŋ] *mst* ~s *pl.* отделка (на платье); приправа, гарнир.
trinket ['triŋkit] безделушка; брелок; ~s *pl. contp.* финтифлюшки *f/pl.*
trip [trip] 1. путешествие; поездка; экскурсия; спотыкание; *fig.* обмолвка, ошибка; 2. *v/i.* идти легко и быстро; спотыкаться [споткнуться]; обмолвиться *pf.*; *v/t.* подставлять ножку (Д).
tripartite ['trai'pɑ:tait] тройственный; состоящий из трёх частей.
tripe [traip] *cook.* рубец.
triple ['tripl] тройной; утроенный; **~ts** ['triplits] *pl.* тройня *sg.*
tripper [tripə] F экскурсант(ка).
trite [trait] □ банальный, избитый.
triturate ['tritjəreit] растирать в порошок.
triumph ['traiəmf] 1. триумф; торжество; 2. праздновать победу, триумф; торжествовать, восторжествовать *pf.* (over над Т); **~al** [trai'ʌmfəl] триумфальный; **~ant** [-fənt] □ победоносный; торжествующий.
trivial ['triviəl] □ обыденный; мелкий, пустой; тривиальный.
trod [trɔd] *pt.* от tread; **~den** ['trɔdn] *p. pt.* от tread.
troll [troul] напевать.
troll(e)y ['trɔli] вагонетка; 🚂 дрезина; *Am.* трамвай.
trollop ['trɔləp] *contp.* неряха *m/f*; проститутка.
trombone [trɔm'boun] ♪ тромбон.
troop [tru:p] 1. толпа; отряд; ⚔ кавалерийский или танковый взвод; *Am.* эскадрон; 2. двигаться или собираться толпой; ~ away, ~ off удаляться [-литься]; **~er** ['tru:pə] (рядовой) кавалерист; рядовой-танкист; **~s** *pl.* войска *n/pl.*
trophy ['troufi] трофей, добыча.
tropic ['trɔpik] тропик; ~s *pl.* тропики *m/pl.* (зона); **~(al** □) [~-pikəl] тропический.
trot [trɔt] 1. рысь (лошади); быстрый ход (человека); 2. бегать рысью; пускать рысью; [по]спешить.
trouble ['trʌbl] 1. беспокойство; волнение; заботы *f/pl.*, хлопоты *f/pl.*; затруднения *n/pl.*; горе, беда; take ~ утруждаться; 2. [по-] беспокоить(ся); [по]просить; утруждать [-удить]; don't ~! не трудитесь!; **~some** [-səm] трудный; причиняющий беспокойство.
trough [trɔf] корыто, кормушка; квашня; жёлоб.
trounce [trauns] F [по]бить, [вы-] пороть.
troupe [tru:p] *thea.* труппа.
trousers ['trauzəz] *pl.* брюки *f/pl.*
trout [traut] форель *f.*
trowel ['trauəl] лопатка (штукатура).
truant ['tru:ənt] 1. лентяй; прогульщик; ученик, прогулявший уроки; 2. ленивый; праздный.
truce [tru:s] перемирие.
truck [trʌk] 1. вагонетка; тележка; *Am.* грузовик; 🚂 (открытая) товарная платформа; мена; товарообмен; 2. перевозить на грузовиках; вести меновую торговлю; обменивать [-нять]; **~-farmer** *Am.* огородник.
truckle ['trʌkl] раболепствовать.
truculent ['trʌkjulənt] свирепый; грубый.
trudge [trʌdʒ] идти с трудом; таскаться, [по]тащиться.
true [tru:] верный; правильный; настоящий; it is ~ правда; come ~ сбы(ва)ться; ~ to nature точно такой, как в натуре.
truism ['tru:izm] трюизм.
truly ['tru:li] правдиво; лояльно; поистине; точно; yours ~ преданный (-ная) вам.
trump [trʌmp] 1. козырь *m*; 2. козырять [-рнуть]; бить козырем; ~ up выдумывать [выдумать]; **~ery** ['trʌmpəri] мишура; дрянь *f.*
trumpet ['trʌmpit] 1. труба; 2. [за-, про]трубить; *fig.* возвещать [-естить].
truncheon ['trʌntʃən] ⚔ (маршальский) жезл; дубинка (полицейского).
trundle ['trʌndl] катать(ся), [по-] катить(ся).
trunk [trʌŋk] ствол (дерева); туловище; хобот (слона); дорожный сундук; **~-call** *teleph.* вызов по междугородному телефону; **~-line** 🚂 магистраль *f*; *teleph.* междугородная линия.
truss [trʌs] 1. связка; большой пук; ⚕ бандаж; ⚠ стропильная ферма; 2. увязывать в пуки; скручивать руки (Д); ⚠ связывать [-зать]; укреплять [-пить].
trust [trʌst] 1. доверие; вера; ответственное положение; ✝ кредит; трест; on ~ в кредит; на веру; 2. *v/t.* доверять, [по]верить (Д); вверять [вверить], доверять [-ерить] (Д with В); *v/i.* полагаться [положиться] (in, to на В); надеяться (in, to на В); **~ee** [trʌs'ti:] ⚖ опекун; попечитель *m*; **~ful** ['trʌstful] □, **~ing** ['trʌstiŋ] □ доверчивый; **~worthy** [-wə:ði] заслуживающий доверия.
truth [tru:θ] правда; истина; **~ful** ['tru:θful] □ правдивый; верный.
try [trai] 1. испытывать [испы-

тать]; [по]пробовать; [по]пытаться; [по]стараться; утомлять [-мить]; ⚖ судить; ~ on примерять [-ерить] (на себя); 2. попытка; **~ing** ['traiiŋ] □ трудный; тяжёлый; раздражающий.

tub [tʌb] кадка; лохань *f*; бадья; F ванна.

tube [tju:b] труба, трубка; F метро *n indecl.* (в Лондоне).

tuber ['tju:bə] ♀ клубень *m*; **~culous** [tju:'bə:kjuləs] ⚕ туберкулёзный.

tubular ['tju:bjulə] □ трубчатый, цилиндрический.

tuck [tʌk] 1. складка, сборка (на платье); 2. делать складки; подбирать под себя; запрят(ыв)ать; ~ up подвёртывать [-вернуть] (подол); засучивать [-чить] (рукава).

Tuesday ['tju:zdi] вторник.

tuft [tʌft] пучок (травы); хохолок; бородка клинышком.

tug [tʌg] 1. рывок; гуж; ⚓ буксир; 2. тащить с усилием; дёргать [дёрнуть] (изо всех сил); ⚓ буксировать.

tuition [tju'iʃən] обучение.

tulip ['tju:lip] тюльпан.

tumble ['tʌmbl] 1. *v/i.* падать [упасть] (споткнувшись); кувыркаться [-кнуться]; опрокидываться [-инуться]; метаться (в постели); *v/t.* приводить в беспорядок, [по]мять; 2. падение; беспорядок; **~-down** [-daun] полуразрушенный; **~r** [-ə] акробат; бокал, (высокий) стакан.

tumid ['tju:mid] □ распухший; *fig.* напыщенный.

tumo(u)r ['tju:mə] опухоль *f*.

tumult ['tju:mʌlt] шум и крики; буйство; душевное возбуждение; **~uous** [tju'mʌltjuəs] шумный, буйный; возбуждённый.

tun [tʌn] большая бочка.

tuna ['tju:nə] тунец.

tune [tju:n] 1. мелодия, мотив; тон; строй; звук; in ~ настроенный (рояль); в тон; out of ~ расстроенный (рояль); не в тон; 2. настраивать[-роить](инструмент); ~ in *radio* настраивать приёмник (to на В); **~ful** ['tju:nful] □ мелодичный, гармоничный; **~less** ['tju:nlis] □ немелодичный.

tunnel ['tʌnl] 1. туннель *m* (*a.* тоннель *m*); ⚒ штольня; 2. проводить туннель через (В).

turbid ['tə:bid] мутный; туманный.

turbulent ['tə:bjulənt] бурный; буйный, непокорный.

tureen [tə'ri:n, tju'r-] суповая миска.

turf [tə:f] 1. дёрн; торф; конный спорт, скачки *f/pl.*; 2. обдернять [-нить]; **~y** ['tə:fi] покрытый дёрном, дернистый; торфяной.

turgid ['tə:dʒid] □ опухший; *fig.* напыщенный.

Turk [tə:k] турок, турчанка.

turkey ['tə:ki] индюк, индейка.

Turkish ['tə:kiʃ] 1. турецкий; 2. турецкий язык.

turmoil ['tə:mɔil] шум, суматоха; беспорядок.

turn [tə:n] 1. *v/t.* вращать, вертеть; поворачивать [повернуть]; оборачивать [обернуть]; точить (на токарном станке); превращать [-ратить]; направлять [-равить]; ~ a corner завернуть за угол; ~ down отвергать [-ергнуть] (предложение); загибать [загнуть]; ~ off закры(ва)ть (кран); выключать [выключить]; ~ on откры(ва)ть (кран); включать [-чить]; ~ out выгонять [выгнать]; увольнять [уволить]; выпускать [выпустить] (изделия); ~ over перевёртывать [-вернуть]; *fig.* перед(ав)ать (доверенность и т. п.); ~ up поднимать вверх; 2. *v/i.* вращаться, вертеться; поворачиваться [повернуться]; [с]делаться, становиться [стать]; превращаться [-вратиться]; ~ about обёртываться [обернуться]; ⚔ поворачиваться кругом; ~ in заходить мимоходом; F ложиться спать; ~ out оказываться [-заться]; ~ to приниматься [-няться] за (В); обращаться [обратиться] к (Д); ~ up появляться [-виться]; случаться [-читься]; ~ upon обращаться [обратиться] против (Р); 3. *su.* оборот; поворот; изгиб; перемена; очередь *f*; услуга; оборот (речи); F испуг; at every ~ на каждом шагу, постоянно; by или in **~s** по очереди; it is my ~ моя очередь *f*; take **~s** делать поочерёдно; does it serve your ~? это вам подходит?, это вам годится?; **~coat** перебежчик, хамелеон *fig.*; **~er** ['tə:nə] токарь *m*; **~ery** [-ri] токарное ремесло; токарные изделия *n/pl.*

turning ['tə:niŋ] поворот (улицы и т. п.); вращение; токарное ремесло; **~-point** *fig.* поворотный пункт; перелом.

turnip ['tə:nip] ♀ репа.

turn|key ['tə:nki:] тюремщик; **~out** ['tə:n'aut] ✝ выпуск продукции; **~over** ['tə:nouvə] ✝ оборот; **~pike** шлагбаум; **~stile** турникет.

turpentine ['tə:pəntain] скипидар.

turpitude ['tə:pitju:d] позор; низость *f*.

turret ['tʌrit] башенка; ✈ турель *f*; ⚔, ⚓ орудийная башня.

turtle ['tə:tl] *zo.* черепаха.

tusk [tʌsk] клык (слона, моржа).

tussle ['tʌsl] 1. борьба, драка; 2. (упорно) бороться, [по]драться.

tussock ['tʌsək] кочка.

tutelage ['tju:tilidʒ] опекунство; опека.

tutor ['tju:tə] **1.** домáшний учи́тель *m*; репети́тор; ⚖ опеку́н; **2.** обучáть [-чи́ть]; наставля́ть [настáвить].
tuxedo [tʌk'si:dou] *Am.* смóкинг.
twaddle ['twɔdl] **1.** пустáя болтовня́; **2.** пустослóвить.
twang [twæŋ] **1.** звук натя́нутой струны́; (*mst* nasal ~) гнусáвый вы́говор; **2.** звенéть (о струнé); гнусáвить.
tweak [twi:k] щипáть [щипну́ть].
tweezers ['twi:zəz] *pl.* пинцéт.
twelfth [twelfθ] двенáдцатый.
twelve [twelv] двенáдцать.
twent|ieth ['twentiiθ] двадцáтый; ~**y** ['twenti] двáдцать.
twice [twais] двáжды; вдвóе.
twiddle ['twidl] вертéть (в рукáх); игрáть (T); *fig.* бездéльничать.
twig [twig] вéточка, прут.
twilight ['twailait] су́мерки *f/pl.*
twin [twin] **1.** близнéц; двойни́к; пáрная вещь *f*; **2.** двойнóй; пáрный.
twine [twain] **1.** бечёвка, шпагáт, шнурóк; **2.** [с]вить; [с]плести́; обви́(вá)ть(ся).
twinge [twindʒ] при́ступ бóли.
twinkle ['twiŋkl] **1.** мерцáние; мигáние; мелькáние; **2.** [за]мерцáть; [за]сверкáть; мигáть [мигну́ть].
twirl [twə:l] **1.** кручéние; вращéние; **2.** вертéть; закру́чивать [-ути́ть].
twist [twist] **1.** кручéние; скру́чивание; сучéние; изги́б; поворóт; вы́вих; **2.** [с]крути́ть; [с]сучи́ть; [с]ви́ть(ся); сплетáть(ся) [-ести́(сь)].
twit [twit]: ~ a p. with a th. попрекáть [-кну́ть] когó-либо (T).
twitch [twitʃ] **1.** подёргивание, су́дорога; **2.** дёргать(ся) [дёрнуть (-ся)].
twitter ['twitə] **1.** щéбет; **2.** [за-] щебетáть; чири́кать [-кнуть]; be in a ~ дрожáть.
two [tu:] **1.** два, две; двóе; пáра; in ~ нáдвое, пополáм; **2.** двóйка; in ~s попáрно; ~**fold** ['tu:fould] **1.** двойнóй; **2.** *adv.* вдвóе; ~**pence** ['tʌpəns] два пéнса; ~**-storey** двухэтáжный; ~**-way** двусторóнний; ~ plug двойнóй штéпсель *m*.
tyke [taik] дворня́жка; шу́стрый ребёнок.
type [taip] тип; типи́чный представи́тель *m*; *typ.* ли́тера; шрифт; true to ~ типи́чный; set in ~ *typ.* наб(и)рáть; ~**write** [*irr.* (write)] писáть на маши́нке; ~**writer** пи́шущая маши́нка.
typhoid ['taifɔid] ⚕ (*a.* ~ fever) брюшнóй тиф.
typhoon [tai'fu:n] тайфу́н.
typhus ['taifəs] ⚕ сыпнóй тиф.
typi|cal ['tipikəl] □ типи́чный; ~**fy** [-fai] служи́ть типи́чным примéром для (P); ~**st** ['taipist] перепи́счик (-чица) (на маши́нке), машини́стка; shorthand ~ стенографи́ст(ка).
tyrann|ic(al □) [ti'rænik, -ikəl] тирани́ческий; ~**ize** ['tirənaiz] тирáнить; ~**y** [-ni] тирани́я, деспоти́зм.
tyrant ['taiərənt] тирáн, дéспот.
tyre ['taiə] ши́на (колесá).
tyro ['taiərou] новичóк.

U

ubiquitous [ju:'bikwitəs] □ вездесу́щий.
udder ['ʌdə] вы́мя *n*.
ugly ['ʌgli] □ безобрáзный; дурнóй; проти́вный.
ulcer ['ʌlsə] ⚕ я́зва; ~**ate** [-reit] изъязвля́ть(ся) [-ви́ть(ся)]; ~**ous** [-rəs] изъязвлённый; я́звенный.
ulterior [ʌl'tiəriə] □ бóлее отдалённый; *fig.* дальнéйший; скры́тый (моти́в и т. п.).
ultimate ['ʌltimit] □ послéдний; конéчный; максимáльный; ~**ly** [-li] в концé концóв.
ultimo ['ʌltimou] *adv.* истéкшего мéсяца
ultra[1] ['ʌltrə] крáйний.
ultra[2]... [~...] *pref.* сверх..., ультра-...
umbel ['ʌmbəl] ♆ зóнтик.
umbrage ['ʌmbridʒ] оби́да; *poet.* тень *f*, сень *f*.
umbrella [ʌm'brelə] зóнтик.
umpire ['ʌmpaiə] **1.** посрéдник; третéйский судья́ *m*; *sport* судья́ *m*; **2.** быть (третéйским) судьёй; быть посрéдником.
un... [ʌn...] *pref.* (придаёт отрицáтельное и́ли противополóжное значéние) не..., без...
unable ['ʌn'eibl] неспосóбный; be ~ не быть в состоя́нии, не [с]мочь.
unaccountable ['ʌnə'kauntəbl] □ необъясни́мый; безответственный.
unaccustomed ['ʌnə'kʌstəmd] не привы́кший; непривы́чный.
unacquainted [-'kweintid]: ~ with незнакóмый с (T); не знáющий (P).
unadvised ['ʌnəd'vaizd] □ неблагоразу́мный; необду́манный.
unaffected ['ʌnə'fektid] □ непритвóрный, и́скренний; не(за)трóнутый (by T).
unaided ['ʌn'eidid] лишённый пóмощи; без посторóнней пóмощи.
unalterable [ʌn'ɔ:ltərəbl] □ неизмéнный.

unanim|ity [ju:nə'nimiti] единоду́шие; **~ous** [ju:'nænimәs] □ единоду́шный, единогла́сный.
unanswerable [ʌn'ɑ:nsәrәbl] □ неопровержи́мый.
unapproachable [ʌnә'proutʃәbl] □ непристу́пный; недосту́пный.
unapt [ʌ'næpt] □ неподходя́щий; неспосо́бный, неуме́лый.
unasked ['ʌn'ɑ:skt] непро́шенный.
unassisted ['ʌnә'sistid] без по́мощи.
unassuming ['ʌnә'sju:miŋ] скро́мный, непритяза́тельный.
unattractive ['ʌnә'træktiv] □ непривлека́тельный.
unauthorized ['ʌn'ɔ:θәraizd] неразрешённый; неправомо́чный.
unavail|able ['ʌnә'veilәbl] не име́ющийся в распоряже́нии; **~ing** [-liŋ] бесполе́зный.
unavoidable [ʌnә'vɔidebl] □ неизбе́жный.
unaware ['ʌnә'weә] не зна́ющий, не подозрева́ющий (of P); be ~ of ничего́ не знать о (П); не замеча́ть [-е́тить] (P); **~s** [-z] неожи́данно, врасплóх; нечáянно.
unbacked [ʌn'bækt] *fig.* не име́ющий подде́ржки.
unbalanced ['ʌn'bælәnst] неуравнове́шенный.
unbearable [ʌn'beәrәbl] □ невыноси́мый.
unbecoming ['ʌnbi'kʌmiŋ] □ неподходя́щий; не иду́щий к лицу́; неприли́чный.
unbelie|f ['ʌnbi'li:f] неве́рие; **~vable** ['ʌnbi'li:vәbl] □ невероя́тный; **~ving** [-iŋ] □ неве́рующий.
unbend ['ʌn'bend] [*irr.* (bend)] выпрямля́ть(ся) [вы́прямить(ся)]; станови́ться непринуждённым; **~ing** [-iŋ] □ негну́щийся; *fig.* непреклóнный.
unbias(s)ed ['ʌn'baiәst] □ беспристра́стный.
unbind ['ʌn'baind] [*irr.* (bind)] развя́зывать [-за́ть]; *fig.* освобожда́ть [-боди́ть].
unblushing [ʌn'blʌʃiŋ] бессты́дный.
unbosom [ʌn'buzәm] поверя́ть [-е́рить] (та́йну); ~ o. s. излива́ть ду́шу.
unbounded [ʌn'baundid] □ неограни́ченный; беспреде́льный.
unbroken ['ʌn'broukn] неразби́тый; не поби́тый (реко́рд); непреры́вный.
unbutton ['ʌn'bʌtn] расстёгивать [расстегну́ть].
uncalled [ʌn'kɔ:ld]: ~-for непро́шенный; неуме́стный.
uncanny [ʌn'kæni] □ жу́ткий, сверхъесте́ственный.
uncared ['ʌn'keәd]: ~-for забро́шенный.
unceasing [ʌn'si:siŋ] □ непрекраща́ющийся, безостано́вочный.
unceremonious ['ʌnseri'mounjәs] □ бесцеремо́нный.
uncertain [ʌn'sә:tn] □ неуве́ренный; неопределённый; неизве́стный; **~ty** [-ti] неуве́ренность *f*; неизве́стность *f*; неопределённость *f*.
unchang|eable [ʌn'tʃeindʒәbl] □, **~ing** [-iŋ] неизме́нный; неизменя́емый.
uncharitable [ʌn'tʃæritәbl] □ немилосе́рдный.
unchecked ['ʌn'tʃekt] беспрепя́тственный; непрове́ренный.
uncivil ['ʌn'sivl] □ неве́жливый; **~ized** ['ʌn'sivilaizd] нецивилизо́ванный.
uncle ['ʌŋkl] дя́дя *m*.
unclean ['ʌn'kli:n] □ нечи́стый.
unclose ['ʌn'klouz] откры́(ва́)ть (-ся).
uncomfortable [ʌn'kʌmfәtәbl] □ неудо́бный; нело́вкий.
uncommon [ʌn'kɔmәn] □ необыкнове́нный; замеча́тельный.
uncommunicative ['ʌnkә'mju:nikeitiv] необщи́тельный, неразгово́рчивый.
uncomplaining ['ʌnkәm'pleiniŋ] □ безро́потный.
uncompromising [ʌn'kɔmprәmaiziŋ] □ бескомпроми́ссный.
unconcern ['ʌnkәn'sә:n] беззабо́тность *f*; беспе́чность *f*; **~ed** [-d] □ беззабо́тный; беспе́чный.
unconditional ['ʌnkәn'diʃnl] □ безогово́рочный, безусло́вный.
unconquerable [ʌn'kɔŋkәrәbl] □ непобеди́мый.
unconscionable [ʌn'kɔnʃnәbl] □ бессо́вестный.
unconscious [ʌn'kɔnʃәs] □ бессозна́тельный; потеря́вший созна́ние; be ~ of не созн(ав)а́ть (P); **~ness** [-nis] бессозна́тельность *f*.
unconstitutional ['ʌnkɔnsti'tju:ʃnl] □ противоре́чащий конститу́ции.
uncontrollable [ʌnkәn'troulәbl] □ неудержи́мый; не поддаю́щийся контро́лю.
unconventional ['ʌnkәn'venʃәnl] □ чу́ждый усло́вности; необы́чный; нешабло́нный.
uncork ['ʌn'kɔ:k] отку́пори(ва)ть.
uncount|able ['ʌn'kauntәbl] бесчи́сленный; **~ed** [-tid] несчётный.
uncouple ['ʌn'kʌpl] расцепля́ть [-пи́ть].
uncouth [ʌn'ku:θ] неуклю́жий.
uncover [ʌn'kʌvә] откры́(ва́)ть (лицо́ и т. п.); снима́ть кры́шку с (P); обнажа́ть [-жи́ть] (го́лову).
unct|ion ['ʌŋkʃәn] пома́зание; мазь *f*; **~uous** ['ʌŋktjuәs] □ масляни́стый; *fig.* еле́йный.
uncult|ivated ['ʌn'kʌltiveitid] невозде́ланный; некульту́рный.
undamaged ['ʌn'dæmidʒd] неповреждённый.

undaunted [ʌn'dɔ:ntid] □ неустраши́мый.
undeceive ['ʌndi'si:v] выводи́ть из заблужде́ния.
undecided ['ʌndi'saidid] □ нерешённый; нереши́тельный.
undefined ['ʌndi'faind] □ неопределённый.
undeniable [ʌndi'naiəbl] □ неоспори́мый; несомне́нный.
under ['ʌndə] **1.** *adv.* ни́же; внизу́, вниз; **2.** *prp.* под (В, Т); ни́же (Р); ме́ньше (Р); при (П); **3.** *pref.* ниже..., под..., недо...; **4.** ни́жний; ни́зший; **~bid** ['ʌndə'bid] [*irr.* (bid)] предлага́ть бо́лее ни́зкую це́ну чем (И); **~brush** [-brʌʃ] подле́сок; **~carriage** [-'kæridʒ] шасси́ *n indecl.*; **~clothing** [-klouðiŋ] ни́жнее бельё; **~cut** [-kʌt] сбива́ть це́ны; подреза́ть [-е́зать]; **~done** [-dʌn] недожа́ренный; **~estimate** [-r'estimeit] недооце́нивать [-и́ть]; **~fed** [-fed] истощённый от недоеда́ния; **~go** [-'gou] [*irr.* (go)] испы́тывать [испыта́ть]; подверга́ться [-е́ргнуться] (Д); **~graduate** [-'grædjuit] студе́нт(ка) после́днего ку́рса; **~ground** ['ʌndəgraund] **1.** подзе́мный; подпо́льный; **2.** метро́(полите́н) *n indecl.*; подпо́лье; **~hand** [-hænd] **1.** та́йный, закули́сный; **2.** *adv.* та́йно, «за спино́й»; **~lie** [ʌndə'lai] [*irr.* (lie)] лежа́ть в основа́нии (Р); **~line** [-'lain] подчёркивать [-черкну́ть]; **~ling** [-liŋ] подчинённый; **~mine** [ʌndə'main] [за]мини́ровать (*im*)*pf.*; подка́пывать [-копа́ть] (*a. fig.*); *fig.* подрыва́ть [подорва́ть]; **~most** ['ʌndəmoust] са́мый ни́жний; ни́зший; **~neath** [ʌndə'ni:θ] **1.** *prp.* под (Т/В); **2.** *adv.* вниз, внизу́; **~privileged** [-'privilidʒd] лишённый привиле́гий; **~rate** [ʌndə'reit] недооце́нивать [-и́ть]; **~secretary** ['ʌndə'sekrətəri] замести́тель мини́стра (в Англии и США); **~sell** [-'sel] [*irr.* (sell)] † продава́ть деше́вле други́х; **~signed** [-'saind] нижеподписа́вшийся; **~stand** [ʌndə'stænd] [*irr.* (stand)] *com.* понима́ть [поня́ть]; подразумева́ть (by под Т); make o. s. understood уме́ть объясни́ться; an understood thing решённое де́ло; **~standable** [-əbl] поня́тный; **~standing** [-iŋ] понима́ние; соглаше́ние; взаимопонима́ние; **~state** ['ʌndə'steit] преуменьша́ть [-ме́ньши́ть]; **~stood** [ʌndə'stud] *pt.* и *p. pt.* от understand; **~take** [ʌndə'teik] [*irr.* (take)] предпринима́ть [-ня́ть]; бра́ть на себя́; обя́зываться [-за́ться]; **~taker** **1.** [ʌndə'teikə] предпринима́тель *m*; **2.** ['ʌndəteikə] содержа́тель похоро́нного бюро́; **~taking** **1.** [ʌndə'teikiŋ] предприя́тие; обяза́тельство; **2.** ['ʌndəteikiŋ] похоро́нное бюро́; **~tone** [-toun]: in an ~ вполго́лоса; **~value** [-'vælju:] недооце́нивать [-и́ть]; **~wear** [-wɛə] ни́жнее бельё; **~wood** [-wud] подле́сок; **~write** [-rait] [*irr.* (write)] подпи́сывать поли́с морско́го страхова́ния; принима́ть в страхо́вку; **~writer** [-raitə] морско́й страхо́вщик.
undeserved ['ʌndi'zə:vd] □ незаслу́женный.
undesirable [-'zaiərəbl] □ нежела́тельный; неудо́бный, неподходя́щий.
undisciplined [ʌn'disiplind] недисциплини́рованный.
undisguised ['ʌndis'gaizd] □ незамаскиро́ванный; я́вный.
undo ['ʌn'du:, ʌn'du:] [*irr.* (do)] уничтожа́ть [-о́жить] (сде́ланное); развя́зывать [-за́ть]; расстёгивать [расстегну́ть]; расторга́ть [-о́ргнуть] (догово́р и т. п.); **~ing** [-iŋ] уничтоже́ние; ги́бель *f*; развя́зывание; расстёгивание и т. д.
undoubted [ʌn'dautid] □ несомне́нный, бесспо́рный.
undreamt [ʌn'dremt]: ~-of невообрази́мый, неожи́данный.
undress ['ʌn'dres] **1.** дома́шний костю́м; **2.** разде́(ва́)ть(ся); **~ed** ['ʌn'drest] неоде́тый; невы́деланный (о ко́же).
undue ['ʌn'dju:] □ неподходя́щий; чрезме́рный; ненадлежа́щий; ещё не подлежа́щий опла́те.
undulat|e ['ʌndjuleit] быть волни́стым, волнообра́зным; **~ion** [ʌndju'leiʃən] волнообра́зное движе́ние; неро́вность пове́рхности.
unearth ['ʌn'ə:θ] вырыва́ть из земли́; *fig.* раска́пывать [-копа́ть]; **~ly** [ʌn'ə:θli] неземно́й; стра́нный, ди́кий.
uneas|iness [ʌn'i:zinis] беспоко́йство; трево́жность *f*; стесне́ние; **~y** [ʌn'i:zi] □ беспоко́йный, трево́жный; стеснённый (о движе́ниях и т. п.).
uneducated ['ʌn'edjukeitid] необразо́ванный; невоспи́танный.
unemotional ['ʌni'mouʃnl] □ пасси́вный; бесстра́стный; сухо́й *fig.*
unemploy|ed ['ʌnim'plɔid] безрабо́тный; неза́нятый; **~ment** [-'plɔimənt] безрабо́тица.
unending [ʌn'endiŋ] □ несконча́емый, бесконе́чный.
unendurable ['ʌnin'djuərəbl] нестерпи́мый.
unengaged ['ʌnin'geidʒd] неза́нятый; свобо́дный.
unequal ['ʌn'i:kwəl] □ нера́вный; неро́вный; **~led** [-d] непревзойдённый.
unerring ['ʌn'ə:riŋ] □ непогреши́мый; безоши́бочный.

unessential ['ʌni'senʃəl] □ несущественный (to для P).
uneven ['ʌn'i:vn] □ неровный; шероховатый (*a. fig.*).
uneventful ['ʌni'ventful] □ без особых событий.
unexampled [ʌnig'zɑ:mpld] беспримерный.
unexpected ['ʌniks'pektid] □ неожиданный.
unfailing [ʌn'feiliŋ] □ неизменный; неисчерпаемый.
unfair ['ʌn'fɛə] □ несправедливый; нечестный (о спортсмене, игре и т. п.).
unfaithful ['ʌn'feiθful] □ неверный, вероломный; неточный.
unfamiliar ['ʌnfə'miljə] незнакомый; непривычный.
unfasten ['ʌn'fɑ:sn] откреплять [-пить]; расстёгивать [расстегнуть]; **~ed** [-d] расстёгнутый; неприкреплённый.
unfavo(u)rable ['ʌn'feivərəbl] □ неблагоприятный; невыгодный.
unfeeling [ʌn'fi:liŋ] □ бесчувственный.
unfinished ['ʌn'finiʃt] незаконченный.
unfit 1. ['ʌn'fit] □ негодный, неподходящий; 2. [ʌn'fit] делать непригодным.
unfix ['ʌn'fiks] откреплять [-пить]; делать неустойчивым.
unfledged ['ʌn'fledʒd] неоперившийся (*a. fig.*).
unflinching [ʌn'flintʃiŋ] □ неуклонный.
unfold [ʌn'fould] развёртывать(ся) [-вернуть(ся)]; откры(ва)ть (тайну и т. п.).
unforced ['ʌn'fɔ:st] □ непринуждённый.
unforgettable ['ʌnfə'getəbl] □ незабвенный.
unfortunate [ʌn'fɔ:tʃnit] 1. несчастный; неудачный; неудачливый; 2. неудачник (-ица); **~ly** [-li] к несчастью; к сожалению.
unfounded ['ʌn'faundid] □ необоснованный; неосновательный.
unfriendly ['ʌn'frendli] недружелюбный; неприветливый.
unfurl [ʌn'fə:l] развёртывать [развернуть].
unfurnished ['ʌn'fə:niʃt] немеблированный.
ungainly [ʌn'geinli] нескладный.
ungenerous ['ʌn'dʒenərəs] □ не великодушный, не щедрый.
ungentle ['ʌn'dʒentl] □ неделикатный, неучтивый.
ungodly [ʌn'gɔdli] □ безбожный.
ungovern|able [ʌn'gʌvənəbl] □ неукротимый; распущенный.
ungraceful ['ʌn'greisful] □ неизящный, неграциозный.
ungracious ['ʌn'greiʃəs] □ немилостивый.
ungrateful [ʌn'greitful] □ неблагодарный.
unguarded ['ʌn'gɑ:did] □ неохраняемый; неосторожный; незащищённый.
unguent ['ʌŋgwənt] мазь *f*.
unhampered ['ʌn'hæmpəd] беспрепятственный.
unhandsome [ʌn'hænsəm] □ некрасивый.
unhandy [ʌn'hændi] □ неудобный; неловкий.
unhappy [ʌn'hæpi] □ несчастный.
unharmed ['ʌn'hɑ:md] благополучный; невредимый.
unhealthy [ʌn'helθi] □ нездоровый, болезненный; вредный.
unheard-of [ʌn'hə:dɔv] неслыханный.
unhesitating [ʌn'heziteitiŋ] □ неколеблющийся, решительный.
unholy [ʌn'houli] безбожный; дьявольский.
unhonoured ['ʌn'ɔnəd] не уважаемый; неоплаченный.
unhope|d-for [ʌn'houpt'fɔ:] неожиданный; **~ful** [-ful] не подающий надежды, безнадёжный.
unhurt ['ʌn'hə:t] невредимый, целый.
uniform ['ju:nifɔ:m] 1. □ однообразный; однородный; 2. форма, мундир; 3. делать однообразным; обмундировывать [-ровать]; **~ity** [ju:ni'fɔ:miti] единообразие, однообразие.
unify ['ju:nifai] объединять [-нить]; унифицировать (*im*)*pf*.
unilateral ['ju:ni'lætərəl] односторонний.
unimaginable [ʌni'mædʒinəbl] □ невообразимый.
unimportant ['ʌnim'pɔ:tənt] □ неважный.
uninformed ['ʌnin'fɔ:md] несведущий; неосведомлённый.
uninhabit|able ['ʌnin'hæbitəbl] негодный для жилья; **~ed** [-tid] нежилой; необитаемый.
uninjured ['ʌn'indʒəd] неповреждённый, невредимый.
unintelligible ['ʌnin'telidʒəbl] □ непонятный.
unintentional ['ʌnin'tenʃnl] □ непреднамеренный, неумышленный.
uninteresting ['ʌn'intristiŋ] □ неинтересный, безынтересный.
uninterrupted ['ʌnintə'rʌptid] □ непрерывный, беспрерывный.
union ['ju:njən] объединение; соединение (*a.* ⊕); союз, федерация; профсоюз; ♀ Jack британский национальный флаг; **~ist** [-ist] член профсоюза.
unique [ju:'ni:k] единственный в своём роде; бесподобный.
unison ['ju:nizn] ♪ унисон; *fig.* согласие.

unit ['ju:nit] ⚔ часть *f*, подразделéние; 𝔄 единица; ⊕ агрегáт; **~e** [ju:'nait] соединя́ть(ся) [-ни́ть (-ся)]; объединя́ть(ся) [-ни́ть(ся)]; **~y** ['ju:niti] единéние; еди́нство.
univers|al [juni'və:sl] □ всеóбщий; всеми́рный; универсáльный; **~ality** [ju:nivə:'sæliti] универсáльность *f*; **~e** ['ju:nivə:s] мир, вселéнная; **~ity** [juni'və:siti] университéт.
unjust ['ʌn'dʒʌst] □ несправедли́вый; **~ified** [ʌn'dʒʌstifaid] неопрáвданный.
unkempt ['ʌn'kempt] нечёсаный; неопря́тный.
unkind [ʌn'kaind] □ недóбрый.
unknown ['ʌn'noun] **1.** неизвéстный; **~** to me *adv.* тáйно от меня́; **2.** незнакóмец (-мка).
unlace ['ʌn'leis] расшнурóвывать [-овáть].
unlawful ['ʌn'lɔ:ful] □ незакóнный.
unlearn ['ʌn'lə:n] разу́чиваться [(-и́ться].
unless [ən'les, ʌn'les] *cj.* éсли ... не.
unlike ['ʌn'laik] **1.** непохóжий на (B); **2.** *prp.* в отли́чие от (P); **~ly** [ʌn'laikli] неправдоподóбный; невероя́тный.
unlimited [ʌn'limitid] безграни́чный, неограни́ченный.
unload ['ʌn'loud] выгружáть [вы́грузить], разгружáть [-узи́ть]; ⚔ разряжáть [-яди́ть].
unlock ['ʌn'lɔk] отпирáть [отперéть]; **~ed** [-t] незáпертый.
unlooked-for [ʌn'lukt'fɔ:] неожи́данный, непредви́денный.
unlovely ['ʌn'lʌvli] некраси́вый, непривлекáтельный.
unlucky [ʌn'lʌki] □ неудáчный, несчастли́вый.
unman ['ʌn'mæn] лишáть му́жественности.
unmanageable [ʌn'mænidʒəbl] □ тру́дно поддаю́щийся контрóлю; непокóрный.
unmarried ['ʌn'mærid] неженáтый, холостóй; незаму́жняя.
unmask ['ʌn'mɑ:sk] снимáть мáску с (P); *fig.* разоблачáть [-чи́ть].
unmatched ['ʌn'mætʃt] бесподóбный.
unmeaning [ʌn'mi:niŋ] □ бессмы́сленный.
unmeasured [ʌn'meʒəd] неизмéренный; неизмери́мый.
unmeet ['ʌn'mi:t] неподходя́щий.
unmentionable [ʌn'menʃnəbl] невырази́мый; нецензу́рный.
unmerited ['ʌn'meritid] незаслу́женный.
unmindful [ʌn'maindful] □ забы́вчивый; невнимáтельный (of к Д).
unmistakable ['ʌnmis'teikəbl] □ несомнéнный; легкó узнавáемый.
unmitigated [ʌn'mitigeitid] несмягчённый; *fig.* абсолю́тный.
unmounted ['ʌn'mauntid] пéший; неопрáвленный (драгоцéнный кáмень); не смонти́рованный.
unmoved ['ʌn'mu:ved] нетрóнутый.
unnamed ['ʌn'neimd] безымя́нный; неупомя́нутый.
unnatural [ʌn'nætʃrəl] □ неестéственный; противоестéственный.
unnecessary [ʌn'nesisəri] □ нену́жный, изли́шний.
unnerve ['ʌn'nə:v] лишáть прису́тствия ду́ха.
unnoticed ['ʌn'noutist] незамéченный.
unobjectionable ['ʌnəb'dʒekʃnəbl] □ безукори́зненный.
unobserved ['ʌnəb'zə:vd] □ незамéченный.
unobtainable ['ʌnəb'teinəbl]: **~** thing вещь, котóрой нельзя́ достáть и́ли получи́ть.
unoccupied ['ʌn'ɔkjupaid] незáнятый.
unoffending ['ʌnə'fendiŋ] безоби́дный.
unofficial ['ʌnə'fiʃəl] □ неофициáльный.
unopposed ['ʌnə'pouzd] не встречáющий сопротивлéния.
unostentatious ['ʌnɔstən'teiʃəs] □ скрóмный; не показнóй.
unpack ['ʌn'pæk] распакóвывать [-овáть].
unpaid ['ʌn'peid] неуплáченный, неоплáченный.
unparalleled [ʌn'pærəleld] несравнéнный, беспримéрный.
unpeople ['ʌn'pi:pl] обезлю́дить *pf.*
unpleasant [ʌn'pleznt] □ непри-я́тный; **~ness** [-nis] неприя́тность *f*.
unpolished ['ʌn'pɔliʃt] неотполирóванный; *fig.* неотёсанный.
unpolluted ['ʌnpə'lu:tid] незапя́тнанный, непорóчный.
unpopular ['ʌn'pɔpjulə] □ непопуля́рный, нелюби́мый.
unpracti|cal ['ʌn'præktikəl] □ непракти́чный; **~sed** [-tist] неóпытный; неприменённый.
unprecedented [ʌn'presidəntid] □ беспрецедéнтный; беспримéрный.
unprejudiced [ʌn'predʒudist] □ непредубеждённый, беспристрáстный.
unprepared ['ʌnpri'pεəd] □ неподготóвленный; без подготóвки.
unpreten|ding ['ʌnpri'tendiŋ] □, **~tious** [-ʃəs] □ скрóмный, без претéнзий.
unprincipled ['ʌn'prinsəpld] беспринци́пный; безнрáвственный.
unprofitable [ʌn'prɔfitəbl] невы́годный; нерентáбельный.
unproved ['ʌn'pru:vd] недокáзанный.

unprovided ['ʌnprə'vaidid] не обеспе́ченный, не снабже́нный (with T); **~for** непредви́денный.
unprovoked ['ʌnprə'voukt] □ ничём не вы́званный.
unqualified ['ʌn'kwɔlifaid] □ неквалифици́рованный; безогово́рочный.
unquestionable [ʌn'kwestʃənəbl] □ несомне́нный, неоспори́мый.
unravel [ʌn'rævəl] распу́т(ыв)ать; разга́дывать [-да́ть].
unready ['ʌn'redi] □ негото́вый.
unreal ['ʌn'riəl] □ ненастоя́щий; нереа́льный.
unreasonable [ʌn'ri:znəbl] □ не(благо)разу́мный; безрассу́дный; непоме́рный.
unrecognizable ['ʌn'rekəgnaizəbl] □ неузнава́емый.
unredeemed ['ʌnri'di:md] □ неиспо́лненный (об обеща́нии); невы́купленный (закла́д); неопла́ченный (долг).
unrefined ['ʌnri'faind] неочи́щенный.
unreflecting ['ʌnri'flektiŋ] □ легкомы́сленный, не размышля́ющий.
unregarded ['ʌnri'gɑ:did] не при́нятый в расчёт.
unrelenting [ʌnri'lentiŋ] □ безжа́лостный.
unreliable ['ʌnri'laiəbl] ненадёжный.
unrelieved ['ʌnri'li:vd] □ необлегчённый; не получа́ющий по́мощи.
unremitting [ʌnri'mitiŋ] □ беспреры́вный; неосла́бный.
unreserved ['ʌnri'zə:vd] □ открове́нный; невозде́ржанный; безогово́рочный.
unresisting ['ʌnri'zistiŋ] □ не сопротивля́ющийся.
unrest ['ʌn'rest] беспоко́йство, волне́ние.
unrestrained ['ʌnris'treind] □ несде́ржанный; необу́зданный.
unrestricted ['ʌnris'triktid] □ неограни́ченный.
unriddle [ʌn'ridl] разга́дывать [-да́ть].
unrighteous [ʌn'raitʃəs] □ непра́ведный; несправедли́вый.
unripe ['ʌn'raip] незре́лый, неспе́лый.
unrival(l)ed [ʌn'raivəld] непревзойдённый; без сопе́рника.
unroll ['ʌn'roul] развёртывать [-верну́ть].
unruffled ['ʌn'rʌfld] гла́дкий (о мо́ре и т. п.); невозмути́мый.
unruly [ʌn'ruli] непоко́рный.
unsafe ['ʌn'seif] □ ненадёжный, опа́сный.
unsal(e)able ['ʌn'seiləbl] неходово́й (това́р); непрода́жный.
unsanitary ['ʌn'sænitəri] негигиени́чный; антисанита́рный.
unsatisfactory ['ʌnsætis'fæktəri] □ неудовлетвори́тельный.
unsavo(u)ry ['ʌn'seivəri] □ невку́сный; непривлека́тельный.
unsay ['ʌn'sei] [*irr.* (say)] брать наза́д (ска́занное).
unscathed ['ʌn'skeiðd] невреди́мый.
unschooled ['ʌn'sku:ld] необу́ченный; недисциплини́рованный.
unscrew ['ʌn'skru:] отви́нчивать (-ся) [-нти́ть(ся)].
unscrupulous [ʌn'skru:pjuləs] □ беспринци́пный; бессо́вестный; неразбо́рчивый (в сре́дствах).
unsearchable [ʌn'sə:tʃəbl] □ непостижи́мый, необъясни́мый.
unseasonable [ʌn'si:znəbl] □ несвоевре́менный.
unseemly [ʌn'si:mli] неподоба́ющий; непристо́йный.
unseen ['ʌn'si:n] неви́димый; неви́данный.
unselfish ['ʌn'seilfiʃ] □ бескоры́стный.
unsettle ['ʌn'setl] приводи́ть в беспоря́док; расстра́ивать [-ро́ить]; **~d** [-d] неустро́енный; неустанови́вшийся; не решённый; неопла́ченный (счёт).
unshaken ['ʌn'ʃeikən] непоколе́бленный.
unshaven ['ʌn'ʃeivn] небри́тый.
unship ['ʌn'ʃip] сгружа́ть с корабля́.
unshrink|able ['ʌn'ʃriŋkəbl] не садя́щийся при сти́рке (о мате́рии); **~ing** [-iŋ] □ непоколеби́мый, бесстра́шный.
unsightly [ʌn'saitli] непригля́дный.
unskil|ful ['ʌn'skilful] □ неуме́лый, неиску́сный; **~led** ['ʌn'skild] неквалифици́рованный.
unsoci|able [ʌn'souʃəbl] необщи́тельный.
unsolder ['ʌn'sɔldə] распа́ивать [-пая́ть].
unsolicited ['ʌnsə'lisitid] непро́шенный, невостре́бованный.
unsophisticated ['ʌnsə'fistikeitid] безыску́ственный; бесхи́тростный.
unsound ['ʌn'saund] □ нездоро́вый; испо́рченный; необосно́ванный.
unsparing [ʌn'speəriŋ] □ беспоща́дный; ще́дрый.
unspeakable [ʌn'spi:kəbl] □ невырази́мый.
unspent ['ʌn'spent] неистра́ченный; неутомлённый.
unstable ['ʌn'steibl] □ нетвёрдый, неусто́йчивый; *phys.*, ⚗ несто́йкий.
unsteady ['ʌn'stedi] □ *s.* unstable; ша́ткий; непостоя́нный.
unstring ['ʌn'striŋ] [*irr.* (string)] снима́ть стру́ны с (P); распуска́ть

[-устить] (бусы и т. п.); расшатывать [-шатать] (нервы).
unstudied ['ʌn'stʌdid] естественный, непринуждённый.
unsubstantial ['ʌnsəb'stænʃəl] □ нереальный; несущественный.
unsuccessful ['ʌnsək'sesful] □ неудачный, безуспешный; неудачливый.
unsuitable ['ʌn'sju:təbl] □ неподходящий.
unsurpassable ['ʌnsə'pɑ:səbl] □ не могущий быть превзойдённым.
unsuspect|ed ['ʌnsəs'pektid] неподозреваемый; неожиданный; **~ing** [-iŋ] неподозревающий (of о П).
unsuspicious ['ʌnsəs'piʃəs] □ неподозревающий; не вызывающий подозрений.
unswerving [ʌn'swə:viŋ] □ неуклонный.
untangle ['ʌn'tæŋgl] распут(ыв)ать.
untarnished ['ʌn'tɑ:niʃt] неопорóченный.
unthink|able ['ʌn'θiŋkəbl] невообразимый; немыслимый; **~ing** [-iŋ] □ опрометчивый.
unthought ['ʌn'θɔ:t](или **~-of**) неожиданный.
untidy [ʌn'taidi] □ неопрятный, неаккуратный; неубранный.
untie ['ʌn'tai] развязывать [-зать]
until [ən'til, ʌn'til] **1.** *prp.* до (Р); **2.** *cj.* (до тех пор) пока ... (не) ...
untimely [ʌn'taimli] несвоевременный.
untiring [ʌn'taiəriŋ] □ неутомимый.
untold ['ʌn'tould] нерассказанный; несчётный.
untouched ['ʌn'tʌtʃt] нетронутый (*a. fig.*); *phot.* неретушированный.
untried ['ʌn'traid] неиспытанный; ⚖ недопрошенный.
untroubled ['ʌn'trʌbld] беспрепятственный; ненарушенный.
untrue ['ʌn'tru:] □ неправильный; неверный.
untrustworthy ['ʌn'trʌstwə:ði] □ не заслуживающий доверия.
unus|ed 1. ['ʌn'ju:zd] неупотребительный; не бывший в употреблении; неиспользованный; **2.** ['ʌn'ju:st] непривыкший (to к Д); **~ual** [ʌn'ju:ʒuəl] □ необыкновенный, необычный.
unutterable [ʌn'ʌtərəbl] □ невыразимый.
unvarnished ['ʌn'vɑ:niʃt] *fig.* неприкрашенный.
unvarying [ʌn'veəriiŋ] □ неизменяющийся, неизменный.
unveil [ʌn'veil] снимать покрывало с (Р); откры(ва)ть (памятник, тайну).
unwanted ['ʌn'wɔntid] нежеланный; ненужный.
unwarrant|able [ʌn'wɔrəntəbl] □ недопустимый; **~ed** [-tid] ничем не оправданный; негарантированный.
unwary [ʌn'weəri] □ необдуманный, неосторожный.
unwholesome ['ʌn'houlsəm] нездоровый, неблаготворный.
unwieldy [ʌn'wi:ldi] □ неуклюжий; громоздкий.
unwilling ['ʌn'wiliŋ] □ несклонный, нерасположенный.
unwise ['ʌn'waiz] □ неразумный.
unwitting [ʌn'witiŋ] □ невольный, непреднамеренный.
unworkable [ʌn'wə:kəbl] неприменимый, негодный для работы.
unworthy [ʌn'wə:ði] □ недостойный.
unwrap ['ʌn'ræp] развёртывать (-ся) [-вернуть(ся)].
unyielding [ʌn'ji:ldiŋ] □ неподатливый, неуступчивый.
up [ʌp] **1.** *adv.* вверх, наверх; вверху, наверху; выше; *fig.* be **~** to the mark быть на должной высоте (науки и т. п.); be **~** against a task стоять перед задачей; **~** to вплоть до (Р); it is **~** to me (to do) мне приходится (делать); what's **~**? *sl.* что случилось?, в чём дело?; **2.** *prp.* вверх по (Д); по направлению к (Д); вдоль по (Д); **~** the river вверх по реке; **3.** *adj.* **~** train поезд, идущий в город; **4.** *su.* the **~**s and downs *fig.* превратности судьбы; **5.** *vb.* F поднимать [-нять]; повышать [-высить]; вст(ав)ать.
up|braid [ʌp'breid] [вы]бранить; **~bringing** ['ʌpbriŋiŋ] воспитание; **~heaval** [ʌp'hi:vl] переворот; **~hill** ['ʌp'hil] (идущий) в гору; *fig.* тяжёлый; **~hold** [ʌp'hould] [*irr.* (hold)] поддерживать [-жать]; придерживаться (взгляда) **~holster** [ʌp'houlstə] оби(ва)ть (мебель); [за]драпировать (комнату); **~holsterer** [-rə] обойщик; драпировщик; **~holstery** [-ri] ремесло драпировщика или обойщика.
up|keep ['ʌpki:p] содержание; стоимость содержания; **~land** ['ʌplənd] нагорная страна; **~lift 1.** ['ʌplift] (духовный) подъём; **2.** [ʌp'lift] поднимать [-нять]; возвышать [-высить].
upon [ə'pɔn] *s.* on.
upper ['ʌpə] верхний; высший; **~most** [-moust] самый верхний; наивысший.
up|raise [ʌp'reiz] возвышать [-высить]; **~right** ['ʌp'rait] **1.** □ прямой, вертикальный; *adv. a.* стоймя; **2.** стойка; (*a.* **~** piano) пианино *n indecl.*; **~rising** [ʌp'raiziŋ] восстание.
uproar ['ʌprɔ:] шум, гам, волне-

ние; ~ious [ʌp'rɔ:riəs] □ шу́мный, бу́йный.
up|root [ʌp'ru:t] искореня́ть [-ни́ть]; вырыва́ть с ко́рнем; **~set** [ʌp'set] [*irr.* (set)] опроки́дывать(ся) [-и́нуть(ся)]; расстра́ивать [-ро́ить]; выводи́ть из (душе́вного) равнове́сия; **~shot** ['ʌpʃɔt] развя́зка; заключе́ние; **~side** ['ʌpsaid] *adv.*: ~ down вверх дном; **~stairs** ['ʌp'stɛəz] вверх (по ле́стнице), наве́рх(у́); **~start** ['ʌpstɑ:t] вы́скочка *m/f*; **~stream** ['ʌp'stri:m] вве́рх по тече́нию; **~turn** [ʌp'tə:n] переве́ртывать [переверну́ть]; **~ward(s)** ['ʌpwəd(z)] вверх, наве́рх.
urban ['ə:bən] городско́й; **~e** [ə:'bein] □ ве́жливый; изы́сканный.
urchin ['ə:tʃin] постре́л, мальчи́шка *m*.
urge [ə:dʒ] **1.** понужда́ть [-у́дить]; подгоня́ть [подогна́ть] (*often* ~ on); **2.** стремле́ние, толчо́к *fig.*; **~ncy** ['ə:dʒənsi] насто́йтельность *f*; сро́чность *f*; насто́йчивость *f*; **~nt** ['ə:dʒənt] □ сро́чный; настоя́тельный, насто́йчивый.
urin|al ['juərinl] писсуа́р; **~ate** [-rineit] [по]мочи́ться; **~e** [-rin] [моча́.
urn [ə:n] у́рна.
us [ʌs; əs] *pron. pers.* (ко́свенный паде́ж от we) нас, нам, на́ми.
usage ['ju:zidʒ] употребле́ние; обы́чай.
usance ['ju:zəns] ✝: bill at ~ ве́ксель на срок, устано́вленный торго́вым обы́чаем.
use 1. [ju:s] употребле́ние; примене́ние; по́льзование; по́льза; привы́чка; (of) no ~ бесполе́зный; **2.** [ju:z] употребля́ть [-би́ть]; по́льзоваться (Т); воспо́льзоваться (Т) *pf.*; испо́льзовать (*im*)*pf.*; обраща́ться [обрати́ться] с (Т), обходи́ться [обойти́сь] с (Т); I ~d [ju:s(t)] to do я, быва́ло, ча́сто де́лал; **~d** [ju:st]: ~ to привы́кший к (Д); **~ful** ['ju:sful] □ поле́зный; приго́дный; **~less** ['ju:slis] □ бесполе́зный; неприго́дный, него́дный.
usher ['ʌʃə] **1.** капельди́нер; швейца́р; при́став (в суде́); **2.** проводи́ть [-вести́] (на ме́сто); вводи́ть [ввести́].
usual ['ju:ʒuəl] □ обыкнове́нный, обы́чный.
usurer ['ju:ʒərə] ростовщи́к.
usurp [ju:'zə:p] узурпи́ровать (*im*)*pf.*; **~er** [ju:'zə:pə] узурпа́тор.
usury ['ju:ʒuri] ростовщи́чество.
utensil [ju:'tensl] (*mst pl.* ~s) посу́да, у́тварь *f*; принадле́жность *f*.
utility [ju:'tiliti] поле́зность *f*; вы́годность *f*; public ~ коммуна́льное предприя́тие; *pl.* предприя́тия обще́ственного по́льзования; коммуна́льные услу́ги *f/pl.*
utiliz|ation [ju:tilai'zeiʃən] испо́льзование, утилиза́ция; **~e** ['ju:tilaiz] испо́льзовать (*im*)*pf.*, утилизи́ровать (*im*)*pf.*
utmost ['ʌtmoust] кра́йний, преде́льный.
utter ['ʌtə] **1.** □ *fig.* по́лный; кра́йний; абсолю́тный; **2.** изд(ав)а́ть (зву́ки); выража́ть слова́ми; **~ance** [-rəns] выраже́ние; произнесе́ние; выска́зывание; **~most** [-moust] кра́йний; преде́льный.

V

vacan|cy ['veikənsi] пустота́; вака́нсия, свобо́дное ме́сто; пробе́л; рассе́янность *f*; **~t** ['veikənt] □ неза́нятый, вака́нтный; пусто́й; рассе́янный (взгляд и т. п.).
vacat|e [və'keit, *Am.* 'veikeit] освобожда́ть [-боди́ть] (дом и т. п.); покида́ть [-и́нуть], оставля́ть [-а́вить] (до́лжность); упраздня́ть [-ни́ть]; **~ion** [və'keiʃən, *Am.* vei'keiʃən] оставле́ние; кани́кулы *f/pl.*; о́тпуск.
vaccin|ate ['væksineit] ⚕ приви́(ва́)ть; **~ation** [væksi'neiʃən] ⚕ приви́вка; **~e** ['væksi:n] ⚕ вакци́на.
vacillate ['væsileit] колеба́ться.
vacuum ['vækjuəm] *phys.* ва́куум; пустота́; ~ cleaner пылесо́с; ~ flask, ~ bottle те́рмос.
vagabond ['vægəbənd] **1.** бродя́га *m*; **2.** бродя́жничать.
vagrant ['veigrənt] **1.** бродя́га *m*; праздношата́ющийся; **2.** стра́нствующий; бродя́чий.
vague [veig] неопределённый, нея́сный, сму́тный.
vain [vein] □ тще́тный, напра́сный; пусто́й, су́етный; тщесла́вный; in ~ напра́сно, тще́тно; **~glorious** [vein'glɔ:riəs] тщесла́вный; хвастли́вый.
valediction [væli'dikʃən] проща́ние; проща́льная речь *f*.
valet ['vælit] **1.** камерди́нер; **2.** служи́ть камерди́нером.
valiant ['væljənt] □ *rhet.* хра́брый, до́блестный.
valid ['vælid] ⚖ действи́тельный, име́ющий си́лу; ве́ский; обосно́ванный; **~ity** [və'liditi] действи́тельность *f* и т. д.
valley ['væli] доли́на.
valo(u)r ['vælə] *rhet.* до́блесть *f*.

valuable ['væljuəbl] 1. □ це́нный; 2. ~s *pl.* це́нности *f/pl.*
valuation [vælju'eiʃən] оце́нка (иму́щества).
value ['vælju:] 1. це́нность *f*; цена́; † сто́имость *f*; † валю́та; значе́ние; 2. оце́нивать [-и́ть] (В); [о-] цени́ть (В); дорожи́ть (Т); ~less ['vælju:lis] ничего́ не сто́ящий.
valve ['vælv] ⊕ кла́пан, ве́нтиль *m*; *radio* электро́нная ла́мпа.
van [væn] фурго́н; 🚃 бага́жный и́ли това́рный ваго́н; ⚔ аванга́рд.
vane [vein] флю́гер; крыло́ (ветряно́й ме́льницы); ло́пасть *f* (винта́); лопа́тка (турби́ны).
vanguard ['vængɑ:d] ⚔ аванга́рд.
vanish ['væniʃ] исчеза́ть [-е́знуть].
vanity ['væniti] су́етность *f*; тщесла́вие; ~ bag да́мская су́мочка.
vanquish ['væŋkwiʃ] побежда́ть [-еди́ть].
vantage ['vɑ:ntidʒ] преиму́щество.
vapid ['væpid] □ безвку́сный, пре́сный; *fig.* ску́чный.
vapor|ize ['veipəraiz] испаря́ть(ся) [-ри́ть(ся)]; ~ous [-rəs] парообра́зный; (*mst fig.*) тума́нный.
vapo(u)r ['veipə] 1. пар; пары́; тума́н; *fig.* химе́ра, фанта́зия; 2. бахва́литься.
varia|ble ['vɛəriəbl] □ непостоя́нный, изме́нчивый; переме́нный; ~nce [-riəns] разногла́сие; ссо́ра; be at ~ расходи́ться во мне́ниях; находи́ться в противоре́чии; ~nt [-riənt] 1. ино́й; разли́чный; 2. вариа́нт; ~tion [vɛəri'eiʃən] измене́ние; отклоне́ние; ♪ вариа́ция.
varie|d ['vɛərid] □ *s.* various; ~gate ['vɛərigeit] де́лать пёстрым; разнообра́зить; ~ty [və'raiəti] разнообра́зие; многосторо́нность *f*; разнови́дность *f*; ряд, мно́жество; ~ show варьете́ *n indecl.*
various ['vɛəriəs] ра́зный; различ́ный; разнообра́зный.
varnish ['vɑ:niʃ] 1. лак; оли́фа; лакиро́вка (*a. fig.*); *fig.* прикра́са; 2. [от]лакирова́ть; придава́ть лоск (Д); *fig.* прикра́шивать [-ра́сить] (недоста́тки).
vary ['vɛəri] изменя́ть(ся) [-ни́ть (-ся)]; ра́зниться; расходи́ться [разойти́сь] (о мне́ниях); разнообра́зить.
vase [vɑ:z] ва́за.
vast [vɑ:st] □ обши́рный, грома́дный.
vat [væt] чан; бо́чка, ка́дка.
vault [vɔ:lt] 1. свод; склеп; подва́л, по́греб; *sport* прыжо́к (с упо́ром); 2. выводи́ть свод над (Т); перепры́гивать [-гнуть].
vaunt [vɔ:nt] [по]хва́статься (of Т).
veal [vi:l] теля́тина; *attr.* теля́чий.
veer [viə] меня́ть направле́ние (о ве́тре); *fig.* изменя́ть взгля́ды и т. п.
vegeta|ble ['vedʒitəbl] 1. о́вощ; ~s *pl.* зе́лень *f*, о́вощи *m/pl.*; 2. расти́тельный; овощно́й; ~rian [vedʒi'tɛəriən] 1. вегетариа́нец (-нка); 2. вегетариа́нский; ~te ['vedʒiteit] *fig.* прозяба́ть.
vehemen|ce ['vi:iməns] си́ла; стреми́тельность *f*; стра́стность *f*; ~t [-t] стреми́тельный; стра́стный.
vehicle ['vi:ikl] экипа́ж, пово́зка (и любо́е друго́е сре́дство тра́нспорта и́ли передвиже́ния); *fig.* сре́дство выраже́ния (мы́слей); проводни́к (зара́зы и т. п.).
veil [veil] 1. покрыва́ло; вуа́ль *f*; *fig.* заве́са; 2. закрыва́ть покрыва́лом, вуа́лью; *fig.* [за]маскирова́ть.
vein [vein] ве́на; жи́ла (*a.* ⚒); *fig.* [жи́лка; настрое́ние.]
velocity [vi'lɔsiti] ско́рость *f*.
velvet ['velvit] ба́рхат; *attr.* ба́рхатный; ~y [-i] ба́рхатный (*fig.*); бархати́стый.
venal ['vi:nl] прода́жный, подкупно́й (*a.* подку́пный).
vend [vend] прод(ав)а́ть; ~er, ~or ['vendə] продаве́ц.
veneer [və'niə] 1. фане́ра; 2. обкле́ивать фане́рой; *fig.* придава́ть (Д) вне́шний лоск.
venera|ble ['venərəbl] □ почте́нный; ~te [-reit] благогове́ть пе́ред (Т); ~tion [venə'reiʃən] благогове́ние, почита́ние.
venereal [vi'niəriəl] венери́ческий.
Venetian [vi'ni:ʃən] венециа́нский; ~ blind жалюзи́ *n indecl.*
vengeance ['vendʒəns] месть *f*, мще́ние.
venison ['venzn] оле́нина.
venom ['venəm] (*part.* змеи́ный) яд (*a. fig.*); ~ous [-əs] □ ядови́тый (*a. fig.*).
vent [vent] 1. отве́рстие; отду́шина; give ~ to изли́(ва́)ть (В); 2. *fig.* изли́(ва́)ть (В), дава́ть вы́ход (Д).
ventilat|e ['ventileit] прове́три(ва)ть; [про]вентили́ровать; *fig.* обсужда́ть [-уди́ть], выясня́ть [вы́яснить] (вопро́с); ~ion [venti'leiʃən] прове́тривание; вентиля́ция; *fig.* выясне́ние, обсужде́ние (вопро́са).
venture ['ventʃə] 1. риско́ванное предприя́тие; спекуля́ция; at a ~ науга́д, наудачу; 2. рискова́ть [-кну́ть] (Т); отва́жи(ва)ться на (В) (*a.* ~ upon); ~some [-səm] □, venturous [-rəs] □ сме́лый; риско́ванный.
veracious [və'reiʃəs] правди́вый.
verb|al ['və:bəl] □ слове́сный; у́стный; *gr.* глаго́льный; ~iage ['və:biidʒ] многосло́вие; ~ose [və:'bous] □ многосло́вный.
verdant ['və:dənt] □ зелене́ющий, зелёный.

verdict ['və:dikt] ⚖ верди́кт; пригово́р (прися́жных) (*a. fig.*).
verdigris ['və:digris] ярь-медя́нка.
verdure ['və:dʒə] зе́лень *f*.
verge [və:dʒ] **1.** край; кайма́ (вокру́г клу́мбы); *fig.* грань *f*; on the ~ of на гра́ни (P); **2.** клони́ться (to к Д); приближа́ться [-ли́зиться] (to к Д); ~ (up)on грани́чить с (T).
veri|fy ['verifai] проверя́ть [-е́рить]; подтвержда́ть [-рди́ть]; **~table** ['veritəbl] □ настоя́щий, и́стинный.
vermin ['və:min] *coll.* вреди́тели *m/pl.*, парази́ты *m/pl.*; **~ous** ['və:minəs] кишащий парази́тами.
vernacular [və'nækjulə] **1.** □ наро́дный (о выраже́нии); родно́й (о языке́); ме́стный (о диале́кте); **2.** наро́дный язы́к; ме́стный диале́кт; жарго́н.
versatile ['və:sətail] □ многосторо́нний; подвижно́й.
verse [və:s] стих; стихи́ *m/pl.*; поэ́зия; строфа́; **~d** [və:st] о́пытный, све́дущий.
versify ['və:sifai] *v/t.* перелага́ть на стихи́; *v/i.* писа́ть стихи́.
version ['və:ʃən] вариа́нт; ве́рсия; перево́д.
vertebral ['və:tibrəl] позвоно́чный.
vertical ['və:tikəl] □ вертика́льный; отве́сный.
vertig|inous [və:'tidʒinəs] □ головокружи́тельный.
verve [vεəv] жи́вость *f* (изображе́ния); разма́х.
very ['veri] **1.** *adv.* о́чень; the ~ best са́мое лу́чшее; **2.** *adj.* настоя́щий, су́щий; са́мый (как усиле́ние); the ~ same тот са́мый; the ~ thing и́менно то, что ну́жно; the ~ thought уже́ одна́ мысль *f*, сама́ мысль *f*; the ~ stones да́же ка́мни *m/pl.*; the veriest rascal после́дний негодя́й.
vesicle ['vesikl] пузырёк.
vessel ['vesl] сосу́д; су́дно, кора́бль *m*.
vest [vest] **1.** жиле́т; нате́льная фуфа́йка; вста́вка (в пла́тье); **2.** *v/t.* облека́ть [-е́чь] (with T); *v/i.* переходи́ть во владе́ние (in P).
vestibule ['vestibju:l] вестибю́ль *m*.
vestige ['vestidʒ] след.
vestment ['vestmənt] одея́ние; *eccl.* облаче́ние, ри́за.
vestry ['vestri] *eccl.* ри́зница; **~man** [-mən] член прихо́дского управле́ния.
veteran ['vetərən] **1.** ветера́н; быва́лый солда́т; **2.** *attr.* ста́рый, о́пытный.
veterinary ['vetnri] **1.** ветерина́р (*mst* ~ surgeon); **2.** ветерина́рный.
veto ['vi:tou] **1.** ве́то *n indecl.*; **2.** налага́ть ве́то на (B).
vex [veks] досажда́ть [досади́ть], раздража́ть [-жи́ть]; **~ation** [vek'seiʃən] доса́да, неприя́тность *f*; **~atious** [-ʃəs] доса́дный.
via ['vaiə] че́рез (B) (на пи́сьмах и т. п.).
vial ['vaiəl] пузырёк, буты́лочка.
viands ['vaiəndz] *pl.* я́ства *n/pl.*
vibrat|e [vai'breit] [по]колеба́ться, вибри́ровать; **~ion** [-ʃən] вибра́ция.
vice [vais] **1.** поро́к; недоста́ток; ⊕ тиски́ *m/pl.*; **2.** *pref.* ви́це...; **~roy** ['vaisrɔi] ви́це-коро́ль *m*.
vice versa ['vaisi'və:sə] наоборо́т.
vicinity [vi'siniti] окре́стность *f*; бли́зость *f*.
vicious ['viʃəs] □ поро́чный; зло́й.
vicissitude [vi'sisitju:d] : *mst* ~s *pl.* превра́тности *f/pl.*
victim ['viktim] же́ртва; **~ize** [-timaiz] де́лать свое́й же́ртвой; [за]му́чить.
victor ['viktə] победи́тель *m*; **~ious** [vik'tɔ:riəs] □ победоно́сный; **~y** ['viktəri] побе́да.
victual ['vitl] **1.** *v/i.* запаса́ться прови́зией; *v/t.* снабжа́ть прови́зией; **2.** *mst* ~s *pl.* продово́льствие, прови́зия; **~ler** ['vitlə] поставщи́к продово́льствия.
video ['vidiou] *adj.* телевизио́нный.
vie [vai] сопе́рничать.
view [vju:] **1.** вид (of на B); по́ле зре́ния, кругозо́р; взгляд; наме́рение; осмо́тр; in ~ of ввиду́ (P); on ~ (вы́ставленный) для обозре́ния; with a ~ to *or* of + *ger.* с наме́рением (+ *inf.*); have in ~ име́ть в виду́; **2.** осма́тривать [осмотре́ть]; рассма́тривать [-мотре́ть]; [по]смотре́ть на (B); **~point** то́чка зре́ния.
vigil|ance ['vidʒiləns] бди́тельность *f*; **~ant** [-lənt] □ бди́тельный.
vigo|rous ['vigərəs] □ си́льный, энерги́чный; **~(u)r** ['vigə] си́ла, эне́ргия.
vile [vail] □ ме́рзкий, ни́зкий.
vilify ['vilifai] поно́сить, [о]черни́ть.
village ['vilidʒ] село́, дере́вня; *attr.* се́льский, дереве́нский; **~r** [-ə] се́льский (-кая) жи́тель(ница *f*) *m*.
villain ['vilən] злоде́й, негодя́й; **~ous** [-əs] злоде́йский; по́длый; **~y** [-i] злоде́йство; по́длость *f*.
vim [vim] F эне́ргия, си́ла.
vindic|ate ['vindikeit] отста́ивать [отстоя́ть] (пра́во и т. п.); реабилити́ровать (*im*)*pf.*; опра́вдывать [-да́ть]; **~tive** [vin'diktiv] □ мсти́тельный.
vine [vain] виногра́дная лоза́; **~gar** ['vinigə] у́ксус; **~-growing** виногра́дарство; **~yard** ['vinjəd] виногра́дник.

vintage ['vintidʒ] сбор виногра́да; вино́ (из сбо́ра определённого го́да).
violat|e ['vaiəleit] наруша́ть [-у́шить], преступа́ть [-пи́ть] (кля́тву, зако́н и т. п.); [из]наси́ловать; **~ion** [vaiə'leiʃən] наруше́ние; изнаси́лование.
violen|ce ['vaiələns] неи́стовство; наси́лие; **~t** [-t] □ неи́стовый; я́ростный; наси́льственный.
violet ['vaiəlit] фиа́лка; фиоле́товый цвет.
violin [vaiə'lin] ♪ скри́пка.
viper ['vaipə] гадю́ка.
virago [vi'reigou] сварли́вая же́нщина.
virgin ['vəːdʒin] **1.** де́вственница; *poet. a. eccl.* де́ва; **2.** □ де́вственный (*a.* **~al**); **~ity** [vəː'dʒiniti] де́вственность *f*.
viril|e ['virail] возмужа́лый; му́жественный; **~ity** [vi'riliti] му́жество; возмужа́лость *f*.
virtu ['vəːtuː] понима́ние то́нкостей иску́сства; article of ~ худо́жественная ре́дкость *f*; **~al** ['vəːtjuəl] □ факти́ческий; **~e** ['vəːtjuː] доброде́тель *f*; досто́инство; in ~ of посре́дством (P); в си́лу (P); **~ous** ['vəːtjuəs] □ доброде́тельный; целому́дренный.
virulent ['virulənt] вируле́нтный (яд); опа́сный (о боле́зни); *fig.* зло́бный.
visa ['viːzə] *s.* visé.
viscount ['vaikaunt] вико́нт.
viscous ['viskəs] □ вя́зкий; тягу́чий (о жи́дкости).
visé ['viːzei] **1.** ви́за; **2.** визи́ровать (*im*)*pf.*, *pf. a.* [за-].
visible ['vizəbl] □ ви́димый; ви́дный; *fig.* я́вный, очеви́дный; *pred.* is he ~? принима́ет ли он?
vision ['viʒən] зре́ние; вид; виде́ние; *fig.* проница́тельность *f*; **~ary** ['viʒənəri] **1.** при́зрачный; фантасти́ческий; мечта́тельный; **2.** прови́дец (-дица); мечта́тель(ница *f*) *m*.
visit ['vizit] **1.** *v/t.* навеща́ть [-ести́ть]; посеща́ть [-ети́ть]; осма́тривать [-мотре́ть]; *fig.* постига́ть [-и́гнуть] *or* [-и́чь]; *v/i.* де́лать визи́ты; гости́ть; **2.** посеще́ние, визи́т; **~ation** [vizi'teiʃən] официа́льное посеще́ние; *fig.* испыта́ние, ка́ра; **~or** ['vizitə] посети́тель (-ница *f*) *m*, го́сть(я *f*) *m*; инспе́ктор.
vista ['vistə] перспекти́ва; вид.
visual ['vizjuəl] □ зри́тельный; нагля́дный; опти́ческий; **~ize** [-aiz] нагля́дно представля́ть себе́, мы́сленно ви́деть.
vital ['vaitl] □ жи́зненный; насу́щный, суще́ственный; живо́й (стиль); **~s**, ~ parts *pl.* жи́зненно ва́жные о́рганы *m/pl.*; **~ity** [vai'tæliti] жизнеспосо́бность *f*, жи́зненность *f*, живу́честь *f*; **~ize** ['vaitəlaiz] оживля́ть [-ви́ть].
vitamin(e) ['vaitəmin] витами́н.
vitiate ['viʃieit] [ис]по́ртить; де́лать недействи́тельным.
vivaci|ous [vi'veiʃəs] □ живо́й, оживлённый; **~ty** [-'væsiti] жи́вость *f*, оживлённость *f*.
vivid ['vivid] □ *fig.* живо́й, я́ркий.
vivify ['vivifai] оживля́ть [-ви́ть].
vixen ['viksn] лиси́ца-са́мка.
vocabulary [və'kæbjuləri] слова́рь *m*, спи́сок слов; запа́с слов.
vocal ['voukəl] □ голосово́й; звуча́щий; ♪ вока́льный.
vocation [vou'keiʃən] призва́ние; профе́ссия; **~al** [-l] □ профессиона́льный.
vociferate [vou'sifəreit] гро́мко крича́ть, горла́нить.
vogue [voug] мо́да; популя́рность *f*.
voice [vɔis] **1.** го́лос; give ~ to выража́ть [вы́разить] (B); **2.** выража́ть [вы́разить] (слова́ми).
void [vɔid] **1.** пусто́й; лишённый (of P); недействи́тельный; **2.** пустота́; ва́куум; **3.** ⚕ опорожня́ть [-ро́жнить]; де́лать недействи́тельным.
volatile ['vɔlətail] ⚗ летучий (*a. fig.*); *fig.* изме́нчивый.
volcano [vɔl'keinou] (*pl.*: volcanoes) вулка́н.
volition [vou'liʃən] волево́й акт, хоте́ние; во́ля.
volley ['vɔli] **1.** залп; *fig.* град (упрёков и т. п.); **2.** стреля́ть за́лпами; сы́паться гра́дом; *fig.* испуска́ть [-усти́ть] (кри́ки, жа́лобы).
voltage ['voultidʒ] ⚡ напряже́ние.
voluble ['vɔljubl] речи́стый, многоречи́вый.
volum|e ['vɔljum] том; объём; ёмкость *f*, вмести́тельность *f*; *fig.* си́ла, полнота́ (зву́ка и т. п.); **~inous** [və'ljuːminəs] □ объёмистый; многото́мный; обши́рный.
volunt|ary ['vɔləntəri] □ доброво́льный; доброво́льческий; **~eer** [vɔlən'tiə] **1.** доброво́лец; **2.** *v/i.* вызыва́ться [вы́зваться] (for на B); идти́ доброво́льцем; *v/t.* предлага́ть [-ложи́ть] (свою́ по́мощь и т. п.).
voluptu|ary [və'lʌptjuəri] сладостра́стник, сластолю́бец; **~ous** [-s] сладостра́стный; (*of people*) сластолюби́вый.
vomit ['vɔmit] **1.** рво́та; **2.** [вы́-]рвать: he ~s его́ рвёт; *fig.* изверга́ть [-е́ргнуть].
voraci|ous [vo'reiʃəs] □ прожо́рливый, жа́дный; **~ty** [vo'ræsiti] прожо́рливость *f*.
vortex ['vɔːteks] *mst fig.* водоворо́т; *mst fig.* вихрь *m*.

vote [vout] **1.** голосова́ние; баллотиро́вка; (избира́тельный) го́лос; пра́во го́лоса; во́тум; реше́ние; cast a ~ отдава́ть го́лос (for за В; against про́тив Р); **2.** *v/i.* голосова́ть (*im*)*pf.*, *pf. a.* [про-] (for за В; against про́тив Р); *v/t.* голосова́ть (*im*)*pf.*, *pf. a.* [про-]; **~r** ['voutə] избира́тель(ница *f*) *m.*

voting... ['voutiŋ] избира́тельный.

vouch [vautʃ]: ~ for руча́ться [поручи́ться] за (В); **~er** ['vautʃə] распи́ска; оправда́тельный докуме́нт; поручи́тель *m*; **~safe** [vautʃ'seif] удоста́ивать [-сто́ить] (В/Т).

vow [vau] **1.** обе́т, кля́тва; **2.** *v/t.* [по]кля́сться в (П).

vowel ['vauəl] гла́сный (звук).

voyage [vɔidʒ] **1.** путеше́ствие (мо́рем); **2.** путеше́ствовать (по́ морю).

vulgar ['vʌlgə] □ гру́бый, вульга́рный; по́шлый; широко́ распространённый; ~ tongue наро́дный язы́к; **~ize** [-raiz] опошля́ть [опо́шлить]; вульгаризи́ровать (*im*)*pf.*

vulnerable ['vʌlnərəbl] □ *fig.* уязви́мый.

vulture ['vʌltʃə] *zo.* стервя́тник; *fig.* хи́щник.

W

wad [wɔd] **1.** клочо́к ва́ты, ше́рсти и т. п.; пыж; **2.** набива́ть и́ли подбива́ть ва́той; забива́ть пыжо́м; **~ding** ['wɔdiŋ] наби́вка, подби́вка.

waddle ['wɔdl] ходи́ть вперева́лку.

wade [weid] *v/t.* переходи́ть вброд; *v/i.* проб(и)ра́ться (through по Д *or* че́рез В).

wafer ['weifə] обла́тка; ва́фля.

waffle ['wɔfl] *part. Am.* ва́фля.

waft [wɑ:ft] **1.** дунове́ние (ве́тра); струя́ (за́паха); **2.** носи́ть(ся), [по-] нести́(сь) (по во́здуху).

wag [wæg] **1.** шутни́к; **2.** маха́ть [махну́ть] (Т), виля́ть [вильну́ть] (Т); ~ one's finger грози́ть па́льцем.

wage [weidʒ] **1.** вести́ (войну́); **2.** *mst* **~s** ['weidʒiz] *pl.* за́работная пла́та.

waggish ['wægiʃ] □ шаловли́вый; заба́вный, коми́чный.

waggle ['wægl] F пома́хивать (Т); пока́чивать(ся).

wag(g)on ['wægən] пово́зка, теле́га; F де́тская коля́ска; 🚂 *Brit.* ваго́н-платфо́рма; **~er** [-ə] во́зчик.

waif [weif] беспризо́рник; бездо́мный челове́к; бро́шенная вещь *f.*

wail [weil] **1.** вопль *m*; вой (ве́тра); причита́ние; **2.** [за]вопи́ть; вы́ть, завы́(ва́)ть; причита́ть.

waist [weist] та́лия; ⚓ шкафу́т; **~coat** ['weiskout, 'weskət] жиле́т.

wait [weit] *v/i.* жда́ть (for В *or* Р), ожида́ть (for Р), подожда́ть *pf.* (for В *or* Р); (ча́сто: ~ at table) прислу́живать [-жи́ть] (за столо́м); ~ (up)on прислу́живать (Д); ~ and see занима́ть выжида́тельную пози́цию; *v/t.* выжида́ть [вы́ждать] (В); ~ dinner подожда́ть с обе́дом (for В); **~er** ['weitə] официа́нт.

waiting ['weitiŋ] ожида́ние; **~-room** приёмная; 🚂 зал ожида́ния.

waitress ['weitris] официа́нтка.

waive [weiv] отка́зываться [-за́ться] от (пра́ва и т. п.); **~r** ['weivə] ⚖ отка́з (от пра́ва, тре́бования).

wake [weik] **1.** ⚓ кильва́тер; **2.** [*irr.*] *v/i.* бо́дрствовать; (*mst* ~ up) просыпа́ться [просну́ться], пробужда́ться [-уди́ться]; *v/t.* [раз]буди́ть, пробужда́ть [-уди́ть]; возбужда́ть [-уди́ть] (жела́ния и т. п.); **~ful** ['weikful] □ бессо́нный; бди́тельный; **~n** ['weikən] *s.* wake 2.

wale [weil] полоса́, рубе́ц.

walk [wɔ:k] **1.** *v/i.* ходи́ть, идти́ [пойти́] (пешко́м); [по]гуля́ть; появля́ться [-ви́ться] (о привиде́нии); *v/t.* прогу́ливать (ло́шадь и т. п.); обходи́ть [обойти́]; **2.** ходьба́; похо́дка; прогу́лка пешко́м; тропа́, алле́я; ~ of life обще́ственное положе́ние; профе́ссия.

walking ['wɔ:kiŋ] **1.** ходьба́; **2.** гуля́ющий; ходя́чий; ~ tour экску́рсия пешко́м; **~-stick** трость *f.*

walk|-out ['wɔ:k'aut] *Am.* забасто́вка; **~-over** лёгкая побе́да.

wall [wɔ:l] **1.** стена́; сте́нка (сосу́да); **2.** обноси́ть стено́й; ~ up заде́л(ыв)ать (дверь и т. п.).

wallet ['wɔlit] бума́жник.

wallflower ⚘ желтофио́ль *f*; *fig.* де́вушка, оста́вшаяся без кавале́ра (на балу́).

wallop ['wɔləp] F [по]би́ть, [поот]колоти́ть.

wallow ['wɔlou] валя́ться, бара́хтаться.

wall|-paper ['wɔ:lpeipə] обо́и *m/pl.*; **~-socket** ⚡ ште́псельная розе́тка.

walnut [-nət] ⚘ гре́цкий оре́х.

walrus ['wɔ:lrəs] *zo.* морж.

waltz [wɔ:ls] **1.** вальс; **2.** вальси́ровать.

wan [wɔn] □ бле́дный; изнурённый; ту́склый.

wand [wɔnd] (волшéбная) пáлочка.
wander ['wɔ:ndə] бродúть; стрáнствовать; блуждáть (тáкже о взгля́де, мы́слях и т. п.).
wane [wein] **1.** убывáние (луны́); **2.** уменьшáться [умéньшиться]; убы́(вá)ть, быть на ущéрбе (о лунé); подходúть к концу́.
wangle ['wæŋgl] *sl.* ухитря́ться получúть.
want [wɔnt] **1.** недостáток (of P *or* в П); нуждá; потрéбность *f*; бéдность *f*; **2.** *v/i.* be ~ing: he is ~ing in patience емý недостаёт терпéния; ~ for нуждáться в (П); *v/t.* [за]хотéть (P *a.* B); [по]желáть (P *a.* B); нуждáться в (Д); he ~s energy емý недостаёт энéргии; what do you ~? что вам нýжно?; ~ed (в объявлéниях) трéбуется, ⚖ разы́скивается.
wanton ['wɔntən] **1.** □ рéзвый; произвóльный; бýйный (о рóсте); похотлúвый; распýтный; **2.** резвúться.
war [wɔ:] **1.** войнá; *fig.* борьбá; make ~ вестú войнý ([up]on с Т); **2.** *attr.* воéнный; **3.** воевáть.
warble ['wɔ:bl] издавáть трéли; [с]пéть (о птúцах).
ward [wɔ:d] **1.** опекáемый; райóн (гóрода); (больнúчная) палáта; (тюрéмная) кáмера; ~s *pl.* борóдка (ключá); **2.** ~ (off) отражáть [отразúть], отвращáть [-ратúть] (удáр); ~**er** ['wɔ:də] тюрéмщик; ~**robe** ['wɔ:droub] гардерóб; ~ trunk чемодáн-шкаф.
ware [wɛə] (в слóжный словáх) посýда; ~s *pl.* товáр(ы *pl.*).
warehouse 1. ['wɛəhaus] товáрный склад; пакгáуз; **2.** [-hauz] помещáть в склад; хранúть на склáде.
warfare ['wɔ:fɛə] войнá, ведéние войны́.
wariness ['wɛərinis] осторóжность *f*.
warlike ['wɔ:laik] воúнственный.
warm [wɔ:m] **1.** □ тёплый (*a. fig.*); *fig.* горя́чий; **2.** согревáние; **3.** [на-, со]грéть, нагрé(вá)ть(ся), согрé(вá)ть(ся) (*a.* ~ up); ~**th** [-θ] теплó; теплотá (*a. fig.*).
warn [wɔ:n] предупреждáть [-редúть] (of, against o П); предостерегáть [-стерéчь] (of, against от P); ~**ing** ['wɔ:niŋ] предупреждéние; предостережéние.
warp [wɔ:p] [по]корóбить(ся) (о дéреве); *fig.* извращáть [-ратúть], искажáть [исказúть] (взгля́ды и т. п.).
warrant ['wɔrənt] **1.** правомóчие; ручáтельство; ⚖ довéренность *f*; ~ of arrest прикáз об арéсте; **2.** опрáвдывать [-дáть]; ручáться [поручúться] за (B); † гарантúровать (*im*)*pf.*; ~**y** [-i] гарáнтия; ручáтельство.
warrior ['wɔriə] *poet.* боéц, вóин.
wart [wɔ:t] бородáвка; нарóст (на стволé дéрева).
wary ['wɛəri] □ осторóжный.
was [wɔz, wəz] *pt.* от be.
wash [wɔʃ] **1.** *v/t.* [вы́]мыть; обмы́(вá)ть; промы́(вá)ть; [вы́]стирáть; *v/i.* [вы́]мы́ться; стирáться (о матéрии); плескáться; **2.** мытьё; стúрка; бельё (для стúрки); прибóй; помóи *m/pl.*; *pharm.* примóчка; ~**able** ['wɔʃəbl] (хорошó) стирáющийся; ~**-basin** ['wɔʃbeisn] таз; умывáльная рáковина; ~**-cloth** тря́почка для мытья́; ~**er** ['wɔʃə] мóйщик (-ица); промывáтель *m*; стирáльная машúна; ⊕ шáйба, проклáдка; ~**(er)woman** прáчка; ~**ing** ['wɔʃiŋ] **1.** мытьё; стúрка; бельё (для стúрки); **2.** стирáльный; стирáющийся; ~**y** ['wɔʃi] жúдкий, водянúстый.
wasp [wɔsp] осá.
wastage ['weistidʒ] изнáшивание; потéри утéчкой, усýшкой и т. п.
waste [weist] **1.** пусты́ня; потéря; излúшняя трáта; отбрóсы *m/pl.*; ⊕ отхóды *m/pl.*; угáр; lay ~ опустошáть [-шúть]; **2.** пусты́нный; невоздéланный; опустошённый; **3.** *v/t.* расточáть [-чúть] (дéньги и т. п.); [по]теря́ть (врéмя); опустошáть [-шúть]; изнуря́ть [-рúть] (органúзм); *v/i.* истощáться [-щúться]; ~**ful** ['weistful] □ расточúтельный; ~**-paper:** ~ basket корзúна для бумáги.
watch [wɔtʃ] **1.** стрáжа; стóрож; ⚓ вáхта; (кармáнные úли нарýчные) часы́ *m/pl.*; **2.** *v/i.* [по]караýлить (over B); стоя́ть на стрáже; бóдрствовать; ~ for выжидáть [вы́ждать] (B); *v/t.* [по]сторожúть; наблюдáть, следúть за (T); выжидáть [вы́ждать]; ~**-dog** сторожевóй пёс; ~**ful** ['wɔtʃful] □ бдúтельный; ~**maker** часовщúк; ~**man** [-mən] (ночнóй) стóрож; ~**word** парóль *m*; лóзунг.
water ['wɔ:tə] **1.** водá; ~s *pl.* вóды *f/pl.*; drink the ~s пить целéбные вóды; *attr.* водянóй; вóдный; водо...; **2.** *v/t.* орошáть [оросúть]; [на]поúть (живóтных); полú(вá)ть; (*a.* ~ down) разбавля́ть водóй; *fig.* чересчýр смягчáть; *v/i.* слезúться; ходúть на водопóй; набирáть вóду (оораблé); ~**fall** водопáд; ~**-gauge** водомéр.
watering ['wɔ:təriŋ]: ~**-can**, ~**-pot** лéйка; ~**-place** водопóй; вóды *f/pl.*, курóрт с минирáльными вóдами; морскóй курóрт.
water|-level ýровень воды́; ⊕ ватерпáс; ~**man** ['wɔ:təmən] лóдочник, перевóзчик; ~**proof 1.** непромокáемый; **2.** непромокáемый плащ *m*; **3.** придавáть водонепроницáемость (Д); ~**shed**

водораздéл; бассéйн реки́; **~-side** бéрег; *attr.* располóженный на берегý; **~tight** водонепроницáемый; *fig.* выдéрживающий кри́тику; **~-way** вóдный путь *m*; фарвáтер; **~works** *pl.*, *a. sg.* водопровóдная стáнция; **~y** ['wɔ:təri] водяни́стый (*a. fig.*).

wattle ['wɔtl] **1.** плетéнь *m*; **2.** [с]плести́; стрóить из плетня́.

wave (weiv) **1.** волнá; знак (рукóй); зави́вка (причёски); **2.** *v/t.* [по-] махáть, дéлать знак (T); зави́(вá)ть (вóлосы); ~ a p. away дéлать знак комý-либо, чтóбы он удали́лся; ~ aside *fig.* отмáхиваться [-хнýться] от (P); *v/i.* развевáться (о знамёнах); волновáться (о ни́ве); качáться (о вéтке); ви́ться (о волосáх); **~-length** длинá волны́.

waver ['weivə] [по]колебáться; колыхáться [-хнýться] (о плáмени); дрóгнуть (о войскáх) *pf.*

wavy ['weivi] волни́стый.

wax[1] [wæks] **1.** воск; сургýч; ушнáя сéра; *attr.* восковóй; **2.** [на-] вощи́ть.

wax[2] [~] [*irr.*] прибы́(вá)ть (о лунé).

wax|en ['wæksən] (*mst fig.*) восковóй; *fig.* мя́гкий как воск; **~y** ['wæksi] □ восковóй; похóжий на воск.

way [wei] *mst* дорóга, путь *m*; сторонá, направлéние; мéтод; срéдство; обы́чай, привы́чка; óбласть *f*, сфéра; состоя́ние; отношéние; (*a.* ~s *pl.*) óбраз (жи́зни, мы́слей); ~ in, out вход, вы́ход; this ~ сюдá; by the ~ кстáти, мéжду прóчим; по дорóге; by ~ of рáди (P); в кáчестве (P); on the ~ в пути́; по дорóге; out of the ~ находя́щийся в сторонé; необы́чный; необыкновéнный; under ~ ⚓ на ходý (*a. fig.*); give ~ уступáть [-пи́ть] (Д); have one's ~ добивáться своегó; настáивать на своём; lead the ~ идти́ во главé; покáзывать примéр; **~-bill** накладнáя; спи́сок пассажи́ров; **~farer** пýтник; **~lay** [wei'lei] [*irr.* (lay)] подстерегáть [-рéчь]; **~side 1.** обóчина; **2.** придорóжный; **~ward** ['weiwəd] □ своенрáвный; капри́зный.

we [wi:, wi] *pron. pers.* мы.

weak [wi:k] □ слáбый; **~en** ['wi:kən] *v/t.* ослабля́ть [-áбить]; *v/i.* [о]слабéть; **~ly** [-li] хи́лый; *adv.* слáбо; **~-minded** ['wi:k'maindid] слабоýмный; **~ness** [-nis] слáбость *f.*

weal[1] [wi:l] бла́го.

weal[2] [~] *s.* wale.

wealth [welθ] богáтство; изоби́лие; **~y** ['welθi] □ богáтый.

wean [wi:n] отнимáть от груди́; отучáть [-чи́ть] (from, of от P).

weapon ['wepən] орýжие; *fig.* срéдство (самозащи́ты).

wear [weə] **1.** [*irr.*] *v/t.* носи́ть (одéжду); (*a.* ~ away, down, off) стирáть [стерéть], изнáшивать [износи́ть]; *fig.* изнуря́ть [-ри́ть], истощáть [-щи́ть] (*mst* ~ out); *v/i.* носи́ться (о плáтье); ~ on мéдленно тянýться (о врéмени); **2.** ношéние, нóска (одéжды); одéжда, плáтье; (*a.* ~ and tear, *part.* ⊕) изнóс, изнáшивание; be the ~ быть в мóде.

wear|iness ['wiərinis] устáлость *f*; утомлённость *f*; **~isome** [-səm] □ утоми́тельный; **~y** ['wiəri] **1.** □ утомлённый; утоми́тельный; **2.** утомля́ть(ся) [-ми́ть(ся)].

weasel ['wi:zl] *zo.* лáска.

weather ['weðə] **1.** погóда; **2.** *v/t.* вывéтривать [вы́ветрить]; выдéрживать [вы́держать] (бýрю) (*a. fig.*); подвергáть атмосфéрному влия́нию; *v/i.* вывéтриваться [вы́ветриться]; подвергáться атмосфéрному влия́нию; **~-beaten, ~-worn** обвéтренный; закалённый (о человéке); повреждённый бýрями.

weav|e [wi:v] [*irr.*] [со]ткáть; [с]плести́; *fig.* сочиня́ть [-ни́ть]; **~er** ['wi:və] ткач, ткачи́ха.

web [web] ткань *f*; паути́на; (плáвательная) перепóнка; **~bing** ['webiŋ] ткáная тесьмá.

wed [wed] выдавáть зáмуж; жени́ть (*im*)*pf.*; сочетáть брáком; **~ding** ['wediŋ] **1.** свáдьба; **2.** свáдебный.

wedge [wedʒ] **1.** клин; **2.** закрепля́ть кли́ном; раскáлывать при пóмощи кли́на; (*a.* ~ in) вкли́нивать(ся) [-ни́ть(ся)]; ~ o. s. in вти́скиваться [вти́снуться].

wedlock ['wedlɔk] брак.

Wednesday ['wenzdi] средá (день).

wee [wi:] крóшечный, мáленький.

weed [wi:d] **1.** сóрная травá, сорня́к; **2.** [вы́]полóть; **~s** [-z] *pl.* вдóвий трáур; **~y** ['wi:di] зарóсший сóрной травóй; F *fig.* долговя́зый, тóщий.

week [wi:k] недéля; by the ~ понедéльно; this day ~ недéлю томý назáд; чéрез недéлю; **~-day** бýдний день *m*; **~-end** нерабóчее врéмя от суббóты до понедéльника; **~ly** ['wi:kli] **1.** еженедéльный; недéльный; **2.** еженедéльник.

weep [wi:p] [*irr.*] [за]плáкать; покрывáться кáплями; **~ing** ['wi:piŋ] плакýчий (об и́ве, берёзе).

weigh [wei] *v/t.* взвéшивать [-éсить] (*a. fig.*); ~ anchor поднимáть я́корь; **~ed** down отягощённый; *v/i.* вéсить; взвéшиваться [-éситься]; *fig.* имéть вес, значéние; ~ (up)on тяготéть над (T).

weight [weit] **1.** вес; тя́жесть *f*; ги́ря; *sport* штáнга; брéмя *n*; влия́ние; 2. отягоща́ть [-готи́ть]; *fig.* обременя́ть [-ни́ть]; ~y ['weiti] □ тяжёлый; *fig.* ва́жный, ве́ский.

weird [wiəd] таи́нственный; роково́й; F стра́нный, непоня́тный.

welcome ['welkəm] 1. приве́тствие; you are ~ to *inf.* я охо́тно позволя́ю вам (+ *inf.*); (you are) ~ не́ за что!; ~! добро́ пожа́ловать!; 2. жела́нный; прия́тный; 3. приве́тствовать (*a. fig.*); раду́шно принима́ть.

weld [weld] ⊕ сва́ривать(ся) [-и́ть (-ся)].

welfare ['welfɛə] благосостоя́ние; ~ work рабо́та по улучше́нию бытовы́х усло́вий населе́ния.

well[1] [wel] 1. коло́дец; родни́к; *fig.* исто́чник; пролёт (ле́стницы); ⊕ бурова́я сква́жина; 2. хлы́нуть *pf.*; бить ключо́м.

well[2] [~] 1. хорошо́; ~ off состоя́тельный; I am not ~ мне нездоро́вится; 2. *int.* ну! or ну, ...; **~-being** благополу́чие; **~-bred** благовоспи́танный; **~-favo(u)red** привлека́тельный; **~-mannered** с хоро́шими мане́рами; **~-timed** своевре́менный; **~-to-do** [-tə'du:] состоя́тельный, зажи́точный; **~-worn** поно́шенный; *fig.* изби́тый.

Welsh [welʃ] 1. уэ́льский, валли́йский; 2. валли́йский язы́к; the ~ валли́йцы *m/pl.*

welt [welt] рант (на о́буви); полоса́ (от уда́ра кнуто́м и т. п.).

welter ['weltə] 1. сумато́ха, сумбу́р; 2. валя́ться, бара́хтаться.

wench [wentʃ] де́вка, (крестья́нская) де́вушка.

went [went] *pt.* от **go.**

wept [wept] *pt.* и *p. pt.* от **weep.**

were [wə:, wə] *pt. pl.* от **be.**

west [west] 1. за́пад; 2. за́падный; 3. *adv.* к за́паду, на за́пад; ~ of к за́паду от (Р); **~erly** ['westəli], **~ern** ['westən] за́падный; **~ward(s)** ['westwəd(z)] на за́пад.

wet [wet] 1. дождли́вая пого́да; мокрота́; 2. мо́крый; вла́жный, сыро́й; дождли́вый; 3. [*irr.*] [на-] мочи́ть, нама́чивать [-мочи́ть]; увлажня́ть [-ни́ть].

wether ['weðə] кастри́рованный бара́н.

wet-nurse ['wetnə:s] корми́лица.

whale [weil] кит; **~bone** ['weilboun] кито́вый ус; **~r** ['weilə] китобо́йное су́дно; китоло́в.

whaling ['weiliŋ] охо́та на кито́в.

wharf [wɔ:f] (това́рная) при́стань *f*; на́бережная.

what [wɔt] 1. что?; ско́лько ...?; 2. то, что; что; ~ about ...? что но́вого о ...?; ну, как ...?; ~ for? заче́м?; ~ a blessing! кака́я благода́ть!; 3. ~ with ... ~ with отча́сти от (Р) ... отча́сти от (Р); **~(so)ever** [wɔt(sou)'evə] како́й бы ни; что бы ни; there is no doubt whatever нет никако́го сомне́ния.

wheat [wi:t] пшени́ца.

wheel [wi:l] 1. колесо́; гонча́рный круг; *mot.* руль *m*; 2. ката́ть, [по-] кати́ть (коля́ску и т. п.); е́хать на велосипе́де; опи́сывать круги́; повора́чивать(ся) [поверну́ть(ся)]; ⚔ заходи́ть фла́нгом; ⚔ right ~! ле́вое плечо́ вперёд — марш!; **~-barrow** та́чка; **~-chair** кре́сло на колёсах (для инвали́да); **~ed** [wi:ld] колёсный, на колёсах.

wheeze [wi:z] дыша́ть с при́свистом.

when [wen] 1. когда́?; 2. *conj.* когда́, в то вре́мя как, как то́лько; тогда́ как.

whence [wens] отку́да.

when(so)ever [wen(sou)'evə] вся́кий раз когда́; когда́ бы ни.

where [wɛə] где, куда́; from ~ отку́да; **~about(s)** 1. ['wɛərə'baut(s)] где?, о́коло како́го ме́ста?; 2. ['wɛərəbaut(s)] местонахожде́ние; **~as** [wɛər'æz] тогда́ как; поско́льку; **~by** [wɛə'bai] посре́дством чего́; **~fore** ['wɛəfɔ:] почему́?; **~in** [wɛər'in] в чём; **~of** [wɛər'ɔv] из кото́рого; о кото́ром; о чём; **~upon** [wɛərə'pɔn] по́сле чего́; **~ver** [wɛər'evə] где бы ни, куда́ бы ни; **~withal** [-wi'ðɔ:l] необходи́мые сре́дства *n/pl.*

whet [wet] [на]точи́ть (на оселке́).

whether ['weðə] ... ли; ~ or по так и́ли и́наче; во вся́ком слу́чае.

whetstone ['wetstoun] точи́льный ка́мень *m.*

whey [wei] сы́воротка.

which [witʃ] 1. кото́рый?; како́й?; 2. кото́рый; что; **~ever** [-'evə] како́й уго́дно, како́й бы ни ...

whiff [wif] 1. дунове́ние, струя́ (во́здуха); дымо́к; затя́жка (при куре́нии); 2. пуска́ть клубы́ (ды́ма); попы́хивать (Т).

while [wail] 1. вре́мя *n*, промежу́ток вре́мени; for a ~ на вре́мя; F worth ~ сто́ящий затра́ченного труда́; 2. ~ away проводи́ть [-вести́] (вре́мя); 3. (*a.* whilst [wailst]) пока́, в то вре́мя как; тогда́ как.

whim [wim] при́хоть *f*, капри́з.

whimper ['wimpə] [за]хны́кать.

whim|sical ['wimzikəl] □ прихотли́вый, причу́дливый; **~sy** ['wimzi] при́хоть *f*; причу́да.

whine [wain] [за]скули́ть; [за]хны́кать.

whip [wip] 1. *v/t.* хлеста́ть [-стну́ть]; [вы́]сечь; сби(ва́)ть (сли́вки, я́йца и т. п.); *pol.* ~ in co-з(ы)ва́ть]; ~ up распеве́ливать [-ли́ть]; подстёгивать [-стегну́ть]; *v/i.* ю́ркать [юркну́ть]; трепа́ться (о па́русе); 2. кнут (*a.* riding-~) хлыст; ку́чер; *parl.* организа́тор па́ртии.

whippet *zo.* ['wipit] гóнчая собáка.
whipping ['wipiŋ] подстёгивание (кнутóм); взбýчка; **~-top** волчóк.
whirl [wə:l] 1. вихревóе движéние; вихрь *m*; кружéние; 2. кружи́ть(ся); **~-pool** водоворóт; **~-wind** вихрь *m*.
whisk [wisk] 1. вéничек, метёлочка; мутóвка; 2. *v/t.* сби(вá)ть (сли́вки и т. п.); смáхивать [-хнýть]; помáхивать (хвостóм); *v/i.* ю́ркать [юркнýть]; **~ers** ['wiskəz] *pl. zo.* усы́ (кóшки и т. п.) *m/pl.*; бакенбáрды *f/pl.*
whisper ['wispə] 1. шёпот; 2. шептáть [шепнýть].
whistle ['wisl] 1. сви ·; свистóк; 2. свистáть, свистéть [сви́стнуть].
white [wait] 1. *com.* бéлый; блéдный; F чéстный; неви́нный, чи́стый; ~ heat бéлое калéние; ~ lie неви́нная (*or* святáя) ложь *f*; 2. бéлый цвет; белизнá; белóк (глáза, яйцá); бели́ла *n/pl.*; **~n** ['waitn] [по]бели́ть; [по]белéть; **~ness** ['waitnis] белизнá; **~wash** 1. побéлка; 2. [по]бели́ть; *fig.* обеля́ть [ли́ть].
whither *lit.* ['wiðə] кудá.
whitish ['waitiʃ] бел(ес)овáтый.
Whitsun ['witsn] *eccl.* трóица.
whittle ['witl] строгáть и́ли оттáчивать ножóм; *fig.* ~ away свести́ на нет.
whiz(z) [wiz] свистéть (о пýлях и т. п.).
who [hu:] *pron.* 1. кто?; 2. котóрый; кто; тот, кто ...; *pl.*: те, кто.
whoever [hu:'evə] *pron.* кто бы ни ...; котóрый бы ни ...
whole [houl] 1. □ цéлый, весь; невреди́мый; ~ milk цéльное молокó; 2. цéлое; всё *n*; итóг; (up)on the ~ в цéлом; в óбщем; **~-hearted** □ и́скренний, от всегó сéрдца; **~sale** 1. (*mst* ~ trade) оптóвая торгóвля; 2. оптóвый; *fig.* в больши́х размéрах; ~ dealer оптóвый торгóвец; 3. óптом; **~some** [houlsəm'] □ полéзный, здорóвый.
wholly ['houli] *adv.* целикóм, всецéло.
whom [hu:m] *pron.* (вини́тельный падéж от who) когó и т. д.; котóрого и т. д.
whoop [hu:p] 1. ги́канье; 2. ги́кать [ги́кнуть]; **~ing-cough** ['hu:piŋkɔf] ⚕ коклю́ш.
whose [hu:z] (роди́тельный падéж от who) чей *m*, чья *f*, чьё *n*, чьи *pl.*; *rel. pron. mst*: котóрого, котóрой: ~ father отéц котóрого ...
why [wai] 1. почемý?, отчегó?, зачéм?; 2. да ведь ...; что же...
wick [wik] фити́ль *m*.
wicked ['wikid] □ злой, злóбный; безнрáвственный; **~ness** [-nis] злóбность *f*; безнрáвственность *f*.
wicker ['wikə] прýтья для плетéния; ~ basket плетёная корзи́нка; ~ chair плетёный стул.
wicket ['wikit] кали́тка; ворóтца *n/pl.* (в кри́кете).
wide [waid] *a.* □ *and adv.* ширóкий; простóрный; далёкий; ширóкó; далекó, далёко (of от P); ~ awake бди́тельный; осмотри́тельный; 3 feet ~ три фýта в ширинý, шириной в три фýта; **~n** ['waidn] расширя́ть(ся) [-и́рить (-ся)] **~-spread** широкó распространённый.
widow ['widou] вдовá; *attr.* вдóвий; **~er** [-ə] вдовéц.
width [widθ] ширинá; широтá.
wield [wi:ld] *lit.* владéть (T); имéть в рукáх.
wife [waif] женá; **~ly** ['waifli] свóйственный женé.
wig [wig] пари́к.
wild [waild] 1. □ ди́кий; бýрный; бýйный; run ~ расти́ без присмóтра; talk ~ говори́ть не дýмая; 2. ~, ~s [-z] ди́кая мéстность *f*; дéбри *f/pl.*; **~cat** *zo.* ди́кая кóшка; *fig.* недобросóвестное рискóванное предприя́тие; *attr.* рискóванный; нелегáльный; **~erness** ['wildənis] пусты́ня, ди́кая мéстность *f*; **~-fire**: like ~ с быстротóй мóлнии.
wile [wail] *mst* ~s *pl.* хи́трость *f*; улóвка.
wil(l)ful ['wilful] □ упря́мый, своевóльный; преднамéренный.
will [wil] 1. вóля; си́ла вóли; желáние; завещáние; with a ~ энерги́чно; 2. [*irr.*] *v/aux.*: he ~ come он придёт; he ~ do it он э́то сдéлает; он хóчет э́то сдéлать; он обы́чно э́то дéлает; 3. завещáть (*im*)*pf.*; [по]желáть, [за]хотéть; ~ o. s. заставля́ть [-стáвить] себя́.
willing ['wiliŋ] □ охóтно готóвый (to на В *or* + *inf.*); **~ness** [nis] готóвность *f*.
will-o-the-wisp ['wilәðәwisp] блуждáющий огонёк.
willow ['wilou] ♀ и́ва.
wily ['waili] □ хи́трый, ковáрный.
win [win] [*irr.*] *v/t.* выи́грывать [вы́играть]; одéрживать [-жáть] (побéду); получáть [-чи́ть]; снискáть *pf.*; (to do) с‹лоня́ть [-ни́ть] (сдéлать); ~ a p. ‹ver склони́ть когó-либо на свою́ стóрону; *v/i.* выи́грывать [вы́играть]; одéрживать побéду.
wince [wins] вздрáгивать [вздрóгнуть].
winch [wintʃ] лебёдка; вóрот.
wind[1] [wind, *poet.* waind] 1. вéтер; дыхáние; ⚕ гáзы *m/pl.*; ♪ духовы́е инструмéнты *m/pl.*; 2. заставля́ть запыхáться; давáть перевести́ дух; [по]чýять.
wind[2] [waind] [*irr.*] *v/t.* намáтывать [намотáть]; обмáтывать [об-

мота́ть]; обви́(ва́)ть; ~ up заводи́ть [завести́] (часы́); † ликвиди́ровать (*im*)*pf.*; зака́нчивать [зако́нчить] (де́ло, пре́ния и т. п.); *v/i.* нама́тываться [намота́ться]; обви́(ва́)ться.

wind|bag ['windbæg] *sl.* болту́н, пустозво́н; **~fall** па́данец; бурело́м; *fig.* неожи́данное сча́стье.

winding ['waindiŋ] **1.** изги́б, изви́лина; нама́тывание; ⚡ обмо́тка; **2.** изви́листый; спира́льный; ~ stairs *pl.* винтова́я ле́стница; **~-sheet** са́ван.

wind-instrument ['windinstrumənt] ♪ духово́й инструме́нт.

windlass ['windləs] ⚓ бра́шпиль *m*; ⊕ во́рот.

windmill [-mil] ветряна́я ме́льница.

window ['windou] окно́; витри́на; **~-dressing** декори́рование витри́ны; *fig.* пока́з в лу́чшем ви́де.

wind|pipe ['windpaip] *anat.* трахе́я; **~-screen** *mot.* ветрово́е стекло́.

windy ['windi] □ ве́треный; *fig.* несерьёзный; многосло́вный.

wine [wain] вино́; **~press** виноде́льный пресс.

wing [wiŋ] **1.** крыло́; *co.* рука́; ✈, ⚔ авиапо́лк, *Am.* авиабрига́да; ⚔ фланг; ⚓ фли́гель *m*; *thea.* **~s** *pl.* кули́сы *f/pl.*; take ~ полете́ть *pf.*; on the ~ на лету́; **2.** *fig.* окрыля́ть [-ли́ть]; ускоря́ть [-о́рить]; [по]лете́ть.

wink [wiŋk] **1.** морга́ние; миг; F not get a ~ of sleep не смыка́ть глаз; **2.** морга́ть [-гну́ть], мига́ть [мигну́ть]; ~ at подми́гивать [-гну́ть] (Д); смотре́ть сквозь па́льцы на (В).

win|ner ['winə] победи́тель(ница *f*) *m*; призёр; **~ning** ['winiŋ] **1.** вы́игрывающий; побежда́ющий; *fig.* привлека́тельный (*a.* **~some** [-səm]); **2.** **~s** *pl.* вы́игрыш.

wint|er ['wintə] **1.** зима́; *attr.* зи́мний; **2.** проводи́ть зи́му, [пере-, про]зимова́ть; **~ry** ['wintri] зи́мний; холо́дный; *fig.* неприве́тливый.

wipe [waip] вытира́ть [вы́тереть]; утира́ть [утере́ть]; ~ out *fig.* смы(ва́)ть (позо́р); уничтожа́ть [-о́жить].

wire ['waiə] **1.** про́волока; про́вод; F телегра́мма; **2.** монти́ровать провода́ на (П); телеграфи́ровать (*im*)*pf.*; скрепля́ть и́ли свя́зывать про́волокой; **~drawn** ['waiə'drɔːn] то́нкий, казуисти́ческий; **~less** ['waiəlis] **1.** □ беспро́волочный; *attr.* ра́дио...; **2.** ра́дио *n indecl.*; on the ~ по ра́дио; ~ (message) радиогра́мма; ~ (telegraphy) беспро́волочный телегра́ф, радиотелеграфи́я; ~ operator ради́ст; ~ pirate радиоза́яц; ~ (set) радиоприёмник; **2.** передава́ть по ра́дио; **~-netting** про́волочная се́тка.

wiry ['waiəri] про́волочный; *fig.* жи́листый; выно́сливый.

wisdom ['wizdəm] му́дрость *f*; ~ tooth зуб му́дрости.

wise [waiz] **1.** му́дрый; благоразу́мный; **~crack** *Am.* уда́чное и́ли саркасти́ческое замеча́ние; **2.** о́браз, спо́соб.

wish [wiʃ] **1.** жела́ние; пожела́ние; **2.** [по]жела́ть (Р) (*a.* ~ for); ~ well (ill) (не) благоволи́ть (к Д); **~ful** ['wiʃful] □ жела́ющий, жа́ждущий; тоскли́вый.

wisp [wisp] пучо́к (соло́мы, се́на и т. п.).

wistful ['wistful] □ заду́мчивый, тоскли́вый.

wit [wit] **1.** остроу́мие; ра́зум (*a.* **~s** *pl.*); остря́к; be at one's **~'s** end быть в тупике́; **2.** to ~ то́ есть, а и́менно.

witch [witʃ] колду́нья, ве́дьма; *fig.* чароде́йка; **~craft** ['witʃkrɑːft] колдовство́.

with [wið] с (Т), со (Т); от (Р); у (Р); при (П); ~ a knife ножо́м, ~ a pen перо́м и т. д.

withdraw [wið'drɔː] [*irr.* (draw)] *v/t.* отдёргивать [-рнуть]; брать наза́д; изыма́ть [изъя́ть] (кни́гу из прода́жи, де́ньги из обраще́ния); *v/i.* удаля́ться [-ли́ться]; ретирова́ться (*im*)*pf.*; ⚔ отходи́ть [отойти́]; **~al** [-əl] отдёргивание; изъя́тие; удале́ние; ⚔ отхо́д.

wither ['wiðə] *v/i.* [за]вя́нуть; [по-] блёкнуть; *v/t.* иссуша́ть [-ши́ть].

with|hold [wið'hould] [*irr.* (hold)] уде́рживать(ся) [-жа́ть(ся)]; отка́зывать [-за́ть] в (П); скры(ва́)ть (from от Р); **~in** [-'in] **1.** *lit. adv.* внутри́; **2.** *prp.* в (П), в преде́лах (Р); внутри́ (Р); ~ doors в до́ме; ~ call в преде́лах слы́шимости; **~out** [-'aut] **1.** *lit. adv.* вне, снару́жи; **2.** *prp.* без (Р); вне (Р); **~stand** [-'stænd] [*irr.* (stand)] противостоя́ть (Д).

witness ['witnis] **1.** свиде́тель(ница *f*) *m*; очеви́дец (-дица); bear ~ свиде́тельствовать (to, of о П); in ~ of в доказа́тельство (Р); **2.** свиде́тельствовать о (П); засвиде́тельствовать (В) *pf.*; быть свиде́телем (Р); заверя́ть [-е́рить] (по́дпись и т. п.).

wit|ticism ['witisizm] остро́та, шу́тка; **~ty** ['witi] □ остроу́мный.

wives [waivz] *pl.* от wife.

wizard ['wizəd] волше́бник, маг.

wizen(ed) ['wizn(d)] вы́сохший; смо́рщенный.

wobble ['wɔbl] кача́ться [качну́ться]; ковыля́ть [-льну́ть].

woe [wou] го́ре, скорбь *f*; ~ is me! го́ре мне!; **~begone** ['woubigɔn] удручённый го́рем; мра́чный;

~ful ['woufuI] □ скóрбный, гóрестный; жáлкий.
woke [wouk] *pt.* от wake; **~n** ['woukən] *p. pt.* от wake.
wolf [wulf] **1.** волк; **2.** пожирáть с жáдностью; **~ish** ['wulfiʃ] вóлчий; хи́щный.
wolves [wulvz] *pl.* от wolf 1.
woman ['wumən] **1.** жéнщина; **2.** жéнский; ~ doctor жéнщина-врач; ~ student студéнтка; **~hood** [-hud] жéнский пол; жéнственность *f*; **~ish** [-iʃ] □ женоподóбный, бáбий; **~kind** [-'kaind] *coll.* жéнщины *f/pl.*; **~like** [-laik] женоподóбный; **~ly** [-li] жéнственный.
womb [wu:m] *anat.* мáтка; чрéво (мáтери); *fig.* лóно.
women ['wimin] *pl.* от woman; **~folk** [-fouk] жéнщины *f/pl.*
won [wʌn] *pt.* и *p. pt.* от win.
wonder ['wʌndə] **1.** удивлéние, изумлéние; чýдо; дикóвина; **2.** удивля́ться [-ви́ться] (at Д); I ~ (мне) интерéсно знать; **~ful** [-ful] □ удиви́тельный, замечáтельный.
won't [wount] не бýду и т. д.; не хочý и т. д.
wont [~] **1.** be ~ имéть обыкновéние; **2.** обыкновéние, привы́чка; **~ed** привы́чный.
woo [wu:] ухáживать за (Т); [по-] свáтаться за (В).
wood [wud] лес; дéрево, лесоматериáл; дровá *n/pl.*; *attr.* леснóй; деревя́нный; дровянóй; ♪ деревя́нные духовы́е инструменты *m/pl.*; **~cut** гравю́ра на дéреве; **~-cutter** дровосéк; гравёр по дéреву; **~ed** ['wudid] леси́стый; **~en** ['wudn] деревя́нный; *fig.* безжи́зненный; **~man** [-mən] лесни́к; лесорýб; **~pecker** ['pekə] дя́тел; **~-winds** [-windz] деревя́нные духовы́е инструмéнты *m/pl.*; **~work** деревя́нные издéлия *n/pl.*; деревя́нные чáсти *f/pl.* (строéния); **~y** ['wudi] леси́стый; *fig.* деревяни́стый.
wool [wul] шерсть *f*; *attr.* шерстянóй; **~-gathering** ['wulgæðəriŋ] витáние в облакáх; **~(l)en** ['wulin] **1.** шерстянóй; **2.** шерстянáя матéрия; **~ly** ['wuli] **1.** покры́тый шéрстью; шерсти́стый; си́плый; **2.** wollies *pl.* шерстяны́е вéщи *f/pl.*
word [wə:d] **1.** *mst* слóво; разговóр; вéсть *f*; сообщéние; ⚔ парóль *m*; **~s** *pl.* ♪ словá (пéсни) *n/pl.*; *fig.* крýпный разговóр; **2.** выражáть словáми; формули́ровать (*im*)*pf.*, *pf. a.* [c-]; **~ing** ['wə:diŋ] формулирóвка; **~-splitting** софи́стика; буквоéдство.
wordy ['wə:di] □ многослóвный; словéсный.
wore [wɔ:] *pt.* от wear 1.
work [wə:k] **1.** рабóта; труд; дéло; заня́тие; произведéние, сочинéние; *attr.* рабóто...; рабóчий; **~s** *pl.* механи́зм; строи́тельные рабóты *f/pl.*; завóд; мастерски́е *f/pl.*; be in (out of) ~ имéть рабóту (быть безрабóтным); set to ~ брáться за рабóту; **~s** council произвóдственный совéт; **2.** *v/i.* рабóтать; занимáться [-ня́ться]; дéйствовать; *v/t.* [*irr.*] обрабáтывать [-бóтать]; отдéл(ыв)ать; [*regular vb.*] разрабáтывать [-бóтать] (рудни́к и т. п.); приводи́ть в дéйствие; ~ one's way проби́(вá)ться; ~ off отрабáтывать [-бóтать]; отдéл(ыв)аться от (Р); ✝ распрод(ав)áть; ~ out решáть [реши́ть] (задáчу); разрабáтывать [-бóтать] (план) [*a. irr.*]; ~ up отдéл(ыв)ать; взбудорáжи(ва)ть; подстрекáть [-кнýть] на (В).
work|able ['wə:kəbl] □ примени́мый; выполни́мый; пригóдный для рабóты; **~aday** ['wə:kədai] бýдничный; **~day** бýдний (*or* рабóчий) день *m*; **~er** ['wə:kə] рабóчий; рабóтник (-ица); **~-house** рабóтный дом; *Am.* исправи́тельный дом; **~ing** ['wə:kiŋ] **1.** рабóта, дéйствие; разрабóтка; обрабóтка; **2.** рабóтающий; рабóчий; дéйствующий.
workman ['wə:kmən] рабóчий; рабóтник; **~like** [-laik] искýсный; **~ship** мастерствó (ремéсленника); отдéлка (рабóты).
work|shop ['wə:kʃɔp] мастерскáя; цех; **~woman** рабóтница.
world [wə:ld] *com.* мир, свет; *attr.* мировóй; всеми́рный; *fig.* a ~ of мнóжество, кýча (Р); bring (come) into the ~ рождáть [роди́ть] (рождáться [роди́ться]); champion of the ~ чемпиóн ми́ра.
wordly ['wə:ldli] мирскóй; свéтский; **~-wise** ['wə:ldli'waiz] óпытный, бывáлый.
world-power мировáя держáва.
worm [wə:m] **1.** червя́к, червь *m*; ⚕ глист; **2.** вывéдывать [вы́ведать], выпы́тывать [вы́пытать] (out of у Р); ~ o. s. *fig.* вкрáдываться [вкрáсться] (into в В); **~eaten** источенный червя́ми; *fig.* устарéлый.
worn [wɔ:n] *p. pt.* от wear 1; **~-out** [wɔ:n'aut] изнóшенный; *fig.* измýченный.
worry ['wʌri] **1.** беспокóйство; тревóга; забóта; **2.** беспокóить(ся); надоедáть [-éсть] (Д); прист(ав)áть к (Д); [за]мýчить
worse [wə:s] хýдший; *adv.* хýже; сильнéе; from bad to ~ всё хýже и хýже; **~n** ['wə:sn] ухудшáть(ся) [ухýдшить(ся)].
worship ['wə:ʃip] **1.** культ; почитáние; поклонéние; богослужéние; **2.** поклоня́ться (Д); почитáть; обожáть; **~per** [-ə] поклóнник (-ица); почитáтель(ница *f*) *m*.

worst [wə:st] 1. (са́мый) ху́дший, наиху́дший; *adv.* ху́же всего́; 2. оде́рживать верх над (T), побежда́ть [-еди́ть].

worsted ['wustid] 1. *attr.* камво́льный; 2. га́рус; камво́льная пря́жа.

worth [wə:θ] 1. сто́ящий; заслу́живающий; be ~ заслу́живать, сто́ить; 2. цена́, сто́имость *f*; це́нность *f*; досто́инство; **~less** ['wə:θlis] □ ничего́ не сто́ящий; **~-while** ['wə:θ'wail] F сто́ящий; be ~ име́ть смысл; be not ~ не сто́ить труда́; **~y** ['wə:ði] □ досто́йный (of P); заслу́живающий (of B).

would [wud] (*pt.* от will) *v/aux.*: he ~ do it он сде́лал бы э́то; он обы́чно э́то де́лал; **~-be** ['wudbi] мни́мый; так называ́емый; самозва́нный.

wound[1] [wu:nd] 1. ра́на, ране́ние; 2. ра́нить (*im*)*pf.*; *fig.* заде́(ва́)ть.

wound[2] [waund] *pt.* и *p. pt.* от wind.

wove ['wouv] *pt.* от weave; **~n** ['wouvn] *p. pt.* от weave.

wrangle ['ræŋgl] 1. препрека́ния *n/pl.*, 2. пререка́ться.

wrap [ræp] 1. *v/t.* (ча́сто ~ up) завёртывать [заверну́ть]; обёртывать [оберну́ть] (бума́гой); заку́т(ыв)ать; оку́т(ыв)ать (*a. fig.*); be **~ped** up in быть погружённым в (B); *v/i.* ~ up заку́т(ыв)аться; 2. обёртка; шаль *f*; плед; **~per** ['ræpə] обёртка; хала́т, капо́т; бандеро́ль *f*; супероблóжка (кни́ги); **~ping** ['ræpiŋ] упако́вка; обёртка.

wrath [rɔ:θ] гнев.

wreath [ri:θ], *pl.* **~s** [ri:ðz] вено́к; гирля́нда; *fig.* кольцо́, коле́чко (ды́ма); **~e** [ri:ð] [*irr.*] *v/t.* сви(ва́)ть; сплета́ть [сплести́]; *v/i.* обви́(ва́)ться; клуби́ться.

wreck [rek] 1. ⚓ обло́мки су́дна; круше́ние, ава́рия; разва́лина (о челове́ке); 2. разруша́ть [-у́шить]; [по]топи́ть (су́дно); be **~ed** потерпе́ть ава́рию, круше́ние; *fig.* разруша́ться [-у́шиться] (о пла́нах); **~age** ['rekidʒ] обло́мки (су́дна и т. п. по́сле круше́ния); круше́ние; крах; **~er** ['rekə] граби́тель разби́тых судо́в; рабо́чий авари́йной кома́нды и́ли ремо́нтной брига́ды.

wrench [rentʃ] 1. дёрганье; скру́чивание; вы́вих; *fig.* тоска́, боль *f*; искаже́ние; ⊕ га́ечный ключ; 2. вывёртывать [вы́вернуть]; выви́хивать [вы́вихнуть]; *fig.* искажа́ть [искази́ть] (факт, и́стину); ~ open взла́мывать [взлома́ть].

wrest [rest] вырыва́ть [вы́рвать] (from у P) (*a. fig.*); истолко́вывать в свою́ по́льзу; **~le** ['resl] *mst sport* боро́ться; **~ling** [-liŋ] борьба́.

wretch [retʃ] негодя́й; несча́стный.

wretched ['retʃid] □ несча́стный; жа́лкий.

wriggle ['rigl] изви́(ва́)ться (о червяке́ и т. п.); ~ out of уклоня́ться [-ни́ться] от (P).

wright [rait]: ship~ кораблестрои́тель *m*; cart~ каре́тник; play~ драмату́рг.

wring [riŋ] [*irr.*] скру́чивать [-ути́ть]; лома́ть (ру́ки); (*a.* ~ out) выжима́ть [вы́жать] (бельё и т. п.); вымога́ть (from у P).

wrinkle ['riŋkl] 1. морщи́на; скла́дка; 2. [с]мо́рщить(ся).

wrist [rist] запя́стье; ~ watch ручны́е (*or* нару́чные) часы́ *m/pl.*

writ [rit] ⚖ предписа́ние, пове́стка; Holy ♀ Свяще́нное писа́ние.

write [rait] [*irr.*] [на]писа́ть; ~ up подро́бно опи́сывать; допи́сывать [-са́ть]; восхваля́ть в печа́ти; **~r** ['raitə] писа́тель(ница *f*) *m*; письмоводи́тель *m*.

writhe [raið] [с]ко́рчиться (от бо́ли).

writing ['raitiŋ] 1. писа́ние; (литерату́рное) произведе́ние, сочине́ние; (*a* hand~) по́черк; докуме́нт; in ~ пи́сьменно; 2. пи́сьменный; пи́счий; **~-case** несессе́р для пи́сьменных принадле́жностей; **~-paper** почто́вая (*or* пи́счая) бума́га.

written ['ritn] 1. *p. pt.* от write; 2. пи́сьменный.

wrong [rɔŋ] 1. □ непра́вильный, оши́бочный; не тот (,кото́рый ну́жен); be ~ быть непра́вым; go ~ уклоня́ться от пра́вильного пути́; не получа́ться [-чи́ться], срыва́ться [сорва́ться] (о де́ле); *adv.* непра́вильно, не так; 2. неправота́; непра́вильность *f*; оби́да; несправедли́вость *f*; зло; 3. поступа́ть несправедли́во с (T); причиня́ть зло (Д); обижа́ть [оби́деть]; **~doer** злоде́й(ка); **~ful** ['rɔŋful] □ незако́нный (посту́пок); несправедли́вый.

wrote [rout] *pt.* от write.

wrought [rɔ:t] *pt.* и *p. pt.* от work 2 [irr.]: ~ goods гото́вые изде́лия *n/pl.*; ~ iron ⊕ сва́рочное желе́зо.

wrung [rʌŋ] *pt.* и *p. pt.* от wring.

wry [rai] □ криво́й, перекошенный; искажённый.

X

X-ray ['eks'rei] 1. **~s** *pl.* рентге́новские лучи́ *m/pl.*; 2. просве́чивать рентге́новскими луча́ми; 3. рентге́новский.

xylophone ['zailəfoun] ♪ ксилофо́н.

Y

yacht [jɔt] ⚓ 1. я́хта; 2. плы́ть на я́хте; **~ing** ['jɔtiŋ] я́хтенный спорт.
yankee ['jæŋki] F америка́нец, я́нки *m indecl.*
yap [jæp] 1. тя́вкать [-кнуть]; *Am. sl.* болта́ть.
yard [jɑ:d] ярд (о́коло 91 см); двор; лесно́й склад; **~stick** измери́тельная лине́йка длино́й в 1 ярд; *fig.* ме́рка, «арши́н».
yarn [jɑ:n] 1. пря́жа; F *fig.* расска́з; (фантасти́ческая) исто́рия; 2. F расска́зывать ска́зки, небыли́цы.
yawn [jɔ:n] 1. зево́та; 2. зева́ть [зевну́ть]; *fig.* зия́ть.
year [jə:, jiə] год (*pl.* года́, го́ды, лета́ *n/pl.*); **~ly** ежего́дный.
yearn [jə:n] томи́ться, тоскова́ть (for, after по Д).
yeast [ji:st] дро́жжи *f/pl.*
yell [jel] 1. пронзи́тельный крик; 2. пронзи́тельно крича́ть, [за]вопи́ть.
yellow ['jelou] 1. жёлтый; F трусли́вый; ~ press жёлтая пре́сса, бульва́рная пре́сса; 2. [по]желте́ть; [за]желти́ть; **~ed** пожелте́вший; **~ish** ['jelouiʃ] желтова́тый.
yelp [jelp] 1. лай, визг; 2. [за]визжа́ть, [за]ла́ять.
yes [jes] 1. да; 2. согла́сие.
yesterday ['jestədi] вчера́.
yet [jet] 1. *adv.* ещё, всё ещё; уже́; до сих пор; да́же; тем не ме́нее; as ~ пока́, до сих пор; not ~ ещё не(т); 2. *cj.* одна́ко, всё же, несмотря́ на э́то.
yield [ji:ld] 1. *v/t.* приноси́ть [-нести́] (плоды́, урожа́й, дохо́д и т. п.); сда(ва́)ть; *v/i.* уступа́ть [-пи́ть] (to Д); подд(ав)а́ться; сд(ав)а́ться; 2. урожа́й, (урожа́йный) сбор; ⚒ вы́ход; дохо́д; **~ing** ['ji:ldiŋ] □ *fig.* усту́пчивый.
yoke [jouk] 1. ярмо́ (*a. fig.*); па́ра запряжённых воло́в; коромы́сло; *fig.* и́го; 2. впряга́ть в ярмо́; *fig.* спа́ри(ва)ть; подходи́ть друг к дру́гу.
yolk [jouk] желто́к.
yonder ['jɔndə] *lit.* 1. вон тот, вон та и т. д.; 2. *adv.* вон там.
you [ju:, ju] *pron. pers.* ты, вы; тебя́, вас; тебе́, вам (ча́сто to ~) и т. д.
young [jʌŋ] 1. □ молодо́й; ю́ный; 2. the ~ молодёжь *f*; *zo.* детёныши *m/pl.*; with ~ супоро́с(н)ая, сте́льная и т. п.; **~ster** ['jʌŋstə] F подро́сток, ю́ноша *m.*
your [jɔ:, juə] *pron. poss.* твой *m*, твоя́ *f*, твоё *n*, твои́ *pl.*; ваш *m*, ва́ша *f*, ва́ше *n*, ва́ши *pl.*; **~s** [jɔ:z, juəz] *pron. poss. absolute form* твой *m*, твоя́ *f* и т. д.; **~self** [jɔ:'self], *pl.* **~selves** [-'selvz] сам *m*, сама́ *f*, само́ *n*, са́ми *pl.*; себя́, -ся.
youth [ju:θ] *coll.* молодёжь *f*; ю́ноша *m*; мо́лодость *f*; **~ful** ['ju:θful] □ ю́ношеский; моложа́вый.
yule [ju:l] *lit.* свя́тки *f/pl.*

Z

zeal [zi:l] рве́ние, усе́рдие; **~ot** ['zelət] ревни́тель *m*; **~ous** ['zeləs] □ рья́ный, усе́рдный, ре́вностный.
zenith ['zeniθ] зени́т (*a. fig.*).
zero ['ziərou] нуль *m* (*a.* ноль *m*); нулева́я то́чка.
zest [zest] 1. пика́нтность *f*, «изю́минка»; F наслажде́ние, жар; 2. придава́ть пика́нтность (Д), де́лать пика́нтным.
zigzag ['zigzæg] зигза́г.
zinc [ziŋk] 1. цинк; 2. оцинко́вывать [-ова́ть].
zip [zip] свист (пу́ли); F эне́ргия; ~ fastener = **~per** ['zipə] (застёжка-)мо́лния.
zone [zoun] зо́на (*a. pol.*); по́яс; райо́н.
zoolog|ical [zouə'lɔdʒikəl] □ зоологи́ческий; **~y** [zou'ɔlədʒi] зооло́гия.

APPENDIX

Grammatical Tables

Грамматические таблицы

Conjugation and Declension

The following two rules relative to the spelling of endings in Russian inflected words must be observed:

1. Stems terminating in г, к, х, ж, ш, ч, щ are never followed by ы, ю, я, but by и, у, а.

2. Stems terminating in ц are never followed by и, ю, я, but by ы, у, а.

Besides these, a third spelling rule, dependent on phonetic conditions, viz. position of stress, is likewise important:

3. Stems terminating in ж, ш, ч, щ, ц can be followed by an о in the ending only if the syllable in question bears the stress; otherwise, i. e. in unstressed position, е is used instead.

A. Conjugation

Prefixed forms of the perfective aspect are represented by adding the prefix in square brackets, e. g.: [про]читáть = читáть *impf.*, прочитáть *pf.*

Personal endings of the present (and perfective future) tense:

1st conjugation:	-ю (-у)	-ешь	-ет	-ем	-ете	-ют (-ут)
(stressed)		(-ёшь)	(-ёт)	(-ём)	(-ёте)	
2nd conjugation:	-ю (-у)	-ишь	-ит	-им	-ите	-ят (-ат)

Reflexive:

1st conjugation:	-юсь (-усь)	-ешься	-ется	-емся	-етесь	-ются	(-утся)
2nd conjugation:	-юсь (-усь)	-ишься	-ится	-имся	-итесь	-ятся	(-атся)

Suffixes and endings of the other verbal forms:

imp.	-й(те)	-и(те)	-ь(те)	
reflexive	-йся (-йтесь)	-ись (-итесь)	-ься (-ьтесь)	
	m	*f*	*n*	*pl.*
p.pr.a.	-щий(ся)	-щая(ся)	-щее(ся)	-щие(ся)
p.pr.p.	-мый	-мая	-мое	-мые
short form	-м	-ма	-мо	-мы
g.pr.	-я(сь), after ж, ш, ч, щ: -а(сь)			
pt.	-л	-ла	-ло	-ли
refl.	-лся	-лась	-лось	-лись
p.pt.a.	-вший(ся)	-вшая(ся)	-вшее(ся)	-вшие(ся)

p.pt.p.	-нный -тый	-нная -тая	-нное -тое	-нные -тые
short form	-н -т	-на -та	-но -то	-ны -ты
g.pt.	-в, -вши(сь)			

Stress:

a) There is *no change of stress unless the final syllable of the infinitive is stressed,* i. e. in all forms of the respective verb stress remains invariably on the root syllable accentuated in the infinitive, e. g.: пла́кать. The forms of пла́кать correspond to paradigm [3], except for the stress, which is always on пла́-. The imperative of such verbs also differs from the paradigms concerned: it is in -ь(те) provided their stem ends in one consonant only, e. g.: пла́кать — пла́чь(те), ве́рить — ве́рь(те); and in -и(те) (unstressed!) in cases of two and more consonants preceding the imperative ending, e. g.: по́мнить — по́мни(те). Verbs with a vowel stem termination, however, generally form their imperative in -й(те): успоко́ить — успоко́й(те).

b) The prefix вы- in perfective verbs always bears the stress: вы́полнить (but *impf.*: выполня́ть). Imperfective (iterative) verbs with the suffix -ыв-/-ив- are always stressed on the syllable preceding the suffix: пока́зывать (but *pf.* показа́ть), спра́шивать (but *pf.* спроси́ть).

c) In the past participle passive of verbs in -а́ть (-я́ть), there is usually a shift of stress back onto the root syllable as compared with the infinitive (see paradigms [1]—[4], [6], [7], [28]). With verbs in -е́ть and -и́ть such a shift may occur as well, very often in agreement with a parallel accent shift in the 2nd p. sg. present tense, e. g.: [про]смотре́ть: [про]смотрю́, смо́тришь — просмо́тренный; see also paradigms [14] — [16] as against [13]: [по]мири́ть: [по]мирю́, -и́шь — помирённый. In this latter case the short forms of the participles are stressed on the last syllable throughout: -ённый: -ён, -ена́, -ено́, -ены́. In the former examples, however, stress remains on the same root syllable as in the long form: -'енный: -'ен, -'ена, -'ено, -'ены.

Any details differingf rom the following paradigms and not explained in the foregoing notes are either mentioned in special remarks attached to the individual paradigms or, if not, pointed out after the entry word itself.

Verbs in -ать

1 [про]**чита́ть**

pr. [*ft.*]	[про]чита́ю, -а́ешь, -а́ют
imp.	[про]чита́й(те)
p.pr.a.	чита́ющий
p.pr.p.	чита́емый
g.pr.	чита́я
pt.	[про]чита́л, -а, -о, -и
p.pt.a.	[про]чита́вший
p.pt.p.	прочи́танный
g.pt.	прочита́в(ши)

2 [по]**трепа́ть**
(with л after б, в, м, п, ф)

pr. [*ft.*]	[по]треплю́, -е́плешь, -е́плют
imp.	[по]трепли́(те)
p.pr.a.	тре́плющий
p.pr.p.	—
g.pr.	трепля́
pt.	[по]трепа́л, -а, -о, -и
p.pt.a.	[по]трепа́вший
p.pt.p.	потрёпанный
g.pt.	потрепа́в(ши)

3 [об]**глода́ть**
(with changing consonant:
г, д, з > ж
к, т > ч
х, с > ш
ск, ст > щ)

pr. [*ft.*] [об]гложу́, -о́жешь, -о́жут
imp. [об]гложи́(те)
p.pr.a. гло́жущий
p.pr.p. —
g.pr. гложа́
pt. [об]глода́л, -а, -о, -и
p.pt.a. [об]глода́вший
p.pt.p. обгло́данный
g.pt. обглода́в(ши)

---

4 **[по]держа́ть**
(with preceding ж, ш, ч, щ)

pr. [*ft.*] [по]держу́, -е́ржишь, -е́ржат
imp. [по]держи́(те)
p.pr.a. держа́щий
p.pr.p. —
g.pr. держа́
pt. [по]держа́л, -а, -о, -и
p.pt.a. [по]держа́вший
p.pt.p. поде́ржанный
g.pt. подержа́в(ши)

Verbs in -авать

5 **дава́ть**
(*st.* = -ешь, -ет, *etc.*)

pr. [*ft.*] даю́, даёшь, даю́т
imp. дава́й(те)
p.pr.a. даю́щий
p.pr.p. дава́емый
g.pr. дава́я
pt. дава́л, -а, -о, -и
p.pt.a. дава́вший
p.pt.p. —
g.pt. —

Verbs in -евать

6 **[на]малева́ть**
(*e.* = -ю, -ёшь, *etc.*)

pr. [*ft.*] [на]малю́ю, -ю́ешь, -ю́ют
imp. [на]малю́й(те)
p.pr.a. малю́ющий
p.pr.p. малю́емый
g.pr. малю́я
pt. [на]малева́л, -а, -о, -и
p.pt.a. [на]малева́вший
p.pt.p. намалёванный
g.pt. намалева́в(ши)

Verbs in -овать (and in -евать with preceding ж, ш, ч, щ, ц)

7 **[на]рисова́ть**
(*e.* = -ю, -ёшь, *etc.*)

pr. [*ft.*] [на]рису́ю, -у́ешь, -у́ют
imp. [на]рису́й(те)
p.pr.a. рису́ющий
p.pr.p. рису́емый
g.pr. рису́я
pt. [на]рисова́л, -а, -о, -и
p.pt.a. [на]рисова́вший
p.pt.p. нарисо́ванный
g.pt. нарисова́в(ши)

Verbs in -еть

8 **[по]жале́ть**

pr. [*ft.*] [по]жале́ю, -е́ешь, -е́ют
imp. [по]жале́й(те)
p.pr.a. жале́ющий
p.pr.p. жале́емый
g.pr. жале́я
pt. [по]жале́л, -а, -о, -и
p.pt.a. [по]жале́вший
p.pt.p. ...ённый (*e.g.* одолённый)
g.pt. пожале́в(ши)

---

9 **[с]горе́ть**

pr. [*ft.*] [с]горю́, -и́шь, -я́т
imp. [с]гори́(те)
p.pr.a. горя́щий
p.pr.p. —
g.pr. горя́
pt. [с]горе́л, -а, -о, -и
p.pt.a. [с]горе́вший
p.pt.p. ...е́нный (*e.g.* презре́нный)
g.pt. сгоре́в(ши)

---

10 **[по]терпе́ть**

pr. [*ft.*] [по]терплю́, -е́рпишь, -е́рпят
imp. [по]терпи́(те)
p.pr.a. терпя́щий
p.pr.p. терпи́мый
g.pr. терпя́
pt. [по]терпе́л, -а, -о, -и
p.pt.a. [по]терпе́вший
p.pt.a. ...енный (*e.g.* претерпенный)
g.pt. потерпе́в(ши)

---

11 **[по]лете́ть**
(with changing consonant:
д, з > ж
к, т > ч
х, с > ш
ск, ст > щ)

pr. [*ft.*] [по]лечу́, -ети́шь, -етя́т
imp. [по]лети́(те)
p.pr.a. летя́щий
p.pr.p. —
g.pr. летя́
pt. [по]лете́л, -а, -о, -и

p.pt.a. [по]лете́вший
p.pt.p. ...енный (*e. g.* ве́рченный)
g.pt. полете́в(ши)

Verbs in -ере́ть

12 **[по]тере́ть**
(*st.* = -ешь, -ет, *etc.*)

pr. [*ft.*] [по]тру́, -трёшь, -тру́т
imp. [по]три́(те)
p.pr.a. тру́щий
p.pr.p. —
g.pr. —
pt. [по]тёр, -рла, -о, -и
p.pt.a. [по]тёрший
p.pt.p. [по]тёртый
g.pt. потере́в *or* потёрши

Verbs in -ить

13 **[по]мири́ть**

pr. [*ft.*] [по]мирю́, -ри́шь, -ря́т
imp. [по]мири́(те)
p.pr.a. миря́щий
p.pr.p. мири́мый
g.pr. миря́
pt. [по]мири́л, -а, -о, -и
p.pt.a. [по]мири́вший
p.pt.p. помирённый
g.pt. помири́в(ши)

14 **[на]корми́ть**
(with л after б, в, м, п, ф)

pr. [*ft.*] [на]кормлю́, -о́рмишь, -о́рмят
imp. [на]корми́(те)
p.pr.a. ко́рмящий
p.pr.p. корми́мый
g.pr. кормя́
pt. [на]корми́л, -а, -о, -и
p.pt.a. [на]корми́вший
p.pt.p. нако́рмленный
g.pt. накорми́в(ши)

15 **[по]проси́ть**
(with changing consonant:

д, з > ж
к, т > ч
х, с > ш
ск, ст > щ)

pr. [*ft.*] [по]прошу́, -о́сишь, -о́сят
imp. [по]проси́(те)
p.pr.a. прося́щий
p.pr.p. проси́мый
g.pr. прося́
pt. [по]проси́л, -а, -о, -и
p.pt.a. [по]проси́вший
p.pt.p. попро́шенный
g.pt. попроси́в(ши)

16 **[на]точи́ть**
(with preceding ж, ш, ч, щ)

pr. [*ft.*] [на]точу́, -о́чишь, -о́чат
imp. [на]точи́(те)
p.pr.a. точа́щий
p.pr.p. точи́мый
g.pr. точа́
pt. [на]точи́л, -а, -о, -и
p.pt.a. [на]точи́вший
p.pt.p. нато́ченный
g.pt. наточи́в(ши)

Verbs in -оть

17 **[рас]коло́ть**

pr. [*ft.*] [рас]колю́, -о́лешь, -о́лют
imp. [рас]коли́(те)
p.pr.a. ко́лющий
p.pr.p. —
g.pr. ко́ля
pt. [рас]коло́л, -а, -о, -и
p.pt.a. [рас]коло́вший
p.pt.p. раско́лотый
g.pt. расколо́в(ши)

Verbs in -уть

18 **[по]ду́ть**

pr. [*ft.*] [по]ду́ю, -у́ешь, -у́ют
imp. [по]ду́й(те)
p.pr.a. ду́ющий
p.pr.p. —
g.pr. ду́я
pt. [по]ду́л, -а, -о, -и
p.pt.a. [по]ду́вший
p.pt.p. ду́тый
g.pt. поду́в(ши)

19 **[по]тяну́ть**

pr. [*ft.*] [по]тяну́, -я́нешь, -я́нут
imp. [по]тяни́(те)
p.pr.a. тя́нущий
p.pr.p. —
g.pr. —
pt. [по]тяну́л, -а, -о, -и
p.pt.a. [по]тяну́вший
p.pt.p. [по]тя́нутый
g.pt. потяну́в(ши)

20 **[со]гну́ть**
(*st.* = -ешь, -ет, *etc.*)

pr. [*ft.*] [со]гну́, -нёшь, -ну́т
imp. [со]гни́(те)
p.pr.a. гну́щий
p.pr.p. —
g.pr. —

pt. [со]гну́л, -а, -о, -и
p.pt.a. [со]гну́вший
p.pt.p. [со́]гнутый
g.pt. согну́в(ши)

---

21 [по]**ту́хнуть**
(-г- = -г- instead of -х- throughout)
pr. [*ft.*] [по]ту́хну, -нешь, -нут
imp. [по]ту́хни(те)
p.pr.a. ту́хнущий
p.pr.p. —
g.pr. —
pt. [по]ту́х, -хла, -о, -и
p.pt.a. [по]ту́хший
p.pt.p. ...нутый (*e. g.* дости́гнутый)
g.pt. поту́хши

Verbs in -ыть

22 [по]**кры́ть**
pr. [*ft.*] [по]кро́ю, -о́ешь, -о́ют
imp. [по]кро́й(те)
p.pr.a. кро́ющий
p.pr.p. —
g.pr. кро́я
pt. [по]кры́л, -а, -о, -и
p.pt.a. [по]кры́вший
p.pt.p. [по]кры́тый
g.pt. покры́в(ши)

---

23 [по]**плы́ть**
(*st.* = -ешь, -ет, *etc.*)
pr. [*ft.*] [по]плыву́, -вёшь, -ву́т
imp. [по]плыви́(те)
p.pr.a. плыву́щий
p.pr.p. —
g.pr. плывя́
pt. [по]плы́л, -а́, -о, -и
p.pt.a. [по]плы́вший
p.pt.p. ...ы́тый (*e.g.* проплы́тый)
g.pt. поплы́вши

Verbs in -зти, -зть, (-сти)

24 [по]**везти́**
(-с[т]- = -с[т]- instead of -з- throughout)
(*st.* = -ешь, -ет, *etc.*)
pr. [*ft.*] [по]везу́, -зёшь, -зу́т
imp. [по]вези́(те)
p.pr.a. везу́щий
p.pr.p. везо́мый
g.pr. везя́
pt. [по]вёз, -везла́, -о́, -и́
p.pt.a. [по]вёзший
p.pt.p. повезённый
g.pt. повёзши

Verbs in -сти, -сть

25 [по]**вести́**
(-т- = -т- instead of -д- throughout)
(*st.* = -ешь, -ет, *etc.*)
pr. [*ft.*] [по]веду́, -дёшь, -ду́т
imp. [по]веди́(те)
p.pr.a. веду́щий
p.pr.p. ведо́мый
pt. [по]вёл, -вела́, -о́, -и́
p.pt.a. [по]ве́дший
p.pt.p. поведённый
g.pt. поведя́

Verbs in -чь

26 [по]**вле́чь**
(г/ж = г instead of к, and ж instead of ч) (-б- = -б- instead of к/ч)
(*st.* = -ешь, -ет, *etc.*)
pr. [*ft.*] [по]влеку́, -ечёшь, -еку́т
imp. [по]влеки́(те)
p.pr.a. влеку́щий
p.pr.p. влеко́мый
g.pr. —
pt. [по]влёк, -екла́, -о́, -и́
p.pt.a. [по]влёкший
p.pt.p. повлечённый
g.pt. повлёкши

Verbs in -ять

27 [рас]**та́ять**
(*e.* = -ю́, -ёшь, -ёт, *etc.*)
pr. [*ft.*] [рас]та́ю, -а́ешь, -а́ют
imp. [рас]та́й(те)
p.pr.a. та́ющий
p.pr.p. —
g.pr. та́я
pt. [рас]та́ял, -а, -о, -и
p.pt.a. [рас]та́явший
p.pt.p. ...янный (*e. g.* обла́янный)
g.pt. раста́яв(ши)

---

28 [по]**теря́ть**
pr. [*ft.*] [по]теря́ю, -я́ешь, -я́ют
imp. [по]теря́й(те)
p.pr.a. теря́ющий
p.pr.p. теря́емый
g.pr. теря́я
pt. [по]теря́л, -а, -о, -и
p.pt.a. [по]теря́вший
p.pt.p. поте́рянный
g.pt. потеря́в(ши)

B. Declension

Noun

a) Succession of the six cases (horizontally): nominative, genitive, dative, accusative, instrumental and prepositional in the singular and (thereunder) the plural. *With nouns denoting animate beings (persons and animals) there is a coincidence of endings in the accusative and genitive both singular and plural of the masculine, but only in the plural of the feminine and neuter genders.* This rule also applies, of course, to adjectives as well as various pronouns and numerals that must in syntactical connections agree with their respective nouns.

b) Variants of the following paradigms are pointed out in notes added to the individual declension types or, if not, mentioned after the entry word itself.

Masculine nouns:

1	ви́д	—	-а	-у	—	-ом	о -е
		-ы	-ов	-ам	-ы	-ами	о -ах

Note: Nouns in -ж, -ш, -ч, -щ have in the *g/pl.* the ending -ей.

2	реб	-ёнок	-ёнка	-ёнку	-ёнка	-ёнком	о -ёнке
		-я́та	-я́т	-я́там	-я́т	-я́тами	о -я́тах

3	слу́ча	-й	-я	-ю	-й	-ем	о -е
		-и	-ев	-ям	-и	-ями	о -ях

Notes: Nouns in -ий have in the *prpos/sg.* the ending -ии.
When *e.*, the ending of the *instr/sg.* is -ём, and of the *g/pl.* -ёв.

4	про́фил	-ь	-я	-ю	-ь	-ем	о -е
		-и	-ей	-ям	-и	-ями	о -ях

Note: When *e.*, the ending of the *instr/sg.* is -ём.

Feminine nouns:

5	рабо́т	-а	-ы	-е	-у	-ой (-ою)	о -е
		-ы	—	-ам	-ы	-ами	о -ах

Note: In the *g/pl.* with many nouns having two final stem consonants -о- or -е- is inserted between these (cf. p. 15 and entry words concerned).

6	неде́л	-я	-и	-е	-ю	-ей (-ею)	о -е
		-и	-ь	-ям	-и	-ями	о -ях

Notes: Nouns in -ья have in the *g/pl.* the ending -ий (unstressed) or -е́й (stressed), the latter being also the termination of nouns in -е́я. Nouns in -я with preceding vowel terminate in the *g/pl.* in -й (for -ий see also No. 7).
When *e.*, the ending of the *instr/sg.* is -ёй (-ёю).
For the insertion of -е-, -о- in the *g/pl.* cf. note with No. 5.

7	áрми	-я	-и	-и	-ю	-ей (-ею)	об -и
		-и	-й	-ям	-и	-ями	об -ях
8	тетрáд	-ь	-и	-и	-ь	-ью	о -и
		-и	-ей	-ям	-и	-ями	о -ях

Neuter nouns:

9	блю́д	-о	-а	-у	-о	-ом	о -е
		-а	—	-ам	-а	-ами	о -ах

Note: For the insertion of -о-, -е- in the *g/pl.* cf. note with No. 5.

10	пóл	-е	-я	-ю	-е	-ем	о -е
		-я́	-éй	-я́м	-я́	-я́ми	о -я́х

Note: Nouns in -ье have in the *g/pl.* the ending -ий. Besides, they do not shift their stress.

11	жили́щ	-е	-а	-у	-е	-ем	о -е
		-а	—	-ам	-а	-ами	о -ах
12	желáни	-е	-я	-ю	-е	-ем	о -и
		-я	-й	-ям	-я	-ями	о -ях
13	врéм	-я	-ени	-ени	-я	-енем	о -ени
		-енá	-ён	-енáм	-енá	-енáми	о -енáх

Adjective

(also ordinal numbers, etc.)

Notes

a) Adjectives in -ский have no predicative (short) forms.

b) Variants of the following paradigms have been recorded with the individual entry words. See also p. 15.

		m	*f*	*n*	*pl.*	
14	бéл	-ый (-óй)	-ая	-ое	-ые	long form
		-ого	-ой	-ого	-ых	
		-ому	-ой	-ому	-ым	
		-ый (-ого)	-ую	-ое	-ые (-ых)	
		-ым	-ой (-ою)	-ым	-ыми	
		о -ом	о -ой	о -ом	о -ых	
		—*	-á	-о(*а.*: -ó)	-ы (*а.*: -ы́)	short form
15	си́н	-ий	-яя	-ее	-ие	long form
		-его	-ей	-его	-их	
		-ему	-ей	-ему	-им	
		-ий (-его)	-юю	-ее	-ие (-их)	
		-им	-ей (-ею)	-им	-ими	
		о -ем	о -ей	о -ем	о -их	
		-(ь)*	-я́	-е	-и	short form
16	стрóг	-ий	-ая	-ое	-ие	long form
		-ого	-ой	-ого	-их	
		-ому	-ой	-ому	-им	
		-ий (-ого)	-ую	-ое	-ие (-их)	
		-им	-ой (-ою)	-им	-ими	
		о -ом	о -ой	о -ом	о -их	
		—*	-á	-о	-и	short form

17	тóщ	-ий	-ая	-ее	-ие	long form
		-его	-ей	-его	-их	
		-ему	-ей	-ему	-им	
		-ий (-его)	-ую	-ее	-ие (-их)	
		-им	-ей (-ею)	-им	-ими	
		о -ем	о -ей	о -ем	о -их	
		—	-á	-е(ó)	-и	short form
18	олéн	-ий	-ья	-ье	-ьи	
		-ьего	-ьей	-ьего	-ьих	
		-ьему	-ьей	-ьему	-ьим	
		-ий(-ьего)	-ью	-ье	-ьи (-ьих)	
		-ьим	-ьей (-ьею)	-ьим	-ьими	
		об -ьем	об -ьей	об -ьем	об -ьих	
19	дя́дин	—	-а	-о	-ы	
		-а	-ой	-а	-ых	
		-у	-ой	-у	-ым	
		— (-а)	-у	-о	-ы (-ых)	
		-ым	-ой (-ою)	-ым	-ыми	
		о -ом**	о -ой	о -ом	о -ых	

* In the masculine short form of many adjectives having two final stem consonants -о- or -е- is inserted between these (cf. p. 15 and entry words concerned).

** Masculine surnames in -ов, -ев, -ин, -ын have the ending -е.

Pronoun

20	я	меня́	мне	меня́	мной (мно́ю)	обо мне
	мы	нас	нам	нас	на́ми	о нас
21	ты	тебя́	тебé	тебя́	тобóй (тобóю)	о тебé
	вы	вас	вам	вас	ва́ми	о вас
22	он	его́	ему́	его́	им	о нём
	онá	её	ей	её	éю (ей)	о ней
	онó	его́	ему́	его́	им	о нём
	они́	их	им	их	и́ми	о них

Note: After prepositions the oblique forms receive an н-prothesis, e.g.: для негó, с нéю (ней).

23	кто	когó	кому́	когó	кем	о ком
	что	чегó	чему́	что	чем	о чём

Note: In combinations with ни-, не- a preposition separates such compounds, e.g. ничтó: ни от чегó, ни к чему́.

24	мой	моегó	моему́	мой (моегó)	мои́м	о моём
	моя́	моéй	моéй	мою́	моéй (моéю)	о моéй
	моё	моегó	моему́	моё	мои́м	о моём
	мои́	мои́х	мои́м	мои́ (мои́х)	мои́ми	о мои́х
25	наш	нáшего	нáшему	наш (нáшего)	нáшим	о нáшем
	нáша	нáшей	нáшей	нáшу	нáшей (нáшею)	о нáшей
	нáше	нáшего	нáшему	нáше	нáшим	о нáшем
	нáши	нáших	нáшим	нáши (нáших)	нáшими	о нáших

26	чей	чьегó	чьемý	чей (чьегó)	чьим	о чьём
	чья	чьей	чьей	чью	чьей (чьéю)	о чьей
	чьё	чьегó	чьемý	чьё	чьим	о чьём
	чьи	чьих	чьим	чьи (чьих)	чьи́ми	о чьих
27	э́тот	э́того	э́тому	э́тот (э́того)	э́тим	об э́том
	э́та	э́той	э́той	э́ту	э́той(э́тою)	об э́той
	э́то	э́того	э́тому	э́то	э́тим	об э́том
	э́ти	э́тих	э́тим	э́ти (э́тих)	э́тими	об э́тих
28	тот	тогó	томý	тот (тогó)	тем	о том
	та	той	той	ту	той (тóю)	о той
	то	тогó	томý	то	тем	о том
	те	тех	тем	те (тех)	тéми	о тех
29	сей	сегó	семý	сей (сегó)	сим	о сём
	сия́	сей	сей	сию́	сей (сéю)	о сей
	сиé	сегó	семý	сиé	сим	о сём
	сии́	сих	сим	сии́ (сих)	си́ми	о сих
30	сам	самогó	самомý	самогó	сами́м	о самóм
	самá	самóй	самóй	самоё	самóй (самóю)	о самóй
	самó	самогó	самомý	самó	сами́м	о самóм
	сáми	сами́х	сами́м	сами́х	сами́ми	о сами́х
31	весь	всегó	всемý	весь (всегó)	всем	обо всём
	вся	всей	всей	всю	всей (всéю)	обо всей
	всё	всегó	всемý	всё	всем	обо всём
	все	всех	всем	все (всех)	всéми	обо всех
32	нéсколько	нéскольких	нéскольким	нéсколько (нéскольких)	нéсколькими	о нéскольких

Numeral

33	оди́н	одногó	одномý	оди́н (одногó)	одни́м	об однóм
	однá	однóй	однóй	однý	однóй (однóю)	об однóй
	однó	одногó	одномý	однó	одни́м	об однóм
	одни́	одни́х	одни́м	одни́ (одни́х)	одни́ми	об одни́х

34	два	две	три	четы́ре
	двух	двух	трёх	четырёх
	двум	двум	трём	четырём
	два (двух)	две (двух)	три (трёх)	четы́ре (четырёх)
	двумя́	двумя́	тремя́	четырьмя́
	о двух	о двух	о трёх	о четырёх

35	пять	пятнáдцать	пятьдеся́т	сто	сóрок
	пяти́	пятнáдцати	пяти́десяти	ста	сорокá
	пяти́	пятнáдцати	пяти́десяти	ста	сорокá
	пять	пятнáдцать	пятьдеся́т	сто	сóрок
	пятью́	пятнáдцатью	пятью́десятью	ста	сорокá
	о пяти́	о пятнáдцати	о пяти́десяти	о ста	о сорокá

36	**две́сти**	**три́ста**	**четы́реста**	**пятьсо́т**
	двухсо́т	трёхсо́т	четырёхсо́т	пятисо́т
	двумста́м	трёмста́м	четырёмста́м	пятиста́м
	две́сти	три́ста	четы́реста	пятьсо́т
	двумяста́ми	тремяста́ми	четырьмяста́ми	пятьюста́ми
	о двухста́х	о трёхста́х	о четырёхста́х	о пятиста́х
37	**о́ба**	**о́бе**	**двое́**	**че́тверо**
	обо́их	обе́их	двои́х	четверы́х
	обо́им	обе́им	двои́м	четверы́м
	о́ба (обо́их)	о́бе (обе́их)	дво́е (двои́х)	че́тверо (четве- ры́х)
	обо́ими	обе́ими	двои́ми	четверы́ми
	об обо́их	об обе́их	о двои́х	о четверы́х

American and British Geographical Names

Американские и британские географические названия

A

Aberdeen (æbə'di:n) г. Абердин.
Adelaide ('ædəleid) г. Аделаида.
Aden ('eidn) г. 'Аден.
Africa ('æfrikə) 'Африка.
Alabama (ælə'ba:mə) Алабама.
Alaska (ə'læskə) Аляска.
Albany ('ɔ:lbəni) 'Олбани.
Alleghany ('æligeini) 1. Аллеганы *pl.* (горы); 2. Аллегейни (река).
America (ə'merikə) Америка.
Antilles (æn'tili:z) Антильские острова.
Antwerp ('æntwə:p) Антверпен.
Arabia (ə'reibjə) Аравия.
Argentina (a:dʒən'ti:nə) Аргентина.
Arizona (æri'zounə) Аризона.
Arkansas ('a:kənsɔ: штат в США, a:'kænsəs река в США) Арканзас.
Ascot ('æskət) г. 'Эскот.
Asia ('eiʃə) 'Азия; ~ *Minor* Малая 'Азия.
Auckland ('ɔ:klənd) г. 'Окленд (порт в Новой Зеландии).
Australia (ɔ:s'treiljə) Австралия.
Austria ('ɔ:striə) 'Австрия.
Azores (ə'zɔ:z) Азорские острова.

B

Bahamas (bə'ha:məz) Багамские острова.
Balkans ('bɔ:lkənz): *the* ~ Балканы.
Baltic Sea ('bɔ:ltik'si:) Балтийское море.
Baltimore ('bɔ:ltimɔ:) г. Балтимор.
Barents Sea ('ba:rənts'si:) Баренцово море.
Bavaria (bə'veəriə) Бавария.
Belfast ('belfa:st) г. Белфаст (столица Северной Ирландии).
Belgium ('beldʒəm) Бельгия.
Bengal (beŋ'gɔ:l) Бенгалия.
Berlin ('bə:'lin, bə:'lin) г. Берлин.
Bermudas (bə[:]'mju:dəz) Бермудские острова.
Birmingham ('bə:miŋəm) г. Бирмингем.
Biscay ('biskei): *Bay of* ~ Бискайский залив.
Black Sea ('blæk'si:) Чёрное море.
Boston ('bɔstən) г. Бостон.
Brazil (brə'zil) Бразилия.
Brighton ('braitn) г. Брайтон.
Bristol ('bristl) г. Бристоль (порт и торговый город на юге Англии).
Britain ('britən) (*Great* Великобритания; *Greater* ~ Великобритания с колониями, Британская империя.
Brooklyn ('bruklin) Бруклин.
Brussels ('brʌslz) г. Брюссель.
Burma ('bə:mə) Бирма.
Bulgaria (bʌl'gɛəriə) Болгария.
Byelorussia (bjelou'rʌʃə) Белоруссия.

C

Calcutta (kæl'kʌtə) г. Калькутта.
California (kæli'fɔ:njə) Калифорния.
Cambridge ('keimbridʒ) г. Кембридж.
Canada ('kænədə) Канада.
Canary (kə'nɛəri): ~ *Islands* Канарские острова.
Canterbury ('kæntəbəri) г. Кентербери.
Capetown ('keiptaun) г. Кейптаун.
Cardiff ('ka:dif) г. Кардифф.
Caribbean Sea (kæ'ribi:ən'si:) Карибское море.
Carolina (kærə'lainə) Каролина (*North* Северная, *South* 'Южная).
Ceylon (si'lɔn) о-в Цейлон.
Chesterfield ('tʃestəfi:ld) г. Честерфильд.
Cheviot ('tʃeviət): ~ *Hills* Чевиотские горы.
Chicago (ʃi'ka:gou, *a.* ʃi'kɔ:gou) г. Чикаго.
Chile ('tʃili) Чили.
China ('tʃainə) Китай.
Cincinnati (sinsi'næti) г. Цинциннати.
Cleveland ('kli:vlənd) г. Кливленд.
Clyde (klaid) р. Клайд.
Colorado (kɔlə'ra:dou) Колорадо.
Columbia (kə'lʌmbiə) Колумбия (река, город, адм. округ).
Connecticut (kə'nektikət) Коннектикут (река и штат в США).
Cordilleras (kɔ:di'ljeərəz) Кордильеры (горы).
Coventry ('kɔvəntri) г. Ковентри.
Cyprus ('saiprəs) о-в Кипр.

D

Dakota (də'koutə) Дакóта (*North* Сéверная, *South* 'Южная).
Denmark ('denmɑ:rk) Дáния.
Danube ('dænju:b) р. Дунáй.
Delhi ('deli) г. Дéли.
Detroit (də'trɔit) г. Детрóйт.
Dover ('douvə) г. Дувр.
Dublin ('dʌblin) г. Дýблин.
Dunkirk (dʌn'kə:k) г. Дюнкéрк.

E

Edinburgh ('edinbərə) г. 'Эдинбург.
Egypt ('i:dʒipt) Еги́пет.
Eire ('ɛərə) 'Эйре.
England ('iŋglənd) 'Англия.
Erie ('iəri): *Lake* ~ óзеро 'Эри.
Eton ('i:tn) г. 'Итон.
Europe ('juərəp) Еврóпа.

F

Falkland ('fɔ:klənd): ~ *Islands* Фолклéндские островá.
Florida ('flɔridə) Флори́да.
Folkestone ('foukstən) г. Фóлкстон.
France (frɑ:ns) Фрáнция.

G

Galveston(e) ('gælvistən) г. Гáлвестон.
Geneva (dʒi'ni:və) г. Женéва.
Georgia ('dʒɔ:dʒiə) Джóрджия (штат в США).
Germany ('dʒə:məni) Гермáния.
Gettysburg ('getizbə:g) г. Гéттисберг.
Ghana (gɑ:nə) Гáна.
Glasgow ('glɑ:sgou) г. Глáзго.
Gloucester ('glɔstə) г. Глóстер.
Greenwich ('grinidʒ) г. Гри́н(в)ич.
Guernsey ('gə:nzi) о-в Гéрнси.
Guiana (gi'ɑ:nə) Гвиáна.
Guinea ('gini) Гвинéя.

H

Haiti ('heiti) Гаи́ти.
Halifax ('hælifæks) г. Гáлифакс.
Harwich ('hæridʒ) г. Хáридж.
Hawaii (hɑ:'waii) о-в Гавáйи.
Hebrides ('hebridi:z) Гебри́дские островá.
Heligoland ('heligoulænd) о-в Гéльголанд.
Hindustan (hindu'stæn, -'stɑ:n) Индостáн.
Hollywood ('hɔliwud) г. Гóлливуд.
Hudson ('hʌdsn) р. Гýдзóн.
Hull (hʌl) г. Гулль.
Hungary ('hʌŋgəri) Вéнгрия.
Huron ('hjuərən): *Lake* ~ óзеро Гýрóн.

I

Iceland ('aislənd) Ислáндия.
Idaho ('aidəhou) Айдáхо.
Illinois (ili'nɔi) 'Иллинóйс.
India ('indjə) 'Индия.
Indiana (indi'ænə) Индиáна.
Iowa ('aiouə) 'Айова.
Irak, Iraq (i'rɑ:k) Ирáк.
Iran (iə'rɑ:n) Ирáн.
Ireland ('aiələnd) Ирлáндия.
Italy ('itəli) Итáлия.

J

Jersey ('dʒə:zi) 1. о-в Джéрси; 2. ~ *City* г. Джéрси-Си́ти.

K

Kansas ('kænzəs) Кáнзáс.
Karachi (kə'rɑ:tʃi) г. Карáчи.
Kashmir (kæʃ'miə) Кашми́р.
Kentucky (ken'tʌki) Кентýкки.
Kenya ('ki:njə, 'kenjə) Кéния.
Klondike ('klɔndaik) Клóндайк.
Korea (ko'riə) Корéя.

L

Labrador ('læbrədɔ:) п-в Лабрадóр.
Lancaster ('læŋkəstə) г. Лáнкáстер.
Leeds (li:dz) г. Лидс.
Leicester ('lestə) Лéстер.
Lincoln ('liŋkən) г. Линкольн.
Liverpool ('livəpu:l) г. Ли́верпýл(ь).
London ('lʌndən) г. Лóндон.
Los Angeles (lɔs'ændʒili:z) г. Лос-'Анжелос.
Louisiana (lu[:]i:zi'ænə) Луизиáна.

M

Mackenzie (mə'kenzi) р. Макéнзи.
Madras (mə'dræs) г. Мадрáс.
Maine (mein) Мэн (штат в США).
Malta ('mɔ:ltə) о-в Мáльта.
Manchester ('mæntʃistə) г. Мáнчестер.
Manhattan (mæn'hætən) Манхáттан.
Manitoba (mæni'toubə) Манитóба.
Maryland ('merilənd, *Brt.* mɛəri-) Мэ́риленд.
Massachusetts (mæsə'tʃu:sets) Массачýсетс.
Melbourne ('melbən) г. Мéльбурн.
Miami (mai'æmi) г. Майáми.
Michigan ('miʃigən) Ми́чиган (штат в США); *Lake* ~ óзеро Ми́чиган.
Milwaukee (mil'wɔ:ki[:]) г. Милуóки.
Minneapolis (mini'æpəlis) г. Миннеáполис.
Minnesota (mini'soutə) Миннесóта.

Mississippi (misi'sipi) Миссиси́пи (река и штат).
Missouri (mi'zuəri, *Brt.* mi'suəri) Миссу́ри (река и штат).
Montana (mɔn'tɑ:nə) Монта́на (штат в США).
Montreal (mɔntri'ɔ:l) г. Монреа́ль.
Moscow ('mɔskou) г. Москва́.
Munich ('mju:nik) г. Мю́нхен.
Murray ('mʌri) р. Му́ррей (Ма́рри).

N

Natal (nə'tæl) Ната́ль.
Nebraska (ni'bræskə) Небра́ска (штат в США).
Nevada (ne'vɑ:də) Нева́да (штат в США).
Newcastle ('nju:kɑ:sl) г. Нька́сл.
Newfoundland (nju:'faundlənd, ⊕ nju:fənd'lænd) о-в Ньюфаундле́нд.
New Hampshire (nju:'hæmpʃiə) Нью-Хэ́мпшир (штат в США).
New Jersey (nju:'dʒə:zi) Нью-Дже́рси (штат в США).
New Mexico (nju:'meksikou) Нью-Ме́ксико (штат в США).
New Orleans (nju:'ɔ:liənz) г. Но́вый Орлеа́н.
New York ('nju:'jɔ:k) Нью-Йо́рк (город и штат).
New Zealand (nju:'zi:lənd) Но́вая Зела́ндия.
Niagara (nai'ægərə) р. Ниага́ра, ~ *Falls* Ниага́рские водопа́ды.
Nigeria (nai'dʒiəriə) Ниге́рия.
Northampton (nɔ:'θæmptən) Нортге́мптон.
Norway ('nɔ:wei) Норве́гия.
Nottingham ('nɔtiŋəm) Но́ттингем.

O

Oceania (ouʃi'einiə) Океа́ния.
Ohio (ou'haiou) Ога́йо (река и штат).
Oklahoma (ouklə'houmə) Оклахо́ма (штат в США).
Ontario (ɔn'tɛəriou) Онта́рио; *Lake* ~ о́зеро Онта́рио.
Oregon ('ɔrigən) Орего́н (штат в США).
Orkney ('ɔ:kni): ~ *Islands* Оркне́йские острова́.
Ottawa ('ɔtəwə) г. Отта́ва.
Oxford ('ɔksfəd) г. 'Оксфорд.

P

Pakistan ('pɑ:kis'tɑ:n) Пакиста́н.
Paris ('pæris) г. Пари́ж.
Pennsylvania (pensil'veinjə) Пенсильва́ния (штат в США).
Philadelphia (filə'delfjə) г. Филаде́льфия.
Philippines ('filipi:nz) Филиппи́ны.
Pittsburg(h) ('pitsbə:g) г. Пи́ттсбург.
Plymouth ('pliməθ) г. Пли́мут.
Poland ('poulənd) По́льша.
Portsmouth ('pɔ:tsməθ) г. По́ртсмут.
Portugal ('pɔ:tjugəl) Португа́лия.
Punjab (pʌn'dʒɑ:b) Пенджа́б.

Q

Quebec (kwi'bek) Квебе́к.

R

Rhine (rain) р. Рейн.
Richmond ('ritʃmənd) г. Ри́чмонд.
Rhode Island (roud'ailənd) Род-'Айленд (штат в США).
Rhodes (roudz) о-в Ро́дос.
Rhodesia (rou'di:ziə) Родe'зия.
Rome (roum) г. Рим.
Russia ('rʌʃə) Росси́я.

S

Scandinavia (skændi'neivjə) Скандина́вия.
Scotland ('skɔtlənd) Шотла́ндия.
Seattle (si'ætl) г. Сиэ́тл.
Seoul (soul) г. Сеу́л.
Sheffield ('ʃefi:ld) г. Ше́ффилд.
Shetland ('ʃetlənd): *the* ~ *Islands* Шетла́ндские острова́.
Siberia (sai'biəriə) Сиби́рь.
Singapore (siŋgə'pɔ:) г. Сингапу́р.
Soudan (su[:]'dæn) Суда́н.
Southampton (sauθ'æmptən) г. Саутге́мптон.
Spain (spein) Испа́ния.
St. Louis (snt'luis) г. Сент-Лу́ис.
Stratford ('strætfəd): ~ **on Avon** г. Стра́тфорд-на-'Эйвоне.
Sweden ('swi:dn) Шве́ция.
Switzerland ('switsələnd) Швейца́рия.
Sydney ('sidni) г. Си́дней.

T

Tennessee (tene'si:) Теннесси́ (река и штат в США).
Texas ('teksəs) Теха́с (штат в США).
Thames (temz) р. Те́мза.
Toronto (tə'rɔntou) г. Торо́нто.
Trafalgar (trə'fælgə) Трафальга́р.
Transvaal ('trænzvɑ:l) Трансваа́ль.
Turkey ('tə:ki) Ту́рция.

U

Utah ('ju:tɑ:) 'Юта (штат в США).

V

Vancouver (væn'ku:və) г. Ванку́вер.
Vermont (və:'mɔnt) Вермо́нт (штат в США).

Vienna (vi'enə) г. Ве́на.
Virginia (və'dʒinjə) Вирги́ния (штат в США).

W

Wales (weilz) Уэ́льс.
Washington ('wɔʃiŋtən) Ва́шингто́н (город и штат в США).
Wellington ('weliŋtən) г. Ве́ллингтон (столица Новой Зеландии).
West Virginia ('westvə'dʒinjə) За́падная Вирги́ния (штат в США).
Winnipeg ('winipeg) Ви́ннипег (город и озеро в Канаде).
Wisconsin (wis'kɔnsin) Виско́нсин (река и штат в США).
Worcester ('wustə) г. Ву́стер.
Wyoming (wai'oumiŋ) Вайо́минг (штат в США).

Y

York (jɔ:k) Йорк.
Yugoslavia ('ju:gou'slɑ:viə) Югосла́вия.

Наиболее употребительные сокращения, принятые в СССР

Current Russian Abbreviations

авт. (автóбус) (motor) bus
Азербайджáнская ССР (Совéтская Социалистúческая Респýблика) Azerbaijan S.S.R. (Soviet Socialist Republic)
акад. (акадéмик) academician
АН СССР (Акадéмия наýк Союза Совéтских Социалистúческих Респýблик) Academy of Sciences of the U.S.S.R. (Union of Soviet Socialist Republics)
Армя́нская ССР (Совéтская Социалистúческая Респýблика) Armenian S.S.R. (Soviet Socialist Republic)
арх. (архитéктор) architect
АССР (Автонóмная Совéтская Социалистúческая Респýблика) Autonomous Soviet Socialist Republic
АТС (автоматúческая телефóнная стáнция) telephone exchange

б-ка (библиотéка) library
БССР (Белорýсская Совéтская Социалистúческая Респýблика) Byelorussian S.S.R. (Soviet Socialist Republic)
БСЭ (Большáя Совéтская Энциклопéдия) Big Soviet Encyclopedia

в. (век) century
вв. (векá) centuries
ВВА (Воéнно-воздýшная акадéмия) Air Force College
ВВС (Воéнно-воздýшные сúлы) Air Forces
ВЛКСМ (Всесоюзный Лéнинский Коммунистúческий Союз Молодёжи) Leninist Young Communist League of the Soviet Union
вм. (вмéсто) instead of
ВС (Верхóвный Совéт) Supreme Soviet
ВСХВ (Всесоюзная сельскохозя́йственная вы́ставка) Agricultural Fair of the U.S.S.R.
втуз (вы́сшее технúческое учéбное заведéние) technical college, institute of technology
вуз (вы́сшее учéбное заведéние) university, college
ВЦИК (Всероссúйский Центрáльный Исполнúтельный Комитéт) All-Russian Central Executive Committee
ВЦСПС (Всесоюзный Центрáльный Совéт Профессионáльный Союзов) the All-Union Central Council of Trade Unions
ВЧК (Всероссúйская Чрезвычáйная Комúссия по борьбé с контрреволю́цией, саботáжем и спекуля́цией) All-Russian Special Committee for the Suppression of Counter-Revolution, Sabotage, and Black Marketeering (*historical*)

г (грамм) gram(me)
г. 1. (год) year; 2. (гóрод) city
га (гектáр) hectare
гг. (гóды) years
ГДР (Гермáнская Демократúческая Респýблика) German Democratic Republic
г-жа (госпожá) Mrs.
глав... in compounds (глáвный)
главврáч (глáвный врач) head physician
г-н (господúн) Mr.
гос... in compounds (госудáрственный)
Госбáнк (госудáрственный банк) State Bank
Гослитиздáт (Госудáрственное издáтельство худóжественной литератýры) State Publishing House for Literature
Госполитиздáт (Госудáрственное издáтельство политúческой литератýры) State Publishing House for Political Literature

ГПУ (Госуда́рственное полити́ческое управле́ние) G.P.U. Political State Administration (*historical*)
гр. (граждани́н) citizen
Грузи́нская ССР (Сове́тская Социалисти́ческая Респу́блика) Georgian S.S.R. (Soviet Socialist Republic)
ГСО (Гото́в к санита́рной оборо́не) Ready to do medical service
ГТО (Гото́в к труду́ и оборо́не) Ready to work and defend
ГУМ (Госуда́рственный универса́льный магази́н) department store
ГУС (Госуда́рственный учёный сове́т) State Advisory Board of Scholars

Детги́з (Госуда́рственное изда́тельство де́тской литерату́ры) State Publishing House for Children's Books
дир. (дире́ктор) director
ДКА (Дом Кра́сной Армии) House of the Red Army
доб. (доба́вочный) additional
Донба́сс (Доне́цкий бассе́йн) Donets Basin
доц. (доце́нт) lecturer, instructor
д-р (до́ктор) doctor

ж. д. (желе́зная доро́га) railroad, railway
ж.-д. (железнодоро́жный) relating to railroads *or* railways

завко́м (заводско́й комите́т) works council
загс (отде́л за́писей а́ктов гражда́нского состоя́ния) registrar's (registry) office

и др. (и други́е) etc.
им. (и́мени) called
и мн. др. (и мно́гие други́е) and many (much) more
и пр., и проч. (и про́чее) etc.
и т. д. (и так да́лее) and so on
и т. п. (и тому́ подо́бное) etc.

к. (копе́йка) kopeck
Каза́хская ССР (Сове́тская Социалисти́ческая Респу́блика) Kazak S.S.R. (Soviet Socialist Republic)
кв. **1.** (квадра́тный) square; **2.** (кварти́ра) apartment, flat
кг (килогра́мм) kg (kilogram[me])
КИМ (Коммунисти́ческий интернациона́л молодёжи) Communist Youth International
Кирги́зская ССР (Сове́тская Социалисти́ческая Респу́блика) Kirghiz S.S.R. (Soviet Socialist Republic)
км/час (киломе́тров в час) km/h (kilometers per hour)
колхо́з (коллекти́вное хозя́йство) collective farm, kolkhoz
комсомо́л (Коммунисти́ческий Сою́з Молодёжи) Young Communist League
коп. (копе́йка) kopeck
КПСС (Коммунисти́ческая па́ртия Сове́тского Сою́за) C.P.S.U. (Communist Party of the Soviet Union)
куб. (куби́ческий) cubic

Латви́йская ССР (Сове́тская Социалисти́ческая Респу́блика) Latvian S.S.R. (Soviet Socialist Republic)
Лито́вская ССР (Сове́тская Социалисти́ческая Респу́блика) Lithuanian S.S.R. (Soviet Socialist Republic)
л. с. (лошади́ная си́ла) h.p. (horse power)

МВД (Министе́рство вну́тренних дел) Ministry of Internal Affairs
МГУ (Моско́вский госуда́рственный университе́т) Moscow State University
МГФ (Моско́вская городска́я филармо́ния) Moscow Municipal Philharmonic Hall
Молда́вская ССР (Сове́тская Социалисти́ческая Респу́блика) Moldavian S.S.R. (Soviet Socialist Republic)
м. пр. (ме́жду про́чим) by the way, incidentally; among other things
МТС (маши́нно-тра́кторная ста́нция) machine and tractor station (*hist.*)
Музги́з (Музыка́льное госуда́рственное изда́тельство) State Publishing House for Music
МХАТ (Моско́вский худо́жественный академи́ческий теа́тр) Academic Artists' Theater, Moscow

напр. (наприме́р) for instance

НКВД (Наро́дный комиссариа́т вну́тренних дел) People's Commissariat of Internal Affairs (*1935 to 1946; since 1946* МВД, *cf.*)
№ (но́мер) number
н. ст. (но́вый стиль) new style (*Gregorian calendar*)
н. э. (на́шей э́ры) A. D.
нэп (но́вая экономи́ческая поли́тика) New Economic Policy

о. (о́стров) island
обл. (о́бласть) region; province, sphere, field (*fig.*)
о-во (о́бщество) society
ОГИЗ (Объедине́ние госуда́рственных изда́тельств) Union of the State Publishing Houses
оз. (о́зеро) lake
ОНО (отде́л наро́дного образова́ния) Department of Popular Education
ООН (Организа́ция Объединённых На́ций) United Nations Organization
отд. (отде́л) section, (отделе́ние) department

п. (пункт) point, paragraph
п. г. (про́шлого го́да) of last year
пер. (переу́лок) lane, alleyway, side street
пл. (пло́щадь *f*) square; area (*a.* ♣); (*living*) space
п. м. (про́шлого ме́сяца) of last month
проф. (профе́ссор) professor

р. **1.** (река́) river; **2.** (ру́бль *m*) r(o)uble
райко́м (райо́нный комите́т) district committee (*Sov.*)
РСФСР (Росси́йская Сове́тская Федерати́вная Социалисти́ческая Респу́блика) Russian Soviet Federative Socialist Republic

с. г. (сего́ го́да) (of) this year
след. (сле́дующий) following
см (сантиме́тр) cm. (centimeter)
с. м. (сего́ ме́сяца) (of) this month
см. (смотри́) see
совхо́з (сове́тское хозя́йство) state farm
ср. (сравни́) cf. (compare)
СССР (Сою́з Сове́тских Социалисти́ческих Респу́блик) U.S.S.R. (Union of Soviet Socialist Republics)
ст. **1.** (ста́нция) station; **2.** (стани́ца) Cossack village
стенгазе́та (стенна́я газе́та) wall newspaper
стр. (страни́ца) page
ст. ст. (ста́рый стиль) old style (*Julian calendar*)
с. х. (се́льское хозя́йство) agriculture
с.-х. (сельскохозя́йственный) agricultural
с. ч. (сего́ числа́) this day's
США (Соединённые Шта́ты Аме́рики) U.S.A. (United States of America)

т (то́нна) ton
т. **1.** (това́рищ) comrade; **2.** (том) volume
Таджи́кская ССР (Сове́тская Социалисти́ческая Респу́блика) Tadzhik S.S.R. (Soviet Socialist Republic)
ТАСС (Телегра́фное Аге́нтство Сове́тского Сою́за) TASS (Telegraph Agency of the Soviet Union)
т-во (това́рищество) company, association
т. г. (теку́щего го́да) of the current year
т. е. (то́ есть) i. e. (that is)
тел. (телефо́н) telephone
тел. комм. (телефо́нный коммута́тор) telephone switchboard
т. к. (та́к как) *cf.* так
т. м. (теку́щего ме́сяца) instant
т. наз. (так называ́емый) so-called
тов. *s.* т. 1.
торгпре́дство (торго́вое представи́тельство) trade agency of the U.S.S.R.
тролл. (тролле́йбус) trolley bus
тт. (тома́) volumes
Туркме́нская ССР (Сове́тская Социалисти́ческая Респу́блика) Turkmen S.S.R. (Soviet Socialist Republic)
тыс. (ты́сяча) thousand

Узбе́кская ССР (Сове́тская Социалисти́ческая Респу́блика) Uzbek S.S.R. (Soviet Socialist Republic)
ул. (у́лица) street
УССР (Украи́нская Сове́тская Социалисти́ческая Респу́блика) Ukrainian S.S.R. (Soviet Socialist Republic)
Учпедги́з (Госуда́рственное изда́тельство уче́бно-педагоги́ческой литерату́ры) State Publishing House for Educational Books

ФРГ (Федерати́вная Респу́блика Герма́нии) Federal Republic of Germany

ЦИК (Центра́льный Исполни́тельный Комите́т) Central Executive Committee (*Sov.*); *cf.* ЦК
ЦК (Центра́льный Комите́т) Central Committee
ЦПКиО (Центра́льный парк культу́ры и о́тдыха) Central Park for Culture and Recreation

ч. (час) hour, (часть) part
ЧК (Чрезвыча́йная коми́ссия...) Cheka (*predecessor, 1917—22,* of the ГПУ, *cf.*)

Эсто́нская ССР (Сове́тская Социалисти́ческая Респу́блика) Estonian S.S.R. (Soviet Socialist Republic)

Current American and British Abbreviations

Наиболее употребительные сокращения, принятые в США и Великобритании

A

A.B.C. *American Broadcasting Company* Америка́нская радиовеща́тельная корпора́ция.

A-bomb *atomic bomb* а́томная бо́мба.

A.C. *alternating current* переме́нный ток.

A/C *account (current)* контокорре́нт, теку́щий счёт.

acc(t). *account* отчёт; счёт.

A.E.C. *Atomic Energy Commission* Коми́ссия по а́томной эне́ргии.

AFL-CIO *American Federation of Labor & Congress of Industrial Organizations* Америка́нская федера́ция труда́ и Конгре́сс произво́дственных профсою́зов, АФТ/КПП.

A.F.N. *American Forces Network* радиосе́ть америка́нских войск (в Европе).

Ala. *Alabama* Алаба́ма (штат в США).

Alas. *Alaska* Аля́ска (территория в США).

a.m. *ante meridiem* (лат. = *before noon*) до полу́дня.

A.P. *Associated Press* Ассо́шиэйтед пресс.

A.R.C. *American Red Cross* Америка́нский Кра́сный Крест.

Ariz. *Arizona* Аризо́на (штат в США).

Ark. *Arkansas* Арка́нза́с (штат в США).

A.R.P. *Air-Raid Precautions* гражда́нская ПВО (противовозду́шная оборо́на).

B

B.A. *Bachelor of Arts* бакала́вр филосо́фии.

B.B.C. *British Broadcasting Corporation* Брита́нская радиовеща́тельная корпора́ция.

B/E *Bill of Exchange* ве́ксель *m*, тра́тта.

B.E.A.C. *British European Airways Corporation* Брита́нская корпора́ция европе́йских возду́шных сообще́ний.

Benelux *Belgium, Netherlands, Luxemburg* экономи́ческий и тамо́женный сою́з, БЕНИЛЮКС.

B.F.B.S. *British Forces Broadcasting Service* радиовеща́тельная организа́ция брита́нских вооружённых сил.

B.L. *Bachelor of Law* бакала́вр пра́ва.

B/L *bill of lading* коносаме́нт; тра́нспортная накладна́я.

B.M. *Bachelor of Medicine* бакала́вр медици́ны.

B.O.A.C. *British Overseas Airways Corporation* Брита́нская корпора́ция трансокеа́нских возду́шных сообще́ний.

B.O.T. *Board of Trade* министе́рство торго́вли (в Англии).

B.R. *British Railways* Брита́нская желе́зная доро́га.

Br(it). *Britain* Великобрита́ния; *British* брита́нский, англи́йский.

Bros. *brothers* бра́тья *pl.* (в названиях фирм).

B.S.A. *British South Africa* Брита́нская 'Южная 'Африка.

B.T.U. *British Thermal Unit(s)* брита́нская теплова́я едини́ца.

B.U.P. *British United Press* информацио́нное аге́нтство „Бри́тиш Юна́йтед Пресс“.

C

c. 1. *cent(s)* цент (американская монета); 2. *circa* приблизи́тельно, о́коло; 3. *cubic* куби́ческий.

C/A *current account* теку́щий счёт.

Cal(if). *California* Калифо́рния (штат в США).

Can. *Canada* Кана́да; *Canadian* кана́дский.

C.C. *continuous current* постоя́нный ток.

C.I.C. *Counter Intelligence Corps* слу́жба контрразве́дки США.

C.I.D. *Criminal Investigation Division* кримина́льная поли́ция.

c.i.f. *cost, insurance, freight* цена́, включа́ющая сто́имость, расхо́ды по страхова́нию и фрахт.

c/o *care of* че́рез, по а́дресу (надпись на конвертах).

Co. 1. *company* о́бщество, компа́ния; 2. (в США и Ирландии также) *County* о́круг.

C.O.D. *cash* (ам. *collect.*) *on delivery* налóженный платёж, уплáта при достáвке.
Col. *Colorado* Колорáдо (штат в США).
Conn. *Connecticut* Коннéктикут (штат в США).
c.w.o. *cash with order* нали́чный расчёт при вы́даче закáза.
cwt. *hundredweight* цéнтнер.

D

d. *penny* (*pence pl.*) (условное обозначение английской монеты) пéнни (пéнс[ы] *pl.*).
D.C. 1. *direct current* постоя́нный ток; 2. *District of Columbia* федерáльный óкруг Колу́мбия (с американской столицей).
Del. *Delaware* Дéлавэр (штат в США).
Dept. *Department* отдéл; управлéние; министéрство; вéдомство.
disc(t). *discount* ски́дка; дискóнт, учёт векселéй.
div(d). *dividend* дивидéнд.
dol. *dollar* дóллар.
doz. *dozen* дюжина.
D.P. *Displaced Person* перемещённое лицó.
d/p *documents against payment* докумéнты за нали́чный расчёт.
Dpt. *Department* отдéл; управлéние; министéрство; вéдомство.

E

E. 1. *East* востóк; *Eastern* востóчный; 2. *English* англи́йский.
E. & O.E. *errors and omissions excepted* исключáя оши́бки и прóпуски.
E.C.E. *Economic Commission for Europe* Экономи́ческая коми́ссия ООН для Еврóпы.
ECOSOC *Economic and Social Council* Экономи́ческий и социáльный совéт ООН.
EE., E./E. *errors excepted* исключáя оши́бки.
e.g. *exempli gratia* (лат. = *for instance*) напр. (напримéр).
Enc. *enclosure(s)* приложéние (-ния).
E.R.P. *European Recovery Program(me)* прогрáмма „восстановлéния Еврóпы", т. наз. „план Мáршалла".
Esq. *Esquire* эсквáйр (титул дворянина, должностного лица; обычно ставится в письме после фамилии).

F

f. 1. *farthing* (брит. монета) чéтверть пéнса, фáртинг; 2. *fathom* морскáя сажéнь f; 3. *feminine* жéнский; *gram.* жéнский род; 4. *foot* фут, *feet* фу́ты; 5. *following* слéдующий.
FBI *Federal Bureau of Investigation* федерáльное бюрó расслéдований (в США).
FIFA *Fédération Internationale de Football Association* Междунарóдная федерáция футбóльных óбществ, ФИФА.
Fla. *Florida* Флори́да (штат в США).
F.O. *Foreign Office* министéрство инострáнных дел.
fo(l). *folio* фóлио *indecl. n* (формат в пол-листа); лист (бухгалтерской книги).
f.o.b. *free on board* фрáнко-борт, ФОБ.
f.o.q. *free on quay* фрáнко-нáбережная.
f.o.r. *free on rail* фрáнко-рéльсы, фрáнко желéзная дорóга.
f.o.t. *free on truck* фрáнко ж.-д. платфóрма; фрáнко-грузови́к.
f.o.w. *free on waggon* фрáнко-вагóн.
fr. *franc(s)* фрáнк(и).
ft. *foot* фут, *feet* фу́ты.

G

g. 1. *gram(me)* грамм; 2. *guinea* гинéя (денежная единица = 21 шиллингу).
Ga. *Georgia* Гeóргия (штат в США).
G.A.T.T. *General Agreement on Tariffs and Trade* 'Общее соглашéние по тамóженным тари́фам и торгóвле.
G.I. *government issue* казённый; госудáрственная сóбственность f; *fig.* америкáнский солдáт.
G.M.T. *Greenwich Mean Time* срéднее врéмя по гри́нвичскому меридиáну.
gns. *guineas* гинéи.
gr. *gross* бру́тто.
gr.wt. *gross weight* вес бру́тто.
Gt.Br. *Great Britain* Великобритáния.

H

h. *hour(s)* час(ы́).
H.B.M. *His (Her) Britannic Majesty* Егó (Её) Британское Вели́чество.
H-bomb *hydrogen bomb* водорóдная бóмба.
H.C. *House of Commons* палáта óбщин (в Англии).
hf. *half* полови́на.
H.L. *House of Lords* палáта лóрдов (в Англии).
H.M. *His (Her) Majesty* Егó (Её) Вели́чество.
H.M.S. 1. *His (Her) Majesty's Service* на слу́жбе Егó (Её) Вели́чества; ✉ служéбное дéло; 2. *His (Her)*

Majesty's Ship кора́бль англи́йского вое́нно-морско́го фло́та.
H.O. *Home Office* министе́рство вну́тренних дел (в Англии).
H.P., h.p. *horse-power* лошади́ная си́ла (единица мощности).
H.Q., Hq. *Headquarters* штаб.
H.R. *House of Representatives* пала́та представи́телей (в США).
H.R.H. *His (Her) Royal Highness* Его́ (Её) Короле́вское Высо́чество.
hrs. *hours* часы́.

I

Ia. *Iowa* 'Айова (штат в США).
Id. *Idaho* Айда́хо (штат в США).
I.D. *Intelligence Department* разве́дывательное управле́ние.
i.e. *id est* (лат. = *that is to say*) т. е. (то́ есть).
Ill. *Illinois* 'Иллино́йс (штат в США).
I.M.F. *International Monetary Fund* Междунаро́дный валю́тный фонд ООН.
in. *inch(es)* дюйм(ы).
Inc. 1. *Incorporated* объединённый; зарегистри́рованный как корпора́ция; **2.** *Including* включи́тельно; **3.** *Inclosure* приложе́ние.
Ind. *Indiana* Индиа́на (штат в США).
I.N.S. *International News Service* Междунаро́дное телегра́фное аге́нтство.
inst. (лат. = *instant*) с. м. (сего́ ме́сяца).
Ir. *Ireland* Ирла́ндия; *Irish* ирла́ндский.

J

J.P. *Justice of the Peace* мирово́й судья́ *m.*
Jr. *junior* мла́дший.

K

Kan(s). *Kansas* Ка́нза́с (штат в США).
k.o. *knock(ed) out* спорт.: нока́ут; *fig.* (окончательно) разде́латься с ке́м-либо.
Ky. *Kentucky* Кенту́кки (штат в США).

L

l. *litre* литр.
£ *pound sterling* фунт сте́рлингов.
La. *Louisiana* Луизиа́на (штат в США).
£A *Australian pound* австрали́йский фунт (денежная единица).
lb. *pound* фунт (мера веса).
L/C *letter of credit* аккредити́в.
£E *Egyptian pound* еги́петский фунт (денежная единица).
L.P. *Labour Party* лейбори́стская па́ртия.
LP *long-playing* долгоигра́ющий; ~ *record* долгоигра́ющая пласти́нка.
Ltd. *limited* с ограни́ченной отве́тственностью.

M

m. 1. *male* мужско́й; **2.** *metre* метр; **3.** *mile* ми́ля; **4.** *minute* мину́та.
M.A. *Master of Arts* маги́стр филосо́фии.
Man. *Manitoba* Манито́ба (провинция Канады).
Mass. *Massachusetts* Массачу́сетс (штат в США).
M.D. *medicinae doctor* (лат. = *Doctor of Medicine*) до́ктор медици́ны.
Md. *Maryland* Мэ́риленд (штат в США).
Me. *Maine* Мэн (штат в США).
mg. *milligramme* миллигра́мм.
Mich. *Michigan* Ми́чига́н (штат в США).
Minn. *Minnesota* Миннесо́та (штат в США).
Miss. *Mississippi* Миссиси́пи (штат в США).
mm. *millimetre* миллиме́тр.
Mo. *Missouri* Миссу́ри (штат в США).
M.O. *money order* де́нежный перево́д по по́чте.
Mont. *Montana* Монта́на (штат в США).
MP, M.P. 1. *Member of Parliament* член парла́мента; **2.** *Military Police* вое́нная поли́ция.
m.p.h. *miles per hour* (сто́лько-то) миль в час.
Mr. *Mister* ми́стер, господи́н.
Mrs. *Mistress* ми́ссис, госпожа́.
MS. *manuscript* ру́копись f.
M.S. *motorship* теплохо́д.

N

N. *North* се́вер; *Northern* се́верный.
N.A.A.F.I. *Navy, Army, and Air Force Institutes* вое́нно-торго́вая слу́жба ВМС (вое́нно-морски́х сил), ВВС (вое́нно-возду́шных сил) и сухопу́тных войск.
NATO *North Atlantic Treaty Organization* Североатланти́ческий сою́з, НАТО.
N.C. *North Carolina* Се́верная Кароли́на (штат в США).
N.Dak. *North Dakota* Се́верная Дако́та (штат в США).
N.E. *Northeast* се́веро-восто́к.
Neb. *Nebraska* Небра́ска (штат в США).
Nev. *Nevada* Нева́да (штат в США).
N.H. *New Hampshire* Нью-Хэ́мпшир (штат в США).
N.J. *New Jersey* Нью-Дже́рси (штат в США).

N.Mex. *New Mexico* Нью-Ме́ксико (штат в США).
nt.wt. *net weight* вес не́тто, чи́стый вес.
N.W. *Northwestern* се́веро-за́падный.
N.Y. *New York* Нью-Йо́рк (штат в США).
N.Y.C. *New York City* Нью-Йо́рк (го́род).

O

O. 1. *Ohio* Ога́йо (штат в США); 2. *order* поруче́ние, зака́з.
o/a *on account of* за (чей-либо) счёт.
O.E.E.C. *Organization of European Economic Co-operation* Организа́ция европе́йского экономи́ческого сотру́дничества.
O.H.M.S. *On His (Her) Majesty's Service* состоя́щий на короле́вской (госуда́рственной или вое́нной) слу́жбе; ✎ служе́бное де́ло.
O.K. *all correct* всё в поря́дке, всё пра́вильно; утверждено́, согласо́вано.
Okla. *Oklahoma* Оклахо́ма (штат в США).
Ore(g). *Oregon* Оре́го́н (штат в США).

P

p.a. *per annum* (лат.) в год; ежего́дно.
Pa. *Pennsylvania* Пенсильва́ния (штат в США).
P.A.A. *Pan American Airways* Панамерика́нская авиакомпа́ния.
P.C. 1. *post-card* почто́вая ка́рточка, откры́тка; 2. *police constable* полице́йский.
p.c. *per cent* проце́нт, проце́нты.
pd. *paid* упла́чено; опла́ченный.
Penn(a). *Pennsylvania* Пенсильва́ния (штат в США).
per pro(c). *per procurationem* (лат. = *by proxy*) по дове́ренности.
p.m. *post meridiem* (лат. = *after noon*) ... часо́в (часа́) дня.
P.O. 1. *Post Office* почто́вое отделе́ние; 2. *postal order* де́нежный перево́д по по́чте.
P.O.B. *Post Office Box* почто́вый абонеме́нтный я́щик.
p.o.d. *pay on delivery* нало́женный платёж.
P.O.S.B. *Post Office Savings Bank* сберега́тельная ка́сса при почто́вом отделе́нии.
P.S. *Postscript* постскри́птум, припи́ска.
P.T.O., p.t.o. *please turn over* см. н/об. (смотри́ на оборо́те).
PX *Post Exchange* вое́нно-торго́вый магази́н.

Q

quot. *quotation* котиро́вка.

R

R.A.F. *Royal Air Force* вое́нно-возду́шные си́лы Великобрита́нии.
ref(c). *reference* ссы́лка, указа́ние.
regd. *registered* зарегистри́рованный; ✎ заказно́й.
reg. ton *register ton* реги́стровая то́нна.
ret. *retired* изъя́тый из обраще́ния; вы́купленный, опла́ченный.
Rev. *Reverend* преподо́бный.
R.I. *Rhode Island* Род-'Айленд (штат в США).
R.N. *Royal Navy* англи́йский вое́нно-морско́й флот Великобрита́нии.
R.P. *reply paid* отве́т опла́чен.
R.R. *Railroad Am.* желе́зная доро́га.

S

S. *South* юг; *Southern* ю́жный.
s. 1. *second* секу́нда; 2. *shilling* ши́ллинг.
S.A. 1. *South Africa* 'Южная 'Африка; 2. *South America* 'Южная Аме́рика; 3. *Salvation Army* 'Армия спасе́ния.
S.C. 1. *South Carolina* 'Южная Кароли́на (штат в США); 2. *Security Council* Сове́т Безопа́сности ООН.
S.Dak. *South Dakota* 'Южная Дако́та (штат в США).
S.E. 1. *Southeast* юго-восто́к; *Southeastern* юго-восто́чный; 2. *Stock Exchange* фо́ндовая би́ржа (в Ло́ндоне).
sh. *shilling* ши́ллинг.
Soc. *society* о́бщество.
sov. *sovereign* совере́н (золота́я моне́та в оди́н фунт сте́рлингов).
Sq. *Square* пло́щадь f.
sq. *square...* квадра́тный.
S.S. *steamship* парохо́д.
St. *Station* ста́нция; вокза́л.
St. Ex. *Stock Exchange* фо́ндовая би́ржа.
stg. *sterling* фунт сте́рлингов.
suppl. *supplement* дополне́ние, приложе́ние.
S.W. *Southwest* юго-восто́к; *Southwestern* юго-восто́чный.

T

t. *ton* то́нна.
T.D. *Treasury Department* министе́рство фина́нсов (в США).
Tenn. *Tennessee* Теннесси́ (штат в США).
Tex. *Texas* Теха́с (штат в США).
T.M.O. *telegraphic money order* де́нежный перево́д по телегра́фу.
T.O. *Telegraph (Telephone) Office* телегра́фное (телефо́нное) отделе́ние.
T.U. *Trade Union* тред-юнио́н, профессиона́льный сою́з.

T.U.C. *Trade Unions Congress* конгре́сс (брита́нских) тред-юнио́нов.

U

U.K. *United Kingdom* Соединённое Королéвство (Англия, Шотландия, Уэльс и Северная Ирландия).
U.N. *United Nations* Объединённые На́ции.
UNESCO *United Nations Educational, Scientific, and Cultural Organization* Организа́ция Объединённых На́ций по вопро́сам просвеще́ния, нау́ки и культу́ры, ЮНЕСКО.
U.N.S.C. *United Nations Security Council* Сове́т Безопа́сности ООН.
U.P. *United Press* телегра́фное аге́нтство „Юна́йтед Пресс".
U.S.(A.) *United States (of America)* Соединённые Шта́ты (Аме́рики).
Ut. *Utah* 'Юта (штат в США).

V

Va. *Virginia* Вирги́ния (штат в США).
VE-day *Victory in Europe-day* День побе́ды в Евро́пе (над Германией в 1945).
viz. *videlicet* (лат.) а и́менно.
vol. *volume* том.
vols. *volumes* тома́ *pl.*
Vt. *Vermont* Вермо́нт (штат в США).

W

W. *West* за́пад; *Western* за́падный.
Wash. *Washington* Ва́шингто́н (штат в США).
W.D. *War Department* вое́нное министе́рство США.
W.F.T.U. *World Federation of Trade Unions* Всеми́рная федера́ция профессиона́льных сою́зов, ВФП.
W.H.O. *World Health Organization* Всеми́рная организа́ция здравоохране́ния, ВОЗ.
W.I. *West Indies* Вест-'Индия.
Wis. *Wisconsin* Виско́нсин (штат в США).
W.O. *War Office* (британское) вое́нное министе́рство.
wt. *weight* вес.
W.Va. *West Virginia* За́падная Вирги́ния (штат в США).
Wyo. *Wyoming* Вайо́минг (штат в США).

X

Xmas *Christmas* рождество́.

Y

yd(s). *yard(s)* я́рд(ы).
Y.M.C.A. *Young Men's Christian Association* Христиа́нская ассоциа́ция молоды́х людей.
Y.W.C.A. *Young Women's Christian Association* Христиа́нская ассоциа́ция (молоды́х) де́вушек.

Числительные — Numerals

Количественные
Cardinals

0 ноль & нуль *m* naught, zero, cipher
1 оди́н *m*, одна́ *f*, одно́ *n* one
2 два *m/n*, две *f* two
3 три three
4 четы́ре four
5 пять five
6 шесть six
7 семь seven
8 во́семь eight
9 де́вять nine
10 де́сять ten
11 оди́ннадцать eleven
12 двена́дцать twelve
13 трина́дцать thirteen
14 четы́рнадцать fourteen
15 пятна́дцать fifteen
16 шестна́дцать sixteen
17 семна́дцать seventeen
18 восемна́дцать eighteen
19 девятна́дцать nineteen
20 два́дцать twenty
21 два́дцать оди́н *m* (одна́ *f*, одно́ *n*) twenty-one
22 два́дцать два *m/n* (две *f*) twenty-two
23 два́дцать три twenty-three
30 три́дцать thirty
40 со́рок forty
50 пятьдеся́т fifty
60 шестьдеся́т sixty
70 се́мьдесят seventy
80 во́семьдесят eighty
90 девяно́сто ninety
100 сто (а и́ли one) hundred
200 две́сти two hundred
300 три́ста three hundred
400 четы́реста four hundred
500 пятьсо́т five hundred
600 шестьсо́т six hundred
700 семьсо́т seven hundred
800 восемьсо́т eight hundred
900 девятьсо́т nine hundred
1000 (одна́) ты́сяча *f* (а и́ли one) thousand
60 140 шестьдеся́т ты́сяч сто со́рок sixty thousand one hundred and forty
1 000 000 (оди́н) миллио́н *m* (а и́ли one) million
1 000 000 000 (оди́н) *миллиа́рд or* биллио́н *m* milliard, *Am.* billion

Порядковые
Ordinals

1st пе́рвый first
2nd второ́й second
3rd тре́тий third
4th четвёртый fourth
5th пя́тый fifth
6th шесто́й sixth
7th седьмо́й seventh
8th восьмо́й eighth
9th девя́тый ninth
10th деся́тый tenth
11th оди́ннадцатый eleventh
12th двена́дцатый twelfth
13th трина́дцатый thirteenth
14th четы́рнадцатый fourteenth
15th пятна́дцатый fifteenth
16th шестна́дцатый sixteenth
17th семна́дцатый seventeenth
18th восемна́дцатый eighteenth
19th девятна́дцатый nineteenth
20th двадца́тый twentieth
21st два́дцать пе́рвый twenty-first
22nd два́дцать второ́й twenty-second
23rd два́дцать тре́тий twenty-third
30th тридца́тый thirtieth
40th сороково́й fortieth
50th пятидеся́тый fiftieth
60th шестидеся́тый sixtieth
70th семидеся́тый seventieth
80th восьмидеся́тый eightieth
90th девяно́стый ninetieth
100th со́тый (one) hundredth
200th двухсо́тый two hundredth
300th трёхсо́тый three hundredth
400th четырёхсо́тый four hundredth
500th пятисо́тый five hundredth
600th шестисо́тый six hundredth
700th семисо́тый seven hundredth
800th восьмисо́тый eight hundredth
900th девятисо́тый nine hundredth
1000th ты́сячный (one) thousandth
60 140th шестьдеся́т ты́сяч сто сороково́й sixty thousand one hundred and fortieth
1 000 000th миллио́нный millionth

Русские меры длины и веса

Russian Measures and Weights

In the U.S.S.R. the metric system is in force since January 1st, 1927. Hence measures and weights are in accordance with the international metric system.

Moreover the following old Russian measures and weights are occasionally still used within the Soviet Union:

1. Ме́ры длины́. Long measures

1 верста́ (verst) = 500 саже́ням (саже́нь, fathom) = 1500 арши́нам (arshin) = 1066.78 m.

1 арши́н (arshin) = 2.333 фу́та (фут, foot) = 16 вершка́м (вершо́к, vershock) = 28 дю́ймам (дюйм, inch) = 0.71 m.

2. Квадра́тные ме́ры. Square measures

1 квадра́тная верста́ (square verst) = 104.167 десяти́ны (dessiatine) = 250 000 квадра́тным саже́ням (square sagene)

1 десяти́на (dessiatine) = 2400 кв. саже́ням (square sagene) = 109.254 acres

3. Ме́ры объёма. Cubic measures

кубический фут (cubic foot); куби́ческая саже́нь (cubic sagene); куби́ческий арши́н (cubic arshin)

4. Хле́бные ме́ры. Dry measures

1 че́тверть (chetvert) = 2 осьми́нам (осьми́на, osmina, eighth) = 4 полуосьми́нам (poluosmina) = 8 четверика́м (четвери́к, chetverik) = 64 га́рнцам (га́рнец, garnetz) = 209.9 l.

5. Ме́ры жи́дкостей. Liquid measures

1 ведро́ (bucket) = 10 кру́жкам (кру́жка, mug) = 100 ча́ркам (ча́рка, cup, gin-glas) = 12.30 l.

6. Ме́ры ма́ссы (ве́са). Weights

1 пуд (pood) = 40 фу́нтам (фунт, pound) = 1280 ло́там (small weight) = 16.38 kg.

1 лот (small weight) = 3 золотника́м (золотни́к, zolotnick) = 288 до́лям (до́ля, dolya)

Валю́та. Currency

1 рубль (rouble) = 100 копе́йкам (копе́йка, copeck)

American and British Measures and Weights

Американские и британские меры длины и веса

1. Ме́ры длины́

1 **line (l.)** ли́ния = 2,12 мм
1 **inch (in.)** дюйм = 2,54 см
1 **foot (ft.)** фут = 30,48 см
1 **yard (yd.)** ярд = 91,44 см

2. Морски́е ме́ры

1 **fathom (f., fm.)** морска́я саже́нь = 1,83 м
1 **cable('s) length** ка́бельтов = 183 м, в США = 120 морски́м саже́ням = 219 м
1 **nautical mile (n. m.)** *or* **1 knot** морска́я ми́ля = 1852 м

3. Квадра́тные ме́ры

1 **square inch (sq. in.)** квадра́тный дюйм = 6,45 кв. см
1 **square foot (sq. ft.)** квадра́тный фут = 929,03 кв. см
1 **square yard (sq. yd.)** квадра́тный ярд = 8361,26 кв. см
1 **square rod (sq. rd.)** квадра́тный род = 25,29 кв. м
1 **rood (ro.)** руд = 0,25 а́кра
1 **acre (a.)** акр = 0,4 га
1 **square mile (sq. mi.)** квадра́тная ми́ля = 259 га

4. Ме́ры объёма

1 **cubic inch (cu. in.)** куби́ческий дюйм = 16,387 куб. см
1 **cubic foot (cu. ft.)** куби́ческий фут = 28316,75 куб. см
1 **cubic yard (cu. yd.)** куби́ческий ярд = 0,765 куб. м
1 **register ton (reg. ton)** реги́стровая то́нна = 2,832 куб. м

5. Ме́ры ёмкости

Ме́ры жи́дких и сыпу́чих тел

1 **British** *or* **Imperial gill (gl., gi.)** станда́ртный и́ли англи́йский джилл = 0,142 л
1 **British** *or* **Imperial pint (pt.)** станда́ртная и́ли англи́йская пи́нта = 0,568 л
1 **British** *or* **Imperial quart (qt.)** станда́ртная и́ли англи́йская ква́рта = 1,136 л
1 **British** *or* **Imp. gallon (Imp. gal.)** станда́ртный и́ли англи́йский галло́н = 4,546 л

6. Ме́ры сыпу́чих тел

1 **British** *or* **Imperial peck (pk.)** станда́ртный и́ли англи́йский пек = 9,086 л
1 **Brit.** *or* **Imp. bushel (bu., bus.)** станда́ртный и́ли англи́йский бу́шель = 36,35 л
1 **Brit.** *or* **Imperial quarter (qr.)** станда́ртная и́ли англи́йская че́тверть = 290,8 л

7. Ме́ры жи́дких тел

1 **Brit.** *or* **Imperial barrel (bbl., bl.)** станда́ртный и́ли англи́йский ба́ррель = 1,636 гл

Америка́нские ме́ры жи́дких и сыпу́чих тел

Ме́ры сыпу́чих тел

1 **U.S. dry pint** америка́нская суха́я пи́нта = 0,551 л
1 **U.S. dry quart** америка́нская суха́я ква́рта = 1,1 л
1 **U.S. dry gallon** америка́нский сухо́й галло́н = 4,4 л
1 **U.S. peck** америка́нский пек = 8,81 л
1 **U.S. bushel** америка́нский бу́шель = 35,24 л

Ме́ры жи́дких тел

1 **U.S. liquid gill** америка́нский джилл (жи́дкости) = 0,118 л
1 **U.S. liquid pint** америка́нская пи́нта (жи́дкости) = 0,473 л
1 **U.S. liquid quart** америка́нская ква́рта (жи́дкости) = 0,946 л
1 **U.S. liquid gallon** америка́нский галло́н (жи́дкости) = 3,785 л
1 **U.S. barrel** америка́нский ба́ррель = 119 л
1 **U.S. barrel petroleum** америка́нский ба́ррель не́фти = 158,97 л

8. Торго́вые ме́ры ве́са

1 **grain (gr.)** гран = 0,0648 г
1 **dram (dr.)** дра́хма = 1,77 г
1 **ounce (oz.)** у́нция = 28,35 г
1 **pound (lb.)** фунт = 453,59 г
1 **quarter (qr.)** че́тверть = 12,7 кг, в США = 11,34 кг
1 **hundredweight (cwt.)** це́нтнер = 50,8 кг, в США = 45,36 кг
1 **stone (st.)** стон = 6,35 кг
1 **ton (tn., t.)** = 1016 кг (тж long ton: tn. l.), в США = 907,18 кг (тж short ton: tn. sh.)